Russia & Belarus

Simon Richmond
Mark Elliott
Patrick Horton
Steve Kokker
Baty Landis
Wendy Taylor
Mara Vorhees

LONELY PLANET PUBLICATIONS
Melbourne • Oakland • London • Paris

ARCTIC OCEAN

ARCTIC

BRITAIN

NORTH SEA

NORWAY

Oslo

DENMARK

Copenhagen

SWEDEN

Stockholm

Norwegian Sea

Svalbard

Zemlya Frantsa-Iosifa

BELARUS
This developing Eastern European country is worth visiting for its charming towns, including Brest, Hrodna and Vitsebsk, and for a taste of life in the old Soviet days

ST PETERSBURG
Russia's most elegant city is home to splendid tsarist palaces, the sites of the revolution, the treasures of the State Hermitage and many excellent museums, theatres and restaurants

Murmansk

Novaya Zemlya

BARENTS SEA

KARA SEA

Dixon

Baltic Sea

Tallinn

Helsinki

Riga

ESTONIA

FINLAND

White Sea

Lake Ladoga

Petrozavodsk

Arkhangelsk

Amderma

Yamal Peninsula

Gydansky Peninsula

Warsaw

RUSSIA

LATVIA

LITHUANIA

Vilnius

Pskov

St Petersburg

Novgorod

Vorkuta

Dudinka

Norilsk

POLAND

BELARUS

Polatsk

Vitsebsk

MINSK

Smolensk

Tver

Vologda

Salekhard

ARCTIC

Igarka

Kiev

Homel

MOSCOW

Bryansk

Ivanovo

Yaroslavl

Suzdal

R U S S I A

Syktyvkar

Siberian Lowland

UKRAINE

Tula

Vladimir

Ryazan

Vyatka (Kirov)

MOSCOW
How could you miss out on Red Square, the Kremlin, the Bolshoi Ballet and Russia's best restaurants and nightlife?

Oryol

Kursk

Nizhny Novgorod

Khanty-Mansiysk

Surgut

Nizhnevartovsk

Voronezh

Cheboxary

Kazan

Perm

Tambov

Izhevsk

Nizhniy Tagil

Yeniseysk

Ulyanovsk

Syzran

Yekaterinburg

Tobolsk

Saratov

Samara

Ufa

Tyumen

Tomsk

Mariinsk

Volgograd

Magnitogorsk

Chelyabinsk

Kurgan

Omsk

Kemerovo

Sea of Azov

Orenburg

Petropavl (Petropavlovsk)

Novosibirsk

Elbrus (5642m)

Rostov-on-Don

Orsk

Barnaul

Abakan

Novokuznetsk

BLACK SEA

Astrakhan

Grozny

GEORGIA

YEKATERINBURG
Historic Yekaterinburg makes an ideal base for exploring the gently rolling Ural Mountains

Astana

Gorno-Altaysk

Tbilisi

CASPIAN SEA

KAZAKHSTAN

Karaganda

ALTAY MOUNTAINS

ARMENIA

Yerevan

Aral Sea

ALTAY REPUBLIC & REPUBLIC OF TUVA
These picturesque, intriguing regions offer great opportunities for outdoor activities

Semey (Sem Ipalatinsk)

Belukha (4506m)

AZERBAIJAN

Baku

Nukus

Balkhash

Aktogay

CAUCASUS MOUNTAINS
Amid this stunning range, carpeted with wild flowers in summer and snow in winter, you'll find relics of little-known ancient cultures and a fascinating ethnic mix

TURANIAN PLATEAU

Lake Balkhash

Urumqi

Tashauz

UZBEKISTAN

Almaty

Bishkek

ZAGROS MOUNTAINS

Ashkabad

Bukhara

Tashkent

KYRGYZSTAN

CHINA

Tehran

TURKMENISTAN

Dushanbe

IRAN

TAJIKISTAN

Tarim Basin

AFGHANISTAN

Kabul

PAKISTAN

0 500 1000km
0 300 600mi

KAMCHATKA
This 'land of fire and ice', one of Russia's least charted regions but among the most attractive, has over 200 volcanoes – several still very active

LAKE BAIKAL
The 'Pearl of Siberia', with its crystal-clear water, is the world's deepest lake, surrounded by mountains and delightful small log cabin settlements

TRANS-SIBERIAN RAILWAY
Probably the world's most famous and certainly its longest continuous rail route, the Trans-Siberian crosses murky swamps and mighty rivers, and traverses mountains and vast steppes during its 9289km journey from Moscow to Vladivostok

VLADIVOSTOK & KHABAROVSK
These major cities, closer to Beijing than Moscow, offer cosmopolitan diversions but are also perfect for exploring the desolate Russian Far East

KRASNOYARSK
This pleasant city, with one of the region's most impressive museums, is an excellent place to embark on a trip along the mighty Yenisey River, flowing through the heart of Siberia to the Arctic

OCEAN

CHUKCHI SEA

USA

St Lawrence Island

Wrangel Island

Providenia

Chukotka Peninsula

EAST SIBERIAN SEA

Anadyr

BERING SEA

Severnaya Zemlya

Novosibirskiye Ostrova

LAPTEV SEA

RUSSIA

Komandorskiye Island

Taymyr Peninsula

Nordvik

Tixi

Khatanga

Klyuchevskaya (4750m)

Shelekhov Gulf

KOLYMSKY MOUNTAINS

Magadan

Petropavlovsk-Kamchatsky

CENTRAL SIBERIAN PLATEAU

Kamchatka Peninsula

Putorana Plateau

CIRCLE

VERKHOYANSKY

Yakutsk

Okhotsk

SEA OF OKHOTSK

S I B E R I A

Olekminsk

Lensk

Bratsk

Krasnoyarsk

Tayshet

Severobaikalsk

Tynda

STANOVOY MOUNTAINS

Komsomolsk-on-Amur

Sakhalin Island

Vanino

Sovetskaya Gavan

Yuzhno-Sakhalinsk

UDOKAN MOUNTAINS

Birobidzhan

Khabarovsk

Blagoveshchensk

Chita

Manchurian Plain

Irkutsk

YABLONOVY MOUNTAINS

Sapporo

Hakodate

Kyzyl

EASTERN SAYAN MOUNTAINS

Ulan Ude

WESTERN SAYAN MOUNTAINS

Darkhan

Harbin

Ussuriysk

Vladivostok

SEA OF JAPAN

JAPAN

Ulaan Baatar

Changchun

Sainshand

C H I N A

Shenyang

NORTH KOREA

Kyoto

Osaka

M O N G O L I A

Erlian

Pyongyang

Gobi Desert

Shanhaiguan

Seoul

Zhangjiakou

Hohhot

Datong

Beijing

Tianjin

SOUTH KOREA

Baotou

Yellow Sea

Yumen

Jiayuguan

Great Basin

Qingdao

Nagasaki

East China Sea

Russia & Belarus
3rd edition – June 2003
First published – January 1996

Published by
Lonely Planet Publications Pty Ltd ABN 36 005 607 983
90 Maribyrnong St, Footscray, Victoria 3011, Australia

Lonely Planet Offices
Australia Locked Bag 1, Footscray, Victoria 3011
USA 150 Linden St, Oakland, CA 94607
UK 72 – 82 Rosebery Ave, Clerkenwell, London EC1R 4RW
France 1 rue du Dahomey, 75011 Paris

Photographs
Many of the images in this guide are available for licensing from
Lonely Planet Images.
w www.lonelyplanetimages.com

Front cover photograph
New Jerusalem Monastery, Moscow (1658–1698), modelled after
the Church of the Holy Sepulchre in Jerusalem (Christina Dameyer)

Russia's Top 50 Experiences Title Page
Church on Spilled Blood, St Petersburg (Stephen Saks)

European Russia Title Page
Main door to the 100-year-old Naval St Nicholas Cathedral of the
Epiphany, St Petersburg (Steve Kokker)

Siberia & the Russian Far East Title Page
Door carved in traditional style at the Ethnographic Museum, Ulan
Ude (John S King)

Belarus Title Page
War-damaged facade of Kholmskie Gate, Brest Fortress
(Steve Kokker)

ISBN 1 74059 265 4

Printed by The Bookmaker International Ltd
Printed in China

Although the authors and Lonely Planet try to make the information as accurate as possible, we accept no responsibility for any loss, injury or inconvenience sustained by anyone using this book.

Contents – Text

THE RUSSIAN FAR EAST

BELARUS

FACTS ABOUT BELARUS

FACTS FOR THE VISITOR

Contents – Maps

SIBERIA & THE RUSSIAN FAR EAST

SIBERIA

RUSSIAN FAR EAST

BELARUS

FACTS ABOUT BELARUS

MINSK

ELSEWHERE IN BELARUS

RUSSIA & BELARUS MAP INDEX

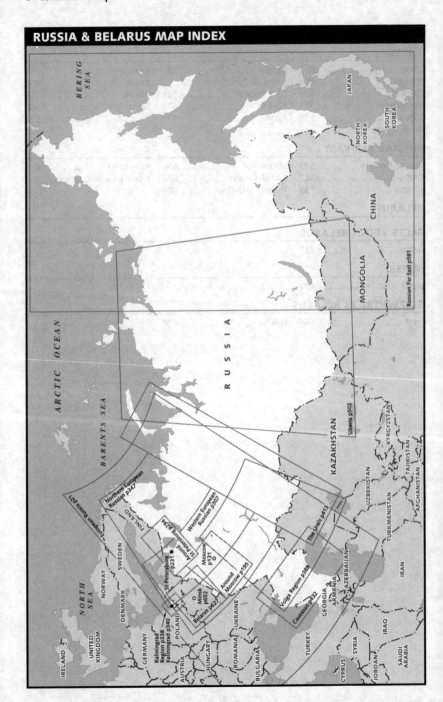

The Authors

Simon Richmond

Blame it on the white vodka-fuelled nights and all that tsarist opulence, but after his first visit to St Petersburg in 1994, Simon knew this would not be his last encounter with this beguiling city and the fascinating country to which it belongs. The award-winning writer travelled from St Petersburg to Vladivostok for Lonely Planet's *Trans-Siberian Railway* guide in 2001 and returned in 2002 to coordinate this, the *War & Peace* of travel guides. Co-author of other Lonely Planet titles including *Istanbul to Kathmandu*, *South Africa*, *Cape Town*, *Central Asia* and *Walking in Australia*, Simon also writes for several other guidebook publishers, magazines and newspapers. He likes to call Sydney home, but seldom seems to be there.

Mark Elliott

Mark updated the Siberia section and researched parts of the new Urals chapter. He first fell in love with Eastern Europe when dragged most willingly by parental caravan to Romania aged 11. Since joining in Prague's 1989 Velvet Revolution, he has been venturing ever further east, criss-crossing the former Soviet Union where the warm-hearted welcome far outweighs the physical cold. He has hitchhiked across Kyrgyzstan with gun-toting drunkards and survived silly spying allegations while writing guidebooks to Azerbaijan. He now lives with the lovely Danielle, who he met while playing blues harmonica in a Turkmenistan club.

Patrick Horton

Patrick, travel writer and photographer, was born with restless feet. He travelled extensively in his native Britain before venturing on the around-the-world trail in 1985.

Fresh from delving into the mysteries of Serbia, Kosovo and Montenegro for Lonely Planet's *Eastern Europe* guide, he slipped into Russia's Caucasus region to research for this book.

Addicted to the arcane, Patrick's travels lead him to lesser-visited countries of the world such as North Korea, Eritrea, East Timor, Cuba and Tonga – or to a motorcycle ride over the Himalaya. Some day he aims to find the world's longest railway journey. His record so far is Helsinki (Finland) to Guilin (southern China), covering the epic Trans-Siberian Railway through Russia and Mongolia for another travel organisation on the way.

Patrick has contributed as an author to Lonely Planet's *Australia*, *Eastern Europe*, *Ireland*, *Delhi* and *India*, and has had many photographs published in other Lonely Planet guides. When there, he calls Melbourne home.

Steve Kokker

Steve wrote the Belarus chapters and the Kaliningrad section of this book and calls Montreal, Tallinn and St Petersburg home. Born in Montreal, he studied and worked in psychology before becoming a film critic for several newspapers. Figuring it's best to

live directly, not virtually, he moved to Tallinn, Estonia, his ances-
tral home. He's been with Lonely Planet since 1998, writing about
Russia, Estonia, Latvia and Lithuania, and has written guides to
Russia's culture capital St Petersburg and Canada's French capital
Quebec.

Baty Landis

Baty updated the Western European Russia chapter of this book. A
native of New Orleans, Baty has recently moved back to her home-
town to dig into her writing and complete a dissertation on Soviet
opera. Her musical passions were amply rewarded in Russia, where
she was thrilled to find local orchestras in the smallest towns and
to walk along paths once trod by the great Russian and Soviet composers. Having recently discovered that her great-grandmother was
from Russia, Baty also spent long hours peering into the eyes of
portraits lining the Hermitage hallways, looking for family resem-
blances she fully expected to find among the nobility.

Wendy Taylor

Born in Anchorage, Alaska, Wendy's affinity for vast snowy landscapes started at an early age. But it was not until the mid-to late
1980s, when her sense of humour gradually became black and
sick, and her penchant for high drama skyrocketed, that she ful-
filled all requirements for the perfect Russophile.

After studying in Moscow and graduating from UC Berkeley with
a degree in Slavic Languages & Literatures, she returned to live in
Moscow, working as an editor for the *Moscow Times*, the *Moscow
Tribune* and the Russian Academy of Sciences. Then she came
home and joined the LP forces, ending her three-year in-house appearance as an editor with this writing assignment, updating the
Northern European Russia chapter. She now devotes her drama-
queen sensibilities to acting, and somehow cobbles together an
existence with freelance work and unemployment cheques – as well
as the occasional acting or stand-up comedy stint.

Mara Vorhees

Mara updated Moscow, Around Moscow, the Volga Region, and
parts of The Urals chapters. Mara was born and raised in St Clair
Shores, Michigan. Her fascination with world cultures and her
penchant for good deeds led her into the field of international development and she set out to assist Russia in its economic
transition. After two years in the field, mainly spent fighting with
the tax police (and losing), she resorted to seeing and saving
the world by other means. The pen-wielding traveller has since
worked on Lonely Planet guides to the *Trans-Siberian Railway*,
Eastern Europe and *Moscow*. When not traipsing around the
former Soviet bloc, she resides in Somerville, Massachusetts,
with her husband and her cat. She still dabbles in international
development.

FROM THE AUTHORS

Simon Richmond

A hearty thanks to my fellow authors and the team of editors who've all contributed their considerable knowledge of Russia to help make this edition the best ever. Well done comrades! Mara and Wendy – I'll particularly cherish our mini-Moscow summit and toasting dawn over the Kremlin. Also a special thanks to Leonid Ragozin, Man about Moscow and best fact-checker in all of Russia – *spasibo* for keeping it all *pravda*.

In St Petersburg, many thanks to the following for their help, various insights and fun times: Peter Kozyrev, Steve Caron, Valudya Kovalev, Paul and Erica Marsh, Jan Krc, James Doty, Irina Volkova, Yegor Churakov, Nikolay Zag, Peter Morley and Chris Hamilton.

In the Russian Far East, the following helped make a challenging trip go all that more smoothly and enjoyably: Alden Green, Alex Hamilton, Eugene Degtyarev, Marina, Irina, Dasha and Zina in Vladivostok; Nikolay, Andrei and Yelena at Lost World and (most of) my fellow Kamchatka tour companions; Mikhail Radokhleb and Viktor in Komsomolsk; Irina and Yevgeny for being such good company on the way to Tynda; Vyacheslav Ipatiev, Dennis and Tanya in Yakutsk; Kristina, Yelena, Galina and Seriyosha in Sakhalin. Finally, many thanks to Natasha and doctors Igor and Victor in Khabarovsk for coming to the rescue of my crook arm.

Mark Elliott

Thank you Paul, Ruslan and the lovely Dasha in Ufa; Igor in Chelyabinsk; Leonid in Magnitogorsk; Konstantin and Ernie in Yekaterinburg; Ludmila, Michael and the irrepressible Igor in Omsk; Shamil, Sergey, Jenny and the inspiring Nastya in Novosibirsk; meditative Minsalim, Yulia and the staff of Radio Ekspres in Tobolsk (yes, that's me on the jingle!); the two Olgas, Dmitry and Tihon in Tomsk; Alla in Barnaul; Dmitri from Biysk; Tole in Aktash; Valery and Vladimir in Onguday; Vitaly in Balyktuyul; Leonid in Tyungur; Milan and friends in Artybash; Lyuba and friends in Petropavlovka; Andrej, Urii, Vladimir, Yana, Dina and Yury in Krasnoyarsk; Irina in Norilsk; Maria, Aleksandr and Vasilly in Igarka; Rada, Vladik, Stefan, Hans and dozens more in Tuva; Natalya at Snow Leopard Camp; Valery in Abaza; Tatiana, Sergei and Matos in Abakan; Lidya in Bratsk; Rashit, Peter, Vladimir, Linny and Nikolai in Severobaikalsk; Viktor in Nizhneangarsk; Yury and Justyna in Irkutsk; Galina, Luda and the two Alyoshas in Ulan Ude; Sergei, Oleg and Jennifer in Chita; Jessica in Aginskoe; Neil in Moscow; Wieland in Brussels; the team at LP; the 'kids' in Shoreham and Dani everywhere.

Patrick Horton

My work would not have been possible without several people who acted as translators and guides to their cities and surroundings. I'd like to say a big thank you to the following people.

Anastasiya Glebova in Krasnodar, and her brother who tracked down Sergae Belov in Sochi for me.

Dan Hites in Sochi who through email suggested that Luba might translate for me. Luba was wonderful and packed me off to Pyatigorsk with enough sandwiches and boiled eggs for three days. Sergae Belov took me out to lunch and gave me the unattributable low-down on how Sochi really works.

By luck I met Nonna Kerkis in Pyatigorsk who introduced me to her sons Roman and Sergae Kerkis in Pyatigorsk, who study English at the local university. I went to their end-of-year concert and drinks party which ended with some unusual explanations of Australian life. Roman led me around the Mineral Spa Towns and I exhausted Sergae on the slopes of Dombay.

Also by luck I came across Aslam Tukhuzhev and Ivan Yarapolsky in a computer-game room in Nalchik; both helped me around Nalchik and in the Elbrus region.

Through Roman in Pyatigorsk, I met Galina Klinchaeva in Vladikavkaz. She took me out into the wilderness of North Ossetia's mountains, where we explored ancient burial tombs and were given fresh Ossetian beer by a very elderly schoolteacher in the Tsmity settlement. Lastly, I'd like to pay thanks to Liz Filleul, who gave me some interesting and challenging assignments in her time at Lonely Planet.

Steve Kokker

In Kaliningrad, thanks to Misha and Albert at Baltma Tours, to Olga Danilov, a most delightful travel companion, and to Natasha at the newspaper kiosk in Hotel Kaliningrad. In Brest, hats off to the incredible Zhanna Volkovicha at Belintourist, and thanks to Dennis Voronov. In Hrodna, heartfelt appreciation to Deacon Valera, a model for me of the near-perfect human being, and to Igor. In Turov, thanks to Natalia Bambiza, to the fun and helpful trio Sergei Uglanets, Vladimir Struk and Aleksander Komar, and to Sergei Bashkov and the others who do such good work for poor children at the local church. In Minsk, thanks to Tatyana Shevstova and to Igor Popov who was a big help before his bizarre, ill-timed Great Disappearing Act. In Vitsebsk, thanks to Zhenya and Galina for an Easter that I'll never forget. Ever. Final thanks to Etienne and Nick from London for being great companions and moonshine-drinking partners.

Baty Landis

Thanks first of all to my hosts in Moscow and St Petersburg: Olga Frolova, Kostya Kalinin, Victor Peters, Yulia Berba, Robert Mulcahy, and Lena, Regina, and Dina Strona – and to Simon Morrison for setting me up with all of them. Briefer but equally crucial assistance came from Ina Zelenina (Novgorod), Irina Gutman (who treated me to my one true Russian *banya*, in Pskov), the ladies at the Khrennikov Museum in Yelets, Svetlana Khadrankova (Smolensk), and the Fredel family (Yelets). I'd also like to thank my mum, who critically contributed cold-weather wear, bought at the 11th hour, made of fabrics I had never heard of but without which a southern girl like me could never have survived the Russian thaw.

Wendy Taylor

I'd like to thank coauthors Simon Richmond and Mara Vorhees for that raucous last night in Moscow. (Simon: I don't think I'll ever get that stain out of my skirt.) Also, many thanks to Liz Filleul of the Melbourne Lonely Planet office and sweetheart Imogen Franks in the London office for their patience and support during this project.

On the road, I discovered many little treasures: JJ Gurga and Lucinda Grynzenia made a day spent in Kem an unforgettable adventure in saunas and vodka; they also were great for tips on Petrozavodsk. Lisa, Adam and Attila (aka Buddha) got me drunk and kept me company after a lonely week on the Kola Peninsula in return for getting them across the Norwegian border. (Sorry I don't have your last names – it was that kind of night.) Also, I'd like to thank expert travelers Peter and Liza Brandt, a lovely older British couple who – undaunted by freezing temperatures, unpredictable flights on a Yak-40, and no indoor plumbing – managed to spend a couple of exciting days on Solovki with me. My old pal and scoop *Moscow Times* reporter Simon Saradhzyan was a great source of information for the Kursk boxed text, and my dear friend and unsinkable Muscovite Andrei Sinelnikov helped me with all sorts of things on this project. Olga at Pasvikturist and the women of Petrozavodsk's Intourist office saved the day for me on more than one occasion.

Speaking of friends, I'd like to thank the following for their indispensable and well-timed morale boosts: Jared Matt 'Sleeves' Greenberg, for his sudden bursts of Mattliness and late-night pep talks; Joseph Barry 'the Barrister' Sollenberger, known for giving last-minute rides to the airport and for having a remarkable talent for mesmerising re-enactments of the final minutes of *Rocky II*; Tammy 'the Terror' Fortin, for her impromptu drumming lessons and never-ending ability to find a way to laugh at everything; and famed LP author and editor Vivek Wagle for listening to me worry about things nonstop and then uttering a few choice words to make me realise I'm just being daft. And to my mummy: thank you for not drowning me in the bathtub when I was six. I love you.

Mara Vorhees

Many thanks to Simon Richmond and coauthors for sharing the trials and triumphs (and vodka shots) that were required to produce this tome. Thanks also to Ryan Ver Berkmoes and Alevtina Chernorukova for their efforts on the second edition.

I am grateful for the loads of ideas, information and memories contributed by friends from Yekaterinburg, including Nadia Altukhova, Steve Harrison, Brook Hefright, Tim O'Brien, Bob Post, Tom Toomey, Samantha Yates and Pavel Yesin. Despite our rocky history, that place still holds a special place in my heart, and I hope I did it justice in this guide. I also received helpful hints and

14 The Authors

hospitality from Victor Orekhov and Natasha Ludosovaya in Moscow; Konstantin Brylyakov and colleagues in Yekaterinburg; Elizabeth Buchanan in Saratov; Benjamin Hanson, Anna Larina and Olga in Samara; Lola Hermasillo in Volgograd; and Mark Strong and Karla Ragland in Rostov.

Thanks to friends and family at home, especially Roy and Ruth Vorhees, for keeping me in your thoughts while I am away; and to Rob Faris and Theo Panayotou at CID, for letting me get away. And finally, to Jerry Easter, who may lose patience with Russia but never seems to lose it with me: спасибо и целую.

This Book

The coordinating author for this 3rd edition of *Russia & Belarus* was Simon Richmond. Simon updated the introductory chapters for European Russia and Siberia & the Russian Far East, as well as the St Petersburg, Around St Petersburg and Russian Far East chapters. Baty Landis contributed the Russian Arts section to the Facts about European Russia chapter and updated Western European Russia with Steve Kokker (who did the Kaliningrad section). Steve updated the introductory Belarus chapters, as well as Minsk and Elsewhere in Belarus. Mara Vorhees updated the Moscow, Around Moscow and Volga Region chapters as well as the first half of The Urals chapter and the Rostov-on-Don section of the Caucasus chapter. Patrick Horton updated the rest of the Caucasus chapter. Mark Elliott updated the Siberia chapter and the second half of The Urals chapter. Wendy Taylor updated the Northern European Russia chapter. All authors contributed to the Russia's Top 50 Experiences special section.

FROM THE PUBLISHER

This 3rd edition of *Russia & Belarus* was produced at Lonely Planet's Melbourne office. Simon Sellars coordinated the editing and proofing and Jack Gavran coordinated the mapping. Tamsin Wilson was the layout designer and and Simon Bracken designed the cover. Quentin Frayne compiled the language chapter.

Assisting Simon with editing and proofing were Carolyn Bain, Carolyn Boicos, Francesca Coles, Melanie Dankel, Bruce Evans, Martin Heng, Evan Jones, Craig MacKenzie, Anne Mulvaney, Diana Saad, Elizabeth Swan, Helen Yeates and Isabelle Young.

Assisting Jack with mapping were Csanad Csutoros, Hunor Csutoros, James Ellis, Tony Fankhauser, Cris Gibcus, Mark Griffiths, Valentina Kremenchutskaya, Kusnandar, Adrian Persoglia, Jolyon Philcox, Jacqui Saunders, Julie Sheridan, Amanda Sierp, Linda Suttie, Chris Thomas, Natasha Velleley and Jodie Whiteoak.

The book was commissioned by Liz Filleul in the Melbourne office, with subsequent development by Imogen Franks in the London office. Eoin Dunlevy was the project manager, assisted by Huw Fowles. Special thanks to managing editors Bruce Evans and Martin Heng, layout managers Kate McDonald and Adriana Mammarella, and managing cartographer Mark Griffiths for expertly shepherding the book through the various stages of production.

THANKS
Many thanks to the travellers who used the last edition and wrote to us with helpful hints, advice and interesting anecdotes. Your names appear in the back of this book.

15

Foreword

ABOUT LONELY PLANET GUIDEBOOKS

The story begins with a classic travel adventure: Tony and Maureen Wheeler's 1972 journey across Europe and Asia to Australia. There was no useful information about the overland trail then, so Tony and Maureen published the first Lonely Planet guidebook to meet a growing need.

From a kitchen table, Lonely Planet has grown to become the largest independent travel publisher in the world, with offices in Melbourne (Australia), Oakland (USA), London (UK) and Paris (France).

Today Lonely Planet guidebooks cover the globe. There is an ever-growing list of books and information in a variety of media. Some things haven't changed. The main aim is still to make it possible for adventurous travellers to get out there – to explore and better understand the world.

At Lonely Planet we believe travellers can make a positive contribution to the countries they visit – if they respect their host communities and spend their money wisely. Since 1986 a percentage of the income from each book has been donated to aid projects and human rights campaigns, and, more recently, to wildlife conservation.

> Although inclusion in a guidebook usually implies a recommendation we cannot list every good place. Exclusion does not necessarily imply criticism. In fact there are a number of reasons why we might exclude a place – sometimes it is simply inappropriate to encourage an influx of travellers.

UPDATES & READER FEEDBACK

Things change – prices go up, schedules change, good places go bad and bad places go bankrupt. Nothing stays the same. So, if you find things better or worse, recently opened or long-since closed, please tell us and help make the next edition even more accurate and useful.

Lonely Planet thoroughly updates each guidebook as often as possible – usually every two years, although for some destinations the gap can be longer. Between editions, up-to-date information is available in our free, monthly email bulletin *Comet* (**w** www.lonelyplanet.com/newsletters). You can also check out the *Thorn Tree* bulletin board and *Postcards* section of our website, which carry unverified, but fascinating, reports from travellers.

Tell us about it! We genuinely value your feedback. A well-travelled team at Lonely Planet reads and acknowledges every email and letter we receive and ensures that every morsel of information finds its way to the relevant authors, editors and cartographers.

Everyone who writes to us will find their name listed in the next edition of the appropriate guide-book. The very best contributions will be rewarded with a free guidebook.

We may edit, reproduce and incorporate your comments in Lonely Planet products such as guidebooks, websites and digital products, so let us know if you don't want your comments reproduced or your name acknowledged.

How to contact Lonely Planet:
Online: **e** talk2us@lonelyplanet.com.au, **w** www.lonelyplanet.com
Australia: Locked Bag 1, Footscray, Victoria 3011
UK: 72 – 82 Rosebery Ave, Clerkenwell, London EC1R 4RW
USA: 150 Linden St, Oakland, CA 94607

Russia's Top 50 Experiences

MARK NEWMAN

Breathtaking crater lake, Kamchatka Peninsula

As you'd expect of the world's largest country, Russia is not short on interesting places to visit and things to do. Here we nominate our 50 favourite Russian experiences – for other great ideas on what to do check the highlights at the start of each of the destination chapters.

MUST-SEE CITIES

Moscow Witness modern Russia in the nation's sacred and profane capital. Tick off the historic sights and museums, party at the latest club or sup at its excellent range of restaurants – just don't miss out on the Moscow experience.

St Petersburg Peter the Great's city on the Neva River is a world-class beauty. Grand architecture, cultural refinement and the hedonistic, sophisticated and resilient residents will all leave a lasting impression.

Irkutsk Once known as the Paris of Siberia, Irkutsk still has considerable charm and grace. Here you'll find many wooden gingerbread houses and museums dedicated to the exiled Decembrists.

Yekaterinburg Packed with museums, a fine range of hotels and restaurants, and interesting architecture, this Urals city is where some of the most important scenes in modern Russian history were played out.

Novgorod Crucible of Russian history, Novgorod has some diverse and beautiful architecture, the best examples being within its restored kremlin, where the Byzantine Cathedral of St Sophia is possibly the oldest building in Russia.

NATURAL WONDERS

Lake Baikal, Eastern Siberia The world's oldest and deepest lake is the sapphire jewel of Siberia. Head to the remote northern end, fringed by jagged mountains, to see Baikal at its most beautiful.

Lapland Biosphere Reserve, Kola Peninsula If you want to experience the Arctic tundra at its most pristine, head to this Unesco-protected reserve, home to Europe's largest concentration of reindeer.

Kamchatka At Russia's far eastern extremity, this 'land of fire and ice' lives up to its reputation, with some 200-plus snowcapped volcanoes, many still bubbling away, and vast areas of unexplored wilderness.

JOHN S KING

St Basil's Cathedral, Moscow

JEFF GREENBERG

Grand Cascade, St Petersburg

SIMON RICHMOND

Reindeer, Lake Baikal

CHRISTINA DAMEYER

Church of Emperor Constantine, Suzdal

JONATHAN SMITH

Mosaic on a St Petersburg mosque

JEFF GREENBERG

Transfiguration Cathedral, Kizhi Island

Altay Mountains, Altay Republic This remote World Heritage–listed mountain range is a kind of Central Asian Shangri-la. Rafting and hiking are the main reasons for visiting; the intrepid traveller will want to tackle Mt Belukha, Siberia's highest peak at 4506m.

Caucasus Mountains Rustic Dombay is the base for this spectacular mountain range, which includes the 5642m Mt Elbrus. Come for the scenery, the superb summer wildflowers, and the fascinating mix of ancient and modern cultures.

RELIGIOUS SITES

Suzdal The centuries seem to have bypassed this lovely Golden Ring town, set beside the gracefully meandering Kamenka River, and chock-full of dazzling onion-domed churches and ancient monasteries.

Involginsk Datsan, Ulan Ude This riotously colourful temple is the centre of Buddhism in Russia and a focal point for the Buryat people of Siberia. Other *datsans* at Tsugol and Anginskoe can be visited from Chita.

Mosques, Kazan & St Petersburg Within the white-washed walls of the kremlin, the enormous Kul Sharif Mosque is a recent addition to the World Heritage–listed fortress. Equally impressive is the the turquoise-tiled mosque in St Petersburg modelled on Samarkand's Gur Emir Mausoleum.

Trinity Monastery of St Sergius, Sergiev Posad Immerse yourself in the heady atmosphere of the Russian Orthodox Church at this spiritual and historical place of pilgrimage, an easy day trip from Moscow.

Kizhi Island, Lake Onega, Karelia Republic Once a pagan ritual site, it is now home to the remarkable, Unesco-proected Transfiguration Cathedral, a fairy-tale marvel of traditional wooden architecture.

ARTISTIC TREASURES

The Hermitage, St Petersburg It will take you several days to do justice to the huge and justifiably famous collection of art based in several splendid tsarist palaces along the Neva River.

Russian Museum, St Petersburg Another must-see gallery, in the former Mikhailovsky Palace, focussing on Russian masterpieces, including classic works by Ivanov, Surikov and Repin.

Tretyakov Gallery, Moscow Home to the world's best collection of Russian icons, plus an outstanding collection of pre-revolutionary art, the Tretyakov is housed in a striking building inspired by the design of an old Russian castle.

Dostoevsky Museums, St Petersburg & Omsk You've read the books, now find out more about one of the giants of Russian literature at the Dostoevsky Museum in St Petersburg, where the writer died in 1881, and the quirky Literature Museum in the Western Siberian city of Omsk, where he was exiled for four years.

Pogankin Chambers & Museum, Pskov In the fortresslike home of a 17th-century merchant, view a remarkable series of icons depicting the life of Christ, most from Pskov churches that have been shut down.

State Hermitage, St Petersburg

MARVELLOUS MUSEUMS

Krasnoyarsk Regional Museum, Krasnoyarsk Housed in an incongruous Egyptian-style building is this ultracontemporary museum, dominated by a full-sized replica of a Cossack boat. It also has excellent displays on the various peoples of the region.

Kremlin's Armoury, Moscow Comprising an eye-boggling collection of treasures and baubles amassed through the centuries, the armoury includes tsarist regalia, Fabergé eggs and a hoard of multi-carat diamonds.

Permafrost Museum, Igarka Go 10m deep into the frozen earth at this almost unique museum (there's also the Permafrost Institute in Yakutsk) in a small town on the Yenisey River, within the Arctic Circle.

Architecture Museum, Nizhnyaya Sinyachikha, Ural Mountains The stone cathedral amid this group of traditional Siberian log buildings displays a remarkable folk art collection. Visit other good open-air ethnographic museums in Nizhny Novgorod, Bratsk, Listvyanka and Ulan Ude.

Tretyakov Gallery, Moscow

Museum of Youth, Yekaterinburg Among Yekaterinburg's many museums, this is the most original. The surreal displays, created by local art students, tell the traumatic story of Russia's contemporary history.

HERITAGE SITES

All-Russia Exhibition Centre (VDNKh), Moscow The socialist-dream pavilions and enormous kitsch statues of this monument to the USSR's achievements provide a

Tsar Cannon, Kremlin, Moscow

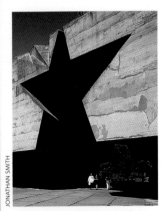

JONATHAN SMITH

Brest Fortress WWII Memorial

SIMON RICHMOND

Stone kremlin, Tobolsk

MARTIN MOOS

Part of the Trans-Siberian, Irkutsk

fascinating contrast to the discount shops and fun fair, which now inhabit the site.

Yusopov Palace, St Petersburg Among the many grand tsarist-era palaces in Russia, this jewel-box of a residence is a standout example of restoration and conservation. Plus it has the delicious notoriety of being the scene of Rasputin's gruesome assassination.

WWII Memorials Volgograd's towering Mamaev Kurgan (Mother Russia) statue, standing guard for the victims of the Battle of Stalingrad, is one of the most impressive of Russia's many WWII memorials. Also pay your respects at St Petersburg's Monument to the Heroic Defenders of Leningrad, and the Brest Fortress in Belarus.

Vladivostok's Fortresses Several in this series of early-20th-century fortresses surrounding the Russian Far East port and naval base can now be explored. Vladivostok itself, a raffish, bustling place, has one of the most striking locations of any city in Russia.

Tomsk & Tobolsk Bypassed by the Trans-Siberian Railway, these historic Siberian towns shed light on the region's heritage. Tomsk has an incredible collection of ornate wooden buildings and Siberia's oldest university; Tobolsk's jewel is its handsome stone kremlin.

GREAT JOURNEYS

Cross Russia on the Trans-Siberian Railway Take time out to enjoy a memorable week travelling across Russia on the Trans-Siberian Railway between Moscow and Vladivostok, or head to Beijing on the weekly Trans-Mongolian Railway (via Ulan Baatar, Mongolia) or the Trans-Manchurian Railway (via Harbin, China).

Discover Deep Siberia on the BAM Beginning west of Irkutsk and passing north of Lake Baikal on its slow, slow journey to the Pacific coast, the Baikal–Amur Mainline (BAM) passes through some of the remotest and most scenic parts of Siberia. Crossing the 1km-long Bratsk Dam is a highlight.

Chug along the Circumbaikal Railway This 94km-long track along the southern shore of Lake Baikal is an engineering wonder, taking in 39 tunnels and 200 bridges. Now a neglected branch line, it's possible to hike part or all of its length.

Cruise the Volga River A cruise down the languid Volga, the mother of all Russian rivers, will take you past some key Russian cities, including Nizhny Novgorod, Kazan, Volgograd and Astrakhan.

Sail to the Solovetsky Islands Understand the meaning of exile as you journey to these far northern Russian islands, scene of Alexander Solzhenitsyn's *Gulag Archipelago*. Their haunting, remote beauty is a counterpoint to their troubled history.

OUTDOOR ACTIVITIES

Watch the Birds The Unesco-recognised Kurshkaya Kosa, in the Kaliningrad region, is a beautiful spit of sand dunes and pine forests. It's home to Russia's first national park and a fascinating bird-ringing centre on the site of the world's first ornithological station.

Setting sun, Volga River

Raft the Rivers The Katun River in the Altay Republic provides some of Russia's most challenging white-water rafting, with rapids up to grade 4. Other rafting hot spots include those around Vladivostok and Kamchatka.

Ski the Hills Cross-country skiing is popular everywhere in winter, but for some downhill action head to Kirovsk in northern European Russia, Magnitogorsk in the southern Ural Mountains, and Krasnaya Polyana in the Caucasus. For the ultimate thrill go heli-skiing on Kamchatka's volcanoes.

Take a Hike There's ideal hiking country in the Caucasus or Altay Mountains, and around Lake Baikal, with beautiful scenery and largely unspoiled tracts of nature.

Alibek River, Dombay

Cast a Line The Russian Far East, in particular, is an angler's paradise, with rivers swollen with grayling and various species of salmon. Fishing excursions can be arranged departing from Khabarovsk, Vladivostok and Petropavlovsk-Kamchatsky.

INDULGENCES & SPECIAL EVENTS

White Nights in St Petersburg Join the native revellers as they party away the white nights of June and July on the banks of the Neva, watching the bridges rise in the small hours to let the ships sail by.

A Night at the Ballet or Opera Soak up the glittering decor and electric atmosphere of Moscow's Bolshoi, St Petersburg's Mariinksy, or Novosibirsk's Opera & Ballet Theatre (Russia's largest), then settle back to enjoy world-class performances.

Azau cable car, Mt Elbrus

JONATHAN SMITH

Victory Day poster, St Petersburg

Victory Day Parades The days of tanks and cruise missiles trundling through Red Square may be over, but your blood will still be stirred by the military and citizens marching together on 9 May to celebrate Russia's proud triumph in WWII.

Naadym in Tuva Long-distance horse-racing, wrestling and the beguiling throat-singing of the Tuvans are all part of this colourful festival held in July.

Dine on Caviar, Astrakhan Take a 'delicacy tour' from Astrakhan into the Volga River delta – a treasure trove of flora and fauna, where you can sample black sturgeon caviar fresh from the Caspian Sea.

QUINTESSENTIAL RUSSIAN EXPERIENCES

Sweat it Out in a *Banya* A combination of dry sauna, steam bath, massage and plunges into ice-cold water, the *banya* is a weekly event that is a regular part of Russian life. Moscow's Sandunovskiye Baths are among the grandest.

SIMON RICHMOND

Sandunovskiye Baths, Moscow

Meet Father Frost Journey back in time to the quaint town of Veliky Ustiug, the picture-perfect home of Father Frost, Russia's own Santa Claus. Audiences with the mighty wizard are granted by appointment.

Eat, Drink & Be Merry! Across the country one of your more memorable experiences will be partying Russian-style. Break open the vodka, dig into the *zakuski* (appetisers) and get ready to dance, sing and generally let your hair down.

Go Mushroom Picking near a Dacha A weekend trip to the country home – the dacha – is a Russian ritual. If you receive an invitation, expect to take part in the hunt for edible fungi, another Slavic passion.

Relax at a Sochi Sanatorium If you want to experience a holiday as many Russians do, check into one of Sochi's grand sanatoriums; you'll need to book. Some are mini-Romanov palaces, with manicured grounds, private beaches, swimming pools and tennis courts.

GEORGI S SHABLOVSKY

Russian alcohol on display

Introduction

You can't understand Russia with reason...you can only believe in her.

Fyodor Tyutchev

There's something about Russia that requires blind faith. How to get your head around a country where the rusting remains of a Gulag death camp lie eight time zones (half the world) away from St Petersburg's glittering palaces? How to compare the lives of a Tuva shaman with a night-clubbing computer programmer in Moscow? Don't try – just believe.

The world's largest country encompasses all the pleasure and pain of the human condition, with the last decade's social and economic revolutions giving a dynamic – and disastrous – spin to Russian lives. A solid middle class, bubbling with energetic, broad-minded entrepreneurs, is firmly entrenched in the major cities, but you certainly don't have to go far to find poverty, corruption, disillusionment and conflict.

Travellers passing through Russia's dramatic human landscape will also be confronted by equally show-stopping physical elements: Europe's tallest peak, Mt Elbrus, in the spectacular Caucasus; the fertile plains alongside the Volga, Europe's longest river; Siberia's endless taiga (forests), home to

Lake Baikal's azure jewel; Kamchatka's bubbling volcanoes and spurting geysers.

For the first time in Russian history, the country is wide open for anyone to visit. From ballet at the Bolshoi in Moscow, to whitewater rafting in the Altay Mountains (or trundling across country on a Trans-Siberian train), Russia's range of holiday possibilities is limitless. While President Putin's economic can-do ethos hasn't entirely supplanted the bureaucratic Soviet mentality of yesteryear, your biggest challenge will be budgeting – not so much your money, but your time. With patience, diligence and a big sense of adventure you can get almost anywhere.

This book comes in three parts: European Russia, covering the area west of the Ural Mountains; Siberia and the Russian Far East; and Belarus, a core republic of the old Soviet Union and the nation with arguably the closest geographical and cultural ties to Russia.

European Russia contains four-fifths of Russia's population, as well as Moscow and St Petersburg, the country's two major cities. It stretches from the Arctic Kola Peninsula – a land of 24-hour sunlight in summer and deeply frozen winters – to the Caucasus mountains, striding from the Black Sea to the Caspian Sea. A composite of old Russia's

RUSSIA & BELARUS

1	Estonia	10	Moldova
2	Latvia	11	Georgia
3	Lithuania	12	Azerbaijan
4	Minsk	13	Armenia
5	Poland	14	Uzbekistan
6	Kyiv	15	Turkmenistan
7	Slovakia	16	Kyrgyzstan
8	Hungary	17	Tajikistan
9	Romania	18	Afghanistan

extravagant glories and communism's drab legacy, European Russia is the birthplace of the Orthodox Church and rusting industrial cities, millions of people who still work the land, and flashy capitalists making the most of the anything-goes post-Soviet era.

Siberia, a place of snowbound exile for generations, has its share of industrial development and cities, but remains mostly untamed and empty of people. The home of the world's longest train ride, Siberia is also dotted with some of the planet's natural wonders: the exquisite Altay Mountains; serene Lake Baikal, the world's deepest, perhaps most beautiful lake; the primeval land of Kamchatka; and unexpected pockets of non-Russian culture, such as the Buddhist Buryats or the shamanist Yakuts and Tuvans.

Belarus shares a heritage with Russia dating to the 9th century and the founding of the Kyivan Rus state. Most of Belarus was part of the Russian Empire for over a century before it became one of the founding members of the USSR in 1922, and an independent state in 1991. While Alexander Lukashenka's authoritarian presidency makes the country an unlikely place for a holiday, its capital, Minsk, is an increasingly cosmopolitan city; Hrodna, Vitsebsk and Brest have a timeless charm; and the countryside retains a haunting, old-fashioned beauty.

To explore both Russia and Belarus, all you need is a sense of curiosity and, when appropriate, small measures of caution, determination and tolerance of discomfort. Take heart: you'll not only share Russia's famous love of suffering, but also its devotion to partying and hospitality.

It is precisely the Russian people's endearing combination of gloom and high spirits, rudeness and warmth, secrecy and openness that makes journeying through their country such a different experience. So leave behind your preconceptions – come shed your own shaft of light on the country famously described by Winston Churchill as 'a riddle wrapped in a mystery inside an enigma'.

Facts about European Russia

European Russia – west of the Ural Mountains – comprises only a quarter of Russia but is still bigger than any other European country. Four-fifths of Russia's population lives here on terrain stretching from the frozen tundra that borders the Arctic Ocean to the peaks of the Caucasus, Europe's highest mountains, 3000km south. Between these extremes lie Russia's two greatest cities: Moscow, in the historic heartland at the centre of European Russia, and St Petersburg, established 300 years ago on the Gulf of Finland as the country's gateway to Europe. In these two places tsars reigned and the world's greatest communist state was born, Russia's unique architecture developed, and the Russian Orthodox Church flourished.

Here too, the impact of all the recent modern changes is most evident – as any traveller can experience in hotels, shops and restaurants or while sampling the nightlife. Within a few hundred kilometres of these cities are dozens of smaller places where you can witness the country's historic grandeur together with the beauty of its gentle landscape and the perennial, bitter hardness of Russian life.

To the north lie tracts of forest, lakes, marshes and tundra – a vast and largely unexplored world for hikers, skiers and campers. As well, the north has the intriguing Arctic ports of Murmansk and Arkhangelsk, Kizhi Island with its extraordinary assemblage of old wooden architecture, remnants of Gulag labour camps and the venerable churches and monasteries of Vologda and elsewhere.

East from Moscow, then south, flows the Volga River. One of Russia's historic highways, the Volga links many cities of both ancient and modern importance – among them Yaroslavl, Nizhny Novgorod, Kazan, Saratov, Ulyanovsk, Volgograd (once Stalingrad) and Astrakhan – along its course to the Caspian Sea. Numerous ethnic minorities, whose religious beliefs range from Islam to Buddhism to animism, live in or near to the Volga basin, reminders of European Russia's proximity to Asia and the many former Soviet republics.

Forming a low barrier between European Russia and Siberia, the Ural Mountains stretch from Kazakhstan in the south to the Arctic Kara Sea in the north. Apart from opportunities to hike and undertake some gentle river rafting, here you'll find major cities such as historic Yekaterinburg and Chelyabinsk, from where you can travel to Russia's main downhill ski centre at Magnitogorsk.

The other great European Russian waterway, the Don River, flows south, from near Moscow to the Sea of Azov (an offshoot of the Black Sea, near Rostov-on-Don). South of here is a coastal riviera, along the Black Sea, to which Russians flock for summer holidays, while heading east is Russia's steppe, part of the great rolling grasslands (now largely given over to agriculture) that continue through to Mongolia.

The steppe gives way on European Russia's southern fringe to the Caucasus Mountains, a range of spectacular beauty and home to an incredible jigsaw of ethnic groups. Many of these people were not conquered by Russia until the 19th century; today, some are tragically mired in bloody conflicts with each other or with Russia, putting part of this region firmly off-limits to tourism.

HISTORY
Early History
European Russia's earliest known people inhabited the basin of the Don River around 20,000 BC. By 2000 BC a basic agriculture, relying on hardy cereals, had penetrated from the Danube region as far east as the Moscow area and the southern Ural Mountains. At about the same time, peoples in Ukraine and southern areas of European Russia domesticated the horse and developed a nomadic, pastoral lifestyle.

While central and northern European Russia remained a complete backwater for

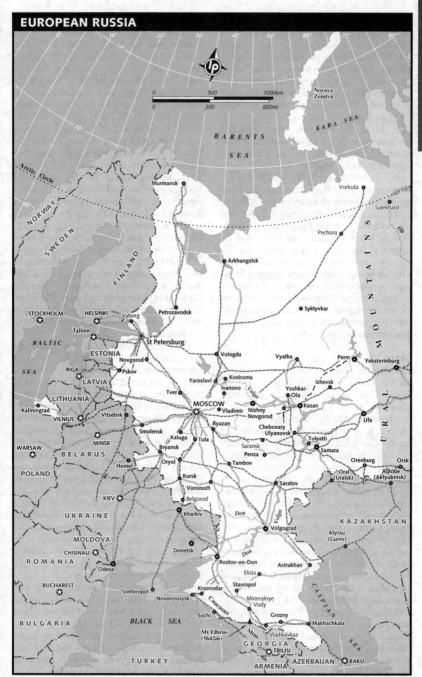

EUROPEAN RUSSIA

almost 3000 years, the south was subject to a succession of invasions by nomads from the east. The first written records, by the 5th century BC Greek historian Herodotus, concern a people called the Scythians, who probably originated in the Altay region of Siberia and Mongolia and were feared for their riding and battle skills. They spread as far west as southern Russia and Ukraine by the 7th century BC. The Scythian empire, which stretched south as far as Egypt, ended with the arrival of another people from the east, the Sarmatians, in the 3rd century BC.

The Sarmatians were followed in the 4th century AD by the Huns, also from the Altay region, then by the Huns' relations the Avars, then by the Khazars, a grouping of Turkic and Iranian tribes from the Caucasus, who occupied the lower Volga and Don basins and the steppes to the east and west between the 7th and 10th centuries. The crafty and talented Khazars brought stability and religious tolerance to areas under their control. Their capital was Itil, near the mouth of the Volga. In the 9th century they converted to Judaism. By the 10th century they had mostly settled down to farming and trade.

Slavs

The migrants who were to give Russia its predominant character, however, were the Slavs. There is some disagreement about where the Slavs originated, but in the first few centuries AD they expanded rapidly to the east, west and south from the vicinity of present-day northern Ukraine and southern Belarus. The Eastern Slavs were the ancestors of the Russians; they were still spreading eastward across the central Russian woodland belt in the 9th century. From the Western Slavs came the Poles, Czechs, Slovaks and others. The Southern Slavs became the Serbs, Croats, Slovenes and Bulgarians.

The Slavs' conversion to Christianity in the 9th and 10th centuries was accompanied by the introduction of an alphabet devised by Cyril, a Greek missionary (now St Cyril), and simplified a few decades later by a fellow missionary, Methodius. The forerunner of Cyrillic, it was based on the Greek alphabet, with a dozen or so additional characters. The Bible was translated into the Southern Slav dialect, which became known as Church Slavonic and is the language of the Russian Orthodox Church's liturgy to this day.

Vikings & Kyivan Rus

The crucial factor in the creation of the first Russian state was the potential for trade on river routes across Eastern Slavic areas – between the Baltic and Black Seas and, to a lesser extent, between the Baltic Sea and the Volga River. Vikings from Scandinavia, called Varyagi (Varangians) by the Slavs, had been nosing east from the Baltic since the 6th century AD, trading and raiding for furs, slaves and amber, and coming into conflict with the Khazars and with Constantinople (Istanbul), the eastern centre of Christianity, as they went. To secure their hold on the trade routes, the Vikings made themselves masters of settlements in key areas – places such as Novgorod, Smolensk and Kiev. Though by no means united themselves, they created a loose confederation of city-states in the Eastern Slavic areas.

The founding of Novgorod in 862 by Rurik of Jutland is traditionally taken as the birth of the Russian state. Rurik's successor, Oleg, became Kiev's ruler two decades later, and the Rurikid dynasty, though soon Slavicised, maintained its hold to produce the dominant rulers in Eastern Slavic areas until the end of the 16th century.

The name Rus may have been that of the dominant Kyivan Viking clan. In later years the term Russian or Great Russian came to be used for Eastern Slavs in the north, while those to the south or west were identified as Ukrainians or Belarusians.

Prince Svyatoslav made Kiev the dominant regional power by campaigning against quarrelling Varangian princes and dealing the Khazars a series of fatal blows. After his death, his son Vladimir made further conquests, and persuaded the Patriarch of Constantinople to establish an episcopal see – a Church 'branch' – in Kiev in 988, marking the birth of the Russian Orthodox Church. He also introduced the beginnings of a feudal structure to replace clan allegiances, though some principalities – including Novgorod, Pskov and Vyatka (north of Kazan) – were ruled democratically by popular *veches* (assemblies).

Kiev's supremacy was broken by new invaders from the east – first the Pechenegs, then the Polovtsy, who sacked Kiev in 1093 – and by the effects of European crusades from the late 11th century onwards, which broke the Arab hold on southern Europe and the Mediterranean, reviving west–east trade routes and making Rus a commercial backwater.

Rulers of Russia – Rurik to Putin

Following is a list of the major rulers of Russia and the Soviet Union. In line with common usage, rulers' names before 1700 are directly transliterated, but are anglicised from Peter the Great until 1917, and transliterated after that – thus Vasily not Basil, Mikhail not Michael, Alexey not Alexis; but Peter not Pyotr, Catherine not Yekaterina etc.

Ivan the Great was the first ruler to have himself formally called tsar. Peter the Great began using emperor, though tsar remained in use. In this book we use empress for a female ruler; a tsar's wife who does not become ruler is a *tsaritsa* (in English, tsarina). A tsar's son is a *tsarevich* and his daughter a *tsarevna*.

Rurik of Novgorod	862–82	Peter I & Ivan V	1689–96
Oleg of Kiev	882–912	Peter I (the Great)	1696–1725
Svyatoslav	962–72	Catherine I	1725–27
Vladimir I	980–1015	Peter II	1727–30
Yaroslav the Wise	1019–54	Anna	1730–40
Vladimir II Monomakh	1113–25	Elizabeth	1741–61
Yury Dolgoruky	1149–57	Peter III	1761–62
Andrey Bogolyubov	1157–74	Catherine II (the Great)	1762–96
Alexander Nevsky	1252–63	Paul I	1796–1801
Daniil of Moscow	1276–1303	Alexander I	1801–25
Ivan I (Kalita)	1325–40	Nicholas I	1825–55
Dmitry Donskoy	1359–89	Alexander II	1855–81
Ivan III (the Great)	1462–1505	Alexander III	1881–94
Vasily III	1505–33	Nicholas II	1894–1917
Yelena (Regent)	1533–47	Alexander Kerensky	1917
Ivan IV (the Terrible)	1547–84	Vladimir Lenin	1917–24
Fyodor I	1584–98	Josef Stalin	1929–53
Boris Godunov	1598–1605	Nikita Khrushchev	1957–64
False Dmitry	1605–06	Leonid Brezhnev	1964–82
Vasily Shuysky	1606–10	Yury Andropov	1982–84
Mikhail Romanov	1613–45	Konstantin Chernenko	1984–85
Alexey	1645–76	Mikhail Gorbachev	1985–91
Fyodor III	1676–82	Boris Yeltsin	1991–99
Peter I & Ivan V (Regent: Sofia)	1682–89	Vladimir Putin	2000–

Novgorod & Rostov-Suzdal

The northern Rus principalities began breaking from Kiev after about 1050. The merchants of Novgorod joined the emerging Hanseatic League, a federation of city-states that controlled Baltic and North Sea trade. Novgorod became the League's gateway to the lands east and southeast.

As Kiev declined, the Russian population shifted northwards and the fertile Rostov-Suzdal region northeast of Moscow began to be developed. Vladimir Monomakh of Kiev founded the town of Vladimir there in 1108 and gave the Rostov-Suzdal principality to his son Yury Dolgoruky, who is credited with founding the little settlement of Moscow in 1147.

Rostov-Suzdal grew so rich and strong that Yury's son Andrey Bogolyubov sacked Kiev in 1169 and moved the court to Vladimir. The Church's headquarters remained in Kiev until 1300. Rostov-Suzdal began to gear up for a challenge to the hold on the Volga-Ural Mountains region of the Bulgars. The Bulgars were a people who had originated farther east several centuries before and had since converted to Islam. Their capital, Bolgar, was near modern Kazan, on the Volga.

Tatars & the Golden Horde

It's hard to overstate the fear instilled by the Mongol-led Golden Horde, who thundered out of Asia in the 13th century. Within 30 years these horsemen built the largest land empire the world had ever seen, slaughtering as many as a quarter of their new subjects in the process.

Russians often refer to these mainly Mongol invaders as Tatars, when in fact the Tatars were simply one particularly powerful tribe that joined the Mongol bandwagon. The Tatars of Tatarstan actually descended from the Bulgars and are related to the Bulgarians of the Balkans. The leader was the Mongolian warlord Temuchin (1167–1227), from south of Lake Baikal in present-day eastern Siberia, who by 1206 had forged a powerful tribal alliance centred at Karakorum in present-day Mongolia, naming himself Jenghis Khan (Great Ruler).

After his armies overran north China and Korea they went west through Central Asia, Afghanistan, Iran and the Caucasus and into the plains between the Volga and the Don Rivers. There they met the armies of the Russian princes and thrashed them at the Battle of Kalka River in 1223. This push was cut short by the death of Jenghis Khan, but his grandson Batu Khan returned in 1236 to finish the job, laying waste to Bolgar and Rostov-Suzdal and annihilating most of the other Russian principalities, including Kiev, within four years. Novgorod was saved only by spring floods that prevented the invaders from crossing the marshes around the city.

Batu and his successors ruled the Golden Horde (one of the khanates into which the empire of Jenghis had broken) from Saray on the Volga, near modern Volgograd. The Horde's control over its subjects was indirect: although it raided them in traditional fashion if they grew uppity, it mainly used local princes to keep order, provide soldiers and collect taxes.

Alexander Nevsky & the Rise of Moscow

One such 'collaborator' was the Prince of Novgorod, Alexander Nevsky, a Russian hero (and later a saint of the Russian Church) for his resistance to invaders from the west (German crusaders and Swedes). His victory in 1240 over the Swedes on the Neva River, near present-day St Petersburg, earned him his nickname, 'Nevsky'. Later, Batu Khan put him on the throne as Grand Prince of Vladimir in 1252.

Nevsky and his successors acted as intermediaries between the Tatars and other Russian princes. With shrewd diplomacy, the princes of Moscow obtained and hung on to the title of Grand Prince from the early 14th century while other princes resumed their feuding. The Church provided backing to Moscow by moving there from Vladimir in the 1320s, and was in turn favoured with exemption from Tatar taxation.

But Moscow proved to be the Tatars' nemesis. With a new-found Russian confidence, Grand Prince Dmitry put Moscow at the head of a coalition of princes and took on the Tatars, defeating them in the Kulikovo Pole battle on the Don River in 1380. For this he became Dmitry Donskoy ('of the Don') and was canonised after his death.

The Tatars crushed this uprising in a three-year campaign but their days were numbered. Weakened by internal dissension, they fell at the end of the 14th century to the Turkic empire of Timur (Tamerlane), which was based in Samarkand. Yet the Russians, themselves divided as usual, remained Tatar vassals until 1480.

Moscow vs Lithuania

Moscow (or Muscovy, as its expanding lands came to be known) was champion of the Russian cause after Kulikovo, though it had rivals, especially Novgorod and Tver. More ominous was the rise of the Grand Duchy of Lithuania, which had started to expand into old Kyivan Rus lands in the 14th century. At first just a headache for Moscow, it became a threat in 1386 when the Lithuanian ruler Jogaila married the Polish queen Jadwiga and became king of Poland, thus joining two of Europe's most powerful states.

With Jogaila's coronation as Wladyslaw II of Poland, the previously pagan Lithuanian ruling class embraced Catholicism. The Russian Church portrayed the struggle against Lithuania as one against the Pope in Rome. After Constantinople (centre of the Greek Orthodox Church) was taken by the Turks in 1453, the metropolitan or head of the Russian Church declared Moscow the 'third Rome', the true heir of Christianity.

Meanwhile, with the death of Dmitry Donskoy's son in 1425, Muscovy suffered a dynastic war. The old Rurikids got the upper hand – ironically with Lithuanian and Tatar help – but it was only with Ivan III's forceful reign from 1462 to 1505 that the other principalities ceased to oppose Muscovy.

Ivan III (the Great)

Ivan III brought most of the Great Russian principalities to heel. Novgorod was first, in 1478, as it was no longer able to rely on the Tatars as a diversion. Two years later a Russian army faced the Tatars at the Ugra River southwest of Moscow. Though they parted without a fight, after that Ivan simply stopped paying tribute to the Golden Horde.

Tver fell to Moscow in 1485, and far-flung Vyatka in 1489. Pskov and Ryazan, the only states still independent at the end of Ivan's reign, were mopped up by his successor, Vasily III. Lithuania and Poland, however, remained thorns in Russia's side.

Servants & Serfs

When Ivan III took Novgorod he installed a governor, exiled the city's influential families and ejected the Hanseatic merchants, closing Russia's 'window on the West' for two centuries. The exiles were replaced with Ivan's administrators, who got temporary title to confiscated lands for good performance. This new approach to land tenure, called *pomestie* (estate), characterised Ivan's rule. Previously, the *boyars* (feudal landholders) had held land under a *votchina* (system of patrimony) giving them unlimited control and inheritance rights over their lands and the people on them. The freedom to shift allegiance to other princes had given them political clout, too. Now, with few alternative princes left, the influence of the *boyars* declined in favour of the new landholding civil servants.

This increased central control spread to the lower levels of society with the growth of serfdom. Before the 1500s, peasants could work for themselves after meeting their masters' needs, and could even change jobs during the two weeks around St George's Day in November. These rights were less frequently bestowed by the new masters, who lacked the old sense of obligation, and peasants became a permanent fixture on the land.

Ivan IV (the Terrible)

Vasily III's son, Ivan IV, took the throne in 1533 at age three, with his mother as regent. After 13 years of court intrigues he had himself crowned 'Tsar of all the Russias'. The word 'tsar', from the Latin *caesar*, had pre-

viously been used only for a Great Khan or for the Emperor of Constantinople.

Ivan IV's marriage to Anastasia, from the Romanov *boyar* family, was a happy one (unlike the five that followed her death in 1560, a turning point in his life). Believing her to have been poisoned, he instituted a reign of terror that earned him the sobriquet *grozny* (literally 'awesome' but in this case translated as 'Terrible') and nearly destroyed all his earlier good works. In a fit of rage he even killed his eldest son and heir, Ivan.

His subsequent career was indeed terrible, though he was admired for upholding Russian interests and tradition. During his active reign (1547–84) Russia defeated the surviving Tatar khanates of Kazan and Astrakhan, thus acquiring the whole Volga region and a chunk of the Caspian Sea coast and opening the way to Siberia. His campaign against the Crimean Tatars, however, nearly ended with the loss of Moscow.

Ivan's interest in the West and obsession with reaching the Baltic Sea foreshadowed Peter the Great, but he failed to break through, only antagonising the Lithuanians, Poles and Swedes, and setting the stage for the Time of Troubles. His growing paranoia led to a savage attack on Novgorod that finally snuffed out that city's golden age.

Boris Godunov & the Time of Troubles

When Ivan died of poisoning in 1584, rule passed to his second son, the hopeless Fyodor I, who had the sense to leave government to his brother-in-law, Boris Godunov, a skilled 'prime minister' who repaired much of Ivan's damage. Fyodor died childless in 1598, ending the 700-year Rurikid dynasty, and Boris ruled as tsar for seven more years.

Then a Polish-backed Catholic pretender arrived on the scene claiming to be Dmitry, another son of Ivan the Terrible, who had died in obscure circumstances – murdered on Boris Godunov's orders, some said. This 'False Dmitry' gathered a huge ragtag army as he advanced on Moscow. Boris Godunov conveniently died, his son was lynched and the *boyars* acclaimed the pretender tsar.

Thus began the Time of Troubles, or Smuta (1606–13), a spell of anarchy, dynastic chaos and foreign invasions. At its heart was a struggle between the *boyars* and central government (the tsar). The False Dmitry

The Cossacks

The word 'Cossack' (from the Turkic *kazak*, meaning free man, adventurer or horseman) was originally applied to residual Tatar groups and later to serfs, paupers and dropouts who fled south from Russia, Poland and Lithuania in the 15th century. They organised themselves into self-governing communities in the Don basin, on the Dnipro (Dnepr in Russian) River in Ukraine, and in western Kazakhstan. Those in a given region, eg, the Don Cossacks, were not just a tribe; its men constituted a *voysko* (army), within which each *stanitsa* (village-regiment) elected an ataman, or leader.

Mindful of their skill as fighters, the Russian government treated the Cossacks carefully, offering autonomy in return for military service. Cossacks were the wedge that opened Siberia in the 17th century. By the 19th century there were a dozen Cossack armies from Ukraine to the Russian Far East.

But they still raised hell when things didn't suit them. Three peasant uprisings in the Volga-Don region – 1670, 1707 and 1773 – were Cossack-led. After 1917 the Bolsheviks abolished Cossack institutions, though some cavalry units were revived in WWII.

★★★

was murdered in a popular revolt and succeeded by Vasily Shuysky (1606–10), another *boyar* puppet. A second False Dmitry (claiming to be both the previous Dmitrys) challenged Shuysky; Swedish and Polish invaders fought each other over claims to the Russian throne; Shuysky was dethroned by the *boyars*; and from 1610 to 1612 the Poles occupied Moscow.

Eventually a popular army, rallied by merchant Kuzma Minin and noble Dmitry Pozharsky, both from Nizhny Novgorod, with support from the Church, removed the Poles. In 1613 a Zemsky Sobor, or Assembly of the Land, with representatives of the political classes of the day, elected 16-year-old Mikhail Romanov tsar, the first of a new dynasty that was to rule until 1917.

17th-Century Russia

Though the first three Romanov rulers – Mikhail (1613–45), Alexey (1645–76) and Fyodor III (1676–82) – provided continuity and stability, there were also big changes that foretold the downfall of 'old' Russia.

Acquisitions The 17th century saw a huge growth in Russian lands. The 'opening' of Siberia, begun by the Stroganov merchant family and Cossack mercenaries under Ataman Yermak Timofeevich, remains one of history's biggest and most explosive territorial expansions. For more information, see Facts about Siberia & the Russian Far East for more details.

Additionally, when Cossacks in Ukraine appealed for help against the Poles, Tsar Alexey came to their aid, and in 1667 Kiev,

Smolensk and lands east of the Dnepr came under Russian control.

Serfdom Authority in the countryside collapsed during the Time of Troubles, with thousands of peasants fleeing to Cossack areas or to Siberia, where serfdom was unknown. Landlords, in despair, found support from the government. The peasants' right to move freely was abolished in 1646. In 1675 they lost all land rights and, in a uniquely Russian version of serfdom, could be sold separately from the estates they worked – slavery, in effect.

In 1670–71 Cossacks, runaway serfs and adventurers joined in a huge uprising in the Volga-Don region, led by the Cossack Stepan (Stenka) Razin. Razin's army of 200,000 seized the entire lower Volga basin before he was captured and killed. He remains a folk hero today.

The Church Internal conflicts transformed the Church into a friend of authority, distrusted as much as the government was. In the mid-17th century, Patriarch Nikon tried to bring rituals and texts into line with the 'pure' Greek Orthodox Church, horrifying those attached to traditional Russian forms.

The result was a bitter schism between Nikon's New Believers and Old Believers who, under government persecution, formed a widespread, occasionally fanatical religious underground. In the end Nikon himself was sacked by Tsar Alexey over the issue of Church authority in the newly acquired Ukrainian territories, while Old Believers survive to this day (for more information see Religion later in this chapter).

Peter the Great

Peter I, known as 'the Great' for his commanding 2.24m frame and his equally commanding victory over the Swedes, dragged Russia kicking and screaming into Europe, made it a major world power and insulted all his administrators and soldiers by shaving off their beards.

Born to Tsar Alexey's second wife in 1672, Peter spent much of his youth in royal residences in the countryside, organising his playmates into military regiments. Energetic, inquisitive and comfortable in any circle, he often visited Moscow's European district to learn about the West. Dutch and British ship captains in Arkhangelsk gave him navigation lessons on the White Sea.

When Fyodor III died in 1682, Peter became tsar, along with his feeble-minded half-brother Ivan V, under the regency of Ivan's ambitious sister, Sofia. She had the support of a leading statesman of the day, Prince Vasily Golitsyn. The *boyars*, annoyed by Golitsyn's institution of a stringent ranking system, schemed successfully to have Sofia sent to a monastery in 1689 and replaced as regent by Peter's unambitious mother.

Few doubted Peter as the true monarch, and when he became sole ruler, after his mother's death in 1694 and Ivan's in 1696, he embarked on a modernisation campaign, symbolised by his fact-finding mission to Europe in 1697–98 – he was the first Muscovite ruler ever to go there. Historical literature abounds with tales of his spirited visits to hospitals, workshops and trading houses, his stint as a ship's carpenter in Amsterdam and his hiring of some 1000 experts for service in Russia.

He was also busy negotiating alliances. In 1695 he had sent Russia's first navy down the Don River and captured the Black Sea port of Azov from the Crimean Tatars, vassals of the Ottoman Turks. His European allies weren't interested in the Turks but shared his concern about the Swedes, who held most of the Baltic coast and had penetrated deep into Europe.

Peter's alliance with Poland and Denmark led to the Great Northern War against Sweden (1700–21), the focal point of his career. The rout of Charles XII's forces at the Battle of Poltava (1709) heralded Russia's power and the collapse of the Swedish Empire. The Treaty of Nystadt (1721) gave Peter control of the Gulf of Finland and the eastern shores of the Baltic Sea and in the midst of this (1707), he put down another peasant rebellion, led by Don Cossack Kondraty Bulavin.

On land taken from the Swedes, Peter founded a new city, which he named St Petersburg after his patron saint. In 1712 he made it the capital, symbol of a new, Europe-facing Russia.

Peter's Legacy Peter succeeded in mobilising Russian resources to compete on equal terms with the West – a startling achievement. His territorial gains were small, but the strategic Baltic territories also added ethnic variety, including a new upper class of German traders and administrators who formed the backbone of Russia's commercial and military expansion.

Peter was also to have the last word on the authority of the Church. When it resisted his reforms he simply blocked the appointment of a new patriarch, put bishops under a government department and in effect became head of the Church himself.

Vast sums were needed to build St Petersburg, pay a growing civil service, modernise the army and launch naval and commercial fleets. But money was scarce in an economy based on serf labour, so Peter slapped taxes on everything from coffins to beards, including an infamous 'Soul Tax' on all lower-class adult males. The lot of serfs worsened, as they bore the main tax burden.

Even the upper classes had to chip in: aristocrats could either serve in the army or the civil service, or lose their titles and land. Birth counted for little, with state servants subject to Peter's Table of Ranks, a performance-based ladder of promotion, with the upper grades conferring hereditary nobility. Some aristocrats lost all they had, while capable state employees of humble origin, and even foreigners, became Russian nobles.

Peter died in 1725 without naming a successor, and the matter was again decided by intrigue and force. If it hadn't been for a government structure built on the Table of Ranks and a professional bureaucracy with a vested interest in its preservation, Peter's reforms might well have died with him.

After Peter

For 37 years after Peter's death, Russia suffered ineffectual rulers. Day-to-day administration was handled by a governing body called the Supreme Privy Council, staffed by many of Peter's leading administrators. Dominated by the Dolgoruky and Golitsyn *boyar* families, the council elected Peter's niece Anna of Courland (a small principality in present-day Latvia) to the throne, with a contract stating that the council had the final say in policy decisions. Anna ended this experiment in constitutional monarchy by disbanding the council.

Anna ruled from 1730 to 1740, appointing a Baltic German baron, Ernst Johann von Bühren, to handle affairs of state. His name was Russified to Biron, but his heavy-handed, corrupt style came to symbolise the German influence on the royal family that had begun with Peter the Great.

During the reign of Peter's daughter, Elizabeth (1741–61), German influence waned and restrictions on the nobility were loosened. Some aristocrats began to dabble in manufacture and trade.

Catherine II (the Great)

Daughter of a German prince, Catherine came to Russia at the age of 15 to marry Empress Elizabeth's heir-apparent, her nephew Peter III. Intelligent and ambitious, Catherine learned Russian, embraced the Orthodox Church and devoured the writings of European political philosophers. This was the time of the Enlightenment, when talk of human rights, social contracts and the separation of powers abounded.

Catherine later said of Peter III, 'I believe the Crown of Russia attracted me more than his person'. Six months after he ascended the throne she had him overthrown in a palace coup led by her current lover (it has been said that she had more lovers than the average serf had hot dinners); he was murdered shortly afterwards.

Enlightened Despotism Catherine embarked on a programme of reforms, though she made it clear that she had no intention of limiting her own authority. She drafted a new legal code, limited the use of torture and supported religious tolerance. But any ideas she might have had of improving the lot of serfs went overboard with the rebellion of 1773–74, led by the Don Cossack Yemelyan Pugachev.

Pugachev claimed he was Peter III. His rebellion, which spread from the Ural Mountains to the Caspian Sea and along the Volga,

was Russia's most violent peasant uprising. Hundreds of thousands responded to his promises to end serfdom and taxation, but were beaten by famine and government armies. Pugachev was executed and Catherine put an end to Cossack autonomy.

In the cultural sphere, Catherine increased the number of schools and colleges and expanded publishing. Her vast collection of paintings forms the core of the present-day Hermitage collection. A critical elite gradually developed, alienated from most uneducated Russians but also increasingly at odds with central authority – a 'split personality' common among future Russian radicals.

Territorial Gains Catherine's reign saw major expansion at the expense of the weakened Ottoman Turks and Poles, engineered by her 'prime minister' and foremost lover, Grigory Potyomkin. War with the Turks began in 1768, peaked with the naval victory at Çesme (Chesma) and ended with a 1774 treaty giving Russia control of the north coast of the Black Sea, freedom of shipping through the Dardanelles to the Mediterranean and 'protectorship' of Christian interests in the Ottoman Empire – a pretext for later incursions into the Balkans. Crimea was annexed in 1783.

Poland had spent the previous century collapsing into semi-independent units with a figurehead king in Warsaw. Catherine manipulated events with divide-and-rule tactics and even had a former lover, Stanislas Poniatowski, installed as king. Austria and Prussia proposed sharing Poland among the three powers, and in 1772, 1793 and 1795 the country was carved up, ceasing to exist as an independent state until 1918. Eastern Poland and the Grand Duchy of Lithuania – roughly, present-day Lithuania, Belarus and western Ukraine – came under Russian rule.

Alexander I

When Catherine died in 1796 the throne passed to her son, Paul I. A mysterious figure in Russian history (often called the Russian Hamlet by Western scholars), he antagonised the gentry with attempts to reimpose compulsory state service, and was killed in a coup in 1801.

Paul's son and successor, Alexander I, Catherine's favourite grandson, who had been trained by the best European tutors, kicked off his reign with several reforms, including an expansion of the school system that brought education within reach of the lower middle classes. But he was soon preoccupied with the wars against Napoleon, which were to dominate his career.

After Napoleon defeated him at Austerlitz, north of Vienna, in 1805 and then at Friedland, near modern Kaliningrad, Alexander came to the negotiating table. The Treaty of Tilsit (1807) left Napoleon in charge as Emperor of the West and Alexander as Emperor of the East, united (in theory) against England.

1812 & Aftermath The alliance lasted only until 1810, when Russia resumed trade with England. With his Grand Army of 700,000 – the largest force the world had ever seen for a single military operation – a furious Napoleon decided to crush the tsar.

The vastly outnumbered Russian forces retreated across their own countryside through the summer of 1812, scorching the earth in an attempt to deny the French sustenance and fighting some successful rearguard actions. Napoleon set his sights on Moscow, the symbolic heart of Russia. In September, with the lack of provisions beginning to bite on the French, the Russian general Mikhail Kutuzov finally decided to turn and fight at Borodino, 130km from Moscow. The battle was extremely bloody, but inconclusive, with the Russians withdrawing in good order.

Before the month was out, Napoleon entered a deserted Moscow; the same day, the city began to burn down around him (whether by Russian or French hand, or by accident, has never been established). Alexander ignored his overtures to negotiate. With winter coming and his supply lines overstretched, Napoleon ordered a retreat – he was unable to do anything else. His troops starved and were picked off by Russian partisans. Only one in 20 made it back to the relative safety of Poland, and the Russians pursued them all the way to Paris.

At the Congress of Vienna, where the victors met in 1814–15 to establish a new order after Napoleon's final defeat, Alexander championed the cause of the old monarchies. His legacies were a hazy Christian fellowship of European kings, called the Holy Alliance, and a system of pacts to guard against future Napoleons – or any revolutionary change.

More Territorial Gains Meanwhile the Russian Empire was inching outwards. Russian merchants had arrived in Alaska in 1784 and established a solid trading community. Russian ships dropped anchor in San Francisco Bay in 1806, capping their explorations of the Pacific coast.

The kingdom of Georgia united with Russia in 1801. After a war with Sweden in 1807–09, Alexander became Grand Duke of Finland. Russia argued with Turkey over the Danube principalities of Bessarabia (essentially, modern Moldova) and Wallachia (now in Romania), taking Bessarabia in 1812. Persia ceded northern Azerbaijan a year later and Yerevan (in Armenia) in 1828.

Decembrists

Alexander died in 1825 without leaving a clear heir, sparking the usual crisis. His reform-minded brother Constantine, married to a Pole and living happily in Warsaw, had no interest in the throne.

Officers who had brought back liberal ideas from Paris in 1815 preferred Constantine to Alexander's youngest brother, the militaristic Nicholas, who was due to be crowned on 26 December 1825. Their rally in St Petersburg was squashed by troops loyal to Nicholas; several of these so-called Decembrists (Dekabristy) were executed and over 100 – mostly aristocrats and officers – were sent into Siberian exile.

This was the tsarist elite's first cry for change. Officers, intellectuals and children of the clergy formed secret societies. Many looked to the American and French revolutions for inspiration. Others drifted towards the typically Russian solution of anarchism – which would in the future be represented by gurus such as Mikhail Bakunin and Pyotr Kropotkin, who loathed all authority and upheld the virtues of the village commune.

Political debate revealed two trends: 'Westernisers' wanted to rebuild Russia on European lines; and Orthodox 'Slavophiles' believed the tsarist tradition could be revitalised with the old idea of the Zemsky Sobor consultative assembly.

Nicholas I

The reign of Nicholas I (1825–55) was a time of stagnation and repression under a tsar who put his faith in his army. The social revolutions that were shaking Europe passed Russia by.

There were positive developments, however. The economy grew, and grain exports increased. Nicholas detested serfdom, if only because he detested the serf-owning class. As a result, peasants on state lands, nearly half the total, were given title to the land and, in effect, freed.

In foreign policy, Nicholas' meddling in the Balkans was eventually to destroy Russian credibility in Europe. Bad diplomacy led to the Crimean War of 1854–56 against the Ottoman Empire, Britain and France, who declared war after Russian troops marched into the Ottoman provinces of Moldavia and Wallachia – ostensibly to protect Christian communities there. At Sevastopol an Anglo-French-Turkish force besieged the Russian naval headquarters. Inept command on both sides led to a bloody, stalemated war.

Alexander II & Alexander III
The 'Great Reforms' Nicholas died in 1855. His son, Alexander II, saw the Crimean War stirring up discontent within Russia and accepted peace on unfavourable terms. The war had revealed the backwardness behind the post-1812 imperial glory, and the time for reform had come.

The serfs were freed in 1861. Of the land they had worked, roughly a third was kept by established landholders. The rest went to village communes, which assigned it to the individual ex-serfs in return for 'redemption payments' to compensate former landholders – a system that pleased nobody.

The abolition of serfdom opened the way for a market economy, capitalism and an industrial revolution. Railways and factories were built, and cities expanded as peasants left the land. Foreign investment in Russia grew during the 1880s and 1890s, but nothing was done to modernise farming, and very little to help the peasants. By 1914, 85% of the Russian population was still rural, but their lot had barely improved in 50 years.

Revolutionary Movements The reforms raised hopes that were not satisfied. The tsar refused to set up a representative assembly for all of Russia. Peasants were angry at having to pay for land they considered theirs by right. Radical students, known as *narodniki* or Populists, took to the countryside in the 1870s to rouse the peasants, but the students

and the peasants proved to be worlds apart and the campaign failed.

Other Populists saw more value in cultivating revolution among the growing urban working class, or proletariat, while yet others turned to terrorism: one secret society, the People's Will, blew up Alexander II in 1881.

Not all opponents to tsarism were radical revolutionaries. Some moderates, well off and with much to lose from a revolution, called themselves liberals and advocated constitutional reform along Western European lines, with universal suffrage and a *duma* (national parliament).

The terrorist groups were genuinely surprised that there was no uprising after Alexander II's assassination. Most were rounded up and executed or exiled, and the reign of his son Alexander III was marked by repression of revolutionaries and liberals alike.

Discontent was sometimes directed at Jews and took the form of violent mass attacks, or pogroms. At their height in the 1880s, these were often fanned by the authorities to unload social tension onto a convenient scapegoat. Tending towards intellectual and commercial professions, Jews were hated as shopkeepers and industrialists by the lower classes and as political radicals by the authorities.

Territorial Expansion During the reigns of Alexander II (1855–81) and Alexander III (1881–94), Central Asia (modern Kazakhstan, Uzbekistan, Turkmenistan, Kyrgyzstan and Tajikistan) came fully under Russian control.

In the east, Russia acquired a long strip of Pacific coast from China and built the port of Vladivostok. At the same time it was forced to sell the Alaskan territories to the USA in 1867 (for the then enormous amount of US$7.2 million), in the wake of the economic crisis following the Crimean War.

Marxism Many revolutionaries fled abroad. Georgy Plekhanov and Pavel Axelrod went to Switzerland; they were converted to Marxism, founding the Russian Social Democratic Party in 1883. As Marxists they believed that Russia was passing through a capitalist phase on its way to socialism, and that the urban proletariat was the only class with revolutionary potential.

One of their converts was young, upper-middle-class Vladimir Ulyanov, better known by his later pseudonym, Lenin. In 1895 he took charge of Russia's first Marxist cell in St Petersburg, which earned him three years of Siberian exile. On his release in 1899 he went to Europe, where he remained (except for a few secret visits) until 1917, rising to joint leadership of the Communist Party with Plekhanov.

Social democrats in Europe were being elected to parliaments and developing Marxism into 'parliamentary socialism', improving the lot of workers through legislation. The question of what to do in Russia, where there was no parliament, only an active secret police, came to a head at a meeting of the Socialist International movement in London in 1903.

Among Russian socialists, Lenin stood for violent overthrow of the government by a small, committed, well-organised Party, while Plekhanov stood for mass membership and cooperation with other political forces. Lenin won the vote through clever manoeuvring, and his faction came to be known as the Bolsheviks, or majority people; Plekhanov's faction became the Mensheviks, or minority people. The Mensheviks actually outnumbered the Bolsheviks in the Party, but Lenin clung to the name, for obvious reasons. The two factions coexisted until 1912, when the Bolsheviks set up their own party.

Back at home, in 1900 the Populist movement became the Social Revolutionary Party, which was the main revolutionary force in rural Russia. Liberal politicians formed the Union of Liberation in 1903, and this soon became the Constitutional Democrats (Kadets).

Russo-Japanese War

Nicholas II, who succeeded his father, Alexander III, in 1894, was a weak man who commanded less respect than his father, but was equally in opposition to representative government.

The first serious blow to his position was a humiliating defeat by Japan. Though in 1875 Russia and Japan had managed to agree on who should have Sakhalin Island (Russia) and who should get the Kuril Islands (Japan), by the turn of the century they were at odds over their respective 'spheres of influence' – Russia's in Manchuria, Japan's in Korea. As in the Crimea 50 years before, poor diplomacy led to war. In 1904 Japan attacked the Russian naval base at Port Arthur (near Dalian in present-day China).

Defeat followed defeat for Russia on land and sea. The ultimate disaster came in May 1905, when the entire Baltic fleet, which had sailed halfway around the world to relieve Port Arthur, was sunk in the Tsushima Straits off Japan.

1905 Revolution

In Russia, unrest became widespread after the fall of Port Arthur. On 9 January 1905, a priest named Georgy Gapon led a crowd of 200,000 workers – men, women and children – to the Winter Palace in St Petersburg to petition the tsar for better working conditions. Singing 'God Save the Tsar', they were met by imperial guards, who opened fire and killed several hundred. This was 'Bloody Sunday'.

After the Tsushima Straits debacle the country broke into anarchy, with wild strikes, pogroms, mutinies and killings of landowners and industrialists. Social democrat activists formed soviets (workers' councils) in St Petersburg and Moscow. These councils, with representatives chosen by acclaim, proved remarkably successful: the St Petersburg Soviet, led by Mensheviks under Leon Trotsky, declared a general strike, which brought the whole country to a standstill in October.

The tsar gave in and promised a *duma*. General elections in April 1906 gave it a leftist majority and it demanded further reforms. The tsar disbanded it. New elections in 1907 pushed the *duma* further to the left. It was again disbanded and a new electoral law, limiting the vote to the upper classes and ethnic Russians, ensured that the third and fourth *duma* were more cooperative with the tsar, who continued to choose the prime minister and cabinet.

The capable prime minister, Pyotr Stolypin, abolished the hated redemption payments in the countryside. Enterprising peasants were now able to buy decent parcels of land, which could be worked efficiently; this led to the creation of a new class of *kulaks* ('big farmers'), and to a series of good harvests. It also made it easier for peasants to leave their villages, providing a mobile labour force for industry. Russia enjoyed unprecedented economic growth and radical activists lost their following.

Still, Stolypin was assassinated in 1911, and the tsarist regime again lost touch with the people. Nicholas became a puppet of his strong-willed, eccentric wife, Alexandra, who herself fell under the spell of the sinister Siberian mystic Rasputin (see the boxed text 'The Priest of Sex' in the St Petersburg chapter).

WWI

Russia's involvement with the Balkans made it a main player in the world war that began there in 1914. The Russian campaign went badly from the start. Heavy defeats in Prussia were followed in 1915 by German advances deep into Russia itself. By the time the Germans halted, to concentrate on trench warfare in France, an estimated two million Russian troops had been killed and Germany controlled Poland and much of the Baltic coast, Belarus and Ukraine.

The tsar responded to protests by disbanding the *duma* and assuming personal command in the field, where he couldn't make much headway. At home, the disorganised government failed to introduce rationing, and in February 1917 in Petrograd (the new, less 'German' name for St Petersburg), discontent in the food queues turned to riots. Soldiers and police mutinied, refusing to fire on demonstrators. A new Petrograd Soviet of Workers' & Soldiers' Deputies was formed on the 1905 model, and more sprang up elsewhere. The reconvened *duma* ignored an order to disband itself and set up a committee to assume government.

Now there were two alternative power bases in the capital. The soviet was a rallying and debating point for factory workers and soldiers; the *duma* committee attracted the educated and commercial elite. In February the two reached agreement on a provisional government that would demand the tsar's abdication. The tsar tried to return to Petrograd but was blocked by his own troops. On 1 March he abdicated.

1917 Revolution

The provisional government announced general elections for November, and continued the war despite a collapse of discipline in the army and popular demands for peace. On 3 April Lenin and other exiled Bolsheviks returned to Petrograd via Scandinavia in a sealed railway carriage provided by the German army. Though well and truly in the minority in the soviets, the Bolsheviks were organised and committed. They won over many with a demand for immediate 'peace, land and bread', and believed the soviets

should seize power at once. But a series of violent mass demonstrations in July (the 'July Days'), inspired by the Bolsheviks, was in the end not fully backed by them and was quelled. Lenin fled to Finland, and Alexander Kerensky, a moderate Social Revolutionary, became prime minister.

In September the Russian military chief of staff, General Kornilov, sent cavalry to Petrograd to crush the soviets. Kerensky turned to the left for support against this insubordination, even courting the Bolsheviks, and the counter-revolution was defeated. After this, public opinion massively favoured the Bolsheviks, who quickly took control of the Petrograd Soviet (chaired by Trotsky, who had joined them) and, by extension, all the soviets in the land. Lenin decided it was time to seize power, and returned from Finland in October.

During the night of 24–25 October 1917, Bolshevik workers and soldiers in Petrograd seized government buildings and communication centres, and arrested the provisional government, which was meeting in the Winter Palace. (Kerensky managed to escape, eventually dying in the USA in 1970.) Within hours, an All-Russian Congress of Soviets, meeting in Petrograd, made the soviets the ruling councils in Russia, headed by a 'parliament' called the Soviet Central Executive Committee. A Council of People's Commissars became the government, headed by Lenin, with Trotsky as commissar for foreign affairs and the Georgian Josef Stalin as commissar for nationalities.

Local soviets elsewhere in Russia seized power relatively easily, but the coup in Moscow took six days of fighting. The general elections scheduled for November could not be stopped, however. More than half of Russia's male population voted. Roughly 55% chose Kerensky's rural Socialist party and only 25% voted for the Bolsheviks – so, when the new assembly met in January, the Bolsheviks disbanded it after its first day in session.

Civil War

The Soviet government wasted no time introducing sweeping measures. It redistributed land to those who worked it, signed an armistice with the Germans in December 1917 and set up the Cheka, a secret police force; Trotsky, now military commissar, founded the

Red Army in January 1918. In March the Bolshevik Party renamed itself the Communist Party and moved the capital to Moscow.

Straight after the revolution Lenin proclaimed the independence of Finland and Poland, and the Founding Assembly gave independence to Ukraine and the Baltic states. Further territorial concessions were made in the Treaty of Brest-Litovsk in March 1918 so the Soviet regime could concentrate on internal enemies. These were becoming numerous in the countryside because of food requisitions by armed trade-union detachments.

In July 1918 the former tsar and his family, who had been interned for months, were killed by their Communist guards in Yekaterinburg. Two months later, the Cheka began a systematic programme of arrest, torture and execution of anyone opposed to them.

Those hostile to the Bolsheviks, collectively termed 'Whites', had developed strongholds in the south and east of the country. But they lacked unity, including tsarist stalwarts, landlord-killing Social Revolutionaries (who were opposed to the Treaty of Brest-Litovsk), Finnish partisans and Japanese troops. The Bolsheviks had the advantage of controlling the heart of Russia, including its war industry and communications. Full-scale civil war broke out in early 1918 and lasted almost three years. The main centres of opposition to the Bolsheviks were:

- In the south, tsarist and liberal sympathisers under generals Kornilov and Denikin, plus Cossacks clamouring for autonomy.
- Ukraine, which was under German control until November 1918, and then was occupied variously by nationalists, the army of newly independent Poland, and Denikin's troops.
- Admiral Kolchak's government of 'all Russia' in Omsk, Siberia, which was supported by 40,000 Czech prisoners of war, the most formidable fighting force the Red Army had to deal with.
- The Baltic provinces and Finland, which waged successful wars of independence.
- British, French, US and Japanese troops who made mischief round the periphery. The Japanese were the biggest threat as they established themselves in large tracts of the Russian Far East, but they eventually pulled out in 1922.
- Uprisings by peasants, as a result of famine in 1920–21; and by sailors at the Kronshtadt naval base near Petrograd in 1921 (see the boxed text 'The Kronshtadt Mutiny' in the Around St Petersburg chapter). These sailors had been among the first supporters of the revolution, but the Cheka executed them in their thousands.

By 1921 the Communist Party had firmly established one-party rule, thanks to the Red Army and the Cheka, which continued to eliminate opponents. Some of them escaped, joining an estimated 1.5 million citizens in exile.

'War Communism'

During the civil war, a system called 'War Communism' subjected every aspect of society to the aim of victory. This meant sweeping nationalisations in all economic sectors and strict administrative control by the Soviet government, which in turn was controlled by the Communist Party.

The Party itself was restructured to reflect Lenin's creed of 'Democratic Centralism', which held that Party decisions should be obeyed all the way down the line. A new political bureau, the Politburo, was created for Party decision-making, and a new secretariat supervised Party appointments, ensuring that only loyal members were given responsibility (Stalin became Party general secretary in 1922).

War Communism was also a form of social engineering to create a classless society. Many 'class enemies' were eliminated by execution or exile, but the economic consequences were disastrous. Forced food requisitions and hostility towards the larger, more efficient farmers, combined with drought and a breakdown of infrastructure, led to the enormous famine of 1920–21, when between four and five million people died.

The New Economic Policy

Lenin suggested a strategic compromise with capitalism. The New Economic Policy, or NEP, was adopted by the 10th Party Congress in 1921 and remained in force until 1927. The state continued to own the 'commanding heights' of the economy – large-scale industry, banks, transport – but allowed private enterprise to re-emerge. Farm output improved as the *kulaks* consolidated their holdings and employed landless peasants as wage earners. Farm surplus was sold to the cities in return for industrial products, giving rise to a new class of traders and small-scale industrialists called 'Nepmen'.

In the state sectors, wages were allowed to reflect effort as professional managers replaced Party administrators. By the late 1920s, agricultural and industrial production had reached prewar levels.

But the political tide was set the other way. At the 1921 Party congress, Lenin outlawed debate within the Party as 'factionalism', launching the first systematic purge among Party members. The Cheka was reorganised as the GPU (State Political Administration) in 1922, gaining much greater powers to operate outside the law; for the time being it limited itself to targeting political opponents.

The Union of Soviet Socialist Republics (USSR), a federation of theoretically independent Soviet Socialist Republics (SSRs), was established in 1922. The initial members were the Russian, Ukrainian, Belarusian and Transcaucasian SSRs. By 1940 the number had reached 11, with the splitting of the Transcaucasian SSR into Georgian, Armenian and Azerbaijani SSRs and the addition of five Central Asian republics.

Stalin vs Trotsky

In May 1922 Lenin suffered the first of a series of paralysing strokes that removed him from effective control of Party and government. He died aged 54 in January 1924. His embalmed remains were put on display in Moscow, Petrograd became Leningrad and a personality cult was built around him – all orchestrated by Stalin.

But Lenin had failed to name a successor, and had expressed a low opinion of 'too rude' Stalin. The charismatic Trotsky, hero of the civil war and second only to Lenin as an architect of the revolution, wanted collectivisation of agriculture – an extension of War Communism – and worldwide revolution. He attacked Party 'bureaucrats' who wished to concentrate on socialism in the Soviet Union.

But even before Lenin's death, the powers that mattered in the Party and soviets had backed a three-man leadership of Zinoviev, Kamenev and Stalin, in which Stalin already pulled the strings. As Party general secretary, he controlled all appointments and had installed his supporters wherever it mattered. His influence grew, with a recruiting drive that doubled Party membership to over a million.

Trotsky, along with his diminishing group of supporters were expelled from the Party in 1927. In 1929 Trotsky went into exile and ended up in Mexico, where an agent of Stalin wielding an ice pick finished him off in 1940.

Five-Year Plans & Farm Collectivisation

With Trotsky out of the way, Stalin took up Trotsky's farm collectivisation idea as part of a grand plan to turn the USSR into an industrial power. The first Five-Year Plan, launched in 1929, called for a quadrupling of output by heavy industry, such as power stations, mines, steelworks and railways. Agriculture was to be collectivised to get the peasants to fulfil production quotas, which would feed the growing cities and provide food exports to pay for imported heavy machinery.

The forced collectivisation of agriculture destroyed the country's peasantry (who were still 80% of the population) as a class and as a way of life. Farmers were required to pool their land and resources into *kolkhozy* (collective farms), usually consisting of about 75 households and dozens of square kilometres in area, which became their collective property, in return for compulsory quotas of produce. These *kolkhozy* covered two-thirds of all farmland, supported by a network of Machine Tractor Stations that dispensed machinery and advice (political or otherwise). Another farm organisation was the *sovkhoz*, a state-owned business for large-scale farming of single crops by paid staff.

Farmers who resisted – and most *kulaks* did, especially in Ukraine and the Volga and Don regions, which had the biggest grain surpluses – were killed or deported to labour camps in their millions. Farmers slaughtered their animals rather than hand them over, leading to the loss of half the national livestock. A drought and continued grain requisitions led to famine in the same three regions in 1932–33, in which a further six million or more people died. Some say Stalin deliberately orchestrated this to wipe out opposition. An estimated 20 million country people had left for the cities by 1939, by which time virtually all those left were 'collectivised'.

In heavy industry, if not in consumer goods, the first two Five-Year Plans produced faster growth than any Western country ever showed. By 1939 only the USA and Germany had higher industrial output.

The Gulag & Purges

Many of these new mines and factories were in Central Asia or the resource-rich, but thinly populated, region of Siberia. A key labour force was provided by the network of concentration camps – begun under Lenin and now referred to as the Gulag, from the initial letters of Glavnoe Upravlenie Lagerey (Main Administration for Camps), which stretched from the north of European Russia through Siberia and Central Asia to the Far East (see the Facts about Siberia & the Russian Far East chapter for more on the Gulag).

Many of the early camp inmates were farmers caught up in the collectivisation, but in the 1930s the terror shifted to Party members and other influential people not enthusiastic enough about Stalin. In 1934 the popular Leningrad Party secretary and Stalin's second-in-command, Sergey Kirov, who favoured alleviating the lot of the peasants and producing more consumer goods for urban workers, was murdered by an agent of the secret police (now called the NKVD, the People's Commissariat of Internal Affairs).

This launched the biggest series of purges yet. That year 100,000 Party members, intellectuals and 'enemies of the people' disappeared or were executed in Leningrad alone. In 1936 the former Party leaders Zinoviev and Kamenev made absurd public confessions, admitting to murdering Kirov and plotting to kill Stalin, and were executed.

This was the first of the Moscow show trials, whose charges ranged from murder plots and capitalist sympathies to Trotskyist conspiracies. The biggest was staged in 1938 against 17 leading Bolsheviks, including the Party theoretician Bukharin. Throughout 1937 and 1938, NKVD 'black raven' vans continued quietly to take victims from their homes at night; most were never heard of again. In the non-Russian republics of the USSR, virtually the whole Party apparatus was eliminated for 'bourgeois nationalism'. The ghastly business clawed its way into all sectors and levels of society – even 400 of the Red Army's 700 generals were shot. Its victims are thought to have totalled 8.5 million.

The German–Soviet Pact

In 1939 the UK and France tried to persuade Stalin to join them in declaring war on Germany if it should invade Poland. They were coolly received. If the Germans were to walk into Poland they would be on the Soviet border, not far from Minsk, and ready, if the USSR was hostile, to roll on to Moscow. Stalin needed time to prepare his country for war, and saw a deal with the Germans as a route to making territorial gains in Poland.

On 23 August 1939, the Soviet and German foreign ministers, Molotov and Ribbentrop, stunned the world by signing a nonaggression pact. A secret protocol stated that any future rearrangement would divide Poland between them; Germany would have a free hand in Lithuania, and the Soviet Union in Estonia, Latvia, Finland and Bessarabia, which had been lost to Romania in 1918.

Germany invaded Poland on 1 September; the UK and France declared war on Germany on 3 September. Stalin traded the Polish provinces of Warsaw and Lublin with Hitler for most of Lithuania, and the Red Army marched into the newly acquired territories less than three weeks later. The Soviet gains in Poland, many of which were areas inhabited by non-Polish speakers and had been under Russian control before WWI, were quickly incorporated into the Belarusian and Ukrainian republics of the USSR.

The Baltic states were made republics of the USSR in 1940 (along with Moldavia, they brought the total of SSRs up to its final number of 15). But the Finns offered fierce resistance, fighting the Red Army to a standstill.

The Great Patriotic War

When Hitler put his secret plans for an invasion of the Soviet Union into effect as 'Operation Barbarossa' on 22 June 1941, the Soviet Union was not completely unprepared for war. The second and third Five-Year Plans had given priority to arms industries, the army budget had increased 40-fold between 1933 and 1940, and universal military service had been introduced in 1939. But Stalin in one of the great blunders of all time refused to believe that the Germans were preparing to attack, even as reports came to Moscow of massive German preparations along the border. The disorganised Red Army was no match for the German war machine, which advanced on three fronts. Within four months the Germans had overrun Minsk and Smolensk and were just outside Moscow; they had marched through the Baltic states and laid siege to Leningrad; and had captured Kiev and most of Ukraine. Only an early, severe winter halted the advance.

The Soviet commander, General Zhukov, used the winter to push the Germans back from Moscow. Leningrad held out – and continued to do so for 2¼ years, during which over half a million of its civilians died, mainly from hunger. In 1942 Hitler ordered a new southern offensive towards the Caucasus oilfields, which became bogged down in the battle for Stalingrad (now Volgograd). Well aware of the symbolism of a city named after the Great Leader, both Hitler and Stalin ordered that there be no retreat (see the boxed text 'A Battle to the Death' in the Volga Region chapter).

The Germans, with insecure supply lines along a front that stretched more than 1600km from north to south, also faced scorched earth and guerrilla warfare. Their atrocities against the population stiffened resistance. Stalin appealed to old-fashioned patriotism and eased restrictions on the Church, ensuring that the whole country rallied to the cause with incredible endurance. Military goods supplied by the Allies through the northern ports of Murmansk and Arkhangelsk were invaluable in the early days of the war. All Soviet military industry was packed up, moved east of the Ural Mountains, and worked by women and Gulag labour.

The Soviet forces slowly gained the upper hand at Stalingrad, and on 2 February 1943 Field Marshal von Paulus surrendered what was left of the encircled German Sixth Army. It was the turning point of the war. The Red Army had driven the Germans out of most of the Soviet Union by the end of the year; it reached Berlin in April 1945.

The USSR had borne the brunt of the war. Its total losses, civilian and military, may never be known, but they probably reached at least 26 million. The battle for Stalingrad alone cost an estimated one million Soviet troops, more than the combined US casualties in all theatres of the war, and the Smolensk-Moscow campaign of 1941 took the lives of 1.5 million.

The successes of the Red Army meant that the US and British leaders, Roosevelt and Churchill, had to observe Stalin's wishes in the postwar settlement. At Tehran (November 1943) and Yalta (February 1945), the three agreed each to govern the areas they liberated until free elections could be held.

Soviet troops liberating Eastern Europe propped up local communist movements, which formed 'action committees' that either manipulated the elections or simply seized power when the election results were unfavourable.

Postwar Stalinism

Control over Eastern Europe, and a postwar modernisation of industry with the aid of German factories and engineers seized as war booty, made the Soviet Union one of the two major world powers. The development of a Soviet atomic bomb as early as September 1949 demonstrated industry's new power. But the first postwar Five-Year Plan was military and strategic (more heavy industry); consumer goods and agriculture remained low priorities.

A Cold War was shaping up between the communist and capitalist worlds, and in the USSR the new demon became 'cosmopolitanism' – warm feelings towards the West. The first victims were the estimated two million Soviet citizens repatriated by the Allies in 1945 and 1946. Some were former prisoners of war or forced labourers taken by the Germans; others were refugees or people who had taken the chance of war to escape the USSR. They were sent straight to the Gulag in case their stay abroad had contaminated them.

Party and government purges continued as Stalin's reign came to resemble that of Ivan the Terrible, with unpredictable, often shattering decisions.

In 1947 US President Harry Truman initiated a policy of 'containment' of Soviet influence within its 1947 limits. The US, British and French forces occupying western zones of Germany unified their areas. The Soviet troops in eastern Germany retaliated by blockading western Berlin, controlled by the Western powers, in 1948; it had to be supplied from the air for a year. This led to the long-term division of Germany.

In 1949 the North Atlantic Treaty Organization (NATO) was set up to protect Western Europe against invasion. The Soviet Union replied with a series of military alliances that led to the Warsaw Pact in 1955.

The Khrushchev Era

Stalin died, allegedly of a stroke, in 1953. An estimated 20 million people had died in his purges, forced famines and labour camps, yet he had become something of a god in his own lifetime. Churchill commented that when Stalin took Russia on, it only had the wooden plough, but he left it with nuclear weapons.

Power passed to a combined leadership of five Politburo members. One, Lavrenty Beria, the NKVD boss responsible under Stalin for killing millions of people, was secretly tried and shot (and the NKVD was reorganised as the KGB, the Committee for State Security, which was to remain firmly under Party control). In 1954 another, Nikita Khrushchev, a pragmatic Ukrainian who had helped carry out 1930s purges, launched the Virgin Lands campaign, bringing vast tracts of Kazakhstan and Central Asia under cultivation. A series of good harvests did his reputation no harm.

During the 20th Party congress in 1956, Khrushchev made a famous 'secret speech' about crimes committed under Stalin. It was the beginning of de-Stalinisation, marked by the release of millions of Gulag prisoners and a thaw in the political and intellectual climate. The congress also approved peaceful coexistence between communist and non-communist regimes. The Soviet Union, Khrushchev argued, would soon triumph over the 'imperialists' by economic means. Despite the setback of the 1956 Hungarian rebellion, which was put down by Soviet troops, in 1957 he emerged the unchallenged leader of the USSR.

In October 1957, the world listened to radio 'blips' from the first space satellite, Sputnik 1, and in 1961 Yuri Gagarin became the first person in space. The Soviet Union seemed to be going places. But foreign crises undermined Khrushchev. In 1961 Berlin was divided by the Wall to stop an exodus from East Germany. In 1962, on the pretext of supplying the USSR's Caribbean ally Cuba with defensive weapons, Khrushchev stationed medium-range missiles with nuclear capability on the US doorstep. After some tense calling of bluff that brought the world to the brink of nuclear war, he withdrew the missiles.

A rift opened between the Soviet Union and China, itself now on the road to superpower status. The two competed for the allegiance of newly independent Third World nations and came into conflict over areas in Central Asia and the Far East that had been conquered by the tsars.

At home, the agricultural sector performed poorly and Khrushchev upset Party colleagues by decentralising economic decision-making. After a disastrous harvest in 1963 forced the Soviet Union to buy wheat from Canada, the Central Committee relieved Khrushchev of his posts in 1964, because of 'advanced age and poor health'.

The Brezhnev Reaction

The new 'collective' leadership of Leonid Brezhnev (first secretary) and Alexey Kosygin (premier) soon devolved into a one-man show under conservative Brezhnev. Khrushchev's administrative reforms were rolled back. Economic stagnation was the predictable result, despite the exploitation of huge Siberian oil and gas reserves. But despite increased repression, the 'dissident' movement grew, along with *samizdat* (underground publications). Prison terms and forced labour did not seem to have the desired effect, and in 1972 the KGB chief, Yury Andropov, introduced new measures that included forced emigration and the use of psychiatric institutions.

The growing government and Party elite, known as *nomenklatura* (literally, 'list of nominees'), enjoyed lavish lifestyles, with access to goods that were unavailable to the average citizen. So did military leaders and some approved engineers and artists. But the ponderous, overcentralised economy, with its suffocating bureaucracy, was providing fewer and fewer improvements in general living standards. Incentive and initiative were dead; corruption began to spread in the Party and a cynical malaise seeped through society.

Repression extended to countries under the Soviet wing. The 1968 Prague Spring, when new Czechoslovak Party leader Alexander Dubcek promised 'socialism with a human face', was crushed by Soviet troops. The invasion was later defended by the 'Brezhnev Doctrine' that the Soviet Union had the right to defend its interests among countries that fell within its sphere of influence. In 1979 Afghanistan would be one such country. Relations with China fell to an all-time low with border clashes in 1969. The military build-up between the two countries was only toned down in the late 1980s.

Ironically, the Brezhnev era also included the easing of superpower tensions, known as detente. US president Richard Nixon visited Moscow and the two superpowers signed the first Strategic Arms Limitation Talks (SALT) treaty, restricting the number of nuclear ballistic weapons.

Andropov & Chernenko

Brezhnev was rarely seen in public after his health declined in 1979. Before he died in 1982, he came to symbolise the lifeless state of affairs in the country. The average age of Politburo members was 69.

Brezhnev's successor, the former KGB chief Yury Andropov, replaced some officials with young technocrats and began campaigns against alcoholism (which was costing the economy dearly) and corruption. He also clamped down on dissidents and increased defence spending, while the economy continued to decline.

Andropov died in February 1984, only 14 months after coming to power. The geriatric generation tried to cling to power by choosing the frail, 72-year-old Konstantin Chernenko as his successor. But Chernenko had only a year to live.

Gorbachev

Glasnost Mikhail Gorbachev, a 54-year-old Andropov protégé, was waiting to step up as general secretary. Articulate and energetic, he understood that the Soviet economy badly needed sparking back into life, and soon departed radically from past policies. He launched an immediate turnover in the Politburo, bureaucracy and military, replacing many of the Brezhnevite 'old guard' with his own, younger supporters, and he clamped down vigorously on alcohol abuse.

'Acceleration' in the economy, and *glasnost* (openness), first manifested in press criticism of poor economic management and past Party failings, were his initial slogans. The aim was to spur the dangerously stagnant economy by encouraging some management initiative, rewarding efficiency and letting bad practices be criticised.

However, the bloody clampdowns on nationalist rallies in Alma-Ata (now called Almaty) in 1986, Tbilisi in 1989, and Vilnius and Riga in early 1991 made an alliance between Gorbachev and the interregional group in the parliament and the Democratic Russia movement impossible.

Foreign Affairs In foreign policy, Gorbachev discontinued the isolationist, confrontational and economically costly policies of his predecessors. Most of the world was delighted to find an active intelligence at the helm of the Soviet Union. The constructive Georgian Eduard Shevardnadze replaced the dour Andrey Gromyko as foreign minister. At his first meeting with US president Ronald Reagan in Geneva in 1985, Gorbachev

suggested a 50% cut in long-range nuclear weaponry. By 1987 the two superpowers had agreed to remove all medium-range missiles from Europe, with other significant cuts in arms and troop numbers following. During 1988–89 the 'new thinking' also put an end to the now-unpopular Afghan War – the Soviet Union's 'Vietnam'. Relations with China improved, too.

Perestroika At home, Gorbachev quickly found that he could not expect a programme of limited reform to proceed smoothly and that he had some hard choices to make. The Chernobyl (Chornobyl in Ukrainian) nuclear disaster in April 1986 led to one step along this road. Gorbachev announced there would be greater openness in reporting embarrassing things such as disasters; it had taken the authorities 18 days to admit the extent of the disaster at the power station in Ukraine, and even when they did, it was in a heavily expurgated form.

The anti-alcohol campaign was very unpopular and won little support. The end result was a huge growth in illegal distilling. Before long the campaign was abandoned.

But above all it was becoming clear that no leader who relied on the Party could survive as a reformer. Many Party officials, with their privileged positions and opportunities for corruption, were a hindrance to, not a force for, change. In the economy, *perestroika* (restructuring) became the new slogan. This meant limited private enterprise and private property, not unlike Lenin's NEP, plus further efforts to push decision-making and responsibility out towards the grass roots. New laws were enacted in both these fields in 1988, but their application met resistance from the centralised bureaucracy.

Glasnost was supposed to tie in with *perestroika* as a way to encourage new ideas and counter the Brezhnev legacy of cynicism. The release at the end of 1986 of a famous dissident, Nobel Peace Prize-winner Andrey Sakharov, from internal exile in Nizhny Novgorod was the start of a general freeing of political prisoners. Religions were allowed to operate more and more freely.

Political Reform In 1988 Gorbachev appealed over the Party's head to the people by announcing a new 'parliament', the Congress of People's Deputies, with two-thirds of its members to be elected directly by the people, thus reducing the power of the bureaucracy and Party. The elections were held and the congress convened, to outspoken debate and national fascination, in 1989. Though dominated by Party apparatchiks (members), the parliament also contained outspoken critics of the government such as Sakharov.

End of the Empire Gorbachev sprang repeated surprises, including sudden purges of difficult opponents, but the forces unleashed by his opening up of society grew impossible to control. From 1988 onwards, the reduced threat of repression and the experience of electing even semirepresentative assemblies spurred a growing clamour for independence in the Soviet satellite states. The Eastern European countries threw off their Soviet puppet regimes one by one in the autumn of 1989. The Berlin Wall fell on 9 November. The Brezhnev Doctrine, Gorbachev's spokesperson said, had given way to the 'Sinatra Doctrine' – letting them do it *their* way. The formal reunification of Germany on 3 October 1990 marked the effective end of the Cold War.

In 1990 the three Baltic states of the USSR also declared (or, as they would have it, reaffirmed) their independence – an independence that for the time being remained more theoretical than real. Before long, most other Soviet republics either followed suit or declared 'sovereignty' – the precedence of their own laws over the Soviet Union's. Gorbachev's proposal for an ill-defined new federal system, to hold the Soviet Union together, won few friends.

The Rise of Yeltsin Also in 1990, the populist reformer Boris Yeltsin won the chairmanship of the parliament of the giant Russian Republic, which had three-quarters of the USSR's area and more than half its population. Soon after coming to power, Gorbachev had promoted Yeltsin to head the Communist Party in Moscow, but had then dumped him in 1987–88 in the face of opposition to his reforms there from the Party's old guard. Yeltsin had already by that time declared *perestroika* a failure, and these events produced a lasting personal enmity between the two men. Gorbachev struggled increasingly from then on to hold together the radical reformers and the conservative old guard in the Party.

Once chosen as chairman of the Russian parliament, Yeltsin proceeded to taunt and jockey for power with Gorbachev. He seemed already to have concluded that real change was impossible not only under the Communist Party but also within a centrally controlled Soviet Union, the members of which were in any case showing severe centrifugal tendencies. Yeltsin resigned from the Communist Party and his parliament proclaimed the sovereignty of the Russian Republic.

At street level, organised crime and blackmarketeering boomed, profiting from a slackening of the law-and-order system, and preying on many of the fledgling private businesses by running protection rackets.

In early 1990 Gorbachev persuaded the Communist Party to vote away its own constitutional monopoly on power, and parliament chose him for the newly created post of executive president, which further distanced the organs of government from the Party. But these events made little difference to the crisis into which the USSR was sliding.

The Economic Collapse & Old-Guard Reaction Gorbachev's economic reforms proved too little to yield a healthy private sector or a sound, decentralised state sector. Prices went up, supplies of goods fell, people got angry. Some wanted all-out capitalism immediately; others wanted to go back to the suddenly rosy old days. Gorbachev tried to steer a middle course to prevent a showdown between the radical reformers and the conservatives in the Party and the armed forces – a tack that achieved nothing and pleased no-one.

Much of the record 1990 harvest was left to rot in fields and warehouses because the Party could no longer mobilise the machinery and hands to bring it in, while private enterprise was not yet advanced enough to do so. When Gorbachev, still trying to keep a balance, backed down in September 1990 from implementing the radical '500 Day Plan' – to shift to a fully fledged market economy within 500 days – many saw it as submission to the growing displeasure of the old guard, and the loss of his last chance to save reform.

His Nobel Peace Prize, awarded in the bleak winter of 1990–91, when fuel and food were disappearing from many shops, left the average Soviet citizen literally cold. The army, the security forces and the Party hardliners called with growing confidence for the restoration of law and order to save the country. Foreign minister Shevardnadze, long one of Gorbachev's staunchest partners but now under constant old-guard sniping for 'losing Eastern Europe', resigned, warning of impending hardline dictatorship.

Fall of the Soviet Union

By spring 1991 Gorbachev appeared increasingly weak, directionless and under the old-guard's thumb, with his popularity at an all-time low. Boris Yeltsin, committed to ending Communist power and resigned to letting the republics (many of which now demanded full independence) go their own way, was already arguably more powerful than Gorbachev. In June, Yeltsin was voted president of the Russian Republic in the country's first-ever direct presidential elections. Yeltsin demanded devolution of power from the Soviet Union to the republics, and banned Communist Party cells from government offices and workplaces in Russia. Gorbachev won some respite by fashioning a new union treaty, transferring greater power to the republics, which was to be signed on 20 August.

The Coup Matters were taken out of Gorbachev's hands, however, on 18 August, when a delegation from the 'Committee for the State of Emergency in the USSR' arrived at the Crimean dacha where he was taking a holiday and demanded that he declare a state of emergency and transfer power to the vice-president, Gennady Yanayev. Gorbachev refused and was put under house arrest. The old-guard coup had begun.

The eight-person Committee for the State of Emergency, which included Gorbachev's defence minister, his prime minister and his KGB chief, planned to restore the Communist Party and the Soviet Union to their former status. On 19 August, the coup leaders sought to arrest Yeltsin, tanks appeared on Moscow's streets and it was announced that Yanayev had assumed the president's powers.

But Boris Yeltsin escaped arrest and went to the Moscow 'White House', seat of the Russian parliament, to rally opposition. Crowds gathered at the White House, persuaded some of the tank crews to switch sides, and started to build barricades. Yeltsin climbed on a tank to declare the coup illegal and call for a general strike. Troops that had been ordered to storm the White House refused to do so.

The following day huge crowds opposed to the coup gathered in Moscow and Leningrad. The leaders of Ukraine and Kazakhstan rejected the coup. Estonia declared full independence from the Soviet Union. Coup leaders started to quit or fall ill. On 21 August the tanks withdrew; the coup leaders fled and were arrested.

Demolition Gorbachev flew back to Moscow on 22 August 1991, but his time was up. The old-style Soviet Union and the Communist Party were already suffering the consequences of their humiliation in the failed coup. Yeltsin had announced that all state property in the Russian Republic was under the control of Russia, not the Soviet Union. On 23 August he banned the Communist Party in Russia. Gorbachev resigned as the USSR Party's leader the following day, ordering that its property be transferred to the Soviet parliament.

Latvia followed Estonia by declaring independence on 21 August; Lithuania had already done so. Most of the other republics of the USSR did likewise. International, and finally Soviet, recognition of the Baltic states' independence came by early September.

Gorbachev embarked on a last-ditch bid to save the Soviet Union with proposals for a looser union of independent states. In September the Soviet parliament abolished the centralised Soviet state, vesting power in three temporary governing bodies until a new union treaty could be signed. But Yeltsin was steadily transferring control over everything that mattered in Russia from Soviet hands into Russian ones.

On 8 December Yeltsin and the leaders of Ukraine and Belarus, meeting near Brest in Belarus, announced that the USSR no longer existed. They proclaimed a new Commonwealth of Independent States (CIS), a vague alliance of fully independent states with no central authority. Russia kicked the Soviet government out of the Kremlin on 19 December. Two days later, at a meeting in Alma-Ata, eight more republics joined the CIS, and the USSR was pronounced finally dead. (The only absentees among the 15 republics of the USSR were the three Baltic states and Georgia, the latter joining the CIS later.)

Gorbachev, a president without a country, formally resigned on 25 December, the day the white, blue and red Russian flag replaced the Soviet red flag over the Kremlin.

Russia under Yeltsin
Economic Reform & Regional Tensions
Yeltsin was quick to announce plans to move to a free-market economy and in November 1991 appointed a reforming government to carry this out. Changes included the phasing out of state subsidies, freeing of prices, reduction in government spending, and privatisation of state businesses, housing, land and agriculture. Yeltsin took on the jobs of prime minister and defence minister, as well as president, as an emergency measure.

With the economy already in chaos, and the 1991 harvest the lowest in years because the distribution system had broken down, some local regions of Russia started hoarding scarce foodstuffs or declaring autonomy and control over their own economic resources. All the 20 nominally autonomous ethnic regions scattered across Russia, some of them rich in resources vital to the Russian economy, declared themselves autonomous republics, leading to fears that Russia might disintegrate as the USSR had just done. These worries were eventually defused, however, by a 1992 treaty between the central government and the republics; by a new constitution in 1993, which handed the other regions increased rights; and by changes in the tax system. (For more information see the Government & Politics section later in this chapter.)

Conflict with the Old Guard
The parliament, although it had supported Yeltsin against the coup in 1991, could not tolerate the fast pace of his economic reforms, the weakening of Russian power that stemmed from his demolition of the Soviet Union, his arms-reduction agreements with the USA and his need for Western economic aid. Elected in 1990 under Gorbachev-era voting rules, the parliament was dominated by communists and Russian nationalists, both opposed to the course events were taking.

As early as April 1991, Yeltsin's ministers were complaining that their reforms were being stymied by contradictory legislation from the parliament. As the austerity caused by economic reform continued to bite –

though there was more in the shops, ordinary people could buy less because they had no money – Yeltsin's popularity began to fall and his opponents in parliament launched a series of increasingly serious challenges to his position. Organised crime was steadily rising and corruption at all levels seemed more prevalent than before.

Yeltsin sacrificed key ministers and compromised on the pace of reform, but the parliament continued to issue resolutions contradicting his presidential decrees, leaving overall policy heading nowhere. In April 1993 a national referendum gave Yeltsin a big vote of confidence, both in his presidency and in his economic reform policies. But the National Salvation Front, an aggressive communist-nationalist group with strong links to parliament, continued to stir trouble, including May Day riots in Moscow that left 600 people injured. Yeltsin began framing a new constitution that would kill off the existing parliament and define more clearly the roles of president and legislature.

Finally, matters came down to a trial of strength. In September 1993 Yeltsin 'dissolved' the parliament, which in turn 'stripped' the president of all his powers. Yeltsin sent troops to blockade the White House, ordering the members to leave it by 4 October. Many did, but on 2 and 3 October the National Salvation Front attempted an insurrection, overwhelming the troops around the White House and attacking Moscow's Ostankino TV centre, where 62 people died. Though Yeltsin enjoyed only patchy support from the armed forces, next morning loyal troops stormed the White House, leaving at least 70 dead. Yeltsin's use of force won him few friends.

1993 Elections
Elections to a new form of parliament were held in December 1993. The name of the more influential lower house, the State Duma, consciously echoed that of tsarist Russia's parliaments. The so-called Liberal Democratic Party, led by the neofascist Vladimir Zhirinovsky, won a sizable chunk of seats, though not enough to dominate the Duma, which was split between Communists (whose party had been legalised again in 1992), nationalists and reformers. The size of Zhirinovsky's vote was interpreted more as a protest against falling living standards and rising crime than as a positive endorsement of his radical views.

At the same time as the elections, a national referendum endorsed the new Yeltsin-drafted constitution, which gave the president a clear upper hand over parliament. The constitution also enshrines the rights to free trade and competition, private ownership of land and property, freedom of conscience, and free movement in and out of Russia, and bans censorship, torture and the establishment of any official ideology.

Some benefits of economic reform took hold during 1994 in a few big cities, notably Moscow and St Petersburg (the name to which Leningrad had reverted in 1991), where a market economy was taking root and an enterprise culture was developing among the younger generations. At the same time crime and corruption seemed to be spiralling out of control. One of Yeltsin's advisers reported in 1994: 'Every, repeat every, owner of a shop or kiosk pays a racketeer.'

War in Chechnya Foreign policy reflected the growing mood of conservative nationalism at home. The perceived need for a buffer zone between Russia and the outside world, and the millions of ethnic Russians living in the former Soviet republics (many already moving to Russia as political tides turned against them), were chief concerns. Russian troops intervened in fighting in Tajikistan, Georgia and Moldova with the aim of strengthening Russia's hand in those regions, and by early 1995 Russian forces were stationed in varying numbers in all the other former republics except Estonia and Lithuania.

But the war with Chechnya proved a disaster. Russia wanted to bring to heel the Muslim republic of around one million people in the Caucasus, which had declared independence from Russia in 1991. Chechnya, prone to internal conflicts and noted as the homeland of many of the most powerful and violent gangsters in Russia, also sits across the routes of the pipelines that bring oil from the Caspian Sea to Russia. Its leader, Jokar Dudaev, seemed to enjoy taunting Moscow and flouting its laws.

Attempts to negotiate a settlement or have Dudaev deposed had got nowhere by the end of 1994. Yeltsin ordered the army and air force into Chechnya for what was meant to be a quick operation to restore Russian control. But the Chechens fought bitterly, their resistance fuelled by anti-Russian resentments

stemming from 1943–45, when the Chechens were deported en masse from the Caucasus to Central Asia for alleged collaboration with the invading Germans (the surviving Chechens were allowed back in the 1950s).

By mid-1995 at least 25,000 people, mostly civilians, were dead, and the Russians had only just gained full control of the Chechen capital, Grozny, which had been reduced to rubble. Some 300,000 or more people fled their homes, Dudaev was still holding out in southern Chechnya, and the guerrilla warfare was continuing unabated. Criticism of Yeltsin surged and in national elections in December 1995, Communists and nationalists won control of 45% of the Duma.

1996 Elections

By early 1996, Yeltsin seemed a shadow of the man who had leapt into world prominence by leaping atop a tank in August 1991. Frequent bouts of various ill-defined sicknesses kept him from public view. Worse for his hold on power, when he was seen in public he often seemed confused and unstable.

But even as the Communists under Gennady Zyuganov seemed set to rise from the dead on a wave of discontent, the powers that had grown rich under Russia's five-year flirtation with capitalism came to Yeltsin's aid. The media moguls and financiers made certain that the only message the Russian voters received was Yeltsin's. The Communists were kept off television. Meanwhile one of Yeltsin's young proteges – Anatoly Chubais – ran a brilliant campaign that among other things had a temporarily revived Yeltsin appear on stage dancing at a rock concert to show his supposed strength.

In the June 1996 elections, Zyuganov and a tough-talking ex-general, Alexander Lebed, split the opposition vote and Yeltsin easily defeated Zyuganov in a run-off in early July (although the strain of dancing at concerts and other stunts had taken their toll because Yeltsin again disappeared from view for several weeks). The Communists and other opposition parties returned to their grousing in the Duma, while Lebed unwisely accepted an offer from Yeltsin to try to negotiate an end to the fighting in Chechnya. Given little leeway, Lebed proved to be the fall guy for the entire botched affair and his political star was greatly dimmed by the time a peace settlement was reached and Russian troops began withdrawing in late 1996.

Meanwhile Yeltsin's health deteriorated to the point where even the Kremlin had to admit he might be suffering from something worse than 'a cold'. In November quintuple heart bypass surgery was carried out on him by an American-led team of surgeons. While Yeltsin slowly recuperated, much of 1997 saw a series of financial shenanigans and deals that became known variously as the 'War of the Oligarchs' or the 'War of the Bankers'. These were nothing more than power grabs by the various Russian billionaires, the most prominent of whom was Boris Berezovsky, a media tycoon who seemed to have his hands in every deal. On occasion Yeltsin would make a grand show of exerting his authority, as he did in 1998 when he sacked the government for its bad economic management.

Economic Collapse
In the spring of 1998, signs that the Russian economy was in deep trouble were everywhere. Coal miners went on strike over months of unpaid wages that were part of more than US$300 billion owed to workers across the country. This, added to well over US$100 billion in foreign debt, meant that Russia was effectively bankrupt. Proposals by the Yeltsin government to stave off default were largely ridiculed by the Communists in the Duma.

During the summer of 1998, the foreign investors who had propped up the Russian economy fled. On 17 August, the Yeltsin government took the inevitable but fateful step of devaluing the rouble. In a repeat of scenes that had shaken the West during the Depression of 1929, many Russian banks closed, leaving their depositors with nothing.

The economy would eventually benefit from the rouble devaluation (see Economy later in this chapter), but late 1998 was a grim time throughout Russia. Sporadic government aid that had kept remote communities afloat dried up. In the north and in Siberia whole towns had to be evacuated because there was no food or fuel for heat.

As the economic situation worsened, old allies in the Yeltsin government took to sniping at each other. Berezovsky was accused of corruption, a development that reminded many people of the scene in *Casablanca* in which Claude Raines declares his 'shock' that

there is gambling at Rick's even as he is being handed his winnings.

In May 1999 Yeltsin fired Yevgeny Primakov (the third prime minister dismissed in 14 months), replacing him with Sergei Stephashin, who was in turn sacked after only 82 days in office. Veteran KGB officer Vladimir Putin was named the fifth prime minister in 17 months.

Rise of the Nationalists
Given the circumstances it was no surprise that various nationalist groups like the Communists would enjoy growing support. Their cause received a major boost on 24 March 1999 when NATO forces led by the USA began bombing Yugoslavia over the Kosovo crisis. This attack on the Serbs, who are regarded by Russians as ethnic kin, inflamed long-dormant passions among Russians, who turned out in Moscow to stone the US embassy.

Prior to the NATO attacks, a poll had shown that 57% of Russians had favourable feelings about the Western democracies. After 24 March, that figure fell to 14%. The nationalists are leading a campaign to recreate a part of the old Soviet Union by reuniting with Ukraine and Belarus (such a coupling might come about – see the Facts about Belarus chapter for more details).

In September 1999 a series of explosions in Moscow left more than 200 people dead. This unprecedented terrorism in the nation's capital fuelled unease and xenophobia. The Moscow government introduced oppressive measures against ethnic minorities, especially those from the southern republics such as Chechnya. There was a widespread belief, although unproven, that Chechen terrorists were responsible for the bombings.

Seizing upon public opinion, the Russian government launched a brutal new military campaign centred on Grozny, the Chechen capital. Tens of thousands of civilians fled to the countryside to escape the bombardment and there was a huge number of casualties. Human rights abuses on both sides have been rampant and the ongoing conflict threatens to eclipse the Afghan War as Russia's Vietnam (see the Caucasus chapter for more details).

Yeltsin's Millennium Surprise
Russian parliamentary elections were held in December 1999, with surprise successes for the newly formed Unity Party (winning 72 of

'Who Is Vladimir Putin?'

When the US journalist Trudy Rubin asked this question of Russia's president at a press conference in Moscow in July 2001, Putin answered: 'One should judge a person not by what he speaks of himself, but by what he does.' This, of course, deliberately misses the point: in the Machiavellian world of Russian politics, who on earth is Vladimir Putin that he has risen so fast from such relative obscurity to Russia's top job?

For a man schooled in the arts of espionage and state control it is perhaps little wonder that Putin comes across as a shady figure. In an effort to strip away some of the mystery, a group of journalists interviewed Putin, family members, friends and acquaintances in 2000. The resulting book, published in English under the title *First Person: An Astonishingly Frank Self-Portrait by Russia's President Vladimir Putin* sheds some light, but ultimately poses more questions than it answers.

Born in St Petersburg in 1952 to a toolmaker (father) and janitor (mother), Putin suffered a poor childhood living in a communal apartment where he poked away at rats in the stairwell for fun. Initially disinterested in school, Putin settled down once he discovered martial arts (he's a judo black belt) and a burning desire to join the KGB. After completing a law degree at university he was indeed hired by the KGB, who only took the brightest and best. There, as he later told a friend, he became 'a specialist in human relations'.

In 1983 he married Lyudmila, an air stewardess. Masha, the first of his two daughters (the other is Katya) was born in 1985, the year he was transferred to Dresden in the former East Germany. This is where he stayed, gathering information, until the fall of the Berlin Wall in 1990. Claiming disillusion with the crumbling Soviet Union and the rejection of all it had stood for, Putin tried to resign from the KGB in 1991 (it's never clear whether he actually did or not), eventually joining the fiercely pro-democratic government of St Petersburg under one of the main leaders of the Russian democratic movement, Anatoly Sobchak.

His quiet achievements in St Petersburg saw him called to Moscow in 1996, where he progressed steadily through a series of important posts to become the director of the FSB (the successor to the KGB) in 1998. In August the following year he was appointed prime minister and by the year's end Yeltsin was announcing Putin as acting president.

Since then Putin's approval rating with Russian voters, typically cynical of politicians, has stayed at a remarkable 70%. Resolving the war in the north Caucuses, he claims, is his 'historical mission' (seemingly at almost any cost). He also talks about the need to make Russia a civil society, integrated with Europe, where the rule of law holds sway: some might say that this is an even tougher proposition than sorting out Chechnya. Some of his views can be read in 'Russia at the Turn of the Millennium' on the website W www.publicaffairsbooks.com.

the 450 seats) and the Union of Right Wing Forces (29 seats). Though the Communists, with 113 seats, remained the largest single parliamentary faction, for the first time they were outnumbered by representatives of centrist and pro-reform parties.

Then on New Year's Eve 1999, in a move that caught everyone on the hop, Russian president Boris Yeltsin announced his immediate resignation, entrusting the caretaker duties of the president to the prime minister Vladimir Putin. In his speech, Yeltsin said he was not leaving for health reasons but because of the need for Russia to 'enter the new millennium with new politicians, new faces, new intelligent, strong and energetic people'.

Putin's sweeping victory in the March 2000 presidential elections did not surprise anyone. He wasted no time in establishing his strongman credentials by boosting military spending, clawing back power to the Kremlin from the regions (see Government & Politics later in this chapter) and cracking down hard on the critical media. Despite the international protests that accompanied such actions as the closure of the independent television station NTV and the increasingly bloody conflict in Chechnya, Putin's home support remained solid, particularly as the economy began to recover on the back of rising oil and gas prices.

Kursk Tragedy & Beyond

As if the Chechnya war wasn't bad enough, Russia's military suffered a humiliating tragedy in 2001 when the nuclear submarine

Kursk exploded in the Barents Sea, taking its crew of 118 to a watery grave (see the boxed text 'The Kursk Tragedy' in the Northern European Russia chapter). Much national soul-searching ensued at the decrepit state of the nation's infrastructure, a situation only underscored by the devastating blaze at Moscow's Ostankino TV tower.

Just as negotiations with the US were looking sticky over the questions of arms reductions and an expanded NATO, Russia – along with the rest of the world – was forced to pause by the events of 11 September in New York. Putin's immediately cooperative stance and support for the US-led assault on Afghanistan won him increased respect in the West. Subsequent meetings with President George W Bush were notably friendly and relaxed, and if there was ever a doubt that the Cold War was really over, then it was squashed in February 2002 when Russia was invited to join NATO discussions on significant issues of mutual concern.

The tragic events at Moscow's Palace of Culture Theatre in October 2002, when Chechen guerrillas held over 700 people hostage, underlined Putin's uncompromising stance on terrorism. Security forces stormed the building, leaving over 100 of the hostages dead from the same nerve gas used to subdue the terrorists.

GEOGRAPHY

European Russia dwarfs all other European countries in size but still makes up only a quarter of the 17 million-sq-km area of Russia – the world's biggest country. The border between Europe and Asia runs down the western side of the Ural Mountains, 1300km east of Moscow. Cities and towns are concentrated chiefly across the middle half of European Russia, thinning out in the frozen north and the southern steppe.

Boundaries

In the north, European Russia faces the Arctic Kara and Barents Seas and the White Sea (an inlet of the Barents Sea), and has a short border with Norway and a longer one with Finland. The Novaya Zemlya and Zemlya Frantsa-Iosifa island groups, the latter stretching to the edge of the permanent Arctic icecap, are also part of European Russia. South of Finland, Russia opens on the Gulf of Finland, an inlet of the Baltic Sea; St Petersburg

stands at the eastern end of this gulf. In the west and southwest, Russia borders Estonia, Latvia, Belarus and Ukraine. The small Kaliningrad region of Russia lies disconnected from the rest of the country, between Lithuania, Poland and the Baltic Sea. East of Ukraine, stretches of Russian coast on the Sea of Azov, an inlet of the Black Sea, and on the Black Sea itself, intervene before Russia's borders with Georgia and Azerbaijan in the Caucasus Mountains. East of the Caucasus, Russia faces the Caspian Sea, and north of the Caspian its border with Kazakhstan runs up to the Ural Mountains.

Topography

Most of the country is flat, with the Ural Mountains rising no higher than 1900m; the plains to their west, never more than 500m high, average 170m. Only in the Caucasus, stretching between the Black and Caspian Seas on European Russia's southern fringe, are major elevations reached. Here, on the Russian side of the Georgian border, stands Mt Elbrus, Europe's highest peak at 5642m.

Rivers & Lakes

Hundreds of rivers snake across the plains. The biggest is the 3690km Volga, Europe's longest river and until the 20th century one of Russia's major highways. The Volga rises northwest of Moscow, then flows eastward for about half its length before turning south at Kazan and emptying into the Caspian Sea near Astrakhan. Long stretches of the river are now reservoirs for hydroelectric purposes. The Volga also has the biggest drainage basin (1.38 million sq km) of any European river. The next-longest rivers are the 1870km Don, which rises south of Moscow and flows south into the Sea of Azov, and the 1810km Pechora, which flows from the Ural Mountains to the Barents Sea.

With all these 'highests' and 'longests', you might bet on Europe's biggest lake being in Russia, too. In fact Russia contains the two biggest, both northeast of St Petersburg: Lake Onega (9600 sq km) and Lake Ladoga (18,390 sq km).

CLIMATE

The central fact of the Russian climate, which has a deep effect on the national psyche, is its long, dark, very cold winters, whose severity is explained by the fact that so much of the

EUROPEAN RUSSIA

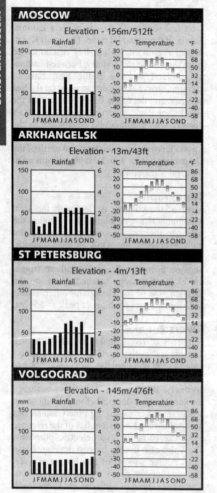

stays until late March/early April. St Petersburg, beside an arm of the Baltic Sea, is a few degrees milder than Moscow in winter but in midwinter is reduced to about five hours of murky light per day. Spring arrives fast, with a great thaw a month or so long, in March and April, and people go a touch crazy. Thousands of extra cars emerge from winter storage onto city streets.

The South
South of Moscow the inland climate is similar to that in Moscow, though perhaps a few degrees warmer in summer. The Black Sea coast is mild – it rarely freezes, and typical mid-May to early September temperatures reach between 20°C and 27°C. Coastal waters of the Black Sea itself are usually in the low 20°Cs from June to September.

The North
Up north, as you'd expect, it gets even colder than in Moscow. Arkhangelsk, despite being on the coast, averages around 5°C below Moscow's temperatures, and inland it's even more bitter. Murmansk, which benefits from the dying eddies of the Gulf Stream, is a bit warmer, and its port is ice-free all year round – but here, 200km inside the Arctic Circle, there's permanent darkness in December and January.

Rainfall
July and August, the warmest months, are also the wettest months in most places, with as many as one rainy day in three. But only the Caucasus region receives really serious precipitation.

The area between Moscow and St Petersburg is marginally wetter than most of the rest of European Russia, but it still gets only half as much rain in a year as New York, and even receives less than Rome. The lower Volga region, from around Saratov, is a bit drier.

ECOLOGY & ENVIRONMENT
In 1999 the Organisation for Economic Cooperation & Development (OECD) concluded that despite many new laws being passed since the collapse of the USSR, environmental trends in Russia are still negative. The fact is that care for the environment has long had a low priority among Russia's rulers.

The Soviet Union's penchant for massive economy-boosting projects was matched

country is so far north and so far from the open sea. The same geographical factors also create light, hot summer days. For weather forecasts for most Russian cities, check online at w http://meteo.infospace.ru.

Moscow & St Petersburg
The two main cities are warm from about mid-May to early September. Summer days in these northern latitudes are long – so long that at midsummer in St Petersburg there's no real darkness. Autumn is brief, and by the end of November Moscow is frozen most of the time. Serious snow arrives in December and

only by its wilful ignorance of these projects' often devastating environmental side effects – think of the draining of the Aral Sea. Mistakes were seldom admitted and, as the 1986 Chernobyl disaster in the Ukraine most famously showed, people were not told when their lives were in danger.

The post-Soviet market economy has scarcely been better for the environment. Many of the most polluting factories have gone bankrupt, yet still the air quality in over 200 cities often exceeds Russian pollution limits, a figure that is likely to worsen. Higher standards of living have put more cars on the roads and substantially increased solid waste generation – there is no management expertise or landfill capacity to deal with this. Less than half of Russia's population has access to safe drinking water. Russia's nuclear power stations are widely regarded as accidents waiting to happen, especially as money to run and maintain them becomes scarce.

Among many other problems are:

- Up to 2.7 million people still living in areas of Russia affected by the Chernobyl disaster (mostly in the west around Bryansk); 400,000 of them are in areas from which it is recognised they should be moved; there are increased rates of cancer and heart problems among these people.
- At least 120 underground and atmospheric nuclear tests on the Arctic Novaya Zemlya Islands, and abnormally high cancer rates among the local Nentsy people and their reindeer herds.
- Desertification of the Kalmyk Steppe areas around the northern Caspian Sea because of overgrazing by sheep.
- Erosion of fertile black-earth steppe lands because of excessive cultivation.
- Severe pollution of the Volga by industrial waste, sewage, pesticides and fertilisers; and a chain of hydroelectric dams along the river, blocking fish spawning routes and slowing the current, which encourages fish parasites. (It now takes water 18 months to flow from Rybinsk to Volgograd, instead of the one month it used to take.)
- All main rivers, including the Volga, Don, Kama, Kuban and Oka, have 10 to 100 times the permitted viral and bacterial levels.
- Chronic overfishing of the Arctic Barents Sea, pollution of both the Baltic and Black Seas, and the near extermination of life in the Sea of Azov as a result of overfishing, salination and industrial pollution.

FLORA & FAUNA
European Russia's natural vegetation falls into several east–west bands. Northernmost is the tundra, which covers the northern 150km or so of mainland and southern Novaya Zemlya. (Northern Novaya Zemlya and Zemlya Frantsa-Iosifa Islands are mostly ice-covered.) Delicate lichens, mosses, grasses, flowers and a few low shrubs and trees grow in the tundra on the permafrost, a frozen bog hundreds of metres deep. Seals, walruses and polar bears live on or near the coasts; lemmings, polar foxes, wolves and (sometimes domesticated) reindeer live inland.

Next is the taiga, the northern pine, fir, spruce and larch forest, that stretches from the Arctic Circle to the latitudes of St Petersburg and Yaroslavl. The vast stretches of forest and tundra across the country serve as a major carbon sink, which helps to minimise the release of carbon compounds that contribute to global warming. It is estimated that the taiga removes 500 million tonnes of carbon from the atmosphere each year. These huge forests shelter elk, some reindeer, wolves, brown bears (also native to the mixed forest farther south), beavers, lynx, foxes and many smaller furry animals.

Farther south, stretching in the west from around St Petersburg almost to Ukraine, is a band of mixed forest roughly 500km wide, in which broad-leaved species (predominantly birch) steadily replace conifers as you move south. Deer, wolves, lynx and foxes are among its fauna. Moscow lies in this belt.

From the latitudes of Voronezh and Saratov down into the Kuban area north of the Caucasus stretches the steppe (from *stepi*, meaning plain), the flat or gently rolling band of low grassland, mostly treeless except along river banks, which runs intermittently all the way from Mongolia to Hungary. Since much of the steppe is on humus-rich *chernozyom* (black earth), superb for grain growing, most of it is cultivated and no longer in its natural state. Fauna of the steppe are mostly small, but herds of the small saygak (a type of antelope), an ancient animal that once grazed all the way from Britain to Alaska, still roam the more arid steppe regions around the northern Caspian Sea. These areas are being desertified because of the huge herds of sheep grazed on them.

The delta through which the Volga River enters the Caspian is, in contrast to the surrounding area, very rich in flora and fauna. Huge carpets of the pink or white Caspian lotus flower spread across the waters in summer, many millions of birds of over 200 species frequent the delta, and wild boar and 30 other mammal species roam the land.

The steppe gives way to alpine regions in the Caucasus, a botanist's wonderland with 6000 highly varied plant species and glorious wild flowers in summer. Among the animals of the Caucasus are the tur (a mountain goat), the bezoar (wild goat), endangered mouflon (mountain sheep), chamois (an antelope), brown bear and reintroduced European bison. The lammergeier (bearded vulture), endangered griffon vulture, imperial eagle, peregrine falcon, goshawk and snowcock are among the Caucasus' most spectacular birds. Both types of vulture will occasionally attack a live tur.

State Nature Reserves

Many of the former USSR's 160 state nature reserves, ranging in size up to several thousand square kilometres, are in European Russia. These are areas set aside to protect fauna and flora, often habitats of endangered or unique species, where controls are very strict. There's also a class of *zakazniki*, areas where protection is limited to specific species or seasons.

These reserves were once the pride of the Soviet government, and were – by Russian standards – lavished with resources. Scientists had ample funding to study the biological diversity of the reserves and conservation laws were strictly enforced.

But, as with reserves in developing countries, the entire network is in danger of collapse due to a shortage of funds. The remaining conservation officers and scientists often grow their own food so they can eat. Some reserves are open to visitors; and unlike in the old days, when your ramblings were strictly controlled, today you can often hire the staff to show you around. Information on some reserves and how to visit them is included in regional sections of this book.

GOVERNMENT & POLITICS

Russia is governed by an executive president and a two-house parliament (*duma*). This system, ushered in by the new constitution of 1993, has potential flaws in that the president and the parliament can (and do) both make laws and can effectively block each other's actions. In practice, the president can usually get his way through issuing presidential decrees. During Yeltsin's time this happened

often. Putin has worked harmoniously with the Duma.

The president is the head of state and has broad powers. He or she appoints all government ministers, including the prime minister, who is effectively number two and who would assume the presidency should the president die or become incapacitated. The *duma* has to approve the president's appointees, which can and has led to showdowns. Presidential elections are held every four years – the next one is due in 2004.

The *duma*'s upper house, the Federation Council (Sovet Federatsii), has 178 seats, occupied by two representatives from each of Russia's 89 administrative districts, including small regions, autonomous areas and the cities of Moscow and St Petersburg. Representatives are the top officials from these areas and as such are not elected to this body (although Putin wants them to be in the future). It legislates the relationship between central government and the regions.

The lower house, the State Duma (Gosudarstvennaya Duma), oversees all legislation. Its 450 members are equally divided between representatives elected from single-member districts and those elected from party lists. Obviously this gives extra clout to the major parties, and efforts to replace its system of representation with a purely proportional system have been shunned. Elections are held every four years in the December preceding the presidential elections.

Political Parties

Although the Communist Party received the largest single share of the vote (24%) in the 1999 elections, it was not a convincing victory being only 1% more than the hastily formed pro-Putin (though not Putin's) Unity Party headed by charismatic Emergencies Minister Sergey Shoygu, an ethnic Tyvan.

The third-place Fatherland-All Russia Party headed by the trio of ex-premier Yevgeny Primakov, Moscow mayor Yuriy Luzhkov and Tatarstan president Mentimer Shaymiyev was in opposition to Putin at the time of elections when Primakov was still deemed one of the main presidential hopefuls. But after Putin became president it reconciled with Unity to the extent that in early 2002 these movements merged to form the United Russia Party.

With two liberal, pro-Western parties also having sizable representation in the Duma,

Putin was ensured a smooth passage of his reform programme of laws in 2001 and 2002. The misleadingly named Liberal Democratic Party headed by maverick right-winger Vladimir Zhirinovsky (who is nevertheless extremely pro-Putin), came fifth with only 6% of the vote.

After the Duma first convened, Unity and the Communists created a kind of unholy alliance against Primakov (who was still Putin's main rival) and the liberals and took most of key posts in parliamentary committees. Moderate Communist Gennady Seleznev became the chairman of the Duma. But once Unity merged with Fatherland-All Russia in early 2002, the posts were redistributed, with the liberals benefiting most. Seleznev was urged by angry comrades to resign, but he stayed and was subsequently expelled from the Communist Party, creating the largest crisis in it since 1991.

Even though, according to opinion polls, the Communists remain the nation's most popular party, in the American-style democracy that Russia now has, the president still matters much more than the parliament. According to rumours, Putin's dream is that Russia evolves into a two-party system comprising United Russia and the liberal Union of Right Forces, headed by charismatic reformer Boris Nemtsov and Irina Khakamada, the daughter of a Japanese communist, with the Communists dumped for good.

Republics & Regions

Russia is officially known as the Russian Federation, a name that acknowledges the existence of 89 constituent parts, including 21 semi-autonomous *respubliki* (republics), and 68 *oblasti* (regions) and *kraya* (territories). About two-thirds of the republics, regions and territories are in European Russia; the rest fall east of the Ural Mountains.

The republics exist as a result of the old Soviet system of nominally autonomous republics for many minority ethnic groups. In Soviet times those autonomous republics that lay surrounded by, or next to, Russia were grouped with it in a 'federation' that made up the USSR's Russian Republic. After the collapse of the Soviet Union, all these republics declared varying degrees of autonomy from Russia, the most extreme being Chechnya, in the Caucasus, which unilaterally declared full independence.

Yeltsin struck deals with the republics, which largely pacified them, and the 1993 constitution awarded regions and territories much the same status as republics and declared that federal laws always took precedence over local ones. Putin has endeavoured to bring control back to the Kremlin by creating seven large federal districts – Central, South, North West, Volga, Ural, Siberia and Far East – each with an appointed envoy.

ECONOMY

Over a decade on from the economic shambles Russia was left with on the disintegration of the Soviet Union, its economy is now looking comparatively healthy. In 2001 Russia saw its third consecutive year of real growth with Gross Domestic Product (GDP) up by 5%, fuelled mainly by high oil prices. Inflation – rampant in the 1990s – is now under control, with a consequent stabilisation of the rouble. Three-quarters of state enterprises have either fully or partly been privatised (with much corruption along the way), and the days of central planning are more-or-less over. In Moscow, St Petersburg and several other major cities you'll notice a burgeoning middle class with the economic trappings that go with it.

The effect of the 1998 rouble devaluation was far less terrible for the economy and the middle class than originally thought. Following the initial shock, the middle class, which was mostly paid in untaxed cash dollars, suddenly realised that their salaries had increased threefold overnight (if counted in roubles) while prices largely remained the same. This led to a huge boom in consumer goods and services. Things such as dining out, fitness clubs and mortgage schemes that were previously only for the rich, suddenly became available to many more people. The situation also gave a great chance to Russian consumer goods producers; 1999 saw imported products being rapidly substituted by high-quality local ones.

Still, despite these improvements and the attempts of Putin at better economic management and introducing the rule of law, Russia's economy still has a long way to go before it can be said to have fully capitalised on its astonishing natural resources. The country's debt still hovers around US$150 billion, and corrupt, inefficient bureaucracy deters all but the most bullish of foreign investors.

The boom and bust period of the late 1990s as well as the abandonment of the social safety net provided by communism has left many people worse off. An estimated 20 million Russians live below the official poverty line, with salaries of US$31 per month, and at least nine million people are unemployed, although many others considered 'employed' have jobs with little work and less pay. One consequence of these declining living standards is that the best and brightest young Russians are emigrating with their talents. Many Russians get by as they did for decades under the Soviet system by growing their own food at their dachas and bartering various goods and services.

POPULATION & PEOPLE

Some 112 million of Russia's 147 million people live in European Russia. Three-quarters of European Russia's people live in towns and cities, the most densely populated areas being around Moscow (population nine million) and St Petersburg (four million), and the areas stretching east of Moscow as far as Kazan and Samara, and south to Voronezh and Saratov. The biggest cities after Moscow and St Petersburg, all with populations of one to 1.5 million, are Nizhny Novgorod, Samara, Kazan, Perm, Ufa, Rostov-on-Don and Volgograd.

Life expectancy of Russians continues to fall: at current rates the population will decline to 123 million by 2030. Much of this is due to the population's staggering health problems. Alcoholism is rampant – as you may notice when it seems as though everybody over the age of 10 is wandering around with a beer on a warm day or clutching a bottle of vodka on a cold day. According to the Russian Ministry of Health, Russians consume on average 12L of pure alcohol a year, which is three times the average for the rest of the developed world. Besides the many health problems inherent to a diet high in alcohol and fat, accidental deaths due to drunkenness are frequent. On a warm summer weekend people drown in the rivers and lakes at a rate four times greater than anywhere else in the West, primarily because of drunkenness. The average life expectancy for a Russian man is 58 years, for a woman 71.

About 81% of European Russia's people are Russians. The rest belong to dozens of smaller ethnic groups, all with their own languages and cultural traditions (in varying degrees of usage), and varied religions. Their complex distribution has been shaped by war, forced movements and migration over many thousands of years. Many ethnic groups have their own republics within Russia, some of which – notably Tatarstan – have developed societies with a character different from the rest of European Russia.

More information on minority peoples can be found in the regional chapters.

Middle Volga Minorities

The region east of Moscow, around the middle section of the Volga River and its tributaries, contains the biggest ethnic minorities, though they're still outnumbered about three to one in the region by Russians. The system of republics in this region stems from Soviet attempts to limit the influence of the Tatars, historical rivals of the Russians.

The region's, and European Russia's, biggest minority is the Tatars themselves, who are descended from the Mongol-Tatar armies of Jenghis Khan and his successors, and from earlier Hunnic, Turkic and Finno-Ugric settlers on the middle Volga. The Tatars are mostly Muslim, and some 1.8 million of them form nearly half the population of the Tatarstan Republic, whose capital is Kazan, on the Volga River. A million or so Tatars live in other parts of European Russia, while a further million or so live elsewhere in the CIS.

Two other important groups in the middle Volga region are the Chuvash (1.8 million) and the Bashkirs (1.5 million). The Chuvash, descendants of the pre-Mongol-Tatar settlers in the region, are Orthodox Christian and form a majority in Chuvashia (capital: Cheboxary). The Bashkirs are a partly Turkic people, nominally Muslim, about half of whom live in the Bashkortostan Republic (capital: Ufa). Here, however, they are outnumbered both by Russians and by Tatars.

The other four major groups of the region are Finno-Ugric peoples, descendants of its earliest known inhabitants, and distant relatives of the Estonians, Hungarians and Finns: the 1.2 million Orthodox or Muslim Mordvins, a quarter of whom live in Mordovia (capital: Saransk); the 800,000 Udmurts or Votyaks, predominantly Orthodox, two-thirds of whom live in Udmurtia (capital: Izhevsk); the 700,000 Mari or Cheremys, with an animist/shamanist religion, nearly half of whom live in Mary-El (capital: Yoshkar-Ola); and the 350,000 Komi, who are Orthodox, most of whom live in the Komi Republic (capital: Syktyvkar).

Northern Minorities
About 140,000 members of another Finno-Ugric people, the Karelians, live in European Russia. Some 80,000 of them form 10% of the population of the Karelia Republic north of St Petersburg. More Karelians live across the border in Finland.

Southern Minorities
The northern Caucasus, which is in Russia, is a real ethnic jigsaw of at least 19 local nationalities. Several of them have been involved in ethnic conflicts in recent years, some of which stem from Stalinist gerrymandering of their territories. Resentments were also fuelled by Stalin's deportation of four entire Caucasus peoples – the Chechens, Ingush, Balkars and Karachay – to Central Asia in 1943–45, allegedly for collaboration with the German invaders. Those who had not died were allowed to return in the 1950s.

The Chechens, a Muslim people almost one million strong, are renowned for their fierce nationalism. This prompted Chechnya to declare independence from Russia in 1991 and, four years later, led to a savage war, in which Russia attempted to regain control of Chechnya. (For more information see the Caucasus chapter.)

Cossacks
The Cossacks, particularly in places north of the Caucasus such as Krasnodar, Stavropol and Novocherkassk, have been reasserting their identity. After the Bolshevik Revolution the Cossacks, who had mostly sided with the Whites in the civil war, suffered massacres, deportations and victimisation and were not recognised as a separate ethnic group. They were registered under other nationalities, usually Russian or Ukrainian. Cossacks are trying to revive their military traditions and have strong Russian nationalist tendencies, merging into xenophobia and anti-Semitism. In 1920 there were about four million Cossacks, but it's difficult to estimate the number of Cossacks today.

Jews
Of the approximately one million Jews in Russia in 1989, only some 500,000 remained

in 1998. Most are in urban European Russia, but there's also a small, conservative community of 17,000 'Mountain Jews' in the Caucasus. A relaxation of exit rules since the mid-1980s has sparked an exodus of Russian Jews to Germany and the USA, and also to Israel, where they have become a sizable force in Israeli politics.

After Kiev's destruction of the Judaic Khazar empire, Russia had few Jews until the 1772–95 partitions of Poland brought in half a million, who were confined by law to the occupied lands – roughly, present-day Ukraine, Belarus, Lithuania and eastern Poland, the so-called Pale of Settlement. The notion of a 'Jewish problem' grew in the 19th century, exploding in the 1880s into pogroms and massive emigration to Western Europe and the USA.

On top of Soviet antireligious policies, Stalin devoted himself after WWII to the destruction of Jewish cultural life, shutting schools, theatres and publishing houses. The denial of Jewish applications for emigration in the early 1980s gave rise to the issue of 'refuseniks'. With its new religious freedoms, *glasnost* also brought an upsurge in grassroots anti-Semitism, and emigration grew to a flood.

EDUCATION
One of the Soviet Union's greatest achievements was education. From an agrarian society in which literacy was limited to the few in the upper classes, the USSR achieved a literacy rate of 98%, among the best in the world. Russia continues to benefit from this legacy, although mandatory schooling has fallen to eight years from the Soviet Union's 11. However, this has been in part attributed to the fact that fully 25% of coursework under the Soviet system involved ideological subjects such as Marxism and the like.

Russian schools today emphasise basics such as reading and mathematics, and the high literacy rate has been maintained. Students wishing to attend a further two years of secondary education must pass rigorous tests. The hurdles are even tougher for those wishing to attend a university. Technical subjects such as science and mathematics are valued and bright students are encouraged to specialise in a particular area from a young age. This has been criticised because it limits a student's educational choice. While Russian teachers and professors are held in high regard by their international peers, at home they are among the worst victims of the economic hardships. Their government-paid salaries are among the lowest in the land.

SCIENCE & PHILOSOPHY

Russia's history of scientific achievement has very much been that of brilliant, capable individuals limited by the whims of the state and by prevailing, ever-shifting ideologies. Its homegrown philosophies – in particular the political philosophies of the 20th century – have also had a profound effect not only on the nation, but the world.

The Russian Academy of Sciences was established in 1726 and has since produced great results. Students the world over learn about the conditional reflex experiments on Pavlov's puppies, and about Dmitry Mendeleyev's 1869 discovery of the Periodic Table of Elements. (Russians often say, with a sigh, 'Russia's lands have everything in Mendeleyev's Table and yet we live so poorly!') Yet visitors may be surprised to hear from locals about Russia's invention of the telephone and radio (didn't you know?).

In the USSR, science hampered by secrecy, bureaucracy and lack of technology was dependent on the ruling Party. Funding was sporadic, often coming in great bursts for projects that served propaganda or militaristic concerns. Thus the space race received lots of money, and even though little of scientific consequence was achieved during the first missions, the public relations was priceless. In other fields, however, the USSR lagged behind the West; genetics, cybernetics and the theory of relativity all at one point were deemed anathema to communism.

Physics – especially theoretical and nuclear – was supported and Russia has produced some of the world's brightest scientists in the field. Andrei Sakharov (1921–89), 'father of the H-bomb', was exiled to Gorky (now Nizhny Novgorod) in 1980, five years after receiving the Nobel Peace Prize for his vocal denunciations of the Soviet nuclear programme and the Afghan War. He was one of the most influential dissidents of his time.

Russian scientists have also been known to be distracted by the enthusiastic pursuit of less than realistic, even mystical goals. For example, after wrapping up the Periodic Table, Mendeleyev, a fan of science fiction, devoted much of his remaining 38 years of life to searching for the universal ethers and rarefied gases that allegedly rule interactions between all bodies.

RUSSIAN ARTS: MASTERS & MASTERPIECES

The history of Russian arts is every bit as complicated and dramatic as the arts themselves. It is a history of abrupt shifts and authoritarian decrees; artistic successes marred by political disgrace; masterpieces created and destroyed; strokes of genius, policies of mediocrity, and entire aesthetic movements swept in and out on the coat tails of yesterday's rulers.

Art in the Service of the Church

The excitement began in the 10th century, when Prince Vladimir of Kiev adopted Christianity on behalf of the Russian state. The decision brought artists and artisans pouring in from Byzantium to help build the infrastructure of the new religion. The earliest of these artists are anonymous to us, but the Russian religious aesthetic was sufficiently developed by the 14th century to warrant the fame of certain masters.

Theophanes the Greek came from Byzantium in the 1370s and brought with him a mystical aesthetic, with frescoes that seemed like constellations of eyes. His most famous Russian student, Andrey Rublyov, is considered the greatest of medieval Russian painters. The wistful, elongated figures in Rublyov's icons are gracefully balanced, particularly in The Trinity (1411), his masterpiece. He blended the classical heritage of Theophanes – the mystical emphasis on symmetry, the focus on eyes – with his own instinct of figuration and earth tones, drawn from his Russian roots.

The Russian icon was much more than a painting; it was thought to actually stand in for the particular saint depicted, which appealed to the taste for mysticism that Russia inherited from Byzantium. Pskov, Novgorod, Kiev and Moscow all had their own styles, and the early icons that survive in these cities today provide tantalising clues to their one-time spiritual atmospheres.

Early Russian architecture, too, was distinctive by city. From the time of Prince Vladimir's adoption of Christianity in 988, the church became the most important building in a Russian town. In fact, legend holds that Vladimir's choice of Orthodox Christianity as the state religion relied heavily upon tales of the beauty of St Sophia in Constantinople (Istanbul).

As Christianity moved into Russia, careful attention was paid to church construction. Churches were the first structures to be built from stone, rather than wood, and as such they became mini-fortresses, harbouring grain and important civic documents in addition to religious services and iconography. Exterior ornamentation detracted from the stability implied by simple, sturdy structures, so in many cases ornamentation was reserved for the interior.

Novgorod's St Sophia (1045), for instance, was built along fortress-like lines, with tiny slits for windows and a hulking, simple exterior. The one detail on the outside, however, is a significant one: the onion domes atop St Sophia are thought to have been Russia's first, replacing tent roofs that burned during the 14th century. The onion shape was apparently chosen for its practicality, as it evenly distributed the weight of the timbers.

As architects grew more confident, designs began to reach further upwards, the number of windows increased, entryways became more decorative. This later style is typified in the churches of Vladimir, such as the Uspensky Cathedral (1158–60), decorated with icons by Rublyov, among other artists.

The beauty of the Vladimir churches became so renowned that Ivan III sent architects to study them and return to Moscow with fresh ideas. His architects then combined the Byzantine-influenced styles they found in Vladimir's designs with Russian additions and the increased decoration demanded by the nobility. St Basil's Cathedral in Moscow is one result of this blending and is emblematic of what came to be known as the 'Moscow style': a combination of domed and tent roofs, exterior decoration to the point of whimsy, and a smattering of massed gables.

The written word in early Russia was not treated to such decoration; it was regarded merely as a means of transmitting information and teaching. Chronicles of early Russian history, the lives of saints, and biblical stories were written down, often in quite beautiful verse versions of the Church Slavonic language. Yet the authors of these works (known as 'bookmen') were regarded merely as conduits for the recording and spreading of information and spiritual truths. One chronicle, *The Campaign of Igor* (13th century; anonymous) relates the story of Prince Igor's campaign against the invading Polovtsy. The stylistic blend of epic style, patriotic hymn and rhythmic verse demonstrates the range of techniques used in the early era, even though writing was not acknowledged as an art.

The rhythmic nature of chronicles such as *The Campaign of Igor* prompts speculation about the incorporation of song, although no traces of musical settings exist. The scant evidence of earlier, pre-Christian artistic activity also points to music: the *skomorokhi*, or minstrels, were pre-Christian itinerant entertainers who plied their trade in villages and courts, singing, dancing, and performing comedic skits. Christianity was not kind to these players: the Orthodox Church regarded theatrical activity as evil, and the *skomorokhi* were eventually outlawed.

The State Strikes Back

In 1652, the patriarch Nikon cracked down on what he perceived to be excessive Western influence in Russian iconography: realistic details and secular backgrounds betrayed the influence of visiting German artists and an unacceptable degree of individual artistic expression. These innovations, according to Nikon, threatened the absolute, objective truth the icons were meant to represent, and he called for their suppression. This gesture amounted to the first public recognition of Western influence in Russia.

At the time of Nikon's pronouncements, it had been six centuries since Russia had experienced active cultural exchange with the West. Tsar Alexey (r. 1645–76), however, turned a more sympathetic eye to Western culture, and his son Peter (the Great), who travelled extensively in Western Europe, loved it. Far from fretting about individual consciousness in art, upon coming to the throne Peter (r. 1682–1725) would rip art – and culture more generally – forcibly from the didactic and religious purposes it had long served.

In 1712, Peter moved the Russian court northward from Moscow to a brand-new city, named St Petersburg after his patron saint. The move would significantly affect every aspect of Russian culture, but the single most important work of art it would spawn was the city of St Petersburg itself. Peter ordered that the city be built along a European model favouring wide boulevards, clean lines and stately grandeur, as opposed to the dense, mazelike Moscow. He traded in the lush splendours of the Kremlin for the more austere elegance of the palaces he had seen in France and especially in Amsterdam.

St Petersburg is no less the creation of Peter's successors, particularly the empresses Elizabeth and Catherine. Elizabeth (r. 1741–61) reverted to more ornate architecture in her commissions, favouring the designs of Bartolomeo Rastrelli, born in Italy and raised amid the creation of Versailles. Among numerous creations throughout Russia, Rastrelli was responsible for the rococo Winter Palace (1754–62) now the home of the Hermitage Museum.

Catherine the Great (r. 1762–96), on the other hand, clung closer to Peter's preference for the simple and elegant. Upon coming to power, she demoted Rastrelli and hired a handful of neoclassicists to continue the development of St Petersburg in more restrained fashion. Yet despite their individual preferences, one trait is common to Peter, Elizabeth and Catherine, the three great builders of St Petersburg: all three placed the State ahead of the Church, reversing the legitimising structure that had been in place since Russia's founding. From now on, the church would have to answer to the State, and not the reverse, and artistic production would focus increasingly on the secular.

The Influence of the West

Peter and his successors brought artists of every discipline from Western Europe to mould Russian aesthetics in the secularist tradition. Naturalism was in fashion in France, Germany and Italy; soon, it was fashionable in Russia, too. Russian artists travelled through Europe for training, and in 1757 the Academy of Fine Arts was founded in St Petersburg, staffed by Western-born teachers. Carefully trained in classical principles, some artists, including Karl Bryullov and Alexander Ivanov, managed to imbue their works with animation and spirit but most art of the time was painfully academic.

The bulk of 18th-century Russian writers, too, struggled to produce pieces that were better than imitative of their Western models. They started by attacking the stilted and chaotic condition of the Russian language, which was trapped somewhere between Church Slavonic and uneducated dialects. During the mid-18th century, Mikhail Lomonosov, philosopher, scientist and author, standardised Russian literary language, classifying it into generic styles. Vasily Trediakovsky joined him in establishing versification guidelines; and Alexander Sumarokov pitched in to systematise literary genres.

All three men practised what they preached, writing in the forms they theorised. In fact, Lomonosov, Trediakovsky and Sumarokov were largely responsible for dragging Russian literature through all the phases of Western European literature and onto its own feet in the span of 50 years, an historical blink of the eye. Despite various false leads and much mediocrity, at the end of the 18th century, Russian literature as such existed, where before it had not.

Taking advantage of the newly available Russian literary language, Nikolai Karamzin, author of plays, novels and poetry, also produced the weighty *History of the Russian State* (1826). It was the first serious attempt to account for the nation's evolution. In his work, Karamzin acknowledged the rich contributions of the Russian folk, providing a foundation for many folk-oriented pieces of literature in the 19th century.

Music lagged behind literature in finding its Russian idioms. Art music (sometimes referred to as 'classical music' – neither traditional/folk music, nor popular music) was simply imported wholesale from Western Europe throughout the 18th century. Even Orthodox chant took a turn westward; Dmitry Bortniansky, the most successful composer for the Church during his time, was sent to Italy for his training and wrote in distinctly Italian style. Orthodox chant was gradually forgotten, and Western-style polyphony came to be regarded as appropriate to the Russian Orthodox Church.

Peter's reforms – and specifically his very deliberate embracing of the West – would set the tone for all aesthetic activity to follow, into the present day. Peter's reforms at one and the same time opened Russia to the West and prompted fresh perspective on the native cultural idioms of Russia itself. Entering the 19th century, artists were self-consciously aware – for the first time since early Christian art and architecture – of those traits that defined Russian culture.

In the process, Peter set in place the enduring concern of Russian art over its relationship to the West. After Peter, an artist could welcome Western influence into his work or resist it, but he could not ignore it. Though Russia is often regarded as ever lagging just behind the latest trends in art, in a way Peter anticipated the tenets of 19th-century modernism by instilling in the artist a self-conscious awareness of his place in aesthetic history and cultural development. The materials of tradition and culture writ large became equally as significant, and just as readily recognised, as the materials of paint, word, or note.

Finding Russia in the Folk

As the cultural eye of Russia, having witnessed the world beyond, turned purposefully inward, the 'folk' – the Russian peasant, the villages, the age-old traditions that had always been inextricable from daily life – became commodities of the highest aesthetic order.

The valuation of Russian folk life appeared in every artistic discipline, but none so famously as literature. Building upon the tremendous strides made by the linguistic and literary innovators of the 18th century, Russian authors of the early 19th century began composing works that had no parallel in Western Europe. They were too clean and structured to be called simply romantic, yet their freedom of expression and attachment to the Russian folk moved them beyond 18th-century classicism. They summed up the classical lessons learned during the 18th century, welcomed the romantic trends from the West, and anticipated the realism that would soon take hold, all at once. And so began the Golden Age in Russian literature.

Without question the biggest name in the early Golden Age was Alexander Pushkin. Pushkin's most successful works were his verse-form dramas, including his 'novel in verse', *Yevgeny Onegin* (1833). Onegin is one of the original 'superfluous men' who would become such a literary presence through the rest of the 19th century. He trifles with a country maiden, kills her sister's fiancé in a duel, and generally seems intent upon pricking at his ennui until he succeeds in making himself really suffer. Pushkin played the part not only in literature but also in life: his passionate personality and pen often got him into trouble, including exile and, tragically, death by duel.

To this day, Pushkin is so revered in Russia that he can seem to tower far above and even outside his era, but in fact he was decidedly a man of his time. Other members of the romantic movement – Lermontov, Griboyedov and Zhukovsky – wrote works in similar style and lived similarly tumultuous, rosmantic lives. But Pushkin is the one generally credited with having set the dynamic force of modern Russian literature in motion. For more details about Pushkin, see the boxed text 'Duels, Fools and Poets' in the Western European Russian chapter.

Pushkin had a foil and a successor in Nikolai Gogol, a mysterious wordsmith whose almost absurdist style was both far ahead of its time and a predecessor of later 19th-century realism. In *The Overcoat* (1842), *Dead Souls* (1842) and other works, Gogol reduced the Russian experience to its external appearances, thereby both drawing attention to influences and cultures that had created the modern Russian world and trivialising the whole package.

Dostoevsky once said, 'We all come out of Gogol's overcoat'. This comment acknowledges the way in which Gogol's seemingly superficial, trivial style, cast in an intuitively textural Russian language, in fact cut deep to the heart of the Russian condition.

Fyodor Dostoevsky himself approached that condition from the opposite direction: while hardly shying from the physical realities of his characters, the great Dostoevsky novels (*Notes from Underground*, 1864; *Crime and Punishment*, 1866; *Brothers Karamazov*, 1880) have psychology as their starting point. These books are directly concerned with the psychological, emotional and spiritual experiences of their characters, even as those experiences are reflected in – and often fed by – physical surroundings.

Leo Tolstoy was more balanced in his portrayal of Russia and Russians. In his novels *Anna Karenina* (1873) and *War and Peace* (1869), he creates characters who are sympathetic and true to a general reader, as opposed to Dostoevsky's dark, voyeuristic realism. Tolstoy does not shy from the beautiful in his novels, in addition to the ugly; in Dostoevsky, moments of beauty must be sought in glimmers through the cracks of the relentless challenge he poses to life: to demonstrate meaning.

The novels of Ivan Turgenev have a still softer edge. Turgenev, decidedly a realist, nonetheless blended elements of romanticism into works such as the novel *Fathers and Sons* (1862).

In music, the turn to the 'folk' was the work of Mikhail Glinka, father of Russian art music. During the 18th century, some references to peasant song begin to appear in letters and small publications, but it was not until Glinka's groundbreaking operas of the mid-19th century that these songs achieved high artistic status. Glinka wove folk songs into the very fabric of *A Life for the Tsar* (1836) and *Ruslan and Lyudmila* (1842), the first Russian operas. In so doing, he inaugurated the 'New Russian School' of composition that would dominate Russian music through most of the 19th century.

Glinka's progeny includes Modest Musorgsky, composer of the intensely folk-oriented operas *Boris Godunov* (1869; the second version 1872) and *Khovanshchina* (1886). Of all Russian nationalist composers, Musorgsky was the most tragic. An artist of indisputable genius, he was too impatient to study orchestration techniques, and as a result many of his pieces had to be completed by others. Increasingly tormented in life, he eventually drank himself to death. Musorgsky's prolific colleague Nikolai Rimsky-Korsakov would eventually take a position at the St Petersburg Conservatory, belying the rogue reputation of the New Russian School and forming a link into the 20th century.

Peter Tchaikovsky, though he had his tensions with the nationalist school, shared with them the valuation of 'folk' materials and themes. In the West, however, Tchaikovsky is best known for his generally romantic ballet scores, through which Western Europe came to know the prestigious St Petersburg Imperial Ballet. The scores of *Sleeping Beauty* (1890), *The Nutcracker* (1892) and *Swan Lake* (1895) were all choreographed by Marius Petipa to worldwide acclaim.

Just as the New Russian School of music was coming into currency in the mid-19th century, a handful of visual artists split from the Academy of Fine Arts to embark on a similar path. They called themselves the *peredvizhniki* (wanderers), and they ventured back through Russian history and deep into the Russian countryside in search of realistic Russian themes, styles and techniques. Artists including Ilya Repin cast their rural subject matter in passionate, realist tones; Repin's *Barge Haulers on the Volga* (1870–73), in St Petersburg's Russian Museum, takes on physical labour with unstylised directness.

20th Century: Age of the Isms

As the 20th century arrived, the artistic movements that had brandished the sharpest edge in the 19th century had dulled, essentially becoming the new academy. The New Russian School of music, led by Rimsky-Korsakov, was 'securely locked in the conservatory': what had been a somewhat subversive trend, resistant to the mainstream, had now become the standard – the Academy itself. In the visual arts, the *peredvizhniki* increasingly repeated themselves, succumbing to the demands of their patrons. The fragmented plays of Anton Chekhov represented the last, though powerful, gasp of Russian literary realism.

In the waning years of the century, modernism began to take hold and soon gave rise to a succession of big-name movements: symbolism, futurism, suprematism, constructivism. These were the aesthetic concepts that would accompany the fall of the Romanov dynasty, the tumultuous years of revolution, and the dawn of the Bolshevik state.

Early symbolist writer Valery Briusov stuck close to a French model of symbolism, but his successors – especially Viacheslav Ivanov, Alexander Blok and Andrey Bely – developed a more distinct Russian symbolist idiom. By creating superior realities in art and then reading that art back onto life, these authors believed that reality itself would become better. Blok and Bely, in particular, pursued their principles to the point of writing poetic death into their works.

Vladimir Mayakovsky (1893–1930) was the primary practitioner of futurism, abstracting and schematising language in his efforts to release its creationary power. Originally enthusiastic about the Soviet project, Mayakovsky became so disillusioned that he committed suicide in 1930.

These literary movements had parallels in music and the visual arts. In music, the dominant figure of the Russian avant-garde was Alexander Scriabin. An avowed symbolist, Scriabin devised a system attaching specific colours to certain sounds. His music was essentially atonal and completely different from anything else being composed at the

Who Put the Pop in Russian Pop Culture?

The top-down genesis of a popular culture is an odd but not unusual phenomenon. The entire romantic movement, for instance, relied upon imagining the lives of the lower classes in art and then expecting the members of the lower classes to adhere to the cultural tendencies invented for them.

And so it has been in Russia: 'folk art' and 'popular culture' connote elaborate idioms not necessarily developed by the peasant classes, but associated with them and thereby legitimised. These contrivances often contain a kernel of 'authenticity': Milii Balakirev did go into the countryside to collect Russian folk songs, from which he and his colleagues drew the handful of musical gestures that came to identify 'Russian' highbrow composition. Ilya Repin observed peasants in the fields in preparation for such classically 'Russian' paintings as *Barge Haulers on the Volga*. But the following generation merely distilled further the first-hand observations of these more or less genuine folklorists, and the next generation was further still from the source. And by the time Stalin announced the adoption of socialist realism as the official state aesthetic, with Russian romanticism as its model and popular socialism as its goal, the threads connecting the style to anything popular or even anything inherently Russian were very, very thin.

And yet, Soviet citizens, more so than any Russian citizens before them, were commanded to identify with the complicated cultural language presented to them as their own. They were educated and were expected to become thereby uniformly cultured, sharing universal aesthetic tastes – the opposite of the norm in democratic societies where individual taste and creativity is valued and encouraged.

The great shift implied by Khrushchev's thaw and, more so, by Gorbachev's *glasnost* was the acknowledgement and allowance of the individual. In the late 1980s, *glasnost* brought a flood of all things Western, similar in its force to the influx of Western influence during the reign of Peter the Great. The irresistible reaction, fully in evidence by the mid-1990s, was a deliberate seeking out and nurturing of distinctly 'Russian' cultural preferences. Yet absent a dictatorship, what constitutes 'Russian' is no longer so tidily constructed.

The result of the disorientation of the 1980s and 1990s in the arts has been a dizzying rush through the various Western forms previously forbidden; through various elements of Russian heritage long suppressed, such as religion; and on to a questioning of the tenacity and value of any of it. *Matryoshka* dolls and lacquer boxes, those seemingly unassailable symbols of old Russian heritage, date only to the early 20th century.

Many Russian visual artists, in particular, have been re-exploring religious themes for painterly inspiration: Irina Gladun, for instance, seeks in her paintings to draw out and develop the essence of the medieval Pskov school of iconography. In literature, writers such as Venedikt Erofeev and Viktor Pelevin represent the all-questioning, all-deconstructing tendencies born of confrontation with the widespread fictions and fictitiousness of the Soviet era.

In all of the arts, this questioning is combined with a growing savvy about consumerism. Russian mysteries, adventures, and sci-fi novels now stand alongside translations of John Grisham; billboards aspire to street art; and designer logos find their way onto highbrow canvases as critical motifs. Music, as usual, lags woefully behind the other arts in moving beyond simplistic imitation: Russian covers of Western pop tunes fill the air of nearly every bar and restaurant. The occasional singer-songwriter or small group achieves an appealing rock-new age fusion with poignant lyrics focussed on Russian, rather than American, realities.

And so, the country that was to be *the* popular culture, by means of socialism, ironically now finds its own pop defined according to the capitalist West, as once again, what is popular descends on the populace from above.

Baty Landis

★★★

time; in fact, in 1961 it was regarded as sufficiently futuristic to serve as the soundtrack to Gagarin's inaugural space flight.

In painting, as in literature, the tenets of symbolism were idealistic and focussed on the perfectibility of life through art. The fantastical abstractions of Vasili Kandinsky embraced spirituality rather than materialism. In reference to their nonrepresentational forms, as well as his sense of music in his work,

Kandinsky generically titled many of his works *Improvisations* and *Compositions*.

Kandinsky belonged to a broad, concept-bound group formed in 1898, Mir Iskusstva (The World of Art). While Mir Iskusstva encompassed a variety of aesthetic styles, most members were sympathetic to the symbolist project. Artists Leonty Benois and Lev Bakst were involved in Mir Iskusstva's most enduring project, the Ballets Russes, as set designers. As such, they brought their visual interpretations of Russian culture to the Parisian stage and were among the elite group that introduced the Russian version of Richard Wagner's *Gesamtkunstwerk* (Total Artwork) to the West.

Sergei Diaghilev, impresario of the Ballets Russes, shared the Symbolist belief in the superiority of art to reality. Unlike hardcore Symbolists, however, Diaghilev allowed art to remain in a specialised space, without asking it to improve upon life itself. With the help of artists from every discipline, including the folk song–derived scores of Igor Stravinsky, Diaghilev orchestrated every aspect of meticulous ballet productions such as *The Firebird* (1910) and *The Rite of Spring* (1913), to rousing success in Paris. Blok, Bely and Scriabin, meanwhile, in trying to draw more from art than it was able to give, drowned in their own symbolist projects.

Partially out of Symbolism and partially in contrast to it grew the Russian avant-garde. Kazimir Malevich, Natalia Goncharova and Vladimir Tatlin were among the major artists who emerged in the 1910s, adopting the primitivist tendencies and folk source materials of the symbolists, yet pushing them ever further towards abstraction and political message. Malevich's suprematist painting *Black Square* (1913), on display at the Tretyakov Gallery in Moscow, took the final step toward abstraction by eliminating all representation from the canvas, as form triumphed over content.

Once the materials of representation had been broken down into their component parts of shape and colour, there was nothing to do but recombine them. Thus arrived constructivism, in quick succession to suprematism.

From Beatles Covers to MTV: The Story of Russian Rock

Russian rock was born in the 1960s when the 'bourgeois' Beatles filtered through, despite official disapproval. Starved of decent equipment and the chance to record or perform to big audiences, Russian rock groups developed underground. By the 1970s – the Soviet hippy era – the music had developed a huge following among the disaffected, distrustful youth. Although bands initially imitated their Western counterparts, by the 1980s a home-grown sound was emerging and in Leningrad (St Petersburg), in particular, many influential bands sprung up.

Mitki were a band of artists, poets and musicians, self-styled Russian hippies donning sailor gear, drinking fantastic amounts of alcohol and putting a Russian accent on the term 'bohemian'. Yury Shevchuk and his band DDT, also from Leningrad and penning very strong lyrics, emerged as the country's main rock band. Boris Grebenshikov and his band Akvarium (Aquarium) from Yekaterinburg caused sensations wherever they performed; his folk rock and introspective lyrics became the emotional cry of a generation. At first, all their music was circulated by illegal tapes known as *magizdat*, passed from listener to listener; concerts were held, if at all, in remote halls in city suburbs, and even to attend them could be risky. All three bands continue to record to this day.

The god of Russian rock, though, was Viktor Tsoy, originally from Kazakhstan. His group Kino was the stuff of legends. A few appearances in kung-fu-type flicks helped make Tsoy the King of Cool, and his early death in a 1990 car crash ensured the legend a long life. To this day, fans gather on the anniversary of his death (August 15) and play his music. His grave, at the Bogoslovskogo Cemetery in St Petersburg, has been turned into a shrine.

Mainstream Russian pop today is on the whole awful; a few minutes of Russian MTV will leave you clambering for Roxette, Celine Dion and others you thought were bad. But standing just outside the mainstream are interesting rock bands like Mumii Troll, led by the literate, androgynous Ilya Lagushenko; Alicia, a more heavy-rock group who put on kick-ass concerts; Splin; and the talented pop-folk singer Pavel Kashin.

Steve Kokker

Malevich turned to constructivism, and Tatlin was a pioneer in the style. Along with other revolution-minded artists, Tatlin demanded that form follow function in art; there was no room in a revolutionary world for wasted ideas. For the most part, however, Tatlin's projects turned out to be exceedingly idealistic and were never built, and we are left with so many models, including *Monument to the Third International* (1919–20).

Constructivism did, however, leave a mark on the built architectural environment of the Soviet Union. Determinedly geometric forms became the structural components of public buildings in which form strove to demonstrably follow function. The offices of *Pravda* in Moscow were one famous example.

Stalinism & Beyond

All of this furious artistic experimentation came crashing to a halt in the late 1920s, as Stalin's repressive stance towards aesthetics became clear. In 1932, an official state aesthetic was announced: socialist realism. While the tenets of socialist realism remained treacherously ill-defined (an artist could be exiled or worse for failing to adhere to them, however earnest the intent), they involved a return to realism along the lines of the 19th-century *peredvizhniki*, as well as a depiction of 'reality in its revolutionary development', as it was infamously decreed.

Experimentation in architecture was an immediate casualty of the socialist realist doctrine, as monumental neoclassicism replaced constructivism. Ironically, the functional, structure-baring aesthetic basic to architectural constructivism would find new voice internationally during the mid-20th century. While the tendency produced such landmarks as the Pompidou Centre in Paris, however, in Russia it was now stripped of artistry and resulted in the characterless blocks that cover much of the modern Russian cityscape.

A number of artists managed to produce quality work under these difficult circumstances. From its introduction to Russia in 1898, film had become a favourite art form with Sergei Eisenstein and Lev Kuleshov among the most famous practitioners.

The preferred technique was for many years that of montage, or rapid editing cuts. The artistry of Eisenstein and his montage technique in films such as *Battleship Potempkin* (1925) endured into the Stalinist era, and

Ivan the Terrible, parts one and two (1944–46) is regarded by many as his greatest work.

The majority of films produced during the 1930s and 1940s were propagandist, or at least were strictly in line with the Party's socialist realist ideals. However, the film idiom was by this time so dominated by montage that even these conformist films provide an interesting and artistically convincing portrait of the aesthetic age. In an art form as young as film, it was difficult for the authorities to sift the contrived from the natural, which in theory they privileged; all film was both contrived and naturalistic to the developing audience. Thus Fridrikh Ermler's film *Counterplan* (1932), considered an important influence on the development of socialist realist doctrine, is nonetheless quite powerful artistically.

Among Soviet writers, Sergei Bulgakov, with his fabulously popular novel *The Master and Margarita* (1940; published 1967) sustained the mystical strains of Russian literature within the framework of a classic romance. In *Doctor Zhivago*, Boris Pasternak casts the Revolution in powerfully mythical terms. Poet Anna Akhmatova lived tragically long while witnessing many of her contemporaries being hauled off to prison or death. The elegant clarity of her poetry is a crucial document of the age.

Perhaps the most sobering written account of the Stalinist age is *The Gulag Archipelago* (published 1973), by Alexander Solzhenitsyn. Solzhenitsyn spent eight years in the Stalinist Gulag, wrote about it in three volumes, then spent the remainder of his life in exile, following the publication of his work abroad.

Musically, the compositions of Dmitry Shostakovich and the Soviet-era works of Sergei Prokofiev are currently regaining favour as critics realise that political exigencies do not automatically spell artistic staleness. And visual artists, including Alexander Gerasimov and Alexander Deineka, managed to create paintings of immediacy and power even within the confines of socialist realism.

With Stalin's death in 1953, the artistic atmosphere in Russia eased up a bit and freer expression crept back into the arts. In the late 20th century, Russian artists were playing a familiar game of catch-up, as they finally explored the artistic innovations and experiments that had been taking place in the West during their long years of isolation and repression. Abstraction and references to previously taboo forms such as the religious icon began to reappear on canvases. The progressive musical practices of Western composers found their way into the compositions of such prominent late- and post-Soviet composers as Alfred Schnittke and Sophia Gubaidulina.

In film and literature, the portrayal of individuals with individual consciousnesses regained legitimacy. Oleg Kovalov is among the film directors who have returned to the subjectivities of the earlier 20th century and put them to the task of social critique; his *Concert for a Rat* (1995) re-examines montage techniques but in order to undermine, rather than prop up, supposed Soviet realities. Nikita Mikhalkov's *Burnt by the Sun*, which won an Oscar in 1994, poignantly treats the Stalinist purges.

The philosophical novels of Viktor Pelevin are among those historicising the concept of the individual and questioning modern perspectives, testing them against the demonstrably failed Soviet perspectives.

As Russian artists enter the 21st century, they once again find themselves in a period of dramatic change, again faced with the task of aesthetically sorting through the cultural, social and historical legacies of their country. Perhaps what is most amazing in the Russian arts is that in the face of these pressures and this complexity of creative circumstance, artists, writers and musicians time and again have made astonishing stylistic moves, often ushering in new aesthetic eras with a single gesture. No doubt the Russian artist of today, too, will manage to press materials and ideas borrowed from others or imposed by tradition far beyond what anyone could imagine.

SOCIETY & CONDUCT
Traditional Culture
With its myriad ethnic groups, Russia has a rich stew of cultures, many of which are discussed in the relevant regional chapters of this book. Many old customs are being revived through the Russian Orthodox Church: Russian women are liable to be pointed at or given a tongue lashing by a babushka if they don't cover their heads in a church. (Tourists, however, will not be expected to follow this custom.)

Hospitality is a delightful tradition. If you are offered some you can expect to be regaled with stories, to be drowned in vodka, to offer and receive many toasts and to eat loads of food off small plates. This may seem foreign if the only Russians you've met previously have been gruff bureaucrats, but if a Russian decides to invite you into his or her home, you can expect a bear hug of an embrace, both physically and mentally. This can be especially true far from the big cities, where you'll meet locals determined to share everything they have with you, however meagre.

The Dacha
At least 30% of Russians have one of these small country homes. Often little more than a bare bones hut (but sometimes quite luxurious) these retreats offer Russians refuge from city life and as such figure prominently in the national psyche. On half-warm weekends, places such as Moscow begin to empty out early on Friday as people head to the country.

One of the most important aspects of dacha life is gardening. Families grow all manner of vegetables and fruits to eat over the winter. A cherry tree will be fussed over for years; hearty crops of potatoes and cabbage will be nurtured through the summer. Flowers also play an important part in creating the proper dacha ambience, and even among people who have no need to grow food the contact with the soil provides an important balm for the Russian soul.

Dos & Don'ts
My first experience of Russia was going for my visa at the Russian consulate in Edinburgh – I dined out on the story of the incredibly blunt attitude... However, the bluntness is a front. Russians are warm-hearted people, and I thought them as hospitable as the Irish. Like most places in the world the locals are forgiving if visitors make an honest attempt to conform to local customs.

Christopher Reeves

Should you be lucky enough to be invited to a Russian's home, bring a gift, such as wine or a cake. Flowers are also suitable but make certain there's an odd number because even numbers are for funerals. Also be prepared to remove your shoes once inside the door. Once the festivities begin you can't refuse any food or drink offered unless you wish to cause grave offence. When you are in any setting with other people, even strangers such as those in a train compartment, you should

Weddings Russian Style

During any trip to Russia you will not fail to notice the number of people getting hitched, particularly on a Friday and Saturday when the registry offices (called ZAGS) are open for business. Wedding parties are particularly conspicuous as they tear around town in convoys of cars making lots of noise and having their photos taken at the official beauty and historical spots. We asked Leonid Ragozin, who married Masha Makeyeva in 1999, to clue us in to some of the other rituals of a Russian wedding. According to Leonid:

'Church weddings are fairly common, but if you want your marriage to be known to the state you need to get a stamp in your passport at a ZAGS. Most ZAGS offices are drab Soviet buildings with a ceremonial hall designed like a modern Protestant church less the crucifix, but there are also *dvortsy brakosochetaniy* (purpose-built wedding palaces), and a few in actual old palaces of extraordinary elegance.

'The ZAGS ceremony is notoriously stupid and has been mocked numerous times in Russian films. The registrar is typically an ageing woman with a funny hairstyle. She reads an extremely solemn speech about the virtues of marriage with an intonation leaving no doubt that a happy marriage is something well beyond her real life experience. The speech is accompanied by usually recorded classical music of the couple's choice, though in wedding palaces there are often live musicians.

'At the end of the ceremony the couple and two witnesses from both sides sign some papers, then the bride and the groom exchange rings (which in the Orthodox tradition you wear on your right hand) and the registrar pronounces them husband and wife. The witnesses each wear a red sash around their shoulders with the word "witness" written on it in golden letters. The groom's best friend takes care of all tips and other payments since it's traditional for the groom not to spend a single kopeck during the wedding. Another tradition is that the bride's mother does not attend the wedding ceremony, although she goes to the party.

'The wedding party, which usually takes place in a restaurant, is presided over by a host (*tamada*; a Georgian word), and all the guests get very, very drunk. The bride's father plays a special role in this, since he should "squander his daughter on drink". Almost every guest proposes a toast, usually long and preferably witty and funny – another Georgian influence. There's also a saying that a wedding is not a wedding without a fist fight!

'Russian Orthodox Church weddings go on for ages, especially for the best friends who have to hold crowns above the heads of the bride and the groom during the whole ceremony. Traditional Russian village weddings last for three whole days.'

★★★

offer to share anything you have to eat, drink or smoke.

Men will find that traditional gentlemanly behaviour is not just appreciated but expected, as you will notice when you see women standing in front of closed doors waiting for something to happen. Giving up your seat on the metro or a bus will also garner many favourable nods except from the dolts not giving up theirs.

RELIGION

The Russian constitution enshrines religious freedom. A law passed in 1997 recognises the Russian Orthodox Church as the leading faith and promises to respect Islam, Judaism and Buddhism. A clause gives courts the power to ban groups inciting hatred or intolerant behaviour.

Russian Orthodox Church

After decades of closures and confiscations of property, victimisation, deportations and executions of believers under the Soviet regime, the Russian Orthodox Church (Russkaya Pravoslavnaya Tserkov) is enjoying a big revival. By 1991 it already had an estimated 50 million members. The rise in churchgoers has been linked to the growth of Russian nationalism, for the Church is an intimate part of many Russians' notions of Russia and 'Russianness'.

Closed and neglected churches are being restored all over the country, and churches and monasteries that had been turned into museums, archive stores, even prisons, have been returned to Church hands. There are probably now close to 25,000 active churches in the whole country, as against fewer than

Miss Manners' Guide to Russian Etiquette

• Don't shake hands across a threshold. An interesting feature of this is that some pizza delivery guys refuse to conduct a transaction across a threshold; you either have to go out to the hall or invite them just inside the door.

• When entering a row in a theatre, face the people you're passing in the same row. Transgressors will be grumbled at and females will probably get their bottoms pinched or slapped by opportunistic Russian guys.

• When sitting on benches keep your feet on the ground. Anyone attempting sideways lounging or picturesque knee-hugging poses is risking death by babushka laser vision.

• Girls especially should never sit on the ground or railings no matter how tired they are. Complete strangers will approach to warn them that they will catch a cold 'down there' and never have children – even in the summer, when heat prostration seems more likely. Since Russians never do this, it's a dead giveaway that you're a foreigner.

Rebekka Chaplin, student in Moscow, 2001

7000 in 1988, and 480 working monasteries, up from 18 in 1980. For more information check the Church website at **w** www.russian-orthodox-church.org.ru/en.htm.

History & Hierarchy Constantinople (modern Istanbul, ancient Byzantium, the capital of the Eastern Roman Empire after AD 395) was the eastern centre of Christianity in the Middle Ages, while Rome was the western centre. For doctrinal, cultural and political reasons, the two gradually drew apart. The final date of the split between the 'Eastern Orthodox' and 'Roman Catholic' churches is usually put at 1054.

Prince Vladimir of Kiev effectively founded the Russian Orthodox Church in AD 988 by adopting Christianity from Constantinople. The Church's headquarters stayed at Kiev until 1300, when it moved north to Vladimir. In the 1320s it moved again, from Vladimir to Moscow.

In 1917 Russia had over 50,000 churches. Lenin adapted Marx's view of religion as 'the opium of the people' to a Russian context, and likened it to home brew. Stalin seemed to be trying to wipe it out altogether until 1941, when he decided the war effort needed the patriotism religion could stir up. Khrushchev returned to the attack in the 1950s, closing about 15,000 churches.

Patriarch Alexy of Moscow & All Russia is head of the Church. The Patriarch's residence is the Danilov Monastery in Moscow, though some Church business is still conducted at the Trinity Monastery of St Sergius at Sergiev Posad, his residence until the late 1980s. The Yelokhovsky Cathedral is currently the senior church in Moscow. The Church's senior bishops bear the title Metropolitan. The Russian Orthodox Church is one of the main fellowships of 15 autocephalous ('self-headed') Orthodox churches, in which Istanbul is a kind of first among equals.

Beliefs & Practice Russian Orthodoxy is highly traditional, and the atmosphere inside a church is formal and solemn. Priests dress imposingly, the smell of candles and incense permeates the air, old women bustle about sweeping and polishing. Churches have no seats, no music (only melodic chanting) and no statues – but many icons (see the Russian Arts: Masters & Masterpieces section earlier in this chapter), before which people will often be seen praying, and even kissing the ground. Men bare their heads and women usually cover theirs.

As a rule, working churches are open to one and all, but as a visitor take care not to disturb any devotions or offend sensibilities. Hands in pockets or legs or arms crossed may attract frowns. Women visitors can often get away without covering their heads, but miniskirts are unwelcome and even trousers sometimes attract disapproval. Photography at services is generally not welcome, though you might get a yes if you ask. At other times you should still feel out the situation first and ask if in doubt.

The Virgin Mary (*Bogomater*, Mother of God) is greatly honoured; the language of the liturgy is 'Church Slavonic', the old Bulgarian dialect into which the Bible was first translated for Slavs. *Paskha* (Easter) is the focus of the Church year, with festive midnight services launching Easter Day.

Christmas *(Rozhdestvo)* falls on 7 January because the Church still uses the Julian calendar that the Soviet state abandoned in 1918.

In most churches, Divine Liturgy (Bozhestvennaya Liturgia), lasting about two hours, is held at 8am, 9am or 10am Monday to Saturday, and usually at 7am and 10am on Sunday and festival days. Most churches also hold services at 5pm or 6pm daily. Some include an *akafist* (akathistos), a series of chants to the Virgin or saints.

Church Design Churches are decorated with frescoes, mosaics and icons, with the aim of conveying Christian teachings and assisting veneration. Different subjects are assigned traditional places in the church (the Last Judgement, for instance, appears on the western wall). An often elaborately decorated iconostasis (icon stand) divides the main body of the church from the sanctuary, or altar area, at the eastern end, which is off limits to all but the priest. During a service the priest comes and goes through the Holy or Royal Door, an opening in the middle of the iconostasis.

The iconostasis is composed of up to six tiers of icons. The biggest is the *deisusnyy ryad* (deesis row), whose central group of icons, known as the deesis, consists of Christ enthroned as the judge of the world, with the Virgin and John the Baptist interceding for humanity on either side. Archangels, apostles and Eastern Church fathers may also appear on this row. Below the deesis row are one or two rows of smaller icons: the bottom one is the *mestnyy ryad* (local row) showing saints with local links. Above the deesis row are the *prazdnichnyy ryad* (festival row) showing the annual festivals of the Church, then the *prorocheskiy ryad* (prophet row) showing Old Testament prophets, and sometimes a further *praotecheskyy ryad* (patriarch row) showing the Old Testament patriarchs.

Church Names In Russian, *sobor* means cathedral, *tserkov* church and *khram* chapel. Common church names include:

Blagoveshchenskaya	(Annunciation)
Благовещенская	
Borisoglebskaya	(SS Boris & Gleb)
Борисоглебская	
Nikolskaya	(St Nicholas)
Никольская	
Petropavlovskaya	(SS Peter & Paul)
Петропавловская	
Pokrovskaya	(Intercession of the Virgin)
Покровская	
Preobrazhenskaya	(Transfiguration)
Преображенская	
Rizopolozhenskaya	(Deposition of the Holy Robe)
Ризоположенская	
Rozhdestvenskaya	(Nativity)
Рождественская	
Troitskaya	(Trinity)
Троицкая	
Uspenskaya	(Assumption or Dormition)
Успенская	
Vladimirskaya	(St Vladimir)
Владимирская	
Voskresenskaya	(Resurrection)
Воскресенская	
Voznesenskaya	(Ascension)
Вознесенская	
Znamenskaya	(Holy Sign)
Знаменская	

Old Believers The Russian Church was split in 1653 by the reforms of Patriarch Nikon, who thought it had departed from its roots. He insisted, among other things, that the translation of the Bible be altered to conform with the Greek original, and that the sign of the cross be made with three fingers, not two. Those who couldn't accept these changes became known as *Starovery* (Old Believers) and came in for persecution. Some fled to the Siberian forests or remote parts of Central Asia, where one group who had never heard of Lenin, electricity or the revolution was found in the 1980s. Only in 1771–1827, 1905–18 and again recently have Old Believers had real freedom of worship. They probably now number over one million, but in 1917 there were as many as 20 million.

Other Christian Churches

Russia has small numbers of Roman Catholics, and Lutheran and Baptist Protestants, mostly among the German and other non-Russian ethnic groups. Other groups such as the Mormons, Seventh-Day Adventists and the Salvation Army are sending hordes of missionaries. Not all groups are being welcomed. Courts have tried to use the 1997 religion law to ban the Pentecostalist Church, the Jehovah's Witnesses and other Christian faiths seen as threats by the Russian Orthodox Church.

Islam

European Russia has about 12 million active and nominal Muslims, mainly among the Tatar and Bashkir peoples east of Moscow and several of the Caucasus ethnic groups (see Population & People earlier in this chapter). Nearly all are Sunni Muslims, except for some Shiah in Dagestan. Soviet 'militant atheism' led to the closure of nearly all the mosques and *madrassas* (Muslim religious schools) in Russia. Under Stalin there were mass deportations and liquidation of the Muslim elite. Policies eased marginally after WWII.

Islam has, like Christianity, enjoyed growth since the mid-1980s. Some Muslim peoples – notably the Chechens and Tatars – have been the most resistant of Russia's minorities to being brought within the Russian national fold since the fall of the Soviet Union in 1991, but nationalism has played at least as big a part as religion in this.

Islam in Russia is fairly secularised – women are not veiled, for example; the Friday Sabbath is not a commercial holiday.

Working mosques are closed to women and often to non-Muslim men, though the latter may occasionally be invited in. There seems to be no way around this. If you are asked in, you'll have to take off your shoes (and hope your socks are clean! – dirty socks, like dirty feet, may be an insult to the mosque).

Judaism

Many of Russia's 500,000 or so Jews have been assimilated into Russian culture and do not seriously practise Judaism; however, there are approximately 30 synagogues. Unlike the country's other religious groups, Jews have no central coordinating body, though a yeshiva, or rabbinical academy, opened in Moscow in 1956. There are two competing chief rabbis, Russian-born Adolf Shayevich and Italian-born Berl Lazar, who is backed by Putin and is becoming increasingly influential.

There has been a disturbing rise in anti-Semitism not only in far-right political groups with neo-Nazi overtones but also in the Communist Party. In 1998, party leader Gennady Zyuganov, who finished second in the 1996 presidential election, accused Jews of causing 'mass impoverishment' and 'extinction' in Russia. However, to date, these sentiments have not swept the populace. A poll taken after Zyuganov's statements showed that 83% of people had found them 'unacceptable'.

Buddhism

The 145,000 Kalmyks – the largest ethnic group in the Kalmyk Republic, northwest of the Caspian Sea – are traditionally members of the Gelugpa or 'Yellow-Hat' sect of Tibetan Buddhism, whose spiritual leader is the Dalai Lama. The Kalmyks fled to their present region in the 17th century from wars in western Mongolia, where Buddhism had reached them not long before. Buddhism was tolerated by the Soviet state until Stalin nearly wiped it out in the 1930s. Today, temples are being rebuilt throughout the Kalmyk Republic. You'll also find a Yellow-Hat sect temple in St Petersburg, dating from the early 20th century.

Shamanism

The religion of most of the 700,000 Mari and some of the 800,000 Udmurts, both Finno-Ugric peoples in the middle Volga region, remains largely animist and shamanist. Animism is a belief in the presence of spirits or spiritual qualities in objects of the natural world. People contact these spirits for guidance through a medium or shaman ('witch doctor').

LANGUAGE

Just about everyone in Russia speaks Russian, although there are also dozens of other languages spoken by ethnic minorities. Russian and most of the other languages are written in variants of the Cyrillic alphabet. Russian grammar is daunting, but your travels will be far more interesting if you at least take the time to learn the Cyrillic alphabet, so that you can read maps and street signs.

It's easy to find English-speakers in the big cities, but not so easy in small towns (sometimes not even in tourist hotels). If you know German, try that because many older Russians have learnt this language in the past. For more information, as well as a list of useful Russian words and phrases, see the Language chapter at the back of this book.

Facts for the Visitor

SUGGESTED ITINERARIES

When planning a trip, remember that transport between sights that seem close can be very slow or infrequent. See the special section on Russia's Top 50 Experiences for more information on the best places to visit.

One week

Visit Moscow and St Petersburg, ideally beginning in one and ending in the other. There will, perhaps, be time to stop off in one of the cities within close range of Moscow, such as Novgorod, which is on the train line linking the two major cities.

Two weeks

As for one week, with an extra day in Moscow and St Petersburg and a few days exploring the historic Golden Ring towns around Moscow.

One month

Allows a more leisurely exploration of the Golden Ring, as well as journeys into parts of western or northern European Russia. Alternatively, combine the two-week itinerary with a journey east on one of the Trans-Siberian routes, taking in cities such as Yekaterinburg, or relaxing on a Volga River cruise.

Two months

In the summer, consider visiting Northern European Russia, perhaps for a month. The second month could be spent in the Ural Mountains and Siberia, even travelling as far as the Russian Far East. Off the beaten track, places to consider include the Altay, Tuva and Kamchatka regions (see the Siberia and Russian Far East chapters).

Six months

Such a trip would be a major adventure *and* an endurance test. You could count on seeing many of the destinations described in this book.

PLANNING

When to Go

July and August are the warmest months and the main holiday season for both foreigners and Russians (which means securing train tickets at short notice can sometimes be a problem). They're also the dampest months in most parts of European Russia, with as many as one rainy day in three. For these reasons, early summer (May and June) and late summer/early autumn (September and the first half of October) are many people's favourite seasons. Early autumn is stunning as the leaves change colour, with locals disappearing into the forests to gather buckets of mushrooms and berries.

Winter, if you're prepared for it, is recommended: the theatres open, the furs and vodka come out, the snow makes everything picturesque, and the insides of buildings are kept warm. (But then there's the first snows and the spring thaw, which turn everything to slush and mud.)

What Kind of Trip

Try to see at least a bit of Russia outside Moscow or St Petersburg. Even the historic towns of the Golden Ring are relatively tourist-free and you will be rewarded with a slice of rural Russian life far from the frenetic city pace.

Independent vs Group Tour Independent travel in Russia can be a lot of fun, although you shouldn't expect it to be necessarily cheap or, indeed, easy to organise. The important factor to note is that your enjoyment will be directly in proportion to your ability to speak and read Russian. Away from the major cities, your odds of meeting anyone who speaks English are slim. With limited language skills, everything you attempt will likely be more costly and difficult. However, it's far from impossible; if you really want to meet locals and have a flexible itinerary, independent travel is the way to go.

To smooth the way, it's a good idea to consider using a specialist travel agency to arrange your visa and make some of your transport and accommodation bookings along the way. Most will be happy to work on any itinerary. It's also possible to arrange guides and transfers – the prices can sometimes be better than those you'd be able to negotiate yourself (with or without language skills).

Once in Russia, excursions and trips can be booked through agencies in all large cities; elsewhere it's usually not too difficult to find locals ready to escort you on nature expeditions, treks and the like. Many interesting places are far off the beaten path and the best way to reach them is often through a local guide or travel agent. We have noted some examples in the various destination listings.

On group tours everything is taken care of; all you need to do is pay and turn up. Tours can cater to special interests and range from backpacker basics to full-on tsarist luxury. Bear in mind you'll seldom be alone, which can be a curse as well as a blessing (depending on the company). This will also reduce your chances of interacting with locals, with opportunities to head off the beaten track or alter the itinerary limited, if not impossible. For information on companies offering group tours, see Travel Agencies & Organised Tours in the Getting There & Away chapter.

Maps

Moscow and St Petersburg maps are available from many outlets in the respective cities, and outside the country. Russia country maps are also readily available. For other city maps, as well as detailed regional maps useful for hiking and other activities, the choices are limited – check this book's listings for each individual destination.

Good overseas sources include a bilingual wall map of Russia from RIS Publications; the CIS (Commonwealth of Independent States) map from German publisher Hallwag (one of the clearest all-Russia maps, covering the whole country and the rest of the CIS – main roads and railways included – on one sheet) at a scale of 1:7,000,000; and *Hildebrand's Travel Map CIS*. Bartholomew publishes a map covering European Russia at 1:2,000,000, while Freytag & Berndt's CIS map has European Russia at 1:2,000,000 on one side, and the whole country at 1:8,000,000 on the other. National Geographic produces far and away the best-looking wall map of Russia.

The most accurate commercial maps of smaller regions, produced by the United States Defense Mapping Agency, depict parts of rural Russia in unmatched detail; they are available for US$13.95 each (divided into many sections) from **A Galaxy of Maps** (☎ 800-388 6588, fax 954-267 9007; e *sales@galaxymaps.com*) in Tampa, USA.

What to Bring

Luggage Unless trekking, it doesn't much matter what you carry it all in. As always, the less you have the better, as train and bus storage can be tight and you'll find no-one to help you. A light day-pack is very useful for excursions. But strap-on bum bags (fanny packs), flags, English-language patches and other 'Hi, I'm a foreigner' accoutrements

should not be used. To really fit in, use a plastic bag as a day-pack.

Clothing Brightly coloured clothes can mark you out as a foreigner and may attract unwanted attention. That said, in the trendy big cities, such as Moscow and St Petersburg, dressing shabbily may also get you picked up by the police. (We're told that's because they may think you're from the Caucasus, rather than any affront to their fashion sense!)

For winter you'll need a thick, windproof coat (preferably long), a hat with ear-flaps (to guard against frostbite), as well as gloves, scarf and thermal underwear. Because buildings are well heated inside, many light, removable layers work better than a few heavy ones. Footwear should be warm, thick-soled and waterproof (even insulated, for the north or Siberia).

In spring, summer and autumn come equipped for sudden chills and rain. In autumn you'll need a hat and a raincoat or light overcoat. Late autumn and early winter tend to be wet and slushy, so shoes should be stout and water-resistant. When it's hot Russians wear as little as possible, although shorts are less common in rural areas.

Except for some posh restaurants in Moscow and St Petersburg, you can dress casually for evenings out. Wear something modest for visiting churches and mosques, possibly including a headscarf for women.

Other Items Western toiletries, tampons and condoms are readily available, even in small towns, so you should pack extra only if there's a brand you must have.

Unless you are going to spend all your nights in four-star Western hotels, bring a small towel for trains or hotels that lack such a luxury. By all means carry toilet paper with you as you will rarely find any when you need it, but you won't need to bring a lot from home as adequate brands (ie, soft) are widely sold.

An electric water-heating element enables you to purify water and make inexpensive hot drinks at will; a Thermos flask, mug and spoon are a boon for long train or road journeys. Other items to consider are a bottle opener and corkscrew, a small torch (flashlight), matches, Swiss army knife, universal bathroom plug, laundry soap, washing line and a few clothes pegs, sunglasses, compass (for hiking), sunscreen and lip salve, and a travel alarm clock.

In summer you'll need strong insect repellent at almost any latitude. St Petersburg is renowned for its huge mosquitoes, as is most of the countryside such as northern Karelia and the Kola Peninsula. Make certain that whatever brand you bring has a high concentration of DEET (diethyl-m-toluamid).

For further health-related information, see the Health section later in this chapter.

RESPONSIBLE TOURISM

As closely as some Russians live with nature, they don't always respect it: littering and poaching are everyday pastimes. As a responsible traveller, you're probably going to be appalled by the mess left in parts of the countryside and at how easily rubbish is thrown out of train windows. Accept that you're not going to change how Russians live, but that you might be able to make a small impression by your own thoughtful behaviour.

An example is to buy food and souvenirs from locals during your travels – this is often the only income those babushkas on the train platforms or town markets might have. But don't buy goods made from endangered species, such as the Siberian or Amur tiger.

TOURIST OFFICES
Local

The tourist offices you may be used to in the West do not exist in Russia (St Petersburg is an exception, and even that's not great). Instead you're mainly dependent for information on the moods of hotel receptionists and administrators, service bureaus and travel firms. The latter two exist primarily to sell accommodation, excursions and transport – if you don't look like you want to book something, staff may or may not answer questions.

Abroad

Russia has no overseas tourist offices and most of its consulates and embassies have little practical information. Foreign travel agencies specialising in Russian travel can be useful (see the European Russia Getting There & Away chapter).

VISAS

All foreigners visiting Russia need visas. Technically, you must confirm accommoda-

Immigration Cards

One of the most important changes to Russia's visa rules is the requirement that all foreigners carry immigration cards at all times; in theory, the cards should be available at all border points. You won't be able to check into a hotel without one, and the fine for being caught without is between 2,250 to 5000 roubles ($70 to $140). The card, divided into two identical sections, records information about a holder's name, age, sex and purpose of stay. Half the card stays at the point of issue, the other is given up when you leave the country.

★★★★★★★★★★★★★★★★★★★★★

tion for every night you'll be in the country, although in practice there are ways to get around this.

In October 2002 the Russian parliament passed laws radically changing the country's visa-issuing system. The aim is to crack down on illegal immigration for work, but the fallout from the changes has also caused chaos among travel agencies and companies applying for tourist and business visas for regular travellers.

OVIR, the Interior Ministry's passport and visa agency, has been renamed PVU (*passportno-vizovoye upravleniy*), although outside of Moscow it's likely that the acronym OVIR will continue to be used. All travel agencies wanting to issue business visas must register with the Interior Ministry; with tens of thousands of agencies in Russia this will inevitably take some time. The new types of visa, as we understand them, are discussed in the section below, but the upshot is that getting anything other than a straight tourist visa might be more tricky and certainly more time-consuming than in the past.

A Russian visa can be a passport-sized paper document separate from your passport, a sticker in your passport, or both. Both the separate form and the sticker list entry/exit dates, your passport number, children travelling with you, and visa type (see Types of Visa later). It's an exit permit too, so if you lose it (or overstay), leaving the country can be harder than getting in.

Some cities in Russia (places of strategic importance, such as Norilsk in Siberia) are still off-limits to foreigners but these are few and far between.

If you turn up in a city that is not listed on your tourist visa, it's possible you may encounter difficulties either at your hotel when you check in or later with the visa registration authorities, though this can usually be talked around. If you do venture from the main routes, it's best to play it safe and get a business visa – its authoritative appearance effectively grants you the run of the country.

Types of Visa

The new visa laws create a 'regular visa' category with eight types. The main ones affecting travellers are 'tourist', 'tourist group', 'business', 'student', 'private' and 'on-the-spot'.

For all visas you'll need

- a passport valid for at least a month beyond your return date – usually only a photocopy of the data pages of your passport are required, but some consulates may want to see the original;
- three passport-size (4cm by 4.5cm) full-face photos, not more than a year old. Vending-machine photos with white background are fine if they're identical;
- a completed application form, including entry/exit dates;
- handling fee (see Processing Fees later in this section).

You're also going to need a visa support letter of some kind. This will be arranged by your tourist operator or, if you're applying for a visa independently, from various organisations in Russia – see Travel Agencies and Organised Tours in the Getting There & Away chapter for details.

Tourist Visas/Tourist Group Visas These are the most straightforward and inflexible visas available. In theory you're supposed to have booked accommodation for every night in Russia, but in practice you can often get away with booking only a few (perhaps just one). Once you've had your visa registered, you can stay where you like.

Extending a tourist visa is a hassle and the extension, if granted, will usually be only for a short time. Tourist visas are best for trips when you know exactly what you're doing and when, where and for how long you'll be doing it. To obtain a tourist visa you'll need the items previously mentioned, as well as one of the following:

- confirmation of hotel reservations, which can be a faxed copy on hotel letterhead signed and stamped by the hotel;
- confirmation of bookings from a travel agent; or
- a visa-support letter from a youth hostel/guesthouse (see the Business Visa section for tourist-visa support fees charged by some hostels and guesthouses).

Business Visa A business (or commercial) visa supported by a Russian company is far more flexible and desirable for the independent traveller. These can be issued for three months, six months or two years, and are available as single-entry, double-entry or multiple-entry visas. Business visas eliminate the need for pre-arranged hotel confirmations, as the company inviting you ostensibly puts you up for the duration of your stay. While a visa to Russia supposedly allows you to travel anywhere, holders of tourist visas may have a harder time getting accommodation in smaller regional cities not listed on their visas than holders of business visas.

To obtain a business visa you must have a letter of invitation from a registered Russian company guaranteeing to provide accommodation during the entire length of your stay, and a covering letter from your company (or you) stating the purpose of your trip.

There are many organisations that will send you a business invitation for a fee, usually around US$50 (see Visa Agencies later in this chapter, the Travel Agencies & Organised Tours section of the Getting There and Away chapter, and the various destination chapters for suggestions) You will need to send a fax or email containing your name as it appears in your passport, date and place of birth, nationality, passport number and expiry date, dates of entry to and exit from Russia (these can be approximate) and the name of the consulate at which you intend to apply for your visa.

Student Visa These are flexible, extendable and even entitle you to pay Russian prices for items affected under the country's dual-pricing system (see Costs under Money later in this chapter). You'll need proof of enrolment at an accredited Russian school or university, which usually requires prepayment.

Private Visa This is the visa you get for a visit by personal invitation, and it's also referred to as an 'ordinary' visa by some authorities. The visa itself is as easy to obtain as a tourist visa but getting the invitation is a complex matter.

The person who is inviting you must go to their local PVU office and fill out an invitation form for approval of the invitation. Approval, which takes several weeks, comes in the form of an *izveshchenie, or* notice of permission, good for one year, which the person inviting you must then send to you. You will need this invitation approval notice together with the standard application form to apply for the visa, which is valid for as many as 60 days in your host's town. On arrival in Russia you will also have to go to the local PVU office to register your visa (see Registration later on in this section).

On-the-Spot Visa These fast-track business visas don't require an advance invitation, and individuals arriving at Moscow's Sheremetevo-2 or St Petersburg's Pulkovo-2 airports can get them at a special consular office before going through passport control. You'll need a copy of a Ministry of Foreign Affairs (MID) invitation and a representative of your inviting company to meet you at the airport. Note, however, that airlines may not necessarily let you board your flight to Russia, because if you're turned down for the fast-track visa the airline is responsible for bringing you out again – so check with the airlines in advance.

This kind of visa is good for up to a month and attracts fees from about US$150 to US$250. Though expensive and problematic, it may be one way around the paper chase.

St Petersburg & Moscow 72-hour Stay Visa Since February 2002, Russia has been running a trial scheme: tourists from Schengen countries and Britain, Switzerland and Japan, who wish to visit St Petersburg and Moscow for less than 72 hours, can receive their visas directly upon entry. Travellers must apply at one of 29 authorised tour operators in their home country 48 hours before departure, where they fill in an application, pay a fee of US$35 and then collect the visa on arrival at one of six entry points: Sheremetevo Airport Terminal 2; St Petersburg's Pulkovo International Airport; the Bagrationovsk and Mamonovo points on the Polish border in the Kaliningrad region; and the Brusnichnoe and Torfyanovka points

on the Finnish border in the Leningrad region.

The aim is to increase Russia's tourist intake from non-CIS countries. For the time being, US citizens are not eligible for the new visas because the Tourism Ministry believes that few US tourists would travel to Russia for less than a week. The government hopes the scheme, scheduled initially to run for a year, will make Russia's major cities more attractive to Europeans seeking weekend getaways.

There are also plans to waive visas for tourists visiting Russia for less than 72 hours on cruises; this will mainly affect visitors to St Petersburg on cruises from Finland.

Transit Visa This is for 'passing through', which is loosely interpreted. For transit by air it's usually good for 48 hours. For a nonstop Trans-Siberian Railway journey it's valid for 10 days, giving westbound passengers a few days in Moscow without the obligatory hotel prebooking (those heading east can't linger in Moscow). Under certain circumstances, travellers transiting Russia and holding valid entry/exit visas to Armenia, Belarus, Kazakhstan, Kyrgyzstan, Tajikistan or Uzbekistan need not apply for a Russian transit visa. The requirements on this are sketchy, and while a Russian consulate may say it's unnecessary, the odds of being allowed into or out of Russia on the premise that you're holding a Tajik visa are slim. Many border guards are not familiar with the latest regulations handed down in Moscow, so it's always best to play it safe, especially when travelling to border crossings in remote areas.

HIV/AIDS Testing
At the time of writing, HIV/AIDS testing was required for foreigners staying in the Russian Federation longer than three months. By definition, this does not affect tourist visas, which are only issued for shorter stays. The medical certificate must be in English and in Russian. Consult the company sponsoring your business visa for the latest regulations.

When to Apply
Apply as soon as you have all the documents you need. Any number of unforseen circumstances can arise to delay the processing of your visa, so try to be patient if things don't go according to plan or what you perceive to be the rules. Business, tourist, private and

student visas all take the same amount of time to process once you have the paperwork – be it invitation, confirmation or *izveshchenie*. This ought to be 10 working days, but can vary. You can pay a higher fee for quicker service at most embassies.

Transit visas normally take seven working days but may take as little as a few hours at the Russian embassy in Beijing.

How to Apply

Individuals can arrange their own visas, though long queues at embassies and consulates are common in the high season and Russian consular officials are sometimes less than bright and perky – and they rarely answer the telephone. If you're booking your flight or accommodation through a travel agency, they'll get your visa too for an extra fee, usually between US$5 and US$30 (agencies in Hong Kong, which must go through the embassy in Bangkok for visas, charge you more) For group tours, the work is done by the agency.

When applying, bear in mind that it's usually a nightmare for a Russian to get a Western visa – the day you'll spend at a Russian embassy or consulate is a picnic in comparison.

Visa Agencies If you're really pressed for time, or especially if badly affected by impersonal bureaucracies, there are agencies that specialise in getting visas. In the USA, try **Visa Services, Inc** (☎ 202-387 0300; 1519 Connecticut Ave NW, Washington DC 20036) and **Travel Document Systems** (☎ 202-638 3800, 800-874 5100; e info@traveldocs.com; 734 15th St NW, Suite 400, Washington DC 20005).

In the UK, **Thames Consular Services** (☎ 020-8995 2492, fax 020-8742 1285; w www .visapassport.com) has a branch at the British Airways Travel Shop, 156 Regent St. They charge £40 (plus VAT) on top of the Russian visa fees, and if you want them to arrange the necessary documents for your tourist or business visa, it's an extra £35 (plus VAT).

Processing Fees

Each Russian consulate charges as much as it can, so rates fluctuate depending on where and when you apply, and how quickly you need the visa. At the time of research, for example, in the UK fees for either a tourist or business visa were £30 for processing in 10 working days, rising to £80 for a one-day ser-

vice. Australian citizens pay anything from AU$85 for a tourist visa processed in 15 working days to AU$400 for overnight processing; business visas cost AU$95 for 20 business days processing to AUS$420 for same-day service.

Registration

When you check in at a hotel, camping ground or hostel, you surrender your passport and visa so the hotel can register you with PVU. You'll get your documents back the next morning, if not the same day, although you'll usually need to ask, as nobody seems to remember to return them to you. A safer alternative is to tell staff at the front desk you need your passport back in five minutes so you can change some money. They'll usually register it right then.

All Russian visas must be registered with PVU within three business days of your arrival in Russia, and again each time you move city. No ifs or buts about it. Some travel agencies claim that their visas don't need to be registered. This is not true, so be highly suspicious of any company that tells you it is. Sometimes you have to pay a registration fee of US$5 to US$10.

The company or organisation that invites you to Russia is responsible for your initial registration, and no other company can support your visa. You can't take a visa issued on the invitation of, say, the HI Hostel in St Petersburg and have it registered in Moscow by the Travellers Guest House.

If you're not sure which organisation invited you (if the sponsorship line – on tourist visas this begins with the words *V uchrezhdenie* – has a name you've never heard of), the simplest option is to spend a night at one of the major hotels, which will register your visa for you right at the front desk; there may be a fee, but usually the cost of the room will suffice.

Extending a visa that's not registered can be impossible, and getting out of the country with an unregistered visa could be a very expensive proposition. You may be lucky and just receive a lecture or even be allowed to leave unhindered, although travellers have reported fines of up to US$500 levied at the Finnish and Norwegian borders.

Visa Extensions & Changes

Extensions are time-consuming, if not downright difficult, as the above anecdote indicates.

Try to avoid the need for an extension by asking for a longer visa than you might need – you can always leave earlier but leaving later than the visa allows will waste time and money. Many trains out of St Petersburg and Moscow to Eastern Europe cross the border after midnight, so make sure your visa is valid up to and including this day. Don't give border guards any excuses for making trouble.

DOCUMENTS

It's vital to carry photocopies of your documents, especially your Russian visa (see Photocopies later for further hints). Otherwise, replacing a lost or stolen visa can be a nightmare; sometimes you'll even have to contact the issuing embassy and ask it to track down your visa number. Good luck.

Your embassy or consulate in Russia can replace a lost or stolen passport, but if you lose your visa you must go to the local PVU office. Russian travel agents, hotel service bureaus and youth hostels can also help, including reporting the loss to the police. Again, procedures are much easier if you've stashed away a few passport-sized photos, your visa number and photocopies of your visa, and your passport's personal information and validity pages.

Travel Insurance

It's wise to take out travel insurance to cover theft, loss and medical problems. There are many policies available, so check the small print for things like ambulance cover or an emergency flight home. Note: some policies specifically exclude 'dangerous activities', which can include scuba diving, motorcycling and trekking.

You may prefer the policy to pay doctors or hospitals directly, rather than paying on the spot and claiming later (if you have to claim later make sure you keep all documentation). Some policies ask you to call back (reverse charge) to a centre in your home country, where an immediate assessment of your problem is made.

Youth & Student Cards

Full-time students and people aged under 26 can get a substantial discount on admissions – always flash your ID before paying.

For about US$6, full-time students can get an International Student Identity Card (ISIC) from student agencies worldwide. If you're not a student but are under 26, ask a student agency at home for an ISIC Youth Card.

Photocopies

All important documents (passport data page and visa page, credit cards, travel insurance policy, air/bus/train tickets, driving licence and so on) should be photocopied before you depart. Leave one copy with someone at home and keep another with you, separate from the originals. Take spare passport photos, and after you have entered Russia try to get a photocopy of your *deklaratsia* (customs declaration). All these will be very useful if your documents go astray.

It's also a good idea to store details of your vital travel documents in Lonely Planet's free online Travel Vault, in case you lose the photocopies or can't be bothered with them. Your password-protected Travel Vault is accessible online anywhere in the world and can be created at **w** www.ekno.lonelyplanet.com.

EMBASSIES & CONSULATES

Generally speaking, embassies won't be much help if you are in some kind of trouble and are at fault. Remember: you are bound by Russian law and embassies will not be sympathetic if you end up in jail after committing a crime locally, even if such actions are legal in your own country.

In genuine emergencies you might get some assistance, but only if other channels have been exhausted. For example, if you need to get home urgently, a free ticket is exceedingly unlikely – the embassy would expect you to have insurance. If you have all your money and documents stolen, the embassy might assist with getting a new passport, but a loan for onward travel is out of the question.

If you will be travelling in Russia for a long period of time (say a month or over) and particularly if you're heading to remote locations, it's wise to register with your embassy. This can be done over the telephone or by email.

Check **w** www.russianembassy.net for a full list of overseas Russian embassies.

Russian Embassies Abroad

Australia (☎ 02-6295 9033/9474, fax 6295 1847, **e** rusemb@dynamite.com.au) 78 Canberra Ave, Griffith, ACT 2603 *Consulate* (☎ 02-9326 1188, fax 9327 5065, **e** russcon@ozemail.com.au) 7 Fullerton St, Woollahra, NSW 2025

EUROPEAN RUSSIA

Belarus (☎ 0172-503 666, fax 503 664,
ⓔ karp@rusamb.belpak.minsk.by) vulitsa
Staravilenskaya 48, 220002 Minsk;
there's also a consulate general in Brest

Canada (☎ 613-235 4341, fax 236 6342,
ⓔ rusemb@intranet.ca) 285 Charlotte St,
Ottawa, Canada.
Visa Department (☎ 613-336 7220,
fax 238 6158)
Consulate (☎ 514-843 5901 or ☎ 842 5343,
fax 842 2012, ⓔ consulat@dsuper.net) 3685
Ave Du Musée, Montreal, Quebec, H3G 2EI

France (☎ 1-45 04 05 50 or ☎ 45 03 40 20,
fax 45 04 17 65, ⓔ rusembfr@club-internet.fr)
40-50 Boulevard Lannes, 75116 Paris
Consulate (☎ 91-77 15 15, fax 77 34 54,
ⓔ consrus@aix.pacwan.net) 8 Ave Ambrois
Pare, 13008 Marseilles; also consulate in
Strasbourg

Germany (☎ 030 220 2821 or ☎ 226 6320,
fax 229 9397, ⓔ russembassyg@trionet.de)
Unter den Linden 63-65, 10117 Berlin
Consulate (☎ 0228-312 085, fax 312 164,
ⓔ bonn@russische-botschaft.de) Waldstrasse
42, 53177 Bonn.
Consular affairs (☎ 0228-312 083, fax 384
561); also consulates in Hamburg, Leipzig,
Munich & Rostok

Japan (☎ 03-3583 4224, fax 3505 0593,
ⓔ rosconsl@ma.kcom.ne.jp) 2-1-1 Azabudai,
Minato-ku, Tokyo 106-0041.
Consular section (☎ 03-3583 4445, fax 3586
0407)
Consulate (☎ 06-6848 3452, fax 848 3453,
ⓔ ruson@mb.kcom.ne.jp) 1-2-2 Nishi Midori-
gaoka, Toyonaka-shi, Osaka-fu 560-0005;
also consulates in Niigata & Sapporo

New Zealand (☎ 04-476 6113, fax 476 3843)
57 Messines Rd, Karori, Wellington

UK (☎ 020-7229 3628, fax 7727 8625,
ⓦ www.russialink.org.uk.com/embassy)
13 Kensington Palace Gardens, London W8 4QX
Consular Section (☎ 020-7229 8027, visa
information message ☎ 0891-171 271, fax
020-7229 3215) 5 Kensington Palace Gardens,
London W8 4QS
Consulate (☎ 0131-225 7121, fax 225 9587,
ⓔ visa@edconsul.demon.co.uk) 58 Melville St,
Edinburgh E13 7HL

Ukraine (☎ 044-244 0961, fax 246 3469,
ⓔ embrus@public.icyb.kiev.ua) 27
Vozduhoflotskiy prospekt, Kiev

USA (☎ 202-298 5700/01, fax 628 0252) 2641
Wisconsin Ave, NW, Washington DC 20007
Visa Department (☎ 202-939 8907, fax 939
8909) 1825 Phelps Place NW, Washington DC
20008
Consulate (☎ 212-348 0926, fax 831 9162)
9 East 91 St, New York, NY 10128
Consulate (☎ 415-928 6878, fax 929 0306)

2790 Green St, San Francisco, CA 94123
Consulate (☎ 206-728 1910, fax 728 1871,
ⓦ www.ruscon.com) 2323 Westin Building,
2001 Sixth Ave, Seattle, WA 98121-2617

Embassies in Moscow

The area code for the following numbers is
☎ 095. For more information, check online
at ⓦ www.themoscowtimes.ru/travel/facts
/embassies.

Australia (☎ 956 60 70, fax 956 61 70,
ⓦ www.australianembassy.ru) Kropotkinsky
per 2

Belarus (☎ 924 70 31, visa inquiries ☎ 924 70
95) ul Maroseyka 17/6

Canada (☎ 956 66 66, fax 232 99 48)
Starokonyushenny per 23

France (☎ 937 15 00, fax 937 15 77,
ⓦ www.ambafrance.ru) ul Bolshaya
Yakimanka 45

Germany (☎ 937 95 00, fax 936 21 43,
ⓦ www.germany.org.ru) Mosfilmovskaya ul 56
Consular section (☎ 936 24 01) Leninsky pr 95A

Japan (☎ 291 85 00, fax 200 12 40) Kalashny
per 12

New Zealand (☎ 956 35 79, fax 956 35 83,
ⓦ www.nzembassy.msk.ru) ul Povarskaya 44

South Africa (☎ 230 68 69) Bolshoy
Strochenovsky per 22/25

UK (☎ 956 72 00 fax 956 72 01,
ⓦ www.britemb.msk.ru) Smolenskaya nab 10

Ukraine (☎ 229 35 42) ul Stanislavskogo 18

USA (☎ 728 50 00, fax 728 50 90,
ⓦ www.usembassy.state.gov/moscow)
Novinsky bulvar 19/23

Consulates in St Petersburg

The area code for St Petersburg is ☎ 812.

Belarus (☎ 273 00 78) Office 66, nab
Robespiera 8

Canada (☎ 325 84 48 or 316 72 22, fax 316 72
22) Malodetskoselsky pr 32

France (☎ 312 11 30, fax 311 72 83) nab reki
Moyki 15

Germany (☎ 327 24 00, fax 327 31 17) ul
Furshtadtskaya 39

UK (☎ 320 32 00, fax 325 31 11) pl
Proletarskoy Diktatury 5

USA (☎ 275 17 01, fax 110 70 22) ul
Furshtadtskaya 15

Consulates in Yekaterinburg

The area code for Yekaterinburg is ☎ 3432.

UK (☎ 3432-56 4931, fax 59 2901,
ⓦ www.britain.sky.ru) Gogolya ul 15A

USA (☎ 3432-62 98 88, fax 56 4515,
ⓦ www.uscgyekat.ur.ru) Gogolya ul 15A

CUSTOMS

You may be asked to fill in a *deklaratsia* upon arrival, which you should keep until departure. If you're bringing in currency and goods valued in excess of US$1500, you *must* follow this procedure; it's recommended even if you have less than that. Several travellers have told us that all their cash was confiscated by customs officers at the Chinese and Mongolian borders because they didn't have the form; even at other border crossings, it is just not worth the risk of being caught out by light-fingered customs officers.

If you are arriving by air, the airline will probably give you two declaration forms in English – keep one to fill out when you leave, as border posts and airports rarely have them in English. The form asks for various details, including name, citizenship and destination; purpose of visit; declarations of weapons and narcotics; currency brought into the country, and so on. You must also list how many pieces of luggage you've sent separately.

When you leave Russia, you will have to fill out an identical form declaring anything removed from the country. If you have a stamped customs form, your exit customs form cannot show you are leaving with more than you brought in. If you did not get your form stamped on the way in, your exit form cannot show you are taking out items with a total value of more than US$500.

Lost Customs Form

Treat a stamped customs declaration as carefully as your passport. If you lose it then you'll need to get a police report confirming the loss, to be presented to customs when you leave Russia.

What You Can Bring In

You may bring in modest amounts of anything for personal use, except illegal drugs and weapons, and GPS (Global Positioning System) devices. If you're travelling with hypodermic needles, bring a prescription and declare them under 'Narcotics and appliances for use thereof'.

Up to 1000 cigarettes and 5L of alcohol are allowed (but bear in mind that prices for such items in Russia will almost certainly be cheaper than abroad) but large amounts of anything saleable are suspect. Food is allowed (except for some fresh fruit and vegetables).

What You Can Take Out

Anything bought from a legitimate shop or department store can be removed from the country, but save your receipts. Leaving with modest amounts of roubles isn't a problem, but change large sums beforehand.

Anything vaguely 'arty' – manuscripts, instruments, coins, jewellery, antiques, antiquarian books (meaning those published before 1975) – must be assessed by the **Committee for Culture** in Moscow (Map 2, Moscow chapter; ☎ 921 32 58; ul Neglinnaya 8/10, room 298) and St Petersburg (Map 6, St Petersburg chapter; ☎ 311 51 96; Malaya Morskaya ul 17). The bureaucrats will issue a receipt for tax paid (usually 100% of the purchase price; bring your sales docket), presented to customs on your way out. If you buy something large, a photograph is usually fine for assessment purposes.

Paintings bought at tourist art markets, department stores or commercial galleries should be declared; keep all receipts. Generally, airport customs are much stricter and more thorough than at any border crossing.

MONEY

Since the economic crash in 1998 the rouble has become much more stable. We've listed most prices in this book in roubles (abbreviated to R), with the main exceptions being some (but not all) hotel prices, which are often quoted in US dollars and tied to that currency.

For rules on taking money in or out of the country, see Customs earlier.

Currency

Russian currency is the rouble (**roo**-bl), written as рубль or abbreviated as ру or р. There are 100 kopecks in a rouble and these come in coin denominations of one (rarely seen), five, 10 and 50.

Also issued in coins, roubles come in amounts of one, two and five, with banknotes in values of 10, 50, 100, 500 and 1000 roubles. In practice the 500 notes are the easiest to carry, but they will be hard to use for small purchases as the seller may not have change. Finding change can be a real problem – while it's wise to hang on to a stash of smaller notes and coins, be insistent at shops, restaurants and so on if the staff are doubtful about giving change for larger notes.

It's illegal to make purchases in any currency other than roubles. When you run into prices in dollars (or the pseudonym 'units', often written as ye – the abbreviation for *uslovnye yedenitsy*, standard units) in expensive restaurants and hotels you will still be presented with a final bill in roubles.

Exchange Rates

The exchange rate used throughout this book is US$1=R30. The exchange rates below were valid at the time of research but are likely to change:

country	unit		rouble
Australia	A$	=	R18.84
Canada	C$	=	R21.03
China	Y10	=	R38.51
Euro zone	€1	=	R34.66
Finland	FIM1	=	R58.30
Japan	¥100	=	R26.60
New Zealand	NZ$1	=	R17.52
UK	UK£1	=	R52.53
Ukraine	10 hv	=	R61.58
USA	US$1	=	R31.85

Exchanging Money

Cash You'll get the best rates for US dollars, which can be exchanged anywhere. Other major currencies, such as the British pound or the euro, can be easily changed in Moscow and St Petersburg, but elsewhere you're likely to run into difficulties.

Any currency you bring should be in pristine condition: banks and exchange bureaus do not accept old, tatty bills with rips or tears. For US dollars make certain they are the new design, with the large offset portrait, and are looking and smelling newly minted.

Every town of any size will have at least one bank or exchange office – be prepared to fill out a lengthy form and show your passport. Your receipt is for your own records as customs officials no longer require documentation of your currency transactions. As anywhere, rates can vary from one establishment to the next so it's always worth shopping around.

Travellers Cheques It can be difficult to exchange travellers cheques outside the largest cities and the process can be lengthy, involving trips to numerous different cashiers in the bank, each responsible for a different part of the transaction. Expect to pay 1% to 2% commission. Unless you spend all your time in Moscow and St Petersburg, it is not

a good idea to carry your fortune in travellers cheques – you might not be able to use them.

Not all travellers cheques are treated as equal by Russian establishments willing to handle them. In descending order of acceptance are American Express (AmEx), Thomas Cook and Visa; you'll have little or no luck with other brands.

ATMs Automated teller machines (ATMs), linked to international networks such as AmEx, Cirrus, Eurocard, MasterCard and Visa, are now quite common across Russia – look for signs that say *bankomat* (БАНК-ОМАТ). Using a credit card or the card you use in ATMs at home, you can obtain cash as you need it – usually in roubles, but sometimes in dollars, too.

If you are going to rely on ATMs, make certain you have a few days' supply of cash at hand in case you can't find a machine to accept your card. Memorise PINs for all cards you intend to carry and check Dangers & Annoyances later in this chapter for ATM scams.

Credit Cards In Moscow and St Petersburg Credit cards are becoming more accepted. Elsewhere, don't rely on them. Most sizable cities have banks or exchange bureaus that will give you a cash advance on your credit card, but be prepared for a tangle of paperwork.

International Transfers Larger cities will have at least one bank that can handle Western Union money wires. Ask at any bank for this information – they will be happy to steer you to a bank in town that can handle wire transfers.

Black Market Don't risk changing money on the street – there are plenty of exchange bureaus and banks where you'll get a decent rate. Should some shadowy character offer to exchange money for you, remember that they can't give you a substantially better rate than banks and still make a profit.

Security

Don't leave money lying around your room – keep it in several different places about your person and baggage. When you go out, carry what you'll need in your pockets (but avoid eye-catching wallet bulges) and tuck any extra away under your clothing (use a money belt, shoulder wallet or ankle pouch). Or wrap the cash carefully in plastic and tuck it under the insole of your shoe.

Costs

Although it's possible to travel in Russia on very little (see the boxed text 'Travelling the Scientific Way' in the Getting Around chapter), for most visitors a reasonable budget is around US$50 a day.

Moscow and St Petersburg are the two most expensive cities. With serious economising you could scrape by on US$30 a day in Moscow, but if you visit museums, take excursions and indulge in the nightlife you're heading towards US$100 a day; prices are marginally lower in St Petersburg. The only bargain you'll share with the locals in either city is riding the metro for R6. The cheapest accommodation in either city won't be much under US$20 a day.

Prices drop away from the metropolises, but not significantly: you can still be up for US$50 a night or more at a decent hotel in major cities, including Yekaterinburg, Nizhny and Novgorod. It's possible to dine out at under US$5 per head, but then your choices will be more limited than in the big cities.

Dual-Pricing System Although dual pricing for airplane and train tickets has ended, as a foreigner you'll still find yourself paying more than a Russian. Hotels (except the most expensive Western-style ones) and museums all frequently have two-tier pricing systems, with foreigners paying more. In hotels the difference can be as much as 50%, although if the room costs only US$10 to begin with that's not too bad. Often, the only rooms available to foreigners will be the better-appointed ones.

It's often fair game for taxi drivers and sometimes market sellers to think they can charge foreigners more – check with locals for prices, but don't expect that knowledge to be much use unless you can bargain in Russian.

Museums have the highest mark-up, percentage wise – it's not unusual for it to be 10 times what Russians pay. There's a certain fairness here, given the vast disparity between Western and Russian incomes. Take heart that your extra money is desperately needed to protect the very works of art and artefacts you've come to see.

Tipping & Bargaining

Tipping is standard in the better restaurants, about 10%; elsewhere, 5% to 10% is fine. It's accepted practice to tip your guide, if you have one, at around US$5 to US$10 a day; a small gift (skin cream, imported chocolates, CDs) is appropriate if service is high.

Prices in stores are usually firm; for goods at markets and souvenir stalls, make a counter bid somewhat lower than the merchant's price. But remember: Russia is not really the place for protracted haggling.

Taxes

The Value Added Tax (VAT, or NDS in Russia) is 20% and is usually included in the listed price for purchases – ask to make sure. In Moscow and St Petersburg there's also a 5% sales tax, ususally only encountered in top hotels.

POST & COMMUNICATIONS
Post

Pochta (ПОЧТАМТ) refers to any post office, *glavpochtamt* to a main post office, and *mezhdunarodnyy glavpochtamt* to an international one. The main offices are open from 8am to 8pm or 9pm, with shorter hours on Saturday and Sunday; in big cities one office will possibly stay open 24 hours a day.

Sending Mail Outward post is slow but fairly reliable; if you want to be certain, use registered post *(zakaznaya pochta;* zakaz-**noi** po-cht). Airmail letters take two to three weeks from Moscow and St Petersburg to the UK, longer from other cities, and three to four weeks to the USA or Australasia. For airmail letters under 20g, the cost is R10/16 for regular/registered post to practically everywhere abroad.

You can address outgoing international mail as you would from any country, in your own language, though it might help to *precede* it with the country name in Cyrillic.

Some Cyrillic country names are

America (USA)	Америка (США)
Australia	Австралия
Canada	Канада
France	Франция
Germany	Германия
Great Britain	Великобритания
Ireland	Ирландия
New Zealand	Новая Зеландия

In major cities you can usually find the services of at least one of the international express carriers, such as FedEx or DHL.

Receiving Mail Incoming mail is so unreliable that many companies, hotels and individuals use private services with addresses in Germany or Finland (a private carrier completes the mail's journey to its Russian destination). Other than this, your *reliable* options for receiving mail in Russia are nil: anything addressed to poste restante should be considered lost before it is sent, and embassies and consulates won't hold mail for transient visitors.

If sending mail to Russia or trying to receive it, note that addresses should be in reverse order: Russia (Россия), postal code (if known), city, street address, name.

Telephone

Russian city codes are listed in this book under the relevant section heading. The country code for Russia is ☎ 7.

Russian telecommunication services have improved no end since 1991, but there's also been an explosion of providers, which can be confusing and, if you're not careful, expensive.

Private Telephones From a private phone in Russia, dialling outside the country is very simple, but the prices keep rising and are now even higher than those for equivalent calls from the West to Russia. To call internationally dial ☎ 8, wait for the second tone, then dial ☎ 10 and the country and city codes, then the number. Omit any zeroes from the city code (eg, to call Sydney, it's ☎ 8 10 61 2, and then the phone number).

At the time of writing, daytime (8am to 8pm, Monday to Friday) telephone prices for Moscow and St Petersburg were R15 per minute to Europe, R19.5 to the USA and Canada, and R35.4 to Australasia. Calls are cheaper from 8pm to 8am weekdays and all day on weekends.

Some useful country codes are

Australia	☎ 61
Belarus	☎ 375
Canada	☎ 1
China	☎ 86
Estonia	☎ 372
Finland	☎ 358
France	☎ 33
Germany	☎ 49
Ireland	☎ 353
Japan	☎ 81
Latvia	☎ 371
Lithuania	☎ 370

Netherlands	☎ 31
New Zealand	☎ 64
Norway	☎ 47
UK	☎ 44
Ukraine	☎ 380
USA	☎ 1

Pay Phones *Taksofon* (pay phones, таксофон) are located throughout most cities, usually in working order. Most take prepaid phonecards, available from metro token booths or kiosks. There are several types of cardphones, and not all cards are interchangeable. Cardphones can be used for local and domestic or international long-distance calls.

Some older phone booths accept *zhetony* (metal tokens) as payment. Place the token in the slot on top of the phone and dial; when the party answers, the token should drop. A series of beeps means you must insert another token.

'Domestic' calls (ie, long-distance calls within Russia or to any former Soviet republic) can be made from *mezhdugorodnyy* (pay phones marked Междугородный), using different, wrinkled-metal tokens available only from telephone offices. They work on a similar principle, but you need to push the *otvet* button (Ответ) on the phone's face when your party answers. Dial ☎ 8, wait for the second tone, then dial the city code (including zeros) and the number.

State/Central Telephone Offices State-run long-distance telephone offices are found in almost all towns and cities, usually in the same building as (or near) a post office. In most, you leave a deposit with an attendant and are assigned a private booth where you dial your number directly. In a few instances, you still give your number to an attendant who dials the number and then sends you to a booth to take the call. Either way, you pay an outstanding balance or collect change from your deposit when you leave. Rates are similar to home services.

Satellite Phone Centres In many cities, you can now find privately run phone centres boasting satellite links to the outside world. These have an advantage over state offices because they offer much more reliable connections, comfortable surroundings and competitive rates.

Country Direct This service allows you to dial a toll-free number in Moscow or St

Petersburg for connection with a service provider such as AT&T, MCI or Sprint, which can put through collect or calling-card calls to numbers outside Russia. (Note: you pay for this reliability and convenience with high rates.) The access numbers for these services change frequently, so check the number with the provider before you leave for Russia.

Hotel Phones At most traditional Russian hotels local calls are free. Placing long-distance calls can be more difficult and you'll have to work the details out with the front desk. Calls from pricey Western hotels are expensive: a direct-dialled call abroad from your room can cost over US$100 for 20 minutes. If you or your company don't want to pay such a rate, use a country direct service or go outside.

Most hotel-room telephones have a direct-dial number for incoming calls, which saves you having to be connected through the switchboard. However, this can lead to unwanted disturbances: see Dangers & Annoyances later in this chapter.

Cellular Service Mobile (cellular) phones are becoming increasingly popular with Russians who want to bypass the antiquated state system. In Moscow and St Petersburg, they are as common as in most major Western cities, although coverage gets a lot patchier the further east you head, until you hit the major Far East urban centres of Khabarovsk and Vladivostok. There are several different systems and you may be able to use your regular cell phone while you are in Russia – check with your service provider for details.

Fax
Faxes can be sent from most post offices and the better hotels. Post office rates are usually around R60 a page to Europe, the US and Canada, and R90 a page to Australia.

Email & Internet Access
It's no problem finding Internet cafés across Russia – even the smallest towns have connections. The best place to start is the main post office or telephone office, as they often have the cheapest rates, around R30 an hour or less.

To access your home email account, you'll need your incoming (POP or IMAP) mail server name, your account name, and your

password; your ISP or network supervisor will be able to give you these. It also pays to become familiar with the process for accessing mail from a net-connected machine before you leave home.

An even easier option is a free ekno Web-based email account, available at **w** www.ekno.lonelyplanet.com, allowing email access from computers running a standard Web browser.

DIGITAL RESOURCES
For links about Russia, the **Lonely Planet website** (**w** www.lonelyplanet.com) has destination profiles, feature stories, reports from travellers on the road, and more.

The following sites are also useful:

w **www.departments.bucknell.edu/russian** The USA's Bucknell University runs this huge award-winning site, with links to just about any Russian topic

w **www.rol.ru** With links to Russian Web cams, Internet radio stations, news and services; Russian-only

w **http://travel.state.gov/russia.html** The US State Department's information page on Russia, with up-to-date information on visas, safety issues, trouble spots and other practical matters

w **www.interknowledge.com/russia** Official site of the Russian National Tourist Office, with information on Lake Baikal and the Arctic region

w **www.infoservices.com** Travellers' Yellow Pages for Moscow and St Petersburg

w **www.waytorussia.net** Useful site run by students from Moscow University, with links to travel agencies in Russia; it also sells Trans-Siberian tickets and arranges visas

w **www.russiajournal.com** Site of an English-language business-orientated weekly newspaper, with some good features

w **www.parovoz.com/cgi-bin/rrr.cgi?lang=eng** Brings together Internet resources about Russian railways, subways and tramways; most sites are in Cyrillic

BOOKS
Lonely Planet
Lonely Planet's *St Petersburg* and *Moscow* books contain all you need to know about those cities, while the *Trans-Siberian Railway* is a guide to the world's most famous train route; the *Russian phrasebook* has detailed language information geared to the traveller. Lonely Planet also publishes guides to many neighbouring countries and regions,

including Finland, Norway, Scandinavian Europe, Estonia, Latvia and Lithuania, Eastern Europe, Poland, the Czech and Slovak Republics, Hungary, Romania and Moldova, Georgia, Armenia and Azerbaijan, Central Asia, Mongolia and China.

Other Guidebooks

Russia by Rail, by Athol Yates, follows several major train routes radiating from Moscow, listing sights viewable by train. *A Travel Guide to Jewish Russia & Ukraine*, by Ben G Frank, is an impressive work documenting the effect of the Jewish culture on these lands. *Live & Work in Russia and Eastern Europe*, by Jonathan Packer, is a good reference for people hoping to find a job or start a business in Russia.

Travel

Among the most recently published travel books on Russia, Charlotte Hobson's *Black Earth City* is one of the best. This eloquent account of her year studying in Voronezh, in the turbulent period following September 1991's attempted coup and subsequent dissolution of the Soviet Union, captures much that is true about the Russian way of life today, over a decade later.

Hooked is by skilled writer Fen Montaigne, who uses the excuse that he wants to fly-fish rural Russia's untamed wild rivers to explore the psyche and lives of people far removed from Moscow and St Petersburg. Or, if an evocative (at times sexually feverish) account of modern city life is what you're after, try Duncan Farrell's *One Hot Night in St Petersburg*.

Several years before glasnost, Colin Thubron taught himself Russian and drove solo across almost every open motor route in the country, visiting many of today's most frequented destinations. The result, *Among the Russians* (published in some countries as *Where Nights Are Longest*), is a precise and eloquent (although rather humourless) personal account of Soviet times – a lot hasn't changed since.

Similarly, there's still a lot to recognise about the 1960s Russia encountered by Laurens van der Post in *Journey into Russia*, an intelligent, insightful account of travel throughout the Soviet Union.

Going even further back, *Letters from Russia*, by the Marquis de Custine, is a

French aristocrat's jolly account of hobnobbing with tsar and the high society in St Petersburg and Moscow in 1839. The Marquis' description of St Basil's Cathedral has never been bettered: '...a sort of irregular fruit bristling with excrescences, a cantaloup melon with embroidered edges...a crystallisation of a thousand colours...this confectionery box.'

Caucasian Journey, by wandering fisherman Negley Farson, describes journeys among the northern Caucasian tribal people in the 1920s, before the full force of Bolshevism hit them. In the 1990s, Negley's son Daniel Farson took off down the Volga to the same destination, and the result is *A Dry Ship to the Mountains*.

The Spirit-Wrestlers, by Philip Marsden, delves into the spiritual world of southern Russia, where mystics and miracle workers are part of life and the secular state is a mere distraction. Mark Taplin's *Open Lands – Travels through Russia's Once Forbidden Places* is an engrossing read, covering some of Russia's once off-limits cities, including Vladivostok and Nizhny Novgorod.

History, Politics & Culture

General & Pre-Soviet Era

Sir Fitzroy Maclean – a Scot whose lifetime affair with Russia and other ex-Soviet republics goes back to his days as a Moscow diplomat in the 1930s – has written several entertaining, intelligent books on the country. *Holy Russia* is a good, short Russian history, while *All the Russias: The End of an Empire* covers the whole of the former USSR; the USSR section of Maclean's *Eastern Approaches* (which also covers WWII adventures elsewhere) focuses mainly on travels in outlying republics but does include a chilling account of the 1938 show trial of veteran revolutionary Bukharin.

A History of Russia, by Nicholas Riasanovsky, is one of the best single-volume versions of the whole Russian story through to the end of the Soviet Union. *A Traveller's History of Russia & the USSR*, by Peter Neville, is good on pre-Gorbachev Russia.

One of the best books on any single strand of pre-Soviet history is *Peter the Great – His Life & World* by Robert K Massie, a good read about one of Russia's most influential rulers. *Catherine the Great: Life and Legend*, by John T Alexander, is a highly readable account of the famous empress, making a case for the veracity of some of the more salacious tales of her life.

Soviet Era Edmund Wilson's *To the Finland Station* (1940) is the most authoritative account of the development of socialism and communism.

The Rise & Fall of the Soviet Empire, by Stephen Dalziel, describes exactly that in lively style, covering the years 1917 to 1992; there are some good photos, too. *A History of the Soviet Union*, by Geoffrey Hosking, is a dense, analytical look at the Soviet era up to 1985 – if you need to know why Kamenev fell out with Kalinin or why Left SRs ('social revolutioners') loathed Kadets, Hosking's your man.

Ten Days That Shook the World, by US journalist John Reed, is a melodramatic, enthusiastic and contemporary account of the Bolsheviks' 1917 power grab. (Reed actually ended up entombed on Red Square.)

The 900 Days: The Siege of Leningrad, by Harrison Salisbury, tells of that city's sufferings in WWII. *Stalingrad*, by Anthony Beevor, a superb work based on new access to long-secret archives, concentrates on the human cost of the war.

Recent History & Politics Because so many foreign correspondents in Russia marked the end of their assignment with a book, new publications about recent events continue to hit the shelves

Dominic Lieven's *Empire* is an astute, scholarly book written with great love and understanding of Russia. *Night of Stone: Death and Memory in Russia*, by Catherine Merridale, is equally enthralling, mixing the country's bleak recent history with psychology and philosophy.

David Remnick's *Lenin's Tomb* and *Resurrection: The Struggle for a New Russia* are both notable volumes by the *Washington Post*'s award-winning ex-Moscow correspondent.

Eternal Russia, by Jonathan Steele, the *Guardian*'s Moscow correspondent from 1988, covers the Gorbachev years and continues up to the 1993 White House shoot-out and subsequent elections.

Martin Walker's Russia, a collection of articles by Steele's *Guardian* predecessor in Moscow, is worth reading for the excitement it conveys of early glasnost, and for its snapshots of daily life.

Vladimir Putin has allowed some of his carefully chosen thoughts and biographical details to be put to paper in *First Person*, but it sadly doesn't live up to its subtitle, *An Astonishingly Frank Self-Portrait*.

General Much of *USSR: From an Original Idea by Karl Marx*, by Marc Polonsky & Russell Taylor, is a streetwise 1980s look at the headaches of Russian travel – the authors, experienced in organising 'real life' Soviet tours, are funny enough to keep you up when the trip gets you down.

Imperium, by Ryszard Kapuscinski, the Polish correspondent and travel writer, is a 1994 collection of essays, journalism and recollections of the Soviet empire. Kapuscinski's boyhood town, Pinsk, was in the part of Poland taken over by the USSR in 1939 (it's in Belarus today). Later, his teacher and some classmates were deported, and the experience left him with a clear loathing of the Soviet system.

Women's Glasnost vs Naglost, by Tatyana Mamonova, combines essays by this Russian women's movement leader with interviews of a cross-section of women in a country where wife-beating and abortion reach incredible levels.

A History of Russian Architecture, by William Craft Brumfield, is the definitive work on the topic, from wooden huts to the bombastic last gasps of the Soviet Union. *Russian Art of the Avant-Garde* is a collection of essays demonstrating that Soviet artists weren't painting in a vacuum and in fact led the West in many trends.

Towards Another Shore, by Aileen M Kelly, is a brilliant examination of the development of Russian ideological thinking. *The Sexual Revolution in Russia*, by Igor S Kon, is considered the authoritative history of sexual mores and habits among Russians throughout history. *Pushkin's Button*, by Serena Vitale, is a fascinating recounting of the duel that killed the writer/poet Pushkin.

NEWSPAPERS & MAGAZINES
Russian-Language
The freeing of the press in Russia throughout the 1990s paved the way for brave journalistic investigations of scandals, high-level corruption, government cover-ups and gross mismanagement. Many of these journalists paid for their daring with their lives, others with forced silence.

Though a far cry from the one-note news days of the Soviet era, most of Russia's biggest papers are, to some degree, mouthpieces for the various powerful bodies that own them, be they political parties or rich businessmen. The public, already used to reading between the lines in the Soviet days, know how to take a bit from here, a bit from there, and imagine a truth that's somewhere in between.

The most popular Russian dailies are *Izvestia*, *Kommersant* and *Komsomolskaya Pravda*. The government's official newspaper is the *Rossiyskaya Gazeta*, while the tabloids are represented by *Moskovsky Komsomolets Versiya*, *Sovershenno Sekretno* and the anti-Putin *Novaya Gazeta*. The weekly *Argumenty I Fakty* is one of the most popular papers in the country, selling over 30 million copies a week. Reputed to be relatively free from outside influences, it covers politics, economics and the social scene.

The magazine market is similarly flooded with local titles and Russian-language versions of popular Western ones, including *Cosmopolitan* and *GQ*. In Moscow, *Afisha* is a trendy *Time Out*–style monthly and worth a look.

English-Language

Top hotels in Moscow and St Petersburg usually have day-old copies of the main dailies, such as the *International Herald-Tribune* and *Financial Times*, as well as news weeklies, including the *Economist*, *Time* and *Newsweek*. Elsewhere, imported English-language newspapers and magazines are a rarity due to high cover prices and Russia's paucity of English speakers.

In Moscow, the locally published *Moscow Times* (**w** www.themoscowtimes.ru) is a first-rate daily staffed by top-notch journalists and editors, covering Russian and international issues – it's available by subscription and is free at hotels, business centres and restaurants. The same company is behind *St Petersburg Times* (**w** www.sptimesrussia.com), a biweekly with the same high standards as its Moscow sibling.

A few other English-language business journals and newspapers come and go from the Moscow and St Petersburg scene, but they mostly dish up the same tepid stories designed to appeal to advertisers while not challenging the readers.

RADIO & TV
Russian-Language Radio
Radio in Russia is broken into three bands: AM, UKV (66MHz to 77MHz) and FM (100MHz to 107MHz). A Western-made FM radio usually won't go lower than 85MHz.

Although the most popular radio stations play a mix of ear-curdling Euro-pop and the even trashier Russian variant, there's enough programming variety for you to find something worth listening to.

English-Language Radio
The clearest BBC World Service short-wave (SW) frequencies in the morning, late evening and night are near 9410kHz, 12,095kHz (the best) and 15,070kHz, though the exact setting varies with Russian locations. The BBC broadcasts as follows:

2am to 5am & 3pm to 9pm at 9410kHz
2am to 5am & 6pm to 8pm at 6195kHz
5am to 9pm at 12,095kHz
6am to 3pm at 15,565kHz
7am to 3pm at 17,640kHz
8pm to midnight at 5930kHz, 6180kHz and 7325kHz

Russian-Language TV
In recent years Russian TV has been rapidly developing, causing a clash of interests between the state, the bankrolling tycoons who own some stations, and journalists. In 2001 the controversial take over of NTV, Russia's first truly professional station (and, crucially, critical of the government), by the state-controlled natural gas monopoly, Gazprom, led to demonstrations on the Moscow streets and a walk-out by the station's top journalists; many went to work for another independent station, TV6, but in January 2002 it too was shut down.

In an interesting turn of events, the ex-NTV journalists, led by Yevgeny Kiselyov (who also spent time at TV6) were awarded the licence to broadcast on TVS, TV6's successor, but only because they agreed to work in alliance with various Putin and government supporters. Still, Kiselyov and his team are back on air, doing pretty much what they did before, which undermines the prevailing Western view that Putin is out to control the media at all costs.

Media insiders tell us that what Russia is left with after all these shenanigans is effectively three clones of the old NTV: RTR

(Channel 2), the new NTV and TVS. ORT (Channel 1, the state channel) is also working hard to match NTV's standards, and RenTV (effectively a mouthpiece for right-wing politicians) is moving in the same direction. Amid all the badly dubbed films, soap operas and cheesy game shows, you will find programmes that are sometimes critical of the powers that be. Kultura (Channel 5) remains outside such politics, showing a mix of new and old films from many countries, as well as plays, concerts and historical and educational programmes; the first half of Channel 5's day is occupied by Russia's version of Euronews, another news programme not censored by the Kremlin. If none of that grabs you, there's also Russia's own MTV, dishing up a hi-energy mix of local and international pop videos.

English-Language TV

In the major hotels you'll have access to those modern-day staples of international travel, CNN and BBC World, and most likely a range of other satellite channels broadcasting in English and other languages.

VIDEO SYSTEMS

Russia's predominant video format, SECAM, is incompatible with the system used in Australia and most of Europe (France and Greece are among the exceptions), and North America's NTSC.

Hi8 and SVHS cassettes are easy to find in most big cities. If your camera records in NTSC, Hi8 and SVHS cassettes will be fine, even if they say PAL on them. You might have a hard time, however, connecting your camera to a TV or transferring onto VHS, depending on whether or not the TV reads, or the VCR records, NTSC.

PHOTOGRAPHY & VIDEO
Film & Equipment

Major brands of print film are widely available throughout Russia at Western European prices, although slide film is not widely sold so bring plenty of rolls with you. (Whatever film you purchase, check the expiration date carefully.) Any town or city of any size will have several places to get your film processed.

The same uncommon specialist shops that sell slide film will also have a smattering of camera gear by leading brands such as Nikon and Canon.

Technical Tips

Avoid running films through airport X-ray machines. No matter what the attendant says, these machines are not film-safe: effects are cumulative and too much will fog your pictures. Lead 'film-safe' pouches help, but the best solution is to have your film and camera inspected by hand. You can minimise officials' annoyance by having all film in clear plastic bags.

For tips on taking decent photos, read Lonely Planet's *Travel Photography*, by Richard I'Anson.

Cold Weather Camera batteries get sluggish in the cold, so carry your camera inside your coat and keep spare batteries warm in your pocket. In the prolonged Siberian winter, you may be better off with a manual camera rather than an automatic battery-operated one – film gets brittle at very low temperatures and a motor drive's fast advance or rewind can break it and leave static marks. Frame-filling expanses of snow come out a bit grey unless you deliberately *overexpose* about one-half to one stop. Deep cold can play tricks with exposure, so 'bracket' your best pictures with additional shots about one stop underexposed and overexposed each.

Hot Weather In hot territories, avoid magenta-tinted pictures by protecting your film from fierce summer heat. Leave it at the hotel, or line a stuff-sack with a piece cut from an aluminised Mylar 'survival blanket' – your film will stay cool inside all day.

Restrictions

You need to be particularly careful about photographing stations, official-looking buildings and any type of military/security structure – if in doubt, don't snap! Travellers have been arrested for such innocent behaviour, including an author of this book.

Some museums and galleries forbid flash pictures, some ban all photos and most will charge you extra to snap away. Some caretakers in historical buildings and churches charge mercilessly for the privilege of using a still or video camera.

Photographing People

As anywhere, use good judgement and discretion when taking photos of people. It's always better to ask first and if the person

EUROPEAN RUSSIA

doesn't want to be photographed, respect their privacy; a lifetime living with the KGB may make older people uneasy about being photographed, although a genuine offer to send on a copy can loosen your subject up. Remember that many people will be touchy if you photograph 'embarrassments' such as drunks, run-down housing and other signs of social decay.

In Russian, 'May I take a photograph of you?' is *Mozhno vas sfotografirovat?* (**mozh**-na sfa-ta-gruh-**fee**-ra-vut?).

TIME

From the early hours of the last Sunday in September to the early hours of the last Sunday in March, Moscow and St Petersburg time is GMT/UTC plus three hours. From the last Sunday in March to the last Sunday in September, 'summer time' is in force: GMT/UTC plus four hours.

Most of European Russia is in the same time zone as Moscow and St Petersburg, exceptions being the Kaliningrad region in the west (Moscow time minus one hour) and some regions in the east: Samara and Izhevsk are on Moscow time plus one hour, while Orenburg, Perm, Ufa and Yekaterinburg operate on Moscow time plus two hours.

East of the Ural Mountains, Irkutsk is on Moscow time plus five hours, Vladivostok on Moscow time plus seven hours, and Petropavlovsk-Kamchatsky on Moscow time plus nine hours.

Russian train timetables (except for suburban services) are mostly on Moscow time everywhere, as are station clocks in most places.

The following international relationships will be wrong by an hour for short periods when other cities change to 'summer time' on different dates.

The rest of the time, when it's noon in Moscow and St Petersburg, it's...

1am in San Francisco
4am in New York and Toronto
9am in London
10am in Paris, Berlin, Vilnius, Warsaw, Prague and Budapest
11am in Helsinki, Tallinn, Riga, Minsk, Kiev, Chisinau, Bucharest and Ankara
1pm in Tbilisi, Yerevan and Baku
2pm in Bishkek and Tashkent
5pm in Beijing and Ulaan Baatar
7pm in Sydney
9pm in Auckland

ELECTRICITY

Standard voltage is 220V, 50Hz AC, although a few places still have the old 127V system. Sockets require a continental or European plug with two round pins; travel adapters enable appliances from countries with different electrical setups to work in Russia. Some trains and hotel bathrooms have 110V and 220V shaver plugs.

WEIGHTS & MEASURES

Russia operates on the metric system (see the back of the book for conversions from other units). Restaurant menus often list the weight of food and drink servings in grams, and you order drinks by weight: a teacup is about 200g, a shot-glass about 50g. The unit of items sold by the piece, such as eggs, is *shtuka* or *sht*, which literally means 'thing' or 'piece'.

LAUNDRY

While self-service laundries are almost unheard of, you can get laundry done in most hotels: ask the floor attendant. It usually takes at least a day and costs around R200 a load, but if you plan on doing it yourself, bring along a universal sink plug.

TOILETS

Pay toilets are identified by the words платный (*platny tualet*). In any toilet Ж (*zhenskiy*) stands for women's, while М (*muzhskoy*) stands for men's.

In cities, you'll now find clusters of temporary plastic toilets in popular public places, although other public toilets are rare and often dingy and uninviting. If you can hold on, use the loos in major hotels or in modern food outlets such as McDonald's.

In all public toilets, the babushka who you pay your R5 to will have toilet paper; still, it's always a good idea to carry your own.

HEALTH

Travel health depends on your predeparture preparations, your daily health care while travelling and how you handle any medical problem that does develop. While the potential dangers can seem quite frightening, in reality few travellers experience anything more than flu or an upset stomach.

Predeparture Planning

Immunisations There are no vaccination requirements for travel to Russia, but some vaccinations are recommended for a healthy trip. Apart from the vaccinations following, consider asking your doctor for a flu jab – flu is the most likely health threat in Russia, particularly in late autumn or early spring, with virulent epidemics frequently appearing in major cities.

Plan ahead: some vaccinations require more than one injection, while some should not be given together (seek medical advice at least six weeks before travel). You should consider vaccinations for the following:

Diphtheria & Tetanus Recommended for everyone, vaccinations for these two diseases are usually combined.

Hepatitis A Vaccines including Avaxim, Havrix 1440 and VAQTA provide long-term immunity after an initial injection, then a booster at six to 12 months. Alternatively, an injection of gamma globulin can provide short-term protection against hepatitis A. Protective immediately, it is reasonably effective, unlike the vaccine, but because it is a blood product, there are current concerns about its long-term safety. Hepatitis A vaccine is also available as Twinrix, combined with hepatitis B vaccine. Three injections over a six-month period are required, the first two providing substantial protection against hepatitis A.

Hepatitis B Consider vaccination if you are on a long trip; visiting countries with high levels of hepatitis B infection, or where blood transfusions may not be adequately screened; or visiting regions where sexual contact or needle sharing is a possibility. Vaccination involves three injections, with a booster at 12 months. Rapid courses are available.

Japanese B Encephalitis Consider vaccination if spending a month or longer in a high-risk area, such as parts of the Russian Far East and Siberia, or if making repeated trips to risk areas, or visiting during an epidemic. It involves three injections over 30 days.

Polio Everyone should keep up to date with this vaccination, normally given in childhood – a booster every 10 years maintains immunity.

Rabies Vaccination should be considered if spending a month or longer in a country where rabies is common, especially if cycling, handling animals, caving or travelling to remote areas; children should also have it. Pretravel rabies vaccination involves three injections over 21 to 28 days. If someone who has been vaccinated is bitten or scratched by an animal, they will require two booster injections of vaccine; those not vaccinated require more.

Tuberculosis The risk of TB to travellers is usually very low, unless you will be living among local people in high-risk areas. Vaccination against TB (BCG) is recommended for children and young adults living in these areas for three months or more.

Typhoid Vaccination, which may be required if travelling for more than a couple of weeks in most parts of Asia and Central and Eastern Europe, is now available as an injection or oral capsules. A combined hepatitis A/typhoid vaccine was launched recently but availability is limited: check with your doctor.

Health Insurance Make sure you have adequate health insurance: see Travel Insurance earlier in this chapter for details.

Other Preparations If on a long trip, make sure your teeth are OK. If you wear glasses, take a spare pair and your prescription. If you require a particular medication, take an adequate supply as it may not be available locally, and bring part of the packaging showing the generic name rather than the brand to enable easier replacement. (It's also a good idea to have a legible prescription or letter from your doctor to avoid any legal problems.)

Basic Rules

Food Vegetables and fruit should be washed with purified water or peeled where possible. Beware of ice cream sold on the street, or melted and refrozen – if there's any doubt (eg, during a power cut), steer well clear. Shellfish such as mussels, oysters and clams should be avoided, as well as undercooked meat, particularly mince. Steaming does not make shellfish safe for eating.

If a place looks clean, well run and busy with customers, with the vendor clean and healthy, then the food is probably safe.

Drinks Note the number one rule: *be careful of the water and especially ice.* If you don't know for certain that the water is safe, assume the worst – we note in the destination chapters where it isn't safe to drink (St Petersburg, for example).

Reputable brands of bottled water (one popular one is blessed by the patriarch of the Orthodox church!) or soft drinks are generally fine, but check the seal to make sure the bottle hasn't been refilled with tap water. Take care with fruit juice, particularly if water has been added. Milk should be treated with suspicion as it is often unpasteurised, though boiled milk is fine if kept hygienically. Tea or coffee should also be OK, if the water has been boiled.

Cheap (and fake) vodka can make you very ill. Look for name brands in unopened bottles and check for a red-and-white licence stamp attached to the cap. Make sure to err on the side of caution, as there have been some serious incidents.

Water Purification The simplest way of purifying water is to boil it thoroughly. At high altitude water boils at a lower temperature, so germs are less likely to be killed – boil it for longer in these environments.

Consider purchasing a water filter for a long trip – there are two main kinds. Total filters take out all parasites, bacteria and viruses and make water safe to drink; while they are often expensive, they can be more cost-effective than bottled water. Simple filters (which can even be a nylon mesh bag) take out dirt and larger foreign bodies from the water so that chemical solutions work much more effectively (if water is dirty, chemical solutions may not work at all). It's very important when buying a filter to read the specifications. Simple filtering will not remove all dangerous organisms, so if you cannot boil water it should be treated chemically. Chlorine tablets will kill many pathogens, but not some parasites like giardia and amoebic cysts. Iodine, available in tablet form, is more effective – follow the directions carefully and remember that too much iodine can be harmful.

Medical Problems & Treatment

Self-diagnosis and treatment can be risky, so always seek medical help. Embassies, consulates or five-star hotels can usually recommend local doctors or clinics. Although we give drug dosages in this section, they are for emergency use only. Correct diagnosis is vital. (We have used generic names for medications; check with a pharmacist for local brands.)

Note that antibiotics should ideally be administered under medical supervision. Take only the recommended dose at the prescribed intervals and use the whole course, even if the illness seems to be cured. Stop immediately if there are any serious reactions, and don't use the antibiotic at all if you are unsure that you have the correct one. If you are allergic to commonly prescribed antibiotics such as penicillin, carry that information when travelling (eg, on a bracelet).

Environmental Hazards

Altitude Sickness Lack of oxygen at high altitudes (over 2500m) affects most people to some extent. The effect may be mild or severe and occurs because less oxygen reaches the muscles and the brain at high altitude, requiring the heart and lungs to compensate by working harder. Symptoms of Acute Mountain Sickness (AMS) usually develop during the first 24 hours at altitude but may be delayed up to three weeks. Mild symptoms include headache, lethargy, dizziness, difficulty sleeping and loss of appetite. AMS may become more severe without warning and can be fatal. Severe symptoms include breathlessness, a dry, irritative cough (which may progress to the production of pink, frothy sputum), severe headache, lack of coordination and balance, confusion, irrational behaviour, vomiting, drowsiness and unconsciousness. There is no hard-and-fast rule as to what altitude is too high: AMS has been fatal at 3000m, although 3500 to 4500m is the usual range.

Treat mild symptoms by resting at the same altitude until recovery, usually a day or two. Paracetamol or aspirin can be taken for headaches. If symptoms persist or become worse, however, *immediate descent is necessary* – even 500m can help. Drug treatments should never be used to avoid descent or to enable further ascent.

The drugs acetazolamide and dexamethasone are recommended by some doctors for the prevention of AMS. However, while they can reduce the symptoms, they may also mask warning signs. Severe and fatal AMS has occurred in people taking these drugs, and we do generally not recommend them for travellers.

To prevent AMS:

- Ascend slowly and have frequent rest days, spending two to three nights at each rise of 1000m. If you reach a high altitude by trekking, acclimatisation takes place gradually and you are less likely to be affected than if you directly reach high altitude.
- If possible, sleep at a lower altitude than the greatest height reached during the day. Once above 3000m, care should be taken not to increase the sleeping altitude by more than 300m per day.
- Drink extra fluids. Mountain air is dry and cold, and moisture will be lost as you breathe. Evaporation of sweat may occur unnoticed and result in dehydration.

- Eat light, high-carbohydrate meals for energy.
- Avoid alcohol as it may increase the risk of dehydration.
- Avoid sedatives.

Heat Exhaustion Dehydration and salt deficiency can cause heat exhaustion. Take time to acclimatise to high temperatures, drink sufficient liquids and don't do anything too physically demanding.

Salt deficiency is characterised by fatigue, lethargy, headaches, giddiness and muscle cramps; salt tablets may help, but adding extra salt to your food is better.

Anhidrotic heat exhaustion, a rare condition caused by an inability to sweat, tends to affect people who have been in a hot climate for some time and can progress to heatstroke. Treatment involves removal to a cooler climate.

Heatstroke This serious, occasionally fatal condition can occur if the body's heat-regulating mechanism breaks down and body temperature rises to dangerous levels. Long, continuous periods of exposure to high temperatures and insufficient fluids can leave you vulnerable to heatstroke.

The symptoms are feeling unwell, not sweating very much (or at all), and a high body temperature (39° to 41°C, or 102° to 106°F). Where sweating has ceased, the skin becomes flushed and red. Severe, throbbing headaches and lack of coordination will also occur, and the sufferer may be confused or aggressive, eventually becoming delirious or convulsive. Hospitalisation is essential but in the interim, get victims out of the sun, remove their clothing, cover them with a wet sheet or towel and fan continually. Give fluids if they are conscious.

Hypothermia Too much cold can be just as dangerous as too much heat. If you are trekking at high altitudes or simply taking a long bus trip over mountains, particularly at night, be prepared.

Hypothermia occurs when the body loses heat faster than it can produce it and the core temperature of the body falls. It is surprisingly easy to progress from very cold to dangerously cold due to a combination of wind, wet clothing, fatigue and hunger, even if the air temperature is above freezing. It is best to dress in layers, with silk, wool and some of

the new artificial fibres all good insulating materials. A hat is important, as a lot of heat is lost through the head. A strong, waterproof outer layer (and a 'space' blanket for emergencies) is essential. Carry basic supplies, including food containing simple sugars (to generate heat quickly) and fluid to drink.

Symptoms of hypothermia are exhaustion, numb skin (particularly toes and fingers), shivering, slurred speech, irrational or violent behaviour, lethargy, stumbling, dizzy spells, muscle cramps and violent bursts of energy. Irrationality may take the form of sufferers claiming they are warm and trying to take off their clothes.

For mild hypothermia, get the person out of the wind or rain, remove their clothing (if wet) and replace with dry, warm clothes. Give them hot liquids – not alcohol – and some high-kilojoule, easily digestible food. Do not rub victims: instead, allow them to slowly warm themselves. This should be enough to treat the early stages of hypothermia. Early recognition and treatment of mild hypothermia is the only way to prevent severe hypothermia, which is a critical condition.

Motion Sickness Eating lightly before and during a trip will reduce the chances of motion sickness. If prone to motion sickness, try to find a place that minimises movement: near the wing on aircraft, close to midships on boats, near the centre of buses. Fresh air usually helps; reading and cigarette smoke don't. Commercial motion-sickness preparations, which can cause drowsiness, have to be taken before the trip commences. Ginger (available in capsule form) and peppermint (including mint-flavoured sweets) are natural preventives.

Sunburn In the tropics, the desert or at high altitude you can get sunburnt surprisingly quickly, even through cloud. Use a sunscreen, a hat, and barrier cream for your nose and lips. Calamine lotion and commercial after-sun preparations are good for mild sunburn. Protect your eyes with good quality sunglasses, particularly if you will be near water, sand or snow.

Infectious Diseases
Diarrhoea Simple things like a change of water, food or climate can all cause a mild bout of diarrhoea, but a few rushed toilet trips

with no other symptoms is not indicative of a major problem.

Dehydration is the main danger with any diarrhoea, particularly in children or the elderly, as dehydration can occur quite quickly. Under all circumstances, *fluid replacement* (at least equal to the volume being lost) is the most important thing to remember. Weak black tea with a little sugar, soda water, or soft drinks allowed to go flat and diluted 50% with clean water are all good. With severe diarrhoea a rehydrating solution is preferable to replace minerals and salts lost. Commercially available oral rehydration salts (ORS) are very useful; add them to boiled or bottled water. In an emergency you can make up a solution of six teaspoons of sugar and a half teaspoon of salt to a litre of boiled or bottled water. You need to drink at least the same volume of fluid that you are losing in bowel movements and vomiting. Urine is the best guide to the adequacy of replacement – if you have small amounts of concentrated urine, you need to drink more. Keep drinking small amounts often. Stick to a bland diet as you recover.

Gut-paralysing drugs such as loperamide or diphenoxylate can be used to bring relief from the symptoms, although they do not actually cure the problem. Only use these drugs if you do not have access to toilets, eg, if you *must* travel. Note that these drugs are not recommended for children under 12 years.

In certain situations antibiotics may be required: diarrhoea with blood or mucus (dysentery), any diarrhoea with fever, profuse watery diarrhoea, persistent diarrhoea not improving after 48 hours, and severe diarrhoea. In these situations, gut-paralysing drugs should be avoided.

In these situations, a stool test may be necessary to diagnose the bug causing your diarrhoea, so seek medical help urgently. Where this is not possible, the recommended drugs for bacterial diarrhoea (the most likely cause of severe diarrhoea in travellers) are norfloxacin (400mg twice daily for three days) or ciprofloxacin (500mg twice daily for five days). They're not recommended for pregnant women, or for children; ampicillin or amoxicillin may be given in pregnancy (medical care is necessary), while children should be given co-trimoxazole (five-day course) with dosage dependent on weight.

Two other causes of persistent diarrhoea in travellers are giardiasis and amoebic dysen-

tery. Giardiasis is caused by a common parasite, *Giardia lamblia*. Symptoms include stomach cramps, nausea, a bloated stomach, watery, foul-smelling diarrhoea and frequent gas. It can appear several weeks after you have been exposed to the parasite. The symptoms may disappear for a few days and then return; this can go on for several weeks.

Amoebic dysentery, caused by the protozoan *Entamoeba histolytica*, is characterised by a gradual onset of low-grade diarrhoea, often with blood and mucus. Cramping abdominal pain and vomiting are less likely than in other types of diarrhoea; fever may not be present. It will persist until treated and can recur and cause other health problems.

You should seek medical advice if you think you have giardiasis or amoebic dysentery, but where this is not possible, tinidazole or metronidazole are the recommended drugs. Treatment is a 2g single dose of tinidazole or 250mg of metronidazole three times daily for five to 10 days.

Hepatitis Inflammation of the liver is covered by the general term hepatitis. There are several different viruses that cause hepatitis, and they differ in the way that they are transmitted. The symptoms are similar in all forms of the illness, and include fever, chills, headache, fatigue, feelings of weakness and aches and pains, followed by loss of appetite, nausea, vomiting, abdominal pain, dark urine, light-coloured faeces, jaundiced (yellow) skin and yellowing of the whites of the eyes. People who have had hepatitis should avoid alcohol for some time after the illness, as the liver needs time to recover.

Hepatitis A is transmitted by contaminated food and drinking water. You should seek medical advice, but there is not much you can do apart from resting, drinking lots of fluids, eating lightly and avoiding fatty foods. Hepatitis E is transmitted in the same way as hepatitis A; it can be particularly serious in pregnant women.

There are almost 300 million chronic carriers of hepatitis B in the world. It is spread through contact with infected blood, blood products or body fluids, for example through sexual contact, unsterilised needles and blood transfusions, or contact with blood via small breaks in the skin. Other risk situations include having a shave, tattoo or body piercing with contaminated equipment. The symptoms of hepatitis B may be more severe than type A and the disease can lead to long-term problems such as chronic liver damage, liver cancer or a long-term carrier state. Hepatitis C and D are spread in the same way as hepatitis B and can also lead to long-term complications.

There are vaccines against hepatitis A and B, but there are currently no vaccines against the other types of hepatitis. Following the basic rules about food and water (hepatitis A and E) and avoiding risk situations (hepatitis B, C and D) are important preventative measures.

HIV & AIDS Infection with the human immunodeficiency virus (HIV) may lead to acquired immune deficiency syndrome (AIDS), which is a fatal disease. Russia is experiencing one of the fastest rise of reported HIV and AIDS cases in the world. Official figures put HIV/AIDS cases at 130,000, but some say that up to one million Russians could die of AIDS by the year 2010.

Any exposure to blood, blood products or body fluids may put the individual at risk. The disease is often transmitted through sexual contact or dirty needles – vaccinations, acupuncture, tattooing and body piercing can be potentially as dangerous as intravenous drug use. HIV/AIDS can also be spread through infected blood transfusions; Russia's record of blood screening is not perfect. If you do need an injection, ask to see the syringe unwrapped in front of you, or take a needle and syringe pack with you.

Sexually Transmitted Infections HIV/AIDS and hepatitis B can be transmitted through sexual contact; see the relevant sections earlier for more details. Other STIs include gonorrhoea, herpes and syphilis; sores, blisters or rashes around the genitals and discharges or pain when urinating are common symptoms. In some STIs, such as wart virus or chlamydia, symptoms may be less marked or not observed at all, especially in women. Chlamydia infection can cause infertility in men and women before any symptoms have been noticed. Syphilis symptoms eventually disappear completely but the disease continues and can cause severe problems in later years. While abstinence from sexual contact is the only 100% effective prevention, using condoms is also effective. The treatment of gonorrhoea and syphilis is with antibiotics. The different sexually transmitted diseases each require specific antibiotics.

Insect-Borne Diseases

Ticks You should always check all over your body if you have been walking through a potentially tick-infested area as ticks can cause skin infections and other more serious diseases. If a tick is found attached, press down around the tick's head with tweezers, grab the head and gently pull upwards. Avoid pulling the rear of the body as this may squeeze the tick's gut contents through the attached mouth parts into the skin, increasing the risk of infection and disease. Smearing chemicals on the tick will not make it let go and is not recommended.

You may want to consider a vaccination against tick-borne encephalitis if you plan to do extensive hiking between May and September. See the Health section of Facts for Visitors in the Siberia and Far East section of the book for more information on what to do to prevent tick-borne encephalitis.

Lyme Disease This is a tick-transmitted infection that may be acquired throughout the region. The illness usually begins with a spreading rash at the site of the tick bite, accompanied by fever, headache, extreme fatigue, aching joints and muscles and mild neck stiffness. If untreated, these symptoms usually resolve over several weeks, but over subsequent months disorders of the nervous system, heart and joints may develop. There is no vaccination against the disease. Treatment should be sought as soon possible for best results.

Cuts, Bites & Stings

Leeches You'll often find leeches in damp forest conditions; they attach themselves to your skin to suck your blood. Trekkers often get them on their legs or in their boots. Salt or a lighted cigarette end will make them fall off. Do not pull them off, as the bite is then more likely to become infected. Clean and apply pressure if the point of attachment is bleeding. An insect repellent may keep them away.

Rabies This fatal viral infection occurs in many animals (usually, but not always, in the countryside) and it is their saliva that is infectious. Any bite or scratch or even lick from an animal should be cleaned immediately and thoroughly with soap and water, with alcohol or iodine solution applied after if the skin has been broken. Medical help should be sought promptly to receive a course of injections to prevent the onset of symptoms and further complications.

Snakes To minimise your chances of being bitten always wear boots, socks and long trousers when walking through undergrowth where snakes may be present. Don't put your hands into holes and crevices, and be careful when collecting firewood.

Snake bites do not cause instantaneous death and antivenins are usually available. Immediately wrap the bitten limb tightly, as you would for a sprained ankle, and then attach a splint to immobilise it. Keep the victim still and seek medical help, if possible with the dead snake for identification. Don't attempt to catch the snake if there is a possibility of being bitten again. Tourniquets and sucking out the poison are now comprehensively discredited.

WOMEN TRAVELLERS

Although sexual harassment on Russian streets is rare, be prepared for it elsewhere. This is what one of our authors had to say about her trip:

Women are very likely to be followed and propositioned; I encountered this especially in Moscow. Eye contact is enough of an invitation for many men. Men in cars, on foot, on the subway are all potential threats. Although I don't think the threat itself is very severe, it was certainly disconcerting for the first few days, until I had developed my hardened 'Russia' face (extensive practice in front of the mirror).

Baty Landis

Sexual stereotyping remains strong. If you're with a man, finer restaurants may hand you a 'ladies' menu' without prices. Russian men have heard that 'American feminists' get upset when a man opens a door for a woman, or helps her with her coat – as is customary for Russian men to do – and cannot comprehend this. On a date, expect the Russian man to act like a 'traditional' gentleman – he may be expecting you to act like a 'traditional' lady.

Russian and International Women's Rights organisations, however, highlight severe domestic violence in Russia: some estimate as many as 12,000 to 16,000 women a year die

at the hands of their partners. (Alcoholism, unemployment and male feelings of passivity and impotence are related problems.) Activists therefore ridicule Women's Day (8 March) as hypocritical – one of Russia's major celebrations, it's a national holiday when businesses shut down for as many as three days and women are traditionally presented with flowers.

Any young or youngish woman alone in (or near) flashy bars full of foreigners risks being mistaken for a prostitute. With lawlessness and crime on the rise, you need to be wary: a woman alone should certainly avoid private taxis at night.

Russian women dress up and wear lots of make-up on nights out. If you wear casual gear, you might feel uncomfortable at a restaurant, a theatre or the ballet; in rural areas, revealing clothing will probably attract unwanted attention.

GAY & LESBIAN TRAVELLERS

While girls holding hands and drunken men showing affection towards each other are common sights throughout Russia, open displays of same-sex love are not condoned. In general, however, the idea of homosexuality is well tolerated by the younger generation, although overt gay behaviour is frowned upon. Indeed, in 2002 a group of publicity-seeking MPs in the State Duma attempted (and failed) to recriminalise homosexuality.

There is an active gay and lesbian scene in Moscow and St Petersburg, and newspapers such as the *Moscow Times* and *St Petersburg Times* feature articles and listings on gay and lesbian issues, clubs and bars and events (don't expect anything near as organised as you might find in other major world centres). Away from the two major cities, the gay scene is much less open – even in Moscow, the founder of the Gay & Lesbian Archive (a centre for gay literature and writing) prefers to remain anonymous for fear of being sacked from her regular job.

For a good overview, visit **w** www.gay.ru /english, with up-to-date information, good links and a resource to put you in touch with personal guides for Moscow and St Petersburg. St Petersburg's **Krilija** *(Wings;* ☎ 812-312 31 80; **e** *krilija@ilga.org;* **w** *www.krilija .sp.ru)* is Russia's oldest officially registered gay and lesbian community organisation. It also runs the Neva Banks Gay Travel Agency

A Woman's Work Is Never Done

In her difficult procession to the bright future the woman proletarian learns to throw off all the virtues imposed on her by slavery; step by step she becomes an autonomous worker, an independent personality, a free lover.

Alexandra Kollontai, feminist and communist heroine

In the Soviet past, women were primarily responsible for household concerns, from serving vodka to their husbands to teaching Pushkin to their children. Women also held full-time jobs outside the home, with Soviet propaganda boasting that the high percentage of women in the labour force demonstrated equality of the sexes. These figures, however, belied the real disparity between sexes in the Soviet work place. Women worked out of economic necessity and were relegated to non-technical factory work, meagre-wage service positions and low-status professions. The job sectors dominated by women included textiles, food processing and health care.

The past decade has dramatically transformed the labour market, and there are career opportunities available to women like never before. Russia's new economy has particularly benefited young, university-educated women, who are gaining valued skills, professional experience and access to information, yielding greater economic independence and self-confidence. For example, 26-year-old Victoria claims she learned the importance of sales (not only selling products and services to clients) but also selling her own work and ideas to her superiors. Alyona, also 26, explains that she used to be intimidated by a closed door in an office building or an uncooperative face at the checkout counter. Her job improved her communication skills, and she now commands the respect she deserves from people in day-to-day life, as well as on the job.

As women succeed in the workplace, it leads inevitably to changes at home. Ten years ago, Tanya was married at the age of 19; one year later she was home with a child, and two years later she was divorced. Tanya's situation was not unusual for young women in the Soviet Union: in 1985, the average female age at marriage was 22 years.

Today, 22-year-old Vera is single, newly graduated from university, and gainfully employed in a promising job. On her 22nd birthday, a friend teased: 'According to Russian custom you should be getting married now.' Her retort: 'According to Russian custom I should be getting divorced now!' Women Vera's age are rejecting the traditional ideas about marriage that Tanya once embraced. Meanwhile, many women who are in Tanya's position have also had a change of heart: they are going back to school, concentrating on their careers and supporting families on their own.

Unfortunately, not all women are able to take advantage of these changes. The transition has been especially severe for pensioners, with some taking to begging. Career shifts have not come easily for middle-aged or unskilled women; women represent two-thirds of the unemployed. Some women have survived by finding work in Russia's seamy sex trade, while others have sought to leave the country: marriage agencies, which hook up Russian women with foreign men, do a bustling business.

Madame Kollontai's hopes for women were left unfulfilled by Communist Russia. Whether they will be realised in the New Russia remains to be seen.

Mara Vorhees

★★

and is happy to assist travellers with information (in English), accommodation and tours.

Cracks in the Iron Closet: Travels in Gay & Lesbian Russia, by David Tuller & Frank Browning, is a fascinating account of modern Russia's gay and lesbian scene. A combination of travel memoir and social commentary, it reveals an emerging homosexual culture surprisingly different from its US counterpart.

DISABLED TRAVELLERS

Inaccessible transport, lack of ramps and lifts and no centralised policy for people with physical limitations make Russia a challenging destination for wheelchair-bound visitors. Keep in mind the various obstacles: distances are great; in restaurants and museums, toilets are frequently accessed from stairs; public transport is extremely crowded; and many footpaths are in poor condition, hazardous even for the mobile.

Readers who use wheelchairs report that Russians are anxious to help but don't know how – it's therefore essential to speak Russian or have a translator. Museum staff may say that most floors are inaccessible, as they don't want to suggest the freight elevator for fear of offending.

Before setting off get in touch with your national support organisation (preferably with the travel officer, if there is one). In the UK contact **Radar** (☎ 020-7250 3222; **w** www .radar.org.uk; 250 City Rd, London EC1V 8AF) or the **Holiday Care Service** (☎ 01293-774 535). In the USA, contact **Mobility International USA** (☎ 541-343 1284; **w** www.miusa.org; PO Box 10767, Eugene, Oregon, 974400).

SENIOR TRAVELLERS
Respect for the elderly is far more ingrained in Russia than in some countries – older people may even get admission discounts at some facilities (but don't count on it). Organisations in your home country, such as the **American Association of Retired Persons** (**w** www.aarp.org), can assist with age-specific information before you leave.

TRAVEL WITH CHILDREN
Travelling in Russia with children can be fun as long as you come well prepared with the right attitudes, equipment and patience. Moscow and St Petersburg have a fair number of attractions to entertain children; elsewhere, finding English-language kids' publications will be a challenge, although there's no shortage of toy shops.

Lonely Planet's *Travel with Children* contains useful advice on how to cope with kids on the road and what to bring to make things go more smoothly.

DANGERS & ANNOYANCES
Danger Regions
Heading to parts of Russia afflicted by war or bandits on the loose is obviously a dumb idea. We're talking about Chechnya here, but Dagestan has also been a scene of civil unrest and general lawlessness. Check with your government's foreign affairs ministry at home or your embassy in Russia for the latest danger zones.

Transport & Road Safety
See the Getting Around European Russia chapter for information on flying hazards and precautions to take on trains.

Take care when crossing the road in large cities: some crazy drivers ignore completely traffic lights, while others tear off immediately the lights change (which can be suddenly), leaving you stranded in the middle of the road.

Crime
The Mafia In Russia, 'Mafia' is a broad term encompassing the country's small- and big-time gangsters, as well as the many thousands of corrupt officials, businesspeople, financiers and police. However, they will be the least of your problems while travelling in the country. Despite occasional beat-ups in the Western media, the lawless situation of the early 1990s has largely disappeared – big-time crime's impact on tourists is now pretty much nonexistent.

Street Crime Moscow and St Petersburg streets are about as safe (or as dangerous) as those of New York and London: there's petty theft, pocket-picking, purse-snatching and all the other crimes endemic to big cities anywhere. Travellers have reported problems with groups of children who surround foreigners, ostensibly to beg, closing in with dozens of hands probing pockets (or worse).

The key is to be neither paranoid nor insouciant – use common sense and be aware that it can be pretty obvious you're a Westerner. Try to fit in: shun bum bags (fanny packs) and bright Western clothes, and scrap the day-pack and carry your goods in a plastic bag.

Scams We've been alerted to several current scams. Be wary of officials, such as police (or people posing as police), asking to see your papers or tickets at stations – they might be on the lookout for a bribe and will try to find anything wrong with your documents. The only course of action is to remain calm, polite and stand your ground. Try to enlist the help of a passer-by to translate (or at least witness what is going on).

Another scam involves the use of devices in ATMs that read credit card and PIN details when you withdraw money from the machines, enabling accounts to be accessed and additional funds withdrawn. In general, it is safest to use ATMs in carefully guarded public places such as major hotels and restaurants.

There have been reports on the Trans-Siberian and Trans-Mongolian railway routes of official-looking men or women requesting that you buy insurance for around US$10 – there is no need to do this.

Burglary Break-ins are epidemic. Don't leave anything of worth in a car, including sunglasses, cassette tapes and cigarettes. Valuables lying around hotel rooms also tempt providence. At camp sites, watch for items on clotheslines and in cabins. If you stay in a flat, make sure it has a well-bolted steel door.

Annoyances

Generally, customer service is improving. However, the single most annoying thing the majority of travellers encounter in Russia is the combination of bureaucracy and apathy that turns some people in 'service' industries into surly, ill-mannered, obstructive goblins. At times you still have to contend with hotel-desk staff struck deaf (or, at best, monosyllabic) by your arrival, as well as shop 'assistants' with strange paralyses that make them unable to turn to face customers.

Then there's the tangle of opening hours whereby every shop, museum and café seems to be having its lunch or afternoon break, or the day off; or is *remont* (closed for repairs); or is simply closed full stop, just when you want to visit.

Russians also have very specific rules for queuing (holding someone's place in the line while they shop or whatever for several hours is common, as is pushing in at the last minute if you're at the train station, say, and the train is about to go). In most cases, neither politeness nor anger will help. If you have the head for it, sharpen your elbows, learn a few scowling phrases, and plough head first through the throng. Good luck.

Prostitution is common, and unsolicited prostitutes still visit or telephone hotel rooms offering sex. Be prepared for strip shows, male and female, at many nightclubs and some restaurants.

Racism & Discrimination

A disturbingly high level of entrenched racism exists in Russia, despite decades of 'let's-all-love-our-comrades' communism. In recent years some embassies have issued warnings to foreigners to stay off the streets around Hitler's birthday (20 April), when bands of right-wing thugs have been known to roam around spoiling for a fight with anyone who doesn't look Russian. Frightening reports of racial violence appear from time to time in the media, and it's a sure thing that if you look like a foreigner you'll be targeted with suspicion by many (the police, in particular).

What is most surprising is that racist attitudes or statements can come from otherwise highly educated Russians. Jews, targets of state-sponsored anti-Semitism during the Communist reign, are more distrusted than hated, although the hatred certainly exists, especially when stirred up by right-wing political parties.

LEGAL MATTERS

Do your best to avoid contact with the myriad types of police. Some are known to bolster their puny incomes by robbing foreigners – either outright or through sham 'fines'. The legal age for alcohol consumption is 18, although you'll see plenty of younger people drinking. There is zero tolerance for alcohol consumption by drivers, and the age of consent for both sexes is 16.

Arrest

If you are arrested, the Russian authorities are obliged to inform your embassy or consulate immediately and allow you to communicate with it without delay. Although you can insist on seeing an embassy or consular official straight away, you can't count on the rules being followed, so be polite and respectful towards officials and hopefully things will go far more smoothly for you. In Russian, the phrase 'I'd like to call my embassy' is 'Pa-**zhahl**-stuh, ya kha-**tyel** bi pahz-vah-**neet** v pah-**solst**-va ma-**yey strahn**-ih'. *(Ya khotel by pozvonit v posolstvo moyey strany).*

BUSINESS HOURS

Government offices, should you need them, open from 9am or 10am to 5pm or 6pm weekdays. Banks usually open from 9am to noon Monday to Friday; those in major cities often also open from 1pm to 6pm. Currency-exchange booths open long hours, and on Saturday and sometimes Sunday too.

Most shops are open Monday to Saturday. Food shops tend to open from 8am to 8pm, except for a *pereryv* (break) from 1pm to 2pm or 2pm to 3pm; some close later, some open Sunday until 5pm. Other shops mostly operate from 10am or 11am to 7pm or 8pm, with a 2pm to 3pm break. Department stores may run from 8am to 8pm or 9pm without a break. A few shops stay open through the weekend and close on Monday.

In major cities there are more and more 24-hour kiosks selling food and drink. Restaurants typically open from noon to midnight except for a break between afternoon and evening meals.

Museum hours change often, as do the weekly days off. Most museums shut entrance doors 30 minutes or an hour before closing time, and may have shorter hours on the day before their day off.

PUBLIC HOLIDAYS & SPECIAL EVENTS
Public Holidays
The main public holidays are:

New Year's Day 1 January
Russian Orthodox Christmas Day 7 January
International Women's Day 8 March
International Labour Day/Spring Festival 1 & 2 May
Victory Day (1945) 9 May
Russian Independence Day (when the Russian republic inside the USSR proclaimed its sovereignty in June 1991) 12 June
Day of Reconciliation and Accord (the rebranded Revolution Day) 7 November

Other widely celebrated holidays are Defenders of the Motherland Day (23 February), Easter Monday and Constitution Day (12 December). Much of Russia shuts down for the first half of May.

Special Events
The Russians do a delightful job of finding reasons to hold a festival. Some of the more important are as follows:

January
Russian Orthodox Christmas (Rozhdestvo; 7 January). Begins with midnight church services

February to April
Pancake Week (Maslenitsa; late February and/or early March). Folk shows and games celebrate the end of winter, with lots of pancake-eating before Lent (pancakes were a pagan symbol of the sun)
Festival of the North (last week of March). Murmansk and other northern towns hold reindeer races, ski marathons and so on

Easter (Paskha; March/April). The main festival of the Orthodox Church year. Easter Day begins with celebratory midnight services. Afterwards, people eat *kulichy* (dome-shaped cakes) and *paskha* (curd cakes), and may exchange painted wooden Easter eggs. The devout deny themselves meat, milk, alcohol and sex during Lent's 40-day pre-Easter fasting period

May
Graduates Day (traditionally 25 May). A day for those finishing school, who parade about their hometowns in traditional student garb

June
St Petersburg White Nights (June). Involves general merrymaking and staying out late, as well as a dance festival. Many other northern towns have their own version

November
National Reconciliation Day (7 November). The old Great October Socialist Revolution Anniversary – still a big day for Communist Party marches. Otherwise, monarchists mourn and others drink while closing down their dachas for winter.

December
Sylvester and New Year (31 December & 1 January). The main winter and gift-giving festival, when gifts are put under the *yolka*, the traditional fir tree. See out the old year with vodka and welcome in the new one with champagne while listening to the Kremlin chimes on TV.

ACTIVITIES
Camping, hiking, skiing, canoeing and other outdoor activities are all popular with Russians. However, unlike Western countries, the infrastructure for most activities is rudimentary, with sporting goods stores, adventure travel firms, organised tours and the like hard to find. See Organised Tours in the European Russia Getting There & Away chapter for details on adventure travel companies inside and outside Russia.

For information about outdoor activities, it's best to inquire locally. There will often be a group of enthusiasts more than happy to share their knowledge and even equipment with a visitor; you might also be able to locate guides for trekking and other activities where detailed local knowledge is essential.

Cycling
Deteriorated roads and manic drivers are two of the main hazards for cyclists. Otherwise, rural

Steaming: The Joys of the *Banya*

For centuries, travellers to Russia have commented on the particular (in many people's eyes, peculiar) traditions of the *banya*; the closest English equivalents, 'bathhouse' and 'sauna', don't quite sum it up. To this day, Russians make it an important part of their week (though more men than women seem to go to public city *banya*) and you can't say you've really been to Russia unless you've visited one.

The main element of the *banya* is the *parilka* (steam room), which can get so hot it makes Finnish saunas wussy in comparison. Here, rocks are heated by a furnace, with water poured onto them using a long-handled ladle. Often, a few drops of eucalyptus or pine oil (sometimes even beer) is added to the water, creating a scent in the burst of scalding steam released into the room. After this some people stand up, grab hold of a *venik* (a tied bundle of birch branches) and beat themselves or each other with it.

It does appear sadomasochistic, and there are theories tying the practice to other masochistic elements of Russian culture. At the very least it's painful, although the effect is pleasant and cleansing: apparently, the birch leaves (sometimes oak or, agonisingly, juniper branches) and their secretions help rid the skin of toxins.

The *banya* tradition is deeply ingrained in the Russian culture that emerged from ancient Novgorod, with the Kievan Slavs making fun of their northern brothers for all that steamy whipping. In folk traditions, it has been customary for bride and groom to take separate *banyas* with their friends the night before the wedding, with the *banya* itself the bridge to marriage; a modern version of this custom is depicted humorously in every Russian's favourite film, *Ironia Sudba* ('Ironic Fate'). Husband and wife would also customarily bathe together after the ceremony, and midwives used to administer a steam bath to women during delivery. (It was not uncommon to give a hot birch mini-massage to the newborn.) The *banya*, in short, is a place for physical and moral purification.

This said, many city *banya* are run down and unappealing (with a few classy exceptions, including Moscow's splendid Sandunovskiye *banya*); grab any chance you get to try a traditional one in a countryside log cabin.

Everywhere, the modern tradition goes like this: at the same time every week, people head out to their favourite *banya* to meet up with the same people they see each week (the Western equivalent would be your gym buddies). Many bring along a thermos filled with tea which is mixed with jams, spices and heaps of sugar. (A few bottles of beer and some dried fish also do nicely.)

After stripping down in the sex-segregated changing room, wishing *Lyokogo para* to their mates (meaning something like 'May your steam be easy!'), bathers head off into a dry sauna – just to get the skin nice and hot – then the *parilka*. After the birch branch (best experienced lying down on a bench, with someone else administering the 'beating'), bathers run outside and, depending on their nerve, plunge into the *basseyn* (ice-cold pool). With eyelids draped back over their skull, they stammer back into the changing room to their mates' wishes of *S lyogkim parom* ('Hope your steam was easy!'). Finally, they drape themselves in sheets and discuss world issues before repeating the process (most *banya* experts go through the motions about five to 10 times over a two-hour period).

Steve Kokker

★★★

Russians are quite fascinated with and friendly towards long-distance riders. Just make certain you have a bike designed for the harshest conditions and carry plenty of spare parts.

Several local agencies run cycle tours, including Team Gorky in Nizhny Novgorod which offers a programme peddling around the Golden Ring towns.

Skiing

Downhill ski slopes are scattered throughout the country (see Around Magnitogorsk in the

Urals chapter and Kirovsk in the Northern European Russia chapter), although cross-country skiing is more common, attracting legions of skiers during the long winters. Given the wealth of open space (even near Moscow), you won't have a problem finding a place to hit the trail. The few sporting goods stores carry decent, inexpensive Russian-made equipment.

Hiking

Those same open lands that are good for cross-country skiing are also perfect for hiking:

Space Tourism Russian Style

Ever fancied flying into space, or at twice the speed of sound? In Russia, it can be arranged – at a price. In April 2001, American billionaire Dennis Tito made history as the first paying customer of the Russian Space Agency, forking out a cool US$20 million to take a shot at space travel.

After several months of training at Star City, Zvezdny Gorodok (30km from Moscow), Tito joined cosmonauts Talgat Musabayev and Yuri Baturin on board a Russian Soyuz spacecraft to pay a week-long visit to the International Space Station. Tito's trip, initially opposed by NASA, was considered a success and in April 2002 another millionaire, South African Mark Shuttleworth, followed in Tito's space boots.

Not everyone has US$20 million to spare, so the Russian aerospace company Sub-Orbital Corporation is working together with the US-based Space Adventures (which arranged the Tito and Shuttleworth jaunts) on its C-21 shuttle, designed to take one pilot and two passengers on brief trips into space. For around US$100,000 passengers will zoom 100km, leaving the atmosphere for about five minutes and experiencing weightlessness and the blackness of space. The round trip will take about an hour and, according to reports, between 100 and 250 people have put deposits on tickets for flights that are hoped to start in 2005.

If you can't wait that long for a space flight, Space Adventures can arrange (for US$12,595) for you to co-pilot a MiG-25 'Foxbat', a fighter jet that can fly at over 3000km/h (more than twice the speed of sound) to an altitude of 80,000 feet (the outer limit of the atmosphere, from where you can see the earth curve). The flights take off from the formerly top-secret Zhukovsky Air Base, an hour's drive southeast of Moscow (Zhukovsky, the testing ground for Russia's newest aircraft, is home to the Gromov Flight Research Institute, one of the country's largest centres for aviation science research and testing).

For your money you get two nights at one of Moscow's premier hotels (including breakfast), transfers between airport, hotel and Zhukovsky Air Base, an English-speaking guide, a flight suit, a model of the plane, flight instructions, training and a medical check. If you can't quite afford the MiG-25 experience, Space Adventures offer a range of flight programmes (including one to experience zero gravity) in other military aircraft. The cheapest is US$3395 for a chance to fly the L-39, the standard Russian Air Force trainer with a maximum speed of 781km/h.

For full details contact **Space Adventures** (in US ☎ 888-85-SPACE, outside US ☎ 703-524-7172; W www.spaceadventures.com; 4350 Fairfax Dr, Arlington, Virginia 22203).

★★

among the best areas to road-test your boots are the Lapland Nature Reserve in Northern European Russia, the Elbrus area of the Caucasus, and the western Ural Mountains. See the relevant chapters for more details.

The difficulty in finding reliable topographical maps means it's especially important to seek out local advice, information and even guides.

Mountaineering

The dramatic peaks of the Elbrus area are a natural magnet for climbers. See the Caucasus chapter for more, and note that these types of trip are best organised before arrival.

Boating

Although many rivers have water quality that discourages even getting near the water, the coasts offer many canoeing and kayaking possibilities. The Solovetsky Islands in Northern European Russia are an example of the remote and fascinating places that can be explored by boat during the summer. The Volga River delta, with its fascinating flora and fauna below Astrakhan, is another good place for exploring.

In towns and parks with clean lakes, there are usually rowing boats available for rent during the warmer months, with yacht clubs in St Petersburg and Moscow.

Ice Skating

Russians skate with abandon during the long winter. Outdoor rinks are common and easy to find and equipment rentals are cheap. There are also many indoor rinks open throughout the year.

LANGUAGE COURSES

Although it's useful to speak Russian before you arrive, there are plenty of opportunities for language study once there. The English-language publications in Moscow and St Petersburg regularly carry listings and advertisements for Russian-language schools and tutors. The cost of formal coursework varies widely, but one-on-one tutoring can be a bargain given the low local wage levels. Numerous professors and other highly skilled people are anxious to augment their incomes teaching you Russian.

Another option for learning Russian is through one of the many international universities operating in Moscow and St Petersburg. These are usually affiliated with a school in either Britain or the USA. To find out about programmes, inquire at any college or university. They will have reams of information on international study programmes worldwide.

WORK

Given the vast number of unemployed and well-educated Russians, the chances of foreigners finding work in the country are slim. However, your odds will be slightly increased if you speak fluent Russian. In addition, starting your own business will also be a hassle given the amount of bureaucracy involved, although the government says it would actually like to increase the level of foreign investment in the country.

In the event that you do find work in Russia or are sent there by your company, it would be wise to use a professional relocation firm to navigate the country's thicket of rules and regulations surrounding foreign employment.

ACCOMMODATION

Long gone are the days when visitors to Russia were restricted to specified hotels and a few grotty camp sites, all of which had to be booked before you could even get a visa. It's a good idea to book a few nights in advance for Moscow and St Petersburg, but elsewhere it's usually not necessary. Make bookings by fax rather than email or telephone, and note that some hotels have a small surcharge for the first night's accommodation.

Camping

Camping in the wild is legal in many places, except those signposted Не разбивать палатку (No putting up of tents) and/or Не разжигать костров (No camp fires); if you're off the beaten track it is usually fine just to put up a tent and hit the hay. Check with locals if you're in doubt.

Kempingi – organised camp sites – are increasingly rare and, usually, only open from some time in June to some time in September. They are not quite like Western camp sites: small wooden cabins often take up much of the space, leaving little room for tents. While some *kempingi* are on the city fringes, they may be in quite attractive woodland settings (although communal toilets and washrooms are often in poor condition and other facilities few).

Tourbases, Rest Houses & Sanatoriums

There are lots of these Soviet-era relics around Russia; some are worth searching out, others not.

A *turbaza* (tourbase) is a holiday camp for Russians, usually owned by a factory or large company for the use of its employees. They're often spartan and lodging options are usually a large common room with six or more beds, smaller doubles and private cottages. All are cheap – from as little as R300 per person – and there are reasons for this: many *turbaza* have no indoor plumbing, with the *stolovaya* (canteen) the only place to eat. But if you bring a good supply of food and a sense of adventure, *turbazy* are a great way to get a feel for the average Russian's holiday. At some, you can arrange boating, skiing, hiking or mountaineering.

Doma otdykha (rest houses) are similar to *turbazy*, although generally more luxurious. Some are now privatised, but many retain original owners. They're cheap, popular with Russians and expats alike, and can be booked through travel agencies in big cities. It's always worth asking about 'elite' *doma otdykha*, belonging to the presidential administration, the various government ministries (especially the Foreign Ministry), and major plants.

Sanatorii (sanatoriums), usually booked through local travel agencies, have professional medical staff on hand to treat your illnesses, design your diet and advise you on correct rest. *Sanatorii* can be spas, sea resorts (there are several good ones in Sochi), or resorts where you can get some kind of nontraditional treatment (for instance with *kumys*, fermented mare's milk of Central Asia).

Resting Rooms

Komnaty otdykha (resting rooms) are found at all major train stations and several smaller ones. Generally, they have basic (but often quite clean) shared accommodation with communal sink and toilet (but no shower). Sometimes there are single and double rooms and, rarely, more luxurious ones. The beds are usually rented by the half-day and their cheap price means they are often full; *komnaty otdykha* are worth trying on the off-chance, or if you're stuck for cheap accommodation. Some will ask to see your train ticket before allowing you to stay.

Hostels

There are several youth or backpacker hostels in Moscow and St Petersburg, all more or less in the international mould and able to offer visa support. (See the individual city listings for details.) The rest of Russia is ripe for development (for foreigners and locals), but so far no hostel movement has emerged (although there are plenty of cheap hotels).

University Accommodation

In Moscow, St Petersburg and other cities with large universities, it's possible to stay in Russian student accommodation, sometimes for as little as R300 a night (the conditions are not unlike the kind you find in hostels and guesthouses). Getting in can sometimes be a bit iffy, dependent upon availability or even the administrator's mood – a student card, and looking like a student, certainly helps. See the city listings for further information or ask around at campuses.

Hotels

Russian hotels run the gamut from dirt-cheap flophouses to megabuck five-star palaces. Most hotels have one price for Russians and a higher price for foreigners (less common in Moscow and St Petersburg) – there is little you can do about this, even if you arrive with Russian friends. The only exceptions are a few, mostly out-of-the-way places that get very few foreigners, or haven't heard of such things as 'foreigner prices'. In this book we list the prices hotels charge foreigners.

At most hotels, you can just walk in and get a room on the spot. If you can't, it will probably be because the hotel is genuinely full (rare); or because they say they don't take foreigners (sometimes receptionists think the hotel is not up to your impeccable Western standards, although they can usually be persuaded otherwise; when you've seen around some places you might agree with them); or because they didn't take foreigners in the Soviet era and don't know times have changed.

Procedures At virtually all hotels you have to show your passport and visa when you check in – staff may keep it till next day to register your presence with the local PVU. Don't worry about this – it's normal – but do remember to get your passport and visa back before you leave. Better yet, tell them you need your passport to change money; they should then complete the paperwork in five minutes.

In most hotels (except the cheapest and the expensive new foreign ones), each floor has a *dezhurnaya* (floor lady); they're well worth making friends with. Often, the *dezhurnaya* and the room cleaners will be the nicest people in the place, almost always able to supply you with snacks, bottled drinks and boiled water. (Also remember that hotels with significant numbers of foreigners attract prostitutes.)

Checkout time is usually noon, but it's unlikely that anyone will mind if you stay an extra hour or two. If you want to store your luggage somewhere safe for a late departure, arrange it with the *dezhurnaya* or front desk staff.

Rooms While many hotels have a range of rooms at widely differing prices, they may automatically offer foreigners the most expensive ones, often claiming that cheaper rooms are 'not suitable'. Given that away from the major cities room prices average about R300, you may be happy with their idea of 'best'. But feel free to look around and ask about cheaper options.

Not all hotels have genuine single rooms and 'single' prices often refer to single occupancy of a double room. Some hotels, mainly in the bottom-end and lower-middle ranges, have rooms for three or four people where the price per person comes to much less than a single or double. Beds are typically single.

Hot water supplies are fairly reliable, but since hot water is supplied on a district basis, whole neighbourhoods can be without it for a month or more in summer when the system is shut down for maintenance (the best hotels are able to avoid this by having their own hot water systems).

A *lyux* room is a suite with a sitting room in addition to the bedroom and bathroom. A *polu-lyux* suite is less spacious.

Budget Rooms may have their own toilet, washbasin or shower, or you may have to use facilities shared by the whole corridor. Some places are clean, if musty, and even include a TV or huge, Soviet-era fridge in the rooms; others are decaying, dirty and smelly and lack decent toilets and washing facilities. Take care with security in some cheap hotels. Prices range from R600 in Moscow to less than R100 elsewhere.

Mid-Range These mainly Soviet-era tourist hotels are typically concrete-and-glass rectangles, though some of the older ones have a bit of style. They have clean, reasonably comfortable rooms with bathrooms (and often small balconies), and there'll be a restaurant along with a bar or *bufety* (snack bar); a casino haunted by mafiosi is another common feature. These are the most common hotels in the country and you'll pay R300 to R600 for a mid-range single (except in Moscow and St Petersburg, where it's R2100 to R3000).

To date, Russia has disappointingly few of the small, cosy, moderately priced hotels found elsewhere in Europe.

Top End The top end consists largely of Western-run luxury hotels in Moscow and St Petersburg. These are up to the best international standards, with very comfortable rooms boasting satellite TV, minibars, fawning service, fine restaurants, health clubs, and prices to match, from around US$200/250 to US$350/ 400 for singles/doubles. (Prices will always be quoted in dollars, on top of which you'll typically pay 20% VAT and 5% local tax.)

Outside the two big cities, the 'top end' (where it exists) is composed mainly of the very best Soviet-era tourist hotels, along with the occasional former Communist Party hotel or smaller, newer private venture. Expect to pay from R2100 to R4500, although you may get better prices through a travel agent.

Private Homes

It's not hard to find a room in a private flat, shared with the owners. This type of accommodation – often referred to as 'bed & breakfast' (B&B) or 'homestay' – enables you to glimpse how Russians really live. Most flats that take in guests are clean and respectable, though rarely large! If you stay in a few you'll be surprised, despite outward similarities, how different their owners can make them.

Moscow and St Petersburg have organisations specifically geared to accommodate foreign visitors in private flats at around US$20 or US$30 per person, normally with English-speaking hosts, breakfast and other services, such as excursions and extra meals. Many travel agencies and tourism firms in these and other cities can also find you a place for around US$25 per person, but the price may depend on things like how far the flat is from the city centre, whether the hosts speak English, and whether any meals are provided.

It's also possible to pay less by going with one of the people who approach travellers arriving off major trains in Moscow and St Petersburg. But be sure you can trust them, establishing how far from the city centre their place is – you'll find many such people are genuine, and just in need of some extra cash. It's better to avoid committing yourself before you actually see the place.

You can contact many Russian homestay agents from overseas (if you do, check they provide visa support), and can even book through travel agencies in your own country.

One reliable Russian organisation is the St Petersburg-based **Host Families Association** (HOFA; ☎/fax 812-275 1992; W *http://www .hofa.us*), which can provide accommodation with English-speaking families throughout Russia and the former Soviet Union, from around US$25/40 for singles/doubles, including breakfast. It charges US$30 to US$50 for a visa invitation and registration.

In Australia Eastern European Travel Bureau, Gateway Travel and Passport Travel Services can book rooms in Russia (see Travel Agents and Organised Tours in the Getting There & Away chapter). In the UK try **Interchange** (☎ 020-8681 3612, fax 8760 0031), which offers homestays in Moscow (£43 a night) and St Petersburg (£34 a night).

In the USA **Russian Home Travel** (☎ 800-861 9335; e *russiahome@aol.com*) offers visa support and represents hosts in Moscow and St Petersburg.

Some of these companies offer more expensive packages, including excursions, all meals, and so on, as well as discounts for longer stays. It's worth knowing that your host family usually only gets a small fraction of the price you pay the agent.

FOOD

So you thought you'd be on a diet of cabbage, potatoes and sloppy stews during your travels? Think again: Russian food is not nearly as bad as you may fear. The local cuisine is undoubtedly on the heavy side, favouring fat-loaded but delicious bliny (pancakes with savoury or sweet fillings), creams and hearty meat dishes. This is fine in winter, though less palatable in summer, when Russia's colourful and tasty range of salads and zakuski (appetizers) come into their own; the wonderful, unique soups are a delight any time.

In the major cities you'll find a decent range of restaurants, with Moscow and St Petersburg particularly well served; there, you can feast on anything ranging from sushi (a favourite repast of the ritziest Russians) to Brazilian barbecue. The most common foreign cuisine is that of the Caucasus, particularly Georgia – their spicy meat and vegetable dishes can be excellent.

This said, only a small percentage of the population eat more than one meal at a restaurant each year, so outside of the main cities the choice of places to dine is limited. Dress is informal in all but the top-end restaurants.

Food Shops

All large cities now have Western-style supermarkets and food stores, with a large range of Russian and imported goods. The old food stores (with their infuriating system of queuing three times for each purchase: once to find out the price, once to pay, once to collect) are fast converting to one-stop service (if not to full supermarket-style shopping). Many places are now open 24 hours.

As well as the supermarkets, there are smaller food stores specialising in particular products, such as bliny or pelmeni, Russian-style ravioli dumplings. And then there are the ubiquitous food-and-drink kiosks, generally located around parks and markets, on streets and near train and bus stations – their products are usually poor, but the kiosks are handy and reasonably cheap.

Every sizable town has a colourful market (Рынок, **rih**-nuk), where locals sell spare potatoes and carrots from their dacha plots (check the market fringes), while bigger traders offload trucks full of fruit, vegetables, meat, dried and dairy goods – you name it – often from the Transcaucasus or Central Asia. Take your own shopping bag and go early in the morning for the liveliest scene and best selection; a certain amount of bargaining is acceptable, and it's a good idea to check prices with a trustworthy local first.

Places to Eat

With so many restaurants and cafés around the major cities and towns, it's not necessary to endure poor hotel food and service. The Western-run luxury hotels will usually have a decent restaurant or two, and sometimes offer good-value lunch deals or buffets.

If you fancy a snack in an old-style hotel its bufet is often a better bet and far cheaper than its restaurant. Bufety are also found in stations and serve a range of simple snacks: open sandwiches, boiled eggs, salads, pastries, drinks.

The stolovaya, the Russian version of the canteen, is the common person's eatery: sometimes decent, often dreary, always cheap. For little more than a couple of dollars you can take your pick from a range of small dishes and drinks (some of them less than mouthwatering). Slide your tray along the counter and point to the food, and the staff will ladle it out. Stolovaya will often be found in market or station areas, with poetic names such as 'Stolovaya No 32'.

Western fast-food chains have hit Moscow, St Petersburg and other cities and are incredibly popular. McDonald's is expanding rapidly and Russian imitators are getting in on the act, with street kiosks, vans and cafés with tables. Pizza and kebabs (often the Caucasian shashlyk form) are common fare.

Ordering & Paying

It's always worth asking if a restaurant has an English-language menu (Anglesky menu, an-**glay**-ski **mozh**-na). If the menu is in Russian only, you may in some places get translation help from the waiter. Otherwise you're on your own, especially at some of the new places away from the major cities, where they never see non-Russians.

Even armed with a dictionary and this book's food glossary, it can be difficult deciphering Russian menus (the different styles of printed Cyrillic are a challenge), although they typically follow a standard form.

If the menu leaves you flummoxed, look around at what the other diners are eating and point out what takes your fancy to the staff. If a waiter – or the food – takes an eternity to appear, ponder on a Russian word given to dining's universal vocabulary, After the victory over Napoleon, impatient Russian soldiers in Paris cafés would bang their tables and shout *Bystro, bystro!*, meaning 'Quickly, quickly!' – from this came the word 'bistro'.

If there's a service charge – noted on the menu with the words За обслуживание (*za obslyzhivaniye*) – there's no need to tip further, unless the service has been exceptional.

For more words to help you order, check out the Language chapter and the Food & Drink Glossary.

Meals

Breakfast (*zavtrak*, **zahf**-truk) in a hotel can range from a large help-yourself buffet spread to simple bread, butter, jam, tea and boiled egg. Try bliny, kasha (various types of porridge, sometimes made from buckwheat or other grains) and *syrniki* (cottage cheese fritters), which are delicious with jam, sugar and the universal Russian condiment, sour cream (*smetana*, smi-**tah**-nuh).

Russians often like a fairly heavy early-afternoon meal (*obed*, ah-**byet**) and a lighter evening meal (*uzhin*, **oo**-zhin). Night-out suppers can go on and on.

Meals (and menus) are divided into courses. First come *zakuski*, appetisers often grouped into cold and hot dishes. The fancier *zakuski* rival main courses for price and include caviar, the most expensive of which is black, or sturgeon (*ikra chyornaya*, also called *zernistaya*). Cheaper and saltier is red (salmon) caviar (*ikra krasnaya*, also called *ketovaya*), traditionally served with buttered toast or bliny and washed down with a slug of vodka. There's also ersatz caviar made entirely from eggplant or other vegetables.

Salads are included with *zakuski*. Old favourites include *olivie*, a chopped-meat and vegetable salad smothered in sour cream, and *selyodka pod shyuboi*, from the Soviet era of cooking – known as 'herrings in fur coats', this is a fish salad with all but the kitchen sink thrown in (both dishes are making a retro comeback across the country). Discovering what's actually under all the creamy mayonnaise of these and other exotic concoctions is often part of the fun, unless you happen to be vegetarian: salads often include shredded meat, fish or seafood.

After *zakuski* come the soups, sometimes listed under *pervyye blyuda* (first courses). They are the pinnacle of Slavic cooking, with dozens of varieties often served with a dollop of sour cream. Most Russian soups are made from meat stock and ones to try include *borshch* (beetroot), *lapsha* (chicken noodle), *okroshka* (a cold vegetable soup made with *kvas*, a beer-like drink) and *solyanka* (a hearty meat or fish soup with vegetables).

Vtoryye blyuda (second courses, or 'mains') are also known as *goryachiye blyuda* (hot courses). They can be divided into *firmenniye* (house specials, often listed at the front of the menu), *myasniye* (meat), *ribniye* (fish), *ptitsa* (poultry) and *ovoshchniye* (vegetable). If it's not already on the table, you might want to ask for *khleb* (bread), which comes in a wide variety of styles – a favourite is 'black' bread made with vitamin-rich sour rye dough.

Perhaps most Russians are exhausted or drunk by *deserty* (dessert, also known as *sladkiye blyuda*), since this is generally the least imaginative course. Most likely there will be ice cream (*morozhenoe*, ma-**roh**-zhi-nah-yuh), which Russians love with a passion (it's not unusual to see people gobbling dishfuls at outdoor tables, even in freezing weather). Weirdly coloured cakes are also popular.

Russia is rough on vegetarians and nonmeat-eaters, though some restaurants have caught on, particularly in Moscow, St Petersburg and other large cities. Main dishes are heavy on meat and poultry, vegetables are often boiled to death, and even the good vegetable and fish soups are usually made from meat stock. If you're vegetarian say so, early and often. You'll see a lot of cucumber and tomato salads, and – if so inclined – will develop an eagle eye for the rare good fish and dairy dishes. *Zakuski* include quite a lot of meatless ingredients such as eggs, salted fish and mushrooms. During Lent, many restaurants have special nonmeat menus. A useful local website for vegetarians is ⓦ www.vegrussia.org.

By the way, potatoes *(kartoshka, kartofel)* aren't filed under 'vegetable' in the Russian mentality, so you must order them separately.

DRINKS

'Drinking is the joy of the Rus. We cannot live without it' – with these words Vladimir of

Kyiv, the father of the Russian state, is said to have rejected abstinent Islam on his people's behalf in the 10th century. And who wouldn't want to bend their minds now and then during those long, cold, dark winters? Russians sometimes drink vodka in moderation, but more often it's tipped down in swift shots, with a beer, and with the aim of getting legless.

The *average* Russian drinks more than 12L of pure alcohol a year, equivalent to over a bottle of vodka a week; men drink much more than women.

The nearest thing to a pub is a *traktir* (tavern), becoming more common as the Russian taste for beer exceeds the love of vodka. A lot of public drinking (other than on park benches) goes on in restaurants and cafés – since many of these are in hotels, the average tourist is likely to encounter quite a lot of it.

Alcohol

Foreign brands are common, but be very suspicious of cheap spirits – there's a lot of bad stuff around that can make you very ill. Only buy screw-top bottles and always check the seal is not broken.

Vodka The classic Russian alcoholic drink is distilled from wheat, rye or occasionally potatoes. The word comes from *voda* (water), and means something like 'a wee drop'. Its flavour comes from what's added after distillation, so as well as 'plain' vodka you'll find Pertsovka (pepper vodka), Starka (apple and pear leaves), Limonnaya (lemon), and Okhotnichya (Hunter's, with about a dozen ingredients, including peppers, juniper berries, ginger and cloves).

Two common 'plain' vodkas are Stolichnaya (perhaps the most famous Russia vodka), which is in fact slightly sweetened with sugar, and Moskovskaya, with a touch of sodium bicarbonate. Don't get excited when you see how cheap Stoli is here – the stuff made for export is way better than the domestic version. Better brands include Flagman, Gzhelka and Russky Standart (Russian Standard).

Supermarket and liquor store prices range from around R50 to R150 for half a litre of regular brands, more for flavoured, and Western prices for imports.

Beer These days beer is much more popular than vodka among Russians, not least because it's cheap (around R10 a bottle) and

---

Drinking Etiquette in Russia

If you find yourself sharing a table at a bar or restaurant with locals, it's odds-on they'll press you to drink with them. Even people from distant tables, spotting foreigners, may be seized with hospitable urges.

If it's vodka being drunk, they'll want a man to down the shot in one, neat of course; women are usually excused. This can be fun as you toast international friendship and so on, but vodka has a knack of creeping up on you from behind and the consequences can be appalling. It's traditional (and good sense) to eat a little something after each shot.

Refusing a drink can be very difficult, and Russians may continue to insist until they win you over. If you can't quite stand firm, take it in small gulps with copious thanks, while saying how you'd love to indulge but you have to be up early in the morning (or something similar). If you're really not in the mood, the only tested and true method of warding off all offers (as well as making people feel quite awful) is to say *Ya alkogolik* (*Ya alkogolichka* for women): 'I'm an alcoholic'.

★★★★★★★★★★★★★★★★★★★★

---

very palatable. There are now scores of breweries across the country pumping out dozens of tasty local brands, as well as Western brands including Stella Artois, Efes and Holsten.

The local market leader is Baltika, a Scandinavian joint venture (with Russian management) based in St Petersburg. You're bound to find something to like among its 12 different kinds of beer: No 3, a light beer, is the most popular; No 10 has natural almond and basil aromas; No 7 is fine, but only found in bars; Medovoye is supposedly made with a taste of honey; No 0 is alcohol-free; and No 9 is a lethal 16.5% proof.

Other brands to look out for include Stepan Razin, Nevskoye and Bochkaryov (all produced in St Petersburg), Staryy Melnik (a product of the Turkish-owned Efes brewery), Klinskoye and Sibirskaya Korona.

Wines & Brandy *Shampanskoye*, sparkling wine, is popular and comes as *bryut* (very dry), *sukhoe* (dry), *polusukhoe* (semidry), *polusladkoe* (semisweet) and *sladkoe* (sweet). Anything above dry is sweet enough to turn your mouth inside out. A 750g bottle is about R240 in a restaurant and R120 in a supermarket, kiosk or liquor store.

Most other wine comes from outside the CIS, with Eastern European brands the cheapest, although you can find Georgian, Moldovan and Crimean wine, some passable.

Brandy is popular and it's all called *konyak*, though local varieties certainly aren't Cognac. The best non-Western *konyak* in Russia is Armenian, and anything classified five-star is usually fine.

Nonalcoholic Drinks

Water & Mineral Water Tap water is suspect in some cities and should definitely be avoided in St Petersburg. Many people stick to ubiquitous, cheap mineral or bottled water – a couple of tasty local brands are Borzhomi from Georgia, and Narzan, both carbonated.

Tea & Coffee The traditional Russian tea-making method is to brew an extremely strong pot, pour small shots of it into glasses, and fill the glasses with hot water from the samovar, an urn with an inner tube filled with hot charcoal; the pot is kept warm on top of the samovar. Modern samovars have electric elements, like a kettle, instead of the charcoal tube. Putting jam instead of sugar in tea is quite common.

Coffee comes in small cups; unless you buy it at kiosks and stand-up eateries, it's usually good. There's been an explosion of Starbucks-style cafés across Moscow and St Petersburg (but not yet Starbucks itself) – cappuccino, espresso and mocha are now as much part of the average Russian lexicon as elsewhere. (In other cities, you might want to check that the cappuccino you order isn't the instant powdered kind.)

Other Drinks *Kvas*, fermented rye bread water, is dispensed on the street, for a few roubles a dose, from big, wheeled tanks with Квас printed on the side. *Kvas* tastes not unlike ginger beer and is cool and refreshing in summer.

Sok is fruit juice, usually sweetened and flavoured, and sometimes heavily diluted. It seldom resembles the original fruit, although a jugful with meals often goes down a treat. *Mors*, made from all types of red berries, is a popular and refreshing *sok*. *Napitok* means

'drink' – it's often a cheaper and weaker version of *sok*, maybe with some real fruit thrown in. *Limonad* (literally 'lemonade'), a fizzy drink rumoured to be made from industrial waste, tastes like mouthwash.

Jugs of *kefir* (yogurt-like sour milk) are served as a breakfast drink, and are also recommended as a hangover cure. Milk, common and cheap in *moloko* (dairy shops), is often unpasteurised. Pepsi, Coke and their fizzy relatives are widely available.

ENTERTAINMENT

There's no shortage of entertainment in the major cities, although options are limited elsewhere. See the relevant chapters for listings and sources of local information about what's on.

Note that much cultural entertainment lies dormant between about June and September as performance companies go away on tour or holiday.

Information & Tickets

The entertainment listings in Moscow and St Petersburg's English-language publications greatly simplify the process of finding out what's on in those cities. There are also websites in Russian only – try ⓦ www.parter.ru and ⓦ www.biletik.ru.

Keep an eye out around town for music and sporting-event posters (the ability to decipher Cyrillic is a huge advantage); you can also learn a lot from the what's-on charts in hotel service bureaus, at concierge desks and in the ticket kiosks that dot sizable cities (the kiosks can be identified by the words Театральная касса *(teatralnaya kassa)* or just Театр *(teatr)*.

It's not difficult to buy face-value tickets from the *kassa* (ticket office) at the venue itself (typically open for advance or same-day sales from early afternoon till the start of the evening show); or a *teatralnaya kassa*, or any other outlets listed on posters. Look for words such as 'sale' (продажа, *prodazha*) and 'tickets' (билеты, *bilyet*).

If you fall back on a hotel service bureau or a ticket agency, be prepared to pay a huge premium over the face value of the ticket – for the Bolshoi Ballet, R1500 for a R450 ticket is not unusual. However, service bureaus and concierges generally get better tickets than you otherwise could, and for some events they might be the only places able to sell you one. In Moscow and St Petersburg, foreigners pay a much higher price than locals for tickets anyway.

Then there are the touts, not only professionals, but also people with spares. It's standard practice to sell tickets outside the main entrance before starting time. Remember that prices are a free-for-all and you run the risk of obstructed views, wrong dates and other hazards, although sellers will normally let you have a look at the ticket before you hand over any money. Make sure that the ticket actually has the date, performance and section you want.

Music

Classical, ballet, opera and dramatic variants all thrive in Russia, the cultural flagships being St Petersburg's Kirov Ballet and Opera, Moscow's Bolshoi Ballet and Opera, and the State Symphony Orchestra, the Russian National Symphony Orchestra and the St Peters-

burg Philharmonic. Many major cities have their own ballet and opera companies and orchestras.

Rock and pop music are popular and you'll see posters for local performances at clubs, bars and stadiums in every town. Live jazz is limited to the largest cities, while finding authentic folk music can be more of a challenge. Outside Moscow and St Petersburg, the best way to track down more esoteric music is to ask around.

Theatre

Live theatre is popular throughout Russia, and you can find companies performing in all but the smallest towns. Obviously, with the exception of a few places in the major cities, the performances will be in Russian, but really that's the best way to see Chekhov or a host of other Russian playwrights. The works range from Russian classics, Soviet standards, and new works, to translated foreign plays.

Useful Theatre Words & Phrases

theatre	teatr	театр
opera & ballet theatre	teatr opery i baleta	театр оперы и балета
drama theatre	dramaticheskiy teatr	драматический театр
concert hall	kontsertnyy zal	концертный зал
circus	tsirk	цирк
cinema	kinoteatr, kino	кинотеатр, кино
Have you got tickets for...?	yest li u vas bily (bil-**yet**-i) na...?	У вас билеты на...?
Extra tickets?	Lishniye bilety?	Лишние билеты?
cheap tickets	deshyovye bilety	дешёвые билеты
best tickets	luchshchiye bilety	лучшие билеты
stalls, lowest tier of seating	amfiteatr, parter, kresla	амфитеатр, партер, кресла
dress circle (one tier up from stalls)	bel-etazh	бель-этаж
box	lozha	ложа
balcony	balkon	балкон
first tier (eg of balcony)	pervy yarus	первый (1-й) ярус
second tier	vtoroy (fta-**roy**) yarus	второй (2-ой) ярус
third tier	tretiy yarus	третий (3-й) ярус
row	ryad (ryat)	ряд
inconvenient place (eg, obstructed view)	neudobnoye mesto (nye-oo-**dobh**-nah-yeh **myest**-ah)	неудобное место
matinee	utrenniy kontsert	утренний концерт
cloakroom	garderob (gar-di-**rop**)	гардероб
guest stars	gastroli	гастроли
Swan Lake	Lebedinoye ozero	Лебединое озеро
Sleeping Beauty	Spyachshchaya krasavitsa	Спячкая красавица
The Nutcracker	Shchelkunchik	Щелкунчик

★★

Bars & Clubs

Friendly bars and clubs abound in Moscow and St Petersburg, as do unfriendly ones. Many of the latter are overrun by goons with IQs matching their neck size (in inches, not centimetres). If you're in a place with these unsavoury gentlemen, ignore them, or find somewhere more convivial. Another phenomenon: otherwise low-key places often stage strip shows aimed at both sexes.

Many bars and clubs have live music most nights, with the quality ranging from dreadful to inspired, and running the gamut from pop to techno.

Finding a quiet place to sip a beer and have a chat may be a challenge (in summer, the outdoor beer and shashlyk stands will do fine), but if you're looking for places where the mood builds to wild abandon, then you will have no problems. There are no real serving hours (if there were, they'd just be bribed away) so many places are open 24 hours.

Away from Moscow and St Petersburg it can be hard to find bars, given that Russia has no pub tradition. Clubs are another matter, with most cities having several places of varying character and respectability where people can party until dawn; there will be a cover charge, as much as R200 at weekends.

SPECTATOR SPORTS

Once-proud sports facilities dot Russia, a huge infrastructure developed during Soviet times for the scores of semi-professional and amateur sports clubs and youth leagues that propelled the USSR's dominance of the Olympics. But it's going to seed in a hurry: many of the sports halls and stadiums have found new uses as shopping complexes, nightclubs and other decidedly unhealthy pursuits.

This primarily limits spectator opportunities to football and ice hockey. Vysshaya Liga, the premier football league, consists of 16 teams, including Moscow's Spartak, Lokomotiv, TsSKA, Torpedo and Dinamo; as well as Alaniya (Vladikavkaz), Rostselmash (Rostov-on-Don), Zenit (St Petersburg), and another Lokomotiv (Nizhni Novgorod). Seemingly unbeatable, Spartak Moscow has won the premier league every year since 1996.

Super Liga, the top ice hockey league, has 20 teams, with the perennial top 10 being Ak Bars (Kazan), Amur (Khabarovsk), Metallurg (Magnitogorsk), Dinamo (Moscow), Metallurg (Novokuznetsk), Avangard (Omsk), Molot-Prikamye (Perm), Lada (Tolyatti), Salavat Yulayev (Ufa) and Torpedo (Yaroslavl). Russia is considered one of the strongest ice hockey countries, although recent performances have been bitterly disappointing. At the 2002 Winter Olympics they beat Belarus to the bronze medal, having lost to the USA in the semifinal. Watch listings for word of ice-skating competitions for both genders; the best talent performs in Russia as part of the never-ending world tours.

There are also traditional Russian sports to look out for, including lapta (like cricket) and nordic hockey.

SHOPPING

Just about anything you can buy in Western cities can be bought in comparable-sized Russian equivalents. There are plenty of attractive souvenirs, if you know where to look (the shopping sections in each chapter of this book will help), and most regions still have some local craft specialities, even if the Soviet years have killed off others.

Traditional Souvenirs

Few visitors leave Russia without a *matryoshka*, the set of wooden dolls within dolls. In recent years they've become a true folk art, with all manner of intricate painted designs, some witty and humorous, others more traditional. Hunt around: some of these dolls can be poorly painted caricatures of Soviet and Russian leaders, the Keystone Cops – you name it. Small, mass-produced sets can go for a couple of dollars, but the best could set you back US$100 – for this price you can take along a family photo to Moscow's Izmaylovsky Park and come back the following week to collect your own personalised *matryoshka* set.

Palekh (named after the town east of Moscow where they originated) are also of variable quality, although they're usually even more expensive. These enamelled wooden boxes have intricate scenes painted in the lid, with the best costing several hundred dollars. Cheaper, but cheerful, are the gold, red and black wooden bowls, mugs and spoons from Khokhloma, a bit farther east, which are widely available.

Another attractive Russian craft is Gzhel, the blue-and-white ornamental china also named after its home town east of Moscow.

Russia's trademark textile is the babushka scarf (officially the 'Pavlovsky Posad kerchief' – or *pavlovoposadsky platok* – once again named after a home town east of Moscow). These fine woollen scarves with floral designs go for R300 or more in shops, but you may find cheaper ones in markets. Other Russian textiles include wool shawls so fine they look like lace.

Yantar (amber) from the Baltic coast is a jewellery speciality, but beware of fake stuff in St Petersburg and Moscow markets and shops. A good necklace or ring might be US$50 to US$200.

Other Items

Russian records and cassettes – rock, jazz, classical – are a bargain at less than R100.

However, Russia is also one of the world's largest markets for bootleg recorded music, videos and computer software, with all manner of pirated versions available for sale in kiosks, underground passageways, markets and stores. Just remember: you get what you pay for. Be especially wary of cheap software, as it's rumoured that 75% of all CD ROMs sold in Russia contain a defect or virus.

More souvenir ideas: paintings from street artists and art markets (there's some talent amid the kitsch); art and children's books from bookshops; posters (old Socialist exhortation *and* modern social commentary) from bookshops or specialist *plakat* (poster) shops; and little Lenin busts sold at street stands and tourist markets.

Getting There & Away

With land borders with nine other countries and flight connections to many more around the world, there are plenty of options for getting to and from European Russia.

Unless you have a transit visa, you can enter the country on a one-way ticket (even if your visa is only good for one day, it's unlikely anyone will ask to see your outgoing ticket), so you have a great deal of flexibility once inside Russia to determine the best way of getting out again.

Information on travel between European Russia and Belarus is given in the Belarus Getting There & Away chapter; information on travel between European Russia and Siberia, the Russian Far East, Mongolia and China is given in the Siberia & the Russian Far East Getting There & Away chapter.

AIR

It's most likely you will fly into Moscow's Sheremetevo-2 or Domodedovo airports, but there are also daily services from several European cities to St Petersburg. Other entry options include Yekaterinburg, Perm, Krasnodar and Mineralnye Vody all served by direct flights from Germany, the last two with occasional flights to Istanbul. Note there aren't any direct services to European Russia from Australasia; go to an Asian, European or US gateway and proceed from there.

Warning

The information in this chapter is particularly vulnerable to change: Prices for international travel are volatile, routes are introduced and cancelled, schedules change, special deals come and go, and rules and visa requirements are amended. You should check directly with the airline or a travel agent to make sure you understand how a fare (and ticket you may buy) works and be aware of the security requirements for international travel.

The upshot of this is that you should get opinions, quotes and advice from as many airlines and travel agents as possible before you part with your hard-earned cash. The details given in this chapter should be regarded as pointers and are not a substitute for your own careful, up-to-date research.

If you are flying to another city in European Russia or elsewhere in the nation your best connection will be through Moscow, which has the bulk of domestic flights. However, this will inevitably require a change of airports, which can mean a potentially costly, inconvenient and time-consuming adventure.

Airlines

Aeroflot Russian International Airlines (w *www.aeroflot.org*) is the main Russian carrier to the rest of the world. It has improved a fair amount from its notorious Soviet days. It flies a large fleet with many Boeings and Airbuses, and has a passable business class and acceptable economy class. It should not be confused with the scores of domestic airlines cast off from the old Aeroflot.

Transaero Airlines (w *www.transaero.com/noframes/eng/home.htm*) is a private Russian airline offering Western-style service on mostly Western-made aircraft. It has a limited schedule of flights to Europe.

Other major airlines flying into Moscow include:

Air China	w www.airchina.com.cn
Air France	w www.airfrance.com
Alitalia	w www.alitalia.it
American Airlines	w www.aa.com
Austrian Airlines	w www.aua.com
British Airways	w www.britishairways.com
CSA Czech Airlines	w www.csa.cz/intro.htm
Delta Airlines	w www.delta.com
Dragonair	w www.dragonair.com
El Al Israel Airlines	w www.elal.co.il
Finnair	w www.finnair.com
Japan Airlines	w www.jal.co.jp
KLM	w www.klm.nl
Korean Air	w www.koreanair.com
LOT Polish Airlines	w www.lot.com
Lufthansa	w www.lufthansa.com
MIAT Mongolian Airlines	w www.miat.com
Qantas	w www.qantas.com.au
Singapore Airlines	w www.singaporeair.com
Swissair	w www.swissair.com
Turkish Airlines	w www.turkishairlines.com

Buying Tickets

The plane ticket will probably be the single most expensive item in your budget, and buying it can be an intimidating business. There is likely to be a multitude of airlines and travel agencies hoping to separate you from your money and you're going to want to get the best deal possible, so it's always worth putting aside time to research the current state of the market.

Use the fares quoted in this book as a guide only. They are approximate and based on the rates advertised by travel agencies at the time of going to press. Quoted airfares do not necessarily constitute a recommendation for the carrier.

Once you have your ticket, write its number down, together with the flight number and other details, and keep the information separate from your ticket. If the ticket is lost or stolen, this will help you get a replacement.

Open-Jaw Tickets These are return tickets that allow you to fly out to one destination but return from another, and can save you backtracking to your arrival point. Even if the same airline doesn't fly into, for example, both Moscow and Yekaterinburg, travel agencies will certainly be able to put together two one-way tickets with different airlines.

While open-jaw tickets may give you peace of mind and something to show immigration officials, they can sacrifice flexibility. You'll have to be at the other end on a certain date, or go through the hassle of changing your flight en route. Also, it unlikely to be any cheaper to do it this way as one-way tickets to major destinations can be purchased reasonably cheaply and at short notice in Moscow, St Petersburg, and elsewhere. Generally, you will be better off buying a one-way ticket into your destination and another one-way ticket out when you finish the trip.

Buying Tickets Online There are many websites specifically aimed at selling flights, where you can look up fares and timetables by selecting your departure point and destination, then book a ticket online using your credit card. Your ticket will (hopefully) be mailed out to you, or it may be an 'electronic ticket' that you claim at the airport before checking in for your flight.

Sometimes these fares are cheap, often they're no cheaper than those sold at a standard travel agency, and occasionally they're way too expensive – but it's certainly a convenient way of researching flights from the comfort of your own home or office. Many

large travel agencies also have websites, but not all of them allow you to look up fares and schedules.

Websites worth checking include:

w www.cheapestflights.co.uk This site really does post some of the cheapest flights (out of the UK only), but you have to get in early to get the bargains.

w www.dialaflight.com This site offers worldwide flights out of Europe and the UK.

w www.expedia.msn.com A good site for checking worldwide flight prices.

w www.flifo.com The official site of One Travel .Com.

w www.lastminute.com This site deals mainly in European flights, but does have worldwide flights, mostly package returns. There's also a link to an Australian version.

w www.statravel.com STA Travel's US website. There are also UK and Australian sites (**w** www .statravel.co.uk and **w** www.statravel.com .au).

w www.travel.com.au A good site for Australians to find cheap flights, although some prices may turn out to be too good to be true.

w www.travelonline.co.nz A good site for New Zealanders to find worldwide fares from their part of the world.

Travellers with Special Needs

Most international airlines can cater for people with special needs – travellers with disabilities, people with young children and even children travelling alone.

Special dietary preferences (vegetarian, kosher etc) can be catered for with advance notice. If you are travelling in a wheelchair, most international airports can provide an escort from check-in desk to plane where needed, and ramps, lifts, toilets and phones are generally available.

Airlines usually carry babies up to two years of age at 10% of the adult fare, although a few may carry them free of charge. Reputable international airlines usually provide nappies (diapers), tissues, talcum powder and all the other paraphernalia needed to keep babies clean, dry and at least half-happy. For children between the ages of two and 12, the fare on international flights is usually 50% of the regular fare or 67% of a discounted fare.

Departure Tax

Russian departure taxes are usually included in the price of the ticket.

The USA

Discount travel agencies in the USA are known as consolidators (although you won't see a sign on the door saying 'Consolidator'), and they can be found in the *Yellow Pages* or the travel sections of major daily newspapers such as the *New York Times*, the *Los Angeles Times*, and the *San Francisco Examiner*. Good deals can generally be found at agencies in San Francisco, Los Angeles, New York and other big cities. A good place to start is **STA Travel** (☎ 800-781 4040; **W** *www.statravel.com*), which has a wide network of offices.

Economy class air fares from New York to Moscow can go as low as one-way/return US$450/550 with Aeroflot. From Los Angeles you're looking at one-way/return fares to Moscow of US$550/960.

Canada

Canadian discount agencies, also known as consolidators, advertise their flight specials in major newspapers such as the *Toronto Star* and the *Vancouver Sun*. The national student travel agency is **Travel CUTS** (☎ 866-246 9762; **W** *www.travelcuts.com*).

In general, fares from Canada to Russia cost 10% more than from the USA. For a one-way/return flight from Vancouver to Moscow the cost is C$1124/1796; from Montreal C$1203/1468.

Australia

Cheap flights from Australia to Europe generally go via South-East Asian capitals, involving stopovers at Kuala Lumpur, Bangkok or Singapore. If a long stopover between connections becomes a necessity, transit accommodation is sometimes included in the price of the ticket. If the fare means you have to pay for transit accommodation yourself, it may be worth your while upgrading to a more expensive ticket.

Quite a few travel offices specialise in discount air tickets. Some travel agencies, particularly smaller ones, advertise cheap air fares in the travel sections of weekend newspapers, such as the *Age* in Melbourne and the *Sydney Morning Herald*.

Two well-known agencies for cheap fares, with offices throughout Australia, are **Flight Centre** (☎ 131 600 Australia-wide; **W** *www.flightcentre.com.au*) and **STA Travel** (☎ 131 776; **W** *www.statravel.com.au*).

The most direct flight you're going to get would be something like Sydney to Bangkok and then Bangkok to Moscow: a Qantas/Aeroflot deal starts at one-way/return A$1100/1450.

New Zealand

The *New Zealand Herald* has a travel section in which travel agencies advertise fares. **Flight Centre** (☎ 0800 243 544; **W** *www.flightcentre.co.nz*) and **STA Travel** (☎ 0508 782 872; **W** *www.statravel.co.nz*); have branches in Auckland and elsewhere in the country; check the websites for complete listings.

Air fares from New Zealand to Russia are similar to those from Australia.

The UK

Newspapers and magazines such as *Time Out* and *TNT Magazine* in London regularly advertise very low fares to places such as Moscow and Beijing. A good place to start shopping for fares is with the major student or backpacker oriented travel agencies such as STA and Trailfinders. Through these reliable agents you can get an idea of what's available and how much you're going to pay – although a bit of ringing around to the smaller agencies afterwards will often turn up cheaper fares.

Addresses of reputable agencies in London include:

Bridge the World (☎ 0870-444 7474 or ☎ 020-7813 3350, **W** www.b-t-w.co.uk) 4 Regent Place, London W1R 5FB
Flightbookers (☎ 0870-010 7000, **W** www.ebookers.co.uk) 34–42 Woburn Place, London WC1H 0TA
STA Travel (☎ 0870-1600 599, **W** www.statravel.co.uk) 40 Bernard Street, London WC1N 1LJ
Trailfinders (☎ 020-7938 3939, **W** www.trailfinders.co.uk) 194 Kensington High St, London W8 7RG

Shop around and you might get a low-season one-way/return fare to Moscow for UK£150/200. Flights to St Petersburg are a bit more expensive at around UK£200/250. Aeroflot generally offer the cheapest deals.

Continental Europe

Though London is the travel discount capital of Europe, there are several other European cities in which you will find a range of good deals. Generally, there is not much variation in air fare prices from the main European cities. All the major airlines are usually offering some sort of deal and travel agencies generally have a number of deals on offer, so shop around. Aeroflot has daily flights between most of the major cities in Europe and Moscow and limited service to/from St Petersburg.

Travel agencies in France specialising in youth and student fares include **OTU Voyages** (☎ 01 40 29 12 12; W www.otu.fr; 39 Ave Georges Bernanos, 75005 Paris). Another general travel agency offering good services and deals is **Nouvelles Frontières** (☎ 01 45 68 70 00; W www.nouvelles-frontieres.fr; 87 blvd de Grenelle, 75015 Paris). Both agencies have branches around the country.

Agencies in Germany include **STA Travel** (☎ 01805-456 422; W www.statravel.de), and **Travel Overland** (☎ 089-27 27 63 00; W www .travel-overland.de; Barerstrasse 73, 80799 Munich); for a list of its offices contact its Munich branch.

Asia

Although most Asian countries are now offering fairly competitive deals, Bangkok and Singapore are still the best places to shop around for discount tickets.

Khao San Rd in Bangkok is the budget travellers' headquarters. Bangkok has a number of excellent travel agencies but there are also some suspect ones; ask the advice of other travellers before handing over your cash. **STA Travel** (☎ 02-236 0262; 33/70 Surawong Rd) is a reliable place to start. Aeroflot has direct flights to Moscow from Bangkok.

In Singapore, **STA Travel** (☎ 737 7188; 33A Cuppage Rd, Cuppage Terrace) offers competitive discount fares for Asian destinations and beyond. Singapore, like Bangkok, has hundreds of travel agents, so you can compare prices on flights.

In Japan there are several branches of **STA Travel** (☎ 03-5485 8380, fax 5485 8373; W www.statravel.co.jp; 1st floor, Star Plaza Aoyama Bldg, 1-10-3 Shibuya, Tokyo) and in Osaka (☎ 06-6262 7066; 6th floor, Honmachi Meidai Bldg, 2-5-5 Azuchi-Machi, Osaka). Other reliable discount agencies in Japan include **No 1 Travel** (☎ 03-3200 8871; W www .no1-travel.com) and **Across Travellers Bureau** (☎ 03-3373 9040; W www.across-travel.com). Generally, one-way/return flights from Tokyo to Moscow are around ¥130,000/221,000, although at certain times of the year 60-day excursion fares on Aeroflot can go as low as ¥60,000 return.

Rest of the World

Aeroflot has infrequent flights to a few cities in South America and Africa. If you intend to use other airlines you'll have to travel via a European hub airport.

There are also frequent flights to/from the capitals of the countries of the former Soviet Union and Moscow. Sample economy ticket fares include the following:

destination	cost (US$)	duration (hrs)	frequency (daily)
Almaty	175	5	2
Baku	113	3	5
Kiev	81	1½	2
Minsk	97	2	1
Tashkent	153	4	2
Yerevan	135	2½	4

LAND
Border Crossings

Except for 72-hour visas for certain citizens (see Visas in the European Russia Facts for the Visitor chapter) Russian visas aren't issued at the border. Upon entry and exit you will have to fill out a *deklaratsia* (customs declaration form; see Customs in the European Russia Facts for the Visitor chapter for details).

On trains, border crossings are a straightforward but drawn-out affair, with a steady stream of customs and ticket personnel scrutinising your passport and visa.

If you're arriving by car or motorcycle, you'll need to show your vehicle registration and insurance papers, your driving licence, passport and visa. These formalities are usually minimal for Western citizens.

On the Russian side, chances are your vehicle will be subjected to a cursory inspection by border guards (your life will be made much easier if you open all doors and the boot yourself, and shine a torch for the guards at night). You pass through customs separately from your car, walking through a metal detector and possibly having hand luggage X-rayed.

Train fares for trips to/from Russia listed under individual countries in this section are for a *kupe* (compartment) in a four-berth compartment.

Azerbaijan

All travellers need a visa to enter Azerbaijan.

Although there are regular trains and buses between Moscow and Baku, plus buses between Baku and Makhachkala, the Russo-Azeri border is currently closed to foreigners. The Dagestan region through which all such

Driving in Russia: the Basics

Russia is open for car or motorcycle tourists, but you may want to pause for consideration before embarking on that road tour. Poorly maintained roads, maddeningly inadequate signposting, low-quality petrol and keen and rapacious highway patrolmen can lead to frustration and dismay. For specific driving tips and information on road rules and fuel, see the European Russia Getting Around chapter.

To legally drive your own or a rented car/motorcycle in Russia you'll need to be over 18 years old and have a full driving licence. In addition, you'll need an International Driving Permit with a Russian translation of your licence, or a certified Russian translation of your full licence (you can certify translations at a Russian embassy or consulate).

You will also need your vehicle's registration papers and proof of insurance. Be sure your insurance covers you in Russia. A customs declaration promising that you will take your vehicle with you when you leave is also required. A departure road tax of about US$10 is also collected at the border.

★★

transport must pass is a dangerous area (see Caucasus chapter for details) and we don't advise travelling there.

Belarus
For details on visas and getting there and away by train and road, see the Belarus Facts for the Visitor and Getting There & Away chapters, respectively.

Estonia
US, UK, Irish, Australian and New Zealand citizens do not need a visa to enter Estonia. Canadians do.

There's a daily train between Moscow and Tallinn (US$42, 16 hours) and one every other day between Tallinn and St Petersburg (US$24, nine hours). Daily express buses from St Petersburg are cheaper (US$10, seven to eight hours).

The nearest border crossing from Tallinn is at Narva, and the road from there to St Petersburg is uneventful, if not particularly fast.

Finland
US, Canadian, UK, Irish, Australian and New Zealand citizens do not need a visa to enter Finland.

Train There are two daily daytime trains between St Petersburg and Helsinki: the *Repin* is the Russian-run service and the *Sibelius* is the Finnish-run service. The trips take five hours and 4½ hours respectively, and both cost sitting/*kupe* US$54/83 Moscow is also connected with Helsinki by nightly trains (US$105, 16 hours).

Bus There are daily buses between Helsinki and St Petersburg (about US$35, seven hours)

with **Finnord** (☎ 812-314 89 51) and **Sovavto** (☎ 812-123 51 25; W *www.pohjolanliikenne .fi*). For more details see the St Petersburg chapter.

Car & Motorcycle Highways cross at the Finnish border posts of Nuijamaa and Vaalimaa (Brusnichnoe and Torfyanovka, respectively, on the Russian side). From these towns to St Petersburg the road is said to be infested with modern-day highwaymen; we've driven it dozens of times and never had any difficulties. Don't stop for anyone, and fill up with petrol on the Finnish side (preferably before you get to the border filling station, which is more expensive than others and closes early). There's a radar speed-trap just outside the St Petersburg city line where the limit is 60km/h (hint: radar detectors are legal in Russia). Be sure and watch for all road signs; a few roads involve tricky curves and signposting is not all it should be. It's best to make this drive for the first time during daylight hours.

Georgia
Although Georgia shares a spectacular mountain border with Russia, the only practicable road across it (the Georgian military highway) is presently closed to foreigners. The coastal road and railway via Sochi has been unusable for a decade as it passes through breakaway Abkhazia a de facto independent state which is blockaded by Georgia and half-heartedly isolated by its erstwhile Russian protectors. To reach Georgia overland the easiest route is by daily boat from Sochi to Trabzon (Turkey), where there's a Georgian consulate. From there it's about four hours to the Georgian border at Sarp via Hopa.

Kazakhstan

All travellers need a visa to enter Kazakhstan, for which a letter of invitation is generally required. There are no conveniently situated Kazakhstan consulates anywhere in Ural or Siberian Russia – the nearest is in Moscow or Ulaan Baatar (Mongolia).

There are trains every two days between Moscow and Almaty (R3456, 50 hours) and daily from Astrakhan to Atyrau/Guriyev, in addition to a variety of services from Siberia. Beware that some trains cut through Kazakhstan en route, including Chelyabinsk–Omsk, Chelyabinsk–Magnitogorsk and Yekaterinburg–Omsk. Visa checks are not always made leaving Russia, but coming back in you may find yourself in serious trouble if you don't have a Kazakhstan visa and double/multiple entry Russian one, too.

Roads into Kazakhstan head east from Astrakhan, and south from Samara, Chelyabinsk and Omsk.

Latvia

US, UK and Irish citizens do not need a visa to enter Latvia. Canadians, Australians and New Zealanders need a visa if they do not already have one for Estonia or Lithuania.

Train From Latvia trains run daily between Riga and Moscow (US$97, 15 hours) and St Petersburg (US$32, 13 hours).

Bus There are daily buses from Riga to St Petersburg (US$17, 11 hours); see the St Petersburg chapter for details. There are also daily buses between Riga and Kaliningrad (10 hours) and a weekly service to Moscow (18 hours).

Car & Motorcycle The M9 Riga–Moscow road crosses the border east of Rezekne (Latvia). The A212 road from Riga leads to Pskov, crossing a corner of Estonia en route.

Lithuania

US, Canadian, UK, Irish and Australian citizens do not need a visa to enter Lithuania; New Zealand citizens do.

Train A service leaves Vilnius for Kaliningrad (seven hours) five times a week, for Moscow (US$103, 15 hours) three times a week and for St Petersburg (US$21, 14 hours) every other day. The St Petersburg

trains cross Latvia, and the Moscow ones cross Belarus (see the Transit Visas section of the Belarus Facts for the Visitor chapter for transit visa information).

Car & Motorcycle The A229 to Kaliningrad crosses the border at Kybartai. Most roads to the rest of Russia cross Belarus.

Norway

US, Canadian, UK, Irish, Australian and New Zealand citizens do not need a visa to enter Norway.

For details of bus connections between Norway and Russia, see the Getting There & Away section of the Kola Peninsula in the Northern European Russia chapter.

Poland

US, UK and Irish citizens do not need a visa to enter Poland; Canadians, Australians and New Zealanders do.

Train There are daily services linking Warsaw with Moscow (US$94, 21 hours) and St Petersburg (US$57, 27 to 31 hours). The Moscow trains enter Belarus near Brest. The St Petersburg trains leave Poland at Kuznica, which is near Hrodna (Grodno in Russian) in Belarus. Changing the wheels to/from Russia's wider gauge adds three hours to the journey.

Bus There are two daily buses between Kaliningrad and each of Gdansk and Oltshyn as well as five weekly buses to/from Warsaw. For further details on buses to/from towns in Poland, see Getting There & Away in the Kaliningrad section of the Western European Russia chapter.

Car & Motorcycle The main border crossing between Poland and Kaliningrad is near Bagrationovsk on the A195 highway. Queues can be very long.

The UK & Europe

Travelling overland from the UK or Europe will be no cheaper than flying (in most cases it will be considerably more) and, from London, takes a minimum of two days and nights. It is, however, a great way of easing yourself into the rhythm of a long Russian journey, such as the Trans-Siberian Railway. If you have time, there are many interesting places to stop along the way, especially in

Eastern Europe, from where the direct train connections to Russia are the best.

Train There are no direct trains from the UK to Russia. The most straightforward route is on the **Eurostar** (w *www.eurostar.com*) to Brussels, from where you can transfer to a train to Cologne and the service that goes straight through to Moscow via Warsaw and Minsk (Belarus). The total cost will be around UK£280.

Crossing the Poland–Belarus border at Brest takes several hours while the wheels are changed for the Russian track. All foreigners visiting Belarus need a visa, including those transiting by train – it's best to sort this out before arriving in Belarus otherwise you're likely to be fined. For more details on visas, see the Belarus Facts for the Visitor chapter.

To avoid this hassle consider taking the train to St Petersburg from Vilnius in Lithuania, which runs several times a week via Latvia. There are daily connections between Vilnius and Warsaw.

From Moscow there are also regular international services to Belgrade, Berlin, Bratislava, Budapest, Prague, Sofia, Vienna, Venice and Warsaw, and from St Petersburg to Berlin and Budapest.

For full European rail timetables check w http://mercurio.iet.unipi.it/misc/timetabl.html, which provides a central link to all of Europe's national railways. Most (but not the Russian Railways site) can be converted to English.

Bus There's twice-weekly direct buses to Moscow from London's Victoria Coach station, via Berlin (where the bus pauses for 13 hours), Barisov in Belarus and Smolensk. The entire trip takes over 2½ days and costs one-way/return UK£92/167 Contact **Eastern European Travel Ltd** (☎ *0161-2023594, fax 0161 2036502;* w *www.ee-travel.com.ua; St. Wilfred's House, 929 Oldham Road, Manchester M40 2EB)* for details.

From Berlin, Cologne, Hamburg, Munich and Stuttgart it's also possible to take a coach to Riga or Tallinn, from where there are direct bus connections to Moscow. For details contact **Eurolines** (w *www.eurolines.com*).

Ukraine

Ukrainian visas are *not* issued at any border crossing; travellers who arrive visa-less will be refused entry into Ukraine.

Train Most major Ukrainian cities have daily services to Moscow, with two border crossings: one used by trains heading to Kiev, the other by trains passing through Kharkiv.

Trains between Kiev and Moscow (US$23, 14 hours, 10 services daily) go via Bryansk (Russia) and Konotop (Ukraine), crossing at the Ukrainian border town of Seredyna-Buda. The best trains to take (numbers are southbound/northbound) between Moscow and Kiev are No 1/2, the *Ukrainia*, or No 3/4, the *Kyiv*; both travel overnight. The best train between Moscow and Lviv (28 hours, daily via Kiev) is No 73/74. Between Moscow and Odessa (28 hours, daily via Kiev) there's the No 23/24, the *Odesa*. There are also daily trains to/from St Petersburg to Lviv (30 hours via Vilnius) and Kiev (23 to 30 hours).

Trains between Kharkiv and Moscow (13 hours, about 14 daily via Kursk) cross the border just 40km north of Kharkiv. The best train is the night train, the *Kharkiv*, No 19/20. Between Moscow and Simferopol (26 hours, daily via Kharkiv), the best train is No 67/68, the *Simferopol*. Trains between Moscow and Donetsk (22 hours, three daily), Dnipropetrovsk (20 hours, twice daily), Zaporizhzhya (19 hours, twice daily) and Sevastopol (29½ hours, daily) all go through Kharkiv.

Many trains travelling between Moscow and the Caucasus go through Kharkiv, including a daily service to Rostov-on-Don (12 hours), and seasonal services to Tbilisi (31 hours, once a week).

There are daily international trains passing through Ukraine to/from Moscow's Kyivsky Vokzal. These include the No 15/16 Kiev–Lviv–Chop–Budapest, with a carriage to Venice twice a week.

Bus There is a handful of weekly buses travelling from Kharkiv across the border into Russia on the E95 (M2) road. The official frontier crossing is 40km north of Kharkiv, and is near the Russian border town of Zhuravlevka.

Car & Motorcycle The main auto-route between Kiev and Moscow starts as the E93 (M20) north of Kiev, but becomes the M3 when it branches off to the east some 50km south of Chernihiv.

Driving from Ukraine to the Caucasus, the border frontier point is on the E40 (M19) road crossing just before the Russian town of

Novoshakhtinsk at the Ukrainian border village of Dovzhansky, about 150km east of Donetsk.

SEA

Opportunities to reach European Russia by sea have all but dried up, the only services being a 'mini-cruise' between Helsinki and St Petersburg (see the St Petersburg chapter) and the occasional ferry from either Istanbul or Trabzon in Turkey to Sochi and Novorossiysk (see the Caucasus chapter).

TRAVEL AGENCIES & ORGANISED TOURS

If you have time, and a certain degree of determination, organising your own trip to Russia is easily done. But for many travellers, opting for the assistance of an agency in drawing up an itinerary, booking train tickets and accommodation, not to mention helping with the visa paperwork, will be preferable.

Also you might want to arrange an outdoor activity, such as hiking or rafting, for which the services of an expert agency is almost always required. Or you may choose to go the whole hog and have everything taken care of on a fully organised tour.

The following agencies and tour companies provide a range of travel services. Numerous more locally based agencies can provide tours once you're in Russia (a few are listed below; for others see the destination chapters), and many work in conjunction with overseas agencies so if you go to them directly you'll usually pay less.

Note that Intourist is no longer the monolithic monopoly it once was (although a few bureaus may still act like it). We list some companies related to the surviving Intourist structure to some extent, which usually have an extensive selection of tours and other services available.

Some agencies that can arrange Trans-Siberian tours are listed below; you'll find other Siberian and Russian Far East specialists in the Getting There & Away chapter of the Siberia & Russian Far East section.

Russia

Len-Alp Tours (☎ 812-279 07 16, fax 279 06 51, Ⓦ www.russia-climbing.com) ulitsa Vosstania 9/4, St Petersburg. This agency specialises in climbing tours, including trips to Mt Elbrus and the Altay region.

Marlis Travel (☎ 095-453 43 68, fax 456 66 06, Ⓦ www.marlis.ru). This Moscow operation of UK-based tour agency The Russia Experience receives recommendations from locals for booking train tickets and making other travel arrangements.

The USA

Cruise Marketing International (toll-free ☎ 800-578 7742, Ⓦ www.cruiserussia.com) Suite 3, 3401 Investment Rd, Hayward, CA 94545. It books tours on cruises along Russian waterways such as the Volga River.

Mir Corporation (☎ 206-624 7289, fax 624 7360, Ⓦ www.mircorp.com) Suite 210, 85 South Washington St, Seattle, WA 98104. Among many other trips around Russia, this agency offers upmarket private train tours along the Trans-Siberian route in Pullman-style carriages from US$4495 for a 15-day Moscow to Vladivostok itinerary.

Russiatours (☎ 800-633 1008, fax 251 6685, Ⓦ www.russiatours.com) Suite 102, 13312 N 56th St, Tampa, FL 33617. This agency specialises in luxurious group tours to Moscow and St Petersburg.

Sokol Tours (☎/fax 617-269 2659, toll-free in USA & Canada 1-800-55-RUSSIA, Ⓦ www.sokoltours.com) PO Box 382385, Cambridge, MA 02238-2385. A Canadian-Russian joint venture company offering a range of Siberian tours, including train trips, and rafting in the Altay.

White Nights (☎/fax 916-979 9381, Ⓦ www.concourse.net/bus/wnights) 610 La Sierra Drive, Sacramento CA 95864. It will assist with purchasing tickets or obtaining visas without requiring clients to book an entire tour. It also has offices in Netherlands, Germany and Switzerland.

Canada

The Adventure Centre (☎ 416-922 7584, fax 922 8136, Ⓦ www.theadventurecentre.com) 25 Bellair St, Toronto, Ontario M5R 3L3. Canada's top adventure tour agency offers Sundowners' Trans-Siberian packages (see also Australia later). It also has branches Calgary, Edmonton and Vancouver.

Australia

Eastern Europe Travel Bureau (☎ 02-9262 1144, fax 9262 4479, Ⓔ eetb@optusnet.com.au) Level 5, 75 King St, Sydney, NSW 2000. Can arrange train tickets, homestays and visas, and put together individual itineraries throughout Russia.

Passport Travel (☎ 03-9867 3888, fax 9867 1055, Ⓦ www.travelcentre.com.au) Suite 11A, 401 St Kilda Rd, Melbourne, Vic 3004. A respected agency that can arrange visa invitations, independent itineraries, language courses, and more.

Russian Gateway Tours (☎ 02-9745 3333, fax 9745 3237, **W** www.russian-gateway.com.au) 48 The Boulevarde, Strathfield, NSW 2135. An experienced Russia specialist, with its own range of Trans-Siberian tours as well as a host of accommodation packages for the major cities. It arranges visas and individual tickets, too.

Sundowners (☎ 03-9672 5300, fax 9672 5311, **W** www.sundowners-travel.com) Suite 15, 600 Lonsdale St, Melbourne, Vic 3000. One of the premier Trans-Siberian tour operators offering both small group tours ranging from eight to 25 days at various levels of comfort, as well as unescorted trips. Its budget eight-day Trans-Mongolia package, including two nights in Moscow, costs from A$1200; it can also book individual tickets and homestays.

Travel Directors (☎ 1800 641 236, fax 08-9322 1310, **W** www.traveldirectors.com.au) Shop 30B, Raine Square, Perth. Specialises in upmarket Trans-Siberian tours, including crossing into Russia from Helsinki, with stops in Irkutsk and St Petersburg and. Its 24-day 'Beyond the Trans-Siberian' tour costs around A$8950, including flights from Australia.

The UK

GW Travel Ltd (☎ 0161-928 9410, fax 941 6101, **W** www.gwtravel.co.uk) 6 Old Market Place, Altringham, Cheshire WA14 4NP. If you're looking to travel the Trans-Siberian route in luxury, these are the people to hook up with. Tours on private Pullman-style carriages with restaurants, showers and lectures start from US$4495. It occasionally runs steam-train tours, including one scheduled for the Trans-Siberian centenary celebrations in 2003.

The Imaginative Traveller (☎ 020-8742 3049, fax 8742 3045, **W** www.imaginative-traveller.com) 14 Barley Mow Passage, Chiswick, London W4 4PH. UK agent for Sundowners' Trans-Siberian tours (see Australia).

Intourist Travel (☎ 020-7538 8600 or 020 7727 4100, fax 7727 8090, **W** www.intourist.co.uk) 7 Wellington Terrace, Notting Hill, London W2 4LW. The old monopoly Russian bureau is no longer the only kid on the Russian tourism block, but it still knows the scene well and offers all manner of packages and services.

Page & Moy Holidays (☎ 0116-250 7979, fax 0870-010 6449, **W** www.page-moy.co.uk) 136–140 London Rd, Leicester LE2 1EN. Specialises in river cruises.

Regent Holidays (☎ 0117-921 1711, fax 925 4866, **W** www.regent-holidays.co.uk) 15 John St, Bristol BS1 2HR. This much-recommended

agency has a wealth of experience in arranging tours and individual trips in and around this part of the world.

The Russia Experience (☎ 020-8566 8846, fax 8566 8843 **W** www.trans-siberian.co.uk) Research House, Fraser Rd, Perivale, Middlesex UB6 7AQ. An agency with years of experience in Russia, which can help with transport, tours and bookings, or put together an all-inclusive adventure. It also runs the Beetroot Bus (**W** www.beetroot.org), a backpacker-style tour between St Petersburg and Moscow, as well as adventurous programs in the Altay and Tuva.

Russian Gateway (☎ 07951-694 620, fax 07050 803 161, **W** www.russiangateway.co.uk) Web-based agency offering ticketing services for the Trans-Siberian route on all available trains between Russia, China and Mongolia. It also provides hotel and excursion add-ons in all three countries and full visa support.

Steppes East (☎ 01285-65 1010, fax 88 5888, **W** www.steppeseast.co.uk) The Travel House, 51 Castle St, Cirencester, Gloucestershire GL7 1QD. It specialises in catering to offbeat requirements and has plenty of experience in the region.

Travel For The Arts (☎ 020-8799 8350, fax 8998 7965, **W** www.travelforthearts.co.uk) 12–15 Hangar Green, London W5 3EL. Specialises in luxury culture-based tours to Russia (particularly St Petersburg) and other European destinations for people with a specific interest in opera and ballet.

Voyages Jules Verne (☎ 020-7616, fax 7723 8629, **W** www.vjv.co.uk) 21 Dorset Square, London NW1 6QG. Its upmarket 'Central Kingdom Express' tour uses private Pullman-style carriages to cover the 15-night journey between Moscow and Beijing. Prices start at around UK£2795.

Wallace Arnold Tours (☎ 0113-231 0739, fax 231 0563, **W** www.wallacearnold.co.uk) Operates bus tours between the UK and Russia aimed at older travellers.

Germany

Lernidee Reisen (☎ 030-786 0000, fax 786 5596, **W** www.lernidee-reisen.de) Dudenstrasse 78, 10965 Berlin. Has over 15 years of experience of arranging Trans-Siberian Railway trips.

Travel Service Asia (☎ 7351-37 3210, fax 37 3211, **W** www.travel-service.asia.de) Schmelzweg 10, 88400 Biberach/Riss. Apart from arranging small group tours along the Trans-Siberian/Mongolian Railway routes this agency specialises in arranging homestays and offers a range of activities around Lake Baikal.

Getting Around

AIR

Flying in Russia is like the country itself – a unique experience. Timetables, generally posted up or available at all ticket offices (of which there are now many), are often based on fantasy. Many flights (except those between major cities) are delayed, often for hours and with no explanation offered.

Buying Tickets

Tickets for all domestic Russian airlines and airlines of former Soviet republics can be purchased from offices in cities all over Russia (see city chapters for locations) and through travel agents in Russia or abroad. Note that some city ticket offices still have a huge Aeroflot sign over the door even if none of the airlines serving that town actually uses that name.

Generally speaking, you'll do better booking internal flights once you arrive in Russia, where more flights and flight information are available, and where prices may be lower.

Whenever you book airline tickets in Russia you'll need to show your passport and visa. Tickets can also be purchased at the airport right up to the departure of the flight and sometimes even if the city centre office says that the plane is full.

Costs

The following are the maximum economy one-way fares from Moscow, valid at the time of research. Return fares are usually just double the one-way fares.

destination	cost (r)	duration (hrs)	frequency (daily)
Arkhangelsk	2820	3	2
Astrakhan	3300	2¼	2
Irkutsk	3300	7½	4
Kaliningrad	2700	1	2
Kazan	3090	1½	1
Krasnoyarsk	5610	4	2
Murmansk	2460	3	3
Nizhny Novgorod	1740	1	2
Novgorod	1530	1½	2
Novosibirsk	4650	4	2
Omsk	3920	3	4
Perm	3090	2½	2
Rostov-on-Don	2520	1½	1
Samara	2310	1½	2
Sochi	2910	2½	5

destination	cost (r)	duration (hrs)	frequency (daily)
St Petersburg	2100	1½	5
Tomsk	2430	5	2
Tyumen	3870	3	2
Ulan Ude	4440	8	1
Vladivostok	7560	9	2
Yekaterinburg	3570	2½	2

Check-In & Luggage

Check-in is 90 to 40 minutes before departure and airlines are entitled to bump you if you come later than that. To minimise the danger of loss or theft, try not to check in any baggage: many planes have special stowage areas for large carry-on pieces. Also note that you put your carry-on luggage under your own seat, not the one in front of you.

Have your passport and ticket handy throughout the various security and ticket checks that can occur right up until you find a seat. Some flights have assigned seats, others do not. On the latter, seating is a free-for-all.

TRAIN

European Russia is crisscrossed with an extensive rail network that makes rail a viable means of getting to practically anywhere. Train journeys can be cheap and relatively comfortable but they usually take a long, long time. If you like trains, and if you or your travelling partner speak good Russian, they're an excellent way to get around, see the countryside and meet Russians from all walks of life. A good 1st- or 2nd-class berth on a Russian sleeper train could prove more civilised than one in Western Europe, as they're often larger and more comfortable.

Trains have a remarkable record for punctuality, with most departing each station on their route to the minute allotted on the timetable, something British and American train travellers may marvel at. However, there are underlying reasons for this punctuality: managers have a large portion of their pay determined by the timeliness of their trains. This not only inspires promptness, but it results in the creation of schedules that are at best forgiving. You'll notice this when you find your train stationary for hours in the middle of nowhere only suddenly to start up and roll into the next station right on time.

Airline Safety in Russia

Since the break up of Aeroflot, the former Soviet state airline, Russia has witnessed the boom and bust of hundreds of smaller airlines ('baby-flots').

Obtaining reliable statistics about all these new airlines is difficult, but people familiar with the Russian aviation scene say that the safety of domestic airlines varies widely.

Tales of Russian airline-safety lapses are common, though often apocryphal. The vast majority of crashes involve small airlines in Siberia (connecting district centres with remote villages or mines) or military planes. A recent exception was the Vladavia crash in Irkutsk in August 2001 in which 145 people died. Almost half of the total number of Russian airlines lost their licences as a result of a purge ordered by President Putin following the Irkutsk crash, reducing your chance of flying with some company that owns only one poorly maintained Antonov-24. Planes owned by major commercial airlines seldom, if ever, crash. For information on flight accidents in Russia check **W** http://aviation-safety.net.

Generally, **Aeroflot Russian Airlines** (**W** *www.aeroflot.com)* is considered to have the highest standards. This airline took over the old international routes of the Soviet-era Aeroflot and today offers Western-style services on mostly Western-made aircraft such as Boeing 757s and 737s. The airline also offers domestic services on many routes; check out the website for further information. Transaero is another Russian airline with a consistent safety record. Sibir and Krasair are another two airlines that are considered quite safe.

Apart from something going wrong with the aeroplane there's also the threat of hijacking to consider; there were a spate of these, mainly involving Chechen fighters and sympathisers, in the 1990s. Again, there's little you can do about this other than avoid flights to the Caucasus and between Russia and Muslim countries.

If you're worried about airline safety, the good news is that for many destinations in Russia, if you have the time, getting there by train or bus is practical, and often preferable. Also, on routes between major cities it's possible that you may have a choice of airlines (although given the dearth of hard information and continually changing circumstances it's impossible to recommend one operator over another). But in some cases – where you're short of time or where your intended destination doesn't have reliable rail or road connections – you will have no choice but to take a flight.

★★★

Another inconvenience of Russian train travel is that, like roads and Rome, many train lines lead to Moscow. Thus journeys to cities that are geographically close but lie on two different lines can be very long, as the train goes part of the way to Moscow before joining the line to its destination.

Types of Train

All trains have numbers. The lower the number, the better the train; if you want the best trains look for numbers under 100. Odd-numbered trains head towards Moscow, even-numbered ones head east of the capital.

Long Distance The regular long-distance service is a *skoryy poyezd* (fast train). It stops more often than the typical intercity train in the West and rarely gets up enough speed really to merit the 'fast' label. Foreigners booking rail tickets through agencies are usually put on a *skoryy* train. The best *skoryy* trains often have

names, eg, the *Rossiya* (the Moscow to Vladivostok service) and the *Baikal* (the Moscow to Irkutsk service). These 'name trains', or *firmennye poyezda*, generally have cleaner cars, polite(r) attendants and more convenient arrival/departure hours; they sometimes also have fewer stops, more 1st-class accommodation and functioning restaurants.

A *passazhirskiy poyezd* (passenger train) is an intercity stopping train, found mostly on routes of 1000km or less. Journeys on these can take an awfully long time, as the trains clank and lurch from one small town to the next.

Short Distance A *prigorodnyy poyezd*, also called an *elektrichka* (suburban train), is a local service linking a city and its suburbs or nearby towns, or groups of adjacent towns – often useful for day trips, though they can be fearfully crowded. There's no need to book ahead for these – just buy your ticket and go.

In bigger stations there may be separate timetables, in addition to *prigorodnyy zal* (the usual name for ticket halls) and platforms for these trains.

Classes

In Europe and America people travel in a train fully aware that it belongs either to a state or company and that their ticket grants them only temporary occupation and certain restricted rights. In Russia people just take them over.

Laurens van der Post, *Journey into Russia*

Russians have the knack of making themselves very much at home on trains. This often means that they'll be travelling with plenty of luggage. It also means some juggling of the available space in all classes of compartment will become inevitable.

In both 1st- and 2nd-class compartments (see below) there's a luggage bin underneath each of the lower berths that will hold a medium-sized backpack or small suitcase. There's also enough space beside the bin to squeeze in another medium-sized canvas bag. Above the doorway there's a gap, which at a push, kick and shove will accommodate a couple of rucksacks. In 3rd-class compartments you'll have to cooperate with everyone else to find a space for your luggage.

In all classes of carriage with sleeping accommodation you'll be given two sheets, a washcloth, a pillowcase and a blanket; you'll usually have to pay extra (around R30) for this to the *provodnitsa* (the carriage attendant; see the boxed text 'She Who Must Be Obeyed' later in this chapter). Your mattress will be rolled up on the seats at the beginning of the journey (in 1st class the bed is often made up). On some name trains an amenity kit and packed breakfast now come as part of the fare.

1st Class/SV Most often called SV (which is short for *spalnyy vagon*, or sleeping wagon), 1st-class compartments are also called *myagkiy* (soft class) or *lyux*. They are the same size as 2nd class but have only two berths, so there's more room and more privacy for double the cost. Some 1st-class compartments now also have TVs on which it's possible to watch videos supplied by the *provodnitsa* for a small fee (there's nothing to stop you from bringing your own). You could also unplug the TV and plug in your computer. These carriages also have the edge in

that there are only half as many people queuing to use the toilet every morning.

2nd Class/Kupe The compartments in a *kupeyny* (2nd-class, also called 'compartmentalised') carriage (commonly shortened to *kupe*) are the standard accommodation on all long-distance trains. These carriages are divided into nine enclosed compartments, each with four reasonably comfortable berths, a fold-down table and just enough room between the bunks to turn around.

In every carriage there's also one half-sized compartment with just two berths. This is usually occupied by the *provodnitsa*, or reserved for railway employees, but there's a slim chance that you may end up in it, particularly if you do a deal directly with a *provodnitsa* for a train ticket (see Buying Tickets later).

3rd Class/Platskartny A reserved-place *platskartny* carriage, sometimes also called *zhyostkiy* ('hard class', or 3rd class), is essentially a dorm carriage sleeping 54. The bunks are uncompartmentalised and are arranged in blocks of four down one side of the corridor and in twos on the other, with the lower bunk on this side converting to a table and chairs during the day.

Privacy is out of the question. The scene often resembles a refugee camp, with clothing strung between bunks, a great swapping of bread, fish and jars of tea, and babies sitting on potties while their snot-nosed siblings tear up and down the corridor. That said, many travellers (women in particular) find this a better option than being cooped up with three (possibly drunken) Russian men. It's also a great way to meet ordinary Russians. *Platskartny* tickets cost half to two-thirds the price of a 2nd-class berth.

If you do travel *platskartny*, it's worth requesting specific numbered seats when booking your ticket – the prime ones are 39 to 52, which are the doubles with the bunk that converts to a table. The ones to avoid are 1 to 4, 33 to 38, 53 and 54, found at each end of the carriage, close to the samovar and toilets, where people are constantly coming and going.

4th Class/Obshchiy Also called 4th class, *obshchiy* (general) is unreserved bench-type seating. At times there might be room to lie down, while at other times there might not be

How to Read Your Ticket

When buying a ticket in Russia you'll always be asked for your passport so that its number and your name can be printed on your ticket. The ticket and passport will be matched up by the *provodnitsa* before you're allowed on the train – so make sure the ticket-seller gets these details correct.

Most tickets are printed by computer and come with a duplicate. Shortly after you've boarded the train the *provodnitsa* will come around and collect the tickets: sometimes they will take both copies and give you one back just before your final destination, sometimes they will leave you with the copy. It's a good idea to hang on to this ticket, especially if you're hopping on and off trains, since it provides evidence of how long you've been in a particular place if you're stopped by police.

Sometimes tickets are also sold with a chit for insurance in the event of a fatal accident (this is a small payment, usually less than R30), and an advance payment for linen, again around R30. The following is a guide for deciphering the rest of what your Russian train ticket is about:

1 Train number
2 Train type
3 Departure date – day and month
4 Departure time – always Moscow time for long-distance trains
5 Carriage number and class: Л = 2-bed SV, M = 4-bed SV, К = *kupe*, П = *platskartny*,
   O = *obshchiy*
6 Supplement for class of ticket above *platskartny*
7 Cost for *platskartny* ticket
8 Number of people travelling on ticket
9 Type of passenger: полный (*polny*, adult); детский (*detsky*, child); студенческий
   (*studenchesky*, student)
10 From/to
11 Bed number
12 Passport number and name
13 Total cost of ticket
14 Tax and service fee
15 Arrival date
16 Arrival time – always Moscow time for long-distance trains

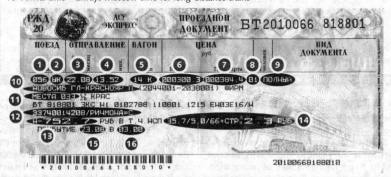

enough room to sit. *Prigorodnyy* trains normally have only this type of accommodation. On a few daytime-only intercity trains there are higher grade *obshchiy* carriages with more comfortable, reserved chairs. *Obshchiy* is rare on *skoryy* trains.

Timetables

Timetables are posted in stations and are revised twice a year. It's vital to note that the whole Russian rail network mostly runs on Moscow time, so timetables and station clocks from St Petersburg to Vladivostok will

A Russian Farce in One Act

After 'enjoying' some sweet-and-sour chicken tasting of ketchup at a Chinese restaurant in St Petersburg, I went to the train station to catch the overnight to Petrozavodsk (I'd already bought my ticket the day before). The train was leaving in 30 minutes, so I had plenty of time: as I ambled along the full length of the train for a good 10 minutes with my monstrous backpack and two handbags, I realised my wagon was the very last. Sweating and eagerly anticipating shucking my burden and kicking out on the overnight bunk, I handed my ticket and passport to the wagon attendant. Glancing at it carelessly, she was about to hand it back when she took a closer look. 'Wait. This ticket is for tomorrow.' I calmly studied the orange slip. 'No, you must be mistaken.' But she was right – it was for the next day.

'Well I bought a ticket for today – the ticket-booth lady made a mistake.' The attendant switched from bored, vain young woman to official bureaucratic robot. 'You'll have to go to the main ticket booth and have *them* change the ticket.' I looked at my watch: 20 minutes until departure. 'I'm worried I don't have the time to do that.' She crossed her arms and looked away. 'What can I do? Isn't there some other way?' I sweetly asked, trying to intercept her gaze. A bystander said to her, 'Miss, why don't you tell her to talk to the train boss?' Turning to me blankly, the attendant said, 'Go to wagon 9. The boss is there. He has the authority to let you on.' Yes! My personal travelogic had again been confirmed: with a little determination, a good attitude and a touch of charm you can get anywhere.

I jogged over to wagon 9, my backpack swinging violently, and asked for the boss. As I explained the situation, he also switched to robot mode. 'No. I can't help you. You have to go to the main ticket booth.' Struggling to smile, I exclaimed, 'But they said *you* could help me, and I don't think I have time to redo my ticket.' He looked at his watch. 'You have 15 minutes. There's time.' I looked at the station building in the distance and the mobs of obstructive people. In a strained, saccharine tone, I again asked the boss to just let me on the train. Crossing his arms and looking away, he mumbled, 'I don't have the authority.' I offered to pay him. He didn't appear to hear. I looked at my watch: 10 minutes to go. I took a deep breath, and began jostling to the main ticket booth and yelling at people to move out of the way.

I made it in about seven minutes and amazingly there was *no line*. 'I can do it!' I felt truly blessed. Sweating, panting and so confused that my Russian reverted to the level of a beginner, I handed the woman my ticket and passport and explained the situation, even managing a smile. This was not returned, although my ticket and passport were, along with the rejoinder, 'It's too late. My computer won't let me generate any new tickets with less than 15 minutes until departure. And you have the gall to show up five minutes beforehand.'

Shocked, feverish, and nearly defeated, I pleaded, 'Isn't there anything you can do? I can't spend the night here. I have to be in Petrozavodsk tomorrow.' She replied, 'Go to the boss of the train, on wagon 9. He has the authority to make an exception.' Holding back tears of frustration, I exclaimed,

★★★

be written in and set to Moscow time. The only general exception is suburban rail services, which are listed in local time.

Most stations have an information window; expect the attendant to speak only Russian and to give a bare minimum of information. Sometimes you may have to pay a small fee (around R5) for information. See the boxed text 'Reading a Train Timetable' later for ways to crack the timetable code on your own.

Buying Tickets

At any station you'll be confronted by several ticket windows. Some are special windows reserved exclusively for the use of the elderly or infirm, heroes of the Great Patriotic War or members of the armed forces. Very occasionally there are special windows where foreigners have to buy tickets, even though Russians and foreigners now pay exactly the same fare. The destination chapters will point out if there is a special ticket window at a station you should go to.

Otherwise, the sensible option, especially if there are horrendous queues, is to avail yourself of the *servis tsentr* (service centre) now found at most major stations. At these air-conditioned centres – a godsend in summer – you'll generally encounter helpful, sometimes English-speaking staff who, for a small fee

A Russian Farce in One Act

'But *he's* the one who sent me to *you* – he said he can't help me!' She retorted, 'Yes he can, he's the boss of the train. *I* can't help you. *He* can.'

Feeling persecuted, I started the long, exhausting jog back to cursed wagon 9. Stammering like Captain Kirk on his deathbed, I panted to the boss, 'She...she...couldn't...do...anything...computer...too...late...please....' He replied with logical stoicism worthy of Mr Spock. 'This ticket is for tomorrow. To take today's train, you must have a ticket for today. This ticket is for tomorrow. The ticket must be redone.' Now the tears began to flow and I lost all semblance of shame. 'But I've just run there and back with this *huge backpack* (what I actually said, in my frantic exhaustion, was 'huge bitch,' which didn't help the matter at all; the boss' brows rose with indignation) and it's *not my fault!* The ticket lady made a mistake!' He crossed his arms, stared into the distance, and slowly and deliberately stepped back onto the wagon.

Then out of the garbled noise of the crowd, a young woman tenderly spoke: 'Girl, there are other trains that stop in Petrozavodsk. Maybe you could catch a train later tonight.' I looked up at her adoringly. What a brilliant, obvious idea! Although I had been defeated in this battle, my goal of reaching Petrozavodsk by the next day was *still possible*. I slowly made my way back through the crowds to the main ticket booth. Streaming sweat and tears of self-pity, I felt like a freak. People were looking at me – they must have thought I was a homeless girl who had fallen into a canal.

I approached the window, but this time there was a line. As I waited, I could smell something interesting – something other than my own sweat and stress pheromones – a heady, cloying odour, with a sharp edge to it. Something not unlike...sweet-and-sour chicken. Sure enough, my leftovers had burst in my bag, drenching my books, my Walkman, my tapes and my packet of Kleenex (which were expressly kept for such an unfortunate circumstance). 'Fuck!' I loudly exclaimed and immediately felt better. Once at the front of the line, the woman in the booth barked, 'I already *told* you, my computer can't *make* you a new ticket!'

I smiled – she could no longer offend me. I guess she hadn't heard. The war was over: Russia had won, I had lost. Her cruelty was only ridiculous to me now. I laughed softly and gently said, 'Yes, I understand. Would you please be so kind as to tell me the departure time of the next train to stop in Petrozavodsk?' She violently pounded her fat fingers on the keyboard. 'The next train leaves at 5pm tomorrow and arrives at midnight.'

The difference in arrival time between that and my original ticket was only a few hours. As I don't particularly like to show up at train stations at midnight, I realised I was going to be using my original ticket after all. Straightening my overburdened posture as best as I could, I walked away, back into the recklessly churning crowd.

The moral of the story is: '*Always* check your ticket immediately after purchase. And double-bag your Chinese leftovers.'

Wendy Taylor

★★★

(typically around R100), can book your ticket. In big cities and towns it's also usually possible to buy tickets at special offices and some travel agencies away from the station; again, individual chapters provide details.

Whoever you end up buying your ticket from, it's a good idea to have the following written down, preferably in Cyrillic, to hand over to the sales assistant:

- your destination
- the train number, if you know it
- date and time of departure
- type of accommodation wanted
- number of tickets

When writing dates, use ordinary (Arabic) numerals for the day of the month and Roman numerals for the month. See the boxed text 'Reading a Train Timetable' for more information.

Even if the ticket-sellers tell you a particular service is sold out, it still might be possible to get on the train by speaking with the chief *provodnitsa*. Tell her your destination, offer the face ticket price first, and move slowly upwards from there. You can usually come to some sort of agreement.

Suburban Trains Tickets for these – which are very cheap – are often sold at separate

EUROPEAN RUSSIA

windows or from *avtomaticheskie kassy* machines. A table beside the machine tells you which price zone your destination is in.

Costs

In this book we typically quote 2nd-class/*kupe* fares. Expect 1st-class/SV fares to be double this, and 3rd-class/*platskartny* about 40% less. Children under five travel free if they share a berth with an adult, otherwise children under 10 pay half fare for their own berth.

It's important to note that fares are frequently hiked upward by large amounts, so please treat the fares provided in this section, valid at the time of research, as a general guide only.

At the time of writing, these were the lowest prices for 2nd-class fares from Moscow – expect to pay more for a berth on name trains such as the *Rossiya* to Vladivostok, the *Baikal* to Irkutsk, and the *Nikolaevsky Express* to St Petersburg.

destination	cost (r)	duration (hrs)	frequency (daily)
Arkhangelsk	870	22	2
Astrakhan	1440	28	4
Irkutsk	3450	75	4
Kaliningrad	1025	22	2
Kazan	660	12	5
Khabarovsk	3050	146½	1
Krasnoyarsk	2160	60	1
Kursk	370	8½	1
Murmansk	1260	42	1
Nizhny Novgorod	360	8	7
Novgorod	420	8	1
Novosibirsk	1650	47½	1
Oryol	455	4½	1
Perm	780	21	8
Pskov	681	12	2
Rostov-on-Don	1110	20	8
Samara	960	18	7
Saratov	600	26	1
Smolensk	318	7½	1
Sochi	1050	30	3
St Petersburg	1050	4½–7	11
Ulan-Ude	2361	93	1
Vladikavkaz	3456	36	1
Vladivostok	3100	160	1
Vologda	960	93	1
Yekaterinburg	990	29	11

On the Journey

There is nothing quite like the smell of a Russian train: coal smoke and coffee, cigarettes and sweat, sausage and vodka, garlic and beef pie, and dozens of other elements

combine to form an aroma that's neither bad nor good but so distinctive it will be permanently etched in your mind's nose.

Smoking is forbidden in the compartments, but permitted in the spaces at the ends of the cars, past the toilets.

Sleeping compartments are mixed sex; when women indicate that they want to change clothing or get out of bed, men go out and loiter in the corridor. Be aware that toilets can be locked long before and after station stops and that there are no shower facilities – improvise with a sponge, flannel, or a short length of garden hose that you can attach to the tap for a dowsing.

Food & Drink It's a safe bet you won't go hungry. On long trips Russian travellers bring great bundles of food that they spread out and, as dictated by railway etiquette, offer to each other; you should do the same. Always

Reading a Train Timetable

Russian train timetables vary from place to place but generally list a destination; train number; category of train; frequency of service; and time of departure and arrival, in Moscow time unless otherwise noted (see the following information on arrival and departure times).

Trains in smaller city stations generally begin somewhere else, so you'll see a starting point and a destination on the timetable. For example, when catching a train from Yekaterinburg to Irkutsk, the timetable may list Moscow as an origination point and Irkutsk as the destination. The following are a few key points to look out for.

Number Номер *(nomer)*. The higher the number of a train, the slower it is; anything over 900 is likely to be a mail train.

Category Скорый Пассажирский Почтовый-багажный Пригородный *(Skoryy, Passazhirskiy, Pochtovo-bagazhny, Prigorodnyy* – and various abbreviations thereof). These are train categories and refer, respectively, to fast, passenger, post-cargo and suburban trains. There may also be the name of the train, usually in Russian quotation marks, eg, 'Россия' ('Rossiya').

Frequency Ежедневно *(yezhednevno,* daily); чётные *(chyotnye,* even-numbered dates); нечётные *(nechyotnye,* odd-numbered dates); отменён *(otmenyon,* cancelled). All of these, as well, can appear in various abbreviations. Days of the week are listed usually as numbers (where 1 is Monday and 7 Sunday) or as abbreviations of the name of the day (Пон, Вт, Ср, Чт, Пт, Сб and Вск are, respectively, Monday to Sunday).

On some trains, frequency depends on the time of year, in which case details are usually given in hard-to-decipher, abbreviated, small print: eg, '27/VI – 31/VIII Ч; 1/IX – 25/VI 2,5' means that from 27 June to 31 August the train runs on even dates, while from 1 September to 25 June it runs on Tuesday and Friday.

Arrival & Departure Times Most train times are given in a 24-hour time format, and almost always in Moscow time (Московское время, *Moskovskoe vremya).* But suburban trains are usually marked in local time (местное время, *mestnoe vremya).* From here on it gets tricky (as though the rest wasn't), so don't confuse the following:

время отправления *(vremya otpravleniya),* which means time of departure;
время отправления с началного пункта *(vremya otpravleniya s nachalnogo punkta),* the time of departure from the train's starting point;
время прибытия *(vremya pribytiya),* the time of arrival at the station you're in;
время прибытия на конечный пункт *(vremya pribytiya na konechny punkt),* the time of arrival at the destination;
время в пути *(vremya v puti),* the duration of the journey.

Corresponding trains running in opposite directions on the same route may appear on the same line of the timetable. In this case you may find route entries like время отправления с конечного пункта *(vremya otpravlenia s konechnogo punkta),* or the time the return train leaves its station of origin.

Distance You may sometimes see the растояние *(rastoyaniye)* – distance in kilometres from the point of departure – on the timetable as well. These are rarely accurate and usually refer to the kilometre distance used to calculate the fare.

Note that if you want to calculate where you are while on a journey, keep a close look out for the small black-and-white kilometre posts generally on the southern side of the track. These mark the distance to and from Moscow. In between each kilometre marker are smaller posts counting down roughly every 100m. The distances on train timetables don't always correspond to these marker posts (usually because the timetable distances are ones used to calculate fares).

★★★

remember to bring along bottled water for the trip, although every sleeping carriage has a samovar filled with boiling water that's safe to drink.

The dining car is favoured more for its makeshift role as a social centre than for any gastronomic qualities. It becomes the place to hang out, drink beer and play cards, particularly on the long Trans-Siberian trip. Note also on the Trans-Mongolian and Trans-Manchurian trains that the dining cars are changed at each border, so en route to Beijing you get Russian, Chinese and possibly Mongolian versions. Occasionally, between the Russian border and Ulaan Baatar there is no dining car.

A meal in a restaurant car will rarely cost more than R200. If you don't fancy what's on offer – which is highly likely – there's often a table of pot noodles, chocolate, alcohol, juice and the like being peddled by the staff. They sometimes make the rounds of the carriages, too, with a trolley of snacks and drinks. Prices are cheap but still more than what you'd pay at the kiosks or to the babushkas at the station halts.

Shopping for supplies at the stations is part of the fun of any long-distance Russian train trip. The choice of items – all incredibly cheap – is often excellent, with fresh milk, ice cream, grilled chicken, boiled potatoes, home cooking such as *pelmeni* (dumplings) or *pirozhki* (savoury pies), buckets of forest berries and smoked fish all on offer. It's a good idea to have plenty of small change to hand, but you rarely have to worry about being overcharged.

Left Luggage
Many train stations have either a left-luggage room (камера хранения, *kamera khraneniya*) or left-luggage lockers (автоматические камеры хранения, *avtomaticheskiye kamery khraneniya*). These are generally secure, but make sure you note down the room's opening and closing hours and, if in doubt, establish how long you can leave your stuff for.

Here is how to work the left-luggage lockers (they're generally the same everywhere). Be suspicious of people who offer to help you work them, above all when it comes to selecting your combination.

1. Buy two *zhetony* (tokens) from the attendant.
2. Put your stuff in an empty locker.
3. Decide on a combination of one Russian letter and three numbers and write it down.
4. Set the combination on the inside of the locker door.
5. Put one token in the slot.
6. Close the locker.

To open the locker, set your combination on the outside of your locker door. Note that even though it seems as if the knobs on the outside of the door should correspond directly with those on the inside, the letter is always the left-most knob, followed by three numbers, on both the inside and the outside. After you've set your combination, put a token in the slot, wait a second or two for the electrical humming sound and then pull open the locker.

Dangers & Annoyances
Make certain on all sleeper trains that your baggage is safely stowed, preferably in the steel bins beneath the lower bunks. When you lock your door, remember that it can be unlocked with a rather simple key; on the left side of the door about three-quarters of the way up there's a small steel switch that flips up, blocking the door from opening more than a few centimetres. Flip this switch up and make sure to stuff a piece of cork in the cavity so it can't be flipped back down by a bent coat-hanger. At station halts it's also a good idea to ask the *provodnitsa* to lock your compartment while you go down to stretch your legs on the platform.

Generally, Russians love speaking with foreigners; on long train rides, they love drinking with them as well. Avoiding this is not always as easy as it would seem. Choose your drinking partners very carefully on trains, and only drink from new bottles and only when you can watch the seal being broken.

BUS
Russian buses are a great but slow way to travel between small towns, although sometimes they can be faster than an equivalent *elektrichka* train. In some regions, such as central Karelia, southwestern Russia and the Kola Peninsula, bus travel may be the only public-transport option you have. Russia's long-distance bus stations – like those everywhere – are scoundrel magnets, and are rarely pleasant places to visit after dark.

Most cities have a main intercity bus station (автовокзал, *avtovokzal*, af-tah-vahkzahl). Prices are comparable to 2nd-class train fares; journey times depend on road conditions.

Tickets are sold at the station or on the bus. Ticket prices are normally listed on the timetable and posted on a wall. As often as not you'll get a ticket with a seat assignment.

HIRED CARS

These are private cars operating as cabs over long distances and can be a great deal if there's a group of you to share the cost. Since they take the most direct route between cities the savings in time can be considerable over slow trains and meandering buses.

Typically you will find drivers offering this service outside bus terminals. Someone in your party must speak Russian to negotiate a price with the driver that typically works out to about R5 per kilometre.

Select your driver carefully, look over his car and try to assess his sobriety before setting off.

CAR & MOTORCYCLE

Driving in Russia isn't everybody's cup of tea but if you've got a sense of humour and don't mind some fairly rugged road conditions, a few hassles finding petrol, and getting lost now and then, it's an adventurous way to go. You experience at least one aspect of Russian reality as the locals do, see more of the countryside, and have total independence from the Russian transportation system.

Motorbikes will undergo vigorous scrutiny by border officials and highway police, especially if you're riding anything vaguely Ninja-ish. But one traveller reported that while riding his hand-built motorcycle across Russia, the only attention he attracted from the police consisted of admiring questions and comments.

Motorcyclists should note that while foreign automobile companies now have an established presence in Moscow, St Petersburg and other major cities, motorcycles in the former Soviet Union are almost exclusively Russian or East German-made – it is to be doubted that a Ural-brand carb will fit your Hog.

See the Car & Motorcycle section of the European Russia Getting There & Away chapter for information on planning and preparing a trip to Russia with your own vehicle and details on border crossings.

Road Rules

Russians drive on the right and traffic coming from the right has the right of way. Speed limits are generally 60km/h in towns and between 80 and 110km/h on highways. There may be a 90km/h zone, enforced by speed traps, as you leave a city. Children under 12 may not travel in the front seat, and safety belt use is mandatory (though few motorists seem to realise this!). Motorcycle riders (and passengers) must wear crash helmets.

Technically the maximum legal blood-alcohol content is 0.04%, but in practice it is illegal to drive after consuming *any* alcohol at all. This is a rule that is strictly enforced. Police will first use a breathalyser test to check blood-alcohol levels – in Moscow and other big cities the equipment is fairly reliable, but old Soviet test kits are not. You have the legal right to insist on a blood test (which involves the police taking you to a hospital). Traffic lights that flicker green are about to change to yellow, then red.

The GAI The State Automobile Inspectorate, GAI (**gah-yee**, short for Gosudarstvennaya Avtomobilnaya Inspektsia), skulks about on the roadsides, waiting for speeding, headlightless or other miscreant vehicles. Officers of the GAI are authorised to stop you, issue on-the-spot fines and, worst of all, shoot at your car if you refuse to pull over.

The GAI also hosts the occasional speed trap – the Moscow–Brest, Moscow–Oryol and Vyborg–St Petersburg roads have reputations for this. In cities, the GAI is everywhere, stopping cars for no discernible reason and collecting 'fines' on the spot.

There are permanent GAI checkpoints at the boundary of many Russian cities and towns. For serious infractions, the GAI can confiscate your licence, which you'll have to retrieve from the main station. GAI guys have been known to shake down foreigners. Don't give them any hard currency. Get receipts for any fine you pay (which should always be in roubles) and if you think you've been ripped off, head for the nearest GAI office and complain. Get the shield number of the 'arresting' officer. (By law GAI officers are not allowed to take any money at all – fines should be paid via Sberbank. However in reality Russian drivers normally pay the GAI officer approximately half the official fine, thus saving money and avoiding a trip to the bank.)

On the Road

Russian main roads are a mixed bag – sometimes smooth, straight dual carriageways, sometimes rough, narrow, winding and choked with the diesel fumes of the slow, heavy vehicles that make up a high proportion of Russian traffic. Driving much more than 300km in a day is pretty tiring.

Russian drivers use indicators far less than they should, and like to overtake everything on the road – on the inside. Priority rules at roundabouts seem to vary from area to area: all you can do is follow local practice. Russian drivers rarely switch on anything more than sidelights – and often not even those – until it's pitch black at night. Some say this is to avoid dazzling others, as for some reason dipping headlights is not common practice.

If you use a hired driver or taxi, the driver will probably be offended if you wear your seat belt. Even if you say, 'It's not your driving, it's those other crazies I'm worried about,' male drivers will often request you leave it off. Of course, you have the final word, but it's not unheard of for passengers to get a new driver who won't mind if the seatbelt is fastened.

Fuel

Joint-venture and other Western-style gas stations are common. Petrol will come in four main grades: 76, 93, 95 and 98 octane. And prices are cheap by European standards: R8 a litre for 76 octane and R10 a litre for 98 octane. Unleaded gas is available in major cities; BP or Castrol gas stations usually always sell it. *Dizel* (diesel) is also available. In the countryside petrol stations are usually not more than 100km apart, but you shouldn't rely on this.

Car Rental

You can rent self-drive cars in Moscow and St Petersburg – see the relevant city chapters for details. Elsewhere, renting a car that comes with a driver is the norm. This can be a blessing given the nature of Russian roads. Away from the largest cities you can rent a car and driver for about R150 an hour through hotels and travel agencies.

HITCHING

Hitching is never entirely safe in any country in the world, and Lonely Planet doesn't recommend it. Travellers who hitch should understand that they are taking a small but potentially serious risk. People who do choose to hitch will be safer if they travel in pairs and let someone know where they are planning to go.

That said, hitching in Russia is a very common method of getting around (see the boxed text 'Travelling the Scientific Way'). In cities, hitching rides is called hailing a cab, no matter what type of vehicle stops (see Taxi in the Local Transport section later in this chapter). In the countryside, especially in remote areas not well served by public transport, hitching is a major mode of transport.

Rides are hailed by standing at the side of the road and flagging passing vehicles with a low, up-and-down wave (not an extended thumb). You are expected to pitch in for petrol; paying what would be the normal bus fare for a long-haul ride is considered appropriate.

While hitching is widely accepted here – and therefore safer than in some other countries – there are always yahoos and lunatics puttering down the nation's highways and byways. Use common sense and keep safe. Avoid hitching at night. Women should exercise extreme caution and everyone should avoid hitching alone.

BOAT

The great rivers that wind across Russia are the country's oldest highways. A millennium ago the early Russians based their power on control of the waterborne trade between the Baltic and Black Seas. River transport remains important and in summer it's possible to travel long distances across Russia on passenger boats. You can do this either by taking a cruise, which you can book through agencies in the West, although it's often expensive, or in Russia, or by using scheduled river passenger services. The season runs from late May through to mid-October, but is shorter on some routes.

To find out what's running, go down to the *rechnoy vokzal* (river station), where you can check timetables and fares. Note that Raketa, Kometa and Meteor are all types of hydrofoil. *Skoraya* (fast) usually refers to steamships; *gidrofoyl* and *skorostnaya* (high-speed), and *na podvodnykh krylyakh* (underwater-winged), to hydrofoils. *Vverkh* means upstream and *vnizu* downstream, while *tuda* means one-way and *krugovoy* return.

Travelling the Scientific Way

Four floors up in an identikit Soviet apartment block in the north of Moscow I find the **Academy of Free Travels** (☎ 095-457 89 49, 458 37 71; Ⓦ www.avp.travel.ru; apt 547, Leningradskoe shosse 112-2), the home of Russian hitchhiker extraordinaire Anton Krotov. Plastered in maps outlining his travels and full of photographs and small souvenirs, with a bed in one corner, a heavily laden desk in another and stockpiles of the 17 books he's written and published, Krotov's world is a fascinating one.

Over ice-cream cornets and tea, the bushy-bearded 26-year-old, who began hitching at age 14, tells me about his travels. These have taken him from one end of Russia to the other on less than an old Soviet 10-kopeck coin, not to mention to India, the Middle East, Central Asia and Africa on little more. In his idiosyncratic English, he declaims his travelling philosophy: 'The world is good and belongs to everyone. There are many cars, many empty seats, many empty houses, food for all to eat, many possibilities! We try to use it!'

Krotov's 'scientific' method of travelling assumes that most people are kind and happy to give bed and board to a traveller – you only need to find the key to their heart. How to do that is the subject of his books, containing frequently hilarious accounts of his travels in which you'll discover that the Russian approach to hitch-hiking includes scrounging lifts not only in cars, but also cargo trains, ships, military planes – basically anything that moves.

Although there's plenty of the tang of the late 1960s and '70s about all this, Krotov is more than a throwback hippie. It actually takes some organisation, and not a little guts, to undertake the type of expeditions Krotov and his followers do: to the geographical centre of Russia, for example, 1200km north of Krasnoyarsk and only accessible in winter because there are no permanent roads, just tracks in the snow; or through some of the most war-torn, poverty-ridden and disease-stricken parts of Africa and Central Asia. So impressed is Krotov by the hospitality of the people in Islamic countries he has passed through that he has become a Muslim himself – the prelude, one feels, for his desire to try hitching through Saudi Arabia to Mecca.

Krotov disdains travelling in the comfortable parts of the world (because he realises that in Europe and the USA people might not be so willing to put him up every step of the way?), but he's certainly not above practising what he preaches. Any traveller who calls in advance and sincerely wants to tap into his and his followers' principles of 'free' travel is welcome to turn up at his flat, buy one of his books (all in Russian), have a cup of tea, even crash for the night. Assuming that he's not on the road, of course.

Simon Richmond

★★★

Major Routes

European Russia's main waterway network extends from St Petersburg to Astrakhan, near the Volga's delta on the Caspian Sea, via the Neva, Svir and Volga Rivers and a series of linking canals. Moscow is part of this system.

Moscow to St Petersburg
There are numerous boats plying the routes between Moscow and St Petersburg. Many of these boats stop at some of the Golden Ring cities on the way.

Most of the trips are aimed at foreign tourists. See the Travel Agencies & Organised Tours section of the European Russia Getting There & Away chapter for the names of travel companies that can book such trips.

You can also sail on a boat aimed at Russian holiday-makers. The price is much less than for the foreigner cruises but the food and accommodation are also less lavish. **Liko-Tour** (☎ 095-921 87 61 or ☎ 095-925 43 63; Ⓦ www.liko.al.ru; ul Petrovka 3/6, apt 115, Moscow) and **Solnechny Parus** (☎ 812-279 43 10; Ⓦ www.solpar.ru; ul Vosstania 55, St Petersburg) both sell tickets for cruises from Moscow to St Petersburg as well as further south along the Volga.

South of Moscow
See the boxed text 'Cruising the Volga' in the Volga chapter.

Other Routes
Other river or sea-passenger services in Russia, some served by hydrofoil, include: along the Neva River and the Gulf of Finland from St Petersburg to Petrodvorets, Kronstadt and Lomonosov; from St Petersburg to Valaam in Lake Ladoga; on Lake Onega, from Petrozavodsk to Kizhi; from Kem (Karelia) and Arkhangelsk to the Solovetsky

Islands; from Pskov to Tartu (Estonia); between Novgorod and Staraya Russa; along the Kuban River from Krasnodar; and along the Black Sea coast between Sochi, Novorossiysk and other places.

LOCAL TRANSPORT

Most cities have good public transport systems combining bus, trolleybus and tram; the biggest cities also have metro systems. Public transport is very cheap and easy to use, but you'll need to be able to decipher some Cyrillic. Taxis are fairly plentiful and usually cheap by Western standards.

Metro

Moscow, St Petersburg, Nizhny Novgorod and Yekaterinburg have metro systems, all of which leave their Western counterparts in the dust. The only confusing element is that a metro station can have several names – one for each different line that crosses at that station. See the Getting Around sections of the relevant city chapters for details on riding these systems.

Bus, Trolleybus & Tram

Even in cities with metros you'll often need to use these above-ground forms of public transport, too. Services are frequent in city centres but more erratic as you move out towards the edges. They can get jam-packed in the late afternoon or on poorly served routes.

A stop is usually marked by a roadside A (uf-**toh**-boos) sign for buses, T for trolleybuses (tra-**ley**-boos), and ТРАМВАЙ (trum-**vai**) or a T hanging over the road for trams. The normal fare (R5 to R10) is usually paid to the conductor on the bus (on trolleybuses it is the same, if there is no conductor pass the money to the driver); you may be charged extra if you have a large bag.

Taxi

There are two main types of taxis in Russia: the official ones (four-door sedans with a chequerboard strip down the side and a green light in the front window); and 'private' taxis (any other vehicle on the road).

Official taxis have a meter that they sometimes use, though you can always negotiate an off-the-meter price. There's a flag fall, and the number on the meter must be multiplied by the multiplier listed on a sign that *should* be on the dashboard or somewhere visible. Extra

charges are incurred for radio calls and some night-time calls. The official taxis outside of luxury hotels often demand usurious rates.

To hail a private taxi stand at the side of the road, extend your arm and wait until something stops. When someone stops for you, state your destination and be prepared to negotiate the fare – it's always a good idea to fix this before getting in. If the driver's game, they'll ask you to get in *(saditse),* but always act on the cautious side before doing this.

Check with locals to determine the average taxi fare in that city at the time of your visit; taxi prices around the country vary widely. Practise saying your destination and the amount you want to pay so it comes out properly. The better your Russian, generally the lower the fare. If possible, let a Russian friend negotiate for you: they'll do better than you will.

Risks & Precautions Avoid taxis lurking outside foreign-run establishments, luxury hotels etc. They charge far too much and get uppity when you try to talk them down. Know your route: be familiar with how to get there and how long it should take. Never get into a taxi with more than one person in it, especially after dark.

Keep your fare money in a separate pocket to avoid flashing large wads of cash. Have the taxi stop at the corner nearest your destination, not the exact address, if you're staying at a private residence. Trust your instincts. If a driver looks creepy, take the next car. Check the back seat of the car for hidden people before you get in.

Boat

In St Petersburg, Moscow and several other cities on rivers, coasts, lakes or reservoirs, public ferries and water excursions give a different perspective on the place. For details, see Getting Around in the relevant chapters or sections.

ORGANISED TOURS

Once in Russia, you'll find many travel agencies specialising in city tours and excursions. Sometimes these are the best way to visit out-of-the-way sights. See the travel agencies listed in the relevant city sections and the list of Russian-based companies specialising in adventure travel under Travel Agencies & Organised Tours in the European Russia Getting There & Away chapter.

Moscow Москва

☎ 095 • pop 9 million

How many times in my sorrowful separation
In my wandering fate,
Have I thought of you, O Moscow!
Moscow...how much there is in that sound
That flows together for the heart of the Russian.

A Pushkin, from *Yevgeny Onegin*

Some people love Moscow. Some hate it. Most do both. It is glittering and grey, beautiful and bleak, pious and hedonistic. Moscow is the epicentre of the 'New Russia' and everything that represents. Its commerce and culture are characteristics that most provincial Russians can still only dream about. Plagued by soaring prices, riddled with corruption, and spattered with beggars, it also epitomises the seamier side of postcommunist Russia.

Nowhere are Russia's contrasts more apparent than in Moscow where ancient monasteries and ultramodern monoliths stand side by side and where New Russian millionaires and poverty-stricken pensioners walk the same streets. This one city captures much of Russian history and culture – and contemporary life.

Despite all its present-day sophistication, Moscow began its life in 1147 as a provincial outpost of the Vladimir-Suzdal princedom. From the Kremlin which was its heart, the city expanded in all directions. The new settlements developed distinct identities depending on their inhabitants. Kitai Gorod, home of craftspeople and merchants, was the centre of trade; Zamoskvorechie was the locale of quarters servicing the royal court; and Zauzie developed around a blacksmith guild in the 17th century. The streets around Tverskoy attracted 18th-century nobility, while the Arbat claimed the artists and writers who were the intellectual elite of the 19th century.

Modern-day Moscow reflects this development. It is a network of neighbourhoods, each with its own flavour. Each street, courtyard and staircase has its own character. Moscow has always been a living city – thus its spirit stems from its inhabitants. As you admire the crumbling architecture on a quiet corner, watch the playful children in a leafy park, barter for beets at a farmers market...there you will find the heart and soul of Moscow.

- Catch rays and go people-watching along Kamergersky pereulok
- Hear them hit the high notes at a Tchaikovsky opera
- Bargain for trash and treasure at Izmaylovsky Park's Vernisazh Market
- Pay your respects to Vladimir Ilych in Red Square
- Sweat off your city smut at the Sandunovskiye Baths

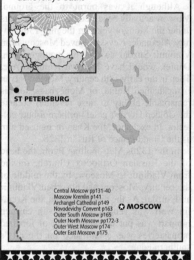

ST PETERSBURG

★★★★★★★★★★★★★★★★★★★★★

HISTORY

In the 10th century, Slavic tribes migrated eastward from their home base along the Dnepr River to settle the forest region of the upper Volga, where Ugro-Finnic hunters and herders had long dwelled. These small agrarian communities grew into fortified towns, ruled by the offspring of Prince Vsevolod, of the Kyivan Rurik dynasty. Sometimes allies and sometimes rivals, these medieval princedoms composed the northeastern territory of the earliest Russian state, Kyivan Rus.

The founding of Moscow is attributed to the Grand Prince of Vladimir-Suzdal, at the time the most powerful of the Rus principalities. Moscow is first mentioned in the historic

MOSCOW

chronicles in 1147, when prince Yury Dolgoruky invited his allies to a banquet there. Moscow village – located atop Borovitsky Hill, at the confluence of the Moscow and Neglinnaya Rivers – was soon reinforced with a wooden palisade and enriched by a merchants row. The site would eventually become Russia's most recognisable setting, housing the Kremlin and Red Square.

The Golden Horde

In 1237 the Slavic principalities were savagely attacked by the Golden Horde, a Mongol-led army of steppe nomads, and forced to pay homage to the Horde's leader, Baty Khan, grandson of Jenghis Khan.

Although it was burnt to the ground, Moscow actually benefited from its long years under the Mongol yoke. In the mid-13th century, Alexander Nevsky cleaved Moscow from Vladimir-Suzdal so that his youngest son, Daniel, would have his own realm to rule. Then in the early 14th century, Moscow's Ivan I (nicknamed Kalita, or Moneybags, for his remarkable ability to raise revenue) became the Golden Horde's chief northern tribute collector. In exchange, the Khan recognised him as the Grand Prince of Rus in 1328.

In the 1320s Metropolitan Pyotr, the head of the Russian Orthodox Church, moved from Vladimir to Moscow; by the middle of the century, Moscow had absorbed Vladimir and Suzdal. As the city prospered, the Kremlin wall was rebuilt in stone, an earthen rampart was put up, and a ring of fortified monasteries was established on the city's southern edge.

The Rise of Muscovy

An emboldened Moscow came to lead the fight against the Golden Horde. Grand Prince Dmitry, Ivan Kalita's grandson, dealt the Horde a rare defeat at Kulikovo on the Don in 1380, earning him the name Dmitry Donskoy. But two years later, the Horde put Moscow to the torch again.

It was not until the late 15th century that Moscow was strong enough to renounce its allegiance to the Golden Horde for good. Under the reign of Ivan III (Ivan the Great), Moscow's control stretched from Novgorod in the west to Tula in the south and the Urals in the east. (Ivan imported Milanese masons to erect commemorative cathedrals and renovate the Kremlin for the occasion.)

Muscovy principality was now the core of a new Russian state – the self-proclaimed 'Third Rome'. In the mid-16th century, Ivan IV, who earned the nickname Grozny (or 'Terrible'), became grand prince at the age of three, spending his childhood amid vicious palace power struggles in which his mother was murdered. Crowning himself tsar ('caesar') at 16, he went on to marry six times (though Elizabeth I of England turned him down), while terrorising the nobles and killing his eldest son in a fit of rage.

Ivan the Terrible expanded Muscovite territory by launching the conquest of Siberia and winning control of the Volga from the Golden Horde khanates of Kazan and Astrakhan. (St Basil's Cathedral was built in celebration.)

By 1571, when the Crimean Tatars burnt all Moscow except the Kremlin, the city had over 100,000 people and was one of the biggest in the world; the Kitai Gorod area, east of the Kremlin, was the main part of town.

By 1600, a 9km white stone wall with 27 towers stood round the line of the Boulevard Ring, with a 16km rampart around the Garden Ring. The area inside the white wall came to be known as the Bely Gorod (White City).

The Time of Troubles

After the mysterious death of Ivan the Terrible's son, Tsarevich Dmitry, a former advisor to the tsarevich took the throne. Tsar Boris Godunov (1598–1605) faced both famine and invasion during his reign, and the years following his death are known as the Time of Troubles. Backed by the Polish army, a pretender to the throne known as False Dmitry claimed himself tsar and was promptly murdered; a second False Dmitry popped up; civil wars and invasions ensued; and Moscow was occupied by Poland. Finally, the Poles were driven out and 16-year-old Mikhail Romanov was elected tsar by a council of nobles launching the 300-year Romanov dynasty.

18th-Century Moscow

Peter I (Peter the Great) dragged Russia kicking and screaming into modern Europe. In 1712, he startled the country by announcing the relocation of the capital to a swampland recently acquired from Sweden in the Great Northern War. St Petersburg would be Russia's

'Window on the West', and everything that Moscow was not: modern, scientific and cultured. The jilted ex-capital went into decline as its prestige and population shrivelled. In the second half of the 18th century, the city suffered from fires, plagues and riots.

Yet Muscovites proved resilient, as well as resentful: the Kremlin remained a seat of government and the site of royal coronations; merchants continued to make money; Russia's first university was founded by academician Mikhail Lomonsov in Moscow; and by 1800 the population had recovered to its previous level.

The rivalry led Muscovites to distinguish themselves from Peter's 'German' city. It was said that 'St Petersburg chatters, while Moscow gets things done'.

19th-Century Moscow

Moscow remained significant enough to be Napoleon's main goal when his troops marched on Russia in 1812. After the bloody Battle of Borodino, 130km west of the city, the Russians abandoned Moscow and allowed Napoleon to march in and install himself in the Kremlin. The night he arrived a great fire broke out that burnt most of the city. With winter coming, the French had to pull out little more than a month after arriving.

The city was rebuilt yet again in just a few frenetic years. In the second half of the 19th century, Moscow underwent a boom: a flourishing textile industry created a class of newly rich entrepreneurs, attracted a wave of peasant migrant labourers, financed grandiose building projects, and prompted the sobriquet, 'Calico Moscow'.

The two outer defensive rings were replaced by the tree-lined Boulevard Ring and Garden Ring roads, and as new industrial suburbs grew up beyond the 'class barrier' of the Garden Ring, the city's population increased from 350,000 in the 1840s to 1.4 million in 1914.

Revolutionary Moscow

The social discontent spawned in sweatshops and squalor spilled onto Moscow streets several times in the early 20th century. In 1905 workers and students erected barricades along the major roads into the city to defend the revolutionary movement; clashes with imperial troops left 800 protesters dead.

In 1917 Moscow was one of the pockets of Bolshevik support, experiencing some of the most intense fighting during the October seizure of power. Fearing a renewed German offensive, Bolshevik leader Vladimir Lenin announced that the capital would be moved back to Moscow after two centuries.

Under Stalin, one of the world's first comprehensive urban plans was devised for Moscow. The first line of the metro was completed in 1935; the broad thoroughfares he deemed necessary for his capital were also created in the 1930s. In the late 1940s and early 1950s, the 'Seven Sisters' – seven great, grey neo-Gothic skyscrapers (see the boxed text 'Stalin's Seven Sisters' later in this chapter) – were erected. Meanwhile, by some estimates, Stalin had demolished half of Moscow's artistic and historical landmarks, most notoriously, the enormous Cathedral of Christ the Saviour, a major city landmark now rebuilt.

20th-Century Moscow

During WWII German troops came within about 30km of the Kremlin in December 1941; a huge monument marks the spot where they were halted, near the entrance road to Sheremetevo-2 airport. The defence of the city was organised by Georgy Zhukov, the Red Army's master strategist of tank warfare. The Battle of Moscow raged through bitter winter cold before an exhausted, extended German army was routed by Zhukov's counteroffensive.

After WWII, huge housing estates grew up round the outskirts. The lesser ones, hurriedly erected under Khrushchev in the mid-1950s, are nicknamed *khrushchoby* (after *trushchoby* – slums), while later blocks were built higher as planners tried to keep the city within its Outer Ring road.

Revolutionary Moscow Returns

Moscow has been at the forefront of political change – and a thorn in the flesh of national leaders – since the first whispers of *glasnost* in the mid-1980s. Boris Yeltsin was made the city's new Communist Party chief in 1985, becoming hugely popular as he sacked hundreds of corrupt commercial managers and permitted demonstrations to be held in the city. This was too much for the Communist old guard and led to Yeltsin's forced resignation in 1987.

Then Moscow elected a new, reforming city council in 1990, with the economist Gavriil Popov as mayor. Popov started the 'decommunisation' of the city, selling off housing and state businesses and restoring prerevolutionary street names.

In 1991 Muscovites rallied behind Yeltsin in front of Moscow's White House (the seat of the Russian Parliament), thus foiling the old-guard coup and precipitating the ultimate collapse of the Soviet Union. Two years later, when disenchantment with Yeltsin and politics had set in, Muscovites attended another confrontation at the White House, between the tanks sent by Yeltsin, now Russian president, and his obstructive foes in parliament. This time the people were spectators, not participants.

Moscow in New Russia

By the mid-1990s Moscow was the vanguard of the New Russia, filling up with all the things Russians had expected of capitalism, but which had barely begun to percolate down to the provinces: stock markets, glittering casinos, luxury cars, neon lights, fashionable shops, posh hotels and pulsing nightlife. While the New Russians luxuriated in excess, most of the population was unable to afford these diversions and could only look on with wonder and envy.

In 1992, the election of Yuri Luzhkov as mayor set the stage for the creation of a big city boss in the grandest of traditions – through a web of financial and real estate interests, Luzhkov acted as both populist and CEO. The bubble finally burst in August 1998, when the government defaulted on its debts and devalued the rouble (the city economy has since rebounded, minus a bit of the earlier brashness).

Moscow remains a free-wheeling city. To a jaded population, there are no surprises, and to the ambitious, no limits.

ORIENTATION

Picture Moscow as four ring roads spreading out from the centre; radial roads spoke out across the rings, and the Moscow River meanders across everything from northwest to southeast.

The Kremlin, a north-pointing triangle with 750m sides, is at Moscow's heart in every way; Red Square lies along the city's eastern side, the Moscow River flowing to the south.

Four Rings

The first of the four rings, a semicircle about 500m north of the Kremlin, is the Inner Ring road formed by Mokhovaya ulitsa, Okhotny ryad, Teatralny proezd, Novaya ploshchad and Staraya ploshchad. Three other important squares, Manezhnaya ploshchad, Teatralnaya ploshchad and Lubyanskaya ploshchad, punctuate this ring.

The second is the Boulevard Ring (Bulvarnoe Koltso), three-quarters of a circle about 1km from the Kremlin, and mostly dual carriageway with a park strip down the middle; each section has a different name, always ending in 'bulvar'. The Boulevard Ring ends as it approaches the Moscow River in the southwest and southeast.

Third is the Garden Ring (Sadovoe Koltso), a full circle about 2km out, which crosses the river twice. Most of its northern sections are called Sadovaya-something (Garden-something) ulitsa; several of its southern sections are called ulitsa-something-val, recalling its origins as a *val* (rampart). And the difference between the Garden and Boulevard Rings? The Garden Ring is actually the one *without* any gardens.

The fourth, much farther out, is Moscow's Outer Ring road, the Moskovskaya Koltsovaya Avtomobilnaya Doroga, some 15km from the Kremlin in the east and west, and 19km north and south. A few protuberances apart, it forms the city limits.

Landmarks

The only elevation worth the name in the whole flat expanse is the Sparrow Hills, 6km southwest of the Kremlin, topped by the Moscow University skyscraper and affording the most panoramic view the city has to offer.

Moscow's most prominent buildings are the 'Seven Sisters' skyscrapers, the Ukraina and Leningradsky hotels, the university tower on the Sparrow Hills, the Foreign Affairs and Transport ministries, Kudrinskaya ploshchad, and the Kotelnicheskaya apartment buildings – but you could easily mistake one for another.

Maps

It is a challenge to find up-to-date, non-Cyrillic Moscow maps reflecting all the street-name changes from the early 1990s. Cartographia and Kummerly & Frey both

[Continued on page 143]

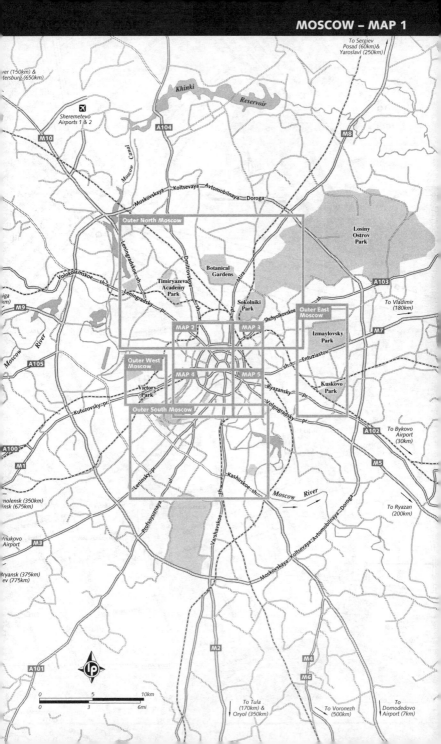

MAP 2 – CENTRAL MOSCOW

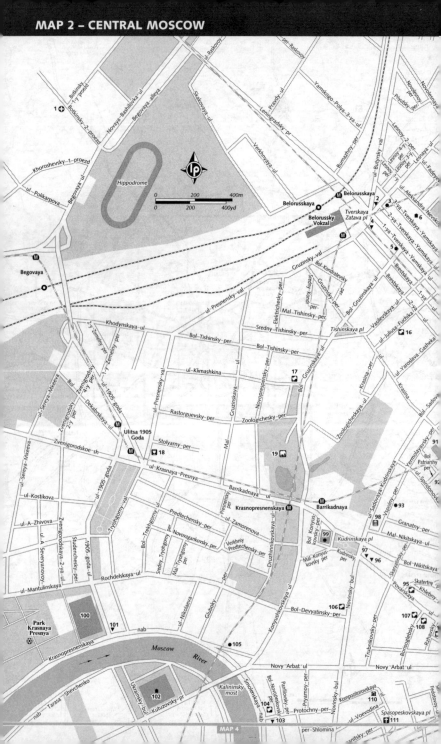

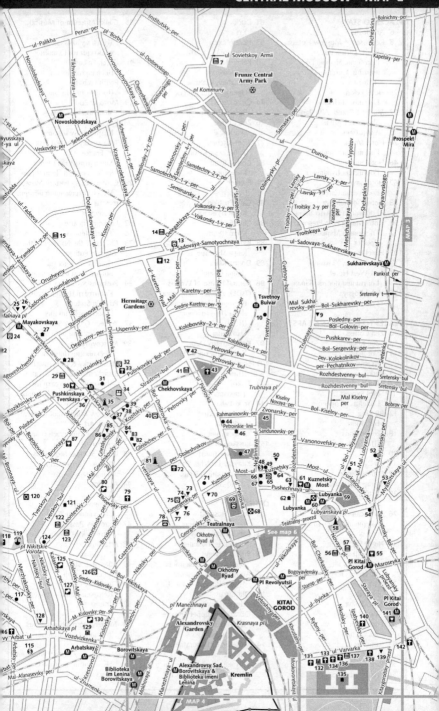

MAP 2

PLACES TO STAY
6 Art Hostel
8 Renaissance Moscow Hotel;
Alitalia; Lufthansa
Ренессанс Москва Гост
иница и Алиталия и
Луфтганса
23 Hotel Pekin
Гостиница Пекин
27 Marriott Grand; Alfa Bank
Марриот Гранд;
Альфабанк
28 Hotel Minsk
Гостиница Минск
46 Hotel Budapest
Гостиница Будапешт
62 Hotel Savoy
Гостиница Савой
83 Hotel Tsentralnaya
Гостиница Центральная
90 Hotel Marco Polo Presnya
Гостиница Марко Поло
Пресня
102 Hotel Ukrainia
Гостиница Украина
121 East-West Hotel
Гостиница Восток Запад
135 Hotel Rossiya
Гостиница Россия

PLACES TO EAT, CAFES & BARS
2 Zen Coffee
Зен Кофе
4 Yakitoria
Якитория
9 York
Йорк
11 Soleil Express
Солейл Экспресс
12 BB King
Б.Б. Кинг
18 Sixteen Tons
Шестнадцать Тоннов
20 B2
Б-2
22 Starlite Diner
Старлайт Дайнер
25 Rostik's
Ростикс
26 American Bar & Grill
Американский бар и
гриль
30 Night Flight
Найт Флайт
36 McDonald's
Макдоналдс
38 Garage
Гараж
42 Taras Bulba
Тарас Бульба
50 Jagannath
Джаганнат
53 Samovar
Самовар
55 Propaganda
Пропаганда

61 Duck
Утка
63 Hola Mexico
Привет Мексико
70 Pelmeshka
Пельмешка
73 Oranzhevy Galstuk
Оранжевый Галстук
74 Cicco Pizza
Чикко Пицца
76 Zen Coffee
Зен Кофе
77 Tibet Kitchen
Тибетская Кухня
82 Coffee Bean
Кофе бин
84 Bunker
Бункер
85 Café Pushkin
Кафе Пушкин
87 Club Forte
Клуб Форте
88 Kafe Margarita
Кафе Маргарита
89 Donna Klara
Донна Клара
96 Central House of Writers
(TsDL); Zapisky Okhotnika
Ресторан Центрального
Дома Литераторов
(ЦДЛ) и Записки
Охотника
97 Kafe Karetny Dvor
Кафе Каретный Двор
101 Shinook
Шинук
103 Tinkoff
Тинкофф
114 Yolki-Palki
Ёлки-Палки
128 Dioskuriya
Диоскурия
139 Russkoe Bistro
Русское бистро
141 Kitaysky Lyotchik Dzhao-Da
Китайский Лётчик
Джао-Да

OTHER
1 Botkin Hospital
Боткина больница
3 Czech Airlines
Чешские Авиалинии
5 British Airways
Британская Авиалиния
7 Armed Forces Museum
Музей Вооруженных Сил
10 Old Circus
Цирк Никулина
13 Obraztsov Puppet Theatre
Кукольный театр им
Образцова
14 Museum of Decorative &
Folk Art
Музей декоративного и
прикладного искусства

15 Glinka Museum of Musical
Culture
Музей музыкальной
культуры им Глинки
16 Czech Embassy
Посольство Чехии
17 Polish Embassy
Посольство Польши
19 Moscow Zoo
Московский зоопарк
21 Bulgakov's flat
Квартира Булгакова
24 Tchaikovsky Concert Hall;
Deli France
Концертный зал имени
Чайковского и Дели Франс
29 Contemporary History Museum
Музей современной истории
31 Izvestia
Известия
32 Lenkom Theatre
Театр Ленком
33 Church of the Nativity of the
Virgin in Putinki
Церковь Рождества
Богородины в Путинках
34 Pushkinsky Cinema
Кинотеатр Пушкинский
35 Pushkin Statue
Памятник Пушкину
37 Yeliseev Grocery Store
Елисеевский магазин
39 Moscow News
Московские Новости
40 Stanislavsky & Nemirovich-
Danchenko Musical Theatre
Музыкальный театр им
Станиславского и Немиров-
ича-Данченко
41 Moscow Museum of Contem-
porary Art
Московский музей соврем-
енного искусства
43 Upper St Peter Monastery
Высоко-Петровский
Монастырь
44 Aeroflot
Аэрофлот
45 Sandunovskiye Baths
Сандуновские бани
47 Petrovsky Passazh
Петровский Пассаж
48 Alfa Bank
Альфабанк
49 Atlas Map Store
Атлас магазин
51 Tsentralny Gastronom
Центральный гастроном
52 Intourist
Интурист
54 Torgovy Dom Biblio-Globus
Торговый дом Библио-
Глобус
56 Moscow City History Museum
Музей истории города
Москвы

MAP 2

Composition at the Sculpture Park, representing victims of Stalin

SIMON RICHMOND

Pelmeshka restaurant, Kuznetsky most

JONATHAN SMITH

Russian State Ballet posters, Bolshoi Theatre

SIMON RICHMOND

Art Deco detail, Moscow house

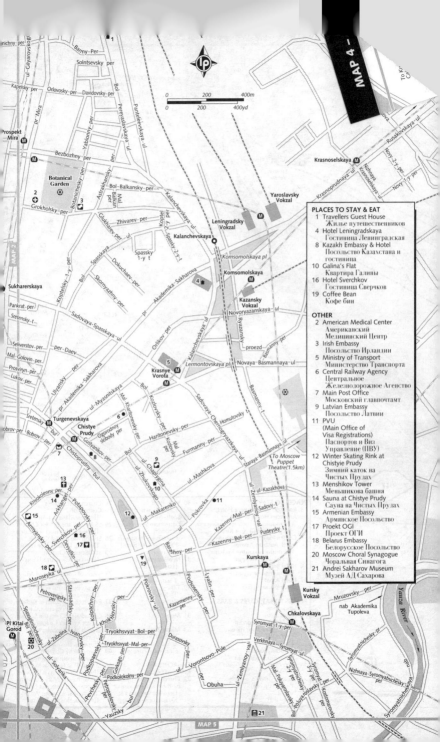

MAP 4 –

PLACES TO STAY & EAT
1 Travellers Guest House
  Жильё путешественников
4 Hotel Leningradskaya
  Гостиница Ленинградская
8 Kazakh Embassy & Hotel
  Посольство Казахстана и
  гостиница
10 Galina's Flat
  Квартира Галины
16 Hotel Sverchkov
  Гостиница Сверчков
19 Coffee Bean
  Кофе бин

OTHER
2 American Medical Center
  Американский
  Медицинский Центр
3 Irish Embassy
  Посольство Ирландии
5 Ministry of Transport
  Министерство Транспорта
6 Central Railway Agency
  Центральное
  Железнодорожное Агенство
7 Main Post Office
  Московский главпочтамт
9 Latvian Embassy
  Посольство Латвии
11 PVU
  (Main Office of
  Visa Registrations)
  Паспортов и Виз
  Управление (ПВУ)
12 Winter Skating Rink at
  Chistiye Prudy
  Зимний каток на
  Чистых Прудах
13 Menshikov Tower
  Меньшикова башня
14 Sauna at Chistye Prudy
  Сауна на Чистых Прудах
15 Armenian Embassy
  Армянское Посольство
17 Proekt OGI
  Проект ОГИ
18 Belarus Embassy
  Белорусское Посольство
20 Moscow Choral Synagogue
  Чоральная Синагога
21 Andrei Sakharov Museum
  Музей А.Д.Сахарова

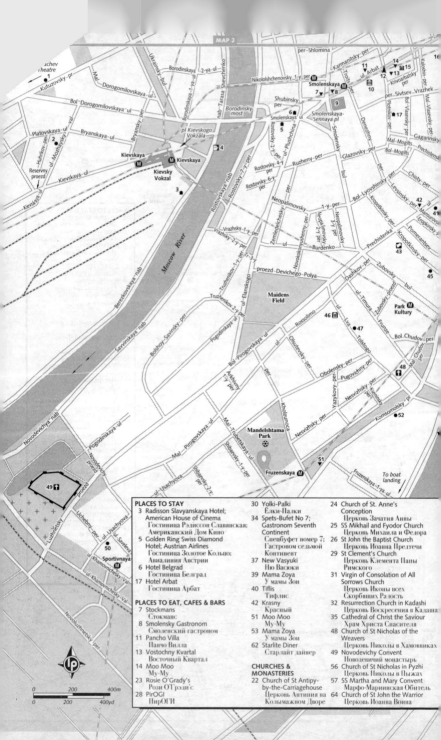

MAP 2

Borodinskaya 2-ya-ul
Ukrainsky bul
Borodinsky most
Borodinsky most
per-Shlomina
Karmanitsky-per
Nikololshchenovsky-1-yi per
Smolenskaya

pl Kievskogo Vokzala

Kievskaya
Kievskaya
Kievskaya-ul
Kievsky Vokzal

Reservny proezd
Kievskaya-ul

Moscow River

Smolenskaya-2-ya-ul-Plushchina
Smolenskaya-Sennaya pl
Rostovsky nab
Rostovsky-2-y-per
Rostovsky-4-y per
Rostovsky-6-y per
Ruzheny-per
Glazovsky-per
Denezhny-per

Neopalimovsky
1-y-per
Neopalimovsky
3-y-per
Neopalimovsky
2-y-per
Burdenko
Prechistenka

Vrazhsky-1-y-per
Vrazhsky-2-y-per
Zemledelchesky-per
Novokonnomolovsky-per
proezd-Devichego-Polya

Maidens Field

Dachkov-per
Zubovsky-bul
Park Kultury

Bol-Pirogovskaya-ul
Pogodinskaya-ul
Trubetskaya-ul-Elanskogo
Truzhenkov-1-y-per

Rossolimo

Ulva
Tolstogo
Bol-Chudov-per
Mal-Chudov-per

Savvinskaya nab
Bozhoy-Savvinsky-per

Oboldevsky-per
Oboldensky-per
Kholzunova
Pugovidny-per
Nesvizhsky-per
Yazykovy-per

Komsomolsky-per

Novodevichy nab
Novodevichy proezd
Pogodinskaya-ul

Mandelshtama Park

Mal-Pirogovskaya-ul
Mal-Tiuberlskaya-ul
Shabeva-2-y-per
Shabeva-1-y-per
ul-Usachova
Nesvizhsky-per

Fruzenskaya
Fruzenskaya-1-ya-ul
To boat landing

Uchebny-per-Usachyova
Luzhnetsky-per
Sportivnaya
ul-Khamovnichesky-Val
Novoluzhnetsky-per

49

50

0   200   400m
0   200   400yd

PLACES TO STAY

3 Radisson Slavyanskaya Hotel;
   American House of Cinema
   Гостиница Рэдиссон Славянская;
   Американский Дом Кино
5 Golden Ring Swiss Diamond
   Hotel; Austrian Airlines
   Гостиница Золотое Кольцо;
   Авиалиния Австрии
6 Hotel Belgrad
   Гостиница Белград
17 Hotel Arbat
   Гостиница Арбат

PLACES TO EAT, CAFES & BARS

7 Stockmans
   Стокманс
8 Smolensky Gastronom
   Смоленский гастроном
11 Pancho Villa
   Панчо Вилла
13 Vostochny Kvartal
   Восточный Квартал
14 Moo Moo
   Му-Му
23 Rosie O'Grady's
   Рози ОТрэди'с
28 PirOGI
   ПирОГИ

30 Yolki-Palki
   Ёлки-Палки
34 Spets-Bufet No 7;
   Gastronom Seventh
   Continent
   Спецбуфет номер 7;
   Гастроном седьмой
   Континент
37 New Vasyuki
   Нью Васюки
39 Mama Zoya
   У мамы Зои
40 Tiflis
   Тифлис
42 Krasny
   Красный
51 Moo Moo
   Му-Му
53 Mama Zoya
   У мамы Зои
62 Starlite Diner
   Старлайт дайнер

CHURCHES &
MONASTERIES

22 Church of St Antipy-
   by-the-Carriagehouse
   Церковь Антипия на
   Колымажном Дворе

24 Church of St. Anne's
   Conception
   Церковь Зачатия Анны
25 SS Mikhail and Fyodor Church
   Церковь Михаила и Федора
26 St John the Baptist Church
   Церковь Иоанна Предтечи
29 St Clement's Church
   Церковь Клемента Папы
   Римского
31 Virgin of Consolation of All
   Sorrows Church
   Церковь Иконы всех
   Скорбящих Радость
32 Resurrection Church in Kadashi
   Церковь Воскресения в Кадаши
35 Cathedral of Christ the Saviour
   Храм Христа Спасителя
48 Church of St Nicholas of the
   Weavers
   Церковь Николы в Хамовниках
49 Novodevichy Convent
   Новодевичий монастырь
56 Church of St Nicholas in Pyzhi
   Церковь Николы в Пыжах
57 SS Martha and Mary Convent
   Марфо-Мариинская Обитель
64 Church of St John the Warrior
   Церковь Иоанна Воина

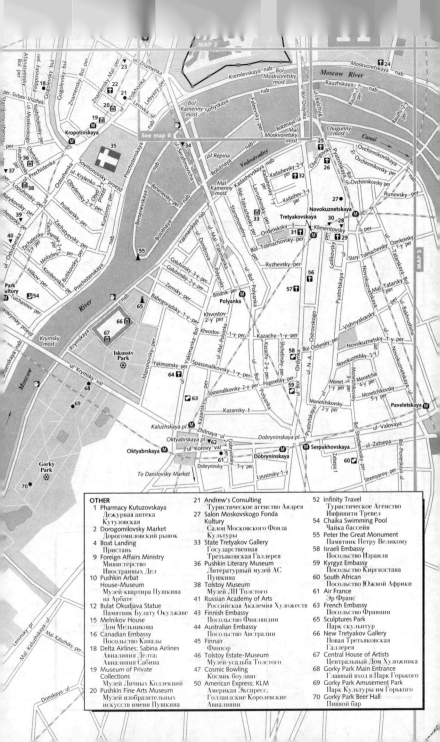

OTHER

1 Pharmacy Kutuzovskaya Дежурная аптека Кутузовская	21 Andrew's Consulting Туристическое агенство Андрея
2 Dorogomilovsky Market Дорогомиловский рынок	27 Salon Moskovskogo Fonda Kultury Салон Московского Фонда Культуры
4 Boat Landing Пристань	33 State Tretyakov Gallery Государственная Третьяковская Галлерея
9 Foreign Affairs Ministry Министерство Иностранных Дел	36 Pushkin Literary Museum Литературный музей АС Пушкина
10 Pushkin Arbat House-Museum Музей-квартира Пушкина на Арбате	38 Tolstoy Museum Музей ЛН Толстого
12 Bulat Okudjava Statue Памятник Булату Окуджаве	41 Russian Academy of Arts Российская Академия Художеств
15 Melnikov House Дом Мельникова	43 Finnish Embassy Посольство Финляндии
16 Canadian Embassy Посольство Канады	44 Australian Embassy Посольство Австралии
19 Museum of Private Collections Музей Личных Коллекций	45 Finnair Финнэр
20 Pushkin Fine Arts Museum Музей изобразительных искусств имени Пушкина	46 Tolstoy Estate-Museum Толстого-усадьба Толстого
	47 Cosmic Bowling Космик боулинг
	50 American Express; KLM Американ Экспресс; Голландские Королевские Авиалинии

52 Infinity Travel Туристическое Агенство Инфинити Тревел
54 Chaika Swimming Pool Чайка бассейн
58 Peter the Great Monument Памятник Петру Великому
59 Israeli Embassy Посольство Израиля
60 Kyrgyz Embassy Посольство Киргизстана
61 South African Посольство Южной Африки
62 Air France Эр Франс
63 French Embassy Посольство Франции
65 Sculptures Park Парк скульптур
66 New Tretyakov Gallery Новая Третьяковская Галлерея
67 Central House of Artists Центральный Дом Художника
68 Gorky Park Main Entrance Главный вход в Парк Горького
69 Gorky Park Amusement Park Парк Культуры им Горького
70 Gorky Park Beer Hall Пивной бар

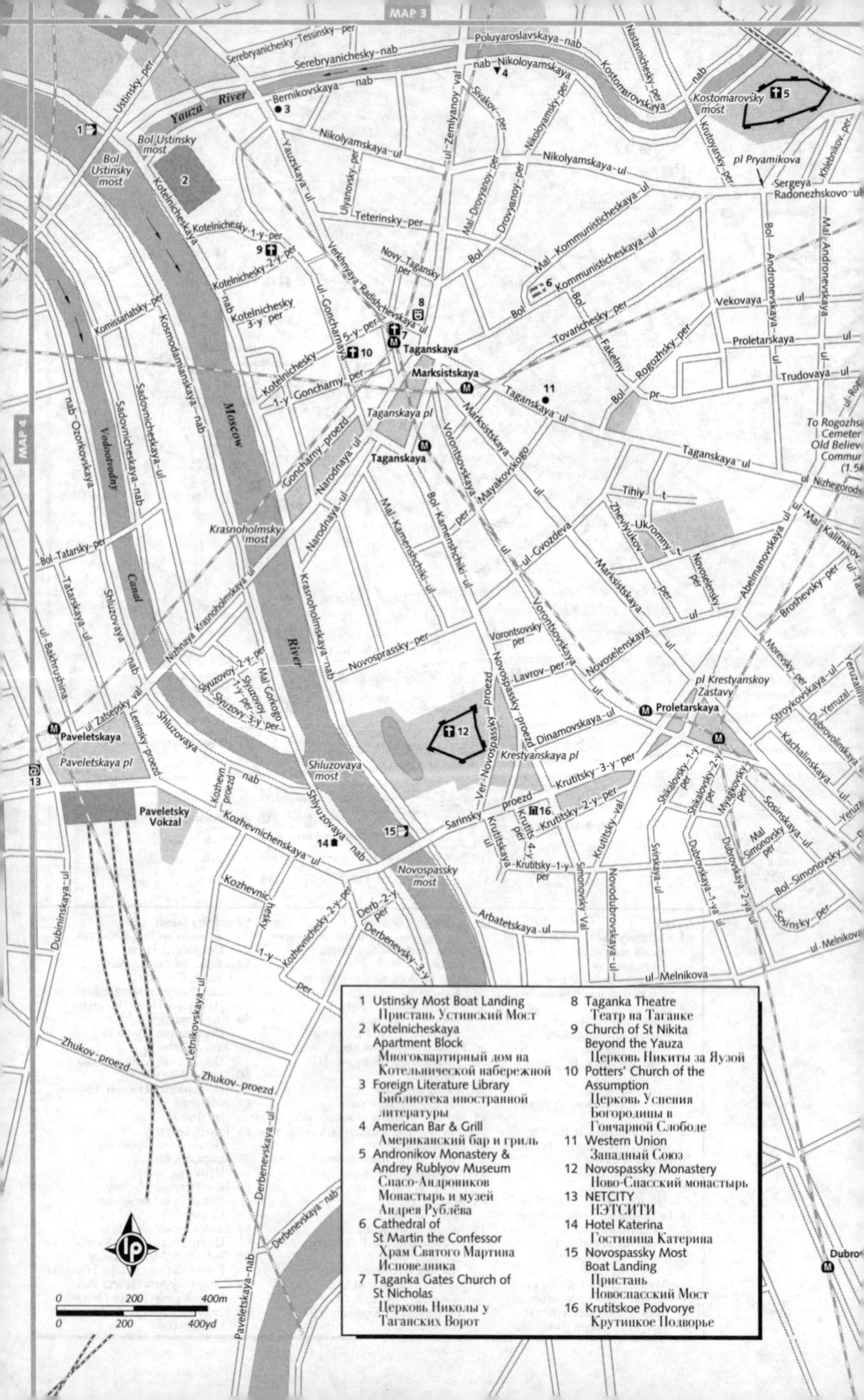

MAP 3

MAP 4

1 Ustinsky Most Boat Landing
   Пристань Устинский Мост
2 Kotelnicheskaya
   Apartment Block
   Многоквартирный дом на
   Котельнической набережной
3 Foreign Literature Library
   Библиотека иностранной
   литературы
4 American Bar & Grill
   Американский бар и гриль
5 Andronikov Monastery &
   Andrey Rublyov Museum
   Спасо-Андроников
   Монастырь и музей
   Андрея Рублёва
6 Cathedral of
   St Martin the Confessor
   Храм Святого Мартина
   Исповедника
7 Taganka Gates Church of
   St Nicholas
   Церковь Николы у
   Таганских Ворот

8 Taganka Theatre
   Театр на Таганке
9 Church of St Nikita
   Beyond the Yauza
   Церковь Никиты за Яузой
10 Potters' Church of the
   Assumption
   Церковь Успения
   Богородицы в
   Гончарной Слободе
11 Western Union
   Западный Союз
12 Novospassky Monastery
   Ново-Спасский монастырь
13 NETCITY
   НЭТСИТИ
14 Hotel Katerina
   Гостиница Катерина
15 Novospassky Most
   Boat Landing
   Пристань
   Новоспасский Мост
16 Krutitskoe Podvorye
   Крутицкое Подворье

Yauza River
Moscow River
Canal

Serebryanichesky-Tesinsky-per
Serebryanichesky-nab
Poluyaroslavskaya-nab
Nastasinsky-per
Kostomarovsky
most
Kostomarovsky
pl Pryamikova
Sergeya-
Radonezhskovo-ul
nab-Nikoloyamskaya
Nikolyamsky-per
val-Zemlyanoy
Nikolyamskaya-ul
Nikolyamskaya-ul
Ustinsky-per
Bernikovskaya-nab
Bol
Ustinsky
most
Bol Ustinsky
most
Kotelnicheskaya
Kotelnicheskaya-nab
Yauzskaya-ul
Ulyanovsky-per
Nikolyamskaya-ul
Drovyanoy-per
Bol-Drovyanoy-per
Mal-Andronevskaya
Bol-Andronevskaya
Kostomarovsky-per
Kotelbakov-per
Vekovaya
Proletarskaya
ul
Teterinsky-per
Novy-Tagansky
per
Bol-Kommunisticheskaya-ul
Mal-Kommunisticheskaya
Tovarishchesky-per
Faletny
Rogozhsky-per
Trudovaya-ul
Kotelnichesky-1-y-per
Kotelnichesky-2-y-per
Kotelnichesky-3-y-per
Kotelnichesky-3-y-per
Verkhnyaya-Radishchevskaya-ul
5-y-Kotelnichesky-per
Bol-Gonchary
Taganskaya
Marksistskaya
To Rogozhskoe
Cemeter
Old Believ
Commun
(1.5M)
Kotelnichesky-1-y-Goncharny-per
Taganskaya pl
Taganskaya-ul
Taganskaya-ul
ul-Nizhegorod
Komsomolsky-per
Kosmodamianskaya-nab
Goncharny-proezd
Narodnaya
Marksistskaya
Bol-Maslovskogo
Voronovsky
per
Mal-Kalitnikov
Brosnevsky-per
Sadovnicheskaya-nab
Vodootvodny
Sadovnicheskaya-nab
Narodnaya-ul
Krasnoholmsky
most
Bol-Kamenshchiki
Bol-Kamenshchiki
Bol-Gvozdeva
Tihiy
Ukromny
Zholobov-per
Marksistskaya
Abelmanovsky-per
Moredvy-per
Proletarskaya
Abelmanovsky-val
Voronovsky-per
Novospassky-per
Lavrov-per
Novoyelemskaya
Dinamovskaya-ul
pl Krestyanskoy
Zastavy
Stroykovsky-per
Dubrovsky-per
Remzud
Krasnoholmsky
River
Novospassky-proezd
Ver-Novospassky-proezd
Krestyanskaya pl
Krutitsky-3-y-per
Kachalinskaya
Dubrovsky-per
Bol-Tatarsky-per
ul-Bakhrushina
Shluzovaya
nab
Shluzovy-1-y-per
Shluzovy-2-y-per
Mal-Gorkogo
Shluzovy-3-y-per
Shluzovaya
most
Krutitsky-val
Krutitsky-2-y-per
Sarinsky
proezd
Shokalsky-1-y-per
Sorinsky-per
Mal-
Simonovsky
Bol-Simonovsky
Vorontsovskaya-nab
Leninsky-proezd
Pavuletskaya
Pavuletskaya pl
Kozhevnichesky-proezd
Kozhevnicheskaya-ul
Kozhevnichenskaya-ul
Kozhevnicheskaya-nab
Novospassky
most
Krutitsky-1-y-
per
Novodubrovskaya-ul
Dubrovsky-per
Yenza
Pavuletsky
Vokzal
Dubininsky-1-y-per
Kozhevnic
Novospassky
most
Arbatetskaya-ul
ul-Melnikova
Dubininsky-1-y-per
1-y-Kozhevnichesky-2-y-per
Derb-2-y-per
Derbenevsky-3-y-
per
Derbenevskaya-nab
ul-Melnikova
Zhukov-proezd
Zhukov-proezd
Derbenevskaya-nab
Dubro
LP

0   200   400m
0   200   400yd

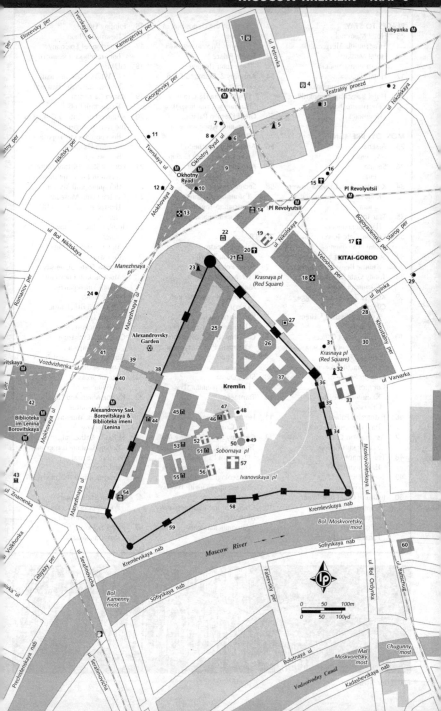

MAP 6

Moscow Kremlin

ALAIN TOMASINI

[Continued from page 130]

have good versions, sensibly called the *Moscow City Map*; another good option is the second edition of the *New Moscow City Map and Guide*, published by Russia Information Services in the USA.

Accurate Cyrillic maps are easily available in Moscow, and good sources include **Atlas** *(Map 2; ☎ 928 6109; Kuznetsky most 9)* and **Torgovy Dom Biblio-Globus** *(Map 2; ☎ 928 3567; ul Myasnitskaya 6)*.

INFORMATION
Tourist Offices
Moscow still has no official tourist offices, but you can get information from travel agencies or upscale hotels.

Visas & Documents
You are required to register your visa within three days of arrival in Moscow (see the boxed text 'The Great Moscow Police Tourist Rip-Off' later). Normally your visa's sponsor or your hotel will do this for you, but you should double-check to make sure.

Otherwise, register yourself at the main branch of **PVU** *(formerly OVIR; Map 3; ☎ 200 8497; ul Pokrovka 42; open 9am-1pm, 2pm-6pm Mon-Fri)*, the city's main visa and registration office; it also deals with visa extensions and can replace lost visas.

For embassies, see the Embassies & Consulates section in the earlier European Russia Facts for the Visitor chapter.

Money
Banks, exchange counters and ATMs are ubiquitous in Moscow, starting at Sheremetevo-2 airport. Rates do vary, so it may be worthwhile shopping around if you are changing a large sum. The best rates are usually offered by individuals on the street. As always, exercise due caution and avoid any deals that seem too good to be true.

Currencies other than US dollars and euros are difficult to exchange and yield bad rates. Travellers cheques can also be problematic, although you can usually change them at **Alfa Bank** *(Map 2; ul Arbat 4/1 • Map 2; Kuznetsky Most 7 • Map 2; Marriott Grand Hotel, ul Tverskaya 26; all open 8.30am-8pm Mon-Sat)*. There are locations all over the city and the ATMs at the branches listed dispense roubles and US dollars.

Credit cards, especially Visa and Master-Card, are becoming more widely accepted in upscale hotels, restaurants and stores. You can also use your credit card to get a cash advance at most major banks in Moscow.

American Express *(Map 4; ☎ 933 6636, fax 933 6635; ul Usachyova 33)* is the most reliable place to cash American Express travellers cheques. It also offers ATM, mail holding and travel services for AmEx card holders.

Contact **Western Union** *(Map 5; ☎ 797 2194; ul Taganskaya 17-23)* for wire transfers of money.

Post
Although service has improved dramatically in recent years, the usual warnings about delays and disappearances of incoming and outgoing mail apply to Moscow. Note that mail to Europe and the USA can take two to six weeks to arrive.

The convenient **Central Telegraph** *(Tsentralny Telegraf; Map 2; ul Tverskaya 7; postal counters open 8am-10pm daily)* offers telephone, fax and Internet services; the telephone office is open 24 hours. Moscow's main post office, **Moskovsky Glavpochtamt**, *(Map 3; ul Myasnitskaya 26; open 8am-8pm Mon-Fri, 9am-7pm Sat & Sun)* is on the corner of Chistoprudny bulvar.

The major air courier services operating in Moscow include **DHL Worldwide Express** *(☎ 956 1000)*, **Fedex** *(☎ 234 3400)*, **TNT** *(☎ 797 2777)* and **UPS** *(☎ 961 2211)*. They can advise on drop-off locations and arrange pick-ups.

Telephone
Major Western telephone service companies have access code telephone numbers for Moscow that allow you to call home using your own long-distance service. These include **MCI** *(☎ 747 3322, 960 2222)*, **AT&T** *(☎ 755 5042)* and **Sprint** *(☎ 747 3324)*. These can change frequently, so check before you leave.

Moscow pay phones operate with cards that are widely available in shops, kiosks and metro stations. The cards are available in a range of units; international calls require at least 50 units.

The phones are fairly user-friendly, and most of them have an option for directions in English. Make sure you press the button with the speaker symbol when your party answers the phone.

MOSCOW

The Great Moscow Police Tourist Rip-Off

Red Square is rife with policemen who stop unsuspecting tourists to 'check' their documents. These diligent law enforcers invariably find something wrong with their victim's visa or registration, even if it really is in perfect order, and the fine for this imaginary crime is often as much as R2000.

If the policeman is feeling magnanimous, he may give you the option of appearing at the police station to pay the fine, but only if he knows it is impossible for you to do so. (One reader was booked on a train out of Moscow within two hours. The officer informed him that he could pay his fine at the station, but only after four hours. Otherwise, he should pay on the spot.) This scam is big business for police officers – it's an entrepreneurial way to supplement their meagre salaries, and they may even furnish you with a (totally meaningless) receipt for your troubles.

What should you do when these humourless cops demand to see your documents?

- To avoid potential problems, get your visa registered in Moscow, even if it has already been registered in another city. Interpretation and enforcement of the policy is inconsistent, but as a rule you can never have too many stamps and signatures.
- Never volunteer your time or date of intended departure.
- Before handing over your documents, ask to see the officer's identification and write down the seven-digit number. Make sure he knows that you know who he is.
- Show the officer a photocopy of your passport and visa (made after you arrive in Moscow, so that your visa registration is visible). Do not give up your passport.
- If you have a mobile (cell) phone, pull it out and tell the officer you would like to ring your embassy to have somebody meet you at the station. One reader writes: 'This exact situation has happened to me four times. Once it cost me 1500 roubles; since the mobile it has cost nothing at all.'

MOSCOW

Email & Internet Access

Time Online *(Map 6; ☎ 363 0060; W www.timeonline.ru; open 24hrs)*, on the lower level of the Okhotny Ryad shopping mall near Red Square, claims to be the largest Internet café in Eastern Europe, with over 200 zippy terminals. It charges from R33 to R60 per hour; after normal business times, enter from the Kuznetsky most underground station.

Drinks and competitive rates (R60 per hour) are available at the equally central **Internet Club** *(Map 2; ☎ 924 2140; Kuznetsky most 12; open 9am-midnight daily)*.

Nearby **NetLand** *(Map 2; ☎ 105 0021; Teatralny proezd 5)* is on the 4th floor of Detsky Mir children's store.

NETCITY *(Map 5; ☎ 969 2125; Paveletskaya pl 2)* has fast terminals, and more of a café feel, with drinks and music.

Digital Resources

See Digital Resources in the European Russia Facts for the Visitor chapter for a list of mostly Moscow-based sites. The *Moscow Times* and the *Exile* (see Newspapers & Magazines later in this section) have electronic versions of their print papers. Other useful resources include the following:

W **www.waytorussia.net** Restaurant and accommodation options and lots of information about local events, sights and transportation

W **www.moscow-guide.ru** Official website run by the Moscow government, frequently updated with a range of topics from transport to culture

W **www.interknowledge.com/russia/moscow01.htm** Another official-type page with a photographic tour of the city

W **www.whererussia.com** Online version of the magazine *Where Moscow*, with restaurants, museums and entertainment listings

Travel Agencies

Infinity Travel *(Map 4; ☎ 234 6555, fax 234 6556; W www.infinity.ru; Komsomolsky pr 13)*, formerly IRO Travel, is affiliated with the Travellers Guest House. It offers rail and air tickets, a visa support service, and trans-Siberian and Central Asia packages. It's a great source for cheap international and domestic airline tickets.

Andrew's Consulting *(Map 4; ☎ 916 9898, fax 916 9828; e recept@88.ru; ul Volkhonka 18/2)* offers a full range of services aimed at business travellers.

G&R International *(Outer East Moscow Map; ☎ 378 0001, fax 378 2866; W www.hostels.ru; ul Zelenodolskaya 3/2, 15th floor)* is located in the G&R Asia Hostel and is an efficient, convenient organisation offering all the normal services, including international airline tickets.

Bookshops

Anglia British Bookshop (Map 2; ☎ 203 5802; Khlebny per 2/3; open 10am-7pm Mon-Sat, 10am-5pm Sun) has Moscow's best selection of books in English, including Lonely Planet travel titles. Another option is **Angliskaya Kniga po Kuznetskom** (Map 2; ☎ 928 2021; ul Kuznetsky most 18/7; open 10am-7pm Mon-Fri, 10am-6pm Sat).

Torgovy Dom Biblio-Globus (Map 2; ☎ 928 3567; ul Myasnitskaya 6) is a Russian bookshop with lots of reference and souvenir books on language, art and history, and a good selection of maps and travel guides.

Newspapers & Magazines

The undisputed king of the hill in locally published English-language news is the *Moscow Times* (W www.moscowtimes.ru), a first-rate daily covering Russian and international issues and staffed by top-notch journalists and editors. Available by subscription, it's free at hotels, business centres and restaurants. The Thursday edition is a great source for what's happening at the weekend (another Moscow daily, the *Moscow Tribune*, always seems to be on the verge of closing).

The Exile (W www.exile.ru) is an irreverent, free weekly, with extensive entertainment listings.

Numerous other English-language weeklies and monthlies seem to appear at random, lasting a few issues and then vanishing. One very useful established monthly is the *Moscow Business Telephone Guide*, a free, invaluable, bilingual phone book. *Capital Perspective* is a glossy bimonthly with great photos and in-depth articles about cultural events and places around Moscow. Both can be found in the same places as the aforementioned publications.

Libraries & Cultural Centres

The **Foreign Literature Library** (Map 5; ☎ 915 3669; ul Nikoloyamskaya 1; open 10am-8pm Mon-Fri, 10am-6pm Sat) is home to several international libraries and cultural centres, including the American Cultural Center Library, the French Cultural Centre, and the **British Council Resource Centre** (☎ 782 0200, fax 782 0201; open noon-7pm Mon-Fri). Take your passport.

The **Russian State Library** (Rossiyskaya Gosudarstvennaya Biblioteka; Map 6; ul Vozdvizhenka 3; open 9am-9pm daily), on the corner of Mokhovaya ulitsa, is one of the world's largest libraries, with over 20 million volumes. If you want to peruse any of these, take along your passport and one passport photo, and fill in some forms at the information office to get a free *chitatelsky bilet* (reader's card). The library is closed the last Monday of each month.

Laundry

Although such facilities are still a rarity in Moscow, there is a **self-service laundry** (Outer South Moscow Map; ul Vavilova 11; open 7am-10pm Mon-Sat) which charges R60 per load. Take tram 39 from Leninsky prospekt or Universitetskaya, head up the short flight of stairs and enter through the unmarked white door. Many places to stay also offer laundry services.

Medical Services

Several foreign-run health services offer Western standards of treatment, but they are very expensive and can be fiscally ruinous without valid insurance coverage.

American Medical Center (Map 3; ☎ 933 7700, fax 933 7701; Grokholsky per 1) offers 24-hour emergency service, consultations (from US$175), a full range of specialists (including paediatricians and dentists), and an English-speaking **pharmacy** (open 8am-8pm Mon-Fri, 9am-5pm Sat & Sun).

European Medical Center (Map 2; ☎ 787 7000; Spiridonovsky per 5) has similar service and costs.

The best Russian facility is **Botkin Hospital** (Map 2; ☎ 945 0045; 2-y Botkinsky proezd 5).

Pharmacy Kutuzovskaya (Map 4; ☎ 243 1601; Kutuzovsky pr 19-21; open 24hrs) stocks Russian and Western medicines.

Emergency

The emergency telephone numbers are **fire** (☎ 01), **police** (☎ 02) and **ambulance** (☎ 03). They have Russian-speaking operators only.

Dangers & Annoyances

Despite Muscovite paranoia about rising crime, visitors will mostly have little to fear. As in any big city, be on your guard against pickpockets and muggers, and watch out especially for gangs of children (generally referred to as 'gypsy kids'), who are after anything they can get their hands on.

Certain members of the police will also bug anybody who doesn't look like a fair-haired Muscovite – practical advice from a Moscow synagogue is 'cover your kippa'. Other members of the police force target tourists (see the earlier boxed text 'The Great Moscow Police Tourist Rip-Off').

The most common hazard is violent and xenophobic drunks. Or even worse, overly friendly drunks.

KREMLIN (MAP 6)

The apex of political power, the **Kremlin** (*☎ 203 0349; W www.kremlin.museum.ru; adult/student R200/100; open 10am-6pm Fri-Wed*) is the kernel not only of Moscow but of the whole country. From here Ivan the Terrible and Stalin orchestrated their terrors; Napoleon watched Moscow burn; Lenin fashioned the proletariat dictatorship; Khrushchev fought the Cold War; Gorbachev unleashed *perestroika*; and Yeltsin concocted the New Russia.

It may come as a surprise that the Kremlin's chief glories – the bases from which most of its famous gold domes rise – are actually cathedrals (the Kremlin was also once the centre of Russia's Church).

The Kremlin occupies a roughly triangular plot of land covering little Borovitsky Hill on the north bank of the Moscow River, probably first settled in the 11th century. Today it's enclosed by high walls 2.25km long, with Red Square outside the east wall. The best views of the Kremlin are from Sofiyskaya naberezhnaya, across the river, and from the upper floors of Hotel Rossiya.

A 'kremlin' is a town's fortified stronghold, and the first low, wooden wall around Moscow was built in the 1150s. The Kremlin grew with the importance of Moscow's princes and in the 1320s became the headquarters of the Russian Church, which had shifted from Vladimir.

The 'White Stone Kremlin' – which had limestone walls – was built in the 1360s, with almost the same boundaries as today. This lasted until Ivan the Great commenced rebuilding from 1475 to 1516, when master builders from Pskov and Italy came to supervise new walls and towers (most of which still stand), as well as the three great cathedrals and more. Other buildings have been added piecemeal since then.

Although Peter the Great shifted the capital to St Petersburg, the tsars continued to show up here for coronations and other celebrations. Nonetheless, today's Kremlin still stands thanks to several twists of fate. Catherine the Great had plans drawn up for a new classical Kremlin in the 1770s, but ran out of money before construction; and Napoleon blew up parts of it before his retreat in 1812, although the timely arrival of Russian troops prevented total destruction (the citadel wouldn't be breached again until the Bolsheviks stormed the place in November 1917).

Until 1955 the Kremlin remained closed to the public, most of whom would have feared for their lives upon entering Stalin's terrifying lair. (It was Stalin who, in 1935, had the imperial double-headed eagles removed from the wall's five tallest towers, replacing them with the distinctive red-glass stars still there today.)

Admission

Before entering the Kremlin, deposit bags for R60 each at the **left luggage office** (*open 9am-6.30pm*), beneath the Kutafya Tower just north of the main ticket office.

The main ticket office closes at 4.30pm and is in the Alexandrovsky Garden, just off Manezhnaya ploshchad (metro Aleksandrovsky Sad, Borovitskaya or Biblioteka imeni Lenina). The ticket covers entry to all buildings except the Armoury and Diamond Fund Exhibition; it's a good idea to buy tickets for these two here as well, to avoid having to queue up again once inside the Kremlin. (A photography permit costs R50 and there's also an entrance at the southern Borovitskaya Gate, mainly used by those heading straight to the Armoury.) Inside the Kremlin, police will keep you from straying into the out-of-bounds areas. Visitors wearing shorts will be refused entry.

Tours Numerous freelance guides tout their services near the Kutafya Tower, with prices ranging from US$10 to US$20 per hour, and the quality varying widely. Dom Patriarshy (see Organised Tours later in this chapter) offers regular tours of the main sights, and occasional ones of the off-limits Great Kremlin Palace.

Northern & Western Buildings

The **Kutafya Tower** (Kutafya bashnya) forms the main visitors' entrance today; it stands away from the Kremlin's west wall, at the end of a ramp over the Alexandrovsky Garden. The ramp was once a bridge over the Neglinnaya River, which used to be part of the Kremlin's defences; it has flowed underground, beneath the Alexandrovsky Garden, since the early 19th century. The Kutafya Tower is the last survivor of a number of outer bridge towers that once stood this side of the Kremlin.

From the Kutafya Tower, walk up the ramp and pass through the Kremlin walls beneath the **Trinity Gate Tower** (Troitskaya bashnya). The lane to the right (south), immediately inside the Trinity Gate Tower, passes the 17th-century **Poteshny Palace** (Poteshny dvorets) where Stalin lived. East of here, the bombastic marble, glass and concrete **Kremlin Palace of Congresses** (Kremlyovksy Dvorets Syezdov), built in 1960–61 for Communist Party congresses, is also a concert and ballet auditorium seating 6000. North is the 18th-century **Arsenal**, ringed with 800 captured Napoleonic cannons.

To the east of the Arsenal, the offices of the Russian president are in the yellow former **Senate** (Senat) building, a fine, triangular 18th-century classical edifice. Next to the Senate is the 1930s **Supreme Soviet** (Verkhovny Soviet) building.

Patriarch's Palace

This palace was mostly built in the mid-17th century for Patriarch Nikon, whose reforms sparked the break with the Old Believers. Inside, the **Museum of 17th Century Russian Applied Art and Life** houses mostly church vestments, icons, illuminated books and so on. From here you can access the five-domed **Church of the Twelve Apostles** (Tserkov Dvenadtsati Apostolov), which Nikon had built as a new patriarch's chapel, and the large **Hall of the Cross** (Krestovaya Palata), once the patriarch's official reception hall.

Assumption Cathedral

At the Kremlin's heart, Sobornaya ploshchad is surrounded by magnificent buildings, including the Assumption Cathedral (Uspensky sobor) on its northern side, with five golden helmet domes and four semicircular gables facing the square. As the focal church of pre-revolutionary Russia, it's the burial place of most of Russian Orthodox Church heads from the 1320s to 1700. The tombs are against the north, west and south walls.

The cathedral was built between 1475 and 1479 after the Bolognese architect Aristotle Fioravanti had toured Novgorod, Suzdal and Vladimir to acquaint himself with Russian architecture. His design is based on the Assumption Cathedral at Vladimir, with some Western features. It replaced a smaller 1326 cathedral on the same site. The church closed in 1918.

In 1812 French troops used the cathedral as a stable, looting 295kg of gold and over five tonnes of silver, although much of it was recovered. According to some accounts, when the Nazis were in the outskirts of Moscow in 1941, Stalin secretly ordered a service in the Assumption Cathedral to protect the city from the enemy. The cathedral was officially returned to the Church in 1989, but still operates as a museum.

A striking 1660s fresco of the Virgin Mary faces Sobornaya ploshchad, above the door once used for royal processions. The visitors' entrance is at the western end, and the interior is unusually bright and spacious, full of warm golds, reds and blues.

Near the south wall is a tent-roofed wooden throne, made in 1551 for Ivan the Terrible; it's commonly known as the **Throne of Monomakh** because of its carved scenes from the career of 12th-century Grand Prince, Vladimir Monomakh of Kyiv.

The **iconostasis** dates from 1652, although its lowest level contains some older icons, among them (second from the right) *Saviour with the Angry Eye* (Spas yaroe oko) from the 1340s. On the left of the central door, the *Virgin of Vladimir* (Vladimirskaya Bogomater) is an early-15th-century Rublyov-school copy of Russia's most revered image; the 12th-century original, *Vladimir Icon of the Mother of God* (now in the Tretyakov Gallery), stood in the Assumption Cathedral from the 1480s to 1930. One of the oldest Russian icons, the 12th-century red-clothed *St George* (Svyatoy Georgy) from Novgorod, is positioned by the north wall.

Most of the existing murals on the cathedral walls were painted on a gilt base in the 1640s, but three grouped together on the south wall – *The Apocalypse* (Apokalipsis), *The Life of Metropolitan Pyotr* (Zhitie Mitropolita Petra) and *All Creatures Rejoice in Thee*

(O tebe raduetsya) – are attributed to Diony-sius and his followers, the cathedral's original 15th-century mural painters.

Church of the Deposition of the Robe

This delicate little single-domed church – Tserkov Rizpolozhenia – beside the west door of the Assumption Cathedral, was built be-tween 1484 and 1486. As the private chapel of the heads of the church, it was built in exclu-sively Russian style (the heads tended to be highly suspicious of Italian architects, for ex-ample); the interior walls, ceilings and pillars are covered with 17th-century frescoes. It houses an exhibition of 15th- to 17th-century woodcarvings.

The Ivan the Great Bell Tower

With its two golden domes rising above the eastern side of Sobornaya ploshchad, the Ivan the Great Bell Tower (Kolokolnya Ivana Ve-likogo) is the Kremlin's tallest structure, a Moscow landmark visible 30km away. (Be-fore the 20th century it was forbidden to build any higher in Moscow.)

When designed by Italian Marco Bono in 1508, the southern tower had just two octag-onal tiers beneath a drum and dome. Boris Godunov raised the tower to 81m, a public works project designed to employ the thou-sands of people who came to Moscow during a famine. The building's central section, with a gilded single dome and a 65-tonne bell, dates from the 1530s, while the tent-roofed annexe next to the belfry was commissioned by Patriarch Filaret in 1642 and bears his name. Exhibitions from the Kremlin collec-tions are shown on the ground level.

Tsar Bell

Beside the bell tower, not inside it, stands the Tsar Bell (Tsar-kolokol), the world's biggest bell, a 202-tonne monster that never rang. In a 1701 fire, an earlier 130-tonne version fell from its belfry and shattered; with these re-mains, the current Tsar Bell was cast in the 1730s for Empress Anna Ivanovna. The bell was cooling off in the foundry casting pit in 1737 when it came into contact with water, causing an 11-tonne chunk to chip off.

Tsar Cannon

North of the bell tower is the Tsar Cannon (Tsar-pushka), cast in 1586 for Fyodor I, whose portrait is on the barrel. Shot has never sullied its 89cm bore – and certainly not the cannonballs beside it, which are too big even for this elephantine firearm.

Archangel Cathedral

The cathedral (Arkhangelsky sobor) at the square's southeastern corner was, for cen-turies, the coronation, wedding and burial church of tsars. The tombs of all Muscovy's rulers from the 1320s to the 1690s are here, bar one – Boris Godunov is buried at Sergiev Posad.

The cathedral, built between 1505 and 1508 by the Italian Alevisio Novi, is dedi-cated to the Archangel Michael, guardian of Moscow's princes. Like the Assumption Cathedral, it is essentially Byzantine-Russian in style, although the exterior has many Venetian Renaissance features, notably the distinctive scallop-shell gables.

Tsarevich Dmitry – Ivan the Terrible's son, who died mysteriously in 1591 – lies beneath a painted stone canopy. Ivan's own tomb is out of sight behind the iconostasis, along with those of his other sons: Ivan (whom he killed) and Fyodor (who succeeded him). From Peter the Great onwards, emperors and empresses were buried in St Petersburg; the exception was Peter II, who died in Moscow in 1730 and is here.

During restorations in the 1950s the cathe-dral's 17th-century murals were uncovered. The south wall depicts many of those buried here, and on the pillars are some of their pre-decessors, including Andrey Bogolyubsky, Prince Daniil and his father, Alexander Nevsky.

Annunciation Cathedral

Dating from 1489, the Annunciation Cathe-dral (Blagoveshchensky sobor) at the south-west corner of Sobornaya ploshchad contains the celebrated icons of master painter Theo-phanes the Greek. Their timeless beauty ap-peals even to those usually left cold by icons.

The cathedral, built between 1484 and 1489 by Pskov masters, was the royal fam-ily's private chapel. Originally, it had just three domes and an open gallery around three sides. Ivan the Terrible, whose taste was more elaborate, added six more domes and chapels at each corner, and enclosed the gallery and gilded the roof.

Ivan's fourth marriage disqualified him under Orthodox law from entering the church

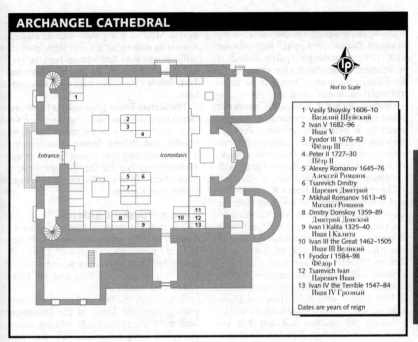

ARCHANGEL CATHEDRAL

Not to Scale

1 Vasily Shuysky 1606–10
Василий Шуйский
2 Ivan V 1682–96
Иван V
3 Fyodor III 1676–82
Фёдор III
4 Peter II 1727–30
Пётр II
5 Alexey Romanov 1645–76
Алексей Романов
6 Tsarevich Dmitry
Царевич Дмитрий
7 Mikhail Romanov 1613–45
Михаил Романов
8 Dmitry Donskoy 1359–89
Дмитрий Донской
9 Ivan I Kalita 1325–40
Иван I Калита
10 Ivan III the Great 1462–1505
Иван III Великий
11 Fyodor I 1584–98
Фёдор I
12 Tsarevich Ivan
Царевич Иван
13 Ivan IV the Terrible 1547–84
Иван IV Грозный

Dates are years of reign

Entrance

Iconostasis

MOSCOW

proper, so he had the southern arm of the gallery converted into the **Archangel Gabriel Chapel** (Pridel Arkhangela Gavriila), from which he could watch services through a grille. The chapel has a colourful iconostasis dating from its consecration in 1564, and an exhibition of icons.

Many of the murals in the gallery date from the 1560s. Among them are the *Capture of Jericho* in the porch, *Jonah and the Whale* in the northern arm, and the *Tree of Jesus* on the ceiling.

The cathedral's small central part has a lovely jasper floor, and the 16th-century frescoes include Russian princes on the north pillar and Byzantine emperors on the south, both with Apocalypse scenes above. But the chapel's real treasure is the **iconostasis**, where restorers in the 1920s uncovered early-15th-century icons by three of the greatest medieval Russian artists.

Theophanes likely painted most of the six icons at the right-hand end of the deesis row, the biggest of the six tiers of the iconostasis. From left to right, these are the *Virgin Mary, Christ Enthroned, St John the Baptist*, the *Archangel Gabriel*, the *Apostle Paul*, and *St*

John Chrysostom. These icons are set apart from most others by way of Theophanes' mastery at portraying visible pathos in facial expressions sets.

Archangel Michael is ascribed to Andrey Rublyov, who may also have painted the adjacent *St Peter*. Rublyov is also reckoned to be the artist of the first, second, sixth and seventh (and probably the third and fifth) icons from the left of the festival row, above the deesis row. The seven at the right-hand end are attributed to Prokhor of Gorodets.

Hall of Facets & Terem Palace

On the western side, named after its facing Italian Renaissance stone, is the square Hall of Facets; its upper floor housed the tsar's throne room, scene of banquets and ceremonies, and was reached by outside staircases from the square below.

The 16th- and 17th-century Terem Palace is the most splendid of all the Kremlin palaces. Catch a glimpse of its sumptuous cluster of golden domes and chequered roof behind and above the Church of the Deposition of the Robe. Both buildings are closed to the public.

Armoury

In the Kremlin's southwestern corner is the Armoury (Oruzheynaya palata; adult/student R300/175), a numbingly opulent collection of treasures accumulated over centuries by the Russian State and Church. Your ticket will specify a time of entry.

Upstairs, **Room 2** houses the renowned Easter eggs made from precious metals and jewels by St Petersburg jewellers, Fabergé. Each egg opens to reveal amazingly detailed miniature objects – most famous is a clockwork trans-Siberian train made of gold, with a platinum locomotive and ruby headlamp.

The royal regalia in **Room 6** contains the joint coronation throne of boy tsars Peter the Great and his half-brother, Ivan V (with a secret compartment from which Regent Sofia prompted them); the 800-diamond throne of Tsar Alexey, Peter's father; the gold Cap of Monomakhsable, jewel-studded and sable-trimmed, and worn for two centuries of coronations until 1682; and the coronation dresses of 18th-century empresses (Empress Elizabeth, we're told, had 15,000 other dresses).

Among the coaches in **Room 9** is the sleigh which Elizabeth rode from St Petersburg to Moscow for her coronation, pulled by 23 horses at a time – about 800 in all.

Between the Armoury and the Annunciation Cathedral stretches the 700-room **Great Kremlin Palace** (Bolshoy Kremlyovsky dvorets), built in the period from 1838 to 1849 as an imperial residence. Now it is an official residence of the Russian president and is used for state visits and receptions. It's not open to the public.

Diamond Fund Exhibition

If the Armoury doesn't sate your diamond lust, there's more in the separate Diamond Fund Exhibition (Vystavka almaznogo fonda; adult/student R300/175); it's in the same building as the Armoury. The collection, mainly of precious stones and jewellery garnered by tsars and empresses, includes such weighty beasts as the 190-carat diamond given to Catherine the Great by her lover Grigory Orlov.

Towers

The Kremlin walls have 19 distinctive towers, mostly built between 1485 and 1500, with tent roofs added in the 17th century. Some towers had to be rebuilt after Napoleonic vandalism.

The **Saviour Gate Tower** (Spasskaya bashnya) is Moscow's Big Ben, with its chimes relayed by state radio; it's over the Kremlin's 'official' exit onto Red Square. Ivan the Terrible watched executions nearby, where the **Tsar Tower** (Tsarskaya bashnya) was later built.

The **Secrets Tower** (Taynitskaya bashnya), facing the river, was both a gate and the start of a secret passage to the river. The **Konstantin and Yelena Tower** (Konstantino-Yeleninskaya bashnya) is also known as the Torture Tower. Ivan the Terrible used the **Annunciation Tower** (Blagoveshchenskaya bashnya) as a prison.

Alexandrovsky Garden

The first public park in Moscow, Alexandrovsky Garden (Alexandrovsky Sad) sits along the Kremlin's western wall. Colourful flower beds and impressive Kremlin views make it a favourite strolling spot for Muscovites and tourists alike.

At the north end is a kind of national pilgrimage spot, the **Tomb of the Unknown Soldier** (Mogila neizvestnogo soldata), where newlyweds bring flowers and have their pictures taken. The tomb contains the remains of one soldier who died in December 1941 at Km 41 of Leningradskoe shosse (the nearest the Nazis came to Moscow). The inscription reads, 'Your name is unknown, your deeds immortal', along with an eternal flame and other inscriptions listing the Soviet hero cities of WWII, honouring 'those who fell for the motherland' between 1941 and 1945. The changing of the guard happens every hour.

CITY CENTRE

The heart of the city lies in the arc around the Kremlin bound by Mokhovaya ulitsa, Okhotny ryad, Teatralny proezd and Lubyansky proezd.

Red Square (Map 6)

Krasnaya ploshchad, Red Square, lies immediately outside the Kremlin's northeastern wall. Commanding the square from the southern end is the building that, more than any other, says 'Russia' – St Basil's Cathedral (see that entry later in this chapter).

Red Square used to be a market square adjoining the merchants area in Kitai Gorod. It has always been a place where occupants of the Kremlin chose to congregate, celebrate and castigate for all the people to see. Here, Ivan the Terrible publicly confessed his misdeeds in 1547, built St Basil's to commemorate his victories in the 1550s, and later had numerous perceived enemies executed. Red Square also saw the dismembering of the Cossack rebel Stepan Razin in 1671, as well as the en masse execution in 1698 of 2000 members of the Streltsy, Peter the Great's mutinous palace guard.

Soviet rulers chose Red Square for their military parades, perhaps most poignantly on 7 November 1941, when tanks rolled straight off to the front line outside Moscow; and during the Cold War, when lines of ICBMs rumbled across the square to remind the West of Soviet military might.

Incidentally, the name 'Krasnaya ploshchad' has nothing to do with communism or the blood that flowed here: *krasnyy* in old Russian meant 'beautiful' and only in the 20th century did it come to mean 'red', too.

Red Square is closed to traffic, except for the limousines that whiz in and out of the Kremlin's Saviour Gate from time to time. Most people here are sightseers, but that doesn't reduce the thrill of walking on this 400m by 150m area of cobbles, so central to Russian history. It's particularly atmospheric when floodlit at night.

The best way to enter Red Square is through the **Resurrection Gate** (Voskresenskiye Vorota). Rebuilt in 1995, it's an exact copy of the original completed on this site in 1680, with its twin red towers topped by green tent spires. The first gateway was destroyed in 1931 because Stalin considered it an impediment to the parades and demonstrations held in Red Square.

Within the gateway is the bright **Chapel of the Iverian Virgin** (Chasovnya Iverskoy Boromateri), originally built in the late 18th century to house the icon.

Lenin's Tomb The granite tomb *(Mavzoley VI Lenina; ☎ 923 5527; admission free; open 10am-1pm Tues-Thur, Sat & Sun)* standing at the foot of the Kremlin wall is another Red Square must-see (especially since the former leader may eventually end up beside his mum in St Petersburg). For now, the embalmed leader remains as he has been since 1924 (apart from a retreat to Siberia during WWII). From 1953 to 1961 Lenin

Lenin under Glass

Red Square is home to the world's most famous mummy, that of Vladimir Lenin. When he died of a massive stroke (on 22 January 1924, aged 53), a long line of mourners patiently gathered in winter's harshness for weeks to glimpse the body as it lay in state. Inspired by the spectacle, Stalin proposed that the father of Soviet communism should continue to serve the cause as a holy relic. So the decision was made to preserve Lenin's corpse for perpetuity, against the vehement protests of his widow, as well as his own expressed desire to be buried next to his mother in St Petersburg.

Boris Zbarsky, a biochemist, and Vladimir Voribov, an anatomist, were issued a political order to put a stop to the natural decomposition of the body. The pair worked frantically in a secret laboratory in search of a long-term chemical solution. In the meantime, the body's dark spots were bleached, and lips and eyes sewn tight. The brain was removed and taken to another secret laboratory, to be sliced and diced by scientists for the next 40 years in the hope of uncovering its hidden genius.

In July 1924, the scientists hit upon a formula to successfully arrest the decaying process, a closely guarded state secret. This necrotic craft was passed on to Zbarsky's son, who ran the Kremlin's covert embalming lab for decades. After the fall of communism, Zbarsky came clean: the body is wiped down every few days, and then, every 18 months, thoroughly examined and submerged in a tub of chemicals, including paraffin wax. The institute has now gone commercial, offering its services and secrets to wannabe immortals for a mere million dollars.

In the early 1990s, Boris Yeltsin expressed his intention to heed Lenin's request and bury him in St Petersburg, setting off a furore from the political left as well as more muted objections from Moscow tour operators. It seems that the mausoleum, the most sacred shrine of Soviet Communism, and the mummy, the literal embodiment of the Russian Revolution, will remain in place for at least several more years.

★★★★★★★★★★★★★★★★★★★★

shared the tomb with Stalin. In 1961, at the 22nd Party Congress, the esteemed (and by then ancient) Bolshevik Madame Spiridonova announced that Vladimir Ilych had

MOSCOW

Kremlin Wall

Some of the worthies given the honour of burial beneath the Kremlin Wall include:

Felix Dzerzhinsky	The founder of the Cheka (forerunner of the KGB)
Yakov Sverdlov	Key organiser of the revolution and the first official head of the Soviet state
Andrey Zhdanov	Stalin's cultural chief and, immediately after WWII, the second most powerful man in the USSR
Mikhail Frunze	Red Army leader; secured Central Asia for the Soviet Union in the 1920s
Inessa Armand	Lenin's rumoured lover
John Reed (Dzhon Rid)	The American author of Ten Days that Shook the World, a first-hand account of the revolution

Plaques in the wall mark the spots where the ashes of many more heroes lie, including:

Yuri Gagarin	The first person in space
Marshal Georgy Zhukov	The commander who defeated Hitler
Alexey Kosygin	Brezhnev's initial partner in power in the 1960s
Igor Kurchatov	The leader of the team that developed the Soviet hydrogen bomb

★★

appeared to her in a dream, insisting that he did not like spending eternity with his successor. With that, Stalin was removed, and given a place of honour immediately behind the mausoleum.

Before joining the queue at the northwestern corner of Red Square, drop your camera at the left-luggage office beneath Kutafya Tower, as you will not be allowed to take it with you. Humourless guards ensure that visitors remain respectful.

After trouping past the embalmed, oddly waxy figure, emerge from the mausoleum and inspect the burial places along the Kremlin wall of Stalin, Brezhnev and other Communist heavy hitters.

St Basil's Cathedral No picture can prepare you for the crazy confusion of colours and shapes that is St Basil's Cathedral *(Sobor Vasilia Blazhennogo; ☎ 298 3304; admission R100; open 11am-5pm Wed-Mon)*. This ultimate symbol of Russia was created between 1555 and 1561 (replacing an existing church on the site) to celebrate Ivan the Terrible's capture of the Tatar stronghold, Kazan. Its design is the culmination of a wholly Russian style that had been developed building wooden churches; legend has it that Ivan had the cathedral's architect blinded so that he could never build anything comparable.

The cathedral owes its name to the barefoot holy fool Vasily (Basil) the Blessed, who predicted Ivan's damnation and added correctly, as the army left for Kazan, that Ivan would murder a son. Vasily, who died while Kazan was under siege, was buried beside the church which St Basil's soon replaced. He was later canonised.

St Basil's apparent anarchy of shapes hides a comprehensible plan of nine main chapels: the tall, tent-roofed one in the centre; four big, octagonal-towered ones, topped with the four biggest domes; and four smaller ones in between. An extra northeastern chapel over Vasily the Blessed's grave and a tent-roofed southeastern bell tower were added later. In the 1670s the domes were patterned, giving St Basil's its present, multicoloured appearance.

The interior is open to visitors. The ground level holds a small exhibition on St Basil's itself, and there are some lovely frescoes of flower patterns and saints.

Out front of St Basil's is a **statue of the butcher Kuzma Minin and Prince Dmitry Pozharsky** (pamyatnik Mininu i Pozharskomu), who together raised and led the army that ejected occupying Poles from the Kremlin in 1612. Up the slope is the round, walled **Place of Skulls** (Lobnoe Mesto), where Ivan the Terrible made his public confession and Peter the Great executed the Streltsy.

GUM The Gosudarstvenny Universalny Magazin (State Department Store) – GUM – lines the northeastern side of Red Square and was built in the 19th century; it houses over 1000 shops. GUM once symbolised all that was bad about Soviet shopping: long queues and shelves empty of all but a few drab goods.

A remarkable transformation has taken place since *perestroika* and today GUM is a

St Basil's Cathedral, Moscow

Lenin's Tomb and the Kremlin, Moscow

Half-constructivist, half-Stalinist Hotel Moskva

Icon of St George, patron saint of Moscow

Street traders with figurines, Moscow

St George's Church, Moscow

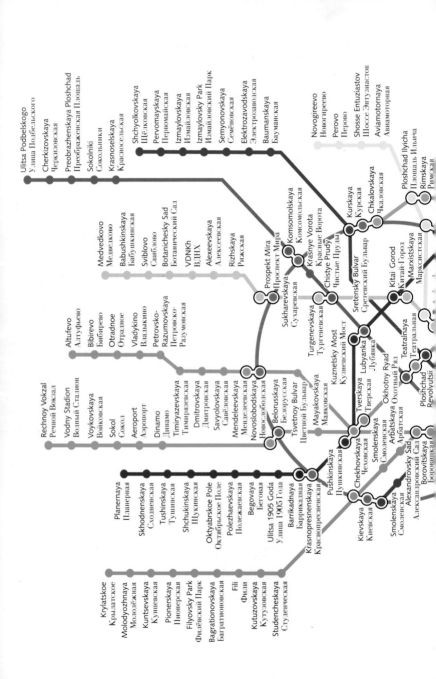

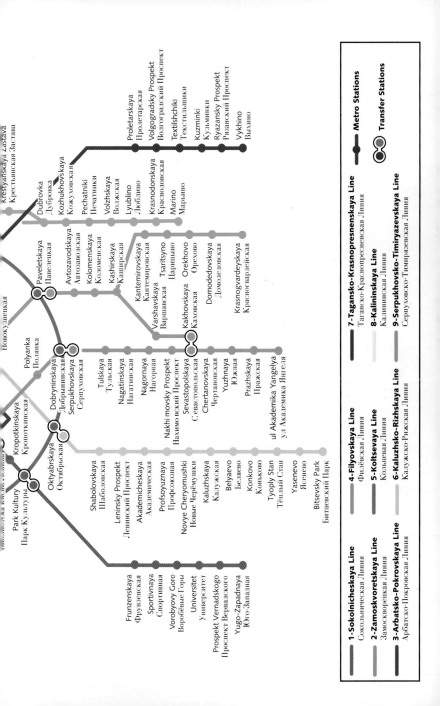

Krestyanskaya zastava
Крестьянская Застава

Novokuznetska

Dubrovka
Дубровка

Kozhukhovskaya
Кожуховская

Pechatniki
Печатники

Volzhskaya
Волжская

Lyublino
Люблино

Krasnodonskaya
Краснодонская

Marino
Марьино

Proletarskaya
Пролетарская

Volgogradsky Prospekt
Волгоградский Проспект

Textilshchiki
Текстильщики

Kuzminki
Кузьминки

Ryazansky Prospekt
Рязанский Проспект

Vykhino
Выхино

Paveletskaya
Павелецкая

Avtozavodskaya
Автозаводская

Kolomenskaya
Коломенская

Kashirskaya
Каширская

Kantemirovskaya
Кантемировская

Tsaritsyno
Царицыно

Orekhovo
Орехово

Domodedovskaya
Домодедовская

Krasnogvardeyskaya
Красногвардейская

Varshavskaya
Варшавская

Kakhovskaya
Каховская

Novokuznetska

Polyanka
Полянка

Kropotkinskaya
Кропоткинская

Dobryninskaya
Добрынинская

Serpukhovskaya
Серпуховская

Tulskaya
Тульская

Nagatinskaya
Нагатинская

Nagornaya
Нагорная

Nakhimovsky Prospekt
Нахимовский Проспект

Sevastopolskaya
Севастопольская

Chertanovskaya
Чертановская

Yuzhnaya
Южная

Prazhskaya
Пражская

Oktyabrskaya
Октябрьская

Park Kultury
Парк Культуры

Shabolovskaya
Шаболовская

Leninsky Prospekt
Ленинский Проспект

Akademicheskaya
Академическая

Profsoyuznaya
Профсоюзная

Novye Cheryomushki
Новые Черёмушки

Kaluzhskaya
Калужская

Belyaevo
Беляево

Konkovo
Коньково

Tyoply Stan
Тёплый Стан

Yasenevo
Ясенево

Bitsevsky Park
Битцевский Парк

ul Akademika Yangelya
ул Академика Янгеля

Frunzenskaya
Фрунзенская

Sportivnaya
Спортивная

Vorobyovy Goro
Воробьёвы Горы

Universitet
Университет

Prospekt Vernadskogo
Проспект Вернадского

Yugo-Zapadnaya
Юго-Западная

Early evening sunlight on a building facade near the Neva River, St Petersburg

May Day performance at the Winter Palace, St Petersburg

Peter & Paul Fortress

Church of Our Lady of Assumption, St Petersburg

The State Hermitage, St Petersburg

bright, bustling place full of attractive shops stocked with Russian and imported goods of all kinds, including Benetton, Yves Rocher, Galerie Lafayette and many other big names. There are a few snack places, and pay toilets at the southern end of the ground level.

Kazan Cathedral The tiny Kazan Cathedral *(Kazansky sobor; Nikolskaya ul 3; admission free; open 8am-7pm, evening service 8pm Mon)* opposite the northern end of GUM is a 1993 replica of the original, which was founded in 1636 in thanks for the 1612 expulsion of Polish invaders (for two centuries it housed the *Virgin of Kazan* icon, which supposedly helped to rout the Poles).

Three hundred years later the cathedral was completely demolished, allegedly because it impeded the flow of celebrating workers in May Day and Revolution Day parades.

State History Museum The State History Museum *(Gosudarstvenny Istorichesky Muzey; ☎ 292 4019; Red Square; adult/student R150/ 75; open 11am-7pm Wed-Mon)* at the northern end of the square has an enormous collection covering the whole Russian empire from the Stone Age on. The building, dating from the late 19th century, is itself an attraction – each room is in the style of a different period or region, some with highly decorated walls echoing old Russian churches. Reopened in 1997, each year sees the addition of a few more galleries.

Across the street, the former **Central Lenin Museum** *(pl Revolyutsii 2)* was once the big daddy of all the Lenin museums, but was closed in 1993 after the White House shootout. Communist rabble rousers still congregate here.

Around Manezhnaya Ploshchad (Map 6)

Manezhnaya ploshchad at the northern end of Red Square has been transformed with the vast underground **Okhotny Ryad Shopping Mall** *(☎ 737 8409)*, which makes its presence known with a series of half-domes and balustrades, and a network of fountains and sculptures.

The long, low building on the southwestern side of the square is the **Manezh Central Exhibition Hall** *(☎ 202 8976; open 11am-8pm daily)*, home to some of Moscow's most popular art exhibitions. On the northwestern side of the square are the fine old edifices,

Moscow State University (built in 1793) and Hotel National (built in 1903).

Hotel Moskva, from the 1930s and fronting the square's northeastern side, is half-constructivist, half-Stalinist. Apparently Stalin was shown two possible designs for the hotel and not realising they were alternatives, approved both. Not daring to point out his error, the builders built half in each style, with predictably incongruous results. Rumours are flying that this place will soon go the way of its former neighbour, the Intourist Hotel (now closed and soon to be demolished).

The entrance to the new **Archaeological Museum** *(☎ 292 4171; Manezhnaya pl 1; admission R30; open 10am-6pm Tues-Sun)* is at the base of Hotel Moskva, facing the square. An excavation of the Voskresensky Bridge (which used to cross the Neglinnaya River and commence the road to Tver) uncovered coins, clothing and other artefacts now displayed in the museum, which is situated in an underground pavilion remaining from the excavation itself.

The **Russian State Library** *(cnr uls Mokhovaya & Vozdvizhenka)* is among the world's biggest, with over 20 million volumes. One of Moscow's finest classical buildings, the 1784–87 **Pashkov House** (Dom Pashkova) holds part of the collection. For details on visiting the grand but financially troubled Russian State Library, see Libraries under Information earlier in this chapter.

Northeast of Manezhnaya ploshchad, Okhotny ryad passes between Hotel Moskva and the glowering **State Duma** (Gosudarstvennaya duma), where Russia's parliament now sits. This building was erected in the 1930s for Gosplan (the Soviet State Planning Department), and was the source of the USSR's Five-Year Plans. The green-columned **House of Unions** (Dom Soyuzov) is next door, dating from the 1780s and formerly the Nobles' Club. Its Hall of Columns (originally a ballroom, now a concert hall) was in 1938 the scene of one of Stalin's most grotesque show trials, that of Nikolai Bukharin, a leading Communist Party theorist who had been a close associate of Lenin.

Teatralnaya Ploshchad (Map 6)

Teatralnaya ploshchad opens out on both sides of Okhotny ryad, 200m from Manezhnaya ploshchad. The northern half of the square is dominated by the **Bolshoi Theatre**, where

MOSCOW

Tchaikovsky's *Swan Lake* was premiered (unsuccessfully) in 1877. Initially overshadowed by St Petersburg's Mariinsky Theatre, the Bolshoi didn't really hit the high notes until the 1950s, when foreign tours won great acclaim for its ballet and opera companies.

The busy streets behind the Bolshoi constitute Moscow's main shopping centre (see Tverskoy Region); across ulitsa Petrovka from the 'big' Bolshoi is the 'small' **Maly Theatre**, a drama establishment. On Teatralnaya ploshchad's southern half is the tiled, sculptured facade of luxurious **Hotel Metropol**.

Around Lubyanskaya Ploshchad (Map 2)

For several decades the broad square at the top of Teatralny proezd was a chilling symbol of the Komitet Gosudarstvennoy Bezopasnosti (Committee for State Security), more commonly known as the KGB.

In the 1930s, **Lubyanka Prison** was the feared destination of thousands of innocent victims of Stalin's purges, but today the grey building is the headquarters of the KGB's successor, the FSB (Federal Security Service). The FSB doesn't operate foreign spies (that's now done by a separate External Intelligence Service, the SVR), but still keeps a sharp eye on domestic affairs. The building is not open to the public.

Behind Lubyanka is the four-room **KGB Museum** *(ul Bolshaya Lubyanka 12/1)*, devoted to the history, propaganda and paraphernalia of the Soviet intelligence services. The museum is not open to casual callers, but Dom Patriarshy Tours (see Organised Tours in this chapter) occasionally takes groups there.

From 1926 to 1990, Lubyanskaya ploshchad was called ploshchad Dzerzhinskogo, after Felix Dzerzhinsky, who founded the Cheka (the KGB's ancestor). A tall statue of Dzerzhinsky which dominated the square was memorably removed by angry crowds (with the assistance of a couple of cranes) when the 1991 coup collapsed. Now you can see the statue in all its (somewhat reduced) glory in the Sculpture Park, where it stands among others fallen from grace.

The much humbler **Memorial to the Victims of Totalitarianism** stands in the little garden on the southeastern side of the square. This single stone slab comes from the territory of an infamous 1930s labour camp on the Solovetsky Islands in the White Sea.

The little **Moscow City History Museum** *(☎ 924 8490; Novaya pl 12; admission R15; open 10am-6pm Tues-Sun)* shows how the city has spread from its starting point at the Kremlin. Across the street, the huge **Polytechnical Museum** *(☎ 923 0756; Novaya pl 3/4; admission R100; open 10am-5pm Tues-Sun)* covers the history of Russian science, technology and industry.

KITAI GOROD

The narrow old streets east of Red Square are known as Kitai Gorod, which literally means 'Chinatown', although the area has nothing to do with China. The name actually derives from *kita*, which means wattle, after the palisades that reinforced the earthen ramp erected around this early Kremlin suburb. Kitai Gorod is one of the oldest parts of Moscow, settled in the 13th century as a trade and financial centre.

Along Teatralnaya proezd, archaeologists uncovered the 16th-century fortified wall which used to surround Kitai Gorod, as well as the foundations of the 1493 Trinity Church. Coins, jewellery and tombstones were also excavated from the site, called **Starie Polya** *(Old Fields; Map 6)*. Besides the remains of the wall and the church, you can now see the memorial statue of Ivan Fyodorov, the 16th-century printer responsible for Russia's first book. The gated walkway **Tretyakovsky proezd** *(Map 6)* leads into Kitai Gorod.

Nikolskaya ulitsa, Kitai Gorod's busiest street, was once the main road to Vladimir and used to be the centre of a busy trade in icons. The dilapidated, occasionally active, **Church of the Zaikonospassky Monastery** *(Zaikonospassky monastyr; Map 6)*, built between 1661 and 1720, stands in the courtyard of No 9. The ornate green-and-white building at No 15 is the old **Printing House** *(Pechatny Dvor; Map 6)*. It was here in 1563 that Ivan Fyodorov reputedly produced Russia's first printed book, *The Apostle*. (The first Russian newspaper, *Vedomosti*, was also printed here in 1703.)

The **Monastery of Epiphany** *(Bogoyavlensky Monastyr; Map 6; Bogoyavlensky per)* is just up the road and around the corner. Its Epiphany Cathedral was constructed in the 1690s, while the monastery itself dates to the 13th century and is the second oldest in Moscow.

Judaism in Moscow

Moscow's Jewish population has experienced long periods of repression, punctuated by short intervals of opportunity. In the Middle Ages, Muscovite princes considered Jews as enemies of Christianity and forbade them from entering the realm. The Jewish population only became statistically notable in the late 18th century, when Imperial Russia annexed the eastern part of the Polish kingdom. Several centuries earlier, Europe's Jews had been welcomed in the Poland-Lithuanian Republic after their expulsion from the Western European states. In this community – known as the Jewish Pale – were the roots of the Jewish population in the Russian Empire.

Jewish trades and traditions were regarded as a threat to the social order of the empire. Official policy fluctuated from forced assimilation to social isolation. A brief respite occurred under Alexander II, the Tsar Reformer, who lifted residential restrictions on Jews with 'useful' talents (merchants, doctors, artisans and so on). Jews were allowed to enter new professions, such as banking and industry, and Moscow's small Jewish community flourished during these years.

But a wave of anti-Semitism accompanied the political reaction that came in the wake of Alexander's assassination. Authorities looked the other way when Jewish communities were overrun by pogroms of looting and violence. Tens of thousands of Moscow Jews were rounded up and expelled back to the Pale; at the outset of the 20th century, less than 1% of the empire's five million Jews lived in Moscow.

Lenin once said, 'Scratch a Bolshevik and you'll find a Russian chauvinist'. While the revolution provided another period of opportunity for individual Jews, the socialist regime was not tolerant toward Jewish language and customs. In the mid-1920s, Jews were the second-largest ethnic group in the capital, composing 6.5% of the city population. In 1930, Lazar Kaganovich, an ethnic Jew and Stalin crony, was made mayor of Moscow. He pleaded against the destruction of the Cathedral of Christ the Saviour, out of fear that he would be personally blamed and it would provoke popular anti-Semitism (both of which happened).

Anti-Semitism became official policy again in the late Stalin period: the Jewish quarter in the Dorogomilova neighbourhood was levelled for new building projects; and two huge apartment houses were constructed for the Communist elite, at 24 and 26 Kutuzov prospekt, on top of the city's old Jewish cemetery. Systematic discrimination finally prompted the rise of a dissident movement which battled Soviet officialdom for the right to leave the country.

In 1986, Mikhail Gorbachev announced that refusenik Anatoly Scharansky was permitted to emigrate, signalling a more relaxed official stance. Between 1987 and 1991, half a million Soviet Jews emigrated to Israel and 150,000 to the USA. Moscow's Jewish community declined as a result, and in 1970 Jews accounted for 3.6% of the city's population (second after ethnic Russians); by 1989, their number made up only 2% (Ukrainians were now the second-largest ethnic group in the capital).

Today, Judaism in Moscow is enjoying a modest revival as believers reconnect with their ancestry and traditions. As in earlier times, the new opportunities for Jews in postcommunist Russia have also stirred anti-Semitism. For more information, contact the **Committee on Soviet Jewry** (e *mucsj@rambler.ru*).

The **Moscow Choral Synagogue** (*Choralnaya Synagoga; Map 3; Bolshoy Spasoglinishchevsky per 10*) was built in 1891 by the businessman Polyakov, who made his fortune in the sugar industry; the interior is exquisite. It was the only synagogue which continued to operate throughout the Soviet period, in spite of Bolshevik demands to convert it to a workers' club. Recently a **Weeping Wall** (*Stena Placha*) was built nearby.

Lyubavicheskaya Synagogue (*Map 2; ul Bolshaya Bronnaya 6*), built in 1902, was converted to a theatre in the 1930s, although the building was still used for gatherings by the Jewish community. The rug on the altar hides a trapdoor leading to a small cell, where Jews used to hide from the Communists or the Nazis – or both. The building has since been returned to the Jewish community, operating as a synagogue since 1991.

The **Memorial Synagogue at Poklyonnaya Mountain** houses the **Museum of Jewish Legacy History and Holocaust** (☎ 148 1907; ul Minskaya; bus No 130 from Universitetskaya; open 10am-6pm Tues-Thur, noon-7pm Sun). Admission is free, but only with a guide, so make arrangements in advance, especially if you want a tour in English. Otherwise you can join an existing group – usually children – at noon, 2pm or 4pm.

From the 16th century, Kitai Gorod was exclusively the home of merchants and craftsmen, as evidenced by the present-day names of its lanes: Khrustalny (crystal), Rybny (fish) and Vetoshny (rugs). Along ulitsa Ilyinka, a block south, the **old stock exchange** *(byvshaya birzha; Map 6; ul Ilyinka 2)* designates Moscow's financial heart.

Ulitsa Varvarka has Kitai Gorod's greatest concentration of interesting buildings, though they're dwarfed by Hotel Rossiya (see Places to Stay later in this chapter). The pink-and-white **St Barbara's Church** *(Tserkov Varvary; Map 2)* dates from the years 1795 to 1804 and is now given over to government offices. The reconstructed 16th-century **English House** *(Palaty starogo angliyskogo dvora; Map 2; ☎ 298 3952; admission R20; open 11am-6pm Tues-Sun)*, white with peaked wooden roofs, was the residence of England's first emissaries to Russia (sent by Elizabeth I to Ivan the Terrible). It also served as the base for English merchants, who were allowed to trade duty free in exchange for providing military supplies to Ivan.

Built in 1698, **St Maxim the Blessed's Church** *(Tserkov Maxima Blazhennogo; Map 2; ul Varvarka 4)* is now a folk-art exhibition hall. Next along is the pointed bell tower of the 17th-century **Monastery of the Sign** *(Znamensky monastyr; Map 2; ul Varvarka 8)*. The **monastery monks' building** and a **golden domed cathedral** are between the street and the western half of Hotel Rossiya's access ramp.

Between the street and the eastern half of the ramp is the small, but interesting, **Chambers in Zaryadie Museum** *(Muzey Palaty v Zaryadie; Map 2; ul Varvarka 10; admission R100; open 10am-5pm Thur-Mon, 11am-6pm Wed)*, devoted to the lives of the Romanov family, who were mere *boyars* (nobles) before they became tsars. The house was built by Nikita Romanov, whose grandson Mikhail later became the first tsar of the 300-year Romanov dynasty. The entrance is on the Hotel Rossiya side and the museum is closed on the first Monday of the month.

The colourful **St George's Church** *(Tserkov Georgiya; Map 2; ul Varvarka 12)*, another crafts gallery, dates from 1658. Off the southeastern corner of Hotel Rossiya is the pretty little 15th- and 16th- century Pskov-style **Church of St Anne's Conception** *(Tserkov Zachatiya Anny; Map 4)*. From here there are

incredible views of the Kremlin, the Moscow River and the Kotelnicheskaya apartment complex.

Opposite St George's Church, Ipatyevsky pereulok leads to the 1630s **Church of the Trinity in Nikitniki** *(Tserkov Troitsy v Nikitnikakh; Map 2)*, one of Moscow's finest (it was closed for renovation at the time of research). The church's onion domes and lovely tiers of red-and-white spade gables rise from a square tower, while the interior is covered with 1650s gospel frescoes by Simon Ushakov and others. A carved doorway leads into St Nikita the Martyr's chapel, above the vault of the Nikitnikov merchant family, one of whom built the church.

At the southern end of Staraya ploshchad, **All Saints Cathedral on the Kulishka** *(Khram vsekh svyatikh na Kulishkakh; Map 2)* was built in 1687. In 1380, Dmitry Donskoy built the original wooden church on this site, commemorating those who died in the battle of Kulikovo.

Hidden among the narrow alleyways of Kitai Gorod are more tiny churches, and ongoing renovations should produce delightful results over the next few years.

TVERSKOY REGION (MAP 2)

In spite of soulless reconstruction in the 1930s, it's hard to imagine Moscow without Tverskaya ulitsa, the beginning of the road to Tver, and therefore to St Petersburg. The bottom end of the street, by Hotel National, is the city's hub: numerous places to eat and some of Moscow's classier shops dot the slope up to Pushkinskaya ploshchad. Trolleybus Nos 12 and 20 go up and down Tverskaya ulitsa as far as Belorus Station (Belorussky vokzal).

The streets around ulitsa Tverskaya comprise the vibrant Tverskoy Region, characterised by old architecture and new commerce. Small lanes such as Kamergersky pereulok are among Moscow's trendiest places to sip a coffee or a beer and watch the big-city bustle.

Inner Tverskaya Ulitsa

Through the arch across the start of Bryusov pereulok is the unexpected little gold-domed **Church of the Resurrection** *(Tserkov Voskresenia)*. The main building, built in 1629, is full of fine icons saved from churches torn down during the Soviet era; the refectory and bell tower date from 1820.

Tverskaya ploshchad is recognisable by its **statue of Yury Dolgoruky**, traditionally considered Moscow's founder. The buffed-up five-storey building that faces it is the **Moscow Mayor's Office**. Behind the statue to the right is the 17th-century **Church of SS Cosma and Damian**.

On the eastern side of Tverskaya ulitsa, shortly before Pushkinskaya ploshchad, is the ornate **Yeliseev Grocery Store** (☎ 229 5562; 14 ul Tverskaya) named after its founding owner, Pyotr Yeliseev, whose bust can be seen in the central hall. Originally a mansion, the store has been restored to its former splendour with chandeliers, stained glass and marble columns.

Around Pushkinskaya Ploshchad

From the square that bears his name, a **Pushkin statue** surveys his domain. It seems Pushkin has been chosen to take the place of Lenin in the New Russian ideology. Behind the statue, the recently renamed **Pushkinsky Cinema** – formerly the Rossiya – is the main venue of Russian film makers and celebrities; Pushkinskaya metro station is underneath.

The square is also famous as the site of Russia's first **McDonald's**, still popular for its predictable food and predictably clean toilets.

Pushkinskaya ploshchad is the nearest thing to a Russian Fleet Street. On the northern side, east of ulitsa Tverskaya, are the **Izvestia offices** (Izvestia, formerly the newspaper of the USSR Supreme Soviet, is now a bland daily). Opposite (physically and politically) is the **Moskovskie Novosti** (Moscow News), a weekly published in several languages and a standard-bearer of reform.

Just off Pushkinskaya ploshchad stand the multiple tent roofs of the **Church of the Nativity of the Virgin in Putinki** (Map 2; ul Malaya Dmitrovka 4), which curiously contributed to a ban on tent roofs on churches by Patriarch Nikon in 1652 (the year this church was completed). Nikon thought them too Russian and secular – too far from the Church's Byzantine roots.

Boulevard Ring

Pushkinskaya ploshchad forms part of Moscow's oddest-shaped park, 8km long and 20m wide, between the two carriageways of the Boulevard Ring. Though hemmed in by traffic, the shady path down the middle of the road makes for a pleasant stroll, with many statues of Russian cultural greats. Present-day Russian culture is also represented by the street performers and phone users enjoying the park.

The Boulevard Ring was created in the late 18th and early 19th centuries, replacing Moscow's old defensive walls with boulevards and terraces of handsome buildings. Some of that era's elegance lingers in the neighbourhoods southwest of Pushkinskaya ploshchad, off Tverskoy bulvar and Nikitsky bulvar.

Trolleybus Nos 15 and 31 run both ways along the ring between Trubnaya ploshchad and Kropotkinskaya metro.

Ulitsa Petrovka

Now restored to its prerevolutionary fashionable status, ulitsa Petrovka constitutes Moscow's glossiest central shopping area (see Shopping later in this chapter).

Moscow's swankiest bathhouse, the grand 19th-century **Sandunovskiye Baths** (Sandunovskie bany, or Sanduny; Zvonarsky per), is just off ulitsa Petrovka . The historic building and luxurious setting make for a very memorable, very sensuous and very Russian experience (see Banya later in this chapter).

The **Upper St Peter Monastery** (cnr ul Petrovka & Petrovsky bulvar; admission free; open 9am-7pm daily) was founded in the 1380s, part of an early defensive ring around Moscow. The grounds are pleasant in a peaceful, near-deserted way. Churches are open only for services.

The main onion-domed **Virgin of Bogolyubovo Church** dates from the late 17th century. The loveliest structure is the brick **Cathedral of Metropolitan Pyotr** in the middle of the grounds, restored with a shingle roof. (When Peter the Great ousted the Regent Sofia in 1690, his mother was so pleased she built him this church.)

The **Moscow Museum of Contemporary Art** (☎ 231 4405; ul Petrovka 25; adult/student R90/45; open noon-8pm Wed-Fri, noon-7pm Sat-Mon) is housed in a classical 18th-century merchant's home. It contains all kinds of 20th-century paintings, sculptures and graphics, including a lovely sculpture garden in the courtyard.

Just beyond the Garden Ring, the **Museum of Decorative and Folk Art** (☎ 923 7725; ul Delegatskaya 3 & 5; admission R30; open 10am-5pm Sat-Thur) has a good two-room Palekh collection, as well as lots of regional folk art.

MOSCOW

The **Glinka Museum of Musical Culture** (☎ 972 3237; ul Fadeeva 4; admission R20; open 11am-6pm Tues-Sun), named for one of Russia's greatest nationalist composers, has over 3000 musical instruments, including 13th-century Novgorod lutes and beautiful old balalaikas.

Outer Tverskaya Ulitsa

North of Pushkinskaya ploshchad is the **Contemporary History Museum** (Muzey sovremennoy istorii; ☎ 299 6724; ul Tverskaya 21; admission R25; open 10am-6pm Tues-Sun), which provides a pretty honest account of Soviet history from the 1905 and 1917 revolutions up to the 1980s. The highlight is the extensive collection of propaganda posters, in addition to all the Bolshevik paraphernalia. Look for the picture of the giant Palace of Soviets (Dvorets Sovietov) that Stalin was going to build on the site of the blown-up – and now rebuilt – Cathedral of Christ the Saviour. English-language tours are available for R700 with advance notice.

Tverskaya ulitsa crosses the Garden Ring at Triumfalnaya ploshchad, where the **Tchaikovsky Concert Hall** and a few other theatres are clustered. Though revolutionary bard Vladimir Mayakovsky no longer lends his name to the square, his statue still surveys it and the metro station beneath is still called Mayakovskaya.

Patriarch's Pond

This peaceful fishpond, Patriarshy prudy, was immortalised by writer Mikhail Bulgakov, who had the devil appear here in The Master and Margarita, one of the most loved 20th-century Russian novels. **Bulgakov's flat** (ul Bolshaya Sadovaya 10), where he wrote the novel and lived up until his death, is around the corner on the Garden Ring. Although the empty flat used to be a hang-out for dissidents and hooligans, it now has tight security appropriate to this high-rent district.

Bolshaya Nikitskaya Ulitsa

Bolshaya Nikitskaya ulitsa runs from the Moscow State University building, on Mokhovaya ulitsa, out to the Garden Ring. In the back streets many old mansions have survived, some renovated, some dilapidated. Most of those inside the Boulevard Ring were built by the 18th-century aristocracy, outside by rising 19th-century industrialists.

With little traffic, Bolshaya Nikitskaya ulitsa is excellent for a quiet ramble.

The **Museum of Folk Art** (☎ 202 7316; Leontevsky per 7; admission free; open 11am-5pm Mon-Sat) is a one-room sampler of traditional and contemporary Russian handicrafts. Across the street, the **Stanislavsky House-Museum** (☎ 229 2855; Leontevsky per 6; admission R50; open 2pm-6pm Wed-Sun) has longer hours varying from day to day (see the boxed text 'Stanislavsky's Methods' later in this chapter).

Ploshchad Nikitskie Vorota, where Bolshaya Nikitskaya ulitsa crosses the Boulevard Ring, is named after the Nikitsky Gates in the city walls, which the ring has replaced. On its eastern side is the headquarters of the Russian news agency **ITAR-TASS**, with its windows full of news photos.

In 1831, the poet Alexander Pushkin married Natalia Goncharova in the **Church of the Grand Ascension** (Tserkov Bolshogo Voznesenia) on the western side of ploshchad Nikitskie Vorota. Six years later, he died in St Petersburg defending her honour in a duel; the **Rotunda Fountain**, erected in 1999 to commemorate the poet's 100th birthday, features the couple.

Immediately north is the fascinating 1906 Art Nouveau **Gorky House-Museum** (☎ 290 5113; ul Malaya Nikitskaya 6/2; admission free; open 10am-5pm Thur, Sat & Sun, noon-7pm Wed & Fri), which can be entered at the back. Designed by Fyodor Shekhtel and given to Gorky in 1931, the house is a visual fantasy with sculpted doorways, ceiling murals, stained glass, a carved stone staircase, and exterior tilework. There's a tale that Stalin hastened Gorky's death in 1936 by having the walls of the small ground-level bedroom covered with toxic paint.

BARRIKADNAYA (MAP 2)

The neighbourhood surrounding the intersection of Bolshaya Nikitskaya ulitsa with the Garden Ring at Kudrinskaya ploshchad is known as Barrikadnaya (barricade), so-called because it saw heavy streetfighting during the 1905 and 1917 uprisings.

Just north, on the inner side of the Garden Ring, is the **Chekhov House-Museum** (☎ 291 6154; Sadovaya-Kudrinskaya ul 6), which was closed for renovations at the time of research.

Behind Kudrinskaya ploshchad is the main entrance to the big **Moscow Zoo** (☎ 255

Stalin's Seven Sisters

The foundations for the Seven Sisters were laid in 1947 to mark Moscow's 800th anniversary. Stalin had decided that Moscow suffered from a 'skyscraper gap' compared to the USA and ordered the construction of these seven behemoths to enhance the city's skyline.

One of the main architects, Vyacheslav Oltarzhevsky, had worked in New York during that city's skyscraper boom of the 1930s and his experience proved essential. Fortunately he'd been released from a Gulag in time to help.

With their widely scattered sites, the towers provide a unique visual look and reference for Moscow. Their official name in Russia is *vystony dom* (high-rise) as opposed to *neboskryob* (foreign skyscraper), and they have been variously nicknamed 'Seven Sisters', 'wedding cakes', 'Stalin's sisters' and so on.

The seven buildings are:

Kudrinskaya apartment block (Map 2), Kudrinskaya ploshchad. Completed in 1954, it's 160m high and popular with government officials.

Kotelnicheskaya apartment block (Map 5), Kotelnicheskaya nab 17/1. Completed in 1952, this one is very ornate with multiple towers, turrets and pinnacles.

Transport Ministry (Map 3), ul Sadovaya-Spasskaya. Dates from 1953 and is 133m high.

Foreign Affairs Ministry (Map 4), Smolenskaya-Sennaya ploshchad 32/34. Completed in 1952 with 27 floors, polished granite pylons and entrance portals, and a facade with the USSR coat of arms on it.

Hotel Ukraina (Map 2), Kutuzovsky prospekt 2/1. Completed in 1957, it's 200m high with 29 floors.

Hotel Leningradskaya (Map 3), ul Kalanchevskaya 21/40. From 1954, this one is the smallest of the seven.

Moscow State University (Outer South Moscow Map), Universitetskaya ploshchad 1. Completed in 1953, it has 36 floors and is 236m high, with four huge wings.

★★★

5375; cnr uls Barrikadnaya & Bolshaya Gruzinskaya; admission R60; open 9am-8pm daily in summer, earlier off-season). Popular with families, the highlight is the big cats exhibit, although the domestic animals and the kids are fun to watch too.

The Garden Ring was created as a tree-lined boulevard in place of Moscow's old outer rampart. Today, this wide, noisy stretch of the Garden Ring makes it easy to believe the story that the ring's widening and tree-felling in the 1930s was done to enable warplanes to land.

The skyscraper at the intersection of Bolshaya Nikitskaya ulitsa with the Garden Ring is one of the Stalinist 'Seven Sisters' neo-Gothic monstrosities.

White House

Moscow's White House (Bely dom; Krasno-presnenskaya nab 2), scene of two crucial episodes in recent Russian history, stands just north of Kalininsky, a short walk west of the US embassy (Krasnopresnenskaya and Barrikadnaya are the nearest metro stations).

It was here that Boris Yeltsin rallied the opposition to confound the 1991 hardline coup, then two years later sent in tanks and troops to blast out conservative rivals – some of them the same people who backed him in 1991. The images of Yeltsin climbing onto a tank in front of the White House in 1991 and of the same building ablaze after the 1993 assault are among the most unforgettable from those tumultuous years.

The White House – now back to its original colour and officially called the House of Government of the Russian Federation (Dom pravitelstva Rossiyskoy federatsii) – fronts one of the Moscow River's stateliest bends, with the Stalinist Hotel Ukraina rising on the far bank. This corner of Moscow is particularly appealing when these buildings and Kalininsky most are lit up at night.

ARBAT REGION

Bound by the Moscow River on both sides, the region includes the area south of ulitsa Novy Arbat and north of the Garden Ring.

Ulitsa Vozdvizhenka & Ulitsa Novy Arbat (Map 2)

The start of the road west to Smolenskis formed by ulitsa Vozdvizhenka (running west

Arbat, My Arbat

Arbat, my Arbat, You are my calling
You are my happiness and my misfortune.

Bulat Okudjava

For Moscow's beloved bard Bulat Okudjava, the Arbat was not only his home, it was his inspiration. Although he spent his university years in Georgia dabbling in harmless verse, it was only upon his return to Moscow – and to his cherished Arbat – that his poetry adopted the freethinking character for which it is known.

He gradually made the transition from poet to songwriter, stating that, 'Once I had the desire to accompany one of my satirical verses with music. I only knew three chords; now, 27 years later, I know seven chords, then I knew three. I sang, my friends liked it, and I liked it... Gradually a scandal began. The composers hated me. The singers detested me. The guitarists were terrified by me. And that is how it went on, until a very well-known poet of ours announced: 'Calm down, these are not songs. This is just another way of presenting poetry.'

And so a new form of art was born. The 1960s were heady times – in Moscow as elsewhere – and Okudjava inspired a whole movement of liberal-thinking poets to take their ideas to the streets. Vladimir Vysotsky and others – some political, some not – all followed in Okudjava's footsteps, their iconoclastic lyrics and simple melodies drawing enthusiastic crowds all around Moscow.

The Arbat today – crowded with tacky souvenir stands and overpriced cafés – bears little resemblance to the hallowed haunt of Okudjava's youth. But its memory lives on in the bards and buskers, painters and poets who still perform for strolling crowds on summer evenings.

★★★★★★★★★★★★★★★★★★★★★

from the Kremlin) and ulitsa Novy Arbat (the continuation to the Moscow River).

The 'Moorish Castle' studded with seashells was built in 1899 for Arseny Morozov, an eccentric merchant, who was inspired by the real thing in Spain; the inside is sumptuous and equally over the top. Morozov's home is now the **House of Friendship with Peoples of Foreign Countries** (ul Vozdvizhenka 16), which is not normally open to the public, although exhibitions are sometimes held here. The 'castle' apparently inspired Morozov's mother to declare to him, 'Until now, only I knew you were mad; now everyone will'.

Ulitsa Novy Arbat, which begins beyond the Boulevard Ring, was created in the 1960s, with four matching ministry highrises. At the corner of ulitsas Novy Arbat and Povarskaya, the 24-storey high-rise overwhelms the small **Church of St Simeon the Stylite** (Tserkov Simeona Stolpnika), built in the middle of the 17th century.

Ulitsa Arbat

Ulitsa Arbat is a 1.25km pedestrian mall stretching from Arbatskaya ploshchad (metro Arbatskaya) on the Boulevard Ring to Smolenskaya ploshchad (metro Smolenskaya) on the Garden Ring. Moscow's most famous street, it's something of an art market, complete with instant portrait painters, soapbox poets, jugglers and buskers (as well as some pickpockets). The Arbat is an interesting walk, dotted with old pastel-coloured merchant houses and tourist-oriented shops and cafés.

Until the 1960s, ulitsa Arbat was Moscow's main westward artery. Then a swathe was bulldozed through streets to its north to create the present ulitsa Novy Arbat, taking out the old Arbatskaya ploshchad, a monastery and half-a-dozen churches. Ulitsa Arbat itself lay like a severed limb, until restored as a pedestrian precinct in the 1980s.

The evocative names of nearby lanes – Khlebny (Bread), Skatertny (Tablecloth), Serebryany (Silver), Plotnikov (Carpenters') – and that of the peaceful quarter south of the Arbat, called Staraya Konyushennaya (Old Stables), identify the area as an old settlement of court attendants (who were eventually displaced by artists and aristocrats).

At Spasopeskosky pereulok, one of the side lanes, there is the 17th-century **Church of the Saviour in Peski** (Tserkov Spasa na Peskakh; Map 2). At the far end of the lane is the elegant **Spaso House** (Map 2), the residence of the US ambassador. Near ulitsa Arbat's eastern end is the **Wall of Peace** (Stena Mira; Map 2), composed of hundreds of individually painted tiles on a theme of international friendship.

In a side street stands the refreshingly bizarre **Melnikov House** (Dom Melnikova;

Map 4; Krivoarbatsky per 10). This concoction of brick, plaster and diamond-shaped windows was built in 1927 by Konstantin Melnikov, the great constructivist architect who, despite being denounced in the 1930s, was respected around the world. Melnikov continued to live in the house (which was one of the few privately owned in the USSR) until his death in 1974.

The statue at the corner of Plotnikov pereulok is of **Bulat Okudjava** *(Map 4)*, a 1960s cult poet, singer and songwriter, much of whose work was dedicated to the Arbat (he lived at No 43; see the earlier boxed text 'Arbat, My Arbat').

At the western end of the street is the **Pushkin Arbat House-Museum** *(Map 4; ☎ 241 4212; ul Arbat 53; admission R25; open 11am-6pm Tues-Sun),* a house where the Pushkins lived after they married. The street ends with one of Stalin's 'Seven Sisters', the **Foreign Affairs Ministry** *(Ministerstvo innostrannykh del; Map 4).*

Pushkin Fine Arts Museum

Moscow's premier foreign-art museum is just a skip from the southwestern corner of the Kremlin. The Pushkin Fine Arts Museum *(Map 4; ☎ 203 7412; ul Volkhonka 12; metro Kropotkinskaya; adult/student R160/60; open 10am-6pm Tues-Sun)* is famous for its impressionist and postimpressionist paintings, but also has a broad selection of European works from the Renaissance onwards, mostly appropriated from private collections after the revolution. There is also an amazing (read: mind-numbing) array of statues through the ages. An audio guide will cost you R100.

Keep an eye open for any special exhibitions at the Pushkin. In recent years – like the Hermitage in St Petersburg – it has revealed some fabulous art hoards kept secret since seizure by the Red Army from Germany at the end of WWII. The museum is also making an effort to mount some ambitious temporary exhibitions from its vast legitimate holdings.

The highlight of the Pushkin's permanent display is the four incredible rooms of impressionist and postimpressionist paintings and sculpture. **Room 22** has Monets and Renoirs; **room 18** has many Gauguins and Cézannes; **room 17** has Picasso, Matisse and Rousseau; and **room 21** has several Van Goghs and Degas. But don't neglect the 17th-century Dutch and Flemish paintings, including several Rembrandt portraits in **room 10**. The ancient Egyptian collection in **room 1** is also very impressive; enter via rooms 3, 4 and 2. Some rooms have labels in English.

Around the Pushkin Fine Arts Museum (Map 4)

Next door to the Pushkin is the **Museum of Private Collections** *(☎ 203 1546; ul Volkhonka 14; admission R40; open noon-7pm Wed-Sun),* with art collections donated by private individuals, many of whom amassed the works during the Soviet era. The collectors/donors are featured along with the art.

The lopsided church beside the Pushkin is **St Antipy-by-the-Carriagehouse** *(Tserkov Antipia na kolymazhnom dvore; ul Kolymazhnaya 8),* supposedly commissioned by Malyuta Skuratov, the psychopath who ran the secret police for Ivan the Terrible.

Nearby, the gargantuan **Cathedral of Christ the Saviour** *(Khram Khrista Spasitelya; ☎ 201 3847; open 10am-5pm daily)* is a dream come true for Moscow mayor Yuri Luzhkov. It sits on the site of an earlier and similar church of the same name, built in 1839–83 to commemorate Russia's victory over Napoleon; this was destroyed during Stalin's orgy of explosive secularism. Stalin planned to replace the church with a 315m-high 'Palace of Soviets' (including a 100m statue of Lenin) but the project never got off the ground – literally. Instead, for 50 years the site served an important purpose: as the world's largest swimming pool.

This time around, the church was completed in a mere two years and at an estimated cost of US$350 million, in time for Moscow's 850th birthday in 1997. Much of the work was done by Luzhkov's favourite architect Zarub Tsereteli, and it has aroused a range of reactions from Muscovites, from pious devotion to abject horror. If they are missing their swimming pool, however, Muscovites should at least be grateful they can admire the shiny domes of a church instead of the shiny dome of Lenin's head.

Prechistenka Ulitsa & Beyond (Map 4)

Prechistenka ulitsa, heading southwest from Kropotkinskaya metro, is virtually a classical mansion museum; most date from empire-style rebuilding after the great fire of 1812.

MOSCOW

MOSCOW

Yuri Luzhkov, Christopher Columbus & Princess Diana

Zarub Tsereteli is nothing if not controversial. As the chief architect of the Okhotny Ryad shopping mall and the massive Cathedral of Christ the Saviour, he has been criticised for being too ostentatious, gaudy, overbearing – and just plain too much.

The most despised of Tsereteli's masterpieces is the gargantuan statue of Peter the Great, which now stands in front of the Krasny Oktyabr chocolate factory. At 94.5m (that's twice the size of the Statue of Liberty without her pedestal), Peter towers over the city. Questions of taste aside, Muscovites were sceptical of the whole idea – why pay tribute to Peter the Great, who loathed Moscow, and even moved the capital away to St Petersburg? Some radicals even attempted (unsuccessfully) to blow the thing up. Today, a 24-hour guard stands watch.

Mixed reactions (to put it mildly) are nothing new to Tsereteli. An earlier sculpture of Christopher Columbus has been rejected by five North American cities for reasons of cost, size and aesthetics. Some believe that the Peter the Great statue is actually a reincarnation of homeless Chris.

Despite his critics, who launched a 'Stop Tsereteli' website, the favourite artist of Moscow Mayor Yuri Luzhkov just does not stop. In 2001 he unveiled a 2m bronze statue of Princess Diana, in honour of her 40th birthday. The Princess of Wales – decked out in a ruffled gown and tiara – was supposed to appear in an unnamed Moscow museum, but she seems to have skipped town.

Tsereteli's latest subject is Mayor Luzhkov himself: this 3m bronze statue has a tennis racket in his hand and a ball at his feet. Tsereteli said that he hopes the statue will be mounted in one of Moscow's parks, where the mayor can inspire Muscovites to adopt a more active and sporty lifestyle.

Rumour has it that Tsereteli's next project will be a theme park in the northwest suburb of Nizhni Mnevniki. Apparently, a 280-hectare plot has already been designated for the so-called 'Park of Wonders', which will be based on Russian fairy tales. As one Moscow journalist observed, 'For the sake of the children, let's hope Tsereteli's fairy tale heroes are not as scary as his Peter the Great'.

★★

The **Pushkin Literary Museum** (☎ 201 3256; Prechistenka ul 12; admission R25; open 11am-6pm Tues, Wed & Fri-Sun; 2pm-7pm Thur) is devoted to Pushkin's life and work. Across the street, the **Tolstoy Museum** (☎ 202 2190; Prechistenka ul 11; adult/student R100/50; open 11am-6pm Tues-Sun) contains Tolstoy's manuscripts, letters and sketches. The **Russian Academy of Art** (Prechistenka ul 19-21) has an exhibition hall.

KHAMOVNIKI REGION

The Moscow River surrounds this region on three sides, as it dips down south and loops back up to the north. The northern boundary is the Garden Ring, and across from it (from the Prechistenka ulitsa end) is the shady **Skver Devichego Polya** (Maiden's Field) park, with its brooding Tolstoy statue.

The interesting **Tolstoy Estate-Museum** (Map 4; ☎ 246 9444; ul Lva Tolstogo 21) was the writer's winter home during the 1880s and 1890s. While it's not particularly big or opulent, it is fitting for junior nobility – which Tolstoy was. Upstairs, Rachmaninov and Rimsky-Korsakov played piano in the reception room. Tolstoy's training weights and bicycle repose outside the study. The house was redone in 2002, and it has English-language notices of exploration.

At the southern end of ulitsa Lva Tolstogo, the beautiful **Church of St Nicholas of the Weavers** (Tserkov Nikoli v Khamovnikakh; Map 4; ul Lva Tolstogo) vies with St Basil's Cathedral as the most colourful in Moscow. Commissioned by the Moscow weavers guild in 1676, it indeed looks like a great, jolly green-and-orange tapestry. Inside are equally rich frescoes and icons.

Novodevichy Convent (Novodevichy Convent Map)

A cluster of sparkling domes behind turreted walls on the Moscow River, Novodevichy Convent (Novodevichy monastyr; ☎ 246 8526; admission R30; open 10am-5pm Wed-Mon) is rich with history and treasures. The adjacent Novodevichy Cemetery is Moscow's most prestigious resting place after the Kremlin wall, with many famous tombs. The name 'Novodevichy' (New Maidens) probably originates from a market, once held in the

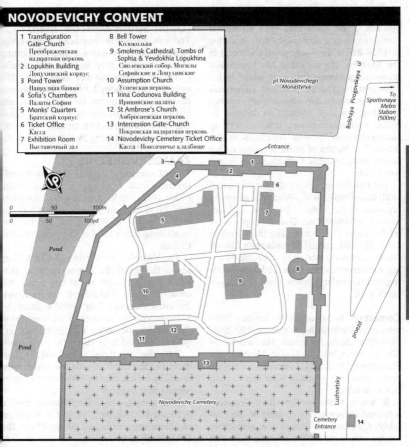

NOVODEVICHY CONVENT

1 Transfiguration
  Gate-Church
  Преображенская
  надвратная церковь
2 Lopukhin Building
  Лопухинский корпус
3 Pond Tower
  Напрудная башня
4 Sofia's Chambers
  Палаты Софии
5 Monks' Quarters
  Братский корпус
6 Ticket Office
  Касса
7 Exhibition Room
  Выставочный зал

8 Bell Tower
  Колокольня
9 Smolensk Cathedral; Tombs of
  Sofia & Yevdokia Lopukhina
  Смоленский собор. Могилы
  Софийские и Лопухинские
10 Assumption Church
  Успенская церковь
11 Irina Godunova Building
  Иринниские палаты
12 St Ambrose's Church
  Амбросиевская церковь
13 Intercession Gate-Church
  Покровская надвратная церковь
14 Novodevichy Cemetery Ticket Office
  Касса - Новодевичье кладбище

pl Novodevichego
Monastyrya

Bolshaya Pirogovskaya ul

To
Sportivnaya
Metro
Station
(500m)

Entrance

Pond

Pond

Novodevichy Cemetery

Cemetery
Entrance

Luzhnetsky

proezd

0   50   100m
0   50   100yd

MOSCOW

locality, where Tatars bought Russian girls to sell to Muslim harems.

Trolleybus Nos 5 and 15 come here down Prechistenka ulitsa and ulitsa Bolshaya Pirogovskaya from Kropotkinskaya metro station. Sportivnaya metro is 500m to the south.

Convent The convent was founded in 1524 to celebrate the taking of Smolensk from Lithuania, an important step in Moscow's conquest of the old Kyivan Rus lands. Novodevichy was rebuilt by Peter the Great's half-sister Sofia, who used it as a second residence when she ruled Russia as regent in the 1680s.

When Peter, aged 17, deposed Sofia in 1689, he confined her to Novodevichy; in 1698 she was imprisoned here for life after being implicated in the Streltsy rebellion (it's said Peter had some of her supporters hanged outside her window to remind her not to meddle). Sofia was joined in her retirement by Yevdokia Lopukhina, Peter's first wife, whom he considered a nag.

You can enter the convent through the red-and-white Moscow-baroque **Transfiguration Gate-Church** (Preobrazhenskaya nadvratnaya Tserkov), built in the north wall between 1687 and 1689. The first building on the left contains a room for temporary exhibitions. Yevdokia Lopukhina lived in the **Lopukhin Building** (Lopukhinsky korpus) against the north wall and Sofia, probably, in the chambers adjoining the **Pond Tower** (Naprudnaya bashnya).

The oldest and dominant building in the grounds is the white **Smolensk Cathedral** *(Smolensky sobor; admission R60)*. Modelled in 1524–25 on the Assumption Cathedral in the Kremlin, the cathedral has beautifully proportioned domes that were added in the 17th century. The walls of the sumptuous interior are covered in 16th-century frescoes and there's a huge iconostasis donated by Sofia, with contemporary icons as well as some more icons from the time of Boris Godunov. The **tombs** of Sofia, a couple of her sisters and Yevdokia Lopukhina are in the south nave.

The **bell tower**, against the convent's east wall, was completed in 1690 and is generally regarded as the finest in Moscow. The red-and-white **Assumption Church** (Uspenskaya tserkov) and its refectory date from 1685 to 1687. The 16th-century **St Ambrose's Church** (Ambrosievskaya tserkov) is adjoined by another refectory and the **Irina Godunov Building** (Irinskie palaty), where Boris Godunov's sister lived.

Cemetery The Novodevichy Cemetery *(Novodevichiye kladbishche; admission R30; open 9am-6pm daily)* contains the tombs of Khrushchev, Chekhov, Gogol, Mayakovsky, Stanislavsky, Prokofiev, Eisenstein, Gromyko, and a mixed bag of many other Russian and Soviet notables.

In Soviet times Novodevichy Cemetery was used for some very eminent people (notably Khrushchev), whom the authorities judged unsuitable for the Kremlin wall. The intertwined white-and-black blocks round Khrushchev's bust were intended by sculptor Ernst Neizvestny to represent Khrushchev's good and bad sides.

The tombstone of Nadezhda Allilueva, Stalin's second wife, is surrounded by unbreakable glass to prevent vandalism; apparently, her nose was once broken off. Allilueva committed suicide in 1932.

A recent addition is Raisa Gorbachev, the sophisticated wife of the last Soviet premier. She died of leukaemia in 1999.

Tickets to the cemetery are sold at a **kiosk** across the street from the entrance on Luzhnetsky proezd (the continuation of ulitsa Bolshaya Pirogovskaya). If you want to investigate this place in depth, buy the Russian map on sale at the kiosk, which pinpoints nearly 200 graves.

Luzhniki (Outer South Moscow Map)

The area within the river bend southwest o Novodevichy contains a group of sportin stadiums collectively known as Luzhnik ('Marshes' – what the area used to be). Th main 80,000 capacity **Luzhniki Stadium** wa the chief venue for the 1980 Olympics, an had a huge renovation in the late 1990s. Coin cidentally, the contract for the new seats wen to a company controlled by the mayor's wife

ZAMOSKVORECHIE

Zamoskvorechie ('Beyond-Moscow-River' stretches south from opposite the Kremlin inside a big river loop. In this part of the cit you'll find Moscow's most famous park, it premier gallery of Russian art, and the cur rent headquarters of the Russian Orthodo> Church.

The Vodootvodny (Drainage) Canal slice across the top of the Zamoskvorechie, pre venting spring floods in the city centre an creating a sliver of island opposite the Krem lin. From the south, Tatars used to attack, s Moscow's defensive forces were stationed i Zamoskvorechie, along with merchants an quarters devoted to servicing the royal court

After the Tatar threat abated and the cour moved to St Petersburg, the merchants were joined by nobles, then by 19th-century factor ies and their workers.

Little damaged by Stalin, Zamoskvorechi is a varied, intriguing area, and from almos any place here you can see the giant **Peter the Great sculpture** (for more on this modern monolith, see the earlier boxed text 'Yur Luzhkov, Christopher Columbus & Princes Diana').

Gorky Park (Map 4)

Stretching almost 3km along the river up stream of Krymsky most, Gorky Park is ful of that (sometimes) rare species, the happy Russian. Officially the 'Park of Culture' *(Parl Kultury imeni A M Gorkogo;* ☎ *237 1266 ul Krymsky val; admission R25; open 10am sundown)*, it's named after Maxim Gorky The main entrance is 500m from either Parl Kultury or Oktyabrskaya metro.

Part ornamental park, part funfair, it's ¿ good place to escape the hubbub of the city In winter the ponds freeze and the paths are flooded to make a giant skating rink; you cai rent skates if you take along ID.

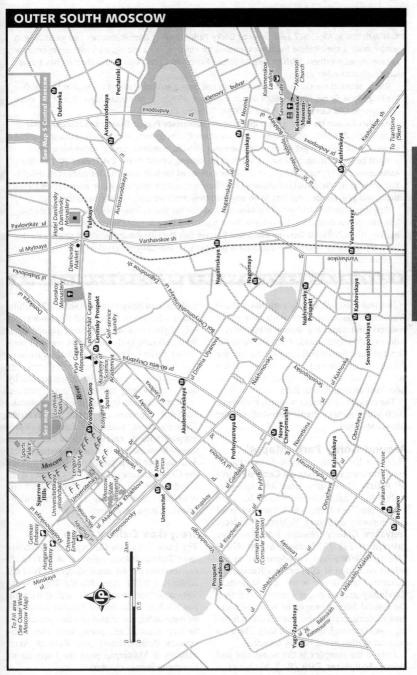

OUTER SOUTH MOSCOW

MOSCOW

Moscow for Children

Kids with you in Moscow? Take them to **Gorky Park** – thrilling rides in summer and ice skating in winter make it the ultimate Russian experience for children. For a more post-Soviet experience (or in case of bad weather), **VDNKh** (see All-Russia Exhibition Centre later in this chapter) has a pavilion devoted to video games.

Russia excels at the circus, and crazy clowns and daring acrobatics are all the rage at two locales: the huge **New Circus** (Outer South Moscow Map; ☎ 930 2815; pr Vernadskogo 7), and the more atmospheric **Old Circus** (Map 2; ☎ 200 0068; Tsvetnoy bulvar 13).

Another Russian favourite is the puppet theatre. **Obraztsov Puppet Theatre and Museum** (Map 2; ☎ 299 3310, 299 5563; ul Sadovaya Samotyochnaya 3) runs colourful Russian folk tales and adapted classical plays; kids can get up-close and personal with the incredible puppets at the museum.

What better entertainment for kiddies than performing kitties? At the **Cat Theatre** (☎ 249 2907; Kutuzovsky pr 25), Yuri Kuklachev's acrobatic cats do all kinds of stunts to the audience's delight. Kuklachev says, 'We do not use the word *train* here because it implies forcing an animal to do something; and you cannot force cats to do anything they don't want to. We *play* with the cats.'

Bigger cats are the highlight of the **Moscow Zoo** (see the Barrikadnaya section earlier in this chapter), an obvious destination for children. For a trip out of the city, take the young ones to the bison nursery at the **Prioksko-Terrasny Biosphere Reserve** (see the later Around Moscow chapter for details), where highly informative educational programs are especially designed for kids.

Have fun!

★★

But that's not all: Gorky Park has a small Western amusement park with two roller coasters and almost a dozen other terror-inducing attractions (aside from the Peter the Great statue). Space buffs can shed a tear for the *Buran*, the Soviet space shuttle which never carried anyone into space. Most of the rides cost around R10 to R20.

The park has a number of snack bars and a 2000-seat German **beer hall** behind the amusement park.

Around Gorky Park (Map 4)

There's a big block opposite Gorky Park's main entrance, containing the **Central House of Artists** (Tsentralny dom khudozhnika; ☎ 238 9634; adult/student R220/110; open 11am-7pm Tues-Sun), which puts on good contemporary art shows. Behind it, the **New Tretyakov Gallery** (Novaya Tretyakovskaya galereya; ☎ 238 1378; adult/student R220/110; open 10am-7pm Tues-Sun) has an excellent collection of 20th-century Russian art featuring innovative work by Malevich, Kandinsky and others; it's much more than the typical heroic images of muscle-bound men wielding scythes and busty women milking cows (although there's that too). There's a busy art market in the nearby arcade.

Behind the complex is the wonderful and moody **Sculptures Park** (Park Skulptur), a collection of Soviet statues (Stalin, Dzerzhinsky, a selection of Lenins and Brezhnevs) put out to pasture when they were ripped from their pedestals in the post-1991 wave of anti-Soviet feeling. These discredited icons have now been joined by contemporary work, including an eerie bust of Stalin surrounded by heads representing millions of purge victims.

Nearby stands the finest of all Zamoskvorechie churches, **St John the Warrior** (Tserkov Ivana voina; ul Bolshaya Yakimanka), with its colourful, tiled domes and mix of Moscow and European baroque styles. Said to have been partly designed by Peter the Great in thanks for his 1709 victory over Sweden at Poltava, it's a working church but is often locked. The big 17th-century iconostasis is reputedly a masterpiece.

Tretyakov Gallery (Map 4)

The State Tretyakov Gallery (Gosudarstvennaya Tretyakovskaya galereya; ☎ 951 1362; Lavrushinsky per 10; adult/student R220/110, audio tour R120; open 10am-6.30pm Tues-Sun) is nothing short of spectacular, with the world's best collection of Russian icons and an outstanding collection of other prerevolutionary Russian art, particularly the 19th-century Peredvizhniki (see Russian Arts: Masters & Masterpieces in the Facts about European Russia chapter).

The collection is based on that of the 19th-century industrialist brothers Pavel and Sergey Tretyakov (Pavel was a patron of the Peredvizhniki). The original part of the building was created in the likeness of an old boyar castle by Viktor Vasnetsov between 1900 and 1905.

Much of the Tretyakov's collection of religious art was confiscated from churches during the Soviet era; now that the Church wants its icons back, the Tretyakov has had to battle to keep its most precious treasures. For the moment at least, it has fended off the pressure by also restoring the **Church of St Nicholas** within its grounds. About 200 icons are displayed there, and the building functions as both church and museum.

Orientation The 62 rooms are numbered and progress in chronological order from rooms 1 to 54, followed by eight rooms holding icons and jewellery. The exhibits begin on the ground level. Most Peredvizhniki are in **rooms 20, 23 and 24**, except in those cases where an artist has a hall to himself. Icons reside on the ground floor in **rooms 55 to 62**. Rublyov's *Holy Trinity* (1420s) from Sergiev Posad, widely regarded as Russia's greatest icon, is in **room 60**. Vrubel's masterpieces, including *Demon Seated* (1890), are in **room 33**.

The entrance to the gallery is through a lovely courtyard; show up early to beat the queues. Thanks to a lavish renovation during the early 1990s, the entire gallery is accessible to wheelchairs.

Ulitsa Bolshaya Ordynka & Ulitsa Pyatnitskaya (Map 4)

The atmosphere of 19th-century Moscow lives on in the low buildings, old courtyards and clusters of onion domes along narrow ulitsa Bolshaya Ordynka, which runs 2km down the middle of Zamoskvorechie to Serpukhovskaya ploshchad. Ulitsa Pyatnitskaya is roughly parallel 200m to the east. The many churches make up a scrapbook of Muscovite architectural styles. The name 'Ordynka' comes from *orda* (horde); until the 16th century, this was the start of the road to the Golden Horde's capital on the Volga, where Tatar ambassadors lived.

If you head south from Maly Moskvoretsky most, the first lane on the right contains the tall **Resurrection Church in Kadashi**, a

restoration centre for other churches. Its rich, late-17th-century decoration is a fine example of so-called Moscow baroque. The tall and elegant belfry earned the nickname 'the candle'.

The small, white **SS Mikhail and Fyodor Church** *(Chernigovsky per)*, dating from the late 17th century, has two rows of spade gables and five domes on a thin tower. The larger **St John the Baptist Church**, from the same period, houses an exhibition of unusual Russian glassware; St John's **bell tower**, a Zamoskvorechie landmark fronting ulitsa Pyatnitskaya, was added in 1753.

The empire-style **Virgin of Consolation of All Sorrows Church** *(ul Bolshaya Ordynka 20)*, mostly dates from between 1828 and 1833. Klimentovsky pereulok leads to **St Clement's Church** *(ul Pyatnitskaya 26)*, built between 1742 and 1774, a rare Moscow example of the true baroque style favoured by Empress Elizabeth.

The blue-and-white **Church of St Nicholas in Pyzhi** *(ul Bolshaya Ordynka 27A)*, a working church, is a typical five-domed, mid-17th-century church, with spade gables and thin onion domes. **SS Martha and Mary Convent** *(ul Bolshaya Ordynka 34A)*, with its pretty, single-domed Intercession Church, now houses church restoration offices. The church and gates were built between 1908 and 1912 in neo-Russian style. At the beginning of the 20th century, the convent was famous for charity work; it has recently reopened. The church is open only for services, but the interior frescoes are worth a visit.

Danilovsky Monastery (Outer South Moscow Map)

The headquarters of the Russian Orthodox Church stands behind white fortress walls, a five-minute walk east of Tulskaya metro. The Danilovsky Monastery *(Danilovsky Monastyr; ☎ 955 6757; Danilovsky val; admission free; open 7am-7pm daily)* was built in the late 13th century by Daniil, the first Prince of Moscow, as an outer city defence. It was repeatedly altered over the next several hundred years, and served as a factory and a detention centre during the Soviet period.

However, it was restored in time to replace Sergiev Posad as the Church's spiritual and administrative centre and become the official residence of the Patriarch during the Russian Orthodoxy's millennium celebrations in 1988.

Today, it radiates an air of purpose befitting the Church's role in modern Russia.

On holy days in particular, the place seethes with worshippers murmuring prayers, lighting candles and ladling holy water into jugs at the tiny chapel inside the gates. Enter beneath the pink **St Simeon Stylites Gate-Church** on the north wall. Its bells are the first in Moscow to ring on holy days.

The monastery's oldest and busiest church is the **Church of the Holy Fathers of the Seven Ecumenical Councils**, where worship is held continuously from 10am to 5pm daily. Founded in the 17th century and rebuilt repeatedly, the church contains several chapels on two floors: the main one upstairs is flanked by side chapels to St Daniil (on the northern side) and SS Boris and Gleb (south). On the ground level the small main chapel is dedicated to the Protecting Veil, and the northern one to the prophet Daniil.

The yellow, neoclassical **Trinity Cathedral**, built in the 1830s, is an austere counterpart to the other buildings.

Donskoy Monastery (Outer South Moscow Map)

Founded in 1591, the Donskoy Monastery *(Donskoy monastyr; ☎ 952 1646)*, the youngest of Moscow's fortified monasteries, is a five-minute walk from Shabolovskaya metro. It was built to house the *Virgin of the Don* icon (now in the Tretyakov Gallery), which was credited with victory in the 1380 battle of Kulikovo. It's also said that in 1591, the Tatar Khan Giri retreated without a fight after the icon showered him with burning arrows in a dream.

Most of the monastery, surrounded by a brick wall with 12 towers, was built between 1684 and 1733 under Regent Sofia and Peter the Great. From 1918 to 1927, it was the Russian Orthodox Church headquarters; later, it was closed as a monastery, falling into neglect despite being used as an architecture museum. Restored in 1990 and 1991, it's now back in Church hands.

The **Virgin of Tikhvin Church** over the north gate, built in 1713 and 1714, is one of the last examples of Moscow baroque. In the centre of the grounds is the large, brick **New Cathedral**, built between 1684 and 1693; just to its south is the smaller **Old Cathedral**, dating from 1591 to 1593.

When burials in central Moscow were banned after a 1771 plague, the Donskoy Monastery became a graveyard for the nobility, and it is littered with elaborate tombs and chapels. At ulitsa Donskaya, leading north from the monastery, there is the **Church of the Deposition of the Robe**, built in 1701.

ZAYAUZIE
Around Taganskaya Ploshchad (Map 5)

Taganskaya ploshchad on the Garden Ring is a monster intersection – loud, dusty and crowded. It's the hub of Zayauzie, the area south of the little Yauza River, and the territory of the 17th-century blacksmiths guild; later it became an Old Believers' quarter. The square's character disappeared with reconstruction in the 1970s and 1980s, but traces remain in the streets radiating from it.

The great block is the **Taganka Theatre** *(cnr Taganskaya pl & Verkhnyaya Radishchevskaya ul)*, famous in the Soviet era for director Yury Lyubimov's vaguely subversive repertoire – ranging from updated Chekhov to modern Russian and Western works, this annoyed the Soviet authorities and delighted everyone else.

Behind metro Taganskaya is the sombre **Taganka Gates Church of St Nicholas**, from 1712. More fetching is the **Potters' Church of the Assumption** *(ul Goncharnaya 29)*, built in 1654, with its star-spangled domes. Note the tile work under the 'extra' refectory dome.

Ulitsa Goncharnaya leads north to two impressive classical mansions at Nos 12 and 16, and to the **Church of St Nikita Beyond the Yauza**, which has 15th-century foundations, 16th-century walls, 17th-century chapels and an 18th-century bell tower. The church is dwarfed by the **Kotelnicheskaya apartment block**, one of the Stalinist Gothic 'Seven Sisters' skyscrapers built around 1950 (see the earlier boxed text 'Stalin's Seven Sisters').

Northeast of Taganskaya, you can't miss the grand **Cathedral of St Martin the Confessor** *(ul Bolshaya Kommunisticheskaya 15)*, built in 1792 in shameless imitation of London's St Paul's Cathedral. Though it was badly neglected during the Soviet period, it's now open and being renovated. This whole neighbourhood has a look of abandoned grace.

Andronikov Monastery & Andrey Rublyov Museum (Map 5)

The fortified, 1360 Andronikov Monastery *(Spaso-Andronikov monastyr; Andronyevskaya pl)* is on the banks of the Yauza – just over a kilometre northeast of Taganskaya ploshchad, near the Ploshchad Ilyicha metro. Andrey Rublyov, the master of icon painting, was a monk here in the 15th century; he's buried in the grounds, but no-one knows quite where.

In the centre of the grounds is the compact **Saviour's Cathedral**, built in 1427, the oldest stone building in Moscow. The posy of *kokoshniki*, or tiers of colourful tiles and brick patterns, is typical of Russian architecture from the era. To the left is the combined rectory and 17th-century Moscow-baroque **Church of the Archangel Michael**. To the right, in the old monks' quarters, is the **Andrey Rublyov Museum of Early Russian Culture and Art** (☎ 278 1467; *Andronyevskaya pl 10; admission R60; open 11am-6pm Thur-Tues*), an icon museum with nothing by Rublyov himself. What is there, however, is lovely, including a few strong, luminous 14th- to 16th-century works interestingly juxtaposed.

Novospassky Monastery (Map 5)
One kilometre south of Taganskaya ploshchad is the **New Monastery of the Saviour** (*Novospassky Monastyr; ☎ 276 9570; Verkhny Novospassky proezd; metro Proletarskaya; admission free; open 7am-7pm Mon-Sat, 8am-7pm Sun*), another of Moscow's fort-monasteries. It dates from the 15th century, when it was relocated from inside the Kremlin. Under restoration for at least 30 years, it became a working monastery again in the early 1990s.

The centrepiece, the **Transfiguration Cathedral**, was built by the imperial Romanov family in the 1640s in imitation of the Kremlin's Assumption Cathedral. Frescoes depict the history of Christianity in Russia, and the Romanov family tree, which goes as far back as the Viking Prince Rurik, climbs one wall.

To the left is the **Intercession Church** (1675), joined to the refectory and bakery buildings. Under the river bank, beneath one of the monastery towers, is the site of a mass grave for thousands of Stalin's victims.

Across the road, south of Novospassky, is the sumptuous **Krutitskoe Podvorye** (*ecclesiastical residence; admission free; open 10am-6pm Wed-Mon*), used by the Moscow metropolitans from the 16th century, when they lost their place in the Kremlin after the founding of the Russian patriarchate. At the northern end of the grounds is the brick **Assumption Cathedral** and an extraordinary

Moscow-baroque **gate tower**, with friezes in unexpected yellows and blues.

Rogozhskoe Cemetery & Old Believers' Community (Map 5)
One of Russia's most atmospheric religious centres is the **Old Believers' Community** (*Staroobryadcheskaya Obshchina; admission free; open 9am-6pm Tues-Sun*), located at Rogozhskoe, 3km east of Taganskaya ploshchad. The Old Believers split from the main Russian Orthodox Church in 1653 when they refused to accept certain reforms. They have maintained old forms of worship and customs ever since.

In the late 18th century, during a brief period free of persecution, rich Old Believer merchants set up what is perhaps the most important Old Believers' community – around their **Rogozhskoe Cemetery** (Rogozhskoe kladbishche). The place remains an island of old Russia to this day, with dark, mysterious churches.

To get there, take trolleybus No 16 or 26, or bus No 51, east from Taganskaya ploshchad along ulitsa Taganskaya and ulitsa Nizhegorodskaya; get off after crossing a railway. Rogozhskoe's tall, green-domed 20th-century **bell tower** is clearly visible to the north (left). The yellow classical-style **Intercession Church** contains one of Moscow's finest collections of icons, all dating from before 1653, with the oldest being the 14th-century *Saviour with the Angry Eye* (Spas yaroe oko), protected under glass near the south door.

The icons in the deesis row (the biggest row) of the iconostasis are supposed to represent the Rublyov school, while the seventh, *The Saviour*, is attributed to Rublyov himself.

CHISTYE PRUDY (MAP 3)
This area encompasses the streets off Chistoprudny bulvar, between ulitsas Myasnitskaya and Pokrovka to the northeast of the Kremlin. Myasnitskaya means 'butchers' and in the late 17th century the area was known for this profession; logically, its ponds were filthy. Peter the Great gave the area to his pal Alexander Menshikov, who launched a bit of a PR campaign, renaming it Chistye Prudy (Clean Ponds). Apparently, he did actually have them cleaned first.

The area boasts the first Moscow post office, founded in 1783 in one of the houses of the former Menshikov estate. Hidden behind

MOSCOW

the post office is the famous **Menshikov Tower** (Menshikova bashnya), built in 1704–06 by the order of Menshikov at his newly founded estate. The tower was originally 3m taller than the Ivan the Great Bell Tower in the Kremlin and was one of Moscow's first baroque buildings. In 1723 it was hit by lightning during a thunderstorm and seriously damaged by fire.

Trouble plagued the owner as well: Menshikov fell from grace after Peter the Great's death and was exiled to Siberia. The tower was neglected for several decades and when finally repaired in the 1780s, it lost much of its height and elegance. Today it houses the working **Church of Archangel Gabriel**.

Chistoprudny bulvar is a pleasant stroll in itself. The pond has paddle boats in summer and an **ice-skating rink** in winter, or you can simply pick a café and (depending on the season) sip a beer or coffee while watching the boats or skaters go by.

Komsomolskaya Ploshchad

From Chistye Prudy, prospekt Akademika Sakharova leads northeast to Komsomolskaya ploshchad, Moscow's transportation hub. In one square the three main railway stations capture Moscow's architectural diversity, along with diverse and dubious crowds; it's among the city's busiest and hairiest centres.

Leningrad Station (Leningradsky vokzal), with its tall clock tower, is on the northern side of the square and is Moscow's oldest railway station (built in 1851). It's very similar to its opposite number at the far end of the line, the Moscow Station in St Petersburg.

Yaroslavl Station (Yaroslavsky vokzal) is next door. The start of the Trans-Siberian Railway, it's a 1902–04 Art Nouveau fantasy by Fyodor Shekhtel.

Kazan Station (Kazansky vokzal), on the southern side of the square, was built between 1912 and 1926 and serves Central Asia and western Siberia. It's a retrospective of seven building styles, going back to a 16th-century Tatar tower in Kazan. (The style of its architect, Alexey Shchusev, transformed over the years – his later work includes Lenin's mausoleum.)

The 26-storey 'wedding cake' west of Komsomolskaya ploshchad is **Hotel Leningradskaya** (Gostinitsa Leningradskaya). Another of Stalin's 'Seven Sisters' is now home to the **Transport Ministry** (Ministerstvo selskogo khozyaystva), 600m south on the Garden Ring. The **Kursk Station** (Kursky vokzal), a further 1.5km south, is Moscow's biggest, with trains to eastern Ukraine, Crimea and the Caucasus.

Andrei Sakharov Museum

Southeast of Chistye Prudy, not far from Kursk Station, is a two-storey house in a small park, containing the Andrei Sakharov Museum *(Muzey A D Sakharova; Map 3; ☎ 923 4115; ul Zemlyanoy val 57; admission free; open 11am-7pm Wed-Sun)*. Its displays cover the life of Sakharov, the nuclear-physicist-turned-human-rights advocate, detailing the years of repression in Russia and providing a history of the dissident movement. Temporary expositions cover current human-rights issues. There are signs in English and audio guides are planned. Watch for a piece of genuine Berlin Wall in front of the building.

MOSCOW OUTSKIRTS
Armed Forces Museum (Map 2)

The Armed Forces Museum *(☎ 281 4877; ul Sovietskoy Armii 2; admission R20; open 10am-4.30pm Wed-Sun)* contains the history of Soviet and Russian forces since 1917. Among the highlights are parts of the American U2 spy plane brought down over Siberia in 1960, plus many tanks, planes, guns, and so on. Take trolleybus No 69 (or walk) 1.25km west from the Novoslobodskaya metro.

All-Russia Exhibition Centre (VDNKh; Outer North Moscow Map)

No other place sums up the rise and fall of the Soviet dream quite as well as the All-Russia Exhibition Centre (Vserossiysky Vystavochny Tsentr, or VVTs). The old initials by which it's still commonly known, VDNKh, tell half the story – they stand for Vystavka Dostizheny Narodnogo Khozyaystva SSSR (USSR Economic Achievements Exhibition).

Originally created in the 1930s, VDNKh was expanded in the '50s and '60s to impress upon one and all the success of the Soviet economic system. Two kilometres long and 1km wide, it is composed of wide pedestrian avenues and grandiose pavilions, glorifying every aspect of socialist construction from education and health to agriculture, technology and science. The pavilions represent a huge variety of architectural styles, symbolic of the contributions from diverse ethnic and artistic movements to the common goal. Here you will find the kitschiest socialist realism, the most inspiring of socialist optimism and, now, the tackiest of capitalist consumerism.

VDNKh was an early casualty when those in power finally admitted that the Soviet economy had become a disaster – funds were cut off by 1990. Today, it's a commercial centre, its pavilions given over to sales of the very imported goods which were supposed to be inferior; much of the merchandise on sale is low-priced clothing and the like from China. The domed Kosmos (Space) pavilion towards the far end became a wholesaler for TV sets and VCRs, while Lenin's slogan 'Socialism is Soviet power plus electrification' still adorns the electrification pavilion to its right. Although you may not want to do your shopping here, VDNKh does host international trade exhibitions.

For tourists, it's a fascinating visit to see the remnants of socialism's achievements. The main entrance, 500m from prospekt Mira, is approached by its own imposing avenues from Hotel Kosmos or VDNKh metro.

The soaring 100m titanium obelisk beside VDNKh metro is a monument to Soviet space flight. In its base is the **Cosmonautics Museum** (*Muzey kosmonavtiki; ☎ 283 7914; admission R30; open 10am-7pm Tues-Sun*), a high-concept series of displays from the glory days of the Soviet space program.

Ostankino (Outer North Moscow Map)

The pink-and-white **Ostankino Palace** (Ostankinsky dvorets), a wooden mansion with a stucco exterior made to resemble stone, was built in the 1790s as the summer pad of Count Nikolai Sheremetev, probably Russia's richest aristocrat of the time. Its lavish interior, with hand-painted wallpaper and intricate parquet floors, houses the count's art treasures. The centrepiece is the oval theatre-ballroom built for the Sheremetev troupe of 250 serf actors (see Kuskovo Park later). In 1801 Count Nikolai married one of the troupe, Praskovia Zhemchugova, and the two retired to Ostankino to avoid court gossip.

Only the **Italian Pavilion** (*☎ 286 6288; admission R40; open 10am-6pm Wed-Sun 18 May-1 Oct*) is open for visits. The hours are limited and it's closed on days when it rains or when humidity is over 80%.

After a fire in the late 1990s, the 540m **Ostankino TV Tower** is no longer open to the public, although it still provides a distinctive landmark for the area.

To reach the Ostankino Palace, walk west from VDNKh metro, across the car parks, to pick up tram No 7 or 11, or trolleybus No 13, 36, 69 or 73 west along ulitsa Akademika Korolyova.

Petrovsky Road-Palace (Outer North Moscow Map)

Leningradsky prospekt, which slices northwest through the suburbs towards Sheremetevo airports and St Petersburg, is a fairly uninspiring avenue. The oddest sight along it, just north of Dinamo Stadium, is the Petrovsky Road-Palace (Petrovsky dvorets), one of the many staging posts Catherine the Great had built for her St Petersburg–Moscow trips. This one (also Napoleon's headquarters after Moscow burned down) is a fantastic blend of pseudo-Gothic, Moorish and traditional Russian styles. For about 50 years it housed the Air Force Engineering Academy, and it is now being restored as (yet another) luxury hotel.

Victory Park & Around (Outer West Moscow Map)

Following a vicious but inconclusive battle at Borodino (see Borodino in the later Around Moscow chapter) in August 1812, Moscow's defenders retreated along what are now Kutuzovsky prospekt and ulitsa Arbat, pursued by Napoleon's Grand Army. Today, about 3km west of Kalininsky most and Hotel Ukraina (where Russian commander Mikhail Kutuzov stopped for a war council) is the **Borodino Panorama** (*Muzey-panorama Borodinskaya bitva; ☎ 148 1927; Kutuzovsky pr 38; admission R60; open 10am-5pm Sat-Thur*), a pavilion with a giant 360° painting of the Borodino battle. Standing inside this tableau of bloodshed (as many as 100,000 were killed in 15 hours) is an impressive, if idealised, way to visualise the event. See if you can spot Napoleon on his white horse.

The **Triumphal Arch**, farther out, celebrates Napoleon's eventual defeat. It was demolished at its original site in front of Belorus Station in the 1930s and reconstructed here in a fit of post-WWII public spirit.

From here it is a short distance west to **Victory Park** (Park Pobedy), a huge memorial complex celebrating the Great Patriotic

MOSCOW

OUTER NORTH MOSCOW

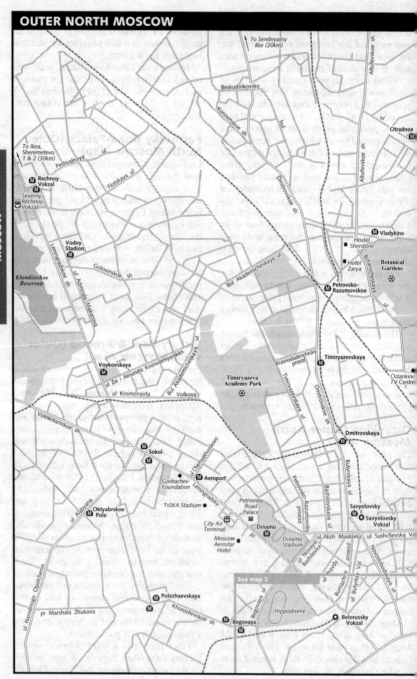

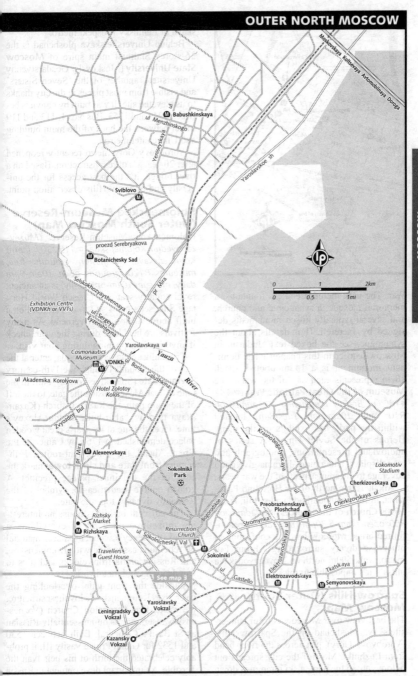

OUTER NORTH MOSCOW

MOSCOW

Moskovskaya Kolbsevaya Avtomobilnaya Doroga

ul Menzhinskogo

Yenisejskaya ul

M Babushkinskaya

Yaroslavskoe sh

Sviblovo M

proezd Serebryakova

M Botanichesky Sad

Selskokhozyaystvennaya ul

pr Mira

*Exhibition Centre
(VDNKh or VVTs)*

ul Sergeya
Eyzenshteyna

Yaroslavskaya ul

*Cosmonautics
Museum*

VDNKh M

ul Akademika Korolyova

Yauza

ul Borisa Galushkina

River

*Hotel Zolotoy
Kolos*

Zvyozdny bul

pr Mira

M Alexeevskaya

Krasnobogatyrskaya

*Sokolniki
Park*

Bogorodskoe sh

Lokomotiv
Stadium

Cherkizovskaya M

Preobrazhenskaya
Ploshchad

Bol Cherkizovskaya ul

M

Stromynka

*Rizhsky
Market*

M Rizhskaya

ul Sokolnichesky Val

*Resurrection
Church*

Sokolniki

*Travellers'
Guest House*

pr Mira

Elektrozavodskaya ul

ul Gastello

Elektrozavodskaya M

Tkatskaya ul

Semyonovskaya M

See map 3

Yaroslavsky
Vokzal

Leningradsky
Vokzal

Kazansky
Vokzal

0   1   2km
0   0.5   1mi

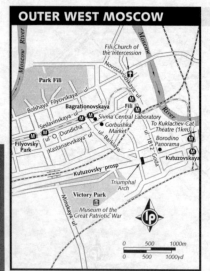

OUTER WEST MOSCOW

Moscow River

Fili Church of the Intercession

Novozavodskaya

Park Fili

Bolshaya Filyovskaya-ul

Bagrationovskaya

Fili

Seslavinskaya-ul

Sivma Central Laboratory

Gorbushka

Gorbushka Market

To Kuklachev Cat Theatre (1km)

ul O Dundicha

Filyovsky Park

Kastanaevskaya-ul

Kutuzovsky-prosp

Borodino Panorama

Kutuzovskaya

Triumphal Arch

Victory Park

Museum of the Great Patriotic War

Minskaya-ul

0   500   1000m
0   500   1000yd

War. The park includes endless fountains, a memorial mosque, a synagogue and church, and several typically kitsch monuments designed by Tsereteli. (For details about the synagogue, see the boxed text 'Judaism in Moscow' earlier in this chapter.) The dominant monument is a 142m obelisk (each 10cm represents each day of the war). The **Museum of the Great Patriotic War** (☎ 142 4185; ul Bratiev Fonchenko 10; admission R10; open 10am-5pm Tues-Sun), located within the park, has exhibits on the many Heroes of the Soviet Union. A series of audiovisual presentations, photograph and map displays, and a huge diorama give good coverage to different aspects of the war years.

About 1.5km north of the Borodino Panorama, in the neighbourhood called Fili, is the 1690s **Church of the Intercession** (admission R50; open 11am-5.30pm Thur-Tues), a beautiful red-brick, Moscow-baroque confection in otherwise dreary surroundings. From Fili metro, walk 500m north on Novozavodskaya ulitsa – it's impossible to miss.

Sparrow Hills (Outer South Moscow Map)

The best view over Moscow is from Universitetskaya ploshchad on the Sparrow Hills (Vorobyovy Gory), just across the river bend from Luzhniki. Most of the city spreads out before you; in the park, a ski jump runs down

to the river. Take trolleybus No 7 from Kievskaya or Leninsky Prospekt metro.

Behind Universitetskaya ploshchad is the 36-storey Stalinist main spire of **Moscow State University** (Moskovsky Gosdarstvenny Universitet), another of the 'Seven Sisters' and visible from most places in the city thanks to its elevated site. It was built by convicts between 1949 and 1953. Bus Nos 1, 113 and 119 travel between the back of the main building and Universitet metro.

Vorobyovy Gory metro recently reopened after 20 years(!) of reconstruction. Based on a river bridge, it's the best access for the university and Sparrow Hills observation point.

Kolomenskoe Museum-Reserve (Outer South Moscow Map)

Kolomenskoe Museum-Reserve (Muzey-zapovednik Kolomenskoe; ☎ 115 2309; metro Kolomenskaya; admission grounds free, museums R120; grounds open 10am-9pm daily, museum 10am-5pm daily) is an ancient royal country seat and Unesco World Heritage Site, set amid 4 sq km of parkland on a bluff above a Moscow Riverbend. As many festivals are held here during the year, check if anything is happening during your visit.

From ulitsa Shtatnaya Sloboda, enter at the rear of the grounds through the 17th-century **Saviour Gate** (Spasskiye Vorota), built in the time of Tsar Alexey. Inside the gate, to the left of the main path, the **Kazan Church** (Kazanskaya tserkov), also built during Alexey's time, faces the site of the tsar's great wooden palace demolished in 1768 by Catherine the Great. Ahead, the white, tent-roofed 17th-century **front gate and clock tower** mark the edge of the old inner palace precinct. A golden double-headed eagle, symbol of the Romanov dynasty, tops the gate.

The adjacent buildings house an interesting **museum** with a bit of everything: a model of Alexey's wooden palace, material on rebellions associated with Kolomenskoe, and Russian crafts from clocks and tiles to woodcarving and metalwork.

Outside the front gate, overlooking the river, rises Kolomenskoe's loveliest structure, the rocket-like **Ascension Church** (Voznesenskaya tserkov), as quintessentially Russian as St Basil's Cathedral. Built between 1530 and 1532 for Grand Prince Vasily III, it probably celebrated the birth of his heir Ivan the Terrible. An important development in Russia architecture, paving the way for St Basil's 25 years later by reproducing the shapes of wooden churches in brick for the first time. Immediately south of it are the round 16th-century **St George's Bell Tower** (Kolokolnya Georgia) and another 17th-century tower.

Some 300m farther south across a gully, the white **St John the Baptist Church** (Tserkov Ianna Predtechi) was built for Ivan the Terrible in the 1540s or 1550s. It has four corner chapels which make it a stylistic 'quarter-way house' between the Ascension Church and St Basil's. Old **wooden buildings** from elsewhere have been collected in the old palace area, among them the cabin where Peter the Great lived while supervising ship and fort building at Arkhangelsk in the 1700s.

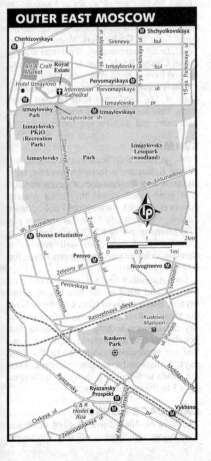

OUTER EAST MOSCOW

Kuskovo Park (Outer East Moscow Map)

When Count Pyotr Sheremetev married Varvara Cherkassakava in 1743, their joint property amounted to 1200 villages and 200,000 serfs. They turned their country estate at Kuskovo, 12km east of the Kremlin, into a mini-Versailles, with elegant buildings scattered around formal gardens, as well as an informal park. It's a pleasant trip out from central Moscow.

Kuskovo Mansion (Usadba Kuskovo; ☎ 370 0160; ul Yunosti 2; admission R10-100 for each exhibit; open 10am-6pm Wed-Sun), the wooden main mansion, was built in the 1770s and overlooks a lake where the count staged mock sea battles to entertain Moscow society. Across the lake to the south is the informal park. North of the mansion in the formal grounds are an **orangery**, now housing an exhibition of 18th- to 20th-century Russian ceramics; an open-air **theatre**, where the Sheremetev troupe of serf actors performed twice weekly; a pond-side grotto with exotic 'sea caverns'; a **Dutch house**, glazed inside with Delft tiles; an **Italian villa**; a **hermitage** for private parties; and a **church** with a wooden bell tower.

Bus Nos 133 and 208 from Ryazansky Prospekt metro go to the main entrance. Buildings are closed when humidity exceeds 80% or when it's very cold, counting out much of the winter.

Izmaylovo (Outer East Moscow Map)

Izmaylovo is best known for its extensive art and craft market (see Markets under Shopping later in this chapter), held every weekend. After shopping, however, Izmaylovsky Park and the crumbling royal estate are nice for a picnic or more serious outdoor activity.

A former royal hunting preserve 10km east of the Kremlin, **Izmaylovsky Park** is the nearest large tract of undeveloped land to central Moscow. Its 15 sq km contain a recreation park at the western end, and a much larger expanse of **woodland** (Izmaylovsky Lesopark) east of Glavnaya alleya, the road which cuts north–south across the park. Trails wind around this park, making it a good place to escape the city for hiking or biking. To get there, head south (away from the giant Hotel Izmaylovo) from Izmaylovsky Park metro.

MOSCOW

The **royal estate** is on a small, moated island. Tsar Alexey had an experimental farm here in the 17th century, where Western farming methods and cottage industries were sampled. It was on the farm ponds that his son Peter learnt to sail in a little boat, which came to be called the Grandfather of the Russian Navy.

Past an extensive 18th-century barracks (now partly occupied by the police) is the beautiful, five-domed 1679 **Intercession Cathedral** (Pokrovsky Sobor), an early example of Moscow baroque. The nearby triple-arched, tent-roofed **Ceremonial Gates** (1682) and the squat brick **bridge tower** (1671) are the only other original buildings remaining. The latter contains an exhibition hall.

RIVER TRIPS

For new perspectives on Moscow neighbourhoods, fine views of the Kremlin, or just good old-fashioned transportation, a boat ride on the Moscow River is one of the city's highlights. The main route runs between the boat landings at **Kiev Station** (Map 4), and **Novospassky most** (Map 5), 1km west of Proletarskaya metro (near the Novospassky Monastery). There are six intermediate stops: at the foot of Sparrow Hills (Outer South Moscow Map); Frunzenskaya, towards the southern end of Frunzenskaya naberezhnaya; Gorky Park (Map 4); Krymsky most; Bolshoy Kamenny most opposite the Kremlin (Map 6); and Ustinsky most near Hotel Rossiya and Red Square (Map 5).

The boats seat around 200 (most Muscovite passengers are actually going somewhere, not just enjoying the ride) and are operated by the **Capital Shipping Company** (☎ 277 3902). They run from late April to early October and weekday/weekend tickets cost R70/140. Check at the landings for the limited weekday schedules; on weekends they run as often as every 20 minutes in either direction.

BANYA

What better way to cope with Moscow than to have it steamed, washed and beaten out of you? There are traditional *banya* (Russian baths) all over town. The oldest and most luxurious are the **Sandunovskiye Baths** (Map 2; ☎ 925 4631; ul Neglinnaya 14; 2-person banya per hr without/with pool R1000/1300; open 8am-10pm Wed-Mon), a work of art in themselves. The Gothic Room has rich wood carving and the main shower room has an almost aristocratic Roman feel to it. If you aren't shy, general admission to shared facilities is cheaper. Either way, the *banya* is a sensuous, exhilarating and uniquely Russian experience.

For a less historic, New Russian experience, try the **Sauna at Chistye Prudy** (Map 3; ☎ 923 5854; Krivokolenny per 14/2; open 24hrs). The facility has a Jacuzzi and billiards, in addition to its Finnish sauna.

For a detailed look at the traditions and workings of a Russian *banya*, see the boxed text 'Steaming: The Joys of the Banya' in the European Russia Facts for the Visitor chapter.

WINTER SPORTS

There's no shortage of winter in Moscow, so take advantage of it. You can rent ice skates and see where all those great Russian figure skaters come from at **Gorky Park** (Map 4; ☎ 237 1266). Bring your passport. The winter skating rink at **Chistye Prudy** (Map 3) is also pleasant, but you have to bring your own skates.

Izmaylovsky Park (Outer East Moscow Map; ☎ 166 8690) has both ski and skate rental. Take bus No 7 or 131 from Izmaylovsky Park metro and get off at the third stop.

SWIMMING

Public pools are difficult places to take the plunge if you are a foreigner because they all insist on a Russian doctor's certificate of your good health before they'll let you in. However, **Chaika Swimming Pool** (Chaika Bassein; Map 4; ☎ 246 1344; Turchaninov per 1/3; admission per hr R150; open 7am-10pm Mon-Sat, 8am-7pm Sun) will provide a checkup, complete with health certificate, for R100 on the spot.

On hot summer days you can join much of the city and head to the beaches at **Serebryaniy Bor**, a series of lakes and channels on the Moscow River, 20km north of the city (a key detail since nothing from Moscow has yet *flushed* into the water). There are areas that are unofficially dedicated to families, gays, nudists and even disco dancers. Take the metro to Sokol and then ride trolleybus No 65 to the end of the line.

LANGUAGE COURSES

The *Moscow Times* carries lots of small ads from tutors and colleges offering short-term

Russian-language lessons. Many will teach you their Russian in return for sharing your English.

ORGANISED TOURS

Dom Patriarshy Tours (Map 2; ☎/fax 795 0927; e alanskaya@co.ru; Vspolny per 6, Moscow school No 1239) provides useful English-language tours on just about any specialised subject; some provide access to otherwise closed museums. Day tours range from US$8 to US$20 per person. Look for the monthly schedule at Western hotels and American restaurants.

Its spin-off **Capital Tours** (Map 6; ☎ 232 2442; w www.capitaltours.ru; Gostiny Dvor, ul Ilyinka 4) offers a twice-daily Moscow city tour (adult/child US$18/10) and Kremlin/Armoury tour (US$30/20).

Sputnik (Outer South Moscow Map; ☎ 939 8310; ul Kosygina 15) specialises in more outdoorsy tours, such as camping, fishing and spas outside the city. Prices average R300 per day, including meals.

Intourist (Map 2; ☎ 956 8844; Milyutinsky per 13/1) runs several mainstream tours, geared for large groups and visiting places like the Kremlin and Pushkin Museum.

SPECIAL EVENTS

See Special Events in the earlier European Russia Facts for the Visitor chapter for a list of Russian spectaculars.

While Mayor Luzhkov is a keen proponent of bread and circuses for the masses, the festivals are an ever-changing lot from year to year; consult the Moscow newspapers for what's on.

For details on the International Tchaikovsky Competition, see Classical Music under Entertainment later in this chapter. Otherwise, three long-established festivals are:

Contemporary Music Festival Held at venues all over the city for a few weeks in late May and early June. Top Russian and international acts perform.

December Nights Festival Held at the main performance halls, theatres and museums from mid-December to early January. Classical music at its best, performed in classy surroundings by the best Russian and foreign talent.

Winter Festival An outdoor funfest during early January for those with antifreeze in their veins (you can bet plenty of people use vodka for this purpose). Teams compete to build elaborate ice sculptures in front of the Pushkin

Museum and on Red Square; the real hard core can be found punching holes in the ice on the Moscow River and plunging in for a dip (do this, become a member of the 'Walrus Club', and take consolation that it's probably too cold for the usual legions of germs).

PLACES TO STAY

Moscow is not a cheap place to stay – the small, simple hotels found elsewhere in Europe just don't exist yet, while those in the mid-price and budget range are mainly older Soviet-era properties that have weathered the transition to a market economy with varying degrees of grace. Many are huge labyrinths (like the Rossiya) lacking any charm; however, with a bit of spirit, a stay in these places can be part of the Russian adventure.

Moscow has no central homestay agency, but you can arrange to stay in private homes before you arrive by booking from abroad – see Private Homes under Accommodation in the European Russia Facts for the Visitor chapter for agency details.

A few words of caution – many hotels, especially the less expensive options, have dual pricing and you will pay more than your Russian or Kazakh counterpart; prices quoted are for foreign visitors. Some cheaper hotels may also charge a 'reservation fee' – as much as 50% – for the first night's stay (even if you do not make an advance reservation). Prices listed include the 20% VAT tax, but not the 5% sales tax which is charged mainly at luxury hotels.

PLACES TO STAY – BUDGET
Camping

There are no camping grounds around Moscow, but take heart – staying at many of the cheaper hotels is much like camping.

Guesthouses

Galina's Flat (Map 3; ☎ 921 6038; e galinas.flat@mtu-net.ru; ul Chaplygina 8, No 35; dorm beds/singles/doubles US$8/15/20) is just that – a private flat with a few extra rooms that Galina rents out. She has a total of six beds (but apparently she can make arrangements with her neighbours if her place is full). Kitchen and Internet facilities are available at this hospitable place.

G&R Hostel Asia (Outer East Moscow Map; ☎ 378 0001, fax 378 2866; w www.hostels.ru; ul Zelenodolskaya 2/3; dorm beds/singles/doubles with breakfast US$16/30/44), on the top floors of an old hotel, is one of the best budget options. The management is clued up and runs a travel agency that can book train tickets and the like. Leave Ryazansky Prospekt metro from the end of the train and look for the tallest building around – that's the hostel.

Hostel Sherstone (*Outer North Moscow Map;* ☎/fax 797 8075; *w www.sherstone.ru; Gostinichny proezd 8/1; dorm beds/singles/doubles US$14/25/40*) is a branch of the G&R. Services include visa support, free transfers from the railway station and discounts for International Youth Hostel Federation (IYHF) cards. It's 10 minutes' walk from Vladykino metro.

Art Hostel (*Map 2; hostel* ☎ *251 2837, central reservations* ☎ *275 1513, fax 275 4581;* w *www.arthostel.net; ul Tverskaya Yamskaya 3-ya 58/5; dorm beds/singles/doubles with breakfast US$15/20/30*) has a prime location two minutes' walk from Belorusskaya metro, in a student hostel run by kindly babushkas. Rooms are well furnished and facilities include a modern kitchen with microwave and washing machine. The catch is the hostel is only open 15 December to 1 March and 1 July to 10 September (when prices are about US$5 higher per person). The entrance is on Aleksandra Nevskogo pereulok, the third door on the left. There's a 1am curfew.

Travellers Guest House (*Outer North Moscow Map;* ☎ *951 4059, fax 280 7686; ul Bolshaya Pereyaslavskaya 50, floor 10; dorm beds US$18, rooms with private/shared bathroom US$48/55*) calls itself Moscow's 'first and only' budget accommodation. Perhaps the first but no longer the only, this lacklustre place is a 10-minute walk north of Prospekt Mira metro. Rooms and shared toilets are basic but clean and there's almost always space. The affiliated Infinity Travel Agency offers all kinds of useful services.

Prakash Guest House (*Outer South Moscow Map;* ☎ *334 8201, fax 334 2598; ul Profsoyuznaya 83/1; dorm beds/doubles US$18/50*), run by an Indian team, is just a minute's walk north of Belyaevo metro. Private rooms come with breakfast, TV and phone and some pairs of rooms share a bathroom and toilet. Use entrance two on the south side of the building; there are no signs.

Hotels

Hotels in the cheapest price range are mostly grey places, poor relations even in Soviet times. Note that the following prices are subject to fluctuation.

Centre A pretty crummy option is **Hotel Tsentralnaya** (*Map 2;* ☎ *229 8957, fax 292 1221; ul Tverskaya 10; singles/doubles R1150/ 1750*), but you can't beat the location and the prices aren't bad either. You may not get a smile from some surly staff.

Hotel Minsk (*Map 2;* ☎ *299 1213, fax 299 0362; ul Tverskaya 22; singles/doubles R700/ 1050*) has the same features: prime location, shabby rooms, and some staff that could be cheerier. The ticket office in the lobby is useful for train and air tickets.

North The shortest of Stalin's 'Seven Sisters' is **Hotel Leningradskaya** (*Map 3;* ☎ *975 1815, fax 975 1802; Kalanchevskaya ul 21/ 40; singles/doubles from R900/1600*). Arriving at this looming skyscraper in the dead of night is likely to strike fear into your heart, but in daylight this showpiece Soviet hotel retains much of its grand 1950s style. It's worth considering as your base for a couple of nights.

Hotel Zarya (*Outer North Moscow Map;* ☎/fax *482 2458; ul Gostinichnaya 4/9; singles/doubles from R700/800*) is a large complex of short brick buildings, located along the tree-lined streets near Petrovsko-Razumovskaya metro. Rooms are nothing special, but the place has a cosy atmosphere.

Zolotoy Kolos (*Outer North Moscow Map;* ☎ *217 4355, fax 286 2703; ul Yaroslavskaya 15; rooms from R600*) is an adequate hotel near VDNKh. Rooms have phones, TVs and private bathrooms.

East Built for the 1980 Olympics, **Hotel Izmaylovo** (*Outer East Moscow Map; Izmaylovskoe shosse 71*) has 8000 beds, apparently making it Europe's biggest hotel. It's divided into five blocks with the facilities managed by a thicket of organisations, some more upstanding than others. However, the atmosphere is brighter than other budget hotels and it's right outside Izmaylovsky Park metro. The rooms are decent and all have bathroom, TV and phone.

The cheapest (and sketchiest) of the five is **Korpus Beta** (☎/fax *792 9898; singles/ doubles from R660/792*).

Korpus Alfa (☎ *166 0163, fax 166 00 60; singles/doubles from R1115/1490*) and

Korpus Vega (☎ 956 0640, fax 956 2850; singles/doubles R1000/1500) are one step up.

Korpus Gamma (☎ 166 3736, fax 166 7758; singles/doubles R1880/2080) and **Korpus Delta** (☎ 166 4127, fax 737 7000; singles/doubles R1880/2080 with breakfast) share the building closest to the market and have slightly snazzier rooms. All the towers have restaurants, cafés and other services.

PLACES TO STAY – MID-RANGE

Twenty years ago, these hotels were the best Moscow had to offer. Today, their prices have been kept in check and the service standards pepped by competition from the wave of superior top-end hotels. This is the category where prices vary the widest, even within individual facilities, and can fluctuate with no warning.

Centre

Hotel Moskva (Map 6; ☎ 960 2020, fax 960 5938; Okhotny ryad 2; singles/doubles R1600/2500) occupies the block between Manezhnaya ploshchad and Teatralnaya ploshchad. Here you can feel like a member of the Politburo as this was the accommodation of choice for visiting Communist Party apparatchiks. The atmosphere is appropriately sombre, but the rooms are tolerable and some have marvellous views of the Kremlin. Rumours are flying that this place will soon go the way of its former neighbour, the Intourist Hotel (now closed and soon-to-be demolished).

Hotel Rossiya (Map 2; ☎ 232 6046, 232 6248; ul Varvarka 6; singles/doubles from R1500/1600) has literally thousands of rooms (some better than others, but you pay more for them). The Rossiya gets a bad rap because it is so big and ugly, but some swear by its unbeatable location and reasonable prices. Besides, you can't see it if you are inside.

Hotel Belgrad (Map 4; ☎ 248 2841, fax 248 2896; ul Smolenskaya 8; singles/doubles R1500/1950) has poky but functional rooms. While the location is noisy, it's convenient to the western end of ulitsa Arbat.

Hotel Pekin (Map 2; ☎ 209 2215, fax 200 1420; w www.hotelpekin.ringnet.ru; ul Bolshaya Sadovaya 5/1; doubles from US$62) has cheesy Oriental decor and a noisy casino. However, it's better than it looks, the staff are helpful, rooms are comfortable, and the location is convenient. It's a good-value option.

Hotel Sverchkov (Map 3; ☎ 925 4978; Sverchkov per 8; rooms with breakfast from R2500), on a quiet lane near Chistye Prudy, is a tiny 11-room hotel in a graceful 18th-century building. Rooms are pretty rundown, but the place is kind of homey.

East-West Hotel (Map 2; ☎ 290 0404, fax 291 4606; w www.col.ru/east-west; Tverskoy bulvar 14/4; singles/doubles with breakfast from US$100/130) is a kitsch but rather charming small hotel on one of central Moscow's most pleasant streets. It has a quiet, secure courtyard and a sauna for warming up in winter.

Kazakh Embassy Hotel (Map 3; ☎ 208 0994; Chistoprudny bulvar 3; singles/doubles US$102/120 with breakfast) caters – as you might guess – to guests and workers of the nearby Kazakh embassy, but others can stay in this interesting, modern building. The rooms and location are good value.

Hotel Budapest (Map 2; ☎ 923 2356, fax 921 1266; w www.hotel-budapest.ru; Petrovskie linii 2/18; singles/doubles US$105/147 with breakfast) is the top pick in the mid-range. This elegant, central hotel has friendly management and 125 stylish rooms.

Hotel Arbat (Map 4; ☎ 244 7628, fax 244 0093; e hotelarbat@hotmail.com; Plotnikov per 12; singles/doubles from US$120/135 with breakfast) has a prime location on a quiet street just off the Arbat. This comfortable, 105-room hotel has a decent restaurant and a lovely courtyard.

Sheremetevo-2 (☎ 578 5753/4, fax 753 8091; Sheremetevo-2 airport; rooms from R2000), near the airport of the same name, is a good option if you are between flights. It's a 10-minute walk; there's also a free shuttle to the Novotel, from where you can walk across the street to here.

Hotel Ukraina (Map 2; ☎ 243 3030, fax 956 2078; Kutuzovsky pr 2/1; singles/doubles R2100/2500) faces the White House across the Moscow River. This giant hotel, popular with tour groups, echoes Stalinist pomp in its hallways and old-fashioned, stately rooms (many with terrific views).

Hotel Danilovsky (Outer South Moscow Map; ☎ 954 0503; e hotdanil@cityline.ru; singles/doubles US$110/130) is Moscow's holiest hotel (in a good way) – it's on the monastery grounds, where the exquisite setting comes complete with 18th-century churches and well-maintained gardens. The hotel itself is comfortable and has its own restaurant.

PLACES TO STAY – TOP END

Moscow's top-end hotels offer international-standard comfort and service, with most managed by Western hotel chains catering mainly to business people. Expect satellite TV, international direct-dial phones, air-conditioning, minibars and room service, as well as a range of expensive restaurants, shops, bars and services. Many hotels have health clubs or exercise rooms with pool, sauna, massage and so on.

Hotel Savoy (Map 2; ☎ 929 8500/8558, fax 230 2186; ul Rozhdestvenka 3; singles/doubles from US$180/230) was the first of Moscow's new-wave luxury hotels when it reopened in 1989. The gilt, murals and chandeliers maintain the atmosphere of prerevolutionary privilege. There are just 86 rooms and suites and the tariff includes buffet breakfast.

Hotel National (Map 6; ☎ 258 7000, fax 258 7100; e hotel@national.ru; Okhotny ryad 14/1; old-wing rooms US$300-450, new-wing rooms US$350-390) occupies the choicest location, facing the Kremlin across Manezhnaya ploshchad, at the foot of Tverskaya ulitsa. Built in 1903, its chandeliers and frescoed ceilings survived the revolution, and after a careful renovation it has become one of the best hotels. Many of the rooms in the old wing are museums in themselves – the hotel publishes a guide to its antiques. Rooms in the old wing, while slightly smaller than standard rooms in the new wing, warrant a sometimes higher tariff for their spectacular Red Square views.

Hotel Metropol (Map 6; ☎ 927 6000, fax 927 6010; e moscow@interconti.com; Teatralny proezd 1/4; rooms US$360), another reborn classic, has a choice position across from the Bolshoi Theatre. Rooms have high ceilings and furniture recalling the early 1900s, when the hotel was first in its prime. Fittings in the public areas are lavish, and the main restaurant has a famous stained-glass ceiling.

Hotel Baltschug Kempinski (Map 6; ☎ 230 6500, fax 230 6502; w www.kempinskimos cow.com; ul Baltschug 1; singles/doubles from US$320/350) is on the Moscow River, opposite the Kremlin, where it commands spectacular views. First built in 1898, it has 234 high-ceilinged rooms filled with state-of-the-art facilities. There's a pool, a basement casino, and a breakfast buffet with food to match the views.

Hotel Marco Polo Presnya (Map 2; ☎ 244 3631, fax 956 5637; Spiridonyevsky per 9; singles/doubles US$215/245 with breakfast), a small hotel, is in the quiet Patriarch's Pond area 2km northwest of the Kremlin.

Marriott Grand Hotel (Map 2; ☎ 937 0000, fax 937 0001; w www.marriott.com; ul Tverskaya 26; singles/doubles US$295/305) has a large atrium, a rooftop patio with excellent views, and a lavish buffet breakfast included in the price. President Bush stayed here recently, so security must be OK.

Radisson Slavyanskaya Hotel (Map 4; ☎ 941 8020, fax 240 6915; w www.radisson .com; Berezhkovskaya nab 2; singles/doubles from US$180/210), a bright and modern place, is 3.5km west of the Kremlin by Kiev Station. It's almost a village in itself with 430 rooms, a large business centre, its own shopping mall, a host of cafés and restaurants, a big pool and the American House of Cinema. If you do venture out of the hotel, you can walk across the modern, glass pedestrian bridge to the Arbat.

Hotel Katerina (Map 5; ☎ 795 2444, fax 795 2443; Shlyuzovaya nab 6; singles/doubles US$165/205) is a welcome addition. With its Scandinavian management, it's Moscow's closest equivalent to an intimate European-style hotel. The small lobby has a comfy fireplace where you can get a glass of wine, and the neighbourhood itself is quiet and leafy. Room rates include buffet breakfast.

Novotel (☎ 926 5900, fax 926 5903; w www.novotel-moscow.ru; singles/doubles weekends from US$160/180, weekdays US$230/260), at Sheremetevo-2 airport, is a good place to stay if stuck between flights; otherwise it's a long trek to the centre, even with free shuttle bus. Discounts abound here.

PLACES TO EAT

You can get any kind of meal in Moscow, as long as you're willing to pay for it. Sticker shock is common at Moscow restaurants, where prices are geared to free-spending New Russians and flush expats rather than the average person. The situation is improving, however, and many new affordable places are opening.

Unfortunately, the places to eat that are geared to the masses typically embody the old motto, 'You get what you pay for': they can be nameless canteens or shabby cafés which your nose will find faster than your

Mamontov's Metropol

Hotel Metropol, among Moscow's finest examples of Art Nouveau architecture, is another contribution of the famed philanthropist and patron of the arts, Savva Mamontov. The decorative panel on the hotel's central facade facing Teatralny proezd is based on a sketch by the artist Vrubel. It depicts the legend of the *Princess of Dreams*, in which a troubadour falls in love with a kind and beautiful princess and travels across the seas to find her. He falls ill during the voyage and is near death when he finds his love. The princess embraces him, but he dies in her arms. Naturally, the princess renounces her worldly life. The ceramic panels were made at the pottery workshop at Mamontov's Abramtsevo estate.

The ceramic work on the side of the hotel facing Teatralnaya ploshchad is by the artist Golovin. The script is a quote from Nietzsche: 'Again the same story: when you build a house you notice that you have learned something.' During the Soviet period, these wise words were replaced with something more appropriate for the time: 'Only the dictatorship of the proletariat can liberate mankind from the oppression of capitalism.' Lenin, of course.

★★

eyes. Times are a-changin', however – Muscovites are eating out in droves, and restaurants, cafés and kiosks are opening up left and right to cater to them.

More and more places are beginning to accept credit cards, but it's best to check first if you don't want to end up doing the dishes. Most places are open from noon to midnight daily, often with later hours on weekends. Discounts of up to 25% are often available before 5pm. Alternatively, many places offer a 'business lunch' special for a fixed price. This is a great way to sample some of the pricier restaurants around town.

Cafeterias

Moo-Moo (*Map 4*; ☎ *241 1364; ul Arbat 45/23 • Map 4*; ☎ *245 7820; Komsomolsky pr 26; meals R150; open 10am-11pm*) offers an easy serve-yourself approach to Russian standards, including borscht, *pelmeni* (small dumplings usually filled with meat) and violently coloured desserts. Dig that spotted-cow decor.

Pelmeshka (*Map 2*; ☎ *292 8392; ul Kuznetsky most 4/3; meals R100; open 11am-midnight*), clean and modern, serves *pelmeni*, the most filling of Russian favourites.

Restaurants

Places in this category are listed by cuisine and in roughly ascending order of price.

Russian There are several outlets for the excellent country-cottage-style Russian chain **Yolki-Palki** (*Map 4*; ☎ *953 9130; Klimentovsky per 14 • Map 2*; ☎ *291 6888; ul Novy Arbat 11; meals R150, salad bar R120; open*

11am-midnight) which specialises in simple, traditional dishes, with cheap beer and a blessed salad bar.

Kafe Karetny Dvor (*Map 2*; ☎ *291 6376; ul Povarskaya 52; meals R300*) offers a wide range of Russian and Georgian dishes, all reasonably priced. The interior is cheerful and relaxed; enjoy the courtyard if the weather's fine.

Kafe Margarita (*Map 2*; ☎ *299 6534; Malaya Bronnaya 28; business lunches R160, mains R280*), right across the street from Patriarch's Ponds, is popular with a well-read young crowd. The place is very lively in the evenings when folk bands play.

Spets-Bufet No 7 (*Map 4*; ☎ *959 3135; ul Serafimovicha 2; meals R300; open noon-6am*) is located in the basement of a once-prestigious apartment block that was home to many Communist Party apparatchiks. This 'Special Buffet' re-creates the forum where the bigwigs may have eaten, and is decked out with propaganda posters and potted plants. The food is decidedly mediocre (thus making the place more authentic).

Samovar (*Map 2*; ☎ *921 4688; ul Myasnitskaya 13; business lunches R250, mains R300-500*) has a menu heavy with delicious classics such as *pelmeni* and bliny. Other dishes, like the fish in champagne sauce, are not so classic.

New Vasyuki (*Map 4*; ☎ *201 3888; Starokonyushenny per 2/2; dinners US$15*), its name taken from the novel *Twelve Chairs*, is a mixture of several kitsch styles. Food is reliably good, and the place specialises in lamb barbecues and pig roasts. Try to ignore the cheesy band and the 'wall o' video' behind.

MOSCOW

When money is no object, try **TsDL** *(Map 2;* ☎ *291 1515; ul Povarskaya 50; meals US$50)*, with its grand decor and expensive modern Russian cuisine. It's in one part of the historic House of Writers, as is the less expensive and atmospheric **Zapisky Okhotnika** (Hunter's Sketches). The latter's name refers both to the historic graffiti-clad walls in the dining room, and its extraordinary stuffed menagerie (the present owners are hunters).

The queen mother of *haute russe* dining is **Café Pushkin** *(Map 2;* ☎ *229 5590; Tverskoy bulvar 26a; meals US$50)*, with an exquisite blend of Russian and French cuisines; service and food are done to perfection. The lovely 19th-century building has created a different atmosphere on each floor, including a richly decorated library and a pleasant rooftop café.

Ukrainian With several branches around the city, **Taras Bulba** *(Map 2;* ☎ *200 6082; ul Petrovka 30/7; meals R600; open noon-midnight)* is the Ukrainian version of Yolki-Palki. There's no salad bar, but the food is good and the atmosphere homey.

In case you did not think Moscow's theme dining was over the top, **Shinook** *(Map 2;* ☎ *255 0204; ul 1905 goda 2; meals US$30)* has re-created a Ukrainian peasant farm near the city centre. The staff wear colourfully embroidered shirts, speak with Ukrainian accents (probably lost on most tourists), and serve up the house speciality, *vareniki* (the Ukrainian version of *pelmeni*). As you dine, you can look out the window at a cheerful babushka tending the farmyard animals (who are very well taken care of, we are assured).

Caucasian & Central Asian The food from the southern Soviet states is very popular in Moscow – probably because it's usually spicy and the wines are cheap.

There are two branches of the Georgian restaurant **Mama Zoya** *(Map 4;* ☎ *201 7743; Sechenovsky per 8; meals R200* • *Map 4;* ☎ *242 8550; Frunzenskaya nab 16; open noon-11pm)*, the latter on a boat, where fleet-footed dancers and musicians accompany the delicious shashlyk and *khachi puri* (rich, cheesy bread).

Dioskuriya *(Map 2;* ☎ *290 6908; Merzlyakovsky per 2; meals R350)* is in a small house just off ulitsa Novy Arbat. The food is delicious and the music – a trio of a capella vocalists – even better.

Vostochny Kvartal *(Map 4;* ☎ *241 3803; ul Arbat 42/24; meals R500)* is a modern Uzbek place with a chic interior and tasty rice *plov* (pilaf rice with diced mutton and vegetables).

Tiflis *(Map 4;* ☎ *290 2897; ul Ostozhenka 32; meals with wine US$35)* is housed in a traditional grand Georgian house, with airy balconies and indoor courtyards. Don't miss the Tiflis wine, produced in Georgia at the restaurateur's winery.

American Of the two **Starlite Diner** locations *(Map 2;* ☎ *290 9638; ul Bolshaya Sadovaya 16* • *Map 4;* ☎ *959 8919; ul Korovy val 9 A)*, the original on the Garden Ring is best, with its wonderful, leafy outdoor seating area. Year-round (and around the clock), you can't beat this ersatz American diner's thick and creamy milkshakes (US$5), cheese fries (US$3), chicken chilli (US$5) and more.

American Bar and Grill 1 & 2 *(Map 2;* ☎ *250 9525; ul 1st Tverskaya-Yamskaya 2/1* • *Map 5;* ☎ *912 3615; ul Zemlyanoy val 59)*, both open 24 hours, are known for good breakfasts (US$8), large lunches, excellent steaks (US$15) and renowned vegetarian lasagne (US$11). The Yauza River location has an outdoor summer garden; in both cases, the bar area hops at night.

Mexican For some top-notch Mexican food, try **Hola Mexico** *(Map 2;* ☎ *925 8251; ul Pushechnaya 7/5; business lunches R180, mains R300; open noon-5am)*. The band gets a little loud, but after a few margaritas, you probably won't care.

Pancho Villa *(Map 4;* ☎ *241 9835; ul Arbat; meals R500; open 24hrs)* claims to be Moscow's first (and still the best) Mexican restaurant. We can vouch that its sidewalk café, right on the Arbat, is an ideal place to sip margaritas and pretend to be in Mexico.

Asian On one of the trendiest streets in Moscow, **Tibet Kitchen** *(Map 2;* ☎ *923 2422; Kamergersky per 5/6)* is a basement place with a cosy interior that will whisk you to Lhasa.

Krasny *(Map 4;* ☎ *202 5649; Prechistenka ul 30; mains R400-600, Mongolian barbecues R800)* has all kinds of Asian food, but the speciality is *shanaga* (Mongolian barbecue), where you choose your own ingredients and fill up your plate (the chefs then stir-fry it for you) – when in doubt, stick with the recommended combinations.

Yakitoria *(Map 2;* ☎ *250 5385; 1-ya Tverskaya-Yamskaya 1/29; open 11am-6am; sushi R60-150 each)* is a good place to join Moscow's ongoing sushi craze.

European If you are in need of vitamins, **Jagannat** *(Map 2;* ☎ *928 3580; Kuznetsky most 11; mains R150)* is a funky, vegetarian café, restaurant and store. Service is slow but sublime, and the food is worth the wait.

Cheap and cheery, **Soleil Express** *(Map 2;* ☎ *725 6474, 725 6474; ul Sadovaya Samotyochnaya 24/27; meals R100; open 8.30am-11pm)* has fresh sandwiches and salads, and cheap coffee.

York *(Map 2;* ☎ *208 2229; ul Trubnaya 20/2; fish & chips R360)* is an English restaurant upstairs and an English pub downstairs; you can get a Guinness for R170. If not eating, you might engage in a game of backgammon.

Cicco Pizza *(Map 2;* ☎ *229 7361; Kamergersky per 5/7; meals R500)* has delicious thincrust pizzas with all kinds of traditional and exotic toppings (none of which is canned peas), as well as salads and pastas. In summer you can dine at the outdoor café.

Tinkoff *(Map 2;* ☎ *777 3300; Protochny per 11; meals R600; open noon-2am)* is Moscow's first branch of the St Petersburg microbrewery, featuring live sports on TV, lagers and pilsners on draught, and a metre-long sausage on the menu (yikes). Beers are R120.

Brunch Sunday brunch at luxury hotels is an institution for many expats and wealthy Russians – while away the hours gorging yourself on an orgy of international foods.

Moscow Aerostar Hotel *(Outer North Moscow Map;* ☎ *213 9000; Leningradsky pr 37, korpus 9)* has an excellent brunch for US$30 in its **Café Taiga**, where there are more Asian selections than many other places.

Hotel Baltschug Kempinski *(Map 6;* ☎ *230 6500; ul Baltschug 1; brunch US$30)* has the best view and, like the others, includes champagne in the price.

Cafés

Moscow's booming café scene is beginning to make long-running imports such as **DeliFrance** *(Map 2; lobby of the Tchaikovsky Concert Hall, Triumfalnaya pl 4)* look decidedly old hat.

Coffee Bean *(Map 3;* ☎ *923 9793; ul Pokrovka 18; open 8am-10pm • Map 2;* ☎ *788 6357; ul Tverskaya 10; open 8am-11pm)* is a classic coffee bar, with high ceilings, newspapers lying around and nice mugs of Joe (R500). There's no smoking here.

Zen Coffee *(Map 2;* ☎ *234 1784; ul Lesnaya 1/2 • Map 2;* ☎ *292 5114; Kamergersky per 6; open 9am-11pm)* also has several outlets. The first of these modern, pleasant cafés is opposite Belorus Station; the second is on the popular pedestrian boulevard, leading off from Tverskaya to Kuznetsky most.

PirOGI *(Map 4;* ☎ *951 7596; ul Pyatnitskaya 29/8; open 24hrs)* is a low-key, bohemian place. It serves coffee, beers and even books (which you can buy, or just peruse while you have a drink).

Donna Klara *(Map 2;* ☎ *290 6974; ul Malaya Bronnaya 21/13; meals R400; open 10am-midnight)*, specialising in flaky pastries and dark coffee, is a great place for breakfast.

Oranzhevy Galstuk *(Map 2;* ☎ *229 1952; Kamergersky per 5; snacks & drinks R600)* is the trendiest café on this trendy lane. Appetisers and salads are scrumptious, beer is cold, and people-watching is tops. At night it's a happening club with live music.

Fast Food

Fighting for prime retail space with McDonald's is **Russkoe Bistro**, an equally omnipresent local chain endorsed (and co-owned) by Mayor Luzhkov. It serves cheap, traditional goodies such as *pirozhki* (pies) and bliny.

McDonald's has many locations; you will pass four between central Moscow and Sheremetevo-2. The original branch *(Map 2; ul Bolshaya Bronnaya 29)* is the most famous, but is now simply another busy outlet. Prices are similar to the West, so the real allure lies in two areas: familiar fare and clean toilets.

Rostik's *(Map 2;* ☎ *251 4950; ul Pervaya Tverskaya-Yamskaya 2/1; open 9am-9pm daily; meals R100)* is another fast-food chain serving very American food: burgers, fried chicken and the like. There's another location on the 2nd floor of the department store **GUM** *(Map 6; Red Square; meals R100; open 9am-9pm daily)*. Both have clean toilets.

Patio Pizza *(Map 4;* ☎ *201 5626; ul Volkhonka 13a; pizzas from R200)* also has branches all over town, but this branch – across from the Pushkin Museum – is considered the best. The pizzas come hot from wood ovens and the salad bar is huge. Often you'll find Patio Pizza and Rostik next to each other, as they are run by the same company.

There's a handy, but pricey food court in the basement of the Okhotny Ryad shopping mall.

Self-Catering

If you want to eat like a Muscovite, you'll buy your food, take it home and cook it there. While this may not be feasible if you're staying in a hotel, Russian food markets can be entertaining; if nothing else you can buy the ingredients for a good picnic.

Supermarkets Carrying mainly the local brands and some Western ones are **Sedmoy Kontinent** *(Seventh Continent; open 24hrs)* supermarkets. The most central locations are as follows (we've given the names as seen on the exteriors):

Gastronom Seventh Continent *(Map 4,* ☎ *959 0342)* ul Serafimovicha 2
Okhotny Ryad Gastronom *(Map 6,* ☎ *292 2248)* ul Okhotny ryad 2
Smolensky Gastronom *(Map 4,* ☎ *241 3581)* ul Arbat 54/2
Tsentralny Gastronom *(Map 2,* ☎ *928 9577)* ul Bolshaya Lubyanka 12/1

Other convenient places are **Stockmans** *(Map 4; Smolensky Passage, Smolenskaya pl 3/5; open 10am-10pm daily)*, with a foreign-goods supermarket in the basement, and **Yeliseev Grocery Store** *(Map 2; Tverskaya ul 14; open 8am-9pm Mon-Sat, 10am-6pm Sun)*, an old-school Soviet market with luxurious prerevolutionary decor.

Markets Moscow's *rynky* (food markets) are full of interest – as well as fruit, vegetables, cheese, honey and meat. Many of the traders and goods are from the Caucasus region republics; take your own bag. Prices are reasonable if you bargain a bit; keep an eye on the quality of the items that are being popped into your bag. The most central markets are:

Danilovsky Market *(Outer South Moscow Map; Mytnaya ul 74; metro Tulskaya)*
Dorogomilovsky Market *(Map 4; ul Mozhaysky val 10); there's an overflow section along Kievskaya ulitsa to Kiev Station*
Rizhsky Market *(Outer North Moscow Map; pr Mira 94-96; metro Rizhskaya)*

ENTERTAINMENT

Moscow can keep anyone entertained for months. The key to finding out what's on is

the comprehensive weekly entertainment section in Thursday's *Moscow Times*. For a laugh, try *Exile*.

The classical performing arts remain an incredible bargain. Highly acclaimed professionals stage productions in a number of elegant theatres around the city. While the Bolshoi is Moscow's most famous theatre, other venues host productions of comparable quality, with tickets a fraction of Bolshoi prices and the theatres themselves often in better shape.

Theatre and concert programs are displayed at venues and on street posters and charts at ticket kiosks. Aside from the Bolshoi, you can usually purchase tickets directly from box offices on the day of the performance.

Most theatres are closed between late June and early September.

Classical Music

Tchaikovsky Concert Hall *(Map 2;* ☎ *299 0378; Triumfalnaya pl 4/31)*, Moscow's largest concert venue, is home to the famous State Symphony Orchestra.

Moscow Tchaikovsky Conservatoire *(Map 2;* ☎ *229 8183; Bolshaya Nikitskaya ul 13)* is Russia's largest music school and has two venues: the Great Hall (Bolshoy Zal) and the Small Hall (Maly Zal). Every four years, hundreds of musicians gather at the Conservatoire to compete for the titles of top pianist, singer, cellist and violinist at the prestigious International Tchaikovsky Competition. The next competition will held in summer 2006.

A huge new musical centre recently opened near Paveletsk Vokzal, with many major classical music events due to move there from the Conservatoire.

Opera & Ballet

An evening at the **Bolshoi** *(Map 2;* ☎ *292 0050;* ☒ *www.bolshoi.ru; Teatralnaya pl 1)* is still one of Moscow's most romantic options, with an electric atmosphere in the glittering six-tier auditorium. Both the ballet and opera companies, with several hundred artistes between them, perform a range of Russian and foreign works.

Since the Soviet collapse (and even before) the Bolshoi has been marred by politics, scandal and frequent turnover. Yet the show must go on – and it does. At the time of research, the Bolshoi was looking forward to an exciting season, including fresh productions of Russian classic operas, as well as visits by foreign opera and ballet companies. A second, smaller stage at the theatre is scheduled to open in 2003. Closure of the theatre for renovations – long talked about, but never undertaken – has been put off for at least another year.

The easiest way to get tickets to the Bolshoi is to go there on the day of the performance and buy them from a tout. Expect to pay upwards of US\$40. Exercise caution so that you don't buy tickets for a show that was, say, last year. Service bureaus and concierges in hotels may also sell tickets to the Bolshoi. But they often charge very hefty commissions on what are usually very cheap face values.

The Bolshoi does not have a monopoly on ballet and opera in Moscow. Leading dancers also appear with the Kremlin Ballet and the Moscow Classical Ballet Theatre, both of which perform in the **Kremlin Palace of Congresses** (Map 6; ☎ 928 5232; ul Vozdvizhenka 1).

Stanislavsky & Nemirovich-Danchenko Musical Theatre (Map 2; ☎ 229 0649; ⓦ www.stanislavsky.ru; ul Bolshaya Dmitrovka 17) is another opera and ballet theatre with a similar classical repertoire and high-quality performances.

Theatre

Moscow has around 40 professional and numerous amateur theatres (the number changes every season), with a wide range of plays – contemporary and classic, Russian and foreign – staged at the majority (most performances in Russian). Some of the best drama can be seen at these venues:

Chekhov Moscow Art Theatre (Map 2, ☎ 229 8760) Kamergersky per 3. Also known as MKhAT, this is where method acting was founded over 100 years ago (see the boxed text 'Stanislavsky's Methods'). Watch for English-language versions of Russian classics performed by the American Studio (☎ 292 0941).
Lenkom Theatre (Map 2, ☎ 299 0708) ul Malaya Dmitrovka 6. Flashy productions and a lot of musicals keep non-Russian-speakers happy.
Maly Theatre (Map 6, ☎ 923 2621) Teatralnaya ploshchad 1/6. A lovely theatre founded in 1824, performing mainly 19th-century works.

Circus

Moscow has two separate circuses, putting on glittering shows for Muscovites of all ages. The first half of the show is usually a modern mix of dance, cabaret and rock music, before animals and acrobats reassert themselves. Both

---

Stanislavsky's Methods

In 1898, over an 18-hour restaurant lunch, playwright-director Vladimir Nemirovich-Danchenko and actor-director Konstantin Stanislavsky founded the Moscow Art Academic Theatre as the forum for method acting. (The theatre is known by its Russian initials, MKhAT – Moskovsky Khudozhestvenny Akademichesky Teatr.)

More than just another stage, the Art Theatre adopted a 'realist' approach stressing truthful portrayal of characters and society, teamwork by the cast (not relying on stars), and respect for the writer. 'We declared war on all the conventionalities of the theatre...in the acting, the properties, the scenery, or the interpretation of the play,' Stanislavsky wrote.

Such treatment of *The Seagull* rescued Anton Chekhov from despair, after the play had flopped in St Petersburg, *Uncle Vanya*, *Three Sisters* and *The Cherry Orchard* all premiered at the MKhAT. Gorky's *The Lower Depths* was another success. In short, the theatre revolutionised Russian drama.

Method acting's influence in Western theatre has been enormous: in the USA, Stanislavsky's theories are the primary source of study for many actors, including such greats as Stella Adler, Marlon Brando, Sanford Meisner, Lee Strasberg, Harold Clurman and Gregory Peck.

MKhAT, now technically called the Chekhov Moscow Art Theatre, still stages regular performances of Chekhov, among others.

★★★★★★★★★★★★★★★★★★

circuses perform at 7pm Wednesday to Sunday, with additional daytime weekend shows.

New Circus (Outer South Moscow Map; ☎ 930 2815; pr Vernadskogo 7), with 3400 seats, is near Moscow University and has the best reputation, especially for its animal acts and clowns.

Old Circus at Tsvetnoy Boulevard (Map 2; ☎ 200 6889; Tsvetnoy bulvar 13), more central than the New Circus, is in a modernised 19th-century building and produces shows around a central theme.

Bars & Clubs

During summer, outdoor beer tents and shashlyk stands pop up all over the city. One of the most pleasant places to head is the **Hermitage Gardens** (Pushkinskaya or Tverskaya metro). You can dress and look how you want at such venues, unlike some of Moscow's trendier clubs where 'face control' rules are arbitrarily supervised by thuggish bouncers.

Kitaisky Lyotchik Dzhao-Da *(Map 2; ☎ 924 5611;* **W** *www.jao-da.ru; Lubyansky proezd 25; cover charge R150)*, in a basement close by Kitai Gorod metro, is one of the best and most relaxed club/restaurants, often with live music.

Proekt OGI *(Map 3; ☎ 229 5489;* **W** *proekt .ogi.ru; Potapovsky per 8/12; cover charge R50-80; open 8am-11pm)* is a vaguely hippy (but definitely hip) place for student types; enter through the unmarked door in the corner of the courtyard. There's live music most nights.

Propaganda *(Map 2; ☎ 924 5732;* **W** *www .propagandamoscow.com; Bolshoy Zlatoustinsky per 7)* is happening, especially on Thursday, when DJs spin a cool mix for the beautiful people to dance to.

Both **Bunker** *(Map 2; ☎ 200 1506; ul Tverskaya 12; open 10pm-7am)* and its successor **B-2** *(Map 2; ☎ 209 9918; ul Bolshaya Sadovaya 8; cover charge R100)* have cheap food and drinks, and live music almost every night.

Sixteen Tons *(Map 2; ☎ 253 5300;* **W** *www .16tons.ru; Presnensky val 6; cover charge R100-200; open 11am-6am daily)* has a brassy English pub/restaurant downstairs, with an excellent house-brewed bitter. Upstairs, the club gets some of the best local and foreign bands that play in Moscow.

Garage *(Map 2; ☎ 209 1848; ul Tverskaya 16/2; open 24hrs)* is a funky Soviet-theme underground bar on Pushkinskaya ploshchad. There's a bit of a biker overlay, with an old BMW protruding from over the bar; after 3am anything goes. There's no cover charge, but strict face control.

Duck *(Map 2; ☎ 923 6158; ul Pushechnaya 9/6; open noon-6am daily)* is a successor to the Hungry Duck, a bar that was often described as the wildest in Europe. Apparently most people lose their clothes by midnight and every woman dances on the bar – this may have something to do with the policy of free drinks for women until 11pm on some nights.

Akademiya *(Outer South Moscow Map; ☎ 938 5775; Academy of Sciences, Leninsky pr 32A)*, on the 22nd floor of the Academy of Sciences, boasts a magnificent view of the city. This retro bar is popularly known as 'The Brains', after the surreal metallic structure topping the building.

As for expat bars, you can't go wrong at **American Bar and Grill** *(Map 2; ☎ 250 9525; ul 1st Tverskaya-Yamskaya 2/1 • Map 5; ☎ 912 3615; ul Zemlyanoy val 59)* or **Rosie O'Grady's** *(Map 4; ☎ 203 9087; ul Znamenka 9/12; open noon-1am)*.

Jazz & Blues The best venue for live jazz and blues is **BB King** *(Map 2; ☎ 299 8206; ul Sadovaya Samotyochnaya 4/2; noon-2am)*. It goes into the wee hours.

Club Forte *(Map 2; ☎ 202 8833; ul Bolshaya Bronnaya 18; cover charge Thur-Sat R300)* is known for the jazz band Arsenal, which plays here on Friday night. The jazzy, intellectual atmosphere is fun, although the music is rather bland. Book ahead; concerts start at 9pm.

Gay & Lesbian Venues

The Moscow gay scene is becoming more open all the time.

The appropriately named **Elf Café** *(Map 3; ☎ 917 2014; ul Zemlyanoy val 13/1; open 11am-midnight Mon-Thur, 11am-3am Fri-Sun)* is a tiny gay bar with an even tinier dance floor, lending it a cosy feel.

Samovolka *(Map 3; ☎ 261 7844; ul Novaya Basmannaya 9; open 10pm-6am daily)*, meaning 'AWOL', connotes freedom, sex and booze to Russian military men. Decor at this gay club follows the military theme and male bar staff sport fatigues (at least at the start of the night).

Bowling & Booze

In a country where some famous guy once said religion was the opium of the masses, the opium of the suburbs has now arrived.

Cosmic Bowling *(Map 4; ☎ 246 3666; ul Lva Tolstogo 18; bowling per hr R600; open noon-5am daily)* is the place to head if you fancy a spot of high-tech bowling – there are several psychedelic fluorescent lanes – or a game of pool.

Cinemas

American House of Cinema *(Map 4; ☎ 941 8747; Berezhkovskaya nab 2)*, inside the Radisson Slavyanskaya Hotel, shows major Hollywood movies in English.

SPECTATOR SPORTS

Vysshaya Liga, the premier football league, has five Moscow teams: Spartak, Lokomotiv,

TsSKA, Torpedo and Dinamo, each with a loyal following. You can often buy tickets immediately before games, played at these venues:

Dinamo Stadium (Outer North Moscow Map; ☎ 212 3132; Leningradsky pr 36; metro Dinamo) Seats 51,000 and hosts Dinamo and TsSKA.

Lokomotiv Stadium (Outer North Moscow Map; ☎ 161 4283; Bolshaya Cherkizovskaya ul 125; metro Cherkizovskaya) Reconstructed in 2002 and seats 30,000.

Luzhniki Stadium (Outer South Moscow Map; ☎ 201 1164; Luzhnetskaya nab 24; metro Sportivnaya) Gleams from its rebuilding, seats 80,000 and hosts Torpedo and Spartak.

Moscow's main entrant in the Super Liga, the top ice-hockey league, is **Dinamo**, which plays at the stadium of the same name.

Since the days of Olympic glory, men's basketball is a distant third to football and ice hockey in popularity. Moscow's top basketball team, **TsSKA** (Outer North Moscow Map; ☎ 213 2288; Leningradsky pr 39A; metro Aeroport), which plays at TsSKA Stadium, does well in European league play, but all too often serves as a retirement home for the NBA, which also poaches the best players. In contrast, some of the best games come from the TsSKA women's team, which plays from September to May.

SHOPPING
Foreign goods are priced the same or more than they would be in their home countries; if the item seems like a steal, it's probably a bargain-basement counterfeit. Local items you may want to purchase are caviar, vodka, linens, traditional crafts and brightly coloured woollen shawls.

For antiques and anything else more than 25 years old, see the Customs section of the earlier European Russia Facts for the Visitor chapter for details on export restrictions.

Shopping Streets
Novy Arbat is Moscow's equivalent of London's Oxford St or an American suburban mall – it's the place for mid-range shops, and is also equally unattractive. The streets around Kuznetsky most, just east of the Bolshoi, and those around GUM are home to the most upmarket shops.

Now restored to its prerevolutionary fashionable status, ulitsa Petrovka begins beside the Bolshoi Theatre. The big department store

TsUM (see Stores later in this section) which stands for Central Department Store (Tsentralny Universalny Magazin), is, like GUM, a bright, busy place now given over to multitudes of separate shops. It was built in 1909 as the Scottish-owned Muir & Merrilees and was the first department store aimed at middle-class shoppers. **Petrovsky Passazh** (Map 2; ul Petrovka 10) has become Moscow's sleekest shopping arcade. A smaller, glitzier version of GUM, it too is dominated by foreign names and dates from the 1900s.

Markets
The weekend **Vernisazh market** (Outer East Moscow Map) at Izmaylovsky Park is a sprawling area packed with art and handmade crafts. You'll find Moscow's biggest original range of matryoshka, Palekh and Khokhloma ware, and dozens of artists selling their own work. There are also rugs from the Caucasus and Central Asia, some very attractive pottery, antique samovars, handmade clothes, jewellery, fur hats, chess sets, toys, Soviet posters and much more. Quality is mostly high, many of the items are truly original, and prices can be reasonable (but you have to bargain for them). The market is two minutes' walk from Izmaylovksy Park metro – follow the crowds past the big hotel complex outside the station.

Many other artists set up their stalls on ulitsa Krymsky val, opposite the entrance to **Gorky Park** (Map 4), particularly on Saturday and Sunday. The art here is a mite less commercial than Izmaylovksy Park's, and there are only a few crafts.

Malls
GUM (see that entry under Red Square earlier in this chapter), on the eastern side of Red Square, has made the transition to a market economy in fine form. It's buffed up and the 19th-century building is a sight in itself. It's often called a 'department store', but that's a misnomer as it is really a huge collection of individual shops spread over several floors.

Okhotny Ryad shopping mall (Map 6; ☎ 737 8409; Manezhnaya pl; open 10am-10pm daily) is the zillion-dollar mall built in the 1990s. Although originally filled with expensive boutiques and no people, times have changed. Now the stores cater to all income levels and they are usually packed. There is a big, crowded food court on the ground floor.

MOSCOW

Stores

TsUM (Map 2; ☎ 292 1157; ul Petrovka 2; open 9am-8pm Mon-Sat, 9am-6pm Sun) is a real department store, stocking everything from perfume to clothes, electronics to sporting goods.

Detsky Mir (Children's World; Map 2; ☎ 238 0096; open 9am-8pm Mon-Sat) was the premier toy store during Soviet times. It now has a fun mix of imported and Russian-produced toys, along with well-stocked sporting goods and housewares departments (and other toys for adults).

Focus Photoshop (Map 6; ul Tverskaya 4; open 8am-8pm daily), conveniently located, is well stocked with photographic equipment, slide film, camcorder tapes and other items to help you record your Russian visit. Developing facilities are reliable.

La Casa de Cuba (☎ 737 8409), deep in the Okhotny Ryad shopping mall, sells a wide range of Cuban cigars.

Salon Moskovskogo Fonda Kultury (Moscow Culture Foundation Salon; Map 4; ☎ 951 3302; ul Pyatnitskaya 16; open 10am-8pm Mon-Sat) is one of the most authentic places to buy Russian arts and crafts. There are also many antiques, but watch those export rules.

Novikh Russkikh Mir (World of New Russians; Map 2; ☎ 241 0081; ☒ www.new russian.net; ul Arbat 36; open 10am-9pm) has a wide range of overpriced but amusing gifts, mostly traditional Russian items with a New Russian theme (the Gzhel mobile phone, for example).

Vologda Linen (Map 6; ☎ 232 9463; Gostiny Dvor; ul Ilinka 4; open 10am-8pm) has fine clothes and linens made according to traditional Russian methods. The stuff is beautiful and reasonably priced.

GETTING THERE & AWAY

For an overview of international air and train routes to Moscow, see the European Russia Getting There & Away chapter.

Air

Moscow has five airports, each with a range of flights to specific sets of places.

To/From Russia Sheremetevo-2 airport, 30km northwest of the city centre, handles most flights to/from places outside the former Soviet Union. This is a major international airport which offers all of the services that one would expect. For flight information call ☎ 956 4666.

Arriving at Sheremetevo-2, passing through passport control can be time-consuming, sometimes taking more than an hour. Checked luggage is also slow, although reports of theft have declined.

The only problem with departing from Sheremetevo-2 is the customs checks you must endure before departure – waiting in disorganised queues can last more than an hour on a busy day. For this reason you should plan to be at Sheremetevo-2 about two hours before your flight departs. Fill out a customs form before inspection (see Customs in the earlier European Russia Facts for the Visitor chapter).

International flights from Moscow's airports incur a departure tax, which is sometimes split between arrival and departure. In any case the taxes are included in the price of the airline ticket.

Domodedovo airport, 40km south of the city centre, has undergone extensive upgrades in recent years. Most notably, the express train from Paveletsky station facilitates access to this airport. As a result, more flights are going in and out of Domodedovo, including some international flights. At the time of writing, Domodedovo serviced Transaero and Swiss Airlines while British Airways have transferred some flights and Lufthansa all their Moscow flights to the new upgraded Domodedovo. For flight information, call ☎ 933 6666.

Within Russia Moscow has four airports handling flights within Russia and the CIS. Arrive at least 90 minutes before your flight in order to navigate check-in formalities and security. Although the airports handle a set range of services, there are exceptions, so confirm where your flight departs from. Services are very basic – buy that magazine before you leave your hotel.

The four airports and the destinations they serve are:

Bykovo (☎ 558 4738) Serves miscellaneous medium-range destinations, including Petrozavodsk, Nalchik and Penza. It's about 30km southeast of the city centre.

Domodedovo (☎ 933 6666) Serves most flights to/from the east (including the Volga cities and Siberia) and the Central Asian states. It's 40km south of the city centre.

Sheremetevo-1 (☎ 232 6565) Most flights are to/from St Petersburg, the Baltic States, Belarus and northern European Russia, with some to Ukraine, Armenia and Georgia. The airport is across the runways from Sheremetevo-2; to journey between them you have to take a bus (see Getting Around later in this chapter).

Vnukovo (☎ 941 9999) Serves most flights to/from the Russian Caucasus, Moldova and Kaliningrad, with some flights to/from Ukraine, Georgia and Armenia. It's about 30km southwest of the city centre.

Tickets You can buy domestic airline tickets at most travel agents and Aeroflot offices all over town. There's a convenient **Aeroflot office** (*Map 2;* ☎ *753 5555; ul Petrovka 20/1; open 9am-7pm Mon-Sat, 9am-3.30pm Sun*) with friendly and helpful staff, and Transaero airlines also has several ticket outlets, such as the very convenient **Transaero office** (*Map 6;* ☎ *241 4800; Okhotny ryad 2; open 9am-9pm daily*) in the corner of Hotel Moskva.

Train

Moscow has rail links to most parts of Russia, most former Soviet states, many Eastern and Western Europe countries and China and Mongolia. See the European Russia Getting Around chapter for general information on train travel, fares, and deciphering timetables.

When taking trains from Moscow, note the difference between long-distance and 'suburban' trains. Long-distance trains run to places at least three or four hours out of Moscow, with limited stops and a range of accommodation classes. Suburban trains, known as *prigorodnye poezdy* or *elektrichka*, run to within just 100km or 200km of Moscow, stop almost everywhere, and have a single class of hard bench seats. You simply buy your ticket before the train leaves, and there's no capacity limit – so you may have to stand part of the way. Most Moscow stations have a separate ticket hall for suburban trains, usually called the Prigorodny Zal and often tucked away at the side or back of the station building. Suburban trains are usually listed on separate timetables, and may go from a separate group of platforms.

Note that the fine for travelling without a ticket in Moscow is R100.

Stations Moscow's nine main stations, all with accompanying metro stops, are:

Belorus Station (Belorussky vokzal; Map 2; metro Belorusskaya; Tverskaya Zastava pl) Serves trains to/from Smolensk, Kaliningrad, Belarus, Lithuania, Poland, Germany; some trains to/from the Czech Republic; and suburban trains to/from the west including Mozhaysk, Borodino, Zvenigorod.

Kazan Station (Kazansky vokzal; Map 3; metro Komsomolskaya; Komsomolskaya pl). Serves trains to/from Cheboxary, Yoshkar-Ola, Kazan, Izhevsk, Ufa, Ryazan, Penza, Ulyanovsk, Samara, Novorossiysk, Central Asia; some trains to/from Vladimir, Nizhny Novgorod, the Ural Mountains, Siberia, Saratov, Rostov-on-Don; and suburban trains to/from the south-east, including Bykovo airport, Kolomna, Gzhel, Ryazan.

Kiev Station (Kievsky vokzal; Map 4; metro Kievskaya; pl Kievskogo vokzala) Serves Bryansk, Kiev, western Ukraine, Moldova, Slovakia, Hungary, Austria, Romania, Bulgaria, Croatia, Serbia, Greece, Venice. There are some trains to/from the Czech Republic, and suburban trains to/from the southwest, including Peredelkino and Kaluga.

Kursk Station (Kursky vokzal; Map 3; metro Kurskaya; pl Kurskogo Vokzala) Serves Oryol, Kursk, Krasnodar, Adler, the Caucasus, eastern Ukraine, Crimea, Georgia, Azerbaijan. It also has some trains to/from Rostov-on-Don, Vladimir, Nizhny Novgorod, Perm; and suburban trains to/from the east and south, including Petushki, Vladimir, Podolsk, Chekhov, Serpukhov, Tula.

Leningrad Station (Leningradsky vokzal; Map 3; metro Komsomolskaya; Komsomolskaya pl) Serves Tver, Novgorod, Pskov, St Petersburg, Vyborg, Murmansk, Estonia, Helsinki; and suburban trains to/from the northwest including Klin, Tver.

Pavelets Station (Paveletsky vokzal; Map 5; metro Paveletskaya; Paveletskaya pl) Serves Yelets, Lipetsk, Voronezh, Tambov, Volgograd, Astrakhan; some trains to/from Saratov; and suburban trains to/from the southeast, including Leninskaya.

Riga Station (Rizhsky vokzal; Outer North Moscow Map; metro Rizhskaya; Rizhskaya pl) Serves Latvia, with suburban trains to/from the northwest, including Istra and Novoierusalimskaya.

Savyolov Station (Savyolovsky vokzal; Outer North Moscow Map; metro Savyolovskaya; pl Savyolovskogo vokzala) Serves Cherepovets; some trains to/from Kostroma, Vologda; and suburban trains to/from the north.

Yaroslavl Station (Yaroslavsky vokzal; Map 3; metro Komsomolskaya; Komsomolskaya pl) Serves Yaroslavl, Arkhangelsk, Vorkuta, the Russian Far East, Mongolia, China, North Korea; with some trains to/from Vladimir, Nizhny Novgorod, Kostroma, Vologda, Perm, Urals, Siberia; and suburban trains to/from the northeast, including Abramtsevo, Khotkovo, Sergiev Posad, Alexandrov.

MOSCOW

Tickets For long-distance trains it's best to buy your tickets in advance. Tickets on some trains may be available on the day of departure, but this is less likely in summer. Always take your passport along when buying a ticket.

Besides train stations, tickets are sold throughout the city at *kassa zheleznoy dorogi* (ticket offices) of the **Central Railway Agency** *(Tsentralnoe Zheleznodorozhnoe Agentstvo; Map 3; ☎ 262 2566; Maly Kharitonevsky per 6; open 8am-1pm & 2pm-7pm daily)*. Alternative options are travel agents and other ticket offices, which will sometimes charge a small commission – frankly, it's worth it.

Bus

Buses run to a number of towns and cities within 700km of Moscow. Bus fares are similar to *kupeynyy* (2nd-class) train fares. The buses tend to be crowded, although they are usually faster than the *prigorodnye* trains, and are convenient for some destinations.

To book a seat go out to the long-distance bus terminal, the Shchyolkovsky Avtovokzal (Щёлковский Автовокзал), beside Shchyolkovskaya metro station in the east of the city. Queues can be bad, so it's advisable to book ahead, especially for travel on Friday, Saturday or Sunday.

Buses are best for those destinations with poor train services. These include Pereslavl-Zalessky (not on a railway) and Vladimir (with few afternoon trains from Moscow).

Car & Motorcycle

See the Car & Motorcycle section in the earlier European Russia Getting Around chapter for general advice.

Ten major highways, numbered M1 to M10 (but not in any logical order), fan out from Moscow to all points of the compass. Most are in fairly good condition near the city, but some get pretty bad farther out. The main road from Western Europe, the M1 from Poland via Brest, Minsk and Smolensk, is straight and dull but fairly quick. The M10 to St Petersburg is dual carriageway for much of the way to Tver, 145km out, although there are narrow stretches beyond. The first 110km of the M2 to Oryol and Ukraine are excellent dual carriageway – something you'll remember like a dream as you hit some of the bumpy, narrow roads farther south. The M7 east to Vladimir and the M8 northeast to

Yaroslavl are in reasonable condition, but are busy and slow.

Moscow has no shortage of gas stations selling all grades of petrol. Most are open 24 hours, are affiliated with Western oil companies, and can be found on the major roads in and out of town. There are parts, service and repair specialists for many Western makes of car in Moscow. See the *Moscow Business Telephone Guide* for listings.

Car Rental While there's little reason for the average traveller to rent a car for getting about Moscow (as public transport is quite adequate), you might want to consider it for trips out of the city.

There are lots of car rental firms in Moscow, and most tourist hotels have a rental desk of some kind, but the scene has two special features: many firms won't let you take their cars out of the city, and others will only rent a car with a driver. Company policies change frequently, so the only answer is to ring round to try to find what you want. Cars with drivers aren't always more expensive, and they save you the trouble of coping with Russian roads.

The major international rental firms have outlets in Moscow. Generally it is best to reserve your car before you arrive – advance reservations and special offers can reduce the price by 50% or more. Prices quoted are for on-the-spot rental of the cheapest car available.

The 'Big Three' have desks at Sheremetevo-2 airport and will usually pick up or drop off the car at your hotel. **Avis** *(☎ 578 7179)* charges US$62 per day, **Budget** *(☎ 737 0407)* US$68 per day, and **Hertz** *(☎ 937 3274)* US$90 per day.

Boat

In summer, passenger boats from Moscow ply the rivers and canals of Russia all the way north to St Petersburg, and south to Astrakhan on the Volga Delta near the Caspian Sea.

The St Petersburg route follows the Moscow Canal and then the Volga River to the Rybinsk Reservoir; then the Volga–Baltic Canal to Lake Onega; the Svir River to Lake Ladoga; and the Neva River to St Petersburg.

The main southbound route takes the Moscow Canal north to the Volga. It then follows the Volga east before heading south all the way downstream to Astrakhan (which is nine days from Moscow), via Uglich,

Yaroslavl, Kostroma, Nizhny Novgorod, Kazan, Ulyanovsk, Samara, Saratov and Volgograd.

The Moscow terminus for these sailings is the **Northern River Station** (Severny Rechnoy Vokzal; Outer North Moscow Map; ☎ 459 7476; Leningradskoe shosse 51). To get there take the metro to Rechnoy Vokzal, then walk 15 minutes due west, passing under Leningradskoe shosse and through a nice park.

The navigation season depends on the route. Sailings between Moscow and Astrakhan via Yaroslavl, Nizhny Novgorod and Kazan leave a few times a week from early June to mid-October. The ships are operated by the **Capital Shipping Company** (☎/fax 458 9163) and tickets are sold at the Northern River Station; sometimes the easiest way to obtain reliable schedule information is to visit the office in person. (See the boxed text 'Cruising the Volga' in the later Volga Region chapter.)

Capital Shipping – and other boat and tour companies – schedule ships between Moscow and St Petersburg, stopping at some of the Golden Ring cities: see Boat in the earlier European Russia Getting Around chapter for details.

GETTING AROUND

The central area around the Kremlin, Kitai Gorod and the Bolshoi Theatre are best seen on foot. Otherwise, the fastest, cheapest and easiest way to get around is almost always on the metro, though buses, trolleybuses and trams are useful sometimes.

To/From the Airports

If you're in a hurry, or travelling at odd hours, or have a lot of baggage, you may want to hire a taxi to get to/from the airport.

However, the easiest and surest way to get from any airport into the city is to book your transfer in advance through a travel agent (see Travel Agencies under Information earlier in this chapter). This means you will be driven straight to your destination in the city and you may not have to pay any more than a normal taxi fare.

Leaving Moscow, your hotel or accommodation will always be able to arrange a taxi for you, although you can get one cheaper yourself – see Taxi later in this section. Don't rely on flagging one down on the street, as it may take a long time to find a driver prepared to drive that far.

Avoid the hassle of a taxi by using metro or suburban trains in conjunction with minivan services for all five airports. Not only do you save a huge amount of money, but during times of heavy traffic you save a lot of time as well. The only disadvantage is that the minivans leave only when full and don't have much room for luggage.

Sheremetevo At Sheremetevo-2, the minibuses leave from a special area 200m in front of the terminal. Walk straight out of the arrivals area to the right around the car park, staying inside the auto ramp. The bus stop has a small shelter and lies between the auto ramps leading to/from the upper departures level.

Minibuses travel between Rechnoy Vokzal and Sheremetevo-1, with Sheremetevo-2 the middle stop in either direction (make certain you get a minibus going in the right direction from Sheremetevo-2). They make the journey as soon as they are full, which is about every 30 minutes or less.

At Rechnoy Vokzal, leave the metro platform by the exit at the front end of your train. Walk 100m straight ahead out of the metro station to the road, where the minivans will be waiting. The combined metro and minivan trip to/from Sheremetevo-2 takes about one hour; to/from Sheremetevo-1 is 70 minutes.

Large, blue Aeroflot buses follow the same route and charge about the same, but they run less often. City bus No 551 also follows this route, but takes much longer.

A taxi arranged on the spot between Sheremetevo airport and the city centre takes about 45 minutes and should cost around R1000, although absurd prices may be asked of tourists. A better bet is to arrange one in advance from **Logus 88** (☎ 911 9747), which charges R500/800 for a prebooked car to/from the Sheremetevo airports. **Taxi Bistro** (☎ 324 9974, 324 5144) is even cheaper, charging R450 to the airport, or R120 per hour otherwise.

Domodedovo As of 2002, a new express train leaves Pavelets Station every two hours for Domodedovo airport. A one-way trip costs RR30 and takes about 45 minutes. This route is particularly convenient, as you can check into your flight at the train station.

From about 7am to 9pm, the airport is linked to Domodedovskaya metro by minibus, taking 30 to 40 minutes. Going out to the

MOSCOW

airport, you should allow 90 minutes for the combined metro and minibus trip.

A taxi to/from the city centre should cost about R1000, with the trip taking one to 1½ hours, depending on traffic.

Vnukovo Minibuses link the airport with Yugo-Zapadnaya metro from about 7am to 9pm. The trip takes 30 minutes and costs R15.

A taxi to/from the city centre can take over an hour and costs about R1000.

Bykovo *Prigorodnye* trains run between Bykovo train station, 400m from the airport, and Kazan Station in the city. One of their stops en route is Vykhino, by Vykhino metro.

Going out to the airport, most trains heading for Vinogradovo, Shifernaya or Golutvin stop at Bykovo, but just a few go straight through; always check. These trains take about one hour and leave about every 20 minutes, from 5am to 10pm.

A taxi to/from the city centre is about R1000 and can take 1½ hours.

Metro

The metro is the easiest, quickest and cheapest way of getting around Moscow. With elegant, graffiti-free stations, many featuring marble-faced, frescoed, gilded works of art, this is one Stalinist project Muscovites are proud of. The stations were meant to double

Underground Art

The Moscow metro is justly famous for the art and design of many of its stations, with the circular line a tourist attraction in its own right. All the stations are done in marble and decorated in bas-reliefs, stucco, mosaics and chandeliers. But diversity of theme is not their strongest point – rather, it's history, war, the happy life of the Soviet people, or a mix of all.

The highlights of the circular line stations are:

Taganskaya Features a war theme, with the heads of unknown war heroes set in luscious, floral stucco frames made of white-and-blue porcelain with gold linings.

Prospekt Mira Also decorated in elegant gold-trimmed white porcelain, although the bas-reliefs receive some development and action. Rather than motionless heads, there are happy farmers picking fruit, children reading books, and so on.

Novoslobodskaya Features brightly illuminated stained-glass panels with happy workers, farmers and even more flowers. There's also a pianist, an artist, and someone sitting at a desk by a globe (who might that be?).

Belorusskaya Mosaics on the ceiling depict yet more happy workers, along with farmers milking cows, dancing, taking oaths. All wear Belarusian national shirts for the occasion.

Komsomolskaya Features a huge stuccoed hall, its ceiling featuring the mosaics of past Russian military heroes: Peter the Great, Dmitry Donskoy, Alexander Suvorov and more.

Barrikadnaya Done in dramatic red-and-white marble, it features bas-reliefs depicting the fateful events of 1905 and 1917.

Kievskaya The hall is decorated with labelled mosaics, among them *Friendship of Russian and Ukrainian Farmers*, *Pushkin in Ukraine* (featuring Pushkin among Ukrainian folk singers), and *Chernyshevsky, Dobrolyubov, Nekrasov and Shevtchenko in St Petersburg* (the first three are Russian writers, the last Ukrainian). Other mosaics feature the events of significant dates, such as *1905 in Donbass* or *The Battle of Poltava, 1709*.

The most decorated of the radial line stations (most near the centre) include:

Mayakovskaya Grand Prize winner at the 1938 World's Fair in New York. It has a central hall that's all stainless steel and marble.

Novokuznetskaya Features military bas-reliefs done in sober khaki and colourful ceiling mosaics depicting pictures of the happy life. The elegant marble benches came from the first Church of Christ the Saviour.

Ploshchad Revolyutsii Life-size bronze statues in the main hall and beside the escalators illustrate the idealised roles of common men and women. Heading up the escalators the themes, in order, are revolution, industry, agriculture, hunting, education, sport and child-rearing.

Izmaylovsky Park Features floral bas-reliefs decorated with AK-47 machine guns.

★★★

as air-raid shelters, which is why the escalators seem to plunge halfway to the centre of the earth.

The 150-plus stations are marked outside with big 'M' signs. Magnetic tickets are sold at ticket booths for one, two or more rides, and each ride costs R5, unless you buy in bulk (10 rides for R35, 20 for R70, 60 for R150).

Stations have maps of the system and signs on each platform showing the destination. Interchange stations are linked by underground passages, indicated by *perekhod* (crossover) signs, usually blue with a stick figure running up the stairs. Once you've figured out which train you need, you'll rarely wait more than two minutes for it. With elementary Cyrillic and by counting stops, you can manage very well. If you get lost, the kindly women who supervise the escalators can point you in the right direction.

These days, the Moscow metro has implemented a sort of public-relations campaign. You will notice posters decorated by pretty, smiling, young ladies in uniform promising 'Good weather, any time of year.' These *devushki* (young women) bear little resemblance to the babushkas sitting at the bottom of the escalators, but let's not mull over a technicality.

The carriages now have maps inside that show the stops for that line in both Roman and Cyrillic letters. The biggest confusion you may find is that often when two or more lines meet, each line's interchange station has a different name.

Here are some other metro facts:

- The first station opened in 1935, with early work driven on by project manager Nikita Khrushchev (and we mean *driven* as thousands toiled around the clock under dire conditions).
- Up to nine million people a day ride the metro, more than the London and New York City systems combined.
- The first stations are so deep because they were designed to double as bomb shelters (you'll notice the newer stations aren't as deep after it was realised you just couldn't dig down far enough to escape a hail of American nuclear bombs).

Bus, Trolleybus & Tram

Buses, trolleybuses and trams are useful along a few radial or cross-town routes that the metro misses, and are necessary for reaching sights away from the city centre.

To ride them, you need a ticket to stick in one of the ticket-punchers inside the vehicle. *Talony* (tickets; R5) can be purchased from drivers, street kiosks, and (sometimes) metro stations – they can be used for all three types of vehicle (some vehicles have their very own *provodnitsa* or conductor). Riding without a ticket is punishable by a fine of about US$5.

Taxi

Almost any car in Moscow could be a taxi if the price is right, so get on the street and stick your arm out. Before too long, you'll be on your way. Many private cars cruise around as unofficial taxis, known as 'gypsy cabs', and other drivers will often take you if they're going in roughly the same direction.

Although the price for such services varies according to time of day, traffic conditions and distance, expect to pay anywhere from R50 to R150. You may want to fix the fare before you get in, thereby avoiding any disagreements with your driver at the end of the ride.

Official taxis have a little chequerboard logo on the side and/or a small green light in the windscreen. They charge about the same. No driver uses a meter (even if the cab has one) and few ever admit to having any change. You'll pay more if you catch a taxi right in front of a hotel.

Don't hesitate to wave on a car if you don't like the look of its occupants; you may not want to ride with more than one person. Problems are more likely to crop up if you take a street cab waiting outside a nightclub, or perhaps a tourist hotel or restaurant at night.

To book in advance, call the **Central Taxi Reservation Office** (*Tsentralnoe Byuro Zakazov Taxi;* ☎ 927 0000); the service operates 24 hours. You should give them at least one, and preferably two or more, hours' notice. Usually the phone dispatcher will speak a bit of English, though it may help if you speak some Russian. They'll ring you back a few minutes before pick-up to confirm you still want the booking and to give you the car's registration number. You'll be charged R50 for the booking, then around R10 per kilometre.

Around Moscow Подмосковье

This region is in many ways the heartland of Russia, with a subtly changing landscape crossed by winding rivers and dotted by peasant villages, the typical provincial scene immortalised by so many artists and writers. The towns and villages are an equally typical mixture of the ancient and picturesque, the modern and drab.

As soon as you leave Moscow, the contrasts between the fast-paced, modern capital and the slower, old-fashioned and often poorer provincial world become apparent. Even one trip out of the big city will provide a glimpse of the life that the majority of Russians lead.

This chapter covers places within about 300 km of Moscow. Most are a feasible day trip from the capital, but some of the more distant places are easier with an overnight (or longer) stop. The 'Golden Ring' of historic towns and villages northeast of Moscow is well worth a few days of your time.

GETTING THERE & AWAY

Many places in this chapter can be reached by *elektrichka* (suburban train) from Moscow, among the easiest and quickest forms of Russian transport to use. At the appropriate Moscow station, find the *prigorodnyy zal* (suburban ticket hall, пригородный зал) check the timetable for a train going where you want, buy your ticket and you're off. All carriages are one class and no advance bookings or compartment reservations are needed. Buses often run the same routes and take less time than the suburban trains.

The most efficient, albeit most expensive, way to visit the destinations around Moscow is by car. Renting a car in Moscow will allow you to visit more than one destination in a day, or to take a tour around the Golden Ring in a few days. Alternatively, you can often hire cars with drivers at the local bus stations. Rates are about R10 per kilometre from Moscow, but less around the smaller towns, which may be cost-effective if you're travelling in a group or on a tight schedule.

Local Moscow-based tour agencies such as **Dom Patriarshy Tours** (*☎/fax 795 0927; e alanskaya@co.ru; Vspolny per 6, Moscow school No 1239*) also organise excursions to most of these destinations.

Highlights

- Wander through the Russian fairy-tale landscape of Suzdal
- Climb the Golden Gate and relive the siege of Vladimir by the Mongol-led Golden Horde
- Be treated to a concert from the Rostov-Veliky bell tower
- Admire the collaborative perfection of the Saviour Church at Abramtsevo
- Contemplate the devastation of the Battle of Borodino

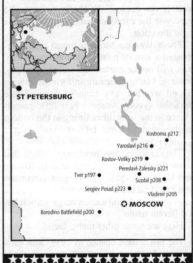

ST PETERSBURG

Kostroma p212
Yaroslavl p216
Rostov-Veliky p219
Tver p197
Pereslavl-Zalessky p221
Suzdal p208
Sergiev Posad p223
Vladimir p205
○ MOSCOW
Borodino Battlefield p200

★★★★★★★★★★★★★★★★★★

Northwest

KLIN
КЛИН

Tchaikovsky lived in Klin, 90km northwest of central Moscow, from 1885 until he died in 1893. Here he wrote his *Pathetique* symphony (the Sixth), as well as the *Nutcracker* and *Sleeping Beauty*. His last residence has become a **museum** (*Dom-Muzey Chaykovskogo; ☎ 224-581 96; ul Chaykovskogo 48; admission R60; open 10am-6pm Fri-Tues*), kept much as it was when Tchaikovsky lived here. You can browse through the documents

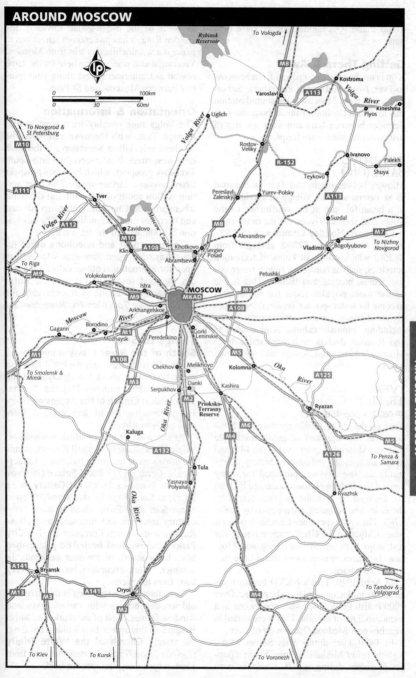

AROUND MOSCOW

AROUND MOSCOW

and personal effects, including his Becker grand piano. Occasional concerts are held here.

Getting There & Away

Klin is on the road and railway from Moscow to Tver, Novgorod and St Petersburg. Suburban trains from Moscow's Leningrad Station run to Klin (1½ hours) throughout the day. Services between Klin and Tver – a trip of just over one hour – are frequent.

ZAVIDOVO
ЗАВИДОВО

Midway between Klin and Tver on the road to St Petersburg, the village of Zavidovo is in a beautiful spot at the confluence of the Volga and Shosha Rivers. On the outskirts is the **Zavidovo Holiday Complex** (☎ 095-937 99 44; hotel rooms R3900, cottages from R6300) which offers all kinds of recreation activities, such as horseback riding, water skiing, tennis, boating and fishing. This is one of the most popular spots for Muscovites to come for water sports. Comfortable cottages are available in various architectural styles, including Finnish cabins, Alpine chalets and Russian dachas. Suburban trains from Moscow's Leningrad Station take about two hours.

TVER
ТВЕРЬ

☎ 0822 • pop 450,000

Tver, on the Volga 150km northwest of Moscow, was the capital of an unruly mini-state that was Moscow's chief rival in the 14th and 15th centuries. Its subsequent history is less fortuitous: the city was punished for rising against the Golden Horde, conquered by Ivan III, savaged by Ivan the Terrible, seized by the Poles and completely destroyed by fire in 1763. The city experienced a rebirth of sorts when Catherine the Great made it one of her rest stops between St Petersburg and Moscow. In places, it now looks like a little rustic St Petersburg.

In April 1940, Tver's NKVD headquarters hosted a murder, or murders to be precise. Over 6000 Polish POWs were shot one by one in a soundproof room at night. They were buried in trenches near Mednoe, 20km west of Tver.

In 1990 Tver dumped its Soviet name, Kalinin (after Mikhail Kalinin, Stalin's puppet president during WWII, who was born here). Though Tver is not in the same league as some of the old Russian towns of the Golden Ring, it has just enough attractions to make it a worthwhile day trip from Moscow. You might also want to stop here for the same reason as Catherine: to rest along your journey between Moscow and St Pete.

Orientation & Information

The Volga runs roughly from west to east through Tver, with the town centre on the southern side. Ulitsa Sovetskaya is the main east–west street. It intersects the north–south Tverskoy prospekt, which becomes prospekt Chaykovskogo farther south. The train station is 4km south of the centre, at the point where prospekt Chaykovskogo turns 90° east and becomes ulitsa Kominterna. The bus station is 300m east of the train station.

The main **post and telephone office** (ul Sovetskaya 31; open 8am-8pm Mon-Sat) is open for international phone calls 24 hours a day. A good source of maps is the **Knigi bookshop** (☎ 33 20 70; ul Tryokhsvyatskaya 28; open 10am-7pm Mon-Fri, 10am-5pm Sat & Sun).

Things to See

South of the River Classical townhouses and public buildings from the late 1700s and early 1800s line **ulitsa Sovetskaya** and the riverfront **naberezhnaya Stepana Razina**. The classical **Church of the Ascension** (Tserkov Voznesenia; cnr ul Sovetskaya & Tverskoy pr) is nearby.

At the western end of ulitsa Sovetskaya, fronted by a statue of Mikhail Kalinin, stands the town's most imposing building – Catherine the Great's 1775 **Road Palace** (Putevoy dvorets). It houses Tver's **Art Gallery** (☎ 33 35 31; ul Sovetskaya 5; admission R10; open 11am-5pm Wed-Sun), which features 18th-century interiors and furniture, as well as Russian and Western European art. The **City Park** on the river bank behind the palace often hosts live concerts on summer weekends. In summer, Volga excursion boats sail every hour from the piers.

The quaintest part of town is the streets of old wooden houses with carved eaves and window frames, west of the market on ulitsa Bragina. In this area is Tver's oldest building, the stately **Church of the White Trinity** (Tserkov Beloy Troitsy; Trudolyubia per), from 1564, where daily services are held.

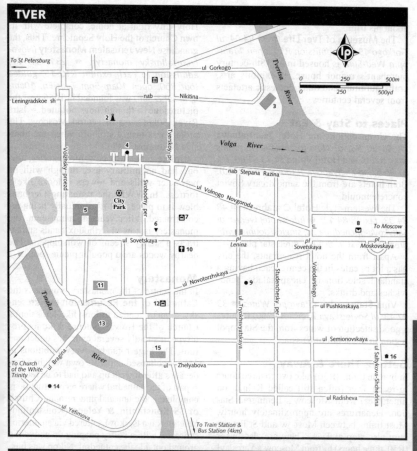

TVER

PLACES TO STAY & EAT
6 Vina Stavropolya
  Вина Ставрополья
11 Hotel Tsentralnaya
  Гостиница Центральная
15 Hotel Volga
  Гостиница Волга
16 Hotel Osnabruck
  Гостиница Оснабрюк

OTHER
1 Museum of Tver Life
  Музей тверского быта

2 Afanasy Nikitin Statue
  Памятник Афанасию
  Никитину
3 River Station
  Речной вокзал
4 Excursion-Boat
  Landings
  Пристань для речных
  экскурсий
5 Road Palace; Art Gallery
  Путевой Дворец
7 Tram Stop
  Трамвайная остановка

8 Post and Telephone Office
  Почтамт и переговорный
  пункт
9 Knigi Bookshop
  Магазин Книги
10 Church of the Ascension
  Церковь Вознесения
12 Tram Stop
  Остановка трамваев
13 Circus
  Цирк
14 Market
  Рынок

AROUND MOSCOW

North of the River A promenade stretches along the north bank of the Volga, providing lovely views of the old houses on the south- ern bank. The **statue** in the park here is of Afanasy Nikitin, a local merchant who went overland to India 30 years before Vasco da

Gama sailed there, and wrote a bestseller about his trip.

The **Museum of Tver Life** (☎ 31 84 04; ul Gorkogo 19/14; admission R15; open 11am-5pm Wed-Sun) is housed in an 18th-century merchant's manor house. It exhibits arts, crafts, furniture and other domestic artefacts from several centuries.

Places to Stay & Eat
The cheap options are **Hotel Tsentralnaya** (☎ 48 90 93; ul Novotorzhskaya 1; rooms from R200) and **Hotel Volga** (☎ 33 81 00, fax 37 95 57; ul Zhelyabova 1; rooms from R360). Both hotels are from the same dreary Soviet concrete mould.

The Western-style **Hotel Osnabruck** (☎ 48 84 33, fax 48 84 12; e info@hotel.tver.ru; ul Saltykova-Shchedrina 20; singles/doubles with breakfast US$60/ 80) is a three-star place.

Apart from the hotel restaurants, the city has a lot of cafés in the centre, each having a standard selection of cheap salads, sandwiches and drinks.

Vina Stavropolya (Stavropol Wines; ☎ 33 37 48; ul Sovietskaya 7; dishes R150) features a good selection of wines from the Stavropol region in the south of Russia.

Getting There & Away
Suburban trains (R30) take two to three hours to reach Tver (often still called Kalinin on timetables) from Moscow's Leningrad Station. Departures are approximately hourly. Most trains between Moscow and St Petersburg also stop at Tver. There are also buses (R50, three hours) to/from Moscow's Yaroslavl Station.

Getting Around
Tram Nos 2, 5, 6 and 11 run from the bus and train stations up Tchaikovskogo and Tverskoy prospekts to the town centre.

West

ISTRA & NEW JERUSALEM MONASTERY
ИСТРА И НОВО-ИЕРУСАЛИМСКИЙ МОНАСТЫРЬ
In the 17th century, Nikon, the patriarch whose reforms drove the Old Believers from the Orthodox Church, decided to show one and all that Russia deserved to be the centre of the Christian world by building a little Holy City right at home, complete with its own Church of the Holy Sepulchre. Thus, the grandiose **New Jerusalem Monastery** (Novo-Iyerusalimsky monastyr; ☎ 231-497 87; admission to each exhibit R10-15; guided tour R50; open 10am-5pm Tues-Fri, 10am-6pm Sat & Sun) was founded in 1656 near the picturesque – though now polluted – Istra River, 50km west of central Moscow. The project was nearly stillborn when the abrasive Nikon lost his job.

Unlike other Moscow monasteries, this one had no military use, though with its perimeter walls and towers it looks like a fortress. In WWII, the retreating Germans blew it to pieces but it's gradually being reconstructed. After years as a museum, the monastery is now in Orthodox hands and attracts a steady stream of worshippers. The nearby woods are a popular picnic spot.

Monastery
In the centre of the monastery grounds is the **Cathedral of the Resurrection** (Voskresensky sobor) intended to look like Jerusalem's Church of the Holy Sepulchre. Like its prototype, it's really several churches under one roof. The huge rotunda – very ambitious in 1685 – collapsed under its own weight a few decades after it went up and had to be rebuilt. A part of the cathedral where reconstruction is complete is the unusual underground **Church of SS Konstantin & Yelena** (Konstantino-Yeleninskaya tserkov), entered via an interior staircase, with a belfry peeping up above the ground outside the cathedral. Nikon was buried in the cathedral, beneath the **Church of John the Baptist** (Tserkov Ioanna Predtechi).

At the rear of the grounds is the Moscow baroque **Nativity Church** (Rozhdestvenskaya tserkov), with chambers for the tsar on the left and the abbot on the right. It houses a **museum** with books, porcelain, paintings, icons, old armour and a section on the history of the monastery. Behind the monastery near the river is Nikon's former 'hermitage', a rather unmonastic three-storey affair.

Museum of Wooden Architecture
Just outside the monastery's north wall, the Moscow region's Museum of Wooden Architecture (☎ 231-497 87; admission R8; open 10am-5pm Tues-Fri, 10am-6pm Sat & Sun) is a collection of renovated 17th- to 19th-

century buildings. Outside they display the traditional 'gingerbread' woodwork, inside they give a glimpse of old rural life.

Getting There & Away

Suburban trains run about twice an hour from Moscow's Riga Station to Istra (about one hour), from where buses run to the Muzey stop by the monastery.

By car, leave Moscow by Leningradsky prospekt and its continuation, Volokolamskoe shosse, and continue through Dedovsk to Istra. The monastery is 2km west of the town centre.

ARKHANGELSKOE
АРХАНГЕЛЬСКОЕ

On the Moscow River a short distance west of Moscow's outer ring road, Arkhangelskoe (☎ 095-363 13 75; admission to grounds/exhibits R35/35; open 10am-5pm Wed-Sun) is one of the grandest estates in the region. A grandson of Dmitry Golitsyn, a statesman under Peter the Great, started work on a palace in the 1780s but lost interest and sold it all to Prince Nikolay Yusupov, one of the richest Russians of that time or since.

During several ambassadorships and as Director of the Imperial Museums, Yusupov accumulated a private art collection that outclassed many European museums. After a rough start – the house was pillaged by Napoleon's troops, trashed in a serfs' revolt and nearly burnt down – Yusupov fixed it up and filled it with his treasures. The grounds and buildings are beautiful.

The **main house** of the palace consists of a series of elegant halls that display Yusupov's paintings, furniture, sculptures, glass, tapestries and porcelain. His paintings include an entire room devoted to the Italian master Tiepolo; according to one source, there are also portraits of every one of Yusupov's 300 mistresses.

The multilevel, Italianate **gardens** are full of 18th-century copies of classical statues. A colonnade on the eastern side was meant to be a Yusupov family mausoleum, but was never finished. Yusupov also organised a troupe of serf actors that eventually became one of the best known of its kind, and built them a **theatre** just west of the gardens. Predating everything else is the little white **Church of the Archangel Michael** (Arkhangelskaya tserkov; 1667).

Getting There & Away

The estate is 22km west of central Moscow. Bus Nos 151 or 62 from Moscow's Tushinskaya Metro Station stop at Arkhangelskoe.

If you're driving, head northwest on Leningradsky prospekt, stay to the left as it becomes Volokolamskoe shosse, then beyond the outer ring road, fork left into Ilinskoe shosse.

BORODINO
БОРОДИНО

In 1812 Napoleon invaded Russia, lured by the prospect of taking Moscow. For three months the Russians retreated, until on 26 August the two armies met in a bloody battle of attrition at the village of Borodino, 130km west of Moscow. In 15 hours, more than one-third of each army was killed – over 100,000 soldiers in all. Europe would know nothing as terrible until WWI.

The French seemed to be the winners, as the Russians withdrew and abandoned Moscow. But Borodino was in fact the beginning of the end for Napoleon, who was soon in full, disastrous retreat.

The entire battlefield – more than 100 sq km – is now the **Borodino Field Museum-Preserve**, basically vast fields dotted with dozens of memorials to specific divisions and generals (most erected at the centenary of the battle in 1912). It includes a **museum** (☎ 238-515 46; **w** www.borodino.ru; open 10am-6pm Tues-Sun), recently renovated to honour the battle's 90th anniversary in 2002.

The front line was roughly along the 4km road from Borodino village to the train station. The French were to its west, the Russians to its east. Most of the monuments are close to the road. The hilltop monument about 400m in front of the museum is the **grave** of Prince Bagration, a heroic Georgian infantry general who was mortally wounded in battle.

Farther south, a concentration of monuments around Semyonovskoe village marks the battle's most frenzied fighting; here Bagration's heroic Second Army, opposing far larger French forces, was virtually obliterated. The redoubts around Semyonovskoe changed hands eight times in the battle. Apparently Russian commander Mikhail Kutuzov deliberately sacrificed Bagration's army to save his larger First Army, opposing lighter French forces in the northern part of the battlefield. Kutuzov's headquarters are marked by an obelisk in the village of Gorki. Another

AROUND MOSCOW

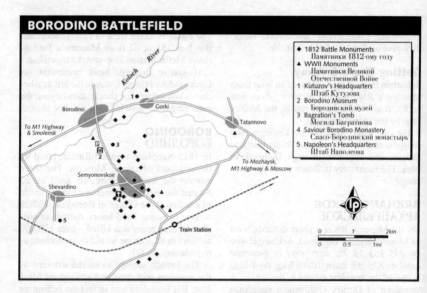

BORODINO BATTLEFIELD

River
Koloch

Borodino

Gorki

To M1 Highway
& Smolensk

Tatarinovo

To Mozhaysk,
M1 Highway & Moscow

Semyonovskoe

Shevardino

Train Station

◆ 1812 Battle Monuments
   Памятники 1812-ому году
▲ WWII Monuments
   Памятники Великой
   Отечественной Войне
1 Kutuzov's Headquarters
   Штаб Кутузова
2 Borodino Museum
   Бородинский музей
3 Bagration's Tomb
   Могила Багратиона
4 Saviour Borodino Monastery
   Спасо-Бородинский монастырь
5 Napoleon's Headquarters
   Штаб Наполеона

obelisk near Shevardino to the southwest, paid for in 1912 with French donations, marks Napoleon's camp.

Ironically, this battle scene was recreated during WWII, when the Red Army confronted the Nazis on this very site. Memorials to this battle also dot the fields, and WWII trenches surround the monument to Bagration. Near the train station are two WWII mass graves. The **Saviour Borodino Monastery** (☎ 238-510 57; admission R15; open 10am-5pm Tues-Sun) has a small exhibit on the WWII battle.

The rolling hills around Borodino and Semyonovskoe are largely undeveloped, due to their historic status. Facilities are extremely limited; be sure to bring a picnic lunch.

Getting There & Away

Suburban trains leave in the morning from Moscow's Belorus Station to Borodino (R20, two hours). A few trains return to Moscow in the evening, but be prepared to spend some time waiting. If you miss the train, you may be able to catch a bus to nearby Mozhaysk, from where there are frequent trains and buses.

Since the area is rural, visiting by car is more convenient and probably more rewarding. If driving from Moscow, stay on the M1 highway (Minskoe shosse) till the Mozhaysk turn-off, 95km beyond the Moscow outer ring road. It's 5km north to Mozhaysk, then 13km west to Borodino village.

PEREDELKINO
ПЕРЕДЕЛКИНО

Boris Pasternak – poet, author of *Doctor Zhivago* and winner of the 1958 Nobel Prize for literature – lived for a long time in a dacha in this now-trendy writers' colony on Moscow's southwestern outskirts, just 5km beyond the city's outer ring road. Pasternak's dacha is now a museum, the **Dom-Muzey Pasternaka** (☎ 095-934 51 75; Pavlenko 3; admission R25, guided tour R50; open 10am-4pm Thur-Sun). The museum features the room where he finished *Doctor Zhivago* and the room where he died.

Though officially in disgrace when he died in 1960, thousands of people came to Pasternak's funeral, and even before *perestroika* his grave had a steady stream of visitors. Follow the main road to the cemetery; in a little pine grove towards the rear on the right-hand side, you will see the stone slab bearing Pasternak's profile. Above the graveyard sits the tiny 15th-century **Transfiguration Church** (Preobrazhenskaya tserkov), which conducted religious services throughout the Soviet period.

Getting There & Away

Frequent suburban trains go from Moscow's Kiev Station to Peredelkino (20 minutes) on the line to Kaluga-II station.

If you're driving, take Kutuzovsky prospekt, which becomes Mozhayskoe shosse.

Beyond the outer ring road, continue on the M1 highway (Minskoe shosse) and at the 21km post turn left to Peredelkino.

South

GORKI LENINSKIE
ГОРКИ ЛЕНИНСКИЕ

After Lenin narrowly survived an assassination attempt in 1918, he and his family took occasional rests at the lovely 1830s manor house on this wooded estate, 32km southeast of the Kremlin. The estate was redesigned in neoclassical style by the Art Nouveau architect Fyodor Shekhtel. Lenin spent more and more time at Gorki Leninskie after suffering strokes in 1922 and 1923. He left only once in the eight months before he died here on 21 January 1924.

Now this **museum** (☎ 095-548 93 09; admission R10; guided tour R120; open 10am-4pm Wed-Mon) maintains some of the rooms as they were, and the clocks still read 6.50 (am), the time of Lenin's death. You can also see a large collection of Lenin's personal items which were moved from his Kremlin office in 1994. There is a decent **café** on the grounds.

Getting There & Away
Bus No 439 (30 minutes to one hour) leaves every 30 minutes for the estate from the Domodedovskaya metro station in Moscow. By car, follow the M4 highway (Kashirskoe shosse) for about 8km to 11km beyond the Moscow outer ring road, then turn left to Gorki Leninskie.

MELIKHOVO
МЕЛИХОВО

The estate south of Moscow where Anton Chekhov lived from 1892 until 1899 is now open as a **museum** (Muzey A P Chekhova; ☎ 272-236 10) dedicated to the playwright. Chekhov wrote The Seagull and Uncle Vanya here. 'My estate's not much,' he wrote of Melikhovo, 'but the surroundings are magnificent'. Visitors today can wander around the village and peek in the 18th-century **wooden church**.

Chekhov was something of a legendary figure in the town, where he built three local schools and a fire station. When he was in residence, he flew a red flag above his home,

notifying peasants that they could come for medical advice and treatment.

Suburban trains (one hour) run from Moscow's Kursk Station to the town of Chekhov, 12km west of Melikhovo. Occasional buses run between Chekhov and Melikhovo. By car, Melikhovo is about 7km east of the dual carriageway that parallels the old M2 Moscow–Oryol road, signposted 50km south of Moscow's outer ring road.

PRIOKSKO-TERRASNY RESERVE
ПРИОКСКО-ТЕРРАСНЫЙ
ЗАПОВЕДНИК

The Priokso-Terrasny Biosphere Reserve (☎ 27-70 71 45; admission R25, guided tour R45; open 9am-4pm daily) covers 50 sq km bordering the northern flood plain of the Oka River, a tributary of the Volga. It's a meeting point of northern fir groves and marshes with typical southern meadow steppe. The Reserve's varied fauna includes a herd of European bison, brought back from near extinction since WWII.

You cannot wander freely around the reserve by yourself, so it's best to make advance arrangements for one of the informative tours. There's a small **museum** near the office with stuffed specimens of the reserve's fauna, typical of European Russia, including beavers, elk, deer and boar. You're unlikely to see the real thing outside, except maybe elk or deer in winter.

The reserve's pride, and the focus of most visits, is its **European bison nursery** (pitomnik zubrov). Two pairs of bison, one of Europe's largest mammals (some weigh over a tonne), were brought from Poland in 1948. Now there are about 60 and more than 200 have been sent out to other parts of the country. The bison come into the nursery in greatest numbers at feeding time, which is early morning and early evening. For this reason, it's worth spending the night at the **Kordon Hotel** on the grounds of the reserve. You can make bookings through the Reserve.

Getting There & Away
Public transport is difficult. If you leave before 8am, you can take a suburban train from Moscow's Kursk Station to Serpukhov (two hours), then a rare bus to the village of Danki, 1km from the reserve's excursion bureau. You might also be able to negotiate a ride from the station.

AROUND MOSCOW

For drivers, the turn-off from the Moscow–Oryol highway is 76km south of Moscow's outer ring road. Driving from Moscow, you have to turn west and then double back under the highway. Go through Danki then turn right to the reserve. It's 5km from the highway to the excursion bureau.

YASNAYA POLYANA
ЯСНАЯ ПОЛЯНА

Located 14km south of central Tula and around 240km from Moscow, Yasnaya Polyana (☎ 087-513 5425; admission R160; open 9.30am-6pm Wed-Sun) is the estate where the great Russian writer Count Leo Tolstoy was born and buried.

Tolstoy spent much of his life in this house, which is a simple place filled with many of his possessions. His nearby grave is unmarked except for the bouquets of flowers left by newlyweds. In autumn, the apple trees are laden with fruit, which visitors can pick and snack on.

Getting There & Away

The new express suburban train from Moscow's Kursk Station is the easiest way to get to Yasnaya Polyana. Otherwise, you have to go to Tula then take bus No 114 to Shchekino, which stops at the Yasnaya Polyana turn-off. Look for the blue 'Yasnaya Polyana' sign on the main road south from central Tula. From here it's 1km west (right) to the estate entrance.

If you're driving from Moscow, it's easiest to follow Tula's western bypass all the way to its southern end and then turn back north towards Tula. The Yasnaya Polyana turn-off is about 24km from the southern end of the bypass on the road back towards central Tula.

Northeast – The Golden Ring
Северовосток – Золотое Кольцо

The Golden Ring (Zolotoe Koltso) is a modern name for a loop of very old towns northeast of Moscow that preceded the present capital as the political and cultural heart of

Russia. The towns' churches, monasteries, kremlins (city forts) and museums make a picturesque portfolio of early Russian art, architecture and history. Some of the towns are little more than villages, providing a glimpse of peaceful country life as it is lived all over European Russia.

Visitors do run the risk of 'old Russian church' overload, so it pays to travel selectively. The most visited places are Sergiev Posad and Suzdal, as they are accessible from Moscow and artistically exquisite. Other places are less touristy and generally more run down, which can be appealing in its own way.

Some places in the Golden Ring can be visited on day or overnight trips from Moscow. Alternatively, if you have time, devote a few days to visiting several of these ancient gems. Transport and accommodation are easy enough to find along the way. One- or two-day excursions are also available from Moscow. For more information, see Organised Tours in the Moscow chapter.

VLADIMIR
ВЛАДИМИР
☎ 09222 • pop 360,000

Little remains in Vladimir, 178km northeast of Moscow, from its medieval heyday when it was Russia's capital. However, what does remain – several examples of Russia's most ancient and formative architecture – is worth pausing to see en route to or from the more charming town of Suzdal.

History

Vladimir was founded by Vladimir Monomakh of Kiev in 1108 as a fort in the Rostov-Suzdal principality, which he later gave to his son Yury Dolgoruky. Under Yury's son Andrey Bogolyubsky, it became capital of the principality, and capital of all Kyivan Rus after Kiev was sacked in 1169. Andrey and his brother Vsevolod III (1176–1212) consolidated themselves as the strongest Russian princes and brought builders and artists from as far away as Western Europe to give Vladimir a Kiev-like splendour.

Devastated by the Nomadic raiders in 1238 and 1293, the city recovered each time, but its realm disintegrated into small principalities, with Moscow increasingly dominant. The head of the Russian Church resided here from 1300 to 1326, but then moved to Moscow. Worldly power finally shifted to Moscow around this

History of the Golden Ring

The Golden Ring's main towns were founded as outposts of the Kyivan Rus state. At the start of the 12th century, Prince Vladimir Monomakh of Kiev founded a fort at Vladimir. He gave the Rostov-Suzdal principality in which it lay to his son Yury Dolgoruky. Yury made Suzdal his capital but concentrated his energies down south, eventually winning the title of Grand Prince of Kiev and installing himself there. He still took the precaution of fortifying the settlements of Pereslavl-Zalessky and Kostroma in his original territory, along with a small western outpost called Moscow.

After Yury died in 1157, his son and successor, Andrey Bogolyubsky, moved back to the more secure northern territories and based himself at Vladimir. Vladimir became the effective capital of Russia in 1169 when Andrey sacked Kiev, taking the Grand Prince title north. Under these princes and their successors, Suzdal grew rich as a commercial centre and Vladimir sprouted cathedrals, monasteries and massive city walls. Rostov, Yaroslavl and other centres later split off as separate principalities.

In 1237, darkness fell as the Mongol-led Golden Horde invaded Russia, sacking and burning everything. Having made their point, they were mostly content to rule and collect taxes through local princes, which they did for the next 250 years. The region again prospered under Andrey's nephew Yaroslav, and his son Alexander Nevsky of Novgorod.

Moscow was given independence by Alexander Nevsky in 1252. This principality grew in influence as an intermediary between the nomadic tribes and the other Russian princes. Moscow absorbed Pereslavl-Zalessky, Vladimir and Suzdal in the 14th century; the headquarters of the Russian Orthodox Church was transferred from Vladimir in the 1320s; and by the end of the 15th century the entire region was part of Muscovy, the Moscow state.

★★★

time too. Even so, the rulers remained nominally Grand Princes of Vladimir until the 15th century.

In the 20th century, Vladimir prospered anew on the back of textile, mechanical engineering and chemical industries.

Orientation

Vladimir's main street is ulitsa Bolshaya Moskovskaya, although it sometimes goes by its former name, ulitsa III Internatsionala. To make matters more confusing, other segments of the street go by different names, including simply ulitsa Moskovskaya, which is just west of the Golden Gate. Ulitsa Bolshaya Moskovskaya is where you'll find the main attractions such as the Golden Gate and the Cathedrals of the Assumption and St Dmitry. The cathedrals stand impressively at the top of a tree-covered slope looking over the Klyazma River to the south. The train and bus stations are on Vokzalnaya ulitsa at the bottom of the slope and 500m east. The M7 Moscow–Nizhny Novgorod road makes a loop round the northern side of the city.

Information

Hotel Vladimir has an ATM in the lobby. There's a **post and telephone office** (ul Podbelskogo; open 8am-8pm Mon-Fri) and an **Internet Café** (☎ 32 52 57; ul Bolshaya Moskovskaya 51; R30 per hour; open 8am-9pm Mon-Sat).

Assumption Cathedral

Begun in 1158, the Assumption Cathedral (Uspensky sobor; admission R30; open 1.30pm-5pm daily) is a white-stone echo of Kiev's brick Byzantine churches. Its simple but majestic form is adorned with fine carving, innovative for the time. Extended on all sides after a fire in the 1180s, and at the same time gaining four outer domes, the cathedral has changed little since.

The cathedral used to house the *Vladimir Icon of the Mother of God*, brought from Kiev by Andrey Bogolyubsky. A national protector bestowing supreme status to its city of residence, the icon was moved to Moscow in 1390 and is now kept in the Tretyakov Gallery.

Inside the working church a few restored 12th-century murals of peacocks and prophets holding scrolls can be deciphered about halfway up the inner wall of the outer north aisle; this was originally an outside wall. The real treasures are the *Last Judgment* frescoes by Andrey Rublyov and Daniil Chyorny, painted in 1408 in the central nave and inner

Art & Architecture of the Golden Ring

The majority of the Golden Ring's surviving architectural monuments date from spurts of building and rebuilding after the collapse of the Golden Horde. Most were built in the 16th and 17th centuries by the Moscow princes, the Church and a new class of rich merchants.

However, the buildings that give the region a key place in the story of Russian architecture were constructed before the Mongols came. Most important are three 12th-century buildings in and near Vladimir: the Cathedrals of the Assumption and St Dmitry, and the Church of the Intercession on the Nerl. These are the vital link between the architecture of 11th-century Kiev and that of 15th-century Moscow – early northern interpretations of Kiev's Byzantine brick churches.

The Vladimir-Suzdal region also inherited Kiev's Byzantine artistic traditions, though only a few fragments of 12th- and 13th-century frescoes survive in the Vladimir and Suzdal cathedrals and in the old church at Kideksha. (Some icons also survive in Moscow and St Petersburg museums.) While still primarily Byzantine, these works employ bold colours and depict empathetic human expressions that herald later Russian developments.

This 'Vladimir-Suzdal school' came to an end with the Mongol-led invasions. Novgorod was left to continue the development of Russian art. Art revived prolifically in the Golden Ring from the 15th century, but never regained its earlier pioneering role. The best examples are the realistic late-17th-century murals by Gury Nikitin of Kostroma and his followers, which adorn several Golden Ring churches.

south aisle, under the choir gallery towards the west end.

The church also contains the original coffin of Alexander Nevsky of Novgorod, the 13th-century military leader who was also Prince of Vladimir. He was buried in the former **Nativity Monastery** east of here, but his remains were moved to St Petersburg in 1724 when Peter the Great allotted him Russian hero status.

Adjoining the cathedral on the northern side are an 1810 **bell tower** and the 1862 **St George's Chapel**.

Cathedral of St Dmitry

A quick stroll to the east of the Assumption Cathedral is the smaller **Cathedral of St Dmitry** (Dmitrievsky sobor; 1193–97), where the art of Vladimir-Suzdal stone carving reached its pinnacle. The church is permanently closed, but the attraction here is its exterior walls, covered in an amazing profusion of images.

The top centre of the north, south and west walls all show King David bewitching the birds and beasts with music. The Kyivan prince Vsevolod III, who had this church built as part of his palace, appears at the top left of the north wall, with a baby son on his knee and other sons kneeling on each side. Above the right-hand window of the south wall, Alexander the Great ascends into

heaven, a symbol of princely might; on the west wall appear the labours of Hercules.

Across the small street, the **Vladimir Region Pre-Revolutionary History Museum** (ul Bolshaya Moskovskaya 64; admission R30; open 10am-4pm Tues-Sun) displays many remains and reproductions of the ornamentation from the Cathedrals of the Assumption and St Dmitry.

Golden Gate

Vladimir's Golden Gate (Zolotye Vorota), part defensive tower, part triumphal arch, was modelled on the very similar structure in Kiev. Originally built by Andrey Bogolyubsky to guard the main, western entrance to his city, it was later restored under Catherine the Great, the Golden Gate now houses a **Military Museum** (☎ 32 25 59; admission R30; open 10am-4pm Wed-Mon), which includes a diorama of old Vladimir being ravaged by the Nomadic raiders.

Across the street to the south you can see a remnant of the old wall that protected the city.

Near the Golden Gate, in the red-brick former Old Believers' Trinity Church (1913–16), is a **Crystal, Lacquer Miniatures & Embroidery Exhibition** (☎ 32 48 72; ul Bolshaya Moskovskaya 2; admission R20; open 10am-4pm Wed-Mon) which features the crafts of Gus-Khrustalny and other nearby towns.

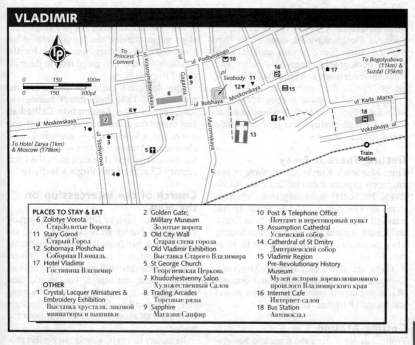

VLADIMIR

0   150   300m
0   150   300yd

To Princess' Convent

ul Podbelskogo

pl Svobody

ul Bolshaya Moskovskaya

ul Moskovskaya

To Hotel Zarya (1km) & Moscow (178km)

To Bogolyubovo (11km) & Suzdal (35km)

ul Karla Marxa

Vokzalnaya ul

Train Station

PLACES TO STAY & EAT
6 Zolotye Vorota
   СтарЗолотые Ворота
11 Stary Gorod
   Старый Город
12 Sobornaya Ploshchad
   Соборная Площадь
17 Hotel Vladimir
   Гостиница Владимир

OTHER
1 Crystal, Lacquer Miniatures & Embroidery Exhibition
   Выставка хрустали, лаковой миниатюры и вышивки

2 Golden Gate; Military Museum
   Золотые ворота
3 Old City Wall
   Старая стена города
4 Old Vladimir Exhibition
   Выставка Старого Владимира
5 St George Church
   Георгиевская Церковь
7 Khudozhestvenny Salon
   Художественный Салон
8 Trading Arcades
   Торговые ряды
9 Sapphire
   Магазин Санфир

10 Post & Telephone Office
   Почтамт и переговорный пункт
13 Assumption Cathedral
   Успенский собор
14 Catherdral of St Dmitry
   Дмитриевский собор
15 Vladimir Region Pre-Revolutionary History Museum
   Музей истории дореволюционного прошлого Владимирского края
16 Internet Cafe
   Интернет-салон
18 Bus Station
   Автовокзал

Other Attractions

Along ulitsa Bolshaya Moskovskaya, the late-18th-century **Trading Arcades** (Torgovye ryady) continue to serve their original purpose, housing shops and cafés.

Down a narrow, winding street dotted with lampposts, **St George Church** (Georgievskaya tserkov; ul Georgievskaya 2A) houses the Vladimir Theatre of Choral Music. Performances are usually held on Saturday and Sunday from September to May. The entrance is at the back of the street.

Just to the south of here, in an old water tower on Kozlov val (part of the old ramparts), the **Old Vladimir Exhibition** (admission R20; open 10am-4pm Tues-Sun) is interesting for its site as well as the old photographs it houses.

The **Princess' Convent** (Knyagnin monastyr), off ulitsa Nekrasova north of the centre, was founded by Vsevolod III's wife, Maria. It is now a convent again after spending recent decades as a museum of orthodoxy and atheism. The only substantial surviving building is its 16th-century **Assumption Cathedral** (Uspensky sobor), with many well-preserved 1640s frescoes.

Places to Stay

Hotel Vladimir (☎ 32 30 42, fax 32 72 01; e tour@gtk.elcom.ru; ul Bolshaya Moskovskaya 74; singles/doubles with shared bathroom R150/290, with private bathroom from R700) is the most pleasant and conveniently located place to stay. As renovations are ongoing, so the quality of the rooms will vary widely.

Hotel Zarya (☎ 22 52 64, fax 22 52 81; Studenaya Gora 36; singles/doubles from R200/300), about 1km west of the cathedrals, is pretty run down.

Places to Eat

Stary Gorod (☎ 32 51 01; ul Bolshaya Moskovskaya 41; mains R100-200; open 11am-2am) is a good, inexpensive place opposite the Cathedral of St Dmitry.

Next door, **Sobornaya Ploshchad** (☎ 32 57 25; ul Bolshaya Moskovskaya 39; mains R50; open 11am-midnight) is a more bar-like version of the same thing.

The town's best restaurant (at least where all tour groups seem to be taken) is **Zolotye Vorota** (☎ 32 31 16; ul Bolshaya Moskovskaya 15; meals R250).

Shopping

Khudozhestvenny Salon (☎ 32 22 11; ul Bolshaya Moskovskaya 26; open 10am-7pm Mon-Fri, 10am-5pm Sat) sells antiques such as old photographs, household items and Russian medals at a fraction of Moscow prices.

Sapphire (ul Gagarina 2; open 10am-7pm Mon-Sat, 10am-4pm Sun) is where you can find some high-quality silver jewellery made to old Russian designs.

Getting There & Away

From Moscow's Kursk Station, there is one afternoon express train (1st/2nd class R130/R115, 2½ hours) and many slow suburban trains to Vladimir every day. Privately run buses (R50) also leave regularly from Kursk and Kazan Stations to Vladimir (three hours). They do not run on a timetable, but leave as they fill up.

There are also buses to/from Moscow's Shchyolkovsky station, as well as Kostroma (R120, five hours), Ivanovo (R60, three hours) and Suzdal (R10, one hour).

Getting Around

Trolleybus No 5 from the train and bus stations runs up to and along ulitsa Bolshaya Moskovskaya. It passes the Hotel Vladimir, the two main cathedrals and the town centre, Hotel Zarya, and then onwards to the western edge of town. Trolleybus No 1 runs from one end of town to the other, along the same street.

BOGOLYUBOVO
БОГОЛЮБОВО

☎ 0922 • pop 3900

There's a story that when Andrey Bogolyubsky was returning north from Kiev in the late 1150s, his horses – so the story continues – stopped where Bogolyubovo now stands, 11km east of Vladimir. Apparently they wouldn't go another step and this is supposedly why Andrey made his capital in nearby Vladimir, and not his father's old base of Suzdal.

Whatever the legend, Andrey built a stone fortified palace that dates from between 1158 and 1165 at this strategic spot near the meeting of the Nerl and Klyazma Rivers. Nearby, in 1165, he built possibly the most perfect of all old Russian buildings, the Church of the Intercession on the Nerl.

Palace & Monastery

A tower and arch from Andrey Bogolyubsky's palace survive amid a dilapidated but reopened 18th-century monastery by the Vladimir–Nizhny Novgorod road in the middle of Bogolyubovo.

The dominant buildings today are the monastery's 1841 **bell tower** beside the road, and its 1866 **Assumption Cathedral**. Just east of the cathedral, there is an arch and tower, on whose stairs – according to a chronicle – Andrey was assassinated by hostile *boyars* (nobles). The arch abuts the 18th-century **Church of the Virgin's Nativity**.

Church of the Intercession on the Nerl

To reach this famous little church (Tserkov Pokrova na Nerli), go back about 200m towards Vladimir from the monastery-palace complex and then turn onto ulitsa Frunze, which winds downhill and under a railway bridge. Under the bridge, you should then take the path to the left that runs along the side of a small wood. The church appears across the meadows, about 1.25km from the bridge.

Its beauty lies in its simple but perfect proportions, a brilliantly chosen waterside site and sparing use of delicate carving. If it looks a mite top-heavy, it's because the original helmet dome was replaced by a cushion dome in 1803.

Legend has it that Andrey had the church built in memory of his favourite son, Izyaslav, who was killed in battle against the Bulgars. As with the Cathedral of St Dmitry in Vladimir, King David sits at the top of three facades, the birds and beasts entranced by his music. The interior has more carving, including 20 pairs of lions. If the church is closed, try asking at the house behind, they may let you in.

Getting There & Away

To get to Bogolyubovo, take trolley bus No 1 east from Vladimir and get off at Khimzavod. Walk along the main road for 100m to the taxi van stop. Taxi vans operate between 7am and 10pm. You will need to get off at the second stop.

Drivers from central Vladimir should head straight out east along the main road. From Suzdal, turn left when you hit Vladimir's northern bypass and go 5km.

IVANOVO
ИВАНОВО
☎ 0932 • pop 550,000

Ivanovo, 78km north of Suzdal on the Suzdal–Kostroma road, is known for two (connected) features: its cotton textiles and its women. The town's female population, swelled by the labour needs of the textile mills, apparently once heavily outnumbered its male population and Ivanovo is still known as the 'town of brides'.

Ivanovo is a drab and dreary industrial town. If you have to change buses here, however, you can easily entertain yourself for an afternoon. Head to the **Art Museum** (☎ 30 16 41; ul Lenina 33; admission R3; open 11am-5pm Wed-Mon) which has a decent collection of Russian works, or to the **Ivanovo Chintz Museum** (☎ 30 06 30; ul Baturina 11/42; admission R3) which illustrates the development of the textile industry to the present. The latter is housed in an Art Nouveau mansion.

Palekh
Палех

Ivanovo is occasionally used as a base for visiting Palekh, the small village famous for icon painters and small lacquer boxes, 65km east on the Nizhny Novgorod road. Palekh has a **museum** (open Tues-Sun) of local icons and boxes, with a gift shop. There are also fine restored 14th- to 19th-century icons in the **Raising of the Cross Church** (Krestovo-Sdvizhenskaya tserkov).

There are frequent buses from Ivanovo and one bus daily from Vladimir via Suzdal.

Places to Stay & Eat

If you must spend the night in Ivanovo, **Hotel Tourist** (☎ 37 64 36; Naberezhnaya 9; singles/doubles R450/700) will put you up. Rooms have bathroom, TV and fridge. The hotel has an acceptable restaurant.

Getting There & Away

In Ivanovo, the train station is at the northern end of ulitsa Engelsa. Trains to Ivanovo run from Moscow's Yaroslavl Station (R100, eight hours). The bus station is several kilometres away in the south of town. Buses run frequently to/from Moscow's Shchyolkovsky Bus Station (R180, 6½ hours), Suzdal (R60, two hours), Vladimir (R100, three hours) and Kostroma (R60, two hours). There a few buses a day to Yaroslavl (R70, two hours).

PLYOS
ПЛЁС
☎ 09339 • pop 40,000

Plyos is a tranquil town of wooden houses and hilly streets winding down to the Volga waterfront, halfway between Ivanovo and Kostroma. Though fortified from the 15th century and later a Volga trade centre, Pylos' renown today stems from its late-19th-century role as an artists' retreat. Isaak Levitan, possibly the greatest Russian landscape artist, found inspiration here in the summers of 1888 to 1890. The playwright Chekhov commented that Plyos 'put a smile in Levitan's paintings'.

Walk along the river front and explore the oldest part of town, as evidenced by the ramparts of the old fort, which date from 1410. The hill is topped by the simple 1699 **Assumption Cathedral** (Uspensky sobor), one of Levitan's favourite painting subjects.

The **Levitan House Museum** (Dom-Muzey Levitana; ☎ 437 82; ul Sovietskaya 11; admission R20; open 10am-5pm Tues-Sun) in the eastern part of the town, across the small Shokhonka River, displays works of Levitan and other artists against the background of the Volga.

You can get here by bus from Ivanovo or Kostroma, or – a better option in summer – by hydrofoil from Kostroma or Yaroslavl (see those cities' Getting There & Away sections).

KOSTROMA
КОСТРОМА
☎ 0942 • pop 300,000

Kostroma, on the Volga River 95km north of Ivanovo and founded in the 1150s, was once one of the Golden Ring's most important cultural and commercial centres. Little remains from these ancient roots, however, as a fire in 1773 destroyed everything wooden, and the centre was rebuilt in Russian classical style. The town's pride is the Monastery of St Ipaty, founded in 1332 by a Tatar ancestor of Boris Godunov and later patronised – like Kostroma in general – by the Romanov dynasty.

Orientation

The main part of the town lies along the northern bank of the Volga, with the bus and train stations some 4km east of the centre. The Monastery of St Ipaty is west of the centre across the Kostroma River, a Volga tributary. The central square is ploshchad Susaninskaya.

AROUND MOSCOW

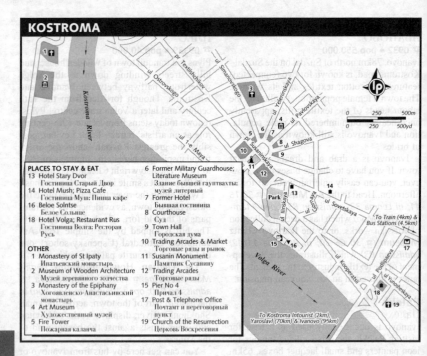

KOSTROMA

Kostroma River

Volga River

PLACES TO STAY & EAT			6	Former Military Guardhouse;
13	Hotel Stary Dvor			Literature Museum
	Гостиница Старый Двор			Здание бывшей гаунтвахты:
14	Hotel Mush; Pizza Cafe			музей литерный
	Гостиница Муш: Пища кафе		7	Former Hotel
16	Beloe Solntse			Бывшая гостиница
	Белое Сольнце		8	Courthouse
18	Hotel Volga; Restaurant Rus			Суд
	Гостиница Волга; Ресторан		9	Town Hall
	Русь			Городская дума
OTHER			10	Trading Arcades & Market
1	Monastery of St Ipaty			Торговые ряды и рынок
	Ипатьевский монастырь		11	Susanin Monument
2	Museum of Wooden Architecture			Памятник Сусанину
	Музей деревянного зодчества		12	Trading Arcades
3	Monastery of the Epiphany			Торговые ряды
	Хогоявленско-Анастасьинский		15	Pier No 4
	монастырь			Причал 4
4	Art Museum		17	Post & Telephone Office
	Художественный музей			Почтамт и переговорный
5	Fire Tower			пункт
	Пожарная каланча		19	Church of the Resurrection
				Церковь Воскресения

To Train (4km) &
Bus Stations (4.5km)

To Kostroma Intourist (2km),
Yaroslavl (70km) & Ivanovo (95km)

Information

The **post and telephone office** (cnr ul Sovietskaya & ul Podlipaeva; open 9am-9pm daily) is southeast of ploshchad Susaninskaya. As part of the same complex, there are **Internet facilities** (☎ 62 10 20; open 9am-9pm).

Monastery of St Ipaty

Legend has it that a Tatar prince named Chet (who later founded the house of Godunovs) was returning to Moscow in 1330 and fell ill. At this time he had a vision of the Virgin Mary and the martyr Ipaty of the Ganges which aided his recovery. When he returned to Moscow he was baptised and founded the Monastery of St Ipaty (Ipatevsky monastyr; ☎ 31 25 89; admission R30; open 9am-5pm daily May-Oct, 10am-5pm Sat-Thur Nov-Apr) to mark the occasion.

The monastery's more recent history is closely tied to the Godunov and Romanov families, fierce rivals in high-level power games before the Romanovs established their 300-year dynasty in the 17th century. In 1590, the Godunovs built the monastery's **Trinity Cathedral** (Troitsky sobor), which contains over 80 old frescoes by a school of

17th-century Kostroma painters, headed by Gury Nikitin (plus some 20th-century additions). The fresco in the southern part of the sanctuary depicts Chet Godunov's baptism by St Ipaty.

The **bell tower**, modelled after the Ivan the Great Bell Tower in Moscow, chimes concerts every hour.

In 1600 Boris Godunov, the only member of his family to become tsar, exiled the head of the Romanov family, Fyodor, and his son Mikhail to this monastery. Mikhail Romanov was in Kostroma when he was elected tsar in 1613, at the end of the Time of Troubles. In honour of the event all his Romanov successors made a point of coming here to visit the monastery's red **Romanov Chambers** (Palaty Romanova), opposite the cathedral.

The monastery is 2.5km west of the town centre. Take bus No 14 from the central ploshchad Susaninskaya and get off once you cross the river; you'll see the monastery to your left.

Museum of Wooden Architecture

Behind the monastery is an attractive outdoor museum (☎ 57 78 72; admission R10, photos

R20; open 9am-5pm daily May-Oct) of northern-style wooden buildings, including peasant houses and churches (one built without nails). Most of the buildings are not open, but the grounds are pleasant for strolling, listening to the chirping of frogs and admiring the handiwork of the artists.

This is a case of the museum being nearly indistinguishable from the village. The surrounding neighbourhood also consists of storybook-like houses, blossoming gardens and picturesque churches, including a **domed wooden church** directly to the north of the monastery.

Town Centre

Ploshchad Susaninskaya was built as an ensemble under Catherine the Great's patronage after the 1773 fire. Clockwise around the northern side are: a 19th-century **fire tower** (still in use and under Unesco protection) with a little museum on fire-fighting; a former military **guardhouse**, housing a small literature museum; an 18th-century **hotel** for members of the royal family; the **palace** of an 1812 war hero, now a courthouse; and the **town hall**.

In the streets between are many merchants townhouses. The **Art Museum** (☎ 51 43 90; pr Mira 5 & 7; admission to each building R30; open 10am-6pm Tues-Sun) comprises two elaborate neo-Russian buildings. No 5 houses a portrait gallery, as well as appropriately decorated 19th-century rooms such as the White Hall (Beliy Zal). No 7, built in 1913 to celebrate 300 years of Romanov rule, contains a collection of mainly 16th- to 19th-century Russian art.

The old **Trading Arcades** on the southern side of ploshchad Susaninskaya now house a bustling **food market**. Sections of the trading rows are named for the products that were traditionally sold here (ie, vegetables, butter, gingerbread). Note the road Molochny Gora (Milk Hill) which leads from the arcades down to the Volga. The **monument** in the park between the arcades is to local hero Ivan Susanin, who guided a Polish detachment hunting for Mikhail Romanov to their deaths, and his own, in a swamp.

Churches

The **Monastery of the Epiphany** (Bogoyavlensko-Anastasinsky monastyr; ul Simanovskogo 26) is now the Archbishop of Kostroma's

residence. The large **cathedral** in this 14th- to 19th-century complex is the city's main working church. The 13th-century icon of Our Lady of St Theodore, on the right-hand side of the iconostasis, is supposedly the source of many miracles.

The 17th-century **Church of the Resurrection** (Tserkov Voskresenia; ul Nizhnaya Debrya 37), near Hotel Volga, has a bright, patterned exterior decoration and was partly financed with a load of gold coins mistakenly shipped from London.

Places to Stay

Hotel Stary Dvor (☎ 31 60 39; ul Sovietskaya 6; rooms with/without bathroom R500/150) is centrally located, but otherwise rather run down.

Hotel Volga (☎ 54 60 62, fax 54 62 62; ul Yunosheskaya 1; singles/doubles with breakfast R500/700) is 2km southeast of the centre; it's just off ulitsa Podlipaeva, near the Volga bridge. Some of the adequately clean rooms have Volga views and the restaurant is passable.

Hotel Mush (☎ 312 400, fax 311 045; w www.mush.com.ru; ul Sovietskaya 29; singles/doubles US$50/60) is the best hotel in town, considering its central location and welcoming atmosphere. There is a pleasant and inexpensive pizza café downstairs.

Kostroma Intourist (☎ 53 36 61, fax 53 23 01; e hotel-in@kosnet.ru; ul Magistralnaya 40; singles/doubles US$49/69) is a modern, Western-style hotel with two good restaurants. Its location, about 2km south of the Volga bridge on the road to Yaroslavl and Ivanovo, is inconvenient unless you are driving. From ulitsa Podlipaeva in front of Hotel Volga, take bus No 10.

The buses that approach Kostroma from Yaroslavl or Ivanovo pass the Intourist and Volga hotels, and drivers may be willing to drop you off at the hotels, saving you a trek back into town from the bus station.

Places to Eat

Restaurant Rus (☎ 54 62 62; ul Yunosheskaya 1; meals R250; open noon-11pm) in Hotel Volga comes highly recommended for Russian food. Besides the hotel restaurants, food options in Kostroma are pretty limited.

Near the river station, **Beloe Solntse** (☎ 57 90 57; ul Lesnaya 2; cover charge R30, mains R300; open noon-midnight) is overpriced, but the food is spicy and the decor colourful. There is live music and dancing most nights.

Getting There & Away

Train The train station is 4km east of ploshchad Susaninskaya. There are three or four daily suburban trains to/from Yaroslavl (R200, three hours), an overnight train to/from Moscow's Yaroslavl Station (R680, 8½ hours) and a daily train to/from Khabarovsk in the Russian Far East.

Bus The bus station can be found 4.5km east of ploshchad Susaninskaya on Kineshemskoe shosse, the continuation of ulitsa Sovetskaya. There are buses to/from Moscow (8½ hours, six daily), Yaroslavl (two hours, eight daily), Ivanovo (two hours, eight daily), Vladimir (5½ hours, daily) via Suzdal (4½ hours), and Vologda (seven hours, daily).

Boat The best way to get between Kostroma and Yaroslavl in summer is by hydrofoil, which runs twice a day in either direction. The hydrofoils depart from the main *prichal* (pier) No 4 to Yaroslavl (1½ hours) and downstream to Plyos (one hour). Timetables are posted at the pier. Long-distance river boats between Moscow and points down the Volga as far as Astrakhan also call at Kostroma.

Getting Around

Bus Nos 1, 2, 9, 9 Expres, 14K, 19 and others run between the bus station and the central ploshchad Susaninskaya, along the full length of ulitsa Sovetskaya. Trolleybus No 2 runs between the train station and ploshchad Susaninskaya.

YAROSLAVL
ЯРОСЛАВЛЬ

☎ 0852 • pop 680,000

Yaroslavl, 250km northeast of Moscow, is the urban counterpart to Suzdal. This is the biggest place between Moscow and Arkhangelsk, and it has a more urban feel than anywhere else in the Golden Ring. Its big-city skyline, however, is dotted with onion domes and towering spires, not smoke stacks and skyscrapers. As a result of a trade boom in the 17th century, churches are hidden around every corner. The poet Grigoriev wrote: 'Yaroslavl is a town of unsurpassed beauty; everywhere is the Volga and everywhere is history.' And everywhere, everywhere, are churches.

History

In 1010, the Kyivan prince Yaroslav the Wise took an interest in a trading post called Medvezhy Ugol (Bear Corner). According to legend, Yaroslav subjugated and converted the locals by killing their sacred bear with his axe. So the town was founded, and its coat of arms bears both the beast and the weapon (no pun intended).

Yaroslavl was the centre of an independent principality by the time the Tatars came. Developed in the 16th and 17th centuries as the Volga's first port, it grew fat on trade with the Middle East and Europe and became Russia's second-biggest city of the time. Rich merchants competed to build churches bigger than those of Moscow, with elaborate decoration and bright frescoes on contemporary themes. Though the city's centrepiece is the Monastery of the Transfiguration of the Saviour, the merchant churches are what makes the city unique.

Orientation

Yaroslavl's centre lies at the crux of the Volga and Kotorosl Rivers, inside the ring road, ulitsa Pervomaiskaya. The centre of the ring is Sovetskaya ploshchad, from which streets radiate out to three squares: Bogoyavlenskaya ploshchad with the landmark Transfiguration Monastery; ploshchad Volkova with the classical facade of the Volkov Theatre; and Krasnaya ploshchad near the river station.

Information

You can change money or use the ATM at **Alfa-Bank** (☎ 73 91 77; ul Svobody 3; open 9am-6pm Mon-Thur, 9am-4.30pm Fri). **Sberbank** (☎ 72 95 18; ul Kirova 6; open 8.30am-4pm Mon-Sat) changes money and gives credit card advances.

The **main post and telephone office** (ul Komsomolskaya 22; open 8am-8pm Mon-Sat, until 6pm Sun) also offers Internet services. The **Internet Club** (☎ 72 68 50; pr Lenina 24; open 9am-11pm) in the Dom Kultury has more facilities.

Dom Knigi (☎ 30 47 51; ul Kirova 18; open 10am-7pm Mon-Fri, 10am-6pm Sat) has a good selection of maps and books, as does **Rospechat** (ul Kirova 10) on the same street.

Monastery & Around

Founded in the 12th century, the **Monastery of the Transfiguration of the Saviour**

(Spaso-Preobrazhensky monastyr; ☎ 30 38 69; Bogoyavlenskaya pl 25; admission free, exhibits R20 each; grounds open 8am-5pm Tues-Sun, museums open 10am-5pm Tues-Sun) was one of Russia's richest and best-fortified monasteries by the 16th century.

The oldest surviving structures, dating from 1516 but heavily altered since then, are the **Holy Gate** (Svyatye vorota), near the main entrance by the river, and the austere **Cathedral of the Transfiguration** (Preobrazhensky sobor), which is under restoration. The north section of the church used to house the monastery library.

To get a new perspective on things, climb the **bell tower** (zvonnitsa). The summit provides a panorama of the city and a close-up view of the spiky gold bulbs that top some of the monastery buildings.

Off Bogoyavlenskaya ploshchad is the vaulted, red-brick **Church of the Epiphany** (Tserkov Bogoyavlenia), which was under restoration at the time of research but is usually open to the public. Built by a wealthy 17th-century merchant, its rich decoration includes bright exterior ceramic tiles (a Yaroslavl speciality), vibrant frescoes and a carved iconostasis.

A statue of Yaroslav the Wise stands in the centre of the square. Past the 19th-century **Trading Arcades** (Gostiny Dvor), is the **Znamenskaya Watchtower** (Znamenskaya bashnya; ul Pervomaiskaya), built in 1658 on what was then the edge of the city.

Church of Elijah the Prophet

This lovely church *(Tserkov Ilyi Proroka; Sovetskaya pl; admission R25; open 10am-1pm & 2pm-6pm daily May-Sept)* was built by prominent 17th-century fur dealers. It has some of the Golden Ring's brightest frescoes by the ubiquitous Yury Nikitin of Kostroma and his school, and detailed exterior tiles. The church is closed during wet spells.

River Embankments

The Volga and Kotorosl embankments from the Church of Elijah the Prophet back to the Monastery of the Transfiguration make an enjoyable 1.5km walk. A pedestrian promenade runs along the bank of the Volga below the level of the street, Volzhskaya naberezhnaya.

From the Church of Elijah the Prophet, head towards the river on Narodny pereulok.

Here, the **Church of St Nicholas the Miracle-Worker** (Tserkov Nikoly Nadeina) was the first of Yaroslavl's stone merchant churches, built in 1622. It has a sparkling baroque iconostasis and frescoes showing the life and works of the popular St Nicholas. It's normally open as a museum.

The unique, private collection **Music & Time** *(☎ 32 86 37; Volzhskaya nab 33a; admission R25; open 10am-7pm Tues-Sun)* is in the little house just north of the church. Here, John Mostoslavsky will enthusiastically guide visitors through his fascinating collection of clocks, musical instruments and various other antiques.

South along the embankment is the old Governor's Mansion that now houses the **Yaroslavl Art Museum** *(☎ 35 33 55; Volzhskaya nab 23; admission R30; open 10am-5pm Tues-Sun)*, with 18th- to 20th-century Russian art. On the next block, the **History of Yaroslavl Museum** *(☎ 30 41 75; Volzhskaya nab 17; open 10am-6pm Wed-Mon)* is in a lovely 19th-century merchant's house. A new **monument** to victims of war and repression in the 20th century is in the peaceful garden. Other surviving merchants' houses are nearby, such as **Dom Matveev** *(cnr Volzhskaya nab & Sovetsky per)*.

A little farther along the embankment are the **Volga Bastion** (Volzhskaya bashnya), built as a watchtower in the 1660s, and a fine early-19th-century church. The 17th-century former Metropolitan's Chambers (Mitropolyichyi Palaty) houses the old Yaroslavl art collection of the **Art Museum** *(☎ 72 92 87; admission R30; open 10am-5pm Sat-Thur)*, with icons and other work from the 13th to 19th centuries.

In the leafy park behind the museum is a stone-slab **monument** marking the spot where Yaroslav founded the city in 1010. The park stretches right out onto the tip of the land between the Volga and the Kotorosl Rivers. Above the Kotorosl, the raised embankments indicate the site of Yaroslavl's old kremlin.

The more time you spend, the more churches you will discover, most dating from the 17th century. There are three more along the embankment, and several south of the Kotorosl River in the settlements of Korovniki and Tolchkovo. Pick up the brochure *Yaroslavl* (available in several languages) at one of the museum gift shops.

YAROSLAVL

PLACES TO STAY
11 Hotel Volga
  Гостиница Волга
16 Hotel Yuta
  Гостиница Юта
24 Hotel Yubileynaya
  Гостиница Юбилейная

PLACES TO EAT
2 Kafe Lira
  Кафе Лира
9 Restaurant/Café Rus
  Ресторан и кафе Русь
14 Café Premyera
  Кафе Премьера
27 Spasskie Palaty
  Спасские Палаты

OTHER
1 River Station
  Речной вокзал
3 Music & Time
  Музыка и Время
4 Church of St Nicholas the
  Miracle-Worker
  Церковь Николы Надеина
5 Yaroslavl Art Museum
  Ярославский
  художественный музей

6 History of Yaroslavl
  Museum
  Музей Истории
  Ярославля
7 Dom Matveev
  Дом Матвеев
8 Church of Elijah the
  Prophet
  Церковь Ильи Пророка
10 Rospechat
  Магазин Роспечать
12 Sberbank
  Сбербанк
13 Dom Knigi
  Дом книги
15 Volkov Theatre
  Театр Волкова
17 Alfa-Bank
  Алфа-банк
18 Znamenskaya
  Watchtower
  Знаменская башня
19 Russian Flax
  Магазин Русский Лён
20 Trading Arcades
  Торговые ряды
21 Yaroslav the Wise Statue
  Памятник Ярославу
  Мудрому

22 Post & Telephone Office
  Почтамт и переговорный
  пункт
23 Tram Terminal
  Трамвайное Кольцо
25 Church of the Epiphany
  Церковь Богоявления
26 Cathedral of the
  Transfiguration and Bell Tower
  Преображенский Собор и Звонница
28 Main Entrance; Holy Gate
  Главный вход
29 Church of the
  Saviour-in-the-Town
  Церковь Спаса-на-Городу
30 Church of the
  Archangel Michael
  Церковь Михаила Архангела
31 Volga Bastion
  Волжская башня
32 Art Museum
  (Former Metropolitan's Palace)
  Художественный музей
  (бывшие митрополичьи палаты)
33 Church of Nikol Rubleny
  Церковь Николы Рубленого
34 Founding of Yaroslavl
  Monument
  Памятник основанию Ярославля

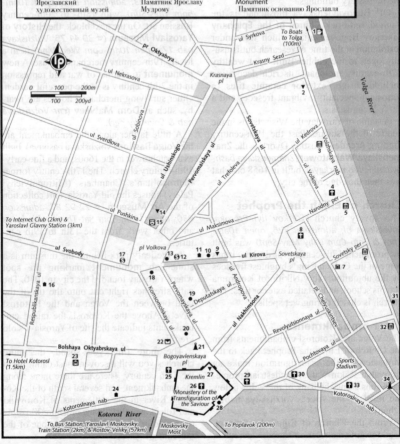

River Trips

There are summer services from the river station on the Volga at the northern end of Pervomaiskaya ulitsa, including a range of slow *prigorodnyy* (suburban) boats to local destinations. The best trip is to **Tolga** (R20), one hour from Yaroslavl on the Konstantinovo route – here, near the river, you'll find a convent with lovely buildings from the 17th-century.

Places to Stay

Hotel Kotorosl (☎ 21 24 15, fax 21 64 68; e kotorosl@yaroslavl.ru; Bolshaya Oktyabrskaya ul 87; singles/doubles R550/800) is the best-value place to stay, within walking distance of the train station and offering modern rooms and decent facilities.

Hotel Yuta (☎ 21 87 93, fax 32 97 86; e utah@yaroslavl.ru; ul Respublikanskaya 79; singles/doubles R600/900) has decent rooms, but management charges a 50% reservation fee the first night (even if you did not make a reservation). The bar with tinted mirrors is too dark to see your food, let alone somebody you might be dining with.

Hotel Volga (☎ 73 11 11, fax 72 82 76; ul Kirova 10; doubles with/without bathroom R1000/600) is located in the very centre of town on a small pedestrian street and has an elegant staircase and furnishings. The nicer rooms come with bathroom, TV, phone and refrigerator; staff are helpful.

Hotel Yubileynaya (☎ 72 65 65; w www.yubil.yar.ru; Kotoroslnaya nab 26; singles/doubles with breakfast from R900/1500), more conventional than Hotel Volga, overlooks the Kotorosl River. It's the usual concrete slab building, but rooms are comfortable. There's a restaurant, bar and business centre with Internet access.

Places to Eat

Café Rus (☎ 72 94 38; meals R50; open 8am-8pm) is perhaps the cheapest and most unpretentious place to eat in town. It's a unique blend of a Soviet eatery and Russian peasant dacha. True to the Soviet eatery, you have to pay first, then pass the receipt to the grumbling serving lady by the counter. Ironically, the **Restaurant Rus** (ul Kirova 8) upstairs is perhaps the most pretentious place in town, but the food is good.

Cosy **Kafe Lira** (☎ 72 79 38; Volzhskaya nab 43; meals R100; open noon-11pm daily) serves soups, salads and drinks at reasonable prices.

Café Premyera (☎ 72 86 01; ul Pervomaiskaya; meals R200) serves Russian food and beer in the small park behind the Volkov Theatre. The place is popular with young families and dating couples.

Spasskie Palaty (☎ 30 48 07; Bogoyavlenskaya pl 25; meals R300) is popular with tourist groups for its atmospheric location (inside the gates of the monastery) and its tasty Russian fare.

Poplavok (☎ 30 36 66; Kotorosl River; open noon-1am) is a new restaurant housed on a boat in the small harbour on the Kotorosl River, below the embankment. The location is ideal for summer dining and drinking.

Shopping

Russian Flax (☎ 30 56 70; ul Pervomaiskaya 51) sells fine linen tablecloths, napkins and bedclothes at remarkably low prices; you can also have items made to order.

Getting There & Away

Boat In summer boats depart from the river station at the northern end of Pervomaiskaya ulitsa. The hydrofoils to downstream destinations will take you to Kostroma (1½ hours) and Plyos (three hours). Tickets go on sale about 30 minutes before departure.

From about early June to early October, long-distance Volga passenger ships stop every couple of days in Yaroslavl on their way between Moscow and cities like Nizhny Novgorod, Kazan and Astrakhan. Timetables are posted at the river station, which also has an information window.

Bus The bus station is on Moskovsky prospekt, 2km south of the Kotorosl River and beside the Yaroslavl Moskovsky train station. One or two buses go daily to/from Moscow's Shchyolkovsky Bus Station (six hours), plus about five buses stopping in transit. Most of these stop at Pereslavl-Zalessky and Sergiev Posad. Other departures include:

destination	duration (hrs)	frequency (daily)
Ivanovo	3	2 or 3
Kostroma	2	10 or 11
Pereslavl-Zalessky	3	3 or 4
Rostov-Veliky	1½	7
Uglich	3	4
Vladimir	6	1 or 2
Vologda	5	2 or 3

AROUND MOSCOW

Train The main station is Yaroslavl Glavny, on ulitsa Svobody 3km west of the centre. The lesser Yaroslavl Moskovsky train station is near the bus station, 2km south of town. Around 20 trains a day run to/from Moscow's Yaroslavl Station, a trip of about five hours. Most of these are headed to destinations farther north (eg, Arkhangelsk) or east (eg, Yekaterinburg, Novosibirsk or Vladivostok). It may be easiest to get tickets on trains that terminate at Yaroslavl.

There's also a daily service to/from St Petersburg and Nizhny Novgorod. For closer destinations such as Rostov (R120, two hours) or Kostroma (R200, three hours), it's easiest to take suburban trains.

Getting Around

The Tram No 3 goes along ulitsa Bolshaya Oktyabrskaya to the tram terminal a short walk west of Bogoyavlenskaya ploshchad. From Yaroslavl Glavny Station, head 200m to the right for the stop on ulitsa Ukhtomskogo; trolleybus No 1 runs between the station and ploshchad Volkova and Krasnaya ploshchad.

From the bus station and Yaroslavl Moskovsky train station, trolleybus No 5 or 9 from the far side of the main road outside will get you to Bogoyavlenskaya ploshchad; No 5 goes on to Krasnaya ploshchad.

UGLICH
УГЛИЧ

Uglich is a quaint but shabby town on the Volga 90km northwest of Rostov-Veliky. A regular stop for Volga cruises, this tiny town has enough attractions to fill a morning.

Here Ivan the Terrible's son Dmitry – later to be impersonated by the string of False Dmitrys in the Time of Troubles – was murdered in 1591, probably on Boris Godunov's orders. Within the waterside kremlin, the 15th-century **Prince's Chambers** (Knyazhyi palaty) house a historical exhibit, including the coffin which carried Dmitry's body to Moscow. The red **Church of St Dmitry on the Blood** (Tserkov Dmitria-na-krovi), with its cluster of spangled blue domes, was built in the 1690s on the spot where the body was found. Its interior is decorated with bright frescoes and the bell that was used to mourn Dmitry's death. (In 1581 the bell was used to call an insurrection on the murder of the tsarevich. In response, Godunov ordered the 300kg bell to be publicly flogged and its tongue to be ripped out before it was banished for many years to the Siberian town of Tobolsk.) The five-domed **Transfiguration Cathedral** (Preobrazhensky sobor) and an **Art Museum** are also in the kremlin (☎ 536 78; each site R20; open 9am-1pm & 2pm-5pm daily).

Opposite each other, along the street from the kremlin, are two other fine buildings from the 1690s: the **Church of the Nativity of John the Baptist** (ul Karla Marxa); and the large but badly dilapidated **Monastery of the Resurrection** (ul Karla Marxa).

When you tire of Dmitry, Uglich boasts a **Vodka Museum** (☎ 235 58; ul Berggolts 9; admission R50), the first in Russia. It's a small but entertaining exhibit with samples!

If you get stuck in Uglich, you can stay at **Hotel Uglich** (☎ 503 70; ul Yaroslavskaya 50; rooms with/without bath per person R170/130), but be prepared for hard beds and cold showers.

Buses go once or twice a day to Yaroslavl. Buses to Rostov-Veliky do not run regularly, so you may have to go via Borisoglebsk. Otherwise, taxis wait outside the tiny bus station if you are short on time.

ROSTOV-VELIKY
РОСТОВ-ВЕЛИКИЙ
☎ 08536 • pop 40,000

After Suzdal, Rostov-Veliky (also known as Rostov-Yaroslavsky) is the prettiest of the Golden Ring towns – a tranquil, rustic place with a magnificent kremlin and beautiful monasteries magically sited by shimmering Lake Nero. It's around 220km northeast of Moscow and is one of Russia's oldest towns, first chronicled in 862.

Perhaps to flatter its home-grown aristocracy, Yury Dolgoruky called Rostov Veliky (Great) in the 12th century, while making Suzdal the capital of his Rostov-Suzdal principality. By the early 13th century, the Rostov region had split first from Suzdal and then into smaller pieces. The Tatars didn't leave much of it standing, and in the late 1600s an ambitious Orthodox Metropolitan, Iona Sysoevich, cleared almost everything else away for a wonderful private kremlin on the shore of Lake Nero.

On the highway in from the south, look out for fairy-tale views across the lake to the kremlin and the Monastery of St Jacob.

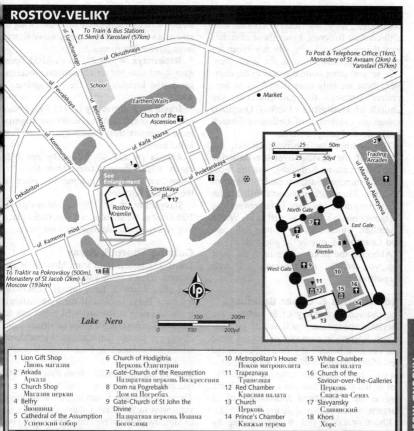

ROSTOV-VELIKY

To Train & Bus Stations
(1.5km) & Yaroslavl (57km)

To Post & Telephone Office (1km),
Monastery of St Avraam (2km) &
Yaroslavl (57km)

ul Lunacharskogo

ul Okruzhnaya

ul Fevralskaya

ul Belinskogo

School

Earthen Walls

Church of the
Ascension

Market

ul Kommunarov

ul Karla Marxa

See
Enlargement

ul Proletarskaya

ul Dekabritov

Sovetskaya
pl.
▼17

Rostov
Kremlin

ul Kamenny most

To Traktir na Pokrovskoy (500m),
Monastery of St Jacob (2km) &
Moscow (193km)

18

Lake Nero

Trading
Arcades

ul Marshala Alexeyeva

North Gate

East Gate

Rostov
Kremlin

West Gate

1	Lion Gift Shop Лионъ магазин	6	Church of Hodigitria Церковь Одигитрии	10	Metropolitan's House Покои митрополита	15	White Chamber Белая палата
2	Arkada Аркада	7	Gate-Church of the Resurrection Надвратная церковь Воскресения	11	Trapeznaya Трапезная	16	Church of the Saviour-over-the-Galleries Церковь Спаса-на-Сенях
3	Church Shop Магазин церкви	8	Dom na Pogrebakh Дом на Погребах	12	Red Chamber Красная палата		
4	Belfry Звонница	9	Gate-Church of St John the Divine Надвратная церковь Иоанна Богослова	13	Church Церковь	17	Slavyansky Славянский
5	Cathedral of the Assumption Успенский собор			14	Prince's Chamber Княжьи терема	18	Khors Хорс

AROUND MOSCOW

Orientation & Information

The train and bus stations are together in the drab modern part of Rostov, 1.5km north of the kremlin. The kremlin sits on the northern shore of Lake Nero; the surrounding town consists mostly of *izbas*, trees and empty grassy spaces.

There is no bank in Rostov-Veliky but you may be able to change money at the Lion gift shop near the old trading arcades next to the kremlin. The main **post and telephone office** *(ul Severnaya 44)* is around 1km east of the kremlin.

Kremlin

The unashamedly photogenic **kremlin** *(☎ 317 17; admission R100; open 10am-5pm daily)* is Rostov's main attraction. Although founded

in the 12th century, nearly all the buildings here date from the 1670s and 1680s.

With its five magnificent domes, The **Cathedral of the Assumption** (Uspensky sobor) dominates the kremlin, although it is just outside its north wall. Outside service hours, you can get inside the cathedral through the door in the **church shop** *(ul Karla Marxa)*. The cathedral was here a century before the kremlin, while the **belfry** (zvonnitsa) was added in the 1680s. The belfry consists of 15 bells, each with its own name. The largest, weighing 32 tonnes, is called Sysoi. The monks play magnificent bell concerts, which can be arranged through the excursions office, in the west gate, for R100.

The west gate (the main entrance) and north gate are straddled by **gate-churches**

(Tserkov Voskreseniya and Tserkov Ioanna Bogoslova); these are richly decorated with 17th-century frescoes. Enter these churches from the monastery walls, which you can access from the stairs next to the north gate. Like several other buildings within the complex, these are only open from May to September. Between the gate-churches, the **Church of Hodigitria** (Tserkov Odigitrii) houses an exhibition of Orthodox Church vestments and paraphernalia.

The metropolitan's private chapel, the **Church of the Saviour-over-the-Galleries** (Tserkov Spasa-na-Senyakh), has the most beautiful interior of all, covered in colourful frescoes. There are museums filled with icons, paintings, and *finift* (enamelware), in the metropolitan's house as well as the **White Chamber,** which was the dining hall, and **Red Chamber,** formerly the guesthouse.

Although the ticket office is in the west gate, you can also enter the kremlin through the north gate.

Monasteries & Other Buildings

The restored **Monastery of St Jacob** is the fairy-tale apparition you'll see as you approach Rostov by road or rail. To get there you can take buses No 1 or 2 1.5km to the west of the kremlin, although it's a very pleasant walk there alongside Lake Nero. Heading east of the kremlin, bus No 1 will also bring you to the dilapidated **Monastery of St Avraam**, with a cathedral dating from 1553.

Khors (π/fax 32483; W www.enamel.by .ru; ul Podozerka 30; admission free; open noon-10pm daily) is a tiny, private museum named after a pagan sun god. Walk towards the lake as you exit the monastery and look for a charming two-storey wooden house with a garden. The eclectic collection includes some antique household items, models of wooden churches and paintings by local artists. The two small rooms are available for rent to 'artists passing through'. The artist who runs the place also hosts workshops on enamel and Rostov artistry.

To enjoy a lovely view of the kremlin from the lake, you may be able to hire a rowing boat from in front of Khors or further east in the park.

Places to Stay & Eat

Dom na Pogrebakh (π 3 12 44; rooms with shared bath from R300) is right inside the kremlin, near the east gate. It has clean, wood-panelled rooms that vary somewhat in size and view. A few more expensive rooms have private bathrooms.

Trapeznaya (π 328 71; meals R200; open 8am-8pm) also has an atmospheric location inside the kremlin, near the metropolitan's house.

Traktir na Pokrovskoy (π 355 74; ul Pokrovskaya; meals around R200) is slightly more expensive than Trapeznaya, but the fare is the same.

Arkada (π 337 05; Sovietsky per 2/3; meals R200; open 11am-11pm Mon-Fri, 11am-2am Sat & Sun) is a pub-like place in the Trading Arcades.

Slavyansky (π 322 28; Sovetskaya pl 8), 100m east of the kremlin, is a new, ritzier place that gets recommendations from the locals.

Getting There & Away

Train The fastest train from Moscow is the express service from Yaroslavl Station (1st/2nd class R100/75, three hours). Otherwise try for a ticket on one of the long-distance trains stopping at Rostov-Veliky en route to Yaroslavl or beyond, or go by suburban train, changing trains halfway at Alexandrov, which takes about five hours.

Bus To get to Yaroslavl from Rostov (R30, one hour 10 minutes) go roughly every hour. These include direct ones and those stopping via Rostov to Yaroslavl. Other transit buses go to Moscow (four to five hours, three daily) via Pereslavl-Zalessky and Sergiev Posad (R100, four to five hours, three daily), Pereslavl-Zalessky (R60, two hours, three daily) and Uglich (R100, three hours, two daily).

Getting Around

Bus No 6 runs between the train station and the town centre.

PERESLAVL-ZALESSKY
ПЕРЕСЛАВЛЬ-ЗАЛЕССКИЙ
π 08535 • pop 45,000

On the shore of Lake Pleshcheevo, almost halfway between Moscow and Yaroslavl, Pereslavl-Zalessky is a popular dacha destination for Muscovites who enjoy the peaceful village atmosphere. The southern half of the town is characterised by narrow dirt lanes lined with carved wooden *izbas* and blossoming gardens.

PERESLAVL-ZALESSKY

1	Hotel Pereslavl	Гостиница Переславль
2	Yartelecom Service Centre	Ярtelecom сервисный центр
3	Taxi Stand	Стоянка такси
4	Zolotoe Koltso	Золотое Кольцо
5	Cathedral of the Transfiguration of the Saviour	Спасо-Преображенский собор
6	Church of Peter the Metropolitan	Церковь Петра митрополита
7	Blinnaya	Блинная
8	Forty Saints' Church	Сорокосвятская церковь
9	Nikolsky Women's Monastery	Никольский женский монастырь
10	Goritsky Monastery	Горицкий монастырь
11	Narrow-guage Train Station	Остановка поезда узкоколейки
12	Danilovsky Monastery	Даниловский монастырь
13	Purification Church of Alexander Nevsky	Церковь Александра Невского Сретенского
14	Bus Station	Автостанция

Pereslavl-Zalessky – 'Pereslavl Beyond the Woods' – was founded in 1152 by Yury Dolgoruky. The town's claim to fame is as the birthplace of Alexander Nevsky. Its earth walls and the little Cathedral of the Transfiguration are as old as the town.

Orientation & Information

Pereslavl is pretty much a one-street town, with the bus station at the southwestern end, 2km from the centre. Apart from the kremlin area, most of the historic sights are out of the centre.

The **Yartelecom Service Centre** (☎ 215 95; Rostovskaya ul 20) has Internet and telephone facilities. Maps are available from the ticket office of the Goritsky Monastery or at Hotel Pereslavl.

Central Area

The walls of Yury Dolgoruky's **kremlin** are now a grassy ring around the central town. Inside is the **Cathedral of the Transfiguration of the Saviour** (Spaso-Preobrazhensky sobor), which was started in 1152 and is one of the oldest standing buildings in Russia. A bust of Alexander Nevsky stands out in front,

while three additional churches across the grassy square make for a picturesque corner. These comprise the tent-roofed **Church of Peter the Metropolitan** (Tserkov Petra mitropolita), built in 1585 and renovated in 1957, and the 18th-century twin churches fronting the road.

The **Trubezh River**, winding 2km from the kremlin to the lake, is fringed by trees and narrow lanes. You can follow the northern riverbank most of the way to the lake by a combination of paths and streets. The **Forty Saints' Church** (Sorokosvyatskaya tserkov) sits picturesquely on the south side of the river mouth.

Southwest of the kremlin, the **Nikolsky Women's Monastery** is undergoing massive renovation. Since its founding in 1350, this monastery has been on the brink of destruction – whether from Tatars, Poles or Communists – more than seems possible to survive. In 1994 four nuns from the Yaroslavl Tolga Convent came to restore the place, and today it looks marvellous. Rumour has it that the rebuilding is being bankrolled by a wealthy Muscovite business person who has benefited from the nuns' blessings.

Nikitsky Monastery

Founded in 1010, this monastery (Nikitsky monastyr) received its current name only in the 12th century, after the death of the martyr St Nikita who lived here. To punish his body for his sins, Nikita clasped his limbs in chains and spent his remaining days in an underground cell on the grounds. The handcuffs, which now hang in the monastery's main **cathedral**, are said to help cure addictions and other worldly vices. Behind the cathedral, a small chapel is being built around the dank cell where Nikita died.

Nikitsky Monastery is about 3km north of the centre on the west side of the main road. Bus Nos 1, 3 and 4 go most of the distance, or you can catch a taxi from Narodnaya ploshchad.

South Pereslavl-Zalessky

The **Goritsky Monastery** (Goritsky monastyr; ☎ 381 00; w museum.pereslavl.ru) was founded in the 14th century, though today the oldest buildings are the 17th-century gates, gate-church and belfry. From the bus station, walk about 1.2km then turn left and it's up on the hill. The centrepiece is the baroque **Assumption Cathedral** (Uspensky sobor) with its beautiful carved iconostasis. In the refectory is a **museum** (admission R10, plus per exhibit R10; open 10am-5pm Wed-Mon) with icons and incredible carved wooden furnishings.

The 1785 **Purification Church of Alexander Nevsky** (Tserkov Alexandra Nevskogo-Sretenskogo) is a working church across the main road from Goritsky. To the east, on a hillock overlooking fields and dachas, is the **Danilovsky Monastery** (Danilovsky monastyr), whose tent-roofed **Trinity Cathedral** (Troitsky sobor) was built in the 1530s. There's another 16th-century walled monastery, the **Fyodorovsky Monastery** (Fyodorovsky monastyr), about 2km south on the Moscow road.

Botik Museum

Lake Pleshcheevo takes credit as one of the birthplaces of the Russian navy. It is one of the places where Peter the Great developed his obsession with the sea, studying navigation and building a flotilla of over 100 little ships by the time he was 20.

Four kilometres along the road past the Goritsky Monastery, at the southern end of the lake, is the small Botik Museum (☎ 227 88; admission R20; open 10am-5pm Tues-Sun). Its highlight is the sailboat *Fortuna*, one of only two of Peter the Great's boats to survive fire and neglect (the other is in the St Petersburg Naval Museum).

In theory, you can reach the Botik on a tiny narrow-gauge train that rattles along its single track from the central ulitsa Kardovskogo. The ride is fun, but the train runs sporadically.

Places to Stay & Eat

Hotel Pereslavl (☎ 217 88, fax 226 87; ul Rostovskaya 27; singles/doubles R420/640, with private bathroom R600/1080), 400m north of the Trubezh River, was built in 1985 but is already falling apart. The rooms are what you would expect for the price. There is quite a pleasant **restaurant** downstairs where everything is under R60.

Blinnaya (ul Sovetskaya 10a; bliny R15; open 9am-9pm daily) offers nothing more than fresh, delicious bliny.

Zolotoe Koltso (☎ 222 49; Narodnaya pl 11; meals R350; open noon-midnight) is a more stylish place with an extensive menu and live music.

Getting There & Away

There is no mainline train station. Buses go to Moscow (2½ hours, three daily), Sergiev Posad (one hour, three daily) and Yaroslavl (three hours, two daily) travelling via Rostov-Veliky (1½ hours); others pass through en route to Moscow, Yaroslavl and Kostroma.

Getting Around

Bus No 1 runs up and down the main street from just south of the bus station; heading out from the centre, you can catch it just north of the river. Taxis wait at Narodnaya ploshchad.

SERGIEV POSAD
СЕРГИЕВ ПОСАД
☎ 254 • pop 100,000

Sergiev Posad is the town built around the Trinity Monastery of St Sergius, one of Russia's most important religious and historical landmarks. Often referred to by its Soviet name Zagorsk, Sergiev Posad is 60km from the edge of Moscow on the Yaroslavl road. If you have time for just one trip out of Moscow, this is the obvious choice.

The monastery was founded in about 1340 by Sergius of Radonezh (now patron saint of

Russia), a monk with enough moral authority to unite the country against Tatar rule, blessing Dmitry Donskoy's army before it gave the Tatars their first beating in 1380. The monastery's status as defender of the motherland grew during the Time of Troubles; it withstood a 16-month siege when Moscow was occupied by the Poles.

As a *lavra* (exalted monastery), it grew enormously wealthy on the gifts of tsars, nobles and merchants looking for divine support. Closed by the Bolsheviks, it was reopened after WWII as a museum, residence of the patriarch and working monastery.

The patriarch and the Church's administrative centre moved to the Danilovsky Monastery in Moscow in 1988, but the Trinity Monastery of St Sergius remains one of the most important spiritual sites in Russia. For its concentrated artistry and its unique role in the interrelated histories of the Russian Church and State, it is well worth a day trip from Moscow.

Orientation & Information

Prospekt Krasnoy Armii is the main street, running north–south through the town centre. The train and bus stations are on opposite corners of a wide square to the east of prospekt Krasnoy Armii. The monastery is about 400m north of here.

For money exchange, **Guta Bank** (☎ 422 28; pr Krasnoy Armii 148; open 9.30am-4.30pm Mon-Sat) is accessible from the car park at the back of the building. There's a **post and telephone office** (pr Krasnoy Armii 127A) outside the southeastern wall of the monastery.

Trinity Monastery of St Sergius

The monastery (Troitse-Sergieva Lavra; ☎ 453 56; admission free, photos R100; grounds open 10am-6pm daily) has additional charges to visit the museums inside.

Tours of the grounds and churches (not the museums), given by English-speaking monks, cost R550 per person. Book tours by phone or at the kiosk next to the Gate-Church of John the Baptist. Female visitors should wear headscarves, and men are required to remove hats in the churches.

Trinity Cathedral Built in the 1420s, this squat, dark yet beautiful church (Troitsky sobor) is the heart of the Trinity Monastery. A memorial service for St Sergius (whose

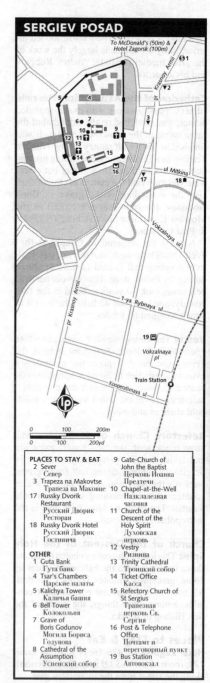

SERGIEV POSAD

To McDonald's (50m) &
Hotel Zagorsk (100m)

ul Mitkina

1-ya Rybnaya ul

Vokzalnaya pl

Train Station

Kooperativnaya ul

| 0 | 100 | 200m |
| 0 | 100 | 200yd |

PLACES TO STAY & EAT
2 Sever
   Север
3 Trapeza na Makovtse
   Трапеза на Маковце
17 Russky Dvorik
   Restaurant
   Русский Дворик
   Ресторан
18 Russky Dvorik Hotel
   Русский Дворик
   Гостиница

OTHER
1 Guta Bank
   Гута банк
4 Tsar's Chambers
   Царские палаты
5 Kalichya Tower
   Каличья башня
6 Bell Tower
   Колокольня
7 Grave of
   Boris Godunov
   Могила Бориса
   Годунова
8 Cathedral of the
   Assumption
   Успенский собор
9 Gate-Church of
   John the Baptist
   Церковь Иоанна
   Предтечи
10 Chapel-at-the-Well
   Надкладезная
   часовня
11 Church of the
   Descent of the
   Holy Spirit
   Духовская
   церковь
12 Vestry
   Ризница
13 Trinity Cathedral
   Троицкий собор
14 Ticket Office
   Касса
15 Refectory Church of
   St Sergius
   Трапезная
   церковь Св.
   Сергия
16 Post & Telephone
   Office
   Почтамт и
   переговорный пункт
19 Bus Station
   Автовокзал

tomb stands in the southeastern corner) goes on all day, every day. The icon-festooned interior, lit by oil lamps, is largely the work of the great medieval painter Andrey Rublyov and his students.

Cathedral of the Assumption This cathedral (Uspensky sobor), with its star-spangled domes, was modelled on the cathedral of the same name in the Moscow Kremlin. It was finished in 1585 with money left by Ivan the Terrible in a fit of remorse for killing his son. Services are held here in summer but otherwise you may find the cathedral closed. Outside the west door is the **grave** of Boris Godunov, the only tsar not buried in the Moscow Kremlin or St Petersburg's SS Peter & Paul Cathedral.

Nearby, the resplendent **Chapel-at-the-Well** (Nadkladeznaya chasovnya) was built over a spring that is said to have appeared during the Polish siege. The five-tier baroque bell tower took 30 years to build in the 18th century, and once had 42 bells, the largest of which weighed 65 tonnes.

Vestry The Vestry (Riznitsa; admission R150; open 10am-5.30pm Tues-Sun) behind the Trinity Cathedral displays the monastery's extraordinarily rich treasury, bulging with 600 years of donations by the rich and powerful – tapestries, jewel-encrusted vestments, solid-gold chalices and more.

Refectory Church of St Sergius The huge block with the 'wallpaper' paint job and lavish interior (Trapeznaya tserkov Sv Sergia) was once a dining hall for pilgrims. Now it's the Assumption Cathedral's winter counterpart, with morning services in cold weather. The green building next door is the metropolitan's residence.

Church of the Descent of the Holy Spirit This little 15th-century church (Dukhovskaya tserkov), with the bell tower under its dome, gracefully imitates Trinity Cathedral. It's used only on special occasions. It contains, among other things, the grave of the first Bishop of Alaska.

Places to Stay & Eat
Hotel Zagorsk (☎ 425 16; pr Krasnoy Armii 171; rooms from US$32) is about 500m north along the street from the monastery gate.

Russky Dvorik (☎ 753 92, fax 7 53 91; e rus_dvorik@conternet.ru; ul Mitkina 14/2; singles/doubles with breakfast from US$50/70) is a delightful small hotel a short walk east of the monastery. It is decorated in rustic style but quite modern. It also has a separate **restaurant** (☎ 4 51 14, pr Krasnoy Armii 134, meals R500) that gets overrun with tour groups at lunch but is otherwise quite pleasant.

The restaurant **Trapeza na Makovtse** (☎ 411 01; pr Krasnoy Armii 131; mains R400; open 9am-9pm) is touristy and a little pricey, but the view of the monastery walls from the outside tables is worth the cost.

Sever (☎ 412 20; pr Krasnoy Armii 141, meals R120; open 10am-9pm) is cheap but the food is as hit and miss as the Soviet-style service. There's also **McDonald's**, further north along prospekt Krasnoy Armii.

Getting There & Away
Train Suburban trains run every half-hour or so to/from Moscow's Yaroslavl Station (1½ hours, R30); take any train bound for Sergiev Posad or Alexandrov. The fastest option is the daily express train to Yaroslavl (1st/ 2nd class R90/60, 55 minutes from Moscow).

To continue on to Rostov-Veliky (3½ hours) or Yaroslavl (five hours), you may have to change at Alexandrov to a Yaroslavl-bound suburban train.

Bus Services to Sergiev Posad from Moscow's Yaroslavl Station (R30) depart every half-hour from 8.30am to 7.30pm (70 minutes). If you're facing Komsomolsky prospekt with Yaroslavl Station behind you, the bus stop is to your left, next to the underground passage.

Three daily buses start at Sergiev Posad and run to Pereslavl-Zalessky (R20, 75 minutes). About nine northbound buses a day stop here in transit to Yaroslavl, Kostroma or Rybinsk; all these will take you to Pereslavl-Zalessky, Rostov-Veliky or Yaroslavl if you can get a ticket.

ABRAMTSEVO
АБРАМЦЕВО
The small Abramtsevo estate, 15km southwest of Sergiev Posad, was a seedbed for several 19th-century movements aiming to preserve nationalistic Russian religious, social and aesthetic values. In the 1840s and 1850s it was the home of Sergey Axakov

ioneer novelist of Russian realism, and a efuge for upper-class intellectuals.

In 1870 Savva Mamontov, a railway ycoon and patron of the arts, bought Abramtevo and turned it into an artists' colony dedcated to a renaissance of traditional Russian rt and architecture which would have a trong influence on painting, sculpture, aplied art and even theatre. The list of resident ainters alone represents a who's who of neo-Russianism': Ilya Repin, landscape artst Isaak Levitan, portraitist Valentin Serov nd the quite un-Slavonic painter and ceramiist Mikhail Vrubel.

Other projects included woodworking and eramics workshops, Mamontov's private pera (where Fyodor Chaliapin made his lebut) and several buildings designed, built nd decorated by group efforts.

All this is now the **Abramtsevo Estate Museum-Preserve** (☎ 254 324 70; admission !35; open 10am-5pm Wed-Sun), which nakes a good addition to a day trip to Sergiev osad. Apart from the highlights below, there re arts and crafts exhibits in the other buildngs on the grounds, which cost extra to enter. he museum is closed the last Friday of each nonth, and sometimes in April and October.

Main House

everal rooms have been preserved intact. Axakov's dining room and study contain aintings and sculptures of family and riends, but most of the house is devoted to he Mamontov years. The main attraction is Mamontov's dining room, featuring Repin's ortraits of the patron and his wife, and erov's luminous *Girl with Peaches*. A strikng majolica bench by Vrubel is in the garden.

Saviour Church 'Not Made by Hand'

he prettiest building in the grounds, this mall church (Tserkov Spasa Nerukotvorny)

seems to symbolise Mamontov's intentions: it's a carefully researched homage by half-a-dozen artists to 14th-century Novgorod architecture. The iconostasis is by Repin and Vasily Polenov. The tiled stove in the corner, still working, is exquisite.

Hut on Chicken Legs

This just goes to show that art doesn't have to be serious. The Slavophile painter Viktor Vasnetsov conjured up the fairy tale of Baba Yaga the witch, with this playhouse with feet (although chicken legs they are not).

Convent of the Intercession

Between Abramtsevo and Sergiev Posad, in the village of Khotkovo, is the Convent of the Intercession (Pokrovsky monastyr); it was founded in 1308 though the present buildings are from the 18th century or later.

The parents of Sergius of Radonezh, Russia's patron saint and founder of the Trinity Monastery of St Sergius at Sergiev Posad, are buried in the convent's recently restored **Intercession Cathedral** (Pokrovsky sobor). The biggest building in the convent is the early-20th-century **St Nicholas' Cathedral** (Nikolsky sobor).

Getting There & Away

Abramtsevo and Khotkovo are just before Sergiev Posad on suburban trains from Moscow's Yaroslavl Station. Most trains heading to Sergiev Posad or Alexandrov stop at both places (but a few skip Abramtsevo, so check). There are regular buses between Abramtsevo and Sergiev Posad (R10, 20 minutes).

By car, turn west off the M8 Moscow–Yaroslavl highway just north of the 61km post. Signs to Khotkovo and Abramtsevo mark the turn-off. For the Khotkovo convent, turn left just before the rail tracks in the village; for Abramtsevo, continue over the railway line for a few more kilometres.

AROUND MOSCOW

St Petersburg Санкт Петербург

☎ 812 • pop 4.2 million

It's almost impossible to believe, but a bare three centuries ago St Petersburg was little more than a giant swamp. Such is the visual power of this handsome city – created by Peter the Great as his 'window on the West' – with a history and European savoir-faire like no other place in Russia.

Apart from the seamless architectural ensemble and languorous canals at the heart of 'Piter' (as it's affectionately known to residents), there are world-class museums – the most famous being, of course, the Hermitage – and stunningly opulent palaces. From here autocratic tsars ruled Russia for two centuries before their downfall in 1917 in a revolution that shook the world.

St Petersburg is the birthplace of Russian ballet and was home to literary giants, including Pushkin and Dostoevsky. The 19th-century flowering of Russian music was centred here, too – a tradition continued today since St Petersburg prides itself on its hedonistic and experimental club scene and the quality of its performing arts.

The city's far northern latitude keeps it bright nearly 24 hours a day in midsummer, a time when its festive spirit is light and carefree. Don't discount the long dark winters, though: the Neva River becomes one giant ice rink, the endless nights have a twinkling magic, and it's the perfect time to take in all those museums, ballets and operas.

Far from perfect – beauty and decay go hand in hand here – St Petersburg, nonetheless, is a consummate charmer that's cosmopolitan in outlook and tourist-friendly. Whenever you choose to visit, don't rush it, because this is a city that demands to be savoured.

HISTORY
Peter the Great

Alexander of Novgorod defeated the Swedes near the mouth of the Neva River in 1240 – earning the title Nevsky (of the Neva). Sweden took control of the region in the 17th century and it was Peter the Great's desire to crush this rival and make Russia a European power that led to the founding of St Petersburg. At the start of the Great Northern War (1700–21) he captured the Swedish outposts

Highlights

- Cruise the canals and admire the city's elegant, crumbling architecture
- Lose yourself amid the artistic riches of the Hermitage or the Russian Museum
- Watch the bridges rise along the Neva during the summer white nights
- Enjoy the opera or ballet at the beautiful Mariinsky Theatre
- Climb the colonnade of St Isaac's Cathedral for panoramic views across the city's skyline

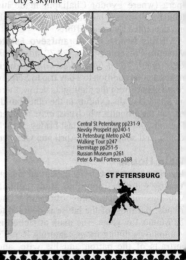

Central St Petersburg pp231-9
Nevsky Prospekt pp240-1
St Petersburg Metro p242
Walking Tour p247
Hermitage pp251-5
Russian Museum p261
Peter & Paul Fortress p268

ST PETERSBURG

★★★★★★★★★★★★★★★★★★

on the Neva, and in 1703 he began his city with the Peter & Paul Fortress.

After Peter trounced the Swedes at Poltava in 1709, the city he named, in Dutch style, Sankt Pieter Burkh (after his patron saint) really began to grow. Canals were dug to drain the marshy south bank and in 1712 Peter made the place his capital, forcing grumbling administrators, nobles and merchants to move here and build new homes. Peasants were drafted as forced labour, many dying of disease and exhaustion; it's still known as the city built upon bones. Architects and artisans came from all over Europe. By Peter's death in 1725 his city had a population of 40,000 and 90% of Russia's foreign trade passed through it.

fter Peter

eter's immediate successors moved the
pital back to Moscow but Empress Anna
anovna (1730–40) returned it to St Peters-
rg. Between 1741 and 1825 under Empress
lizabeth, Catherine the Great and Alexander
it became a cosmopolitan city with a royal
urt of famed splendour. These monarchs
mmissioned great series of palaces, gov-
nment buildings and churches, turning it
to one of Europe's grandest capitals.

The emancipation of the serfs in 1861 and
dustrialisation, which peaked in the 1890s,
rought a flood of poor workers into the city,
ading to squalor, disease and festering dis-
ntent. St Petersburg became a hotbed of
rikes and political violence and was the hub
f the 1905 revolution, sparked by 'Bloody
unday' on 9 January 1905, when a strikers'
arch to petition the tsar in the Winter Palace
as fired on by troops. In 1914, in a wave of
atriotism at the start of WWI, the city's name
as changed to the Russian-style Petrograd.
he population at the time was 2.1 million.

evolution & War

1917 the workers' protests turned into a
eneral strike and troops mutinied, forcing
e end of the monarchy in March. The Petro-
rad Soviet, a socialist focus for workers' and
oldiers' demands, started meeting in the
ity's Tauride Palace alongside the country's
eformist Provisional Government. It was to
etrograd's Finland Station that Lenin trav-
lled in April to organise the Bolshevik Party.

The actual revolution came after Bolshe-
iks occupied key positions in Petrograd on
4 October. The next day, the All-Russian
ongress of Soviets, meeting in the Smolny,
ppointed a Bolshevik government. That
ight, after some exchanges of gunfire and a
lank shot from the cruiser *Aurora* on the
leva, the Provisional Government in the
inter Palace surrendered to the Bolsheviks.

The new government moved the capital back
Moscow in March 1918, fearing a German
ttack on Petrograd. The privations of the Civil
Var caused Petrograd's population to drop to
bout 700,000, and in 1921 strikes in the city
nd a bloodily suppressed revolt by the sailors
f nearby Kronstadt helped to bring about
enin's more liberal New Economic Policy.

Petrograd was renamed Leningrad after
enin's death in 1924. A hub of Stalin's 1930s
dustrialisation program, by 1939 it had 3.1

million people and 11% of Soviet industrial
output. Yet Stalin feared it as a rival power
base and the 1934 assassination of the local
communist chief Sergey Kirov at Smolny was
the start of his 1930s Communist Party purge.

When the Germans attacked the USSR in
June 1941 it took them only two and a half
months to reach Leningrad. As the birthplace
of Bolshevism, Hitler swore to wipe it from
the face of the earth, but not before his
expected New Year's victory ball in Hotel
Astoria. His troops besieged the city from 8
September 1941 until 27 January 1944 (see
the boxed text 'The Leningrad Blockade').

After the war, Leningrad – now proclaimed a 'hero city' – was reconstructed and
reborn, though it took until 1960 for its population to exceed pre-WWII levels.

The Tsar's Return

In 1989, Anatoly Sobchak, a reform-minded
candidate, was elected mayor. Two years later
the city's citizens voted to bring back the
name of St Petersburg (though the region
around the city to this day is still known as
Leningradskaya oblast).

Romanov ghosts returned to the city on 17
July 1998, when the remains of Tsar Nicholas
II, his wife, three of his five children, their
doctor and three servants were buried in the
family crypt at the SS Peter & Paul Cathedral
within the fortress of the same name. President
Boris Yeltsin was in attendance, together with
many Romanov family members, but other
politicians downplayed the event, and Patriarch (head of the Russian Orthodox Church)
Alexey II held his own, rival service in Sergiev
Posad, outside Moscow, along with a few
renegade Romanov descendants (those who
held some pretensions to regaining the throne).
The burial, which Yeltsin called an expiation
of Russia's common guilt, set off touchy de-
bates on monarchism, and on the authenticity
of the royal remains (see the boxed text 'Bones
of Contention: The Romanov Remains' in the
Urals chapter).

300 Years & Going Strong

In 1996 Sobchak was succeeded as governor
by his deputy Vladimir Yakovlev (Yakolev's
first act after his victory was to change the title
from mayor to governor). Sobchak later ended
up in comfortable self-exile in Paris after
serious charges of corruption and fiscal mismanagement.

ST PETERSBURG

The Leningrad Blockade

The Leningrad Blockade was the defining event of the 20th century for the city. Around one million people died from shelling, starvation and disease in what's called the '900 Days' (actually 872). By comparison, the USA and UK suffered about 700,000 dead between them in all of WWII.

After the war began on 22 June 1941, with the Germans fast approaching, many residents fled. Art treasures and precious documents from the Hermitage and other museums were shipped out by the train-load; factories were evacuated and relocated to Siberia; historical sculptures were buried or covered with sandbags. Yet no-one could possibly have predicted the suffering to come.

The Nazi plan, as indicated in a secret directive, was to 'wipe the city of Petersburg from the face of the earth'. A fragile 'Road of Life' across frozen Lake Ladoga was the only (albeit heavily bombed) lifeline the city had for provisions and evacuations.

Food was practically nonexistent, and at one point rations were limited to 175g of sawdust-laden bread a day. People ate their pets, even rats and birds disappeared from the city. The paste behind wallpaper was scraped off and eaten, leather belts were cooked until chewable. Cannibalism started in the shelters for refugees from the neighbouring towns; without ration cards, they were among the first to die. The exhausted and starved literally fell over dead on the streets. There were periods when over 30,000 people per day died of hunger.

More than 150,000 shells and bombs were dropped on the city during the Blockade, the effects of which are still visible on some buildings (notably on the west wall of St Isaac's Cathedral and the northwest corner of the Anichkov bridge). Still, life went on. Concerts and plays were performed in candle-lit halls, lectures given, poetry written, orphanages opened, brigades formed to clean up the city. Most famous was the 9 August 1942 concert of Shostakovich's 7th Symphony by the Leningrad Philharmonic, broadcast nationally by radio from the besieged city.

According to survivors, random acts of kindness outnumbered incidents of robbery and vandalism, and lessons learned about the human spirit would be remembered for a lifetime. From a poem by Olga Berggolts, written after the Blockade was lifted: 'In mud, in darkness, hunger, and sorrow, where death, like a shadow, trod on our heels, we were so happy at times, breathed such turbulent freedom, that our grandchildren would envy us.'

For a detailed, harrowing description of the Blockade, read Harrison Salisbury's *The 900 Days*. Otherwise, a visit to one or all of these Blockade-related sites – St Petersburg History Museum, Blockade Museum, Monument to the Heroic Defenders of Leningrad and Piskaryovskoe Cemetery (all covered later in this chapter) – would greatly enrich your understanding of its history.

Yakovlev hasn't earned himself a lily-white reputation, but his administration has at least spearheaded a beautification policy – particularly in the run-up to the city's 300th birthday celebrations – which has pleased the populace. The US$1.3 billion allocated to St Petersburg for the tricentenary has made it look better now probably than at any other time in its history.

In notable contrast to Moscow's infighting, dirty politics and entrenched lobbyist subculture, St Petersburg has been able to capitalise on the injection of foreign interest in Russia and business is booming. It hasn't harmed matters that President Vladimir Putin wastes no opportunity to return to his birthplace and show it off to visiting heads of state and other dignitaries. Overused as the term may be, St Petersburg has, in fact, re-established itself as Russia's window on the West.

ORIENTATION

St Petersburg sprawls across and around the delta of the Neva River, at the end of the easternmost arm of the Baltic Sea, the Gulf of Finland. Entering St Petersburg at its southeastern corner, the Neva first flows north and then west across the middle of the city, dividing there into several branches and forming the islands making up the delta. The two biggest branches, which diverge where the Winter Palace stands on the south bank, are the Bolshaya (Big) Neva and Malaya (Small) Neva; they flow into the sea either side of Vasilevsky Island.

The heart of St Petersburg is the area spreading back from the Winter Palace and the Admiralty on the south bank, its skyline dominated by the golden dome of St Isaac's Cathedral. Nevsky prospekt, heading east-southeast from here, is the main drag, with many of the sights, shops and restaurants.

The northern side of the city comprises three main areas. Vasilevsky Island is the westernmost, with many of the city's fine early buildings still standing at the eastern end – the Strelka. The middle area is Petrograd Side, a cluster of delta islands whose southern end is marked by the tall gold spire of the SS Peter & Paul Cathedral. The third, eastern, area is Vyborg Side, stretching along the north bank of the Neva.

Maps

There are dozens of maps of St Petersburg available at hotels and bookshops across the city. Lonely Planet's handy *St Petersburg City Map* covers the city centre at a scale of 1:16,000 and features maps of Pushkin, Petrograd and Petrodvorets, a metro map, walking tour and complete index of all streets and sights.

Karta (W *www.karta-ltd.ru*) publishes several useful maps, including a fully indexed *Sankt-Peterburg i prigorody atlas* and the *Marshruty gorodskogo transporta Sankt Peterburg*, which lists all the city's transport routes. Its website is in Russian only.

The best selection of maps, including old, out-of-print maps and those depicting other Russian regions can be found at **Staraya Kniga** (Map 2; ☎ 232 17 65; *Bolshoy pr 57*) on Petrograd Side.

INFORMATION

The Russian-language (and English-indexed) *Luchshee V Sankt Peterburge* and its English-language version, *The Traveller's Yellow Pages*, are comprehensive and accurate yellow pages telephone books. They include good city-centre maps and helpful seating plans for major theatres, opera houses and stadiums. Published by Telinfo, they can be accessed through the website W www.infoservices.com. The official English-language portal for the city is W http://petersburgcity.com/for-tourists.

Tourist Offices

Inside the Beloselsky-Belozersky Palace, the official **Tourist Information Office** (Map 6; ☎ 311 28 43, fax 15 97 96; W *www.spb.ru /eng; Nevsky pr 41; open 10am-7pm Mon-Sat Sept-May, daily June-Aug*) has multilingual staff and can help with individual queries, but staff don't book accommodation and there's little in the way of official literature. There are

plans to open kiosks at Pulkovo-2 airport, Peter & Paul Fortress and Petrodvorets.

Consulates

See the European Russia Facts for the Visitor chapter.

Visa Registration

Your visa should ideally be registered by the hotel or hostel in which you are staying, or through the company that invited you. However, it may be that you might have to go to a local *passportno-vizovoye upravleniye* (PVU; passport and visa department) office to register it yourself. For general inquiries, try your luck at the **main office** (Map 3; ☎ 278 24 81; *Kirochnaya ul 4; open 9am-5pm Mon-Fri*).

Headaches can be minimised by getting your visa registered at any hotel or hostel which can do so, even if you are not staying there, usually for a fee equivalent to the price of one night in its cheapest room. Ost-West Kontaktservice (see Travel Agencies later) can also help with visa registration.

Money

Exchanging Money There are exchange offices all along Nevsky prospekt – shop around since some places offer better rates to foreigners than others. A reliable currency exchange is **Ligovsky** (Map 6; ☎ 325 10 93; *Ligovsky per 2; open 9am-9pm daily*), near the Moscow Station.

ATMs are located inside every metro station, in hotels and department stores, main post offices and along major streets. If you want to get dollars from an ATM, try those in the major hotels.

Note that **American Express** (Map 5; ☎ 326 45 00, fax 326 45 01; *Malaya Morskaya ul 23; open 9am-5pm Mon-Fri*) now only offers travel services.

Post

St Petersburg's **main international and domestic post and telegraph office** (*glavpochtamt; Map 4; Pochtamtskaya ul 9; open 9am-8pm Mon-Sat, 10am-6pm Sun*) is two blocks southwest of St Isaac's Cathedral. All nonbook parcels leaving Russia must be sent from here, from Window 24 (this keeps changing though; just walk to the far left side of the main hall and look for the sign).

There are also 400 branch offices that are scattered throughout the city and these vary in services usually in proportion to size. A particularly friendly **branch** *(Map 6; Stremyannaya ul 14; open 10am-8pm Mon-Fri, 10am-5pm Sat & Sun)* is centrally located (between the Fontanka and ploshchad Vosstania), not very busy, and the motherly staff will wrap your book or souvenir parcels (up to 5kg) and help you fill out those ubiquitous forms.

Express Services Inside the main post office, Window 16 offers a special overnight service to Moscow and Minsk. Euroletter at Window 26 will send letters and parcels up to 2kg, charging US$6 for up to 250g, US$10 for 2kg. It uses express post until Sweden, then Swedish post, and swears it only takes five days to reach the USA or Australia.

Express Mail Service (EMS) is provided by **EMS Garantpost** *(☎ 311 11 20; e ems@comset.net)*. Documents up to 2kg (500g) to the USA costs US$21; to Australia US$30) and packages up to 31kg (5kg to the USA costs US$56; to Australia US$78) take five days to reach their destination (three days to European capitals). It has several outlets in the centre, but the head office is at Konnog-

vardeysky bulvar 4 (Map 4), behind the main post office.

Westpost *(Map 6; ☎ 275 07 84, 327 30 92; w www.westpost.ru; Nevsky pr 86; open 9.30am-8pm Mon-Fri, noon-8pm Sat)* is a privately run, international mail service. Mail is transported daily from St Petersburg to Lappeenranta in Finland, and mailed from there. To the USA, a 20g letter costs US$2.20, and a 2kg parcel costs US$64. It has a full range of delivery and courier services.

DHL *(Map 5; ☎ 326 64 00; Izmailovsky pr 4)*, **Fed Ex** *(Map 6; ☎ 311 98 40; nab kanala Griboedova 16)* and **UPS** *(Map 3; ☎ 327 85 40; Shpalernaya ul 51)* are the main global express mail services in town, offering two-day delivery to Europe and the USA/Canada, and three-day delivery to Australia/New Zealand, all with services starting at US$38 for letters.

Receiving Mail The most reliable option for those not staying in luxury hotels or the HI St Petersburg Hostel (which provide mail service via Finland) is limited to American Express and Optima cardholders. American Express (see Exchanging Money earlier) will hold mail (letters only) for cardholders and holders of travellers cheques for up to 30 days; the mailing address is American Express, PO Box 87, SF-53501 Lappeenranta, Finland.

Westpost (see Express Services earlier) offers post boxes in Lappeenranta, with daily pick-up or delivery to the Westpost office or, for corporate clients, to an address in St Petersburg.

Telephone

Calling from a private phone is the simplest, though no longer necessarily the cheapest, option – except for local calls, which are free.

Payphones *Taksofon* (payphones) are located throughout the city. The green ones are the most common (but not the cheapest), and accept prepaid phonecards (with the letters SNM – CHM in Cyrillic – on them), readily available from metro token booths or, at slightly higher prices, from telephone offices. Occasionally you'll need to press the star button as soon as you hear your party answer (you'll know you'll need to if they scream 'Allo? Allo?' after you start speaking).

Street Names

In the early to mid-1990s, St Petersburg went on a rampage, changing the Soviet-era names of dozens of its streets, bridges and parks back to their prerevolutionary names. Ten years on, only their 'new' names are used, though 'Griboedova Canal' will probably never be changed back to its tsarist-era moniker, Yekaterinsky (Alexander Griboedov was a 19th-century playwright who lived in a house on this canal). Only two fairly recent changes may cause confusion to tourists: Kirochnaya ulitsa and Kazanskaya ulitsa may occasionally be referred to by their Soviet names ulitsa Saltykova-Shchedrina and ulitsa Plekhanova respectively.

St Petersburg has two streets called Bolshoy prospekt: one on Petrograd Side, one on Vasilevsky Island. The two sides of some Vasilevsky Island streets are known as lines (linii) and opposite sides of these streets have different names – thus 4-ya linia (4th line) and 5-ya linia (5th line) are the east and west sides of the same street – which collectively is called 4-ya i 5-ya linii (4th and 5th lines).

★★★★★★★★★★★★★★★★★★★★

[Continued on page 243]

Map labels

Ozerki
pr. Prosveshchenya
A122
pr. Lunacharskogo

Dolgoe Ozero
Komendantsky Aerodrom
Grazhdanka
pr. Toreza
pr. Nauki

Staraya Derevna
Kronshtadt (17km) & ...borg (166km)
Bogatyrsky pr.
Landskoe sh.
pr. Engelsa

Piskaryovka
Piskaryovskoe Cemetery
Nepokoryonnykh pr.
A128

M10
Torzhkovskaya
3
1
5

MAP 2
Primorsky pr.
MAP 3
Vyborg Side
Poluostrovo
Petrograd Side

Dekabristov Island
Malaya Neva
Bolshaya Neva
Bolshoy Sampsonievsky pr.
Kamennoostrovsky pr.
Finland Station
Polyustrovsky pr.
Piskaryovsky pr.

Smolenka River
Neva pr.

MAP 4
Kosygina

Vasilevsky Island
Maly pr.
Bolshoy pr.
Neva
Nevsky pr.
Liteyny pr.
Moscow Station
Zanevsky pr.

Gulf of Finland (Finsky Zaliv)
... Sredny pr.
Nakhimova
Sadovaya ul.
Vitebsk Station
MAP 6
Neva River
Krasnogvardeysky pr.

M18

Baltic Station
Warsaw Station
Ligovsky pr.
MAP 5
Vesyoly Posyolok
To Volkhov & Staraya Ladoga (100km)

...onersky ...land
Baltiyskaya ul.
Moskovsky pr.
pr. Obukhovskoy Oborony
M18

6
7
Obukhovo

pr. Stachek
Avtovo
M11
pr. Yuriya Gagarina
M10

Marshala Kazakova
15
ul Ziny Portnovoy
14
Vitebsky prosp
pr. Slavy
8
9

M11
rgofskoe sh.
Dachnoe
etrodvorets (15km) & ...onoso (27km)
10
11
Moskovskaya pl
13
pl Pobedy
Kupchino

To Tallinn
Ulyanka
M20
Moskovskoe sh.
To Novgorod (190km), & Moscow (670km)

PULKOVO AIRPORT
Pulkovo-2
Pulkovo-1
To Observatory (3km), Pushkin & Pavlovsk (19km)
M10

Legend

1 Kruglye Bani
   Круглые бани
2 Seven Forty
3 Xali Gali
4 Hotel Vyborgskaya
   Гостиница Выборгская
5 Hotel Kareliya
6 Moscow Triumphal Arch
   Московские ворота
7 Shalom
8 Lomonosova China Factory
9 River Terminal
10 Chesma Church
   Чесменская церков
11 Lenin Statue
   Памятник В. И. Ленину
12 Monument to the Heroic
   Defenders of Leningrad
13 Hotel Pulkovskaya
   Гостиница Пулковская
14 Ramses Playground
15 Warehouse Market
   Вещевой рынок

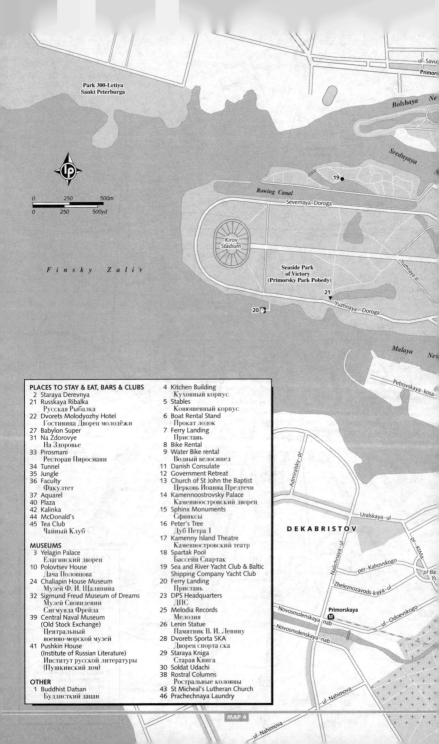

Park 300-Letiya
Sankt Peterburga

Bolshaya Ne

Srednyaya

Rowing Canal

Severnaya-Doroga

Kirov
Stadium

Finsky Zaliv

Seaside Park
of Victory
(Primorsky Park Pobedy)

21

20

Yuzhnaya-Doroga

Yuzhnaya al

Malaya New

Petrovskaya-kosa

Admiralsky-pr

Uralskaya-ul

DEKABRISTOV

per-Kahovskogo

pl-Ba

Nalichnaya-ul

per-KiMa

Zheleznovods-kaya-ul

Primorskaya

ul-Odoevskogo

Novosmolenskaya-nab

Novosmolenskaya-nab

ul-Nahimova

ul-Nahimova

PLACES TO STAY & EAT, BARS & CLUBS
2 Staraya Derevnya
21 Russkaya Ribalka
    Русская Рыбалка
22 Dvorets Molodyozhy Hotel
    Гостиница Дворец молодёжи
27 Babylon Super
31 Na Zdorovye
    На Здоровье
33 Pirosmani
    Ресторан Пиросмани
34 Tunnel
35 Jungle
36 Faculty
    Факултет
37 Aquarel
40 Plaza
42 Kalinka
44 McDonald's
45 Tea Club
    Чайный Клуб

MUSEUMS
3 Yelagin Palace
    Елагинский дворец
10 Polovtsev House
    Дача Половцова
24 Chaliapin House Museum
    Музей Ф. И. Шаляпина
32 Sigmund Freud Museum of Dreams
    Музей Сновидении
    Сигмунда Фрейда
39 Central Naval Museum
    (Old Stock Exchange)
    Центральный
    военно-морской музей
41 Pushkin House
    (Institute of Russian Literature)
    Институт русской литературы
    (Пушкинский дом)

OTHER
1 Buddhist Datsan
    Буддисткий дацан

4 Kitchen Building
    Кухонный корпус
5 Stables
    Конюшенный корпус
6 Boat Rental Stand
    Прокат лодок
7 Ferry Landing
    Пристань
8 Bike Rental
9 Water Bike rental
    Водный велосипед
11 Danish Consulate
12 Government Retreat
13 Church of St John the Baptist
    Церковь Иоанна Предтечи
14 Kamennoostrovsky Palace
    Каменноостровский дворец
15 Sphinx Monuments
    Сфинксы
16 Peter's Tree
    Дуб Петра I
17 Kamenny Island Theatre
    Каменностровский театр
18 Spartak Pool
    Бассейн Спартак
19 Sea and River Yacht Club & Baltic
    Shipping Company Yacht Club
20 Ferry Landing
    Пристань
23 DPS Headquarters
    ДПС
25 Melodia Records
    Мелодия
26 Lenin Statue
    Памятник В. И. Ленину
28 Dvorets Sporta SKA
    Дворец спорта ска
29 Staraya Kniga
    Старая Книга
30 Soldat Udachi
38 Rostral Columns
    Ростральные колонны
43 St Micheal's Lutheran Church
46 Prachechnaya Laundry

MAP 4

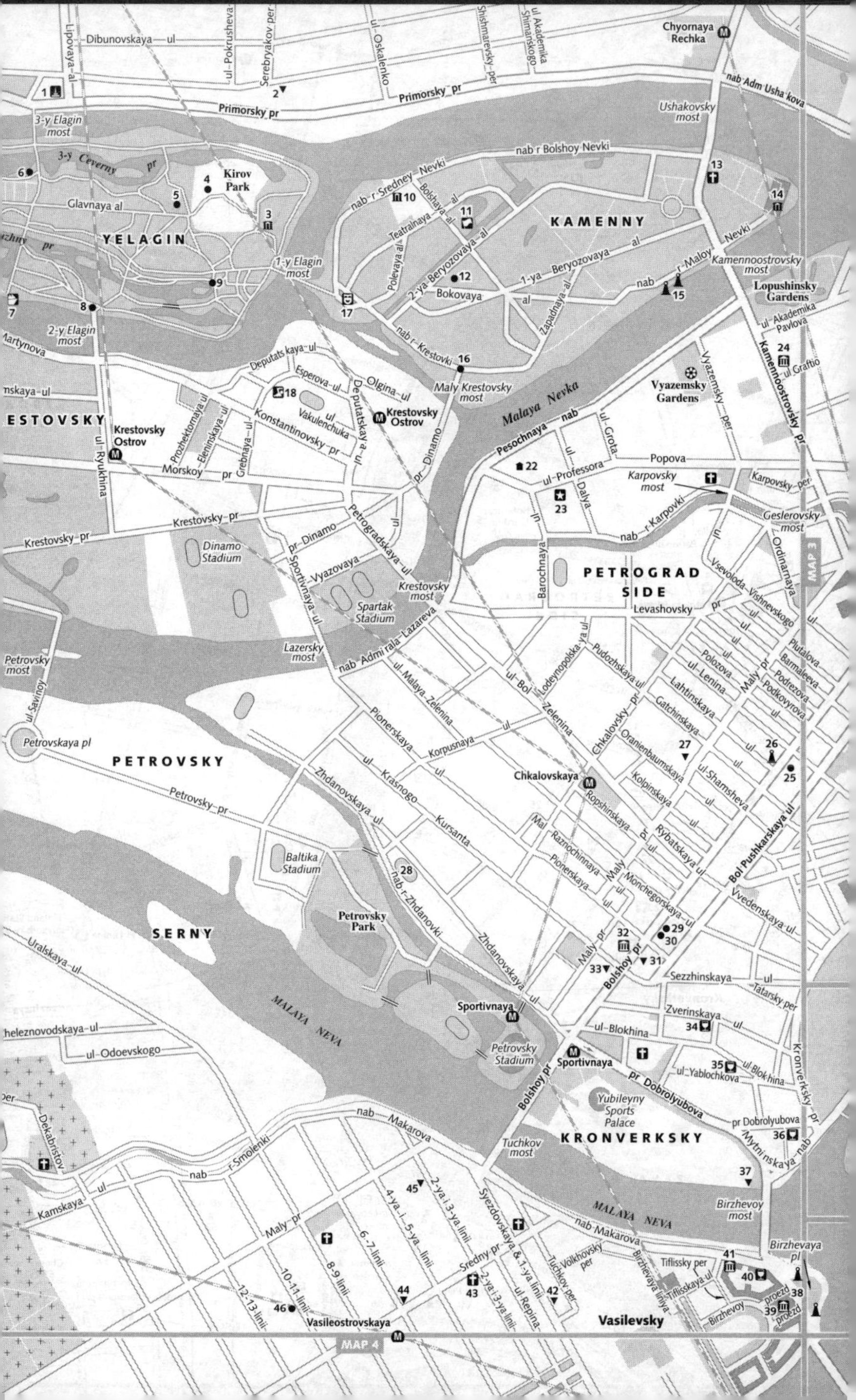

Dibunovskaya—ul

Lipovaya—ul

ul—Pokrusheva

ul—Oskalenko

Serebryakov—per

ul—Akademika
Shmaratsko

Shkiperatsk

Chyornaya
Rechka M

1 🏛

2 ▼

Primorsky—pr

Primorsky—pr

nab Adm Usha'kova

3-y Elagin
most

Ushakovsky
most

3-y Ceverny—pr

nab r Bolshoy Nevki

6 ●

4 ● Kirov
Park

5 ●

13 🏛

Glavnaya al

nab—r—Sredney—Nevki

🏛 10

KAMENNY

14 🏛

YELAGIN

3 🏛

Teatralnaya

11 ▼

Pokrovaya

1-y Elagin
most

2-ya Beryozovaya—a

🏛 12

1-ya—Beryozovaya—

nab—r—Maloy—Nevki

Kamennoostrovsky
most

7 ●

8 ●

9 ●

17 🏛

Bokovaya

15 ▲

Lopushinsky
Gardens

2-y Elagin
most

ul—Akademika
Pavlova

24 ▼

Martynova

nab—r—Krestovki

16 🏛

Maly Krestovsky
most

Malaya Nevka

Vyazemsky
Gardens

🏛

Grafto

nskaya—ul

ESTOVSKY

Esperova—ul

Olgina—ul

Vyazemsky
per

Kamennoostrovsky—pr

MAP 3

Deputatskaya—ul

🏛 18

ul—Dinamo

Pesochnaya—nab

ul—Grota

Krestovsky
Ostrov M

Konstantinovsky—pr

Krestovsky
Ostrov

🏛 22

ul—Professora
Popova

Karpovsky
most

Karpovsky—per

Krestovsky
Ostrov

Vakulenchuka

23 🏛

ul—Dinamo

Geslerovsky
most

Prozhektornaya—ul

Belinskaya—ul

Grebanka—ul

Morskoy—pr

ul—Ryukhina

nab—r—Karpovki

Ordinarnaya—ul

Krestovsky—pr

Petrogradskaya—ul

Barochnaya—ul

PETROGRAD
SIDE

Vsevoloda—Vishnevskogo—ul

Krestovsky—pr

pr—Dinamo

Krestovsky
most

Levashovsky—pr

Plutalova—ul

Dinamo
Stadium

Vyazovaya—ul

Sportivnaya—ul

Spartak
Stadium

Lazersky
most

nab—Adm—rala—Lazareva

ul—Bol—Zelenina

Podrezova—ul

Lenina—ul

Polozova—ul

Petrovsky
most

Pionerskaya—ul

ul—Malaya—Zelenina

Voskova—ul

Lahtinskaya—ul

Petrovskaya—pl

PETROVSKY

Petrovsky—pr

Zhdanovskaya—ul

Korpusnaya—ul

ul—Krasnogo
Kursanta

Chkalovskaya M

Oranienbaumskaya—ul

Pudozhskaya—ul

Gatchinskaya—ul

Shamsheva—ul

27 ▼

26 ▲

25 ●

Baltika
Stadium

28 ▲

Petrovsky
Park

nab—r—Zhdanovki

Zhdanovskaya—ul

Pionerskaya—ul

Maly—pr

Razpochnaya—ul

Ropshinskaya—ul

Maly—Monchegordaya—ul

Kolpinskaya—ul

Rybatskaya—ul

Vvedenskaya—ul

Bol—Pushkarskaya—ul

SERNY

MALAYA—NEVA

32 🏛

29 ●

30 ●

33 ▼

31 ▼

Bolshoy—pr

Sportivnaya M

Sezzhinskaya—ul

Tatarsky—per

34 ▼

Zverinskaya—ul

Petrovsky
Stadium

Sportivnaya M

ul—Blokhina

35 ▼

ul—Blok—hina

Kronverksky—pr

zheleznovodskaya—ul

ul—Odoevskogo

Uralskaya—ul

Pr—Dobrolyubova

Yubileyny
Sports
Palace

pr—Dobrolyubova

36 ▼

KRONVERKSKY

Mytninskaya—nab

Tuchkov
most

37 ▼

Dekabristov

🏛

Kamskaya—ul

nab—r—Smolenki

nab—Makarova

45 ▼

2-ya—i—3-ya—linii

Syezdovskaya—&—1-ya—linii

nab—Makarova

MALAYA—NEVA

Birzhevoy
most

41 ▲

Birzhevaya
pl

🏛

Maly—pr

4-ya—i—5-ya—linii

6-7—linii

8-9—linii

Sredny—pr—&—7-ya—linii

Tuchkov—per

Volkhov—per

Bol—prospekt

40 🏛

38 ▲

44 ●

43 🏛

ul—Repina

42 ▲

Tiflissky—per

39 ▼

proezd—38

proezd

46 ●

12-13—linii

10-11—linii

Vasileostrovskaya M

Vasilevsky

Birzhevoy

MAP 4

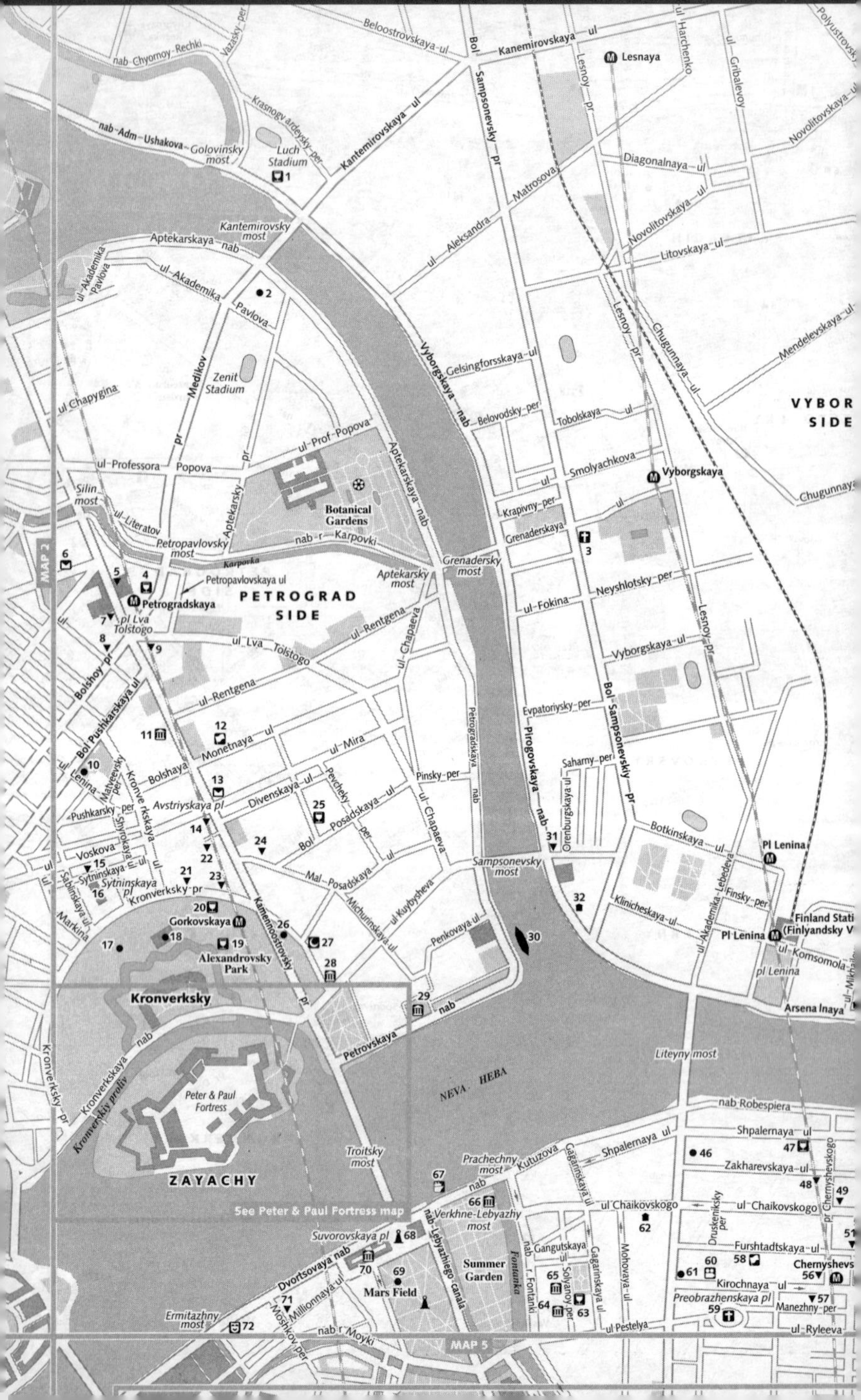

MAP 3 – CENTRAL ST PETERSBURG

Beloostrovskaya-ul

ul-Harchenko

ul-Polyustrovs

Vazelskiy-per

Bol-Kanemirovskaya-ul

Ⓜ Lesnaya

Lesnogo-pr

ul-Gribalevoy

Novolitovskaya-ul

nab-Chyornoy-Rechki

Krasnogo-kursanta-per

nab-Adm-Ushakova-Golovinsky-most

Luch Stadium
1

Diagonalnaya-ul

Kantemirovskaya-ul

Matrosova

Aptekarskaya-nab

Kantemirovsky most

ul-Aleksandra

Novolitovskaya-ul

Litovskaya-ul

ul-Akademika-Pavlova

ul-ul-Akademika-pavlova

● 2

Vyborgskaya-nab

Mendelevskaya-ul

Medikov-pr

Zenit Stadium

Gelsingforsskaya-ul

Chugunnaya-ul

VYBOR SIDE

ul-Chapygina

ul-Prof-Popova

Belovodsky-per

Tobolskaya

ul-Professora-Popova

Aptekarskaya-nab

Smolyachkova

Ⓜ Vyborgskaya

Chugunnay

Silin most

Botkinskaya-pr

Botanical Gardens

nab-r-Karpovki

Krapivny-per

ul-Literatov

Karpovka

Grenaderskiy

✝ 3

Chugunnay

Petropavlovsky most

6
Ⓜ

5 ▼ 4 ▼

Petropavlovskaya ul

Aptekarsky most

ul-Fokina

Neyshlotsky-per

Lesnoy-pr

Ⓜ Petrogradskaya

PETROGRAD SIDE

Grenadersky most

7 ▼
pl-Lva-Tolstogo

ul-Lva-Tolstogo

ul-Rentgena

ul-Chapaeva

Vyborgskaya-ul

8 ▼

9 ▼

Petrogradskaya

Evpatoriysky-per

ul-Rentgena

Bol-Sampsonievsky-pr

ul-Mira

Pirogovskaya-nab

Botkinskaya-ul

Pl Lenina
Ⓜ

11 🏛

12 ▼

Monetnaya

Pinsky-per

Saharny-per

Finsky-per

Bolshoy-pr

10 ▼

Matveeva

Kronve-Kskay

13 ▼

Divenskaya-ul

Pesochny

25 ▼

Bol-Posadskaya

ul-Chapaeva

Orenburgskaya-ul

31 ▼

Klinicheskaya-ul

Pl Lenina
Ⓜ Finland Stati
(Finlyandsky V

Pushkarsky-per

Avstriyskaya pl

Sampsonievsky most

pl-Komsomola

14 ▼

24 ▼

Mal-Posadskaya

32 ●

pl Lenina

Voskova

15 ▼

22 ▼

23 ▼

Mandamskaya-ul

ul-Kurbyheva

Penkovaya-ul

Arsena Inaya

Sytninskaya-ul

21 ▼

S-Sytninskaya

16 ▼

20 🏛

Kamennoostrovskiy

26 ▼

30

Markina

19 🏛

Ⓜ Gorkovskaya

27 🎦

17 ●

18 ●

Alexandrovsky Park

28 🏛

Liteyny most

nab Robespiera

29 ▼
nab

Kronverksky

Petrovskaya

NEVA HEBA

Shpalernaya-ul

47 🛒

● 46

Zakharevskaya-ul

Kronverksky-pr

Kronverkskaya-nab

Kronverksky-prosp

Peter & Paul Fortress

Troitsky most

Prachechny most

Kutuzova

Gagankaya-ul

48 ▼

Drozdeniksky-per

ul-Chaikovskogo

49 ▼

ul-Chernyshevskogo

51

ZAYACHY

See Peter & Paul Fortress map

67 ▼

Verkhne-Lebyazhy most

66 🏛

ul-Chaikovskogo

62 ▼

Furshtadtskaya-ul

58 🛒

60 ▼

Chernyshevs
56 ▼
Ⓜ

Suvorovskaya pl

68 ▼

70 ▼

69 ▼

Dvortsovaya nab

71 ▼

Millionnaya-ul

Mars Field

Lebyazhego-Canala

Summer Garden

r-Fontanki

Gangutskaya

Solyanoy-per

65 ▼

64 🏛

63 🏛

Mohovaya-ul

Kirochnaya-ul

61 ●

Preobrazhenskaya pl

57 ▼

Manezhny-per

59 🕌

Ermitazhny most

72 🛒

nab-r-Moyki

ul-Pestelya

ul-Ryleeva

MAP 5

See MAP 2 (left margin)

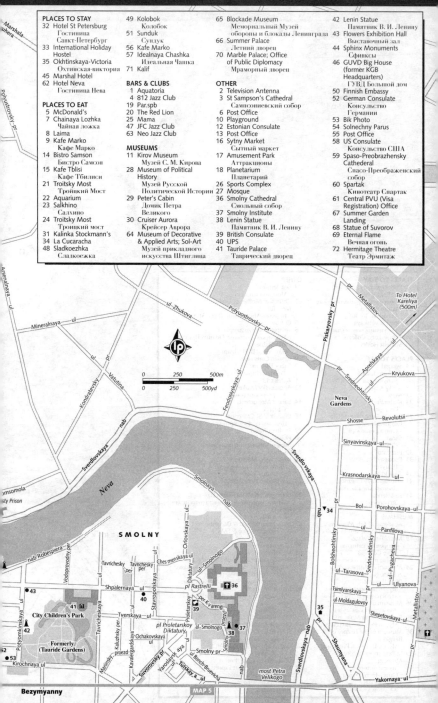

PLACES TO STAY
32 Hotel St Petersburg
   Гостиница
   Санкт-Петербург
33 International Holiday
   Hostel
35 Okhtinskaya-Victoria
   Охтинская-виктория
45 Marshal Hotel
62 Hotel Neva
   Гостиница Нева

PLACES TO EAT
5 McDonald's
7 Chainaya Lozhka
   Чайная ложка
8 Laima
9 Kafe Marko
   Кафе Марко
14 Bistro Samson
   Бистро Самсон
15 Kafe Tblisi
   Кафе Тбилиси
21 Troitsky Most
   Тройкий Мост
22 Aquarium
23 Salkhino
   Салхино
24 Troitsky Most
   Тройкий мост
31 Kalinka Stockmann's
34 La Cucaracha
48 Sladkoezhka
   Сладкоежка

49 Kolobok
   Колобок
51 Sunduk
   Сундук
54 Kafe Marko
57 Idealnaya Chashka
   Идеальная Чашка
71 Kalif

BARS & CLUBS
1 Aquatoria
4 812 Jazz Club
19 Par.spb
20 The Red Lion
32 Mama
47 JFC Jazz Club
63 Neo Jazz Club

MUSEUMS
11 Kirov Museum
   Музей С. М. Кирова
28 Museum of Political
   History
   Музей Русской
   Политической Истории
29 Peter's Cabin
   Домик Петра
   Великого
30 Cruiser Aurora
   Крейсер Аврора
64 Museum of Decorative
   & Applied Arts; Sol-Art
   Музей прикладного
   искусства Штиглица

65 Blockade Museum
   Мемориальный Музей
   обороны и блокады Ленинграда
66 Summer Palace
   Летний дворец
70 Marble Palace; Office
   of Public Diplomacy
   Мраморный дворец

OTHER
2 Television Antenna
3 St Sampson's Cathedral
   Самсониевский собор
6 Post Office
10 Playground
12 Estonian Consulate
13 Post Office
16 Sytny Market
   Сытный маркет
17 Amusement Park
   Аттракционы
18 Planetarium
   Планетарий
26 Sports Complex
27 Mosque
36 Smolny Cathedral
   Смольный собор
37 Smolny Institute
38 Lenin Statue
   Памятник В. И. Ленину
39 British Consulate
40 UPS
41 Tauride Palace
   Таврический дворец

42 Lenin Statue
   Памятник В. И. Ленину
43 Flowers Exhibition Hall
   Выставочный зал
44 Sphinx Monuments
   Сфинксы
46 GUVD Big House
   (former KGB
   Headquarters)
   ГУВД Большой дом
50 Finnish Embassy
52 German Consulate
   Консульство
   Германии
53 Bik Photo
54 Solnechny Parus
55 Post Office
58 US Consulate
   Консульство США
59 Spaso-Preobrazhensky
   Cathedral
   Спасо-Преображенский
   собор
60 Spartak
61 Central PVU (Visa
   Registration) Office
67 Summer Garden
   Landing
68 Statue of Suvorov
69 Eternal Flame
   Вечная огонь
72 Hermitage Theatre
   Театр Эрмитаж

MAP 2

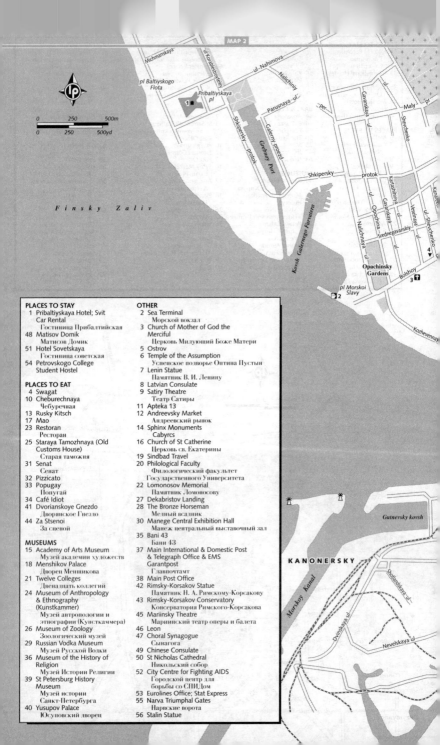

Finsky Zaliv

KANONERSKY

Opachinsky Gardens

Gutnevsky kovsh

PLACES TO STAY
1 Pribaltiyskaya Hotel; Svit
   Car Rental
   Гостиница Прибалтийская
48 Matisov Domik
   Матисов Домик
51 Hotel Sovetskaya
   Гостиница советская
54 Petrovskogo College
   Student Hostel

PLACES TO EAT
4 Swagat
10 Cheburechnaya
   Чебуречная
13 Rusky Kitsch
17 Mao
23 Restoran
   Ресторан
25 Staraya Tamozhnaya (Old
   Customs House)
   Старая таможня
31 Senat
   Сенат
32 Pizzicato
33 Popugay
   Попугай
34 Café Idiot
41 Dvorianskoye Gnezdo
   Дворянское Гнездо
44 Za Stsenoi
   За сценой

MUSEUMS
15 Academy of Arts Museum
   Музей академии художеств
18 Menshikov Palace
   Дворец Меншикова
21 Twelve Colleges
   Двенадцать коллегий
24 Museum of Anthropology
   & Ethnography
   (Kunstkammer)
   Музей антропологии и
   этнографии (Кунсткамера)
26 Museum of Zoology
   Зоологический музей
29 Russian Vodka Museum
   Музей Русской Водки
36 Museum of the History of
   Religion
   Музей Истории Религии
39 St Petersburg History
   Museum
   Музей истории
   Санкт-Петербурга
40 Yusupov Palace
   Юсуповский дворец

OTHER
2 Sea Terminal
   Морской вокзал
3 Church of Mother of God the
   Merciful
   Церковь Милующий Боже Матери
5 Ostrov
6 Temple of the Assumption
   Успенское подворье Оптина Пустын
7 Lenin Statue
   Памятник В. И. Ленину
8 Latvian Consulate
9 Satiry Theatre
   Театр Сатиры
11 Apteka 13
12 Andreevsky Market
   Андреевский рынок
14 Sphinx Monuments
   Сабурсs
16 Church of St Catherine
   Церковь св. Екатерины
19 Sindbad Travel
20 Philological Faculty
   Филологический факультет
   Государственного Университета
22 Lomonosov Memorial
   Памятник Ломоносову
27 Dekabristov Landing
28 The Bronze Horseman
   Медный всадник
30 Manege Central Exhibition Hall
   Манеж центральный выставочный зал
35 Bani 43
   Бани 43
37 Main International & Domestic Post
   & Telegraph Office & EMS
   Garantpost
   Главпочтамт
38 Main Post Office
42 Rimsky-Korsakov Statue
   Памятник Н. А. Римскому-Корсакову
43 Rimsky-Korsakov Conservatory
   Консерватория Римского-Корсакова
45 Mariinsky Theatre
   Мариинский театр оперы и балета
46 Leon
47 Choral Synagogue
   Сынагога
49 Chinese Consulate
50 St Nicholas Cathedral
   Никольский собор
52 City Centre for Fighting AIDS
   Городской центр для
   борьбы со СПИДом
53 Eurolines Office; Stat Express
55 Narva Triumphal Gates
   Нарвские ворота
56 Stalin Statue

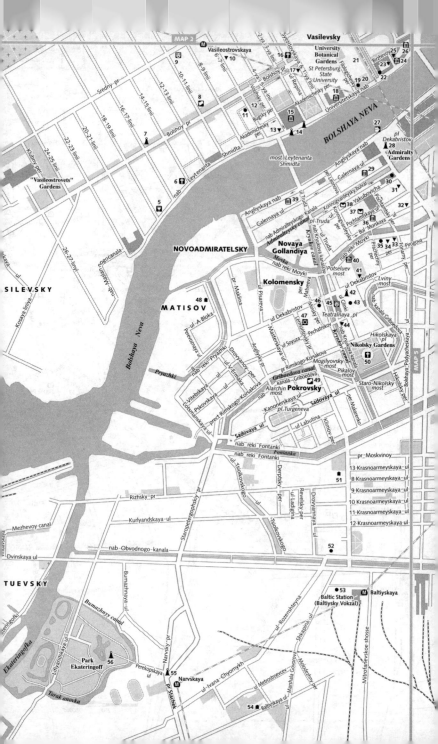

MAP 5 – CENTRAL ST PETERSBURG

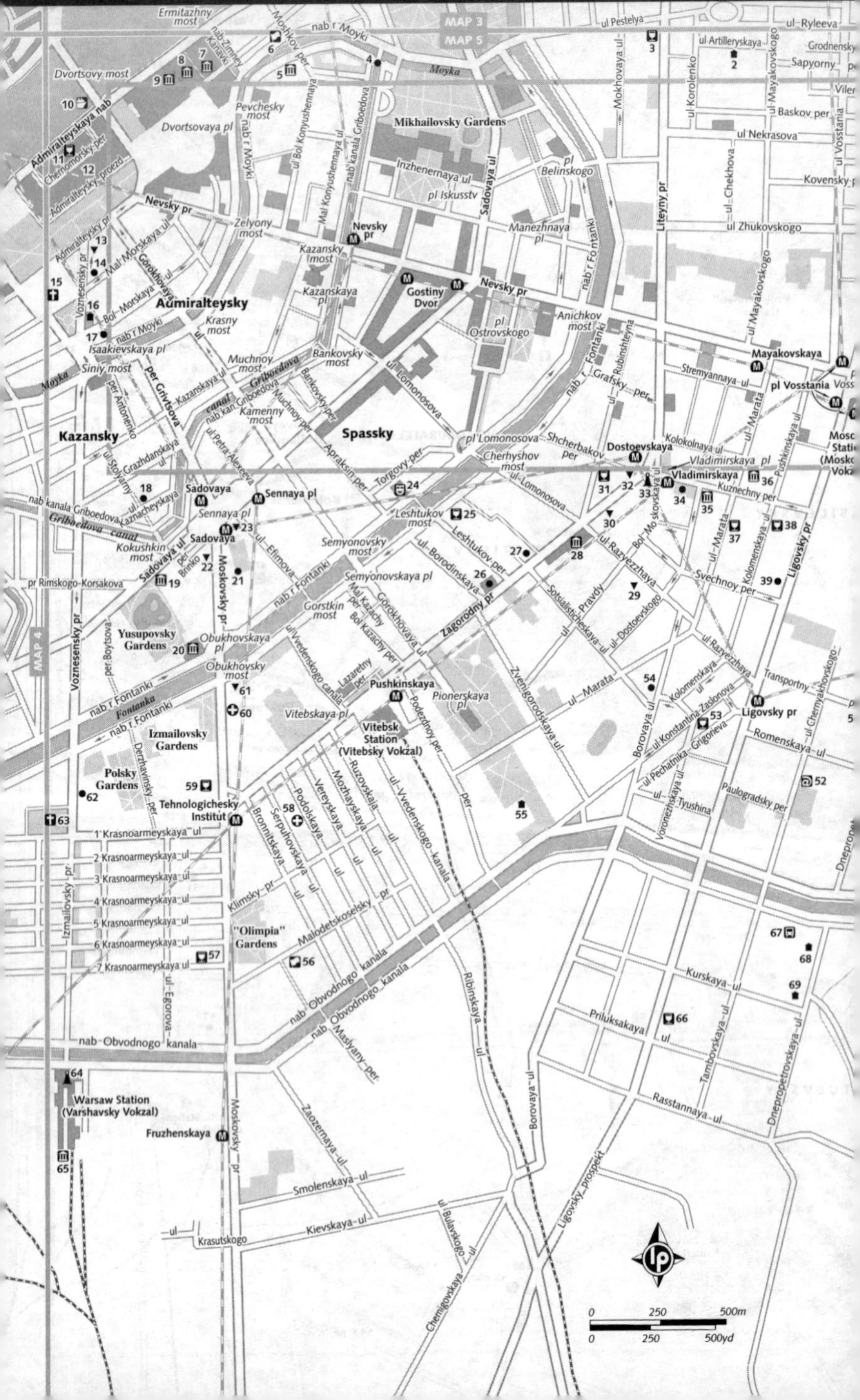

Ermitazhny most
MAP 3
MAP 5
ul Pestelya
ul Ryleeva
ul Artilleryskaya
Grodnensky
Sapyorny
Viler
Mokhovaya ul
ul Korolenko
Mayakovskogo
nab r Moyki
Dvortsovy most
8 7
6
Moykov pro
4
Moyka
3
2
ul Baskov per
9
5
ul Nekrasova
10
Dvortsovaya pl
Pevchesky most
nab r Moyki
ul Chekhova
Kovensky
Admiralteyskaya nab
11
12
Admiralteysky proezd
nab kanal Griboedova
Mal Konyushennaya ul
Bol Konyushennaya ul
Inzhenernaya ul
Belinskogo
pl Iskusstv
Manezhnaya pl
ul Zhukovskogo
Nevsky pr
Zelyony most
13
14
Mal Morskaya ul
Kazansky most
Nevsky pr
Mikhailovsky Gardens
Liteyny pr
nab r Fontanki
Mokhovaya ul
15
16
Admiralteysky
Krasny most
Kazanskaya pl
Gostiny Dvor
Nevsky pr
ul Mayakovskogo
17
Isaakievskaya pl
Bol Morskaya ul
Bankovsky most
pl Ostrovskogo
Anichkov most
Mayakovskaya
Stremyannaya ul
pl Vosstania Voss
Siniy most
Muchnoy most
Gribedova
nab r Fontanki
Grafsky per
Rubinshteina
Kazansky
Griboedova canal
Kamenny most
Spassky
pl Lomonosova
Shcherbatov Per
Cherhyshov most
Dostoevskaya
Vladimirskaya pl
Kolokolnaya ul
Kuznechny per
Mosc Statie (Mosk Voka)
18
Sadovaya
Sennaya pl
24
pl Lomonosova
31 32
33
Vladimirskaya
34 35
36
nab kanala Griboedova
Lachmatova ul
Sennaya pl
23
Leshtukov most
25
30
ul Razyezzhaya
37
38
Griboedova canal
Kokushkin most
Sadovaya
22
Moskovsky pr
21
Semyonovsky most
Leshtukov per
27
28
ul Dostoevsky
Kolomenskaya
39
pr Rimskogo-Korsakova
Sadovaya ul
Brino
19
Semyonovskaya pl
26
Zagorodni pr
Borodinskaya pr
29
Svechnoy per
Yusupovsky Gardens
20
Obukhovskaya pl
Gorstkin most
Bol Kazachy
Mal Kazachy
Sotsialistichestva ul
ul Pravdy
Zvenigorodskaya ul
54
Kolomenskaya
Transportny
Obukhovsky most
61
60
Vitebskaya pl
Pushkinskaya
Pionerskaya
ul Marata
53
Ligovsky pr
Izmailovsky Gardens
Vitebsk Station (Vitebsky Vokzal)
ul Konstantina Grigneva
Romenskaya ul
62
Polsky Gardens
59
Tehnologichesky Institut
58
55
ul Pechatnika Zadorova
ul Tyushina
52
67
63
1' Krasnoarmeyskaya ul
2 Krasnoarmeyskaya-ul
3 Krasnoarmeyskaya-ul
4 Krasnoarmeyskaya-ul
6 Krasnoarmeyskaya-ul
6 Krasnoarmeyskaya-ul
7 Krasnoarmeyskaya ul
57
"Olimpia" Gardens
56
nab Obvodnogo kanala
Priluksakaya ul
66
68
69
Kurskaya-ul
nab Obvodnogo kanala
Rasstannaya-ul
64
Warsaw Station (Varshavsky Vokzal)
Fruzhenskaya
65
Smolenskaya-ul
Kievskaya-ul
ul Krasutskogo

0   250   500m
0   250   500yd

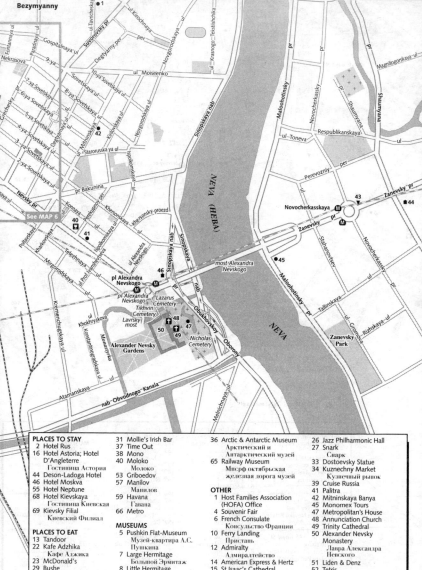

PLACES TO STAY

2 Hotel Rus
16 Hotel Astoria; Hotel
   D'Angleterre
   Гостиница Астория
44 Deson-Ladoga Hotel
46 Hotel Moskva
55 Hotel Neptune
68 Hotel Kievskaya
   Гостиница Киевская
69 Kievsky Filial
   Киевский Филиал

PLACES TO EAT

13 Tandoor
22 Kafe Adzhika
   Кафе Аджика
24 McDonald's
29 Bushe
   Буше
30 U Tyoshi Na Blinakh
   У Тёши на Блинах
32 Teremok
   Теремок
43 Schvabsky Domik
61 Staroe Kafe
   Старое Кафе

BARS & CLUBS

3 Jimi Hendrix Blues Club
12 Decadance
25 Manhattan Club/Katyol

31 Mollie's Irish Bar
37 Time Out
38 Mono
40 Moloko
   Молоко
53 Griboedov
57 Manilov
   Манилов
59 Havana
   Гавана
66 Metro

MUSEUMS

5 Pushkin Flat-Museum
   Музей-квартира А.С.
   Пушкина
7 Large Hermitage
   Большой Эрмитаж
8 Little Hermitage
   Малый Эрмитаж
9 Winter Palace
   Зимний дворец
19 The Museum of Railway
   Transport
   Музей железнодорожного
   транспорта
28 Rimsky-Korsakov
   Flat-Museum
   Музей-квартира
   Римского-Корсакова
35 Dostoevsky Museum
   Музей Ф.М. Достоевского

36 Arctic & Antarctic Museum
   Арктический и
   Антарктический музей
65 Railway Museum
   Мпсрф октябрьская
   железная дорога музей

OTHER

1 Host Families Association
   (HOFA) Office
4 Souvenir Fair
6 French Consulate
   Консульство Франции
10 Ferry Landing
   Пристань
12 Admiralty
   Адмиралтейство
14 American Express & Hertz
15 St Isaac's Cathedral
   Исаакиевский собор
17 Artists' Union of Russia
   Exhibition Center of
   Graphic Arts
18 Dostoevsky Flats
20 Yusupov Palace
   Юсуповский дворец
21 Sennoy Market
   Сенной рынок
24 Tovstonogov Bolshoy
   Dramatic Theatre
   Большой драматический
   театр им Товстопогова

26 Jazz Philharmonic Hall
27 Snark
   Снарк
33 Dostoevsky Statue
34 Kuznechny Market
   Кузнечный рынок
39 Cruise Russia
41 Palitra
42 Mitninskaya Banya
45 Monomex Tours
47 Metropolitan's House
48 Annunciation Church
49 Trinity Cathedral
50 Alexander Nevsky
   Monastery
   Лавра Александра
   Невского
51 Liden & Denz
52 Tetris
54 Astoria-Service
56 Canadian Consulate
58 American Medical Center
60 Poliklinika No 2
   Поликлиника Но 2
62 DHL
63 Trinity Church
   Троицкий собор
64 Lenin Statue
   Памятник В. И. Ленину
67 Bus Station (Avtovokzal
   No 2)
   Автовокзал

MAP 6 – NEVSKY PROSPEKT

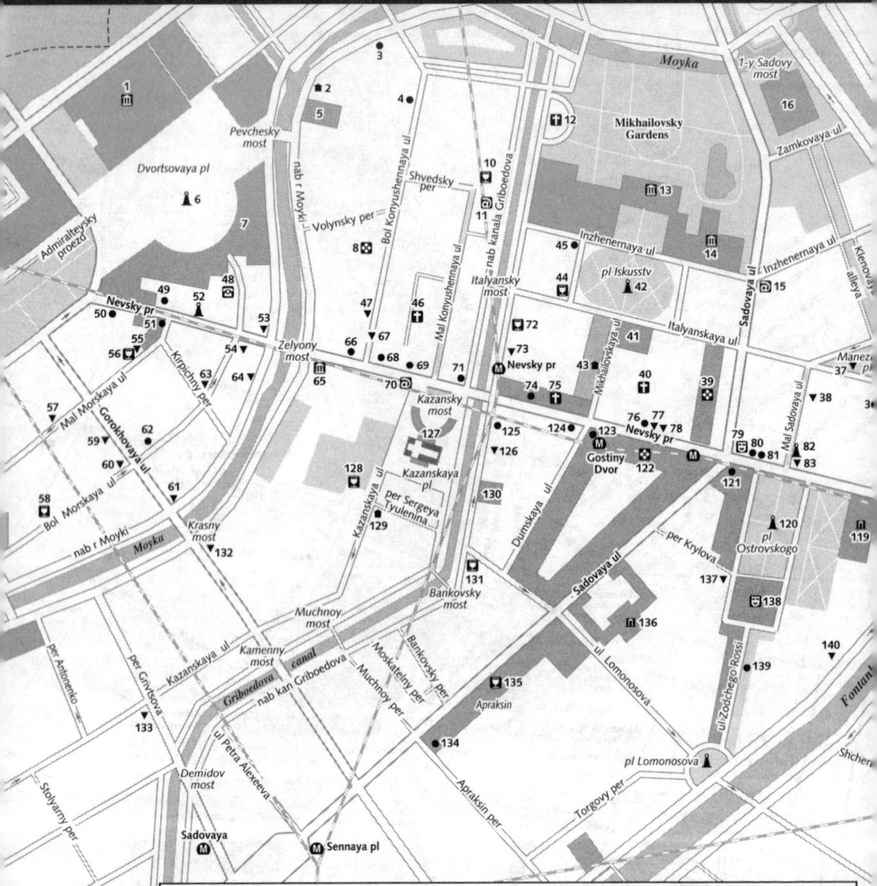

PLACES TO STAY
2 Pushka Inn
23 St Petersburg Puppet Hostel
43 Grand Hotel Europe; Chopsticks; Rossi's
100 Hotel Oktyabrskaya Гостиница Октябрьская
102 HI St Petersburg Hostel & Sindbad Travel
105 Oktyabrsky Filial
112 Corinthia Nevskij Palace Hotel; Landskrona; Admiralty Restaurant
114 Raddison SAS Royal St Petersburg
129 Herzen University Hotel & State Pedagogical University Общежитие Института Герцена

PLACES TO EAT
21 Caravan Sarai
24 Shogun
25 Albina
30 Wendy's Baltic Bread
31 Kharbin
36 Mama Roma
37 Teremok
38 Circus
47 La Strada

53 Kafe Literaturnoe Кафе Литературное
54 Idealnaya Chashka
55 Sladkoezhka
57 Da Vinci
59 Shogun
60 Orient
61 Pizza Hut
63 McDonald's
64 Taleon Club
67 Teremok
73 Laima
78 Grillmaster
83 Sever Гастроном Елисеевский
87 Propaganda
93 Planet Sushi
94 Pizza Hut; KFC
96 Idealnaya Chashka
97 U Tyoshi Na Blinakh
98 Chainaya Lozhka
99 Gresbi
101 Orient
103 Idealnaya Chashka
104 Bistrot Garçon
107 Baskin Robbins
108 Café Rico
110 Kafe Kat
115 Gushe Гуше

116 Green Crest
126 Coffee Break
132 Kharbin
133 Kotletnaya Котлетная
137 Yakitoriya
140 La Cucaracha
145 Bliny Domik Блинный домик
146 Orient Express
147 Sladkoezhka
148 Dzinn 24-hour store Джинн
152 Depo

BARS & CLUBS
10 James Cook Pub
18 Probka
27 Pivnoy Klub
44 The Stray Dog
56 Bar O Meter
58 Ot Zakata do Rasveta От заката до расвета
72 Chayka
84 Psycho Pub
95 Kafe Marko
128 Tinkoff
131 Greshniki Грешники
135 City Club; Money Honey Saloon
150 Fish Fabrique; Free Arts Foundation

153 Che

MUSEUMS
1 Winter Palace Зимний дворен
13 Russian Museum Русский музей
14 Museum of Ethnography Музей этнографии
16 Engineers' Castle Инженерный замок
32 Akhmatova Memorial Museum Музей-квартира Анны Ахматовой
33 Sheremetev Palace; Museum of Theatrical & Musical Arts Шереметьевский дворец
65 Stroganov Palace & Stroganov Yard café
118 Beloselsky-Belozersky Palace; Tourist Information Office & Historical Museum of Wax Figures Дворец Белосельских-Белозерских
119 Anichkov Palace Аничков дворец

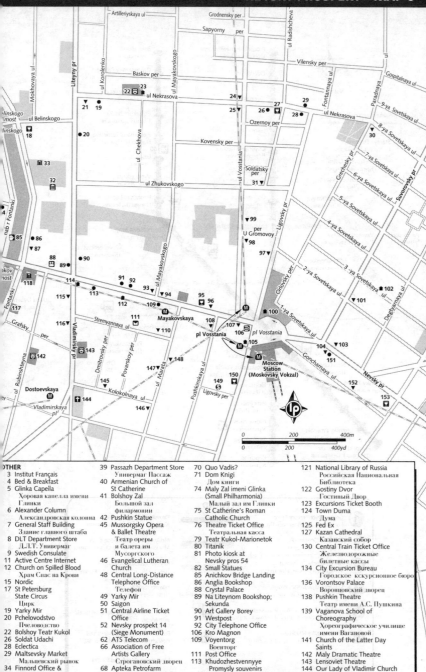

OTHER
3 Institut Français
4 Bed & Breakfast
5 Glinka Capella
   Хоровая капелла имени
   Глинки
6 Alexander Column
   Александровская колонна
7 General Staff Building
   Здание главного штаба
8 DLT Department Store
   Д.Л.Т. Универмаг
9 Swedish Consulate
11 Active Centre Internet
12 Church on Spilled Blood
   Храм Спас на Крови
15 Nordic
17 St Petersburg
   State Circus
   Цирк
19 Yarky Mir
20 Pchelovodstvo
   Пчеловодство
22 Bolshoy Teatr Kukol
28 Eclectica
29 Maltsevsky Market
   Мальцевский рынок
34 Finnord Office &
   Bus station
35 Intendant

39 Passazh Department Store
   Универмаг Пассаж
40 Armenian Church of
   St Catherine
41 Bolshoy Zal
   Большой зал
   филармонии
42 Pushkin Statue
45 Mussorgsky Opera
   & Ballet Theatre
   Театр оперы
   и балета им
   Мусоргского
46 Evangelical Lutheran
   Church
48 Central Long-Distance
   Telephone Office
   Телефон
49 Yarky Mir
50 Saigon
51 Central Airline Ticket
   Office
52 Nevsky prospekt 14
   (Siege Monument)
62 ATS Telecom
66 Association of Free
   Artists Gallery
   Строгановский дворец
68 Apteka Petrofarm
   Аптека Петрофарм
69 Wild Russia

70 Quo Vadis?
71 Dom Knigi
   Дом книги
74 Maly Zal imeni Glinka
   (Small Philharmonia)
   Малый зал им Глинки
75 St Catherine's Roman
   Catholic Church
76 Theatre Ticket Office
   Театральная касса
79 Teatr Kukol-Marionetok
80 Titanik
81 Photo kiosk at
   Nevsky pros 54
82 Small Statues
85 Anichkov Bridge Landing
86 Anglia Bookshop
88 Crystal Palace
89 Na Liteynom Bookshop;
   Sekunda
90 Art Gallery Borey
91 Westpost
92 City Telephone Office
106 Kro Magnon
109 Voyentorg
   Военторг
111 Post Office
113 Khudozhestvennyye
   Promysly souvenirs
117 British Council; Goethe Institute
120 Catherine the Great Statue

121 National Library of Russia
   Российская Национальная
   Библиотека
122 Gostiny Dvor
   Гостиный Двор
123 Excursions Ticket Booth
124 Town Duma
   Дума
125 Fed Ex
127 Kazan Cathedral
   Казанский собор
130 Central Train Ticket Office
   Железнодорожные
   билетные кассы
134 City Excursion Bureau
   Городское кскурсионное бюро
136 Vorontsov Palace
   Воронцовский дворец
138 Pushkin Theatre
   Театр имени А.С. Пушкина
139 Vaganova School of
   Choreography
   Хореографическое училище
   имени Вагановой
141 Church of the Latter Day
   Saints
142 Maly Dramatic Theatre
143 Lensoviet Theatre
144 Our Lady of Vladimir Church
149 Ligovsky
151 Ost-West Kontaktservice

Not to Scale

Prospekt Prosveshchenia
Проспект Просвещения

Devyatkino
Девяткино

Ozerki
Озерки

Grazhdansky Prospect
Гражданский Проспект

Udelnaya
Удельная

Akademicheskaya
Академическая

Kommendantsky Prospekt
Комендантский проспект

Pionerskaya
Пионерская

Politekhnicheskaya
Политехническая

Staraya Derevnaya
Старая Деревня

Chyornaya Rechka
Чёрная Речка

Ploshchad Muzhestva
Площадь Мужества

Krestovsky Ostrov
Крестовский остров

Petrogradskaya
Петроградская

80

Lesnaya
Лесная

Chkalovskaya
Чкаловская

Gorkovskaya
Горьковская

Vyborgskaya
Выборгская

Sportivnaya
Спортивная

Ploshchad Lenina
Площадь Ленина

Primorskaya
Приморская

Vasileostrovskaya
Василеостровская

Chernyshevskaya
Чернышевская

Novocherkasskaya
Новочеркасская

Admiralteyskaya
Адмиралтейская

Ladozhskaya
Ладожская

Prospekt Bolshevikov
Проспект Большеви

Ligovsky Prospekt
Лиговский Проспект

Ulitsa Dybenko
Улица Дыбенко

Elizarovskaya
Елизаровская

Pushkinskaya
Пушкинская

Lomonosovskaya
Ломоносовская

Baltiyskaya
Балтийская

Frunzenskaya
Фрунзенская

Proletarskaya
Пролетарская

Narvskaya
Нарвская

Moskovskie Vorota
Московские Ворота

Kirovsky Zavod
Кировский Завод

Elektrosila
Электросила

Obukhovo
Обухово

Avtovo
Автово

Park Pobedy
Парк Победы

Rybatskoe
Рыбацкое

Moskovskaya
Московская

Leninsky Prospekt
Ленинский Проспект

Zvyozdnaya
Звёздная

Prospekt Veteranov
Проспект Ветеранов

Kupchino
Купчино

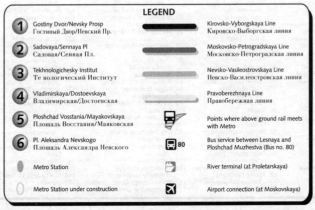

LEGEND

1. Gostiny Dvor/Nevsky Prosp.
Гостиный Двор/Невский Пр.

Kirovsko-Vyborgskaya Line
Кировско-Выборгская линия

2. Sadovaya/Sennaya Pl
Садовая/Сенная Пл.

Moskovsko-Petrogradskaya Line
Московско-Петроградская линия

3. Tekhnologichesky Institut
Те нологический Институт

Nevsko-Vasileostrovskaya Line
Невско-Василеостровская линия

4. Vladimirskaya/Dostoevskaya
Владимирская/Достоевская

Pravoberezhnaya Line
Правобережная линия

5. Ploshchad Vosstania/Mayakovskaya
Площадь Восстания/Маяковская

Points where above ground rail meets
with Metro

6. Pl. Aleksandra Nevskogo
Площадь Александра Невского

80 Bus service between Lesnaya and
Ploshchad Muzhestva (Bus no. 80)

Metro Station

River terminal (at Proletarskaya)

Metro Station under construction

Airport connection (at Moskovskaya)

[Continued from page 230]

Newly installed, coin-operated phones are now quite popular; you can find one inside every metro station. On these, the rate is R1 per minute, though coins seem to disappear quicker than that. They accept 50-kopeck and one-, two- and five-rouble coins.

There are several types of card payphones (Peterstar, ☎ 329 90 90, had better prices but fewer phones at the time of research; BCL charges the highest prices), and cards are not interchangeable.

There has been a recent proliferation of prepaid, pin-code-operated long-distance phonecards. Scan the St Petersburg Times for ads. Pricing systems are mind-boggling, but using one still ends up cheaper than dialling direct or using the SNM cards. These cards can be used from any private or public phone and are very handy. Peterstar has good deals, as does Fon-Mezhsvyaz (☎ 233 65 87). Only thing to note: these cards (at least for the time being) are not available anywhere but directly from the companies themselves. However, representatives of these companies will meet you anywhere in the city and bring cards to you for no extra charge.

State Telephone Offices The **central long-distance telephone office** (Map 6; ul Bolshaya Morskaya 3/5) was indefinitely closed for renovations at the time of research; there are several other branch offices along Nevsky prospekt including at Nos 27 and 88. From these offices you can make direct-dial calls anywhere, or order them through the operator.

Cellular Service Mobile (cellular) phones are fast gaining ground. European mobile phones work here (double-check with your service provider before leaving home), yet the costs will be sky-high, unless you sign up with a local service provider. This is easily done with pay-as-you-go SIM cards for as little as US$30; service providers include Northwest GSM, Biline and MTS – their offices can be found all over the city.

You can rent a cellphone at the most convenient branch of **ATS Telecom** (Map 6; ☎ 326 86 40; Bolshaya Morskaya ul 19). You will need a US$150 deposit and rental is about US$3 a day, on top of the cost of your calls.

Fax & Telegram

Faxes can be sent and received at the branch of the long-distance telephone office on Nevsky prospekt 88 (☎ 314 14 80); the incoming fax number is ☎ 314 33 60 and the cost to retrieve them is R15 per page. Faxes can also be sent and received at the business centres in all major hotels and in the Moscow Station, as well as at the two youth hostels, for much higher prices.

International telegrams can be sent from many of the larger post offices, as well as from Window 38 at the main post office. (See the Post section earlier.)

Email & Internet Access

There are Internet cafés all over the city and many of them are open 24 hours. One of the most prominent is **Quo Vadis?** (Map 6; ☎ 311 8011; Nevsky pr 24), which charges R60 per hour, has 65 terminals and a quiet library in which you can browse foreign newspapers and magazines. **Kro Magnon** (☎ 279 57 26; Nevsky pr 81) is cheaper (R40 per hour); its office is on the right side of the courtyard and on the 2nd floor.

Other handy places at which to surf the Web include **Nordic** (Map 6; ☎ 269 42 22; Sadovaya ul 8/7); **Active Centre Internet** (Map 6; ☎ 311 63 38) on the north side of Griboedova Canal; and **Tetris** (Map 5; ☎ 164 48 77; ul Chernyakhovskogo 33).

Digital Resources

There is no shortage of useful and quirky information about St Petersburg on the Web. The following list provides some of the best, but see individual sections for more suggestions, as well as the European Russia Facts for the Visitor chapter for other handy sites.

w **www.cityvision2000.com** One of the best places to start. There's information on sights, current events and listings, a virtual city tour, online hotel booking, and a great, up-to-date traveller's message board.

w **www.spb.ru** A good general starting point for St Petersburg information, including links to the St Petersburg Times (see Newspapers & Magazines later in this section).

w **www.museum.ru** More detailed information about the city's museums.

w **http://petersburgcity.com/for-tourists** Representing the official English-language portal for St Petersburg.

Travel Agencies

Some of the most reliable include:

Sindbad Travel (Map 6; ☎ 327 83 84, fax 329 80 19; W www.sindbad.ru; 3-ya Sovetskaya ul 28) Owned by the HI St Petersburg Hostel, it has two offices in town. The first is inside the hostel itself; the second (☎ 324 08 80) is inside the St Petersburg Philological Faculty building on Vasilevsky Island, Universitetskaya naberezhnaya 11 (Map 4). Both are genuine Western-style student (and adult) discount air-ticket offices. Staffed by friendly, knowledgeable people, Sindbad operates as a full-service ticketing centre for STA and Kilroy Travel, sells and issues train tickets, can service any student-issued tickets regardless of its source and can book youth hostel accommodation through the IBN system. It also sells ISIC/ITIC cards.

Ost-West Kontaktservice (☎ 327 34 16 or 272 87 61, fax 327 34 17; W www.ostwest.com; Nevsky pr 105; open 10am-6pm Mon-Fri) Here's another winner. Staff can arrange tourist and business visas for you, find you an apartment to rent, organise tours and tickets – heck, they'll even sell you a Lomo (they're the city's official distributor of the nifty little Russian camera). The multilingual staff are down-to-earth, willing and able to help.

Wild Russia (Map 6; ☎/fax 25 93 30; W www .wildrussia.spb.ru; Nevsky pr 22/24) Apart from organising wilderness expeditions in the far reaches of the country, the friendly guys at Wild Russia can also arrange outdoor activity trips in the St Petersburg surrounds, including rock climbing and kayaking around Lake Ladoga.

Bookshops

Books are for sale everywhere – street corners, pedestrian subways, grocery shops – but books in English are scarce. The exception is **Anglia** (Map 6; ☎ 279 82 84; nab reki Fontanki 40), a veritable oasis of Western books, with a dizzying collection of art, history and literature titles at dizzyingly Western prices (but ISIC cardholders get a 5% discount). Get your Lonely Planet guidebooks here too.

Snark (Map 5; ☎ 164 93 66; Zagorodny pr 21) has several locations around the city and was the first Russian bookstore in St Petersburg with a Western look and feel (it's actually possible to browse!). This friendly, well-stocked place gives discounts to members, features monthly themes, and has lots for the children.

Dom Knigi (Map 6; ☎ 219 64 02; Nevsky pr 28), the biggest bookshop in town, is a trip in itself. It's located in the prerevolutionary headquarters of the Singer sewing machine company and has two newly renovated floors of mainly Russian books on every subject imaginable. While choice and availability is small compared to Western abundance, this is as good as it gets. Excellent souvenir books are on the 2nd floor.

Na Liteynom (Map 6; ☎ 275 38 73; Liteyny pr 61) has a good selection of antiquarian books. It's tucked away in a courtyard and is an interesting place to browse for antiques and unusual souvenirs.

Newspapers & Magazines

Published every Tuesday and Friday (when it has an indispensable listings and arts review section), the English-language St Petersburg Times (W sptimesrussia.com) is well worth picking up. It's available at hotels, restaurants and youth hostels, as is the free monthly Pulse, a slick colour monthly with the occasional good feature and review, available in English and Russian editions.

Also monthly is the dull Neva News, which tries hard in a hyper-patriotic way. Still, it often prints useful historical facts about the city.

Radio & TV

Most of St Petersburg's popular radio stations play a mix of trashy Europop and its even more over-the-top Russian variant. Still, their playlists are often unexpectedly eclectic. Some of the more popular FM stations include Eldoradio (101.4 MHz), Radio Hit (90.6 MHz) and the cool Maximum (102.8 MHz). Two stations – Echo Peterburga (91.5 MHz) and Severnaya Stolitsa (105.9 MHz) – focus almost exclusively on St Petersburg-related news, music and features (in Russian only).

As well as the main state TV channels, St Petersburg has several local channels, including Peterburg and Kanal 6. Satellite TV is available at all major hotels, and the British Council (see Cultural Centres below) has a TV perennially tuned to BBC World.

Cultural Centres

St Petersburg's best organised – and busiest – foreign cultural centre is the **British Council** (Map 6; ☎ 325 60 74; W www.britishcouncil .ru; nab reki Fontanki 46; open 12.30pm-7pm Tues-Fri, noon-5pm Sat), which holds classical concerts, theatre and other performances and arranges for exchanges of students and professionals between Russia and the UK. It has a great resource centre for foreign teachers of

English. For use of its excellent library the annual membership fee is R150 for teachers, R300 for everyone else.

The **Goethe Institute St Petersburg** *(Map 6; ☎ 311 21 00)* is in the same building as the British Council and also has a well-stocked German-language library.

The busy **Institut Francais** *(Map 6; ☎ 311 09 95; Ⓦ www.fr.spb.ru; nab reki Moyki 20; open 10am-7pm Mon-Fri)* has a library with over 12,000 French-language books, magazines, videos and CDs. It also organises numerous cultural events.

The US-sponsored **Office of Public Diplomacy** *(Map 3; ☎ 311 89 05; Millionnaya ul 5; open 9am-5.30pm Mon-Fri)* has a small library with Internet terminals.

Laundry

Most hotels offer a laundry service. Otherwise, there is only one Western-style 'beautiful laundrette' in the city, **Prachechnaya** *(Map 2; ☎ 323 74 98; 11-ya linia 46; open 8am-10pm daily)* near metro Vasileostrovskaya. It'll cost about R150 to wash and dry 5kg while you wait, slightly more if you drop off your dirty stuff and pick it up later. All other places in town offer next-day service at best, usually longer.

Toilets

Inexpensive public toilets are scattered around town, marked with the Latin characters 'WC' or the Russian CHM *(platny tualet;* pay toilet). There are also toilets at bus and train stations. Some may even be clean. Your best bet is to use the facilities inside McDonald's, the Idealnaya Chashka coffee shop at Nevsky prospekt 15, or the facilities on the main floor of the Grand Hotel Europe (just stride in meaningfully then turn left).

Left Luggage

All the major train stations have luggage lockers and/or left-luggage services. You can also check your bags in at most of the major hotels (if you're a guest).

Medical Services

Within Russia, St Petersburg is second only to Moscow in medical services and offers adequate routine, and some emergency, treatment. More serious medical emergencies are best treated outside Russia; Finland is the best option.

The best bet for Western-quality treatment in St Petersburg is the US-run **American Medical Center** *(AMC; Map 5; ☎ 326 17 30; Serpuhovskaya ul 10)*, which offers a full range of medical services including gynaecological and paediatric care, dentistry, 24-hour emergency care, ambulance services, house calls and medical evacuations. Prices are stellar; a check-up won't be less than US$100, and an HIV test will cost US$75. Prices are marginally cheaper for members, but they're already paying US$55 a month for the privilege.

For routine matters, a Russian *poliklinika* (medical centre) provides perfectly adequate care. One of the best is **Poliklinika No 2** *(Map 5; ☎ 316 62 72; Moskovsky pr 22)*, the former clinic of choice for diplomatic staff. The clinic charges US$70 for house calls, US$26 for in-house visits with doctors, and US$31 for an HIV test.

Pharmacies *Apteka* are located all over the city and most are well stocked with Western medications and toiletries. **Apteka Petrofarm** *(Map 6; Nevsky pr 22)* is an excellent, all-night pharmacy. After hours, use the side entrance on Bolshaya Konyushennaya ulitsa (under the archway of house No 14 and to the right).

Emergency

Emergency telephone numbers (Russian-speaking operators) are ☎ 01 for fire and ☎ 02 for police. The state-run ambulance service is still free; Russian-speakers can get help by dialling ☎ 03. If you're trying to find out if someone's been in an accident and been picked up by ambulance (and where they were taken), dial ☎ 278 00 55.

Dangers & Annoyances

Every year in early spring and during winter thaws, several people die when child-sized, sword-shaped icicles fall from St Petersburg's rooftops and balconies. Walking a city block at this time can be exhausting: while stepping with trepidation on sheer ice, negotiating potholes and avoiding pedestrians, you must also crane your neck skywards to make sure one of these monsters is not dangling above your head.

Mosquitoes are another nightmare. From May to September, you may wish to leap from the very window that let the bastards in in the first place. Bring along industrial-strength repellent that's at least 95% DEET. The plug-in gizmos which slowly heat repellent-saturated cardboard pads are available everywhere in the city and are pretty effective.

If you're staying in a ground-level apartment in the city centre in early autumn, just before the central heating is turned on and after it starts getting cool, you may have problems with fleas, which come up through floorboards looking for warmth. Yes, they are very happy to feed off humans if rats, their usual sup, are not around. At the first sign of these hopping devils (usually itchy ankles!), get out of the place.

Watch out for pickpockets particularly along Nevsky prospekt around Griboedova Canal. It's also wise to avoid crossing directly in front of Moscow Station, unless you have to, since the police there have a nasty habit of trying to shake down foreigners for supposed infringements of visa registration rules.

If you are a victim of a crime, you can report this to a **police line** (☎ 164 97 87) that supposedly has multilingual staff. Just in case, *vorovstvo* and *krazha* both mean theft in Russian.

WALKING TOUR

This walking tour takes in the highlights of the route between Dvortsovaya ploshchad and Bankovsky most (bridge). It should take about an hour to complete, not including stops along the way.

The most perfect way of seeing **Dvortsovaya ploshchad** (Palace Square) for the first time is to approach it via Bolshaya Morskaya ulitsa. As you turn the corner, behold the **Alexander Column**, with the **Hermitage** in the background, perfectly framed under the triumphal double arch. If you aren't too ga-ga at the sight before you, grab your camera now.

Continue walking towards the square, keeping your eyes fixed on the columns and enjoy the visual magic tricks as the perspective changes the closer you get to the arches' opening. Then head northeast to the start of Millionnaya ulitsa, and into the porch covering the south entrance of the New Hermitage. Here was the museum's first public entrance when it opened in 1852. This is one of several buildings in the city that has a facade supported by semi-clad musclemen. A favourite tourist shot is from here looking west towards St Isaac's Cathedral past the Winter Palace – you can usually fit in a few of the Atlantes, or at least a calf or two.

Walking northeast again, make the first right turn and walk along the **Zimny Canal** the short block to the **Moyka River** (glance behind you towards the Neva for another great view). This stretch of the Moyka is lovely: to your right, Nevsky prospekt is crossed by **Zelyony most**, while diagonally opposite you is **Pushkin's last home** at naberezhnaya reki Moyki No 12, where the poet died in 1837.

Turn left and walk along the side of the river, across which you'll see the former **Court Stables**, dating from Peter the Great's time but completely redone by Stasov between 1817 and 1823. One of imperial St Petersburg's flashiest streets, Bolshaya Konyushennaya ulitsa (the Russian for horse is 'kon'; hence its name) extends south from here. Turgenev, Rimsky-Korsakov and Chernyshevsky all called this street home.

Continue along the river until you come to a very picturesque ensemble of bridges where the Moyka intersects at right angles with the start of the Griboedova Canal. Across the top of the touristy souvenir kiosk canopies you can see the **Church on Spilled Blood** looming

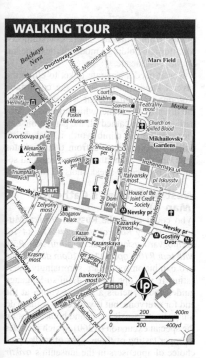

WALKING TOUR

in the foreground. Head towards this, crossing over the **Malo Konyushenny most**, which itself is connected to the pretty **Teatralny most**.

Having run the gauntlet of the souvenir sellers, cross over to the church, circle around it towards your left and admire the striking Style Moderne wrought-iron fence of the **Mikhailovsky Gardens**. Walk south along Griboedova Canal until you reach the sweet footbridge that crosses it. Called the **Italyansky most**, it dates from 1896, but was redesigned in 1955. Its main purpose seems to be to afford photographers a postcard-perfect view of the Church on Spilled Blood. Note the amazing building on the west side of the street at No 13. Originally the **House of the Joint Credit Society** and built in 1890, its central cupola was placed to give the appearance of a grand palace.

Continue down to Nevsky prospekt, where the old Singer sewing company building stands regally on the corner (it's now home to the **Dom Knigi** bookshop). Cross Nevsky prospekt towards the Kazan Cathedral and head to the next bridge, no doubt St Petersburg's most picturesque and most photographed, the **Bankovsky most** (1826). The cables of this 25.2m-long bridge are supported by four cast-iron gryphons with golden wings.

THE HISTORIC HEART
Dvortsovaya Ploshchad (Map 6)

Like most visitors to the city, you're probably going to want to start your explorations at Dvortsovaya ploshchad (Palace Square), where the stunning green, white and gold **Winter Palace** (Zimny dvorets) is a rococo profusion of columns, windows and recesses topped by rows of larger-than-life statues. Home to the tsars from 1762 to 1917, it's now the biggest part of the Hermitage art museum – see later in this chapter for more details. To reach here from Nevsky prospekt or Gostiny Dvor metro, walk 15 minutes west along Nevsky prospekt.

During Bloody Sunday (9 January 1905), tsarist troops fired on workers who had peaceably gathered in the square – the shootings sparked the 1905 revolution. And it was across Dvortsovaya ploshchad that the much exaggerated storming of the Winter Palace took place during the 1917 October Revolution. There *was* gunfire before the Provisional Government in the palace surrendered to the revolutionaries, but the famous charge across the square was largely invented by the film-maker Eisenstein.

The 47.5m **Alexander Column** in the square commemorates the 1812 victory over Napoleon and is named after Alexander I. The former **General Staff Building** of the Russian army (1819–29) curves round the south of the square in two great blocks joined by arches, which are topped by a chariot of victory, another monument to the Napoleonic wars. In the east wing of the building special exhibitions of the Hermitage are mounted.

Admiralty (Map 5)

The gilded spire of the old Admiralty at the western edge of Dvortsovaya ploshchad is an unmistakable St Petersburg landmark. Gorokhovaya ulitsa and Voznesensky and Nevsky prospekts all radiate outwards from it. Here was the headquarters of the Russian navy from 1711 to 1917, and today the building houses the city's largest naval college.

Constructed from 1806 to 1823 to the designs of Andreyan Zakharov, it's a foremost example of the Russian Empire style of classical architecture, with its rows of white columns and plentiful reliefs and statuary. One feature you can get a close look at is the nymphs holding giant globes flanking the main gate.

The gardens and fountain here are particularly lovely in summer.

Ploshchad Dekabristov (Map 4)

West of the Admiralty, ploshchad Dekabristov (Decembrists' Square) is named after the first attempt at a Russian revolution, the Decembrists' Uprising of 14 December 1825. Inspired by radical ideas from France during Napoleonic campaigns, young officers tried to depose the new tsar, Nicholas I, by drawing up troops in the square. But they allowed their opponents to argue with them and were finally dispersed with grapeshot. Most of the leaders ended up on the gallows or in Siberia.

The most famous statue of Peter the Great (practically a trademark image of the city) stands at the river end of the square. The **Bronze Horseman** has Peter's mount rearing above the snake of treason and was sculpted over 12 years for Catherine the Great by Frenchman Etienne Falconet. The inscription reads 'To Peter I from Catherine II – 1782'.

Most of the square's western side is occupied by the Central State Historical Archives in the former Senate and Synod buildings, built in 1829–34. The **Manege Central Exhibition Hall** (☎ 314 82 53; admission R30; open 10am-6pm Fri-Wed) across the street used to be the Horse Guards' Riding School (constructed in 1804–07 from a design by Quarenghi). It now hosts rotating exhibitions.

St Isaac's Cathedral (Map 5)

The golden dome of St Isaac's Cathedral (Isaakievsky sobor; adult/student R240/120; open 11am-6pm Thur-Mon, closed last Mon of the month) looming just south of ploshchad Dekabristov, dominates the St Petersburg skyline. Its obscenely lavish interior is open as a museum and photography is not permitted. Since 1990, after a 62-year gap, services have been held in the cathedral on major religious holidays.

The Frenchman Ricard de Montferrand won a competition organised by Alexander I to design the cathedral in 1818. It took so long to build – until 1858 – that Alexander's successor Nicholas I was able to insist on a more grandiose structure than Montferrand had planned. Special ships and a railway had

to be built to carry the granite for the huge pillars from Finland. There's a statue of Montferrand holding a model of the cathedral on the west facade.

You'll need a separate ticket to climb the several hundred steps up to the **colonnade** (kolonnada; adult/student R100/50) around the drum of the dome, which closes an hour earlier than the cathedral; the panoramic city views make the climb worth it. Babushkas will try to prevent you from taking photos from up there (something about national security), but people sneak shots all the time.

West of St Isaac's Cathedral (Map 4)

Who could resist the **Russian Vodka Museum** (Muzey Russkoi Vodki; ☎ 312 34 16; Konnogvardeysky bulvar 5; admission R50, with tour R100; open 11am-10pm daily)? The two exhibition rooms are surprisingly interesting if you opt for the English-language guided tour. There's a shot of vodka at the end for everyone, but if you really want to do things in style, call ahead and book a spot on the special excursion (R360), which includes a proper tasting of three types of vodka plus choice of appetisers in the museum's traktir (tavern). The food here, incidentally, is pretty good – see Places to Eat later in this chapter.

History buffs will want to check out the **St Petersburg History Museum** (☎ 311 75 44; Angliyskaya nab 44; admission R50; open 11am-5pm Thur-Tues). Housed in the majestic Rumyantsev Mansion (1826), its main focus is the Blockade; it has the city's largest repository of documents from that time.

The **Museum of the History of Religion** (☎ 314 58 38, excursions ☎ 311 04 95; Pochtamtskaya ul 14/5; adult/student R100/50; open 11am-6pm Thur-Tues), opposite the main post office, thoroughly documents the history and infamies of many religions.

THE HERMITAGE (Hermitage Map)

Mainly set in the magnificent Winter Palace, the State Hermitage (Gosudarstvenny ermitazh; ☎ 11 34 65; ⒲ www.hermitagemuseum.org; Dvortsovaya nab 34; open 10.30am-6pm Tues-Sat, 10.30am-5pm Sun) fully lives up to its reputation as one of the country's chief glories. You can be absorbed by its treasures for days and still come out wishing for more.

Friends of the Hermitage

Since 1997, the Friends of the Hermitage Society (☎ *110 90 05, fax 311 95 24;* W *www.hermitagemuseum.org)* has been encouraging membership and donations to help with its restoration and conservation programs. All memberships allow you access to special events hosted by the Hermitage, either at a reduced cost or for free. A US$100 annual donation will get you a free entry to the Hermitage and Menshikov Palace for a year, plus a 20% discount at their shops; for US$200 you can bring a friend along for free as well and get invitations to opening parties; US$500 allows you to bring two friends along for free and even more privileges.

★★★★★★★★★★★★★★★★★★★★★

The enormous collection (over three million items!) almost amounts to a history of Western European art, and as much as you see in the museum, there's about 20 times more in its vaults. The vastness of the place – five main buildings, of which the Winter Palace alone has 1057 rooms and 117 staircases – demands a little planning. Consider making a reconnaissance tour first, then returning another day to enjoy your favourite bits.

The State Hermitage consists of five linked buildings along riverside Dvortsovaya naberezhnaya. From west to east they are the Winter Palace, the Little Hermitage, the Old and New Hermitages (sometimes grouped together and called the Large Hermitage) and the Hermitage Theatre (only open for special events, mainly concerts). The art collection is on all three floors of the Winter Palace and the main two floors of the Little and Large Hermitages. There are also sections of the museum in the east wing of the General Staff Building and the Menshikov Palace on Vasilevsky Island.

History

The present baroque/rococo Winter Palace was commissioned from Rastrelli in 1754 by Empress Elizabeth. Catherine the Great and her successors had most of the interior remodelled in classical style by 1837. It remained an imperial home until 1917, though the last two tsars spent more time in other palaces.

The classical Little Hermitage was built for Catherine the Great as a retreat that would also house the art collection started by Peter the Great, which she significantly expanded. At the river end of the Large Hermitage is the Old Hermitage, which also dates from her time. At its south end, facing Millionnaya ulitsa, is the New Hermitage, which was built for Nicholas II to hold the still-growing art collection and was opened to the public for the first time in 1852. The Hermitage Theatre was built in the 1780s by the classicist Quarenghi, who thought it one of his finest works.

The Hermitage's collection really began with Catherine the Great, one of the greatest art collectors of all time. She pulled off some stunning deals, including famously exchanging one large framed portrait of herself for 15 Van Dykes from the collection of Sir Robert Walpole, Britain's first prime minister. Nicholas I also greatly enriched the Hermitage's collection, which he opened to the public for the first time in 1852. It was the post-revolutionary period that saw the collection increase in size threefold, as many valuable private collections were seized by the state.

Throughout the 1990s, the museum has, partially thanks to partnerships with foreign museums and donors, been able to renovate its heating and temperature control system, install a new fire detection system, fit its windows with a thin sheath of UV-filtering plastic, and to begin the first thorough, digitised inventory of its mammoth collection. Further renovations include moving the main entrance to the Dvortsovaya ploshchad side of the building. The museum is also actively promoting itself abroad: there are now the Hermitage Rooms at Somerset House in London and the Hermitage-Guggenheim Museum at Las Vegas' Venetian Resort-Hotel Casino, with more joint ventures to come.

Admission & Tours

The main ticket hall is inside the main entrance on the river side of the Winter Palace. Summertime queues can be horrendous, so get there early or go late in the day when the queues have died down.

Admission is R300 for adults, 20 times the Russian price – something you'll just have to grin and bear; however, ISIC cardholders and visitors under the age of 17 get in free of charge. Also, foreigners working or residing in Russia (and who can show proof of this) get in for the Russian price – R15. Anyone

[Continued on page 256]

The Hermitage Collection

Hermitage Highlights

If your time in the Hermitage is limited, the following suggested itinerary takes in the major highlights:

Winter Palace, 2nd floor
Room 189 Malachite Hall.
Rooms 190–198 Great state rooms.

Little Hermitage, 2nd floor
Room 204 Pavilion Hall, with its view onto the hanging garden.

Large Hermitage, 1st floor
Rooms 106–109 Ancient classical culture, with gorgeous rooms designed by Leo von Klenze.
Room 128 The jasper Kolyvanskaya Vase.

Large Hermitage, 2nd floor
Rooms 207–215 Florentine art, 13th to 16th centuries.

Rooms 217–222 & 237 Venetian art, 16th century.
Room 229 Raphael and his disciples.
Rooms 239–240 Spanish art, 16th to 18th centuries.
Rooms 244–247 Flemish art, 17th century.
Rooms 249–252 & 254 Dutch art, 17th century.

Winter Palace, 3rd floor
Rooms 315–333 Impressionists and post-impressionists.
Room 334 Vincent van Gogh.
Rooms 343–349 Picasso and Matisse.

The Collection

Winter Palace, 1st floor

Rooms 1–33 (Russian prehistoric artefacts) 11 Palaeolithic (from 500,000 years ago to the 12th millenniums BC) and Mesolithic (12th to 3rd millennium BC); **12** Neolithic (4th millennium BC to 2400 BC) and Bronze Age (2000 to 500 BC), including petroglyphs from 2500 to 2000 BC taken from the northeastern shores of Lake Onega; **13** Bronze Age, western steppes, 4th to 2nd millenniums BC; **14** Bronze Age, southern Siberia and Kazakhstan, 2nd millennium to 9th century BC, fine bronze animals; **15–18** Scythian culture, 7th to 3rd centuries BC – but the best Scythian material is in the Golden Rooms Special Collection; **19 & 20** Forest steppes, 7th to 4th centuries BC; **21–23 & 26** Material from Altay Mountains burial mounds, including human and horse corpses preserved for over 2000 years complete with hair and teeth (Room 26); **24** Iron Age, Eastern Europe, including Finno-Ugrians and Balts, 8th century BC to 12th century AD; **33** Southern steppes tribes, 3rd century BC to 10th century AD – some fine Sarmatian gold.

Rooms 34–39 & 46–69 (The Russian East) Central Asia, 4th century BC to 13th century AD; **(The Russian East continued) 55–66** Caucasus and Transcaucasia, 10th century BC to 16th century AD, including Urartu, 9th to 7th centuries BC (Room 56); Dagestan, 6th to 11th centuries AD (Room 59); 14th-century Italian colonies in Crimea (Room 66); **67–69** Golden Horde, 13th to 14th centuries.

Room 100 (Ancient Egypt) A fine collection, much of it uncovered by Russian archaeologists; there is no English labelling except the signs saying 'Please Do Not Touch'.

The 2-tonne Cauldron of Tamerlane, cast in bronze in 1399 by master smith Abdal-Aziz for a mosque in present-day Kazakhstan, and now part of the Hermitage's Central Asian collection

The Hermitage Collection

The Hermitage Collection

Little Hermitage, 1st floor
Most of this floor is off limits but **Rooms 101 & 102** have displays of Roman marble.

Large Hermitage, 1st floor
Rooms 106–131 (Ancient classical culture) 106–109 & 127 Roman sculpture, 1st century BC to 4th century AD; **111–114** Ancient Greece, 8th to 2nd centuries BC, mostly ceramics and sculpture; **115–117 & 121** Greek colonies around northern Black Sea, 7th century BC to 3rd century AD; **128** The huge 19th-century jasper Kolyvanskaya Vase from Siberia; **130 & 131** Ancient Italy, 7th to 2nd centuries BC, including Etruscan vases and bronze mirrors.

Winter Palace, 2nd floor
Rooms 143–146 (French art, 19th to 20th centuries) This is most of what used to be called the Hidden Treasures Revealed exhibit. It boasts oil paintings captured by the Red Army from private collections in Germany, including works by Monet, Degas, Renoir, Cézanne, Picasso and Matisse, almost all never before publicly displayed.

Rooms 147–189 (Russian culture and art) 147–150 10th to 15th centuries; **151** 15th to 17th centuries; **152** Icons, ceramics, jewellery etc from 'Moscow baroque' period, first half of the 17th century; **153** Items relating to Peter the Great; **155–166** Late 17th and early 18th centuries, including: **155** Moorish Dining Room; **156** Rotunda, with a bust of Peter the Great and a brass Triumphal Pillar, topped by a Rastrelli-created statue of Peter; **157–first half of 161** Petrovskaya Gallereya, including lathing machinery used by Peter; **161** An ivory chandelier partly built by the Great Guy himself; **162** Mosaic of Peter by Lomonosov; **167–173** Mid- to end 18th century (spot the bizarre 1772 tapestry image of Australia); **175–187** (start at Room 187 and work your way back) Rooms occupied by the last imperial family, now displaying 19th-century interior design, including:

178 Nicholas II's English Gothic-style library; **188** Small Dining Room, where the Provisional Government was arrested by the Bolsheviks on 26 October 1917; **189 Malachite Hall** with two tonnes of gorgeous green malachite columns, boxes, bowls and urns – possibly the most impressive of all the palace rooms.

Rooms 190–192 (Neva Enfilade) One of two sets of state rooms for ceremonies and balls. **190** Concert Hall for small balls, with an 18th-century silver tomb for the remains of Alexander Nevsky; **191** Great or Nicholas Hall, scene of great winter balls; **192** The Fore Hall. All these halls are now used for temporary exhibitions.

Rooms 193–198 (Great Enfilade) The second series of state rooms. **193** Field Marshals' Hall; **194** Peter the Great's Hall, with his none-too-comfy-looking throne; **195** Armorial Hall, bright and gilt-encrusted, displaying 16th- to 19th-century Western European silver; **197** The 1812 Gallery, hung with portraits of Russian and allied Napoleonic war leaders; **198** Hall of St George or Great Throne Room – once a state room, now used for temporary exhibitions.

Rooms 200–202 (Western European tapestry, 16th to 19th centuries)

Rooms 263–268 (German art, 15th to 18th centuries) Including Dürer and Lucas Cranach the Elder.

Rooms 269–271 (Western European porcelain, 18th century) Room 271 was the tsars' cathedral.

Rooms 272–289 (French art, 15th to 18th centuries) 272–273 Tapestries, ceramics, metalwork; **279** Paintings by Poussin; **280** Lorrai; **284** Watteau.

British art, 16th to 19th centuries: Room 299 Reynolds **300** Gainsborough's *Lady in Blue*.

Room 303 'Dark Corridor' containing Western European tapestry, 16th to 18th centuries, mainly from Flanders.

Follow the confusing trail through 167 and 308 to get to: **304** A wonderful collection of Western European stone engravings from the 13th to 19th centuries; **305** The Burgundy Hall, containing

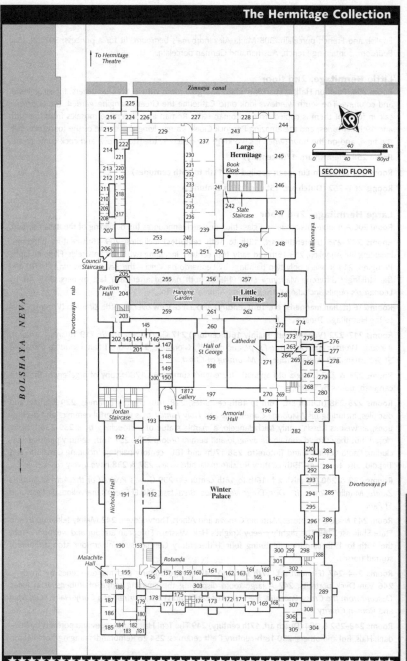

The Hermitage Collection

To Hermitage Theatre

Zimnaya canal

225

216 224 226 227 228
215 229 243 244
214 222 237 245
221 230 **Large**
213 220 219 231 **Hermitage**
212 *Book* 241 246
211 218 233 *Kiosk*
210 209 217 234 235 236 242 *State Staircase* 247
208 253 239
207 240 248
254 252 251 250 249

206
Council Staircase

205

204
Pavilion Hall

Hanging Garden 255 256 257 **Little Hermitage** 258

203 259 261 262

Dvortsovaya nab

BOLSHAYA NEVA

260 274
202 143 144 146 145 272 273 275 276
201 147 *Hall of St George* *Cathedral* 263 277
148 198 271 264 265 266 278
149 267 279
200 150 270 269 268 280

1812 Gallery 197

194
Jordan Staircase 193 195 *Armorial Hall* 196 281

192
282

151

290 283
291 284
Winter Palace 292
293 285
294 286
Nicholas Hall 191 152 295
296 287
297 288

190 153
Malachite Hall *Rotunda* 300 299 298
155 301
189 156 157 158 159 160 161 162 163 164 166 167 302
188 165
187 179 178 175 303 307 308
186 180 177 176 174 173 172 171 170 169 168 306
185 184 182 181 305 289 304
183

SECOND FLOOR

0   40   80m
0   40   80yd

Millionnaya ul

Dvortsovaya pl

ST PETERSBURG

The Hermitage Collection

English and French porcelain; **306** Maria Alexandrovna's bedroom, fit for a princess; **307** the Blue Bedroom, containing French, Austrian and German porcelain.

Little Hermitage, 2nd floor
Room 204 (Pavilion Hall) A sparkling white-and-gold room with lovely chandeliers, tables, galleries and columns. The south windows look onto Catherine the Great's hanging garden; the floor mosaic in front of them is copied from a Roman bath. Roman and Florentine mosaics from the 18th and 19th centuries, and the amazing Peacock Clock – a revolving dial in one of the toadstools tells the time, and on the hour (when it's working) the peacock, toadstools, owl and cock come to life.

Room 258 (Flemish art, 17th century)

Room 259 (Western European applied art, 11th to 15th centuries)

Rooms 261–262 (Dutch art, 15th and 16th centuries)

Large Hermitage, 2nd floor
Room 206 A marble, malachite and glass triumphal arch announces the beginning of the Italian section.

Rooms 207–215 (Florentine art, 13th to 16th centuries) including **209** 15th-century paintings, including Fra Angelico; **213** 15th and early 16th century, including two small Botticellis, Filippino Lippi, Perugino; **214** Russia's only two paintings by Leonardo da Vinci – the *Benois Madonna* (1478) and the strikingly different *Madonna Litta* (1490), both named after their last owners; **215** Art by Leonardo's pupils, including Correggio and Andrea del Sarto.

Room 216 (Italian mannerist art, 16th century) Also a nice view over the little Zimnaya (Winter) Canal to the Hermitage Theatre.

Rooms 217–222 (Venetian art, mainly 16th century) **217** Giorgione's *Judith*; **219** Titian's *Portrait of a Young Woman* and *Flight into Egypt*, and more by Giorgione; **221** More Titian, including *Dana* and *St Sebastian*; **222** Paolo Veronese's *Mourning of Christ*.

Rooms 226 & 227 (Loggia of Raphael) Quarenghi's sumptuous 1780s copy of a gallery in the Vatican with murals by Raphael.

Rooms 228-238 (Italian art, 16th to 18th centuries) **228** 16th-century ceramics; **229** Raphael and disciples, including his *Madonna Conestabile* and *Holy Family*, plus wonderful ceramics and decorations, as well as Russia's only Michelangelo, a marble statue of a crouching boy; **230-236** Usually closed, but they should contain Caravaggio and Bernini (Room 232); **237** 16th-century paintings, including Paolo Veronese and Tintoretto; **238** 17th- and 18th-century painters including Canaletto and Tiepolo; also two huge 19th-century Russian malachite vases; **237 & 238** have lovely ceilings.

Rooms 239 & 240 (Spanish art, 16th to 18th centuries) **239** Goya's *Portrait of the Actress Antonia Zarate*, Murillo's *Boy with a Dog*, Diego Velazquez' *Breakfast*; **240** El Greco's marvellous *St Peter and St Paul*.

Room 241 Marble sculptures, Antonio Canova and Albert Thorwaldsen; **242** Mainly taken up by the State Staircase; **243** The slightly creepy Knight's Hall; Western European armour and weaponry from the 15th to 17th centuries, featuring four 16th-century German suits of armour atop armoured, stuffed horses.

Rooms 244–247 (Flemish art, 17th century) **245** Savage hunting and market scenes by Snyders; **246** Van Dyck portraits; **247** A large room displaying the amazing range of Rubens. It includes *Descent from the Cross*, *Bacchus*, *The Union of Earth and Water*, *Portrait of a Curly-Haired Old Man* and *Roman Charity*.

Rooms 248–252 & 254 (Dutch art, 17th century) **249** The Tent Hall. Landscapes and portraits by Ruisdael, Hals, Bol and others; **250** 18th-century Delft ceramics; **254** 26 Rembrandts ranging from lighter,

The Hermitage Collection

more detailed early canvases such as *Abraham's Sacrifice of Isaac* and *Dana* to *The Holy Family* (1645), and darker, penetrating late works such as *The Return of the Prodigal Son* and two canvases entitled *Portrait of an Old Man*. There's also work by Rembrandt's pupils, including Bol.

Winter Palace, 3rd floor
An approximate chronological order in which to view the French art collection is Rooms 314, 332-328, 325-315 and 343-350. The staircase beside Room 269 on the 2nd floor brings you out by Room 314.

Rooms 314–320, 330–332 (French art, 19th century) 315 Rodin sculptures; **316** Gauguin's Tahitian works; **317** Van Gogh, Rousseau, Forain, Latour; **318** Cézanne, Pissarro; **319** Pissarro, Monet, Sisley.

320 Renoir, Degas; **321 & 322** Corot, Courbet, Rousseau; **333** Kandinsky.

Room 334–342 (European art, 19th century) 334 Vincent van Gogh, and landscapes by Caspar David Friedrich.

Rooms 343–345 (Matisse) 35 canvases in all, including *The Dance* and *Arab Coffeehouse.*

Rooms 346, 347 & 350 (French art, 19th to 20th centuries) Including Bonnard, Vlaminck, Marquet, Leger and others.

Rooms 348 & 349 (Picasso) 348 mainly his blue and cubist periods; **349** cubist and later periods.

Rooms 351–371, 381–396 (Oriental and Middle Eastern culture and art) 351–357, 359–364 Art of China and Tibet, an excellent collection; **358** Indonesia; **365–367** Mongolia; **368–371** India; **381–387** Byzantium, Near and Middle East.

Rooms 398 & 400 Coins.

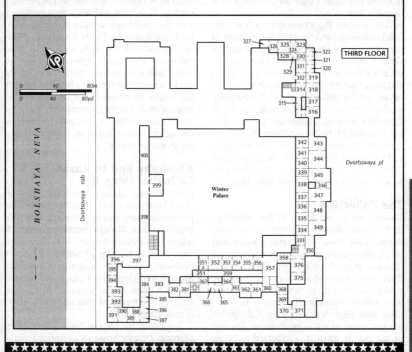

[Continued from page 249]

wishing to take photographs must pay an extra R100; using your camcorder will cost you another R250.

There are also tickets for R500 which give you access to the Hermitage, the General Staff Building, the Menshikov Palace and the Peter the Great Palace, but the ticket is only valid for one day. It is also possible to visit these other places and simply pay a separate admission.

To avoid queues, you can join a tour, which whizzes round the main sections in about 1½ hours but at least provides an introduction to the place in English. It's easy to 'lose' the group and stay on until closing time. The museum's **excursions office** (☎ 311 84 46, 213 11 12; open 11am-1pm & 2pm-4pm) is down the corridor to the right as you enter, up the stairs and straight to the end of the small corridor (don't turn right towards the coat-check). You can either call in advance (suggested) or show up and hope to be able to arrange a guided tour through the museum in English, German or French, or a thematic tour.

Also contact the excursions office, your hotel concierge desk or your travel agent if you plan to visit the **Golden Rooms Special Collection** in Rooms 41 to 45. This costs another R300 (more if booked through an agent) and places are limited, so book early if you're interested. The focus is a hoard of fabulously worked Scythian and Greek gold and silver from the Caucasus, Crimea and Ukraine, dating from the 7th to 2nd centuries BC.

There is a special entrance for the physically disabled from Dvortsovaya ploshchad (the museum also has a few wheelchairs on hand) – call in advance if you need this.

The Collection

Though the rooms listed in this room-by-room guide should in principle be open during your visit, occasionally some will be closed without warning for maintenance or other mysterious reasons. Additionally, there's only space to show up to 10% of the collection at any given time, so the works on view change occasionally. Only a few sections have English labelling, so if the painting you came to see is inaccessible, ask one of the guards when it is expected to be on view again.

Rooms are numbered. From the main ticket hall, the Rastrelli Gallery leads to the white marble Jordan Staircase, with windows and mirrors on all sides, which takes you up to the 2nd floor of the Winter Palace. The staircase is one of the few parts of the interior to maintain its original Rastrelli appearance.

NEVSKY PROSPEKT

Though the Soviets tried renaming it 25th of October Avenue in honour of their revolution, the name never stuck. Nevsky prospekt is and always will be Russia's most famous street, running 4km from the Admiralty to the Alexander Nevsky Monastery, from which it takes its name. The inner 2.5km to Moscow Station is St Petersburg's seething main avenue, the city's shopping centre and focus of its entertainment and street life. Pushing through its crowds is an essential St Petersburg experience, and if you're here on a holiday evening (such as 27 May – City Day), the sight of thousands pouring like a stream down its middle is one you'll not soon forget.

Nevsky prospekt was laid out in the early years of St Petersburg as the start of the main road to Novgorod and soon became dotted with fine buildings, squares and bridges. At the beginning of the 1900s, it was one of Europe's grandest boulevards, with cobblestone sidewalks and a track down the middle for horse-drawn trams. On either side of the tracks were wooden paving blocks to muffle the sound of horse-drawn carriages – an innovation that was apparently the first in the world and for which the prospekt was dubbed the quietest main street in Europe. Today, things are bit noisier.

Admiralty End to Kazan Cathedral (Map 6)

Inner Nevsky, Malaya Morskaya and Bolshaya Morskaya ulitsas were the heart of the prerevolutionary financial district. Points of interest include **Malaya Morskaya ulitsa 13**, where Tchaikovsky died in 1893. The wall of the school at **Nevsky prospekt 14** bears a blue-and-white stencilled sign maintained since WWII. Beginning Гражданe! (*Grazhdane!*) it translates as 'Citizens! At times of artillery bombardment this side of the street is most dangerous!'

Just before the Moyka River is **Kafe Literaturnoe**. Despite being an overpriced tourist trap, it's worth peeping into for its Pushkin associations (he ate his last meal here). Across the Moyka, Rastrelli's green **Stroganov Palace** (☎ 219 16 08; *Nevsky pr 17; adult/ tudent R240/120; open 10am-5pm Tues- un*) has kept most of its original baroque appearance (1752–54). Inside there's a gallery of historical waxworks figures, and an exhibition of Russian decorative and applied arts from the Russian Museum's collection.

A block beyond the Moyka, on the southern side of Nevsky prospekt, the great colonnaded arms of the **Kazan Cathedral** (Kazansky sobor; 1801–11) reach out towards the avenue. Its design, by Andrey Voronikhin, a former serf, was influenced by St Peter's in Rome. His original plan was to build a second, mirror version of the cathedral opposite it on the northern side of Nevsky prospekt. The square in front of it has been a site for political demonstrations since before the revolution.

Opposite the cathedral is St Petersburg's biggest bookshop, **Dom Knigi**, while south of it, along Griboedova Canal, sits **Ban- kovsky most**, one of St Petersburg's loveli- est bridges – see the Walking Tour earlier for details.

Griboedova Canal to the Fontanka (Map 6)

Check out the lavish **Grand Hotel Europe**, built between 1873 and 1875, redone in Style Moderne (Russian Art Nouveau) in the 1910s and completely renovated from 1989 to 1991. Boasting shameless splendour, it's one of the city's architectural gems.

Diagonally across Nevsky prospekt, the fashionable arcades of **Gostiny Dvor** depart- ment store stand facing the clock tower of the former **Town Duma**, seat of the prerevolu- tionary city government. One of the world's first indoor shopping malls, Gostiny Dvor (the 'Merchant Yard') dates from 1757–85, stretches 230m along Nevsky prospekt (its completely restored perimeter is over 1km ong) and is another Rastrelli creation.

On the other side of Nevsky prospekt, the arcade at No 48, the **Passazh** department store is beautiful to look at (notice the glass ceilings) and packed with pricey goods.

Tucked in a recess near Mikhailovskaya ulitsa, the **Armenian Church** (1771–80), one of two in St Petersburg, has been completely renovated and is open to visitors.

On Sadovaya ulitsa, opposite the south- eastern side of Gostiny Dvor, the **Vorontsov**

Palace (1749–57) is another noble town house by Rastrelli. It's now a military school for young cadets; on weekends you can watch mothers pass food parcels to their sons through the wrought-iron front gates.

Worth ducking down is the newly pedes- trianised Malaya Sadovaya ulitsa. A number of statues and sculptures have been placed here (look up near the junction with Nevsky prospekt to see the tiny black-and-white cats poised on ledges on either side of the street), including a marble ball with a fountain un- derneath which makes it spin forever.

Yeliseevsky *(Nevsky pr 56)* is the most sumptuous 'grocery store' you may have ever seen. Built in Style Moderne between 1901 and 1903, it is decorated with sculptures and statues on the outside, and a gorgeous mir- rored ceiling and stained-glass windows on the inside.

Ploshchad Ostrovskogo (Map 6)

An enormous **statue of Catherine the Great** stands amid the chess, backgammon and sometimes even mah jong players that crowd the benches here. At the Empress' heels are some of her renowned statesmen, including her lovers Orlov, Potyomkin and Suvorov.

This airy square, commonly referred to as the Catherine Gardens, was created by Carlo Rossi in the 1820s and 1830s. The square's western side is taken up by the lavish **Na- tional Library of Russia**, St Petersburg's big- gest with some 31 million items, nearly one- sixth of which are in foreign languages.

Rossi's **Pushkin Theatre** (formerly the Alexandrinsky) at the southern end of the square is one of Russia's most important the- atres. In 1896 the opening night of Chekhov's *The Seagull* was so badly received here that the playwright fled to wander anonymously among the crowds on Nevsky prospekt.

Behind the theatre, on ulitsa Zodchego Rossi, is a continuation of Rossi's ensemble. It is proportion deified: it's 22m wide and high and 220m long. The **Vaganova School of Choreography** situated here is the Kirov Ballet's training school where, Pavlova, Nijin- sky, Nureyev and others learned their art.

The **Anichkov Palace** (1741–50, the city's second palace), between ploshchad Ostrov- skogo and the Fontanka River (its main facade faces the river and was once joined to it by a canal), was home to several imperial favourites, including Catherine the Great's lover Grigory Potyomkin. A slew of architects, including Rastrelli and Rossi, worked on it. It became the city's largest Pioneer Club headquarters after 1935 and to this day houses over 100 after-school clubs for over 10,000 children.

Anichkov Bridge & Beyond (Map 6)

Nevsky prospekt crosses the Fontanka on the **Anichkov most**, with famous 1840s statues (sculpted by the German P Klodt) of rearing horses at its four corners. To witness pure artistic revenge, put prudery aside and take note of the southwestern horse's genitals: unlike those of his anatomically correct companions, the genitals of this one are apparently created in the image of the sculptor's unfaithful wife's lover (another version has it that it's Napoleon's profile).

The photogenic backdrop is provided by the 1840s **Beloselsky-Belozersky Palace** (Nevsky pr 41). Apart from the city's tourist office, it now houses the **Historical Museum of Wax Figures** (☎ 312 36 44; adult/student R120/60; open noon-6pm daily), which is a hoot. Concerts are occasionally held here too.

About 200m north along the Fontanka, splendid wrought-iron gates guard the **Sheremetev Palace** (1750–55), which houses two lovely little museums. In the palace itself is a branch of the **Museum of Theatrical and Musical Arts** (☎ 272 38 98; nab reki Fontanki 34; adult/student R80/40; open noon-6pm Wed-Sun), which has a collection of musical instruments from the 19th and 20th centuries, some beautifully decorated. The Sheremetev family was famous for the concerts and theatre it hosted at the palace, which was a centre of musical life in the capital in the 18th century.

Behind the palace is the **Akhmatova Memorial Museum** (☎ 272 22 11; entrance at Liteyny pr 53; adult/student R60/30; open 11am-5.30pm Tues-Sun), celebrating deeply loved and persecuted early 20th-century poet Anna Akhmatova. Her peaceful old apartment is on the 2nd floor, filled with mementos of the poet and her correspondence with Pasternak. Downstairs is a bookshop and video room where you can watch Russian-language documentaries on her life while drinking tea or coffee.

Marking the division of Nevsky prospekt and Stary (old) Nevsky prospekt is **ploshchad Vosstania** (Uprising Square), whose

landmarks are the giant granite pillar with the Commie star, and Moscow Station. Note the writing on top of Hotel Oktyabrskaya across from the station: ГОРОД ГЕРОЙ ЛЕНИНГРАД (Hero City Leningrad); several cities were designated 'hero cities' for heroism, stoicism and losses during WWII.

Stary Nevsky prospekt juts off the northeastern side of the square and heads southeast to the Alexandra Nevskogo most. Its charm is in its relative desolation and laid-back mood.

Alexander Nevsky Monastery (Map 5)

The working monastery (Lavra Alexandra Nevskogo; ☎ 274 04 09; Nevsky pr 179/2; entrance to main complex adult/student R50/25; open 11am-5pm Fri-Wed), with the graves of some of Russia's most famous artistic figures, is entered from ploshchad Alexandra Nevskogo opposite Hotel Moskva. It was founded in 1713 by Peter the Great, who wrongly thought this was the location where Alexander of Novgorod had beaten the Swedes in 1240. In 1797 it became a lavra (superior monastery). Today it is open to the public and, sadly, the courtyard is filled with homeless beggars.

Either side of the main approach to the monastery are two important **graveyards** (adult/student R50/25; open 9.30am-5.30pm Fri-Wed); tickets are sold outside the main gate (to your right as you enter). The **Tikhvin Cemetery** (Tikhvinskoe kladbishche), on the right, contains the most famous graves: Tchaikovsky, Borodin, Mussorgsky, Rimsky-Korsakov (check out his wild tomb!) and Glinka all rest here. Make a right after entering and you'll reach the tomb of Dostoevsky.

The **Lazarus Cemetery** (Lazarevskoe kladbishche), opposite the Tikhvin across the entrance path, contains several late, great St Petersburg architects – among them Starov, Voronikhin, Quarenghi, Zakharov and Rossi.

Across the canal just outside the main lavra complex, the first main building on the left is the 1717–22 baroque **Annunciation Church** (Blagoveshchenskaya tserkov), now the **City Sculpture Museum** (Muzey gorodskoy skulptury; ☎ 274 254 17; adult/student R50/25), featuring a large collection of the original models and designs for the city.

About 100m farther on is the monastery's 1776–90 classical **Trinity Cathedral** (Troitsky sobor; open for worship from 6am Sat, Sun &

iolidays). Hundreds crowd in on 12 September to celebrate the feast of St Alexander Nevsky. His remains are in the silver reliquary in the main iconostasis.

Opposite the cathedral is the St Petersburg **Metropolitan's House** (1775–78). On the far right of the grounds facing the canal you'll see St Petersburg's **Orthodox Academy**, one of only a handful in Russia (the main one is at Sergiev Posad).

NORTH OF NEVSKY PROSPEKT
Ploshchad Iskusstv (Map 6)

Just a block north of Gostiny Dvor metro, quiet ploshchad Iskusstv (Arts Square) is named after its surrounding museums and concert halls. A statue of Pushkin, erected in 1957, stands in the middle of the tree-lined square. Both the square and Mikhailovskaya ulitsa, which joins the square to Nevsky prospekt, were designed as a unit by Rossi in the 1820s and 1830s.

Russian Museum (Map 6)

The former Mikhailovsky Palace, now the Russian Museum *(Gosudarstvenny Russky muzey;* ☎ 311 14 65; *Inzhenernaya ul 4; adult/student R240/120; open 10am-6pm Wed-Mon)*, houses one of the country's two finest collections of Russian art (the other is in Moscow's Tretyakov Gallery). If your time in the city is limited and you think only the Hermitage is a must-see, try your utmost to make some time for this gem of a museum; your appreciation of Russian culture will be deepened by it.

The palace was designed by Carlo Rossi and built between 1819 and 1829 for Grand Duke Mikhail (brother of Tsars Alexander I and Nicholas I) as compensation for not being able to have a chance on the throne. The museum was founded in 1895 under Alexander III and opened three years later.

The Benois building, now connected to the original palace, was constructed between 1914 and 1919. Note that the facade of the palace is illuminated at night, making that a good time to photograph it. The building is also impressively viewed from the back on a stroll through the pleasant **Mikhailovsky Gardens** behind it.

The museum now owns three other city palaces where temporary exhibitions are also held: the Marble Palace, the Stroganov Palace and the Engineer's Castle.

See the boxed text 'The Russian Museum (A Room-by-Room Tour)' later for a straightforward walk through the rooms. The museum's main entrance is through a tiny door on the far right side of the main building, off Inzhenernaya ulitsa. You can also enter via the Benois wing off naberezhnaya kanala Griboedova. English guided tours can be booked on ☎ 314 44 48.

Museum of Ethnography (Map 6)

This worthwhile museum (☎ 313 44 20; *Inzhenernaya ul 4/1; adult/student R100/50; gold & jewellery exhibition R100/50; open 10am-5pm Tues-Sun)* displays traditional crafts, customs and beliefs of the more than 150 peoples who make up Russia's fragile ethnic mosaic. There's a bit of leftover Soviet propaganda going on here, but it's a marvellous collection: the sections on Transcaucasia and Central Asia are fascinating, with rugs and two full-size yurts (nomad's portable tent-houses).

Church on Spilled Blood (Map 6)

Also known as the Church of the Resurrection of Christ, this multi-domed dazzler (☎ 315 16 36; *adult/student R240/120; open 11pm-6pm Thur-Tues)*, partly modelled on St Basil's in Moscow, sits on the Griboedova Canal just near the Mikhailovsky Gardens. It was built between 1883 and 1907 on the spot where Alexander II, despite his reforms, was blown up by the People's Will terrorist group in 1881 (hence its gruesome name).

It's now most commonly known as the church that took 24 years to build and 27 to restore. In August 1997, with much fanfare, it finally opened its doors after painstaking work on the 7000 sq metres of mosaics by over 30 artists which line the walls inside. On the very spot of the assassination is the marble bust *Shatrovy Cen*, a monument to Alexander. Most visitors agree that the church's splendour is much better appreciated from the outside.

Pushkin Flat-Museum (Map 5)

Pushkin's last home (he only lived here for a year) is beside one of the prettiest curves of the Moyka River. This is where the poet died after his duel in 1837. His killer was a French soldier of fortune, Baron d'Anthes, who had

The Russian Museum (A Room-by-Room Tour)

Mikhailovsky Palace, 2nd floor

Rooms 1–4 12th- to 15th-century icons. Apostle Peter and Apostle Paul by students of Andrey Rublyov are particularly good; **5–9** 17th- to 18th-century sculpture, portraits and tapestries, and Rastrelli's pompous *Anna Joannovna and an Arab Boy* (Room 7); **10, 12, 13, 14, 17** Late-18th-century, early-19th-century paintings and sculpture; **11** The White Hall, the most ornate in the palace, with period furniture by Rossi, and where Strauss and Berlioz, as guests, performed concerts; **14** Karl Bryullov's *Last Day of Pompeii* (1827–33), which was, in its time, the most famous Russian painting ever; Pushkin, Gogol, Herzen and other writers rhapsodised over it, and there were queues for months to see it. Petersburgers saw in it a doomsday scenario of their own city, which had a few years earlier been damaged in a huge flood;**15** Big 19th-century canvases mainly by graduates of the official Academy – Aivazovsky's Crimea seascapes stand out, most frighteningly *The Wave*. Here is Ivanov's most famous work, *Christ's Appearance to the People*.

Mikhailovsky Palace, 1st floor

Rooms 18–22 19th-century works focusing (Room 19) on the beginnings of the socially aware 'Realist' tradition and including (Room 21) spectacular works by Semiradsky and Flavitsky, including his gigantic *Christian Martyrs in Colosseum*; **23–38** Peredvizhniki and associated artists, including **25** Kramskoy; **26** Nikolai Ge, including his fearsome *Peter I Prosecuting Tsarevich Alexey in Peterhof*; **27** Shishkin; **31** KA Savitsky's *To the War*; **32** Poleneov, including his *Christ and the Sinner*. Note that in Room 29, there is an interactive computer display, in English, about the museum.

33–35, 54 A permanent exhibition of the work of Repin, probably Russia's best-loved artist; Room 33 has portraits and the incomparable *Barge Haulers on the Volga*, an indictment of Russian 'social justice'; and Room 54 contains the massive *Meeting of the State Council*, Repin's rendering of the meeting at the Mariinsky Palace on 7 May 1901 (it's full of tsarist hotshots; there's a scheme in the room to help you tell who's who); **36, 37** Russian history, portraits by Surikov, a national revivalist, and Mikhail Mikeshin's model of the Millennium of Russia (Room 36); **38** Historical works by Vasnetsov, including *Russian Knight at the Crossroads* and other 'sketches' for his mosaics; **39** Popular 19th-century painter Malyavin's depictions of Russian mothers and maidens; **40 & 41** Unforgettably stunning landscapes by Kuindzhi; **42–47** Works by Levitan and other late-19th-century painters, and (Room 45) Ryabushkin on pre-Peter the Great 17th-century Russian history, including the very telling and humorous *Yedut*, or *They Are Coming*, depicting the perturbed-looking reception committee for the first foreigners allowed in Russia; **48** Antakolski sculptures (Exits straight ahead lead to 10 halls of Russian folk art, including handicrafts, wood work, carvings, pottery, toys etc; exits to the right lead to the Benois building.); **49** A long corridor that houses temporary exhibitions; **50–53** Closed storage area; **55–59** Sculptures from the 18th to 20th centuries, including sensitive works by Matveev and Shubin; **60–65** Temporarily closed for repairs.

Benois Building, 2nd & 1st floors

Rooms 66–79 20th-century art, including **66** Vrubel, with his epic *Russian Hero and Venice*, and Artemiy Ober's terrifying bronze *Calamity*; **67** Nesterov's religious paintings of the history of the Orthodox Church; Konenkov sculptures and Vasnetsov's *The Entombing*; **70 & 71** Serov, portraits of Russian aristocracy and other high-rollers; Trubitskoy sculptures of same including *Isaak Levitan and Children*; **72** Impressionists Korovin, Grabar and Serebryakova; Trubitskoy's *Moscow Carriage Driver* and Boris Kustodiev's *Holiday on the Volga*; **73** Kustodiev's paintings of stereotypical Russians; **74** The Rerikh Room; **75–79** Russian avant-garde, symbolism, neoclassical works by Saryan Kuznetsov, Petrov-Vodkin, Grigoriev, Shukhaev, Altman, Lenturov etc, including Petrov-Vodkin's famous *Mother* (1915) (Room 78).

81–105 Halls for rotating exhibitions; **106–113** Temporarily closed.

The Russian Museum (A Room-by-Room Tour)

First Floor
Первый этаж

nab kanala Griboedova

Entrance

104 | 105 | 106 | 107
103 | | | 108
102 | **Benois** | | 109
101 | | | 110
| | | 111
100 | | | 112
| | | 113

Folk Art

G | F | E | D | C | B | A | 48 | 47
| | | | | | 50a | | 46
| | | | | 50 | 49 | 45
Rossi | | 51 | | 44
65 | | 52 | 43
64 | | 53 | 42
63 | | | 41
62 | 61 | 60 | 59 | 58 | 57 | 56 | 55 | 54 | 40 | 39

36 | 35 | 34 | 33
37 | | 32
38 | | 31
| | 30
| | 29 ●
Mikhailovsky Palace | 28
18 | 27
19 | 26
20 | 25
| Computers
21 | 22 | 23 | 24

Main Entrance

Second Floor
Второй этаж

77 | 76 | 75 | 74 | 73 | 72 | 71
| 92 | | 91 |
78 | 94 | 93 | | 90 | 89 | 70
79 | 95 | **Benois** | | 88 | 69
80 | 96 | | | 68
| 98 | 99 | 86 | 87 | 67
81 | 97 | | | 66
82 | 83 | 84 | 85

Rossi

15
14
16
17 | 13 | 12
11
1
2 | 10
3 | 9
| 8
4 | 5 | 6 | 7

Mikhailovsky Palace

Inzhenernaya ul

0 — 30 — 60m
0 — 30 — 60yd

been publicly courting Pushkin's beautiful wife, Natalia. The affair was widely seen as a put-up job on behalf of Tsar Nicholas I, who found the famed poet's radical politics inconvenient – and who, gossip said, may himself have been the one really stalking Natalia. The little house is now the **Pushkin Flat-Museum** (☎ 311 35 31; nab reki Moyki 12; adult/student R80/40; open 10.30am-5pm Wed-Mon), reconstructed to look as it did in the poet's last days. Entry includes a Russian-language tour (English tours can be arranged in advance). There's a pleasantly quiet courtyard and café in front of the museum if you just want a rest.

Mars Field (Map 3)

The Mars Field (Marsovo pole) is the open space south of the Troitsky most, about 1km north of Nevsky prospekt along Sadovaya ulitsa. Don't take a short cut across the grass – you may be walking on graves from the 1917 revolution, the civil war, or of later communist luminaries also buried here. The field is the scene of 19th-century military parades. An eternal flame burns here for the victims of the revolution and the ensuing civil war.

Between the field and the Neva is the **Marble Palace** (☎ 312 91 96; Millionnaya ul 5; adult/student R160/80; open 10am-5pm Wed-Mon), built for Catherine the Great's lover Grigory Orlov from 1768 to 1785. It's now a branch of the Russian Museum featuring rotating exhibitions.

Summer Garden (Map 3)

Perhaps St Petersburg's loveliest park, the Summer Garden (Letny sad; admission R10; open 9am-10pm daily May-Oct, 10am-6pm daily Oct-mid-Apr, closed mid-end-Apr) is between the Mars Field and the Fontanka River. You can enter at either the north or south ends.

Laid out for Peter the Great with fountains, pavilions and a geometrical plan to resemble the park at Versailles in France, the garden became a strolling place for St Petersburg's 19th-century leisured classes. Though changed since that era, it maintains a formal elegance, with thousands of lime trees shading its straight paths and lines of statues.

The modest, two-storey **Summer Palace** in the northeast corner was St Petersburg's first palace, built for Peter from 1710 to 1714, and is pretty well intact. Little reliefs

around the walls depict Russian naval victories. Today the palace is a **museum** (Muzey letny dvorets Petra I; ☎ 314 04 56; adult/student R50/25; open 11am-6pm Wed-Mon early May-early Nov) stocked with early-18th-century furnishings.

A much greater Summer Palace used to stand across the canal from the southern end of the Summer Garden. But Rastrelli's fairy-tale wooden creation for Empress Elizabeth was knocked down in the 1790s to make way for the bulky, brick **Engineers' Castle** (Map 6) of Paul I, an insanely cruel tsar who lived in fear of assassination and was indeed suffocated in his bed a month after moving into the castle. Later it became a military engineering school (hence the name). One wing is now part of the Russian Museum, which stages occasional exhibitions.

Museum of Decorative & Applied Arts (Map 3)

Otherwise known as the Stieglitz Museum, this must-see establishment (☎ 273 32 58; Solyarnoy per 13; adult/student R150/75; open 11am-5pm Tues-Sat) is in the block opposite the eastern side of the Summer Garden; the entrance is through the Sol-Art gallery (see the Shopping section later in this chapter). The objects displayed are breathtaking, from medieval handcrafted furniture to a rare collection of 18th-century Russian tiled stoves to the contemporary works of the students of the arts school. Their surroundings merely match their magnificence.

In 1878, the millionaire Baron Stieglitz founded the School of Technical Design and wanted to surround his students with world-class art to inspire them. He began a collection, continued by his son, that was to include a unique array of European and Oriental glassware, porcelains, tapestries, furniture and paintings. Between 1885 and 1895, a building designed by architect Messmacher was constructed to house the collection, and this building also became a masterpiece. Each hall is decorated in its own, unique style, including Italian, Renaissance, Flemish and baroque. The Terem Room, in the style of the medieval Terem Palace of Moscow's Kremlin, is an opulent knockout.

After the revolution, the school was closed, the museum's collection redistributed to the Hermitage and Russian Museum, and most of the lavish interiors brutally painted or plastered over, even destroyed (one room was used as a sports hall). The painstaking renovation continues to this day, despite receiving no funding from the Ministry of Education under whose direction it falls (being connected to the Applied Arts School next door). This would be the perfect direction for any philanthropic art-lovers' extra cash.

Blockade Museum (Map 3)

Next door to the Stieglitz Museum is this museum (☎ 275 72 08; Solyarnoy per 9; admission R30; open 10am-4pm Thur-Tues), opened just three months after the Blockade was lifted. At that time it had 37,000 exhibits, including real tanks and aeroplanes, but three years later, during Stalin's repression of the city, the museum was shut, its director shot, and most of the exhibits destroyed or redistributed. It reopened in 1989 and the displays now contain donations from survivors, including propaganda posters from the time, and an example of the sawdust-filled tiny piece of bread Leningraders had to survive on. English excursions are available, if booked in advance.

SMOLNY REGION
Tauride Gardens & Tauride Palace (Map 3)

The former Tauride Gardens, now the City Children's Park, is a great place for a stroll, and there are some rusty rides for the kiddies. The view across the lake towards the Tauride Palace (Tavrichesky dvorets), built between 1783 and 1789 for Catherine the Great's lover Potyomkin, is a fine sight.

The palace takes its name from the Ukrainian region of Crimea (once called Tavria), which Potyomkin was responsible for conquering. Between 1906 and 1917 the State Duma, the Provisional Government and the Petrograd Soviet all met here; in the 1930s it housed the All-Union Agricultural Communist University. Today, it's home to the Parliamentary Assembly of the Member States of the CIS and you can't go in. The gardens are a block-and-a-half east of Chernyshevskaya metro.

Flowers Exhibition Hall (Map 3)

One of the finest ways to escape momentarily from a St Petersburg winter is to head for the Flowers Exhibition Hall (☎ 272 54 48; Potyomkinskaya ul 2; admission R30; open 11am-7pm Tues-Wed & Fri-Sun), an indoor tropical paradise just northwest of the City Children's Park. Check out the 'monster' tree to the right of the entrance. It has a wishing well, and there's a flower-selling stall at the front of the building.

Smolny (Map 3)

About 1km east of the City Children's Park, Smolny Cathedral (pl Proletarskoy diktatury 3) is one of the most fabulous of all Rastrelli's buildings, and the Smolny Institute next door was the hub of the October Revolution. Trolleybus Nos 5 and 7 via much of Nevsky prospekt end up here.

The ice-blue cathedral is the centrepiece of a convent built mostly to Rastrelli's designs from 1748 to 1757. His inspiration was to combine baroque details with the forest of towers and onion domes typical of an old Russian monastery. There's special genius in the proportions of the cathedral (it gives the impression of soaring upward), to which the convent buildings are a perfect foil.

The interior is disappointingly austere. Skip the art gallery (☎ 278 14 61; adult/student R120/60; open 11am-5pm Fri-Wed) and climb one of the 63m belfries (R100); the views are stupendous.

The Smolny Institute (☎ 276 14 61; open by appointment only), built by Quarenghi from 1806 to 1808 as a school for aristocratic girls, had fame thrust upon it in 1917 when Trotsky and Lenin directed the October Revolution from the Bolshevik Central Committee headquarters and the Petrograd Soviet which had been set up here. In its Hall of Acts on 25 October, the All-Russian Congress of Soviets conferred power on a Bolshevik government led by Lenin, which ran the country from here until March 1918.

SOUTH & WEST OF NEVSKY PROSPEKT
Sennaya Ploshchad Area (Map 5)

Wide open Sennaya ploshchad, also known as the Haymarket, has been a construction site for decades. It's also the gateway to Dostoevskyville. The peripatetic writer, who occupied around 20 residences in his 28-year stay in the city, once spent a couple of days in debtors' prison in what is now called the Senior Officer's Barracks, just across the square from the Sennaya Ploshchad metro station. Dostoevsky had been thrown in there by his publisher for missing a deadline ('Had we but thought of it...' – T Wheeler). The site of the metro station was once home to a large cathedral that dominated the square.

Just west of the square, across the river, is the **flat** (ul Kaznacheyskaya 7) where Dostoevsky wrote *Crime and Punishment*; Raskolnikov's route to the murder passed directly under the author's window. The old woman lived at flat 74, naberezhnaya kanala Griboedova 104; you can visit the hallway outside the flat (residents are quite used to it). Entering from the canal side, walk straight back to entrance No 5 (apartments 22-81); the flat's on the 3rd floor.

The Museum of Railway Transport (Map 5)

Every schoolboy's dream is realised at the Museum of Railway Transport *(Muzey Zheleznodorozhnogo Transporta;* ☎ 168 80 05; Sadovaya ul 50; adult/student R30/10; open 11am-5pm Sun-Thur, closed last Thur of month), a fascinating collection of scale locomotives and model railway bridges often made by the engineers that built the real ones. The oldest such collection in the world (the museum was established in 1809, 28 years before Russia had its first working train!), it includes models of Krasnoyarsk's *Yenisey Bridge*, the ship that once carried passengers and trains across Lake Baikal, and a sumptuous 1903 Trans-Siberian wagon complete with piano salon and bathtub.

Trainspotters should note that an impressive collection of full-sized locomotives can be viewed at the **Railway Museum** *(Zheleznaya Doroga muzey; Map 5;* ☎ 168 20 63; nab Obvodnogo Kanala; adult/student R100/50; open 10am-6pm daily), at the old Warsaw Station: some 75 engines and carriages are on display, including one dating from 1897.

Teatralnaya Ploshchad Area (Map 4)

Teatralnaya ploshchad has been an entertainment centre since fairs were held here in the mid-18th century. Bus Nos 3 and 22 from Nevsky prospekt come here.

The **Mariinsky Theatre** *(*☎ 114 12 11; [w] www.mariinsky.spb.ru; Teatralnaya pl; tour R300; box office open 11am-7pm daily) has played a pivotal role in Russian ballet ever since it was built in 1859. Outside performance times you can usually wander into the theatre's foyer, and maybe peep into its lovely

Historic Railway Stations

As the birthplace of Russia's railway system, it's not surprising that St Petersburg has some grand stations. The most elegant is Vitebsk (also the oldest), originally built in 1837 for the line to Tsarskoe Selo. The current building dates from 1904 and is partly graced with gorgeous Style Moderne (Russian Art Nouveau) interior decoration, best appreciated in the café upstairs on the right of the building.

While at Moscow Station, look up at the expansive ceiling mural in the main entrance hall. There's a striking giant bust of Peter the Great in the hall leading to the platforms.

Finland Station was rebuilt after WWII and is famous as the place where, in April 1917, Lenin arrived from exile and gave his legendary speech atop an armoured car in the square. When the progress of the revolution began to look iffy, it was from here that Lenin hightailed it off to Finland, only to return again in October to seize power. Lenin's statue, pointing across the Neva towards the old KGB headquarters, stands outside the station.

★★★★★★★★★★★★★★★★★★★

auditorium. To organise a full tour fax a request to **Dr Yuri Schwartzkopf** *(*☎ 114 12 11; fax 314 17 44) and call back for an answer.

The St Petersburg Conservatory faces the Mariinsky Theatre. A couple of blocks west from here is the **Choral Synagogue** *(*☎ 113 89 74; Lermontovsky pr 2), a 180-year-old Byzantine-styled beauty that has been recently restored to its full glory.

Northeast of Teatralnaya ploshchad, the Griboedova Canal runs under **Lviny most**, another of St Petersburg's beautiful, beast-supported bridges, with cables emerging from the mouths of golden lions.

Yusupov Palace (Map 4)

One good walking route in the area is along the southern side of the Moyka River from Isaakievskaya ploshchad. On the way, you'll pass the original **Yusupov Palace** *(*☎ 314 98 83; nab reki Moyki 94; adult/student R120/60, separate R90/45 ticket to visit cellar rooms where Rasputin had his last meal; open 11am-4pm daily, but advance reservation is required), best known as the place where Rasputin (see the boxed text 'The Priest of Sex') met his untimely end. This notoriety is a shame, since the palace's sumptuously rich

The Priest of Sex

Cult figure of the Russian aristocracy in the early 1900s, Grigory Rasputin was born in the Siberian village of Pokrovskoe in 1869. Though not a monk as is sometimes supposed, Rasputin did pray a lot. In his mid-20s, he experienced a vision of the Virgin while working in the fields and left Pokrovskoe to seek enlightenment. On his wanderings he came to believe, as did the contemporary Khlyst (Whip) sect, that sinning (especially through sex), then repenting, could bring people close to God.

On reaching St Petersburg, Rasputin's racy brand of redemption, along with his soothing talk, compassion and generosity, made him very popular with some aristocratic women. His magnetic personality was apparently heightened by what the French ambassador called 'a strong animal smell, like that of a goat'.

Eventually Rasputin was summoned by Tsarina Alexandra and seemed able, thanks to some kind of hypnotic power, to cure the uncontrollable bleeding of her haemophiliac son, Tsarevich Alexey, the heir to the throne. As he continued his drunken, lecherous life, replete with famous orgies, Rasputin's influence on the royal family grew to the point where he could make or break the careers of ministers and generals. He became increasingly unpopular and many blamed him for the disasters of WWI.

His end finally came late in 1916 when Prince Felix Yusupov and others decided he had to be got rid of. This proved to be easier said than done, as Rasputin lived through being poisoned, shot repeatedly, and beaten with sticks – all in the one evening at St Petersburg's Yusupov Palace. Apparently he only died when pushed through the ice and submerged underwater.

★★★

rooms are quite beautiful; the gilded jewel box of a theatre, where performances are still held, is particularly notable.

Vladimirskaya Ploshchad Area (Map 5)

Some 500m south of Nevsky prospekt is this square dominated by the working, onion-domed, 18th-century **Our Lady of Vladimir Church** *(Map 6)* with its 1783 three-tiered belfry by Quarenghi. Around the corner is the indoor **Kuznechny market** *(Kuznechny per 3; open 8am-4pm daily)*, St Petersburg's best-stocked and most expensive market; it's a great place to browse for photo opportunities and free samples.

Dostoevsky groupies will want to beat a path to the engrossing **Dostoevsky Museum** *(☎ 311 40 31; W www.md.spb.ru; Kuznechny per 5/2; adult/student R60/30; open 11am-5.30pm Tues-Sun, closed last Wed of month)*, where the great writer penned most of *The Brothers Karamazov* before dying here in 1881. There's also a rather gloomy statue of the writer outside the Vladimirskaya metro.

Two other specialist museums in the area are the **Arctic & Antarctic Museum** *(☎ 113 19 98; ul Marata 24A; adult/student R50/25; open 10am-4.15pm Wed-Sun)*, which focuses on Soviet polar explorations and has ratty taxidermy exhibitions; and the charming **Rimsky-Korsakov Flat-Museum** *(☎ 113 32*

08; Zagorodny pr 28; admission R30; open 11am-6pm Wed-Sun), which is open later hours for concerts on Wednesday.

Moskovsky Prospekt (Map 1)

This long avenue, south from Sennaya ploshchad (Map 5), is the start of the main road to Moscow. The iron **Moscow Triumphal Arch**, 3.5km out, was built in 1838 to mark victories over Turks, Persians and Poles, demolished in 1936 then rebuilt from 1959 to 1960.

A couple of kilometres farther south, east off Moskovsky prospekt, is the striking red-and-white 18th-century Gothic **Chesma Church** *(ul Lensoveta 12; admission free; open 10am-7pm daily)* built from 1774 to 1780 in honour of the Battle of Çesme (1770), when the Russian fleet sailed from the Baltic to the Aegean to beat the Turks.

Wide Moskovskaya ploshchad, a little way south of ulitsa Gastello, was intended under a 1930s plan to become the centre of St Petersburg, replacing the old tsarist centre. In a testament to the stubbornness of St Petersburgers during Stalin's terror, this plan was universally ignored.

Monument to the Heroic Defenders of Leningrad (Map 1)

Moskovsky prospekt ends a few hundred metres farther south at the awe-inspiring

Monument to the Heroic Defenders of Leningrad (☎ 293 60 36; pl Pobedy; admission free; open 10am-6pm Thur-Tues). Centred around a 48m-high obelisk, the monument (unveiled in 1975) is a sculptural ensemble of bronze statues symbolising the heavy plight of defence, and eventual victory.

On a lower level, a bronze ring 40m in diameter symbolises the city's encirclement. Haunting symphonic music creates a sombre atmosphere to guide you downstairs to the underground exhibition in a huge, mausoleum-like interior, where 900 bronze lamps create an eeriness matched by the sound of a metronome – the only sound heard by Leningraders on their radios throughout the war save for emergency announcements. Twelve thematically assembled showcases feature items from the war and Blockade. Ask to see the two seven-minute documentary films, played on large screens at the touch of a button.

The monument is a 10-minute walk south of metro Moskovskaya.

VASILEVSKY ISLAND

Some of the best views of the city are from Vasilevsky Island at its eastern 'nose' – the Strelka (Tongue of Land), where Peter the Great first wanted his new city's administrative and intellectual centre. In fact, the Strelka became the focus of St Petersburg's maritime trade, symbolised by the white colonnaded **Stock Exchange**. The two **Rostral Columns** on the point, studded with ships' prows, were oil-fired navigation beacons in the 1800s (on some holidays gas torches are still lit on them). The area remains an intellectual centre, with the St Petersburg State University, the Academy of Arts and a veritable 'museum ghetto'.

Museums near the Strelka

The Stock Exchange is now the **Central Naval Museum** (Tsentralny Voenno-Morskoy muzey; Map 2; ☎ 218 25 02; adult/student R90/30; open 11am-5.15pm Wed-Sun, closed last Thur of the month), full of maps, excellent model ships, flags and photos relating to the Russian navy up to the present.

To the north is the old Customs House, topped with statues and a dome. It's now called **Pushkin House** (Pushkinsky dom; Map 2; ☎ 328 05 02; nab Makarova 4; guided tours R60; open 10am-4pm Mon-Fri) and is home to the **Institute of Russian Literature** and a **Literary Museum** with exhibits on Tolstoy,

Gogol, Lermontov, Turgenev, Gorky and others. They're not particularly welcoming to people dropping in off the street; call ahead to book a tour.

South of the Stock Exchange is the **Museum of Zoology** (Zoologichesky muzey; Map 4; ☎ 218 01 12; adult/child R30/10, free Thur; open 10.30am-4.50pm Sat-Thur), reputed to be among the world's biggest and best. Amid the dioramas and the tens of thousands of mounted beasties from around the globe is a complete woolly mammoth, thawed out of the Siberian ice in 1902, and a live insect zoo! Pay your entrance fee at the microscopic cash window just west of the main entrance.

Museum of Anthropology & Ethnography (Map 4)

Housed in the blue-and-white building with the steeple, this museum (Muzey Antropologii i Etnografii; ☎ 218 14 12; entrance on Tamozhyonny per; adult/student R100/50; open 10.30am-6pm Tues-Sat, 10.30am-5pm Sun) was the city's first, founded in 1714 by Peter himself. Forget the campy exhibits about peoples outside the former USSR – the big draw here is the old anatomy theatre with selections from Peter's original kunstkammer. While this translates from German to 'art chamber', the bloodthirsty crowds are really here to see Peter's collection of monstrosities, notably preserved freaks, two-headed mutant foetuses and odd body parts.

Menshikov Palace (Map 4)

Alexander Menshikov was a close friend (many now say lover) of Peter the Great. In 1707 Menshikov put up one of the city's first buildings, a riverside palace (Dvorets Menshikova; % 23 11 22; Universitetskaya nab 15; adult/student R200/100; open 10.30am-4.30pm Tues-Sun) just west of the Twelve Colleges. He effectively ran Russia from here for three years between Peter's death and his own exile. Later the palace was a military academy and then it went to seed until Lenin suggested it be saved. Now its impressive interiors are again filled with period art and furniture as a branch of the Hermitage. An English-language tour is included in the price.

Twelve Colleges (Map 4)

West of the Museum of Anthropology & Ethnography and marked by a statue of the scientist-poet Mikhail Lomonosov is Mendeleevskaya linia and the skinny, 400m-long Twelve Colleges building. Built originally for Peter's government ministries, it's now part of the university, which stretches out behind it.

Academy of Arts Museum (Map 4)

The Russian Academy of Arts' Research Museum *(Muzey Akademii Khudozhestv; ☎ 213 64 96, excursions ☎ 213 35 78; Universitetskaya nab 17; adult/student R60/30; open 11am-6pm Wed-Sun)* doesn't get many visitors but is well worth exploring. It's guarded by two imported Egyptian sphinxes said to be about 3500 years old. Boys would live in this building from the age of five until they graduated at age 15 – it was an experiment to create a new species of human: the artist. It mostly worked since graduates included Ilya Repin, Karl Bryullov and Anton Losenko.

Inside are works done by academy students and faculty since its founding in 1775, including many studies, plus temporary exhibitions. Visit the 3rd floor, where the models for the original versions of Smolny, St Isaac's, and the Alexander Nevsky monastery are kept, and take a peek into the fabulous old library.

A short walk away, opposite the Andreevsky market, is **Apteka 13** *(☎ 23 13 18; 7-ya linia 16; open 8am-8pm Mon-Fri, 8am-5pm Sat & Sun)*. Built in 1902, the gorgeous interiors will blow away your notion of a drugstore; pharmaceutical tools, jars and porcelain from the 17th and 18th centuries are on display.

Churches (Map 4)

The 1771 **Church of St Catherine** *(Tserkov Yekateriny; Bolshoy pr 1)* is now a sound studio (with purportedly the best acoustics in the city) owned by the record company Melodia.

The stunning 1895 neo-Byzantine **Temple of the Assumption** *(Uspenskoe Podvore Optina Pustin; ☎ 321 74 73; cnr nab Leytenanta Shmidta & 15-ya linia; open daily)* was closed in 1934 and from 1957 was turned into the city's first – and very popular – year-round skating rink. Now a working church, it's still in the process of being reconstructed but is worth a look.

Intriguingly off limits, at the far western end of Bolshoy prospekt and on the grounds of what has always been a military training school, is the **Church of Mother of God the Merciful** (Miluyoushchi Bozhe Materi; 1889–98), designed by V Kosyakov, who also did the Naval Cathedral in Kronshtadt. The Soviets converted it into a surreal training base for future submariners and for life-saving exercises. The Russian Byzantine exterior is more or less intact, but the interior has been completely gutted, and there is now a 26m-high tube filled with 333 tonnes of water, in which young divers practise their craft.

PETROGRAD SIDE

Petrograd Side (Petrogradskaya storona) is a cluster of delta islands between the Malaya Neva and Bolshaya Nevka channels. On little Zayachy Island, Peter the Great first broke ground for St Petersburg, founding the Peter & Paul Fortress. There's some fabulous architecture here, too – just stroll up Kamennoostrovsky prospekt for a Style Moderne treat.

Peter & Paul Fortress

Founded in 1703, the **Peter & Paul Fortress** *(Petropavlovskaya krepost; Peter & Paul Fortress Map; ☎ 238 45 50; free entry to grounds, admission to all buildings adult/student R120/60; open 10am-5pm Thur-Mon, 10am-4pm Tues)* is the oldest building in St Petersburg. Peter planned it as a defence against the Swedes but defeated them before it was finished. Its main use up to 1917 was as a political prison; famous residents included Dostoevsky, Gorky, Trotsky and Lenin's older brother, Alexander. One of the best things you can do here is walk part of the **battlements** *(adult/student R50/30; open 10am-10pm daily)*; the entrance is at the Peter I Bastion.

The 122m-tall, needle-thin spire of the **Cathedral of SS Peter & Paul** remains one of the defining landmarks of St Petersburg. Don't miss the magnificent baroque interior. All of Russia's prerevolutionary rulers from Peter the Great onward, except Peter II and Ivan VI, are buried here.

In the fort's southwest corner are reconstructions of the grim cells of the **Trubetskoy Bastion**; one of its first inmates was Peter's own son Alexey, whose torture Peter is said to have overseen personally.

In the south wall is **Nevsky Gate**, a later addition, where prisoners were loaded onto boats for execution. Notice the plaques showing water levels of famous floods. Outside

ST PETERSBURG

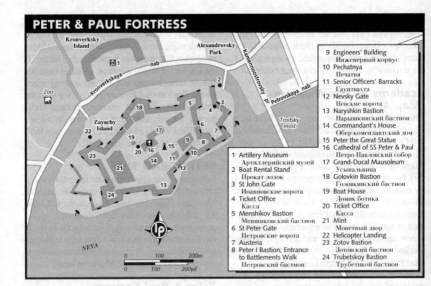

PETER & PAUL FORTRESS

Kronverksky Island
Alexandrovsky Park
Kamennoostrovsky Pr
Petrovskaya nab
nab
Kronverkskaya
Zoo
Zayachy Island
Troitsky most
NEVA

0   100   200m
0   100   200yd

1 Artillery Museum
  Артиллерийский музей
2 Boat Rental Stand
  Прокат лодок
3 St John Gate
  Иоанновские ворота
4 Ticket Office
  Касса
5 Menshikov Bastion
  Меншиковский бастион
6 St Peter Gate
  Петровские ворота
7 Austeria
8 Peter I Bastion; Entrance
  to Battlements Walk
  Петровский бастион

9 Engineers' Building
  Инженерный корпус
10 Pechatnya
   Печатня
11 Senior Officers' Barracks
   Гауптвахта
12 Nevsky Gate
   Невские ворота
13 Naryshkin Bastion
   Нарышкинский бастион
14 Commandant's House
   Обер-комендантский дом
15 Peter the Great Statue
16 Cathedral of SS Peter & Paul
   Петро-Павловский собор
17 Grand-Ducal Mausoleum
   Усыпальница
18 Golovkin Bastion
   Головкинский бастион
19 Boat House
   Домик ботика
20 Ticket Office
   Касса
21 Mint
   Монетный двор
22 Helicopter Landing
23 Zotov Bastion
   Зотовский бастион
24 Trubetskoy Bastion
   Трубетцкой бастион

are fine views of the whole central water-front. Around to the left in summer is a fascinating collection of fishers, joggers and standing sunbathers (standing's said to give you a *proper* tan), and in winter you might see people swimming in holes cut through the ice (an activity that's said to be 'good for the health').

At noon every day a cannon is fired from **Naryshkin Bastion**, scaring the daylights out of the tourists. The **Commandant's House** is a Museum of the History of St Petersburg up to the 1917 revolution, and the **Engineers' Building** has a museum complete with rotating exhibitions.

It's a pleasant walk to the fortress across either Troitsky or Dvortsovy mosts, or across Alexandrovsky Park from metro Gorkovskaya.

Around Alexandrovsky Park

Across the moat, in the fort's original arsenal, is the **Artillery Museum** (*Artilleriysky muzey; Peter & Paul Fortress Map; ☎ 232 02 96; Alexandrovsky park 7; adult/student R90/45; open 11am-6pm Wed-Sun*). It's great if you like weapons.

West of the museum is the **zoo** (*Peter & Paul Fortress Map; ☎ 232 48 28; Alexandrovsky park 1; adult/child R40/10; open 10am-7pm daily May-Sept, 10am-4pm Tues-Sun Oct-Apr*), full of miserable animals. The

lack of funds is pitifully evident, but all things considered, it's pretty well kept. Near the zoo is a large **amusement park** (*Map 3*), complete with bumper cars, a couple of small roller coasters and the like.

East and behind the museum is **Alexandrovsky Park**, a neat hang-out in summer, but too close to traffic and thronged with people to be peaceful. In the northern part of the park, the **Planetarium** (*Map 3; ☎ 233 53 12; Alexandrovsky park 4; shows R30-50; open 10.30am-6pm Tues-Sun*) offers cool 50-minute star shows throughout the day.

Across Kamennoostrovsky prospekt from the park is a working **mosque** (*Map 3*) built from 1910 to 1914 and modelled on Samarkand's Gur Emir Mausoleum where Timur (Tamerlaine) is buried.

Museum of Political History in Russia (Map 3)

East of Kamennoostrovsky prospekt is the Kshesinskaya Palace, which contains the Museum of Political History in Russia (*☎ 233 72 20; ul Kuybysheva 4; adult/child R60/30; open 11am-5pm Sun-Thur*) – way more interesting than it sounds. The Bolsheviks made it their headquarters, and Lenin often gave speeches from the balcony of this elegant Style Moderne palace that once belonged to Matilda Kshesinskaya, famous ballet dancer and one-time lover of Tsar Nicholas II. Go in to see the house itself, the best Soviet kitsch in town (including socialist realist porcelain with workers' slogans), and some incredibly rare satirical caricatures of Lenin published in magazines between the 1917 revolutions (the same drawings a few months later would have got the artist imprisoned, or worse).

Peter's Cabin (Map 3)

St Petersburg's first residence is a log cabin (Domik Petra; ☎ 232 45 76; Petrovskaya nab 6; adult/child R20/10; open 10am-5pm Wed-Mon) where Peter lived in 1703 while supervising the construction of the city. It's preserved in a patch of trees a short walk east of the fortress.

Cruiser Aurora (Map 3)

In the Nevka opposite Hotel St Petersburg is the Aurora (Avrora; ☎ 230 84 40; Petrovskaya nab; admission free; open 10.30am-4pm Tues-Thur & Sat & Sun), a mothballed cruiser from the Russo-Japanese War, built in 1900. From a downstream mooring on the night of 25 October 1917, its crew fired a blank round from the forward gun, demoralising the Winter Palace's defenders and marking the start of the October Revolution. During WWII, the Russians sank it to protect it from German bombs. Now, restored and painted up in pretty colours, it's a museum that is swarming with kids on weekends.

Other Museums

Petrograd Side includes a handful of specialist museums that you might consider visiting. The Kirov Museum (Map 3; ☎ 346 02 89; Kamennoostrovsky pr 26/28; admission R10; open 11am-6pm Thur-Tues) is in the 4th-floor apartment where Sergei Kirov, one of Stalin's henchmen, spent his last days. His murder started a wave of deadly repression throughout Russia. Don't miss the Party leader's death clothes, hung out for reverence: the tiny, bloodstained hole in the back of his cap is where he was shot, and the torn seam on his jacket's left breast is where doctors tried to revive his heart.

A unique conceptual exhibition based on abstractions and ideas, the Sigmund Freud Museum of Dreams (Map 2; ☎ 235 28 57; W www.freud.ru; Bolshoy pr 18A; admission without/with tour R30/140; open noon-5pm Tues & Sun) is an outgrowth of the Psycho-analytic Institute that houses it. It aims to stimulate your subconscious via projection as you struggle to read the display symbolising what Freud himself would have dreamt of in a dimly lit, ambient hall.

Opera buffs will thrill to the lovingly curated Chaliapin House Museum (Map 2; ☎ 234 26 98; ul Graftio 2B; adult/student R30; open noon-6pm Wed-Sun), where the great singer Fyodor Chaliapin last lived before fleeing post-revolutionary Russia in 1922. The kindly babushkas in charge will happily play the singer's recordings as you wander around.

Botanical Gardens (Map 3)

This quiet jungle in eastern Aptekarsky (Apothecary) Island, northeast of the Petrogradskaya metro station and across the Karpovka Canal, was once a garden of medicinal plants that gave the island its name. The botanical gardens (☎ 346 36 39; ul Professora Popova 2; free admission to grounds, all greenhouses R30; open 11am-4pm Sat-Thur) contains 26 greenhouses on a 22-hectare site and, although faded from its glory days, it's still a pleasant place to stroll. In the early 1900s, these were the second-biggest botanical gardens in the world, behind only London's Kew Gardens. One of the highlights is the 'tsaritsa nochi' (selenicereus pteranthus), a flowering cactus which blossoms only one night a year, usually in mid-June. On this night, the gardens stay open until morning for visitors to gawk at the marvel and sip champagne.

Kirovsky Islands (Map 2)

This is the collective name for the outer delta islands of Petrograd Side – Kamenny, Yelagin and Krestovsky. Once marshy jungles, the islands were granted to 18th- and 19th-century court favourites and developed into elegant playgrounds. Still mostly parkland, they're huge leafy venues for picnics, river sports and white-nights cavorting.

Kamenny Island This island's charm, seclusion and century-old dachas (now inhabited by the wealthy), combined with winding lanes and a series of canals, lakes and ponds, make a stroll here pleasant at any time of year. At the eastern end of the island the Church of St John the Baptist (Tserkov Rozhestva Ioanna Predtechi; 1776–81) seems to have found better use as a basketball court.

Behind it the big, classical **Kamennoostrovsky Palace**, built by Catherine the Great for her son, is now a weedy military sanatorium.

The island also boasts a **government retreat** *(Bokovaya al)*, used by the president when he's in town and by other bigwigs when he's not.

Look for the tree, said to have been planted by Peter the Great, almost blocking naberezhnaya reki Krestovki in the southern part of the island near the Maly-Krestovsky most.

Kamenny Island is a short walk south of metro Chyornaya Rechka (turn right as you exit, cross the bridge and you're there).

Yelagin Island The centrepiece of this 2km-long, pedestrian-only island *(admission R10)* is the **Yelagin Palace** *(Yelaginsky dvorets; ☎ 430 11 31; adult/student R90/45; open 10am-6pm Wed-Sun)*, built for his mother by Tsar Alexander I, who had architect Carlo Rossi landscape the entire island while he was at it. The palace, with beautifully restored interiors, is to your right as you cross the footbridge from Kamenny Island.

The rest of the island is a lovely park, with a plaza at the western end looking out to the Gulf of Finland. You can rent rowing boats in the northern part of the island, while at the entrance from Krestovsky Island mountain bikes can be hired *(R500 for the day, with a deposit of your passport or R4000)*.

Krestovsky Island The biggest of the three islands, Krestovsky consists mostly of the vast **Seaside Park of Victory** (Primorsky Park Pobedy), dotted with sports fields and the 100,000-seat **Kirov Stadium**.

Bus Nº 71 from metro Petrogradskaya runs the length of Krestovsky Island to Kirov Stadium. Trolleybus Nº 34 from near metro Petrogradskaya terminates on Krestovsky near the footbridge to Yelagin Island.

VYBORG SIDE (MAP 3)

Peter the Great had no apparent interest in the far side of the Neva, and today, beyond the embankment and Finland Station (see the boxed text 'Historic Railway Stations' earlier in this chapter), there are few attractions among the factories and railway lines.

Kresty Prison

The perfect antidote to all of St Petersburg's high culture is a visit to its dark underbelly: Kresty Prison. This is the city's main holding prison and a deathly grim place it is too. Opened in 1892 with 1150 individual cells (later reconstructed and designed to hold 2065 inmates), these days close to 10,000 poor buggers call it 'home'. Six-bed cells hold 10 to 15 people, sleeping in rotation. Tuberculosis is rife, fleas abound, and there are masked guards with ferocious dogs policing the halls.

Tours are possible of the prison and small museum *(☎ 542 68 61, 542 47 35; Arsenalnaya nab 7; admission R250; tours noon, 1.30pm & 3pm Sat & Sun)*. You'll be led through the church on the premises, through some of the holding areas, and into the inner courtyards where there's an intriguing little museum. Here the guide will tell you about past residents – such as Trotsky and the entire Provisional Government from 1917 – and you can view objects made by prisoners with lots of time on their hands. Most impressive is a chess set with a 'cops and robbers' motif made entirely from glazed bits of hardened, chewed bread. To gain entry you'll need your passport; photography is strictly forbidden.

If you opt out of the tour, on any given day you can see well-wishers lining Arsenalnaya naberezhnaya until they are chased away by police patrols who try to discourage this sort of thing. The visitors' arm-waving may look like intricate dance moves, but it is, in fact, a crude code. The prisoner makes himself known by holding an article of clothing out the window (only their hands are visible, stuck through slats or holes in the steel mesh). When the friend down on the street identifies their man, they start waving their arms about, tracing Cyrillic characters in the air. The prisoner waves up and down to signal 'I understand', and side to side to signal 'repeat'. Under this method, after five minutes of waving, one can clearly discern the message, 'I-c-a-l-l-e-d-M-i-s-h-a'!

The inmates have a better way of communicating. Notice all those bits of folded newspaper littering the footpath? These have all been flown over from inside the prison with a blowpipe, with a written message folded inside. If you see one of these flying towards you, duck – they fly quick and painfully. Police regularly patrol the embankment and will shoo you away if they suspect you are lingering.

St Petersburg for Children

There's heaps to do with kids in St Petersburg – there are even museums your kids will like! For starters, the Kunstkammer in the Museum of Anthropology & Ethnography is an all-time favourite with its display of mutants in jars, as is the Museum of Zoology for its stuffed animals. The Flowers Exhibition Hall near Smolny has great tropical plants to gawk at. Then, of course, there's the zoo and circus, the Peter & Paul Fortress and the Planetarium, all of which have special kids' programs.

The city's parks are first rate; there's a full-scale amusement park right behind the Peter & Paul Fortress, and a smaller one in the City Children's Park. There's a great children's **playground** (Map 3) on the eastern side of ulitsa Bolshaya Pushkarskaya just north of ulitsa Lenina, Petrograd Side. Also check out **Ramses Playground** (Map 1) outside the centre, on ulitsa Ziny Portnovoy between houses No 6 and 8 (from metro Leninsky Prospekt, walk west one block and turn right). Created by retired circus clown Arkady Kontsepolsky and named after his beloved dog Ramses, this is a charming, inventive place that any child will love.

There are rowing boat rental outlets by the Peter & Paul Fortress, and on Yelagin Island, where you can also rent bikes.

A few theatres in town cater to kids, and these can be a real treat, even if children don't understand the language. (See the Theatre section under Entertainment later.)

Piskaryovskoe Cemetery (Map 1)

Some half-million WWII victims are buried in mass graves in this cemetery (☎ 247 57 16; *Nepokoryonnykh pr; admission free; open 10am-6pm daily*). Nearly 200 raised mounds are marked only by simple plaques engraved with a year and either a red star or hammer and sickle (indicating a military or civilian grave mound). At the entrance is an exhibit of photographs from the Blockade that need no captions. The cemetery is about 35 minutes from the city centre on public transport. From metro Ploshchad Muzhestva turn left, cross Nepokoryonnykh prospekt and take bus No 123. It's the sixth stop.

ACTIVITIES
Banya

Tired? Frustrated by Russian bureaucracy? A good beating may be all you need – or all you need to give! Here are a few of the better *banya* (bathhouses; see the boxed text in the European Russia Facts for the Visitor chapter for correct *banya* etiquette):

Bani 43 (Map 4; ☎ 311 70 41; nab reki Moyki 82) You can book this whole place out for R300 per hour at any time, and the friendly guys who run it can arrange for massages (R150) and will get you beer. A Russian and expat crowd often meets here on Sunday nights.

Kruglye Bani (Map 1; ☎ 550 09 85; Karbysheva ul 29A; regular/lyux-class R30/90; open 8am-

9pm Tues-Sun) Expats meet here at 9pm Wednesday and enjoy a co-ed *lyux banya*. The banya is opposite metro Ploshchad Muzhestva – look for the round building.

Mitninskaya Banya (Map 5; ☎ 271 71 19; ul Mitninskaya; admission R30; open 8am-10pm Fri-Tues, last entry 8.30pm) This is the last *banya* in the city to be heated with a wood furnace, just like in the countryside. Experts swear by it. You'll see lots of tattooed bodies here.

Yachting

Yachts and other boats can be rented at negotiated rates from private captains at the **Sea and River Yacht Club** (Map 2; ☎ 235 01 11; nab Martynova 92, Krestovsky Island; open 9am-6pm Mon-Fri). **The Baltic Shipping Company Yacht Club** (Map 2; ☎ 235 39 35) at the same place also arranges tours to Lakes Onega and Ladoga. **Solnechny Parus** (Map 3; ☎ 279 43 10; W www.solpar.ru; ul Vosstania 55) is a recommended agency that organises yacht cruises in the Gulf of Finland.

If you plan on bringing your own vessel into St Petersburg, see W sailing.dkart.ru for detailed information on custom points, anchorage sites etc, in the St Petersburg area.

Ice Skating & Skiing

You can go ice skating at the **Yubileyny Sports Palace** (Map 2; ☎ 119 56 01; Dobrolyubova pr 18, Petrograd Side; admission R150 plus R60 per hour and skate rental) and at **Dvorets Sporta SKA** (Map 2; ☎ 237 00 73;

Zhdanovskaya nab 2; indoor facilities open Fri, Sat, Sun year-round 11pm-5am), which has indoor and outdoor facilities. Both are close to metro Sportivnaya. Yubileyny doesn't rent out skates, and only lets people in (with their own skates) on Sundays around noon.

Ice Palace (☎ 118 66 20; *per hour including skate rental R180, with your own skates R120)*, right near metro Prospekt Bolshevikov, is a recent addition to the scene. Built for the 2000 World Ice Hockey Championships, it's absolutely fancy. Although mainly used for concerts now, it does have a public skating rink. Hours are irregular, so call on the day for more details.

Larger sporting goods shops carry cross-country skiing equipment for about half the price back home. Popular cross-country day-skiing destinations are **Toksovo** and **Tagalovo**, reachable by *elektrichka* from Finland Station, and the raised grounds surrounding Pulkovo Observatory south of the airport.

Sporting Facilities

The best sports complex in the city is called (you'll never guess) **Sports Complex** (*Map 3; ☎ 238 16 32; Kronverksky pr 9A; admission R100 for 90 minutes; open 7am-11pm daily)* on Kamennoostrovsky prospekt's east side, across from metro Gorkovskaya. Its 25m pool, under a glass roof, is heavenly and staff will let you in without the required medical certificate if you look clean. There's also a weights room, and the staff are a good source of information for spectator sporting events in the city.

Diving

Red Shark Dive Club (☎ 271 48 20; W *www .redshark.spb.ru)* offers PADI diving courses in English and can arrange wreck dives for more experienced divers in the Gulf of Finland and Lake Ladoga. The club can be contacted via Sindbad Travel (see Travel Agencies under Information earlier in this chapter).

LANGUAGE COURSES

The *St Petersburg Times* advertises many private tutors and classes, but the **Herzen State Pedagogical University** (*Map 6; ☎ 311 60 88; W www.herzen.spb.ru; Kazanskaya ul 6)* runs excellent courses, from two weeks to graduate programs several years long, 20 hours per week, for US$4 to US$7 an hour in groups of two to eight. **Liden & Denz** (*Map 5;*

☎ 325 22 41; W *www.lidenz.ru; Transportny per 11)* offers well-structured courses from US$650 for a two-week intensive program.

ORGANISED TOURS & GUIDES

Eclectica (*Map 6; ☎/fax 279 77 72; W www .eclectica.spb.ru; Ligovsky pr 1, office #313)* and the **City Excursion Bureau** (*Map 6; ☎ 312 05 27, fax 311 40 19; Sadovaya ul 26/28)* offer a large range of city and suburb tours for groups of two or more in English (and several other languages with advance notice).

For something more exotic, **Monomex Tours** (*Map 5; ☎ 445 01 59, fax 324 73 22; W www.2russia.com; Zanevsky pr 1)* organises conferences for business groups as well as sociological tours, including Russian Child Rearing Practices and Police Enforcement.

Peter Kozyrev runs the excellent **Peter's Tours** (☎ 329 80 18; e *pkozyrev@hotmail. com)*, which offers walking tours that depart the HI St Petersburg Hostel at 10.30am daily. He also offers cool variations, such as a Dostoevsky tour and a food tour of the city. You can customise other tours to suit your interests. It's US$8 per person for a four- to five-hour walk, US$10 per hour for private tours.

Sasha Bogdanov (☎ 356 72 06) is also affable and knowledgeable, offering unique tours. He has encyclopaedic knowledge of the city, equally at home with students and the elderly. His speciality is providing visitors with alternative experiences of the city, taking them to off-beat nooks and crannies tourists rarely see. His rate is US$20 per day.

There's an excursion booth at the corner of Gostiny Dvor (where Nevsky prospekt and Dumskaya ulitsa intersect) that sells tickets for Russian-language tours only.

Helicopter Tours

Baltic Airlines (☎ 311 00 84, 104 16 76) offers helicopter flights over the Neva between the Admiralty and Smolny, which take off from in front of the Peter & Paul Fortress on weekends; just show up and wait for the next tour (US$30 for 10 to 15 minutes). You can also arrange a parachute jump with the same company for US$200.

River & Canal Trips

From May to October excursion boats ply the rivers and canals at all hours. Don't leave without taking one of these tours; it's the ideal way to view the city's romantic architecture.

There are many tours – excursion boats are found at the Anichkov most landing on the Fontanka River, just off Nevsky prospekt; on the Neva outside the Hermitage and the Admiralty; at the Dekabristov landing; along Griboedova Canal, just north of Nevsky prospekt, and one block south near Bankovsky most; and along the Moyka River at Nevsky prospekt and one block south.

Prices and frequency range; expect to pay R150 for 40 minutes. The cheapest tours leave from in front of the Admiralty (R60 for 30 minutes). The tours are longer from the Anichkov most (about 75 minutes for R210). There are also plenty of opportunities to use small boats as your own private water taxis. With boats docked along the Griboedova Canal and Moyka River, and near the Hermitage No 2 landing, you can haggle your way to anywhere you like. Prices may start at US$60 an hour, but you can often get down to around US$40 an hour or less for a small group. You can do whatever you like on these rides – the drivers have already seen it all.

SPECIAL EVENTS

In St Petersburg the **White Nights arts festival** lasts all June. The **Russian Winter** (25 December to 5 January) and **Goodbye Russian Winter** (late February to early March) festivities are centred outside the city, with *troyka* (horse-drawn sleigh) rides, folk shows and performing bears.

The **Mariinsky Ballet Festival** is from 10 to 18 February. The **St Petersburg Music Spring** is an international classical music festival held in April or May. The **Sergey Kuryokhin International Festival** (SKIF), held over three days in late April, has a stunning array of local and international music and dance. Mid-November, **Osenie Ritmy** (Autumn Rhythms) centres around St Petersburg's jazz clubs.

See the European Russia Facts for the Visitor chapter for general Russian holidays.

PLACES TO STAY – BUDGET
Homestays & Private Flats

.The **Host Families Association** (HOFA; Map 5; ☎/fax 275 19 92; ⓦ http://webcenter.ru /~hofa; ul Tavricheskaya 5/25) is the most established and reliable agency for finding private accommodation. Its city centre homestay programs start with basic B&B (singles/doubles from US$25/40). **Ost-West Kontaktservice** (see Travel Agencies under Informa-

tion earlier in this chapter) can arrange homestays and apartment rentals from about US$30 a day.

Pushka Inn (Map 6; ☎ 312 09 57, fax 318 47 12; ⓦ www.pushkainn.ru; nab reki Moyki 14) has very central, modern furnished flats in the building above its popular café-bar. These start at US$60 a night for two and go up to US$180 for a flat sleeping up to six. The rates include continental breakfast, taxes and Internet access.

Among the several accommodation agencies, check **Bed & Breakfast** (Map 6; ☎ 315 19 17; ⓦ www.bednbreakfast.sp.ru; Bolshaya Konyushennaya ul 3), which has good central deals from US$20 per person per night. Also see the listings in the *St Petersburg Times*.

It's also possible to stay in a private flat for about US$10 a night by going with one of the older women who approach travellers arriving off major trains at Moscow Station. Use your judgement about who to trust (many really are genuine folk in need of extra cash) and check how far from the city centre their place is before accompanying them.

Hostels & Student Accommodation

HI St Petersburg Hostel (Map 6; ☎ 329 80 18, fax 329 90 19; ⓦ www.ryh.ru; 3-ya Sovetskaya ul 28; metro Ploshchad Vosstania; dorm beds/ double including breakfast US$19/48) is a longrunning hostel that remains popular and is just a five-minute walk northeast of Moscow Station. Dorms have three to six beds and there's one double; all rates are slightly cheaper from November to March and for ISIC and HI cardholders. This is a clean and friendly place, and although the bathroom situation is far from ideal there's a kitchen for self-catering and a video room. The hostel's visa support service is reliable as is its Sindbad Travel Agency. Reserve by fax or email. Note they don't accept credit card payment in the hostel.

Some people prefer **International Holiday Hostel** (Map 3; ☎/fax 327 10 70 or 327 10 33; e info@hostel.spb.ru; Arsenalnaya nab 9; metro Ploshchad Lenina; dorm beds/singles/doubles including breakfast US$14/37/38, private doubles including bathroom and satellite TV US$50), a convivial place just southeast of Finland Station and next door to Kresty Prison. It's quiet and a little out of the way, but does have a kitchen, video room and the advantage of an outdoor terrace overlooking the Neva – a lovely spot to while away the summer evenings. Management can also arrange visa support (US$30).

St Petersburg Puppet Hostel (Map 6; ☎ 272 54 01, fax 272 8361; w www.hostelling -russia.ru; ul Nekrasova 12; metro Ploshchad Vosstania; dorm beds/doubles including breakfast US$16/42) is a great option if you can get a bed – central, friendly, cosy and clean. You can book directly or via the HI St Petersburg Hostel. It's a great choice if you're travelling with kids because it gives free tickets to the puppet theatre next door.

Petrovskogo College Student Hostel (Map 4; ☎ 252 75 63, fax 252 65 12; Baltiyskaya ul 26; metro Narvskaya; doubles/triples US$4/6), while not close to the centre, is certainly the cheapest deal. Showers and toilets are passable, and there's a cafeteria. Reserve in advance, though, as it's often full. From the metro walk left (south) down prospekt Stachek away from the Narva Triumphal Gates to Baltiyskaya ulitsa, where you turn left and continue another 500m. It's open year-round.

Hotels
City Centre, South & East of Centre
Out of the way in a boring neighbourhood is **Hotel Kievskaya** (Map 5; ☎ 166 82 50, fax 166 56 93; e info@kievskaia.spb.ru; Dnepropetrovskaya ul 49; metro Ligovsky Prospekt; singles/doubles/triples with shared facilities US$17/22/24, singles/doubles with private facilities from US$28/60) and its stable-mate around the corner, the **Kievsky Filial** (Map 5; ☎ 166 58 11, fax 166 56 98; Kurskaya ul 40; same prices as Hotel Kievskaya). Although a little grubby, it's a somewhat friendly Soviet relic slowly undergoing renovation.

Hotel Rus (Map 5; ☎ 273 46 83, fax 279 36 00; Artilleryskaya ul 1; metro Chernyshevskaya; singles/doubles including breakfast US$44/63) is a Soviet relic. It's threadbare in places, but has acceptable rooms and English-speaking staff who are reasonably friendly.

Hotel Neva (Map 3; ☎ 278 05 04, fax 273 25 93; ul Chaikovskogo 17; metro Chernyshevskaya; singles/doubles US$36/52) may have a fancily decorated stairwell (it was once a bordello) but the cheapest rooms here are drab, although they do have TV and fridge and are relatively spacious. Travellers seldom make bad reports on the hotel; it's only a short bus or trolleybus ride from Nevsky prospekt.

Herzen University Hotel (Map 6; ☎ 314 74 72, fax 314 76 59; ul Kazanskaya 6; singles/doubles US$42/96), 120m behind the Kazan Cathedral, has a great location. The old-fashioned rooms, with TV and fridge, are fine, but the hotel cannot register your visa, so you'll have to find alternative ways of doing this. Availability is tight, especially in summer, so it's best to make a reservation, for which there will be a 25% extra charge for the first night.

Petrograd & Vyborg Sides On the mainland, north of Kamenny Island, **Hotel Vyborgskaya** (Map 1; ☎ 246 91 41, fax 246 81 87; Torzhkovskaya ul 3; metro Chyornaya Rechka; singles/doubles with breakfast from US$30/33) is nothing fancy and staff only speak Russian, but it's an otherwise pleasant place. Head left out of the metro, then follow the main road over the little bridge. The hotel is to your right.

Big and Soviet-modern outside, and plain inside, **Dvorets Molodyozhy Hotel** (Palace of Youth; Map 2; ☎ 234 32 78; ul Professora Popova 47; metro Petrogradskaya or Chkalovskaya; singles/doubles/triples including breakfast US$48/50/57) will do, but only if you're really stuck. Call ahead because it's often full (or at least staff claim it is). It's a 20-minute walk to the metro. On the same site is an entertainment emporium including billiards, bowling, crazy golf, sauna, pool and concert hall.

PLACES TO STAY – MID-RANGE
City Centre & South
Hotel Oktyabrskaya (Map 6; ☎ 118 15 15, fax 315 75 01; Ligovsky pr 10; singles/doubles

with breakfast US$50-80/80-110), bang opposite the Moscow Station, has done plenty of upgrading in recent years. It's a sprawling place, but the new rooms are fine and the staff are pleasant. It offers a full range of services, including visa support for US$30. Prices range according to the season, with May to October the most expensive period.

Of a similar standard and just as convenient is the smaller **Oktyabrsky Filial** *(Map 6; ☎ 277 72 81, fax 315 75 01; Ligovsky pr 43/45; singles/doubles with breakfast US$60/ 92)*, sister establishment of the Oktyabrskaya. It's almost always full, so book well in advance.

Matisov Domik *(Map 4; ☎ 318 54 45, fax 318 74 19; nab reki Pryazhki 3/1; singles/ doubles with breakfast US$60/100)* is an excellent choice. About a 10-minute walk west of the Mariinsky Theatre, this family-run place has 24 super-clean rooms, all with phone, TV and free soft drinks, and a secure courtyard for parking. From the Mariinsky Theatre, walk west on ulitsa Dekabristov, up to the canal. Cross it, turn right and the hotel is 250m ahead.

Marshal Hotel *(Map 3; ☎ 279 99 55, fax 279 75 00; e marshal.hotel@tpark.spb.ru; Shpalernaya ul 41; metro Chernyshevskaya; doubles with breakfast from US$80)* is a small, new hotel on the way to Smolny Cathedral. It has reasonably large, modern rooms and is in a quiet location.

Hotel Moskva *(Map 5; ☎ 274 30 01, fax 274 21 30; pl Alexandra Nevskogo 2; metro Ploshchad Alexandra Nevskogo; singles/ doubles including breakfast US$69/91)* is a monstrous, three-star place sitting atop the metro, favoured by package-tour groups. The rooms are not that bad for the price; ask for one at the back where it's quieter.

Hotel Neptune *(Map 5; ☎ 324 4610, fax 324 46 11; w www.neptun.spb.ru; nab Obvodnogo kanala 93A; metro Pushkinskaya; singles/doubles with shower US$80/120, with bathroom US$120/150, all including breakfast)* is managed by Best Western and has stylish, decent-sized rooms. It's great value given that its rates include a morning sauna and a swim. There's a bowling alley in the complex, too, and the walk here from the metro station is pleasant.

Hotel Sovetskaya *(Map 4; ☎ 329 95 99, fax 251 88 90; e hotel@sovetksaya.com; 43/1 Lermontovsky pr; metro Tekhnologich-*

esky Institut; singles/doubles including breakfast US$49/82) is another Soviet behemoth given a flashy makeover, but its spacious, comfortable rooms do have great views across the city. There's a range of restaurants here (including Fontanka, which specialises in traditional Russian grub), a business centre, sauna and cheesy nightclub.

Hotel Pulkovskaya *(Map 1; ☎ 123 51 22, fax 123 51 16; pl Pobedy 1; metro Moskovskaya; singles/doubles/twins with breakfast US$88/103/153)* is a Finnish-built hotel about a 20-minute metro ride south of the centre, and staying here has the main advantage of being close to the airport. It's a pretty anonymous place but a step above other package-tour giants, with comfortable rooms, good service and decent restaurants and lobby bar.

Vyborg Side

Hotel St Petersburg *(Map 3; ☎ 380 19 19, fax 380 19 20; w www.hotel-spb.ru; Pirogovskaya nab 5/2; metro Ploshchad Lenina; singles/ doubles including breakfast from US$50/ 60)*, a big three-star place, has unrenovated but acceptable front rooms with amazing views over the Neva (but also traffic noise if you open the windows). The cheaper rooms, naturally, face away from the river, but all in all it's a good deal for this category.

Deson-Ladoga Hotel *(Map 5; ☎ 528 56 28, fax 528 54 48; pr Shaumyana 26; metro Novocherkasskaya; singles/doubles/twins including breakfast US$108/126/146)* is a smaller, modernised hotel in a quiet area, but reasonably close to the metro. The rooms' decor leaves something to be desired, but the staff are professional and speak English.

Okhtinskaya-Victoria *(Map 3; ☎ 227 44 38, fax 227 26 18; Bolsheohtinsky pr 4; singles/ doubles including breakfast US$83/96)* is on the opposite side of the river to Smolny Cathedral and some of its rooms have great views across to it. Staff at the reception are a bit abrupt, but the rooms are clean and simply decorated. Rates are around US$10 less from November to March and the hotel offers a shuttle bus to the city centre for R20.

Northeast of the centre, **Hotel Kareliya** *(Map 3; ☎ 118 40 48, fax 226 35 11; e b-kar elia@online.ru; ul Marshala Tukhachevskogo 27/2; singles/doubles with breakfast US$31/ 36)* is clean, comfortable and has friendly staff. It's great value, especially if you go for

ST PETERSBURG

the acceptable old-style rooms (the modernised ones are more than twice the price and have tacky furnishings). It's a good option for motorists since there's secure parking near the hotel. Minibus No 28 from Moscow Station and No 320 from Finland Station regularly come here.

Vasilevsky Island

Pribaltiyskaya Hotel (Map 4; ☎ 356 01 58, fax 356 44 96; e market@pribalt.spb.su; ul Korablestroyteley 14; metro Ploshchad Lenina; singles/doubles including breakfast US$160/ 180) is popular with package-tour groups. This behemoth has fair service and big, clean rooms with panoramic views of the Gulf of Finland (ask). There's a bowling alley, billiards hall and sauna on the premises – just as well since it's miles from anywhere. Bus 147 goes here regularly from the city centre.

PLACES TO STAY – TOP END

The following hotels are all on or within easy walking distance of Nevsky prospekt. We list high-season (May to September) prices, onto which you should add 20% VAT and 5% local tax. Winter rates (November to March) are often quite a bit lower and many places will offer discounts for weekend stays and special packages. Investigate booking through a travel agency, since they often get better rates. Note also that at all these hotels the buffet breakfast costs extra, typically US$22 although the Grand Hotel Europe gets away with US$29!

The five-star **Grand Hotel Europe** (Map 6; ☎ 329 60 00, fax 329 60 01; w www.grand -hotel-europe.com; Mikhailovskaya ul 1/7; singles/doubles/suites from US$350/390/ 500) has suitably lavish rooms, some spectacular but also some smaller than you would expect. The original gorgeous Style Moderne interiors, along with a baroque facade designed by Rossi, have been restored to their late-19th-century glory. There are shopping arcades in the lobby, several bars and restaurants, and a harpist strumming away on the mezzanine.

Hotel Astoria (Map 5; ☎ 313 57 57, fax 313 50 59; w www.roccofortehotels.com; ul Bolshaya Morskaya 39; singles/doubles/suites from US$325/350/460), right in front of St Isaac's Cathedral, is the very essence of old-world class. The pricier rooms and suites are decorated with original period antique furniture. Its Davidovs restaurant is very smart and sometimes groups can dine in the glass-roofed Winter Garden; it's easy to see why Hitler wanted to hold his victory celebration here, and why US President Bush checked in during his 2002 summit with Putin. If nothing else, drop by for afternoon tea (daily from 3pm to 6pm, US$12).

Hotel D'Angleterre (Map 5; ☎ 313 56 66, fax 313 51 25; ul Bolshaya Morskaya 39; singles/doubles/suites from US$260/290/ 330) is the four-star (thus slightly cheaper) establishment in the wing adjoining the Astoria, and sharing the same management as its more expensive neighbour. The rooms have an appealing contemporary design with parquet floors; the hotel's Borsalino brasserie is a relaxed place with great views of St Isaac's and live jazz in the evenings. Morbid romantics might like to know that poet Sergei Esenin hung himself on the 2nd floor of this hotel; it's the room whose balcony is closest to the left-hand corner when facing the hotel.

Radisson SAS Royal St Petersburg (Map 6; ☎ 322 50 00, fax 322 50 01; w www .radissonsas.com; Nevsky pr 49/2; singles/ doubles/suites US$330/350/500) is St Pete's newest top-rank addition. It's a good choice with professional staff and comfortable, if unspectacular, rooms. Although it doesn't have the same range of facilities as its rivals, it's better value if you upgrade slightly to the business-class rooms, where the rates include breakfast.

Corinthia Nevskij Palace Hotel (Map 6; ☎ 380 20 01, fax 380 19 37; Nevsky pr 57; singles/doubles/suites from US$336/384/ 600), which has one of the best restaurants in town (Landskrona – see Places to Eat), caters mainly to business clientele and package-tour groups. The rooms, while excellent, are quite forgettable, but the staff are friendly and the executive-class rooms come with extras such as Internet access and breakfast in the Executive Club lounge.

PLACES TO EAT

The choice of dining options in St Petersburg is enormous, with something to suit all budgets. There's been an explosion of cheap cafés over the last few years, many of which serve good food and are also pleasant places for a drink in the evening. Theme restaurants, everything from those styled on King Arthur's

Camelot to famous film sets, have also become popular: just don't expect the food to be as flash as the decor!

Restaurants

Russian There's plenty to choose from on the comprehensive (English) menu and it's all pretty good at **Bliny Domik** (Map 6; ☎ 315 99 15; Kolokolnaya ul; meals R100-200; open 8am-11pm daily), which is set up like a country home but isn't too kitsch like other places. Of course bliny are featured here, but there are also many vegetarian delights, herbal tea concoctions (including one for the libido), a full breakfast menu – and all using low-cholesterol oil! Live piano music adds to the atmosphere in the evenings.

Circus (Map 6; ☎ 310 10 77; 4 Malaya Sadovaya ul; meals R150-300; open 11am-2am daily) is an imaginatively decorated, cosy basement space with a short-but-sweet menu – all Russian favourites such as bliny, beef stew in a pot and cutlets. Prices are keen for this touristy end of town and the service attentive. You're likely to be treated to a complimentary shot of vodka, too.

Na Zdorovye (Map 2; ☎ 232 40 39; Bolshoy pr 13, Petrograd Side; meals R200-300; open noon-11pm Tues-Sun) is fun and colourful; a heady mix of both Soviet and Russian folk culture dictates the decor here. The food, also a combination of traditional Russian and Soviet cuisine, is imaginatively presented and tasty.

If you think you've seen it all at Na Zdorovye, visit its stable-mate **Rusky Kitsch** (Map 4; ☎ 325 11 22; Universitetskaya nab 25; meals R300; open noon-4am daily), the self-proclaimed 'period of perestroika café'. Here bad taste is raised to an ironic art that, against all odds, works. Check out Brezhnev smooching with Castro on the ceiling of the 'kissing room' and a host of other cheeky touches, including menus secreted in works by Lenin and Stalin. The Russian burger (kangaroo and ostrich meat with deep-fried banana) takes the bad-taste joke way too far, but other dishes (especially the salad bowl) are fine. Come for a drink and a gawp, if nothing else.

In comparison to the previous two listings the designer-Soviet decor at **Propaganda** (Map 6; ☎ 275 35 58; nab reki Fontanki 40; meals R300-400; open noon-5am daily) comes across as restrained. The food is fine (though overpriced), with hamburgers (around R150) being the big drawing card. This is a good late-night haunt since there's 20% off prices from 1am to 5am.

Kotletnaya (Map 6; ☎ 318 40 50; per Grivtsova 7; meals around R200) also has Soviet relics as design touches, but overall the decor retains a stylish touch. Its speciality is *kotlets* (meat cutlets) with sauce fillings, but there are plenty of other options.

You don't need to be visiting the **Russian Vodka Museum** (Map 4; ☎ 312 91 78; Konnogvardeysky bulvar 5; meals R200; open 11am-10pm daily) to eat at its simple *traktir* (tavern), which serves appetising Russian soups and dishes.

Worth going out of your way for is the intimate **Staraya Derevnaya** (Map 2; ☎ 431 00 00; ul Savushkina 72; meals R200-300; open 1pm-11pm daily), a first-rate family-run traditional Russian restaurant, which continues to warrant its solid reputation. From metro Chyornaya Rechka, take any tram three stops or grab a taxi.

Caucasian & Central Asian Every local and expat has a favourite Georgian restaurant; there are plenty to choose from in this category, which also covers Uzbek cuisine.

Salkhino (Map 3; ☎ 232 78 91; Kronverksky pr 25; meals R400; open 11am-11pm daily) is currently one of the most popular Georgian restaurants, serving delicious food in a convivial, arty setting enlivened by the motherly service of its owners. It can get pricey, though, especially if you get into the tasty Georgian wines.

Not far away is **Kafe Tbilisi** (Map 3; ☎ 230 93 91; Sytninskaya ul 10; meals R300; open noon-11pm daily), practically a St Petersburg institution. It's nothing flash to look at, but nonetheless serves top-class food. Try the home-made cheese, and the lavash and khachipuri breads.

Kafe Adzhika (Map 5; ☎ 310 26 27; Moskovsky pr 7; meals R150; open 24hrs), a cheap and friendly place with quite funky decor, is a respite from the chaos of nearby Sennaya ploshchad.

Cheburechnaya (Map 4; 6-ya linia 19; meals R150-200; open 11am-11pm Mon-Sat, noon-11pm Sun), just down from metro Vasileostrovskaya, is legendary. Nothing fancy, it's worth visiting if only to try the delicious, thick Georgian soup *chanaxhi* (R45).

Kafe Kat (Map 6; ☎ 311 33 77; Stremyannaya ul 22; meals R150-200; open noon-11pm daily) is a cosy, centrally located Georgian restaurant with fake vines hanging from the ceiling. A selection of appetisers plus the cheese bread will fill you up.

Caravan Sarai (Map 6; ☎ 272 71 29; ul Nekrasova 1; meals R300; open noon-midnight daily) offers tasty Uzbek cuisine in an atmospheric setting with a side order of belly dancing. Similar is **Kalif** (Map 3; ☎ 312 22 65; Millionnaya ul 21; meals R450; open noon-midnight daily), which has hubble-bubble pipes for US$10 a smoke.

Pirosmani (Map 2; ☎ 235 64 56; Bolshoy pr 14, Petrograd Side; meals R400; open noon-midnight daily) has good Georgian food, but it's the decor that is more of an attraction; a stream flows through the dimly lit restaurant. It's walkable from metro Sportivnaya.

Chinese Painted bright red and yellow, **Mao** (Map 4; ☎ 328 44 72; 1-ya linia 18; meals R200) is a jolly place with authentic, tasty and inexpensive Chinese cuisine.

Kharbin has three branches (Map 6; ☎ 279 99 90; ul Nekrasova 58 • ☎ 272 65 08; ul Zhukovskogo 34/2 • ☎ 311 17 32; nab reki Moyki 48), all with great food and good service (locals swear the last branch is best).

Aquarium (Map 3; ☎ 326 82 86; Kamennoostrovsky pr 10; meals R600; open noon-midnight daily) is an upmarket option, but worth the expense. This large, slick emporium has a good range of seafood, including shark fin and abalone, and ridiculously priced bird's nest dishes.

Chopsticks (Map 6; ☎ 329 60 00; Grand Hotel Europe, Mikhailovskaya ul 1/7; meals R600; open noon-midnight daily) specialises in Szechuan and Cantonese dishes but, while the ambience in nice, the food's no better than at more inexpensive venues.

German **Schvabsky Domik** (Map 5; ☎ 528 22 11; Novocherkassky pr 28/19; buffet section meals R150, restaurant meals R200-600; open 11am-1am daily) is a food emporium, done out in hokey Bavarian style and combining three restaurants in one (taking up an entire block). On the menu is schnitzel, sauerkraut, sausages, roasts and potatoes galore (50 potato dishes in its Potato House section!). The food is great and so is the German beer. Visit each of the three dining

halls before deciding where to eat; the menus vary quite a bit between them.

The long-running **Chayka** (also known as Tschaika; Map 6; ☎ 312 46 31; nab kanala Griboedova 14; meals R500; open 11am-3am daily) remains a prostitute-riddled haunt of foreign businessmen. It does, however, serve good German beer and what is regarded as the best German cuisine in St Pete.

Indian The most central Indian place in town, **Tandoor** (Map 5; ☎ 312 38 86; Voznesensky pr 2; meals R300-600; open noon-11pm daily) offers glitzy decor, courteous service and a full, albeit Russianised, Indian menu and a limited wine list. Its R300 business lunch (Monday to Friday) is recommended.

Swagat (Map 4; ☎ 217 21 11; Bolshoy pr 91; meals R400-500; open noon-11pm Tues-Sun), on Vasilevsky Island, is less convenient than Tandoor, but still worth visiting. Its north Indian cuisine, including tandoori, tikka and masala curry dishes, is authentically spicy. There's dancing nightly after 8pm and sometimes sitar music.

Italian & Pizza Some of the best pizza in town can be enjoyed at **La Strada** (Map 6; ☎ 312 47 00; Bolshaya Konyushennaya ul 27; meals R400; open noon-11pm daily). The restaurant has a spacious area with an enormous glass ceiling and an open kitchen area where you can watch the cooks prepare the pizzas. Portions are huge.

Pizzicato (Map 4; ☎ 315 03 19; ul Bolshaya Morskaya 45; meals R450; open noon-midnight daily) is a stylish Italian joint tucked away beneath the House of Composers. It serves excellent pizza, pasta and salads, plus, for unfathomable reasons, 'chicken a la New Delhi'. There's 30% off all prices until 4pm each day.

Ostensibly Italian, **Da Vinci** (Map 6; ☎ 311 01 73; w www.davinci.spb.ru; Malaya Morskaya ul 15; meals R150-600; open noon-6am daily) is one of those collage restaurants so popular in Russia – there's as much American and Mediterranean food on the menu as Italian, and the entertainment runs the gamut of jazz, Russian folk dancing and musclemen strip shows. There's a children's menu too, and the website is a hoot.

Mama Roma (Map 6; ☎ 314 03 47; Karavannaya ul 3/35; meals R300-400; open 9am-2am) has acceptable pizza and pasta dishes and is in a convenient location a hop and a skip from Nevsky prospekt.

Rossi's *(Map 6; ☎ 329 60 00; Mikhailovskaya ul 1/7; meals R500-600; open noon-11pm daily)* is consistently one of the best places in St Pete for fine Italian food. Delicious freshly made pasta is served in very aesthetically presented portions in this casual but elegant hall.

St Petersburg also has two **Pizza Huts** *(Map 6; nab reki Moyki 71/76 • Map 6; Nevsky pr 96)*. Both offer a good variety of pizza (also available by the slice to take away) and have salad bars.

Japanese The sushi craze that has gripped Moscow has, inevitably, spread to St Pete. There's sushi at **Tinkoff** (see Pubs & Bars under Entertainment later in this chapter) and the excellent Moscow-based chain **Yakitoriya** is slated to open a branch at the back of ploshchad Ostrovskogo, on the corner of pereulok Krylova (Map 6).

Planet Sushi *(Map 6; ☎ 273 35 58; Nevsky pr 94; meals R300-600; open noon-midnight daily)* is the best-value Japanese restaurant in town, with set sushi selections from R290. The *bento* lunches (available noon to 5pm Monday to Friday) are excellent value at R315 and the whole place, with waitresses decked out in grey and black kimonos, is very stylish.

Shogun *(Map 6; ☎ 275 32 97; ul Vosstania 26 • Map 6; ☎ 314 74 17; Gorokhovaya ul 11/25; meals R400-600; open noon-11pm daily)* has two branches in the city. The branch on ulitsa Vosstania has beautiful interiors, private shuttered rooms and absolutely lovely staff. At the Gorokhovaya ulitsa location, there's a real sushi bar.

Mexican Tasty enchiladas, burritos and tamales are available at **La Cucaracha** *(Map 6; ☎ 110 40 06; 39 nab reki Fontanki; meals R300; open noon-midnight daily)*, a pleasant and cosy basement space. It also has a drive-in/takeaway outlet *(Map 3; ☎ 222 12 12; Sverdlovskskaya nab 62-64)*, which does free home delivery.

Vegetarian Despite the fact that **Café Idiot** *(Map 4; ☎ 315 16 75; nab reki Moyki 82; meals R300; open noon-11pm daily)* is always packed with expats and is generally overpriced, the atmosphere here is excellent –

funky lamps and tables, couches to lounge on, and several rooms with different ambiences (including one that's nonsmoking). It's a pleasant place to while away an evening as well as try standard Russian vegetarian dishes.

It's hard to believe, but there's not a shred of meat in the delightful **Gushe** *(Map 6; ☎ 113 24 05; Vladimirsky pr 5; meals R90-120; open 9am-11pm daily)*. Many of the dishes, including soya and tofu casseroles, vegetarian lasagne, salads and fresh juices, are on display, and therefore easy to order.

Though the sign out front makes this place look like a pharmacy, inside **Green Crest** *(Map 6; ☎ 113 13 80; Vladimirsky pr 7; meals around R90; open 9am-11.30pm daily)* is a selection of cream-drenched salads (takeaway available) and a great vegetable stew. It also has fish and meat dishes and Tinkoff beer on tap.

Troitsky Most *(Map 3; ☎ 326 82 21; Malaya Posadskaya ul 2 • ☎ 232 66 93; Kronversky pr 9/2; meals R90-120; open 24hrs)*, with two branches, is the original vegetarian operation in town (it used to be the Hare Krishna café). There are vegie burgers, dry soya meals, potato cutlets and lots of salads.

Top-End Offerings One of the most consistently recommended places in town is **Staraya Tamozhnaya** *(Old Customs House; Map 4; ☎ 327 89 80; Tamozhenny per 1; meals R600-800; open 1pm-1am daily)*. The atmosphere is simply delightful, with vaulted brick ceilings, live jazz, fantastic service and large portions of very well-prepared Russian and European specialities, and vegetarian offerings.

Across the street is **Restoran** *(Map 4; ☎ 327 89 79; Tamozhenny per 2; meals R400-600; open noon-midnight daily)*, where the chic minimalist decor provides an ideal setting for the generally well-presented range of traditional Russian dishes. There's a good table of appetisers and salads and some interesting, home-made, flavoured vodkas.

Za Stsenoi *(Backstage; Map 4; ☎ 327 06 84; Teatralnaya pl 18/10; meals R400-600; open noon-midnight daily)*, the official restaurant of the Mariinsky Theatre, has the same designer as Restoran – it's tastefully decorated with props from past productions. The food and desultory service can leave something to be desired; best to stick to the simpler dishes and soups, which are generally well executed.

ST PETERSBURG

Aquarel (Map 2; ☎ 320 86 00; Birzhevoy most, Petrograd Side; meals R600-1000; open noon-6am daily) is the place to come for beautifully presented fusion cuisine. Based on a moored boat with fantastic city views, it's a stylish place with a cheaper café on the top floor and a DJ in the evenings; erratic service is the only letdown.

Seven-Forty (Map 1; ☎ 246 34 44; Bolshoy Sampsonevsky pr 108; meals R500-600; open noon-11pm daily) is an excellent Jewish-themed restaurant with imaginative decor and very tasty, authentic food. The painted wooded plates, each one unique, can be bought for US$100 each, and there's live music at night on weekends. Take any tram three stops heading east from Chyornaya Rechka metro station. Seven-Forty isn't kosher, but if that's what you're after check out **Shalom** (Map 1; ☎ 327 54 75; ul Koli Komchaka 8), a five-minute walk east of Moskovskie Vorota metro station.

Taleon Club (Map 6; ☎ 312 53 73; ⓦ www.taleon.ru; nab reki Moyki 59; Sunday brunch R1100; open noon-3am daily) is the place to splurge on Sunday brunch, a voluptuous affair with as much caviar, oysters and *shampansky* as you can guzzle. Dress smartly and take along some ID so you can be made a member for entry. Sadly the opulent setting is spoiled by a live band playing such incongruities as the Pink Panther theme. The Sunday brunch (from noon to 4pm) at the Corinthia Nevskij Palace Hotel's **Admiralty Restaurant** (Map 6; ☎ 380 20 01; Nevsky pr 57) is more expensive (R1500), but includes free-flowing Moët, vodka or beer and is also recommended.

Bistrot Garçon (Map 6; ☎ 277 24 67; Nevsky pr 95; meals R1000; open 9am-1am daily) is like stepping into a French film set, but is saved from being too kitsch by professional service and delightful, authentic cuisine. The chocolate lamb ragout is delicious. Sometimes the atmosphere is enhanced by an accordion player and a Piaf-wannabe. Breakfast is available too.

A classy number on the 8th floor of the Corinthia Nevskij Palace Hotel, **Landskrona** (Map 6; ☎ 380 20 01; Nevsky pr 57; mains from US$15; open 6pm-midnight daily) hangs onto its reputation as one of the best restaurants in St Petersburg. In addition to the top-class European cuisine there's live classical music and panoramic views of the city.

Austeria (Peter & Paul Fortress Map; ☎ 238 42 62; Peter & Paul Fortress; meals R500-600; open noon-midnight daily) was closed for renovation at the time of research, but it has a great location inside the fortress and in the past the service and solid Russian food have not disappointed.

Kalinka (Map 2; ☎ 323 37 18; Syezdovskaya linia 9; meals R700-800; open noon-midnight daily), on Vasilevsky Island, has a beautiful atmosphere, live music performed on original old instruments and fine food, but it can get packed with tourists, so weekday visits are better.

Russkaya Ribalka (Map 2; ☎ 323 98 13; 11 Yuzhnaya Doroga, Krestovsky Island; meals R600-800; open noon-9pm daily) makes an interesting diversion, if you're exploring Krestovsky Island. The name means Russian fishing and that's exactly what you can do at the pools outside this operation based in a cutely designed wooden building. Its fish include trout, stertlet and several types of sturgeon. Not for those in a rush, though, since service is on a five-year plan.

Senat (Map 4; ☎ 314 92 53; Galernaya ul 1; meals R600; open noon-2am daily) is a smart, convivial place tucked away in the basement of the Senate building near St Isaac's. There's live classical music some nights. President Clinton supped here, as he did also at the charming **Dvorianskoye Gnezdo** (The Noble Nest; Map 4; ☎ 312 32 05; ul Dekabristov 21; meals R1000 plus; open noon-last customer). Set in the summer pavilion of the Yusupov Palace, it serves some of the finest Russian and European cuisine in St Pete in an intimate, tsarist setting (shame about the scrappy park outside).

Café-Bars

The following serve a mix of Russian and international cuisine, and are distinguished by their relaxed, low-key atmosphere. Meals at these venues will cost around R200. They're often good places for a drink at night, too.

Staroe Kafe (Map 5; ☎ 316 51 11; nab reki Fontanki 108; open noon-11pm daily) is a long-time favourite with expats but isn't spoiled by their patronage. It's a tiny, dimly lit space that throws you back a century or so. The food is decent and so are the drinks (watch the prices – some wines are stellar).

For years **Sunduk** (Map 3; ☎ 272 31 00; Furshtadskaya ul 42; open 10am-11pm daily) was the cosiest grotto space with good food and the funkiest bathrooms in the city. Now it has quadrupled its space while retaining the cosiness. The menu's varied, but you don't come here for cuisine – it's the atmosphere that'll keep you lingering. Live music (mainly jazz) is performed nightly after 8.30pm.

There's nothing extraordinary about the (tasty) food at **Depo** (Map 6; ☎ 277 44 51; Goncharnaya ul 14; open 11am-midnight daily) but the decor – train and train-station themed, with an ironic wink – is light and happy. It's the kind of place where you don't notice time passing by.

Popular **Stroganov Yard** (Map 6; ☎ 315 23 15; Nevsky pr 17; buffet lunch R180, dinner R270; open 11am-midnight daily) is in the courtyard of the Stroganov Palace, and you feel like you're in an outdoor café because of the glass walls. The buffet is good but if you don't fancy it there's also a full menu. The novelty factor here is the telephone on each table – if you see someone you fancy, just ring them up and try not to sound too corny.

Popugay (Map 4; ☎ 311 59 71; Fornarny per 1; open 6am-6pm Mon-Sat, noon-midnight Sun) is a new basement place with a laid-back reggae vibe. It's popular with overseas students, who like to veg out over board games.

Orient Express (Map 6; ☎ 325 87 29; ul Marata 21; open noon-midnight daily) is styled after the famous train, with a first-class restaurant section and a more atmospheric (and cheaper) passenger carriage café.

Kafe Literaturnoe (Map 6; ☎ 312 60 57; Nevsky pr 18) is in many other guidebooks, but – trust us – it had its day back in Pushkin's time (his last meal was eaten here) and today is little more than a tourist trap with old-style decor and classical music concerts.

Coffee & Tea Houses A relatively recent explosion of Western-style coffee and tea houses continues to throw up some excellent places.

Idealnaya Chashka (Ideal Cup; ⓦ www .chashka.ru; Map 6; Nevsky pr 15, 112 & 130 & Map 3; Kirochnaya ul 19; open 9am-11pm daily) is the St Pete equivalent of Starbucks. This company kickstarted the craze for caffeine back in 1998. There are dozens of different coffees to choose from, with the garlic-honey coffee a real eye-opener.

Kafe Marko (Map 6; Nevsky pr 108 • Map 3; pr Chernyshevskogo 26 • Map 3; pl Lva

Tolstogo 1) is another good chain with a wider selection of food than Idealnaya Chashka and alcoholic drinks too. Its Nevsky prospekt branch is eternally thronged with teenagers.

Café Rico (Map 6; ☎ 164 72 14; Nevsky pr 77/1, enter on Pushkinskaya ul) has South American-influenced decor. The coffee is good and there's a wide range of coffee cocktails and snacks.

Coffee Break (Map 6; ☎ 314 67 29; nab kanala Griboedova 22; open 7.30am-11pm daily) is not just a good modern café, but also an interesting art gallery infused with chill-out music. You can try the South American tea drink mate here.

Chainaya Lozhka (Teaspoon; Map 6; ☎ 275 05 08; ul Vosstania 13; open 9am-10pm daily) does excellent bliny, but there's also a fine selection of loose-leaf tea by the pot. Decor is refreshingly contemporary. There's also a branch on Kamennoostrovsky prospekt, opposite Petrogradskaya metro station (Map 3).

China Club (Map 2; ☎ 323 92 79; 3-ya linia 48; open 11am-11pm daily), on Vasilevsky Island, is a tranquil place where you can lounge on cushions on the floor and choose from 120 different types of tea; a pot for two starts from R75.

Ice Cream St Petersburg produces some of Russia's finest ice cream and it's highly recommended to try one of the bars or cones on sale at push-cart freezers all over the city. Baltisky and Bely Nochi are particularly good ones to sample.

Baskin Robbins (Map 6; Nevsky pr 79; open 10am-10pm daily) serves up its usual 31 flavours (locally produced).

Sladkoezhka (Map 6; ☎ 312 97 71; Malaya Morskaya ul 9) is a slick ice cream café and pastry shop serving good cappuccino. There are also branches at ulitsa Marata 11 (Map 6) and Zakharevskaya ulitsa 25 (Map 3).

Budget

Fast Food You don't need to bloat up on burger grease just to save pennies in this city. The following four self-service operations are open 24 hours and a meal at one of them won't cost much over R100.

The excellent **Laima** (Map 6; ☎ 232 44 28; nab kanala Griboedova 14 & Map 3; ☎ 315 55 45; Bolshoy pr 88, Petrograd Side) has a vast menu (there's an English one available) including oodles of salads, soups, main dishes and drinks. Similar are **Orient** *(Map 6; ☎ 277 57 15; Suvorovsky pr 1/8 • Map 6; ☎ 314 64 43; Bolshaya Morskaya ul 25)*; **Bistro Samson** *(Map 3; Kamennoostrovsky pr 16)*; and **U Tyoshi Na Blinakh** *(Map 5; Zagorodny pr 18 • Map 6; Ligovsky pr 25)*, which specialises in bliny.

All over the city you'll find the yellow kiosks of **Teremok** *(Map 6; Manezhnaya pl • Map 6; Bolshaya Konyushennaya ul • Map 5; Vladimirskaya pl; open 10.30am-11pm daily)* serving some of the most mouth-watering bliny in town. Made in front of you, they come stuffed with a full range of savoury and sweet things – no wonder there are always queues.

Kolobok *(Map 3; ☎ 275 38 65; ul Chaikovskogo 40)* has a variety of decent-tasting traditional Russian dishes on offer, most of which you can point to (for ease of ordering).

For die-hard Western fast-food fans, McDonald's has oodles of outlets and there's also **KFC** *(Map 6; ☎ 279 61 36; Nevsky pr 96)*. The choice is wider at **Grillmaster** *(Map 6; ☎ 110 40 55; Nevsky pr 46)*.

Self-Catering It's worth visiting **Yeliseevsky** *(Map 6; Nevsky pr 56; open 9am-9pm Mon-Fri, 11am-9pm Sat & Sun)* just to admire the glittering interior. This is Russia's most beautiful, if not most famous, grocer. Prices here are higher than in other shops, but the choice is good.

The **supermarket** *(Map 6; ☎ 312 47 01; Nevsky pr 48; open 10am-10pm daily)* in the basement of Passazh shopping centre will probably stock that special item you've been craving since you left home.

There are dozens of 24-hour supermarkets dotted all over the city. One good central one is **Dzinn** *(Map 6; ☎ 164 10 80; ul Marata 16)*. Another, **Babylon Super** *(Map 2; ☎ 233 35 18; Maly pr 54/56, Petrograd Side)*, has a terrific selection of exotic (for Russia) fresh vegies (such as fresh ginger root and avocado), and an awesome bakery. It accepts credit cards.

Kalinka Stockmann's *(Map 3; ☎ 542 22 97; Finlyandsky pr 1; open 9am-10pm daily)*, near Hotel St Petersburg, is a good place to buy decadent Western luxuries to cook up at the nearby International Holiday Hostel.

Markets These are fascinating venues to visit, and not only for the choice of exotic and fresh produce (the meat is so fresh that in some cases it's still being hacked off the carcass). Bargaining, even if the price is marked, is encouraged, and you'll often be beckoned to try samples of honey, cream products and pickles, with no obligation to buy.

Two of the liveliest, most central and most expensive markets are the **Kuznechny** *(Map 5; Kuznechny per)*, a few steps east of Vladimirskaya metro station, and the **Maltsevsky** *(Map 6; ul Nekrasova 52)*. Also try **Sennoy** *(Map 5; Moskovsky pr 4-6; metro Sennaya Ploshchad)* and **Sytny** *(Map 3; Sytninskaya pl 3/5; metro Gorkovskaya)*, behind Alexandrovsky Park.

Bakeries Head to **Wendy's Baltic Bread** *(Map 6; ☎ 275 64 40; Grechesky pr 25; open 10am-9pm daily)* for by far the city's widest selection of fresh-baked breads, cakes, sweet and savoury pastries, and delicious pizzas.

Bushe *(Map 5; ☎ 312 35 78; Razyezzhaya ul 13; open 10am-9pm daily)* runs a close second to Wendy's in terms of baked-goods paradise. Pumpkin bread is just one of its selected fresh breads, and the entire line-up of filled croissants is just too yummy for words.

Albina *(Map 6; ☎ 273 74 59; ul Vosstania 10; open 8.30am-11.30pm daily)* is a modern bakery and café giving nearby Wendy's a run for its money. It's a quiet, contemporary place to kick back.

The legendary cake shop **Sever** *(Map 6; ☎ 311 25 89; Nevsky pr 44; open 10am-9pm Mon-Sat, 10am-8pm Sun)* is chock-full of cookies and oddly coloured pastries and cakes.

ENTERTAINMENT

Check the Friday *St Petersburg Times* and *Pulse* for up-to-date listings.

Tickets

The box offices at some of the city's largest venues, including the Mariinsky, Mussorgsky, Hermitage and Maly Theatres, charge a separate foreigner's price that is many times the Russian price. It's still cheaper than what you'd pay for the same tickets purchased through a top hotel's concierge or travel agency. If you can prove that you're working or studying in Russia, you'll pay the Russian price.

If you purchase a Russian ticket and your cover is blown inside the theatre (a frustrating and embarrassing experience), you'll be made to pay the difference by rabid babushkas. Scalpers usually sell last-minute tickets out-

Drama at the Mariinsky

St Petersburg's most famous theatre was built in 1859 as the home of the Imperial Russian Opera and Ballet companies. The gilded Italianate house saw the premieres of Tchaikovsky's *Sleeping Beauty* and *The Nutcracker*. In 1935 the Soviets renamed it the Kirov Opera and Ballet Theatre, and while the theatre has reverted to its prerevolutionary name, the company is still called the Kirov. The Kirov Ballet nurtured stars including Nijinsky, Pavlova, Nureyev, Makarova and Baryshnikov.

After hard times in the 1980s, the new Mariinsky has undergone an artistic renaissance under dynamic, workaholic artistic director Valery Gergiev. New productions are paid for by Western benefactors, or staged in conjunction with overseas companies, and these days not everything is sung in Russian (even so, there will be English surtitles).

Despite its revival and the phenomenal success of some of its modern productions, the fact remains that the 19th-century theatre is clapped out and in desperate need of renovation. In January 2002, the Russian government announced that it planned to spend nearly US$130 million on the Mariinsky's reconstruction and expansion – all very much welcomed by St Petersburg's arts community, except for one set of plans submitted by US-based deconstructivist architect Eric Owen Moss.

Moss' vision involves building a strikingly modern theatre in the radical style of Bilbao's Guggenheim Museum on the banks of the Kryukov Canal behind the existing Mariinsky, as well as a correspondingly contemporary business and cultural centre on the nearby (currently off limits) island of Novaya Gollandiya. The plans have caused a storm of controversy. Crucially the Moss concept is supported by Gergiev, but the city's architectural guardians are up in arms.

A commission has been set up to review all the possibilities and it's sure to be the scene of many a drama before the planned completion of the new theatre in 2006 and renovations to the existing Mariinsky in 2008.

★★★

side the theatre an hour before the show. These will be Russian tickets, and if they're for a sold-out show, they can go for up to US$50 each. Check the ticket carefully and see that the date and seat position promised are correct; there are fakes around. First floor is the *parter*; the mezzanine is the *beletazh*; and the balcony is the *balkon* or *yarus*.

There are ticket booking offices and kiosks all over the city; one of the best for classical and rock concerts, plays and ballet performances is the **Theatre Ticket Office** (*Teatralnaya kassa; Map 6; ☎ 314 93 85; Nevsky pr 42*) opposite Gostiny Dvor.

Classical Music, Ballet & Opera

September to the end of June is the main performing season – in summer many companies are away on tour, but plenty of performances are still staged.

The St Petersburg Philharmonica's Symphony Orchestra is particularly renowned. It has two concert halls: the grand **Bolshoy Zal** (*Big Hall; Map 6; ☎ 110 42 57; Mikhailovskaya ul 2*); and the **Maly Zal imeni Glinki** (*Small Philharmonia; Map 6; ☎ 311 83 33; Nevsky pr 30*). The **Glinka Capella** (*Map 6; ☎ 314 10 58; nab reki Moyki 20*) also has

high standards, focusing on choral, chamber and organ concerts.

St Petersburg was the birthplace of Russian ballet back in 1738: the present 1780-seat **Mariinsky Theatre** (*Map 4; ☎ 114 52 64; W www.mariinsky.spb.ru; Teatralnaya pl 1*) is home to the world-famous Kirov Ballet and Opera company and a visit here is a must, if only to wallow in the sparkling glory of the interior (see the boxed text 'Drama at the Mariinsky' for more on the history of this famous theatre).

The Symphony Orchestra and the Kirov Ballet and Opera companies tend to go on tour for about two months in the summer and unpredictably the rest of the year, but they usually stage five ballets and five operas per month. Some are standouts, but standards vary. The ballet's home shows are nearly always booked out; ticket sales from the theatre usually start 20 days in advance. Other visiting companies also perform here.

It's cheaper and easier to get tickets to the ballet and opera performances staged at **Mussorgsky Opera & Ballet Theatre** (*Teatr Opery i Baleta imeni Mussorgskogo; Map 6; ☎ 318 19 78; pl Iskusstv 1*). More contemporary works are also performed here than by the Kirov and standards are respectable. Also worth checking out are the performances at the **Rimsky-Korsakov Conservatory** *(Map 4; ☎ 312 25 19; Teatralnaya pl 3)* and the beautiful **Hermitage Theatre** *(Map 3; ☎ 311 90 25; Dvortsovaya nab 34)*, where occasional concerts and operettas are staged.

Theatre

There are dozens of theatrical performances each night. Tickets are available from the same ticket offices as those for classical music.

The premier drama theatre is the **Pushkin** *(Map 6; ☎ 110 41 03; pl Ostrovskogo 2)*, which stages Russian and foreign plays, usually on a grand scale. The **Tovstonogov Bolshoy Dramatic Theatre** *(Map 5; ☎ 310 04 01; nab reki Fontanki 65)* is another top mainstream theatre.

Even if your Russian isn't great, the plays are so good at the **Lensoviet Theatre** *(Map 6; ☎ 113 21 91; Vladimirsky pr 12)* and at the **Maly Dramatic Theatre** *(Map 6; ☎ 113 20 49; ul Rubinshteyna 18)*, you can't go wrong.

At the Lensoviet, Bruchner's *Voychek*, Beckett's *B Ozhidaniy Godo* (Waiting for Godot) and Pinter's *Lyubovnik* (The Lover) are in the repertoire and are all excellent. There are also frequent performances for children. At the Maly, under the expert direction of Lev Dodin, don't miss *Gaudeamus*, *Claustrophobia*, and Dodin's 9½-hour version of Dostoevsky's *Besy* (The Possessed).

Another particularly good theatre for excellent, off-beat comedies is the **Satiry Theatre** *(Map 4; ☎ 314 70 60; Sredny pr 48)* on Vasilevsky Island.

Circus & Puppets

St Petersburg State Circus *(Map 6; ☎ 314 84 78; W www.ticketsofrussia.ru/theatres /circus; nab reki Fontanki 3; tickets R300; shows 7pm Tues, Wed & Fri, 3pm & 7pm Sat & Sun Sept-June)* has a permanent location here, 500m south of the Summer Garden. Check out the website for the current program.

For puppets, the main venue is the **Bolshoy Teatr Kukol** *(Map 6; ☎ 272 82 15; Nekrasova ul 10; tickets around R30; shows 11.30am & 2pm Sat & Sun)*; there are 16 different shows in the repertoire, including two for adults. The **Teatr Kukol-Marionetok** *(Map 6; ☎ 311 19 00; Nevsky pr 52; tickets about R30)* has, as the name suggests, puppet and marionette shows on a varying schedule.

Pubs & Bars

Also see the Café-Bars section in Places to Eat for more recommended watering holes.

Don't leave St Petersburg without sampling the very quaffable beers of **Tinkoff** *(Map 6; ☎ 118 55 66; Kazanskaya ul 7; open noon–2am daily)*. Set inside a gigantic, contemporary brewery, its large array of fresh microbrewed beers, including the delicious White Unfiltered, go for R60 to R120 a half-litre. There's also good, pricey food, including a sushi bar. The business lunch (from noon to 4.45pm Monday to Friday, European cuisine R250, Japanese R350) includes a mug of beer and is a winner.

Ot Zakata do Rasveta *(From Dusk to Dawn; Map 6; ☎ 314 64 48; Bolshaya Morskaya ul 31; open 24hrs)* is named after the Mexican cowboy/vampire movie and is a dark, fun place. There's lots of wood, swinging doors, interesting toilets, decent chow, a laid-back clientele, lively entertainment and overall good atmosphere.

Time Out *(Map 5; ☎ 113 24 42; ul Marata 36)* is your average sports bar, with pool table and satellite TV, but there's also a foreign book exchange, good pizza and happy hour from 5pm to 8pm.

Among the several things that make **Bar O Meter** *(Map 6; ☎ 315 53 71; Malaya Morskaya ul 7; open 11am–6am daily)* stand out are the incredibly energetic and friendly staff; amazing pasta dishes expertly served (al dente and with a spoon!); and the metre-long 'glasses' of beer from which the bar takes its name.

James Cook Pub *(Map 6; ☎ 312 32 00; Shvedsky per 2; café open from 9am, pub from noon until last customer daily)* is upscale, but anything but elitist. Divided into a café and tavern, this British pub has a wide selection of imported beers. The food is reliable but can get pricey. The café sells coffee beans and exotic loose-leaf tea, including the nearly narcotic silver tea (R1050 for 50g!).

Che *(Map 6; ☎ 277 76 00; Poltavskaya ul 3; open 7am–6am daily)* is where you'll find the smart set, slumped in the comfy sofas. It's one of the most Euro-trendy spaces in the city, serving good coffee, wine and snacks; there's sometimes tango lessons and often live jazz in the evenings. A couple of other chic watering holes, both serving food, are **Manilov** *(Map 5; ☎ 112 78 75; 7 Krasnoarmeyskaya ul 5; open 11am–last customer daily)*; and **Decadance** *(Map 5; ☎ 312 39 44; W www.decadance .spb.ru; Admiralteyskaya nab 12; open 24hrs)*, where some very cool live bands and DJs feature on Friday and Saturday.

Probka (Map 6; ☎ 273 49 04; ul Belingskogo 5; open 5pm-1am daily) is small, romantic and sophisticated – what more could you ask of a wine bar that features bottles from Europe, Chile and Argentina? Some wines are available by the glass (divide the dollar price by four) and there's a menu of light snacks.

The Stray Dog (Map 6; ☎ 312 80 47; pl Iskusstv 5; performances R90-150; open 11am-midnight daily) is a unique space. From late 1912 to 1915, this bar was the focal point of futurist and avant-garde art culture in St Petersburg. Artists were admitted free, all others paid a heavy cover charge to see the likes of Mayakovsky, Akhmatova, Meyerhold and Diaghilev hanging out or expressing themselves. This new version hopes to unite the disjointed world of the city's young creators, as well as host concerts, screenings and exhibitions of all kinds. There's a great bar to hang out at and watch the proceedings.

Manhattan Club/Katyol (Map 5; ☎ 113 19 45; nab reki Fontanki 90; cover R60-100; open 2pm-5am daily) used to be an artsy, 'Nouveaux Bohemian Wannabe' magnet, but now has live music in a good, airy space played to an interesting, mixed crowd.

Fish Fabrique (Map 6; ☎ 164 48 57; Pushkinskaya ul 10, entrance through arch at Ligovsky pr 53; open 3pm-late daily) is set in the building that's the focus of the avant-garde art scene, thus attracting some radical artsies and fun-lovers. The crowd, not the sparse, nonexistent decor, gives this cramped space its edge. Live bands kick up a storm at 10pm nightly.

Psycho Pub (Map 6; nab reki Fontanki 23; cover R40; open 3pm-5am daily) is one for the hard-rockers among you; this grungy, tiny space, located in a dingy courtyard just off Nevsky prospekt, thrives on its unwashed but friendly clientele and energetic bands playing rap, thrash or reggae from 9pm to midnight Wednesday to Sunday.

Pivnoy Klub (Beer Club; Map 6; ☎ 279 18 52; ul Nekrasova 37; open noon-3am daily) is a relaxed place with a pleasant, local feel to it. The decor's subdued, but the atmosphere lively with bands playing most nights.

If you're pining for the familiar then **Mollie's Irish Bar** (Map 5; ☎ 319 97 68; ul Rubinshteyna 36) should do the trick. The

city's long-running Irish pub serves Guinness pints for R120 and remains popular for its classic decor, friendly service and tasty grub.

The Red Lion (Map 3; ☎ 233 93 91; Alexandrovsky Park 4, Petrograd Side; open 24hrs) boasts a menu with over 30 kinds of beer and has a range of theme nights. The outdoor deck is a pleasant place to down a pint if the weather's good. The food, including standards such as fish and chips and Irish stew, isn't bad but comes in small portions.

Nightclubs & Discos
The city's nightclub scene is varied, inventive and perpetually changing – you're bound to find somewhere you like. Also keep your ear to the ground for news of dance parties held out on the Gulf of Finland islands around Kronshtadt (see the Around St Petersburg chapter) in the summer.

Par.spb (Map 3; ☎ 233 33 74; W www.icc.sp.ru; Alexandrovsky Park 5B; cover R100-150; open 11am-6am daily) is the hip club of the moment, with different music each night and a strict door policy. The stripped-back interior is sleek and includes two dance spaces and a chill-out area, but check its website because it may move location.

St Petersburg likes clubs in bunkers and tunnels. One of the best is **Griboedov** (Map 5; ☎ 164 43 55; Voronezhskaya ul 2A; cover R60-80; open 5pm-6am daily), an artfully converted bomb shelter where weekends are stiflingly crowded; the best nights are Wednesday (1970s and 80s disco) and Thursday (trance). The original 'underground' club was **Tunnel** (Map 2; ☎ 233 40 15; W www.tunnelclub.ru; cnr Lyubansky per & Zverinskaya ul; cover R150-300; open noon-6am Fri & Sat), which has recently started up again. Hard-core clubbers should check it out.

The energy at **Mama** (Map 3; ☎ 232 31 37; Malaya Monetnaya ul 3B; cover R60; open 11pm-6am Fri & Sat), a split-level club, can rise to fever pitch (DJ Kefir usually does the trick), but at other times it's just packed with a wild teen crowd.

Faculty (Map 2; ☎ 233 06 72; W www.fakultet.sp.ru; pr Dobrolyubova 6; cover R50-100 after 9pm; open noon-6am daily) has a student union vibe to it – not surprising, since it was opened in cooperation with the St Petersburg State University. It can be a fun place with some unusual acts and a variety of music on the decks.

Moloko (Map 5; ☎ 274 94 67; w www
.molokoclub.ru; Perekupnoy per 12; cover
R40-80; open 7pm-midnight Wed-Sun) is
everything an underground club should be –
dimly lit, modestly decorated and bubbling
with promise. Great bands running the gamut
of genres play here, and it's one of the few
places to get going earlier in the evening.

City Club & Money Honey Saloon (Map
6; ☎ 310 05 49; w www.moneyhoney.org
/cityclub; Apraksin dvor 14; cover around R60;
live shows 8.20pm Mon-Sun & 1am Fri & Sat)
appeal to a wide crowd. Upstairs at City Club
there's a dance floor and pool tables and lots
of space to mingle (the place attracts an over-
20s crowd), and downstairs the Money Honey
Saloon has great live rockabilly and country
bands; the crowds' randiness sometimes spills
over into rowdiness later on. Enter via the
courtyard off Sadovaya ulitsa.

Ostrov (Map 4; ☎ 328 48 57; nab Leytenanta Shmidta 37; cover R300; open 9pm-6am
Fri-Sun) is a funky place where the dance
floor rocks from side to side (not good if
you've had one too many vodkas), a snow
and rainmaking machine douses dancers at
unexpected moments, and there are ham-
mocks in the chill-out room.

Havana (Map 5; ☎ 259 11 55; Moskovsky
pr 21; cover R30-60; open 9pm-6am daily) is
a real salsa and Latin club with Cuban theme
and imported dancers. It's big and fun and
fills up on the weekends.

The big-disco, standard-pop-music thing
is dished up at the following three venues.

Make it past the bouncers at **Plaza** (Map 2;
☎ 323 90 90; nab Makarova 2; cover R300-
600; open 10pm-6am Tues-Sun) and you find
plenty of glitzy chrome and nouveaux Russian posing going on here. Still, the restaurant
(admission free) is an acceptable place to
hang out if you get caught out by the bridges
going up on Vasilevsky Island.

Aquatoria (Map 3; ☎ 118 35 18; w www
.aquatoria.ru; Vyborgskaya nab 61; cover
R120-200; open 10pm-6am Tues-Sun) is a
huge and somewhat overbearing entertainment complex with several dance floors,
theme nights, strip shows, and modern, Euro
decor. If that doesn't grab you, there's also a
bowling alley, casino and pool hall.

There are three dance floors at **Metro**
(Map 5; ☎ 166 02 04; w www.metroclub.ru;
Ligovsky pr 174; cover R60-250; open 10pm-
6am daily), with music on the pop-techno

side, but there's an attempt to keep the young
crowd happy with different events nightly,
from amateur strip contests to lip-synching
teeny pop bands.

The infamous **Xali Gali** (Map 1; ☎ 246 38
27; Lanskoe shosse 15; cover R540; open
9pm-4am daily) is practically in a category of
its own. A wild and foul-mouthed MC
orchestrates the night's strip shows, saucy
comedy and magic acts, and penis-measuring
contests (for each of your centimetres you
get 1% discount off the price of drinks). It
helps if you understand Russian, but either
way get there by 10pm – staff may not let you
in after the show has begun. From metro
Chyornaya Rechka, head north along
naberezhnaya Chyornoy Rechki one block,
turn right onto Lanskoe shosse, and try to
lose your inhibitions along the way.

Gay & Lesbian Venues

The St Petersburg Times has gay venue listings in its Friday edition. Otherwise, contact
Krilija (Wings; ☎ 312 31 80; e krilija@ilga
.org), Russia's oldest officially registered gay
and lesbian community organisation, for general information on the city's gay scene and
tourist services.

There's not much room at **Mono** (Map 5;
☎ 164 36 78; Kolomenskaya ul 4; cover R20-
50 for men, R100 for women; open 10pm-
6am daily) – the dance floor is tiny – but it's
a friendly, pleasantly decorated place with
reasonably priced drinks. Thursday is for
women when the cover prices are reversed.

Greshniki (Sinners; Map 6; ☎ 318 42 91;
nab kanala Griboedova 29; cover free-R70 for
men, R100-200 for women; open 6pm-6am
daily), with its dark leather-and-chains decor
and staff dressed as demons, comes across
like an S&M joint. More downmarket than
other clubs of this ilk, some find it on the
creepy side.

The long-running **Jungle** (Map 2; ☎ 327
07 70; ul Blokhina 8, Petrograd Side; cover
R50 for men, R80 for women; open 11pm-
6am Fri-Sat) keeps plugging away with its
Soviet-era ambience and Russian pop music.
It's only for the curious or desperate.

Jazz

At all the city's jazz clubs, cover charges
range from R60 to R120 depending on the
night and acts. Also check out café-bars such
as Che and Sunduk for free live jazz music.

JFC Jazz Club (Map 3; ☎ 272 98 50; Shpalernaya ul 33; open from 7pm nightly) is probably the best of its kind in the city. Small and New York-styled, it makes you feel like you're in New York's East Village.

Small **812 Jazz Club** (Map 3; ☎ 346 16 31; Bolshoy pr 98, Petrograd Side; open from 8pm nightly) is an alternative jazz club that hosts great jam sessions after its nightly concerts, which start at 8pm. Enter via the courtyard.

Jimi Hendrix Blues Club (Map 5; ☎ 279 88 13; Liteyny pr 33; open 24hrs) can be pretty good, depending on the band (they usually start at 7.30pm).

Jazz Philharmonic Hall (Map 5; ☎ 164 85 65; W www.jazz-hall.spb.ru; Zagorodny pr 27; concerts from 8pm nightly) represents the established, more traditional side of jazz. It has two bands – a straight jazz and a Dixieland – plus foreign guests doing mainstream and modern jazz.

Neo Jazz Club (Map 3; ☎ 273 38 30; Solyanoy per 14; open 9am-midnight daily) is a laid-back place with more mellow live jazz music. Most people go there for supper too (very good Armenian specialities for under R250) and to just chill.

Cinema

Check out Friday's St Petersburg Times for full cinema listings. Movie theatres line Nevsky prospekt, but all the Western films played at them are dubbed. Try **Crystal Palace** (Map 6; ☎ 272 23 82; Nevsky pr 72), which was the first cinema to open in the USSR, in 1929, and which now has Dolby stereo. **Spartak** (Map 3; ☎ 272 78 97; Kirochnaya ul 8) screens older European or lesser-known Russian films.

Billiards & Bowling

Play under chandeliers at **Leon** (Map 4; ☎ 110 83 77; ul Dekabristov 34; open 24hrs), the city's premier pool and bowling hall, in a converted Dom Kultury (House of Culture). It has eight tenpin bowling lanes and over 20 billiard tables in three sizes. Prices vary depending on the time of day but don't rise above R150 per hour.

SPECTATOR SPORTS

Zenith, St Petersburg's popular football team, usually plays at the **Petrovsky Stadium** (Map 2; ☎ 119 57 00; Petrovsky ostrov 2), near metro Sportivnaya. Tickets (from R60 to R300) can be purchased at any Teatralnaya kassa or at the stadium where the game is being held; posters are plastered all over town well beforehand.

SHOPPING
Souvenirs & Soviet Memorabilia

Souvenir stands set up shop around all major tourist attractions, especially at the Hermitage, in front of the Peter & Paul Fortress, and at the **Souvenir Fair** (Map 5), diagonally across the canal from the Church on Spilled Blood. At each of these places, there are matryoshka dolls, palekh painted boxes, military gear, Russian-language T-shirts and watches galore. A certain amount of bartering is perfectly acceptable.

Khudozhestvennyye Promysly (Map 6; ☎ 113 14 95; Nevsky pr 51) is a major souvenir shop that can be pricey, but the selection and quality are good.

Truly beautiful Soviet-era commemorative stamps cost a handful of roubles each at the **philately booth** (window No 11) at the main post office (Map 4; Pochtamtskaya ul 9).

If the army's your thing, **Voyentorg** (Map 6; ☎ 314 62 54; Nevsky pr 67) is the place to come for original military clothing of all types and varieties, from soldiers' underwear (unused!) to officers' caps and parade uniforms.

Sekunda (Map 6; ☎ 275 75 24; Liteyny pr 61, enter through the courtyard) is a small place that sometimes has unusual souvenirs from old postcards to stuffed moose heads.

Lomonosova China Factory (Lomonosova Farforvy Zavod; Map 1; ☎ 560 85 44; pr Obukhovskoy Oborony 151; open 10am-7pm Mon-Sat, 11am-5pm Sun) has an outlet shop on site, where you get anything from the company catalogue at prices lower than in the department stores. From metro Lomonosovskaya, turn left (east), walk under the bridge to the embankment then left – the factory's ahead. The shop is inside the main door and to the right.

Arts & Antiques

There are dozens of art and antique shops throughout the city, but only some of them – generally the more expensive ones – will guide you through the customs-clearing procedures.

Often referred to simply by its address, **Free Arts Foundation** (Map 6; ☎ 164 53 71; Pushkinskaya ul 10, enter through arch at Ligovsky pr 53) is gallery central as far as modern art is concerned. There are lots of separate galleries all with different opening

ST PETERSBURG

times spread throughout the complex, but most are open on Saturday. You'll find anything from paintings and sculpture to digital works. Sometimes the space itself and its denizens are more intriguing than the actual art. Occasionally performance pieces take place, such as poets firing live rounds of ammunition at bottles of Baltika beer.

Sol-Art *(Map 3; ☎ 327 30 82;* **W** *www.solartgallery.com; Solyanoy per 15; open 10am-6pm daily)*, in the sumptuous surroundings of the Museum of Decorative & Applied Arts, is a great place to buy local, contemporary art, with thousands of paintings to rummage through and a large selection of Russian souvenirs, too.

Palitra *(Map 5; ☎ 277 12 16; Nevsky pr 166; open 11am-7pm Tues-Sat)*, a gallery owned and operated by St Petersburg artists is well worth a visit. **Art Gallery Borey** *(Map 6; ☎ 273 36 93; Liteyny pr 58)* is one of the cooler galleries in town.

The **Artists' Union of Russia Exhibition Center of Graphic Arts** *(Map 5; ☎ 24 06 22; Bolshaya Morskaya ul 38; open 1pm-7pm Tues-Sun)* displays the more establishment side of the St Petersburg arts scene. Check out the lovely wooden doors on the 3rd floor.

Pechatnya *(Printing Press; Peter & Paul Fortress Map; ☎ 238 07 42; Peter & Paul Fortress; open 11am-5pm daily)* offers yet another reason for visiting the Fortress. Check out the interesting collection of prints, both new and old and see printers at work.

Music, Video Cassettes & CD-ROMs

Saigon *(Map 6; ☎ 315 58 73; Nevsky pr 7/9)* is the biggest and most crowded music shop in the city, selling bootlegged and licensed tapes, imported CDs, T-shirts and videos.

Titanik *(Map 6; ☎ 310 49 29; Nevsky pr 52/54; open 24hrs)* is a chain store with several locations in the city, all stocking an overwhelming array of music CDs and videos.

Melodia *(Map 2; ☎ 232 11 39; Bolshoy pr 47, Petrograd Side)* stocks mainly CDs of Russian musicians and composers on the original Soviet record label.

Photography

One-hour drop-off places for prints are all over the city centre. For slide flim, professional rolls, equipment and development, your best option is **Yarky Mir** *(Map 6; ☎ 272*

56 41; ul Nekrasova 1; open 9am-9pm daily), which also has a branch at Nevsky prospekt 6.

For good deals on truly cool Soviet photographic equipment try **Bik Photo** *(Map 3; ☎ 272 09 35; Kirochnaya ul 36; open 11am-7pm daily)*, and in the basement **photo kiosk** *(Map 6; Nevsky pr 54)*, where you can also get passport photographs done.

Speciality Shops

Pchelovodstvo *(Map 6; ☎ 273 72 62; Liteyny pr 46; open 10am-7pm Mon-Sat)* is where you'll find many types of fresh honey from Russia's Rostov region, dozens of products, remedies and creams made from bee pollen, as well as unique teas, which make nice gifts.

Apart from selling Spanish reproductions of antique weaponry, **Soldat Udachi** *(Map 6; ☎ 279 18 50; ul Nekrasova 37 & Map 2; ☎ 232 20 03; Bolshoy pr 17, Petrograd Side)* has everything a modern-day Rambo could wish for, including GPS devices, Swiss army knives and camping gizmos.

Intendant *(Map 6; ☎ 311 15 10; Karavannaya ul 18/37)* is St Petersburg's finest wine shop. It stocks everything from fine table wines for R300 to a R68,000 bottle of Chateau Petrus – and the proper glasses to drink them out of.

Markets

Most of the city's markets are for food (see under Places to Eat earlier), but the best for trinkets, clothes, leather, technical appliances, and a huge music selection is **Warehouse Market** *(Map 1; ul Marshala Kazakova; open 9am-4pm Tues-Sun)*, a fair way southwest of the centre. From metro Avtova, cross the street and take express bus No 81 (five to seven minutes) straight there.

GETTING THERE & AWAY
Air

Pulkovo-1 and **Pulkovo-2** *(Map 1)* are, respectively, the domestic and international terminals that serve St Petersburg.

St Petersburg has direct air links with most major European capitals. Airline offices in St Petersburg include:

Aeroflot (☎ 327 38 72) Kazanskaya ulitsa 5
Air France (☎ 325 82 52) Bolshaya Morskaya ulitsa 35
Austrian Airlines (☎ 325 32 60) Corinthia Nevskij Palace Hotel, Nevsky prospekt 57

ritish Airways (☎ 329 25 65) Malaya
Konyushennaya ulitsa 1/3
SA Czech Airlines (☎ 315 52 59) Bolshaya
Morskaya ulitsa 36
elta Airlines (USA) (☎ 311 58 19) Bolshaya
Morskaya ulitsa 36
innair (☎ 326 18 70) Kazanskaya ulitsa 44
LM (☎ 346 68 68) Malaya Morskaya ulitsa 23
OT Polish Airlines (☎ 273 57 21) Karavannaya
ulitsa 1
ufthansa (☎ 320 10 00) Nevsky prospekt 32
Malev Hungarian Airlines (☎ 324 32 43)
Pulkovo-2, office 74
ulkovo Airline (☎ 327 38 72) Kazanskaya
ulitsa 5
candinavian Airlines System (SAS) (☎ 325 32
55) Corinthia Nevskij Palace Hotel, Nevsky
prospekt 57
ansaero (☎ 279 64 63) Liteyny prospekt 48

ickets for all airlines can be purchased from
ravel agencies such as **Sindbad Travel** (see
ravel Agencies under Information earlier
n this chapter) as well as from the **Central
Airline Ticket Office** (Map 6; ☎ 11 80 93;
levsky pr 7), which also has a counter for
ain tickets.

rain

he three major long-distance train stations
re: **Finland Station** (Finlyandsky vokzal; Map
; ☎ 168 76 87; pl Lenina, Vyborg Side), for
aily trains to and from Helsinki; **Moscow
tation** (Moskovsky vokzal; Map 6; ☎ 168 43
4; pl Vosstania), for services to/from Mos-
ow, the far north, the Urals, Siberia, Crimea
nd the Caucasus; and **Vitebsk Station**
Vitebsky vokzal; Map 5; ☎ 055; Zagorodny pr
2), for services to and from the Baltic states,
astern Europe, Ukraine and Belarus. **Baltic
tation** (Baltiysky vokzal; Map 4; ☎ 168 28
9) is for suburban trains.

Tickets can be purchased at the train sta-
ions, the **Central Train Ticket Office** (Map
; ☎ 162 33 44; nab kanala Griboedova 24),
he Central Airline Ticket Office (see Air
bove), Sindbad Travel and, at a huge mark-
p, from any luxury hotel.

Moscow Most of the 12 or so daily trains to
Moscow take seven to 8½ hours to complete
he journey. Several are overnight sleepers,
which save time and a night's accommodation
osts. To and from Moscow, the best overnight
rains are Nos 1/2 Krasnaya Strela (Red Arrow;
eparting from St Petersburg 11.55pm), 3/4
departure 11.59pm) and 5/6 Nikolaevsky

Express (departure 11.35pm/11.10pm). All of
these trains cost from R613.20 for the cheapest
kupe (compartmentalised) berth to R1508.30
for SV (sleeping wagon) class.

If you want to save money, a few services,
including train Nos 27/28 (10.30pm/9.30pm)
have platskartny (dorm) carriages with tickets for R232.70.

The fastest service is No 163/164 ER200,
which covers the 650km between the two
cities in 4½ hours – it leaves from both St
Petersburg and Moscow at 6.30pm on
Wednesday, Thursday, Sunday and Monday.
Kupe/SV tickets cost R602.70/787.70.

Finland There are two daily trains between
St Petersburg and Helsinki. The Repin, a
Russian-operated train, departs from Finland
Station at 7.15am, arriving at 12.03pm. From
Helsinki it leaves at 3.34pm and arrives at
10.37pm.

The Sibelius, a Finnish Railways–run train,
leaves St Petersburg at 5.01pm, arriving in
Helsinki at 9.28pm. It leaves Helsinki at
6.30am and arrives in St Petersburg at 1.07pm.
Tickets for both services are sitting/kupe
R1620/2490.

You can save yourself a few hundred rou-
bles by spending a lot of time: from St
Petersburg's Finland Station, take any train to
Vyborg Station, where you can meet the
Helsinki-bound Repin at 10.44am, or the
Sibelius at 6.52pm. The trip to Vyborg takes
approximately 2½ hours and costs R42 to
R75 depending on the service.

Poland There's a service six times a week
from St Petersburg to Warsaw. On Tuesday,
Thursday and Sunday trains leave at 11.45am,
and on Tuesday, Friday and Sunday at
11.16pm (R1710 kupe, 27 to 31 hours). These
trains pass through Belarus, for which you're
required to hold a transit visa (see ⓦ www
.belarusembassy.org for up-to-date information). A transit visa usually costs about US$15
and must be acquired in advance, not at the
border. Border guards have been known to
force people off trains and back to where they
came from if they don't have a visa.

Other Destinations Kupe fares to other
international destinations include: Berlin
(R3400, 38 hours, odd days); Kiev (R795, 30
hours, daily); Minsk (R990, 15¼ hours,
daily); Riga (R1524, 13 hours, daily); Tallinn

(R706, nine hours, odd days); and Vilnius (R1005, 14½ hours, odd days).

Other destinations served within Russia include: Arkhangelsk (R657 or R927 including sheets and breakfast, 24½ hours, daily); Kaliningrad (R1033, 26½ hours, daily); Murmansk (R814, 29 hours, daily); Nizhny Novgorod (R618, 15½ hours, daily); Novgorod (R107, 3½ hours, three daily); Novosibirsk (R2980, 69 hours, odd days); Petrozavodsk (R487, 8½ hours, daily); and Pskov (R222, 5½ hours, several daily).

Bus

St Petersburg's bus station **Avtovokzal No 2** *(Map 5; ☎ 166 57 77; nab Obvodnogo kanala 36)* – there isn't a No 1 – is 1km from Ligovsky Prospekt metro. It serves Tampere, Vyborg, Pskov, Novgorod, Moscow, Novaya Ladoga, Petrozavodsk and lots of other smaller destinations.

Eurolines *(Map 4; ☎ 168 27 48; W www.eurolines.ru; ul Shkapina 10)* operates four or five daily buses to Tallinn (R270-330, seven to eight hours), and daily buses to Tartu (R300, eight hours) and Riga (R500, 11 hours). It also has two or three buses a week to destinations in Germany. Its head office is 50m west of Baltic Station, but you can also buy tickets at its kiosk inside the Central Airline Ticket Office (see Air earlier) from 11am to 6pm Monday to Friday.

Stat Express *(Map 4; ☎ 168 20 03, fax 316 24 31; ul Shkapina 10)* has twice-weekly buses to Germany, stopping in 20 cities and towns.

Finland Daily buses to Tampere from Avtovokzal No 2 leave at 9.30am (R1140).

Finnord *(Map 6; ☎ 314 89 51; Italyanskaya ul 37)* runs buses to Helsinki via Vyborg and Lahti from its office (R1050 one-way). Buses leave at 3.40pm and 11pm and arrive in Helsinki at 10.30pm and 6am respectively.

Sovavto *(☎ 123 51 25; W www.pohjolan liikenne.fi)* has daily coaches to Helsinki (R1200) and Turku via Lappeenranta, as well as a Vyborg-Lappeenranta service. In St Petersburg, buses leave from the Grand Hotel Europe at 8.40am and 12.15pm, arriving at 3.45pm and 7.15pm respectively.

Car & Motorcycle

See the European Russia Getting Around chapter for general driving information. Always remember to take it slowly; not only

are there numerous speed traps (toward Vyborg, there's one just outside the cit limits, where the speed limit become 60km/h), but the state of some roads ca easily lead you to the repair shop in no time The road to the Estonian border can be par ticularly horrendous in spots.

Car Rental Some agencies offering self drive and chauffeured vehicles include:

Astoria-Service (Map 5; ☎ 112 15 83; Borovay ul 11/13) rents out cars with drivers only for th most reasonable rates – from R100 an hour fo an old Zhiguli to R240 an hour for a Mercede (minimum three hours).

Hertz (Map 5; ☎ 272 50 45; W www.hertz.spb.r Malaya Morskaya ul 23) has offices in the cit as well as at Pulkovo-2 airport. Its cheapes rental is around R2400 per day. Transfer service from the airport to the centre cost around R780

Svit (Map 4; ☎ 356 93 29; Pribaltiyskaya Hotel, Korablestroyteley 14) rents out Fords with dr vers for R600 per hour.

Boat

In 2002 the Finnish firm **Silja** *(W www .silja.com)* started running a 'mini-cruise' be tween St Petersburg and Helsinki. The cruis leaves Helsinki on Wednesday and Friday a 4pm, arriving in St Petersburg at 9am o Thursday and Saturday. Departures back t Helsinki are on the same day at 7pm, givin you around nine hours in the city. This is no intended as a ferry service and you can onl embark from Helsinki – if you leave the shi to tour St Petersburg you'll need to arrange t be on the group visa organised by Silja. Th cruise costs from around US$150 per perso for a basic four-berth cabin (including buffe dinner and breakfast), rising to US$650 for two-berth suite; it berths at the Sea Termina on Vasilevsky Island. There's also a recentl launched ferry service between St Petersbur and Kaliningrad. The boat is called *Georg O* and is supposed to be relatively comfortable if ancient. The cheapest tickets are R1100.

River Cruises In summer (June to August passenger boats ply the rivers and canals be tween Moscow and St Petersburg. The rout follows the Neva River to Lake Ladoga sometimes up to Valaam, to the Svir River an Lake Onega up to Kizhi (see the Norther European Russia chapter for more details the Volga-Baltic Canal to the Rybinsko eservoir and through some of the Golden ing along the Volga River to Moscow.

The **river terminal** (rechnoy vokzal; Map ; ☎ 262 02 39, 262 13 18; pr Obukhovskoy)borony 195), near metro Proletarskaya (turn ight upon exiting and take any tram one op), sells a wide variety of excellent cruises o Moscow, from five to 14 days long, taking n different routes.

Eight- to 12-day trips to Moscow including izhi, Valaam, Yaroslavl and many other tops cost from R7500 to R13,500, depend-ng on the class of cabin, including meals.

You can also check out what's available at ruise Russia (Map 5; ☎ 164 69 47; w www ruise-ru.com; Ligovsky pr 87). Prices are retty much the same as at the river terminal tself; both places book the same boats.

;ETTING AROUND

t Petersburg's excellent public transport sys-em makes getting around simple and inex-ensive. Pack a good pair of walking shoes: he centre is best seen on foot.

o/From the Airport

t Petersburg's airport is at Pulkovo, about 7km south of the centre. This is easily and very) cheaply accessed by metro and bus. rom Moskovskaya metro (not Moskovskie /orota), bus No 39 runs to Pulkovo-1, the omestic terminal, and bus No 13 runs to ulkovo-2, the international terminal. There re also plenty of minibuses. The trip takes bout 15 minutes. A metro and bus combo /ill get you there for under R20. If you're rriving at either of the airport terminals, gnore all enthusiastic offers of a taxi ride and vait at bus stops directly outside.

If you do opt for a taxi it will be cheaper oing from the city to the airport than vice ersa. From the city, hailing down a private ar is your cheapest bet – they'll do it for bout R150. A registered cab will cost you at east R300.

If you're coming from the airport, you'll e introduced to the bunch of thugs who con-rol who can park and wait for fares there. If here's a whiff of accent in your speech, hey'll ask for at least R1000 to get you into own, then bring it down to R900 if you com-lain and walk away (it's 20m on to the stop or bus No 13!).

You can also fax in advance **Astoria-ervice** (☎ 112 15 83), who could take you

---

Raising the Bridges

Many of St Petersburg's main bridges are raised every night when the Neva isn't frozen over (from the end of April to end of September) to let seagoing ships through. The following schedule (which every year changes by five minutes here or there; double-check once you're in the city) governs the lives of the city's motorists and nighthawks trying to get from one area to another. Watching the bridges rise is also a favourite romantic activity of locals and foreigners alike.

Alexandra Nevskogo (Map 5),
  2.30am–5.05am
Birzhevoy (Map 2), 2.10am–4.50am
Dvortsovy (Map 5), 1.35am–2.55am and
  3.15am–4.50am
Leytenanta Shmidta (Map 4),
  1.55am–4.50am
Liteyny (Map 3), 1.50am–4.40am
Petra Velikogo (Map 3), 2am–5am
Troitsky (Map 3), 2am–4.40am
Tuchkov (Map 2), 2.10am–3.05am and
  3.55am–4.45am

---

into town for under R600. If you're staying at any of the city's luxury hotels, or if your hotel package includes transfers, you'll be met by bus or minivan.

To/From Train Stations

Train stations are at or near metro stations, and taxis are easily found at each of them.

Metro

Though less majestic than Moscow's, the St Petersburg metro leaves most of the world's other undergrounds for dead. It's usually the quickest way around the city and you'll rarely wait more than three minutes for a train (even at 6am on a Sunday); the clock at the end of the platform shows time elapsed since the last train departed. The grandest stations are on Line 1. Stations open around 5.30am and close shortly after midnight.

Zhetony (tokens) cost R6 and can be bought from the booths in the stations. More convenient and better value are the magnetic-strip multi-ride pass-cards (for seven, 15 or 30 days with various multiples of rides). All metro stations have card-reading turnstiles –

place your card in the slot and when it comes back out you'll have a green light to proceed if there's sufficient credit left on the card.

Note that due to a cave-in of a section of a tunnel, there is an interruption in the Line 1 service north of the city. Lesnaya and Ploshchad Muzhestva are connected by a free shuttle-bus service (bus No 80). This should affect only those interested in visiting the Piskaryovskoe Cemetery or the Kruglye banya.

Bus, Trolleybus & Tram

Tickets (R5 to R10 depending on the service) are bought from a controller inside the vehicle. Bus stops are marked by roadside 'A' signs (for *avtobus*), trolleybus stops by 'Ш' (representing a handwritten Russian 'T'), tram stops by a 'T', all usually indicating the line numbers too. Stops may also have roadside signs with little pictures of a bus, trolleybus or tram. Most transport runs from 6am to 1am.

The following are some important long routes across the city:

Along Nevsky prospekt between the Admiralty and Moscow Station: bus Nos 7 and 22; trolleybus Nos 1, 5, 7, 10 and 22. Trolleybus Nos 1 and 22 continue out to Hotel Moskva and Alexander Nevsky Monastery. Trolleybus Nos 5 and 7 continue to Smolny.
Around the Sadovaya ulitsa ring road south of Nevsky prospekt: tram Nos 3, 13 and 14. Tram No 3 continues north of Nevsky prospekt and

then crosses the Troitsky most into Petrograd Side.
From the Hermitage to the Pribaltiyskaya Hotel on Vasilevsky Island: bus No 7; trolleybus No 10
To get to the Kamenny Islands, tram No 34 from the Baltic Station or Liteyny prospekt just north of Nevsky prospekt goes along Kamennoostrovsky prospekt and ends up on Krestovsky Island. Bus No 10 from the corner of Bolshaya Morskaya ulitsa and Nevsky prospekt will also get you there
To end up on Petrograd Side at the Botanical Gardens, bus No 128 runs from near Primorskaya metro station along both Bolshoy prospekts.

Taxi

Official taxis (four-door Volga sedans with chequerboard strip down the side and a green light in the front window) have a meter that drivers sometimes use, though you most often pay a negotiated price. If you want to book a taxi in advance try **Peterburgsky Taxi** (☎ *068*), **New Service** (☎ *327 24 00*) or **Taxi na Zakaz** (☎ *100 00 00*).

Most often, though, people use unofficial taxis, ie, any car you can stop. Stand at the side of the road, extend your arm and wait until something stops, which generally is little more than a few seconds. Negotiate the price for your destination before getting in; most short rides around the city centre shouldn't cost more than R50, for longer journeys R100 is acceptable. See the European Russia Getting Around chapter for safety rules on taking unofficial taxis.

Around St Petersburg

St Petersburg has a wealth of options for day-trippers. Between 25km and 45km from the city lie several splendid old tsarist palaces surrounded by lovely parks. In the Gulf of Finland, Kronshtadt, a once-closed naval base, has one of the most striking cathedrals in northern Russia. Farther northwest is the charming old Finnish town of Vyborg, and eastwards, near the banks of Lake Ladoga, are the Nizhnezvirsky Nature Reserve, and what very well could have been Russia's first capital, the sleepy village of Staraya Ladoga. If you have a bit more time, spending a night in a monastery on an island in Lake Ladoga is also possible.

Though all of these are accessible by public transport, tours of the palaces can be booked at the excursion booths at the west end of Gostiny Dvor on Nevsky prospekt. The tours cost around US$4 and are in Russian (English-language ones can be booked in advance for an extra fee: see Organised Tours in the St Petersburg chapter), but they are the simplest way to get there and back if you don't want to deal with public transport.

As for longer excursions from St Petersburg, check out Novgorod and Pskov in the Western European Russia chapter and Valaam and Kizhi islands in the Northern European Russia chapter.

PETRODVORETS
ПЕТРОДВОРЕЦ

This 'Russian Versailles' *(Nizhny Park & Park Aleksandriya; grounds adult/student R120/ 60, free after 4pm; open 9am-9pm daily),* 29km west of St Petersburg on the Gulf of Finland, is arguably the most impressive of St Petersburg's suburban palaces.

It's all a far cry from the original cabin Peter the Great had built here to oversee construction of his Kronshtadt naval base. He liked the place so much he built a villa, Monplaisir, and then a whole series of palaces across an estate originally called Petergof, which has been called Petrodvorets (pet-ra-dvar-**yets**, Peter's Palace) since 1944. All are set within a spectacular ensemble of gravity-powered fountains that are now the site's main attraction.

While Petrodvorets was trashed by the Germans in WWII (what you see is largely a

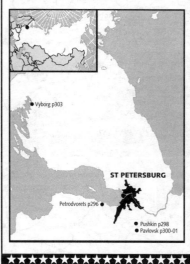

Vyborg p303

ST PETERSBURG

Petrodvorets p296

Pushkin p298
Pavlovsk p300-01

reconstruction), it suffered heaviest damage under Soviet bombing raids in December 1941 and January 1942 (according to more recent historians). Hitler, abandoning his hopes for a New Year's victory celebration inside St Petersburg's Hotel Astoria, planned to throw a party here, and drew up pompous invitations. Stalin ordered the place heavily attacked to thwart this.

Inexplicably, each museum within the estate has different closing days, and some are closed or only open for weekends from October to May. So generally you must try to see everything in a single day on weekends, when the place is swarming with visitors. All

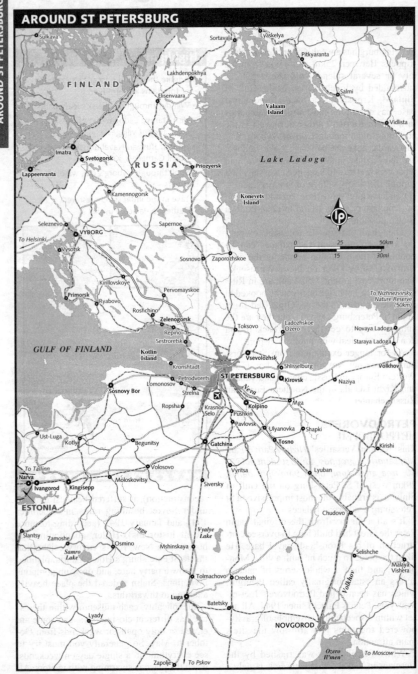

AROUND ST PETERSBURG

FINLAND

RUSSIA

Lake Ladoga

GULF OF FINLAND

Sulkava

Sortavala
Lyaskelya

Pitkyaranta

Lakhdenpokhya

Salmi

Elisenvaara

Vidlista

Valaam Island

Imatra
Svetogorsk

Lappeenranta

Priozyersk

Konevets Island

Kamennogorsk

To Helsinki

Seleznevo
VYBORG

Vysotsk

Sapernoe

To Nizhnezvirsky
Nature Reserve
(50km)

Kirillovskoye

Sosnovo
Zaporozhskoye

Pervomayskoe

Primorsk
Ryabovo

Roshchino

Zelenogorsk

Repino

Toksovo

Ladozhskoye
Ozero

Novaya Ladoga

Staraya Ladoga

Sestroretsk

Kotlin Island

Kronshtadt

Vsevolozhsk

Shlisselburg

Volkhov

ST PETERSBURG

Neva

Kirovsk

Naziya

Lomonosov
Petrodvorets

Kolpino

Mga

Sosnovy Bor

Strelna

Krasnoe
Selo

Pushkin

Ropsha

Pavlovsk

Ulyanovka
Shapki

Kirishi

Ust-Luga

Kotly

Begunitsy

Gatchina

Tosno

Lyuban

Volosovo

To Tallinn

Vyritsa

Narva
Ivangorod
Kingisepp

Moloskovitsy

Siversky

Chudovo

ESTONIA

Luga

Slantsy
Zamoshe

Osmino

Mshinskaya

Vyalye Lake

Selishche

Malaya
Vishera

Samro Lake

Tolmachovo
Oredezh

Luga

Batetsky

Lyady

Zapolje
To Pskov

NOVGOROD

Ozero Il'men'

To Moscow

0   25   50km
0   15   30mi

the attractions charge separate admissions. Admission to the grounds is payable at the cash booths on the jetty and outside the gates leading to the Grand Cascade.

Things to See

Grand Cascade The uncontested centrepiece is the Grand Cascade and Water Avenue, a symphony of (over 140) fountains and canals partly engineered by Peter himself. The central statue of Samson tearing open a lion's jaws celebrates – as so many things in St Petersburg do – Peter's victory over the Swedes.

There are trick fountains – triggered by hidden switches (hidden, that is, by hordes of kids jumping on them) – designed to squirt unsuspecting passers-by. Normally the fountains play from 11am to 7pm daily from the last weekend in May to September.

Grand Palace Between the cascade and the formal Upper Garden is the Grand Palace (*Bolshoy dvorets;* ☎ 427 95 27; adult/student R240/120; open 10am-6pm Tues-Sun, closed last Tues of month). Peter's modest project, finished just before his death, was grossly enlarged by Rastrelli for Empress Elizabeth and later redecorated for Catherine the Great. It's now a vast museum of lavish rooms and galleries – a monument above all to the craft of reconstruction (which is still going on). Anything not nailed down was removed before the Germans arrived, so the paintings, furniture and chandeliers are original.

Highlights include the **Chesma Hall**, full of huge paintings of Russia's destruction of the Turkish fleet at Çesme in 1770. Of some 20 rooms, the last, without a trace of Catherine, is the finest – Peter's simple, beautiful study, apparently the only room to survive the Germans. The study has 14 fantastic carved-wood panels, of which six reconstructions (in lighter wood) are no less impressive; each took 1½ years to do. Peter the Great still looks like the tsar with the best taste.

Tickets are sold inside, near the lobby where you pick up your *tapochki* (slippers worn over shoes to avoid damaging the wooden floors). But be warned: it's almost always packed with tour groups.

Monplaisir Peter's outwardly more humble, sea-facing villa (☎ 427 91 29; admission R100; open 10.30am-4pm Thur-Tues May-Sept, closed last Thur of the month) remained his favourite. It's not hard to see why: it's wood-panelled, snug and elegant, peaceful even when there's a crowd – which there used to be all the time, what with Peter's mandatory partying ('misbehaving' guests were required to gulp down huge quantities of wine).

To the west of Monplaisir is an annexe, called the **Catherine Building** (☎ 427 91 29; admission R100; open 10.30am-5pm Fri-Wed May-Sept, 10.30am-5pm Sat & Sun winter, closed last Fri of month), built by Rastrelli between 1747 and 1755; Catherine the Great was living here (conveniently) when her husband Peter III was overthrown. On the right side is Quarenghi's 1800 **Bath Building** (☎ 427 91 29; admission R60; open 10.30am-4pm Wed-Mon May-Sept, 10.30am-4pm Sat & Sun winter). Tsarist families and their guests once purified body and mind here.

Nizhny Park & Other Pavilions Along the gulf is Nizhny Park, with more fountains (watch out for the trick fountains) and pavilions.

Near the shore, the **Hermitage** (☎ 427 53 25; admission R90; open 10.30am-6pm Sat & Sun) is a two-storey pink-and-white box featuring the ultimate in private dining: special elevators hoist a fully laid table into the imperial presence on the 2nd floor, thereby eliminating any hindrance by servants. The elevators are circular and directly in front of each diner, whose plate would be lowered, replenished and replaced.

Farther west is yet another palace, **Marly** (☎ 427 77 29; admission R75; open 11am-4pm Sat & Sun), inspired by a French hunting lodge. To the east of the Grand Palace, an old orangery houses the **Historical Museum of Wax Figures**, containing 49 ho-hum figures of big-wigged Russians from the 18th and 19th centuries. Better is the **Triton fountain** outside, with its 8m jet of water.

Park Aleksandriya Even on summer weekends, the rambling, overgrown Park Aleksandriya (admission free), built for Tsar Nicholas I (and named for his tsarina), is peaceful and empty. Besides a mock-Gothic chapel, the park's diversions include the ruined **Farmer's Palace** (1831), which vaguely resembles a stone farmstead, and the **Cottage** (1829),

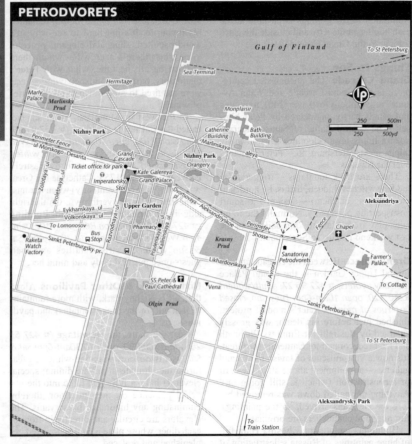

PETRODVORETS

Gulf of Finland

To St Petersburg

Sea Terminal

Hermitage

Marly Palace

Marlinsky Prud

Monplaisir

Nizhny Park

Catherine Building
Bath Building

Perimeter Fence

ul Morskogo-Desanta

Marlinskaya

aleya

Zolotaya ul

Grand Cascade

Ticket office for park

Nizhny Park

Proletarnaya ul

Kafe Galereya

Orangery

Imperatorsky Stol

Grand Palace

Dvortsovaya · Aleksandryskoe

Park Aleksandriya

Eykhanskaya ul

Upper Garden

Volkonskaya ul

To Lomonosov

Pharmacy

Perimeter

Chapel

Razvodnaya ul

Pravlenskaya ul

Shosse

Fence

Kalininskaya pl

Raketa Watch Factory

Bus Stop

Krasny Prud

Sanktu Peterburgsky pr

Sanatoriya Petrodvorets

Farmer's Palace

Likhardovskaya ul

To Cottage

SS Peter & Paul Cathedral

ul. Avrora

Sankt Peterburgsky pr

Vena

Olgin Prud

ul. Avrora

To St Petersburg

Aleksandrysky Park

To Train Station

0   250   500m
0   250   500yd

modelled on an English country cottage, which is now a museum.

Pharmacy Just east of the Upper Garden this renovated old-style **pharmacy** (☎ 427 95 78; open 8am-8pm Mon-Fri, 11am-6pm Sat, 9am-8pm Sun), with drawers full of medicinal plants, looks (and smells) like the real thing. You can sip herbal teas here and, if your Russian's good enough, ask the staff about your medical problem.

Petrodvorets Town The eye-catching five-domed **SS Peter & Paul Cathedral**, across the road and east of the palace grounds, is built in neo-Byzantine style but dates only from the turn of the 20th century. One bus stop west of the main palace entrance is the

Raketa watch factory (☎ 420 50 41; Sankt Peterburgsky pr 60) with a little boutique (open 10am-6pm Mon-Fri, 10am-5pm Sat) selling *very* cool watches.

Six kilometres east of Petrodvorets is **Strelna**, another estate with parklands and two palaces built for Peter (later enlarged for Empress Elizabeth by Rastrelli). One of these, the Konstantinovsky Palace, was chosen by Vladimir Putin as his summer residence.

Places to Eat

There are a few cafés scattered around Nizhny Park, none particularly outstanding and all overpriced: you could try **Kafe Galereya** (☎ 427 70 68), on the west side of Grand Palace, which has caviar-stuffed eggs and strawberries on its menu. Otherwise, you'd do better to pack a picnic.

Getting There & Away

The easiest way here is to hop on the regularly departing double-decker buses from outside the Baltic Station (R30, 40 minutes) and get off at the main entrance to the Upper Garden, on Sankt Peterburgsky prospekt. There's also a suburban train from the Baltic Station to Novy Petrodvorets (not Stary Petrodvorets), departing every 30 to 60 minutes until early evening, but then you'll have to take any bus but No 357 to the fifth stop, another 10 minutes.

From May to September, a fine alternative is the *Meteor* hydrofoil (R300 one way, 30 minutes) from the jetty in front of St Petersburg's Hermitage, which goes every 20 to 30 minutes from 9.30am to at least 7pm.

LOMONOSOV (ORANIENBAUM)
ЛОМОНОСОВ

While Peter was building Monplaisir, his right-hand man, Alexander Menshikov, began his own palace, **Oranienbaum**, 12km down the coast, a grand enterprise that eventually bankrupted him. Following Peter's death and Menshikov's exile, the estate served briefly as a hospital and then passed to Tsar Peter III, who didn't much like ruling Russia and spent a lot of time there before he was dispatched in a coup led by his wife Catherine (the Great).

Spared Nazi occupation, after WWII Oranienbaum was renamed for the scientist-poet Mikhail Lomonosov and now doubles as a **museum** and **public park** (*open 9am-10pm daily*), with boat rentals and carnival rides alongside the remaining buildings, all open 10am to 5pm Wednesday to Monday from May to October. Admission to the park is free.

Menshikov's **Grand Palace** (☎ 423 16 27; *adult/student R50/15*) impresses with its size, though many of its decrepit rooms are still under renovation. Beyond the pond is **Peterstadt** (*admission R50*), Peter III's boxy toy palace, with rich, uncomfortable-looking interiors and some Chinese-style lacquer-on-wood paintings. It is approached through the **Gate of Honour**, all that remains of a toy fortress where he amused himself drilling his soldiers.

Worth a peek also is Catherine's over-the-top **Chinese Palace** (*admission R50*). It's baroque outside and extravagantly rococo inside, with a private retreat designed by Antonio Rinaldi including painted ceilings and fine inlaid-wood floors and walls. Check out the blindingly sumptuous **Large Chinese Room**, done up in the 'Oriental' style of the day.

Perhaps Lomonosov's best feature is the several kilometres of quiet paths through pine woods and sombre gardens, with relatively small crowds; again it's a lovely place for a picnic.

Getting There & Away

The suburban train from St Petersburg's Baltic Station to Petrodvorets continues to Lomonosov. Get off at Oranienbaum-I (not II) Station, an hour from St Petersburg. From the station it's a short walk south, then west at the Archangel Michael Cathedral (Sobor Arkhangela Mikhaila) along Dvortsovy prospekt until you reach the palace entrance. There are also taxi-buses to both Petrodvorets and Lomonosov from outside metro Avtovo.

PUSHKIN & PAVLOVSK
ПУШКИН И ПАВЛОВСК

The sumptuous palaces and sprawling parks at Pushkin (sometimes called by its old tsarist name Tsarskoe Selo) and Pavlovsk, 25km and 29km south of St Petersburg, can be combined in a day's visit (but since they're both good for relaxing, you might take them more slowly).

Pushkin's palaces and parks were created under Empresses Elizabeth and Catherine the Great between 1744 and 1796. The centrepiece is the vast 1752–56 baroque Catherine Palace (Yekaterininsky dvorets), designed by Rastrelli and named after Elizabeth's mother, Peter the Great's second wife. The country's first railway opened in 1837 to carry the royal family between here and St Petersburg. The town changed its name from Tsarskoe Selo (Tsar's Village) to Pushkin in 1937 after Russia's favourite poet, who studied here.

Of the two estates, many find Pavlovsk's park of woodland, rivers, lakes, little valleys, avenues, classical statues and temples one of the most exquisite in Russia, while its Great Palace is a classical contrast to baroque Catherine Palace.

Catherine Palace

As at the Winter Palace, Catherine the Great had many of Rastrelli's original interiors remodelled in classical style. Most of the

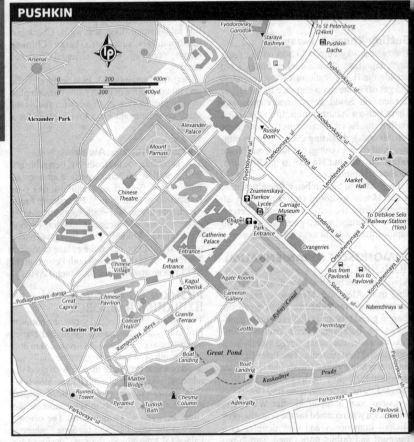

PUSHKIN

wonderful exterior and 20-odd rooms of the palace (☎ 466 66 99; Sadovaya ul 7, Pushkin; adult/student R300/150; open 10am-4.30pm Wed-Mon, closed last Mon of the month) have been beautifully restored – compare them to the photographs of the devastation left by the Germans.

Visits normally start with the white State Staircase (1860). South of here, only two rooms, both by Rastrelli, have been restored: the **Gentlemen-in-Waiting's Dining Room** and, beyond, the **Great Hall**, the largest in the palace, all light and glitter from its mirrors and gilded woodcarvings.

The rooms north of the State Staircase on the courtyard side are the **State Dining Room**, **Crimson** and **Green Pilaster Rooms**, **Portrait Room** and finally **Amber Room** (Yantarnaya

komnata). The latter was decorated by Rastrelli with gilded woodcarvings, mirrors, agate and jasper mosaics, and exquisitely engraved amber panels given to Peter the Great by the King of Prussia in 1716. But its treasures were plundered by the Nazis and went missing in Kaliningrad (then Königsberg) in 1945 (they're still looking for them!).

Most of the north end is the early classical work of Charles Cameron. The elegant proportions of the **Green Dining Room** (Zelyonaya stolovaya) on the courtyard side are typical. Also on the courtyard side are three rooms with fabulous, patterned silk wall-coverings: the **Blue Drawing Room** (Golubaya gostinaya), **Chinese Blue Drawing Room** (Kitayskaya golubaya gostinaya) and **Choir Anteroom** (Predkhornaya), whose gold silk, woven with swans and pheasants, is the original from the 18th century.

Pushkin Parks

Around the Catherine Palace extends the lovely **Catherine Park** (Yekaterininsky Park; adult/student R60/30; open 9am-6pm daily). The main entrance is on Sadovaya ulitsa, next to the palace chapel. The **Cameron Gallery** (adult/student R160/80; open 10am-5pm Wed-Mon) has changing exhibitions. Between the gallery and the palace, notice the south-pointing ramp which Cameron added for the ageing empress to walk down into the park.

The park's outer section focuses on the **Great Pond**, where you can rent boats in summer. This section is dotted with intriguing structures ranging from the **Pyramid**, where Catherine the Great buried her favourite dogs, to the **Chinese Pavilion** (or Creaking Summerhouse), **Marble Bridge** (copied from one in Wilton, England) and **Ruined Tower**, which was built 'ready-ruined' in keeping with a 1770s romantic fashion – an 18th-century empress's equivalent of prefaded denim.

A short distance north of the Catherine Palace, classical **Alexander Palace** (☎ 466 60 71; Dvortsovaya ul 2; adult/student R160/80; open 10am-5pm Wed-Mon, closed last Wed of the month) was built by Quarenghi in 1792–96 for the future Alexander I, but Nicholas II was its main tenant. It's the least touristed palace, so in some ways the most pleasant. The overgrown and empty **Alexander Park** (admission free) surrounds the palace.

Pavlovsk Great Palace & Park

Although designed by Charles Cameron between 1781 and 1786, on Catherine the Great's orders, for her son, the future Paul I, the interiors of Pavlovsk's **Great Palace** (☎ 470 21 55; ul Revolutsii; adult/student R240/120; open 10am-5pm Sat-Thur, closed 1st Fri of the month) were largely orchestrated by Paul's second wife Maria Fyodorovna.

A royal residence until 1917, the original palace was burnt down two weeks after liberation in WWII by a careless Soviet soldier's cigarette which set off German mines (the Soviets blamed the Germans). As at Tsarskoe Selo its restoration is remarkable: for more history check out the official website **w** www.pavlovskart.spb.ru.

The finest rooms are on the middle floor of the central block. Cameron designed the round Italian Hall beneath the dome, and the Grecian Hall to its west, though the lovely green fluted columns were added by his assistant Vincenzo Brenna. Flanking these are two private suites mainly designed by Brenna – Paul's along the north side of the block and Maria Fyodorovna's on the south. The Hall of War of the insane, military-obsessed Paul contrasts with Maria's Hall of Peace, decorated with musical instruments and flowers.

On the middle floor of the south block are Paul's Throne Room and the Hall of the Maltese Knights of St John, of whom he was the Grand Master.

If you skip the palace, it's a delight simply to wander around the serene park grounds (much less crowded than those at Pushkin) and see what you come across.

Places to Eat

Both palaces have tourist-trap, self-service cafeterias. There are other options.

Staraya Bashnya (The Old Tower; ☎ 466 66 98; 14 Akademichesky pr 14, Pushkin; meals US$30; open noon-10pm daily) consists of just four tables shoehorned into an old watchtower at this darling restaurant five minutes' walk north of the Alexander Palace, so you must book. It can be pricey, but you're bound to find something on its extensive menu to please and the atmosphere and service can't be beat.

A relative newcomer is **Russky Dom** (Russian House; ☎ 466 88 38; 3 Malaya ul, Pushkin; meals US$25; open noon-midnight daily). The interior is smartly decorated in a contemporary country Russian style that's all the rage. They serve lots of standard dishes including shashlyk, cooked on wood-fired braziers outside.

Podvorie (☎ 465 13 99; 16 Filtrovskoye Shosse, Pavlovsk; meals around US$25; open daily noon-11pm) looms large like a traditional Russian log house on steroids. This huge tourist-orientated restaurant near Pavlovsk Station has OK food which comes in big portions but is a little overpriced.

Getting There & Away

Get to either Pushkin or Pavlovsk by hopping in one of the many taxi-buses (R15, 30 minutes) that regularly shuttle to both towns from outside metro Moskovskaya.

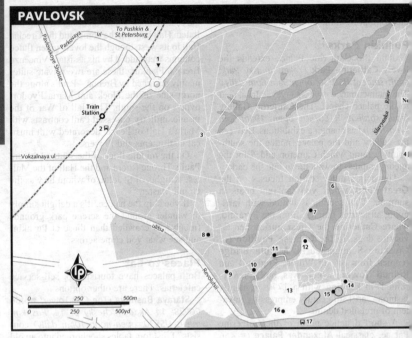

PAVLOVSK

Suburban trains run from Vitebsk Station in St Petersburg, but they're infrequent apart from weekends. For Pushkin get off at Detskoe Selo Station (R9, a zone 3 ticket), and for Pavlovsk (R12, zone 4) Pavlovsk Station. It's about half an hour to either place.

From the Detskoe Selo Station frequent minibuses (R5, 5 minutes) will take you to within two minutes of Pushkin's Catherine Palace. The same minibuses pause in front of Pavlovsk Station to take you to the front of the palace. Far nicer is to enter the park across the road from the station, and walk the 1.5km across to the palace. Walking at least one way across the park is recommended.

GATCHINA
ГАТЧИНА

The palace estate (☎ 271 134 92; admission R240; open 10am-5pm Tues-Sun) at Gatchina, 45km southwest of St Petersburg, was a gift from Catherine the Great to her lover Grigori Orlov for helping her get rid of her husband Peter III. It was later passed on to Catherine's son Paul I.

Today Gatchina is but a shadow of its former self. The palace, shaped in a graceful curve around a central turret, looks fine from the front, but is falling to pieces around the back. Inside, few of the rooms have been restored (work only began in 1985); the most interesting feature is a tunnel running from the palace to the ornamental lake.

Really the best reason for coming here is to wander around the leafy park which has many winding paths through birch groves and across bridges to islands in the lake. Look out for the **Birch House** (Beriozov Dom), with a facade made of birch logs, and the ruined **Eagle Pavilion** (Pavilion Orla).

In the nearby town there are a couple of interesting churches. The baroque **Pavlovsky Sabor** (ul Gobornaya), at the end of the main pedestrianised shopping street, has a grandly restored interior with a soaring central dome. A short walk west is the **Pokrovsky Sabor**, a red-brick building with bright blue domes.

Places to Eat

The excellent bakery and café **Dom Khleba** (ul Gobornaya 2) is one place where you could grab a snack. Across the street is the simple **Kafe Piramida** (ul Gobornaya 3), a friendly place with some outdoor seats, and

1 Podvorie
  Подворье
	10 Cold Baths
	  Холодная баня

2 Bus Stop
  Автобусная остановка
	11 Humpback Bridge
	  Горбатый мостик

3 The Circle Hall
  Круглый зал
	12 Temple of Friendship
	  Храм дружбы

4 Mausoleum
  Мавзолей
	13 Great Palace
	  Большой дворец

6 Visconti Bridge
  Висконтьев мост
	14 Grave of Revolutionaries
	  Могила жертв
	  революции

7 Great Cascade
  Большой каскад
	15 Rossi Pavilion
	  Павильон Росси

8 Rose Pavilion
  Розовый Павильон
	16 Pavilion of the
	  Three Graces

8 Summer Theatre Летний театр	Павильон трёх граций

9 Apollo Colonnade
  Колоннада Аполлона
	17 Bus Stop
	  Автобусная остановка

closer to the church, the Chinese restaurant **Shankhai Kafe** (*ul Gobornaya 15*).

Getting There & Away

Infrequent suburban trains run to Gatchina (R15, one hour) from Baltic Station. The palace is a minute's walk directly east of the station. Easier is to take the metro to Moskovskaya station and then bus No 431 (R20, one hour), which runs roughly every half-hour. In Gatchina the bus stops on prospekt 25 Oktyabrya: the park is immediately to the west.

KRONSHTADT
КРОНШТАДТ
☎ 812 • pop 45,100

Within a year of founding St Petersburg, Peter – desirous of protecting his new Baltic toehold – started work on the fortress of Kronshtadt on Kotlin Island, 29km out in the Gulf of Finland. It's been a pivotal Soviet and Russian naval base ever since, and was closed to foreigners until 1996.

The main reason to visit here is to view up close the exterior of the unusual and beautiful **Naval Cathedral** (*Morskoy Sobor*; 1903–13).

Built to honour Russian naval muscle, this neo-Byzantine-styled wonder stands on Anchor Square (Yakornaya ploshchad), where you'll also find an eternal flame for all of Kronshtadt's sailors, and the florid Art Nouveau monument of Admiral Makarov. The cathedral's intricately detailed facade (anchors and all) has an air of mystery – the off-limits interior has been used as a sailors' club and cinema since 1932. A section of the cathedral houses the mildly interesting **Central Naval Museum** (*☎ 236 47 13; admission R90; open 11am-5.15pm Wed-Sun*).

Otherwise, Kronshtadt is pleasant to stroll around. In the harbourside **Petrovsky Park**, 700m southwest of the cathedral, there's a statue of Peter the Great and you can glimpse Russian warships and even some submarines: be careful about taking photographs though. There are a few cafés along prospekt Lenina, the town's main drag: a good one is **Ckazka** at No 31, decorated with Disney characters.

In recent summers, Kronshtadt and some of the surrounding sea forts have been the scene of big dance parties, something St Petersburg aims to promote in the future – keep an eye out for posters in the city advertising events out here.

The Kronshtadt Mutiny

In 1921 Kronshtadt was the scene of a short-lived mutiny against the Bolsheviks, one of the last overt signs of opposition to the revolution until *perestroika* (restructure). The Red Army sailors stationed there, ironically, were the most revolutionary, pro-Bolshevik element in 1917; Trotsky called them 'the pride and glory of the Russian Revolution'.

Four years later, hungry and poor, the sailors set up a Provisional Revolutionary Committee and drafted a resolution demanding, among other things, an end to Lenin's harsh policy of War Communism. Red Army attempts to stifle the mutiny were at first repulsed, but on 16 March 1921 the mutineers were defeated when 50,000 troops crossed the ice from Petrograd and massacred nearly the entire naval force. Though bloodily suppressed, the event did cause Lenin to relax state pressure and scrap War Communism, marking the end of the Russian revolutionary movement.

★★★★★★★★★★★★★★★★★★★

Getting There & Away

Catch bus No 510 to the island from metro Staraya Derevnya (R20, 30 minutes) or take a taxi bus from metro Chyornaya Rechka; exit the station to your left, cross the street and veer right towards the bus stop where bus No E510 and any number of taxi-buses or private cars will be waiting.

In Kronshtadt, the bus stop is on the corner of ulitsa Grazhdanskaya and prospekt Lenina. From there it's about a 1km walk southeast to the Naval Cathedral.

VYBORG
ВЫБОРГ
☎ 278 • pop 81,000

Like Calais by the British, Vyborg (**vih**-bork) – a Gulf of Finland port, rail junction and the main border town, 174km northwest of St Petersburg – is visited by Finns for its cheap booze and other goods. Consequently you'll find a lot of drunk Finns here; ignore them and come to enjoy the lovely, if dishevelled, 13th-century town dominated by an imposing medieval castle and filled with old buildings and romantic, winding cobblestone streets.

Currently 30km away from Finland, the border has jumped back and forth around Vyborg for most of its history. Peter the Great added it to Russia in 1710. A century later it fell within autonomous Finland, and after the revolution it remained part of independent Finland. Since then the Finns have called it Viipuri. Stalin took Vyborg in 1939, lost it to the Finns and Germans during WWII, and on getting it back deported all the Finns.

Today it's a laid-back, Finnish-looking city full of Russian fishers, timber-haulers, military men, the usual border-town shady types – and carousing Finns. Its compactness makes it easy to walk everywhere. The main street, Leningradsky prospekt, cuts southwest from the railway station at the north to the Pantserlax bastion (1574).

There's a **telephone office** (cnr ul Mira & Moskovsky pr) located in town. The easiest places to change money are at the Druzhba or Vyborg hotels. Maps are available at the **bookshop** (pr Lenina 6), or from kiosks around town.

Things to See

Vyborg Castle (Vyborgsky zamok; ☎ 215 15; admission museum/tower R20/20, special exhibitions R10; museum open 11am-5.30pm Tues-Sun, tower 10am-5pm Tues-Sun), built on a rock in Vyborg Bay, is the city's oldest building, built by the Swedes in 1293 when they first captured Karelia from Novgorod. Most of it is now 16th-century alterations. Inside the castle is a mildly diverting small **museum** on local history, including a hokey set-up of a border post; skip this and climb the many steps of the tower for great views of the town.

Across the bridge is the **Anna Fortress** (Anninskaya Krepost) built in the 18th century as protection against the Swedes and named after Empress Anna Ivanovna. Behind this is **Park Monrepo Reserve** (☎ 205 39), a massive expanse of wooded and lake-dotted parkland one could spend a whole day in. Laid out in a classical style, it also has a forest feel to it; as pretty as Pavlovsk's park, only wilder. Curved bridges, arbours and sculptures complete the picture. To read about the park's interesting history, see ₩ www.obl museums.spb.ru/eng/museums/20/info.html.

Spend some time wandering the evocative streets in the town centre, with centuries-old churches, bell towers and cathedrals, especially along and off ulitsa Krepostnaya. On the way to the castle you'll pass the **Round Tower** (Kruglaya bashnya; 16th century) and the **Cathedral of the Transfiguration** (Spaso-Preobrazhensky sobor; 1787).

Places to Stay & Eat

There's little reason to stay overnight but, if you do, an interesting option is **Korolenko Boat Hostel** (☎/fax 3 44 78; cabins per person R450), opposite Hotel Druzhba. Set on a well-maintained 1957 Volga River cruise boat, the cabins are tiny with just a sink and shared showers and toilets, but they're nicely furnished and the staff are friendly. The 24-hour bar can get rowdy.

The more conventional options are **Hotel Druzhba** (☎/fax 2 57 44; ul Zheleznodorozhnaya 5; singles/doubles with breakfast US$53/66), with an outdoor beer garden, comfortable, if old-fashioned, rooms and a decent restaurant; and **Vyborg Hotel** (☎ 2 23 83, fax 2 80 48; ℮ hotel_vyborg@bcl.ru; Leningradsky pr 19; singles/doubles from R1100/1900), with pleasantly enough renovated rooms (note that the rates here go up by around 50% on weekends).

For a picnic, the **market** just north of the Round Tower has good fresh produce.

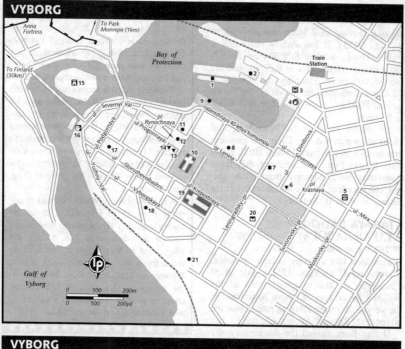

VYBORG

PLACES TO STAY
1 Korolenko Boat Hotel
 Гостиница Короленко
2 Hotel Druzhba
 Гостиница Дружба
7 Vyborg Hotel
 Гостиница Выборг

PLACES TO EAT
6 Champion
 Чэмпион
13 Pizzeria
 Пищерия
14 Bar-Restaurant
 Nordwest
 Бар-Ресторан
 Нордвест

OTHER
3 Bus Station
 Автовокзал
4 Neste Petrol Station
 Несте бензоколонка
5 Telephone Office
 Телефон - Телеграф
8 Book Shop
 Книги
9 Row boat rental
10 Peter & Paul Cathedral
 Собор Св Петра и
 Павла
11 Market
 Рынок
12 Round Tower & Restaurant
 Круглая Башня и Ресторан

15 Vyborg Castle
 Выборгский замок
16 Sea Passenger
 Terminal
17 Clock Tower
 Башня часов
18 City Hall Tower
 Башня ратуши
19 Cathedral of the
 Transfiguration
 Спасо-Преображенский
 Собор
20 Post Office
 Почта
21 Pantserlax Bastion
 Пантсерлакс
 бастион

Round Tower Restaurant (☎ 2 78 38; pl
Rynochnaya), on the top floor of the tower
itself, is the most atmospheric place in town
to eat, with reasonable meals for around
US$4. Across the street, the **Bar-Restaurant
Nordwest** (☎ 2 58 93) looks a bit tacky but
has a longer menu (in English); try its salmon
cream soup for R45. It's also open 24 hours.
If neither of these appeal, there's a **Pizzeria**

next door that does cheap slabs of pizza,
various pastries and salads in a bright setting.

 Champion (cnr ul Dimitrova & pr Lenina;
open noon-2am daily) also serves food and is
hands-down the coolest bar in town.

Getting There & Away

Several suburban trains leave St Petersburg's
Finland Station (R42, 2½ hours), usually

early in the morning and in the late afternoon. The best service is the daily No 87 *Baltika* leaving at 7.54am and arriving at 9.20am (R75). It has comfy seats and a buffet. There's another fast service (No 97) daily except Wednesday at 6.27pm, and the No 95 service on Saturday and Sunday at 12.43pm. Returning from Vyborg, the No 88 goes at 10.03am, No 96 at 2.50pm and No 98 at 8.28pm.

All buses between St Petersburg and Helsinki stop at Vyborg. There are also several buses a day to/from Vyborg (R60, 2½ to three hours). From St Petersburg, they leave Avtovokzal No 2 and stop in front of the western entrance/exit of the Ploshchad Lenina metro, on ulitsa Botkinskaya.

STARAYA LADOGA
СТАРАЯ ЛАДОГА
☎ 263 • pop 3000

It may look like a sleepy village, but once, Staraya (Old) Ladoga, 125km east of St Petersburg on the winding banks of the Volkhov River, was an active participant in the very birth of the Russian nation (see the boxed text 'Russia's Ancient Capital').

Dating from around the 8th century, the town was known only as Ladoga until 1704 when Peter the Great founded Novaya (New) Ladoga to the north, as a transfer point for the materials arriving to build St Petersburg. Protected as a national reserve, the town's basic structure and street patterns have remained virtually unchanged since the 12th century, give or take a few ugly Soviet blocks. The area boasts over a hundred items of archaeological and historical interest, including an ancient fortress and churches. It's a pleasant place to wander for a few hours, particularly in summer when a swim in the river adds to the charm.

Things to See

Within the **fortress** (*Staroladozhskaya Krepost; open 9am-6pm Tues-Sun June-Aug, 9am-4pm Tues-Sun Sept-May*), at the southern end of the village, you'll find the stone **St George's Church** (*Tserkov Georgiya; admission R30*), only open during dry weather, to protect the delicate 12th-century frescoes still visible on its walls, and the wooden **Church of Dimitri Solun**.

The main tower of the fortress is the **Historical-Architectural & Archaeological**

Russia's Ancient Capital

Just as the origins of Rus are continually debated, so will Staraya Ladoga's status as 'Russia's first capital'. Nevertheless, its age (historians have given 753 as the village's birthdate) and significance remain uncontested.

According to some ancient texts, when the Scandinavian Viking Rurik, along with his relatives Truvor and Sineus, swept into ancient Russia in 862, he built a wooden fortress at present-day Staraya Ladoga and made this his base. Locals even claim the tumulus on the banks of the Volkhov River at the northern end of the village is the grave of Oleg, Rurik's successor.

Archaeological expeditions continue to uncover a wealth of information about the town's past. In 1997, a second 9th-century fortress was discovered 2km outside the village, and it's known that at one time, six monasteries worked in this small region. Evidence of Byzantine cultural influences in the frescoes of the village's 12th-century churches point to the town as a cultural as well as historical and commercial crossroad.

★★★★★★★★★★★★★★★★★★★★

Museum (*☎ 4 93 31; admission R15*) housing a retrospective of the area's history.

The **John the Baptist Church** (Ioanna-Predtechi tserkov; 1694), located atop the highest hill in the area at the north end of the village, is the only church with a regular weekend service. On this site was a 13th-century monastery. Nearby, beside the river banks, is an ancient burial mound and, beneath the church, caves where glass was once made.

There are no hotels in Staraya Ladoga, but you can get to eat at **Ladya**, a surprisingly decent restaurant above the general store on the main road through the village.

Getting There & Away

Take one of the frequent *elektrichka* to Volkhov (the Volkhovstroy I station) from Moscow Station in St Petersburg (R30, 2½ hours). From Volkhov, take bus or minibus No 23 (R10, 20 minutes) headed towards Novaya Ladoga from the main bus stop outside the station, just across the square. The second of the three town bus stops lets you off just past the fortress.

NIZHNEZVIRSKY NATURE RESERVE
НИЖНЕЗВИРСКИЙ ГОСУДАРС-ТВЕННЫ ЗАПОВЕДНИК

On the southeastern shore of Lake Ladoga (**lah**-da-ga), the 414 sq km Nizhnezvirsky Nature Reserve (☎ 81264-2 05 21; e orlan@orlan.spb.su), 175km from St Petersburg, is an important stopover for migratory birds and home to a variety of animals, among them the Lake Ladoga ringed seal, a freshwater subspecies peculiar to the area. Arrangements to visit the reserve can be made directly, or through the American Association for the Support of Ecological Initiatives. In St Petersburg call Alexander Karpenko of the AASEI's local branch **ADONIS** (☎ 812-307 09 18; e alexk@aasei.spb.su), or contact director Bill Wasch at its **US headquarters** (☎ 860-346 2967, fax 347 8459; e wwasch@wesleyan.edu).

KONEVETS ISLAND
ОСТРОВ КОНЕВЕЦ

If you have more time, consider taking a boat excursion to Konevets Island, around 100km north of St Petersburg, close to the western shore of Lake Ladoga. The monastery here was founded in 1393 by Arseny Konevetsky. In Soviet times, it was an off-limits military base (some scientific experiments are still conducted here), and the destruction is still visible. Reopened as a monastery in the early 1990s, with Finnish funding, it has undergone massive restoration.

There are several chapels as well as the main Kremlin grounds, near which is a large guesthouse. On a huge boulder sits a lonely chapel; this was the site of pagan horse-slaughtering rituals. It makes a pleasant break for a day or so, with peaceful, clean beaches and lots of forests to wander through.

Getting There & Away

First contact the monastery's **office** (☎ 812-311 71 94; Zagorodny pr 7) in St Petersburg to check the boat schedules and availability to stay overnight. It's about three hours by public transport (suburban train from Finland Station to Gromovo, direction Priozyersk, then bus No 624 one hour to the last stop). One night including vegetarian meals should cost about US$15. More information can be had via w www.orthodoxy.ru/konevitsa.

Western European Russia
Западно-Европейская Россия

Western European Russia, between Moscow and St Petersburg and the borders of Ukraine, Belarus, Latvia and Estonia, is an area of rolling hills, endless steppe and long-contested borders. This area saw the heaviest fighting in the country during WWII; towns in the south of the region such as Kursk, Oryol, Bryansk and Smolensk have all been devastated by war on several occasions. For the most part they have been thoroughly rebuilt, and today you will find everything here from sleepy roadside villages to large industrial cities.

By a quirk of geopolitical fate, this region also includes Kaliningrad, the strategically important wedge of Russia between Lithuania, Poland and the Baltic Sea. Not included in this chapter are European Russia's two largest cities – Moscow and St Petersburg – or the surrounding areas. These are covered in previous chapters.

HISTORY

The region was settled by the Slavs, migrating from the west, in about the 6th to 8th centuries AD. At the same time Varangians (Vikings) from Scandinavia began trading and raiding across the region en route to the Black Sea. In 862, apparently at the invitation of local Slavic tribes, Varangians under Prince Rurik came to rule and establish order in the land of 'Rus'. Their first permanent settlement, Novgorod, is seen by many as the birthplace of Russia. Rurik's successor Oleg founded the Kyivan Rus state, and the upstart principalities of Vladimir and Muscovy are descended from the same line.

By the 12th century, Novgorod was a European political and commercial centre that began expanding aggressively, increasingly attracting the attention of the Swedes, who had held sway in most of present-day northwest Russia. The friction, at first economic, took on a religious tenor as Swedish crusaders tried to push back the Orthodox 'heathens'. Novgorod's Prince Alexander Nevsky is considered a Russian hero for thrashing both the Swedish and Teutonic crusaders in the 1240s, putting an end to Christian intentions in Russia.

Highlights

- Gaze at the centuries-old frescoes of the legendary Theophanes the Greek in Novgorod's 14th-century Church of Our Saviour-at-Ilino

- Breathe the moist air of the marshes during a stroll around Yurev Monastery, near Novgorod

- Descend into the spooky burial caves of the Pechory Monastery, followed by a drive through the surrounding Pskov region

- Pay homage to 19th-century Russian literature at Oryol, Mikhailovskoe, Staraya Russa and Spasskoe-Lutovinovo

- Hear the Smolensk orchestra play in the hall where Russian music patriarch Mikhail Glinka once performed

- Explore the dramatic sand dunes and pine forests of Kurshkaya Kosa, the Kaliningrad region's half of the Curonian Spit

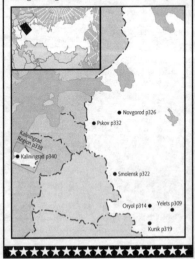

- Novgorod p326
- Pskov p332
- Kaliningrad Region p338
- Kaliningrad p340
- Smolensk p322
- Oryol p314
- Yelets p309
- Kursk p319

★★★★★★★★★★★★★★★★★★★★★★

Though the Mongol Tatars got only as far as the swamps outside Novgorod, the city's princes sensibly accepted the Tatars as rulers. By 1480 Ivan III had driven out the Tatars and annexed Novgorod and all its northern

306

WESTERN EUROPEAN RUSSIA

lands for Moscow. South of Moscow, towns such as Oryol and Voronezh were founded to serve as fortifications against the Tatars.

From 1558 to 1583, Ivan IV (the Terrible) fought Poles, Lithuanians and Swedes in an unsuccessful grab for Baltic real estate. Soon afterwards, with Russia in a shambles during the Time of Troubles, Sweden and Poland took bits of western Russian territory, including Smolensk and the east end of the Gulf of Finland.

Under the reign of the early Romanovs (1613–82), Russia gradually expanded its territories west and south of Moscow, but experienced revolts from Cossack communities, including those from Voronezh, near the Don River.

Determined to defeat the Swedes and reach the Baltic, Peter the Great made an alliance with Poland and Denmark, and forced his way to the Gulf of Finland, pausing only to lay the foundations of St Petersburg. With his new navy, he won the Great Northern War (1700–21), gaining everything back from Sweden, plus the Baltic coastline down to Riga in Latvia. With the Partitions of Poland between 1772 and 1795, Russia's western

territories expanded further to include Lithuania, Belarus and much of Poland.

In 1920 Soviet Russia recognised the independence of Estonia, Latvia and Lithuania. During the early stages of WWII secret deals that had been struck with Nazi Germany allowed the USSR's western European border to expand again. Hitler subsequently invaded the western USSR, including the Baltic States, but lost it all (plus Kaliningrad, a previously German city) to the Red Army towards the end of the war. The tumultuous events of 1990–91 saw the new independence of the Baltic states, Belarus and Ukraine and made Russia's western boundaries into borders between countries, rather than just between republics of the Soviet Union.

South & West of Moscow

Three main routes head southwest from the Moscow region. The eastern route, along the M4 highway, leads to Yelets and Voronezh. The central route, taken by the M2 highway and the railway heading for Kharkiv (Kharkov) in Ukraine, leads through Oryol, Kursk and Belgorod. The southwestern route, heading ultimately for Kiev, leads to Bryansk, just off the M3 highway. All these routes take you over rolling, always-changing steppe. The towns in this region are generally very poor, with large portions of the populace unemployed and given to loitering on street corners, often in Adidas sweatclothes, for some reason. Keeping a low profile will help you to avoid offence or threats, though for the most part the residents are not anti-foreigner or aggressive – they're just bored.

YELETS
ЕЛЕЦ

☎ 07416 • pop 120,000

Yelets was founded along the Sosna River in 1146 as a fortification against the Polovtsy, the invaders from the east. It was sacked by Tatars three times and rebuilt in the 16th century; what remains of the town now is like a perfect movie set of mid-19th-century Russian life. The centre is laid out in a logical grid and the streets are lined with colonnaded buildings, wood and brick 19th-century houses and only the occasional post-war Soviet monstrosity.

The town's showpiece, visible from kilometres around, is the beautiful Ascension Cathedral, which was designed by Konstantin Ton (1794–1881), the architect who brought us St Petersburg's Moscow and Moscow's Leningrad train stations. There's a great view of it from the bridge crossing the Sosna, just east of the town. And tucked into the town's tidy streets are about half a dozen working churches and cathedrals, plus the ruins of several more. A well-stocked regional museum and a museum devoted to Soviet composer Tikhon Khrennikov are other attractions.

Yelets is a charming and relaxing town in the midst of some beautiful countryside, with a surprising number of sights for such a small place. If you do not require much in the way of nightlife or hotel amenities, you might consider staying here and making the far larger and gruffer Voronezh into a day trip.

Orientation & Information

Yelets is 78km west of Lipetsk, 180km south of Tula, 170km east of Oryol and 140km northwest of Voronezh.

Post-Soviet street names, official for nearly a decade now, have not caught on with Yelets locals or cartographers. In this chapter we use the old, more useful street names, with the new names provided in parentheses at the first mention, in case they come into more common usage.

To reach the centre from the train station, walk to the west end of the platform and cross the tracks to the bus stop. Long-distance buses stop a hundred metres or so down the road to the left. Take bus No 1 into the city centre – a seven-minute ride. The bus runs about every 10 to 15 minutes and stops just past Hotel Yelets on ulitsa Kommunarov (Orlovskaya), the city's main street.

Excellent Russian-language maps (R25) are available from kiosks or the café in Hotel Yelets. If you are interested in Russian-language excursions, visit the **tourist office** (☎ 2 06 18; ul Mira 121). You can change money (US dollars and euros only) at the **Lipetsky Oblastoi Bank** (ul Kommunarov) between ulitsa Mira (Torgovaya) and ulitsa Oktyabrskaya (Sobornaya). If you can manage squeeze in among eager Yelets schoolkids, you can log on at the Internet venue at ulitsa Mira 96 for R50 an hour.

Churches

The highlight is the working **Ascension Cathedral** (Voznesensky sobor; foot of ul Kommunarov) which sits at the eastern end of the street. Every wall of the fantastical, multicoloured interior is stacked high with iconography and gilt. Services take place from 8am to 11am and 5pm to 7pm daily.

The **Vvedenskaya Church** (Vvedenskaya tserkov) on ulitsa Shevchenko (Vvedensky spusk) is a tiny, peaceful jewel box of a church near a cluster of photogenic late-17th- and early-18th-century wooden houses. Garden benches line the brief entrance path. At the bottom of the hill, a path under the trees bearing right leads in summer to a floating footbridge over the river to the **local beach**.

Great Count's Church (Velikoknyazheskaya tserkov) on ulitsa Sovietskaya (at ulitsa Tolstogo) has to be one of the most unique of Russia's churches. Built during the early 1900s, it has a distinctly modernist, even Art Nouveau flair. The cross on the top is made of crystal, supposedly donated from the local glassware factory.

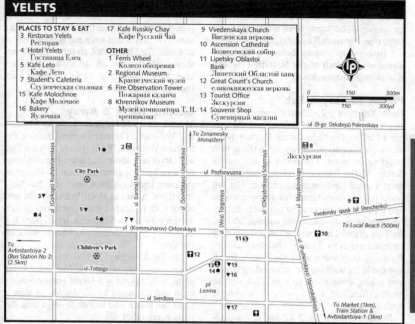

YELETS

PLACES TO STAY & EAT
3 Restoran Yelets
 Ресторан
4 Hotel Yelets
 Гостиница Елец
5 Kafe Leto
 Кафе Лето
7 Student's Cafeteria
 Студенческая столовая
15 Kafe Molochnoe
 Кафе Молочное
16 Bakery
 Яблочная

17 Kafe Russkiy Chay
 Кафе Русский Чай

OTHER
1 Ferris Wheel
 Колесо обозрения
2 Regional Museum
 Краеведческий музей
6 Fire Observation Tower
 Пожарная каланча
8 Khrennikov Museum
 Музей композитора Т. Н.
 зренникова

9 Vvedenskaya Church
 Введенская церковь
10 Ascension Cathedral
 Вознесенский собор
11 Lipetsky Oblastoi
 Bank
 Липетский Областой банк
12 Great Count's Church
 еликокняжеская церковь
13 Tourist Office
 Экскурсии
14 Souvenir Shop
 Сувенирный магазин

WESTERN EUROPEAN RUSSIA

Other Attractions

The town's **City Park** (Gorodskoy Park) is quite relaxing, with a Ferris wheel that spins during summer. There's a small **Children's Park** (Detsky Park) across the street, with basic playground equipment used by lots of smiling kids.

For a great view of the town's gilded cupolas, ask the firefighters at the antique red-brick fire house to let you climb up their **fire observation tower** (ul Kommunarov).

The town's **Regional Museum** (Kraevedchesky muzey; ulitsa Lenina 99 (Manezhnaya); admission R5; open 9am-5pm Tues-Sat), just off ulitsa 9-go Dekabrya (ulitsa Pokrovskaya), houses artefacts from Yelets' colourful past. Particularly interesting are the model of ancient Yelets and the remarkably comprehensive collection of Russian coins from the 4th century BC to the Soviet era. Upstairs is a collection of paintings by local 19th-century artist Meshchkov and information on the WWII experience in the area.

The crisp new **Khrennikov Museum** (Dom-Musey Khrennikova; ☎ 4 94 76; ul Mayakovskovo 16) pays homage to the successful Soviet composer on the site where he

grew up and first studied music. Original furniture, photos and artefacts fill the small house; because Khrennikov was favoured by the Soviet state, the documentation is also interesting in terms of the history of Soviet aesthetics. Writer IA Bunin also spent some of his childhood here, studying at the Yelets gymnasium. A small **museum** (☎ 2 43 29; ul Gorkogo 16) chronicles his life and works.

The main **shopping street**, ulitsa Mira, is perhaps the most picturesque street in town (the kind of street where horse-drawn coal carts would look perfectly appropriate). At the southern end sits the town's main square, **ploshchad Lenina**, which looks like a movie set for an Ostrovsky drama, only all the actors have gone home. On the square, opposite the direction in which Lenin is pointing, is a souvenir shop.

The crumbling tower visible over the town's north end is the early-19th-century **Znamensky Monastery**. For a nice hour-long hike, follow ulitsa Sovietskaya toward the monastery. At the fork in the road, veer right downhill to the water and cross the homemade footbridge. A bit to your left will be the base of a stone stairway leading up to the monastery. All that's left today are remnants of the old wall, the shell of a tower, and an unsurpassed view over all Yelets. The large blue cupolas off to the right, as you look out from the monastery, belong to the now-abandoned **Church of the Nativity** (Tserkov Khristorozhdestvenskaya).

Places to Stay & Eat

Hotel Yelets (☎ 2 22 35; ul Kommunarov 14; singles/doubles from R192/330), on the corner of ulitsa Gorkogo (ulitsa Rozhdestvenskaya), is the only hotel and it's in the ugliest building in town. The doors to the rooms barely fill the frames, leaving space for the hotel's small cockroach population. The hot water is sometimes turned off during summer and toilet paper seems to be rationed. But the rooms have nice views of the cupolas, and the staff are grateful for tourists – so grateful they charge foreigners double what they charge Russians. If by some quirk the hotel is filled, you could try walking the surrounding streets and asking for a room to rent. This will be more difficult in winter, when everyone is huddled inside.

Restoran Yelets (☎ 2 22 96; ul Kommunarov 18), located in the same building as the hotel (go outside and turn left), is a red velvet, disco-light extravaganza. The live music – synchronizer, drum box and schmaltzy vocalist – starts at 8pm. The food, on the other hand, is very good. The *firmennye blyuda* (house specialities) are good bets. Listed on the first page of the menu and changed periodically, they always include some tasty meat dishes (R60 to R100) and bliny (R30 to R100).

The cafeteria-style **Kafe Russkiy Chay** (pl Lenina; open to 8pm) is a wondrous place. There is blissful silence unless a customer requests the Russian pop that plagues every other establishment, and there are actually 'no smoking' signs on the walls! Just don't get your heart set on anything on the menu until you've asked what's available. Each dish tastes much like the next, but you can have a full meal including drinks for well under R50.

Similarly basic fare can be had at the then **Kafe Molochnoe** (98 ul Mira). Why not try the *kasha risov* (boiled rice) for R3, or the beef goulash (R14)?

A central **bakery** (ul Mira at pl Lenina) has croissants and jam-filled *bulochki* (small buns) but no coffee, despite the sign.

Kafe Leto, just inside the park off ulitsa Kommunarov, has the standard *pelmeni* (small dumplings usually filled with meat), shashlyk, salads and soup but is open only in summer. The **Student's Cafeteria** (Studencheskaya Stolovaya; cnr uls Orlovskaya & Lenina; open 11am-6pm daily) backs up to the local university and is sinfully cheap.

Getting There & Away

Yelets is on the M4 highway between Moscow and Voronezh. There are several buses a day to/from Voronezh (R58). Buses to/from Tula and Oryol take about six hours. The two long-distance bus stops are near the train station on the main highway; from here, take bus No 1 into town. A taxi to Hotel Yelets should cost about R40. Buses to local destinations as well as some buses to Voronezh leave from bus stop No 1 (Avtostantsiya-1) next to the train station.

On the Moscow–Donetsk railway, Yelets has several daily services to Moscow (R380, eight to 10 hours) and Oryol (four hours by train and six hours by *elektrichka*, a slower suburban train). The Voronezh–Riga train departs every other day.

The **train station** (☎ 3 31 09) has lockers (R25 per day). While at the station, don't miss the banner-waving collection of Soviet socialist realist oil paintings in the main hall.

VORONEZH
ВОРОНЕЖ
☎ 083 • pop 1,000,000

Voronezh is a city scraping and clawing its way out of the Soviet era, with few immediate signs of success. Construction is rampant in this large, industrial city, giving rise to everything from gleaming new churches to cookie-cutter apartment buildings – but all the scaffolding cannot conceal the poverty that afflicts most citizens here. The city is abysmally poor, and isolated investments that benefit a tiny elite do not begin to touch the population at large.

The Adidas-clad young men who seem to lurk on every corner of provincial European Russia are especially numerous and especially sullen in Voronezh. They are generally harmless, but solo women should step up the usual cautions here. Prostitution may be Voronezh's only booming industry, and any eye contact or other acknowledgement could be taken as an invitation.

Though Voronezh lacks the charm and accessibility of smaller towns in the region, it does contain several interesting sights. The city and the surrounding district are fondly remembered by many Russians for a rich history, which you can sample at a handful of small museums. The beautiful St Alexey monastery is also well worth a visit. Beyond these sights, though, Voronezh, with its overpriced hotels, a dearth of restaurants and generally depressed atmosphere, is not a town for extended lingering.

History

Voronezh was first mentioned in 12th-century chronicles, but it was officially founded in 1585 as a fortress against the invading Tatars. Some *stanitsa* (Cossack villages) were established in this frontier region, and uprisings against Russian domination were common. Some of the more legendary uprisings were led by Stenka Razin in 1670–71 and Kondraty Bulavin in 1707–08.

During the reign of Peter the Great, the first Russian warship, the *Predestinatia*, was built here in 1696; more than 200 warships from the Voronezh dockyards followed to form the new Russian fleet.

During WWII the city suffered frontline fighting for 200 days, when over 90% of its buildings were destroyed (especially during the most intense skirmishes in July and August 1942).

Orientation & Information

The main street is prospekt Revolyutsii; its northern tip is connected to the train station by ulitsa Koltsovskaya, while the southern tip passes through ploshchad Lenina before becoming ulitsa Kirova. The other main street is ulitsa Plekhanovskaya, intersecting at ploshchad Lenina. The eastern bank of Voronezh across the reservoir was founded in 1928. In fact the view across the river is a Soviet dream: factories and smokestacks piled one upon the other and all becloaked in the smog of productivity.

Once they recover from the shock of encountering visitors to their city, the staff at the **Voronezh Office of Travel & Excursions** (☎ 55 25 70; *ul Plekhanovskaya 2*) will offer excursions through town. English-language tours are unlikely, but not impossible; call in advance. There are several places to change US dollars and euros, including **Sberbank** (*ul Ple-*

khanovskaya 12 • pr Revolyutsii 52); it has two convenient locations with 24-hour ATMs. The main **post office** (*pr Revolyutsii 23*) has Internet service to the left inside the entrance, while **Firma Krista** (*pr Revolyutsii 33*) offers telephone, fax and copy services. You can also browse the Internet in the ground-level computer centre at the **public library** (*pl Lenina 2*) for around R30 to R50.

Usable Russian-language maps of the city are available from kiosks at the train station and from **Knizhniy Mir** (*pr Revolyutsii 37*), while **TsUM** on the opposite side of the street can satisfy your department-store needs. For information on goings-on around town, as well as current museum exhibitions, pick up the *Kamelot Programma*, published each Wednesday, at any newsstand.

Museums

The **IN Kramskoy Regional Fine Arts Museum** (*Khudozhestvenny muzey IN Kramskogo;* ☎ 55 38 67; *pr Revolyutsii 18; admission R10; open 10am-6pm Tues-Sun*) is reached through a passage into the courtyard; look for the large green structure. Russian painting and sculpture, Greek and Roman sculpture and an Egyptian sarcophagus form the bulk of the collection, with exhibitions of modern local artists behind the main building.

Well stocked if not well lit, the **Regional Museum** (*Kraevedchesky muzey;* ☎ 52 38 92; *ul Plekhanovskaya 29; admission R5; open 10am-6pm Wed-Sun*) has permanent exhibits on Peter the Great and the history of the region from the pre-Bronze Age to the Soviet era. It is closed on the first Wednesday of each month. Postcards of old Voronezh are on sale at the *kassa* (ticket office).

The large, two-storey **Museum of the Great Patriotic War 1941–1945/Arsenal** (*Muzey Velikoy Otechestvennoy voyny 1941-1945/Arsenal;* ☎ 55 24 21; *ul Stepana Razina 43; admission R10; open 11am-6pm Tues-Sun*) has the usual photos and weapons of destruction found in WWII museums. One of the most interesting exhibits is an *obyavlenie* (a handwritten bulletin) ordering residents to evacuate and leave everything behind except their cows and goats. Outside the museum, about 50m towards the reservoir, are a few tanks and a rocket-launching truck.

IS Nikitin Literary Museum (*Oblastnoy literaturnyy muzey imeni IS Nikitina; ul Plekhanovskaya 3*) includes exhibits on writers

Alexei Koltsov, Ivan Bunin and Andrei Platonov in the former home of Ivan Nikitin, a second-rate realist poet born in Voronezh in the early 19th century. You'll have to delve deep into the backstreets of Voronezh to reach the quirky collection at the **AL Durov House-Museum** (Dom-muzey AL Durova; ☎ 53 03 87; ul Durova 2; admission R40; open approx 10am-6pm Tues-Sat), near the reservoir. The Durovs were Russia's most famous circus stars, and the museum is situated on what were once the grounds of their home-base circus. It showcases photos and costumes. Even if it is closed, you can still admire the grounds, including Durov's grave.

Churches & Monastery

There are a dozen churches, cathedrals and monasteries in town, with more popping up all the time. The large green-domed church in the centre, visible from many points in town, is the brand-new **Voskreseveskii Khram** (ul Ordzhonikidze 15); its exterior was still under construction at the time of writing. The fresco-covered interior is the site of regular choral services.

The recently restored **St Alexey of Akatov women's monastery** (Svyatoy Alexeevsky-Akatova zhenskogo monastyr; ul Osvobozhdeniya Truda 1) is worth visiting. The interior of the monastery church is covered entirely with frescoes; if you come at 7.30am or 5pm you'll hear the intensely beautiful service, sung by nuns. The monastery, founded in 1674, is near the river, on lovely grounds including a tiny graveyard and surrounded by colourful, lopsided cottages.

In a downtrodden part of town, the small 1720 **Nicholas Church** (Nikolskaya tserkov; ul Taranchenko 19-a) has a fresco-covered entryway and an 18th-century iconostasis. In spite of the many icons and ornamentation, it has the feel of a country church and holds frequent Orthodox services.

Walking Tour

To explore working-class Voronezh while taking in a few sights, a good walking route from the centre of town would be to start at the **Arsenal** (take any minibus from ulitsa Plekhanovskaya to the stop just before Chernyavsky bridge), cross ulitsa Stepana Razina and take the narrow, dusty Sacco and Vanzetti ulitsa shooting north. The cross streets off Sacco and Vanzetti are named for

Russian artists (notice dilapidated ulitsa Dostoevsky). Turn right onto ulitsa Durov and follow the dirt road to the Durov Museum. After the museum, go towards the reservoir then turn right and continue about 100m until you see an overgrown stone staircase. This leads to the **St Alexey monastery**, which will emerge on your left. Leaving the monastery, follow the street away from the reservoir, past the 18th-century **Vvedenskaya Church** (Vvedenskaya tserkov; ul Osvobozhdeniya Truda 18) and back to ulitsa Stepana Razina. From the bridge at the foot of Razina, you can see the gold dome of the **Intercession Cathedral**, from where it's a short walk to the café and store-lined prospekt Revolyutsii.

Places to Stay & Eat

Voronezh is an expensive place to stay. **Hotel Don** (☎ 55 53 15; ul Plekhanovskaya 8; singles/doubles from R660/800) is the best option, with large, pleasant rooms. It is often booked, though, with groups or conferences. Even when rooms are available, you'll need to convince the receptionist that you were turned away from the ex-Intourist hotel and will be in town for only one night. If you call ahead, you'll pay a reservation fee, but this is a better bet than the bleak ghost of Intourist, **Hotel Brno** (☎ 50 92 49; ul Plekhanovskaya 9; singles/doubles from R930/1100). The smallish, fairly clean rooms are overpriced. Both hotels are convenient, just off ploshchad Lenina.

Kafe Milan (☎ 55 43 51; pr Revolyutsii 44) offers snacks (individual pizzas R33), gelati and coffee in a simple setting that constitutes the tasteful in Voronezh. Don't let the name lead you to expect much from the espresso.

Yuventa (☎ 55 45 64; pr Revolyutsii 36) is a fast-food place adjoined to a Baskin-Robbins and serving plausible burgers (R14), chicken sandwiches (R35) and salads. Live music sets up in a corner early some evenings, and some of Voronezh's more chatty and cheerful youth are fond of the place.

For a splurge, dine at **Restoran Pushkin** (☎ 53 33 05; ul Pushkinskaya 1; mains R100-250), where the simple, green-toned interior is marred only by the live music. This is a good place to sample black caviar (R480) or specialities such as rabbit salad (R170). A bottle of Veuve Cliquot is R2500. This is where businesspeople dine in Voronezh, and as a result there is an English-language menu.

Street food in Voronezh is exceptionally bland, in particular the ubiquitous **Robin Bobbin**, a chain that has invested all of its energy into colourful carts and none into the pastries like cardboard. A regional speciality, the Voronezh streetside *sosiska* (sausage) is a hot dog wrapped in dough and submitted to a waffle iron. Condiments are provided.

Get your high-end groceries at the **Gastronome** (☎ *39 10 19; pr Revolyutsii 58; open until 10pm daily*).

Entertainment

In addition to the **Regional Philharmonia** (*Oblastnaya filarmoniya;* ☎ *55 48 77; pl Lenina 11*), the **State Theatre of Opera & Ballet** (*Gosudarstvenny teatr opery i baleta;* ☎ *55 39 27; pl Lenina 7*) hosts regional productions, some youth productions and the occasional touring show. One of the few arts truly embraced by the Soviets, quality puppet theatre can be admired at the **Regional Puppet Theatre** (*Oblastnoy teatr kukol; pr Revolyutsii 50*). Tickets for all venues can usually be had for R50 to R70.

Getting There & Away

Voronezh is so well connected by rail and bus, you probably won't be using air. However, there are several daily flights to/from Moscow (Domodedovo).

Trains to Moscow take about 10 hours and cost around R600. Trains to other destinations include Saratov (18 hours), Kislovodsk (25 hours) and St Petersburg (24 hours).

Some sample bus fares are: Moscow (R291, eight hours), Saratov (R270, 12 hours), Volgograd (R345, 12 hours), Oryol (R175, 10 hours) and Yelets (R60, three hours). You may have to pay a small fee (R10 to R50) for your luggage. For Voronezh bus information call ☎ 16 13 78.

Getting Around

Buses to the airport (40 minutes) depart from the train station or near Hotel Brno.

Outside the **train station** (*pl Chernyakhovskogo*) you'll encounter a mess of buses, minibuses and trams. Most have major destination points pasted to the window; to get to the centre look for ploshchad Lenina.

The **main bus station** (*Moskovsky pr 17*) is far from the train station; take tram No 12. To reach the centre from the bus station, exit the station and catch a bus heading right; Nos 6 and 7 are among those that run along ulitsa Plekhanovskaya.

Bus, trolleybus and tram fares cost R3 to R4.50, payable to the driver or conductor.

RAMON
РАМОНЬ

The 19th-century **chateau** of Princess Oldenbruskoy near Ramon, 36km north of Voronezh, off the M4 highway, has a collection of antique furniture and some wonderful scenery. To get there, take one of the buses departing at least hourly from 6.15am to 7.30pm (R15, one hour) from the main bus station in Voronezh. When you arrive at the Ramon bus station (the last stop), continue walking in the direction of the bus five minutes. The chateau is to the right as you stand in front of the bus stop; it faces the road.

ORYOL
ОРЁЛ

☎ 08622 for five-digit numbers ☎ 0862 for six-digit numbers • pop 350,000

Founded in 1566 as a fortress against the Tatars, Oryol (arr-**yol**, meaning eagle) is a lovely, inviting town, rewarding exploration and good for an overnight stay. For Russia it's a visibly wealthy place, with a distinctly European capitalist flavour. The public spaces are neat and planned, the river is lined with parks and paths and condominiums, and the residents are well-heeled and taken to promenading in pleasant weather. In contrast to the sullen, lurky young men who populate most of Western European Russia, Oryol youth are jovial and chatty and tend to move about in mixed-sex groups.

Locals attribute the affluence to Yegor Stroev, an agricultural specialist who happened to be a great chum of Gorbachev. In 1985, Stroev was appointed regional administrator and, confident of his position due to his ties to the Kremlin, he announced that the distribution of Oryol's significant agricultural output would favour Oryol rather than Moscow.

Oryol was also prosperous during the 19th century, when the writer Ivan Turgenev was among a surprising number of gentry that called Oryol home (19,000 out of a population of 32,000 in 1853). Turgenev's literary company was similarly impressive – 12 of the writers who thrived here are remembered in the city's museums.

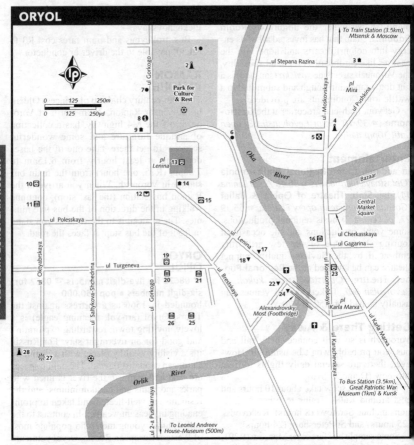

ORYOL

For lovers of 19th-century Russian literature, Oryol is bound to be paradise. To others, the town may seem to be in something of a time warp, with capitalism and communism rather awkwardly commingled.

Orientation & Information

Though the main streets are freshly cobbled and the cupolas newly gilded, most activity still hovers around the less-polished, inner areas of the city. The train station is 3.5km northeast, and the bus station is 3km south of ploshchad Lenina. The pedestrian ulitsa Lenina runs between ploshchad Karla Marksa and ploshchad Lenina, connecting the old city centre to Moskovskaya ulitsa, the main commercial strip today. Both areas are of interest to the visitor, and pleasant footbridges

make crossing back and forth between them easy.

You can change money at Hotel Salyut or at a number of banks, especially on the east side of the river. Hotel Salyut also has convenient train and bus schedules posted in the lobby.

There's a simple **Internet café** on the 2nd floor of the **main post office** (☎ 41 01 47; ul Lenina 43, cnr ul Gorkogo) and a **telephone office** (ul Lenina 34) down the street. Pick up a map at the train station or one of the bookshops that are everywhere in this literary town.

Intourist (☎ 9 59 36; e intourist@orel.ru; ul Gorkogo 39) has a couple of English-speaking staff; English-language tours of town should be arranged in advance.

ORYOL

PLACES TO STAY & EAT		4	Tank Memorial	16	Regional Museum
3	Hotel Oryol		Памятник танкистам		Краеведческий музей
	Гостиница Орёл	5	Orlovsky Univermag	19	Teatr 'Russkiy Stil'
9	Hotel Rus		Орловский универмаг		Театр "Русский стиль"
	Гостиница Русь	6	Rowing Boat Rentals	20	Museum of Oryol Writers
14	Hotel Salyut		Прокат лодок		Музей писателей-орловцев
	Гостиница Салют	7	Bunin Public Library	21	Turgenev Museum
17	Bakery		Библиотека Бунина		Музей Тургенева
	Хлеб	8	Intourist	23	Children's Theatre
18	Bar Pogrebok		Интурист		'Svobodnoye Prostraystvo'
	Бар Погребок	10	Teatr Tyen'		Театр "Свободное
22	Beer Club at the Bridge		Театр Тень		Пространствисво"
	Пивной клуб у моста	11	Dom-Muzey NS Leskova	25	Muzey IA Bunina
24	Kafe Letneye		Дом-Музей Н. С.		Музей Бунина
	Кафе Летнее		Лескова	26	TN Granovskogo
		12	Post & Telegraph Office		House-Museum
OTHER			Главный почтамт		Дом-музей Т.Н. Грановского
1	Amusement Park	13	Turgenev Teatr	27	Garden & Lookout Point
	Аттракционы		Театр имени Тургенева		Сад и видовая площадка
2	Turgenev Statue	15	Telephone Office	28	Turgenev Bust
	Памятник Тургеневу		Переговорный пункт		Бюст Тургенева

Literary Attractions

A cluster of literary museums covers an awkward block off the unwieldy Georgievskiy pereulok. They are all open from 10am to 5pm Saturday to Thursday and closed Friday, and a central organisational **office** (☎ 6 55 20) manages all six. Admission is R30.

The short-story writer Nikolai Leskov (1831–95), who immortalised an English jumping flea, is honoured at the **Dom-Muzey NS Leskova** (☎ 6 33 04; ul Oktyabrskaya 9), a few blocks from the main cluster. Also set a bit apart, across the river, the birthplace of writer and dramatist Leonid Andreev is a sweet, late-19th-century cottage, now the **Leonid Andreev House-Museum** (☎ 5 48 24; 2-ya Pushkarnaya ulitsa 41). The **TN Granovskogo House-Museum** (☎ 6 34 65; ul 7-go Noyabrya 24) presents materials and memorabilia relating to a number of 19th-century revolutionary thinkers.

Though materials on the poet and prose writer and 1933 Nobel Laureate Ivan Bunin (1870–1953) are spread thin through provincial Russia, the Oryol **Muzey IA Bunina** (☎ 9 77 74; per Georgievskiy 1) has a good collection of photos and other documents, as well as a 'Paris Room' devoted to Bunin's years as an emigrant, including the bed in which he died. At the end of the one-hour excursion (the only way you're going to make sense of all the curious photos and yellowed books), the guide flips on a tape player and

the man himself reads one of his last poems, a typed copy of which lays near his typewriter. Still not sated? There's a statue of Bunin (though apparently it bears no resemblance to him) in front of the **Bunin Public Library** (Biblioteka imeni Bunina; ul Gorkogo 43; open 10am-8pm Mon-Thur, 10am-6pm Sat & Sun), opposite the Park of Culture and Rest. The Greek Revival library itself is in beautiful condition and sees a good deal of scholarly activity. It is a good place for a few warm moments with a book during the chilly months.

Turgenev's estate Spasskoe-Lutovinovo (see that entry later in this chapter) is the literary mecca of provincial Russia. Not to be outdone, Oryol has its own **Turgenev Museum** (☎ 6 27 37; ul Turgeneva 11). You will find tributes to Turgenev throughout town, including a big statue of him overlooking the Oka on Turgenevsky spusk, the sloping street off ploshchad Lenina, and a bust in the public garden.

The **Museum of Oryol Writers** (☎ 6 35 28; ul Turgeneva 13), next door to the Turgenev Museum, has small displays on all of the above writers and more, including a good deal of original furniture.

Other Attractions

The **Park of Culture and Rest** (Park Kultury i Otdykha) is a typical small-city park, with an amusement park at the northeastern end. A walk down the steep embankment to the Oka, between the park and junction of the Oka and Orlik Rivers, brings you to the town's **rowing boat rental stand**, open from 9am to 9pm during the warmer months. The banks of the Oka draw huge crowds of bathers and carpet washers on sunny days.

The nonliterary museums in Oryol are decidedly less interesting than the literary ones. The **Regional Museum** (☎ 5 67 91; ul Gastinaya 2, cnr Moskovskaya ul; open 10am-6pm Tues-Sun) on Oryol's fashionable shopping strip holds some good temporary exhibitions.

The **Great Patriotic War Museum** (☎ 9 17 94; cnr uls Komsomolskaya & Normandiya Neman; open 10am-6pm Tues-Sun) has a rather paltry collection of weaponry, recruitment and propaganda posters and a panorama depicting the liberation of Oryol as Red Army troops advanced on Kursk.

Ploshchad Mira (Peace Square; cnr uls Moskovskaya & Pushkina) is easily identified by its WWII tank. The fighting machine, perched atop a granite base, is a time-honoured spot for newlyweds to pose for photos on the big day. It's also the site for city residents to pay their respects to those who fought and died in battle. There is a marble memorial, with maps, behind the tank.

Places to Stay

Hotel Rus (☎ 47 55 50; ul Gorkogo 37; singles/doubles with bath from R320/600) is the best place to stay in town. The rooms are small but clean and comfortable, the staff is friendly and the location is ideal, on ploshchad Lenina across from the park. However, you should heed the sign by the front desk that warns the hotel is 'not responsible for night calls concerning intimate services… we kindly recommend you switch off your telephone…'

Just across the ploshchad is the soulless **Hotel Salyut** (☎ 43 50 40; 36 ul Lenina; singles/ doubles from R375/750).

The dim **Hotel Oryol** (☎ 5 05 25; pl Mira 4; singles/doubles from R320/550) does not readily accept foreigners, though the foreigner price list is prominently posted at the front desk. The trick to getting a room here is to say the other hotels are booked up and/or to show up towards evening when the receptionist is least likely to send you back onto the street. The rooms themselves are brighter and nicer than the lobby.

Places to Eat

For some reason, there are precious few eateries around ulitsa and ploshchad Lenina, with the result that you might have trouble getting a table at dinnertime. On the other hand, you might wind up seated with chatty locals and pick up on the latest Oryol gossip.

Beer Club at the Bridge (Piv-Bar 'Y Mosta'; ☎ 43 56 02; ul Lenina 13) is a mellow basement grotto with a handful of wooden tables and unintrusive music. There's a R100 cover charge at night. If you can get past the attitudinal doorman, appetisers include fried cheese, fried calamari and julienne (mushrooms, cheese, egg whites, onion and sour cream baked in a tin demitasse) for R18 an order. The speciality is locally brewed 'English Ale' for R25 a mug; it tastes like dark Baltika.

Subtract the atmosphere and re-insert the usual pounding pop and you've got **Bar Pogrebok** (☎ 6 28 08; ul Lenina 25; mains around R50), a few doors down and also underground. The traditional Russian main courses are well manoeuvred.

Kafe Letneye (ul Lenina 9) is a snack bar with outdoor seating only, overlooking the footbridge and riverside park. Treat yourself to the marvellous breads at the nearby **bakery** (ul Lenina 26), including caramel eclairs and chocolate croissants. There's a teeming daily **market** on the south bank of the Oka just east of Moskovskaya ulitsa, along with a bazaar selling just about everything from toothpaste and TVs to a large selection of fresh produce from the Caucasus.

Entertainment

Given the literary bent of Oryol, it's no surprise to find a number of quality theatres paying tribute to the works of local luminaries and others. The **Turgenev Teatr** faces Lenin on ploshchad Lenina and hosts highbrow theatre several times a week. It is a clever modernist building, the facade mimicking the effect of a stage with the curtains drawn. **Teatr Tyen'** (☎ 81 35 70; ul Oktyabrskaya 5) hosts both opera and theatre. **Teatr 'Russkiy Stil'** (☎ 6 90 90; ul Turgeneva 18) is a fun, small-scale, occasionally experimental theatre. Most of the offerings are comedies, often with local colour. **Teatr 'Svobodnoye Prostraystvo'** (☎ 6 48 46; pl Karl Marksa) is an excellent children's theatre, both entertaining and good for practising your Russian. Tickets at all theatres cost under R100.

Getting There & Away

Oryol is on the Moscow–Kharkiv (Kharkov) railway, with numerous daily services. The **train station** (☎ 9 21 21) is your first clue to the upscale character of Oryol. It is a clean, attractive, almost fancy place (note the neoclassical colonnades outside) with several appealing waiting areas. Left luggage costs R26 per day, per bag.

Buses heading to Moscow several times a day (six hours) leave from the station at the opposite end of the Moskovskaya ulitsa–Komsomolskaya ulitsa axis through the east bank. To Kursk there is both rail (two hours by train, 3½ hours by *elektrichka*) and bus service (R60, 2½ hours). There is a bus, but no direct rail service, to Smolensk.

Getting Around

The best way to see the city is on foot. From the train station, tram Nos 1 and 2 stop at ulitsa Karla Marksa, on the southeastern end of the Alexandrovsky Most footbridge leading to ulitsa Lenina, before continuing on to the bus station.

A taxi to the train or bus station from ploshchad Lenina should cost about R40.

SPASSKOE-LUTOVINOVO
СПАССКОЕ-ЛУТОВИНОВО

The manor of 19th-century novelist Ivan Turgenev, 6km west of the Moscow–Oryol road from a turn-off 65km north of Oryol, is open as a **museum** (☎ 08646-5 72 47, 2 39 48; admission R20; open 10am-6pm Wed-Mon). It is closed on the last day of each month as well as other days when it is unpredictably shut down for 'technical reasons', so call ahead.

Turgenev, born in Oryol in 1818, grew up at his family's estate here. The land was given to the family by Ivan the Terrible, and the local landscape and people inspired much of Turgenev's writing. Though he spent much of his life in Moscow, St Petersburg, Germany and France, Turgenev thought of Spasskoe-Lutovinovo as his homeland and returned here many times. The beauty of the estate makes this easy to understand.

Turgenev was exiled here from St Petersburg in 1852–53 as a result of his work *The Hunter's Sketches*. He completed his most famous novel, *Fathers and Sons*, at Spasskoe-Lutovinovo.

The main house, restored in the 1970s (which was when the coal stoves were installed), contains a good bit of original furniture, some of the writer's personal items and a substantial percentage of his books. There's an icon hanging in Turgenev's study that was given to the family by Ivan the Terrible. The entrance to the house was formerly the kitchen.

Also on the grounds, the family church has been restored and holds regular services. The big oak tree planted as a sapling by Turgenev and the writer's 'exile house', where he lived in 1852–53, are just away from the main house.

Outside the estate, descendants of the peasant serfs who once belonged to the Turgenevs still live and work on tiny farms. There is a flower-bedecked WWII Memorial among their homes, a five-minute walk to the right as you exit the estate.

Admission to the estate includes a mandatory Russian-language guided tour. Photographers and videographers are charged R100 extra. There are a few small shops outside the grounds selling beer, soda, ice cream and souvenirs, including cassette recordings of the master's works.

Getting There & Away

The bus will be the best way to get here. The Mtsensk bus from Oryol leaves at least hourly from about 6am to 9pm (R27, one hour); switch at Mtsensk's bus station for an hourly Spasskoe–Lutovinovo bus (R9, 40 minutes). On the way back, try hopping onto one of the air-conditioned excursion buses.

If you prefer the train, *elektrichka* leave from Oryol at 9am for Bastyevo (R39, 1½ hours). From the northern end of the train station, cross the tracks and walk west 5km (to the left), or catch the bus that runs from Mtsensk via Bastyevo to the estate about once an hour. The bus stop is to your right (east) from the front of the train station. Trains return to Oryol at 5.30pm.

KURSK
КУРСК

☎ 07100 • pop 430,000

Founded (most likely) in the 9th century, Kursk was destroyed by the Tatars in 1240. It then lay in Lithuanian territory for a couple of centuries before being annexed by Moscow and emerging as a southern frontier fort in the late 16th century. In the 18th and 19th centuries it became a grain-trade and industrial centre and an important railway junction.

Much of its appearance is a result of rebuilding after severe damage during WWII. It's a pretty unappealing place – just a mid-size, working-class city – except for its importance to military history as the base of the WWII Battle of the Kursk Bulge. As such, the Kursk Battle Museum is probably the most interesting sight in town.

Orientation & Information
Kursk's centre is divided by the north–south running ulitsa Lenina, with Krasnaya ploshchad at the southern end. Ulitsa Dzerzhinskogo heads quite steeply downhill from the west side of Krasnaya ploshchad to the valley of a now invisible river, where you'll find the busy central market.

A good bet for changing money is **Sberbank** (ul Lenina 19). At the **post office and 24-hour telephone office** (☎ 2 51 59, 2 48 73; Krasnaya pl), a lone computer terminal features Internet connection for R0.60 a minute from 9am to 7pm Monday to Saturday, until 4pm Sunday.

More than just a bookshop, the grand interior of **Dom Knigi** (ul Lenina 11) stocks a good selection of Russian books as well as snacks, clothing, homewares and toys. The only available city map is a huge, topographically correct affair with far more detail than you will need, but if you are determined, ask for a copy of it at the Xerox counter just inside the door.

Things to See
The foot of ulitsa Lenina opens into **Krasnaya ploshchad**, surrounded by imposing Stalinesque buildings – the House of Soviets on the east side, the post office on the west, the Hotel Tsentralnaya on the northwest and the matching city council building on the northeast. At the south end of the square is Kursk's most distinctive building, the domed 1816–28 **Assumption Cathedral** (Znamensky sobor). The Soviets converted the cathedral into a cinema; at the time of writing, the main church was undergoing restoration, but a smaller upstairs chapel was functioning. There are no signs marking the entrance, and approaching the cathedral feels a bit like trespassing on a construction site, but the chapel is to your right through the main gate.

Around ulitsa Sonina from the Assumption Cathedral is the two-room **Kursk Battle Museum** (Muzey Kurskoy Bitvy; ul Sonina;

admission R30; open 9am-4pm Wed-Sun), upstairs in the ornate red-and-white former House of the Nobles which is now the Officers House (Dom Ofitserov). The museum is devoted to an important Soviet victory over the Germans near Kursk in 1943. Admission buys you good views over town, documentation and artefacts from the battle, and an enthusiastic former Red Army soldier who will tell you all about it and then some. Downstairs, you might be able to stir up a game of billiards with a military man. The tables are available to the public from 1pm to 9pm daily.

A block to the east off ulitsa Lenina, on a pleasant, tree-lined street, is the fine baroque **Sergievo-Kazansky Cathedral** (ul Gorkogo, cnr ul Zolotaya), built in 1752–78 to a design by Elizabeth I's court architect, Rastrelli. The construction was ordered by a wealthy merchant who sought repentance for a murder he committed (more or less in self-defence so the story goes).

A bit farther down, the 1786 **Church of Ascension-Ilinsky** (Voznesensko-Ilinsky khram; ul Lenina) was used during communism as a warehouse for Dom Knigi, a hulking neoclassical structure placed smack in front of the strawberry-milk-hued, 18th-century church. With the end of communism, the books were moved out and the church reopened. When a regional bank was constructed next door in 1997, tinted glass was used to reflect the church, creating the illusion that it is once again part of the main street. Inside, you can see original frescoes by famous icon painter Vasnetsov.

Places to Stay
Hotel Tsentralnaya (☎ 56 90 48; Krasnaya pl; singles/doubles without bath from R170/290) is a grand old place with high ceilings and tiled bathrooms in some rooms.

Hotel Kursk (☎ 2 69 80; ul Lenina, cnr ul Zolotaya; singles/doubles from R385/580) is also quite clean and comfortable, though with a bit less character than the Tsentralnaya.

If you're turned away from the Kursk and Tsentralnaya, you can either take a step up or down – the Tsentralnaya has a bleak second location, **Hotel Tsentralnaya building 2** (☎ 56 65 21; ul Lenina 72; singles/doubles from R200/300, with bath R300/350), near the top of ulitsa Lenina.

Situated in a park some kilometres from the centre, **Motel Solovinaya Roshcha** (☎ 50

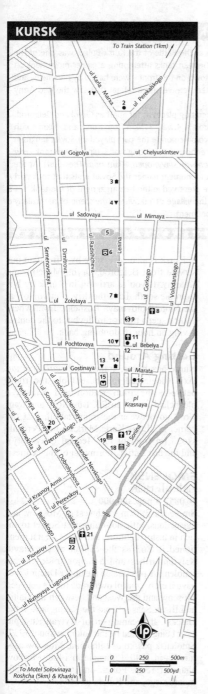

KURSK

PLACES TO STAY & EAT
1 Northern Market
Северный рынок
3 Hotel Tsentralnaya (Building 2)
Гостиница Центральная
4 Restoran Kolizey
Ресторан Колизей
7 Hotel Kursk
Гостиница Курск
10 Pizzeria & Bistro
Пищерия и Бистро
13 Kafe Prirestorani
Кафе Приресторан
14 Hotel Tsentralnaya
Гостиница Центральная
20 Central Market
Центральный рынок

OTHER
2 Medical University
Медицинский университет
5 Stadium
Стадион
6 Pushkin Theatre
Театр Пушкина
8 Sergievo-Kazansky Cathedral
Сергиево-Казанский собор
9 Sberbank
Сбербанк
11 Church of Ascension-Ilinsky
Вознесенско-Ильинский Храм
12 Dom Knigi
Дом книги
15 Post & 24-Hour Telephone Office
Почта и круглосуточный
переговорный пункт
16 House of Soviets
Дом Советов
17 Assumption Cathedral
Вознесенский собор
18 Officers House/Kursk Battle Museum
Дом офицеров
19 Regional Museum
Краеведческий музей
21 Lower Trinity Church
Свято-Троицкий Храм
22 Museum of Archaeology
Археологический музей

40 00, fax 50 40 50; ul Engelsa 142a; singles/
doubles from R900/1200) has simple but
excellent facilities, including sparkling renovated bathrooms. A hearty breakfast is included. From the centre take a taxi (about
R70) or one of a number of buses, including
No 10, 21, or 61, or tram No 4 or 5. Ask for
notice when nearing the hotel; you will have
to walk a few minutes off the road to your
left. A shady, pine-filled park lines one side
of the hotel, lending an almost rural feel.

Kursk Battle Memorial Памятник Курской Битвы

The battle from 5 July to 5 August 1943, known as the Battle of the Kursk Bulge, was one of the Red Army's most important victories in WWII. German tanks attempting a pincer movement on Kursk – at the time the most forward Soviet-held town on this front – were halted by minefields and then driven back, turning Germany's 1943 counteroffensive into a retreat that saw the Red Army pass the Dnepr River by the end of September.

The Kursk battle sprawled over a wide area, liberating places as far apart as Oryol and Belgorod, but the main memorial is beside the Kursk–Belgorod highway, 115km from Kursk and 40km south of Oboyan. A T-34 tank and a Yak fighter plane commemorate the part played by Soviet tankmen and airmen in the battle. Antitank guns stand on either side of a long wall sculpted with tank crew faces, beneath which is the **War Glory Hall** (*Zal boevoy slavy; open 10am-5pm Tues-Sun*). At the north end of the memorial area, past the plane, a monument names the Soviet units that took part in the battle. Gun emplacements and trenches are preserved in the tree area, right of the tank.

About 8km farther south, at the south end of the village of Yakovlevo (the scene of particularly fierce fighting in the battle), there's a cannon monument.

★★

Places to Eat

On ulitsa Lenina next to Detsky Mir is a very popular dual **eatery** (☎ 56 41 51; ul Lenina 12). To the left is a smoky pizzeria where beer sells more than food. Medium-sized pizzas with sausage, mushrooms and vegies cost R51. Across the hall, a less populous bistro serves smaller pizzas for R15 to R20, along with a few other snacks.

Kafe Prirestorani (☎ 56 92 21; ul Lenina 2) is a no-frills café, to the left of the entrance to Hotel Tsentralnaya, offering appetiser beef roulades (R20) and speciality salads (R21 to R27). **Restoran Kolizey** (☎ 2 11 95; ul Lenina 72) is a fancy restaurant serving Euro-dishes like calamari (R80) and steak (R200) along with more traditional Russian fare, all at elevated prices. The food is good, not great, but given the options that might be enough.

The town's two main markets, the central **Tsentralny** (*ul Dzerzhinskogo*) and the northern **Severny** (*ul Karla Marksa*) sell food, produce and clothes (the sort that will make you say, 'So *that*'s where they get it!').

Getting There & Away

Kursk is so well connected by bus and rail you probably will not want to fly. However, there are flights to/from Moscow and St Petersburg.

Like Oryol, Kursk is on the Moscow–Kharkiv railway with trains to Moscow every half hour, sometimes more. It's eight hours to Moscow (R420), three to Kharkiv and there are also daily trains to/from the Caucasus and Crimea. The **station** (*ul Internatsionalnaya*) is about 3km northeast of Krasnaya ploshchad.

Kursk is also accessible by a frequent bus service from Belgorod, Oryol, Moscow and Kharkiv. If you're arriving in Kursk by bus from the south, have the driver let you off at the Motel Solovinaya Roshcha, from where you can get a tram or trolleybus to the centre, saving an hour of doubling back.

Getting Around

Numerous buses, trams, and *marshrutnoe* taxis (dedicated minibuses) ply the route between the train station and Krasnaya ploshchad for R4 to R5. Bus No 1 and tram No 2 go between the train station, past the corner of ulitsas Karla Marksa and Perekalskogo (in front of the Medical University), and the bus station, northwest of the centre.

SMOLENSK
СМОЛЕНСК

☎ 0812 • pop 300,000

Smolensk, 390km southwest of Moscow, is a marvellous, little not-quite-post-Soviet town, rich in history, culture, and beauty. First mentioned in 863 as the capital of the Slavic Krivichi tribes and a major trade centre, Smolensk's position on the upper Dnepr River gave it early control over trade routes between Moscow and the West and between the Baltic and Black Seas – 'from the Varangians to the Greeks'. It became part of Kyivan Rus, but after being sacked by the Tatars in about 1237, Smolensk passed to Lithuania. Moscow captured it in 1340, Lithuania in 1408, Moscow again in 1514, Poland in 1611 after a 20-month siege, and Russia in 1654.

There was a big battle between the Russians and Napoleon's army outside Smolensk n 1812 and more heavy fighting in 1941 and 1943. In a sign of Soviet favour, much of the devastated centre was quickly rebuilt, often along original plans, resulting in the very complete feeling of the central area today. Long sections of the restored city walls boast fine towers reminiscent of the Moscow Kremlin.

Other areas of interest for the visitor include flax production and music. Smolensk was the regional hub of flax production during the Middle Ages, and you can still find fine locally made products. Meanwhile, composer Mikhail Glinka, regarded as the founder of Russian art music, grew up near Smolensk and performed frequently in the Nobles' Hall, facing what is now the Glinka Garden. The statue of Glinka, installed in 1885, is surrounded by a fence with excerpts from his opera *A Life for the Tsar* wrought into the iron. Real music aficionados will want to make the trip out to Glinka's family home, now a museum. Inquire at the Intourist office.

Orientation

Central Smolensk, surrounded by lengths of ancient wall, stands on a hill on the south bank of the Dnepr. The formal city centre is ploshchad Lenina with the Glinka Garden (Gorodskoy sad imeni MI Glinki) on its south side and the House of Soviets, Drama Theatre and Hotel Tsentralnaya on the north side. Venture beyond the walled centre to the south to find the art gallery and a bustling commercial and residential area, with more than a little Soviet residue. The train station and Kolkhoznaya ploshchad, site of the main market, are north of the river. Ulitsa Bolshaya Sovietskaya leads across the river and up the hill from Kolkhoznaya ploshchad to the centre. The Moscow–Minsk highway passes about 13km north of Smolensk.

Information

The local **Intourist office** (☎ 3 14 92; ul Konenkova 3; open 9am-6pm Mon-Fri), a couple of doors down from Hotel Tsentralnaya, is unusually helpful. Staff can arrange a two- to three-hour English-language city tour (R100 per person, R200 individual tour) as well as excursions to Novospasskaya (Glinka's birthplace), about 100km away. You'll probably need to arrange things a day in advance for the city tour and a few days in advance for

Novospasskaya, for which you'll also need to rent a car or hire a taxi. Intourist is also the place to pick up an English-language city map (R30). Russian-language maps are available at either of the two bookshops facing each other across ulitsa Bolshaya Sovietskaya at Nos 12 and 17.

At the **central post, telegraph and telephone office** (ul Oktyabrskoy Revolyutsii 6), Internet access is available from two computers to the right as you enter (R30 per hour; open 8am to 7pm weekdays, to 6pm Saturday). Local calls are free from public phones.

You can change money at any number of banks in the city, including **SKA bank** (ul Lenina 13a) and **Sberegatelniy Bank** (cnr uls Glinki & Communistichesky).

Fortress Walls

The 6.5km-long, 5.5m-thick, 15m-high walls of the Smolensk fortress were built in 1596–1602. Originally they had 38 towers, 17 of which stand today. The **Central Park of Culture and Rest** (Tsentralny Park Kultury i Otdykha) backs onto a longish southwest stretch of the walls. Overlooking the Spartak Stadium just outside the line of the walls on the west side of the park, the Korolevsky Bastion is a high earth rampart built by the Poles who captured Smolensk in 1611. It saw heavy fighting in 1654 and 1812. The park has a 26m-high cast-iron monument to the 1812 defenders.

At the foot of the walls southeast of the Glinka Garden you'll find an eternal flame memorial to the dead of WWII and the graves of some of the Soviet soldiers who died in Smolensk's defence, plus another monument to the heroes of 1812. A **WWII museum** (☎ 3 32 65) within the fortress walls nearby documents the invasion and widespread devastation; it is incredible to see how much of old Smolensk is actually reconstruction.

Assumption Cathedral

Smolensk's big green and white working **Uspensky sobor** rises at the top of a flight of steps off ulitsa Bolshaya Sovietskaya. A cathedral has stood here since 1101 but this one was built in the late-17th and early 18th centuries; it is one of the earliest examples of the Russo-Greek revival in architecture following the Europeanisation trends of Peter the Great's reign. Topped by five domes, it has a spectacular gilded interior. Napoleon is said to have

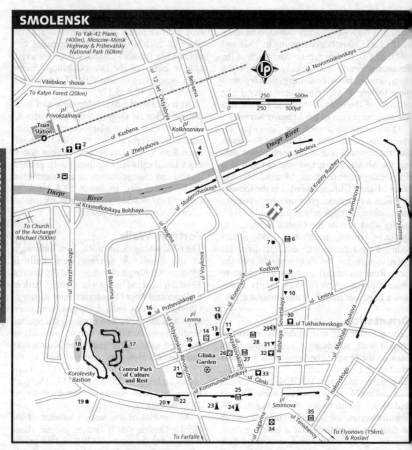

SMOLENSK

been so impressed by it that he set a guard to stop his own men from vandalising it.

Immediately on your left as you enter, an icon of the Virgin is richly encrusted with pearls drawn from the Dnepr around Smolensk. Further on, a cluster of candles marks a supposedly wonder-working icon of the Virgin. This is a 16th-century copy of the original, said to be by St Luke, which had been on this site since 1103 and was stolen in 1923. The cathedral bell tower is to the left of the cathedral. There's a good view of the fortress walls and two towers from the terrace at the eastern end of the cathedral.

Glinka Concert Hall

Attending a concert is the best way to get a look at the reconstructed hall (☎ 3 29 84; ul

Glinki 3) where Glinka once entertained Russian nobility and launched the history of secular art music in Russia. The local orchestra uses balalaiki in lieu of violins and is quite good; tickets run about R50.

Museums

The wealth of Smolensk museums is a blessing for the traveller, except those who have rolled into town on Sunday night; they are all closed on Monday.

The pink former Church of Trinity Monastery now houses a **Flax Museum** (Muzey-Zapoliednik Smolenskiy Lyon; ☎ 3 16 11; ul Bolshaya Sovietskaya 11). Historically, flax production has been one of Smolensk's main industries as the moderate climate sustains soil ideal for flax growth. To get a souvenir

SMOLENSK

PLACES TO STAY & EAT		6	Smolensk Flax Museum	23	Eternal Flame Memorial
4	Zadneprovsky Market		Выставка Смоленский лён		Мемориал Вечный огонь
	Заднепровский рынок	7	Trinity Monastery Bell Tower	24	Monument to the Heroes of
10	Stary Gorod		Колокольня Троицкого		1812
	Старый город		монастыря		Памятник героям 1812г.
11	Grocery Store	8	Bookshop	25	WWII Museum
	Магазин Продукты		Книжный магазин		Музей Великой
13	Hotel Tsentralnaya/	9	Bookshop		Отечественной войны
	Restoran Tsentralnaya		Книжный магазин	26	Glinka Concert Hall
	Гостиница	12	Intourist		Концертный зал им. М. И.
	Центральная		Интурист		Глинки
19	Hotel Rossia	14	Drama Theatre	27	Konenkov Sculpture Museum
	Гостиница Россия		Драматический театр		Музей скульптуры
20	Pizzeria Domino	15	House of Soviets		Коненкова
	Пиццерия Домино		Дом Советов	28	History Museum
31	Ladya	16	Flax Shop		Исторический музей
	Ладья		Магазин Лён	29	SKA Bank
		17	Monument to the 1812		Ска банк
OTHER			Defenders	30	Zakusochnaya
1	St Barbara's Church		Памятник защитникам		Закусочная
	Церковь Св Варвары		Смоленска 1812г.	32	Mir 24
2	SS Peter & Paul Church	18	Spartak Stadium		Мир 24
	Церковь святых		Стадион Спартак	33	Beer Pub
	Петра и Павла	21	Central Post, Telegraph &		Пивной бар
3	Bus Station		Telephone Office	34	Central Department Store
	Автовокзал		Главный почтамт		ЦУМ
5	Assumption Cathedral	22	Gramovaya Tower	35	Art Gallery
	Успенский собор		Громовая башня		Художественная галерея

of the distinctive local style, visit the **flax shop** (ul Przhevalskogo at ul Oktyabrskoy Revolyutsii) near the Central Park of Culture and Rest.

Smolensk's **History Museum** (Muzey istorii; ☎ 3 38 62; ul Lenina 8; admission R10; open 10am-6pm Tues-Sun) doubles as a fine arts museum, displaying 18th- and 19th-century portraiture and 13th-century iconography and graffiti along with battle maps and Soviet paraphernalia.

The town's main **art gallery** (khudozhestvennaya galereya; ☎ 3 27 09; ul Tenishevoy 7/1; admission R10), south of the fortress walls, has paintings by famous painters such as Rerik and Ivanov, a good sampling of socialist realism, 14th- to 18th-century icons, and works by Smolensk artists patronised by Princess Maria Tenisheva (see Flyonovo under Around Smolensk later in this chapter).

The **Konenkov Sculpture Museum** (☎ 3 20 29; ul Mayakovskogo 7; open 10am-6pm Tues-Sun) has some playful woodworks by Sergey Konenkov. Upstairs is a small but very good collection of steel, bronze and aluminium statuettes, and another room housing pure kitsch – if you've been itching to see a matryoshka doll, they have some good ones here.

Yak

Want to see a Yak-42, hoping that you won't have to fly in one? There's a weathered specimen of the **aircraft** (ul Frunze), named for designer Yakovlev and achieving speeds of 900km/hour, in front of the financially struggling Smolensk Aviation Factory. Take tram No 5 from the centre of town.

Places to Stay

The hulking **Hotel Rossia** (☎ 65 56 10; ul Dzerzhinskogo 23/2; singles/doubles from R520/ 800) follows the European supposition that the more stuff a room contains, the more it should cost. If you value a grainy TV, a 'mini-bar' (a plastic basket of candy bars and a wheezing refrigerator filled with dusty bottles) and a one-station radio, this is the place for you.

If, on the other hand, you favour central, clean, and cheap, opt for **Hotel Tsentralnaya** (☎ 3 36 04; cnr pl Lenina & ul Konenkova; singles with/without bath from R300/140, doubles with bath from R400), where the rooms are brighter and cleaner, if smaller, than at the Rossia. Ask for a 'renovated' room to score fresh paint and fixtures. The café downstairs pulls a decent espresso (R30).

WESTERN EUROPEAN RUSSIA

Places to Eat

Dining options in Smolensk are broader than in many provincial towns, but still limited in large part to bar-restaurants, offering standard Russian cuisine. There are plenty of grocery stores – a particularly nice one, with fresh breads, is on the corner of ulitsas Konenkova and Lenina, diagonally across from the Glinka Garden, with the entrance on ulitsa Lenina.

Among the numerous bar-restaurants on ulitsa Bolshaya Sovietskaya, **Ladya** (*ul Bolshaya Sovietskaya 18*) is a stand-out. The menu holds no surprises, but Russian staples such as pork with vegetables (R70) and mushroom-oriented snacks (R20 to R40) are prepared with fresh ingredients, a confident touch, and even some imagination.

Restoran Tsentralnaya (*pl Lenina*), in the same building as the like-named hotel but with an entrance facing the Glinka Garden, is a more formal spot with good service. The intrusion of a DJ and disco in the main dining room keep it from going too far upscale, as do the prices: salads for R30 to R90 and meat dishes R60 to R120, all well prepared in traditional Russian guise. **Stary Gorod** (*ul Bolshaya Sovietskaya 21; entrance through the courtyard*) is a maze of smoky dining rooms. Lights fancifully strung along the walls do not improve the 1960s den interior, but the cheeseburgers (R45), omelettes (R15) and *buterbrod* (open-faced sandwiches, R15 to R30) are passable.

A few blocks south of the Glinka Garden, **Farfalle** (*ul Oktyabrskoy Revolyutsii 7*) is an Italian restaurant that draws a young crowd and strives to play the part, even attempting a ceiling trellis. Though far from authentic, the food is not bad – a good opportunity to break the habit of eggs, mushrooms, and bliny. Pizzas and salads hover around R30 while meat dishes are closer to R60.

Finally, Smolenskers seem certain foreigners will enjoy **Domino** (*ul Dzerzhinskogo*), purveyor of pizzas and fast food in a seemingly caricatured Western setting. It is on an empty stretch of ulitsa Dzerzhinskogo, with no visible address, but you can't miss it as it's lit up like a Christmas tree.

Smolensk's main market is the **Zadneprovsky** (*Kolkhoznaya pl*), north of the river.

Entertainment

Drinking in Smolensk is easier still than eating; there is at least one bar per block in the centre. Near Ladya restaurant, **Mir 24** (*ul Bolshaya Sovietskaya 20*) hosts a young crowd of beer drinkers and chain smokers nightly at its pleasant café tables; it is one of the few bars in town with a good view of the street scene. A **beer pub** (*pivnoi bar; ul Glinka 11*) around the corner is as no-nonsense as its name, serving beer only at two tables and two stools in the former gatehouse to the building beyond. Beer is again the only option at **Kalambur**, down the alley near ul Bolshaya Sovietskaya 14, a tiny cavern of a bar. Cosy, stone-and-wood surroundings, comfortable wooden benches, and R15 beers might convince you of the wisdom of a liquid lunch. **Zakusochnaya** (*behind ul Tukhachevskogo 1*) is a small, friendly bar with basic sandwiches and beers from R8.

Getting There & Away

Smolensk is on the Moscow–Minsk–Warsaw railway with several daily trains to/from Moscow (R500, six hours), Minsk (four hours), Prague (24 hours), Brest (eight hours) and Warsaw (nine hours), as well as regular trains to Berlin (41 hours). The **kassa** (*ticket office, ☎ 9 51 77; open 9am-5pm Mon-Thur, 10am-5pm Fri*) for international rail tickets is to the right as you enter the station. If it's closed when you need to travel, purchase a ticket to Brest, where the trains stop at the border for several hours, time enough to get a cross-border ticket at the 24-hour *kassa*, so we're told.

Smolensk bus station, just south of the train station, serves most of the region's smaller towns with frequent daily services, and daily services to Moscow. Buses to Moscow also leave from the train station across the footbridge.

Getting Around

From the train station, you can take the bus or tram (R3) to the centre of town. Many buses and trams stop in front of the station; choose one that stops by the green structure to the right beyond the parking lot. Some buses stop at the bus station, across the footbridge from the train station. In either case, if your Russian is not up to confirming the direction, take a taxi (R40).

AROUND SMOLENSK
Flyonovo
Флёново

In the late 19th and early 20th centuries, top Russian art and music names such as

Stravinsky, Chaliapin, Vrubel and Serov visited the Flyonovo estate of singer Princess Maria Tenisheva, near Talashkino, 15km southeast of Smolensk on the Roslavl road. The visitors joined in applied-art workshops, which the princess organised for her peasants, and helped in building projects.

The most striking result is dramatic, almost psychedelic murals and mosaics on the brick Holy Spirit Church – particularly the one of Christ over the entrance. Much of the painting is by well-known landscape painter Rerikh. One house called Teremok, decorated with ornate peasant-style carving, is now a **folk-art museum** (☎ 7 21 06; open 10am-4pm Tues-Sun). Take bus No 104 from Smolensk's bus station to Talashkino.

Katyn Forest
Катынский Лес
In 1990 the Soviet authorities finally admitted that the NKVD (predecessor of the KGB) had shot over 6000 Polish officers in the back of the head in the Katyn Forest near Smolensk in 1940. The bodies of the officers, who had been imprisoned by the Soviet occupying troops in Poland in 1939, were left in four mass graves.

Until 1990, Soviet authorities blamed it on the Nazis. Victims were trucked from Gnezdovo, a country station, to Kozi Gory, site of the graves. The graves have not been disturbed and are now marked by memorials. About 11,000 other Polish officers almost certainly suffered similar fates elsewhere in the USSR.

Less well known is the fact that the Katyn Forest was also, according to a 1989 *Moscow News* report, the site of massacres of 135,000 Soviet prisoners of war by the Nazis (out of an estimated one million Soviet POWs shot by the Germans in WWII) and of thousands of Soviet 'enemies of the state' exterminated by the NKVD in the 1930s.

Getting There & Away Getting there on your own is simple; take bus No 101 (direction: Smolensk Smetanino) from the Smolensk bus station to Kozi Gory. It's easy to miss so look for the sign saying 'Memorial Polskim ofitseram pogibshim v Katyni' about 1km past the highway flyover. If you get to Katyn, you've gone too far. The memorial is in two spots. One has a simple wooden cross and a marble headstone dedicated to the Russian dead, while the more impressive Polish one is

farther up the path. The forest is spooky, but the memorials are moving.

Przhevalsky National Park
Национальный парк имени Пржевальского
Lying 60km north of Smolensk, the birthplace of adventurer Nikolai Przhevalsky is a beautiful national park, a favourite spot for locals to spend a long weekend camping by one of the many lakes. The road to the park is asphalt and after that there are dirt roads and footpaths. A park ranger might be at the post at the entrance to the park, where you may have to pay a small fee. If no-one is there, don't be surprised if one of the rangers stops by your campfire to collect the fee, which might be a shot or two of vodka.

South of St Petersburg

NOVGOROD
НОВГОРОД
☎ 8162 for six-digit numbers ☎ 81622 for five-digit numbers • pop 240,000
The name means 'new town', but Novgorod was here by the 9th century and for 600 years was Russia's most pioneering artistic and political centre. Today it's mostly known for its history, and for some of the most diverse and beautiful architecture in the country. Methodically trashed by the Nazis, it's a sign of the city's historical importance that its old kremlin was one of the Soviet government's first reconstruction projects.

In a sense, Russian history began here. This was the first permanent settlement of the Varangian Norsemen who established the embryonic Russian state. By the 12th century the city, called 'Lord Novgorod the Great', was Russia's biggest: an independent quasi-democracy whose princes were hired and fired by an assembly of citizens, and whose strong, spare style of church architecture, icon painting and down-to-earth *byliny* (epic songs) were to become distinct idioms.

Spared from the Mongol Tatars, who got bogged down in the surrounding swamps, Novgorod suffered most at the hands of other Russians. Ivan III of Moscow attacked and annexed it in 1477, and Ivan the Terrible, whose storm troopers razed the city and slaughtered

WESTERN EUROPEAN RUSSIA

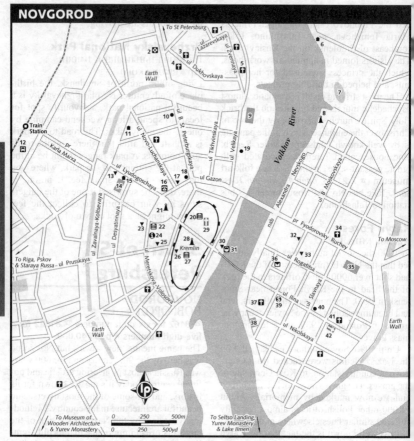

NOVGOROD

60,000 people in a savage pogrom, broke its back. The founding of St Petersburg finished it off as a trading centre.

Novgorod is now an easy, rewarding overnight stop popular with foreign and Russian tourists.

Orientation

Novgorod is only three hours by road from St Petersburg and is just off the M10 highway connecting Moscow and St Petersburg. The town has two main centres: the kremlin on the west bank of the Volkhov River, and the old market district, Yaroslav's Court, on the east bank. The kremlin side sprawls outwards like a pheasant's tail, while the east side is grid-like.

Though the Soviet street names were officially scrapped long ago, some locals still use

them, so we've left the more important ones in parentheses. City maps in Russian and English are available at the tourist office (see the following section) behind the Novgorod Fine Arts Museum, or at bookshops, hotels and museums.

Information

Novgorod is ready and waiting for visitors. You will find English-language menus, hotels that welcome foreigners with open arms – and equitable prices – and plenty of ATMs. There are many **post offices** around town; the branch (☎ 7 35 08; ul Bolshaya Dvortsovaya 2) just east of the bridge offers Internet connection for R90 an hour. The **main telegraph and telephone office** on the corner of ulitsa Lyudogoshchaya (Sovietskaya) and ulitsa Gazon

NOVGOROD

PLACES TO STAY & EAT

6	Beresta Palace Hotel Отель Береста Палас
9	Hotel Intourist Гостиница Интурист
11	Rosa Vetrov Hostel Гостиница Роза Ветров
13	Pri Dvore & Restoran Pri Dvore Ресторан При дворе
14	Hotel Volkhov Гостиница Волхов
15	Hotel Akron Гостиница Акрон
17	Derzhavnyy Cafe-Bar Державный Кафе-Бар
23	Kafe Charodeyka Кафе Чародейка
25	Grill-Bar Гриль бар
26	Restoran Detinets Ресторан Детинец
30	Summer Shashlyk Stand Летний шашлычный киоск
32	Kafe Kauri Кафе Каури
33	Kofeinya Sudarishka Кофейня Сударишка
35	Hotel Sadko Гостиница Садко
38	Hotel Rossia Гостиница Россия

OTHER

1	Zverin Monastery Зверин Монастырь
2	Central Department Store ЦУМ
3	Trinity Church Троицкая церковь
4	St George's Church Церковь Св Георгия
5	Church of Peter & Paul Церковь Петра и Павла
7	Stadium Стадион
8	Alexander Nevsky Statue Памятник Александру Невскому
10	Bookshop Книжный магазин
12	Bus Station Автовокзал
16	Main Telegraph & Telephone Office Главный Телеграф и Телефон
18	Prestige Souvenir Shop "Престиж"
19	Banya Баня
20	Chamber of Facets Грановитая палата
21	Sofiyskaya Ploshchad & Lenin Statue Софийская площадь и памятник Ленину

22	Novgorod Fine Arts Museum Художественная Галерея
24	Tourist Office Бюро Красная Изба
27	Museum of History & Art Музей истории и искусства
28	Millennium of Russia Monument Памятник Тысячелетие России
29	Cathedral of St Sophia Софийский собор
31	Kremlin Landing Причал у Кремля
34	Church of St Theodore Stratelates Церковь Федора Стратилата
36	Post Office Почта
37	Yaroslav's Court Ярославово Дворище
39	Sberbank Сбербанк
40	Servis Tur Сервис Тур
41	Church of Our Saviour- at-Ilino Церковь Спаса на Ильине
42	Cathedral of Our Lady of the Sign Знаменский собор

WESTERN EUROPEAN RUSSIA

(Gorkogo) is at the north end of Sofiyskaya ploshchad. You can change money at hotels, or at **Sberbanks** scattered about town including the branch (ul bolshaya Moskovskaya 20) across from Yaroslav's Court.

Travellers who have been to other Russian towns will not believe their good luck in encountering the central **tourist office** (☎ 13 73 42; e redizba@novline.ru; Sennaya pl), behind the Fine Arts Museum. Staff hand out Russian- and English-language maps and other literature, but the real treat here is the friendly, thorough, English-language advice. At the time of research, staff were trying to arrange English-language tours of town; otherwise, tours in English, French, German and Russian are available through the package-tour-oriented **Servis Tur** (☎ 3 25 17; ul Slavnaya 46, back entrance; e servtour@ telecom.nov.ru; half/full day R310/620).

One thing Novgorod doesn't lack is souvenirs. You'll see woven birch boxes, mini wooden churches, matryoshka dolls and lacquer boxes all over the place. One well-stocked shop is **Prestige** (ul Bolshaya Sankt-Peterburg 1).

Kremlin

Part park, part museum, part archive, the kremlin (☎ 7 36 08, 7 71 87 for information) is worth seeing with a guide. Russian-language guides sometimes hang out at the Millennium of Russia Monument. English-language tours can be arranged, usually a day or two in advance (see Information earlier). The fortress gates themselves are open from 6am to midnight daily; hours for specific sights within the kremlin vary.

Cathedral of St Sophia Finished in 1052, the handsome, Byzantine Cathedral of St Sophia (Sofiysky sobor; open 8am-8pm daily) is the town's centrepiece and one of the oldest buildings in Russia. The simple, fortress-like exterior was designed to withstand attack or fire (flames had taken out an earlier, wooden church on the site); ornamentation was reserved for the interior. The onion domes were probably added during the 14th century – even so, they are perhaps the first example of this most Russian architectural detail. The west doors, dating from the 12th century, have tiny cast-bronze biblical scenes and even portraits of the artists. The icons inside date from the 14th century, and older ones are in the museum. In comparison, the interior frescoes are barely dry, being less than a century old. Services usually take place between 6pm and 8pm daily. Nearby are the 15th-century belfry and a leaning 17th-century clock tower.

Millennium of Russia Monument

Watch the crowds go round and round this bronze birthday cake, unveiled in 1862 on the 1000th anniversary of the Varangian Prince Rurik's arrival. The Nazis cut it up, intending to ship it to Germany, but the Red Army saved the day.

The women at the top are Mother Russia and the Orthodox Church. Around the middle, clockwise from the south, are Rurik, Prince Vladimir of Kyiv (who introduced Christianity), tsars Mikhail Romanov, Peter the Great and Ivan III, and Dmitry Donskoy trampling a Mongol Tatar. In the bottom band on the east side are nobles and rulers, including Catherine the Great with an armload of laurels for all her lovers. Alexander Nevsky and other military heroes are on the north side, and literary and artistic figures are on the west.

Chamber of Facets

The Gothic Chamber of Facets (Granovitaya palata; adult/student R40/20; open 10am-6pm Thur-Tues), part of a palace built in 1433, has a collection of icons and lavish church booty from the region, including some beautiful illuminated manuscripts. It's closed the last Friday of the month.

Museum of History & Art

The Muzey Istorii i Iskusstva (adult/student R48/24; open 10am-6pm Wed-Mon) is said to be one of the best research museums of its kind in Russia, with a huge collection of early icons, birchbark manuscripts, paintings, early wooden sculpture and applied art.

Yaroslav's Court

Across a footbridge from the kremlin is old Novgorod's market, with the remnants of a 17th-century arcade facing the river. Beyond that is the market gatehouse, an array of churches sponsored by 13th- to 16th-century merchant guilds, and a 'road palace' built in the 18th century as a rest stop for Catherine the Great.

Restored between 1995 and 1999, the Kiev-style Court Cathedral of St Nicholas (Nikolo-Dvorishchensky sobor, 1136) is all that remains of the early palace complex of the Novgorod princes, from which the area gets its name of Yaroslav's Court (Yaroslavovo dvorishche). The cathedral itself is closed, but across from the cathedral entrance, an **exhibition hall** (☎ 3 34 65; adult/student R35/17; open 10am-4.30pm Wed-Sun), in the former trading court gate, holds church artefacts and temporary exhibitions of local interest.

Church of Our Saviour-at-Ilino

On the outside, the 14th-century Church of Our Saviour-at-Ilino (Tserkov Spasa-na-Iline; ul Ilina; adult/student R48/24; open 10am-5pm Tues-Sun) has graffiti-like ornaments and lopsided gables which are almost playful. Inside are the only surviving frescoes by legendary Byzantine painter Theophanes the Greek (and they came close to extinction when the church served as a Nazi machine-gun nest). Recent restoration has exposed as much of the frescoes as possible, though they are still faint. A small exhibit upstairs includes reproductions with explanations in Russian. Note Theophanes' signature use of white warlike paint around the eyes and noses of his figures, and his soul-penetrating expressions. The church itself, east of Yaroslav's Court, is pure Novgorod style (in contrast to the more complex 17th-century Moscow-style Cathedral of Our Lady of the Sign across the street).

Other Churches

Another interesting study in contrasting styles, the 1557 Muscovite **Trinity Church** (Tserkov Troitsy; ul Dukhovskaya 20) and Novgorod-style **St George's Church** (ul Dukhovskaya 31) sit directly across the street from one another. Trinity Church was closed and in rather bad shape at the time of research; St George's was open during the day. Other churches in the Novgorod style include the 1406 **Church of Peter and Paul** (Tserkov Petra i Pavla) on ulitsa Zverinskaya (Bredova) near Hotel Intourist. It's a small, crumbling, brick structure occupying its own little field amid a neighbourhood in the process of Euro-transformation. There's also the 1361 **Church of St Theodore Stratelates** *(Tserkov Fyodora Stratilata; open 10am-6pm Thur-Tues)* on ulitsa Fyodorovsky Ruchey 19 (prospekt Yuriya Gagarina). The 1468 **Zverin Monastery** *(open 10am-4pm Sat-Wed)* contains some original frescoes. It is closed the first Monday of the month.

Yurev Monastery & Museum of Wooden Architecture

One of the highlights of a visit to Novgorod is this trip to a working Orthodox monastery and an architectural museum, in the midst of peaceful marshlands. Though these sights feel worlds away from the city, in fact bus No 7 takes just 10 minutes to bring you within walking distance of both. The 12th-century Yurev Monastery *(open 10am-8pm daily)* features the heavily reconstructed Cathedral of St George and a clutch of 19th-century add-ons. Services are held in the Church of Exaltation of the Cross (1761), which is attached to the monks' dorms. The monastery grounds are worth a visit, but what really warrants the trip out here is the windswept river setting, with gorgeous views out across the marshes and toward the centre of Novgorod. There is a nice little **beach** beneath the monastery walls; a café is open in good weather.

Roughly 1km up the road is the beautiful **Vitoslavlitsy Museum of Wooden Architecture** *(adult/student R48/24; park open 10am-5pm daily, houses close at 4pm)*, an open-air museum of peasant houses and intricate, beautiful wooden churches from around the region. The bus back into town stops just outside the park gates; the bus makes a loop out to these sights, so you will be reboarding a bus continuing in the same direction you were heading when you arrived.

Novgorod Fine Arts Museum

The cool halls of Novgorod's **Fine Arts Museum** *(☎ 7 37 70; Sofiyskaya pl 2; adult/student R48/24; open 10am-6pm daily)* showcase paintings by 18th- and 19th-century Russian artists, including Andropov, Brulov and Ivanov. The 3rd floor features Novgorod artists. The collection is a strong provincial one, though not spectacular. Local crafts are among the offerings at the art shop in the lobby.

River Trips

The Volkhov River flows out of Lake Ilmen, about 10km south. On a good day, the surrounding marshes are lovely, with churches sticking up here and there. From the dock below the kremlin, you should be able to catch a boat for a two-hour **cruise** *(adult/student R20/10)*. At the time of research, the tourist office was trying to firm up ferry schedules, but until it does you'll have to negotiate, probably at least a day in advance, with one of the captains to go to Yurev, Staraya Russa (four hours each way) and other destinations around Novgorod.

Gorodki

Sometimes on summer evenings, by the kremlin's north wall, you can watch this violent species of bowling in which wood-and-iron bars are flung at elaborately stacked-up pins.

Banya

For a good sweat with a proletarian price tag, visit the public *banya* *(☎ 7 20 19; ul Velikaya 4)*. It costs R100 per person, or R500 to rent a private cabin for three hours. The cabin provides privacy and comfort for a small group, and you can order in food and drinks. There is an extra charge to rent a *venik* (birch branch) with which to whip yourself, if so inclined.

Places to Stay

The rooms at **Hotel Akron** *(☎ 13 69 18, fax 13 69 34; ul Predtechenskaya 24; singles/doubles from R500/750)* have all the charm of corporate cubicles, but they are at least clean, and the modern bathrooms are about the best you'll see for the price. Next door, the crisp **Hotel Volkhov** *(☎ 11 55 05, fax 11 55 26; W www.novgorod-hotels.com/volkhov-hotel; ul Predtechenskaya 24; singles/doubles from R800/1000)* targets business travellers and charges a bit more. Rates include breakfast.

Decaying is a polite way to describe **Hotel Rossia** *(☎ 3 41 85; nab Alexandra Nevskogo 19/1; singles/doubles from R290/420)* where the riverfront location, with views of the kremlin, and discount price tag can't quite make up for the shabby rooms. The prices are better still at the wilted, but clean, dormitory/hostel **Rosa Vetrov** *(☎ 7 20 33; ul Nonoluchanskaya 27; dorm beds R150, singles/doubles R230/290)*, though space is very limited.

Hotel Sadko (☎ 66 30 04, fax 66 30 17; e sadko@novline.ru; ul Fyodorovsky Ruchey 16; singles/doubles from R400/600) is a bit outside the centre. The spacious rooms are bright enough for heart surgery, but most are overpriced. Rates include breakfast.

Hotel Intourist (☎ 7 50 89, fax 7 41 57; e root@intour.vnov.ru; singles/doubles with breakfast R800/1100), at ulitsa Velikaya (Dmitrievskaya) 16 by the river, has plain rooms. It's overpriced.

Beresta Palace Hotel (☎ 15 80 10, fax 15 80 25; e beresta@novtour.ru; ul Studenche-skaya 2; singles/doubles R2500/3000), a Best Western establishment, is on the east bank of the Volkhov, a bus or taxi ride from the centre. It is a Western-style luxury hotel, with pool, health club, sauna and tennis courts. Breakfast is included.

Places to Eat

Most places to eat are on the west side of town.

Restoran Detinets (☎ 7 46 24; dishes R35-200; open 11am-11pm daily), partly in the kremlin wall, is the place to try for good Russian dishes. Entering the kremlin from the west bank, turn right and follow the wall beyond the WWII memorial and the first few buildings to the restaurant entrance. Down a winding two-lane staircase, the bar serves strong coffee, ice cream topped with Russian balsam (a liquor flavoured with herbs) for R27 and medovukha, a locally brewed mead. The tables are tucked in the brick alcoves of what was the kremlin's Intercession Church.

Pri Dvore (ul Lyudogoshchaya 3) is a cheery little cafeteria with good prepared salads and hot dishes by the kilogram. Designing a full meal costs around R50. Try the tasty pastries or fruit ice creams (R5 a scoop) for dessert. In the same building, around the corner, the **Restoran Pri Dvore** (☎ 7 43 43; mains R100-200) is rather formal, with standard Russian dishes, an English-language menu, and weekly lunch specials. The underground dining room of **Derzhavnyy Cafe-Bar** (☎ 7 30 23; ul Gazon 5) also offers daily specials; the R50 lunchtime prix fixe includes soup, salad, main course, dessert and tea.

Kafe Charodeyka (ul Volosova-Meretskova 1/1), a favourite with homesick foreigners, has Tuborg on tap (R40), Irish coffee (R90) and pizza (R65 to R235). Nearby, a little cabin of a **grill** (☎ 13 23 70; ul Volosova-

Meretskova 4) sits behind the Fine Arts Museum, just off the Kremlin's west wall. The four booths offer a cosy site for tea (R3), beer (R20) and snacks (R10 to R50). In summer, snacks are also available at the **shashlyk stand** just outside the kremlin's east gate before the footbridge.

As for food on the east side of town, there are a couple of good café-restaurants across the street from one another, near Yaroslav's Court. **Kafe Kauri** (☎ 3 48 66; ul bolshaya Moskovskaya 11) is a friendly, blue-toned café serving chicken soup with egg (R10), 'Russian-style' fish (with cream and mushrooms, R38) and tasty onion pirozhky (small pastries, usually with a filling) for R4. **Kofeinya Sudarishka** (ul bolshaya Moskovskaya 32) is a tiny café across the way, with a few barstools and tables and a comfortable pub atmosphere.

Getting There & Away

The **train station** (☎ 9 87 45) is 1.5km west of the kremlin, at the end of prospekt Karla Marksa. A fast train runs daily to St Petersburg's Moscow Station (R108, three hours); a slower train runs to/from St Petersburg's Vitsebsk Station (R55, 4½ hours). There are also trains twice a week to Kiev and three times a week to Murmansk.

The modern **bus station** (☎ 3 42 52), right next to the train station, serves St Petersburg half a dozen times daily (R109, four hours, 190km). There's also direct bus service to/from Pskov twice daily (R130, 4½ hours).

If you're planning on visiting Novgorod en route from Moscow to St Petersburg or vice versa, the **Beetroot Bus** (w www.beetroot .org) might appeal. This offshoot of the UK-based tour operator, The Russia Experience, runs English-language package tours for backpackers during summer; for details check the website.

Getting Around

From the bus and train stations, bus Nos 4 and 20 (R4) pass in range of the Hotel Volkhov (between the first and second stops from the stations, or a 15-minute walk), Intourist (Universam Kremlyovsky/Kremlyovsky Park stop, about 500m from the hotel), Sadko (the stop on the corner of ulitsa Bolshaya Moskovskaya and prospekt Fyodorovsky Ruchey right after the bus crosses the river; the hotel is 200m farther along Fyodorovsky

Ruchey) and Beresta Palace. For the Beresta, get off at the stadium and cut through the park. Returning to the stations, you'll need to catch bus No 4 or 19 instead of No 20. A taxi from the train station to the Beresta or Sadko should cost about R50.

AROUND NOVGOROD
Khutin Monastery
The working **Orthodox convent** *(open 9am-8pm daily)* at Khutin was founded in the 12th century on sinful land. Early nuns prayed long and hard to exorcise evil spirits abiding here, and were so successful the site is now known for miracles and its holy water springs. Buses from Novgorod station (R4, 30 minutes) run from 9am to 2.30pm daily.

STARAYA RUSSA
СТАРАЯ РУССА
☎ 81652 • pop 40,000
Staraya Russa is a small town with major appeal for literary enthusiasts. Here, Dostoevsky spent summers and wrote much of *The Brothers Karamazov*. There's a **tourist office** *(☎ 2 19 40)* on the 1st floor of Hotel Polist, though you won't find a map here or anywhere else in town. You can, however, pick up a book on Staraya Russa's history (in Russian) at the bookshop just off the main square.

Dostoevsky's simple, two-storey house on the small River Pererititsa is now open as a **museum** *(☎ 2 14 77; ul Dostoevskogo 42; adult/student R40/20; open 10am-5.30pm Tues-Sun)*. The house never left the family's possession before becoming a museum, and some original pieces remain. Dostoevsky's desk sports copies from his maze-like drafts, his bookcase holds books from the period, and his wife's bedroom still contains her bed and chest. A keyboard instrument that Dostoevsky supposedly tinkered with sits by a window overlooking the river. Russian-language guides lead you through, pointing out every detail in a half-hour tour. In summer you might be able to arrange an English-language tour (R35) ahead of time by contacting the **Dostoevsky cultural centre** *(☎ 3 72 85; ul Dostoevskogo 8)*. The centre also offers tours of town (R300, two hours). Staraya Russa was also the setting for *The Brothers Karamazov*, and fans will want to visit the streets and churches that the characters frequented.

Ardent war buffs can check out a couple of non-Dostoevsky sights in town, as well: the small but earnest **Museum of the Northwest Front** *(ul Volodarskogo 20)* is a few blocks from the Hotel Polist and directly across the street from a veterans' **memorial**.

Places to Stay & Eat
For those who must wake up to the morning air that inspired the master, **Hotel Polist** *(☎ 8 75 47; ul Engelsya 20; singles/doubles from R100/150, with bath R240/480)* is a serviceable spot with time-worn rooms.

Around the main square are a few places that can feed you, including the Soviet-era cafeteria **Rushanka** *(cnr Filipov & main square)*, where tea costs R1.40, salads hover around the R5 mark, and mains range from R10 to R15.

Getting There & Away
There are buses leaving Novgorod's bus station at 7.25am, 10.15am, 11.15am and once or twice in the afternoon and return at 12.15pm and 3.35pm; the trip takes two hours each way and a round-trip ticket costs R52. From the Staraya Russa bus station, bus Nos 1, 4, 6 and 11 head to the centre, though there can be long waits between buses. Once there, find the river and follow it to your left from the main square to reach Dostoevsky's house. A taxi from the bus station straight to the museum is far simpler and should cost about R40.

PSKOV
ПСКОВ
☎ 8112 • pop 200,000
Situated 265km southwest of St Petersburg and close to both the Latvian and Estonian borders, Pskov is a pretty town that would be beautiful with a little more attention. It's built around a riverside kremlin with a stunning cathedral inside and bursts with churches designed by its own school of architects and icon painters. Unfortunately, almost all of the churches are closed, and almost none marked for renovation. Some comfort in the face of this circumstance is found at the town's excellent museum, the Pogankin Chambers, where a great deal of the iconographic art from these churches has been collected and displayed.

Pskov is also filled with parks; perhaps the most pleasant spot in town is along the river, just upriver from the small spillway near the footbridge and Epiphany Church.

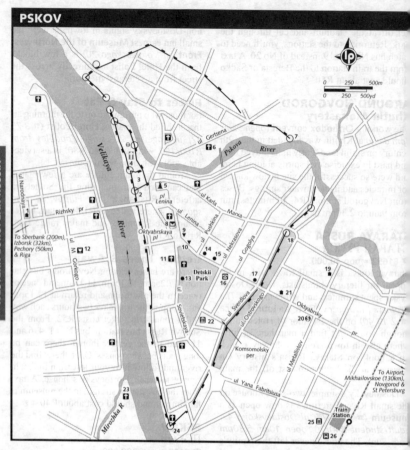

PSKOV

To Sberbank (200m), Izborsk (32km), Pechory (50km) & Riga

To Airport, Mikhailovskoe (130km), Novgorod & St Petersburg

As a border town (30km from Estonia), Pskov's history is saturated with 700 years of war for control of the Baltic coast. German Teutonic Knights captured it in 1240, but Alexander Nevsky routed them two years later in a famous battle on the ice of Lake Peipus. The Poles laid siege to it in the 16th century and the Swedes wrecked it the following century. Peter the Great used it as a base for his drive to the sea, and the Red Army fought its first serious battle with Nazi troops nearby.

This is also Pushkin country. The poet's grave and Mikhailovskoe, his family's estate, are a two-hour drive away.

Orientation & Information

Hotel Rizhskaya is three long blocks west of the Velikaya River, while almost everything else is on the east side. The town's axis is Oktyabrsky prospekt, ending at Oktyabrskaya ploshchad. The helpful **tourist office** (w www.tourism.pskov.ru; pl Lenina 1) can assist with excursions and maps.

There are several bookshops on Oktyabrsky prospekt; **Books for You** (Knigi dlya vas; Oktyabrsky pr 22) has maps of town, or you can buy a map at the train station. A tourist office in the lobby of **Hotel Oktyabrskaya** (Oktyabrsky pr 36) offers excursions through town and day trips to Izborsk and Pushkin's house at Mikhailovskoe.

The hulking **main post office** (☎ 72 47 85; Oktyabrskaya pl) offers **Internet service** (☎ 72 46 85) for R40 per hour. Two blocks up the street, the **telephone office** (Oktyabrsky pr 17) houses a more pleasant **Internet salon**

PSKOV

PLACES TO STAY & EAT
1 Hotel Rizhskaya
   Гостиница Рижская
9 Kafe Cheburechnaya
   Кафе Чебуречная
10 Kafe Snezhinka
   Кафе Снежинка
19 Hotel Krom
   Гостиница Кром
21 Hotel Oktyabrskaya
   Гостиница Октябрьская

OTHER
2 Vlasevskaya Tower
   Власьевская башня
3 Dovmont Town
   Довмонтов город
4 Kremlin & Trinity Cathedral
   Кремль и Троицкий собор

5 Lenin Statue
   Памятник Ленина
6 Epiphany Church
   богоявленская церковь
7 Gremyachaya Tower
   Гремячая Вашня
8 Main Post Office
   Главпочтамт
11 Church of St Nicholas-of-Usokha
   Церковь Николы со Усохи
12 Bingo
   Бинго
13 Merchant Houses
   Торговые дома
14 Gonchar Ceramics Store
   Магазин Гончар
15 Books for You
   Книги для Вас

16 Telephone Office
   Переговорный пункт
17 Souvenir Shop
   Сувенирный магазин
18 Petrovskaya Tower
   Петровская башня
20 Sberbank
   Сбербанк
22 Pogankin Chambers & Museum
   Поганкины палаты и музей
23 Mirozhsky Monastery
   Мирожский монастырь
24 Pokrovskaya Tower
   Покровская башня
25 Railway Museum
   Железнодорожный музей
26 Bus Station
   Автовокзал

(open 8am-10pm Mon-Fri, 11am-9pm Sat)
with access for R30 per hour.

You can change money at a number of
banks, including **Sberbank** (Oktyabrskaya pr
23), or at the main post office.

Old City

Pskov's walls formerly had four layers. The
kremlin or *krom* was the religious and ceremonial centre. Its stone walls and the southern annexe, Dovmont Town (Dovmontov
gorod), date from the 13th century. The Central Town (Sredny gorod), around ulitsa
Pushkina, was the commercial centre, though
little remains of it or its 14th-century walls.
The walls and towers of the 15th- to 16th-
century Outer Town (Okolny gorod) can still
be seen along ulitsa Sverdlova, the Velikaya
River embankment and across the tributary
Pskova River. You can walk along portions of
the ramparts, including behind the kremlin.

Kremlin & Dovmont Town In Dovmont
Town (named after an early prince), the foundations of a dozen 12th- to 15th-century
churches are scattered around like discarded
shoes. Through a passage is the kremlin,
where the *veche* (citizens' assembly) elected
its princes and sent them off to war, and Trinity Cathedral where many of the princes are
buried. Some of the kremlin's towers and galleries are open.

Trinity Cathedral The grandeur of the
1699 Trinity Cathedral (Troitsky sobor),

Pskov's principal sight, is only heightened by
the simplicity of the skeletal kremlin surrounding it. The gilded centre dome, as high
as a 28-storey building, can be seen from
30km away on a clear day. At the time of research the main space was closed for restoration, with services being held in a small
chapel on the ground floor.

Mirozhsky Monastery

The attraction here is the Unesco-protected,
nonworking **Cathedral of the Transfiguration
of the Saviour** (Spaso-Preobrazhensky sobor;
☎ 46 73 02; adult/student R100/80; open
11am-5.30pm Tues-Sun), with 12th-century
frescoes considered to be one of the most complete representations of the biblical narrative to
have survived the Mongols. The frescoes have
been beautifully restored after centuries of
damage from flooding, whitewashing, and
scrubbing; 80% of what you see today is original. The artists are unknown but were almost
certainly from Greece, based on the style of the
frescoes. The guided tour takes 1½ hours and
will fascinate art lovers and historians. The
cathedral itself was also based on a 12th-
century Greek model, formed around a sym-
metrical cross. Later additions and demolitions
have altered the footprint, but you can still see
traces of the original structure along exterior
walls. The church closes often due to incle-
ment weather: too hot, too cold or too wet; call
in advance if you don't want to waste the trip.

The monastery is also a working iconography school; at the time of writing there

was only one student in residence, but ask to see any current activity. The whole complex is across the Velikaya River from the centre; take bus No 2 from the vicinity of Hotel Rizhskaya. The monastery is the first stop across the river.

Pogankin Chambers & Museum

A very rich 17th-century merchant built his fortress-like house and treasury here in the heart of Pskov, with walls 2m thick. The original building and a newer addition now house the rather extensive collections of the **Pskov History Museum & Art Museum** (☎ 16 33 11; ul Nekrasova 7; adult/student R100/60; open 11am-6pm Tues-Sun, closed last Tues of the month). The 2nd floor of the new building usually showcases Soviet-era art, while the Russian avant-garde, including a couple of Petrov-Vodkins, is represented on the 1st floor along with works by Grigoriev and Rerikh.

The original house holds the real gems of the collection – several intact series of icons depicting the life of Christ, most from Pskov churches that have been shut down. It is a rare chance to thoroughly examine one particular style of iconography at close range. Note, for instance, the bulbous noses and otherwise harsh realism that characterises the Pskov school, as well as a predominance of subdued earth tones. One impressive 17th-century icon on display relates the history of Pskov's development. Admission to the museum includes a guided tour, which helps make sense of the icons and artefacts and enriches the history of iconography and iconoclasm in the region. The tours are in Russian, but your guide may speak some English.

Parks

Along the Pskova tributary, near a small spillway and the Epiphany Cathedral, is a lovely stretch of park, nice for strolling, picnicking or short hikes. **Gremyachaya Tower**, a decaying 16th-century fortress tower on the north bank, is open to explorers. The greenery along the south bank is shared by fishers and lovers. **Detskii Park**, right in the centre of town, is less bucolic but still very pleasant. During summer, a handful of adorable children's rides whirl gleeful youngsters around.

Railway Museum

If you've some time to kill while waiting for a train or bus, consider taking in the free

Railway Museum (☎ 9 66 32; ul Vokzalnaya 38; open 11am-5pm Wed-Sun, 11am-3pm Sat Nov-Apr; 10am-6pm daily May-Oct). In addition to chronicling the history of regional rail travel, the museum's three rooms contain all sorts of Pskoviana, including weaponry, writing implements, and the innards of a dissected personal computer. Scrapbooks organised by decade cover civic history still more thoroughly. It's fun.

Places to Stay

The hotels in Pskov are sufficiently unpleasant to warrant consideration of the lovely 10-room motel in Izborsk (see that entry later in this chapter). The bus between the two towns takes 45 minutes and costs R13; a taxi takes 20 minutes and should cost about R150.

The nicest rooms in Pskov – and that's not saying much – are at **Hotel Rizhskaya** (☎ 46 22 23; Rizhsky pr 25; singles/doubles R600/ 900), a bland but quiet Intourist-style place west of the Velikaya River. It's a 15-minute walk from the sights, and farther still from the train station.

Far more convenient is the tired **Hotel Oktyabrskaya** (☎ 16 42 46, fax 16 42 54; Oktyabrsky pr 36; singles/doubles from R140/210, with bath R300/830), between the train and bus stations and the centre. The main problems at the Oktyabrskaya concern the plumbing: smelly taps, dripping pipes and a scarcity of hot water.

Just around the corner, **Hotel Krom** (☎ 3 90 07; ul Metallistov 5; singles/doubles from R120/150, with bath R500/800) has no-frills rooms in a former dormitory.

Places to Eat & Drink

Kafe Cheburechnaya (☎ 6 27 37; Oktyabrsky pr 10; open 12pm-8pm daily) serves delicious Georgian dishes in a pretty, peach dining room. The management is exceedingly pleased to have tourists and will bend over backwards to accommodate you, including seating you – or even accepting a reservation – outside regular opening hours. The best way to order here is to ask for recommendations; expect to spend about R200 per person. The entrance is around the back.

Nearby, **Kafe Snezhinka** (☎ 72 30 86; Oktyabrsky pr 14; open 24 hrs), apparently aiming for minimalism, has turned out just plain uninspired. It's trendy enough for Pskov youth, though, and is a good place for coffee

(R15), beer (R30) and light Russian meals (appetisers R20 to R60, mains R40 to R80). Picture windows look out across Oktyabrsky prospekt onto Detskii Park.

Pskov has a friendly nightlife scene, and clubs have recently been laying claim to some prime properties. **Belaya Rus Plus** (☎ 72 00 90) is a three-tiered operation in the old kremlin tower overlooking Dovmont Town, at the foot of the bridge. The **restaurant** *(open noon-2am daily)* is rather nice and would be downright fancy if it weren't for the cheesy lighting and soft Russian pop. From the tables in the tower's alcoves, you can peek out at the river through crossbow slits. Dishes are unspectacular but fresh: marinated mushrooms and potatoes cost R67, crab and tomato salad costs R58. Downstairs from the restaurant is a cosy bar, upstairs there is a discotheque. The bar and disco are closed Monday and Tuesday.

Bingo (☎ 72 34 54; ul Gorkogo 22) is a laid-back disco and billiards hall in what was not so long ago a working bingo parlour. The cover charge is R30.

Shopping

For souvenirs, there is a **shop** *(Oktyabrsky pr 32; open 10am-9pm Mon-Fri, 10am-4pm Sat)* with scarves, linen tablecloths, so-so lacquer boxes, teaware and enamelled jewellery.

Gonchar *(Oktyabrsky pr 16; open 10am-7pm Mon-Fri, 10am-4pm Sat)*, a bit farther down, has locally made ceramics.

Getting There & Away

The **train station** (☎ 53 62 37) has limited amenities, although you can check a bag here (R26 per bag, per day). The only direct trains to St Petersburg are night trains (R152, six hours) to the Vitebsk Station; during the day you have to travel to Luga and transfer. One night train goes to Moscow (R500, 12 hours) and Riga (R900, 12 hours).

There are no easy train connections to Novgorod, but there are two buses daily (R130, 4½ hours) from the **central bus station** (☎ 2 40 02), near the train station. Buses for Pushkinskie Gory via Izborsk leave regularly (R45, two hours). Buses to Pechory (R33, 1½ hours) also leave every three hours.

Getting Around

For the Hotel Rizhskaya a taxi (about R80) is simplest to the stations; otherwise bus Nos 1, 11 and 17 from the train station run past Hotel Oktyabrskaya and through the centre.

AROUND PSKOV
Izborsk
Изборск

On a ridge with wide views over the countryside, Izborsk was once the equal of Pskov, chosen as a base by one of the original Varangian princes who ruled over early Russia. Now it's a sleepy village by the ruins of the oldest stone fortress in Russia. Inside the ruins are the 14th-century **Church of St Nicholas** – still the parish church – and a stone tower older than the church itself. Outside is the 17th-century **Church of St Sergius**, which has a little exhibit on local archaeology; some pieces date from the 8th century. A path around the back of the walls leads down to a lake. The locals you'll pass toting water bottles are coming from the 12 Springs of Happiness, Love, Health etc. A second museum in town, the **State Historic-Archaeological Museum 'Izborsk'** *(☎ 9 66 96; ul Pechorskaya 39; admission R5; open 10am-6pm Tues-Sun)*, houses archaeological finds from Izborsk and written explanations, in Russian, of the town's extremely rich history.

Places to Stay & Eat A crisp, modern cabin behind the fortress harbours an unlikely **hotel** (☎ 9 66 12) overlooking the valley. Six of the rooms share a very nice bath (singles/doubles R200/400), while the two-room 'lux' suite with a broad private balcony also has a private bath (single/double R600/700).

Beyond the kremlin walls, near the Church of St Sergius, is **Blinnaya** (☎ 9 67 13), a sweet little bliny restaurant boasting 'Izborskian' bliny. With butter they cost R20, with jam R25. Nice outdoor tables and benches provide a good spot for an afternoon beer (R10).

Getting There & Away It's 32km from Pskov to Izborsk on the Riga road. Buses run regularly from Pskov's bus station (R13, 45 minutes); be sure to take the bus towards Stary (Old) Izborsk, not Noviy (New) Izborsk.

Mikhailovskoe
Михайловское

☎ 81146 outside Pskov region, 246 within
The family house of Russia's most loved writer is open as part of the **Pushkin Museum Reserve** *(☎ 2 23 21; admission R150;*

Duels, Fools and Poets

One does not have to be in Russia very long to realise that poets are to this country what baseball stars and presidents are to the USA, or the queen and a foamy pint to England. They're quoted constantly, their birthdays are celebrated as national holidays and there is bound to be a bronze plaque on every house they've ever slept or sneezed in. Even their wives, nannies, mistresses and dogs are caught up and turned into the legend.

On the whole, the poets – from Pushkin and Lermontov to Pasternak and Brodsky – have been heavy drinkers, gamblers, womanisers and troublemakers. Nevertheless, schoolchildren bring flowers to their graves and can recite their poems before they know how to read. On a more sombre note, many a political prisoner sent to Siberia by Stalin has recalled in their memoirs being saved from insanity by methodically reciting all 5000-plus lines of Pushkin's *Eugene Onegin*, by rote.

For visitors to Russia, the veneration and attention enjoyed by the bards can seem almost fanatical. But for Russians, their poets are an untranslatable, inexhaustible source of intrigue, sensual pleasure and spirituality which strikes at the heart of the nation. None of the poets has come as close to expressing the soul of Russia as one young dandy with a protruding jaw and high forehead backed by a mass of curly hair.

Born in 1799, the son of nobility with a dollop of African blood in his lineage, Alexander Pushkin grew up in the French-speaking high society of St Petersburg. He went to school at the Lyceum in the shadow of the royal family's summer palace. Before he reached puberty, this precocious youth was using his perfect pitch, sharp wit and flawless sense of timing to hit on court women, diplomats' wives, peasant girls and the like. He and his school friends, many of them also poets, would spend their idle hours, between balls, composing odes and love poems. A child of his time, the Romantic Age, Pushkin was obsessed with obsessions – war, male honour, and beautiful and unattainable women. He is said to have had a foot fetish; his heroes were Lord Byron and Napoleon.

He wrote everything from classical odes and sonnets to short stories, plays and fairy tales. He is best loved for his poems in verse, *The Bronze Horsemen* and *Eugene Onegin*, in which he nearly answered that eternal question – why do Russians (like to) suffer so much? Politically, he was a hot potato and the tsars exiled him from St Petersburg thrice, once to his home estate in Mikhailovskoe and twice to the Caucasus, where his romping with the local beauties and war-loving men added even more fuel to his poetic fire. At home in Mikhailovskoe, he is said to have spent long evenings drinking with his childhood nanny. Pushkin himself admitted she told him many of the tales which he then turned into national legends. While on long walks, he would compose aloud. To keep his arm in good shape for duelling, he carried a cane filled with rocks.

It did not help. In 1837, Pushkin was mortally wounded in a duel over his wife, Russian beauty queen Natalia Goncharova. He lay dying for two days while all of St Petersburg came to pay homage, dramatically directing taxi drivers, 'To Pushkin!' Even today the Russian rumour mills are producing versions of this 166-year-old scandal; only the theories about JFK's assassination come close in weirdness and speculation. During the night, Pushkin's body was carried from Chyornaya Rechka in St Petersburg and buried at the monastery near his home estate.

Four years later, another Russian bard, 26-year-old Mikhail Lermontov, would also be killed in a duel. Eerily, both poets had written major works in which the highly autobiographical heroes summoned their antitheses to the field. In the fictional versions, however, the heroes lived.

open 10am-8pm Tues-Sun Dec-Mar; Tues-Sun 9am-5pm May-Oct; closed Apr & Nov), a 2½-hour bus ride from Pskov. Alexander Pushkin spent two phenomenally productive years in exile at Mikhailovskoe, his family's estate near the settlement of Pushkinskie Gory (Pushkin Hills), 130km south of Pskov. The family first came to the area in the late 1700s, when Pushkin's great-grandfather Abram Hannibal was given the land by Empress Elizabeth. The family house was destroyed during WWII and has since been rebuilt.

The 20-hectare park is closed on the last Tuesday of the month. The attraction is Pushkin's writing room with his comfy leather chair, portraits of Byron and Zhu-kovsky (Pushkin's mentor, also a poet) and a mini statue of Napoleon. The big, thick, religious book on his writing table he supposedly grabbed from the family bookcase and pretended to be reading when he saw the local priest coming for a visit.

At Pushkinskie Gory, about 800m north of the bus stop, is the **Svyatogorsk Monastery**, where Pushkin is buried. Not far from the monastery is **Hotel Druzhba** (☎ 2 16 51; singles/doubles R160/300) which provides nice rooms with bath and shower. To get to the hotel, walk from the bus stop along the road away from the monastery and bear right.

This is lovely countryside and can be seen as part of a day trip.

Getting There & Away A number of agencies run excursions from Pskov; check with the tourist office (see Orientation & Information under Pskov earlier in this chapter) to find one that matches your schedule. Alternatively, you can do it yourself by catching a bus to Pushkinskie Gory from the Pskov bus station. There are several buses a day (R40, 2½ hours).

The Pushkinskie Gory bus station is 4km from the Pushkin house; there may or may not be a short-distance bus to cover the last leg. The walk is pleasant. Follow the road away from Svyatogorsk Monastery past the bus stop. At the fork in the road, past the shiny Western-style toilets built in celebration of Pushkin's 200th birthday (they will probably be locked), bear left. There will be signs.

You could also try to hitch a ride on an excursion bus leaving from Hotel Druzhba or ask a local driver (it should cost around R50). The last bus back to Pskov from Pushkinskie Gory leaves at around 7pm.

Pechory Monastery
Печорский Монастырь
Founded in 1473 in a ravine full of hermits' caves, this monastery has been a working cloister ever since. With all the high ground outside, it's an improbable stronghold, but several tsars fortified it and depended on it. A path descends under the 1564 St Nicholas Church (Nikolskaya tserkov) into a sea of colours and architectural styles, where several dozen monks still live and study. Taking photos of the buildings is acceptable if you make a contribution at the front gate; photographing the monks is taboo.

The central yellow church is really two buildings. At ground level is the original **Assumption Cathedral** (Uspensky sobor), built into the caves; upstairs is the 18th-century baroque **Intercession Church** (Pokrovskaya tserkov). Below the belfry on the left is the entrance to the caves, where some 10,000 bodies – monks, benefactors and others – are bricked up in vaults, with more dying to get in.

You can wander the monastery grounds and visit most of the churches on your own, but to visit the caves you'll have to find a monk willing to lead you down through the spiderweb of dark, spooky, nearly freezing sand tunnels. Everyone carries a candle, which in places you can thrust through holes in the tunnel walls to see the wooden coffins lying lopsided on top of each other. The monks insist that there has never been the smell of decay. At the exit to the caves, you'll be shown an ancient coffin burned around the edge (supposedly this happened when some evil-doer tried to open it).

On the grounds is the summer carriage of Peter the Great's daughter, the licentious Anna Ioannovna, who – as the story goes – came to have some fun with the monks and didn't leave until winter, on a sleigh. Before WWII, this area was in independent Estonia, thereby avoiding the frequent stripping or destruction of churches during that time; the 16th-century bells in St Nicholas Church are original, a rarity in Russia.

There's a booth outside the monastery gates housing an **excursion office** (☎ 81148-2 14 93; open 9am-1pm & 2pm-6pm daily). The office offers tours in Russian for about R100, depending on the number of people. On the monastery grounds, women must wear skirts and cover their heads; you can borrow wraparound skirts and shawls at the entrance. Men should wear long pants, and both men and women should cover their shoulders. It's possible for men to stay at the monastery and eat with the monks in their modest cafeteria, with special permission. To arrange this, ask for Maxim, and explain why you are interested in staying.

There are several buses a day from Pskov to Pechory (R33, 1½ hours). In addition, one early morning and one evening train run here.

Kaliningrad Region
Калининградская область

The Kaliningrad region is like no other in Russia. Not only is it the country's smallest, newest and most westerly region, it also has a history that differs in all ways from that of the rest of Mother Russia. As such, the mind-set and outlook of its inhabitants are also markedly different and this, along with a landscape that includes some of Europe's highest sand dunes, stretches of deserted sandy beaches and thick forests, make Kaliningrad an intriguing region to explore.

From the 13th century until 1945, the area was German, part of the core territory of the Teutonic knights and their successors the dukes and kings of Prussia. Its capital, now named Kaliningrad, was the famous German city of Königsberg, capital of East Prussia, where Prussian kings were crowned. Scant Prussian legacy remains in the city of Kaliningrad, but the countryside is sprinkled with picturesque, moss-covered ruins of Prussian castles. The world's largest amber mine, in Yantarny, still produces over 90% of the world's amber.

After WWI, East Prussia was separated from the rest of Germany when Poland re-gained statehood. The three-month campaign by which the Red Army took it in 1945 was one of the fiercest of the war, with hundreds of thousands of casualties on both sides.

Russia's Baltic Fleet is headquartered at Baltiysk, and therefore the entire region was closed to Westerners until 1991. Despite a massive military downsizing since the 1990s, the area is still heavily militarised. The area has always been strategically important, now again in light of NATO and EU expansion eastwards. Kaliningrad will soon be surrounded by EU and NATO-member countries (Poland and Lithuania), and providing a visa-free transit corridor from Kaliningrad to 'mainland' Russia has become one of the most contentious topics at Russia–EU meetings.

The fate of this tiny wedge, only 15,100 sq km, with a population of 926,000, is far from clear, but is destined to be interesting. Talk of turning it into a fourth 'Baltic state' still has not died down, while more realistic measures, such as Russia giving it autonomous status, are still on the table. It's plausible that Kaliningrad – and not the Westernized window to the West that St Petersburg has long represented – might ironically be what finally drags Russia into Europe.

Visas

Unless you're flying, to reach the Kaliningrad Region from anywhere else means

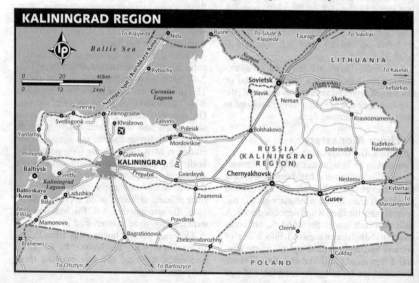

KALININGRAD REGION

you must be in possession of either a double or multiple-entry Russian visa, and/or visas for its neighbouring countries. These must be arranged in advance. In Kaliningrad, the main **PVU office** (☎ 22 82 74, 22 82 82) is at Sovietsky prospekt 13, room 9.

Disabled Travellers

Inaccessible transport, lack of ramps and lifts and no centralised policy for people with physical limitations make the Kaliningrad Region challenging for wheelchair-bound travellers. In Kaliningrad, Hotel Kaliningrad and several restaurants are wheelchair-accessible. Baltma Tours (see Travel Agencies under Information) can provide further information or assistance for disabled tourists.

KALININGRAD
КАЛИНИГРАД
☎ 22 (within the region) ☎ 0112 (from elsewhere) • pop 423,000

Old photos attest that until 1945, Königsberg was one of Europe's finest-looking cities: regal, vibrant, cultured and an architectural gem. But WWII, later Soviet destruction of German-era constructions and misguided building projects saw to it that today's Kaliningrad is not exactly eye-candy.

However, there are lovely residential corners of the city that predate the war, a forest-like park and a few large ponds which work as effective antidotes to all the concrete. A number of central areas have been given a recent and friendly face-lift. It's also a vibrant, fun-loving city that feels larger than its population would suggest.

Founded as a Teutonic Order fort in 1255, Königsberg joined the Hanseatic League in 1340 and from 1457 to 1618 was the residence of the grand masters of the Teutonic order and their successors, the dukes of Prussia. The first king of Prussia was crowned here in 1701. The city centre was flattened by British air raids in August 1944 and the Red Army assault from 6 to 9 April 1945. Many of the surviving Germans were killed or sent to Siberia – the last 25,000 were deported to Germany in 1947–48, one of the most effective ethnic cleansing campaign in European history.

The city was renamed on 4 July 1946 (City Day celebrations are thus held on the first weekend in July) after Mikhail Kalinin, one of Lenin's henchmen who had conveniently died just as a new city name was needed. After opening up in 1991, it struggled through extreme economic difficulties. A wave of elderly German tourists revisiting their *Heimat* (Homeland), often weeping upon seeing what it had become, resulted in a complete reconstruction of Königsberg's cathedral thanks to their donations. Slowly, Kaliningrad has emerged as one of Russia's most Western-minded cities, and due to its mix of historical legacies, one of its most interesting.

Orientation

Leninsky prospekt, a broad north–south avenue, is Kaliningrad's main artery, running over 3km from the bus and main train station, the Yuzhny Vokzal (South Station), to the suburban Severny Vokzal (North Station). About halfway it crosses the Pregolya River and passes the cathedral, the city's major landmark. The city's real heart is further north, around the sprawling ploshchad Pobedy.

Information

A free Russian/English guide to the region and city called *Kaliningrad Travel Guide* is available in hotel lobbies, while the *In Your Pocket* team hasn't produced a guide to Kaliningrad since 2000. However, you can download a free quarterly *Instant Kaliningrad* guide at ⓦ www.inyourpocket.com /instant. Baltma Travel Agency (see Travel Agencies later in this section) has produced a regional guide, available at its office.

Money You can change money and get cash advances at branches of Investbank and other major banks. There are exchange bureaus at most hotels, often with 24-hour service, and along the side of the State Technical University. The best rates are at **Stroivestbank** (ul Gendelya 10). Many shops along Leninsky prospekt and elsewhere have ATM machines.

Post The main **post office** (ul Kosmonavta Leonova 22) is out of the way, about 600m north of prospekt Mira, but try the smaller, more convenient **branch** (☎ 56 33 21; ul Chernyakhovskogo 32) opposite the central market. Both branches offer EMS. There is also a **UPS office** (☎ 55 39 22; ul Chernyakhovskogo 66).

Telephone International phone calls can be made from card-operated public phone booths (St Petersburg cards work in these). Cards are

WESTERN EUROPEAN RUSSIA

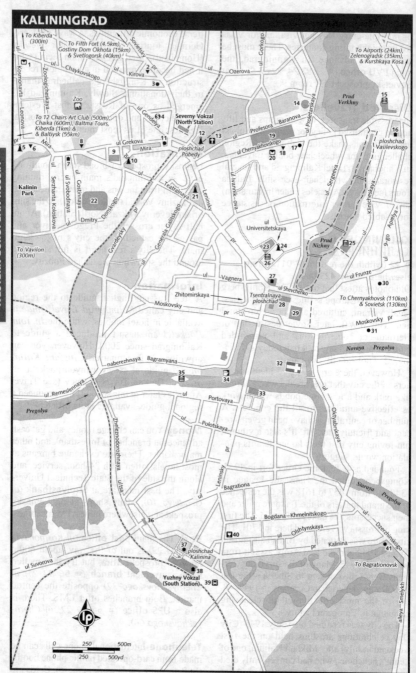

KALININGRAD

KALININGRAD

PLACES TO STAY
7   Hotel Moskva
    Гостиница Москва
16 Dona Hotel
    Дона Отель
27 Hotel Kaliningrad
    Гостиница
    Калининград
38 South Train Station
    Hotel

PLACES TO EAT
2   Razgulyai
    Разгуляй
6   Universal
8   Solyanka
    Солянка
18 Planeta; Taverna
    Diky Dyouk
    Планета; Таверна
    Дикий Дюк
28 Kiosk Village;
    V Teni Zamka
    В Тени Замка

OTHER
1   Main Post Office
    Главпочтамп
3   Main OVIR Office
    ОВИР
4   Stroivestbank
    Стройвестбанк
5   Cosmonaut
    Monument
    Землякам Космонавтам

9   Kaliningrad Drama; Comedy
    Theatre
    Театр драмы и комедии
10 Schiller Statue
    Памятник Шиллеру
11 State Technical University;
    E-Type
    Технический
    Университет
12 Lenin Statue
    Памятник В И Ленину
13 Site of Future Cathedral of
    Christ the Saviour
    Кафедральный собор
    Христа Спасателя
14 Wrangel Tower
    Башня Врангель
15 Amber Museum; Dohna
    Tower; Rossgarten Gate
    Музей Янтаря, Башня
    Дона; Ворота
    Росгартенские
17 UPS
19 Central Market
    Центральный рынок
20 Post Office
    Почта
21 Mother Russia Statue
    Мать Россия
22 Baltika Stadium
    Балтика Стадион
23 University
    Университет
24 Kant Statue
    Памятник Канту

25 History & Art Museum
    Историко Художеств-
    енный музей
26 Bunker Museum
    Блиндаж Ляша
29 Dom Sovietov
    (House of Soviets)
    Дом Советов
30 Golden Orchid
    Travel Agency
31 Kaliningrad Art Gallery
    Художественная
    галерея
32 Cathedral & Kant's Tomb
    Кафедральный собор
    и могила Канта
33 Former Stock Exchange
    Биржа
34 Pier
    Пристань
35 Oceanography
    Museum
    Музей Мирового
    Океана
36 Brandenburg Gate
    Ворота
    Бранденбургские
37 Kaliningrad Airlines &
    Aeroflot
39 Bus Station
    Автовокзал
40 Olshtyn
    Олштын
41 Friedland Gate
    Ворота Фридландские

WESTERN EUROPEAN RUSSIA

available from post offices, kiosks and most major hotels. Hotel Kaliningrad has a handy phone and fax office, open 24 hours. You'll get better rates by ordering calls at the **telephone and fax centre** (*Teatralnaya ul 13/19; open 24hrs*). Self-dial long-distance calls can be made one block south at its second office.

Email & Internet Access In room 155 of the State Technical University there's a busy Internet club, **E-Type** (☎ 44 72 42; *Sovietsky pr 1; open 9am-9pm Mon-Fri, 9am-7pm Sat*), which charges R26 per hour. A funky, grotto-like Internet café, **Kiberda** (☎ 51 18 30; *Komsomolskaya ul 87; open noon-11pm daily*), charges from R32 per hour and also serves decent meals.

Travel Agencies The best travel agency in town is **Baltma Tours** (☎ 21 18 80; **w** *www .baltmatours.com; pr Mira 49*). There's nothing it can't do – from arranging visa support

and accommodation to any kind of tour of the region. It offers boat cruises throughout the region and excursions with friendly, knowledgeable guides to every corner of Kaliningrad. Car rental with a driver is typically US$10 per hour, guides cost about US$40 a day extra. Its office is by far the best source of regional information in town.

Golden Orchid (☎ 53 85 53, 01145-21 098; **w** *www.enet.ru/~goldorch; ul Frunze 6*) specialises in arranging extremely interesting trips to nearby military port Baltiysk (formerly Pillau), with permission, transport, guide and overnight accommodation costing about US$50, or around US$15 for six-hour excursions.

Cathedral & Surroundings

The outstanding German remnant is the red brick Gothic **cathedral** (*Kafedralny Sobor;* ☎ 27 25 83; *adult/student R54/15; open 9am-5pm daily*). Founded in 1333, it was severely damaged during WWII and, since 1992, has been undergoing total reconstruction. On the bottom floor are small Lutheran and Orthodox chapels; upstairs are displays of old Königsberg and objects from archaeological digs. On the top floor is an austere room with the death mask of Emanuel Kant, whose rose marble **tomb** lies outside on the outer north side. The 18th-century philosopher was born, studied and taught in Königsberg.

The fine blue Renaissance-style building, just across the river to the south of the cathedral, is the old **Stock Exchange** (*Leninsky pr 83*) built in the 1870s, now a 'Sailors' Culture Palace'.

West of the cathedral, across the Novaya Pregolya branch of the Pregolya River, is the Petra Velikogo embankment where you'll find the **Oceanography Museum** (☎ *34 02 44; nab Petra Velikogo 1; each of its 3 sections adult/student R30/20; open 10am-5pm Wed-Sun*). It has recently tripled in both size and interest. The *Vityaz* ship is a museum with exhibits on its past scientific expeditions. Newly opened are the *B-413* submarine, a pavilion with the skeleton of a 16.8m-long sperm whale, and the *Leonov*, another ship with exhibits devoted to Soviet space exploration.

Along the same embankment as the museum is a small **pier**, from which pleasant **city boat cruises** are now run. Call Baltma Tours for schedule information.

North of the cathedral is **Tsentralnaya ploshchad** (Central Square) on which sits one of the dourest, ugliest of Soviet creations, the upright H-shaped **Dom Sovietov** (House of Soviets). On this site stood a magnificent 1255 castle, damaged during WWII but dynamited out of existence by narrow-minded Soviet planners in 1967–68 to rid the city of a flagrant reminder of its Germanic past. In its place this eyesore was built (over 10 long years), but which has never even been used. Money ran out, and it was discovered that the land below it was hollow, with a (now flooded) four-level underground passage connecting to the Dom.

Further north, near the university, is the popular **Bunker Museum** (*Blindazh Lyasha;* ☎ *53 65 93; Universitetskaya ul 2; admission R30; open 10am-6pm daily*), the German command post in 1945, and from where the city's last German commander, Otto van Lasch, signed capitulation to the Soviets.

Other Museums

Kaliningrad's outstanding **History & Art Museum** (☎ *45 38 44; ul Klinicheskaya 21; adult/student R30/20; open 10am-6pm Tues-Sun*) is housed in a reconstructed 1912 concert hall by the banks of the pretty Prud Nizhny (Schlossteich, Lower Pond), a favourite recreation spot. The museum displays a fairly open history of the city. Though it mainly focuses on Soviet rule, the German past comes through as the city's spine. There are chilling posters of the castle's destruction.

The **Amber Museum** (☎ *46 15 63; pl Vasilievskogo 1; admission R40; open 10am-5pm Tues-Sun*) is housed in the attractive **Dohna Tower**, a bastion of the city's old defensive ring sitting at the lower end of **Prud Verkhny** (Upper Pond), another mini-lake surrounded by parkland. The adjacent **Rossgarten Gate**, one of the old German city gates, completes the ensemble. Inside the museum are some 6000 examples of amber art works, the most impressive being from the Soviet period.

At the city's northern border, along Sovietsky prospekt, is the **Fifth Fort** (Pyaty Fort). One of the city's 15 forts constructed between 1872 and 1892 as a second line of defence, and the only one open to the public, it's a heavily wooded ruin that's fun to explore for hidden passages. Take trolleybus No 1 to the Pyaty Fort stop.

The **Kaliningrad Art Gallery** (☎ *46 71 66; Moskovsky pr 62; open 11am-7pm Tues-Sun*) features exhibitions by local artists.

Prospekt Mira

Ploshchad Pobedy is the current city centre, still dominated by an awkward-looking **Lenin statue**. He is soon to be dwarfed by a massive cathedral being built behind him. The small, wooden **Church of Christ the Saviour** is a temporary substitute.

Extending west of the square is prospekt Mira, a pleasant artery leading to some of the city's prettiest areas and lined with shops and cafés. Some 300m from ploshchad Pobedy is the 1927 **Kaliningrad Drama and Comedy Theatre** (☎ *21 24 22; pr Mira 4*) restored in 1980.

Another 200m farther on is the **Zoo** (☎ *21 89 24; adult/student R30/15; open 9am-6pm daily*), which before WWII was considered the third best in the world, but is now in a sorry state (donations accepted – and needed!).

Further west is the splendid **Cosmonaut Monument**, a gem of Soviet iconography. This honours the several cosmonauts who hail from the region. Just west, as prospekt Pobedy branches out from prospekt Mira, is the entrance to **Kalinin Park**, an amusement ground and splendid, forest-like park on the grounds of an old German cemetery.

Walks through the linden-scented, tree-lined old German neighbourhoods are the best way to experience old Königsberg. The entire area between prospekts Pobedy and Mira is particularly enchanting (ulitsa Kutuzova especially), despite looking somewhat dishevelled.

Places to Stay

The truly desperate will find themselves at the **South Train Station Hotel** (☎ 49 24 47; pl Kalinina; singles/doubles R150/240) with predictable services (shared showers and toilets).

Otherwise, the most pleasant hotel in town is the 24-room **Chaika** (☎ 21 07 29; ul Pugacheva 13; singles/doubles from R900/1200) nestled in a leafy, residential area. The 171-room **Hotel Moskva** (☎ 27 20 89; pr Mira 19; singles/doubles from R1100/1300) has been reborn after extensive renovations and boasts decent rooms in a friendly atmosphere. The town's principal hotel, **Hotel Kaliningrad** (☎ 46 94 40; w www.hotel .kaliningrad.ru; Leninsky pr 81; singles R800-1340, doubles R1340-1940), is conveniently placed and offers many services, but the rooms are drab and, if facing the city centre, very noisy due to the traffic.

More expensive, but worth the extra, is **Dona Hotel** (☎ 35 16 50; w www.dona.kalinin grad.ru; pl Vasilievskogo 2; singles R1350-3000, doubles R2050-3200), definitely the region's funkiest hotel. Rooms are small but cosy and ultramodern in their pseudo-Philippe Starck design.

For those who don't mind staying out of the city, **Gostivoy Dom Okhota** (☎ 22 69 94; Petrogo village; singles/doubles R500/700), on the main road to Zelenogradsk 15km north along Sovietsky prospekt, is a small slice of paradise. Rooms in this two-floor wooden chalet are modern, bright and clean, and the surroundings peaceful. There's horse-riding nearby and meals can be ordered.

Places to Eat

Cafés & Budget The city's best espresso, coffee cocktails and ice cream are in **V Teni Zamka** (Tsentralnaya pl, kiosk No 63; open 11am-10pm daily), a tiny but charming space seating only 20, inside the so-called kiosk village. More stylish and Western is **Universal** (☎ 21 59 70; pr Mira 43; open 10am-3am daily), a complex comprising a café, restaurant (mains R100 to R150), cinema and upscale nightclub.

There may be a doorman at **Solyanka** (☎ 27 92 03; pr Mira 24; mains R50-70; open 9am-11pm daily), but this setup is basically cafeteria-style (non-Russian speakers can point to what they like) serving tasty dishes at great prices. More great deals can be had at **Planeta** (☎ 46 52 35; ul Chernyakhovskogo 26; mains R25-75; open noon-6am), a youth hang-out decked out like a mall food court; accordingly, pizzas are cheap (R40) and the fast food is, well, fast and filling.

The city's main **market** is almost across the street and is a good place to stock up on fresh produce.

Restaurants The city's absolute must-visit is **12 Chairs Art Club** (☎ 21 09 31; pr Mira 67; mains R70-150; open noon-1am daily), a dark and ambient space filled with antiques and couches. Its extensive menu is sure to please, as will its famous cocktails.

There are generous portions of scrumptious Russian, French and Lithuanian dishes served at the medieval-themed **Taverna Diky Dyouk** (☎ 46 52 35; ul Chernyakhovskogo 26; mains R120-470; open noon-6am daily).

The splendid **Razgulyai** (☎ 21 48 97; Sovietsky pr 13; mains R50-180; open noon-2am daily) is a cheery, tavern-style place with tasty meals.

Entertainment

The city is full of discos and upscale nightclubs. The three-storey **Olshtyn** (☎ 44 46 35; Olshtynskaya ul 1; open noon-5am daily) has been the premier club for years, though it's starting to show its age. **Vavilon** (ul Domskogo 19; open noon-8am daily) is a bowling and pool emporium and also serves 40 kinds of yummy pizza.

Getting There & Away

Air Kaliningrad's **domestic** (☎ 45 94 26) and **international** (☎ 44 13 36) airports are 24km north of the city, near Khrabrovo village. The only international flight is a thrice-weekly flight to Warsaw on LOT; call ahead or contact

Baltma Tours to find out if other routes have been added. **Kaliningrad Airlines** (☎ 44 14 63) has two flights daily to Moscow, three weekly to St Petersburg (Pulkova Airlines flies an additional three to/from St Petersburg), and flights to a host of other cities in Russia and the CIS. **Aeroflot** (☎ 55 53 53) has daily flights to Moscow. The joint offices of Kaliningrad Airlines and Aeroflot are opposite the train station on ploshchad Kalinina.

Train There are two stations in the city: **Severny Vokzal** (North Station; ☎ 49 99 91) and the larger **Yuzhny Vokzal** (South Station; ☎ 49 26 75). All long-distance and many local trains go from Yuzhny Vokzal, passing through but not always stopping at Severny Vokzal.

Local trains include nine a day to Svetlogorsk, six a day to Zelenogradsk and two a day to Chernyakhovsk. There are four trains a day to Vilnius, at least once daily to Moscow, every second day to Brest, Gomel and St Petersburg, and about two per week to Odessa and Kiev. There are no longer any direct trains to Berlin.

Bus The bus station (☎ 44 36 35; pl Kalinina) is next to Yuzhny Vokzal. Buses depart from here to every corner of the region, including one or two per hour to Svetlogorsk, eight daily to Chernyakhovsk and four daily to Smiltyne, Lithuania along the Kurshkaya Kosa. One bus daily goes to Klaipeda via Sovietsk, and there are two daily each to Kaunas and Vilnius. Daily buses go to Riga and Tallinn. There are two daily buses to Gdansk and Olshtyn, five weekly to Warsaw, three weekly to Berlin, Hamburg and Bremen, and once weekly buses to Hanover, Essen and Stuttgart. Buses to Poland and Germany are operated by **König Auto** (☎ 43 04 80).

Car & Motorcycle From the south it is possible to enter Kaliningrad from Poland although the lines at the Lithuanian borders at Kybartai or on the Kurshkaya Kosa at Nida are not as monstrous. Petrol is widely available.

Sea Passengers are accepted by **Trans Exim** (☎ 55 40 27; e office@transexim.ru) on its cargo ship running from Kiel to St Petersburg via Kaliningrad. A ship leaves once a week to either destination and costs US$140 one way to either city. **Anjuta** (☎ 21 07 42) runs a daily hydrofoil service between Kaliningrad

and Elblag in Poland, one-way tickets costing around US$28. **Inflot** (☎ 47 14 42) may restart its services to Germany.

Getting Around

Tickets for trams, trolleybuses, buses and minibuses are sold only by controllers inside. To get to the domestic airport, take bus 128 from the bus station (R30). Taxis ask around R300 for the ride *from* the airport, and less *to* the airport.

SVETLOGORSK
СВЕТЛОГОРСК
☎ 253 (within the region) ☎ 01153 (from elsewhere) • pop 13,000

Svetlogorsk (formerly Rauschen, founded in 1228) is a pleasant, green coastal town, 35km northwest of Kaliningrad. It was not much damaged by WWII. The narrow beach is backed by high, steep sandy slopes and the town is dotted with pretty wooden houses which are the main reason visitors come here; avid sunbathers head to Zelenogradsk or the Kurshkaya Kosa for heavier beach action.

On Oktyabrskaya ulitsa are the 25m **water tower** and the curious red-tile-domed Jugendstil (Art Nouveau) **bathhouse**. Around the corner is a small *bufet* which serves delicious, local spring water to sanatorium residents – but if you ask nicely, they'll let you have a glass. About 200m east of the main beach promenade is an impressive, colourful **sundial**, believed to be the largest in Europe.

At the eastern end of ulitsa Lenina there is a **Commemorative Chapel**, opened in 1994 on the former site of a kindergarten. It is a memorial to the 23 children and 11 adults who died after an A-26 Soviet military transport plane crashed into the building. The tragedy was hushed up for almost 20 years and only came to light when the Orthodox Church built the chapel.

Places to Stay & Eat

There are several hotel options in town, including very inexpensive ex-sanatoriums and a camping ground, all on Kaliningradsky prospekt, about 500m west of the Svetlogorsk II train station.

The **Mebelschik** (☎ 334 78; ul Lenina 1; singles/doubles from R200/400) is a small boarding house with some of the best deals in town.

If you can afford it, **Stary Doktor** (☎ 213 62; ul Gagarina 12; singles/doubles R1200/1800) is worth the extra – warm and cosy in an old German home. One of the town's best restaurants and souvenir shops are also at this address.

The cheapest fill-up is at **Blinnaya** (Oktyabrskaya ul 22; mains R15; open 10am-6pm daily) where yummy bliny start at R6.

There are decent Korean dishes at **Kuk-Si** (☎ 213 64; Oktyabrskaya 3 ul; mains R70-150; open noon-11pm daily).

Getting There & Away

Nine trains a day make the 70-minute trip from Kaliningrad (get off at Svetlogorsk II, not I). More convenient and faster (45 to 60 minutes) are more than 20 buses and taxi buses which make the trip daily leaving from the bus station and stopping outside the Severny Vokzal on Sovietsky prospekt (timetables are posted on the street at the bus stop). Svetlogorsk's bus station is 500m west of the train station, at the corner of ulitsa Lenina and Kaliningradsky prospekt.

KURSHKAYA KOSA
КУРШКАЯ КОСА

☎ 250 (within the region) ☎ 01150 (from elsewhere)

The Kurshkaya Kosa is the Russian half of the thin, 98km-long Curonian Spit, which divides the Curonian lagoon from the Baltic Sea. The area is a Unesco World Heritage Site. It boasts dramatic landscapes – high sand dunes, pine forests, an exposed western coast and a calm lagoon.

Fishing and holiday villages dot the eastern coast. The main ones, from the south to the north, are: Lesnoy (formerly Sarkau); Rybachy (formerly Rossitten), the largest with a population of 1200; and Morskoe (formerly Pillkoppen). Highlights of any visit include admiring the dunes (the most magnificent are just south of Morskoe) and quiet walks by the sea or lagoon and through the pine forests.

The **Kurshkaya Kosa National Park** (☎ 213 46; Lesnaya ul 7), the first national park in Russia, is headquartered in Rybachy, but runs a fascinating bird-ringing centre 7km north of Lesnoy, on the site of what was the world's first ornithological station. Some 25,000

visitors a year come by to see some of the world's largest bird-trapping nets (one is 15m high, 30m wide and 70m long) which trap an average of 1000 birds a day. A highly worthwhile, by-donation tour of the facilities (best prearranged) will show you how they catch and ring hundreds of birds including the bluetit, scarlet chaffinch and middle spotted woodpecker before releasing them. There is also a museum at the headquarters in Rybachy.

In Rybachy, also worth a visit is the red brick church **Temple of Sergei Radonezhsky** (1873), reopened in 1990 after being used as a storage room for fishing equipment. The simple interiors are charming.

The **Ecotourism Information Centre** (☎ 282 75; Tsentralnaya ul) in Lesnoy works in collaboration with the national park and organises excursions, transport and accommodation. You can also rent bikes there – the perfect way to explore the Spit.

Places to Stay & Eat

Kurshkaya Kosa (☎ 482 42; Tsentralnaya ul 17; singles/doubles/2-room suites 15 June-25 Aug US$60/65/70, other times US$25/30/40) in Lesnoy, is one of the best choices, a cheery, modern place a few steps from the beach. The suites fit four people and are great deals. There's also an excellent restaurant here.

Postoyaly Dvor (☎ 212 96, fax 212 90; singles/doubles with breakfast & supper US$44/54) is a popular, comfortable motel on the main road at the turn-off to Rybachy. Its restaurant has a solid reputation throughout the region, but is overpriced with tasty main meals for R150 to R350.

Dom Otdykha (☎ 212 44; Pogranichnaya ul 11; singles/doubles R250/350), in Rybachy has sparse, recently renovated rooms, some overlooking the lagoon. A lady named **Olga** (☎ 211 24) next door at No 13 rents out rooms and a small cabin by the beach for R100 to R150.

Getting There & Away

Four buses a day from Kaliningrad (via Zelenogradsk) take the road to Smiltyne in Lithuania at the northern tip of the peninsula. There are about three others which run daily between Zelenogradsk and Morskoe.

Northern European Russia
Северно-Европейская Россия

Stretching from the Gulf of Finland to the Arctic Barents Sea and from Finland to the Ural Mountains, Northern European Russia is a picture window into the dichotomy that is Russia. While the land's countless centuries-old churches and monasteries chronicle the deeply spiritual nature of its people, its stolid apartment blocks, rusted-metal ports, smoke-stack factories and monolithic monuments recall the staunch Soviet affinity for ideology.

Because the region is well linked by rail and air, travelling here is slowly becoming more popular, especially with all breeds of outdoor enthusiasts, who appreciate the relatively inexpensive cost of stitching through the landscape's richly embroidered fabric of open tundra, snowcapped mountains, innumerable lakes and huge, virginal patches of pine and birch forests.

The larger cities in the region are somewhat small in comparison with other Russian cities, and each has a distinctive character. Petrozavodsk, the capital of the Karelian republic, is a clean, aesthetically pleasing city with lovely parks, a European atmosphere and a unique language and culture that stems from its Finnish past. Almost at the top of the world, hilly and heavily militarised Murmansk is the planet's largest city inside the Arctic Circle and home to the country's nuclear icebreakers; nearby, in the closed city of Severomorsk, is the port of the Northern Fleet. Farther east, Arkhangelsk straddles the Northern Dvina River, which is rife with fishers and rich with the Pomory culture. North of Moscow is Vologda, where people actually live in old wooden buildings, a far cry from the clunky cement apartment blocks found elsewhere: in spots, it is so quaint that it's hard to believe it holds a population of nearly 300,000.

No traveller should leave without touching down on at least one of the area's enchanting islands. Valaam, Kizhi and the Solovetsky Islands (given worldwide infamy by Solzhenitsyn's *Gulag Archipelago*) form a Trinitarian constellation of tranquillity, wondrous architecture and religious history.

But it's not all vodka and roses: amid the nature and the cities are indelible black spots

Highlights

- Stroll with an ice-cream cone through expansive, lovely parks in the friendly Karelian city of Petrozavodsk
- Spend the night in former prisoner barracks at the kremlin/Gulag on Solovetsky Island
- Peer down at a nuclear icebreaker in port from the hilly heights of Murmansk, the Arctic Circle's largest city
- Ski and snowboard down the longest, cheapest runs in Kirovsk
- Meet Father Frost himself in Veliky Ustiug

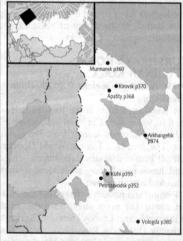

★★★★★★★★★★★★★★★★★★★★★

of ecological devastation, caused by decades of industrial carelessness. These places, which are primarily on the Kola Peninsula, are easily avoided but also easily accessible for those who want to see with their own eyes the extent of humankind's capacity for destruction.

HISTORY
Early Russian incursions into the region came from Novgorod (for more on Novgorod see History in the Western European Russia

346

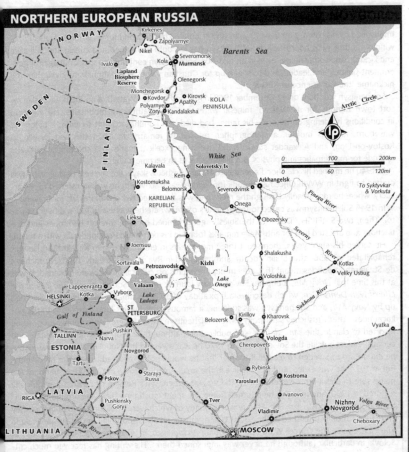

NORTHERN EUROPEAN RUSSIA

chapter). By the 12th century Novgorod was a European political and commercial centre that began expanding aggressively up Karelia's rivers and lakes to the White Sea.

Soon, the Swedes, who held sway in most of present-day northwestern Russia, began to feel the effects of the expansion. The friction, at first economic, became ostensibly religious as Swedish crusaders tried to push back the Orthodox 'heathens'. Novgorod's Prince Alexander Nevsky is considered a Russian hero for thrashing both the Swedish and Teutonic crusaders in the 1240s, putting an end to Western Christian intentions in Russia.

The Norwegians were more easily persuaded to give up claims to the Kola Peninsula. For several centuries, Russians, Finns, Norwegians and Swedes exploited fish, fur and the indigenous Sami reindeer-herders on the peninsula.

During the Time of Troubles (1606–13), a period of domestic anarchy and foreign invasions, Sweden again took over a swathe of territory from the Baltic Sea to the White Sea. Determined to defeat the Swedes and reach the Baltic Sea, Peter the Great made an alliance with Poland and Denmark and forced his way to the Gulf of Finland, pausing only to lay the foundations of St Petersburg. With his new navy, he won the Great Northern War (1700–21), winning everything back from Sweden, plus Vyborg and the Baltic coastline down to Riga. The Swedes were pushed back even farther, and in 1809, they forfeited Finland.

The north rose to prominence again as a WWI supply route. An Arctic port was built

The Russian Gadfly

Imprisoned by his country for over 10 years and celebrated by the world for his writings, Nobel Prize-winning author Alexander Isaevich Solzhenitsyn has led both a charmed and cursed life. Still alive and kicking, and complaining, even in his mid-80s, Solzhenitsyn continues to speak out against government policies and leaders and to speak up for Christian values and nationalism, giving him the nickname 'the Conscience of Russia'.

Solzhenitsyn was born on 11 December 1918 in Kislovodsk ('Sour Water'), a northern Caucasian resort town famous for its 'Narzan' mineral water and its breathtaking mountains. He grew up in conditions bordering on misery – his father had died in a hunting accident six months before he was born, and his mother, a stenographer, refused to remarry. In 1924 the two moved to Rostov-on-Don, and Alexander studied hard, receiving excellent marks and showing a particular aptitude for mathematics and physics. But his dream was to become a writer.

In 1940 he married his childhood sweetheart, Natalia Reshetovskaya. But the very next year, he was drafted to fight in WWII. Once his aptitude for science was discovered, he was transferred to the artillery, where he rose steadily through the ranks and was decorated twice with medals for bravery.

In 1945 Solzhenitsyn was called to the general's office, where he was asked to hand over his pistol. Then, two SMERSH ('Death to the Spies') agents jumped on him, tore off his stripes and distinctions and arrested him for anti-Stalin remarks found in his personal correspondence with a friend.

He served his eight years, then spent three more years in enforced exile in Kazakhstan. He was rehabilitated in 1956, after Stalin's death, and he settled in Ryazan. In the early 1960s Krushchev's de-Stalinisation policies meant that government restraints on cultural media were loosened. It was at this time that *Novy Mir*, a popular Soviet literary journal, received Solzhenitsyn's *One Day in the Life of Ivan Denisovich*, which describes a typical day of a Gulag inmate. The novel was snatched up by *Novy Mir*, and Solzhenitsyn was suddenly a famous man. But his luck changed with the political tides. After Krushchev's fall from power, Solzhenitsyn's works were denied publication, so he resorted to clandestine *samizdat*, or 'self-publication', although his works also reached eager and curious readers outside the Soviet Union. In 1970 he was awarded the Nobel Prize for Literature but he did not go to Sweden to receive it for fear that he would not be allowed to re-enter his country. But in 1974, he was exiled, and went to live in the small American town of Cavendish, Vermont (he made sure to pick up his Nobel Prize on the way). Solzhenitsyn's Russian citizenship was officially restored in 1990, and in 1994, he returned home. He spent much time travelling around the country and speaking to Russians. His literary works, many of which were published abroad before they were ever officially published in the Soviet Union, mostly revolve around life in Gulags and include *The First Circle*, *The Cancer Ward* and *The Gulag Archipelago*, in which he describes conditions at Solovki in particular (although he never was imprisoned there). His writing has received much criticism, due to alleged factual errors about Gulag history and basic readability problems (one Moscow critic said 'Everyone knows his name, but no one reads his books').

Still, you have to hand it to Solzhenitsyn. Even now, he makes his opinions heard – after applauding and then assailing Putin, he was paid a visit by the president himself for a chat and a little vodka, which settled him down a bit. Like the esteemed, curmudgeonly grandfather who has seen much in his long life and who loves his family dearly, the Russian people respectfully listen to Solzhenitsyn and to his impossible notions about the way things ought to be.

★★

at Murmansk and a rail line laid down to Petrozavodsk and St Petersburg. After the October Revolution, the Allies occupied Murmansk and Arkhangelsk for two years, advancing south almost to Petrozavodsk.

Stalin invaded Finland and the Baltic states in 1939–40, confident from his secret pact with Hitler that they were his. Finland, hav-

ing achieved independence after the revolution, fought the Red Army to a standstill but had to give up parts of Karelia and the area around Vyborg. Hoping to retrieve this territory, Finland allied itself with Germany during WWII, and Hitler launched attacks along the entire Soviet–Finnish border. Murmansk again became a supply port, a lifeline from the Allies to Russia's defenders, and was later bombed to rubble for its importance.

CLIMATE

The entire region has a continental climate. In the far north, summers are cool and short, and winters snowy but dry. Petrozavodsk is about 5°C cooler than St Petersburg in any season, while Murmansk and Arkhangelsk can be decidedly winterlike as early as the first week in September. Though Kola Peninsula winters are bitter, the Gulf Stream makes the weather in Murmansk changeable but, on average, less extreme than St Petersburg. Temperatures in Murmansk range from -8°C to 13°C in January, and 8°C to 14°C in July.

PEOPLE

Apart from the majority Russians and representatives of other former Soviet republics, about half the country's 140,000 Karelians, who are cousins of the Finns, are concentrated in the Karelian Republic along the Finnish border. Only about 2000 of the once numerous Sami (less politically correctly known as Lapp) reindeer-herders remain in the far north; most of the other Sami are in northern Scandinavia.

GETTING THERE & AWAY

Most international connections to Northern European Russia are through St Petersburg. There's air service almost daily to Murmansk, Arkhangelsk and Vologda from St Petersburg and Moscow. The area is also well served by trains. There are overland routes to Murmansk from Norway and to Petrozavodsk from Finland (see the Getting There & Away sections for those cities).

GETTING AROUND

If you're not driving, overnight trains are the way to go. In summer it's a beautiful journey across Karelia and the Kola Peninsula – the track is never far from a river bank or lake shore, endless forest and tundra stretch as far as the eye can see, and (industrial centres aside) the air is crystal-clear.

However, intercity flights are surprisingly affordable, and within regions, long-distance buses provide convenient and inexpensive transport.

Buses are frequently available between cities and are the cheapest option.

Driving a car can also be convenient. For most stretches, the St Petersburg–Murmansk highway is a fine road, though car-jacking is not unheard of around Petrozavodsk and on the southern stretch of the Kola Peninsula. If you're in a hurry and not pinching kopecks, hiring someone to drive you to a nearby city is a common alternative. You can usually negotiate a more than fair price, and the driver is bound to have some interesting stories to tell.

Although many highways are in decent condition, you may sometimes find you're in for a bumpy ride.

Karelia Карелия

The republic of Karelia stretches from St Petersburg to the Arctic Circle – half is forest, and much of the rest is water. Its more than 60,000 lakes include Ladoga and Onega, the two largest in Europe.

The original Karelians are related to Finns, and western Karelia has also been part of Sweden and Finland at various times. Finnish, the closest thing outside Russian that the Karelians have to a national language, is commonly used along with Russian (though Karelian, a Finno-Ugric language, is spoken by some); bilingual signs are common.

Many residents of Karelia are the offspring of prisoners and deportees sent by Stalin between 1931 and 1933 to dig the White Sea Canal that links rivers and lakes into a domestic water route to the Arctic.

PETROZAVODSK
ПЕТРОЗАВОДСК
☎ 8142 • pop 280,000

Despite the pleasant, laid-back feel of its present-day, tree-lined avenues and extensive parklands, Petrozavodsk, 420km northeast of St Petersburg, has a short, grim history. It was created in 1703 as an iron foundry and armaments plant for Peter the Great (its name means 'Peter's factory'), and the town was subsequently used by both the tsars and the Bolsheviks as a place of exile for St Petersburg's troublemakers.

The city has the semblance of a small St Petersburg, and is truly worthy of a visit. Many come to Petrozavodsk in order to visit the famous collection of old wooden buildings and churches on Kizhi, an island 66km northeast of the city, in Lake Onega (it's the most famous of the lake's 1368 islands). It's also a starting point for adventure seekers wishing to experience the Karelian wilderness.

Orientation

The city straddles the Lososinka River where it enters Lake Onega (Onyezhskoye Ozero). Its axis, prospekt Marksa, runs all the way to the ferry terminal, and the main drag, prospekt Lenina, stretches from the train station down to the river.

City maps are on sale at **Ex-Libris** *(pr Lenina 13; open 10am-7pm Mon-Fri, 10am-5pm Sat, noon-5pm Sun)*, which also has music, good books on local history, postcards and second-hand books. Intourist, in the Hotel Severnaya, can give you a simplified map in English.

Information

You'll have no trouble finding an ATM or currency exchange in this city. There are two branches of **Sberbank** *(ul Kuybysheva 17 • cnr uls Andropova & Sverdlova)* and Hotel Severnaya has an interesting ATM that looks like a 1970s UNIVAC computer monstrosity but works well.

The 24-hour **telephone and telegraph office** and the **post office** *(cnr uls Dzerzhinskovo & Sverdlova)* are conveniently close to the Hotel Severnaya.

Internet Tsentr *(☎/fax 71 18 54; ul Anokhina 20)* is a nice facility charging R30 between 9am and midnight and R19 from midnight to 9am. It's open 24 hours. **Internet Salon** *(☎ 76 30 88; ul Antikaynena 22)* also offers provider services for R30 per hour. The Hotel Severnaya's **business centre** has only one computer (Internet access is R24 per hour) and a fax/phone (usually free), but the warm and helpful staff make up for the lack of equipment.

Intourist *(☎ 78 13 78, 78 15 49, fax 78 47 57; e intourist@intourist.onego.ru)*, at the Hotel Severnaya, has very friendly staff and they can help with organising any kind of individual or group tour of the area or to Finland.

Lukomorye *(☎ 55 24 29; pr Nevskovo 43)* specialises in group tours to Valaam, Kizhi and the Solovetsky Islands but also offers trips to other destinations. Call in advance to find out about joining a scheduled group if you don't have a dozen or so people to hand over.

Passport/Visa Service *(☎ 71 53 82, 55 03 11; pr Nevskovo 17; open 9am-1pm & 2pm-5pm Mon-Fri)* can help you register your visa if need be.

Things to See & Do

The **Fine Arts Museum** *(pr Marksa 8)* and the classical crescent-shaped structures around ploshchad Lenina are pretty to look at in addition to being the oldest buildings in town (the museum was closed for renovation during research).

In one of the crescent-shaped buildings is the fine **Museum of Local Studies** *(☎ 78 27 02; pl Lenina 1; admission R50; open 10am-5.30pm Tues-Sun)*, which features nicely laid-out displays on the founding of the city and its environs, as well as everything you need to know about the epic poem *The Kalevala*.

Foreign geologists rave about the free museum in the **Geological Institute** *(☎ 78 43 16; ul Pushkinskaya 11)* at the Russian Academy of Sciences. It houses rocks and minerals up to three billion years old, including some indigenous to Karelia. You can't just waltz in off the street, though: when you enter the building, explain that you'd like to see the museum, and they'll get someone to accompany you up to the 5th floor.

Monthly art shows and, at times, Sunday afternoon classical or jazz concerts, are hosted at the **Exhibition Hall** *(vystavochny zal; ☎ 78 16 50; pr Lenina 26; open noon-7pm Tues-Sun)*.

The **Sports Museum** *(dom fiz-kul-tu-ry; ☎ 78 53 69; ul Pushkinskaya 7)* is the place to check out the odd basketball, sambo or children's gymnastics tournament.

Next door is **Akvatika** *(☎ 76 50 05; open 7am-11pm daily)*, an excellent swimming facility charging R150 per 1½-hour session. The pool is large and clean, and even features a waterslide! The facility also offers a solarium, sauna and massage parlour.

It's lovely to stroll along the lake shore, which is dotted with assorted pieces of civic art. One of the most eye-catching is *The Fishermen*. Duluth, Minnesota – Petrozavodsk's US sister city – commissioned Rafael Consuegra for the creation, which seems to be *The Old Man and the Sea* meets Edvard Munch's *The Scream*.

There's a sweet summertime **children's amusement park** behind the ferry terminal. It's got a mini-Ferris wheel and various swing and pony rides. You'll find closer to the lake shore a small roller coaster, a popular tilt-a-whirl and a 25m-high Ferris wheel for grown-ups that is slow and affords no view whatsoever of the city.

The **Alexander Nevsky Cathedral**, built in 1831, was recently restored and is interesting to look at if you're in the area.

An **Afghanistan War Memorial** – one of Russia's few – lists locals who died in the conflict. It's hard to track down though – if you can find the building at Leningradskaya ulitsa 19 (behind which is an awesome **view** of the parks and lake), it's just south of that, on a hill above the river. The adjacent dirt road, Volnaya ulitsa, will lead you to two interesting side-by-side **cemeteries**, one Jewish and one Russian Orthodox.

Places to Stay

Hotel Severnaya (☎ 76 20 80, 78 07 03, fax 76 22 55; w http://severnaja.onego.ru/new/eng; pr Lenina 21; singles with shared bath R200-220, doubles R260-340, singles with private bath R500-720, doubles R600-720, luxes R1500-3200) is without question your best bet: it's clean, smack in the centre and has very affordable rooms. Just beware of paper cuts: it has the roughest loo paper in Russia (A4 writing paper cut into four!). Still, everything works and the staff are great. As it's probably the city's most popular hotel, reservations are a good idea. At the time of research, the hotel couldn't register visas; if this is still the case, and if you're staying longer than three days, take your visa to Passport/Visa Service (see Information earlier).

Karelia Hotel (☎/fax 55 23 06; nab Gyullinga 2; singles R500-700, doubles R1200-1400, polu-lyux R850, lyux R1700), a five-minute walk from the ferry terminal, is a depressing monstrosity with staff to match, but the rooms are clean. Try for a view of the lake.

Hotel Fregat (☎ 76 41 62, 76 41 63; singles/doubles US$45/55, lyux $75) is on the lake side of the ferry-terminal building. If you're going to Kizhi, you couldn't be more conveniently located, but its renovated rooms are on the rip-off end of the scale (and they charge for reservations). Breakfast is included in the cost of the room (woo hoo). The entrance is next to the Fregat restaurant; ring the bell on the left.

Places to Eat

Many bars (see Entertainment later) have decent and well-priced menus. Also, all of the hotels listed earlier have restaurants that are slightly upscale, but if you'd like to venture out, try one of the following.

There is a **market** (ul Antikaynena), which has a good selection of fresh produce and meat (behind is a clothing and gadget market). **Lotus** (ul Anokhina 37; open 9am-midnight daily) is the best-stocked supermarket in town and accepts credit cards. There are two **24-hour shops** opposite the train station, and several more lining ulitsa Lenina.

The **stolovaya** (canteen; pr Lenina 9; mains R9-18; open 10am-7pm Mon-Sat) is always there for a very cheap fill-up. It ain't bad, but bring your own napkins – they evidently use the same A4 paper as the Severnaya!

Gostiny Dvor (☎ 78 13 69; pr Marksa 22; mains R10-45; open 10am-10pm daily) is another cheap and reliable stolovaya option.

Ben & Jerry's Ice Cream (Krasnaya ul 8; R10-100; open noon-6pm Mon, 10am-8pm Tues-Sun) serves up locally produced versions of Cherry Garcia, Chunky Monkey and other favourites. Sundaes, milkshakes and fudge bars – is this heaven? Three scoops for R24 – it is!

Kafe Morozhenoe (cnr pr Marksa & ul Kuybysheva; ice cream R13-30, mains R19-45; open 10am-11pm daily) has a watered-down version of Ben & Jerry's, as well as a few hot meals.

Kafe Tsentralnaya (ul Antikaynena 22; mains R15-30; open 11.15am-3am Mon-Fri), in the same building as the Internet Salon, is popular with the local workforce (always a good sign).

Petrovsky Restoran (ul Andropova 1; mains R70-200; open 11am-2am daily) claims to serve Karelian cuisine but the menu is for the most part standard Russian. However, the local speciality, myaso po medvednoye (a meat casserole with potatoes, cheese and mayo; R114) is worth a try. The dining area is kind of classy, with lots of wood and well-spaced tables.

Kavkaz (ul Andropova 13; mains R50-250; open 11am-10pm daily) is the city's popular Georgian restaurant. The interior is cavernous, with wooden tables and low benches. The service is hit-and-miss, and the menu is usually pretty scarce, but many of the dishes are quite tasty.

Restoran Tok (mains R54-270, lobster R568; open noon-1am daily), in the back of the Karelia Hotel, used to be the top place in town. It seems to have lost this status, but where else are you going to get your lobster fix?

NORTHERN EUROPEAN RUSSIA

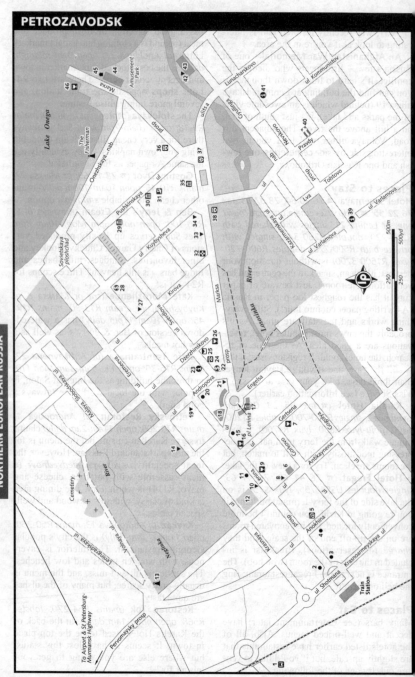

PETROZAVODSK

Lake Onega

Amusement Park

The Fisherman

Train Station

To Airport & St Petersburg-Murmansk Highway

PETROZAVODSK

PLACES TO STAY
18 Hotel Severnaya & Intourist
   Гостиница Северная
43 Karelia Hotel
   Гостиница Карелия
45 Hotel Fregat & Bar
   Гостиница Фрегат

PLACES TO EAT
8 Kafe Tsentralnaya & Internet Salon
   Кафе Центральная Интернет Салон
10 Sanches
   Санчес
14 Ben & Jerry's Ice Cream
   Бэн и Джеррис
19 Kavkaz
   Кавказ
21 Petrovsky Restaurant
   Ресторан Петровский
27 Stolovaya
   Столовая
33 Gostiny Dvor
   Гостинный Двор
34 Kafe Morozhenoe
   Кафе Мороженое
42 Restoran Tok
   Ресторан Ток

OTHER
1 Bus Station
   Автовокзал
2 24-hour Shop
   Кгуглосуточный Магазин

3 24-hour Shop
   Кгуглосуточный Магазин
4 Lotus Supermarket
   Универсам Лотос
5 Internet Tsentr
   Интернет Центр
6 Karelskoye Agenstvo
   Карелское Агенствс
7 Jungli
   Джунгли
9 Karelia
   Карелиа
11 Exhibition Hall
   Выставочный зал
12 Central Market
   Центральный рынок
13 Afghan War Memorial
   Памятник Афганской войны
15 Ex-Libiris Books
   Книги Экс-Либрис
16 Neubrandenburg Bar & Restaurant
   Бар-Ресторан Нойбранденбург
17 Museum of Local Studies
   Краеведческий музей
20 Podarki
   Подарки
22 Sberbank
   Сбербанк
23 Turist
   Турист
24 Telephone & Telegraph Office
   Телефон и телеграф

25 Post Office
   Почта
26 Spartak
28 Sberbank
   Сбербанк
29 Geological Museum
   Геологический музей
30 Sports Museum
   Дом Физкультуры
31 Akvatika (Swimming Pool)
32 Department Store & Rendez-vous
   ЦУМ
35 Fine Arts Museum
   Музей изобразительных искусств
36 Puppet Theatre
   Театр Марионеток
37 Russian Theatre
   Русский театр
38 National Theatre
   Национальный театр
39 Lukomorye
   Лукоморе
40 Alexander Nevsky Cathedral
   Собор Александра Невского
41 Passport/Visa Service
   Служба Пасспортов и Виз
44 Ferry Terminal
   Водный вокзал
46 Kovcheg Odisseev
   Одиссеев

Saloon Sanches (☎ 76 39 77; pr Lenina 26; mains R120-400; open 9am-1am daily) is the place to go if you're into paying big roubles for novelty but mediocre Tex Mex dishes, served by irritated waiters in flimsy blouses. Pluses are the good selection of breakfast omelettes and the menu's fumbling attempt at translating the language of the Wild West into Russian.

Entertainment

Kantele is a jolly Karelian folk ensemble that performs at different venues. You can buy tickets through Intourist and, if you're staying at the Severnaya, you'll see flyers for the next show posted around the lobby. The National Theatre, where its performances are frequently held, was closed for renovation during research but may be open soon.

Russian Drama Theatre (pr Marksa) has light operas, plays and ballets most nights. Check out the wild interior decor: a mix of Ancient Greek, Roman and Soviet styles, with Russian folk maidens dancing on the ceiling around an enormous chandelier.

The **Puppet Theatre** (☎ 78 50 92; pr Marksa 19; ticket office open 1pm-6pm Thur & Fri, 10am-4pm Sat & Sun) has weekend shows at 11am and 1pm.

The **billiard hall** (open noon-3am Mon-Fri, noon-6am Sat & Sun) inside the Karelia Hotel can be a blast. It's less than R100 an hour for tables, and the space is roomy and pleasant.

Bar Fregat (☎ 56 14 98; open noon-3am daily), next to Hotel Fregat, gets mixed reviews for its downstairs restaurant (mains R53-107) but the upstairs bar isn't half-bad, and the live music is worth tuning in to. Erotic dancing is featured at 11pm on many nights.

Bar Neubrandenburg (pr Lenina 23; open 9am-1am Mon-Thur & Sun, 9am-3am Fri & Sat) is comfy enough and good for meeting locals; food is served as well.

Rendez-vous (*pr Marksa; open 10am-midnight Sun-Thur, 10am-2am Fri & Sat*), the best place for a nightcap, is connected to the department store. It has a few hot meals, all good, and the relaxed atmosphere, with large glass windows and indoor street lamps, is unique in the city. It's worth a visit.

Jungli (*ul Gertsena; open until 4am*) is a fun nightclub with 80s music.

Spartak, next to the post office, has a big-screen TV downstairs and a vaguely Western dance floor upstairs.

Karelia (*☎ 76 72 78; pr Lenina; R30 after midnight Mon-Fri, women/men R60/90 Sat & Sun*) is a palatial space that is used as a cinema during the day. On Friday and Saturday nights, there's something resembling a discotheque here. It's the kind of place where the girls dance around their purses, but there are no teeny-boppers, and the upstairs bar has reasonable prices.

Kovcheg Odiseev (*open summer noon-1am*) is a floating bar/restaurant/disco on the lake; it's great for White Night celebrations.

Shopping

Karelian embroidery and traditional-style clothing are sometimes available at nontourist prices in department stores and some kiosks. If you're under the weather, the local firewater Karelsky Balzam, made from 20 herbs, is said to have tremendous powers of healing. And at 45% alcohol it bloody well should!

Podarki (*cnr pr Lenina & ul Andropova*) has the biggest selection of handicrafts and souvenirs.

The **gift shop** inside the Museum of Local Studies has a unique selection of gifts made from Karelian birch (a government-protected tree). However, remember that any untreated or unsealed wood products will be a problem in customs.

Getting There & Away

Surprisingly, it is currently not possible to fly to Petrozavodsk. Contact **Karelskoye Agenstvo** (*☎ 76 59 01; ul Antikaynena 20; open 8am-8pm Mon-Sat, 8am-6pm weekends & holidays*) for any updates on this, or for tickets to and from other cities.

There are several daily trains to/from St Petersburg (*plats/kupe* R176/312, seven to 15 hours), Moscow (R325/569, 15 to 20 hours) and Murmansk (R354/618, 20 to 30 hours). It is also possible to take a train to Arkhangelsk,

but you'll have to transfer in Belomorsk or Volkhovstroi-1 (to the south); both routes take about the same time, but the Volkhovstroi station is cleaner and safer.

If you really want to save money, you can take one of the twice-daily buses to St Petersburg (R180, nine hours).

For destinations in northern Karelia, catch buses at the main bus station, behind the train station. Turistiliikenne, in Kuhmo, Finland operates a daily bus from Kuhmo to Kostomuksha on the western border of Karelia with connecting bus service to Belomorsk.

It's possible to cross the border into Finland at Vyartsilya (500km west from Petrozavodsk via Olonets) to Tohmajrvi and then drive on to Joensuu in Finland.

Getting Around

Trolleybuses Nos 1, 2 and 6 go from the train station to the Hotel Severnaya, though it's not a long walk. To order a taxi, call ☎ 77 51 51, 55 09 71 or 76 76 76. There are always official taxis at the train station and across the street from the Severnaya.

AROUND PETROZAVODSK

To the north and west of the city lies one of the most beautiful and accessible regions for hunting, fishing, hiking and camping in Russia. Finns have been revelling in the area for some time (it used to be theirs, after all), and Finnish tourists can be found all over Karelia.

Other than in small, closed military towns along the border with Finland, you are free to roam at will. Camping and campfires are permitted almost anywhere, except where posted: Не разбивать палатку (No putting up of tents) and/or Не разжигать костров (No campfires). If you're off the beaten track, it's usually legal to put up a tent and hit the hay. Check with locals if you're in doubt.

The Karelian people are keen boaters and the region's lakes and rivers make for great kayaking and rubber-rafting, although there aren't many rapids.

Intourist in Petrozavodsk runs excursions to Russia's first mineral spa, founded by Peter the Great, at **Martsialnye Vody** (55km from Petrozavodsk), and to the 10.7m waterfall and nature reserve at **Kivach** (north of Petrozavodsk). It's difficult to reach either without the help of a tourist agency, but check at the bus station. From Martsialnye Vody, you can hire a taxi to Kivach for about R150.

Kizhi
Кижи

An old pagan ritual site, Kizhi made a natural 'parish' for 12th-century Russian colonists, though none of the early churches remain. The entire island serves as a **museum** (Petrozavodsk ☎/fax 76 70 91, Kizhi ☎ 51 98 25; w http://kizhi.karelia.ru) and has been deemed a Unesco World Heritage Site.

The island's centrepiece is the 1714 fairy-tale **Transfiguration Cathedral** (Preobrazhensky sobor). With its chorus of 22 domes, gables and ingenious decorations to keep water off the walls, it is the gem of Russian wooden architecture. Next door is the nine-domed **Church of the Intercession** (Pokrovskaya tserkov) built in 1764.

The other buildings in the collection were brought from the region around Lake Onega. The 19th-century peasant houses, some more ornate than others, are nicely restored inside. The little **Church of the Resurrection of Lazarus**, from the 14th century, may be the oldest wooden building in Russia. The **Chapel of the Archangel Michael** has an exhibit on Christianity in Karelia, and music students from Petrozavodsk play its bells in summer. There are numerous other houses and windmills open to exploration.

Outside the museum grounds are other churches, and a hamlet with houses like the ones inside, only occupied. The silence, fresh air and views on a sunny day are reason enough to come here (but beware of poisonous snakes in the remoter parts).

Admission is steep for foreigners at around R310 (though the staff often pity students – ISIC cards aren't officially accepted, but they usually take them).

This is a day trip only; there is no accommodation. It's also smart to bring food, although there's a **restaurant** near the landing and, opposite the pier, a small kiosk cluster including an overpriced 'art shop' and **café**, but these open and close at will and sometimes only have yesterday's hot dogs left.

Getting There & Away From June to August, when navigation is open, going on your own is easy – hydrofoils make the trip twice a day from the Petrozavodsk ferry terminal. The cost is R120 each way.

Summertime trips can also be booked through St Petersburg agencies, although similar trips at substantially cheaper rates can

KIZHI

To Hamlet, Village & Other Buildings
Art Shop & Souvenirs
Cafe Kiosk
Kiosks
House
Landing
Kizhi Restaurant
Kiosks
Gate and Cash Desk
Cathedral of the Transfiguration
Bell Tower
Church of the Intercession
Church of the Resurrection of Lazarus
Barn
Lake Onega
House
Windmill
Barn
Chapel of the Archangel Michael
Bathhouse
House
Barn
Bathhouse
House
House
Smithy

0   250   500m
0   250   500yd

be booked through the river terminal in St Petersburg (see Getting There & Away in the St Petersburg chapter).

If you can only go outside of navigation season, you will need to join or form a group and go by charter flight (plane or helicopter) via a tourist agency, such as Lukomorye (see the Petrozavodsk section earlier). Make sure to arrange this well in advance, unless you have the money to book a charter flight for yourself.

Valaam
Валаам

The Valaam Archipelago, which consists of Valaam Island and about 50 smaller islands, sits in northwestern Lake Ladoga. The main attractions here are the 14th-century **Valaam**

NORTHERN EUROPEAN RUSSIA

Transfiguration Monastery (Spaso-Preobrazhensky Valaamsky monastyr), its cathedral and buildings, and the pleasant town that surrounds it.

There is some dispute about the identity of the first settlers – some sources say that they were 10th-century monks – but most agree that the monastery was first settled in the late 14th century as a fortress against Swedish invaders, who managed to destroy it completely in 1611. Rebuilt with money from Peter the Great, the monastery doubled as a prison.

Many of the monks and much of the monastery's treasure were moved to Finland, which controlled the territory between 1918 and 1940. After 1940, when the territory fell back into Soviet hands, the Soviet authorities closed the monastery, took whatever was left and built what they referred to as an 'urban-type settlement' there.

Today the buildings are protected architectural landmarks, but neglect has taken its toll. Many of the buildings are decrepit and in need of repair. There are about 500 residents on the main island, including army service personnel, restoration workers, guides and clergy, most of whom get around in horse-drawn carriages or motorboats.

Getting There & Away Although many people arrange a visit to Valaam via Petrozavodsk, it's also popular among travellers coming from St Petersburg. If it's not mid-May to August, don't count on being able to take a boat to the island. Flights outside of this time may be arranged, but facilities on the island are likely to be closed.

To/From Petrozavodsk From southern Karelia, the gateway to Valaam is the sleepy town of Sortavala, about 300km west of Petrozavodsk. A local bus leaves Petrozavodsk's main station early in the morning and arrives in Sortavala in the afternoon. The cost is under R150.

Trains bound for Kostomuksha leave Petrozavodsk in the evening and arrive in Sortavala early in the morning. Once you get to Sortavala, it's an easy 15-minute walk from the train station to the boat pier. Head north along the tracks – the direction from which the train comes into the station – until you get to the bridge, then turn right, then right again past the (probably nude) Finnish sunbathers to get to the pier.

Three boats are usually docked there: a hydrofoil, which takes 40 minutes; a large boat, which takes a bit more than an hour; and a smaller boat, which takes three hours. The hydrofoil costs about R100 per person.

From the small pier near the main monastery, where you arrive from Sortavala, it's about a 5km walk through forests and meadows to the main harbour where the boats go to and from St Petersburg. It is a blissful walk, but you can always try hitching a ride from the friendly locals along the main road.

To/From St Petersburg Boats of all shapes and sizes leave nearly every day in summer for Valaam on one- to four-day excursions, some of which include Kizhi. A reliable St Petersburg–based agent that specialises in boat tours to Valaam is **Solnechny Parus** (☎/fax 812-327 35 25; W www.solpar.ru; ul Vosstania 55).

If you speak Russian, you can also deal directly with the monastery's centre in St Petersburg (☎ 812-271 22 64; W www .valaam. karelia.ru; nab Sinopskaya 34/36). It organises a full range of year-round excursions (by boat or helicopter) and can set you up with a place to sleep inside the monastery. It also has combined Valaam/Kizhi tours.

KEM
КЕМЬ
☎ 81458 • pop 18,000

The only reason to come to Kem is to use it as a jumping-off point for the Solovetsky Islands in the summer – it is simpler, faster and cheaper than going through Arkhangelsk.

Founded in the 16th century, the history of Kem is as bleak as that of many other towns in the region: prisons and, later, Gulags operated in the area for centuries; during the 1920s and 1930s, prisoners on their one-way trips to the Solovetsky Islands would be herded through this town; the Nazis set up a concentration camp outside the city limits during WWII; and, during the Soviet era, police would arrest undercover monks trying to sneak their way to the monastery on Solovetsky Island.

Today, the town is crumbling, but there are some lovely wooden houses on its outskirts, the villages on the way to the port are picturesque, and the White Nights are unforgettably beautiful.

Don't be caught in Kem without enough roubles for your stay. If you really need to exchange money, discreetly ask at a kiosk, and be alert. Getting cash from a credit card is far from likely. Although there's nothing by the way of useful banks or fancy supermarkets, Kem's **post office** *(cnr uls Proletarskaya & Energetikov; open 9am-6pm Mon-Fri, 9am-2pm Sat)* has Internet access – whaddaya know.

If you're in Kem for a few hours, check out the wooden houses on the southeastern side, near the lovely wooden **Assumption Cathedral** (Uspensky sobor) dating from 1711. The religious staff here are extremely friendly (Sasha's probably the handsomest priest around) and willing to give free tours (but be nice and leave a generous donation). The main priest's wife speaks English, so she could give a tour if advance notice is given. Across from the cathedral is a sorry **Ethnographical Museum** *(open 9am-5pm Wed-Sun; admission R50)*. Just north of the eastern end of the town's main drag, prospekt Proletarskaya, is the crumbling **Annunciation Cathedral** (Blagovyeshchensky sobor), open for services, but only just – its interior and exterior are scaffolded, and you need to walk down a plank to get to the entrance. Inside are some icons of an interesting medium-glazed ceramic.

Places to Stay & Eat

Turbaza Kem *(☎ 2 03 85, fax 2 82 00; ul Energetikov 22)* is a pleasant stone and wood building. Although it seems OK, don't be surprised if they send you across the street to Kem hotel, saying, 'It's a dump here, we don't even have hot water'.

Kem *(☎ 2 08 33, 2 00 26; ul Energetikov 17; singles/doubles R400/800)* does indeed have hot water and decent rooms. Allegedly, you'll receive a 25% discount if you reserve a room in advance.

Prichal *(☎ 3 53 60, fax 2 11 07; e prichal@ onego.ru; ul Naberezhnaya 1; rooms R360-500)* is a new accommodation complex right by the port *(prichal* is 'mooring' in Russian), which means its surroundings leave much to be desired. Still, it's really a great deal: the clean, modern rooms are in lovely, freshly built wooden cottages, and a great sauna (R100 per hour per person) is on the premises, as is a very good restaurant/bar/disco. Staff are very friendly.

Getting There & Around

Kem is a stop on the St Petersburg–Moscow–Murmansk railway.

Bus No 1 runs from Kem's train station to the port (and Hotel Prichal), a 35-minute ride away. From the bus stop, follow the road to your right, cross the train tracks and keep walking to the very end, some 500m. The buses are infrequent, however, so you may want to hire a driver to take you to the port (R100).

Kola Peninsula
Кольский Полуостров

The Kola Peninsula, dominated by the port of Murmansk, is a 100,000 sq km knob of tundra, forest and low mountains between the White Sea and the Barents Sea. It was originally populated only by Sami reindeer-herders and a few Russian trappers and fishers, the discovery of a northern sea route in the 16th century turned the tiny settlement of Kola into an Arctic trading post. In 1916, under pressure from the British to establish a supply port, Murmansk was founded (the first buildings were British-built wooden houses).

The Kola Inlet from the Barents Sea, which is ice-free year-round thanks to an eddy from the Gulf Stream, was the ideal site for the port of Murmansk, and for the Russian Northern Fleet's home base at nearby Severomorsk (see the boxed text 'Closed Cities'). Thanks to the latter, the Kola Peninsula today has the somewhat dubious distinction of being home to the world's greatest concentration of military and naval forces. The discovery of ore and mineral deposits sped up growth and generated an environmental mess in many areas; thousands of square kilometres of forests are dying of sulphur dioxide poisoning from nickel smelters around the towns of Nikel and Monchegorsk. Thanks to an influx of foreign aid, mainly from worried neighbours Norway and Sweden, new facilities are being constructed, resulting in a substantial reduction in emissions. But it will take a long, long time before Mother Nature is back up on her feet again around here.

In addition to its geological interest, the area also offers outdoor activities. The Khibiny Mountains have some fine hiking

Closed Cities

Severomorsk, Severodvinsk and Borisoglebsk – all on the Kola Peninsula – are closed cities, which means no foreigners are allowed to visit. In order to enter a closed city legally, you need special permission, which usually involves an invitation from a resident. It is true that many travellers end up in these cities without any problems, but if you're caught, you're in for a rash of trouble that could include a huge fine or even jail time. Determined folks can do online research to obtain information on visiting and to make connections with residents.

★★★★★★★★★★★★★★★★★★★★★

and mountaineering opportunities (new granite up to 700m high), cross-country skiing is possible anywhere, and skiers and snowboarders will love the long, amazingly affordable downhill runs at Kirovsk. North and west of the ecologically devastated city of Monchegorsk lies the relatively pristine Lapland Biosphere Reserve, a 2784 sq km natural wonderland.

Don't forget to bring sunscreen and sunglasses – an Arctic sunburn can really sneak up on you.

MONEY

For any destination on the peninsula other than Murmansk, it's best to have plenty of roubles with you. Although some banks may be able to give you cash from a credit card or exchange foreign currency, it can be problematic and isn't worth the headache.

GETTING THERE & AWAY

While some curious folks may wander northwards from St Petersburg, most visitors to the Kola Peninsula are making short excursions from the northern regions of Norway (whose time zone is two hours behind Northern European Russia). Flying, if you can afford it, from Norway is the most hassle-free route, but crossing the border by land and seeing the dramatic difference between the two countries is far more interesting.

Note that it is currently not allowed to cross the border on foot. It may be possible to hitch over with some Norwegians or others who can cross the border by car, but the guards can be unpredictable as to whether or not they'll allow it. Your best bet is to make

arrangements with a Norwegian firm (see Organised Tours later in this section) or buy a bus ticket from Murmansk all the way to Kirkenes, the Norwegian border town. (Don't try to buy a bus ticket to Nikel and then find your own way across the border from there – the small savings isn't worth the hassle at customs.) A new Russian border station is under way and rules may change once construction is completed.

In Kirkenes, Pasvikturist or Grenseland/ Sovjetreiser (see Organised Tours later) can help you get a Russian visa. Also in town is a **Russian consulate** (☎ 47-78 99 37 37, fax 78 99 37 42; Rådhusplassen 2; open 9am-noon Mon-Fri). Fees are determined by your nationality and how quickly you want the visa to be processed; all applications require a passport photo.

Air

The Norwegian airline **Arctic Air** (☎ 47-78 94 48 40, fax 78 98 77 68; e vardo@arctic.no) has services between Kirkenes and Murmansk on Monday, Wednesday and Friday (Nkr 717-1627).

Arkhangelsk Airlines (☎ 8182-65 62 16 or 21 88 43, fax 8182-21 88 55; w www.avl .aero) sometimes has twice-weekly flights between Murmansk and Tromsø in Norway. Check the website. Your ticket agent can advise you how to get to the airport (there are buses), which is in Høbuktmoen, about 15 minutes from town.

Bus

Bus rides from Kirkenes to Murmansk last anywhere from five to nine hours, depending on the situation at the border (the difference between Norway and Russia is so visible from the border, like Tijuana). The most convenient bus company to use is Sputnik, which sells its tickets through Grenseland/Sovjetreiser (Nkr 350; see Organised Tours). Its minivans leave Kirkenes Monday to Friday at 2pm (Sunday at 4pm) from the Rica Arctic Hotel; minivans from Murmansk leave from Hotel Polyarnye Zory at 8am Monday to Friday (noon on Sunday).

Organised Tours

Many visitors who have travelled as far as Kirkenes want to visit Russia – or at least sally up to the border – and several local agencies are happy to accommodate them, whether that means just arranging a visa or customising a tour for you.

Pasvikturist (☎ 47-78 99 50 80, fax 78 99 50 57; w www.pasvikturist.no) is an excellent and thoroughly experienced company to work with and has Norwegian and Russian staff. Tours vary but include day trips to Nikel and Zapolyarnye, a historical tour to a WWII battlefield, weekend trips to Murmansk and voyages to the Solovetsky Islands on a replica 18th-century boat.

Grenseland/Sovjetreiser (☎ 47-78 99 25 01, fax 78 99 25 25; w www.grenseland.no) offers all sorts of tours, including trips to Arkhangelsk and Malye Karely, ski trips to Kirovsk and weekends in Murmansk.

MURMANSK
МУРМАНСК
☎ 8152 • pop 380,000

Situated midway between Moscow and the North Pole, Murmansk is the largest city in the world north of the Arctic Circle. It's also different from many other Russian cities in that it's surrounded by hills (Russians call them *sopki*), and you may find yourself walking up a flight of stairs to get from one block to the next. And like many other Russian cities, the administration is beginning to put its face on – half of the city centre facades are now brightly painted (with a paint that won't wash off after the first winter). Nightlife and modern culture still need development but the large number of youth should eventually help with that.

The nearby port of Severomorsk (see the boxed text 'Closed Cities') is home to the Northern Fleet – including nuclear submarines and much of Russia's nuclear arsenal – and the city itself is the home port of Russia's nuclear icebreakers. Perhaps they're hoping the glow will light up the long polar nights!

The indigenous Sami people are generally reclusive, except during the Festival of the North (see Special Events later), when they come to compete in traditional games.

Orientation & Information

The city occupies three levels: the port, the centre and the surrounding heights, crowned with dozens of bland housing blocks. Dominating the centre is ploshchad Sovietskoy Konstitutsii, also known as Five Corners. To the north of the centre lies Lake Semyonovskoe and a truly immense concrete soldier

named 'Alyosha', from which there are spectacular views of the city.

Hotels Polyarnye Zory and Artika are the most convenient places to get roubles, whether it be from an ATM or exchange booth.

The **post and telephone office** is just behind Hotel Arktika. Calls on satellite phones cost about the same price as the state phones and are available to the public on the 4th floor of the Hotel Arktika. NMT-450 standard cellular phones work here, as well as on the rest of the Kola Peninsula. Internet access is available at the Hotel Polyarnye Zory's business centre. Arktika also has a business centre with Internet access but when we visited it was very unprofessional. There is a DHL office in the Arktika.

Limited tourist information is available at **Intourist** (☎ 45 43 86; open 10am-5.30pm Mon-Thur, 10am-5pm Fri), in Hotel Polyarnye Zory (see Places to Stay), but for the best results you'll need to speak Russian. There is a **Kola-Tavs office** (☎ 23 55 10, fax 23 55 13; e kolatavs@murmansk.rosmail .com; pr Lenina 19) and a branch in the lobby of the Hotel Polyarnye Zory as well (open 9am-1pm & 2pm-6pm Mon-Thur, 9am-1pm & 2pm-5pm Fri).

St Nicholas Church

Named for the patron saint of sailors, St Nicholas Church (Svyato-Nikolskaya tserkov) is the Kola Peninsula's religious administrative centre and it has a colourful history. The site was first occupied by a wooden church, built in 1946. In 1984 the rather low-profile congregation decided they needed a new church but thanks to the Soviet government, which allowed no other gods above itself, the work had to progress clandestinely. Not surprisingly, however, it was difficult to hide a cathedral, and when the government learned of the effort in 1985, it sent in miners with orders to dynamite the structure. This raised a holy ruckus, and demonstrators descended upon the site, blocking the miners, while simultaneous protests were held outside the Moscow city executive committee. The government eventually capitulated to some extent, allowing what remained of the building to stand, but forbidding any further work on it. However, in 1987, after perestroika allowed the exiled Christian God back into the Soviet Union, construction resumed, and over the next five summers, the project was completed. The brick structure is

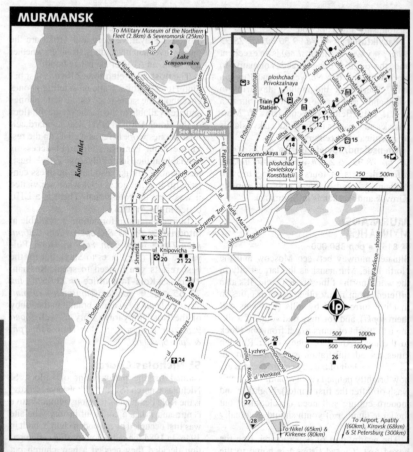

MURMANSK

far from breathtaking, but if you so desire, you can reach it on trolleybus No 4 from the train station; after four stops, walk past the pond and up the stairs, then along a dirt trail to the main road, and the church is to the right.

Museums

The **Fine Arts Museum** (*Khudozhestvenny muzey*; ☎ 45 03 85; *ul Kominterna 13; admission R10; open 11am-6pm Wed-Sun*) was established in Murmansk's oldest stone building in 1989. The collection isn't very inspiring, but ask to see the Boris Nepomnyashchy prints – they'll make your visit worthwhile. The 3rd floor houses temporary exhibitions, which change monthly.

In the **Museum of Regional Studies** (*Krayevyedchesky muzey*; ☎ 42 26 17; *pr*

Lenina 90; admission R10; open 11am-6pm Sat-Wed, ticket office until 5pm*), the 2nd floor features geology, natural history and oceanography. Exhibits on WWII, the Anglo–American occupation, Sami and Pomor history and anthropology occupy the 3rd floor. There's a good souvenir shop inside, and in addition to tours in English (R450), you can negotiate for a city tour with staff here.

On the 2nd floor of the city administration building, the **Regional Centre of Crafts** (*ul Sofi Perovskoy 3; open 10am-6pm Mon-Wed, 10am-5pm Sat & Sun*) holds a permanent exhibition of art by Kola Peninsula artists, including 'paintings' made with powder from crushed stones – a technique developed in Apatity. Admission is free.

MURMANSK

The hard-to-find **Military Museum of the Northern Fleet** (*Voyenno-marskoy muzey severnogo flota;* ☎ 22 14 45; *ul Tortseva 15; admission R50; open 9am-1pm & 2pm-4.30pm Thur-Mon*) is a must if you're a WWII or naval buff. It has six rooms on the Great Patriotic War and one on the modern fleet – torpedos, mines, model ships, and diving and chemical warfare paraphernalia. To get there, take trolleybus No 4 north to the last stop, cross the street, then take bus No 10 for four stops (look for the smokestack). Walk towards the smokestack, and turn left at the shop.

Other Attractions

In front of the stadium on prospekt Lenina is a **statue of Anatoly Bredov,** a hero of the Great Patriotic War. Finding himself surrounded by Nazi troops, Anatoly detonated a grenade, taking several of the bad guys with him. He's considered a hero all over the Kola Peninsula and thanks to this character, Murmansk is one of several Soviet cities that were nicknamed Gorod Geroy (hero city).

In summer you may see one of the four **atomic-powered icebreakers** at the dock. Photography here, except in the port itself, is now permitted.

Lake Semyonovskoe is named after the unfortunate would-be hermit Semyon Korzhnev, an old tsarist soldier who retired at the turn of the 20th century to a cabin on the shore and was the only resident for miles around. Imagine his disappointment when Murmansk appeared on his utopian horizon! You'll see people swimming in the lake in winter, and in summer there's a kiddie amusement park.

Okeanarium (☎ 31 58 84; **e** murocean@ online.ru; *pr Geroyev-Severomortsev 4; adult/ child R60/40*), nearby, is even better and hosts splashy seal shows. If you're at the lake and can't seem to track down the place, just follow the smell of old fish. And vigilantly standing guard over the port is the dizzyingly colossal of statue of **Alyosha,** an unknown WWII soldier. To get to the lake area, take trolleybus No 3 up prospekt Lenina.

Organised Tours

Intourist (☎ 45 43 86, 45 43 85; *ul Knipovicha 17; open 10am-5.30pm Mon-Thur, 10am-5pm Fri*), at Hotel Polyarnye Zory, offers several local tours, but you'll probably need a group before it will organise anything. How about a winter reindeer-sledding expedition, met by a folk ensemble and including an outdoor

NORTHERN EUROPEAN RUSSIA

The Kursk Tragedy

On 12 August 2000 in the Barents Sea, US Navy submarine *Memphis* detected two explosions in the vicinity of the Russian nuclear submarine *Kursk*, the pride and joy of the Northern Fleet. It was the largest attack submarine ever built and was described by its designers as 'unsinkable' (the same label that cursed the *Titanic*).

The media were alerted only after three days (not bad, considering the 18-day delay in Gorbachev's public announcement of the Chernobyl disaster), but once the news hit that the *Kursk* had sunk, chaos ensued. The array of conflicting reports – from how many were on board and how long they suffered to how it happened and what was being done about it – was dizzying.

The confusion was caused by a rash of misinformation, both deliberate and inadvertent. Thanks to haphazard reporting on the part of the impulsive and eager Russian press, as well as the Russian Navy's attempts to evade responsibility and guard military secrets, just what took place on that nuclear vessel is shrouded in an uncertainty that lingers to this day.

Some proposed that the sub hit a floating mine left over from WWII. At one point, Chechen rebel leaders announced that the detonations were the work of two kamikaze Dagestanis on board. More popular was the claim that the nearby Russian warship *Peter the Great* inadvertently destroyed the *Kursk* when it fired an experimental seek-and-destroy missile. Although the Russian Navy claims that its seek-and-destroy missiles do not have the ability to hit underwater targets, and though every indication corroborates this claim, there have been reports that two bodies recovered from the accident bore notes attributing the incident to such missiles.

One conspiracy theory that has drifted to the surface can't seem to be submerged: there is reasonable evidence that the *Kursk* collided with a US submarine. Russian military officials claimed to have found a fragment of a foreign vessel 330m from the scene of the catastrophe. Moreover, the USS *Memphis*, which first detected the explosions, took an abnormally long time to reach the Norwegian port of Bergen, which indicates that it may have been damaged. Both Russian and Norwegian military sources have stated that the *Memphis* underwent repairs in Bergen, and that the wives of 12 of its crewmembers were urgently and secretly flown to Norway.

Such a collision would not be unique. There have been more than a dozen collisions between Russian and US submarines, all of which have been officially denied by the USA. The most harrowing incident took place in 1986 off the US Atlantic coast. The Russian K-219 suffered serious damage: a fire broke out, and a nuclear meltdown was imminent. Sergei Preminin, a 20-year-old sailor from a small town near Kotlas, stayed on board to manually shut down the reactor, ensuring a certain and painful death, but saving the lives of countless Americans living along the eastern seaboard. He was made a Soviet hero, and a monument in his honour, still adorned with flowers, can be seen on the road from Veliky Ustiug to Kotlas. The story is brilliantly told by Peter Huchthausen in his book *Hostile Waters*, which later aired as a made-for-TV movie. In response to the popularity of *Hostile Waters*, the US Navy made the following official announcement:

'The United States Navy categorically denies that any US submarine collided with the Russian Yankee submarine (K-219) or that the Navy had anything to do with the cause of the casualty that resulted in the loss of the Russian Yankee submarine.'

In October 2001, after over a year of delays and technical difficulties, the 18,000-tonne *Kursk*, resting only 108m down, was recovered – a feat that cost the Russian government US$65 million. The official cause of the tragedy has now settled on the accidental detonation of a test torpedo before it left its hatch, which consequently set off another torpedo explosion.

★★★

barbecue accompanied by folk dancing? Alternatively, it will arrange five-day snow-machining tours or cruises on Kola Harbour.

MKTI-Tour (☎ 54 03 90; e *mktitour@ online.ru*) is the place to call for a day of snowmobiling through the surrounding *sopki*.

A day of riding costs between US$22 and US$106, depending on the level of difficulty; there is an additional charge of US$15 for hotel pick-up. For simple city tours, ask at the Museum of Regional Studies (see the Museums section earlier).

Special Events

The annual 10-day **Festival of the North**, held since 1934, takes place at the end of March or beginning of April, with each town in the area hosting its own events. Murmansk has reindeer and deer-plus-ski races (in which a reindeer pulls a contestant on skis), an international ski marathon and biathlon, ice hockey, 'polar-bear' swimming and a general carnival atmosphere. Hotels are booked out well in advance. Most events in Murmansk are held at the south end of town in Dolina Uyuta (Cosy Valley), a 25-minute ride from the train station on bus No 12.

Places to Stay

69th Parallel Hotel (☎ 56 56 45, 56 53 30; Lyzhny proezd 14; singles R400-600, doubles R640-900, polu-luxes R1600) is the cheapest option but it's not central. Take trolleybus No 1 or 6 from the centre for about 10 minutes. Rooms come with phones and TVs (some even have balconies and fridges). The attached nightclub (see Entertainment) is popular.

Moryak (☎ 45 55 27; ul Knipovicha 23; singles R170-750, doubles R620-1500), right next door to Hotel Polyarnye Zory, is more popular with Russians than with foreigners and is great for budget travellers; the rooms are simple but adequate.

Hotel Polyarnye Zory (☎ 28 95 00, 45 02 82, fax 28 95 04; e polarzor@dionis.mels.ru; ul Knipovicha 17; singles R930-3565, doubles R426-4061, luxes with sauna R4340-5146) has large, clean rooms with cable TV and friendly staff. There are many Westerners here – mostly businesspeople and adopting parents – and it has a lively bar and an excellent stolovaya, as well as an upscale **restaurant** (mains R110-320).

Meridian (☎ 28 86 00, 28 86 50; ul Vorovskovo 5/23; standard rooms with breakfast R300-600, remodelled rooms R850-2900) has ho-hum and good-value, nicely remodelled rooms. However, at the time of research, the money used for extra soap and shampoo in the bathroom might have been better spent on an extra month of customer-service training.

Obkomovsk Administratsii Hotel (☎ 45 92 78; ul Sofi Perovskoy 3; singles/doubles R550/800, polu-luxes R900) is a slightly more expensive option with only decent rooms.

Hotel Arktika (☎ 45 79 88; pr Lenina 82; standard singles R350-690, doubles R540-1900, business-class with breakfast R1490-1900, luxes R2990 or R3500) is the most dominant hotel in town; it has overpriced remodelled rooms and dingy standard rooms.

Ogni Murmanska Hotel (☎ 49 08 00, fax 49 10 93; Sankt Peterburg Shosse 8; rooms US$40-80) is far from town but has luxurious rooms (some are bi-level) with a private sauna and a great view.

Places to Eat

Reindeer meat is a popular export for the region but will probably be hard to find in stores and restaurants. Of course, there is lots of fish, especially cod. Try severyanka, which is the local chowder. For self-caterers there's a small **market** at the bottom of ulitsa Volodarskovo.

Dnyom i Nochyu (mains R30-60) is a good stolovaya attached to the Hotel Arktika.

The **pelmennaya** (pr Lenina; mains R45-120; open 11am-10pm daily), next to the shoddy pizzeria, is an excellent find – it's cheap, delicious and packed at lunchtime, where Murmanskians enjoy fresh, made-to-order (you will have to wait for them), piping-hot pelmeni (small dumplings usually filled with meat) and vareniki (curd or fruit dumplings).

Kafe Yunost (pr Lenina; desserts R5-27; open 9am-8pm) has an ice-cream parlour feel with pastries, ice cream, coffee and hot food available.

Medved (☎ 45 34 09; pr Lenina 97; mains R90-160, 3-course lunch R65; open 11am-5am) is relatively posh and enjoyed by local show-offs.

Tsarskaya Okhota (☎ 56 37 09; Kolsky pr 86; meals about R500/person; open noon-late) is considered by many locals to be one of the best places in town. Xena fans will enjoy the mesmerising mural of a naked huntress inside.

Inari (☎ 47 35 80; Teatralny bulvar 8; mains R100-300; open noon-midnight daily) boasts yummy seafood.

Entertainment

The **Puppet Theatre** (☎ 45 81 78; ul Sofi Perovskoy 21A; admission R20-25) holds puppet shows at 11.30am and 2pm on weekends from September to June.

Philharmonic Concert Hall (Kontsertny zal filharmonii; ul Sofi Perovskoy 3), a renovated 700-seat auditorium building, holds

NORTHERN EUROPEAN RUSSIA

classical concerts. Tickets and information are available there.

Nightlife in Murmansk still leaves much to be desired – there are indications however, that some of the clubs' seediness will soon sprout into something better. Both the Meridian and Arktika have dance clubs.

Nightclub 69 (☎ 56 55 88; Lyzhny proezd 14; open Wed-Sun 5pm-6am) has a sauna, restaurant and billiards area, in addition to a dance floor. Don't get your hopes up – the name is in reference to the latitudinal position of the city.

Getting There & Away

For information on crossing the Storskog (Norwegian) border by land, see Getting There & Away, at the beginning of the Kola Peninsula section.

Air There are daily flights to/from Moscow (R2634, two to three hours), St Petersburg (R2860, two hours) and Arkhangelsk (R2444, two hours). Contact **Kola-Tavs** (☎ 23 57 30, 56 05 08; pr Lenina 19; open 8am-8pm Mon-Sat, 8am-6pm Sun) for reservations and purchase; there is also a booth at Hotel Polyarnye Zory (see Places to Stay).

Train There are daily trains to/from Moscow (plats/kupe R767/1280, 36 hours), St Petersburg (R510/950, 28 hours), Petrozavodsk (R351/768, 20 hours) and indirect trains to Arkhangelsk (R345/606, 30 hours). On even dates, there are trains to/from Vologda (R447/782, 36 hours). Trains from Nikel go to Murmansk Monday to Saturday and back to Nikel Sunday to Friday (R60, eight hours). Trains to/from Minsk (R785/1240, 40 to 50 hours) leave Wednesday and Saturday. Train station lines are long and slow, so be prepared to wait, and make doubly sure you're in the right line. The website **w** www.rwzakaz.ru is helpful if you and your computer can read Russian; it posts relatively up-to-date prices and schedules for Murmansk trains, and you can book tickets if you're willing to pay a commission for the convenience.

Bus There is a daily bus service to/from other Kola Peninsula towns: Monchegorsk (R120, 3 hours), Nikel (R140, 3 hours), Kirovsk (R59, 4 hours) and Zapolyarnye (R51, 2½ hours). The bus-station lines are almost as bad as those at the train station next door.

Car & Motorcycle Open all the way, the Murmansk–St Petersburg highway is relatively smooth sailing. You can also drive to or from Kirkenes, Norway, via the Storskog border crossing – see Getting There & Away at the beginning of the Kola Peninsula section.

The only border crossing into Finland is between Lotta and the Finnish town of Raja Jooseppi. Although the road is open, it's used mainly by freight traffic and for independent drivers, and may well prove more difficult than the crossing at Storskog.

Getting Around

The city is well served by a relatively efficient system of trolleybuses, which connect the centre with most outlying areas.

Bus Nos 106 and 106 Э (express) leave the airport every 20 to 30 minutes and cost R16; the express takes half an hour. For hotels Arktika or Meridian, get off at the train station; for Moryak, use the Detsky Mir bus stop.

A taxi from the airport to the centre can cost as much as R500 – it's a long way. In town, rides are about R40 or R140 per hour. Call ☎ 23 77 70, 26 26 77 or 23 70 70 to have a driver pick you up.

NIKEL
НИКЕЛЬ
☎ 8152 • pop 21,000

Named for the rich mineral deposits found in the area, Nikel is far from being as shiny as the polished metal. The land, as in many other places on the peninsula, has been poisoned by emissions from metallurgical plants, and in some cases (although this is often denied) by nuclear detonations, to get at the ore. The result is quite depressing: if Greenpeace needs a poster child or some Hollywood director chooses to film a vision of post-nuclear apocalypse, Nikel is all prepped and ready for the cameras to roll.

In recent years emissions have been reduced drastically, thanks to aid from Norway and Sweden, but it's hard to imagine when the damage will ever reverse itself.

The small **local museum**, in the bright yellow building visible from the hotel, features a collection of minerals from the Kola Peninsula, as well as the historical links between Norway, Finland and northwestern Russia.

If for some reason you want to stay the night, there is the very simple **Nikel Hotel**

(☎ 2 04 66; Gvardeiskii pr 2; rooms with shared bath R322). Across the street is a small **stolovaya**.

From Murmansk you can reach Nikel on the snail train (R60, eight hours) Sunday to Friday. From Murmansk, there are daily buses to Nikel (R140, three hours). See the earlier Getting There & Away section for the Kola Peninsula for details of the Kirkenes–Murmansk bus, which can stop in Nikel.

ZAPOLYARNYE
ЗАПОЛЯРНЫЕ
☎ 81554 • pop 23,000

The nickel-mining town of Zapolyarnye is the proud home of the world's deepest hole, which extends more than 12km beneath the surface and is only about 14cm in diameter at its widest point.

The drilling project started as a seismological experiment, with the aim of testing how the earth conducts soundwaves at deep levels. But once drillers reached a certain point, the challenge of 'how low can we go' became more interesting. Eventually, at about 16km deep, geologists believe drillers will hit the earth's mantle – a substance that has never been seen or touched and whose qualities are still a mystery.

Unless you're part of a group of famous or wealthy geologists, it's very difficult to arrange to view the hole and its facility, but if your Russian is good and you'd like to know more about the project (which is on hold due to a lack of funding), you can arrange to speak to its master: **Dr Guberman** *(☎ 7 26 84 or 7 35 00, fax 7 24 31; ul Yubileinaya 17)*. If you talk to him, make sure to call the hole a '**skva**-zhe-na', not a '**ya**-ma' or '**dir**-ka' – even if it's obvious that your Russian is not native, Dr Guberman is very proud of his hole and may get offended.

Hotel Pechenga *(☎ 3 65 00; ul Mira 9; singles/doubles R1050/1500, luxes R2200)* is quite nice, with a billiards room, solarium and sauna. The high prices are due mainly to the fact that most of the takers are short-term Norwegian visitors (for whom these rates are a bargain). As well as the hotel **dining room**, there's also a basic Russian **stolovaya** in town.

The easiest way to reach here is on the bus between Kirkenes, Norway, and Murmansk. You could also negotiate for someone to drive you here from Murmansk or Nikel.

MONCHEGORSK
МОНЧЕГОРСК
☎ 81536 • pop 75,000

Monchegorsk is yet another dark spot in the midst of natural beauty. The ground here is literally black, sparsely dotted with toothpick-like skeletons of what were once trees. Ironically, the Sami name of the town translates as 'beautiful tundra' (the word 'tundra' is from the Sami language), and as you drive farther from town, the land eventually becomes beautiful again.

In the case of Monchegorsk, the culprit was the Severonikel Kombinat plant. In 1994 and 1995, emissions were cut roughly in half, due to lower production, but given the current state, it was clearly too late to make much of a difference.

The irony is, since the fall of the Soviet Union and the related decline in military orders, the main clients of the plant are now subcontractors for US and Japanese auto manufacturers, who use its products to manufacture catalytic converters that reduce emissions on Western cars. Another irony is that the vicinity's only visitor attraction – unless you're curious about the outer limits of possible ecological devastation – is the nearby Lapland Biosphere Reserve, which is the most accessible nature reserve in Arctic Russia.

Orientation & Information
Nearly everything in town is on the romantically named main drag, prospekt Metallurgov.

The **Sberbank** *(pr Metallurgov 7; open 10am-2pm & 3pm-7pm Mon-Fri, 10am-2pm & 3pm-4pm Sat)* is across from the Sever Hotel. Although it can change currency and give you money off a credit card, you'll find it best to have what you need when you get there.

The nicest Internet centre, **Svyaz-Servis** *(☎ 5 87 00; ul Lesnaya 10; open 10am-10pm)*, charges R40 per hour and is best reached by taxi, but there's also access at the conveniently located **library** *(pr Metallurgov 27; open Sat-Thur noon-9pm)* where the charge is R30 per hour.

Places to Stay & Eat
Sever Hotel *(☎ 7 26 55; pr Metallurgov 4; singles/doubles R570/1140)* is near the bus station and tolerable if you don't mind a cockroach or two.

NORTHERN EUROPEAN RUSSIA

Metallurgov (☎ 7 45 33, 7 20 53; pr Metallurgov 45A; rooms R600-2400) is loads nicer than the Sever, but call ahead – they only accept foreigners who have made reservations. They can probably set you up with hot food.

Otherwise, good luck with getting a hot meal. You can ask staff at the Sever Hotel to direct you to the nearby restaurant of the same name but it's likely to be closed. The **pelmennaya** across from the Sever Hotel is pretty awful. Luckily, there are some **stores** along prospekt Metallurgov that sell sweets and even some fruit.

Getting There & Around

Buses leave to/from Murmansk (R101, three hours, five daily), Kirovsk (R61, 2½ hours, three daily) and Kandalaksha (R82, 2¾ hours, Friday and Sunday only), as well as other, even stranger destinations. The **bus station** (ul Sopchinskaya 6a), housed in a little blue shack, is open from 6.30am to 1pm and 1.30pm to 9pm, although additional 45-minute 'technological' breaks are likely to pop up a few times a day.

LAPLAND BIOSPHERE RESERVE
ЛАПЛАНДСКИЙ ЗАПОВЕДНИК
☎ 81536

North and west of Monchegorsk, and spanning north and west towards Norway and Finland, the Unesco-protected Lapland Biosphere Reserve (Laplandsky zapovyednik; ☎ 5 00 80, fax 5 71 99; e lapland@monch.mels .ru) consists of 2784 sq km of almost pristine wilderness. About half of it is virgin tundra, and the rest consists of alpine grasslands, marshes, rivers, lakes and five small mountain ranges (the highest peak being 1114m). The reserve was founded in 1930 to protect the area's reindeer herds; today over 1000 reindeer live on the biosphere's territory, making it one of the largest concentrations in Europe. Along with 33 species of mammals (including brown bears, elks and wolves), 201 bird species and 15 species of fish, there are more than 900 species of higher plants, mosses and lichens.

The threat to the ecological balance of the flora and fauna of the park is multifaceted: while the Khibiny mountain range manages to stave off most of the damage that Monchegorsk's nickel plant threatens to inflict, the easternmost section of the park has been decimated. Inside the park itself, poachers and careless trespassers inflict damage too (each year fires caused by illegal campfires destroy hectares of forest). These miscreants, along with the usual culprits – local and regional government corruption, lack of funding – make keeping the park alive more difficult. While the Russian government provides minimal funding and the US-based Global Ecological Fund has provided support for an ecological education program, the reserve must mainly rely on itself for maintenance.

Inside, visitors can trek through the wilderness – the best times are March to April, June and August to September – or traverse it on skis, snowshoes or skidoos. The possibilities for adventure tourism are endless, ranging from hiking (the views of seemingly endless stretches of mountains are breathtaking), camping and relaxing nature walks, to winter igloo-building expeditions. There are several waterfalls on the territory, and even a German war plane resting where it fell from the skies during WWII.

Individuals or groups of less than 10 people can visit the reserve any time of the year with advance notice. There are perfectly comfortable **guest cottages** at the reserve's main base on the quiet banks of Chuna Lake, but visitors should expect to rough it in tents on longer expeditions. You can rest those weary bones in the base's heavenly banya (bathhouse) on Friday along with the friendly forest rangers who live and work there. Costs vary depending on the kind of experience you're looking for, but expect to pay US$20 to $40 per day.

What to Bring

It's important to bring layers of warm clothing – the outer layer should be waterproof. You'll also need good, comfortable trekking boots, as much of this landscape is soggy muskeg, and even in the summer it can get mighty wet. Visitors are responsible for their own food and equipment – trail-mix and high-protein snacks work best. Don't expect anything to be available at the reserve (one trekking group ran out of Snickers bars after two days and had to rely on the rangers' and guides' own meagre rations). Locals maintain that most of the surface water here is clean and drinkable – which is hard to believe when you consider the nuclear presence and utter devastation so near at hand – so it is a good idea to carry a means of purification. It's also wise to bring navigational equipment, though the guides are quite well equipped.

Getting There & Away

The easiest access is through Monchegorsk. Arrangements to visit the reserve must be made in advance, either directly (the most effective route) or through **Econord** (see Apatity). Alternatively, try the **American Association for the Support of Ecological Initiatives** (USA ☎ 1-860-346-2967, fax 347-8459; e alexk@aasei.spb.su, wkwasch@william kwaschassociates.com).

APATITY
АПАТИТЫ
☎ 81555 • pop 60,000

Founded in 1966, Apatity is home to the world's greatest source of apatite ore (hence the name) and is the Kola Peninsula's second-largest city. While the city itself isn't that attractive to nonscientific types, Apatity makes an excellent jumping-off point for hiking, climbing and skiing expeditions in the nearby Khibiny Mountains. You may even spot the yeti, the bigfoot-like forest loiterer (42cm-long footprints have been found) that is said to put in an occasional appearance and leave its mark.

Orientation & Information

Apatity has two main sections, the Akademgorodok ('Academic Town') and the city proper. The main shopping streets are ulitsas Fersmana and Lenina. The train station lies southwest of the centre, while the main bus stops lie on ploshchad Lenina (for Monchegorsk and Murmansk) and along ulitsa Fersmana (for Kirovsk). Maps of the region are available from Hotel Ametist.

You can change or withdraw money at **Sberbank** (cnr uls Moskovskaya & Kosmonavtov). ATMs are stationed at the store **Arktika** and at Hotel Ametist, but these don't take all cards. The **post and telephone office** (pl Lenina; open 9am-7pm Mon-Fri, 11am-4pm Sat & Sun) has an **Internet salon** (open noon-7pm Mon-Fri, noon-4pm Sat) in the back charging R25 per hour but it's really just a kid renting out his computer, which has a faulty power connection.

Econord (☎ 7 97 62; e econord@inep .ksc.ru; ul Fersmana 40A; open 10am-5pm Mon-Fri) is a good source of information and

can arrange trips to the Lapland Biosphere Reserve.

Yug-Kola (☎ 7 41 78; w www.kola-penin sula.com), in the Hotel Ametist, does snow-mobiling and fishing trips and can arrange for stays in Sami tepees.

Things to See & Do

There's not a lot for entertainment (it says something when the spiffiest joint in town is the Statoil petrol station).

The **Museum of the History of the Research & Exploration of the North** (☎ 7 92 55; open 2pm-5pm Mon-Fri; admission R15-50) was founded in the 1970s and features exhibits on Russian Arctic expeditions, both scientific and exploratory. There are also exhibits on the Solovetsky Monastery, unique drawings of Novaya Zemlya and 5000-year-old Sami rock carvings, tools and other instruments.

Rock fans may enjoy the user-friendly **Regional Geological Museum** (☎ 3 72 74; ul Fersmana 16; open 9am-6pm Mon-Fri), which has fine exhibitions of local rocks and minerals, and local crafts; the entrance is in back. The **Scientific Mineral Museum** (ul Fersmana 14; open 8.30am-5pm Mon-Fri) is nearby. You may also want to stroll through the **Open-Air Geological Museum** (ul Fersmana), farther west, which features a few paths lined with local rock samples.

At the **swimming pool** (ul Lenina 26; open 8am-10pm Tues-Sun), a 45-minute session costs R30, and the sauna costs R300. Staff may ask for a health certificate, but if you're clean and look healthy, you probably won't have any problems. Another building worth noting is the **library** on ulitsa Lenina which – yes – resembles the pages of an open book. The library also has a museum with changing exhibits.

Apatity is an artistic centre, and a locally invented method of 'painting', using coloured dust from crushed local minerals, is now catching on all over the Russian north. The **Salma Art Salon** (ul Dzerzhinskovo 1; admission R3) is a private cooperative outlet for over 200 Kola Peninsula artists. Prices are low, and the management can arrange the paperwork to expedite customs procedures. **Gallery M** (pl Lenina; admission free; open 2pm-6pm Mon-Sat) is on the 2nd floor of the Polyarnye building and features a changing exhibit of artworks by local artists. The

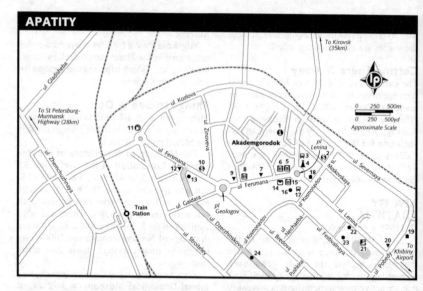

Polyarnye building also has a *bar (open noon-midnight Mon-Fri, noon-7pm Sat).*

Places to Stay & Eat

Hotel Ametist *(☎ 7 45 01; ul Lenina 3; singles/doubles R380/500)* has clean rooms, some of which have a mountain view. There is also a smoky *bufet*/bar on the 2nd floor.

Izovela *(☎ 6 26 66; ul Pobedy 29A; singles/doubles US$10/19, luxes $50)*, at the eastern edge of town, is sometimes known as the *dom otdykha* (rest home, or sanatorium). It formerly served as the rest and health clinic of a construction company and is now open to the public. The resort-like complex features a nice pool and sauna/*banya*, a winter garden, massages and two restaurants, not to mention a dental clinic. To get there from the centre, take bus No 8 from the train station or ploshchad Lenina.

Baza Otdikha Rus *(☎ 6 14 52; rooms R200-700)*, 13km from town, is a real treat – it's a large dacha-like structure that's best for groups, but they're more than happy to make arrangements for individuals. The sauna and meals cost extra, but negotiating a fair price is not a problem. Make arrangements through Izovela, and ask to see the nearby children's sanatorium – it's a lovely and interesting place, with loads of excellent facilities for the kids, who are recuperating from various illnesses.

For snack foods and fruit, try the **kiosk cluster**, which is near the Open-Air Geological Museum.

Restaurant Zapolyarye *(ul Lenina 31A; mains R40-50; open noon-midnight Mon-Thur, noon-1am Fri-Sun)* is a decent place to try and isn't far from Izovela.

Kulinaria *(ul Fersmana 20)* has tasty sweet and savoury pastries.

If you can live by bread alone (a real plus in these parts), look for the locally made, round-loaf bread, *Pomorsky khleb* or the ubiquitous *Rom Baba* (which is notably devoid of rum and normally makes its public debut when it's several days old).

Getting There & Around

Kola-Tavs *(ul Lenina 2A)* is the place to go for air, bus or train tickets.

Apatity's airport is served by Moscow (R2184, four hours, Monday to Wednesday and Friday), St Petersburg (R2527, three hours, Sunday only), Sochi (R4784, six hours, Monday and Wednesday to Saturday) and Cherepovets (R3016, two hours, Saturday only). In summer there are weekly flights from Arkhangelsk (R2028, one hour). There are no flights to or from Murmansk.

Most trains between Moscow, St Petersburg and Murmansk stop at Apatity; take any train headed south from Murmansk (*plats/kupe* R108/194, five to eight hours).

APATITY

PLACES TO STAY
18 Hotel Ametist; Yug-Kola
    Гостиница Аметистж
    Юг-Кола
19 Izovela
    Центр Здоровя
    Апатитстройя

PLACES TO EAT
7 Kulinaria
   Грил-Бар
9 Kiosk Cluster
12 Arktika; ATM
    Арктика
20 Restaurant Zapolyarye
    Ресторан Заполярье

OTHER
1 Econord; Museum of the
   History of Research &
   Exploration of the North
   Эконора Центр интернаци
   ональный Еконорд

2 Sberbank
   Сбербанк
3 Bus Stop for Kirovsk
   Остановка в Кировск
4 Lenin Statue
   Памятник Ленину
5 Scientific Mineralogical
   Museum
   минералогический музей
   Колского научного центра
6 Regional Geological
   Museum
   Геологический музей
8 Open-Air Geological
   Museum
   Открытым Небом
10 Sberbank
    Сбербанк
11 Statoil Petrol Station
    Заправочная станция
13 Salma Arts Centre
    Центр Художественный
    Салма

14 Post & Telephone Office &
    Internet Salon
    Почтамт.
    телефон и
    телеграф
15 Gallery M
    Галерея М
16 Kola-Tavs
    Кола-ТАВС
17 Murmansk/Monchegorsk
    Bus Stop
    Остановка в Мурманск-
    Мончегорск
21 Sports Ground &
    Swimming Pool
    Стадион и
    Бассейн
22 Library
    Библиотека
23 Skating Rink
    Каток
24 Market
    Рынок

There are three daily buses to/from Murmansk, and several to nearby Kirovsk as well.

If you're driving along the St Petersburg–Murmansk highway, Apatity lies 30km down a well-signposted eastwards spur road, 35km south of Monchegorsk.

Bus Nos 5 and 13 (not 13K) run between the train station and the town centre. There's an hourly bus to Khibiny airport. Bus Nos 101, 102 and 105 travel between Apatity and Kirovsk about every half-hour (R10).

KIROVSK
КИРОВСК
☎ 815231

Kirovsk is an attractive town. In fact, if you throw back a couple of shots, squint and look in the right direction, you can almost believe you're in a Swiss alpine village. The reason most visit is for the skiing and snowboarding – the finest in northwestern Russia – with prices that will make you want to stay all season.

Information
Menatep Bank, next to Hotel Ekkos, has a finicky 24-hour ATM and an exchange booth (open 9am-1pm & 2pm-3pm). The **post office** (pr Lenina; open 11am-7pm Mon-Fri, 11am-4pm Sat & Sun) is opposite the bus stop to/from Apatity. **Internet Kafe Vechernee** (ul Khibinogorskaya 29; open 2pm-5pm & 6pm-9pm Mon-Thur & Sun, 2pm-5pm & 6pm-11pm Fri & Sat), also bearing the ambitious name of 'Club New Civilization', has a café/bar for meals.

Things to See
The most interesting building in town is the decrepit **Kirovsk train station**, which like many of the 'Potyomkin villages' that would pop up around Russia (constructed only to impress visiting officials), is a monument to Soviet antilogic. Locals joke that its first and last passenger was Josef Stalin. Now it looks like a bomb was dropped on it. It's fun to explore – you can walk up the staircases that drop off into the garbage and ruins below – just be careful, and don't trust the handrails.

The Kirovsk-25 'microregion' has a few things that are worthy of a visit. To get there and to sites along the way, take bus No 1, 12 or 105. There is a **Regional Museum** that seems to be perpetually closed, but it's still worth a slog out there to see the surrounding mountains – or rather, the awesome gap where they used to be. A veteran geophysicist for a major Western minerals concern said that he knew of no way to accomplish such a neat removal of literally half a mountain other than a nuclear detonation, but local scientists insist the feat was accomplished with earth movers and heavy equipment – right.

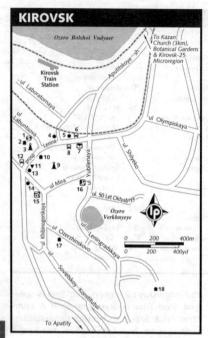

KIROVSK

PLACES TO STAY
2	Hotel Ekkos
	Гостиница Еккос и Касино
	Фортуна
10	Hotel Severnaya & Restaurant
	Гостиница Северная
17	Sport
	Почтамт
18	Khibiny Hotel
	Гостиница Хибины

PLACES TO EAT
11	Kafe Zodiak
	Кафе Зодияк

OTHER
1	Menater Bank
	Менатер Банк
3	Kirov Statue
	Памятник Кирову
4	Bolshevik Theatre
	Рынок
5	Department Store
	Универмаг
6	Bus Stop to/from Apatity
	Остановка автобуса в
	Аратигах и Кировск-25
7	Main Post Office
	Главпочтамт
8	Bus to Slopes
	Автобус на склоны
9	Lenin Statue
	Памятник Ленину
12	Bus Stop to/from Apatity
	Остановка автобуса в
	Аратигах и Кировск-25
13	Library
	Библиотека
14	Pharmacy
	Аптека
15	Internet Cafe Vechernee
	Ресторан Вечернее
16	Swimming Pool
	Бассейн

The new orthodox **Kazan Church** (*Kazanskaya tserkov*), en route to Kirovsk-25, is built on the site of another church that was moved from Kirovsk, and is unorthodox in that it was converted from a typical Northern Russian wooden house. The inside is lovely, however, with an impressive iconostasis and the allegedly miraculous **Icon of St Nicholas** (open 9am-2pm & 3pm-6pm Mon-Fri). On the night of 21 May 1994, the icon reportedly restored itself, and now works its miracles during these hours. Take bus No 1, 12 or 105 from Kirovsk's centre towards Kirovsk-25, and ask for the church. From the bus stop, walk west (back towards Kirovsk), turn south (left), then turn east (left again) and the church is 200m on the right-hand side of the road. Also on the way to Kirovsk-25 are some lovely **Botanical Gardens** (☎ 5 16 46, 5 14 36; open 9.30am-3pm).

Activities

The ski season in Kirovsk is delightfully lengthy – from November to June, with the best months being January to April. Lift tickets are as affordable as they come: half-day/full-day/weekly R200/350/2000. Rentals of skis and snowboards are available for about R100 per hour (bring your passport), but get there early if you want a snowboard. The runs are long and the slope is wide, with plenty of steep parts and moguls for hot dogs and lots of open space for those who need to carve a wide zigzag across the mountain to get down. If you are into **parasailing** or **ski jumping**, there are facilities for that as well. The bus stop to the slopes is in front of the post office; buses come about every half-hour and cost R5.

The Khibiny Mountains also offer the best **hiking** in northwestern Russia. The highest point, Judychvumchorr, rises 1200m above sea level; the Lovozero massif is just to the east. There are several companies that arrange for guided treks; **Geographic Bureau** (**w** www.geographicbureau.com) does trekking, mountaineering and biking trips in the Khibiny and throughout Russia.

Places to Stay & Eat
Sport (☎ 9 26 50, 9 11 45; ul Dzerzhinskovo 7A; singles R240-390, doubles R300-450) is probably the best deal – and staying here will get you discounts on lift tickets. There is a sauna on the premises for R250 and a daily shuttle to the mountain.

Hotel Ekkos (☎ 3 27 16; pr Lenina 12a; beds R300), housed in a cute castle-like building, is not as impressive on the inside, but it's not bad. If alone, you'll be expected to pay for any empty beds in the room. The only rooms are on the 4th floor (there's no lift). Meals carry an additional charge.

Khibiny Hotel (☎ 5 89 02, 5 89 01; ul Leningradskaya 25; singles R425-550, doubles R780-980) is a large turbaza (tourbase) about 1km from the centre. The rooms are very basic, but great views are available.

Hotel Severnaya (☎ 5 44 42; pr Lenina 11; singles/doubles US$80/160), a Hungarian-built place, is more or less a Western-standard hotel (except for the tiny Russian hotel beds) right in the town centre. There's also a lobby bar and a **restaurant** (mains R20-200) with good food, loud music and cold service.

The **market** (pr Lenina; open 11am-7pm) in the Bolshevik Theatre, opposite the Lenin statue, is home to a few tables of produce.

Kafe Zodiak (pr Lenina 13; open 11am-10pm Mon-Sat, 11am-8pm Sun) has one table and some blasé prepared foods. But hey, you can get a (watery) milkshake for R7.

Also try the Internet Kafe Vechernee (see Information earlier); it has a good café.

Getting There & Away
Bus Nos 101, 102 and 105 and minibuses marked Kirovsk–Apatity travel between Apatity and Kirovsk. Bus Nos 1, 12 and 105 run between Kirovsk and Kirovsk-25. Bus, train and plane tickets are sold at ulitsa Yubilenaya.

KANDALAKSHA
КАНДАЛАКША
☎ 81533 • pop 63,000
The Kola Peninsula's most important port after Murmansk, Kandalaksha is home to one

of the military's most important aluminium plants. The Pomory fishing village, around which the town was founded and dating from the 17th century, is still inhabited.

Next to the Byelomorye Hotel, Internet access is available at the **Biznyes Tsentr** (☎ 2 30 15; ul Pervomaiskaya 29) for R50 per hour, there's also a telephone office.

The large **nature reserve and sea-bird sanctuary** (Kandalakhisky gosudarstvenny zapovyednik), on the White Sea Islands, southwest of the town, is home to more than 250 species of sea birds. Most prominent are the eider ducks, gulls, murres, kittiwakes, razorbills and black guillemots, which nest in the rookeries of the Kuvshin and Kharlov Islands. Summer visits can be arranged through the **city administration** (☎ 9 30 11, 9 31 78) or the reserve administration centre, at the southern end of town. To reach the reserve, take bus No 1 from the train station to the last stop and walk towards the port; the administration centre will be on the left, across the river from the Pomory village. For more information, you can contact the **American Association for the Support of Ecological Initiatives** (☎ 1-860-346-2967, fax 347-8459; **e** alexk@aasei.spb.su or **e** wkwasch@william kwaschassociates.com).

Your best option for somewhere to stay is **Byelomorye** (☎ 2 30 15; ul Pervomaiskaya 29; singles/doubles R600/700, polu-lyux R900). There's a **food store** and a **bufet** in the lobby. The **restaurant** of the same name, next door, has good food.

Spolokhi (☎ 5 57 68; ul Naberezhnaya 130; singles/doubles R345/390, luxes R900), east of the centre towards the river bank, is another option. It has rooms, without phones, as well as a **bar** and a **bufet**.

Arkhangelsk Region
Архангельская
Область

The coastal region between the Kama and Onega Rivers on the White Sea is called Pomorye ('along the sea'), and the Pomory people, who have a strongly fishing-based culture, are the descendants of colonists from Novgorod and Nisov who settled the area in the 12th century.

ARKHANGELSK
АРХАНГЕЛЬСК
☎ 8182 • pop 375,400

Arkhangelsk's grim history, a product of its strategic location, has ensured that since its inception many of its residents have worn some sort of uniform.

Unfortunately, this grimness is reflected in the city's modern look; it is not a pretty city by any stretch of the imagination. Despite a few architectural remnants from the past – which are all concentrated along the waterfront – most of Arkhangelsk is a sprawling expanse of concrete. Still, a few century-old wooden houses survive (mainly concentrated on prospekt Chumbarova-Luchinskovo), and the contrast with their next-door Soviet structures is unique.

What it lacks in aesthetics, however, is more than made up for by a populace that is surely among the friendliest of all Russian cities (even the operators don't hang up on you!) and one that is relatively well connected with the world at large. There's a real sense of Arkhangelsk as a 'happening' city if you meet the right people, and to the sensitive person, it has a palpably magical atmosphere.

Many tourists will, however, want to use Arkhangelsk merely as a jumping-off point to one of the region's other offerings, such as the untamed northern wilderness, the open-air museum at Malye Korely, or the Solovetsky Islands.

History

The construction of present-day Arkhangelsk was decreed by Ivan the Terrible in 1574, 21 years after the arrival of the first British traders who – searching for a northern access route to China – ended up in what was then a remote fishing settlement along the Severnaya Dvina River. Ivan, then still in his pre-Terrible period, enthusiastically accepted Britain's advances and established trade ties with England. The Brits, keen to discover an enormous new market for their wool, established the Muscovy Company in late 1553.

In 1693 Peter the Great, fully charged with his vision of a great Russian navy, built an admiralty and seaport at Arkhangelsk, from where he launched the Russian navy's tiny first ship, the *Svyatoy Pavel*, in 1694.

The importance of Arkhangelsk's port as a centre for trade, especially with Western Europe, led to an enormous bazaar, which reached the height of its power in the late 18th century. The 19th century and the early 20th century established Arkhangelsk as a major lumber centre, which it remains today.

Allied troops have twice played an important role in the city's history. During Russia's civil war, the allied 'interventionists' managed to land at Arkhangelsk on 2 August 1918, but otherwise accomplished nothing because of confusion and a breakdown in communication within their own multinational ranks.

During WWII, Arkhangelsk, along with Murmansk, became a key supply port bringing desperately needed foreign equipment to the Russian army, and food to the besieged city of Leningrad. Before and after the war, the region was home to numerous prison camps, and many of today's residents are descendants of prisoners and exiles.

Orientation

Arkhangelsk sits on a peninsula jutting into the Severnaya Dvina River. The city's streets sprawl in a rough 'V' shape with an axis formed by ulitsa Voskresenskaya, which cuts from the river at the southwest to the train and bus stations at the northeast. The most obvious landmark is the 22-storey towering skyscraper on ploshchad Lenina.

City maps are available at the **bookshop** (*ul Voskresenskaya*) opposite the Aeroflot office and are sometimes available at the main **Dom Knigi bookshop** (*pl Lenina*).

Information

Money Nextdoor to the Hotel Dvina, the well-stocked and Western-style department/grocery store **Premier** (*open 9am-9pm daily*) is good for all sorts of things, including its ATM and exchange booth. Most larger stores have an ATM somewhere on the premises. There's also a 24-hour **Sberbank** on ul Voskresenskaya, as well as at several other banks. **Western Union** (*Pomorskaya ul 7*) operates at the Moskovsky Industrialny Bank.

Post & Communications The main post office (*ul Voskresenskaya 5; open 8am-7pm Mon-Fri, 9am-5pm Sat, 10am-5pm Sun*) is on the west side of ploshchad Lenina. For kicks, you can check out the display there on 'the history of email' and send an email to a friend, telegram style (you fill out a slip of paper with a message and they send it for you).

If you're looking for something a little more high-tech than that, there's an **Internet Salon** (☎ 43 73 90; pr Troitsky; open 11am-9pm Mon-Fri, noon-8pm Sat & Sun) in room 424 of the Technical University, just north of ulitsa Svobody (enter from the courtyard on the northern side). The charge there is R20 per hour. The dozen or so computers have a fast connection, and it could be a great way to meet some students.

The **telephone office** (cnr pr Lomonosova & ul Voskresenskaya; open 24hrs) also has photocopy and fax services.

Travel Agencies There are a few good agencies in town, but the most popular is **Pomor Tur** (☎ 20 46 00; e pomortur@atnet .ru; ul Svobody 3; open 10am-6pm Mon-Fri). The company organises city and regional tours, excursions to the Solovetsky Islands by plane and boat (including one from Vologda), and trips to lesser-known islands in the area. Personalised wilderness adventures are also a speciality.

Things to See & Do

In summer the waterfront is teeming with activity – you'll find moored boats with bars, restaurants and dancing.

Fine Arts Museum (☎ 65 36 16; admission R40; open 10am-5pm Wed-Mon), on the northeastern side of ploshchad Lenina, is surprisingly good. It boasts an impressive selection of 14th- to 18th-century icons and other religious artworks on the 2nd floor. Towards the rear of the 2nd floor, you'll also find 19th- and early-20th-century textiles and some applied decorative art. There's also a good selection of paintings and portraits – look for Stanislav Khlebovsky's *Death of Prince Oranskovo* (1861) and IB Lampi's portrait of Catherine the Great (1790s). Guided tours are available (Russian/English R50/60).

Regional Studies Museum (kra-ye-**vyed**-ches-ky mu-**zyey**; ☎ 43 66 79; per exhibit R6; open 10am-6pm Sat-Thur), also on the northeast side of ploshchad Lenina, hosts a sobering 2nd-floor exhibition dedicated to local soldiers who died in the war with Afghanistan. Snapshots taken by Russian soldiers during the conflict give a first-hand view of conditions, and there is a moving display of personal effects and letters sent home from soldiers who died. The 1st floor houses a lumpy taxidermy collection of local sea life

that's interesting in a ghoulish sort of way. The museum is closed on the last Thursday of the month.

State Naval Museum of the North (☎ 43 03 44; admission R8, free Wed; open 10am-4.45pm Tues-Sun), facing the docks at the edge of the water, just east of the Krasnaya Pristan Pier, features a well laid-out exhibit on Soviet polar expeditions (there's lots on the nuclear dump that is now Novaya Zemlya) and models of 18th-century icebreakers.

Severnaya Dvina naberezhnaya makes for a pleasant stroll at any time of year. Between ulitsas Voskresenskaya and Svobody, you'll pass the **Gostiny Dvor** (trading arcade), built at the beginning of the 18th century. This was the largest building in Russia until St Petersburg's Gostiny Dvor was built, but today, only a fraction of the original structure remains. There are sometimes museum exhibits here (admission R6-10). The city's **Great Patriotic War monument**, with its eternal flame, is just to the south of ulitsa Marksa.

Places to Stay

Hotel Dvina (☎ 28 88 88, fax 28 13 11; e dvina@arh.ru; pr Troitsky 52; singles R400-1000, doubles R1000-1400, luxes R1300 or R1800) is the most affordable place, and the service is quite friendly. It's also right next to the Premier store, which is very convenient. Bus No 12 from Talagi airport and bus No 54 from the train station both stop here (get off at ulitsa Pomorskaya).

Hotel Belomorskaya (☎ 66 16 00, 46 26 67, fax 46 53 27; w www.belhotel.ru; ul Ya Timme 3; singles/doubles R450/600, luxes R840-1200) is similar to Dvina, but with less friendly service and an inconvenient location. The business centre staff are quite helpful though (there is Internet access) and can also help you with trip planning.

Pur Navolok Hotel (☎ 65 39 81; w www .arh.ru/~ihotel; nab Severnaya Dvina 88; singles R800-1200, doubles R2500-3200) is the place that most foreigners choose. It has rooms with bay-windows and very nice river views, English-speaking staff and all the services and conveniences.

Zelyony Otel (☎ 26 91 30, fax 47-78 91 61 43; e greentel@atnet.ru; ul Voskresenskaya 8; singles/doubles including breakfast R2277/2645, luxes R3312/3795), around the corner from the telephone office, is a small

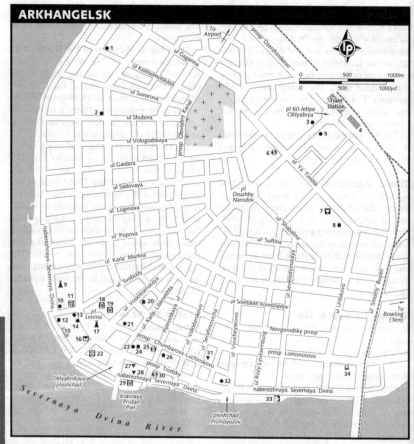

ARKHANGELSK

hotel with small, very expensive Western-style rooms. Its restaurant has the best reputation in the city.

Polina (☎ 26 84 20; ul Chumbarova-Luchinskovo 37; rooms about US$100), in a pastel-green wooden building, sure is pricey, but it sure is nice too. It has a romantic B&B feel, with a beautiful communal kitchen and spacious living rooms with fireplaces. And of course there's a pool and sauna.

Places to Eat

Premier (open 9am-9pm daily), next to Hotel Dvina (see Places to Stay), is a supermarket/department store that has almost anything you could ask for, including some prepared foods. All of the hotels have decent but pricey restaurants.

Solovetsky Podvorye (nab Severnaya Dvina 78; open noon-midnight; mains R30-300) is an absolute must. Take the first door on your left and you're in a friendly and traditional Russian *izba* (cottage), serving delicious variations of national dishes. Save room for the pear in puff pastry, and order some ice cream on the side – you'll cry with joy.

Cafe Yaroslavna (pr Troitsky 37/1), opposite the Dvina, has Georgian food that could use some work (like an attempt to remove bone shards from the soup), but it'll do if you need something Caucasian. It's small and sort of cosy, with wooden furniture.

Pof-Bun Pizzeria (☎ 43 43 61, delivery 20 99 99, fax 20 55 24; pr Chumbarova-Luchinskovo 8; pizzas R90-300; open 11am-11pm daily) serves 25 kinds of pizza; some of

ARKHANGELSK

NORTHERN EUROPEAN RUSSIA

the varieties might make a Sicilian shudder, but if you stick to the tried-and-true, you won't be too disappointed. It's very popular – you might want to call ahead.

Dvina (☎ 20 73 23; ul Pomorskaya 7, 2nd floor; mains R100-400; open noon-1am daily), although an upscale establishment, is reasonably priced; it has Russian and European food.

Pomorsky (☎ 26 81 58; ul Pomorskaya 7, 3rd floor; mains R100-400; open noon-midnight daily) is similar to and affiliated with the Dvina restaurant, only with a maritime theme and a seafood menu.

Entertainment

Many clubs serve as a cinema by day and a dance hall at night.

Modern (☎ 64 60 29; ul Shubina 9; disco R100, films R30-60) is a club that also hosts fashion shows and concerts from time to time.

Snezhok (cnr pr Troitsky & ul Komsomolskaya; disco R100, films R30-60) is similar to Modern in every way, except for the Wednesday night stripteases (R120).

Kristina (☎ 64 29 79; ul Ya Timme 7; films R30-40), next to the Belomorskaya hotel, has

a bar, restaurant and billiards room and also shows films in the daytime. Next door is **Laguna** (☎ 23 96 88), where you can get a sauna.

Bowling (☎ 28 77 77; Moscovsky pr 33; open noon-5am; R350-700/hr), named for the latest pastime of 'New Russia – The Next Generation', is probably the hot spot of the city. It has six lanes, two pool tables, and a lot of black-clad attitude.

Shopping

On the 3rd floor of Detsky Mir is an excellent antique shop, **Russkaya Starina** (☎ 65 18 99), which is full of surprises. Ask the staff to open up the old and rare book section if it's closed. **Dom Knigi** (open 10am-7pm Mon-Fri, 10am-5pm Sat) has a strange selection of English-language books, miniature books in Russian, and Soviet propaganda postcards and posters. More original souvenirs can be found inside the Regional Studies Museum.

Getting There & Away

Air Arkhangelsk has two airports; Talagi is the main one, and Vaskovo is the one you will probably use to go to the Solovetsky Islands.

From Talagi, there is daily service to/from Moscow (R2900) and St Petersburg (R2500), and four times weekly to/from Murmansk (R2350) airports. There are also flights on odd dates to/from Kotlas, near Veliky Ustiug (R1350). Arkhangelsk Airlines has thrice-weekly flights to/from Rovaniemi, in Finland, and a weekly flight to/from Tromsø, in Norway.

You'll find the friendly **Aeroflot office** (☎ 23 80 98; ul Voskresenskaya 116; open 9am-1pm & 2pm-7pm Mon-Fri, 10am-1pm & 2pm-5pm Sat & Sun) just west of the train and bus stations.

Train There is at least one direct train a day to/from Moscow (plats/kupe 475/835, 24 hours). There are four trains a week to/from St Petersburg (plats/kupe 416/775, 28 to 35 hours). There are indirect trains to Murmansk (R345/606, 30 hours) through Moscow or St Petersburg. Call ☎ 23 72 41 for information. In addition to the station, train tickets may also be purchased at the Aeroflot office.

Car & Motorcycle From Moscow, take the M8 north through Vologda, but bring extra shock absorbers. It's about 1100km.

Boat Check with Pomor Tur (see Travel Agencies earlier) about river cruises to Arkhangelsk (and on to the Solovetsky Islands) from Vologda.

Getting Around
The city has an extensive network of buses, trams and taxis. Bus No 54 goes from the bus station to the centre. Bus No 531 runs between the bus station and Arkhangelsk airport about once an hour from 5.55am to 7.30pm. Bus No 12 also runs between the bus station and the airport (R12). For a taxi, call ☎ 65 55 00 or ☎ 20 40 60. A ride from the airport to the centre costs R150 to R200; per hour, taxis are about R140.

MALYE KORELY
МАЛЫЕ КОРЕЛЫ
The open-air **Wooden Architecture Museum** (☎ 25 84 38, tours 25 82 87; admission R30; open 10am-7pm Wed-Sun in summer, 10am-3pm Wed-Sun in winter), 25km east of Arkhangelsk, features 17th- to 19th-century wooden buildings, windmills and watermills and bell towers. Also here is the stand-out **St**

George's Church (Giorgyevskaya tserkov) dating from 1672 and the impressive five-domed **Ascension Church** (Voznyesenskaya tserkov) built in 1669. The exhibits were all brought here from various places throughout the Arkhangelsk region. The architecture and construction are similar to that found in Kizhi, and the natural scenery around the reserve is quite pleasant – bringing a picnic would be a splendid idea (although there are a restaurant and a store just outside the premises, as well as shashlyk and hot-dog stands around the entrance). The Mezensky section of the museum grounds features some of the most interesting structures and the nicest views of the surrounding valleys.

Follow the large map of the grounds to your left as you enter. Most of the buildings, the churches and **chyornye izby** (or 'black cottages', so called because the lack of a full chimney resulted in smoke staining the outside walls) are open to exploration.

At the main museum area **horse rides** are offered every day at midday, though you don't get much time on the beastie.

Getting There & Away
Bus No 104 goes from Arkhangelsk's bus station and bus No 111 from the train station; buses run every half-hour or so until 10.30pm. To catch either (or the faster taxi-bus No 104), wait at the bus stop on prospekt Lomonosova near the southeastern corner of ulitsa Uritskovo, where they all make stops; you shouldn't have to wait much more than 15 minutes. Malye Korely is bus No 104's last stop; on No 111, ask for the museum. The ride is about R10.

SOLOVETSKY ISLANDS
СОЛОВЕЦКИЕ ОСТРОВА
☎ 8183590 • pop 1200
Perched in the forbidding waters of the White Sea's lower reaches, 165km south of the Arctic Circle, are the Solovetsky Islands (often referred to as Solovki). The islands have always been used for exile and retreat: here was one of the most famous monasteries in the Russian Empire, a tsarist-era penal colony, and one of the cruellest Soviet prison camps. For travellers unfazed by remote locations and complications in getting there, the islands offer unparalleled beauty, with frequent reminders of their troubled history to keep one's mood sober.

Expect it to be cool to cold whenever you visit. Though summer days can be as hot as 20°C, if you aren't prepared for cool evenings, or if you forget your mosquito repellent, you too will get to know something about suffering here.

History

Though reconstructed stone labyrinths on the islands, dating from the 1st and 2nd centuries BC, prove that the location was used in ancient times for worship, the modern history of the Solovetsky Islands begins in 1429 when two monks from the Kyrill-Belozersk Monastery, Savvaty and German, founded a wooden monastery in the area now called Savatevo. In the mid-16th century, another monk, Philip (who Ivan the Terrible later had murdered for his outspoken views), founded the stone churches and thick fortress walls that still stand inside today's kremlin.

Solovki has been used as a prison or place of forced exile for political and religious criminals since the 16th century. In 1923, a work camp for 'enemies of the people' was opened. At first, prisoners worked fairly freely, keeping up the Botanical Gardens and libraries. But in 1937 Stalin reorganised it into one of the severest Gulags in his empire. Isolated from central command, officers maintained the prisoners in intolerable conditions, torturing or killing them at will. Some of its most famous inmates were linguist DS Likachov and poet and priest Anatoly Zhurakovsky, along with hundreds of other artists, writers and intelligentsia. The prison was closed in 1939.

During WWII the islands became the base of a special navy youth wing and remained an important Northern Fleet base until recently. The monastery reopened in the early 1990s.

Orientation & Information

The Solovetsky Islands are six separate islands, with a combined land mass of 300 sq km and over 500 lakes. Solovetsky Island is by far the largest (24km north to south and 16km east to west) and all of the islands' services are in the village surrounding the kremlin.

There is a **Sberbank** with mysterious operating hours but it won't be able to change currency. Residents will be happy to change money with you, but it's best to bring enough. A general store with similarly unpredictable opening hours, facing the monastery, has

film, souvenirs, hardware and clothing. Late morning and early afternoon seem the best times to find these spots open.

There is currently no Internet access on the islands but that is bound to change soon.

When to Go

Most people go to Solovki in the summer, when navigation is open and it's not so cold. The downside to this is that the feral mosquitoes and swarms of midges can make you miserable.

Kremlin

You can tour many of the nonresidential kremlin buildings, either on your own or as part of a tour group. The only church with regular services is the **Annunciation Church** (*Blagovyeshchenskaya tserkov; open 8am & 5pm daily*), built from 1596 to 1601. The others have largely been under renovation for the last 30 years. It is nonetheless possible to visit the **Transfiguration Cathedral** (Preobrazhensky sobor), built between 1558 and 1566; the **Assumption Church** (Uspenskaya tserkov), built from 1552 to 1557 and the majestic **St Nicholas Church** (Glavny Nikolsky tserkov), built between 1832 and 1834, with its adjoining **bell tower** (1777) – a climb to the top is a must for the greatest view of the island.

State Historical-Architectural Museum

The most arresting room in this museum (*admission R50; open 9am-5pm Tues-Sun*) focuses on the Gulag period. The walls are lined with official images of smiling workers from the Soviet period, but the detailed exhibits show the unofficial story of pain and suffering in prisons like these.

Private Museum of Crosses

Near the kremlin, in a little wooden building, is a *mastyerskaya* (workshop) where intricately engraved crosses are made for churches throughout Russia. The crosses, some of which take months to complete, are truly beautiful. The museum is free, although donations are gratefully accepted.

Sekirnaya Gora

Literally 'Hatchet Mountain', Sekirnaya Gora is 12km from the kremlin and is infamous thanks to the tortures Alexander Solzhenitsyn alleged took place there in his *Gulag Archipelago* (scholars now dispute many of his claims as unfounded). The unassuming **Ascension Church** (1857–62) at the top of the steep hill was used for solitary confinement; there are spectacular views from here. Many prisoners died here from cold and starvation, and their bodies were thrown down the nearby stairs, which have been renovated with Norwegian funding. At the bottom of the stairs lies a cross in memory of all who died on Solovki, placed there in the late 1980s by the Russian Patriarch. The church is perpetually closed, open only on 4 and 10 June, traditional days for memorial services on the island.

Khutor Gorka Botanical Gardens

Founded by the monastery in 1822, 5km from the kremlin, this is one of the northernmost botanical gardens in the world. Nestled in a heat-trapping valley and interlaced with an intricate system of underground hot-water pipes, the gardens boast trees and plants usually found in more southern climates. In summer there are rowboats you can use to get from one part of the gardens to another. On top of Alexander Hill is the adorably miniature **Alexander Nevsky Church** (1854); find the nearby bench for the most beautiful view – the wind magically seems to ignore this tranquil spot.

Abandoned Prison

On the same territory as Turbaza Solovki (see Places to Stay & Eat) is a vacant ex-prison; roaming freely inside the ruins makes for an even creepier experience than visiting the Peter & Paul Fortress in St Petersburg. Door numbers, markings on walls, and guards' observation windows are still intact. There are plans to turn this into a hotel.

Organised Tours

At the time of research Sasha Ivanovsky was establishing an extreme-adventure tour company. **Dikii Tyen** (*Wild Shadow;* ☎ *314*) will have custom adventure tours of the islands, which will have either an ecological or a military twist to them. He will take you through different challenges on the island and you could end up in a paintball tournament. Travellers will stay in military barracks and also pitch tents. For more mundane tours, check with Pomor Tur (see Information under Arkhangelsk earlier).

Places to Stay & Eat

Although the islands are theoretically accessible year-round, accommodation is only open during navigation season (roughly June to August). Call Vika and Andrei at ☎ 314 for a homestay – they're a great resource and lots of fun. They're also starting a guesthouse in a lovely new wooden house with a great view of the kremlin.

Camping is allowed with permission. Contact the **Solovetsky Leskhoz** (*☎ 312 or 326; ul Severnaya 14*) and ask for Leonid Ivanovich, who'll show you where camping is permitted for R10 per person. As there are no facilities, bring everything you'll need.

Priyut (*☎ 297; Primorskaya 11; rooms R500 plus meals*) is a great deal, with clean, quiet rooms (including modern, shared facilities) for one to four people. Saunas are available for an extra charge and a small car can be rented cheaply to tour the island privately. Also, you can negotiate with the lovely and very helpful staff to prepare hot meals for you. Ask for a room facing the monastery.

Turbaza Solovki (*☎ 214; Varyazheskaya ul 1; rooms with 3 meals per person per day US$50*), the most luxurious place, is worthwhile if you're planning to stay a few days and can afford it. Two kilometres outside the main village, it boasts quiet, renovated lakeside cottages with single, double and triple rooms, and clean, shared facilities. Spacious living rooms have satellite TV and fireplaces. The friendly staff will prepare a traditional Russian *banya* for an additional charge. Pedal-boating and fishing are possible, as is a laundry service, unavailable elsewhere. They can also provide transportation.

There are no restaurants but it is possible to make meal arrangements at any of the hotels without staying there. **Produkty shops** along ulitsa Zaozyora and ulitsa Kavaleva offer a fair selection of goods.

Getting There & Away

Air There are flights to and from Arkhangelsk year-round Monday, Wednesday and Friday. A one-way ticket is R1080. Schedules can be confirmed at the **Vaskovo aerodrome** (*☎ 45 01 65, fax 45 17 94;* e *aoao@mail.sts.ru*) from which flights leave Arkhangelsk; a taxi to Vaskovo should cost around R150. Planes for up to 17 people can also be rented for US$150 each way through the rather pushy **Solovki Tours** (*☎ 8182-44 31 19*) in Arkhangelsk.

It's important to remember that although these flights are scheduled year-round, they may be delayed from a couple hours to as much as a couple of days if the wind is severe – this happens frequently, so make sure there's some leeway in your schedule.

Boat You can reach Solovetsky Island by boat only from June to August. Check with Pomor Tur about boats from Vologda and Arkhangelsk (see that section earlier).

While Turbaz Kem, in Kem, or Pomor Tur, in Arkhangelsk (see those sections) will be happy to book you onto their tours of the islands, the most economical way to go is on your own, through Kem.

In Kem, take bus No 1 across from the train station to the last stop, the village of Rabocheostrovsk, 35 minutes away. Boats leave from the tiny port there; the only sure way to find out when is to ask a hotel in town.

Getting Around
You'll need people's help to see the sites outside the village surrounding the kremlin. Dirt roads are so bumpy that off-road vehicles are required; women should make sure to wear a sports bra. Ask at your accommodation for transportation. There is no official bike rental but if your Russian is good enough, you could try renting one from a villager. The 25km round trip to Sekirnaya Gora and Savatevo makes for a nice afternoon bike ride, if you don't mind dirt roads and mosquitoes.

Vologda Region
Вологодская Область

Due to its prominence up until the 17th century, the Vologda region has a rich history, and plenty of lovely old churches to show for it. Its capital, Vologda, is in itself worth a visit to the region, but the small town of Veliky Ustiug, that is – the *rodina* of Father Frost himself – is an evergrowing attraction.

VOLOGDA
ВОЛОГДА
☎ 8172 • pop 299,500
About 400km northeast of Moscow, Vologda is a pleasant provincial city with a high concentration of churches and monasteries, and many lovely parks and dilapidated wooden

buildings that would make the city a real treasure if someone would only invest in their renovation. Its surrounding areas also hold great monastic treasures.

'Liberated' by Novgorod from the Finns in the 12th century, Vologda thenceforth led a reasonably happy existence thumbing its nose at the Novgorodians. Taking Moscow's side against all comers seemingly from the moment of its inception, Vologda was rewarded by Ivan the Terrible, who deemed the quaint city perhaps worthy of his living there (Vologdians are steadfast in their belief that the city was a contender for Russian capital), and a perfect site for a grand cathedral.

Vologda was an important centre of industry, commerce and arts – Vologda lace is still a coveted luxury item – up to the 17th century, but with the increasing importance of Arkhangelsk as a port and the founding of St Petersburg, its economic powerhouse status was revoked. With the construction in the late 19th century of a railway linking it to Moscow, St Petersburg and Arkhangelsk, Vologda became known more as a gateway between power centres than a force of its own. At the start of the 20th century, many political undesirables (like one Josef Stalin and philosopher Nikolai Berdyaev) were exiled there. And, for a few months in 1918, Vologda became the diplomatic capital of Russia.

Orientation & Information
Vologda straddles the Vologda River, with the town's centre mainly concentrated on the southern side. The town's main axis, ulitsa Mira, runs from the train and bus station north to the junction of ulitsa Oktyabrskaya, where it juts northeast and crosses the Vologda. The **Archbishop's Courtyard** (*kremlyovskaya ploshchad*), which is often referred to as the Vologda Kremlin, is on the south bank of the Vologda, west of the main bridge.

If you have any registration concerns, Vologda has a **PVU** (☎ 23 64 40; ul Maltseva 54; open 2pm-6pm Mon-Wed & Fri, 10am-1pm Sat).

Money There's an ATM at the formidable **Severgazbank**, in the same pedestrian zone as the perky-glum Central Department Store, one block north of ulitsa Mira's northeast tack. Access to the latter seems to be open 24 hours or at least until late. There is also an ATM in Hotel Spasska's lobby.

Post & Communications The main post office (☎ 72 07 51; Sovietsky pr 131; open 8am-2pm & 3pm-7pm Mon-Fri, 10am-5pm Sat) is on ploshchad Babushkina. The 24-hour telephone office (ul Gertsena 29) is on the corner of ulitsas Predtechenskaya and Gertsena. For Internet access, try the central library (☎ 25 18 67; ul MI Ulyanovoy) just off ploshchad Revolyutsii where the charge is R12 per hour, but it's often packed with students eager for time in cyberspace. If you'd rather not wait, go across the street to Uslugi Electrosvyazi. The charge here is R54 per hour.

Travel Agencies & Tour Guides One good place is Sputnik (☎ 25 96 44; e sputnik@vologda.ru; open 9am-6pm Mon-Fri) in room 310 of Zolotoy Yakor (see Places to Stay), which has many different kinds of tours, including literary, children's and lace-making tours, in addition to excursions to ancient cities in the region. All are reasonably priced if you're in a good-sized group.

Intourist (☎ 72 60 63; e intour@vologda .ru; ul Blagoveshchenskaya 26) can also be counted on for efficiency. It offers visa support and city and regional tours, though these are quite pricey.

State Historical, Architectural and Artistic Museum Reserve (☎ 72 22 83; e museum@vologda.ru; ul Orlova 15), in the Archbishop's Courtyard administrative offices in the centre of the kremlin, runs most of the museums in the city and also arranges excellent tours of the kremlin, including buildings closed to the public, as well as city tours.

The best city tours are conducted by Marina Barandina (☎ 75 70 40, 72 20 02; e mus dip@vologda.ru), a curator at the Museum of Diplomatic Corps (see Things to See & Do). Not only is she a specialist in the city's history and points of interest, she speaks English extremely well.

Things to See & Do
Archbishop's Courtyard Vologda's Archbishop's Courtyard is the city's historical centrepiece, a multitowered stone fortress (1671–75) containing several noteworthy buildings. These include the 1659 Treasurer's Palace (Kazenny prikaz); the house of Josef Zolotoy (Iosefsky korpus) built between 1764 and 1769; and the baroque (but not crazily so) Resurrection Cathedral (Voskresensky sobor) which was built from 1772 to

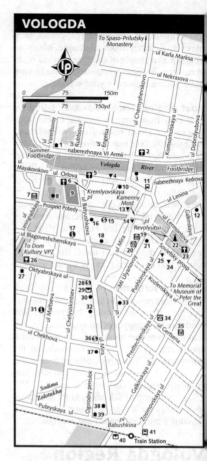

1776 in place of the northeastern tower. It's been an art and picture gallery since 1952. The courtyard also houses the town's Museum of History & Architecture (see later).

The courtyard was, according to the sign above the entrance, 'generously donated' by the church to the victorious Soviet atheists just after the Great October Revolution. The courtyard is open to visitors and the art gallery and café have rotating exhibitions on varying schedules.

St Sofia's Cathedral & Bell Tower Directly outside the courtyard's walls sits Vologda's most famous cathedral, St Sofia's (open 10am-5pm daily), said to be built on the direct orders of Ivan the Terrible. Ivan's ruthlessness at Novgorod – where he sacked his own city

VOLOGDA

PLACES TO STAY
1 Sretenskaya Church Dorm
Сретенская Церковь
Общежитие
27 Hotel Spasska
Гостиница Спасска
38 Hotel Vologda
Гостиница Вологда
39 Sputnik Hotel
Гостиница Спутник

PLACES TO EAT
4 Akvarium Pizzeria
Пиццерия Аквариум
13 Restaurant Mercury
Ресторан Меркурий
14 Pirozhkovaya
Пирожковая
24 Cafe Lesnaya Skazka
Кафе Лесная Сказка
25 Zolotoy Yakor; Sputnik
Гостиница Золотой Якорь

OTHER
2 Church of St Dmitrius of
Preluki
Церковь Дмитрия
Прилуцкого
3 Boat Rental (Summer)
Прокат лодок (летом)
5 Alexander Nevsky Church
Церковь Александра
Невского
6 St Sofia's Cathedral
Софийский Собор

7 Museum of Forgotten
Things
Выставочный зал
8 Kiddie Boat Rental
Прокат лодок
для детей
9 Kremlin (Archbishop's
Courtyard) & Museum of
History & Architecture
Кремль
(Архиерейское подворье)
10 Spice Jam
Спайс Джэм
11 Bus Stop to Spaso-Prilutsky
Monastery
Остановка на Спасо-
Прилутский Монастырь
12 Technical University &
Internet Salon
Технический
Университет
15 Severgazbank
Севергазбанк
16 Central Market
Центральный рынок
17 Intourist
Интурист
18 Department Store
Универмат
19 Afghanistan Hall
Афганский зал
20 Ulsugi Elektrosvyazi
Услуги Электросвязи
21 Central Library
Библиотека

22 Lenin Statue
Памятник В. И.
Ленину
23 Church of St John
the Baptist
Церковь Иоанна
Предтечи
26 Cafe ARS
Кафе АРС
28 Vologda Bank
Вологда банк
29 Post Office
Почта
30 Dom Knigi
Дом Книги
31 OVIR
ОВИР
32 Banya
Баня
33 Stalin's Apartment
Квартира Сталина
34 Telephone Office
Телефон
35 Museum of Diplomatic
Corps
Музей дипломатического
корпуса
36 Sberbank
Сбербанк
37 Souvenir Shop
Сувениры
40 Main Post Office
Главпочтамт
41 Bus Station
Автовокзал

and tortured its inhabitants, even going so far as to roast them on spits and fry them alive in enormous frying pans especially made for the occasion – was well known throughout Russia. So the workers jumped: the massive stone cathedral Ivan wanted so badly was erected in just two years (1568–70) – and they only worked in summer.

But haste, of course, makes waste. Local legend has it that Ivan, upon walking into St Sofia's for the first time, was struck on the head by a 'red tile' that had been carelessly grouted to the ceiling. Ivan angrily stormed out of the cathedral and never returned. The cathedral was finally consecrated after the feisty tsar's death. It was decorated between 1680 and 1686, but the iconostasis you'll see today was made between 1724 and 1738 by designer Maxim Iskritsky. The frescoes were restored from 1962 to 1978. You can gain access to the cathedral by arrangement with the museum's administration.

Next to the cathedral, the 78.5m **St Sofia's Bell Tower** (*Kolokolnya Sofiiskaya sobora; admission R20; open 10am-5pm daily*) is a reconstruction (1869–70) of the original, which was built in 1659.

Alexander Nevsky Church Across the street from St Sofia's, this early-18th-century church (Tserkov Aleksandra Nevskogo) holds daily services at 8am and 5pm and features an excellent choir.

Museum of History & Architecture Housed in the Archbishop's Courtyard, this museum (*admission R10; open 10am-5pm Wed-Sun*) is good fun. Those with a morbid streak will appreciate the female skeleton from the 2nd century BC and the astounding anonymous painting from 1721, *Strashny Sud* (Frightful Trial). Those with an even more morbid streak will love the Soviet hammer and sickle done up in fine, delicate Vologda lace.

NORTHERN EUROPEAN RUSSIA

Museum of Forgotten Things Housed in a restored home with period furniture, the goal of this new interactive museum *(Muzey Zabytykh Vyeshchei; ☎ 25 14 17; ul Leningradskaya 6; admission R50, with tour in Russian R150; open 10am-5pm Wed-Sun)* is to give you an understanding of Russian life in the 19th century. Guests are encouraged to attempt to set the dining-room table with imperial china, play period music on a gramophone and learn the complicated norms of receiving guests.

Memorial Museum of Peter the Great Opened in 1885, this is the oldest of Vologda's museums *(☎ 75 27 59; Sovietsky pr 47; admission R50, with tour in Russian R150; open 10am-5pm Wed-Sun)*. The late-17th-century stone building in which it is housed is where Peter I stayed during his visits to Vologda. Some interesting personal effects of the tsar are on exhibit, as well as his death mask.

Church of St John the Baptist Before the revolution, on ploshchad Revolyutsii there were three churches and one grand cathedral. All were destroyed save the disused Church of St John the Baptist (1710; the bell tower was built in 1717). You'll also find a Great Patriotic War Memorial and eternal flame here. The church makes a truly classy backdrop for the smallest **Lenin statue** around. The very first Lenin statue ever erected in the USSR, back in 1924, this is supposedly life-size (awww). His itty-bittyness stands on a big pedestal – anyone who's seen the Stonehenge scene in the film *Spinal Tap* will appreciate this.

Museum of Diplomatic Corps This unusual museum *(☎ 72 20 02; e musdip@vologda.ru; ul Gertsena 35)* chronicles a little-known blip in WWI history. In February 1918, when Allied ambassadors in Petrograd were ordered to evacuate (Germans were approaching), US ambassador David Francis suggested simply relocating; he studied a map and chose Vologda. The British, Japanese, Chinese, Siamese, Brazilian, Belgian, French, Italian and Serbian embassies followed his lead and set up shop here until July. The eclectic and impressively researched exhibit, housed in the former US 'embassy', is intriguing and full of surprises. It specialises in receiving foreign visitors.

Stalin's Apartment You won't find this on any maps, and tour guides don't mention it, but this two-storey wooden house *(ul Ulyanovoy 33)* was once Stalin's home while on one of his three exiles in the city; after garnering a reputation as a carouser and woman-chaser – some say an illegitimate son still lives in Vologda – he kept escaping. The house was a museum in his honour from 1937 to 1956, housed an exhibition on the revolution until 1967, and is now the office of a rather pathetic real-estate venture. If people are around and in the mood to receive curious visitors, ask to see the *pechka* (stove) on which he slept. It still works – who knows, you may even be invited to have some tea made on it.

Afghanistan Hall The moving Afghanistan Hall *(☎ 72 07 61; ul Ulyanovoy 6, 2nd floor; admission free; open 10am-6pm daily)* commemorates locals who died in the war with that country. Letters and personal effects of the deceased contrast sharply with propaganda posters of the time.

Spaso–Prilutsky Monastery This working monastery, dating from the 14th century, looms on the outskirts of the city. It's a bit muddy, but guests are welcome, and a visit makes for an interesting afternoon, especially if you can get inside its centrepiece, the 16th-century **Cathedral of the Saviour**. If you show up alone, act interested and are polite, the monks will let you walk the grounds unescorted at no cost. Standard modest dress and covered heads for women are required. Take bus No 103 or 133 to the end, or better yet, get off one stop earlier (at the Zheleznodorozhna stop, where the road forks), and cross the railway bridge, from which you can get a great photo of the place (no photos from inside are allowed).

Boat Rental In summer you may be able to rent rowing boats for short cruises up the Vologda. The **rental station** is just east of the ulitsa Chernyshevskovo bridge, across from the Church of St Dmitrius of Preluki. Kiddie boat rentals can be found in the children's playground just behind the kremlin.

Banya The city's largest *banya* *(☎ 72 14 49; ul Mira 40; admission R35; open noon-8pm Wed-Fri, 8am-8pm Sat & Sun)* is clean and its staff are friendly. There are also great massages (R35 to R140) available.

Places to Stay
During research **Sretenskaya Church Dorm** (☎ 72 94 42; nab VI Armii 85), a converted 1731 church directly across the Vologda from the kremlin and **Zolotoy Yakor** (☎ 72 14 54; Sovietsky pr 6), where religious philosopher Nikolai Berdyaev lived while in exile, were both unable to accept foreign visitors due to problems with the PVU office. They're both great budget places though, so it's worth trying to see if the situation's changed.

Hotel Vologda (☎ 72 30 79; ul Mira 92; singles/doubles with shower R360/576, without shower R144/260) has decent rooms and unenthused service.

Hotel Spasska (☎ 72 01 45; ul Oktyabrskaya 25; singles/doubles R550/900) is the town's most expensive offering, but the small amount of added comfort is worthwhile and the buffet breakfast is excellent and includes made-to-order omelettes. In the morning the 2nd-floor **café** serves a true rarity: freshly squeezed orange juice.

Places to Eat
The town's good central **market** is near the corner of prospekt Pobedy and ulitsa Batyushkova. Of the hotel restaurants, **Zolotoy Yakor** has a sort-of-fancy atmosphere and decent dishes around R150. **Spasska** has the fanciest and most expensive restaurant in town, but it's still pretty affordable (mains R100 to R300) and the staff are touchingly servient – your plastic litre of Coke is presented and poured for you as if it were a fine Pinot Noir.

Cafe Lesnaya Skazka (Sovietsky pr 10; mains R90-150; open 11am-3am daily), one of the most pleasant places in town, is within the converted Chapel of the Laying of the White Robes (1911).

Restaurant Mercury (ul Mira 6; mains R80-250) can be a blast with the right company. Very effusive women will guide you to heavily laid-out tables and lavish you with attention while a band plays gypsy tunes (Vologda has a sizable Roma population).

Akvarium Pizzeria (ul Orlova 6; mains R80-250; open 11am-11pm Sun-Thur, 11am-2am Fri & Sat), packed with students from the institute next door, has decidedly so-so pizza, but it has other meals too.

Entertainment
Youths who've decided to skip the weekend beer-and-apathy conventions that take place, ironically, at ploshchad Revolyutsii (Revolution Square) head to **Spice Jam** (Torgovaya pl 8), 200m east of the pizzeria, or **Dom Kulturny VPZ** (☎ 23 42 33; ul Leningradskaya 89; admission R40; open 11pm-5am Sat).

What **Kafe ARS** (across from hotel Spasska; open 11am-10pm daily) lacks in a fortunate name, it makes up for in fresh arcade games. If your performance makes you want to drown your sorrows or feed your pride, the bar/restaurant serves booze/food.

The restaurant at **Hotel Spasska** also has a spacious dance floor for anyone who needs to get down with their bad selves and adult Volodgians to the Russian version of I Will Survive (disco friends: that would be Ya Budu Zheet). And yes, it has the same effect on Russian women as the original does on the English-speaking ladies of the world. Rock on, sisters.

Shopping
Kruzhevo (Vologda lace) is the big hit; you can try the 1st floor of the **central department store** or the great **souvenir shop** (cnr uls Mira & Chekhova).

Another local speciality is Vologda butter, with a slight vanilla-nut flavour. Most restaurants serve it, and local stores sell it.

The **Dom Knigi** (ul Mira) has yet another strange collection of English-language books (who decides what gets translated at these pub houses?).

Getting There & Around
There are regular flights to/from St Petersburg (R5782) and Moscow (R3240). For more information, call the airport on ☎ 79 07 99 or ☎ 72 33 02 or check W www.polets.ru.

There are several daily trains to/from Moscow (plats/kupe R218/534, eight hours), the best of which is the overnight train No 60. There are also many trains to/from St Petersburg (R230/387, 10 hours), as well as daily service to Arkhangelsk (R260/437, 12 hours). Trains to Murmansk leave on even dates (R480/717, 35 hours).

There are no long-distance buses from Moscow or any other major city but there are daily buses to smaller towns in the area including Kirillov, Ferapontov, Cherepovets and Rybinsk.

Call ☎ 77 41 75 or 72 20 00 for a taxi, which will cost about R130 per hour. If you can afford it, this is a great alternative to the bus for visiting the Spaso-Prilutsky Monastery or Kirillov and Ferapontov.

KIRILLOV & FERAPONTOV
КИРИЛЛОВ И ФЕРАПОНТОВ
☎ 8257

The **Kirilla-Belozersky Museum of History, Architecture & Fine Arts** (☎ 3 14 79; admission R50; open 9am-5pm Tues-Sun), housed in a nonworking 14th-century monastery of the same name, is the reason to come to this teensy village about 135km northwest of Vologda. Legend has it that the monastery's founder, Kirill, was living at the Similovsky monastery when he had a vision of the Virgin Mary showing him the towers of a new monastery. There's an icon depicting the vision inside the monastery.

Massive walls surround four main areas: the Large Assumption Monastery, the Small Ivanov Monastery, the Stockaded Town and the New Town. The main exhibition includes a tour of the churches, cathedrals and buildings, a regional history, and history of the monastery.

In the even more tranquil village of **Ferapontov**, 17km west of Kirillov, is another monastery, which has been converted to a branch of the Kirillov museum (☎ 3 14 79; admission R20-75; open 9am-5pm Tues-Sun). Dionysius came here in 1502 to paint frescoes on the church's interior (he did it all in an amazing 34 days) and Ivan the Terrible is said to have frequented and enjoyed this church.

Getting There & Away
From Vologda's bus station, buses leave several times daily to/from Kirillov; it's nearly a three-hour journey. When you arrive in Kirillov, ask the driver to let you off in the centre; you'll see the monastery from there. Buses to Lipinvor stop in Ferapontov. To get to Ferapontov from Vologda, catch a bus or taxi to Lipinvor, which stops right there.

If you hire a driver to take you there, you can count on a total of about six hours to go to both villages, spend a bit of time there, and come back. Although the general rate is about R130 per hour, the roads are hard on cars, so the total charge will be more like around R300 per hour. For the best price, negotiate with a driver you're familiar with instead of ordering a driver directly through a taxi company.

VELIKY USTIUG
ВЕЛИКИЙ УСТИУГ
☎ 81738 • pop 36,000

The name of this provincial village 350km east of Vologda means 'Great Mouth of the Yug' and was recently blessed by a windfall that changed its fate forever.

In 1998 Moscow Mayor Yury Luzhkov officially deemed Veliky Ustiug the home of Ded Moroz, gave the town a large sum of money, and said 'Make it so'. Despite the rather grim-sounding name, Ded Moroz (strikingly similar to 'Dead Morose') translates as Father Frost and is the Russian version of the Finnish St Nicklaus, or Santa Claus. The two are not the same, however, as any Russian will assure you (see the boxed text 'Identifying Your Giftgiver').

The town itself often looks like a children's storybook and the views from the riverfront, freckled with churches, are some of the most epic in Northern European Russia. There are so few cars that it's normal to find all pedestrians walking down the middle of the paved streets.

It's a trek from Vologda, but paying a visit to the home of Father Frost, kitsch as it is, will be loads of fun.

Orientation & Information
Nestled in at the confluence of two rivers (the Sukhona and Yug) that merge into a third (the Northern Dvina), Veliky Ustiug has a history of terrible springtime floods, when the ice on the surrounding rivers begins to melt and large chunks coagulate at the confluence, forming a natural and disastrous dam. Each year, inhabitants hold their breath while local militia do what they can to prevent a flood.

The town is so small that it's hard to get lost. Sovietsky prospekt, also known as ulitsa Uspenskaya, is the main street. The train station is northwest of town.

Obviously, the high season here is around Christmas and New Year – book everything well in advance if you plan to visit during this time.

A **Sberbank** is on ulitsa (not pereulok) Krasnaya; they can change money or give you cash off a card. There are no ATMs in town.

Woman selling *kvas*, a brew made from fermented rye bread, Pskov

Reflection of Sergievo-Kazansky Cathedral, Kursk

Nicholas Church fresco, Voronezh

Ancient windmill, Kizhi Island

Fairy-tale Cathedral of the Transfiguration with its 22 domes and ingenious decorations, Kizhi Island

Visiting Father Frost

Two agencies operate excursions to Votchina, the estate where Father Frost resides in his wooden palace. It's best to go to Votchina through an agency rather than just show up; it's not too expensive, and you'll be sure to catch the wizard when he's ready to receive guests. Besides, they'll provide transportation to the estate, which is 15km from Veliky Ustiug and not particularly easy to find. Both agencies can also arrange accommodation in Votchina if you'd rather stay there than at the single hotel in town. Note that Father Frost is busy travelling during the New Year celebrations and only returns to his palace in March to begin answering children's letters and preparing the next season's gifts.

Ded Moroz (☎ 2 66 73, ☎/fax 2 04 32; w www.dedmoroz.ru; Sovietsky pr 85; 1-/5-day tours R628/1720) is run by young and friendly staff and offers excursions that could include transportation, accommodation, a trip to the post office, a session with Father Frost, and tours of local churches and nature walks.

Travel & Excursions Bureau (☎ 2 45 41, ☎/fax 2 10 10; w www.vologda.ru/~travel; Sovietsky pr 74) has packages and prices similar to Ded Moroz.

Father Frost's Post

You can't pay a visit to Veliky Ustiug without stopping in at the fabulous post office, where boxes and boxes of letters from children all over Russia arrive, are processed and are dutifully answered – it's probably the most efficient post office in the country. And it surely doesn't get the credit it deserves.

One boy named Dima, who lived in the northern Altay region, wrote to say that he couldn't go outside to play because he didn't have a coat, mittens, hat or shoes. The staff at the post office were touched, and went about collecting money to buy the boy some winter clothes. They were able to round up enough funds for everything but the mittens, and so they sent everything else, in a package that said 'From Father Frost'.

Soon, they received another letter from little Dima. It said, 'Thank you for the gifts, Father Frost, but I didn't receive the mittens. They probably stole them at the post office'.

★★★★★★★★★★★★★★★★★★★★

Other Things to See & Do

Apart from the obligatory trip to Votchina, there are definitely sights worth visiting in the town itself.

The **State Historical Art & Architecture Museum** (ul Naberezhnaya; admission R30; open 9am-5pm Wed-Sun) is truly excellent for such a small town. Yury Ivanov, the resident guide, is an amusing and extremely knowledgeable fellow, but you'll need to find an interpreter if you don't speak Russian.

Ascension Church, next to and part of the museum, was built between 1648 and 1649 and is the town's oldest building. The iconostasis is glorious, and explanations in Russian can be arranged. Outside, along the wall facing the river, is a **wishing stone** purported to grant your wish if you sit on it, clear your mind, and look at the huge fresco on the church across the river.

Places to Stay & Eat

Apart from arranging food and accommodation through one of the travel agencies, you can stay at the town's hotel.

Sukhona (☎ 2 25 52; per Krasnaya 12; rooms with/without shower R510/360, luxes R800) has a good and inexpensive **restaurant** (mains R20-40; open 7am-10am, 11am-4pm & 5pm-midnight).

Across the street is a very inexpensive **stolovaya**.

Around the corner is the excellent, lushly decorated **Restoran Na Uspenskoi** (Sovietsky pr 72; open noon-3.30pm & 5pm-2am), next door to which is **Russkoye Kukhnya**, an amazing bakery with fresh pastries.

You can book accommodation in Votchina through one of the travel agents listed earlier.

Shopping

Souvenirs in Veliky Ustiug are unique, lovely and affordable. Silverwork is a speciality, and shops sell everything from rings to silverware collections. Neil metalwork on silver is especially popular. Carved birch crafts are also a local speciality. **Severnaya Churn**, on ulitsa Uspenskaya, is the best place to go for nielloware. There is also a souvenir shop next to the Sukhona hotel.

Getting There & Away

Air Kotlas, about an hour away from Veliky Ustiug, has an airport with flights to/from

Identifying Your Giftgiver

There's no doubt about it – Santa Claus and Father Frost have an awful lot in common. So if you find an old man with a white beard in a red suit leaving a gift under your tree this December, and you're not sure who to send the thank-you card to, try using the following table.

	Father Frost	Santa Claus
Religion	pagan	Christian
Build	tall and mighty	short and fat
Personality	gruff but fair	jolly and kind
Crunch time	New Year's Eve	Christmas Eve
Occupation	wizard	toymaker
Hobby	freezing rivers & lakes	smoking a pipe by the fire
Transport	troika pulled by horses	sleigh pulled by flying reindeer
Vision	20/20	far-sighted; requires glasses
Accessories	carries a big stick	carries a big sack
Assistant(s)	Snegurochka (the snow maiden)	many elves
Marital status	bachelor	happily married to Mrs Claus

★★

Moscow (R3000, two hours, Wednesday and Friday), St Petersburg (R2750, three hours, Wednesday) and Arkhangelsk (R1350, 1–1½ hours, Monday, Wednesday and Friday). There is a daily train and several buses to Kotlas from Veliky Ustiug.

Train Most trains stop in nearby Jahidra, from where you can catch a bus to Veliky Ustiug. The Veliky Ustiug train station is only open from 8am to 4pm.

Daily trains leave from Vologda (R252, 13 hours) and have *platskartny* seats only. There are infrequent trains from Arkhangelsk (*plats/kupe* R277/455, 36 hours), daily trains from St Petersburg via Vologda (R374/625, 23 hours), several daily trains from Moscow

(R350/582, 24 hours), and a long, long train ride from Murmansk (R608/1006, 72 hours), which leaves on even dates.

Bus & Boat Daily buses from Vologda to Veliky Ustiug (12 hours) leave at 9am. Summertime riverboats from Vologda are planned for the future, so if you're interested check with a travel agent.

Car & Motorcycle By car, the best route is from Vologda to Totma, where the road branches into a long road (which is in decent condition) and a short road (which is in worse condition) along the Sukhona River. The drive is long; count on at least one overnight stay somewhere.

Volga Region Поволжье

The Volga region (*Povolzhye*, literally 'Along the Volga River') is the heartland of Russia. Mother Volga', the majestic river that dominates the region, is one of the nation's most enduring and endearing symbols. The cultural legacies of Russian merchants, Tatar tribes and German colonists are displayed in the towns along the river banks. The Volga was home to Russia's most infamous rebels and revolutionaries, and the site of WWII's fiercest battle.

The river is immortalised in the Song of the Volga Boatmen: 'Mighty stream so deep and wide. Volga, Volga our pride.' Today its lush environs attract boaters, bathers, hikers, birders and fishermen.

HISTORY
The Volga is the central artery of Russia's vast river network. Since ancient times, it has supported agricultural settlements and served as a main link in transcontinental commerce. More than a thousand years ago, the Vikings plied its waters, establishing a trade route between Baghdad and the Baltic.

Medieval Volga
In the Middle Ages, the Lower Volga was dominated by the realm of the Khazars, notable among the Turkic tribes for religious tolerance. The Khazar capital stood at Itil (present-day Astrakhan).

The Middle Volga was the domain of another Turkic tribe, the Bulgars. Descendants of the Huns and distant relatives of the Balkan Bulgarians, they migrated eastwards, mixed with local tribes and adopted Islam in the 10th century. Their feudal state was northeastern Europe's most advanced economic and cultural centre at that time.

The forests of the Upper Volga were originally settled by Ugro-Finnic tribes, who were eventually displaced by the migrating Slavs. The river was also a vital conduit in the lucrative fur trade for Novgorod's merchants. These peoples competed with one another for military and commercial advantage along the river.

The Golden Horde
In the 13th century, the entire Volga region was conquered by the heirs of Jenghis Khan,

Highlights

- Walk in the footsteps of Vladimir Lenin in Ulyanovsk, Yuri Gagarin in Saratov and Andrey Sakharov in Nizhny Novgorod
- Discover the Tatar spirit in the mosques and marketplaces of ancient Kazan
- Cruise down the river to Shiryaeva, Ilya Repin's quintessential Volga village
- Be awestruck and inspired at the Mamaev Kurgan memorial to the Battle of Stalingrad
- Follow flocks of waterfowl and feast on fresh fish among the marshy rivers of the Volga Delta

Nizhny Novgorod p392 ●
● Kazan p396
● Ulyanovsk p398
● Samara p400
● Saratov p405
Volgograd p407
Astrakhan p409 ●

the Mongol-led Golden Horde, who made Sarai (near present-day Volgograd) their capital. For the next 200 years, the Volga's Slavic and Turkic communities paid tribute and swore allegiance to the great Khan, or suffered his wrath. Challenged by Tamerlane's marauder armies in the south and upstart Muscovite princes in the north, the Golden Horde eventually fragmented into separate Khanates: Kazan, Astrakhan, Crimea and Sibir. In the 1550s Ivan the Terrible razed Kazan and Astrakhan, and claimed the Middle and Lower Volga for Muscovy, the capital of the new Russian state.

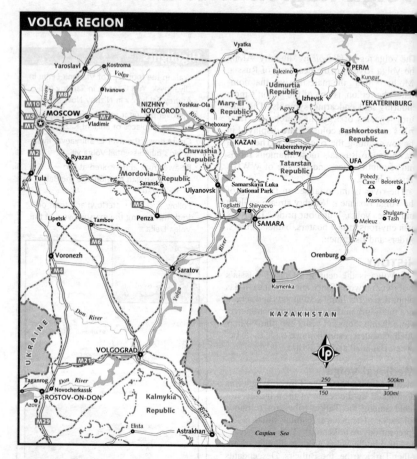

VOLGA REGION

Cossacks

While the river trade was a rich source of income for Muscovy, it also supported the gainful bandit and smuggling ventures. Hostile steppe tribes continued to harass Russian traders and settlers and the region remained an untamed frontier for many years.

In response, the tsar ordered the construction of fortified outposts at strategic points along the river. Serfs, paupers and dropouts fled to the region, thereafter organising semi-autonomous Cossack communities, or 'hosts'. The Cossacks elected their own atamans (leaders) and pledged their swords in service to tsar and Church.

The Cossacks were more like commissioned adventurers than a typical military unit: the name derives from a Turkic word, '*kazakh*', meaning 'freebooter'. The Cossacks not only defended the frontier for the tsar, but also operated their own protection rackets, plundered local natives, and raided Russia's southern neighbours. Their misdeeds would often be placated by gifts of loot or land.

Sabre-rattling Cossacks conducted large-scale peasant uprisings. In 1670 Stepan Razin led a 7000-strong army of the disaffected in a Robin Hood–style campaign, which moved up the Lower Volga before meeting defeat at Simbirsk. In 1773 Emelian Pugachev declared himself tsar and led an even larger contingent of Cossacks and runaway serfs on a riotous march through the Middle Volga region. The bloody revolt was forever romanticised by Pushkin in his novel *The Captain's Daughter*.

Germans in the Volga Region

Astounded by the scale of Pugachev's rebellion, Catherine the Great responded with a plan for economic development in the Volga region, particularly the cultivation of the fertile southern river basin. Russia's peasants, however, were bound to noble estates and had limited opportunity for migration. Instead, Catherine, in 1763, issued an invitation to Germany's peasants to colonise the region.

Eager to escape economic hardship and religious persecution, German Lutherans readily relocated to special settlements along the Volga, with the largest concentration near Saratov. At the end of the 18th century, roughly 50,000 German colonists had moved to the Volga region: by end of the 19th century, the population had reached over 1.5 million ethnic Germans.

In the 1920s a German autonomous republic was established along the Lower Volga. Hitler's blitzkrieg across the Soviet Union's western border in 1941 prompted a vengeful wave of persecution against the Volga Germans, who were collectively branded 'enemies of the state': the German autonomous republic was eliminated, residents were forced into exile and their citizenship revoked. After Stalin's death, nearly a million survivors were liberated from Siberian labour camps, but not allowed to return to their old villages.

Soviet Development

The Soviet state harnessed the mighty Volga for its ambitious development plans. Eight complexes of dams, reservoirs and hydroelectric stations were constructed between the 1930s and 1960s. A network of canals connected Russia's heartland to Moscow, the Baltic Sea and the Black Sea. Smoke-stacked factories, sulphurous petrochemical plants, sprawling collective farms and secret military complexes sprang up along its shores. Provincial trading towns, such as Nizhny Novgorod and Samara, grew into urban industrial centres and became closed off to outsiders. Today the river hosts almost 1000 ports and over 500 industrial docks.

The Volga provided a desperately needed supply line in the war effort against Nazi Germany. The river continues to convey as much as two-thirds of all Russia's overland cargo freight. The Volga Basin supplies one quarter of all Russia's agricultural output and one-fifth of its total fish catch; however, the accumulated effects of Soviet scientific planning inflicted severe harm on the river's fish stocks and posed serious health risks to adjacent communities (see the boxed text 'Roe to Ruin' later in this chapter).

The Volga Today

Although fundamentally transformed by Soviet communism, the Volga has reclaimed some of its historic identity in recent years. Closed cities reopened and river trade resurfaced as military-industrial managers were pushed aside by a new financial-commercial elite. The frontier images of yore reappeared in contemporary guise with organised crime and regional separatists; local khans have revived tribal customs and even the Cossacks have suited up in traditional regalia. Tatarstan, heir to the Kazan Khanate, declared sovereignty and challenged Moscow's authority along the Middle Volga (see Kazan later for more details).

GEOGRAPHY

The Volga's headwaters lie in the Valdai Hills northwest of Moscow. The river flows eastwards to Kazan, from where it bends southwards, making its way unhurriedly to the brackish delta of the Caspian Sea. The Volga is Europe's longest river at 3700km, and has 200 tributaries feeding it along its course, most notably the Kama, Oka and Samara Rivers. Seventy species of fish are found in Volga waters.

A series of hydroelectric dams have turned the Upper and Middle Volga into a chain of stagnant reservoirs; the river flows freely only from Volgograd to the Caspian. The Volga delineates a natural topographical divide: the right (western) bank is high and wooded, while the left (eastern) bank is flat and sandy.

PEOPLE

Bisecting the Eurasian continent, the Volga has brought together different peoples and cultures throughout the centuries. Today the region is among Russia's most ethnically mixed: the river almost resembles a chain of ethnic republics, a political legacy of Soviet federalism. After the Russians, the most populous groups are the descendants of the Turkic tribes: the Volga Tatars (6.6 million), Chuvsh (1.8 million) and Bashkirs (1.4 million). The region is also home to the modern

Cruising the Volga

From June to September cruise ships ply the Volga River from Moscow to Astrakhan. Journey times vary depending on weather and currents and prices vary according to class of service. Average times, distances and prices are listed in the table below.

route	time (hours)	distance (km)	average price (roubles)
Moscow–Nizhny Novgorod	65	860	1800
Nizhny Novgorod–Kazan	20	408	1050
Kazan–Ulyanovsk	10	228	760
Ulyanovsk–Samara	12	216	760
Samara–Saratov	24	429	1100
Saratov–Volgograd	18	385	1050
Volgograd–Astrakhan	20	494	1189

Here is an excerpt from one reader's account of his journey:

The ship was a Russian ship intended for Russians: all signs were Russian only and virtually nobody spoke English. The ship was in poor condition; it was probably not in danger of sinking but it clearly needed major renovations. The toilets on our deck were foul, and later on each day became really objectionable.

The ship headed north from Moscow, through the system of canals that joined a series of lakes and drained marshes, and eventually into the Volga above the reservoir. Thousands of people were swimming on sandy beaches; private yachts, motor boats and jet skis abounded on the lakes; and numerous lakeside dachas dotted the scenery.

On the first night, the sky was bright until 11pm and the scenery gradually changed from city to country. It is astonishing how empty Russia seems once you get outside the big cities.

Fred Thornett, July 2001

If you wish to follow in the wake of the merchants, the Cossacks and Fred Thornett, there are several options.

Capital Shipping Company (☎ 095-458 9163, 458 9624; *Leningradsky pr 1*) operates transit boats (primarily used by Russians for transportation), departing regularly from Moscow's Severny Rechnoy Port (Northern River Station).

Volga Flot (*Volzhskoe Paroxodstvo;* ☎ 8312-31 34 49, fax 30 36 60; **W** *www.volgaflot.com; Rechnoy Vokzal Nizhny Novgorod*) is a Nizhny-based company that also provides transit passenger services; the prices listed earlier in this boxed text are for 'middle class' (1B) quoted by Volga Flot.

Similar to train accommodation, transit ship cabins have two or four bunks, shared toilets and bland, cheap food. Stops along the way are too brief for sightseeing, but if your schedule is flexible, you can certainly purchase tickets for individual segments of your route from river stations at each port of call.

Russian tour companies organise affordable, all-inclusive cruises targeted to Russians (like the one Fred Thornett was on). While accommodation quality varies from ship to ship, the cruises eliminate a lot of hassle and provide an opportunity to call at various ports along the way. **Cruise Company Orthodox** (☎ 095-943 8560, fax 198 1101; **W** *www.cruise.ru; ul Alabyana 5*) is a Russian company also catering to foreigners, with simple variations such as English-speaking staff. Cruises go all the way to Rostov-on-Don, through the locks of the Rostov-Don Canal. Cruise Company Orthodox also has a **Rostov office** (☎ 8632-65 43 64, fax 65 14 86; *ul Bolshaya Sadovaya 87*).

To cruise the Volga in high style, you might consider booking a tour through a Western travel agent. The packages vary, but accommodations are relatively luxurious, and some may provide cultural programs or English-language tour guides. The average price is US$100 per day, including room and board on the ship. **Four Winds Travel** (☎ 630-966 9060; **W** *www.4windstravel.com; 55 South Lucust St, Aurora IL 60506, USA*) offers an 18-day luxury cruise from Moscow to Rostov for US$2800, including air fares from the US.

★★★

descendants of the Ugro-Finnic tribes: the Mordvins (1.2 million) and the Mari (700,000). The Kalmyks of the Lower Volga are of Mongolian origin and practise Buddhism. The Volga Germans remain widely dispersed, although a small enclave still exists near Saratov.

NIZHNY NOVGOROD
НИЖНИЙ НОВГОРОД
☎ 8312 • pop 2 million

On the banks of the mighty Volga, Nizhny Novgorod, Russia's 'third capital', is markedly less cosmopolitan than Moscow and St Petersburg, but has a low-key charm making it a pleasant place to spend a few days. A stroll along the high embankment above the river, or a promenade along the city's central shopping street, demonstrates this provincial capital's appeal.

During Soviet times the city was named Gorky (after the writer Maxim Gorky, who was born here in 1868), and this name is still sometimes used on train timetables.

History
Founded in 1221, Nizhny Novgorod has long been an important trading centre. Barges used to dock on the river and exchange goods; this floating market later became a huge trade fair, the Yarmarka, a tradition that continues to this day. In the 19th century it was said, 'St Petersburg is Russia's head; Moscow its heart; and Nizhny Novgorod, its wallet'.

The presence of many industries connected with the military (submarine construction, for example) meant that Nizhny Novgorod was closed to foreigners for many decades; this is one reason why the late Andrey Sakharov, physicist, dissident and Nobel laureate, was exiled here in the 1980s (see the boxed text 'Andrey Sakharov: Conscience of the Reform Movement' later in this chapter).

Orientation & Information
Nizhny Novgorod lies on the southern bank of the Volga River and is also split by the Oka River. The train station is on the western bank, with the kremlin sitting on the high eastern bank overlooking the Volga. Outside its southern wall, the city's main streets spoke out from ploshchad Minina. From here the pleasant and pedestrian ulitsa Bolshaya Pokrovskaya heads south to ploshchad Gorkogo.

Maps showing local transport routes are widely available. Try **Dom Knigi** (☎ 44 22 73; ploshchad Lenina; open 10am-7pm Mon-Fri, 10am-6pm Sat, 11am-4pm Sun), which also has some English-language books.

Alfa Bank (☎ 30 09 55; ul Semashko 9; open 8am-8pm Mon-Fri) handles cash advances and has an ATM.

Besides the **small post office** (ul Bol Pokrovskaya 7; open 8am-7pm Mon-Sat, 8am-3pm Sun) near the kremlin, the **central post office** on ploshchad Gorkogo is open 24 hours. **Internet Sitek** (☎ 77 58 44; ul Sovetskaya 12; open 24 hrs) is on the 8th floor of Hotel Tsentralnaya.

Kremlin
The mighty walls of the kremlin and its 11 towers date from the 16th century. You may be able to climb up into the ramparts through the Kladovaya Bashnya gate.

Inside, the 17th-century **Cathedral of the Archangel Michael** (Mikhailo-Arkhangelsky sobor; open 9am-2pm) is a functioning church. One of the best views of the city and the Volga is from behind the church, where you will also find an eternal flame and a striking **monument to the heroes of WWII**.

Most of the buildings within the kremlin are government offices. At the northeast end of the grounds, the former governor's house is now home to the impressive **Fine Arts Museum** (Khudozhestvenny muzey; ☎ 39 13 73; admission R40; open 10am-5pm Wed-Mon). Exhibits range from 14th-century icons to 20th-century paintings by artists including Rerikh and Surikov.

Sakharov Museum
A reminder of more repressive times, the **Sakharov Museum** (☎ 66 86 23; pr Gagarina 214; admission R15; open 10am-5pm Sat-Thur) provides a sobering but fascinating view of Andrey Sakharov's life. Located in the actual flat where the physicist lived with his wife Yelena Bonner, the museum documents their lives before and after their exile. To get there catch minibus No 104 or 4 from ploshchad Minina.

Museum of Architecture & Living in the Lower Volga
The name of this museum (☎ 65 15 98; ul Gorbatovskaya 39; admission R50; open 10am-4pm Tues-Sun) is a mouthful, but

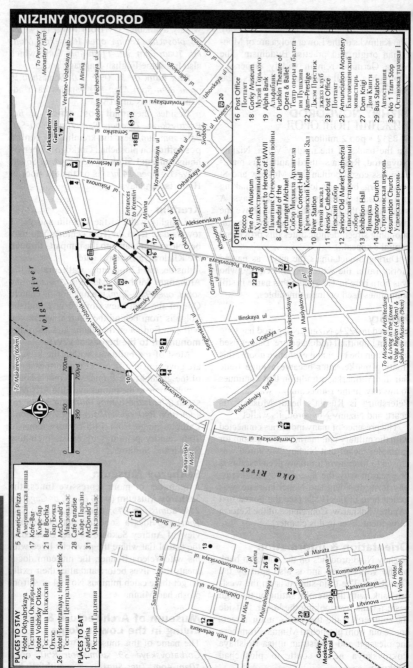

NIZHNY NOVGOROD

PLACES TO STAY
2 Hotel Oktyabrskaya
   Гостиница Октябрьская
4 Hotel Volzhsky Otkos
   Гостиница Волжский
   Откос
26 Hotel Tsentralnaya; Internet Sitek
   Гостиница Центральная

PLACES TO EAT
1 Gardinia
   Ресторан Гардения
5 American Pizza
   Американская пицца
17 Kofe-Bar
   Кофе-бар
21 Bar Bochka
   Бар Бочка
24 McDonald's
   Макдоналдс
28 Cafe Paradise
   Кафе Параdiа
31 McDonald's
   Макдоналдс

OTHER
3 Rocco
6 Fine Arts Museum
   Художественный музей
7 Monument to Heroes of WWII
   Памятник Отечественной войны
8 Cathedral of the
   Archangel Michael
   Собор Михаила Архангела
9 Kremlin Concert Hall
   Кремлёвский Концертный Зал
10 River Station
   Речной вокзал
11 Nevsky Cathedral
   Невский собор
12 Saviour Old Market Cathedral
   Спасский староярмарочный
   собор
13 Exhibition Hall
   Ярмарка
14 Stroganov Church
   Строгановская церковь
15 Assumption Church
   Успенская церковь
16 Post Office
   Почтамт
18 Gorky Museum
   Музей Горького
19 Alpha Bank
   Альфабанк
20 Pushkin Theatre of
   Opera & Ballet
   Театр оперы и балета
   им Пушкина
22 Jam-Prestige
   Джэм Престиж
   джаз клуб
23 Post Office
   Почтамт
25 Annunciation Monastery
   Благовещенский
   монастырь
27 Dom Knigi
   Дом Книги
29 Bus Station
   Автостанция
30 No 1 Tram Stop
   Остановка трамвая 1

pretty well sums up this collection of traditional wooden buildings; only a handful of the 14 structures in this woodland site (a popular spot with locals for swimming in its weedy pond) are open. The highlight is the **Pokrovskaya church** (Pokrovskaya tserkov), a beautiful wooden church dating from 1731.

Gorky Museums

Fans of Maxim Gorky can visit the quaint wooden houses where the writer lived. The best is the **Gorky Museum** (☎ 36 56 29; ul Semashko 19; open 9am-5pm Tues-Wed & Fri-Sun), where he lived during his 30s. **Gorky House** (☎ 34 06 70; Pochtovy sezd 21; open 10am-5pm Thur-Tues) is where he spent his childhood years.

Churches & Monasteries

Nizhny Novgorod has many churches, most of which are nicely restored and functioning. The 17th-century stone **Assumption Church** (Uspenskaya tserkov) is unique in that its design was normally exclusive to wooden churches. The baroque **Stroganov** or **Nativity Church** (Stroganovskaya tserkov) has retained its magnificent stone carvings.

On the west bank of the Oka River is the prominent **Nevsky Cathedral** (Nevsky sobor). The **Saviour Old Market Cathedral** (Spassky Staroyarmarochny sobor) sits behind the **Yarmarka**, the handsomely restored exhibition hall on ploshchad Lenina.

The 13th-century **Annunciation Monastery** (Blagoveshchensky monastyr), above ulitsa Chernigovskaya, and the 17th-century **Pechorsky Monastery** (Pechorsky monastyr), overlooking the Volga, can both be viewed from the outside only.

Places to Stay

Hotel Volzhsky Otkos (☎ 39 19 51, fax 19 48 94; Verkhne-Volzhskaya nab 2a; rooms per person with/without bathroom from R315/210), a Soviet relic, has friendly staff and decent rooms. Nicer rooms overlooking the Volga start at R1050.

Hotel Tsentralnaya (☎ 77 55 00, fax 77 55 66; ul Sovetskaya 12; singles/doubles R700/1000) has helpful staff and a convenient location close to the station; otherwise, the old-style rooms are overpriced.

Hotel Oktyabrskaya (☎ 32 06 70, fax 32 05 50; e oktbr@kis.ru; Verkhne-Volzhskaya nab 9A; singles/doubles with breakfast R1700/

2000) is an acceptable business hotel. It also has cheaper, unrenovated singles/doubles from R700/1500 but they are hard to secure.

Hotel Volna (☎ 96 19 00, fax 96 14 14; w www.volna.nnov.ru; ul Lenina 98; singles/doubles with breakfast from US$120/180), Nizhny's only four-star hotel, offers all the expected facilities. The location, 9km south of the station (but near the end of the metro), is not in its favour.

Places to Eat

Kofe-Bar (☎ 19 29 14; ul Bolshaya Pokrovskaya 6; coffee R30; open 10am-11pm) is a pleasant, trendy place for a coffee or snack.

American Pizza (☎ 39 18 44; Verkhne-Volzhskaya nab 2A; meals R150) offers tasty pizza, salads and beers as well as a view of the Volga.

Gardinia (☎ 19 41 01; Verkhne-Volzhskaya nab; meals R60) is basically a cafeteria, so ordering is as easy as pointing. The Russian food is OK, the river views better.

Bar Bochka (☎ 33 55 61; 14 ul Bolshaya Pokrovskaya; mains around R200) serves excellent Georgian cuisine. The restaurant is hidden behind a convivial bar, where there's often live music.

Café Paradise (☎ 44 52 37; ul Sovetskaya 18; mains from R50; open noon-midnight) is on the west bank near the train station. The place lacks atmosphere but the food is tasty.

McDonald's has a couple of branches, one opposite the station, the other on ploshchad Gorkogo.

Entertainment

Summer evenings in Nizhny are often spent strolling along ulitsa Bolshaya Pokrovskaya or sitting on the terrace above the Alexandrovsky Gardens, a great spot for sunset views and cold beers.

The philharmonic gives concerts in the **Kremlin Concert Hall** (Kremlevsky Kontsertny zal; ☎ 39 08 11), at the west end of the kremlin. The beautiful **Pushkin Theatre of Opera & Ballet** (☎ 35 16 40; ul Belinskogo 59) is also recommended.

Rocco (☎ 36 03 53; ul Minina 10B; admission R120; open 10pm-5am daily) is Nizhny's top nightclub, with dancing, cabaret, laser shows, casino and small bowling alley. **Jam-Prestige** (☎ 33 32 46; Bolshaya Pokrovskaya ul 49A; admission R50) has regular jazz and other musical acts; showtime is at 9pm.

Andrey Sakharov: Conscience of the Reform Movement

Dr Andrey Dmitrievich Sakharov (1921–89) was a leading nuclear physicist who became a human-rights advocate and one of the main figures opposing the Soviet regime from within. He was born in Moscow and followed in his father's footsteps as a physicist. By the age of 32 he was a full member of the Soviet Academy of Sciences, and was one of the two leading scientists involved in developing the Soviet Union's first hydrogen bomb.

In 1961 he landed in official hot water by opposing the Soviet government's intention to violate the Nuclear Test Ban Treaty; he was also vocal in opposing nuclear arms production and human-rights abuse. In 1975 Sakharov was awarded the Nobel Peace Prize but never dared to go and pick it up, fearing the authorities might not let him return to the USSR – once outside the country he would lose the ability to pressure the Communist regime through his dissident activities.

In 1980 Sakharov was exiled to Nizhny Novgorod (then Gorky) after he criticised the Soviet invasion of Afghanistan. His wife, Yelena Bonner, joined him in 1984, by which time he had undertaken several hunger strikes.

Sakharov was released in 1986 by Mikhail Gorbachev, who called him with the news on a phone specially installed for that purpose. He became a member of the Congress of People's Deputies (or Parliament) in 1989, the year it was first established. He continued to criticise the Soviet leadership as a member of the congress, and by the time of his death was widely regarded as the conscience of the reform movement.

Getting There & Away

Air There are daily flights to all three Moscow airports, with prices starting at around US$58. Other daily flights go to Samara, Ufa and Yekaterinburg. Flights go once or twice a week to Baku, Mineralniye Vody, Rostov-on-Don, Saratov, Sochi, St Petersburg, Volgograd and Yerevan. **Lufthansa** (☎ 75 90 85) flies three times a week to/from Frankfurt.

Train Gorky-Moskovsky Vokzal is on the western bank of the Oka River, at ploshchad Revolyutsii. Trains go to all the stops along the Trans-Siberian route, as well as Kazan, Samara, Astrakhan, Nizhny Tagil, Tomsk and Severobaikalsk.

Bus The bus station is across from the train station. There are five daily buses to/from Moscow's Shchyolkovsky bus station (nine hours). Daily buses also go to Vladimir, Ivanovo, Kostroma and Yaroslavl.

Boat The **river station** (☎ 30 36 66) is on Nizhne-Volzhskaya naberezhnaya, below the kremlin. Apart from short trips along the Volga (see Around Nizhny Novgorod later), this is where you can find out about the summer cruises linking Nizhny Novgorod with St Petersburg, Moscow and cities farther down the Volga.

Getting Around

Tram No 1 is convenient, starting from the train station, crossing the Kanavinsky Bridge and climbing the hill to the kremlin. From the train station, cross the street and walk past the kiosks to reach the stop.

There are plans to extend the metro across the river but it's unlikely to happen in the life of this book. Currently you might use it only to get to Hotel Volna.

AROUND NIZHNY NOVGOROD
Makarevo
Макарево

The sleepy village of Makarevo is around 60km east of Nizhny Novgorod along the Volga. The fortified stone walls and church domes of its **Makariev Monastery** (☎ 249-269 67; admission R100; open 9am-5pm) look magnificent on the approach from the river.

The monastery and surrounding village, founded in 1453, thrived on vibrant river trade through the 19th century. The monastery was closed during the Soviet period, but a few nuns returned in 1991 to help restore the churches. Today four churches are working, but only 20 nuns live here. The village of 180 people is made up of rustic wooden cottages, as well as a small **museum** in the old school house. Most locals come here for a day of sunbathing by the river; bring a picnic since there are only a few small shops.

From Nizhny boats to Makarevo (3½ hours) depart in the morning from near the Rechnoy river station and return in the evening.

KAZAN
КАЗАНЬ
☎ 8432 • pop 1.1 million

Famous for its historic kremlin, Kazan has an intriguing atmosphere redolent of Central Asia, particularly around its several mosques. Nearby in the teeming central market, you'll find everything from pineapples to pig heads. Kazan's riverside beaches are fine places to relax, as are the cafés along ulitsa Baumana.

As the capital of Tatarstan, Kazan is the cultural and administrative centre for modern-day Tatars, descendants of a nomadic Turkic tribe that wreaked particular havoc in Russia. Nationalism is strong here – you'll frequently see the Tatar flag with green, white and red stripes, and bilingual signposts on all streets.

History

Kazan, one of Russia's oldest Tatar cities, dates back to around 1005. Capital of the Kazan khanate in the 15th and 16th centuries, it was famously ravaged in 1552 by Ivan the Terrible, who forced the Muslim khan to become Christian. St Basil's Cathedral in Moscow was built to celebrate Kazan's downfall.

The city later flourished as a gateway to Siberia; Leo Tolstoy and Lenin were educated here. During Soviet times, Kazan became the capital of the Tatar Autonomous Republic. In autumn 1990, this oil-rich region (now renamed Tatarstan) declared its autonomy from the rest of Russia, launching several years of political warfare with Moscow. But full independence remains unlikely given that 43% of the population is Russian.

Orientation & Information

Kazan's city centre is flanked in the north by the Kazanka River and in the west by the Volga; the train station is on the east bank of the Volga. The main drag, ulitsa Baumana, is about 500m east of the train station, running from the kremlin in the northwest down to busy ulitsa Tatarstan, which goes to the bus station and river station. There are nice beaches on the north bank of the Kazanka River, which flows into the Volga.

There's a **foreign exchange office** in the lobby of Hotel Tatarstan. **Ak Bars Bank** (☎ 49 35 56; ul Dekabristov 1; open 9am-7pm Mon-Fri, 9am-5pm Sat) cashes travellers cheques. It's five minutes from the train station by trams 14 or 21; get off at the first stop after crossing the causeway.

Besides the main **post and telephone office** (ul Kremlyovskaya 8; open 7am-9pm), another convenient **telephone office** (cnr uls Pushkina & Profsoyuznaya) has Internet facilities. You can also check your email for R30 an hour at the **Komputerny Salon** (☎ 92 14 59; ul Baumana; open 24hrs).

For local excursions or assistance with hotel reservations, contact **Volga Travel Plus** (Volzhskie Puteshestvie Plus; ☎ 99 41 75; w www.volga-travel.ru; ul Dostoevskogo 74).

Kremlin

Declared a Unesco World Heritage site in 2000, Kazan's striking kremlin is pleasant to stroll around, although the buildings were not open to visitors at the time of research. Some of the white limestone walls date from the 16th and 17th centuries.

The **Annunciation Cathedral** (Blagoveshchensky sobor) was designed by the same architect responsible for St Basil's Cathedral in Moscow. Nearby, the slightly leaning 59m-high **Syuyumbike Tower** is named after a long-suffering princess who was married to three successive khans.

Ivan the Terrible launched his siege of Kazan as a result of Syuyumbike's refusal to marry him – according to legend. So to save her city, the princess agreed to marry the tsar, but only if he could build a tower higher than any other mosque in Kazan in a week. Unfortunately for Syuyumbike, the tower was completed, driving her to jump to her death from its upper terrace shortly thereafter.

Today, the tower competes with a rival landmark inside the kremlin. The enormous **Kul Sharif mosque** is being constructed on the site of a mosque by the same name, which was burnt and destroyed after Ivan the Terrible captured the city in 1552.

Other Things to See & Do

Outside the kremlin's main entrance is the **Museum of the Republic of Tatarstan** (☎ 92 89 84; ul Kremlyovskaya 2; admission R40; open 10am-5pm Tues-Sun), in an ornate building dating from 1770. The exhibition of Tatar treasures is worth a look.

Among Kazan's several Russian Orthodox churches, the most attractive is the **SS Peter**

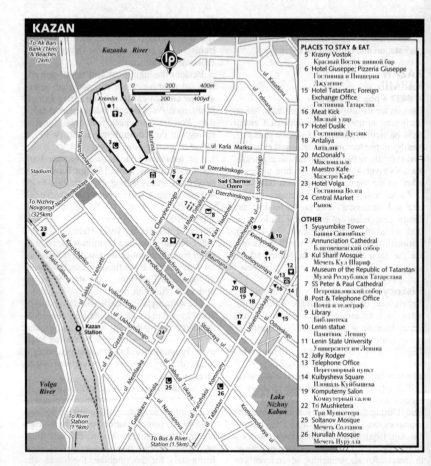

KAZAN

To Ak Bars Bank (1km) & Beaches (2km)

Kazanka River

Kremlin

Yarmaro-chnaya ul

ul Baturina

ul Telmana

ul Kasatkina

ul Karla Marksa

Stadium

To Nizhny Novgorod (325km)

ul Novokremlevskaya ul

ul Chernyshevskogo

ul Dzerzhinskogo

Sad Chernoe Ozero

ul Dzerzhinskogo

ul Lobachevskogo

ul Musy Dzhalilya

ul Kavi Nadzhmi

Kremlyovskaya ul

ul Astronomicheskaya

ul Profsoyuznaya

ul Korotchenko

ul Said-Galeeva

Vaisetti

ul Pravobulachnaya

ul Levobulachnaya

ul Kirova

ul Baumana

ul Sakko i Van;cetti

ul Volodarskogo

ul Ukhtomskogo

Kazan Station

ul Tazi Gizzata

ul Merhlauka

ul Gabdull Tukaya

ul Galiaskara Kamala

ul Narimanova

ul Tatarstan

ul Parizhsko kommuny

ul Universitetskaya

ul Stolovaya ul

ul Ostrovskogo

ul Komsomolskaya

Lake Nizhny Kaban

To River Station (1.5km)

To Bus & River Station (1.5km)

Volga River

PLACES TO STAY & EAT
5 Krasny Vostok
    Красный Восток пивной бар
6 Hotel Giuseppe; Pizzeria Giuseppe
    Гостиница и Пиццерия Джузеппе
15 Hotel Tatarstan; Foreign
    Exchange Office
    Гостиница Татарстан
16 Meat Kick
    Мясный удар
17 Hotel Duslik
    Гостиница Дуслик
18 Antaliya
    Анталия
20 McDonald's
    Макдональдс
21 Maestro Kafe
    Маэстро Кафе
23 Hotel Volga
    Гостиница Волга
24 Central Market
    Рынок

OTHER
1 Syuyumbike Tower
    Башня Сююмбике
2 Annunciation Cathedral
    Благовещенский собор
3 Kul Sharif Mosque
    Мечеть Кул Шариф
4 Museum of the Republic of Tatarstan
    Музей Республики Татарстана
7 SS Peter & Paul Cathedral
    Петропавловский собор
8 Post & Telephone Office
    Почта и телеграф
9 Library
    Библиотека
10 Lenin statue
    Памятник Ленину
11 Lenin State University
    Университет им Ленина
12 Jolly Rodger
13 Telephone Office
    Переговорный пункт
14 Kuibysheva Square
    Площадь Куйбышева
19 Komputerny Salon
    Компьютерный салон
22 Tri Mushketera
    Три Мушкетера
25 Soltanov Mosque
    Мечеть Солтанов
26 Nurullah Mosque
    Мечеть Нурулла

& **Paul Cathedral** (Petropavlovsky Sobor; ul Musy Dzhalilya 21; open 1pm-3pm daily). Built between 1723 and 1726, this baroque cathedral, with its heavily decorated facade and soaring iconstasis, commemorates Tsar Peter I's visit to the city in 1722.

At the foot of ulitsa Kremlyovskaya, you can't miss the overbearing classical facade of the main building of **Lenin State University** (Gosudarstvenny Universitet imeni Lenina). Across the street, the statue of a young Lenin looks like he's on his way to class. However, the plaques don't tell us that he was actually expelled from the university for revolutionary activity and questionable ties. The **university library** (cnr uls Astronomicheskaya & Kremlyovskaya) has an exquisite decorated exterior.

Many of the mosques are clustered in the rather dumpy southwest corner of town. Near the central market is the **Soltanov mosque** (ul Gabdull Tukaya 14), dating from 1867, and the **Nurullah Mosque** (ul Kirova 74), which has been rebuilt several times since 1849.

Places to Stay

Visa registration is a tricky business in Tatarstan, and cheaper hotels may be hesitant to accept foreign guests, especially if staying more than two nights. If you are planning a longer stay, you may want to make arrangements through a local travel agent.

Hotel Volga (☎ 31 64 58, fax 92 14 69; ul Said-Galieva 1A; singles/doubles R300/450) is the best of the cheapies. This clean hotel is closest to the train station (so suffers from

VOLGA REGION

traffic and train noise), but the rooms are acceptable enough for a night or so.

Hotel Tatarstan (☎ 38 83 79, fax 38 85 68; ul Pushkina 4; singles/doubles R550/900) is a hideous, concrete-slab hotel in a good location. Take tram No 2 from the train station.

Hotel Duslik (☎ 92 33 20, fax 92 35 92; ul Pravobulachnaya 49; singles/doubles from R300/600) is smaller and friendlier, despite the stark lobby. The nicely renovated doubles are worth the price.

Hotel Giuseppe (☎ 92 69 34, fax 92 79 15; ul Kremlyovskaya 15/25; singles/doubles from US$65/85) is hidden inside the restaurant of the same name. Rooms are plush and good value if you are willing to spend the money. Book in advance.

Places to Eat

The colourful, sprawling **central market** (ul Mezhlauka) is good for stocking up on snacks or just for browsing.

Maestro Kafe (☎ 92 13 38; ul Baumana 47; breakfast R50; open 24hrs), specialising in *bliny* and coffees, is a great place for breakfast or a late-night snack.

Antaliya (☎ 38 38 03; ul Baumana 74; mains R100-150; open 10am-10pm daily) is popular for Turkish treats, including *shaurma* and Efes beer. Food is plentiful and tasty.

Ironically, **Meat Kick** (☎ 92 93 32; ul Profsoyuznaya 9; mains R250, salad bar R100) also provides a rare chance to get your fill of veggies. Besides the highly sought-after salad bar, this place offers average Western-style steakhouse fare.

Pizzeria Giuseppe (☎ 32 69 34; ul Kremlyovskaya 15; pizza R30) is a lively place for pizza and pastas. Members of the local professional basketball team are known to frequent this place (they must be getting their vitamins because they sure are tall).

Krasny Vostok (☎ 92 91 29; ul Kremlyovskaya 11; 9am-9pm daily) is what's known as a 'beer bar', serving up local brew and not much else. Unless you want beer for breakfast the hours aren't convenient, although it's a colourful place for an afternoon break.

Need we mention that **McDonald's** (ul Baumana 70A) is one of the city's most popular pit stops?

Entertainment

Tri Mushketera (☎ 92 37 11; ul Baumana 42/9; mains around R100-200; lunch 11am-3pm, dinner 7pm-3am) has a menu in English and Russian, but the main attractions at this stylish basement club are the pool tables, dance floor and live music.

Jolly Rodger (☎ 36 63 43; ul Pushkina 15) has an excellent jazz band playing nightly, but we can't make any promises about the badly translated menu items, such as 'chicken chest in woodoo style'.

Getting There & Away

Air Tickets for flights to Moscow's Domodedovo airport (1½ hours, twice daily) and St Petersburg (3¾ hours, three weekly) can be purchased in the long-distance ticket office at the train station. Lufthansa has twice-weekly flights to/from Frankfurt.

Train The beautifully restored original train station, an attraction in itself, is only a waiting room. Just north, the tatty 1960s building handles suburban tickets. Farther north, long-distance tickets are sold in a new building that's sleek inside and out. If the ground-floor ticket counters are busy, try the 2nd floor. Frequent trains link Kazan to Moscow (15 hours), Nizhny Novgorod and Yekaterinburg. Every second day, trains going to Perm travel along a winding, scenic route through the mountains.

Bus Buses go five times a day to Ulyanovsk (five hours), twice daily to Nizhny Novgorod (seven hours), and once to Samara (10 hours). The **long-distance bus station** (☎ 93 04 00) is at the intersection of ulitsas Tatarstan and Portovaya (take tram No 7 from the train station).

Boat The river station for cruises along the Volga is at the end of ulitsa Tatarstan.

Getting Around

A bus to the airport leaves every hour from 4am to 10.30pm; get on at the stop across from the train station. Tram No 7 links the train and river stations. Tram No 2 goes from the station to the bottom of ulitsa Baumana near Hotel Tatarstan.

ULYANOVSK
УЛЬЯНОВСК
☎ 84222 • pop 650,000

Founded as Simbirsk in the 17th century, Ulyanovsk is now a tourist stop for only one

VOLGA REGION

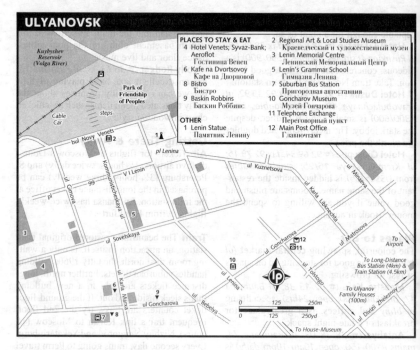

ULYANOVSK

PLACES TO STAY & EAT
4 Hotel Venets; Svyaz-Bank; Aeroflot
  Гостиница Венец
6 Kafe na Dvortsovoy
  Кафе на Дворцовой
8 Bistro
  Бистро
9 Baskin Robbins
  Баскин Роббинс

OTHER
1 Lenin Statue
  Памятник Ленину
2 Regional Art & Local Studies Museum
  Краеведческий и художественный музеи
3 Lenin Memorial Centre
  Ленинский Мемориальный Центр
5 Lenin's Grammar School
  Гимназия Ленина
7 Suburban Bus Station
  Пригородная автостанция
10 Goncharov Museum
  Музей Гончарова
11 Telephone Exchange
  Переговорный пункт
12 Main Post Office
  Главпочтамт

reason: it's the birthplace and boyhood home of Lenin (born Vladimir Ilych Ulyanov).

Initially a fortified town, Simbirsk was Moscow's border guard post and a trade centre. During the 18th century it earned the nickname 'Noble's Nest', as Russia's rich used to retire here for their holidays.

Despite taking its new name upon Lenin's death, the city stayed a backwater until the centenary of his birth in 1970. Then, in a Brezhnevian orgy of development, the city centre became a 'memorial zone', with the construction of a vast museum complex and yawning plaza, and the restoration of an entire neighbourhood, including no less than seven Ulyanov family houses. The city itself is bland, but the quiet, tree-lined streets and brightly painted wooden houses of the restored area hark back to late-19th-century provincial Russia.

Orientation & Information

The main memorial zone occupies the high Volga banks from ploshchad Lenina to the giant Lenin Memorial Centre. Two blocks east is ulitsa Goncharova, the shopping district. The restored neighbourhood is farther east, occupying ulitsa Tolstogo and ulitsa Lenina (of course).

Svyaz-Bank (☎ 39 43 85; ul Sovetskaya 19; open 9am-1pm, 2pm-4pm Mon-Fri) has a foreign-exchange office in Hotel Venets' lobby.

The **main post office** is on the corner of ulitsas Tolstogo and Goncharova and the spiffy **telephone exchange** (open 8am-8.30pm daily) is just around the corner.

Lenin Memorial Centre & Around

The sprawling Memorial Centre is built around two Ulyanov family houses. The **Lenin Flat-Museum** (☎ 39 49 70; open 9am-4.45pm Sun-Wed & Fri) has the expected collection of personal items in the flat where the Ulyanovs lived for several years. The house where Lenin was born is now a **Museum of Folk Art** (☎ 39 49 75; open 9am-5pm Sat-Thur), with a small collection of local paintings and crafts. The gigantic, cement **Historical Cultural Centre** (Istorik-Kulturny Tsentr; ☎ 39 49 04; open 10am-6pm Tues-Sun) contains another museum; enter from ploshchad 99 VI Lenin. Upstairs are a zillion Lenin portraits, dioramas of old Simbirsk and glossy depictions of the revolution.

Down the riverbanks behind the centre is the **Park of Friendship of the Peoples** built by the Soviet republics in 1970. Now weedy and crumbling, it is rich in unintended symbolism. Above, a sometimes-functioning cable car descends to the river.

Just off ploshchad Lenina is the **Regional Art and Local Studies Museum** (☎ *31 37 84; bul Novy Venets 3; art/regional R20/15; open 10am-6pm Tues-Sun*). At the southern end of ulitsa Kommunisticheskaya is **Lenin's grammar school** (*ul Sovetskaya 18*). When young Vlad finished school (with a gold medal, of course), his report card said he was 'highly capable, hard-working and painstaking...a top scholar in all forms'.

Ulitsa Lenina and Around

In 1875 the Ulyanov family moved to Moskovskaya St (now ulitsa Lenina), at the time a rather prestigious street with a cobbled roadway and wooden pavements. These have since been updated, but the leafy trees and cosy wooden houses still evoke the atmosphere of the last century.

The pleasant ulitsa Lenina and neighbouring ulitsa Tolstogo contain four more houses where the Ulyanovs resided (two of which are now museums). The too-perfect **house-museum** (☎ *31 22 22; ul Lenina 68; open 9am-4.30pm Wed-Mon*) is worth a visit for its detailed look at upper-middle-class life of that time. Other buildings from the era include the old Simbirsk police and fire stations (Nos 43 & 47). For a walking tour, pick up the brochure *The Lenin Memorial Complex in Ulyanovsk*, available in English at the Historical Cultural Centre.

For a break from the Lenin idolatry, you might also peek in the **Goncharov Museum** (*ul Lenina 134; open 10am-6pm Tues-Sun*) in the two-storey house where the writer grew up. Goncharov's most famous work is *Oblomov*, the story of a wealthy nobleman who spent most of his life in bed.

Places to Stay & Eat

Hotel Venets (☎ *39 45 76; ul Sovetskaya 15; singles/doubles from R450/800*) is a towering place opposite the Big Hall with standard Soviet fare. Lenin tourism is not a big drawcard; even on Lenin's birthday rooms were available without a reservation.

Kafe na Dvortsovoy (☎ *31 25 51; ul Karla Marxa 9; meals R100; open 11am-11pm daily*) is one of many cafés in the area with a full menu of Russian standards.

Bistro (☎ *31 86 34; meals R50; open 9am-9pm daily*) is a sparkling Russian fast-food place next to the suburban bus station. A well-stocked **produkty** (food store) is next door.

Lenin might be rolling over in his mausoleum with the arrival in Ulyanovsk of **Baskin Robbins** (☎ *31 23 56; ul Goncharova 30; open 10am-11pm daily*), but only because he never got to try cookies and cream.

Getting There & Away

Flights go daily to/from Moscow (Domodedovo); there's an **Aeroflot office** (☎ *39 47 50; ul Sovetskaya 15; open 8am-noon & 1pm-4pm Mon-Sat*) in the lobby of Hotel Venets.

Frequent buses make the journey to Kazan and Samara. Trains go to Moscow (15 hours), Kazan (six hours), Ufa (15 hours), Saratov (11 hours), Samara (five hours) and Volgograd (15 hours).

Getting Around

For the airport, take bus No 6 from the stop on ulitsa Goncharova behind Hotel Venets. Ulyanovsk-Tsentralnaya train station is 4.5km from the centre by bus Nos 1, 2 or 117, or tram No 4. The long-distance bus station is 4km from the centre, served by bus Nos 9 and 20 from the corner of ulitsa Karla Marxa and ulitsa Goncharova.

To get to the river station, take tram No 4 from Hotel Venets, then walk down a lane to the Kuibyshev Reservoir.

SAMARA
САМАРА

☎ 8462 • pop 1.2 million

On a summer day, Samara's riverbanks are packed with bathing beauties, Rollerbladers and beer drinkers. The lazy Volga is indeed inviting on a hot day, and Samara is the place to jump in. If you're not a beachcomber, Samara has a few good museums and also serves as the base for excursions into the Samara Luka, the nearby forest preserve.

History

Samara grew up where the Volga meets the Samara River, at a particularly sharp bend across from the Zhiguli Hills. The site provided a valuable vantage point for monitoring river activity; in 1568 a fortress was constructed here to guard the tsar's recently

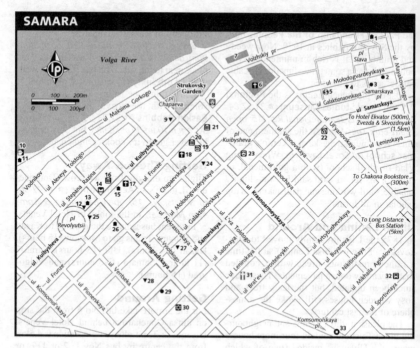

SAMARA

acquired territorial possessions. In 1606 a customs house was built. This enabled the tsar to take a cut of the profitable river trade.

In 1670 Stepan Razin's rebel band came through, pausing to torch the town and drown the military governor. A hundred years later, Pugachev's peasant army also paid a call on Samara. The military governor, apparently a student of history, thought it best to flee on that occasion, leaving the town to the whims of the angry throng.

The Russian Civil War began in Samara, when a unit of Czechoslovak prisoners of war commandeered their train and seized control of the city. They were quickly joined by a contingent of old regime officers, who formed the restorationist White Army.

The name of the city and province was changed in 1935 to Kuibyshev, in honour of a local Bolshevik hero who made it big in Moscow. In WWII, Kuibyshev became the 'second capital', housing much of the relocated central government. Industry developed along the river, oil was discovered in the province and the city was closed. With the fall of Soviet communism, the city was reopened and its original name restored.

Orientation & Information

The centre of Samara is on the left bank of the Volga at its junction with the Samara River. The main street, ulitsa Kuibysheva, runs from ploshchad Revolyutsii in the west (a few blocks south of the river station), then changes name to Volzhsky prospekt as it continues east along the Volga.

The convenient **post office** *(ul Kuibysheva 82; open 8am-8pm Mon-Fri, 9am-6pm Sat & Sun)* has a 24-hour telephone centre. **Svyaz-Service** *(☎ 33 38 65, fax 32 51 66; e pkp@ mail.samtel.ru; ul Krasnoarmeyskaya 17; open 8am-9pm daily)* has a few computers with Internet access. There are better facilities at **Vizit Internet Centre** *(☎ 70 66 71; ul Samarskaya 199; open 9am-10pm daily)*.

There's an ATM at **Alfa Bank** *(☎ 42 06 24; ul Molodogvardeyskaya 151; open noon-8.30pm Tues-Fri, noon-7.30pm Sat)*.

Samara Intour *(☎ 79 20 40, fax 32 60 62; w www.samaraintour.ru; ul Samarskaya 51/ 53)* arranges city tours, river cruises and excursions in the region, including rafting trips in the Samarskaya Luka.

Packed with books and maps, **Chakona** *(☎ 42 96 22; w www.chaconne.ru; ul Chkalova*

SAMARA

PLACES TO STAY
1 Volga Hotel
  Гостиница Волга
11 Hotel Rossiya
  Гостиница Россия
13 Zhiguli Hotel
  Гостиница Жигули -
  филиал
15 Zhiguli Hotel
  Гостиница Жигули
26 National Hotel
  Гостиница Националь

PLACES TO EAT
4 Papa Vito
  Папа Вито
9 U Palycha
  У Палыча
12 Dzhin Dzhu
  Джин Джу
24 Malenkoe Kafe
  Маленькое Кафе
25 Zhili Byli
  Жили были
27 La Cucaracha
  Ла Кукарача

28 Troitsky Market
  Троицкий рынок

OTHER
2 Avia Kassa
  Авиационная касса
3 Gallery Maria
  Мария галерея
5 Alfa Bank
  Альфабанк
6 Iversky Women's Monastery
  Иверский женский
  монастырь
7 Zhiguli Brewery
  Жигулёвское пиво
8 Drama Theatre
  Драматический театр
10 River Station
  Речной вокзал
14 Post Office & Telephone
  Centre
  Почтамт и переговорный
  пункт
16 Samara Art Museum
  Художественный музей
  Самары

17 Lutheran Church
  КирХах
18 Catholic Church
  Костёл
19 Svyaz-Service
  Связь-сервис
20 Alabina Museum
  Музей Алабина
21 Stalin's Bunker
  Бункер Сталина
22 Vizit Internet Centre
  Визит интернет центр
23 Opera & Ballet Theatre
  Театр оперы и балета
29 Samara Intour
  Самара Интур
30 Synagogue
  Синагога
31 Pokrovsky Cathedral
  Покровский собор
32 Suburban Bus Station
  Пригородный автовокзал
33 Train Station; Hotel
  Transit
  Вокзал; Гостиница
  Транзит

100; open 9am-7pm daily) is often packed
with people.

Along the Naberezhnaya
The Volga River is banked by a wide swathe
of lush parks and the city's main attraction:
sandy beaches. Swimming, sunbathing or
simply strolling along the naberezhnaya are
Samara's favourite pastimes.

Ploshchad Slava is a memorial to Samara's role in WWII. The shiny 53m-high
worker is holding a pair of wings, symbolic
of the city's aviation-related contributions:
local factories produced the IL-2, known as
the 'flying tank' during WWII.

The **Iversky Women's Monastery** (Iversky Zhensky monastyr), founded in 1850,
was once home to 360 nuns, mostly daughters of local merchant families.

Walk through **Strukovsky Garden** and up
the steps to Teatralnaya ploshchad, with
its striking monument to Bolshevik hero
Vasily Chapaev, and the ornate 1888 **Drama
Theatre**.

A slow walk from one end of the
naberezhnaya the other takes a few hours,
longer if you stop for a cold drink at one of
the highly recommended *letny kafe* (summer
café). Even better, head to the eastern side of

the **Zhiguli Brewery** and fill your bottle with
fresh local beer for R13 per litre.

Museums
Stalin's Bunker (☎ 33 35 71; *ul Frunze 167;
open 11am-1pm & 2pm-3pm Mon-Fri)*, built
nine storeys below the Academy of Culture
and Art, never actually served its intended purpose, as Stalin decided to stay in Moscow to
direct events. The secret hideaway is nonetheless fascinating. Only guided groups can visit,
so call in advance to make arrangements.

The **Alabin Museum** (☎ 33 03 20; *ul
Frunze 142; open 10am-5pm Tues-Sun)* has
exhibits on regional palaeontology and archaeology, including dinosaur fossils found
in the Zhiguli Hills.

The **Samara Art Museum** (☎ 33 46 50; *ul
Kuibysheva 92; open 10am-6pm Wed-Mon)*
exhibits mainly Russian art, including works
by artists who came to the region to paint.
Look for *Boyarishina*, gifted by Surikov to a
local doctor who treated him when he fell ill.
The museum also holds an impressive collection of over 100 avant garde paintings.

Churches & Synagogues
The **Pokrovsky Cathedral** (*ul Leninskaya
75A)*, built in 1860, was once resplendent in

gold, marble and artistry. Apparently these riches proved their value during the 1920s famine, when they were sold to Finland for 32 wagons of bread for Samaran residents to eat.

After the suppression of Polish uprisings in the Russian empire in 1830, a small group of Polish exiles settled in Samara. In 1902 this community built the Gothic **Catholic Church** (Kostyol; ul Frunze 157).

Reminiscent of a medieval German basilica, the **Lutheran Church** (Kirkha; ul Kuibysheva 115) was built by a growing German population, who settled here from the 1860s under Catherine the Great's agricultural development programme.

When the **synagogue** (ul Sadovaya 49) was built in 1903, it served over 1000 people, the largest Jewish community in the Volga region. The building served as a bread factory during Soviet times, but has been a working synagogue since 1993.

Places to Stay

Samara does not yet have the facilities to manage the hordes of travellers it attracts, and rooms can be hard to come by. Samara Intour can assist with reservations.

Housed in an ornate 19th-century building, the **Zhiguli Hotel** (☎ 32 04 13; ul Kuibysheva 111; singles/doubles with shared bathroom R280/720, with private bathroom R600/1000) is dilapidated and dingy and the staff are cranky. The cheap rooms are in the hotel's second building at ulitsa Kuibysheva 78.

The **National Hotel** (☎ 33 76 95; ul Frunze 91/37; rooms from R600) has a convenient central location that can be noisy. Rooms are functional but tired.

Located at the naberezhnaya's northern end, the **Volga Hotel** (☎ 42 38 25; Volzhsky pr 29; singles/doubles with shared bathroom R340/450, with private bathroom RR1000/1200) is not a bad choice. Some rooms have lovely river views.

Hotel Rossiya (☎ 39 03 11, fax 33 24 41; e hotel-rossia@samtel.ru; ul Maksima Gorkogo 82; singles/doubles from R590/900) has a nice location on the naberezhnaya, near the river station. Although the rooms are nothing fancy, they're good value.

Ekvator (☎ 38 28 77, fax 38 28 85; e equator@samaramail.ru; ul Novo-Sadovaya 18; rooms with breakfast from R1950) is a small, welcoming guesthouse in a quiet neighbourhood. Its 13 comfortable rooms

have double beds, telephones and air con. Take bus No 50 from the train station.

Transit Hotel (☎ 39 30 00, fax 39 41 87; Komsomolskaya ploshchad 2/1; singles/doubles R1500/2000), on the 1st floor of the train station, is sleek and modern (like the station itself). Once you leave the station, this hotel's location is not so pleasant, due to the crime and chaos that normally surround a train station. Smaller singles are R700.

Places to Eat

Malenkoe Kafe (☎ 32 82 58; ul Chapaevskaya 177; salads R50, mains R100; open 10am-10pm daily) is a small café with a cosy atmosphere and a menu of Russian standards.

Zhili Byli (☎ 70 41 32; ul Kuibysheva 81; meals R180; open 11am-midnight) recreates a Russian country inn, complete with convivial atmosphere, reasonable prices and abundant soups and salads.

Papa Vito (☎ 70 43 60; Molodogvardeyskaya 153; pizzas R150, salad bar R190; open noon-midnight) reproduces the atmosphere of an Italian garden, a pleasant place for tasty pizzas and salads.

La Cucaracha (☎ 32 48 78; ul Galaktionovskaya 39/8; meals R300; open noon-midnight) has the best Mexican food east of Moscow. Although some dishes have funny Russian nuances, the guacamole does not disappoint. Live Latin music plays most nights.

Dzhin Dzhu (☎ 32 99 56; ul Kuibysheva 72; mains R200-400; open 24hrs) has stylish Chinese decor complete with bamboo furniture and gold fish ponds. The food is tasty and authentic, if expensive.

U Palycha (☎ 32 36 05; ul Kuibysheva 100; open noon-midnight) is highly recommended for Russian cuisine. This fashionable, pricey restaurant has over 250 dishes and live Russian folk music every night.

For self-caterers, the **Troitsky market** (ul Galaktionovskaya; open 7am-6pm daily) has tables piled high with fresh fruit and veggies, as well as breads, meats and cheeses.

Entertainment

The **Opera & Ballet Theatre** (☎ 32 25 09; ploshchad Kuibysheva 1) is the main venue for classical dance and musical performances.

Zvezda (☎ 70 34 47; w www.zvezda.v63.ru; ul Novo-Sadovaya 106) is a huge entertainment complex with cinemas, bowling and billiards, as well as a pumping nightclub and bar.

Across the street, **Skvozdnyak** (☎ 34 34 02; cnr ul Novo-Sadovaya & pr Masslenikova; open 5pm-3am daily) has live music by local rock and blues groups. You can also play pool or watch extreme sports on TV.

Shopping

Gallery Maria (☎ 42 28 52; ul Galaktionovskaya 132; open 10am-6pm daily) hosts exhibitions by local artists, with paintings and crafts for sale.

Getting There & Away

Air Flights go several times a day to Moscow, Nizhny Novgorod and St Petersburg. There are also daily flights to Irkutsk, Novosibirsk and Baku. Buy tickets at the **Aviakassa** (ul Molodochvardeyskaya 221).

Train As you enter the Samara train station, you may believe you have left Russia and arrived in the future. It is worth leaving Samara by train if only to wait in this ultramodern, clean and efficient station. In addition to the several trains to Moscow (18 to 20 hours), there are also daily trains to Saratov (eight hours), Kazan (13 hours) and Ufa (10 hours). ' Trains to St Petersburg and Volgograd go a few times a week.

Bus The central bus station is 6km southeast of the centre. Buses go to Ulyanovsk six times a day and Kazan once a day.

Boat The river station is at the western end of the naberezhnaya, in front of Hotel Rossiya; long-distance cruises go to Nizhny Novgorod, Ulyanovsk, Volgograd and Astrakhan.

There are also boats leaving for regional destinations including Shiryaevo.

Getting Around

Trolleybus No 2 runs between the train and bus stations. From ulitsa Kuibysheva, take bus No 37, 46, 47 or 57 to the central bus station. Bus No 24 runs from ploshchad Revolyutsii to ploshchad Slavy.

AROUND SAMARA
Shiryaevo
Ширяево
In the 1870s, Ilya Repin spent two years in this village just north of Samara on the west bank of the Volga. Here he completed sketches for his famous painting, the *Volga Boatmen*, which is now in the Russian Museum in St Petersburg. Apparently Repin created somewhat of a scandal when he was here, as local villagers felt objectified when used as models for the artist.

Today, the pleasant village is more welcoming to art lovers. The **Repin museum** (☎ 33 77 12; ul Sovetskaya 14) has a nice selection of Volga River paintings by Repin and other artists. The three-hour trip to Shiryaeva by hydrofoil makes for a pleasant day trip from Samara.

Samarskaya Luka
Самарская Лука
Where Samara sits on the left bank of the Volga, the right bank is dominated by the rocky Zhiguli Hills. The river loops around the hills creating a peninsula, encompassing 32,000 hectares of national forest reserve, known as the Samarskaya Luka (Samara

---

Grushinsky Festival

Every summer, the first Saturday in July kicks off one of Samara's most anticipated events, the Grushinsky Festival. The event has its roots in the 1960s, when the musical poetry known as 'Author's Song' gained popularity among intellectuals and hippy types. Simple melodies, acoustic guitar and poetic lyrics characterise this folksy music, making it difficult for non-Russian speakers to really appreciate it.

Since the 1960s, musicians from all over Russia and the former Soviet bloc collect in the Zhiguli Hills National Park to perform their Authors' Songs, with as many as 100,000 gathering on 'spectator hill'. A stage in the shape of a guitar is set up on the lake below. Besides performances by better-known musicians, there is also a sort of 'open mike' competition, plus campfires, football and general merrymaking.

The festival is named after Valery Grushin, outdoorsman and hiker, student at the local aviation institute, and member of the trio 'Singing Beavers'. Grushin perished in 1967 while saving drowning children from the Uda river in Siberia.

Onion). While undeserving of its nickname 'Russian Switzerland', it's a prime area for hikes along rocky ledges and grand Volga vistas. The peaks – the highest being Strelnaya mountain at 370m – are in the northwest corner of the reserve.

These hills were the hideout of peasant rebel Stepan Razin in the 17th century. He supposedly hid his loot in a large 20-sq-metre cave near the village of Perevoloka, in the southwest corner.

The traditional way to experience the Samarskaya Luka is by boat. Every year, thousands of locals raft Zhigulyovskaya Kruglocvetka – 'Around the World'. The route follows the loop in the river, then cuts back up north via a channel on the west side of the preserve.

Otherwise, the easiest way to reach the reserve is to take a riverboat to any of the villages on the right bank, such as Shiryaevo, Polyana or just across the river to Rozhdestveno. Alexander Gubernatov, Director of the **Samarskaya Luka Ecological Center** (☎ 8466-23 55 02; e orfr@mail.samtel.ru), is an excellent source of information on hiking and camping in the reserve. Local tour agencies such as Samara Intour can arrange this adventure.

SARATOV
САРАТОВ
☎ 8452 • pop 900,000

Although it lacks major tourist attractions, Saratov is a pleasant city with a thriving commercial centre and an attractive green river embankment. Founded in 1590, Saratov was initially a fortress forming a line of defence for the trade route along the Volga.

A large community of ethnic Germans, mostly farmers, settled along the Volga around Saratov in the 18th and 19th centuries and even got their own autonomous republic within Russia in 1924. However, this was abolished during WWII, when Saratov was actually occupied by the Nazis. Emigration and deportation have since decreased their numbers, although Germany still maintains a consulate here.

The first man in space, cosmonaut Yuri Gagarin, lived in Saratov and studied at the local university, which now bears his name. The lively café scene on prospekt Kirova and the town's distinctive German flavour (due mainly to the tourists it attracts) make Saratov an enjoyable place to spend a day.

Orientation & Information

The centre of town is the pedestrian mall on prospekt Kirova, stretching 1km from the market at ulitsa Chapaeva to ulitsa Radishcheva. Three blocks north, busy prospekt Moskovsky links the train station to the river station.

Intourist (☎ 24 18 23; e intour@overta.ru; ul Gorkogo 30; open 9am-6pm Mon-Fri) organises local tours, including one on German history in the Volga region. **Sberbank** (☎ 50 32 95; pr Kirova 7; open 9am-2pm & 3pm-7pm Mon-Fri) has foreign-exchange services and an ATM.

The **post office** (cnr pr Moskovsky & ul Chapaeva; open 9am-6pm daily) is near the market. The most convenient cybercafé is **Beshenaya Mysh** (☎ 27 74 50; pr Kirova 27; open 10am-11pm daily). **Stalker Internet Café** (☎ 48 62 14; Kosmonavtov nab 7; open 8am-10pm daily) is across from the river station.

The **German consulate** (☎ 24 27 29, fax 24 49 39; pr Kirova 34) is in the Volga Hotel.

Dom Knigi (☎ 24 32 92; ul Volskaya 81; open 9am-7pm daily) has a fine collection of maps and reference books.

Things to See

River views and shady walks are the highlights of the **Naberezhnaya Kosmonavtov** (Cosmonaut's Embankment) along the Volga, surveyed by a resolute Yuri Gagarin from the river's shore. The **Regional Museum** (Muzey Kraevedeniya; ☎ 26 45 38; ul Lermontova 34; admission R40; open 10am-5pm daily) has many news clips and photos from Gagarin's life, as well as the airplane in which he learned to fly; typical local nature and history displays are also here. Across the street, the 17th-century **Trinity Cathedral** (Troitsky sobor) is a working church with a heavily decorated interior.

For the full story on Gagarin in Saratov, check out the **Gagarin Museum** (Narodnoy Muzey Gagarina; ☎ 26 76 66; ul Sakko i Venzetti; open 9am-4pm Mon-Fri). Not only did the cosmonaut live and study in Saratov, he also landed (crashed?) his rocket nearby after his much-lauded flight. The crash site, 40km out of town near the village of Kvasnikovka, is marked by a commemorative monument.

The **Radishchev Museum** (☎ 24 36 27; ul Pervomayskaya 75; open 10am-6pm Tues-Sun) is the main branch of the Fine Arts Museum, with a good selection of art from the 18th to the 20th century.

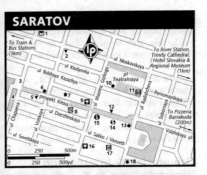

Places to Stay & Eat

Hotel Volga (☎ 24 36 45, fax 24 02 35; pr Kirova 34; singles/doubles with breakfast from R862/1300) is the most atmospheric accommodation option. High-ceilinged rooms and an impressive art collection give the hotel a glorious, prerevolutionary air.

Located on the waterfront, **Hotel Slovakia** (☎ 26 95 01, fax 72 55 73; ul Lermontova 30; singles/doubles from R600/960) is the most common option for visiting business types. You can get renovated singles/doubles for R1280/1600.

Restaurant Bavaria (ul Volskaya 58; open 11am-midnight) is the place to go for wiener schnitzel and ale, Volga-style.

If you want to do the café scene, head directly to **Buratino** (☎ 27 74 79; pr Kirova 10; meals R200-300; open 11am-midnight daily), a favourite of expats.

The ever-popular **Pizzeria Barrakuda** (☎ 72 55 82; ul Volzhskaya 16; pizzas R100-200; open 11am-1am daily) has an airy outdoor eating and drinking area.

Wild West (Dikhii Zapad; ☎ 24 45 87; pr Kirova 43; burgers R100; open noon-midnight) serves up American food and real live brawls.

Entertainment

Grand Michel (☎ 24 36 40; pr Kirova 22; open 1pm-6am daily) is a lively entertainment complex with bowling for about R600 an hour and billiards from R100 to R150 an hour. The stylish **Morskoy Konek** (☎ 73 18 26; ul Maksima Gorkogo 16/20) offers a restaurant, bar and nightclub bordering on swanky.

The **Sobinov Conservatory** (☎ 26 06 52; pr Kirova 1), one of the best in Russia, holds frequent performances by resident and visiting musicians. Other classical venues include the **Philharmonic Theatre** (☎ 26 57 05; Sobornaya ploshchad 9) and the **Opera & Ballet Theatre** (☎ 24 31 64; Teatralnaya ploshchad; show 6pm).

Shopping

Vanka-Vstanka (☎ 21 23 87; ul Maksima Gorkogo 30; open 9am-5pm daily) exhibits and sells beautifully crafted work by local artists.

Getting There & Away & Around

There are two daily flights to Moscow for US$60. The **train station** (Privokzalnaya ploshchad) is at the western end of prospekt Moskovsky. Daily trains go to/from Moscow's Paveletsky station (16 hours), as well as Samara (eight hours), Volgograd (nine hours) and Astrakhan (12 hours).

The regional bus station is on the southern side of the train station.

The **river station** (☎ 26 93 24; *Kosmonavtov nab*) is at the eastern end of prospekt Moskovsky. The friendly port office has schedule details for long-distance and local tour boats.

Trolleybus Nos 2 and 2A stop at the market at the western end of prospekt Kirova. Trolleybus Nos 1 and 9 ply prospekt Moskovsky from the train station to the river station.

VOLGOGRAD
ВОЛГОГРАД
☎ 8442 • pop 1 million

Volgograd was founded in 1589 as Tsaritsyn, a mighty fortress at the convergence of the Volga and Don rivers. Nothing is left of ancient Tsaritsyn, however, due to events in more recent history.

During the Soviet period, the city was renamed Stalingrad to honour the leader who took credit for organising its defences during the Civil War. As the locale of WWII's most decisive battle, the old city was levelled and hundreds of thousands died; for more information, see the boxed text 'A Battle to the Death'.

In 1952 the Lenin Ship Canal (also known as the Volga-Don Canal) was completed, connecting the two rivers and completing an intricate network of waterways from the Arctic

to the Mediterranean. After Stalin's fall from grace, the city was renamed once again in 1961, this time to pay tribute to the river which dominates its geography, economy and culture.

Rebuilt from scratch since WWII, Volgograd is a bit sterile, although memories of the 'Great Patriotic War' are still fresh. Even today Volgograd bears witness to the simultaneously most triumphant and tragic event in Soviet history, the Battle of Stalingrad.

Orientation & Information

Volgograd's main north–south artery is prospekt Lenina. From the central ploshchad, Pavshikh Bortsov (Fallen Warriors' Square), the promenade alleya Geroyev (Avenue of Heroes) crosses prospekt Lenina to the river station on the Volga's west bank.

Hotel Volgograd has a foreign-exchange office in the lobby. There's an ATM in **Minsk Gastronom** (*ul Lenina 16; open 8am-9pm daily*). The **post office** (*ploshchad Pavshikh Bortsov; open 24hrs*) has an adjacent **Service Center** (☎ 32 54 94, fax 36 43 54; e collbox@ avtlg.ru; open 8am-8pm) with fax and Internet facilities.

Mamaev Kurgan (Mamai Mound)

Known as Hill 102 during the Battle of Stalingrad, Mamaev Kurgan was the site of four

A Battle to the Death

Even in a century marked by war, the Battle of Stalingrad is still shocking for its destruction of lives and disregard for humanity. From July 1942, when the German army besieged the city on its thrust to the oil-rich Caucasus region, to February 1943, when the Soviet army captured the last remaining German soldier, the two sides fought a battle to the death. The facts of this hell speak for themselves.

As the two armies dug in across from each other, they made starving children carry their messages between posts. Most were killed before they received the promised food.

The Soviets shot 13,500 of their own troops for actions including cowardice or self-inflicting wounds to escape the front; thousands more escaped from the Germans only to be killed on the grounds they were possible spies. The Germans captured 60,000 Stalingrad civilians and shipped them back to Germany to work and die as slaves.

After the German position became hopeless during the winter, the generals – most of whom survived – were resolute in honouring Hitler's decree against surrender. The battle continued with thousands more dying needlessly.

At least 600,000 German troops died in battle, with a further 180,000 captured by the Soviets; only 6000 went on to survive the Siberian prisoner-of-war camps.

The total number of Russian soldiers killed is unknown but is thought to be around 600,000. Even the Germans were shocked by the Soviet army's tactic of sending swarms of men to be mowed down by machine guns so that their bodies would shield the waves of troops behind.

More than 50 years after the battle, any digging in Volgograd still turns up bodies.

★★★

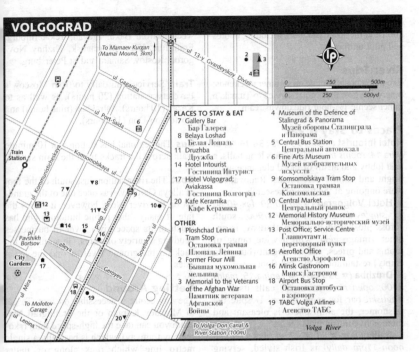

VOLGOGRAD

To Mamaev Kurgan
(Mamai Mound, 3km)

ul 13-y Gvardeyskoy Divizii

ul Gagarina

ul Port-Saida

Komsomolskaya ul

Train
Station

ul Kommunisticheskaya

prosp Lenina

Sovetskaya ul

pl
Pavshikh
Bortsov

alleya

City
Gardens

ul Mira

Geroyev

ul Lenina

To Molotov
Garage

To Volga-Don Canal &
River Station (100m)

Volga River

0   250   500m
0   250   500yd

PLACES TO STAY & EAT
7 Gallery Bar
   Бар Галерея
8 Belaya Loshad
   Белая Лошадь
11 Druzhba
   Дружба
14 Hotel Intourist
   Гостиница Интурист
17 Hotel Volgograd;
   Aviakassa
   Гостиница Волгоград
20 Kafe Keramika
   Кафе Керамика

OTHER
1 Ploshchad Lenina
   Tram Stop
   Остановка трамвая
   Площадь Ленина
2 Former Flour Mill
   Бывшая мукомольная
   мельница
3 Memorial to the Veterans
   of the Afghan War
   Памятник ветеранам
   Афганской
   Войны

4 Museum of the Defence of
   Stalingrad & Panorama
   Музей обороны Сталинграда
   и Панорама
5 Central Bus Station
   Центральный автовокзал
6 Fine Arts Museum
   Музей изобразительных
   искусств
9 Komsomolskaya Tram Stop
   Остановка трамвая
   Комсомольская
10 Central Market
   Центральный рынок
12 Memorial History Museum
   Мемориально-исторический музей
13 Post Office; Service Centre
   Главпочтамт и
   переговорный пункт
15 Aeroflot Office
   Агентство Аэрофлота
16 Minsk Gastronom
   Минск Гастроном
18 Airport Bus Stop
   Остановка автобуса
   в аэропорт
19 TABC Volga Airlines
   Агентство ТАБС

months of fierce fighting. It's now a moving memorial to all who died in this bloody but victorious fight.

The complex's centrepiece is an evocative 72m statue of Mother Russia wielding a sword extending another 11m above her head. The area is covered with statues, memorials and ruined fortifications. The Pantheon is inscribed with the names of 7200 soldiers who died here, which are meant to represent the 600,000 Russian soldiers who were killed in this tragic battle. Take the high-speed tram to the Mamaev Kurgan stop, 3km north of the centre.

Museum of the Defence of Stalingrad & Panorama

This exhaustive museum *(Muzey Oborony Stalingrada; ☎ 34 67 23; admission R40, guided tours R400; open 10am-5pm daily)* has dozens of exhibits on the battle and the soldiers who fought in it. The model of the ruined city (post-battle) is a moving display of human capacity for both destruction and rebuilding. Captions are in Russian only.

Upstairs is the **Panorama 'Stalingradskaya Bitva'**, a 360° illustration of the battle as it might have been seen from atop Mamaev Kur-

gan. Viewers can relive the battle experience literally in the midst of the chaos and carnage. The Panorama is accessible only with a guided group, so listen for the loudspeaker announcements indicating the start of a guided tour.

Below the museum on the riverside is a **Memorial to Veterans of the Afghan War**. The startling ruins nearby are the only evidence of the Battle of Stalingrad left in the centre. Ironically, this former flour mill had been constructed by the Germans in 1893. It has been left as a reminder of the devastating battle.

The complex is two blocks east of ploshchad Lenina high-speed tram stop; otherwise, a 20-minute stroll through the river park from alleya Geroyev gets you there.

Other Museums

The small **Fine Arts Museum** *(Muzey Izobrazitelnykh Iskusstv; ☎ 36 39 06; pr Lenina 21; admission R20; open 10am-5.30pm Thur-Tues)* has a typical collection of Russian paintings, porcelain and carved ivory. Enter from ulitsa Port-Saida. The **Memorial History Museum** *(Memorialno-istorichesky muzey; ☎ 36 17 05; cnr ul Kommunisticheskaya & pl Pavshikh Bortsov; open 10am-5pm Wed-Mon)*

VOLGA REGION

has a collection of artefacts from Russian aviation and the space program, including photos and pilot uniforms.

River Trips

Excursion boats operate on summer weekends; otherwise, take the regular service to Tumak, a rather scenic 1½-hour ride downstream.

Places to Stay & Eat

Hotel Intourist (☎ 36 45 53, fax 36 16 48; ul Mira 14; rooms from R1500) has long halls, a vast lobby and an air of faded elegance, with bright and comfortable rooms. Renovations were ongoing at the time of research.

Hotel Volgograd (☎ 40 80 30, fax 40 80 33; singles/doubles from R750/900), south across ploshchad Pavshikh Bortsov, is another vintage gem, with a wide range of rooms and prices, and an elegant (but often empty) restaurant on the 2nd floor.

Druzhba (☎ 33 71 01; pr Lenina 15; mains R300; open noon–midnight) calls itself an *Angliskii* bar for some reason. Despite the misnomer, the atmosphere is pleasant and there is live music most nights.

Gallery Bar (☎ 33 56 72; ul Mira 11; open noon–11pm daily) is Irish styled, serving Guinness pints for an all-too-authentic R120.

Cheerful, cheap **Kafe Keramika** (☎ 36 22 41; ul Chuykova 9; meals around R100; open 10am–10pm daily) is always busy with Russian families and couples on dates. The decoration, provided by local artists, is for sale.

Belaya Loshad (☎ 36 76 00; ul Ostrovskogo 5; meals R200; open noon–2am) is better for drinking than eating. Local rock bands play nightly.

Stocked with typical fruit, veggies and cheeses, the **central market** (cnr uls Komsomolskaya & Sovetskaya) is the best place for self-caterers.

Entertainment

The top night spot in Volgograd, featuring live music and a laid-back atmosphere, is **Molotov Garage** (☎ 44 22 06; ul Rabochie-Krestyanskaya 2/1),

Getting There & Away

Air Buy all airline tickets at the **Aviakassa** (☎ 40 80 66; Hotel Volgograd; open 9am–5pm Mon-Fri & 9am-3pm Sat) or at the **Aeroflot office** (☎ 30 05 15; alleya Geroyev 6; open 9am-6pm daily). There are seven flights a day

to/from Moscow. Flights go once or twice a week to/from Baku, Erevan, Yekaterinburg, Frankfurt, Kiev, Murmansk, Nizhny Novgorod, Rostov, Samara and St Petersburg.

Train Services run daily to/from Moscow's Paveletsky station (20 hours), as well as to Kazan (10 hours), Astrakhan (nine hours) and Rostov-on-Don (16 hours).

Bus The regional bus station is a 10-minute walk across the tracks from the train station.

Boat The river station, just south of the foot of alleya Geroyev, was once one of the grandest on the river. Now, however, it shares the fate of many other public buildings and has much of its space given over to businesses peddling a variety of wares. Go around to the back on the ground level to find the ticket sales.

Getting Around

The city centre is accessible on foot. To get to Mamaev Kurgan or the Stalingrad Museum you can take the high-speed tram (skorostnoy tramvay), which is basically a single metro line which runs along or under prospekt Lenina. To get to the airport, catch a minibus from the stop in front of the TABC Volga Airlines office. Buses run every 30 minutes or so.

ASTRAKHAN
АСТРАХАНЬ
☎ 8512 • pop 500,000

Situated at the upper end of the Volga River delta, about 100km from the Caspian Sea, Astrakhan is both a river and a sea port. The Golden Horde controlled this area in the 13th century and founded a city on the right bank of the Volga River. After Kazan fell to Ivan the Terrible, however, his troops took over the rest of the Volga River region and destroyed the original Tatar city. In 1558 the Russian troops built the kremlin on the left bank of the river and founded the modern city of Astrakhan.

As a trading centre between Europe, Central Asia and the Caucasus, Astrakhan has always been prosperous. Today its economic role hinges on its dwindling sturgeon population (for caviar production; see the boxed text 'Roe to Ruin' later in this chapter) and its disputed access to the Caspian Sea (for oil

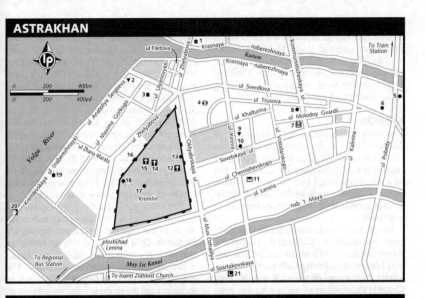

ASTRAKHAN

PLACES TO STAY & EAT
1 Victoria Palace
   Гостиница Виктория Палас
2 Podkova Grill
   Подкова Гриль
3 Hotel Astrakhanskaya;
   Intourist Delta Volga
   Гостиница Астраханская;
   Интурист
9 Picnic
   Пикник
19 Hotel Lotos
   Гостиница Лотос

OTHER
4 Sberbank
   Сбербанк

5 Market
   Рынок
6 Kustodiev Art Gallery
   Художественная галерея
   имени Кустодиева
7 History and Architecture
   Museum
   Историко-архитектурный
   музей
8 Shatrovaya Tower
   Шатровая башня
10 Business Centre
   Бизнес центр
11 Post Office
   Почта
12 Assumption Cathedral
   Успенский собор

13 Prechistenskie Gate
   Пречистенские
   ворота
14 Trinity Cathedral
   Троицкий собор
15 Kirillov Chapel
   Кириловская часовня
16 Nikolsky Gate
   Никольские ворота
17 Cultural Exhibit
   Выставка
18 Red Gate
   Красные ворота
20 River Station
   Речной вокзал
21 Mosque
   Мечеть

production). Astrakhan serves as a gateway to the beautiful Volga Delta and the carefully preserved area of waterways and wetlands leading south to the Caspian.

Marked by canals and bridges, an impressive kremlin and lively markets, Astrakhan is pleasant for wiling away a day.

Orientation & Information

Astrakhan's centre is on an island surrounded by the Volga River, the Kutum Canal and the May 1st Canal. Ulitsa Pobedy, the major thoroughfare, cuts across the eastern end of the island and goes north to the train station. The naberezhnaya, west of the kremlin,

is where locals go to have a drink, or stroll and watch the sun set over the Volga. Maps of Astrakhan exist but they are not widely sold.

Sberbank (☎ 22 93 81; ul Trusova 11; open 8.30am-6pm Mon-Sat) can handle foreign-exchange and cash-advance services. There's a **post office** (cnr uls Kirova & Cherni-shevskogo; open 8am-7pm daily) and the **Business Centre** (☎ 39 12 03, fax 39 07 10; e business@asranet.ru; ul Sovetskaya 5; open 8am-6pm Mon-Fri, 9am-4pm Sat & Sun) with Internet facilities.

Intourist Delta Volga (☎ 24 63 44, fax 22 97 30; w www.deltavolgy.narod.ru; ul

VOLGA REGION

Ulyanovykh 6; open 10am-5pm Mon-Fri), in Hotel Astrakhanskaya, offers a wide range of excursions into the Volga Delta, including bird-watching and fishing. Enthusiastic staff can also arrange a one- to three-day 'Delicacy Tour', visiting local fisheries and sampling caviar and other local treats.

Kremlin

The large 16th-century fortress on top of Zayachy Hill was the realisation of a dream for architect Dorofey Myakishiev. Today the kremlin is a peaceful green haven in what can be a hot, dusty city. Enter through the main, eastern **Prechistenskie Belfry Gate** (Prechistenskie vorota; 1908–12), with its impressive bell tower.

Inside, the main churches are the magnificent **Assumption Cathedral** (Uspensky sobor) (1698–1710) and the lovely (but fading) 18th-century **Trinity Cathedral** (Troitsky sobor). At the time of research, only **Kirillov Chapel** (Kirillovskaya Chasovnya) was open for visitors.

Other buildings, including the Nikolsky Gate in the north wall, house rather mundane cultural and historical **exhibits**. The most interesting is in the Red Gate (Krasniye vorota), in the kremlin's western corner, also provides a panoramic view of city and river.

Other Things to See

The **Kustodiev Art Gallery** (☎ 22 64 09; ul Sverdlova 81; admission R15; open 10am-7pm daily) has an extensive collection of sculptures and paintings by artists including Nesterov, Kustodiev and Levitan.

The **History and Architecture Museum** (☎ 22 14 29; ul Sovetskaya 15; admission R30; open 10am-5pm Sat-Thur) holds special exhibitions on local palaeontology and archaeology, featuring treasures excavated from around the region. Nearby, **Shatrovaya Tower** (cnr uls Trusova & Kommunisticheskaya) is all that remains of the 16th-century Saviour-Transfiguration Monastery (Spaso-preobrazhensky monastyr).

The **Ioann Zlatoust Church** (ul Magnitogorskaya), dating from 1763, is one of the city's few churches to survive the ravages of time and revolution; it has been fully and beautifully restored, including the frescoes. The **mosque** (ul Spartakovskaya), just south of the centre, is evidence of Astrakhan's diverse population.

Places to Stay & Eat

Astrakhansky Hotel (☎ 22 29 88; ul Ulyanovykh 6; singles/doubles with shared bathroom R315/450, with private bathroom RR750/920) is dark and shady (in more ways than one), but it's the cheapest place in town.

The hulking **Hotel Lotos** (☎ 22 95 00, fax 22 99 12; ul Kremlevskaya 4; singles/doubles R1100/1600), at the southern end of the naberezhnaya, is ugly on the outside, but OK on the inside. The river views are a plus.

Victoria Palace (☎ 39 48 01, fax 39 54 90; Krasnaya naberezhnaya; e mellain@astranet.ru; rooms from US$80) is a shiny, new four-star hotel with fancy rooms and prices.

The best meal in town is hot shashlyk and cold beer from a café along the naberezhnaya. If the weather drives you inside, try **Podkova Grill** (☎ 39 50 05; ul Anatoliya Sergeeva 7; mains from R300; open noon-midnight), also along the naberezhnaya. The atmosphere is pleasant (although a bit dark in summer) and the menu is more varied than its outdoor counterparts.

Picnic (☎ 24 48 41; ul Kirova 7; dishes US$1; open 10am-10pm daily) is a bustling Russian fast-food place.

The lively **market** (cnr ul Pobedy & Krasnaya naberezhnaya) is worth a visit to pick up some snacks or to witness the vibrant trade in produce and fish. Try *oblyoma*, the local speciality, a salty fish complemented by beer (or vice versa).

Getting There & Away

Flights go to/from Moscow three times a day for about US$110. Daily trains go to Moscow (30 hours), Volgograd (nine hours), Rostov-on-Don (24 hours) and south to Makhachkala in Dagestan (20 hours). The **regional bus station** (cnr ul Generala Yepisheva & nab Privolzhskoga Zatona) is in an old cathedral.

Astrakhan is the end point of cruises on the Volga; the **river station** (ul Kremlevskaya 1) is located on the naberezhnaya. There are no regular passenger boats to the other Caspian Sea ports.

Getting Around

Bus No 5 and trolleybus No 3 go to/from the airport, train station and ploshchad Lenina. Catch the bus from any stop along ulitsa Pobedy, ulitsa Sverdlova or ulitsa Zhelyabova. Trolleybus Nos 1, 2, 3 and 4 run to/from the train station and ploshchad Lenina.

Roe to Ruin

Caviar: the very word evokes glamorous lifestyles, exotic travel and glittering festivities. But the sturgeon, the source of this luxury item, is in grave danger. Although they have survived since dinosaurs roamed the Earth, the question now is whether these 'living fossils' can withstand the relentless fishing pressure, pollution and habitat destruction that have brought many sturgeon species to the brink of extinction.

Sturgeon are remarkable fish: clad in bony plates and equipped with broad snouts, some species live to be more than 100 years old and can grow to be 2500 pounds and 15 feet long, although the very largest fish are extremely rare today, following decades of overfishing. Like humans, many sturgeon species reproduce relatively late in life; some do not reach sexual maturity until the ages of 15 to 25. A single sturgeon can produce hundreds of pounds of fish eggs, or roe. Sturgeon live in rivers, coastal marine waters and lakes in the northern hemisphere, and feed on organisms dwelling at the bottom of the water, including worms, molluscs, small fish, shrimp and insect larvae.

Sturgeon today face six major problems (for more information, see **W** www.caviaremptor.org).

- **Overharvesting** The global caviar market has placed a premium on sturgeon, prompting overfishing and poaching.
- **Illegal trade** Political turmoil in sturgeon-producing countries, including Russia, has resulted in a flourishing black-market trade.
- **Life history** As sturgeon reproduce more slowly than other fish, their depleted populations can take a century or more to recover.
- **Lack of effective management** Many sturgeon migrate through the waters of different states and countries, often resulting in a patchwork of catch levels, fishing seasons, size limits and other management measures.
- **Loss of habitat** Sturgeon migrate upriver to spawn; dam construction and diversion of river water for irrigation and other purposes have nearly eliminated spawning runs on many large river systems used by the fish.
- **Pollution** Pollutants from urban and agricultural runoff, and industrial discharges, have been linked to significant reproductive problems and other abnormalities in sturgeon, as well as to large fish kills.

★★★

AROUND ASTRAKHAN
Volga Delta
Волга Дельта

The delta of the lower Volga River, where the river divides into thousands of branches, is home to an immense treasure of flora and fauna. Among the reeds here are beavers, racoons, musk rats, foxes and otters. The waterways and marshes are also home to flocks of water fowl and other birds, including herons, swans, cormorants and magnificent bald eagles. Not to mention the fish (for more information see the boxed text 'Roe to Ruin').

About 90% of Volga Delta territory is uninhabited by humans and accessible only by boat. Whether fishing, bird-watching or sunbathing, a cruise through the delta's winding waterways is among the best ways to spend a day in the Volga region.

Fishing season is from April to November. In most cases, anglers will not be allowed to keep their prizes, but should throw the fish back after securing photographic evidence. (Birds abound during these months as they follow the fish.) April can be chilly, but still enjoyable. May and June are apparently unbearable in the delta due to the inescapable swarms of mosquitoes. In August, the area is abloom with floating Lotus flowers, often growing over two metres high and featuring blossoms larger than your head. September and October are also pleasant.

Access to the delta is restricted to tour agencies and fisheries with special permission, so the only way to visit the area is to book a tour with a local agency such as Intourist Delta Volga (see Orientation & Information under Astrakhan earlier in this chapter).

The Urals Урал

The Ural Mountains stretch 2000km from the Arctic Kara Sea in the north to Kazakhstan in the south. They're low as famous mountain ranges go, failing to top 2000m anywhere; if you pass through on the train you'll hardly notice them. Nonetheless, the Urals have been vital to Russia for centuries as a major source of metals and minerals, which gave rise to a number of industrial cities such as Perm, Yekaterinburg and Chelyabinsk. On the western edge of the mountains you'll also find Ufa, capital of the autonomous Bashkortostan Republic.

HISTORY

Nentsy, Khanty and Mansi natives had traded furs, walrus ivory and other products across the Ural Mountains from the 12th century, and early Russian invaders and merchants crossed the Urals from the 1580s, but it was the region's reserves of iron ore, metals, coal and gemstones that first aroused serious Russian interest. Peter the Great sent pioneer industrialists to set up metalworks, with mainly military purposes in mind, in the early 18th century. Industrial centres like Yekaterinburg, Chelyabinsk, Nizhny Tagil, and Perm (to the west of the Ural Mountains) date from that time.

Gold, platinum and ruthenium were found in the region in the 19th century, along with amethyst, topaz and aquamarine. WWII brought a new industrial boom as Stalin moved over 1000 factories east of the Ural Mountains. This growth continued after the war, when more or less the whole region was off limits to foreigners.

Five of the 10 secret cities of the Soviet Union's 'nuclear archipelago' for weapons research and production were in the Urals. One of these, Chelyabinsk-65 (formerly Chelyabinsk-40), was the scene of the world's worst nuclear accident before Chernobyl, back in 1957 (though it wasn't admitted for decades). A nuclear waste tank exploded, severely contaminating an area 8km wide and 100km long, with about 10,000 people eventually moved out and 23 villages bulldozed. The explosion, along with deliberate dumping of radioactive waste during the 1950s into the nearby Techa River and Lake Karachay (which later dried up, allowing the wind

Highlights

- Straddle continents at the Europe–Asia border
- Follow the pilgrims from the Romanovs' execution site in Yekaterinburg to their original burial site at Ganina Yama
- Gawp at Magnitogorsk's *Til Frontu* statue, an awesome Soviet-realist masterpiece with the perfect industrial backdrop
- Enjoy Bashkir hospitality, once you've got a taste for *buza* and *koumys*
- Hike through the gently pleasant scenery around Abzakovo or Minyar

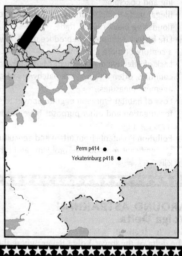

Perm p414
Yekaterinburg p418

★★★★★★★★★★★★★★★★★★★

to scatter the radioactive dust), has led to grave health and environmental problems in the area.

GEOGRAPHY

The Ural Mountains are divided into five sections. Yekaterinburg is on the east side of the longest, broadest and generally lowest stretch, the Middle Urals (Sredny Ural).

The highest mountain in the Southern Urals (Yuzhny Ural) is Mt Yaman Tau (1638m). The Northern Urals (Severny Ural) reach 1617m at Mt Telposiz. North of the Northern Urals (if this makes sense) come the Subarctic Urals (Pripolyarny Ural), a short stretch but with the highest peak in the whole range, 1894m Mt Narodnaya. The Arctic Urals (Polyarny Ural), whose highest peak is 1499m Mt Pay-Yer, take the range almost to the Kara Sea. The Arctic Novaya Zemlya islands, one of the Soviet Union's nuclear bomb testing grounds, are effectively a northern outcrop of the Urals.

Most of the Ural Mountains are covered in taiga, with rocky outcrops forming the peaks, but there are some more dramatic rock walls on the northern peaks.

ACTIVITIES

Frith Maier's *Trekking in Russia & Central Asia* (see Books in the Siberia & the Russian Far East Facts for the Visitor chapter) describes a two- to three-day hike up Konzhakovsky Kamen (1569m), the highest peak in the Middle Urals. It also details a nine- to 10-day trek in the Mt Narodnaya area for those with more time and energy. July and August are the best months for such explorations. The approach to the Mt Narodnaya area is from Pechora on the Moscow–Vorkuta railway on the western side of the Urals, then by hydrofoil up the Pechora River.

Aside from hiking, cross-country skiing and rafting or kayaking are other locally popular activities. Trips on relatively easy rivers like the Chusovaya, Serga, Usva and Vilva in the Middle Urals and the Vishera in the Northern Urals can be arranged through the Ekaterinburg C&V Bureau & Guide Centre (see the Yekaterinburg section later in this chapter for contact details).

PERM
ПЕРМЬ

☎ 3422 • pop 1 million • Moscow time plus 2 hours

Dominated by heavily trafficked avenues and ugly concrete blocks, Perm itself is an industrial city that most travellers could bear to miss. It is, however, a base for several interesting excursions, such as the ice caves at nearby Kungur and the Gulag museum at Perm-36.

By the time Catherine the Great decreed Perm a provincial capital in 1780, it was well on its way to being a major trade gateway to Siberia and Asia. During the Soviet period, however, it was another closed city, renamed Molotov, after the foreign minister who also gave his name to the explosive cocktail.

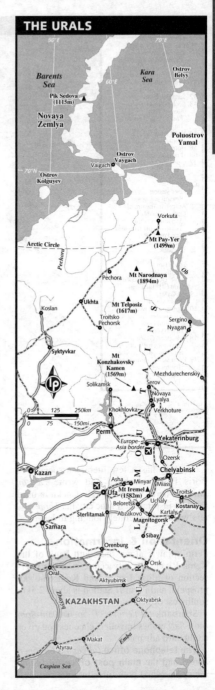

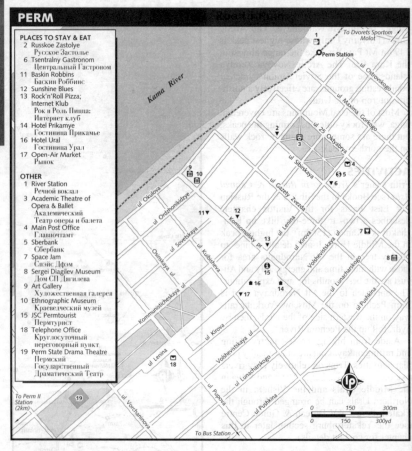

PERM

PLACES TO STAY & EAT
2 Russkoe Zastolye
   Русское Застолье
6 Tsentralny Gastronom
   Центральный Гастроном
11 Baskin Robbins
   Баскин Роббинс
12 Sunshine Blues
13 Rock'n'Roll Pizza;
   Internet Klub
   Рок и Роль Пицца;
   Интернет клуб
14 Hotel Prikamye
   Гостиница Прикамье
16 Hotel Ural
   Гостиница Урал
17 Open-Air Market
   Рынок

OTHER
1 River Station
   Речной вокзал
3 Academic Theatre of
   Opera & Ballet
   Академический
   Театр оперы и балета
4 Main Post Office
   Главпочтамт
5 Sberbank
   Сбербанк
7 Space Jam
   Спэйс Джэм
8 Sergei Diagilev Museum
   Дом СП Дигилева
9 Art Gallery
   Художественная галерея
10 Ethnographic Museum
   Краеведческий музей
15 JSC Permtourist
   Пермтурист
18 Telephone Office
   Круглосуточный
   переговорный пункт
19 Perm State Drama Theatre
   Пермский
   Государственный
   Драматический Театр

The city has a few literary associations: Boris Pasternak lived and wrote *Doctor Zhivago* here; more tellingly Chekhov used Perm as inspiration for the city his *Three Sisters* were so desperately longing to leave.

Orientation & Information

Perm sprawls along the south bank of the Kama River. The city centre is at the intersection of ulitsa Lenina and Komsomolsky prospekt, and Perm II Station is about 2.5km southwest of here.

Sberbank (ul Lenina 31; open 10am-8pm Mon-Sat) cashes travellers cheques and gives credit card advances.

The **telephone office** (ul Lenina 66; open 24hrs) and the **main post office** (ul Lenina 29; open 24hrs) both offer Internet services.

Rates will generally be R20 to R30 per hour. There is also the **Internet Klub** (Komsomolsky pr 34; open 24hrs) upstairs from Rock'n Roll Pizza.

JSC Permtourist (☎ 34 35 60, fax 12 48 43; e travel@permtourist.ru; ul Lenina 58) arranges local excursions as well as cruises along the Kama River and farther to the Volga.

Things to See

Perm has a decent **Art Gallery** (Permskaya Gosudarstvennaya Khudozhestvennaya Galereya; ☎ 12 23 95; Komsomolsky pr 4; admission R15; open 11am- 5.30pm Tues-Sun), easily identified by the spire and cupola of the former cathedral. The gallery, which underwent renovations in 2002, houses one of the largest icon collections in the country.

Next door, the **Ethnographic Museum** (*Permsky oblastnoy kraevedchesky muzey;* ☎ *12 24 56; Komsomolsky pr 6; admission R10; open 10am-6pm Sat-Thur*) features mainly stuffed local animals.

The **Sergei Diaghilev Museum** (*Dom SM Dyagileva;* ☎ *12 06 10; ul Sibirskaya 33; admission free; open 9am-6pm Mon-Fri*) is a small, lovingly curated exhibition on the world-famous ballet and opera impresario (1872–1929), whose family came from the Perm region.

Places to Stay & Eat

Hotel Prikamye (*☎/fax 34 86 62; Komsomolsky pr 27; singles/doubles from R550/ 700*) has friendly service and decent rooms. Cheaper singles with shared bath are also available for R300.

Hotel Ural (*☎ 90 62 20, fax 12 92 17;* e *ural-hotel@permtourist.ru; ul Lenina 58; singles/doubles from R370/740*) is a monolith (average distance from front desk to room is about 1km), but the rooms are fine and cheap. Better rooms with facilities such as a telephone and TV are still reasonably priced.

Russkoe Zastolye (*☎ 12 57 71; ul Sovietskaya 29; meals from R400; open noon-midnight*) is a pricey but pleasant place to get traditional Russian food with a modern twist.

Sunshine Blues (*☎ 12 72 55; Komsomolsky pr 16; lunch R100, dinner R200; open 9am-11pm*) is a convivial blues bar with good food and an outdoor terrace in summer.

Rock'n Roll Pizza (*☎ 22 22 22; Komsomolsky pr 34; pizza R50; open 24hrs*) serves decent pizza with typically Russian, imaginative toppings. For dessert, go for ice cream at **Baskin Robbins** (*☎ 10 31 13; Komsomolsky prospekt 7*).

For self-catering supplies try the daily open-air **market** behind Hotel Ural, or the well-stocked **Tsentralny Gastronom** (*ul Sibirskaya 6; open 8am-9pm Mon-Sat, 9am-6pm Sun*).

Entertainment

The terrace overlooking the Kama River just outside the Art Gallery is a good place for beer and shashlyk from the *letny kafe* (summer café).

The **Academic Theatre of Opera & Ballet** (*Akademichesky teatr opery i baleta;* ☎ *12 30 87; Kommunisticheskaya ul 25*) located in Reshetnikova Garden is one of Russia's top

schools of performing arts. It stages good productions.

The **Perm State Drama Theatre** (*ul Lenina*) is another venue that stages classical performances.

Space Jam (*☎ 12 39 81; ul Sibirskaya 25; open noon-2am*) is a popular nightclub with a dance floor, bar and restaurant.

Perm is home to Russia's most successful basketball team, Ural Great. They play from September to April at the **Dvorets Sportom Molot** (*ul Lebedeva 13*), which seats 9000 people. Tickets, from R100 to R2000, are available at the stadium or the local **Reebok outlet** (*☎/fax 33 49 30; ul Lenina 79; open 10am-8pm Mon-Sat, 11am-6pm Sun*).

Getting There & Away

Air There are two daily Aeroflot flights to/ from Moscow. **Lufthansa** (*☎ 28 44 42*) flies to/from Frankfurt twice a week. There's an airline **ticket office** (*open 9am-8pm daily*) in the lobby of Hotel Ural.

Train Perm II, the city's major train station, is on the Trans-Siberian route from Moscow (R1200, 20 hours). Yekaterinburg (R150, six hours) is the next major city east. Trains to Kazan (R300, 14 hours) depart every other day from the *gorny trakt* (mountain track) on the north side of Perm II, and follow a windy but scenic route through the mountains. The crumbling Perm Station, 1km east of the centre, is used by suburban trains only.

The **ticket office** (*ul Kirsanova 19; open 6am-6pm*) in the city centre has manageable queues and charges a small booking fee.

Boat The **river station** (*☎ 19 93 04*) is at the eastern end of ulitsa Ordzhonikidzye, opposite Perm Station. Boats down the Kama River to the Volga depart about once a week during summer.

Bus The bus station is at the southern end of ulitsa Popova. Daily buses go to Yekaterinburg and to other small towns in the Urals region.

Getting Around

Bus Nos 110, 119 and 120 serve the airport from the centre (35 minutes), or you can take a taxi for about R250. Take any bus or trolleybus, or tram No 7, between Perm II Station and Hotels Ural and Prikamye. A taxi on this route costs around R80.

THE URALS

Tricky Tracks

I arrived at Perm II Station in plenty of time for my train to Kazan. Having spent much of the day securing this ticket, I was starting to feel like those Three Sisters in the Chekhov play. I waited on the platform with a few other people who seemed to be waiting for nothing in particular. The time of my intended departure approached, but my train did not.

Inside the station, the big board gave no indication of a delay. The solitary person responsible for answering questions was swamped – go figure – by people asking questions. My train was nowhere to be found. As precious moments ticked away, I questioned a security guard. Sure, his business was troublemakers not timetables, but he must know something, right?

He shrugged. 'Is your train on the *glavny trakt* or the *gorny trakt*?' he asked me. The main track or the mountain track – good question. I didn't even know there was a mountain track on the opposite side of the station. In fact, I had never even heard of the mountain track. I dashed out onto the mountain track just in time to see my train pull away.

The moral of the story is: 'Don't make a mountain out of a main (or vice versa)'.

Mara Vorhees

★★

AROUND PERM

Khokhlovka
Хохловка

The **Architecture-Ethnography Museum** (☎ 99 71 82; admission R30; open 10am-6pm Mon-Sun late May-Oct) is set in the rolling countryside at Khokhlovka, about 45km north of Perm. Its eight wooden buildings include two churches dating back to the turn of the 18th century, while the other structures are from the 19th or early 20th centuries. During the first weekend of May, a folk and culture festival celebrates the coming of spring. A few buses a day serve Khokhlovka from Perm.

Kungur
Кунгур

Although it's now a backwater, Kungur still has many notable (though dilapidated) buildings, including the **All Saints Church**, a 17th-century **governor's house** and 19th-century arcade, **Gostiny Dvor**. There is also the **Regional Local Studies Museum** (ul Gogolya 36; open 11am-5pm). Admission costs around R15.

The main attraction, however, is the **Kungur Ice Cave** (Ledyanaya peshchera; admission R100; open 10am-5pm daily), 5km out of town, which is famous for unique ice formations with frozen waterfalls and underground lakes. JSC Permtourist (see Orientation & Information in the Perm section earlier) can arrange tours here, as well as accommodation in the adjacent **Stalagmit Hotel** (☎/fax 34271-3 97 23; singles/doubles R150/300).

The train and bus stations in Kungur are on ulitsa Bachurina. There are eight trains a day from Perm II Station (R20, 2½ hours). A day trip is possible if you start early but check the train schedule in advance.

Perm-36
Пермь-36

Perm-36 (Perm tridtsat shest) is about 10km from the town of Chusovoy, which is 100km east of Perm. This was one of the infamous labour camps of the Gulag Archipelago where many dissidents were persecuted. Stalin ordered the camp built in 1946 for the detention of political prisoners, who were confined to small freezing sheds. Perm-36 closed in 1987 and the camp now has a memorial to the victims of the Gulag system and a museum and research centre.

Perm-36 is difficult to reach as it has no public transport connections with Chusovoy; however, you can hire a cab for just a few dollars. Buses and trains run between Chusovoy and Perm.

JSC Permtourist offers tours, arranged in advance and with the price variable according to the number of people in your party.

YEKATERINBURG
ЕКАТЕРИНБУРГ

☎ 3432 • pop 1.37 million • Moscow time plus 2 hours

With a notoriously bloody and secret history (to which high-profile Russian Mafia killings in the 1990s added a contemporary edge) Yekaterinburg is an intriguing place on paper. In reality, this birthplace of Boris

Mamaev Kurgan (Mother Russia), Volgograd

Resurrection Cathedral, Starocherkassk

Fighter plane memorial to the Battle of Stalingrad (Volgograd) on the Volga River

Ornately carved window frames at the Architecture Museum, Nizhnyaya Sinyachikha

Road leading to Gumbashi Pass in the valley between Tereze and Karacajevsk

Yeltsin and focus of the Urals' industrial and mineral wealth is even better: a pleasant city to stroll through, with loads of museums, a fascinating variety of architecture, and a decent range of accommodation, restaurants and entertainment. It's also a good base for trips into the Urals for adventure activities and winter sports.

History

Founded as a factory-fort in 1723 as part of Peter the Great's push to exploit the Ural region's mineral riches, the city was named after two Yekaterinas – Peter's wife (later Empress Catherine I), and the Russian patron saint of mining. A year later, Peter discovered his wife's infidelity and had her lover's head cut off and placed in a jar of surgical spirit in her bedroom.

By the 19th century Yekaterinburg, already wealthy from the machinery it supplied to the Ural mines, became a gold-rush town. Gold is still being discovered here – a find in the 1980s during excavations for the city's metro helped pay for the metro line itself.

Yekaterinburg is most famous, though, as the place where Tsar Nicholas II and his family were murdered by the Bolsheviks in July 1918. Six years later, the town was renamed Sverdlovsk, after Yakov Sverdlov, a leading Bolshevik who was Lenin's right-hand man until he died in the flu epidemic of 1919.

WWII turned the city into a major industrial centre as hundreds of factories were transferred here from vulnerable areas west of the Urals, and it was closed to foreigners until 1990 because of its many defence plants. Remnants of this era still litter the city, with fighter planes proudly displayed in school yards and missiles arranged outside the city's Military History Museum.

It was one such missile that in 1960 brought down the US pilot Gary Powers and his U2 spy plane in this area. Powers, who bailed out successfully, was exchanged for a Soviet spy in 1962. In 1979, 64 people died of anthrax after a leak from a biological weapons plant, Sverdlovsk-19, in the city.

During the late 1970s a civil engineering graduate of the local university, Boris Yeltsin, began to make his political mark, rising to become regional Communist Party boss before being promoted to Moscow in 1985. Russians of a less political bent are equally likely to remember Yekaterinburg during this period

Wet Paint

My fondest memory of Yekaterinburg was the amazing profusion of statues. I found it to be a city that rewards the aimless wanderer. In the park behind the city pond we saw some old babushkas repainting all the benches. No wet paint signs or anything. We saw many people with paint across the back of their trousers and dresses, and mum was one of them!

Brett Hyland, July 2001

as the birthplace of the rock band Nautilus Pompilius.

In 1991, Yekaterinburg took back its original name. After suffering economic depression and Mafia lawlessness in the early 1990s, business is now on the upswing, with the local economy growing by some 20% in 2000.

Orientation

The city centre lies between the main boulevards, prospekt Lenina and ulitsa Malysheva, and runs from ploshchad 1905 goda in the west to ulitsa Lunacharskogo in the east. The train station is 2km north of the centre on ulitsa Sverdlova, which changes its name to ulitsa Karla Libknekhta closer to the centre. Prospekt Lenina crosses the dammed Iset River three blocks west of ulitsa Karla Libknekhta. Although changes to some street names have long been on the cards, the old names are still used by locals.

Information

Money Gutabank (☎ 59 25 21; pr Lenina 27) is one of the few places in the city that accept travellers cheques. **Alfa Bank** (ul Malysheva 33a) has a 24-hour ATM that dispenses roubles or US dollars.

Post & Communications The main **post office** (pr Lenina 39; open 10am-7pm Mon-Fri) offers Internet and international telephone connections. **Poligon Internet Klub** (☎ 77 66 93; ul 8 Marta 13; open 24hrs) is convenient, although it is often overrun by kids playing computer games. Rates are generally R15 to R30 an hour.

Travel Agencies The **Ekaterinburg C&V Bureau & Guide Centre** (☎ 68 16 04, fax 55 60 19; W www.ekaterinburg-guide.com; ul Krasnoarmeyskaya 1, side entrance), in the

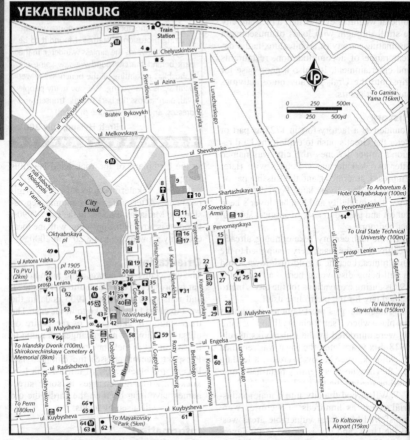

YEKATERINBURG

Bolshoy Ural Hotel, is run by an enthusiastic husband-and-wife team that organises English-language tours of the city and surrounding area, including one-day Urals rafting trips, from US$25 to US$35 per person (depending on numbers). They can also arrange inexpensive hotel/homestay accommodation.

Sputnik (☎ 59 83 00, fax 71 34 83; e sputnik@dialup.mplik.ru; ul Pushkina 5; open 9am-7pm Mon-Sat) is a long-running agency that handles bookings for the major hotels and can arrange all kinds of air tickets. Its tours include a three-hour city tour and a four-hour tour out to the Europe–Asia border.

Bookshops Dom Knigi (☎ 59 42 00; ul Antona Valeka 12; open 9am-7pm) is best for foreign-language and local-interest books.

The Knigi bookshop near the train station opposite the end of ulitsa Sverdlova sells a fairly decent range of local maps, including a bus/tram/trolleybus map. For maps of Yekaterinburg and Sverdlovsk Oblast, try **Karta** (☎ 75 62 90; ul Pervomayskaya 74; open 9am-1pm & 2pm-6pm Mon-Fri).

Visa Registration The passport and visa department office, or **passportno-vizovoye upravleniye** (PVU; ☎ 58 82 59; ul Krylova 2; open 10am-noon & 2pm-4pm Mon, Wed & Fri) is accessible by tram No 2, 13 or 18.

Around the City Centre
Freshly painted benches aside, a walking tour is the ideal way to take in the scope of the city's tumultuous history. Start at **Istorichesky**

YEKATERINBURG

PLACES TO STAY
1 Resting Rooms
Комнаты Отдыха
5 Hotel Sverdlovsk
Гостиница Свердловск
23 Hotel Iset
Гостиница Исет
24 Academy of Geology Hotel
Гостиница Академии
Геологии
29 Bolshoy Ural Hotel; Ekaterin-
burg C&V Bureau & Guide
Centre; Museum of Stones
Гостиница Большой Урал;
Екатеринбургский центр
гилов; Музей Камня
60 Hotel Premier
Гостиница Премьер
61 Atrium Palace Hotel; City Bar
Атриум Палас Отель;
Сити бар
63 Hotel of the Urals Academy
State Service
Гостиница Уральской
Государственной Академии
65 Hotel Magister
Гостиница Магистр

PLACES TO EAT
12 Sem Sorok
Семь Сорок
26 Trali-Bali
Трали-бали
27 Yellow Submarine
Йелоу Субмарин
31 Zolotoy Drakon
Золотой Дракон
32 Friday
Фрайдей
34 Subway
Субуэй
39 Monetny Dvor
Монетный Двор
43 Akvarium
Аквариум
51 Mak Pik
Мак Пик
54 Kafe Pari Klassik
Кафе Пари Классик
56 La Gradara
Ла Градара
58 Kamenny Most
Каменный Мост
66 Kupets
Купец

METRO STATIONS
3 Uralskaya
Уральская
6 Dinamo
Динамо
46 Ploshchad 1905 Goda
Площадь 1905 Года
64 Geologicheskaya
Геологическая

OTHER
2 Bus Station
Автовокзал
4 Knigi Bookshop
Магазин книги
7 Romanov Death Site; Chapel
of the Revered Martyr Grand
Princess Yelisaveta Fyodorovna
Место убийста Романовых
8 Church of Blood
Церковь на Крови
9 Rastorguev-Kharitonov
Mansion
Усадьба Расторгуев-
Харитонов
10 Ascension Church
Вознесенская Церковь
11 Philharmonic
Филармония
13 Military History Museum
Военно-Исторический музей
14 Karta Map Shop
Карта Магазин
15 Malakhit
Малахит
16 Museum of Photography
Музей Фотографии
17 Museum of Youth
Музей Молодёжи
18 Governor's Residence
Резиденция Губернатора
19 Governor's Residence
Резиденция Губернатора
20 Nikolai Sevastianof Mansion
Дом Николая
Севастианофа
21 Post Office
Почтамт
22 Sverdlov Statue
Памятник Свердлову
25 Transaero
Трансаэро
28 Gans
Ганс

30 Opera & Ballet Theatre
Театр оперы и балеты
33 Sputnik; Lufthansa
Спутник; Луфтгаиса
35 Chapel
Часовня
36 Tatishchev & de Gennin Statue
Памятник Татищеву и де
Геннин
37 Order of Lenin
Орден Ленина
38 Water Tower; Blacksmith
Museum
Водонапорная башня
40 Museum of City Architecture
& Urals Industrial Technology
Музей Истории Архит-
ектуры Города и Промышл-
енной Техники Урала
41 Geological Alley
Геологическая аллея
42 Museum of Fine Arts
Музей Изобразительных
Искусств
44 Railway & Air Kassa; Alfa Bank
Железнодорожные и Авиа
кассы; Алфабанк
45 Poligon Internet Klub
Полигон Интернет клуб
47 Lenin Statue
Памятник Ленину
48 Regional Government Building
Дом областной админист-
рации
49 Dom Knigi
Дом книги
50 Gutabank
Гутабанк
52 Toilet
Туалет
53 Tsentralny Univermag (TsUM)
ЦУМ
55 The Old Dublin Pub
Старый Дублин
57 Regional Local Studies
Museum
Краеведческий Музей
59 US & UK Consulates General
Генеральные Консульства
Великобритании и США
62 Circus
Цирк
67 Ural Geology Museum
Уральский Геологический
Музей

skver (Historical Square) where prospekt Lenina crosses a small dam forming the Gorodskoy prud (City Pond) on its north side, with the Iset River funnelled through a narrow channel on the south side. This area, better known as the *plotinka* (little dam), was where Yekaterinburg began back in 1723. Water from the dam (reconstructed twice since that date) powered an iron forge, a mint and a stone-cutting works.

Istorichesky skver is surrounded by a clutch of statues and old buildings (see Museums later), and on its west side is **Geological Alley** (Geologicheskaya alleya), a small park dotted with rocks from the Ural region. The bridge on ulitsa Lenina holds the striking, red, sculpted **Order of Lenin** given to the city for honourable service during WWII.

About 100m west along prospekt Lenina is another square, **ploshchad 1905 goda**. On one side, the department store **Tsentralny Univermag** (TsUM) does brisk business in all kinds of wares. On the other side, the looming statue of Lenin occupies the spot where once stood one of Yekaterinburg's main cathedrals, destroyed in the Soviet period. Farther west, artists sell their wares along the tree-lined strip in the centre of ulitsa Lenina.

Cross the bridge heading east on prospekt Lenina. The **statue** on the south side of the street is of Tatishchev and de Gennin, founders of Yekaterinburg, holding the tsar's decree. The small chapel was built in 1998 on the site of another grand cathedral, which was destroyed during the Soviet period.

Across the street, the architecture demonstrates the radical changes of the 19th and 20th centuries. The eclectic 19th-century **mansion**, which is now a trade union's headquarters, was the exotic creation of Nikolai Sevastianof, a rich merchant who wanted his house to outshine that of the **governor's mansion**, which stands next door. In total contrast are the clean lines of the **central post office** and the **regional government building** across the pond, both prime examples of 1930s constructivism.

Farther east, you will pass the attractive **Opera & Ballet Theatre**. A statue of Yakov Sverdlov stands in front.

At the roundabout, head north on ulitsa Lunacharskogo towards **ploshchad Sovetskoi Armii**, dominated by one of the most powerful statues you're likely to see in Russia. The giant soldier with downcast head primarily commemorates losses in Russia's Afghanistan War (1979–89), but plaques around the statue also note those lost in other conflicts during the Cold War years.

Continue north from the square along ulitsa Mamina-Sibiryaka to the entrance to a pretty **park**, which climbs up the hill known locally as the Yekaterinburg Acropolis. At the top is the ostentatious classical-fronted **mansion** of the rich 19th-century family Rastorguev-Kharitonov, and the restored **Ascension Church** (Voznesenskaya Tserkov; ul Karla Tsetkin 11).

Immediately ahead of the church, across ulitsa Karla Libknekhta, is where Tsar Nicholas II, his wife and children were murdered on the night of 16 July 1918. The house was known as Dom Ipateva, after its owner Nikolay Ipatev, but it was demolished in 1977 by then-governor Boris Yeltsin. Today, the site is marked by an iron cross dating from 1991, and another of marble from 1998 when the Romanovs' remains were sent to St Petersburg for burial in the family vault.

Beside the crosses is the pretty little wooden **Chapel of the Revered Martyr Grand Princess Yelisaveta Fyodorovna** (Chasovnya vo imya Prepodobnomuchenitsy Velikoi Knyagini Yelisavety Fyodorovny; open 9am-5.30pm daily). Grand Princess Yelisaveta was a great-aunt of the royal family and a pious nun who, soon after her relatives' murders, reportedly met an even worse end. When she survived being thrown down a mine, poisonous gas was pumped in and the shaft filled with earth. You can visit this spot, where a monastery has recently been built, on a trip to Nizhnyaya Sinyachikha (see Around Yekaterinburg).

The chapel is already overshadowed by the neighbouring Byzantine-style **Church of the Blood** (Tserkov na Krovi), which should be completed in 2003. This will honour the Romanov family, now elevated to the status of saints.

Head south from here along ulitsa Karla Libknekhta, turn west at ulitsa Pervomayskaya, then north on ulitsa Proletarskaya (also called ulitsa Ofitserskaya), where several of the **wooden buildings** are small museums dedicated to local writers. At No 6 is an old **post house** marked by a pole showing the distances, in the ancient Russian measurement of versts, to Moscow and St Petersburg. From here follow the shoreline south to Istorichesky skver.

Lenin Goes Shopping

According to a local anecdote, the statues of Sverdlov and Lenin are actually supposed to be interacting with each other.

Sverdlov: Vladimir Ilych, where did you get that coat?

Lenin: Over there, at TsUM!

★★★★★★★★★★★★★★★★★★★★★

Bones of Contention: The Romanov Remains

What happened to the bodies of the Romanovs after their deaths is a mixture of the macabre, the mysterious and the plain messy. After decades of rumour and speculation, expert investigations since 1991 have finally pieced the story together.

The Romanov remains actually resurfaced back in 1976, when a group of local scientists discovered them in Porosenkov Log, about 3km from Ganina Yama (see Around Yekaterinburg later). So politically sensitive was this issue during Soviet times that the discovery was kept secret until the remains were finally fully excavated in 1991. The bones of nine people found were tentatively identified as Tsar Nicholas II, his wife Tsarina Alexandra, three of their four daughters, the royal doctor and three servants. Absent were any remains of the royal couple's only son, Tsarevich Alexey, aged 13 at the time of the killings. Also notably absent was the fourth daughter, which gave a new lease of life to theories that the youngest daughter, Anastasia (aged 17 in 1918), had somehow escaped the killings. The best known of several people who had claimed to be Anastasia was Anna Anderson, who appeared in Berlin in 1920 with convincing stories of life among the Romanovs which led many people to believe her claims. She died in the USA in 1984.

In 1992 bone samples from the excavated skeletons were sent to the British government's Forensic Science Service, to be tested by DNA identification techniques pioneered by British scientists. Using blood and hair samples from the Duke of Edinburgh (a grandson of the tsarina's sister) and two descendants of the tsar, the scientists had established with 'more than 98.5%' certainty by 1993 that the bones were those of the tsar, the tsarina and three of their daughters.

An official Russian inquiry team in Yekaterinburg then managed to piece together the skulls found in the pit – some badly damaged by rifle butts, hand grenades and acid – and built plaster models of the faces they had once borne. This, together with the DNA tests and dental records, satisfied them by 1994 that the three daughters found were Olga and Tatyana (the two oldest) – and Anastasia.

The missing daughter was Maria. Her and Alexey's remains were still undiscovered, but the Russians said they at least knew how the family had been disposed of. And what a tale of ghoulish bungling it was. According to the Russian team, all five children had died with their parents in the cellar of Dom Ipateva. The bodies were then dumped in Ganina Yama, an abandoned mine 16km away, followed by several grenades intended to collapse the mine shaft. The mine, however, did not collapse. The bodies were pulled out and an acids expert summoned. He brought 160L of acid but fell off his horse, broke a leg and couldn't help. It was then decided to distribute the bodies among various smaller mines and pour acid on them. But the lorry carrying them became bogged in a swamp, so the disposal team – by now understandably desperate – opted to bury them on the spot. They tried burning Alexey and Maria in preparation, but realised it would take days to burn all the bodies properly, so the others were just put in a pit and doused with acid. Even then, most of the acid soaked away into the ground – leaving the bones to be uncovered 73 years later.

In mid-1998 the royal remains were finally buried at St Petersburg's SS Peter & Paul Cathedral, alongside most of Nicholas II's predecessors dating back to Peter the Great. The Orthodox Church never recognised that these were truly the royal remains that had been removed from Ganina Yama, and church officials were not in attendance at the burial in St Petersburg. The Church recognises Ganina Yama as the final resting place of the royal family.

Museums

Among Yekaterinburg's many museums, our favourite – and one of the most original in Russia – is the **Museum of Youth** (*Muzey Molodyozhy*; ☎ 71 37 61; *ul Karla Libknekhta 32; admission R20; open 10am-7pm Mon-Fri, 2pm-7pm Sat*). The highly imaginative and often surreal displays on 20th-century history were created by local art students.

Almost as good is the neighbouring **Museum of Photography** (*Muzey fotografii*; ☎ 71 38 14; *ul Karla Libknekhta 36; admission R10; open 11am-5.30pm Wed-Mon*). The museum displays evocative photographs of old Yekaterinburg, in addition to modern exhibitions.

The star exhibit of the **Museum of Fine Arts** (*Muzey izobrazitelnykh iskusstvs*; ☎ 71

06 26; ul Voevodina 5; admission R30; open 11am-6pm Wed-Sun), at the south end of Istorichesky skver, is the elaborate Kasli Iron Pavilion that won prizes in the 1900 Paris Expo. On the opposite side of the river, you'll find the **Blacksmith Museum** (ul Vainera 11) in the old water tower and the **Museum of City Architecture & Urals Industrial Technology** (☎ 71 40 45; ul Gorkogo 4 & 5) in the old mining-equipment factory and mint buildings. Admission will be around R15.

The **Military History Museum** (Voenno-istorichesky muzey; ☎ 55 17 42; ul Pervomayskaya 27; admission R10; open 9am-4pm Tues-Sat) is a must for military buffs. It is not always open, so call ahead to check. A few scraps of metal are all that's left on display of Gary Powers' spy plane.

The **Regional Local Studies Museum** (Oblastnoy kraevedchesky muzey; ☎ 76 47 58; ul Malysheva 46; admission R30; open 11am-6pm Mon & Wed-Sat) has some interesting exhibits on the Romanovs and the Old Believers in the Ural region.

Serious geologists will do well to visit the **Ural Geology Museum** (Uralsky Geologichesky Muzey; ☎ 22 31 09; ul Kuybysheva 39; admission R30; open 11am-5pm Tues-Fri), which has over 500 carefully catalogued Ural region minerals and a collection of meteorites. Less specialised is the **Museum of Stones** (Muzey Kaminya; ☎ 55 60 19; ul Krasnoarmeyskaya 1A; admission R30; open 10am-7pm Tues-Sun), which has an impressive, but unimaginatively displayed, collection of rare minerals and semiprecious stones.

University & Arboretum

The Ural State Technical University (Uralsky gosudarstvenny tekhnichesky universitet), an imposing 1930s Soviet classical edifice at the east end of prospekt Lenina, 2km from the centre, is the biggest Russian university east of the Ural Mountains. It's still known as UPI, the initials of its old name, Uralsky Politekhnichesky Institut (Ural Polytechnical Institute), when it was renowned as a stepping stone to high political office – for Boris Yeltsin, among many others.

There's a nice, quiet open-air arboretum (Dendrologichesky Park-Vystavka) a block north of the university, on the corner of ulitsa Pervomayskaya and ulitsa Mira. You can reach the university by tram No 4, 13, 15 or 18 or bus No 28 east along prospekt Lenina.

Get off the tram when it turns right down ulitsa Gagarina, a block before the university.

Winter Sports

Winter in the Urals lasts a long time, making this a terrific place for winter sports. The rolling hills that surround Yekaterinburg are breathtaking when covered with a fresh layer of snow. If there's no time to leave the city, head to **Mayakovsky Park** (☎ 24 30 32), 5km south of town, for cross-country skiing. Take tram No 3 from the train station or No 29 from ulitsa Lenina. Equipment is available to rent.

Places to Stay

Budget You'll be lucky to score a place at the train station's **resting rooms** (komnaty otdykha; level 4, west wing; doubles without/ with bathroom R150/400). The rooms are clean and will do for a night but the station is so busy that they fill up quickly.

Ekaterinburg C&V Bureau & Guide Centre (see Information earlier) arranges **homestays** for US$20/34/48 including breakfast for one/two/three people. It can also book some cheap hotels which are otherwise not available to walk-in guests.

Hotel Sverdlovsk (☎ 53 65 74, fax 53 62 48; ul Chelyuskintsev 106; singles/doubles from US$20/32) gives a choice between cheap and dilapidated rooms or upgraded and overpriced. In its favour is its location opposite the station.

The **Academy of Geology Hotel** (☎ 55 05 08; Bldg 6, pr Lenina 54; singles/doubles with breakfast US$30/40) is the best budget option, with smart, spacious rooms in a quiet complex tucked away off the main road.

The **Hotel of the Urals Academy of State Service** (☎ 29 77 40; ul 8 Marta 70; dorm beds/singles US$14/30) is used by visiting civil servants. The rooms here are old-fashioned but decent enough. Take tram No 15 going west from prospekt Lenina to the Dekabristov stop.

Bolshoy Ural Hotel (☎ 55 68 96, fax 55 05 83; ul Krasnoarmeyskaya 1; e bu@adx.ru; singles/doubles from R243/640) is indeed bolshoy (large). It is also not a small bit seedy, but at least there are always rooms available.

Mid-Range & Top End A comfortable choice with professional staff and service,

Hotel Oktyabrskaya (☎ 74 15 95, fax 74 50 16; e man@gw.ural.ru; ul Sofyi Kovalevskaya 17; singles/doubles from R1000/1500 plus 25% reservation fee on first night) is a former Communist Party hang-out in a leafy neighbourhood 2km east of the centre (north off ulitsa Pervomayskaya).

With bright and comfortable rooms and friendly staff, **Hotel Iset** (☎ 55 69 43, fax 56 24 69; e hotel_is@etel.ru; pr Lenina 69; singles/doubles from R1500/2100) is in a building shaped like a hammer and sickle when seen from the sky.

The small and friendly **Hotel Magister** (☎ 22 42 06, fax 22 56 74; e magister1@etel.ru; ul 8 Marta 50; singles/doubles with breakfast US$88/100) is still the most popular place for businesspeople (so you will need to make a booking well in advance). Tram No 15 running west along prospekt Lenina goes past the door. Get off just before the circus.

Hotel Premier (☎ 56 38 97, fax 56 38 80; ul Krasnoarmeyskaya 23; singles/doubles US$83/117) is a new place with big, stylishly decorated rooms.

The **Atrium Palace Hotel** (☎ 59 60 00, fax 59 60 01; e aph.ektb@aph-ural.ru; ul Kuybysheva 44; singles/doubles with breakfast US$198/251) once claimed to be the only five-star hotel east of Moscow. Lack of competition explains the prices. This snazzy place has a pricey restaurant, popular bar and a nightclub, plus a gym, sauna and pool.

Places to Eat

Restaurants A good re-creation of a hospitable Russian country inn, **Trali-Bali** (☎ 55 17 04; pr Lenina 50; meals from R100; open noon-midnight) also has a salad bar providing the recommended daily allowance of vegies, which you won't get elsewhere.

Yellow Submarine (☎ 55 17 05; pr Lenina 46/2; meals R100; open 11am-11pm) is a funny café that takes on the decor of an actual yellow submarine. You can dine next to a life-size Lennon.

Akvarium (☎ 59 82 19; ul Voevodina 6; mains from R200) features fish swimming in tanks around the restaurant and – surprise, surprise – fish on the menu.

The classy **Sem Sorok** (☎ 55 70 17; ul Pervomayskaya 9; meals R150-300) serves excellent Jewish food, including gefilte fish and cholent (a meat stew).

Kamenny Most (☎ 56 19 55; ul Malysheva 56A; mains from R200) is a stylish Russian restaurant overlooking the Iset River. Across the street, **Monetny Dvor** (☎ 71 24 75; ul Gorkogo 4; mains from RR200; open noon-midnight) is in one of the atmospheric old mint buildings.

Zolotoy Drakon (☎ 71 37 46; ul Karla Libknekhta 13; meals R200; open 10am-2am) represents the latest craze in Russian theme restaurants – Mongolian barbecue. Friendly servers in traditional dress explain how it works.

For reasonably priced Italian food (but expensive wine), try **La Gradara** (☎ 59 83 66; ul Malysheva 36; meals from R300).

Fast Food & Self-Catering Specialising in burgers like the 'Big Mak Pik', **Mak Pik** (☎ 71 68 98; pr Lenina 24/8; meals R100; 9am-10pm) also does pizza, pelmeni and, of all things, sushi. **Friday** (☎ 71 22 53; ul Karla Libknekhta 16/18; meals R100) is similar, but sticks to pizza and salad.

For a taste of home (especially if you're from New York), **Subway** (☎ 71 97 61; pr Lenina 32; meals R100; open 11am-10pm) has all kinds of sandwiches.

Not quite Paris, **Kafe Pari Klassik** (☎ 71 18 25; ul 8 Marta 8b; meals R100; open 11am-midnight) offers light meals and snacks in a more stylish setting.

If you're looking for a large, Western-style supermarket with a wide selection of Russian and imported food items, head to **Kupets** (ul 8 Marta 48; open 24hrs).

Entertainment

Classical Music, Opera & Ballet Attending a performance at the **Opera & Ballet Theatre** (☎ 55 80 57; pr Lenina 45A) is worth the price of the ticket just to see the inside of this grand theatre. Tickets for the **Philharmonic** (☎ 51 73 77; ul Karla Libknekhta 38) tend to be more expensive (from R150) but both institutions put on good shows. Tickets start at R100.

Bars & Clubs Excellent service and food attract a good crowd every night of the week to **The Old Dublin Irish Pub** (☎ 10 91 73; ul Khokhryakova 23; mains from R200, half-litre of Guinness R140; open noon-2am), which is actually owned – partially – by an Irish bloke. Although less authentic, **Irlandsky**

Dvorik (☎ 76 33 18; ul Malysheva 11; mains from R200; open noon-2am) is also a pleasant place with good food and drink.

Gans (☎ 55 90 67; ul Malysheva 63; mains R400-500; open noon-2am) is a German beer bar, with some very quaffable but pricey ales and food.

City Bar (☎ 59 60 00; Atrium Palace Hotel, ul Kuybysheva 44; meals R300; open 11am-1am) is the expatriate hang-out for Friday evening happy hour, between 7pm and 11pm, when fish and chips are served for R150.

Yekaterinburg's top club is **Malakhit** (☎ 56 40 48; ul Lunacharskogo 128; admission Fri & Sat men/women R250/150, Wed-Thur R100; open 9pm-6am Wed-Sun), a typically flash place with plenty of options if you don't want to dance, including a restaurant, strip bar, bowling alley, and even a bucking bronco!

Circus Another entertainment option is that favourite Russian pastime, the circus. In Yekaterinburg, the clowns and lions live in the strangely shaped circus building at the corner of ulitsa Kuibysheva and ulitsa 8 Marta.

Getting There & Away

Air The main airport is **Koltsovo** (☎ 24 99 24), 15km southeast of the city centre. Daily flights go to/from Moscow (US$130, 2½ hours) and Irkutsk (US$120, four hours) and there are services several times a week to/from Rostov (three hours), Samara (two hours), St Petersburg (2½ hours), Novosibirsk (two hours) and Vladivostok (11 hours). Flights go less frequently to Baku, Khabarovsk, Krasnodar, Mineralnye Vody, Odessa, Rostov, Saratov, Sochi, Tashkent, Volgograd and Yerevan. Lufthansa flies to/from Frankfurt three times weekly (six hours).

Lufthansa (☎ 59 83 00) operates from the Sputnik office (see Travel Agencies earlier). **Transaero** (☎ 65 91 65, fax 77 73 97; pr Lenina 50) handles bookings for all airlines.

Train Yekaterinburg is a major rail junction with connections to all stops on the Trans-Siberian route. Additionally, eastbound trains go via Tyumen (R300, 4½ hours) to Omsk (R1200, 12 hours); others go via Kurgan and Petropavlovsk (in Kazakhstan) to Omsk. Westbound, trains to Moscow go via Kazan

(R1050, 15 hours) and Perm (seven hours). There is also a direct service to/from Tobolsk (12½ hours). You can buy tickets at outlets throughout the city, including the convenient **Railway and Air Kassa** (Zheleznodorozhnie i Avia Kassi; ☎ 71 04 00; ul Malysheva 31; open 7am-9pm).

Getting Around

Bus No 1 links the train station and Koltsovo airport (45 minutes) from 5.30am to 11pm. A taxi to/from the airport costs around R240, or double this price at night. Hire a taxi from the stand on ulitsa 8 Marta in front of the shopping centre.

Many trolleybuses (pay on board) run up and down ulitsa Sverdlova/ulitsa Karla Libknekhta between the train station and prospekt Lenina. Tram Nos 4, 13, 15 and 18 and bus No 28 cover long stretches of prospekt Lenina, with tram Nos 4 and 15 also serving the bus station.

The metro currently runs from the Uralmash machine tool factory in the north to the train station (metro: Uralskaya) and into the centre near ploshchad 1905 goda. A new station, Geologicheskaya, near the circus and Hotel Magister, has been under construction for years.

AROUND YEKATERINBURG
Shirokorechinskaya Cemetery & Memorial to the Victims of Political Repression
Широкоречинская кладбище и Мемориальный комплекс Жертв Политических Репрессий

A trip out to Shirokorechinskaya cemetery, 8km west of the city along the Moskovsky Trakt, reveals Yekaterinburg's more recent history. At the entrance you will see monumental graves to casualties of gang warfare in the 1990s; one has a life-size engraving of the 35-year-old gangster, his hand dangling Mercedes car keys as a symbol of his wealth.

On the opposite side of the road nearby is a vast memorial, opened in 1992 and dedicated to victims of the political repression of the 1930s. Some 25,000 people were killed in Yekaterinburg during Stalin's rule, and many of their bodies were later discovered here.

Bus Nos 9 and 24 go from the west end of ulitsa Lenina to nearby ploshchad Kommunarov. Alternatively, catch a taxi from the city to the cemetery for R120 per hour.

If you wish to have one foot in Europe and one in Asia, you can head 32km farther from here to the **Europe–Asia border**. Erected in 1837 at a 413m highpoint in the local Ural Mountains, the marker is a popular spot for wedding parties to visit on their post-nuptial video and photo jaunts.

Ganina Yama
Ганина Яма

After the Romanov family was shot in the cellar of Dom Ipateva, their bodies were discarded in the depths of the forests of Ganina Yama, 16km northeast of Yekaterinburg. The Orthodox Church is now building the exquisite **Monastery of the Holy Martyrs** (Monastyr vo imya Svyatye Tsartvennikh Strastoterptsev) at this pilgrimage site. Set deep in the peaceful birch forest, the wooden buildings are being constructed using ancient methods, which preclude the use of nails. An observation platform overlooks the mine shaft where the remains were deposited and burned. According to the Orthodox Church, this is the final resting place of the Romanov family and therefore sacred ground (see the boxed text 'Bones of Contention: The Romanov Remains' earlier).

Ganina Yama is nearly impossible to reach by public transport. If you hire a taxi from Yekaterinburg, take the road to Nizhny Tagil and look for the wooden signpost in the median 16km out of the city. Follow the signs to the monastery. Alternatively, Ekaterinburg C&V Bureau and Guide Centre (see Information under Yekaterinburg earlier) offers a three-hour tour for US$50, which goes to both Ganina Yama and Porosinkov Log.

Nizhnyaya Sinyachikha & Around
Нижняя Синячиха

The pretty village of Nizhnyaya Sinyachikha, about 150km northeast of Yekaterinburg and 12km north of the town of Alapaevsk, is home to an open-air **Architecture Museum** (Muzey Uralskoi Narodnoy Zhevolisi; ☎ 246-7 51 18; admission R50; open 10am-4pm Thur-Sun). Here there are 15 traditional Siberian log buildings, featuring displays of period furniture, tools and domestic articles. The stone cathedral houses a collection of Ural region folk art, which is one of the best of its kind. This impressive collection of art and architecture was gathered from around

the Urals and recompiled by the single-handed efforts of Ivan Samoylov, an enthusiastic local historian.

About 2km west of Nizhnyaya Sinyachikha is a new monastery dedicated to Grand Princess Yelisaveta (see Around the City Centre in the Yekaterinburg section earlier), on the spot where she died. Back in Alapaevsk there's also a **museum** dedicated to Tchaikovsky, in a house where the composer lived as a child.

There are local trains to Alapaevsk, but they're infrequent; it's better to take a bus from Yekaterinburg or hire a car for the day.

Verkhoturie
Верхотурье

Founded in 1598, Verkhoturie was a mighty 17th-century fortress and monastery, as well as an administrative centre. Today this small town on the Tura River, about 310km north of Yekaterinburg, remains an important religious centre for the Urals and Siberia. Its sights include the Verkhotursky kremlin, a dozen cathedrals and churches, and several museums. The monastery contains the miraculous relics of St Simeon, a local saint.

Verkhoturie was one of the residences and pilgrimage destinations of Grigory Rasputin. He often claimed that a trip here would cure the tsarevich of his haemophilia. Rasputin is still considered by the Orthodox Church to be a holy figure, and his home has been made into a museum.

Verkhoturie is a long trip from Yekaterinburg, so make arrangements to stay at **Gostiny Dvor** (☎ 219-2 14 14). There are no direct trains from Yekaterinburg, so you'll have to go via Nizhny Tagil. Alternatively, Ekaterinburg C&V Bureau & Guide Centre (see Information in the Yekaterinburg section for contact details) runs full-day trips from US$250, which include transport and a knowledgeable English-speaking guide.

CHELYABINSK
ЧЕЛЯБИНСК

☎ 3512 • pop 1.2 million • Moscow time plus 2 hours

Founded in 1736, and prospering as a tea trading city, Chelyabinsk, 199km south of Yekaterinburg, expanded grandly after 1892 with the completion of the railway from Moscow. Eventually the Trans-Siberian mainline was to bypass the city but expansion continued as its arms factories turned out Katyusha rockets and legendary, WWII-winning T34s, for which it was nicknamed 'Tank City'. Despite a heavy mantle of industrial sprawl, Chelyabinsk retains odd hints of former architectural appeal and is a useful transport hub for the southern Urals.

The real centre of this huge, amorphous sprawl is ploshchad Revolutsiy on prospekt Lenina, 1.5km from the joint train and main bus stations. Here a harried-looking Vladimir Ilych paces away from the big 1980s **Drama Theatre** (☎ 63 22 03) for a spot of shopping in patchily attractive ulitsa Kirov. This area is worth a wander and has some scattered late-19th- and early-20th-century mansions (ulitsa Karla Marxa 68, ulitsa Vasenko 41, ulitsa Pushkina 1, ulitsa Tsvillinga 15, ulitsa Kommuny 58).

The finest buildings house the **Glinka Opera House** (ul Jaroslavskogo 1), the **Fine Art Gallery** (ul Truda 92a; open 10am-4.30pm Tues-Sat) opposite, and the nearby **Geology Museum** (ul Truda 98; open 10am-3pm Tues-Sat). Active religious buildings include an early-20th-century **synagogue** (ul Pushkina 6a), several churches and the 1899 **Ake Mosque** (ul Elkina 20), with a lighthouse of a minaret topped with a fine, golden spire. The 1883 **cathedral** (Svyato Simenov sobor; ul Kychtymskaya 32) has a curious exterior featuring lion and dragon ceramics and is lovely inside. It's beside the north bus station; take tram No 6 to ulitsa Kalinina then walk a block east, then south.

Places to Stay & Eat

At the train station **parked rail carriages** (from R91.25 per berth for 12hrs) offer cheap beds but are stiflingly hot in summer.

Hotel Malakhit (☎ 63 54 78; ul Truda 153; singles/doubles from R478/751) has reasonable en-suite Soviet rooms and a few excellent-value, totally remodelled singles for R700.

Viktoria (☎ 98 98 20; ul Moldogvardeytsev 34; rooms from US$120) is the town's top business hotel, way out in the distant north-west suburbs.

The appealing café **Red Cup** (☎ 65 63 54; ul Svobody 139; coffee R40-90) does a mean cappuccino.

Beloe Sontse (☎ 63 07 44; pr Lenina 63; mains R100-300) is a fun, hip, pseudo-desert 'outpost' serving Central Asian cuisine. It's

guarded by an amusingly costumed 'legionnaire'.

Cotton Club (☎ 63 50 92; ul Svobody 80; mains R125-350; open 24hrs) offers a suave jazz ambience and live evening performances, plus meals with creative names featuring song titles.

Bad Gastein (☎ 65 93 92; ul Kommuny 87; mains R300-1000; open noon-midnight) serves mostly Germanic food in an Austrian alpine ambience.

Getting There & Around

Useful overnight rail connections include Ufa (No 181, 9½ hours) and Tobolsk (No 260, 18 hours) via Tyumen (13 hours). For Yekaterinburg (R229, 5¾ hours) it's easier to get tickets on the Purpe-bound train No 190. Beware that most trains heading east from Chelyabinsk to Omsk, Novosibirsk etc, cut through Kazakhstan (visa required).

Bus services are much more useful for Magnitogorsk (R163.50, six hours, 12 daily), Zlatoust (R73, 3½ hours, nine daily) and Miass (R58, 2¼ hours, 14 daily), departing from beside the train station. The **North Bus Station** (Severny avtovokzal; ulitsa Kychtymskaya 30) has afternoon buses to Yekaterinburg (R216, 4½ hours, two daily), Uchaly (R193, five hours, two daily) and Beloretsk (R292, eight hours, one daily).

From the train station, bus No 64 and trolleybus No 17 go up ulitsa Svobody, then turn eastwards along prospekt Lenina, continuing to the post office and beyond. Bus No 18 does the same as far as ploshchad Revolutsiy then turns north up ulitsa Kirova right through the old town. Get off at the river bridge for Hotel Malakhit, the opera house and the art gallery.

AROUND CHELYABINSK
Miass
Миасс
☎ 31535 • pop 180,000 • Moscow time plus 2 hours

Miass struck it rich in an 1820s gold rush. Although it's now a mostly monotonous 20km concrete strip, bus No 1 from prospekt Avtozavodtsev to ulitsa Pushkinskaya takes you to the reasonably intact old town with several fine, if unkempt, mansions and museums surrounded by wooden cottages. Locals rave (somewhat exaggeratedly) about the pleasant nearby lakes, notably Ilmenskoe and

Turgoyak, beside which there are popular *tur-baza* ('tourbases' – holiday camps).

At the new, combined train and bus station there are **resting rooms** *(komnaty otdykha; beds from R58)*. The unmarked **Hotel Ilmeny Plus** *(☎ 6 06 76; pr Avtozavodtsev 34; dorms/singles/twins R130/250/400)* is much less appealing than the grand entrance might suggest. To get there take trolleybus No 3 from the station.

Miass to Beloretsk

Two daily buses and trains link Miass to **Uchaly** (Учалы, population 38,000), the clean but dull 1960s copper- and zinc-processing town, with a very well-kept little **museum** *(ul Karla Marxa 7; admission R7; open 9am-1pm & 2pm-5pm Mon-Fri)*, an unusual green-spired **mosque** *(far end of ul Mutazina)* and a basic hotel on ploshchad Lenina. But the main reason to come is for the gently attractive scenery beyond the town, along the route to Beloretsk (bus R62.70, two hours, four or more daily). You'll pass through Bashkir villages selling fresh *koumys* (fermented mare's milk), with low, forested mountains giving way to parkland in the style of Capability Brown. There's a glimpse of flat-topped 1582m Mt Iremel from Uraz village and the fun of crossing between Asia and Europe: a feat marked by two suitably inscribed obelisks either side of the minuscule Ural River.

Beloretsk (Белорецк, population 74,000) is an insensitive grid of prefabricated concrete apartment blocks in the forested mountains. Though founded in 1776, the only notable historical structure is an old wooden-topped brick watchtower facing the Univermag supermarket (opposite ulitsa Lenina 55). There's a simple **museum** *(ul Lenina 30a; admission R10; open 8am-noon & 1pm-3pm Mon-Fri)* a block farther north, past the Lenin statue, where half-hourly Magnitogorsk minibuses terminate. Other bus services (to/from Uchaly, Ufa etc) use the bus station, two blocks east plus two huge blocks south.

If you choose to stay in town, there's the ropey **Hotel Beloretsk** *(☎ 34792-4 06 80; ul Lenina 39; dorms/singles/twins with shared WC from R65/100/155)*.

Miass to Ufa

The Miass-Ufa train line was once the main Trans-Siberian route across the Urals and links foundry towns and a few modest attractions. Undulating across folds of foothills around a mountain lake, **Zlatoust** (Златоуст, population 212,000) is an economically sagging steel town famous for intricate etching and gold inlay. See classic works by mastersmith Ivan Bushyuev (1800–34) in the appealing **Regional Museum** *(Kraevedchesky muzey; ul Lenina 1a; admission R25; open 10am-5.30pm Tues-Sun)*. It's behind Drakula nightclub just off central Gorodski ploshchad, also snappily known as III Internatsionalskaya. This square is the meeting point for tram No 1 (from the bus station), tram No 3 (from the train station) and bus No 14 from lakeside **Hotel Taganay** *(☎ 35136-5 12 25; pr 30i let Pobedy, 7; singles/twins from R357/230)*. Both tram routes give great views of old wooden cottages.

From the Tesminsky dam at the northern end of Zlatoust are lovely views of the Taganay National Park's forested mountains and modest rocky protrusions. To get to the views, take bus No 6 to Polyklinika, walk down the concrete road (right) and veer left around the NFS (НФС) filtration plant (ask permission!). For the national park, we don't recommend going without a guide, given the bears and the likelihood of getting lost

The nicest scenery en route to Ufa is around the ragged mining village of **Minyar** (Миняр), which sits in two cliff-edged valleys of forested hills punctuated with cedars reminiscent of Van Gogh's famous painting. Minyar's 19th-century **Svyato Vvedenskisi Church** is 4km from the train station, beyond a small reservoir with a *turbaza*. Every 60 to 90 minutes a minibus shuttles 18 attractive kilometres to **Asha** (Аша, population 37,000), a small, drab transport hub and mineralogical factory town with a cheap skiing area and the surprisingly acceptable **Hotel Asha** *(☎ 35139-2 25 19; ul Sovetskaya 4; en-suite singles/twins R266/475)*. *Elektrichka* (suburban trains) continue to Ufa (R26.30, 2½ hours, four daily).

MAGNITOGORSK
МАГНИТОГОРСК
☎ 3511 • pop 439,000 • Moscow time plus 2 hours

Memorable Magnitogorsk is a Frankenstein of a city with prospekt Lenina as its reanimated Stalinist spine. Across the Ural River, the steel mills of the Ordzhonikidze district are magnificently ugly, with snarling, densely packed gangs of chimneys belching dense curtains of smoke in fearfully multifarious colours. This is most photogenically viewed from Park Pobedy, behind the gigantic, 83-tonne, square-jawed colossus of the **Til Frontu** memorial. Over 15m tall, this pair of Soviet archetypes hold aloft an enormous sword, symbolic of the city's industrial support for the WWII patriotic effort.

Three kilometres south on bus No 21, beyond the excellent **museum**, circus and mosque construction site, the splendid new gold, multi-domed **Khram Vozneseniya** is nearing completion.

The main **post office** (ul Lenina 32) has a decent Internet connection for R20 per hour (minimum charge R10).

A nifty fold-out city map with bus and tram routes sells for R50 from kiosks.

Places to Stay & Eat

The cheapest beds are at the **resting rooms** (komnaty otdykha; dorm beds from R85), upstairs at the western end of the combined bus/train station.

Hotel Transagentstvo (☎ 34 45 90; pr Karla Marxa 141; doubles R200 per person) is small and simple, with clean rooms sharing toilets and a powerful if grimy hot shower. Take bus No 7 to the Stalevarov stop.

Hotel Evropa (☎ 21 46 01, fax 21 46 88; ul Zelyonaya 3; rooms from US$115) is an upmarket, low-rise affair set in a quiet, green neighbourhood around a central chalet-style bar and reception block.

Hotel Valentino (☎ 376 766, fax 219 988; ul Gryaznova 24; bus stop Yunost; doubles/ twins with breakfast R1960/2160), two minutes' walk southwest of ploshchad Mira, is an acceptable new business hotel.

Handy for the Hotel Transagentstvo, the building at ulitsa Karla Marksa 143 houses fast-food joint **Grill Master** (open 11am-11pm daily) and a currency exchange booth to pay for it. **Kafe 7 More** (pr Lenina 29; open 11am-11pm daily) is a stylish, central modern café, while **Shale** (Chalet; ☎ 224 489; pr Lenina 46; mains R150-360; open 11am-2am daily) offers pricey French food, including snails in garlic.

Getting There & Away

Trains to Moscow leave on odd days, plus there's an overnight service to Ufa. Without a Kazakhstan visa, buses are more practical for journeys to Chelyabinsk (R163.50, six hours), while minibuses are the best bet for Beloretsk (R40, 2½ hours via Abzakovo).

Getting Around

The bus and train stations are both located at the north end of ul Lenina. From here bus No 21 serves the museum and Khram Vozneseniya; bus No 7 and tram No 17 go down prospekt Karla Marksa past Hotel Valentina, Hotel Transagentstvo and central market. Bus 142 from the Yunost stop (ploshchad Mira on prospekt Karla Marksa) serves the airport twelve times daily. Tram No 6 down ul Leningradskaya takes you across the Tsentralny Perekhod bridge right into the most photogenically nightmarish industrial zone.

AROUND MAGNITOGORSK
Abzakovo
Абзаково

Abzakovo is the most attractive spot in the wooded mountains between Magnitogorsk and Beloretsk, easily accessible by regular minibuses from Magnitogorsk (R35, 1½ hours) and Beloretsk (1 hour). The wooden church and quaint village are 3km west of the well-equipped **MMK Abzakovo Resort** (☎ 3919-25 93 00, fax 3511-33 77 61; singles/ twins from R525/735), a year-round operation that's principally of interest as a ski destination. Skis and ski gear can be hired here. The resort's chair lift (R25 per ride) runs from 3pm to 4pm only outside the ski season.

Also at the resort you can hire horses (R300 per day), kayaks and bicycles (R25 per hour), and there's an **Aquapark** (R180 for 2hrs; open 10am-10pm) complex of indoor swimming pools, as well as several reasonably priced eateries. Book well ahead, especially for the luxurious Western-standard 'cottages' (up to R2625).

To reach the resort, get off the bus or train at Novoabzakovo station (from where there's a useful overnight train to Ufa) and stroll 15 minutes towards the mountains, keeping straight ahead after the river bridge.

Arkaim
Аркаим

The best known of the region's 3500- to 4000-year-old Bronze-Age fortress sites ('Land of Cities') is Arkaim, some 120km south of Magnitogorsk. Considered exciting by archaeologists, it's tough to reach and more visually compelling viewed via the website **w** www.arkaimhome.narod.ru/en/pole02.htm, which has a three-dimensional 'tour'.

UFA
УФА
☎ 3472 • pop 1.1 million • Moscow time plus 2 hours

Ufa is capital of the self-consciously autonomous Bashkortostan Republic. Although the Muslim Turkic Bashkir people now make up barely one-third of Bashkortostan's population of four million, you'll hear their lispy language spoken widely in rural areas and on many city radio programs, along with the curiously oriental-style singing. Written Bashkir requires nine extra Cyrillic letters absent from standard Russian, including two variants of 'th'. 'Hello' in Bashkir is *hau-ma*, 'thank you very much' is *zur rakhmat*.

Orientation & Information
Ufa fills a 20km-long dumbbell-shaped area of land between the meandering Belaya and Ufa Rivers. The smart, economically dynamic southern lobe has a peaceful pedestrianised zone of old wooden cottages (eg, ulitsa Salavata Yulaeva) mixed with gleaming governmental buildings and new theatres (ulitsa Tukaeva). This area culminates in a cliff from which the much-photographed equestrian statue of 18th-century Bashkir hero Salavat Yulaev appears ready to leap the wide Belaya into the forest beyond.

Alfa Bank (*ul Lenina 32*) changes money and has an ATM and the **post office** (*ul Lenina 28*) is nearby. There's a good **Internet club** (*R20 per hour plus R2 per MB; open 24hrs*) attached to Hotel Turist (see Places to Stay). Useful if flawed bus maps, *Skhema Ufy*, cost R15 to R20 from newsstands and the **Znanie Bookshop** (*ul Lenina 26; open 10am-2pm & 3pm-7pm daily*).

Things to See
The focus of sporadically appealing ulitsa Lenina is the 19th-century **Trading Arcade** (Gostiny dvor), set on a fountain-cooled piazza. Behind the renovated facade is a luxuriously marble-lined shopping mall full of boutiques, cafés and carts selling freshly squeezed orange juice.

While the **Regional Museum** (Kraevedchesky muzey) is being rebuilt, you can find its fabulous collection of 4th-century BC *zolotoye oleni* (golden antelopes) and other grave finds displayed in the nicely renovated **Nesterova Art Gallery** (*☎ 23 42 36; ul Gogol 27; admission R50; open 10am-4pm Tues-Sun*).

Incongruously dwarfed by the modern UralSib skyscraper, ulitsa Krupskaya is a short, overgrown street of wooden houses one block east of ulitsa Lenina (between ulitsas Kirova and Dostoevskogo). In the grey, New England–style cottage at No 45, Lenin stayed for three weeks in 1900 awaiting a boat to Pskov. The cottage is now an interesting **Lenin Museum** (*☎ 23 24 39; admission R10; open 10am-6pm Tues-Sun*) and houses an unusually human statue of Vladimir Ilych holding hands with his (diplomatically shortened) wife Nadezhda Krupskaya – in reality she was 3cm taller than petite Lenin.

A mostly downhill half-hour stroll from the Salavat Yulaev horseman statue to the Druzhby obelisk takes you via the imposing university buildings, some grand new government palaces, the giant Bashkortostan drama theatre (between ulitsas Frunze and Tukaeva) and through remnant wooden cottages of ulitsa Salavata Yulaeva for the best available view of the city's historic **mosque** (*ul Tukaeva 52*).

Places to Stay
The train station **resting rooms** (*komnaty otdykha; beds R63-190*) are upstairs beside the Prigorodnyy Kassy (suburban train ticket office).

Superbly central is **Hotel Agidel** (*☎ 22 56 80; ul Lenina 14; unrenovated singles/twins from R390/640*), whose totally remodelled en-suite rooms are worth the R870/1380 asking price.

Four kilometres from the centre but right beside the main (Yuzhny) bus station, **Hotel Turist** (*☎ 25 46 45; ul Zorge 17; singles/twins from R640/1000*) has some partly improved R700/1100 rooms with functional showers and toilets.

The **Bashkortostan** (*☎ 79 00 00, fax 79 00 09; e gkbashkiria@ufacom.ru; ul Lenina 25–29; singles/twins R2085/3380*) is an international styled business hotel.

Places to Eat
Säy Chay (*ul Lenina 24; sandwiches R3-8; open 10am-7pm*) is a handily central grocery-café opposite the Trading Arcades where you

can try the disturbingly viscous Bashkir wheat-drink *buza* for R3 per cup.

Kafehe Kymyz *(end of ul Gafuri; snacks R8-25; open 11am-10pm)* is a summer shashlyk café in the park near the Yulaev horseman statue, with a sideline in classic Bashkir snacks. The best is *gubadiya* (R18), in which rice, crumbled meat, plump moist raisins and chopped egg are layered in a pork-pie-style pastry case. There's a fair chance of finding *buza* and *koumys* here too.

U Babaya *(☎ 23 94 01; ul 50 let Oktyabrya 20; mains R30-60; open 9am-11pm daily)* is a fun, wood-lined café with an excellent salad bar. Take the bus No 101 to the Dom Pechati stop.

Mefistofolya *(☎ 51 61 51 ext 3225; mains R115-200; open noon-4am daily)*, in the historic brick-arched bowels of the Trading Arcades, is a sedate, business-casual restaurant despite the misleading horror-theme entrance.

Portofino *(☎ 24 45 10; pr Oktyabrya 25; beer from R28, meals from R170; open noon-11pm)*, also known as Dasko Pizza, is one large block east of the main bus station. It has an upmarket European restaurant plus a cheaper yurt-style beer garden next door.

Getting There & Away

Overnight trains serve Samara (No 691, nine hours), Ulyanovsk (No 607, 14 hours), Chelyabinsk (No 014, 8½ hours) and Magnitogorsk (No 675, 10 hours) via Abzakovo (7½ hours). There are at least four daily services to Moscow (at least 30 hours) and an occasional No 608 to Uchali via Zlatoust (eight hours) and Miass (10 hours). *Elektrichka* are cheaper for Asha and thence Minyar.

The main **Yuzhny Bus Station** *(ul Zorge 13)* has departures for Beloretsk (two daily), Uchaly (four daily) and Orenburg (three daily). The inconveniently distant north **Severny Bus Station** has morning services to Yekaterinburg and Kazan.

Summer river boats depart regularly from the Monument Druzhby jetty and beach at the east end of ulitsa Frunze (bus No 31) but only as round-trip cruises (eg, to Moscow from R6750, 16 days, two per month). **Belskoe River Transport Company** *(☎ 25 65 56; Russian only* **w** *www.brp-inform.ru/pas_mr.htm)* has prices and departure dates.

Getting Around

The handy if convoluted bus No 101 route snakes between the train station, 3km from the old centre, and the airport via the main bus station, prospekt Oktyabrya, the central market, and ulitsa Lenina. Bus No 2 links the TV transmission station, Teletsentr, near the Salavat Yulaev monument, and the north bus station via ulitsa Frunze (for the art gallery), ulitsa Lenin (Trading Arcades), ulitsa Kirova (for the Lenin Museum and grand new church) and prospekt Oktyabrya.

Caucasus Кавказ

The dramatic Caucasus mountain range, striding from the Black Sea to the Caspian Sea, forms Russia's most southerly border. This chapter covers the northern (Russian) side of the range, the foothills and steppe to the north including Rostov-on-Don, and the Russian coastal strip along the Black Sea. The steeper southern side of the Caucasus lies in the states of Georgia and Azerbaijan, now independent from Russia.

Though parts of the Caucasus region have been tragically beset by war and ethnic conflict, its untroubled areas can make for exciting travel. Not only different from everything to the north, the Caucasus is also immensely varied. Below jagged 3000m, 4000m and 5000m-peaks lie valleys that are home to a varied range of cultures, with dozens of peoples speaking dozens of languages, and practising Christianity, Islam and Judaism.

The Caucasus is the most spectacular part of European Russia. Even if you're no walker or mountaineer, do venture into the hills by visiting Dombay, or the Baxan Valley beneath Mt Elbrus (5642m) – Europe's highest peak. The main northern approach is from Rostov-on-Don across the slowly rising Kuban Steppe, and through the mineral-water spa area in the central Caucasus foothills. Where the Caucasus meets the Black Sea is Russia's holiday coast, centring on the resort of Sochi. At the eastern end of the Caucasus lies Chechnya and Dagestan, a complicated and fractious ethnic jigsaw with an Asiatic atmosphere, extending from the mountains to the Caspian Sea.

One possible route might start with Rostov, from where you could wander down to Krasnodar and then maybe take a day trip to Novorossiysk. Alternatively, take the train and make Sochi your coastal base. An overnight train can then take you to Mineralnye Vody and a base for touring in Kislovodsk or Pyatigorsk. Dombay and Elbrus can be done as side trips with stays in either for hiking, climbing or messing around in the snow. Unexciting Nalchik is a possible base for Elbrus, while another option is to start in Vladikavkaz. Getting to Nalchik and then Vladikavkaz is best done by bus or taxi, but whatever you decide, the Caucasus is a region that rewards the adventurous spirit.

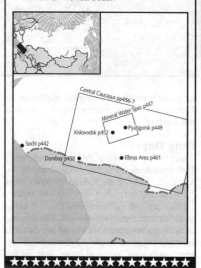

Highlights

- Explore the valleys and gorges of North Ossetia as they slice into the mountain scenery
- Take the chairlift above Dombay to survey all and then discover waterfalls, glaciers, alpine meadows, bears, wild goats – and party with local mountain tribes
- Catch an early morning glimpse of Elbrus from afar
- Take a dip in the Narzan Mineral Baths or a massage in the Hotel Dagomys sanatorium
- Lounge around at sunny Sochi, Russia's version of Florida Beach

Central Caucasus pp456-7
Mineral Water Spas p447
Kislovodsk p452 • Pyatigorsk p449
Sochi p442
Dombay p458
Elbrus Area p461

★★★★★★★★★★★★★★★★★★★★★★

HISTORY

The northern Caucasus has been at the crossroads of Mediterranean, Central Asian, west Asian and Eastern European cultures since the Bronze Age. The result is an extraordinary mix of races with three main linguistic groups: Caucasian, Indo-European and Turkic. Several religions are represented in the region, Islam and Orthodox Christianity having the most adherents. The Caucasus has suffered from many invasions and occupations, having been

431

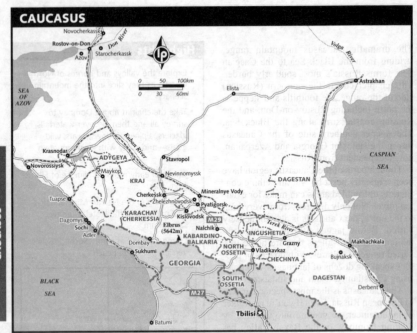

squeezed between rival empires, including the Roman, Byzantine, Persian, Arab, Ottoman and Russian.

Early Days

While little is known of the area's prehistory, there have been several prehistoric and Stone Age finds. Some of the earliest traces are from the Neolithic era, when farming was replacing hunting and gathering and the first communities were being established. These come from Dagestan's dry valleys and are dated to the same era as other early agriculture developments in west Asia and Japan, making the northern Caucasus one of the 'cradles of civilisation'.

The significant post-Neolithic remains are the 3000-plus dolmens scattering the coastal foothills from Novorossiysk to Sochi. These funeral memorials of huge flat stones date from the end of the 4th century BC to the beginning of the 2nd century BC.

Apart from archaeological finds, little else is known of early northern Caucasian people except that they used copper and iron tools around 1000 BC, during the so-called Koban culture. The region had well-established trad-

ing routes to the Greek civilisation, peaking around the 7th century BC.

Early Invasions

The era of the great migrations brought many different peoples to the Caucasus. Scythians arrived from the east along the northern Black Sea coast in the 8th century BC, followed by Sarmatians, also from the east, in about the 3rd century BC. In the 1st millennium AD, groups including the Kipchaks (ancestors of the present-day Balkar), Huns, Pechenegs and Khazars all left their mark, some settling and mixing with the existing inhabitants.

Alans

The Alans, ancestors of modern Ossetians, are thought to be a fusion of Sarmatians with local tribes. The Alan state came to prominence during the 10th century AD and at its peak ruled most of the northern Caucasus with established trade routes to surrounding empires.

During the 11th century, Kipchak, Polovtsy and Nogai Turkic tribes constantly raided the region, with some settling the northern Caucasus. The Mongol Tatars invaded in the early 13th century and destroyed the Alan state. A far more brutal invasion and occupation, destroying any remnants of the Alan state, came with Timur (Tamerlane), who brought a new Asian terror to much of west Asia. Many surviving Alans either left the region or went higher into the mountains.

Arrival of the Russians

Russian peasants and adventurers, escaping the oppressive serf system, had already settled in the lower Terek River region when Russian military power reached the area in the late 1550s – the tsar, Ivan the Terrible, had married Maria Temryukovna, daughter of a Kabardian prince. Russian economic and military influence grew, and eventually the Russians pushed the Ottoman (Turkish) Empire out of the Caucasus.

In the early 19th century, Russian conquest of the Caucasus met with fierce resistance from local tribes, as the predominantly Muslim populace resented being ruled by the European and Christian Russians. Bitter guerrilla-type warfare ensued and lasted several decades.

At several points in history, usually at a time of crisis (such as a foreign invasion), the northern Caucasian tribes have united to form a military alliance. In the 19th century, Imam Shamil brought together the Dagestanis and Chechens for a 30-year fight against the Russians. In 1859 Russian army units surrounded them in Gunib, Dagestan, causing Shamil and his followers to surrender after a 15-day siege. As a result of this defeat, many with strong Muslim beliefs fled to Ottoman territory. The Russians, as Orthodox, were inimical to Muslims who felt that after defeat they would be better off in a Muslim country like Turkey, which was then a strong regional power. The Ossetians were an exception: as Christians they never fought the Russians, apparently because they didn't want to be part of a state governed by Koranic law, the aim of Shamil's proposed northern Caucasian state.

Russian Rule

During the 1917 Russian Revolution, many northern Caucasian tribes united to form the Mountain Republic, but this independence was short-lived: once the Soviet forces had consolidated power over Russia, they conquered much of the former Tsarist Imperial Empire. The Mountain Republic was taken back in 1921 and given the status of an autonomous republic within the Soviet Union, while the various Dagestan nationalities were combined into a new and separate Dagestan Autonomous Republic.

The following year four new autonomous regions – Adygeya, Chechnya, Kabarda-Balkar and Karachay-Cherkessia – were created from the Mountain Autonomous Republic that ceased to exist in 1924. Soviet policy was to divide and rule by creating small autonomous regions, sometimes combining two totally different nationalities. The Soviet regime also used other methods to break the unity of the mountain people, including giving each ethnic group its own national identity by promoting folk traditions and devising a written language. Aligned with increased 'Russification', the Soviets divided the troublesome northern Caucasian groups, intent on pacifying the region. The results can be seen in today's sometimes violent conflicts.

Deportations

In 1944 most of the Balkar, Chechen, Ingush and Karachay peoples were deported to Central Asia and Siberia on Stalin's orders. The official reason was suspicion of collaboration

CAUCASUS

with the German forces, but this was unfounded, although property was still confiscated and the land absorbed into surrounding republics. This fuelled bitterness and hatred towards the Russians and between the nationalities that stayed and those that were deported. The nationalities left behind took the property and land of the deported groups, who were never compensated.

In 1957, when Nikita Khrushchev allowed the exiled groups to return to their former lands, there seemed to be no problems between the various nationalities, mainly due to the oppressive and dictatorial nature of the Soviet regime. Repression of minorities gave little opportunity to form any opposition to Soviet power. This changed very quickly after the failed 1991 coup in Moscow.

Post-Soviet Era

The demise of the Soviet Union led to a political restructuring of Russia, with many autonomous republics and regions transformed into federal republics. Karachay-Cherkessia, Kabardino-Balkaria, Dagestan, North Ossetia, Adygeya and Checheno-Ingushetia became the northern Caucasus, while later, Checheno-Ingushetia became the separate republics of Chechnya and Ingushetia.

CLIMATE

In winter, the Black Sea coast is the mildest place in Russia – it's rarely freezing. In summer the area is warm and humid, reaching around 25°C from June to September. North of the Caucasus there's a continental climate consisting of three or four freezing winter months, then temperatures up to about 30°C from June to August.

The higher you go the cooler it gets – many Caucasus peaks are permanently snow-covered – but on a sunny summer day you'll still be sweating at 3000m. November to April/May is the wettest season. Only on the Black Sea coastal plain (where around 1200mm to 1800mm of rain falls each year) does it get significantly wet.

PEOPLE & LANGUAGE

Around 23 million people inhabit the area covered in this chapter. Most Caucasian societies are strongly patriarchal but the tribal nature of the mountain peoples has been diluted by Soviet education, collectivisation and urbanisation.

The region's ethnic complexity is revealed by its administrative divisions, their names indicating some of the peoples that inhabit them. From west to east, the administrative divisions are Adygeya, Karachay-Cherkess, Kabardino-Balkaria, North Ossetia, Chechnya, Ingushetia and Dagestan.

Classified by language, of which 40 or so are spoken, the region's peoples divide into three main families. Russian is spoken just about everywhere.

Caucasians

About 2.5 million people in the region use some 30 indigenous Caucasian languages, divided into northwestern and northeastern groups. All the written languages use the Cyrillic alphabet.

The northwestern group, with about 750,000 people, includes the Kabardian, the Adygeya, the Abaza in Karachay-Cherkessia (also known as Circassians), as well as the Abkhazians of Abkhazia (a disputed part of Georgia). Many more Circassians now live in Turkey, Syria, Jordan and Iraq.

Northeastern Caucasians divide into speakers of Nakh languages (chiefly 890,000 Chechen and 210,000 Ingush) and speakers of the 30 or so Dagestan languages. All are loosely known as Lezgians. But Lezgi (or Kury) is also the name of one of the more important individual languages, with 260,000 speakers in Dagestan and 172,000 in Azerbaijan. Others are Avar, with about 539,000 speakers, Lakh with 105,000, and Dargwa with 350,000.

Indo-Europeans

The Indo-European language family is thought to have originated in western Turkey, spreading out over most of Europe and south and southwest Asia by 1000 BC. The Slavs, mainly Russians and Ukrainians who make up 80% of the population north of the Caucasus, are Indo-European. Prominent among speakers of other Indo-European languages in the Caucasus are the Ossetians, who number around 700,000. Most Ossetians live on the northern (Russian) side of the Caucasus although significant numbers live in South Ossetia, part of Georgia.

Turks

Turkic peoples in the region include 274,000 Kumyk and 70,000 Nogay in Dagestan, and the 149,000-plus Karachay and 71,000-plus Balkar in the western and central Caucasus.

RELIGION

Most Caucasus mountain peoples, including the Kabardian, Karachay, Chechens and Balkar, are Muslim. There is also a small population of about 19,000 *gorskie yevrie* (Jews) living mostly in the cities of Nalchik, Pyatigorsk and Derbent. Russian Orthodoxy predominates in the *stanitsy* (Cossack villages) along the borders as well as in the cities.

GETTING THERE & AWAY

Air

You can fly to several places in the region, including Rostov, Krasnodar, and Sochi on the Black Sea, and Mineralnye Vody, Nalchik and Vladikavkaz on the edge of the Caucasus.

Train

The main railways funnel through Rostov-on-Don and then diverge – one to Mineralnye Vody, Astrakhan (which is a huge detour around Grozny) and Makhachkala; and the other to Krasnodar and down the Black Sea coast to Sochi and Adler. (Before the Abkhazian–Georgian conflict, trains continued onto Tbilisi.)

There are trains to/from Moscow taking 1½ to two days: some go via the Ukraine, which means obtaining a Ukraine visa.

Car & Motorcycle

The main route through the region runs from Rostov-on-Don to the Georgian capital Tbilisi, via Mineralnye Vody, Nalchik, Vladikavkaz and the spectacular Georgian Military Highway over the Caucasus. This winding, narrow road, open at the time of research, has a constant question mark of safety over it due to its poor condition, as well as highway bandits, including local Mafia, police and border guards, all of whom might extract a *tarify* (tariff) of US$5 to US$20 (and upwards) for passage along 'their' section of the highway.

The road through Chechnya, leading to Dagestan and Baku (Azerbaijan), is absurdly risky even if you're allowed in. The other main north–south road loops round from Rostov through Krasnodar to Sochi on the Black Sea; its continuation to Sukhumi (Abkhazia) and Batumi (western Georgia) is open although not trouble-free, thanks to the Abkhazian–Georgian conflict.

Boat

See the later Novorossiysk and Sochi sections for the irregular passenger ferries that travel to Georgian and Turkish destinations.

Organised Tours

Companies offering trips into Krasnaya Polyana, Dombay, Teberda and the Mt Elbrus area are mentioned in the relevant sections of this chapter.

GETTING AROUND

Travelling from one city to another, although not difficult in the Caucasus, can require a combination of bus, *marshrutki* and train. As schedules and prices fluctuate, it's always best to consult with a local before making your move. Given the terrain, the most obvious way on the map may not be practicable.

Train

It's fairly easy to buy tickets at the station within an hour or two of departure. If you would like to avoid queues, the major stations have service centres where you can arrange your ticket for a charge, usually R50.

Bus

Cars, taxis, buses and minivans are the only transport into the mountainous areas. Usually there are overnight buses between major destinations but train travel is more comfortable.

Car & Motorcycle

Main roads are generally in a decent condition but the many animals wandering over them behave more sensibly than some of the drivers, who sometimes like to overtake in truly lunatic situations. Accidents are common.

Cable Car

One unusual form of transport here is the cable car. Highly exotic to hill-starved northern Russians, these are strung across any landscape, not just mountains but also parks, lakes and even along flat valleys.

Kuban Steppe
Кубанская Степь

From Rostov-on-Don, the overland routes to the Caucasus and the Black Sea coast cross the intensively cultivated Kuban Steppe,

CAUCASUS

named after its major river flowing from El-brus into the Sea of Azov. This region had a high Cossack population and its peasants were among the chief victims of the grain requisitioning and forced collectivisation of the late 1920s and early 1930s – millions were starved, shot or deported.

The trip from Rostov to Pyatigorsk or Kislovodsk on the northern fringe of the Caucasus can be made in a day – by road it's just under 500km. Mikhail Gorbachev, remembered bitterly by many Russians as responsible for the collapse of the Soviet Union, was born near unexciting Stavropol.

ROSTOV-ON-DON
РОСТОВ-НА-ДОНУ
☎ 8632 • pop 1 million

Rostov-on-Don (Rostov-na-Donu), on the right bank of the River Don, is often called the gateway to the northern Caucasus. When serfs, paupers and dropouts fled south in the 15th century, they organised into communities in the Don river basin and established their capital in Starocherkassk, 30km north of Rostov. Known as the Don Cossacks, these communities elected their own ataman (leaders), formed armies and gained a degree of autonomy.

The independent-minded Cossacks went on to lead three major peasant uprisings in the Volga-Don region in the 17th and 18th centuries, and ended up causing trouble for the central Russian government well into the 20th century. The lower Volga and Don basins put up furious resistance to the Great October Revolution, launching a vicious White Army offensive.

The Don – made famous in Mikhail Sholokhov's novels of the Civil War – flows from just south of Moscow to the Sea of Azov. In 1952, the Lenin Ship Canal joined the Volga and the Don near Volgograd, completing an immense network of canals, lakes and rivers. An ocean-going ship can now sail right across Russia from the Arctic to the Mediterranean.

Today, Rostov is a vibrant and prosperous southern city, which also serves as a base for excursions of historical interest.

Orientation & Information
The city's main east–west axis, ulitsa Bolsh-aya Sadovaya, has many of the city's hotels and restaurants; the suburban and long-distance train stations are at its west end. The

pedestrian artery of Pushkinsky bulvar runs parallel.

There is a **post & telegraph office** (cnr per Podbelskogo & ul Serafimovicha), and the computer centre **Invest** (☎ 44 30 30; Budyonovsky pr 97, 2nd floor; open 10am-10pm) has efficient Internet services.

Change money or use the ATM at **Sberbank** (ul Bolshaya Sadovaya 39).

Things to See & Do
Rostov's main attractions are out of town, but the city has some pleasant and interesting spots. The lavish **Nativity of the Virgin Cathedral** (ul Stanislavskogo 58), near pereulok Podbelskogo, is surrounded by a lively open-air market. The **Museum of Local Studies** (☎ 65 55 72; ul Bolshaya Sadovaya 79; open 10am-6pm Tues-Sun) features Cossack history and the peasant rebellions of Bulavin, Razin and Pugachov.

At the west end of town, **Gorky Park** has secluded gardens, men playing dominoes, an observatory and the 19th-century town hall. At the other end of ulitsa Bolshaya Sadovaya, October Revolution Park contains the expected **Memorial to the Liberation of Rostov**. Karaoke and shashlyk attract people in droves on summer evenings.

The **left bank** of the River Don is where Rostovites go when the temperature begins to rise. Beaches along the river bank are dotted with casinos and cafés, and at the outdoor restaurants you can watch the cooks work the mangal (grill), feast on their speciality, shashlyk, and dance under the stars to the local rhythm.

Places to Stay & Eat
The standard Soviet **Intourist hotel** (☎ 65 90 65, fax 65 90 07; e intourist@rostov.ru; 115 ul Bolshaya Sadovaya; singles from R1700) is the obvious place to stay. Renovated 'business' rooms are worth the extra cash if somebody else is paying.

Dokhodny Dom (☎ 65 20 72; 113 ul Bolshaya Sadovaya; singles/doubles with breakfast US$55/64) is a private hotel with five comfortable, air-conditioned rooms.

Hotel Rostov (☎ 34 69 58; 59 Budyonovsky pr; singles/doubles R450/800) is cheap and charmless, although good value for its central location.

Peter Pizza (☎ 67 93 27; 121 ul Maluginoi; pizza & beer R500) is Rostov's most popular pizzeria, especially for the classic Volkswagen Beetle parked in its midst. The pizza is not bad either, save for oddities like canned peas. Enter from behind the *dvorets sporta* (sports palace).

Zelyonaya Gorka (*☎ 40 24 49; Gorky Park; mains R50; open 11am-11pm*) has tasty, cheap Russian food. In summer, try the fish shashlyk at the outdoor café.

Cafe Salvador (*44 ul Universitetskaya; mains from R100; open 11am-11pm*) is a hot spot for local university students. **Cafe Mango** (*49 ul Serafimovicha; mains R100; open 10am-11pm*) is another great place for inexpensive food such as fish and chips.

Pavlin Mavlin (*☎ 62 30 77; 79/81 ul Temernitskaya; dinner from R150, weekend cover charge R30; open 11am-11pm daily*) is Rostov's only vegetarian restaurant. Not unlike Russia's nonvegetarian restaurants, this place specialises in beet salad and borshch. Service is slow but cheerful.

Satisfy your sweet tooth at **Zolotoy Kolos** (*☎ 40 82 90; ul Bolshaya Sadovaya 43; coffee R30; 10am-9pm*) which has mediocre coffee but delicious cakes and home-made ice cream.

Entertainment

The modern, notable **Rostov Musical Theatre** (*Musikalniy Teatr; ☎ 64 07 07; 140 ul Bolshaya Sadovaya*) has an architectural design in the shape of a white concert piano, as well as progressive amenities, including toilets that can accommodate 30 desperate theatre-goers at once.

The friendly **Club Lila** (*☎ 62 38 19; 67 Sotsialisticheskaya ul; R60 cover charge; open 6pm-2am*) features live music by local rock and blues groups.

Guinness Bar (*☎ 40 30 19; 57 ul Bolshaya Sadovaya; beer R100; open 10am-midnight*) attracts businessmen and New Russians, the only people who can afford it.

Getting There & Away

Daily flights to Moscow are R2520. A fast train from Moscow's Kursky station takes 20 hours. Some trains to/from Moscow go via Kharkiv (Kharkov) in Ukraine; be aware of Ukrainian visa requirements. Trains also go daily to Astrakhan (24 hours), Volgograd (16 hours) and Sochi (14 hours). The river station is at the southeastern end of Budyonovsky prospekt. Boats to Volgograd go several times a week from May to September.

Getting Around

Romaks Taxi (*☎ 77 45 99*) is cheap and efficient for the airport or the train station. Bus No 7, 12 or 13 and trolleybus No 1, 9 or 15 ply ulitsa Bolshaya Sadovaya. To reach the left bank, catch a ferry from the dock near Voroshilovsky bridge.

AROUND ROSTOV-ON-DON
Starocherkassk
Старочеркасск

Founded in 1593, Old Cherkassk was the Don Cossack capital for two centuries. Once a fortified town of 20,000, it is now a village of vegetable farmers, with its main street restored to its 19th-century appearance. The remains of a fortress, **Cherkassk Krepost**, are 3km down the River Don.

Allegedly, Peter the Great came across a drunken Cossack sitting on a barrel, wearing only a rifle. This image of a soldier who'd sooner lose his clothes than his gun so impressed the tsar that he had it drawn up as the Don Cossack army seal.

Near the west end of the main street is the fortified house of peasant rebellion leader Kondraty Bulavin (1709). Walk east past the plain **SS Peter & Paul Church** (1751), the old market square, and the sturdy **Cossack fort-houses**. In the brick building, a good **museum** (*☎ 250-297 49 18; admission R10; open 10am-5pm Tues-Sun*) illustrates 16th- to 20th-century Cossack life and rebellions. Next door, the **Church of Our Lady of the Don** (1761) was the private church of a Cossack ataman. Behind it is his classical 'palace'.

In the square at the eastern end, Stepan Razin rallied his followers in 1670 and later was clapped in chains on the same spot. The **Resurrection Cathedral** (Voskresensky sobor) contains an exquisite iconostasis and baroque chandelier. On most summer weekends, Starocherkassk holds a 'Cossack fair', featuring music, dancing, crafts and horseback riding.

Several times a day, a hydrofoil travels the 30km up the Don River to Starocherkassk (40 minutes).

Novocherkassk
Новочеркасск

The Don Cossacks moved their capital in 1805 to New Cherkassk, 40km northeast of Rostov; this is supposedly the setting for

CAUCASUS

Nobel laureate Mikhail Sholokhov's novel, *And Quiet Flows the Don*.

A local hero is Ataman Matvey Platov, a Cossack general whose brigade chased Napoleon back to Paris; a monument commemorates Platov's return. The **History of the Don Cossacks Museum** (☎ 252-2 84 70; ul Sovietskaya; open 10am-5pm Tues-Sun) has a collection of Cossack memorabilia, including a sword presented to Platov in England. From Rostov, buses (40 minutes) and trains (75 minutes) go to Novocherkassk.

Tanaïs & Azov

Танаис и Азов

From the 3rd century BC until the 4th century AD, the Greek colony of Tanaïs flourished on the Sea of Azov at the mouth of the Don. On the road from Rostov to Taganrog (near the village of Nedvigovka) you can see excavations of the original Tanaïs and a relevant **museum** (open May-Oct).

In the 13th century, Genoese merchants established a trading settlement nearby called Tana (now Azov). Later the Turks built a fortress on the site to keep the Russians out of the Black Sea. Now the industrial town of Azov houses **Azov Fort** (Azovskaya Krepost) and yet another **museum** (☎ 242-3 07 71; ul Moskovskaya 38/40; open 10am-5pm Tues-Sun) with exhibits on Cossack life and history. Several times a day, a hydrofoil travels the 45km down to Azov from Rostov.

KRASNODAR

КРАСНОДАР

☎ 8612 • pop 756,000

When Catherine the Great travelled south to tour the lands she'd won from the Turks in the Crimean War, her lover Potemkin had lively facades erected along her route. These aimed to hide the mud-splattered hovels that comprised the newly founded city bearing her name, Yekaterinodar ('Catherine's gift').

Some two centuries later, Krasnodar (the city was renamed after the 1917 Revolution) is resort-like with flowering parks, fountains and old Soviet-era hotels with fresh coats of paint.

You may catch a glimpse of the Kuban Cossacks, whose headquarters are in the city. Sometimes the Cossacks gather in uniform for *krugi* (meetings), and if you're lucky you can even catch a folk festival in a neighbouring *stanitsa* (Cossack village).

Nearby is the Kuban Sea (Kubanskoe More), a huge reservoir created in the 1970s, when the water table rose so high that 3500 sq km of farmland were flooded and the foundations of 27,000 blocks of flats were waterlogged.

Orientation & Information

Krasnaya ulitsa is Krasnodar's 2km-long main street. The road from Rostov-on-Don feeds into its northern end as a tree-lined dual carriageway. Parallel, two blocks east, is ulitsa Kommunarov; one block west is ulitsa Rashpilevskaya. Main cross-streets include, in south–north order, ulitsas Mira, Lenina and Severnaya.

There are several places to change money, including the Hotels Moskva and Intourist. **Alfa Bank** (☎ 37 27 00; ul Krasnaya 124) will cash American Express (AmEx) travellers cheques. There's a **main post office** (ul Karasunskaya 68; open 9am-7pm Mon-Sat, 9am-6pm Sun), and the Hotel Moskva has a **post office counter**. The **telephone office** (ul Krasnaya 118; open 8am-7.45pm daily) provides Internet access from 9am to 1pm and 2pm to 8.45pm daily at R32 an hour. An alternative is the 24-hour **Internet café** (ul Krasnaya 190), also R32 an hour.

A large **department store** (Domknige; ul Krasnaya) opposite Hotel Moskva has a variety of small shops, among them a small bookshop selling titles in English (its fiction is mostly geared to the educational market). Another shop sells bright and cheery lacquer ware but at prices greater than at the art and craft market in Zhukov Square.

Globis Tours (☎ 65 05 33, fax 6 52 14; e globustur@mail.ru; ul Krasnaya 41) organises day trips for R450 per person to the Logamake area, including views of mountains, waterfalls and caves.

Taxi Service (☎ 057) is the cheapest of the taxi firms.

Things to See

You'll find Scythian and ancient Greek figures at the **Regional Museum** (Kraevedchesky muzey; ul Voroshilova 67; admission R30; open 10am-5pm Tues-Sun). Although all captions are in Russian, there's enough of visual interest – natural history, prehistoric items, Cossack items – to make a visit worthwhile. To appreciate the post-revolution displays, you'll need an interpreter.

Zhukov Square accommodates an open-air **art and craft market** selling paintings, embroidery work and lacquer ware. You can also add to your Lenin medal collection here. The nearby **Art Museum** (*Khudozhestvenny muzey; ul Krasnaya 13*) was closed for renovation at the time of research.

Several times a month there's a traditional **circus** (☎ 55 84 89; cnr uls Kalinina & Ok-*yabrskya; admission R70-150; showtime 6pm Mon-Fri, noon & 4pm Sat & Sun*). Concerts are also held at the venue, although you'll be lucky to squeeze information from the indifferent booking office attendant.

Places to Stay & Eat

Hotel Moskva (☎ 53 18 07, fax 53 01 00; ul Krasnaya 66; singles/doubles R600/800) has basic rooms that are pretty tired but if you lash out R1600 you'll get a 'half luxury' apartment way, way up on the quality scale.

Hotel Tsentralnaya (☎ 68 60 57; ul Krasnaya 25; doubles per person R400), on the corner of ulitsa Mira, has decent double rooms and no singles. The rooms are quite basic and worn but each does have a fridge and sink; toilets and showers, an extra R15, are down the corridor.

Hotel Intourist (☎ 68 52 97, fax 59 75 19; ul Krasnaya 109; singles/doubles R1485/1800), a looming place about halfway along the street, is Krasnodar's top hotel with quite acceptable but expensive rooms.

Alionushka Restaurant (☎ 53 23 04; ul Krasnaya 90; dishes R60-100; open 8am-midnight daily) specialises in tasty shashlyks and intimacy. Each dining table is in its own room, just the thing for shady deals or private affairs.

The Hotel Intourist's **Khrustalny Restaurant** (dishes R25-120; open 7am-midnight) is quite a surprise for a three-star hotel in that there's a varied menu, reasonable prices and good food.

There are cafés dotted all around the centre of town selling sandwiches, soups and salads. **Cafe Mur** (cnr uls Kommunarov & Mira; dishes R10-25) is typical: if you haven't tried borshch, this is the place.

There are many other places to eat along ulitsa Krasnaya. If the travel gods are with you, beige-and-brown **ice-cream wagons** will also be on the main drag selling some of Russia's best two-scoop waffle cones (R8).

The **central market** (ul Budyonnogo 129) is opposite the circus, a block west of Hotel Intourist. There's another market on ulitsa Mira, 500 metres west of the bus station on ulitsa Mira (near the junction with ulitsa Suvorovaan; it's an excellent source of fresh fruit and spicy pickled Korean food.

Getting There & Away

Air There are daily Aeroflot flights to/from Moscow (R2239), a weekly flight to Mineralnye Vody (R735), four weekly to Sochi (R435), two weekly to Istanbul (R1405) and one to Frankfurt (€280).

Counters sell airline tickets in the foyers of Hotels Moskva and Tsentralnaya. **Aeroflot** (☎ 64 00 10; ul Krasnaya 43; open 9am-6pm Mon-Fri) is in the Book Store building opposite Hotel Moskva and **Kuban Air** (☎ 55 65 08; ul Krasnaya 129) is just north of Hotel Intourist. The airport is about 15km from the city; take bus No 1 (R4) from the junction of ulitsas Krasnaya and Severnaya, one block north of Hotel Intourist. Taxis cost about R200.

Train There are daily trains to Rostov (R239, seven hours), Sochi (R214, six hours), Moscow (R943, 22 to 30 hours) and twice weekly to Kiev (R811, 27 hours). Many trains serve Novorossiysk (R171, 3¼ hours).

An overnight train on even dates of the month goes to Mineralnye Vody (R266, eight hours) and on to Vladikavkaz (R355, 11 hours).

Krasnodar-I (Privokzalnaya pl), at the eastern end of ulitsa Mira next to the intercity bus station, is the more convenient of Krasnodar's two stations. **Krasnodar-II** (ul Kommunarov 282), two blocks east of the northern end of ulitsa Krasnaya, has the same trains.

Bus For buses to all destinations in the region, the **intercity bus station** (avtovokzal mezhdugorodnyy soobshcheny; Privokzalnaya pl) has a handy touch-screen display with bus times and fares. Trains are better for travelling to the spa towns, Sochi and Vladikavkaz.

Sample destinations are Sochi (R135, eight hours) by overnight bus, Novorossiysk (R65, three hours) and Anapa (R75, four hours).

Car & Motorcycle Krasnodar is 275km from Rostov-on-Don and 435km from Sochi. A main route goes west to the coast at Novorossiysk and another south via Tuapse to Sochi.

CAUCASUS

Black Sea Coast
Побережье Чёрного моря

The foothills among the western 400km of the Caucasus provide a scenic backdrop to Black Sea resorts and ports with a fine sub-tropical climate. In summer it's usually hot, not too humid, and the sea is warm; Sochi and Dagomys are the leading resorts. The region also has some terrific trekking through lake and waterfall-filled valleys, old Cherkess villages and alpine plateaus. Skiing is popular at nearby Krasnaya Polyana and Mt Fisht from about January to April.

NOVOROSSIYSK
НОВОРОССИЙСК
☎ 8617 • pop 220,000

This port on a deep, sheltered bay houses part of the Russian Black Sea Fleet displaced from Ukraine. The road from Krasnodar comes in along Anapskoe shosse, ending with **Hotel Brigantina** (*☎/fax 22 63 73, fax 61 00 79; Anapskoe shosse 18; singles/doubles from R840/1470*), which has cheaply furnished rooms with TV, fridge and phone. The more expensive rooms have been tarted up and the hotel has a restaurant.

Anapskoe shosse then becomes ulitsa Sovietov, with the port just to its east, on the west side of the bay. Just beyond is the **Town History Museum** (*Muzey istorii goroda; ul Sovietov 58; entry R50; open 10am-8pm Sat-Thur*) with a significant collection devoted to WWII and many maritime photographs, artefacts and model ships.

WWII Memorials
Novorossiysk is peppered with WWII memorials. In 1943, a small Soviet landing party heroically held out here for 225 days, forming a bridgehead for the Soviet counteroffensive against the occupying Germans. Their feats are celebrated by the amazing memorial at **Malaya Zemlya**. This huge concrete construction represents the beached prow of a liberating ship disgorging a party of soldiers and sailors, all depicted in chunky bronze. Inside the 'prow' is a walk-through **gallery** (*admission R50; open 10am-5pm daily*), with plaques of heroes and a solemn, deep-voiced Russian choir singing patriotic songs.

There are clusters of memorials at the southern end of prospekt Lenina, where the party landed, and farther round at **Dolina Smerti** (Death Valley), where the Russians came under fiercest bombardment.

Getting There & Away
Apart from a branch line to Anapa, Novorossiysk is the end of the train line. Buses serve many destinations, including Krasnodar (R71, three hours) and Sochi (R135, 8¾ hours).

On the first and third Tuesday of the month, there's a ferry to Istanbul with four-berth cabins (US$263, 36 hours), returning the following Monday. **Novoship** (*☎ 25 15 62, fax 25 15 62; ⓦ www.novoship.ru; 4th floor ul Mira 23*) sells tickets and is in a building with large portico columns.

Between June and September there are frequent hydrofoils to/from Gelendzhik and Sochi.

SOCHI & DAGOMYS
СОЧИ И ДАГОМЫС
☎ 8622 • pop (Sochi) 378,000

While the Black Sea resorts have been compared to Florida, Sochi – despite its arcades, discotheques, Zoom Flumes and beachside cafés – is not quite Daytona Beach. However, it is a relaxing place for seaside recuperation from the ardours of travel in Russia's vast inland or large cities.

This mountainous coast, a sunny and somewhat tacky holiday land, used to belong to the Cherkess (also known as Adygey or Circassians), fierce tribes who farmed the foothills and traded slaves, gold and honey with the Turks in exchange for salt, jewellery and wheat.

By the 1900s, the area was already a prestigious holiday spot and Tsar Nicholas II had a dacha in Dagomys. Famous Russian artists and performers, including opera singer Fyodor Chaliapin, poet Vladimir Mayakovsky and writer Isaac Babel, also came here. The most prestigious resort then was Kavkhazskaya Rivera, now in ruins.

During WWII Sochi became a hospital city, treating over half a million wounded. In its Soviet heyday, Communist elite and workers alike came here to bask on beaches and stroll along cypress- and palm-shaded promenades. Now they're outnumbered by kids in pirated fashion wear, old folk nursing their ailments at the many sanatoria, New Russians in BMWs – and a few foreigners.

The season starts in late May with a loud and messy week-long beer festival; accommodation may be hard to find in July and August. Several hundred Russian and foreign breweries set up pavilions along the sea front and attendees attempt to taste all on offer. A week-long film festival in June attracts the film stars of Russia and outdoor screens have free screenings that attract adolescents with laser pointers. The Winter Theatre also has screenings but you have to pay. In late September Sochi hosts the Velvet Season fashion show, another week-long extravaganza attracting the top names in the Russian fashion industry.

Orientation

Greater Sochi, some 150km long, is the world's second-largest conurbation after Los Angeles. Sochi itself stretches about 7km down the coast from Sochi River to the southern suburb of Matsesta. At the northern end is a cluster of adjacent train and bus stations, the harbour and the shopping centre. Kurortny prospekt, the main north–south street, runs the length of the town a few blocks in from the sea.

Flea markets line ulitsa Moskovskaya, opposite the bus station, ulitsa Voykova near the harbour, and the entire length of ulitsa Navaginskaya. From the harbour, a pedestrian promenade stretches south along the jam-packed beaches, backed for much of their length by steep slopes with a wooded park on top.

The town of Dagomys is 12km north of Sochi on the main coast road. The Dagomys resort comprises the Hotel Dagomys, the Motel Meridian, Camping Dagomys and a couple of restaurants. It stands in its own hilly grounds, between the untidy town centre and the sea. It is reached by a 2km approach road.

Information

Sochi has a **tourist bureau** (☎ 99 20 82, fax 92 87 83; Hotel Zhemchuzhina, Chernomorskaya ul 3; open 10am-6pm daily) that runs tours around Sochi and surrounding regions, and makes theatre, plane and train bookings.

For trips to Krasnaya Polyana, Mt Fisht and Vorontsovskaya Cave, white-water rafting, heliskiing tours and bookings at most of Sochi's sanatoria, contact **Reinfo** (☎ 62 23 65, fax 62 20 42; e reinfo@sochi.ru; office 214, Hotel Sochi-Magnolia). It caters to individual travellers and offers 10-day expeditions involving hiking, sailing and whitewater rafting for US$200 per person. An amicable, knowledgeable colleague of this firm is **Sergei Shuklin** (☎ 31 96 14), a mountain climber who speaks some English.

Aerotour (☎ 92 87 55, fax 92 15 01; e sochi@aerotour.ru; Hotel Moskva, pr Kurortny 18) has helpful English-speaking staff who will book domestic and international airline tickets. **Territory Agency of Air Connections** (☎ 92 29 36; ul Navaginskaya 16) can do the same.

Vneshtorgbank (Karl Libknekhta 10) cashes travellers cheques and gives advances on credit cards. Sochi has a **main post office** (cnr pr Kurortny & ul Vorovskogo; open 8am-7pm daily) but major hotels have their own postal counters. A **bookshop** (ul Navaginskaya 12) sells maps and a decent guide (R200) in English and Russian on the natural history of Sochi and surrounding areas. A useful website is w www.russianriviera.com.

Things to See & Do

The **Art Museum** (Khudozhestvenny muzey; Kurortny pr 51; admission R30; open 10am-5.30pm daily) has special visiting exhibitions and an expansive permanent collection; an English guidebook is available for R5. The classical building – an artwork in itself, with massive columns representing Soviet might – looks out to a statue of comrade Lenin.

The recently moved **Town History Museum** (Gorodskoy Istorichesky Muzey; ul Vorovskogo 54; admission R10; open 9am-5.30pm daily) currently only has a small part of its collection on display. The curators are quite keen on their display of driftwood which has been shaped, with bits added, into various amorphic animal forms.

Sochi's lovely **arboretum** (Dendrariy; pr Kurortny; admission R30; open 10am-7pm), with more than 1500 species of trees and shrubs from the world over, is attractively laid out and well worth seeing. It extends on both sides of Kurortny prospekt, about 2km south of the town centre; there are Mediterranean, Caucasus, Far East, Himalayan, Australian and American sections in the upper part. The best way to see it is to take the **cable car** (single/return R80/100; 1pm-6pm

CAUCASUS

Mon, 9am-1pm & 2pm-6pm Tues-Sun) to the top and walk back down.

The beach, swimming and assorted seaside fun-time activities are the main reason for visiting Sochi and Dagomys. Although the beaches are pebbly wherever you go, Dagomys is less crowded, with somewhat cleaner waters, boards for lying on, and a panoramic lift connecting the beach and Dagomys resort. Wherever you go there's an almost continuous strip of cafés and bars backing the beach.

Park Rivera in Sochi has a fun fair as well as a tacky range of art and craft shops, pony rides and an avenue of magnolias with trees planted by cosmonauts. Gagarin is not represented, as the park was started after his death – but did you know that there was an Afghani cosmonaut (who *is* represented here)?

Places to Stay

Sochi A typical Russian holiday would once have been a month at the sanatorium related to one's profession (for example, the stately Stalinist Metallurg Sanatory for metal workers). Unfortunately you can't just front up and get a room like at a hotel; most likely you'll be given short shrift by security personnel at the front gate. Aerotour in the Hotel Moskva foyer can book sanatoria accommodation, as can Reinfo (see the Information section earlier for details).

Built in the 1930s in Russian Imperial style, some sanatoria are mini Romanov palaces: grounds are beautiful, beaches are private, meals are included and there are pools and tennis courts. Locals say the best sanatoria are the Rus, Sochi, the Voroshilova, Zelyonaya Rosha (where Stalin's dacha is located) and Ordzhonikidze.

At the brand new **Chernomorje Sanatorium** (☎ 60 90 60, fax 62 38 98; ul Ordzhonikidze 27; rooms with full board per week from R5400), the rates include all treatment. If you just want to call in for a medicinal bath the cost is around R130; to use the swimming pool it's R100 an hour.

A popular option is to rent a room in a flat, or rent the entire flat. At the train station, the **Resort Bureau** (Kurortnoe byuro; ☎ 62 28 22, fax 92 29 76; e propan@sochi.ru; open 24hrs) can arrange private rooms from May to June (R100) and from July to August (R150); the apartments, also available from May to June (R400 to R500) and from July to August

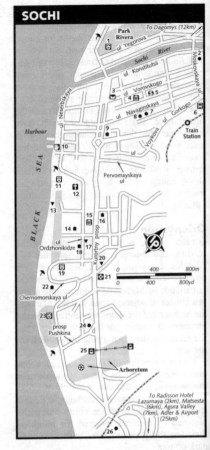

(R600 to R800), take up to three people and have a bedroom, kitchen and bathroom. Train passengers will also be approached by people with rooms or flats to rent.

Sochi has many hotels, with prices increasing about 25% every month from May to August. **Hotel Moskva** (☎ 92 35 32, fax 92 34 10; Kurortny pr 18; singles/doubles off-season R515/800, summer R700/1200), large, noisy and run-down, is smack in the town centre. **Hotel Primorskaya** (☎ 92 57 43; ul Sokolova 1; singles/doubles R450-810/750-1350), a sprawling, pale-yellow hotel with gloomy Soviet-style foyer and cramped but clean rooms, is a better bet than the Moskva. For a month in April there's no hot water while the pipework is overhauled for the seasonal rush starting in June.

SOCHI

PLACES TO STAY

9 Hotel Moskva; Aerotours; Cafe Cinzano
   Гостиница Москва
14 Hotel Primorskaya
   Гостиница Приморская
16 Hotel Sochi-Magnolia; Reinfo
   Гостиница Сочи-Магнолия
18 Chermnomorje Sanatorium
   Черноморье Санаторий имени
22 Hotel Zhemchuzhina; Tourist Bureau; American Diner; Caesar Palace
   Гостиница Жемчужина

PLACES TO EAT

13 Kafe Briz
   Кафе риз
17 Seventh Heaven
   Восьмое Небо
20 Art Pizza
   Арт Пицца

OTHER

1 Zelyony Teatr
  Зелёный театр
2 Market
  Рынок
3 Main Post Office
  Главпочтамт
4 Town History Museum
  Музей истории города
5 Vneshtorgbank
  Внешторгбанк
6 Bus Station
  Автовокзал
7 Aeroflot; Territory Agency of Air Connections
  Аэрофлотж Агентство Территории Воздушны Связей
8 Bookshop
  Книжный магазин
10 Sea Terminal; Ticket Office
   Морской вокзал

11 Festivalny Concert Hall
   Концертный зал Фестивальный
12 Church Of Michael the Archangel
   шхюрам Миаила Ар ангела
15 Art Museum
   шхюудожественный музей
19 Teatralnaya Ploschad
   Театральная Площадь
21 Supermarket
   Универсам
23 Letny Teatr
   Летний театр
24 Circus
   Цирк
25 Cable Car
   Канатно-кресельная дорога
26 Stadium
   Стадион

Hotel Zhemchuzhina (☎ 66 11 88, fax 66 18 88; e zhem@sochi.comstar.ru; Chernomorskaya ul 3; rooms Sept-June/July & Aug R1100/1600), a 965-room place, has its own beach, a pool with heated sea water and tennis courts (for a small fee). It's by the sea, 2km from the centre and a 500m walk past the Zimny Teatr. It's rather timeworn but comfortable standard rooms are attended to by helpful and smiling staff, and hot water is available year-round. The hotel's sales department is open 9am to 8pm daily and sells tickets to theatre productions and excursions, as well as train and plane tickets.

Radisson Hotel Lazurnaya (☎ 66 33 33, fax 66 32 92; Kurortny pr 103; singles/doubles May-June US$135/150, July-Aug US$170/185) is just like other Radissons around the world with similar facilities and service, including a private beach, casino, saunas, health centre and pool (US$20 a day for nonresidents); breakfast is included in the rates. Airport buses go past the hotel, which is 2km south of town on the Adler road, or you can catch the frequent *marshrutki* (dedicated minibuses).

Dagomys The towering, pyramid-like construction hogging the skyline is the four-star, 1800-bed **Hotel Dagomys** (☎ 30 71 27, fax 32 21 00; w www.dagomys.ru; Leningradskaya ul 7; singles/doubles US$40-66/50-76). Rooms range from basic doubles to two-floor apart-

ments with double bathrooms. The hotel has several bars, restaurants, a post office, shopping arcade and a service bureau for excursions, car rental, plane and train tickets. The exchange kiosk will change money and give cash advances on Visa and MasterCard credit cards. The hotel also has extensive sanatoria facilities, as well as resort features including the beach, indoor and outdoor pools, a sports centre with tennis courts, a concert hall-cumcinema and a library. Given such services, the unadventurous need go nowhere else.

En route to Hotel Dagomys is the three-star **Olympic** (☎ 30 76 30, fax 30 76 25; e olimp@ sochi.ru; rooms per person from US$23), with well-equipped rooms of a similar standard to the Dagomys. Air-conditioned rooms are an extra US$4 per person. Like the Dagomys, all rooms face either the sea or mountains.

The adjacent **Motel Meridian** (☎ 30 76 30, fax 30 76 25; rooms from US$27) has motel-style rooms. The cheapest have just two beds and a kitchenette, while the more expensive are on two levels with bedroom, sitting room and kitchenette. All rooms have attached bathrooms.

Camping Dagomys (☎ 32 18 29; caravans R450-530) has bare-bones caravans that sleep two people and have their own toilet. Shower blocks are separate and there's a canteen open from 8am to 8pm (there are no cooking facilities). An area is set aside for tents.

Places to Eat

Sochi You can choose between more expensive hotel restaurants and less expensive seaside cafés. Food everywhere is about the same mix of shashlyk, salads, grilled chicken and fish.

Cafe Cinzano (*dishes R35-90; open 9am-midnight daily*), by Hotel Moskva, has some of the best food in Sochi. Try the succulent pancakes stuffed with mushrooms for R35, or *hachapari*, home-made bread with cheese and egg.

Kafe Briz (*dishes R40-70; open year-round*), below the Park Hotel, is for those who won't make it to Georgia but still want to try Georgian food, including *satsivi* (chicken in garlic and nut sauce), *lobio* (kidney beans in spicy sauce), and eggplant stuffed with garlic, nuts and cilantro. Home-made wine is R28 a glass.

Art Pizza (*☎ 92 52 52; Teatralnaya pl 9; pizzas R80-150; open 10am-midnight daily*), a new addition to Sochi's dining scene, has Baltica beer on tap. If it's too early for beer and pizza, try the cake and coffee.

American Diner (*Hotel Zhemchuzhina; snacks R70-120; open 24hrs*) is a typical American-style diner, with red leatherette bar seats, Harley Davidson motorcycle photographs on the wall and an old jukebox. Sandwiches, salads and steaks are the mainstays of the menu.

Seventh Heaven (*☎ 62 38 88; ul Ordzhonikidze 24; dishes R80-700; open 2pm-3am daily*) is an expensive restaurant with an eclectic menu. Frogs legs braised in Chablis will set you back R220, a seafood platter R370, and venison, rabbit or quail anything between R200 and 700. Service is probably too attentive.

Sochi market (*ul Moskovskaya*), a short walk north of the bus station, has fresh fruit and vegetables, much of it from Turkey. Try the very tasty nut sticks – nuts strung together with cotton and covered with fruit jelly.

Agura Valley For open-air dining, **Salkhino** (*☎ 97 08 17; Agura Valley; dishes R50-100; open 11am-late daily*) has rustic huts in a garden setting accompanied by live music in summer. Their speciality is shashlyk, and inevitably trout, given the major trout farm in nearby Adler. Adjacent is the renowned **Restoran Kavkazsky Aul** (which was undergoing renovation when we were there). Both restaurants are just inland from Matsesta. If you're dining at night your best option would be to take a taxi.

Dagomys There are many restaurants around the Dagomys complex, the more famous being the open-air **Restoran Dubrava**, serving Russian food, and **Kavkazskaya Kukhnya**, with Caucasian food. The popular **Restoran Saturn** (Russian food) and **Restoran Rubin** are both in Hotel Dagomys.

There are so many bars and cafés in Dagomys, with and without alcohol, that you would need a month to try all of them.

Bar Panorama has the freshest of fresh air, being on the roof of Hotel Dagomys, while the bar in the main lobby offers air-conditioned seclusion.

Entertainment

The Dagomys complex has a cinema/concert hall, a disco in the sports centre, several nightclubs, and a few restaurants with shows or live bands.

In Sochi, most hotels have discos that are usually open from 9pm to 4am, with a typical cover charge of R100 to R200. Most restaurants have live music.

A doorman with top hat sets the atmosphere for **Seventh Heaven** (*ul Ordzhonikidze 24; entry R150*), a nightclub with live bands and modern dance music. It's in the same building as the restaurant of the same name.

Visiting rock acts, as well as classical musicians and theatre troupes, perform at Sochi's open-air **Letny Teatr** (Summer Theatre) in Park Frunze or the **Zelyony Teatr** (Green Theatre) in Park Rivera from late May to September. For opera, ballet and drama, check out the huge **Zimny Teatr** (*Winter Theatre; ☎ 99 77 06; Teatralnaya pl; booking office open 10am-7pm daily*), another massive colonnaded building built in a majestic, imperial style.

Caesar Palace Casino (*admission US$40; open 7pm-late daily*), a glitzy, orange-velvet place, is at Hotel Zhemchuzhina. Your admission money will be returned in chips.

Sochi has a **circus** (*☎ 92 03 75; cnr Pushkina and Kurortny prs; box office open 10am-8pm in season*), with Russian and international performances, as well as boxing and other events in season.

Getting There & Away

Air Flights to/from Sochi are more frequent during the May to October season. There are several daily flights to/from Moscow (R2000 to R3000), but only a few a week from November to April. Other services include Mineralnye Vody once a week (R631), Tbilisi (R3660) every Sunday, and Istanbul each Monday for US$184.

Train There are several trains a day between Sochi and Moscow (R1476, about 38 hours), via Rostov-on-Don. Train Nos 11, 12, 79 and 80 – although they take a few hours longer – do not pass through Ukraine, so you won't need an extra set of visas. On even-numbered dates of the month, there's a train to Krasnodar (R214, 6½ hours), and one on odd-numbered days to Vladikavkaz (R550, 17 hours) stopping at Mineralnye Vody (R400, 13 hours).

Bus Services include twice-daily buses to Krasnodar (R129, eight hours), and daily buses to Novorossiysk (R123, nine hours) and Mineralnye Vody (R304, 17 hours).

Boat Although the sea terminal is under restoration, the adjacent **ticket office** (☎ 60 96 03; open 8am–ship sailing) handles tickets and information for daily services to Trabzon in Turkey (US$80, 12 hours) and occasional ferries to Istanbul (R3110, 36 hours).

There are sailings winter Tuesdays and Fridays and summer Mondays, Wednesdays and Fridays to Batumi in Georgia, costing R1500 (six or 12 hours, depending on the boat used).

Getting Around
To/From the Airport The airport is about 30km south of Sochi (near Adler). Bus No 124 from Sochi bus station takes about 50 minutes and costs R7 (plus a small charge for baggage). Local bus Nos 4 and 4C also link the airport and bus station, but are slower. A taxi should cost about R200.

Between Sochi & Dagomys It's a half-hour bus ride to Dagomys from Sochi on Bus No 49, which stops on the main road, about 1km from the resort. A taxi shouldn't be more than R300.

Sochi Bus Nos 3, 4 and 17 travel from the bus station along Kurortny prospekt as far south as Matsesta. Many *marshrutki* ply the main routes for R7 a journey.

AROUND SOCHI & DAGOMYS
Most hotels offer day excursions, and both Agura Valley and Mt Bolshoy Akhun can be done in a day. However, for Krasnaya Polyana, Mt Fisht and the 12km-long Cave Vorontsovskaya, you should allow a couple of days or more. Reinfo (see Information in the Sochi & Dagomys section earlier) can assist you with guides, accommodation and transport.

Dagomys Tea Houses
Dagomys proudly boasts of having the most northerly tea plantations in the world. About 10km on the coast road towards Tuapse, **Tea Houses** (☎ 31 13 54; admission R110; open 10am–5pm daily) puts on song and dance performances depicting Russian customs in a traditional wooden lodge. Tea Houses also brews its own tea and holds tea parties in the lodge's elaborately decorated upper room.

Agura Valley
Áгурское Ущелье
An inland turning at Matsesta takes you to a car park and path, which leads to a small lake and waterfalls, with one of the latter being 30m high; entry is R20. The **Orlinye Skaly** (Eagle Cliffs) tower is above, and endangered flora here include species of cyclamen, box trees and the Pitsunda pines growing high on Orlinye Skaly.

Mt Bolshoy Akhun
Гора Большой Ахун
elevation 662m
An 11km road signposted 'Akhun', just south of the Agura turning, leads up to a 662m hill with a **lookout tower** (admission R20; open 24hrs) on top. The tower gives commanding views of Sochi, Adler, Mt Fisht and Mt Chugsh (3256m), with the latter being the highest mountain in the Sochi region. Just down from the tower is the rustic **Prokhlada Cafe** (dishes R30–60; open 10am–midnight daily), serving excellent shashlyk. You could also also try the *lobio* and the assortment of pickles.

There is a path by the tower that wanders down through the Agura Valley. It's a two-hour descent along the river and waterfalls, longer if you start partaking of the home-made wine sold by locals near the swimming hole. From the main road, take a *marshrutki* back to Sochi.

CAUCASUS

Mt Fisht
Гора Фишт
elevation 2867m

About 50km from Sochi but reachable only by helicopter or a four-day return trek, Mt Fisht is the start of the Caucasus mountain range. The hotel, **Lunnaya Polyana** (US$10 per night), is at 1800m and has basic accommodation; it looks like a two-storey yurt (a nomad's portable, round tent-house).

A helicopter flies here for heliskiing and sightseeing from Krasnaya Polyana. Reinfo (see Information under Sochi & Dagomys) charges US$150 per person for the whole day (minimum groups of 10), although individuals can join an existing group. September hiking is superb.

Krasnaya Polyana
Красная Поляна
elevation 550m

Krasnaya Polyana (Beautiful Glade) is a small settlement surrounded by mountains and alpine meadows, about 70km from Sochi. The spectacular road up from Adler follows the Mzymta River passing through a deep, steep gorge.

Krasnaya Polyana, a candidate for the 2002 Winter Games, is a well-developed ski resort with chairlifts for intermediate skiing and heliskiing for the experienced. The ski season is November to May but the **chairlifts** (sightseeing R300; all-day skiing R450; open 9am-6pm daily Nov-May, 9am-6pm Wed-Sun Jun-Oct) operate year-round. The most beautiful time is May to July, when spring flowers bloom. There are 40/60-minute **jeep rides** (mobile ☎ 08622-39 40 80) available up mountain tracks for R500/600, and a half-day trip up to 2000m for R3186. There's also year-round horse riding available for R200 an hour, with both horse riding and jeeps operating from the base chairlift station (also where a number of stalls sell home-made wine, pickles and Georgian hats).

Most hotels arrange day excursions, and Reinfo can arrange longer overnight hikes, but you need to stay here for several days to get the best out of the area.

For accommodation, ask Reinfo or put yourself up at the expensive **Radisson SAS Lazurnaya Peak Hotel** (☎ 66 36 00, fax 66 36 45; Krasnaya Polyana; singles/doubles US$110-150/140-180). Another hotel, **Krasnaya Polyana 2** (☎ 43 03 45; Krasnaya Polyana; rooms from R550 per person), is owned by the military and requires advance bookings.

From Adler, take the frequent bus No 135 (R15, 1½ hours) and persuade the driver to take you onto the chairlift station for a few extra roubles.

Mineral Water Spas
Минеральные Воды

Here, the central Caucasus begins to rise from the steppe in an eerie landscape studded with dead volcanoes and spouting mineral springs. The curative powers of the springs have attracted unhealthy, hypochondriac or holiday-minded Russians ever since someone noticed in the late 18th century that wounded soldiers appeared to get better quicker when bathing in them. The area had passed from Turkish to Russian hands in 1774 but still came under attack from local tribes. Early patients sometimes had to take refuge in the forts.

Today the area, known as **Kavkazskie Mineralnye Vody** (Caucasian Mineral Waters), is a holiday resort where the healthy seemingly outnumber the ailing. The atmosphere is relaxed, the air fresh and the walks lovely. The parks and elegant but decaying spa buildings recall the 19th century, when fashionable society trekked down from Moscow and St Petersburg to see, be seen, attend balls and look for a spouse.

There are five main towns – the resorts of **Pyatigorsk, Kislovodsk, Yessentuki** (more a city than a resort), **Zheleznovodsk** and the industrial and transport centre, **Mineralnye Vody** (Minvody for short).

The whole area is haunted by the Romantic writer Mikhail Lermontov, whose tale 'Princess Mary', from his novel A Hero of Our Time, is set here. Lermontov, in an uncanny echo of its plot, was killed in a duel at Pyatigorsk in 1841 and many local sites crop up in the book, which also contains an episode set on the Georgian Military Highway. A Hero of Our Time – very short by Russian literary standards – makes a great travelling companion.

There used to be over 130 springs in the region, gushing out 60 million litres of mineral water a day and variously believed to benefit disorders of the muscles, bones, heart,

MINERAL WATER SPAS

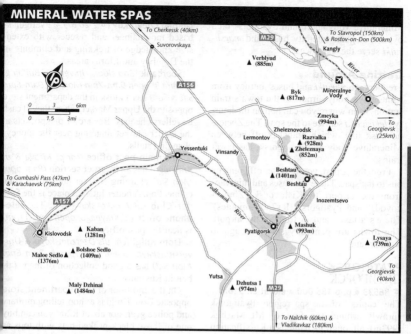

circulation, nervous system and skin. However, many have since fizzled out, mainly due to lack of maintenance.

Tucked away in rambling verdant parks in each town are buildings labelled *istochnik* (spring). Although many are closed with corroded and dry taps, others will be the highlight of the resort experience, where you can enter and drink for free.

For a fee, you can also have a dip in one of the *vanny* (bathhouses), but don't expect Turkish luxury – the baths are strictly medicinal 15-minute plunges, monitored by a nurse. You can also subject yourself to being plastered with supposedly curative mud from Lake Bolshoy Tombukan, near Pyatigorsk. Unfortunately you can't just show up at a sanatorium and ask for a mud bath – you are supposed to be referred by a doctor, which can be organised by Stavropolintour (see information under the Pyatigorsk section later).

Getting There & Away

The airport and train station at Mineralnye Vody are linked to the spa towns by buses and a good local train service.

Air There are several daily services to/from Moscow (R2500), four weekly to/from St Petersburg (R3900) and two weekly to/from Sochi (R700) in summer (less in winter). Weekly flights go to Istanbul (US$170) and Munich (US$380).

Train Mostly likely you'll arrive by train and transfer to a bus or *elektrichka* (suburban train) to carry on to Pyatigorsk or one of the other towns.

Mineralnye Vody has several daily trains to/from Moscow (about 30 hours) originating from Nalchik or Vladikavkaz. Trains on odd-numbered dates of the month go to Krasnodar (R266, eight hours) and then Novorossiysk (11 hours). On odd days there's a service to Sochi (R400, 13 hours). Daily trains travel to Nalchik (3½ hours) and Vladikavkaz (five hours), but buses are quicker. A few mainline trains run along the branch line into Pyatigorsk and Kislovodsk.

The **Servis Centre** (☎ 5 13 34; open 8am-noon & 1pm-8pm daily) of the Mineralnye Vody train station can assist you with ticketing. In addition, you can connect to the Internet here.

Bus The Rostov-Tbilisi road goes through Mineralnye Vody and round Pyatigorsk on a bypass. Regular intercity buses and *marshrutki* serve the spa towns.

Getting Around

Frequent *marshrutki* and buses journey from Mineralnye Vody airport to the town's train station, from where you can hop on the hourly *elektrichka* service to the spas. The Zheleznovodsk line, which branches off between Mineralnye Vody and Pyatigorsk, has fewer trains.

From the airport, you're better off going by bus to the spas. There are buses and minivans from the airport to Kislovodsk, Zheleznovodsk and Pyatigorsk (R17, 35 minutes). There's a taxi stand in front of the airport. The towns are generally small enough to walk around.

PYATIGORSK
ПЯТИГОРСК
☎ 86533 • pop 185,000 • elevation 510m

The 'capital' of the spa region, Pyatigorsk sprawls around the foot of Mt Mashuk (993m), although its name is a Russification of Beshtau (Five Peaks), the Turkish title of the highest mountain in the neighbourhood. Pyatigorsk began life as the fort Konstantinovskaya in 1780.

Orientation

The main street is the tree-lined prospekt Kirova, running west from below the Academic Gallery near the foot of Mashuk through the town centre to the train station. The jagged crags of Mt Beshtau (1400m) rise to the northwest with the town's suburbs stretching to their feet. The twin snow-covered peaks of Mt Elbrus to the south can be seen from several points around town on a clear day.

Information

Stavropolintour (☎ 4 91 76, fax 5 95 57; Hotel Intourist, floor C, pl Lenina 13) can arrange a guided tour (in English) of the city plus medical treatment in the Pyatigorsk's many sanatoria.

Inexpensive day trips (R230 to R250) to Dombay or Elbrus – as well as afternoon trips (R60 to R125) to Kislovodsk, Zheleznovodsk, the Stallion Farm or a local wine factory – are sold from stands around the city.

For more serious adventures, contact **Nikolai Oleynikov** (☎ 7 20 67), a Pyatigorsk-based mountaineer and rescuer with extensive knowledge of trekking and climbing in the Dombay and Elbrus areas.

Sberbank (2nd floor, Univermag Building, ul Mira 3; open 9am-7pm Mon-Fri, 9am-6pm Sat & Sun) has a kiosk in the department store opposite the Upper Market, where they'll cash travellers cheques. Beware of pickpockets at the Upper Market lingering near the money-changing stalls.

The **main post office** (cnr pr Kirova & ul Kraynego) has an **Internet section** (8am-5pm Mon-Sat) charging R50 an hour for a slow connection. A better Internet place is the **Spider Club** (ul Moskovskaya 84). The **telephone office** (ul Kraynego; open 6am-11pm) is near the post office.

Dom Knigi (cnr uls Dzerzhinskogo & Universitetskaya; open 9am-1pm & 2pm-6pm Mon-Sat) has a good collection of maps (albeit in Russian).

On the 2nd floor of the **department store** opposite Dom Knigi is a shop selling military and police gear. For about R200 you can buy one of those black-peaked hats with tops as big as dinner plates, worn by anyone with a uniform in Russia. For a few extra roubles they'll throw in all the badges and gold braid.

Mt Mashuk & Around

A **cable car** (R25 one way; 10am-5pm Tues-Sun) whisks you to the top of Mt Mashuk for fresh breezes and a great panorama – weather permitting. You'll get the best views of Elbrus from here very early in the morning. It's a 35-minute, fairly easy climb but keep a watch for stray dogs.

Just above Krasnoarmeyskaya ulitsa is a little domed pavilion, the **Aeolian Harp**, long a favourite lookout point. It was built in 1831 to replace a real harp plucked by a weather vane. From here you can walk down via **Lermontov's Grotto**, a small cave visited by Lermontov, to the **Academic Gallery** (pr Kirova; open 7am-10am, 11am-3pm & 4pm-6pm daily), formerly the Elizabeth Gallery, built in 1851 by an English architect, Upton, to house one of Pyatigorsk's best known springs – 'No 16'. It was here that Lermontov's antihero, Pechorin, first set eyes on Princess Mary. The small art gallery in the pavilion – closed at the time of research – has a butterfly exhibition. Krasnoarmeyskaya

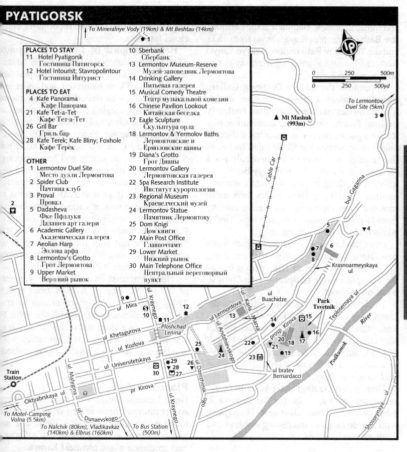

PYATIGORSK

To Mineralnye Vody (19km) & Mt Beshtau (14km)

PLACES TO STAY
11 Hotel Pyatigorsk
    Гостиница Пятигорск
12 Hotel Intourist; Stavropolintour
    Гостиница Интурист

PLACES TO EAT
4   Kafe Panorama
    Кафе Панорама
21 Kafe Tet-a-Tet
    Кафе Тет-а-Тет
26 Gril Bar
    Гриль бар
28 Kafe Terek; Kafe Bliny; Foxhole
    Кафе Терек

OTHER
1   Lermontov Duel Site
    Место дуэли Лермонтова
2   Spider Club
    Паутина клуб
3   Proval
    Провал
5   Dadasheva
    Фке Ффдцукц
    Дадашев арт галери
6   Academic Gallery
    Академическая галерея
7   Aeolian Harp
    Эолова арфа
8   Lermontov's Grotto
    Грот Лермонтова
9   Upper Market
    Верхний рынок

10 Sberbank
    Сбербанк
13 Lermontov Museum-Reserve
    Музей-заповедник Лермонтова
14 Drinking Gallery
    Питьевая галерея
15 Musical Comedy Theatre
    Театр музыкальной комедии
16 Chinese Pavilion Lookout
    Китайская беседка
17 Eagle Sculpture
    Скульптура орла
18 Lermontov & Yermolov Baths
    Лермонтовские и
    Ермоловские ванны
19 Diana's Grotto
    Грот Дианы
20 Lermontov Gallery
    Лермонтовская галерея
22 Spa Research Institute
    Институт курортологии
23 Regional Museum
    Краеведческий музей
24 Lermontov Statue
    Памятник Лермонтову
25 Dom Knigi
    Дом книги
27 Main Post Office
    Главпочтамт
29 Lower Market
    Нижний рынок
30 Main Telephone Office
    Центральный переговорный
    пункт

To Lermontov Duel Site (5km)

▲ Mt Mashuk (993m)

Krasnoarmeyskaya ul

Park Tsvetnik

Train Station

To Motel-Camping Volna (5.5km)

To Nalchik (80km), Vladikavkaz (140km) & Elbrus (160km)

To Bus Station (500m)

---

litsa takes you back down into town, past several more springs squirting out of spouts in walls. About a half-hour walk from the Aeolian Harp, past **Dadasheva Art Gallery** (☎ 5 45 80; bulvar Gagarina 2; entry R10; open 9am-9pm daily), is the **Proval**, a cave open to the sky where 19th-century couples would dance on a bridge over the pond of light blue (and smelly) sulphurous water. Downhill, over the other side of the road, is a small bath where you can immerse yourself for free.

A **monument** marks the site of Lermontov's fatal duel, another hour's walk round the road behind Mt Mashuk. Lermontov had been banished twice from St Petersburg to serve in the Caucasus army: first, after blaming the tsarist authorities for the death in a duel of another 'troublesome' writer, Pushkin, and sec-

ond, for himself duelling. In Pyatigorsk, Lermontov was challenged to another duel for jesting about the clothes of one Major Martynov. Lermontov, firing first, aimed into the air but was in return shot through the heart. Many saw his death, like Pushkin's, as orchestrated by the authorities.

You can reach the cable car, the Aeolian Harp and Proval by bus No 1 from the train station via prospekt Kirova and ulitsa Andzhievskogo, or bus No 15 from the Upper Market; for the duel site take bus No 113 from the Upper Market.

Park Tsvetnik

Central Park Tsvetnik boasts the beautiful blue **Lermontov Gallery** (Lermontovskaya Galereya) from 1901, a sort of glass-and-cast-iron

Brighton Pavilion, now a concert hall for plays and music in season. Behind it is the **Lermontov Bath** (Lermontovskaya Vanyi) from 1831 and the **Yermolov Bath** (Ermolovskiye Vanyi) from 1880, now a gynaecology/fertility clinic, and spring No 2.

Opposite is the modern **Drinking Gallery** (Pitevaya galereya; open 7am-6pm daily), where you can take the waters from endlessly gushing faucets (bring your own cup or pay R1 for a plastic one). The water has a flat and yucky taste, somewhat like diluted bad eggs due to sulphur content (it's supposedly good for stomach complaints, probably because it kills off anything in your stomach). Behind, another drinking gallery offers two more samples from the variety of waters coming from 16 different underground springs. You're advised not to drink too much.

From the Lermontov Gallery, a path leads past **Diana's Grotto**, a small artificial cave, up to Goryachaya (Hot) Hill, with a much-photographed **eagle sculpture** and a **Chinese pavilion lookout**.

The **Spa Research Institute** (Institut Kurortologii; pr Kirova 34), which develops mineral water treatments, is in the classical Institut Kurortologii, Pyatigorsk's first building, built in 1780, and once the Restoratsiya, the town's first hotel and the scene of balls described in A Hero of Our Time.

There's also the **Regional Museum** (Kraevedchesky muzey; ul bratev Bernardacci 2; admission R25; open 10am-6pm Thur-Tues), with a wide range of interesting displays and temporary exhibitions.

Lermontov Statue & Museum

Lermontov himself stares towards Elbrus from his pedestal in the Lermontov Garden, near the foot of ulitsa Andzhievskogo. The thatched cottage where he spent his last two months in 1841 is up the hill in the **Lermontov Museum-Reserve** (Domik Lermontova; ul Buachidze; admission R30; open 10am-5pm Wed-Sun), which is an extended family of Lermontov-related buildings and exhibitions in a beautiful garden. The buildings still have some original furniture and copies of Lermontov's poems, sketches and a collection of water colours of local scenes.

Places to Stay

Sanatoria have the nicest rooms, but you'll need to make advance reservations. Contact Nikolai Oleynikov for help (see the Information section earlier) or Stavropolintour at the Hotel Intourist.

Hotel Pyatigorsk (☎ 3 67 03; ul Kraynego 43/1; singles/doubles R115-550/120-800) isn't pretty but it is inexpensive. The cheapest singles have no TV or bathroom, and toilet and shower facilities are shared. Mid-range rooms come with two single beds, TV and phone. A counter in the foyer sells airline tickets.

Motel-Camping Volna (☎ 5 05 38; ul Ogorodnaya 39; singles/doubles R200/280) is 5.5km west of the centre and has camp site cabins for R25 per person, self-contained and due for replacement; there's little space for tents, but there is a bar and café. Signposts to here are hard to spot; it's about 500m south of ulitsa Tolyatti, which branches south off ulitsa Fevralskaya leading west from the train station. The nearest stop for tram No 2 is on ulitsa Tolyatti, then it's a 500m walk; alternatively, a taxi costs R70 from the train station.

Hotel Intourist (☎ 4 90 18, fax 4 90 36; pl Lenina 13; singles/doubles from R900/1100), despite the gloomy cavernous foyer – oh, for an interior designer with the verve to remodel it – is a clean and comfortable three star place. All rooms have balconies with good views – ask for a room looking toward Elbrus.

Places to Eat

Hotel Intourist, besides its loud and expensive **restaurant**, has a decent **wine bar** in the lobby, which oddly closes at 7.30pm. The last two years have seen an explosion of cafés and bars spreading along prospekt Kirova.

Gril Bar (cnr ul Dzerzhinskogo & pr Kirova; dishes around R30; open noon-11pm daily) is downstairs and has good grilled chicken. Before 7pm it's a quiet place to relax, but then on most nights the live music is revved up and the place takes on a different character.

Kafe Terek (Lower Market; dishes R40-80; open 10am-midnight) is one of three cafés in the same building. This top-floor café offers a fast-food menu until 3pm and then à la carte until closing. The middle-floor **Bliny Kafe** (bliny R7-46; open 7am-10pm) specialises in bliny filled with almost anything – red caviar, jam, meat or bananas – take your pick. **Fox hole** (meals R22-50; open 10am-midnight) in the basement, is a dark hideaway, great for intimate conversations. Try the bliny with salmon caviar and scuttle it down with vodka

Kafe Tet-a-tet *(2nd floor, Tsvetnik Exhibition Hall; pr Kirova 23; open 11am-11pm daily)* is the place for people-watching, as well as good coffee and ice cream.

Cafe Panorama *(off ul Teplosernaya; dishes R30-60; open noon-midnight daily)*, in an old railway carriage part of the way up Mt Mashuk, is an Armenian restaurant specialising in shashlyks and kebabs; try its 'Iulya', a ground mutton kebab that melts in the mouth. There's live music every evening. A taxi is the best way to get there (R50), or take tram No 4 and alight adjacent to 31 ulitsa Teplosernaya, then walk half an hour uphill.

Entertainment
The **Musical Comedy Theatre** *(Teatr muzykalnoy komedii; pr Kirova 17; booking office open 10am-6pm)* puts on light opera from June to August. There's often an evening disco in Park Tsvetnik and one end of the Lermontov Gallery is used for plays and concerts.

Getting There & Away
Frequent *elektrichka* connect Pyatigorsk with the other spa towns and Mineralnye Vody. Travel to Zheleznovodsk is best by *marshrutki* as otherwise you have to change trains at Beshtau; regular *marshrutki* leave from the Upper Market. Long-distance trains originating in Kislovodsk pass through Pyatigorsk. The train station has a service centre where you can buy advance tickets for a small premium. A taxi to the Mineralnye Vody airport should cost R260.

KISLOVODSK
КИСЛОВОДСК
☎ 87937 • pop 187,000 • elevation 822m
Kislovodsk (Sour Waters) is hillier, greener, higher and prettier than Pyatigorsk. It's probably the most popular of the resorts. 'Love affairs that begin at the foot of Mashuk reach happy endings here,' Lermontov wrote. Even if you're not staying in Kislovodsk, the beautiful park alone is worth a day trip.

Orientation & Information
The train station and Narzan Gallery (Narzanaya galereya), at the eastern and western ends of ulitsa Karla Marksa respectively, link the centre with Kurortny Park spreading to the south. The bus station is on the Yessentuki road on the northern edge of town.

The **main post, telephone and telegraph office** *(Oktyabrskaya pl; post office 8am-8pm daily, telephone centre 7am-11pm daily)* is at the northern end of traffic-free bulvar Kurortny, running north from the Narzan Gallery.

For Internet access, try **Narzan Network** *(open 8am-8pm daily)* in the post office, at R40 per hour. There's **KMB** *(☎ 97 60 47; bulvar Kurortny 2; open 8am-7pm daily)* for airline ticketing.

The **bank** on bulvar Kurortny across from Narzan Gallery changes money and has an outside ATM that takes Visa. (When we used it, it would only dish out a maximum of R500, presumably because it all came in R10 notes.) **Sberbank** *(ul Kujbisheva 51)* cashes major travellers cheques.

For maps and art albums go to **Bukinist** *(ul Karla Marksa 3)*. Next door is the **Circus ticket office** *(☎ 5 96 58; ul Karla Marksa 1; tickets R60-120)* for performances on Friday, Saturday and Sunday at 3pm.

Major hotels and stands along bulvar Kurortny should be able to arrange inexpensive day excursions (R250) to Dombay and Elbrus.

Narzan Baths & Gallery
The main Narzan Baths *(bulvar Kurortny 4; admission R95; open 9am-1pm daily)* are in a 1903 Indian temple-style building. Bathing in Narzan – which means 'Drink of Brave Warriors' in Turkish – is said to prolong life and ease pain. You can take a 15-minute relaxing dunk in brownish, tea-warm mineral water.

The rich, carbonic Narzan Spring, around which Kislovodsk was founded, bubbles up inside its own glass dome in a graceful, well-preserved gallery *(Kurortny Park; open 7am-9am, 11.30am-2pm & 4pm-6pm daily)* designed by Upton in the 1850s.

Kurortny Park
Fountain-and flower-filled Kurortny Park dates from the early 19th century. During spa season (June to August), it's cluttered with street artists, musicians and holiday-makers toting plastic water bottles to and from the springs. Numerous stalls selling art and craft make this an open-air art gallery; a local speciality is kitsch decorated china. You'll find many cafés and restaurants here, too.

A few minutes ambling among the stalls will bring you to the **Kislovodsk Resort History Exhibition** *(Istoriya Kislovodskogo*

CAUCASUS

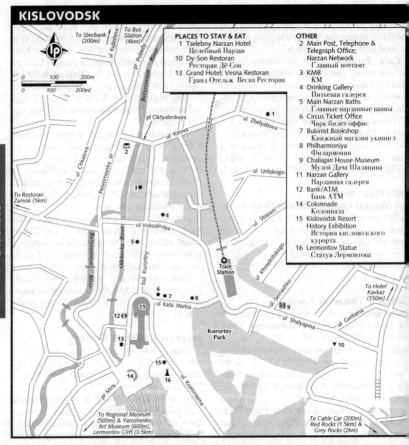

KISLOVODSK

To Sberbank (200m)
To Bus Station (4km)

ul Kulbidova
pr Pobedy

Berzovonaya River

To Restoran Zamok (5km)

ul Chkalova
Pervomaysky pr
pl Oktyabrskaya
ul Kirova

ul Zhelyabova

ul Uritskogo

ul Vokzalnaya

Olkhovka River

Berzovaya River

bul Kurortny

ul Stopani

Train Station

ul Khmelnitskogo

ul Karla Marksa

Kurortny Park

ul Semashko

ul Shalyapina
ul Gertsena

To Hotel Kavkaz (150m)

pr Mira

ul Kominterna

To Regional Museum (500m) & Yaroshenko Art Museum (600m), Lermontov Cliff (3.5km)

To Cable Car (200m), Red Rocks (1.5km) & Grey Rocks (2km)

PLACES TO STAY & EAT
1 Tselebny Narzan Hotel
   Целебный Нарзан
10 Dy-Son Restoran
   Ресторан Дё-Сон
13 Grand Hotel; Vesna Restoran
   Гранд Отель ж Весна Ресторан

OTHER
2 Main Post, Telephone &
   Telegraph Office;
   Narzan Network
   Главный почтамт
3 KMB
   КМ
4 Drinking Gallery
   Питьевая галерея
5 Main Narzan Baths
   Главные нарзанные ванны
6 Circus Ticket Office
   Цирк билет оффис
7 Bukinist Bookshop
   Книжный магазин укинист
8 Philharmoniya
   Филармония
9 Chaliapin House Museum
   Музей Дача Шаляпина
11 Narzan Gallery
   Нарзанная галерея
12 Bank/ATM
   Банк АТМ
14 Colonnade
   Колоннада
15 Kislovodsk Resort
   History Exhibition
   История кисловодского
   курорта
16 Lermontov Statue
   Статуя Лермонтова

kurorta; admission R10; open 10am-6pm Wed-Sun), displaying the history of the resort, mostly in photographs. A little farther on up some steps is a **Lermontov statue**. The fiend behind bars, in the grotto below, is an illustration of Lermontov's famous poem, 'The Demon', while across the way is the **Colonnade**, with a café and benches where older men gather to play chess and backgammon.

A path heads uphill via a rose garden to the **Red Rocks** (Krasnye Kamni), coloured by their iron content. Beyond, 2km from the Narzan Gallery, are the **Grey Rocks** (Serye Kamni) featuring an eagle sculpture and good views. Walking routes of varying lengths are marked around the park.

Just past the Grey Rocks you can wander up to Krasnoe Solnyshko hill, with views of

Elbrus on a good day, or turn right to the **cable car** *(R30 one way; 10am-1pm & 2pm-5pm daily)* that will sweep you over Krasnoe Solnyshko to the top of 1376m-high **Mt Maloe Sedlo** (Little Saddle), with its great panorama of valleys and upland plateaus.

Depending on the weather you can explore the surrounding mountaintop trails by horseback for R50 to R150 (according to the route chosen). If not, it's easy enough to walk 5km southeast along the top to Mt Maly Dzhinal (1484m). Mt Bolshoe Sedlo (1409m) is 1km northeast.

Other Attractions

Prospekts Lenina and Dzerzhinskogo have some grand and curious old houses, many now sanatoria.

The **Regional Museum** *(Kraevedchesky muzey; Krepostnoy pereulok 3; admission R10; open 10am-6pm Tues-Sun)*, in an 1805 fort, has two rooms of photographs and relics of archaeology, history and some pieces on writer and dissident Solzhenitsyn (who was born in Kislovodsk.) To get there, walk about 500m along prospekt Mira, south from the Colonnade, to just before the big church, where you'll see the small fort on the left.

Just past the church is the small **Yaroshenko Art Museum** *(Yaroshenko muzey; ul Yaroshenko 1; admission R30; open 10am-6pm Wed-Mon)*, dedicated to the works of painter Nicolai Yaroshenko who lived in this house surrounded by a pleasant, walled, garden-orchard. Yaroshenko was a portraitist, a painter of genre scenes and a leading proponent of Russian realism in the 1880s and 1890s. A second building houses a collection of works of Yaroshenko's contemporaries who also spent time here.

Other museums include the **Culture Museum of Music & Theatre** *(Muzey muzykalnoy i teatralnoy kultury; admission free; open 9am-1pm Tues, Wed & Fri-Sun)* at the Philharmoniya, a two-room museum mostly containing photographs of artists who have performed at the Philharmoniya. One room, for small concerts, has a white piano once played by Prokofiev and Rachmaninov.

Chaliapin House Museum *(Dom Shalyapina; admission R20; open 10am-6pm Wed-Mon)* is a rickety stained-glass villa near the train station. Chaliapin, the legendary Russian opera singer, lived here in 1917 and the downstairs room is devoted to photographs of him in his various roles. Also of interest are the marvellous plaster ceilings bursting with cherubs and fruit designs, and a lovely glaze-tiled chimney.

The **Lermontov Cliff** (Lermontovskaya Skala), where the climactic duel took place in *A Hero of Our Time*, is about 4km southeast of the town centre in the valley of the Olkhovka River.

Places to Stay

Grand Hotel *(☎ 5 03 42, fax 5 17 83; e grand@narzan.com; bulvar Kurortny 14; singles/doubles including breakfast from R980/1400)* is a most pleasant four-star hotel, recently reopened and the best in Kislovodsk. The rooms are all freshly furnished and the bathrooms have been decked out in some rather expensive-looking tile work.

Tselebny Narzan Hotel *(☎ 6 61 97, fax 5 97 57; e intour@narzan.com; ul Zhelyabova 5; singles/doubles US$60/80)* is a rather pricey reincarnation of a former Intourist hotel with appalling wallpaper in the rooms. Prices include use of the pool and breakfast, although tennis courts are extra. The hotel offers a number of spa-related medical packages. One that caught our eye was for newly-weds: the package, from US$580 per week, entitles the happy couple to romantic dinners, consultations from a gynaecologist/urologist, and an ultrasound screening, in case they start a family.

Hotel Kavkaz *(☎ 97 60 05; pr Dzerzhinskogo 24; singles/doubles from R417/540)* is just acceptable for the price. The attached bathrooms need renovating and there's no restaurant; if you want food, order and have it delivered. Bus No 5 and *marshrutki* Nos 2, 4, 8 and 9 come here from the train station.

There'll be people at the train station with placards offering **rooms and apartments** *(singles/doubles from R250/400)*.

Places to Eat

Restoran Zamok *(☎ 5 98 04; dishes R70-150; open noon-11pm daily)* is on the ground floor of the **Castle of Treachery & Love** (Zamok kovarstva i lyubvi), 7km west of Kislovodsk

---

Love and Treachery, or 'Boy Falls for Wrong Girl'

Local legend tells the story of a girl from a rich family who fell in love with a boy from a poor family. Her father wouldn't let her marry her love as he'd promised her to an old, ugly but rich merchant. She refused the match and ran away with the boy, her family pursuing them to the edge of a cliff just outside Kislovodsk. Faced with a dilemma, the boy suggested jumping off together and ending their lives in love rather than misery. The girl agreed but said she was afraid. Her lover should jump first, she suggested, so he did – and died. Looking down at his splattered body, the girl decided not to join him and ended up marrying the old man.

on Alikonovka River gorge. This modern castle, built to trade on the local legend of treachery and love (see the earlier boxed text), is a favoured place for locals, visitors and wedding parties. The restaurant setting is pseudo-medieval and the dishes Georgian, with an emphasis on seafood; if you've got R550 to spare there's lobster. Taxi is the easiest transport, costing about R70 one way.

Restoran Dy-Son (☎ 6 20 02; ul Shalyapina 22; dishes R60-140; open 11am-11pm daily), if you're tired of shashlyk, is an atmospheric Korean restaurant near Kurortny Park. The house speciality is tempura, a chunk of osetrina (sturgeon) and a slice of tomato in a sleeping-bag of dough (R120). Live music and dancing begins after 7pm.

Vesna Restoran (☎ 6 13 27; bulvar Kurortny; meals R80-250) is the Grand Hotel's restaurant, with first-class food and service. The English menu offered a 'fragrant salting from the chief' for R85, although we didn't investigate further. In the evenings there's live music.

The **Tselebny Narzan Hotel restaurant** (dishes R50-150) has the standard po Kavkazsky, a spicy beef dish, and chicken Kiev. There's a large dance floor to twirl around on and variety shows some evenings.

The **café** on top of Mt Maloe Sedlo does good shashlyk, coffee and biscuits.

Entertainment

The **Philharmoniya** (ul Karla Marksa 1) has concerts, opera, musical and comedy events, while Tselebny Narzan Hotel has a casino. There are a couple of nightclubs/discos in the park.

Getting There & Away

There's a frequent elektrichka service to Pyatigorsk and Mineralnye Vody and daily trains to Moscow (R1550, 27 hours), as well as services to Kiev on odd-numbered dates of the month (30½ hours), St Petersburg four times weekly (R1350, 21 hours) and Minsk, also on odd days (13 hours).

ZHELEZNOVODSK
ЖЕЛЕЗНОВОДСК
☎ 86532 • pop 50,000 • elevation 570m

The smallest spa town, Zheleznovodsk (Iron Waters), lies at the foot of Mt Zheleznaya (852m) on the northern side of Mt Beshtau. It's 6km west of the Mineralnye Vody–

Pyatigorsk road and served by its own branch train line.

It's so local to Pyatigorsk and its attractions not so numerous that it's an ideal day trip, with all the sites of interest able to be visited within a day. Although the town has a train service, the best way from Pyatigorsk is by marshrutki No 113 from the Upper Market (R12, 25 minutes). Get off at the Lenin statue on ulitsa Lenina, where the pleasant park spreads up the mountain towards the natural forest. Zheleznovodsk waters are used for digestive, kidney and metabolic problems, and several springs are in the upper reaches of the park.

Before ascending to the park, have a nose around the red-and-white striped **Ostrovsky Baths** (Ostrovoskie Vanie), dating from 1893. Although they've been closed for a number of years, of particular interest is the Islamic influence in the building's design, featuring arches, a pseudo-minaret and decorative Arabic lettering.

Another beautiful building is the blue-and-white, iron-and-glass **Pushkin Gallery** (Pushkinskaya Gallereya) from 1901, which has been under restoration for several years. Similar to the Lermontov Gallery in Pyatigorsk, it's a prefabricated building made in Warsaw.

Another Islamic-influenced architectural beauty is nearby, the Emir of Bukhara's late-19th-century palace, now the **Sanatory Telmana** (Sanatoriy Telmana).

There are a couple of cafés in the park, including the expensive **Birarov Cafe** with grumpy service.

Of the resort's 54 springs, only four are left, three with the same water. Others have run dry or fallen into disrepair. To see how the place looked in its heyday, visit the **local museum** (Kraevedchesky muzey; admission R5; open 10am-5pm Tues-Sun) across from the Sanatory Telmana. It has a good photograph collection.

From the park, a 3.5km ring road leads round the mountain. There's also a spiral path to the top, a climb of about 1¼ hours.

Central Caucasus
Центральный Кавказ

The spectacular Caucasus mountain range – about 1000km long with peaks of more than

3000m – is a geographical, political and ethnic boundary, its watershed forming the frontier between Russia and Georgia, and Azerbaijan. The two mountain destinations most visited by foreigners are Dombay and Elbrus, accessible from towns in the foothills, such as Pyatigorsk, Kislovodsk and Nalchik. The main road crossing the central Caucasus is the Georgian Military Highway from Vladikavkaz to Tbilisi in Georgia.

The Caucasus is about 25 million years old with over 2000 glaciers, 70% of them on the northern side and some 13km or 14km long. The highest peaks are mostly in the middle third where it's relatively narrow. From west to east they include Dombay-Yolgen, 4046m; Elbrus (Russia), 5642m; Ushba (Georgia), 4700m; Shkhara (Georgia), 5068m; Dykhtau (Russia), 5204m; and Kazbek (Georgia), 5033m. Farther east are Tebulosmta, 4493m, and Bazardyuzyu, 4466m.

The name Caucasus comes from the Greek Kaukasos, and maybe before that from Kazkaz, a Hittite name for people living on the Black Sea.

DOMBAY
ДОМБАЙ
elevation 1600m

Dombay is a small mountain resort in a deep forested valley, surrounded by massive mountains with snowcapped peaks. Three deep valleys watered by glacier-fed torrents – the Alibek from the west, the Amanauz from the south and the Dombay-Yolgen from the east – meet here to flow north, eventually as the Teberda River. The scenery is magnificent and even if you're no hiker or mountaineer, chairlifts will carry you away to wonderful panoramas.

The hiking and climbing from June to August – when the alpine wild flowers are superb – are what attract visitors. Dombay caters for around 2000 people in hotels and camps; during the peak ski season, from late December to April, prices can triple and hotels will be full.

Dombay is at the heart of the **Teberdinsky Nature Reserve** (entry R10), stretching up to 20km either side of a line from Teberda to the crest of the Caucasus main ridge. The reserve has a herd of European bison, reintroduced after being wiped out in the 1920s, plus lynx, bear, deer and unique flora and bird life, including the black griffon.

Guides are genuinely essential on many routes as trails are not marked and permits are needed for being in the vicinity of the border. There are some bureaucratic procedures involved in getting permits. First you must get your visa registered for the Karachay-Cherkess Republic in the main police station in Cherkess. Then, visit the adjacent Border Guard headquarters where you need to obtain permission to be in the border areas. Finally, present your paperwork at the headquarters of the Teberdinsky Nature Reserve (see the Teberda section later), where they will grant you the right to be in their area.

None of this is needed if you go up the Mussa-Achitara ridge for skiing, sightseeing or lower-level trekking. If you are going on an organised trip, all paperwork should be done for you – but check with the organisers.

Information

There's a **money-changing kiosk** at Hotel Gornye Vershiny, but no ATMs or facilities for cashing travellers cheques. Come prepared with enough roubles. There's a **post and telegraph office** in Hotel Dombay.

Kiosks outside some of Dombay's hotels sometimes have district maps, but you are more likely to find maps in Pyatigorsk or Kislovodsk.

For best advice on routes, guides (from R200 to R1200 per day) and equipment rental (around R300 per day), check in at the **rescue post** (spasatelnaya sluzhba; ☎ 5 81 38), which is a three-storey cabin near Hotel Solnechnaya Dolina. You can also spend a night here, in true basic mountaineering style – no bathroom or showers – for R50 to R70.

As most of the walks are a stone's throw from Russia's border with Abkhazia, it's nearly essential to have a guide should you be stopped by Russian border guards. Also, some of the most spectacular sights are tricky to get to, as you need to cross glaciers, torrential rivers and so on. Plus there's a bear population. The hardy, friendly (somewhat English-speaking) guides at the rescue post know the terrain well, but if you stubbornly plan on heading out on your own, at least pop into the post office. Remember, these people are responsible for rescuing you if you get lost.

Mussa-Achitara

On the north side of the Dombay-Yolgen Valley, the 3012m-high Mussa-Achitara (Horse

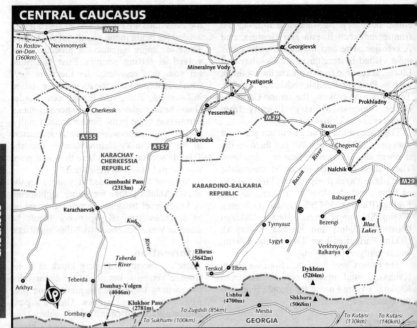

CENTRAL CAUCASUS

Thief) ridge has magnificent views around the Dombay peaks, valleys and glaciers. First, take **chairlift Nos 1 and 2** *(skiers/nonskiers R60/80)*, behind Hotel Krokus, straight up the mountain to the upper cable car station (2260m). Alternatively, take the **cable car** *(skiers/nonskiers R70/80)* from near Hotel Solnechnaya Dolina. Then, **chairlift Nos 3 and 4** *(skiers/nonskiers R60/90)* rise to the ridge where, on a clear day, you can make out Elbrus to the east. Skiers are charged R10 per subsequent chairlift use. The cable car and chairlifts work year-round during daylight hours; the chairlifts are continuous, while the cable car waits for at least 12 passengers.

Walks
Chuchkhur Waterfalls & Ptysh Valley
It's an easy and scenic 6km walk from the start of chairlift No 1 to the two fine waterfalls on the Chuchkhur River. First, follow the vehicle track and then branch across the Russkaya Polyana clearing; it's another two hours and 5km to the first set of waterfalls. Past the waterfalls, a steep path leads towards the Chuchkhur Pass. Twenty minutes downstream from the falls, a path forks south for a steady 2km walk up the Severny (North) Ptysh Valley and another waterfall, this one over 70m high.

Amanauz Valley A marked trail, steep in parts, leads south from the Dombay housing area and goes for about 4km, up through two sets of woods to a waterfall and Chyortova Melnitsa (Devil's Mill) viewpoint.

Alibek Glacier The track behind Hotel Solnechnaya Dolina leads about 6km up the Alibek Valley to a mountaineers' hostel, passing a climbers' cemetery after 2km. From the hostel there's a path up to little Lake Turie near the Alibek Glacier, 9km from Dombay. A strenuous variation is to fork left from the path after the hostel, and head through woods to the dramatic Alibek Falls. If you cross the dodgy bridge at the foot of the falls and then scramble up the left side you can walk on the glacier and up the scree on its right side to Lake Turie.

Other Walks Crystal Pass is a 20km trip and takes around 12 hours, up over the north side of the Alibek Valley, with more great

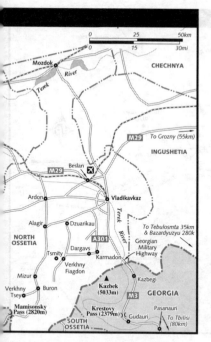

CAUCASUS

views. Treks to the Murudzhinskie and Azgekskie lake groups, in the ranges east and west of the Dombay-Teberda road respectively, involve overnight camping as well as permission from the Teberdinsky Nature Reserve (see the Teberda section later).

Climbs
Peaks that can be tackled from Dombay include Sofrudzhu (3780m), Dombay-Yolgen (4046m), Sulakhat (3409m) and Semyonovbashi (3602m) above the Alibek Valley.

Other Activities
You can swim in the evenings in Hotel Gornye Vershiny's **pool**. Take a **sauna** there or at Hotel Solnechnaya Dolina.

Excellent skiing, similar to the European Alps, is possible from November until late May. There are good, long and steep runs for experienced skiers from the Mussa-Achitara ridge down to 1620m. There is plenty of terrain for ski touring if you have a local guide, but beware of avalanches. Ski equipment and snowboards can be rented at Hotel Dombay, most other hotels and at the rescue post. The going rate is R200 to R350 a day.

Places to Stay & Eat
Just behind the Hotel Solnechnaya Dolina, **Snezhinka** (☎ 5 81 89; 2-room doubles May-Oct/Nov-Apr R1500/US$70, 4-bed units May-Oct/Nov-Apr R1800/US$100) is the nicest of Dombay's hotels. Rooms are doubles only and there is a romantic wood-panelled apartment with open fire for four people (US$100 year-round). This hotel, with the friendliest staff in the village, also has a bar, restaurant, sauna, billiards and, for the tuneful, karaoke sessions.

Hotel Dombay (☎ 5 81 69; doubles per person summer/winter R150/300, meals R50) is a purely functional establishment with clean, standard rooms containing private baths, balconies and great views. Some rooms, with bunk beds and life-expired mattresses, can accommodate five people for the price of a double.

Hotel Gornye Vershiny (Mountain Peaks; ☎/fax 095-255 70 08; doubles per person summer/winter R400/450, plus R100 full board) is less spartan than the Dombay. In summer, the hotel organises free walks and in winter provides skiing and snowboarding instruction from R200.

The picturesque, wooden **Hotel Solnechnaya Dolina** (Sunny Valley; ☎ 5 82 69; per person summer/winter US$15/30, US$5 half-board), a comfortable private hotel, is 100m from the cable car and seems to be a haunt of the local mafiosi. The double rooms are rather cramped, whereas those for four guests have their own sitting area.

Locals will rent their two-room **flats** (per person Jan-Mar R200, whole flat Apr-Dec R500) – just ask around. If you do stay in a flat, you'll need to register at the nearby police station.

During the peak hiking and skiing seasons, there are **cafés** and **stalls** selling shashlyk, sweets and drinks around the village. There are at least 10 cafés at the junction of chair-lifts 3 and 4, and a couple at the top cable car terminus.

Bring some food supplies if you come between peak seasons, otherwise try your luck in the small, overpriced and scantily supplied stores in the residential area.

Entertainment
In winter, the convivial **disco** on the 1st floor of Hotel Gornye Vershiny is the nocturnal hot spot. It also has bowling and billiards.

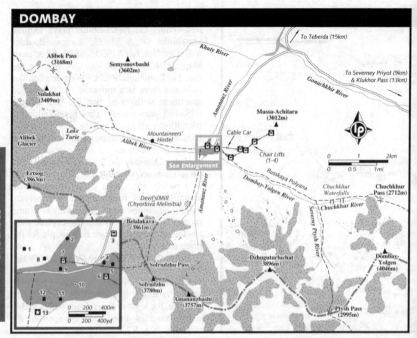

DOMBAY

PLACES TO STAY & EAT	9	Hotel Gornye Vershiny	6	Chairlift #1, Lower Station
1 Hotel Snezhinka		Гостиница Горные		Канатно-кресельная
Гостиница		Вершины		дорога, нижняя станция
Снежинка	12	Flats	7	Cable Car, Lower Station
4 Hotel Krokus		Квартирные дома		Нижняя станция
Гостиница Крокус				канатной дороги
5 Hotel Dombay		OTHER	10	Mineral Water Spring
Гостиница Домбай	2	Rescue Post		Минеральный источник
8 Hotel Solnechnaya		Спасательная	11	Shop
Dolina		станция		Магазин
Гостиница Солнечная	3	Bus Station	13	Police station
Долина		Автобусная остановка		Милицейский участок

Getting There & Away

The only way is by road. Coaches from Pyati-gorsk usually take the 225km, five-hour route through Cherkess and Karachaevsk. A shorter (in distance) route along the A157 road takes you over the 2044m Gumbashi Pass, with gob-smacking views of Elbrus and the whole mountain chain. In early morning light it is an incredible sight, even to those weary of mountain views.

A day trip by tourist coach to Dombay is possible from Pyatigorsk or Kislovodsk, but you won't see much. It's far better to use the tour as a means of transport and come to some arrangement with the driver. Don't forget to have your passport on you, as you'll be crossing borders between republics.

The nearest train station on the main line is Nevinnomyssk, 180km north, with one bus daily between there and Teberda (about five hours). There are no buses between Teberda and Dombay, but it is possible to hitch a ride.

TEBERDA
ТЕВЕРДА

Teberda, 20km north of Dombay, is a provincial city. Although it's not really worth seeing, it is useful as a base for more hiking.

The old Hotel Teberda is a wreck and closed. The new **Hotel Teberda** (☎ 60732-5 18 08; doubles R150-250) is also a wreck, so only stay here if you're desperate.

Better is the **Teberdinsky Nature Reserve headquarters** (☎ 60732-5 12 61), first left after the bridge as you leave Teberda going north, with decent accommodation in pleasant wood-lined rooms that come with a sitting room; the rate is R100 to R150 per person and bathrooms are shared. There is also a **nature museum** (entry R5; open 8.30am-5.30pm daily) at the reserve and a small **zoo** (entry R5; open 8.30am-5.30pm daily).

Walks to the **Dzhamagatskie Narzany mineral springs** – west up the Dzhamagat Valley and around seven hours for the round trip – start here, as do those to the **Mukhinsky Pass** (east). Before setting out, get permission from the Teberdinsky Nature Reserve headquarters for R5. The reserve will also provide guides for groups (five minimum) for R300 a day.

NALCHIK
НАЛЬЧИК
☎ 86622 • pop 300,000 • elevation 550m
Nalchik is the capital of the Kabardino-Balkaria Republic and is in the foothills of the Caucasus; it began life in 1822 as a Russian fort. This is the nearest starting point for a day trip to Mt Elbrus.

Around 60% of the republic's population are Kabardian, while 20% are Balkar, mostly living in the mountains. The Kabardian are the most numerous of the peoples known as Circassian or Adygey. They're famous for horse breeding. In 1557 they united with Russia in the face of a Turkish invasion, the first Caucasus people to do so. Both the Kabardian and the Balkar are Muslim and heavily patriarchal.

Orientation & Information
The main streets are prospekt Lenina, running south from the train station through the town centre, and prospekt Shogentsukova two blocks east.

Phone numbers are being changed from five to six digits – five digits use code 86622, and six digits use 8662. The **main post, telephone and telegraph office** (pr Shogentsukova 5) is near the corner of ulitsa Lermontova. For Internet access, the **Internet Club**

(pr Shogentsukova 25; open 9.30am-8pm daily) charges R30 and has fast connections. The **Grand Caucasus Hotel** (ul Tarchokova 2) will change money, as will **Ecodom** (pr Shogentsukova), a hardware store to the left of the post office.

There's a supermarket just east of the Hotel Rossia on prospekt Lenina, and **Knizhny Magazin Elbrus** (cnr pr Lenina & ul Golovko) has a good stock of maps. **Air Communications Agency** (☎ 42 33 26; ul Lenina 43) deals with all domestic air ticketing, except for Aeroflot. Aeroflot has no office in town, so you will have to go to Vladikavkaz or Pyatigorsk.

Things to See
A large, fine **park** with a permanent fairground stretches over 2km south from the Hotel Nart. From its southern end, a **chairlift** (one way R40; open 11am-7pm Mon, 9am-7pm Tues-Sun) crosses a lake to wooded hills. The interesting **Kabardino-Balkar National Museum** (Natsionalny muzey; ☎ 5 68 80; ul Gorkogo 62; admission R5; open 10am-5.30pm Tues-Sat) has displays on the natural history of the area, as well as mammoth remains, national costumes and artefacts. There's also the **Fine Arts Museum** (pr Lenina 35; admission R5; open 10am-6pm Sat-Thur), with a permanent collection of 18th- to 20th-century works of art.

Chegem Canyon The canyon road turns west at Chegem-2, about 17km north of Nalchik. The spectacular part of the **ushchelie**, or canyon, is about 44km up the valley and just past the 30m **Chegem Waterfall**. The canyon is 250m high but only 20m wide, through which both river and road squeeze; both canyon and waterfall are more spectacular after the snow melts in mid-June.

Around Verkhny Chegem, a farther 20km or so, are several archaeological sites, including **Lygyt village** with stone mausoleums dating back to the 10th and 11th centuries. Within the village is a three-storey defensive tower from the 18th century.

Golubye Ozera The Golubye Ozera (Blue Lakes) are several pretty lakes 39km up the Cherek Valley from Urvan, 13km east of Nalchik. There is no public transport to here and a taxi for the return journey should cost about R600.

Places to Stay & Eat

Grand Caucasus Hotel (☎ 7 72 66, fax 40 00 87; ul Tarchokova 2; singles/doubles including breakfast from R800/1000) is in a wooded suburb west of town and is the poshest hotel in Nalchik. A lushly carpeted grand staircase sweeps you up to the 1st floor and a mixture of rooms. The cheapest rooms are just bedroom and bathroom, while the more expensive ones boast sitting rooms with lounging furniture. The hotel has a restaurant and will change money.

Hotel Nart (☎ 42 10 28; ul Lermontova 2; singles/doubles with shower from R130/220, suites R360) is a medium-sized 1970s tower block near the park, with no-frills rooms. When we visited, all the cheap rooms were occupied by Chechen refugees.

Hotel Rossia (☎ 5 50 46; singles/doubles R210-555/210-648), off the main square, keeps its mangy guard dog locked up in a cupboard in the foyer during the day. Residents fare better. The rooms with shower are adequate, although guests aren't trusted with a water supply at night so it's turned off. At the time of research, there was an evening police raid to check documents, so make sure the hotel has registered your visa. If nothing else this central place has character. There's no restaurant so the best place for breakfast is the nearby **Cafe Darida** (ul Pushkina; breakfast R28; open 8am-late daily), where you can get coffee, eggs, bread and jam.

Choices for dining out are limited but improving. The State Concert Hall **café** (pr Shogentsukova; snacks R60; open 9am-9pm daily) has a good supply of sandwiches, pastries and salads. **Tri Sestri** (Three Sisters; cnr uls Pushkina & Lermontova; dishes R25-60; open 9am-1am daily) is a small, clean café with tables in an open area as well as small private booths. Try its manti, a succulent lamb dish baked inside a dough, and the khichin, a traditional dish of baked dough stuffed with cheese and potato and dressed in butter.

Getting There & Away

There are daily flights to Nalchik from Moscow (US$185, 2½ hours), plus a weekly service to Sochi.

A daily train service to/from Moscow (R1080, 39 hours) runs through Mineralnye Vody and Rostov-on-Don (R500, about 11 hours). Sochi trains travel on even-numbered dates (R500, 15½ hours).

The quickest way to the spa towns or Vladikavkaz is by bus or taxi. There is a daily bus to/from Terskol for Elbrus (R42, 3½ hours), a daily bus to Pyatigorsk (R37 1½ hours) and three to Mineralnye Vody (R50, 2½ hours). There is one daily bus to Vladikavkaz (R51, 2½ hours). A taxi to either Vladikavkaz or Elbrus should cost about R900.

Getting Around

Bus No 17, running between the airport and Dolinsk suburb, stops on prospekt Shogentsukova on the corner of ulitsa Lermontova (close to the centre), near the park chairlift. A taxi ride around town should cost R20 plus R5 per kilometre.

ELBRUS AREA
ПРИЭЛЬБРУСЬЕ

☎ 86639 • elevation (Terskol) 2085m

Elbrus rises on a northern spur of the main Caucasus ridge, at the western end of the Baxan Valley. Tourist facilities littered along the valley floor make it less attractive than Dombay, but the mountains are majestic and there are fine walks, climbs and skiing. The area – known in Russian as Prielbruse – pulls in a more adventurous crowd than Dombay, but day-trippers can use chairlifts or cable cars to reach the slopes of Elbrus, or view its peaks from across the valley. The highest peak on the south side is Ushba at 4700m, with several others exceeding 4000m.

Information

The village of Terskol has several hotels and is at the upper part of the Azau Valley, the head of which has the Azau cable car and the beginning of the Elbrus mountain trail. Peak seasons are December to April and June to August; the former is the busier. Off-season, there may be only one or two hotels open and the chairlifts may not be working. Most foreign tourists come with a tour group. As there are only a few cafés in Terskol everyone, including nonresidents, eats in the hotel cafeterias.

The area by the Azau cable car terminus becomes a market in the snow season with open-air stalls selling the knitting output of the local babushkas: mohair mittens, socks and sweaters. Smoky barbecues turn out enough shashlyks to feed hungry skiers and there are a few ad hoc cafés. Ask around here

ELBRUS AREA

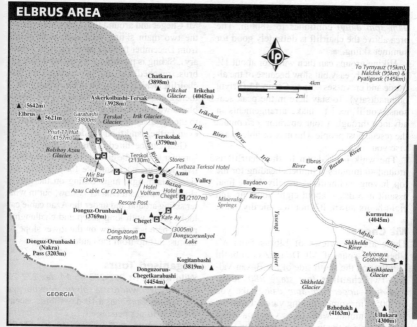

for ski instruction, which can cost about R300 an hour.

Terskol has a **post and telephone office** *(open 9am-4pm Tues-Fri, 9am-3pm Sat)*, although most hotels have international payphones. There are two or three sparsely stocked **general stores** in old train containers, and a fruit and vegetable stall in the courtyard of Turbaza Terskol Hotel. There are no banks but money can be changed at Hotel Cheget.

Guides are advisable and those at the **rescue post** *(☎ 7 14 89; Terskol)* charge US$100 to US$300 (maximum group of five) for trekking and climbing, depending upon what is involved. For a three-day ascent of Mt Elbrus, reckon on US$300 (equipment extra). For base trails, the going rate is about US$25 a day.

Mt Elbrus

Elbrus, a volcanic cone with two peaks – the western at 5642m and the eastern at 5621m – bulges up nearly 1000m above anything else in the vicinity. Elbrus is also Europe's highest mountain, lying on the Caucasus ridge that is the geographical border between Europe and Asia. The upper slopes are said to be coated in ice up to 200m thick; numerous glaciers grind down its flanks and several rivers, including the Kuban, start here. The name 'Elbrus', meaning Two Heads, comes from Persian. In the Balkar language the mountain is called 'Mingi-Tau' (meaning 'thousands' – ie, very big – mountain).

The first unconfirmed climb of Elbrus was in 1829 by a Russian expedition, but it was a lone Circassian hunter named Killar, hired as a guide, who apparently reached the peak on his own. The lower eastern peak was officially climbed on 31 July 1868 and the western peak on 28 July 1874, both by British expeditions. In the 1980s the Soviet regime, showing off for propaganda purposes, had groups of up to 400 climbers reaching the peak at one time. Nowadays, the ascent and descent have been done in many ways: by ski, light aircraft, hang gliding, paragliding, by a motorcycle with skis, and even in a Land Rover.

The **Azau cable car** *(per stage R80; 9am-4.30pm daily)* rises in two stages, from 2350m to the **Mir Bar** at 3500m (open during the main ski season – December to April), from where you can see the twin peaks and the main Caucasus ridge. A **chairlift** *(R80; 9am-3pm daily)* continues to 3800m. The area above the chairlift is definitely good for summer skiing.

Hiking groups can then walk for about 1½ hours – fairly easy but slow because of the altitude and crevasses – up to **Camp 11** (Priyut odinnadtsaty). To stay here in the peak seasons, you'll need to make arrangements in advance through a tour operator, or contact the rescue post people who may be able to advise you.

The walk back down to the chairlift is around 40 minutes. Climbers heading for the top, having acclimatised, usually do the final assault in a day – about eight hours up and eight hours down. It's not, technically, hard.

Mt Cheget
There are fine views of Elbrus from Mt Cheget, a spur of Mt Donguz-Orunbashi (3769m) on the south side of the Baxan Valley. Two **chairlifts** *(per stage R80, lower 9am-4pm, upper 9am-3pm daily)* take you to 3005m for some stunning views. From the top, a 45-minute walk takes you to a small peak. Between the two lifts is **Kafe Ay**, serving drinks, and an easy path of about 7km round the side of Mt Cheget, passing Donguzorunkyol Lake, to Donguzorun Camp North (Severny priyut Donguzorun) at 2500m, south of Mt Donguz-Orunbashi. Mt Donguzorun-Chegetkarabashi (4454m) soars behind the lake. From Camp North it's a steep 3km up to the snow-covered Donguz-Orunbashi, or Nakra Pass on the Georgian border. Check with the rescue post regarding the route and any possible border problems.

Other Walks
An easy, two- to three-hour walk, one way, leads up the Terskol Valley from behind the white obelisk in Terskol village to a dramatic view of Elbrus behind the 'hanging' Terskol Glacier, dripping over a hill's edge.

From the paved road up the Adylsu Valley south of Elbrus village, it's about 1½ hours up a good, gently rising path to the impressive Shkhelda Glacier. **Zelyonaya Gostinitsa** (Green Hotel), a shelter near little Bashkarinskoe Lake at the head of the Adylsu Valley, is a day-walk destination; you'll need a tent. Day-walk valleys with glaciers at the top include the Irikchat, west of Elbrus village, and the Yusengi, south from Baydaevo.

Skiing
Mt Cheget and around the Azau cable car are the two main skiing locations, with skiing from December to May (the best is in February). Skiing is possible year-round on Mt Elbrus, reached via the two cable cars and chairlift (which might be open in summer if there's enough snow). Otherwise, it's possible to walk up a trail alongside the chairlifts to the Garabashi Glacier, the Camp 11 site or even farther, and then ski down.

Gear can be hired at Hotel Cheget but in summer it might be closed. The lifts are primitive, with the accident rate for climbers and skiers alarmingly high. Skiing on the gently sloping Garabashi Glacier is slow, but in winter skiing around and under the Azau cable car looks great, with long, steep and challenging runs. There is a ski tow on the lower slope of Elbrus, just up from the cable car station.

Organised Tours
Wild Russia (☎ 812-273 65 14, fax 279 28 56; ⓦ www.wildrussia.spb.ru; *Mokhovaya 28, St Petersburg*) has a 10-day Elbrus ascent for US$930 per person.

Lenalptours (☎ 812-279 07 16, fax 279 06 51; ⓦ www.russia-climbing.com; *ul Vosstaniya 9-4, St Petersburg*) offers 11-day ascents from US$489/773 per person (for group sizes of 10 to 12 or two to three) from Mineralnye Vody and a 10-day ski tour from US$496/598 for group sizes of 10 to 12 or four to six, from Mineralnye Vody.

Nikolai Oleynikov (see the earlier Pyatigorsk Information section) offers an Elbrus climb for US$300 and a 10-day circumnavigation for US$100 per person.

Stavropolintour (see the Pyatigorsk Information section) also offers a 10-day ascent of Elbrus for US$920/710 per person (groups of two/four).

GoElbrus (☎ 7 13 35, Terskol 5-5; ⓦ www.goelbrus.ru) offers climbing trips, trekking and heliskiing. Although its website is in Russian, it has English-speaking staff.

Places to Stay & Eat
The busy time for Elbrus is winter and the early May holidays when there's still snow around. You might be able to rent a flat for about R100 to R200 per person per day – check at the stores.

Volfram (☎ 7 13 08; Terskol; rooms summer/winter R500/700), the hotel of choice for Western groups and Russian sports teams, is behind the telephone office. The spacious rooms – unheated and without hot water before 9am in the off season – are clean, with views and bathrooms. There are billiards, table tennis and a bar on the 3rd floor. The *stolovaya* (cafeteria) serves hearty meals (R60) to guests and nonguests and is open at 8am for breakfast and 7pm for dinner. The sauna costs an outrageous R600 for two hours.

Turbaza Terskol (*☎ 7 11 40; rooms R640*), the Defence Ministry hotel next to the Volfram, has cosy three-bed rooms in good condition. There's a swimming pool, billiards, a sauna (R400 for 90 minutes), bar and cafeteria. Bathrooms are shared and ski equipment can be hired for R70 to R100 a day. For R150 you can use the minibus shuttle to the Azau chairlift for the length of your stay.

Hotel Cheget (*☎ 7 11 80; singles/doubles per person from R155-400*) has a bar, concert hall, movie theatre and cafeteria. For an extra R144, you get full board (three meals a day). Nonresidents can eat here as well and the rooms are small but satisfactory. Other services include money changing and ski equipment hire. Outside there's a market selling mostly souvenirs and kiosks near the chairlift selling things like shashlyk, *pichin* (a meat-filled flat bread), *shchorpa* (a Balkar soup) and soft drinks.

Getting There & Away

During the peak seasons, there is at least one bus daily to Mineralnye Vody (R65, four hours). Otherwise, you'll have to take the bus to Baxan (R50, 2½ hours) on the Pyatigorsk-Nalchik road, where it is possible to catch a *marshrutki* to many destinations, including Krasnodar, Stavropol and Pyatigorsk.

Getting Around

Many taxis (about R60 from Terskol to the Azau lift) and minivans operate between Cheget and Azau during the peak seasons. During the off season, you'll have to walk or hitch a ride.

VLADIKAVKAZ
ВЛАДИКАВКАЗ

☎ 86722 • pop 330,000 • elevation 740m

The town of Vladikavkaz has a hard, ugly Soviet-era exterior, although the centre is pleasant with many old houses remaining (mostly in a poor state of repair). Vladikavkaz (King of the Caucasus) was called Ordzhonikidze from 1931 to 1944 and from 1954 to 1990, after the Georgian Grigory 'Sergo' Ordzhonikidze, who led the brutal imposition of Bolshevism on the Caucasus region in the 1920s.

Located at the northern end of the Georgian Military Highway, Vladikavkaz is on the mountain-charged Terek River. There have been settlements here intermittently since the 3rd millennium BC. The Russians built a fort in 1784. In WWII, the Germans were stopped just a few kilometres north.

The real attractions of the area are the arcane relics of old Ossetian settlements, out in the valleys to the southwest, and the impressive mountain scenery.

Vladikavkaz is the capital of the republic of North Ossetia. About 700,000 of the republic's population are Ossetians, thought to be descended from Sarmatians, Indo-European people from east Iran who arrived on the steppe in the last centuries BC and were pushed south into the Caucasus by the Huns in the 4th century AD. They assimilated with local tribes to form a people called the Alans, or Alany, whose state lasted from about the 8th to the 13th century, when the Tatars destroyed it. Some escaped deep into the mountains and by the 18th century their descendants – the Ossetians – were mainly found in the valleys west of Vladikavkaz. Ossetia was incorporated into Russia in 1774.

Most Ossetians are now Christian, but maintain some animistic practices such as ram or bull sacrifices during celebrations. Their main traditional festival is Jorguba, lasting for seven days from the second last Sunday of November. More Ossetians are in South Ossetia, across the Caucasus, in Georgia.

The other main people living in eastern North Ossetia were the Ingush. Stalin had most Ingush deported to Siberia in 1944 and incorporated western Ingushetia into North Ossetia. The Ingush were rehabilitated during Khrushchev's rule but returned home to find most of their property occupied by Ossetians.

Under Communist rule both Ossetians and Ingush coexisted peaceably, but this was an illusion. In June 1992 the Russian Duma set up an autonomous Ingushetia, leading to bloody clashes between Ossetians and Ingush on 22 October 1992, with hundreds dying.

CAUCASUS

Russian forces were sent in to try to defuse the conflict and, according to local accounts, sided with the Ossetians, committing atrocities in the process. The combined force of Russians and Ossetians eventually forced the entire Ingush population of over 50,000 into Ingushetia to live in extremely poor conditions. Most of their houses in North Ossetia were destroyed and their property confiscated, but in the last few years the Ingush have been allowed to return.

Orientation & Information

The two main streets, prospekt Mira to the east and prospekt Kosta to the west, strike northeast to southwest flanking each side of the Terek River. The town centre is low-rise, with a number of oldish buildings on ulitsa Gorkogo, ulitsa Butyrina and prospekt Mira, a 1.25km tree-lined boulevard given over to pedestrians and trams. Fortunately the older buildings have escaped replacement by Soviet cement blocks. Most of the locations in this section are around prospekt Mira.

Apart from changing money on the street, (corner of ulitsas Kuvisheva and Druzba, but take care), the only place to do this is the **Moscow Bank** (pr Mira 46; open 9am-1pm & 2pm-4pm daily). There's nowhere to cash travellers cheques and getting an advance against your credit card takes several days. So bring roubles.

Global Alania (ul Lenina 2; open 10am-8pm daily) charges R30 an hour for fast Internet connections.

The two branches of the **post, telephone and telegraph office** (pr Kosta 100; open 9am-5pm Mon-Sat • ul Gorkogo 12; open 8am-9pm daily) are the most central places for post and telephone.

The best shop for maps of Vladikavkaz and North Ossetia is the old-world **Ironchinning** (pr Mira 28; open 9am-6pm daily). There's a **supermarket** on the corner of ulitsas Mira and Gorkogo. Air tickets can be organised at the **ticketing office** (☎ 54 24 97; ul Millera 25).

Things to See

Most postcards of Vladikavkaz show the Sunni **mechet** (mosque), 100m from Hotel Vladikavkaz beside the Terek. It's the most eye-catching building in town with its blue dome, twin towers and 300 Koranic inscriptions on the inner walls depicted in gold, red,

grey, blue and silver. It was built from 1906 to 1908 by a Baku oil magnate with an Ossetian wife. Rules posted by the door require you to enter with your right foot and exit with your left.

The **North Ossetian History, Architecture & Literature Museum** (Severo Osetinski Muzey Architecturi, Istorii i Literaturi; ul Gorkogo; admission R10; open 10am-6pm Tues-Sun) has some amazingly deformed old Alany skulls.

The **North Ossetian Art Museum** (Severo Osetinski Muzey Iskusstti; admission R10; pr Mira 12; open 10am-5pm daily) has a fairly large collection of works by local painters Khetagurov and Tuganov. Especially interesting are the paintings of Ossetian epics and myths. Upstairs is a former merchant's house, a delight with a ceiling painting of bubbly angels and cherubs reminding one of the Sistine Chapel. The walls in a second room are painted in Art Nouveau style.

The **Khetagurov Ossetian Literature Museum** (Muzey Osetinski Literaturi imeni Khetagurova; ul Botoeva 3; admission R10; open 10am-5pm Mon & Wed-Sat) is named after the writer, Kosta Khetagurov (1859–1906). The museum is devoted to Ossetian writings, a culture that once had its own alphabet. There are early Ossetian newspapers and books, as well as information on Pushkin, Lermontov, Tolstoy and Chekhov, all of whom visited Vladikavkaz.

Khetagurov's house is also a **museum** (ul Butyrina 19).

Places to Stay & Eat

The two major hotels, similarly priced, charge a little too much for what's on offer.

Imperial (☎ 76 90 31, fax 75 65 83; pr Mira 19; singles/doubles from US$30/75) is the city's top hotel, with rooms of varying quality dotted around the swanky, rambling old building.

Hotel Vladikavkaz (☎ 75 20 28, fax 53 77 96; ul Kotsoeva 75; singles/doubles US$30/40), overlooking the Terek on one side and the mountains on the other, is tidy and well kept and has rooms with balconies. The hotel **restaurant** (dishes R65-200) has a menu in English and offers a variety of dishes including pasta, expensive fish at R200 and lavash (Ossetian bread).

Bistro (pr Mira 26; meals R35; open 10am-6pm daily) is a breezy café with nautical themes decorating the walls. Apart from drinks and cakes, there's a canteen-style display of hot food, making it easy to point out your selection if your Russian isn't up to scratch.

Cafe 2 by 2 *(ul Butyrina 8; dishes R20-60; open 10am-11pm daily)* is a cosy little café where you have the option of eating in small private cubicles. You should try its *Ossentinsky pirog* (Ossetian pie), a pastry filled with spinach, meat, potato or cheese.

Getting There & Away

Air The airport is at Beslan, 22km north. There are daily flights to/from Moscow (R2600), a Friday flight to St Petersburg (R3050) and a Sochi flight on Monday and Friday (R1200).

Train Vladikavkaz is on a branch railway line, with just one train a day to/from Moscow (R1700, 37 hours) via Rostov-on-Don and Krasnodar (R550, 15 hours).

Road Buses travel every hour to Nalchik (R50, two to 3½ hours) and Pyatigorsk (R85, 3½ to 4½ hours). When the Georgian Military Highway is open, a daily bus travels to Tschinval in South Ossetia (R72, five hours). From there a connecting bus (R40, two hours) goes onto Tbilisi (Georgia).

By car it's an easy 115km from Nalchik. To the south, the spectacular Georgian Military Highway winds over the Caucasus, 70km to Kazbegi and 220km to Tbilisi. Be warned: buses have plunged over the sides and avalanches and falling rocks also make the way hazardous. The road is closed by snow in winter. Foreigners are permitted to travel into Georgia if they have the appropriate visas – that's the theory and we stress the need for current research in Vladikavkaz to find out that day's possibility.

Aside from that, the only worries are highway bandits, border guards and police, all of whom extract tolls at *shlagbaumy* (checkpoints). Travelling by public transportation should give you less problems.

AROUND VLADIKAVKAZ
Dargavs

Significant archaeological sites lie southwest of Vladikavkaz in three valleys striking south into the mountains. You're best hiring a taxi at about R1000 for the day, which should

Mysteries of the Ossetian Pie

The Ossetian pie is an ordinary dish, but one that has a special place in celebrations. No tables are laid without them. The pies come in several guises: *valibach* (cheese), *sacharadzin* (spinach), *kartofchin* (potato) and *fidzin* (meat and onions).

If it's a happy occasion there'll be an odd number of pies per plate and an even number if sad. Three pies represent earth, water and the sun but when a person dies they can't see the sun so there'll be one less pie.

When guests sit down to table, the headman calls for a toast. But before he does, he arranges the pies so God can count the number and gauge the type of celebration. Then a speech is made and a toast of wine or vodka is drunk. The person to the speaker's right, who must be older, then also makes a speech and scuttles a drink. The headman then cuts up the pies, serves them out and the party begins.

★★★★★★★★★★★★★★★★★★★★

give you enough time to visit all the sites. Higher sites may be snowed in before June.

Giseldon Valley

Dargavs, some 40km from Vladikavkaz, has a *mjorti gorodok*, or 'village of the dead'; it's a cemetery of an old Ossetian village with 44 beehive-shaped family tombs scattered up a hillside and dating from the 13th and 14th centuries. Skeletons are visible through holes in the bases of these tombs and several have been buried in boat-shaped coffins.

It's the most spectacular of many similar cemeteries in the district, which are likely to have been established by members of an ancestor cult. The defensive tower and some of the tombs have been restored and the whole site is controlled by the state. To reach Dargavs, turn left at Gizel on the Vladikavkaz–Alagir road, fork left to Karmadon when the valley divides, then cross into the next valley to the west by a dirt road over the top from Karmadon.

Kurtati Valley

You can approach the glacier-watered Kurtati Valley (Kurtatinskoe ushchelie) either from Dzuarikau on the Vladikavkaz–Alagir road, or by a dirt road from near Dargavs in the next valley east. On the slopes west of the small, ugly mining town of Verkhny Fiagdon are the towers and broken buildings of Tsmity, the valley's old settlement. A few people still live here and wandering around the ruins you can appreciate how solidly built walls can withstand centuries of weather and degradation.

More towers and defence works lie around Kharisdzhin, a few kilometres farther up the valley. Down the valley of Verkhny Fiagdon is the small village of Dzvgis, just before the gorge. Look up and you'll see a high stone wall across a cave above the village betraying an old refuge against invaders. Between Verkhny Fiagdon and Dzuarikau the valley narrows to an exciting gorge.

Ardon Valley & Ossetian Military Highway

The Ardon Valley runs south from Alagir, 40km west of Vladikavkaz. About 2km south of the turning, a massive figure on a horse leaps out of the side of a cliff, high above the road – this is St George, patron saint of (male only) travellers. Ossetians come here during the Jorguba festival to pay their respects.

Nuzal, about 30km from Alagir, boasts an old cemetery and towers, plus a tiny frescoed 12th- or 13th- century chapel where David Soslan, husband of Queen Tamara of Georgia, was buried. The chapel is down a lane, just before the village shop on the left-hand side of the road going upvalley. The chapel is usually locked so you'll have to hunt round for someone with a key. On the opposite side of the river, in the middle of the cliff face, is a stone building clinging onto the rock, claimed to be a fortress of Queen Tamara.

The wooden **Rekom Church**, Ossetia's most revered shrine, is a farther 8km up the valley to Buron and about 15km west to Verkhny Tsey in the Tseyadon Valley. Dating from the 15th or 16th century, it's dedicated to St George although it may have originally been a ram-cult shrine. The upper Tseyadon Valley is surrounded by glaciers and the church may be snowed in until late May.

At the top of the Ardon Valley, the road winds over the 2819m Mamisonsky Pass to Kutaisi in Georgia, following the old Ossetian Military Highway (Voenno-Osetinskaya doroga), built to assist Russian control of the region in the 19th century.

Chechnya Чечня

Lonely Planet advises most strongly against travel to Chechnya, due to the civil war and continuing violence.

The Chechens are Sunni Muslims and belong linguistically to the Nakh group. By reputation they are very proud, independently minded and unruly (Chechen means 'unsubjectable' in Turkish). They live by strict codes of honour and revenge, and clan blood feuds are well entrenched in their patriarchal culture.

As a nation they've suffered greatly at the hands of the Russians, who conquered them and other neighbouring nationalities in 1859 after a 30-year war. In 1944, with great loss of life, many Chechens were deported to Siberia for allegedly collaborating with the Germans – this was Stalin's pretext for disposing of potentially troublesome nationalities. The survivors were allowed to return after Khrushchev's amnesty in 1957.

Many Russians regard the Chechens as brutal mafiosi who run a large underworld of organised crime, even though Chechen gangs constitute a very small minority of the population. In fact the majority is still devastated by the war which began when Chechen President, Dzhafar Dudaev, a former Soviet bomber pilot and air-force general, unilaterally declared independence from the Russian Federation in 1991.

Within days of the declaration, which was not recognised internationally, Russian president Boris Yeltsin declared a state of emergency, sending 650 Russian troops to occupy various strategic places. The Russians were soon forced to withdraw not only because the state of emergency was rejected by the Russian parliament, but also because they realised their positions were not defensible against Chechen armed resistance.

On 11 December 1994, in the face of much opposition in Russia and around the world, Russian troops openly invaded Chechnya. They surrounded the capital Grozny and almost bombed it into submission, while Yeltsin tried to negotiate the total surrender of Dudaev's army. The attack on Grozny commenced on 31 December 1994, but the Chechens repulsed it and remained victorious for several days. The demoralised Russian forces suffered heavy losses due to poor planning and ill-equipped, untrained recruits. In 1995, after a new offensive with experienced troops, the Chechen capital fell. The hardy defenders left for the mountains of their homeland, from where they continued to fight.

In June 1995, a group of Chechens bribed their way through Russian checkpoints along the Chechnya border to a hospital in Budyonovsk, more than 100km into southern Russia, where they took about 1000 Russians hostage. Armed confrontations between the Chechens and Russian security forces killed around 120 hostages and 15 Chechens, the Russian forces bungling yet again. The surviving Chechens eventually negotiated their way back home.

Both sides appeared keen on a peace treaty. Talks were supervised by the Organization for Security and Co-operation in Europe and an agreement signed in July 1996. The terms of the agreement were a cease-fire and the release of prisoners and demilitarisation of Chechnya. In parts of the country fighting continued. The major sticking-point – the Chechen demand for total independence, with the Russians only willing to grant autonomy – was barely touched upon in the July agreement.

Many Russians and Chechens viewed the war not as an ethnic conflict but a political one, concerning control over the oil pipelines that pass through Chechnya from Azerbaijan and Kazakhstan to Tuapse and Novorossiysk on Russia's Black Sea coast.

Since 1999, with Dudaev dead and the more flexible and less powerful Aslan Maskhadov as president, Chechen fighters have been trying to form an independent, fundamentalist Islamic state. They are suspected of numerous kidnappings of Russians and foreigners, along with the planting of the bomb which killed some 50 people in a Vladikavkaz marketplace in March 1999, and another in the same city killing seven in April 2002.

In the summer of 1999, after Chechen rebels stirred up fighting in Dagestan and a series of apartment-building bombings in Moscow left many dead and the capital paralysed with fear, Russia again bombed Chechnya. Yeltsin, in his umpteenth cabinet sweep that year, appointed Vladimir Putin, ex-KGB boss, as prime minister and gave him the task of resolving the Chechen crisis once and for all. Putin, having learned from the mistakes of his predecessors in the war of the mid-1990s, took a no-compromise stance, demanding the annihilation of Chechen renegades and complete submission of the republic to Russian control. Unlike the earlier war, with mass protests against the attacks on Chechnya, many Russians, fed up by terrorist acts and other criminal activities attributed to the Chechens, supported this action as the only solution to the Chechen crisis.

Putin's campaign brought him widespread support, helping him to win the presidential election in March 2000, although he's still no nearer to sorting out Chechnya. The Russian army's battle has been at a stalemate, as they are unable to wipe out the rebels whose continuing sporadic attacks kill a high number of troops.

In April 2002, Russia's secret services claimed they had assassinated Chechen warlord Khattab by poisonous letter. Khattab, thought to have been born a Saudi Arabian, had been accused by Russia and America of having links with al-Qaeda, a supposition Putin has been keen to take advantage of. Chechen fighters also fought in Afghanistan alongside their Taliban and al-Qaeda co-believers.

On 10 May 2002, a massive bomb blast in Dagestan killed at least 40 people. It was quickly assumed by Putin that this was the work of Chechen rebels but no responsibility has been claimed. However, on the same day, rebels fired missiles into the VIP stand at a parade in Grozny.

Then in October 2002, 40 Chechen rebels, armed with explosives strapped to their bodies and automatic weapons, entered a Moscow theatre where the musical *Nord-Ost* was in mid-performance. About 800 people inside were taken hostage, with the rebels threatening to blow up the theatre if their demands were not met. These demands included an immediate stop to the war with Russia and the withdrawal of Russian troops from Chechnya within a week.

After three days of negotiations and sporadic violence, Russian commandos fired canisters of sedative gas into the hall, signalling the beginning of a full-blown rescue operation. Around 200 commandos succeeded in recapturing the theatre; 120 hostages and all 40 rebels were killed in the siege.

The Russian authorities have accused Chechen leader Aslan Maskhadov of being involved in the siege, although Maskhadov denies the charges.

CAUCASUS

Dagestan Дагестан

As with Chechnya, Lonely Planet strongly advises against travel in Dagestan. Foreigners especially run a high risk of being held hostage for ransom.

The name Dagestan means 'Mountain Kingdom'. The region stretches deep into the northeast Caucasus from its 400km Caspian coast and is the most complex and traditional part of the Caucasian ethnic jigsaw, with about 30 languages spoken by 81 nationalities, a result of its position on a great migration corridor between the Caspian and the Caucasus. The capital is Makhachkala.

Out of the two million-plus population, over two-thirds live in inland villages. Most Dagestanis are Sunni Muslim. However, in some villages, ultra-orthodox Wahhabis have taken over.

The history of Dagestan reaches back into ancient times. A settlement more than 10,000 years old has been found and Russian biologists and archaeologists assert that Dagestan was one of the first places where cultivation and domestication began, making it a 'cradle of civilisation'.

Dagestan has a bloody history of struggles for independence against Turks and Russians (the latter annexed Dagestan in 1813). But the local tribes did not take to Russian occupation easily. The fight against the Russian Imperial forces during the 19th century was led by Imam Shamil, a Lezgian and local folk hero, from 1845 until his surrender in 1859. Shamil still holds a very romantic, legendary place in the nationalistic hearts of the people. The Russians did not establish full control until 1877 and it is this strong nationalism and independence that caused Stalin to fear them. Along with other Caucasian nationalities, Stalin had the Dagestan people exiled to Siberia at the end of WWII for alleged collaboration with the Germans, a fabricated charge.

The 1994–96 Chechnya war left its mark on Dagestan, with returning Dagestani fighters determined to set up an independent Islamic state. In 1999 they joined with two Chechen warlords, Shamil Basale and Khattab, to achieve that aim.

Violence has continued to be a way of life, both from political and criminal interests. There have been a series of recent bombings – on 10 May 2002, a huge blast at a WWII Victory Day parade in Kaspiysk, Dagestan, killed at least 43 people, including 12 children, and injured more than 150. A Dagestani member of the Wahhabite movement has been accused of leading the attack using a landmine allegedly purchased from Russian soldiers stationed in Dagestan.

Facts about Siberia & the Russian Far East

Gulags, snowbound exile, frozen wastelands – images conjured by the name Siberia and the Russian Far East are somewhat less than welcoming. So it's a great surprise to many Westerners to discover that in summer it can be a blistering 35°C, that there are beachside rave parties in Novosibirsk, great new restaurants in most of the cities, and that icy cold March is actually a fine time to visit as frozen lakes and rivers turn into motorable roads.

Certainly the region has a tragic history. Used by the tsars and then by the Soviet regime to dispose of 'undesirable elements', it took first criminals, then political dissenters, the suspiciously wealthy, the religious, the stubborn citizens of troublesome nationalities and eventually virtually anyone for no reason at all. The writer Maxim Gorky gave voice to the national dread of Siberia when he described the region as 'a land of chains and ice'.

At the same time, though, Russians have also long viewed this vast slab of land as a place of adventure, discovery and immense riches. This was where heroic men such as Yermak, Khabarov and Bering pushed forward the boundaries of the Russian Empire. Of the early exiles, many chose to stay on after their sentences had ended, seduced by the wide open spaces and, strangely enough, the sense of freedom.

Siberia ('Sibir' in Russian, from the Mongolian Altay language, meaning 'Sleeping Land') takes in essentially the entire North Asian continent, east to the Pacific and south to China and Mongolia. This means BIG: 7000km by 3500km, wrapped around a third of the northern hemisphere. Viewed from the air, the flat land goes on and on, punctuated by meandering rivers, slashes of development and long banners of industrial smoke.

The population of this great land is only three times that of metropolitan Moscow, with most of it huddled along the railways in the south. Travellers today still write, not of trips in Siberia, but of odysseys, hypnotised by unending views of taiga (Siberian forest) from the cocoon of a Trans-Siberian Railway carriage.

By magnifying the difficulties for literary effect, such semifactual travelogues have helped to scare tourists into taking the 'rush through' approach. And travel agents are all too happy to oblige by perpetuating the 'tour only' myth. However, it's reasonably straightforward to hop across the region, taking one overnight train at a time, using the railway as a hotel, and spending the long summer days to explore.

There's plenty to discover in this land of mesmerising beauty encompassing the serenity of Lake Baikal, the pristine geometry of the Altay Mountains, the fiery volcanic landscapes of Kamchatka, the sparkling brilliance of the Arctic and the lush semitropical forests of the Pacific coast.

HISTORY
Early History
The first known Siberians were Palaeolithic (early Stone Age) tribes who lived around Lake Baikal and the headwaters of the Ob and Yenisey Rivers. Remains of Neolithic (late Stone Age) settlements have been found all over Siberia. Indeed, many northern tribes were still basically at the Neolithic stage when the Russians arrived. As late as the Iron Age, the steppes and forests from the Ural Mountains to Baikal were populated by tribes of herders whose origins lay in the Caucasus. (Abakan's regional museum contains relics from burial mounds of this period.) Soon afterwards the earliest Mongolians appeared.

By the 3rd century BC, the southern region of what is now Siberia was under the control of the Huns. Descendants of these nomads were later driven west, to the terror of Russia and Europe. In the first few centuries AD, Turkic tribes moved in from Central Asia. Their most prominent descendants were the Khyagas, or 'Yenisey Kyrgyz', whose 6th- to 13th-century empire, which took in much of Central Asia and central Siberia, was the Mongol Tatars' first big conquest. Another Turkic dynasty, the Bohai, dominated the southeast.

The first Russians in Siberia were fur traders from Novgorod, who reached the northern Ob River in the late 11th century.

Mongol Tatars

Jenghis Khan got his start in the early 13th century as a warlord southeast of Lake Baikal. His confederation of armies (called Tatars, after a prominent neighbouring tribe who were among Jenghis' first conquests) pushed the Khyagas into Kyrgyzstan, went on to subdue most of Asia except far northern Siberia and, in the end, crossed Russia into Europe to create history's largest land empire. Of the empire's later fragments, the Golden Horde dominated Russia until the mid-15th century and the Golden Horde's splinters loosely controlled the Volga region and much of Siberia for another century.

The Opening of Siberia

Ivan the Terrible's seizure of the Tatar strongholds of Kazan (in 1552) and Astrakhan (in 1556) put the entire Volga region in Russian hands and swung open the door to Siberia. Seeing the writing on the wall, Yediger, the Khan of the Sibir Tatars, offered Ivan a tribute of sable pelts and became his vassal.

In 1558, the tsar authorised the powerful Stroganov family of merchants to open trading posts east of the Ural Mountains under the protection of Cossack mercenaries. When Yediger's successor, Kuchum, began plundering these settlements, a band of Cossacks and soldiers led by a convict named Yermak Timofeevich set out to teach him a lesson. In 1582, they took the Tatar capital of Kashlyk (present-day Tobolsk).

In recognition of this achievement, Ivan pardoned Yermak for his past crimes and this bandit is now honoured as the 'conqueror of Siberia'. Three years later Yermak plunged into a river to escape a Tatar ambush and was drowned.

Nevertheless, the settlement of Siberia had begun and the next half-century saw one of history's most explosive expansions. Fuelled by a lust for furs, waves of Cossacks, trappers, traders and misfits had reached the Ob River by the 1580s. Until then this had represented the eastern limit of the known world. They had pushed on to the Yenisey by the end of the 16th century, the Lena by the 1620s and, in 1639, they made it to the Pacific coast at Okhotsk.

Behind the pioneers came the tsar's officials and soldiers to exact *yassak* (tributes) in the form of pelts. The export of furs became Russia's biggest moneymaker. Indigenous tribes may have found the newcomers a welcome change from the Tatars but, despite their greater numbers, with only bows and arrows against Russian muskets they had no choice in the matter anyway. Only the Tatars, the Buryats, who lived around Lake Baikal, and the Chukchi in the northeast put up much resistance. Benson Bobrick, in his history of Siberia, *East of the Sun*, likens the scenario to the push across the plains of the American West, with the Cossacks as cowboys, the Buryats etc as Indians and the tsarist army as the cavalry. Instead of a gold rush, Siberia experienced a fur frenzy.

Ostrogs (military stockades) grew into towns: Tyumen in 1586, Tomsk in 1604, Krasnoyarsk in 1627, Yakutsk in 1632, Okhotsk in 1647, Irkutsk in 1651 and Chita in 1655. Settlement was encouraged with promises of easy land and freedom from serfdom. By the late 17th century there were as many settlers, traders, soldiers and missionaries as there were indigenous Siberians. As expeditions began to size up Siberia's huge mineral wealth, Peter the Great also sent engineers and geologists.

Edging into Manchuria

Rumours that the Amur and Ussuri river basins in the east contained desperately scarce arable land were confirmed by an exploratory expedition. In 1650, the tsar commissioned the Cossack trader Yerofey Khabarov (after whom Khabarovsk is named) to open up the region, but his rapacious barbarity was so great that the local tribes appealed to their Manchu overlords for help. Following a Chinese show of might, Khabarov withdrew to a position well north of the Amur.

Like the schoolyard game in which children creep stealthily towards one colleague facing a wall, then freeze when this 'guard' suddenly spins round, the Russians surreptitiously filtered back into Manchu territory. Even allowing for a couple of retreats, the Russians were in occupation of the northern bank of the Amur by 1689. The Manchus, threatened already by the Mongols, could not afford to enter into war on another front, but nor could Russia afford to lose the Chinese market, where most of its furs were sold. The two powers came to terms in the Treaty of Nerchinsk, which sealed a peace that lasted for more than 150 years.

Russians in America

Under the Treaty of Nerchinsk, Russia had to give up all claims to the Amur Valley, and instead the government began to concentrate its efforts on the largely unknown far northeastern territories. In 1648, the Cossack Semyon Dezhnev had been the first to sail round the northeastern corner of Asia, from the Pacific Ocean into the Arctic. However, the glory went to Vitus Bering, a Danish officer in the Russian navy, who discovered the strait (which now bears his name) all over again in 1728. Peter the Great called Bering to head the Great Northern Expedition, which was ostensibly a scientific survey of Kamchatka (claimed for the tsar in 1697 by the explorer Vladimir Atlasov) and the eastern seaboard. In reality the survey's aim was to expand Russia's Pacific sphere of influence as far south as Japan and across to North America.

Bering succeeded in discovering Alaska, landing in 1741. Unfortunately, on the return voyage his ship was wrecked off an island just 250km east of the Kamchatka coast. Bering died on the island, and it, too, now carries his name. (Archaeologists digging on the island in 1991 discovered his grave and the bones were flown to Moscow for scientific examination. They've since been returned to the island and reburied with full naval ceremony.)

Survivors of Bering's crew brought back reports of an abundance of foxes, fur seals and otters inhabiting the islands off the mainland, triggering a fresh wave of fur-inspired expansion. An Irkutsk trader, Grigory Shelekhov, landed on Kodiak Island (in present-day Alaska) in 1784 and, 15 years later, his successor founded Sitka (originally called New Archangel), the capital of Alaska until 1900.

In 1804 the Russians reached Honolulu, and in 1806 Russian ships sailed into San Francisco Bay. Soon afterwards, a fortified outpost was established at what is now called Fort Ross, California, where the imperial flag flew and a marker was buried on which was inscribed 'Land of the Russian Empire'.

Early Exiles

From about 1650, the authorities began dumping criminals in Siberia. In the 1700s, as Siberia's natural wealth became obvious, those dumped there were put to work digging it up. As the demand for labour increased, so did the list of punishable offences: prizefighting, prostitution, vagrancy, even fortunetelling all became grounds for banishment.

The death penalty was abolished and replaced with exile and forced labour, and people were soon being sent to Siberia without trial. POWs, religious dissenters and, more or less, anyone with an irritating opinion was soon joining the criminals on the long trail east. Exile had become big business. The Great Siberian Trakt, or Post Road, along the only route through the Ural Mountains and the taiga beyond, was developed to include a complex system of exile stations and holding prisons. By 1890, some 3400 exiles a week were marched in shackles to Irkutsk, although up to 15% failed to survive the journey.

Once in Siberia, lesser offenders were simply released into villages (exiles were permitted to comprise up to a third of the population of any settlement) though they were forbidden to return west. More serious offenders were set to work in prisons or labour camps, the most notorious of which were the silver mines at Nerchinsk, east of Chita, and the gold mines at Kara, in the Ural Mountains.

Decembrists & Other Political Exiles

The most celebrated exiles were the Dekabristy, or Decembrists, army officers and aristocrats who bungled a revolt against Tsar Nicholas I in December 1825. Five were executed, but 116 were sent to Siberia for terms of hard labour, mostly in rural parts of the Chita region. After serving their sentences, these exiles could move to towns, *personae non gratae* but allowed to carry on as best they could. Their presence had a marked effect on the educational and cultural life in their adopted towns. Pardoned by Tsar Alexander II in 1856,

SIBERIA & THE RUSSIAN FAR EAST

many chose to stay on in Irkutsk and elsewhere.

After Napoleon's defeat in 1812, Russia had taken control of Poland, and in 1863–64 an uprising nearly overthrew the puppet government. Huge numbers of Polish rebels, many well educated, were shipped to Siberia. Other famous exiles over the years included novelist Fyodor Dostoevsky, Leon Trotsky, Josef Stalin and Vladimir Lenin, who spent nearly three years near Abakan.

More Expansion & the Railway

In the mid-1800s, China was racked with civil strife and the Opium Wars, and the Russians, made bold by the concessions Great Britain had wrung from the weakened Manchus, stepped up the pace of expansion in the Russian Far East. In the 1850s, ignoring old treaties, the Governor General of Eastern Siberia, Count Nikolay Muravyov, repossessed and colonised the Amur River Basin (for which the grateful tsar added 'Amursky' to Muravyov's name). Far from precipitating a Sino-Russian war, expansionist Russia also gained the Primorsky region (the dogleg of land between the Ussuri River and the Pacific) as a reward for its help in negotiating the lifting of an Anglo-French siege against Beijing.

Under Muravyov's direction, in 1853 Sakhalin Island had also been added to the Russians' grab bag of territories, though they were forced to share the island with the Japanese, who had already staked a claim to the southern half. In 1875 Japan withdrew its claim in exchange for recognition of its sovereignty over the Kuril Islands. By 1900, the Russians held all of Manchuria and had naval bases at Port Arthur and Dalny (now Lüshen and Dalian).

Siberian development was hamstrung by vast distances and poor communications. It wasn't until 1886, when Tsar Alexander III authorised the building of 7500km of railroad between Chelyabinsk (then Russia's eastern railhead) and Vladivostok, that things shifted up a few gears. Cities grew like mushrooms along the line. In less than 25 years to 1911, the immigrant population leapt above eight million. Most were peasants, who put Siberian agriculture at the head of the class in grain, stock and dairy farming (before the October Revolution, Europeans had Siberian butter on their tables). This growth was to collapse with Stalin's forced collectivisation of agriculture in the 1930s.

The Russo-Japanese War

Feeling threatened by Russian expansion across Manchuria, wary of Slavic ambitions on Korea and keenly aware that the imminent completion of the Trans-Siberian Railway would facilitate rapid troop movement into the Russian Far East, the Japanese launched a sudden naval attack on the Russian fleet at Port Arthur in February 1904. Tsar Nicholas II ordered the Baltic fleet to sail clear around the world to join the battle, where it was immediately annihilated in the Tsushima Straits. In September 1905, a badly beaten Russia signed the Treaty of Portsmouth (New Hampshire), under the terms of which it gave up Port Arthur, Dalny and southern Sakhalin as well as any claims to Korea – but at least retained its pre-eminent position in Manchuria.

Civil War

Soviet rule was proclaimed in Siberia's major towns soon after the October Revolution, but in spite of all those exiled dissidents, this was not fertile ground for the Bolsheviks. Cossacks, merchants and a fairly contented peasantry were uneasy about Lenin's promises. Local heroes tended to be upper-class explorers, scientists or Decembrists.

A general counter-revolution swept across Siberia in May 1918, sparked by a force of 45,000 Czechoslovakian POWs. The Czechoslovaks, who had been fighting alongside the Russians against the Germans, were heading home via Vladivostok when caught out by the revolution and Russia's decision to pull out of WWI. Convinced that the new Soviet government was going to hand them over to the Germans, the fully armed Czechoslovaks seized virtually the entire Trans-Siberian Railway. The regional Bolshevik government in the Russian Far East was thrown into retreat and by mid-September all Siberia was 'White'.

Meanwhile, the tsarist Admiral Alexander Kolchak, stranded in the USA by the revolution, landed at Vladivostok and headed west at the head of a White army. His cause was boosted when the entire area from the Pacific to Lake Baikal was occupied by foreign troops – 72,000 Japanese, 7000 Americans, 6400 British, 4400 Canadians and others – all there, ostensibly, to help the Czechoslovaks.

The Gulag

The exile system was abolished at the turn of the 20th century, but Stalin brought it back with a vengeance, expanding it into a full-blown, homegrown slave trade. It was during his rule that Siberia became synonymous with death. He established a vast bureaucracy of resettlement programmes, labour colonies, concentration camps and special psychiatric hospitals, commonly known as the Gulag (Glavnoe Upravlenie Lagerey, or Main Administration for Camps).

The Gulag's inmates – some of whose only 'offence' was to be Jewish or a modern artist or a high-profile Buryat, or simply to have shaken the hand of such a person – cut trees, dug canals, laid railway tracks and worked in factories in remote areas, especially Siberia and the Russian Far East. A huge slice of the northeast was set aside exclusively for labour camps, and whole cities such as Komsomolsk-on-Amur and Magadan were developed as Gulag centres.

The Gulag population grew from 30,000 in 1928 to eight million in 1938. Prisoners were underfed, mistreated and literally worked to death; the average life expectancy was about two years, and 90% of inmates didn't come out alive. The Gulag continued well after WWII, and Boris Yeltsin announced the release of Russia's 'last 10' political prisoners from a camp near Perm in 1992.

An estimated 20 million people died in the Gulag. Nadezhda Mandelstam, whose husband Osip Mandelstam, a highly regarded poet, was exiled to Siberia in 1934, wrote that a wife considered herself a widow from the moment of her husband's arrest. She was almost right – Osip lasted four years before dying at the Vtoraya Rechka transit camp in Vladivostok.

★★

In November 1918, Kolchak pushed into European Russia. Joining with armies from the Don Basin and northwest Russia, he very nearly overthrew the Bolsheviks before being pushed back to Omsk, where his forces were decisively routed. Kolchak hastily retreated to Irkutsk. There he was captured and shot in 1920, which effectively ended the Civil War – except in the Russian Far East, where it raged on until the Red victory at Volochaevka, west of Khabarovsk, in February 1922.

Soviet Consolidation

At that point almost all the foreign troops withdrew. The Japanese, however, who rather fancied the land they had been occupying from Baikal to the Sea of Japan, stayed put. To keep things cool, the Soviet government made this area into a buffer zone, declaring it the independent Far East Republic, with its capital at Chita. When the Japanese left in 1922, it was promptly absorbed into the USSR. A Canadian expedition that in 1922 had claimed for the British Empire little Wrangel Island (ostrov Vrangelya), north of the Bering Strait, was evicted at gunpoint five years later. No more was said about it.

Siberia was never a battlefield in WWII but in virtually the closing days of the war, with Japan now on its knees, the Soviet Union occupied southern Sakhalin Island and the Kuril Islands. Japan accepted the loss but continues to this day to maintain a claim to the southern islands in the Kuril chain, which at their closest point are approximately 14km from Hokkaido (see Kuril Islands section in the Russian Far East chapter).

From Gulags to Gigantomania

Following Stalin's death in 1953, amnesties freed up to two-thirds of all of Siberia's prisoners. Exile and labour camps remained as corrective tools of the state right up until the dissolution of the USSR, but in a vastly reduced form. 'Gigantomania' would now be the word that replaced 'Gulag' in the Siberian word-association game, as the 1950s saw a proliferation of Olympian schemes that were variously bigger, wider, taller or more powerful than anything that had gone before (and in many cases costlier, less efficient and more environmentally disastrous, too). A series of hydroelectric power plants were constructed along the Angara and Yenisey rivers to supply power for the huge *kombinaty* (plants), such as aluminium smelters and pulp mills, which sprang up in their wake. At one point, Soviet planners even proposed building a barrage of mammoth dams in the upper reaches of rivers flowing to the Arctic, so as to reverse their flow and flood parts of central Siberia. Fortunately, this scheme was abandoned in the mid-1980s following huge pressure from environmentalists.

Shielded from foreign attention, Siberia became a major centre of Cold War activity, with Novaya Zemlya and Kamchatka used for thermonuclear testing, nuclear weapons facilities at Lake Irtysh and Tomsk 7, and a radar station, which in the words of Eduard Shevardnadze was 'the size of the Egyptian pyramids', at Krasnoyarsk. The border with China and the Pacific seaboard bristled with antennae, tank barrels and missiles. So sensitive were these facilities that, in 1983, Russia intercepted and destroyed the off-course Korean Airlines flight 007 just off Sakhalin Island. All 267 on board were killed.

To attract the workforce to Siberia, salaries three times higher than in European Russia were offered, as well as bonus schemes, longer holidays and tax exemptions. But by the end of the 1980s, wages were failing to keep up with inflation, bonuses were cut back and, worst of all, the work was drying up. In 1989, and again in 1991, the miners of Siberia's Kuzbass region went on strike for more money and better conditions. In the history of the Soviet Union they were the first ever to employ such openly defiant tactics. The government was almost brought to its knees.

Contemporary Siberia
In Siberia the dramatic demise of the Soviet Union rekindled the separatist spirit. Siberian Accord, a confederation of regional political actors, was founded in Novosibirsk in 1991. Resentful of Moscow's grabbing hand, they were determined to wrest control of Siberia's natural resources away from central government ministries. President Yeltsin, a former regional governor himself, defused the conflict through negotiated compromises, by which Siberia's regions were granted greater political autonomy and a larger share of the region's wealth. His successor, Vladimir Putin, however, has pursued an incrementally paced policy of recentralisation.

The tawdry privatisation of state property gave rise to a new breed of economic adventurer. Those who have succeeded in gaining control over Siberia's prized natural resources have reaped great fortunes, while the state struggles to provide for the region's pensioners, teachers and academics. Today, oil and mineral towns such as Nizhnevartovsk or Norilsk are booming, while some outlying towns and villages are simply dying. Though sad for residents, these had often been plonked randomly on a map by Gulag planners and simply don't have a chance in the new, unbridled capitalist economy. Meanwhile, in the medium-sized cities, things are generally improving, a middle class has been sneaking into existence and a sudden flurry of new shops, restaurants and cafés has appeared to serve them. Quietly, a European normalcy is threatening to break out.

GEOGRAPHY
Siberia and the Russian Far East, all the land to the east of the Ural Mountains, cover nearly 14 million sq km. The easternmost point, Big Diomede Island (ostrov Ratmanova) in the Bering Strait, is just 45km from the Alaskan mainland.

The dividing line between Siberia and the Russian Far East lies along the borders of the Chita and Amur regions in the south and the Sakha Republic (Yakutia) in the north. The eastern seaboard is 15,500km long, giving Russia more 'Pacific Rim' than any other country.

The region is washed in the north by the Arctic Kara, Laptev and East Siberian Seas, with the Severnaya Zemlya Islands between the first two constituting its northernmost extension. In the south it has land borders with Kazakhstan, Mongolia, China and North Korea.

Rivers & Lakes
Siberia's dominant geographical features are its 53,000 rivers and more than one million lakes. From west to east the major rivers are the Ob, Yenisey and Lena – all of which flow north to the Arctic – and the Amur, which flows east towards the Pacific. These four drain about two-thirds of the entire area of Siberia and the Russian Far East.

The Ob rises in the Altay Republic, flows through Novosibirsk and empties into the Kara Sea via the 960km-long Ob Gulf (Obskaya guba) between the Yamal and Gydansky peninsulas. If the Irtysh, which rises in China and flows through Omsk and Tobolsk, is considered the main stream of the Ob, then the Ob has a length of nearly 6000km to the Kara Sea.

The Yenisey rises in Tuva and flows through Krasnoyarsk to enter the Kara Sea between the Gydansky and Taymyr peninsulas. Its tributary, the Angara, flows out of Lake Baikal and through Irkutsk and Bratsk to join the Yenisey north of Krasnoyarsk.

The 4400km Lena rises in the mountains west of Lake Baikal and flows through Yakutsk to the Laptev Sea. The 4416km Amur forms a long stretch of the Russia-China border before flowing through Khabarovsk and into the Tatar Strait between the mainland and the large island of Sakhalin (which divides the seas of Japan and Okhotsk). The Amur's southern tributary, the Ussuri, which meets it at Khabarovsk, forms another long stretch of the Chinese border.

Siberia's most famous lake is beautiful Lake Baikal, the world's deepest, holding nearly one-fifth of all the world's fresh water.

Mountains & Volcanoes

Another overwhelming impression of Siberia is of its flatness, especially if you travel along the railway that runs near the southern border most of the way. Between the Ural Mountains (which rarely top 1000m and are barely noticeable in their middle reaches west of Yekaterinburg) and the Yenisey River stretches the marshy Western Siberian Plain, all of it below 200m. The Ob River, crossing this plain, falls only 100m in its last 2000km. Between the Yenisey and the Lena is the Central Siberian Plateau, nearly all between 200 and 1000m.

In southern regions, and from Lake Baikal and the Lena eastwards, there's more relief. Southeast of Novosibirsk are the beautiful Altay Mountains, which stretch over into Kazakhstan and Mongolia and peak at 4506m-high Mt Belukha on the Kazakhstan border. A little farther east, the Western and Eastern Sayan ranges, which reach around 3000m, separate the Tuva from the rest of Russia. Mountains surround most of Lake Baikal and continue, occasionally topping 3000m, most of the way to the Sikhote-Alin Range in Ussuriland, east of Khabarovsk.

In the northeast there's a tangle of ranges all the way up to the Chukotka Peninsula facing Alaska, the most dramatic – indeed, probably the most dramatic of all of Russia's mountains – being the 200-odd volcanoes on the 1200km-long Kamchatka Peninsula. Sixty eight of these – including Siberia and the Russian Far East's highest peak, 4750m-high Klyuchevskaya – are active, some highly so. The volcanic chain continues south in the form of the Kuril Islands, strung all the way from Kamchatka to Japan, which contain a further 40 active volcanoes.

CLIMATE

Siberia's climate is sharply continental but not as fearsome as you might imagine. Winter is bitingly cold in Trans-Siberian Railway towns – average January night temperatures are -20° to -25°C, with cold snaps to -35°C – but, from January onwards, is mitigated by low humidity and lots of sun (and a sense that this is, after all, the time to see the 'genuine' Siberia). Siberians claim they feel cold if they go to St Petersburg in winter – where temperatures are a good 10°C higher – because of the humidity there. Spring comes in late April or May, later in the mountains.

July and August can be quite warm months, with temperatures averaging 15° or 20°C and reaching as high as 38°C. There are mosquitoes but, in most areas, not enough to ruin a visit. Of course, if you're hiking or doing anything else at high altitudes in summer, it can still get cold. You can also expect rain (sometimes a lot of it) around Vladivostok. September is the time for mushrooms, wild berries and brilliant foliage; residents claim that this is the most beautiful time of year in the Russian Far East. September and October bring unstable weather. The first frost is usually in October, and most snow falls in November and December.

You'll find it nippier if you stray northwards. In Verkhoyansk, 650km north of Yakutsk, winter temperatures have dropped to -71°C (but summers can be surprisingly warm). And south doesn't necessarily mean warm: the zone of year-round permafrost, a good indicator of nasty cold, reaches right down to east of Lake Baikal.

Ussuriland, southeast of Khabarovsk, has a northern monsoonal climate. This means it has more rain (30% to 40% rainy days from May to September) and slightly milder winters – a balmy -13°C on a typical January day.

For weather forecasts for most Russian cities, see ⓦ http://meteo.infospace.ru.

ECOLOGY & ENVIRONMENT

While it has undoubtedly been a great source of wealth for Russia, the oil and gas industry, through greed, inattention and a failing infrastructure, has been perhaps the country's greatest environmental desecrator. The fragile Arctic tundra has suffered massive degradation from oil spills. In the Western Siberian Plain, environmental loss from oil exploration and production has reached such levels

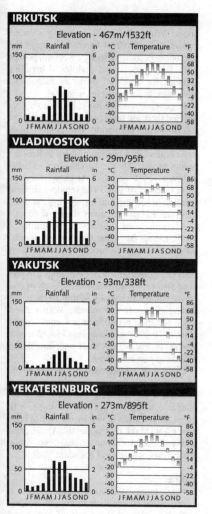

IRKUTSK
Elevation - 467m/1532ft

VLADIVOSTOK
Elevation - 29m/95ft

YAKUTSK
Elevation - 93m/338ft

YEKATERINBURG
Elevation - 273m/895ft

the Nentsy, Khanty, Mansy and Nivkhi, is in danger. The tundra is also suffering the effects of acid rain, most of it the result of metal smelting around Norilsk.

The catalogue of environmental wreckage in Siberia and the Russian Far East is as varied as it is awful. Chukotka in the far northeast is a past nuclear testing site, and the local natives have actually been subjected to as much radiation as they would have if they'd been at Chernobyl in 1986. But in Chukotka there were no warnings and no evacuations. Today, there is close to a 100% incidence of tuberculosis and a child mortality rate of 10%.

Post-glasnost disclosures have revealed that the Russian Navy secretly dumped nuclear waste, including used reactors from submarines, in the Sea of Japan, off Vladivostok, and the Arctic Ocean. Meanwhile, multinational logging concerns from the USA, South Korea and Japan, in partnership with Russia, are queuing up to clear-fell the Siberian forests, which are currently being devoured at an estimated four million hectares a year. And that's not to mention some of the northern hemisphere's worst polluted rivers, swathes of dead taiga, and air around some Siberian industrial towns which is so defiled that there'll never be any need for tinted windscreens.

The most documented instance of environmental degradation has centred on Lake Baikal. When two large pulp and paper plants began using the lake as a dump for waste products, it proved a rallying cause not just for locals but also for concerned parties in all parts of the country. In 1987 Baikal became the focus of the Soviet Union's first and most voluble environmental campaign, and the catalyst for the creation of a Russian green movement. Such was the groundswell of nationwide popular support that the government was forced to act and the offending paper plants were allegedly cleaned up. For an update on the current situation see the boxed text 'Baikal's Environmental Profile' in the Siberia chapter.

The native inhabitants of the Yamal Peninsula, on the Arctic coastline of western Siberia, also managed to halt construction of a railway and gas pipeline that would have interfered with reindeer migration routes.

International agencies are now adding their weight to the Russian environmental cause. For example, Unesco is funding research

that the huge Ob River flowing across it is almost dead.

Less acknowledged, though equally harmful, is the destabilisation of the delicate tundra ecosystem by the construction of buildings, roads and railways and the extraction of underground resources. Parts of the low-lying Yamal Peninsula at the mouth of the Ob, containing some of the world's biggest gas reserves, have been literally melting into the sea as the permafrost melts near gas installations. The traditional hunting and reindeer-herding way of life of Siberian native peoples, such as around Lake Baikal; to find out more contact **Baikal Watch, Earth Island Institute** (w *www.earthisland.org/baikal/*), a Russian-American environmental group active in the protection and preservation of Lake Baikal.

Other international wildlife agencies monitoring and involved in projects in Siberia and the Russian Far East include the **Wild Salmon Centre** (w *www.wildsalmoncenter.org*) – which is endeavouring along with the Moscow State University to save the last wild steelhead salmon in Kamchatka – and the Wisconsin-based **International Crane Foundation** (w *www.savingcranes.com*).

FLORA & FAUNA

Siberia is divided into three distinct, broad east–west bands of vegetation type. In the northernmost extremes, fringed by the Arctic Ocean, is the icy tundra. These bleak, seemingly barren flatlands extend from 60km to 420km south from the coast. They gradually become more amicable to life and build up to taiga, the vast, dense forest that characterises and covers the greater part of Siberia. At its southern fringes, close to the borders with Kazakhstan, Mongolia and, in parts, China, the taiga peters out to become a treeless, gently undulating grassland, or steppe.

Both tundra and taiga extend across to the Pacific coast, but the Russian Far East also has two other unusual vegetative zones. Kamchatka, a peninsula in the far northeast of Russia, is an active volcanic region with, in some places, a moonlike landscape and, elsewhere, weird and wonderful gigantic plant life. Ussuriland, as a result of its lower latitude in the extreme Russian southeast, experiences tropical air and rains. The forests covering this region – and their indigenous animals and vegetation – more closely resemble those of Southeast Asia than anything typically associated with Siberia.

Tundra

Falling almost completely within the Arctic Circle, the tundra is the most inhospitable of Siberian terrain. The ground is permanently frozen (in places recorded to a depth of 1450m) with whole strata of solid ice and just a thin, fragile carpet of vegetation lying on top. The few trees and bushes that manage to cling tenaciously to existence are stunted dwarfs, the permafrost refusing to yield to their roots. For nine months of the year the beleaguered

greenery is also buried beneath a mattress of snow. When the brief, warming summer comes, the permafrost prevents drainage and the tundra becomes a spongy wetland, pocked with lakes, pools and puddles – breeding grounds for clouds of predatory mosquitoes and gnats, and a haven for wildfowl.

In general, wildlife has it hard on the tundra and there are few species that can survive its climate and desolation. The reindeer, however, has few problems and there are thought to be around four million of them in Russia's tundra regions. They can endure temperatures as low as -50°C and, like the camel, they can store reserves of food. The reindeer sustains itself on lichen and grasses, in winter sniffing them out and pawing away the snow cover.

A similar diet sustains the lemming, a small, round, fat rodent fixed in the popular consciousness for its proclivity for launching itself en masse from clifftops. More amazing is its rate of reproduction. Lemmings can produce five or six litters annually, each of five or six young. The young in turn begin reproducing after only two months. With a three-week gestation period, one pair could spawn close to 10,000 more lemmings in a 12-month period. In reality, predators and insufficient food keep numbers down.

Other tundra mammals include the Arctic fox, a smaller, furrier cousin of the European fox and a big lemming fan, and the wolf, which, although it prefers the taiga, will range far and wide drawn by the lure of reindeer meat. Make it as far as the Arctic coast and you could encounter seals, walruses, polar bears, whales and abundant birdlife.

Taiga

Siberia's taiga is the world's largest forest. It covers about five million sq km (an area big enough to blanket the whole of India) and accounts for about 25% of the world's wood reserves. Travelling on the Baikal–Amur Mainline (BAM) through the depths of Siberia, two or three days can go by with nothing but the impenetrable and foreboding dark wall of the forest visible outside the train: 'Where it ends,' wrote Chekhov, 'only the migrating birds know.' Few people choose to live in the gloomy depths of the forest, and the towns and villages cling tightly to the railways and large rivers.

Though the conditions are less severe than in the Arctic region, it's still harsh and bitterly cold in winter. The trees best suited for survival, and the main components of the taiga, are the pine, larch, spruce and firs. In the coldest (eastern) regions the deciduous larch predominates; by shedding its leaves it cuts down on water loss, and its shallow roots give it the best chance of survival in permafrost conditions. Due to the permanent shade, the forest-floor vegetation isn't particularly dense (though it is wiry and spring-loaded, making it difficult for humans to move through), but there is a great variety of grasses, moss, lichens, berries and mushrooms. These provide ample nourishment for the animals at the lower end of the food chain which, in turn, become food for others. Wildlife flourishes. The indigenous cast includes squirrels and chipmunks (which dine well on pine cone seeds), voles and lemmings, as well as small carnivores such as polecats, foxes, wolverines and, less commonly, the sable, a weasel-like creature whose luxuriant pelt played such a great role in the early exploration of Siberia.

The most common species of large mammal in the taiga is the elk, a large deer that can measure over 2m at the shoulder and weighs almost as much as a bear. The brown bear itself is also a Siberian inhabitant that you might come across, despite the Russian penchant for hunting it.

Kamchatka

The fantastic array of vegetation and wildlife on Kamchatka is a result of the geothermal bubbling, brewing and rumbling that goes on below the peninsula's surface and manifests itself periodically in the eruption of one of around 30 active volcanoes. The minerals deposited by these eruptions have produced some incredibly fertile earth, which is capable of nurturing giant plants with accelerated growth rates. John Massey Stewart, in his book *The Nature of Russia*, gives the example of the dropwort, normally a small, unremarkable plant, which in Kamchatka can grow as much as 10cm in 24 hours and reaches a height of up to 4m. This effect is at its most fantastic in the calderas (craters) of collapsed volcanoes. Here, hot springs and thermal vents maintain a high temperature year-round, creating almost greenhouse-like conditions for plants. Waterfowl and all manner of animals make their way here to shelter from the worst of winter, and Massey Stewart likens it to a 'Russian Garden of Eden'.

The volcanic ash also enriches the peninsula's rivers, leading to far greater spawnings of salmon than experienced anywhere else. And in thermally warmed pools the salmon also gain weight at a much increased rate. All of which is good news for the region's predatory mammals and large sea birds (and for local fishermen). The bears, in particular, benefit and the numerous Kamchatkan brown bears are the biggest of their species in Russia: a fully grown male stands at over 3m and weighs close to a tonne. Other well-fed fish eaters are the peninsula's sea otters (a protected species), seals and the great sea eagle, one of the world's largest birds of prey, with a 2.5m wingspan. The coastline is particularly favoured by birds, with over 200 recognised species including auks, tufted puffins and swans.

Ussuriland

Completely different to the taiga, tundra or steppe, Ussuriland is largely covered by a monsoon forest filled with an exotic array of plant life and animals – from tree frogs to tigers – found nowhere else in Russia. The mix of plants and wildlife draws from the taiga to the north, and also from neighbouring China, Korea and the Himalaya. The topography is dominated by the Sikhote-Alin Range, which runs for more than 1000km in a spine parallel to the coast. Unlike the sparsely vegetated woodland floor of the taiga, the forests of Ussuriland have a lush undergrowth, with lianas and vines twined around trunks and draped from branches. However, it's the animal life that arouses the most interest – not so much the wolves, sables or Asian black bears, tree-climbing, herbivorous cousins to the more common brown bears (also found here), as Russia's own tiger, the Siberian or Amur tiger.

The Siberian tiger is the largest subspecies of tiger and the largest member of the cat family. These animals have been measured at up to 3.5m in length. Little wonder that the native Nanai (Nanaytsy in Russian) used to worship this incredible beast. There are estimated to be around 300 of the tigers in Ussuriland (out of a total world population of 350 to 450), which is something of a success considering that they had been hunted down to between 20 and 30 by the 1940s. The tiger was designated a protected species in 1948, and since then six reserves have been set up

SIBERIA & THE RUSSIAN FAR EAST

in the region, partly to help monitor and safeguard the cats. The tigers' favoured prey is boar, though they've been observed to hunt and kill bears, livestock and even humans.

Ussuriland is also home to the Amur leopard, a big cat significantly rarer than the tiger, though less impressive and consequently less often mentioned. Around 30 of these leopards roam the lands bordering China and North Korea.

GOVERNMENT & POLITICS

As with European Russia, Siberia and the Russian Far East is split into *oblasti* (regions), *kray* (territories) and *respubliki* (republics), each with its own local government and administration. Moscow keeps an overview of the whole region through its envoys to the two super regions, Siberia and the Russian Far East. The republics – Altay, Khakassia, Tuva, Buryatia and Sakha (formerly Yakutia) – have significant non-Russian populations and greater powers of self-determination.

Central government is responsible for defence, long-distance communications and the like, while regions are responsible for local services and privatisation. Both, in theory, are jointly responsible for foreign investment and the development of natural resources, the biggest sticking point. Products from Siberia and the Russian Far East – especially timber, minerals, petroleum, gold, diamonds and furs – still generate more than half of Russia's total hard-currency income, but the regions from which this wealth emanates are just starting to see a few of the benefits. Siberians are still worse fed, have a lower life expectancy and produce fewer and less healthy children than their counterparts in western Russia.

ECONOMY

It may well be that in terms of raw materials, Russia is the richest country on earth, and much of this natural wealth lies in Siberia and the Far Eastern territories. The gold and diamond seams there exceed those in South Africa, the oil and gas fields are as bountiful as those in the Arabian Gulf and there is more timber than in all Brazil. The region also holds a third of the world's proven coal reserves.

Traditionally, Siberian society was agrarian, although as early as 1740 its precious-metal mines were making a significant contribution to the wealth of the Russian Empire. Large-scale industrialisation began under the socialist government, facilitated by the development of the Kuzbass-Kuznetsk coal basin, which fuelled growth along the route of the Trans-Siberian Railway. Iron foundries were established at Magnitogorsk in the Urals, an enormous tractor factory at Chelyabinsk. The closed city of Norilsk, now the largest anywhere within the Arctic Circle, was founded in 1922 to exploit the copper, nickel and other deposits of the far northern Taymyr Peninsula. WWII hastened the industrial evolution when many of European Russia's large manufacturing plants were dismantled and moved east of the Urals, well out of reach of the advancing Germans.

Oil was first discovered in Siberia in 1965. Leonid Brezhnev poured billions of roubles into extensive oilfields, principally located north of Tyumen and Omsk. In the 1990s the oil and gas fields of Sakhalin Island began to be developed by international consortiums. The world's largest gas deposits lie even farther north, around Urengoy and Yamburg east of the Ob Gulf and on the Yamal Peninsula to its west. Today, billions of barrels of crude are pumped each year from the region.

The Russian Far East accounts for only 5% of Russia's industrial output but the region contributes in other significant ways. It has a near monopoly on diamonds and gold, as well as antimony and tungsten, and the Pacific seaboard accounts for 60% of Russia's annual fish haul. The government is tight-lipped about the quantity of precious substances the mines of Sakha might yield, but in recent years billions of dollars worth of precious stones originating in Russia have appeared on the international market, seriously challenging South Africa's long-standing primacy.

A combination of counterproductive Soviet-era central planning, daunting physical conditions and inappropriate technology has meant that some of Siberia's resources are only beginning to be tapped – most recently with the help of foreign investors who have faced tremendous bureaucratic hurdles while working in some of Russia's most sensitive niches.

POPULATION & PEOPLE

About 30 million people live in Siberia and the Russian Far East – just 22% of Russia's population in 75% of its territory. The biggest settlements (Novosibirsk and Omsk have populations over a million) are strung along or near the Trans-Siberian Railway. Siberians are ostly ethnic Russians but there are also Ukrainians, Tatars, Germans and most other nationalities of the ex-Soviet Union, who came as pioneers, settlers, exiles or prisoners.

Over 30 original indigenous Siberian peoples now make up only 4% of the total, most numerous being the ethnic Mongol Buryats (480,000), Yakuts of Sakha (380,000), Tuvans (210,000), Khakass (80,000) and Altay (71,000). Each of these has a distinct Turkic-rooted language and their 'own' republic within the Russian Federation, but only Tuvans form a local majority. All were originally shamanist-animists although since the early 19th century many Tuvans and eastern Buryats have overlayed a veneer of Tibetan-style Buddhism. Unless you venture into rural areas, you're unlikely to see (or, at any rate, recognise) any but the more numerous Buryats, Tuvans and Yakuts. Most native peoples have adopted Russian dress.

More on many of the Siberian peoples can be found in the relevant regional chapters, where they are referred to in the Russian plural, Yakuty (Yakuts), Nivkhi (Nivkh), Nanaytsy (Nanai) etc. The **National Museum of Natural History** (W www.mnh.si edu/arctic/features/croads), based in Washington, DC, has an Internet site that provides a virtual exhibition of the peoples of Siberia and Alaska.

Smaller Indigenous Groups

There are eight *okrugi* (districts) named after their native inhabitants, even though most form only a tiny minority of the population. Spread widely but very thinly throughout Siberia the Evenki/Tungusi (30,000) form just 14% of the population of the huge Evenk Autonomous District (Okrug), north of Krasnoyarsk. Related tribes include the Evens (17,000), scattered around the northeast, and the Nanai (12,000) in the lower Amur River basin. The Arctic hunter-herder Nentsy (35,000) are the biggest of the 25 Peoples of the North'. Together with three smaller groups they are called the Samoyed, though the name's not too popular as in Russian it sounds like 'cannibal'. All these tribes face increasing destruction of their reindeer herds' habitat by the oil and gas industries.

Khanty/Ostyak (22,000) are a Finno-Ugric people, the first indigenous people seen by 11th-century Novgorodian explorers. Along with the related Mansi/Voguls (8000) they have a swampy joint Khanty-Mansisk autonomous district on the middle Ob River, where their share in the population has declined to just over 1% and their way of life has been shattered by the massive exploitation of the Samotlor oilfield, discovered in the 1960s.

The Chukchi (15,000) and Koryaks (9000) are the most numerous of six Palaeoasiatic/Palaeosiberian peoples of the far northeast who total some 34,000, with languages that don't belong in any other category. Their Stone Age forebears, who crossed the Bering Strait ice to America and Greenland, may also be remote ancestors of the American Indians. Also in the far northeast are 1700 Eskimos, 700 Aleuts and the Oroks of Sakhalin Island, who counted at just 190 in the 1989 census.

ARTS
Literature

Siberia is associated more with the deaths of writers than with their genesis. In 1938 the poet Osip Mandelstam, exiled for criticism of Stalin, died in a transit camp on the outskirts of Vladivostok. The same year, Ukrainian poet Mikhaylo Dray-Kharma succumbed to the harsh camp conditions at Kolyma. Dostoevsky was among the writers who did survive Siberia, and his four years of hard labour in a camp near Omsk are recounted in *The House of the Dead* (1862).

The novel that etched the Siberian landscape into the hearts and minds of Westerners is *Dr Zhivago*, smuggled into Britain by its author, Boris Pasternak in 1958. In later times, Anatoly Rybakov, author of *Children of the Arbat*, was sentenced to hard labour in Siberia, an experience that, no doubt, provided much source material for his Gulag novel *Fear*, published in 1993.

One writer whose origins are in Siberia is Krasnoyarsk, born Yuz Aleshkovsky, though that still didn't save him from being sent farther east for a period in the camps. A US resident since 1978, Aleshkovsky has published *Kangaroo* (1978) and *The Hand* (1980), both in English.

The most famed native Siberian writer is Valentin Rasputin, known for his stories decrying the destruction of the land and spirit and traditions of the Russian people. His best-known work is *Farewell to Matyora* (1979), about a Siberian village flooded when a hydroelectric dam is built.

SIBERIA & THE RUSSIAN FAR EAST

Architecture

Native Siberian dwellings fall into three main types: tepee-style cones of poles covered with skins or strips of bark (the Evenki *chum*); hexagonal or cylindrical frameworks of poles covered with brush and earth (the Altay *ail* or similar western Buryatian equivalents); and round felt covered tent-houses (the yurts of nomadic Tuvan and Kazakh herders). Yurts and *aily* are still used in rural Tuva and Altay, and examples of all these dwellings can be found in open-air museums including those near Bratsk, Listvyanka and Ulan Ude.

The buildings of the Russian settlers are, not surprisingly, similar to those west of the Ural Mountains but fewer and more functional. Siberian variations on the traditional Russian *izba* (log house), with 'wooden-lace' window frames and eaves can still be seen. Some of the finest examples can be seen in Tomsk, Irkutsk and the villages around Lake Baikal. Both Khabarovsk and Vladivostok retain vestiges of the grand stone-and-brick architecture of the late 19th and early 20th century, while Tobolsk still has a fine kremlin.

Being wooden, very few of Siberia's early churches have survived (there's a rare example near Novosibirsk's Akademgorodok). Soviet-era destruction of the finest cathedrals and Buddhist temples was fairly thorough, but some did survive and are now being painstakingly restored.

Native Culture

Native art was long relegated to dry museum exhibitions, squeezed between the stuffed seals and the railway builders' theodolites. However, there is a minor resurgence of wood and bone carving. A well-established craft is the forming and intricately patterning of birch bark to make containers and decorative objects, colours varying according to the age and season of peeling. These *beresta* items can now be found as souvenirs in most major Siberian cities. In Tuva, soapstone carving and traditional leather forming is being rediscovered.

In Buryatia and Tuva people share a passion for sumo-like Mongolian wrestling. Each group has its own musical styles and instruments, Altay minstrels sing gargled epic ballads and various styles of Tuvan Khöömei throat singing range from the ultra-deep troll-warbling of *kagara* to the superhuman self harmonising of *syrgyt*.

In dance, Buryat peoples retain their unique steps and patterns, which they put on show every summer at the Buryatia festival in Ulan Ude. In northern Kamchatka, the Koryaks and Even use dance to tell stories, not just traditional myths and legends but also contemporary tales and anecdotes – 'the day I got my fingers trapped in the snowmobile tracks', that sort of thing – done as a fluid, ensemble mime. For more details, see the boxed text 'The Dancers of Esso' in the Russian Far East chapter.

RELIGION
Shamanism

Since long before the coming of Christianity the common religion of the indigenous peoples of Siberia has been shamanism, a form of pagan earth-reverence that dates back to the Stone Age. Philosophically the core belief is a need for ecological balance. Every natural object, particularly mountains and springs, are believed to have a spirit which should be consciously thanked with small offerings. This practice remains most visibly apparent in Tuva, Khakassia and Altay with prayer ribbons tied to holy trees and stone cairns beside mountain passes.

Spiritual guidance was traditionally offered by a shaman: a high priest, prophet and doctor rolled into one. Spectacular old shamans' outfits can be seen in several Siberian museums, notably Krasnoyarsk's regional museum, which has examples from many different tribal groups. However, there are still many practising shamans. While they don't advertise, the easiest place to get a consultation is at one of the shamanic schools in Kyzyl (Tuva). Buryat shaman Sarangerel's book *Riding Windhorses* is a great general introduction to the subject.

Christianity

The church made its first appearance in the 1570s in the form of a collapsible tent carried over the Ural Mountains by a mercantile-sponsored band of marauding explorers. The first permanent church structure in Siberia was built in Tyumen in 1586. Soon afterwards, as part of their methods of subjugation, the Russians began forcibly baptising the natives – in some cases, tying a couple to poles and ducking them into water through a hole cut in the ice. Unsurprisingly, Christianity was never a big hit.

The Messiah of Siberia

He was born in Krasnodar, near Russia's Black Sea coast. A former factory worker and traffic cop, he now lives with his five apostles on a roadless mountaintop above Lake Tiberkul (some 200km east of Abakan) where he plans a 'City of the Sun'. To his euphoric followers he is the 'teacher', a second Jesus. Meet Vissarion, formerly Sergei Torop, leader of the 30,000-strong Church of the Last Testament.

Torop realised his divinity in 1991. Perceiving modern society to be on a destructive collision course with nature, he formulated an ecologically based philosophy for a clean-living way of life. Then he moved his nascent community of followers into the remote, beautiful but harsh Siberian countryside to aid their spirituality. Vissarionites are mostly vegan vegetarians. Tobacco and alcohol are considered unacceptable vices, and a woman's place is considered very traditionally as homemaker and loyal supporter for her husband. Horse carts are preferred over polluting tractors, and low technology agriculture is encouraged both as meditation and for its ecological sustainability. Despite an eventual goal of independence from the global energy-financial system, the community has its own computers, TV and recording studios, and doctors from Western, herbal and Oriental traditions.

The Church has a new calendar dating from the holy one's birth in 1961, and Christmas has been replaced by a feast on 14 January, Torop's birthday. However, the best time to visit Petropavlovka is during its main summer festival on 18 August.

Interestingly the villages in which the Vissarionites live – Kuragino, Imisskoye, Petropavlovka and Cheremshanka – are also where many of the descendants of the original Old Believers settled. In a flight similar to that of the schismatics 350 years ago, many European Russians, as well as a few Western Europeans, are now heading to Siberia to be close to this Siberian messiah, including computer scientists, TV producers and even a former Ukrainian pop star. They all seem radiantly happy...unlike the families they left behind.

★★★

The state initially backed the Church in Siberia, perceiving it as an excellent tool of colonisation. But eventually, as the wealth and influence of the Church grew, it came to be viewed as a threat to secular power and a determined attempt was made to subordinate it to the state.

After the Russian Church reforms of 1653, there were those who couldn't accept the changes and continued to worship in the old ways: most symbolically by crossing themselves using two instead of three fingers. To avoid persecution many of these Old Believers fled to Siberia where in remote villages their beliefs still survive. Their villages tend to be neat with many wooden cottages, but part from a preponderance of long beards, are not immediately different from other old rural Russian settlements. Relatively accessible examples lie within 40km of Ulan Ude.

As well as the Old Believers, many other religious communities were exiled to Siberia or simply settled there hoping to find freedom of worship. The Skoptsy were a fanatical Christian sect exiled to Olekminsk in Yakutia during the 18th century. They believed in sexual abstinence, and to remove the threat of temptation, young males were castrated.

Many Russian Orthodox churches were destroyed in the civil war, or at least suffered some damage, which gave the Bolsheviks an excellent excuse to complete the demolition. The surviving churches were usually converted to some secular use: the Church of the Trinity in Irkutsk became a planetarium; a Lutheran church in Vladivostok was commandeered for a naval museum; and the Orthodox Hodigitria Cathedral in Ulan Ude was designated a museum of atheism. In recent years most of these have been re-sanctified and reopened. Meanwhile throughout Siberia and the Russian Far East one can gauge a town's perceived prosperity by the size of the new church(es) that are under (re)construction.

For further details on Christianity in Russia, see the Facts about European Russia chapter.

Buddhism

The Gelugpa or 'Yellow Hat' sect of Tibetan Buddhism (whose spiritual leader is the Dalai Lama) reached eastern Buryatia and Tuva via Mongolia in the 18th century, but only really took root in the 19th. Contemplative and essentially atheistic, Buddhism was never a direct threat to the Soviet state and was tolerated until Stalin attempted to wipe it out in the 1930s. During this time 150 temples and 46 monasteries (*datsan* in Buryat, *khuree* in Tuvan) were levelled and thousands of peaceable lamas (Buddhist priests) were exiled or executed. At the end of WWII, two *datsan* were opened, a new one at Ivolginsk near Ulan Ude and an old one at Aginskoe, southeast of Chita.

Since 1950 Buddhism has been organised under a Buddhist Religious Board based at Ivolginsk. Until the era of glasnost the only approved work for Buddhist organisations was to maintain a profile in various world peace movements. Now they are free to reopen monasteries, and are doing so. The Russian Federation now has an estimated half a million Buddhists, a figure that has been growing steadily in the years since glasnost. The 14th (present) Dalai Lama has visited both Buryatia and Tuva, though his 2002 trip was thwarted by visa refusals.

Judaism
Even before the Soviet creation of the Jewish Autonomous Region centred on Birobidzhan, Siberia was home to large numbers of Jewish people. At one time they accounted for one-third of the population of Sretensk (a port town on the Shilka River, 300km east of Chita) and in the 1880s Kansk, near Krasnoyarsk, was so predominantly Jewish that it was known as the Jerusalem of Siberia.

There was also a synagogue in Verkhneudinsk (later Ulan Ude), and the one in Irkutsk is still standing and now operates as a Jewish cultural centre.

Islam
Muslim Kazakhs, a small minority in southeast Altay, are the only long-term Islamic group east of Bashkortostan. However, significant summer populations of migrant workers from Tajikistan and Azerbaijan now work in the booming northern cities.

LANGUAGE
Russian is the predominant tongue and everywhere it is not the first language (Tuva, rural Buryatia and corners of Altay), everyone has learnt it at school. The Turkic-Mongol languages of Buryatia, Tuva, Altay and Sakha are all distantly related, but only the numbers are easily recognisable between all four. If you don't speak any Russian be sure to invest in a good phrasebook and dictionary, and learn the alphabet as quickly as possible.

Facts for the Visitor

Information in this chapter is largely specific to Siberia and the Russian Far East. See the European Russia Facts for the Visitor chapter for general information on travel in Russia.

SUGGESTED ITINERARIES

The best way to explore this huge chunk of the world is from east to west or west to east: along the Trans-Siberian Railway or the Baikal–Amur Mainline (BAM). Venturing beyond the railway lines depends on how much time and money you have.

You can have a great trip just by hopping from one Trans-Siberian city to the next. Tobolsk, Omsk, Novosibirsk, Tomsk, Krasnoyarsk, Irkutsk, Ulan Ude, Khabarovsk and Vladivostok all have things going for them. You certainly won't want to miss out on Lake Baikal either, if only to squeeze in a trip to its touristy southern half. In two or three weeks you could visit all these places.

More intrepid travellers will be drawn to the vast and varied wilderness regions. Khakassia and Altay, south of the Trans-Siberian Railway, are relatively accessible and a week or two should be enough to get a basic feel for either. Sakha, Tuva, Sakhalin and Kamchatka are wilder and emptier. Visits to Taymyr, Kolyma and Chukotka require very serious planning; ideally, you'd need a month to explore each of these.

Two months is enough to do the Trans-Siberian Railway or BAM at leisure, allowing around a week to explore Lake Baikal or Kamchatka, while still finding the time to take in one other region. Don't be too rigid about your schedule and allow for the unexpected, whether it's an invitation to a dacha or a roundabout route from point A to B. Siberia is one of the last territories in the world where you can venture to areas few other foreigners (if any) have been.

PLANNING
When to Go

This depends a great deal on what you want to see and do. In summer getting around is easier, boat tours are available and the bustle of street life and pavement traders adds an upbeat air to cities and towns.

Winter brings the Siberia of the imagination to life: starkly beautiful, snow-dusted landscapes resemble Christmas-card scenes, with much of the urban grime hidden beneath a great white cloak. Temperatures as low as minus 25°C might not be to everybody's liking, although rural land transport becomes easier in winter as muddy tracks solidify, potholes are evened out by fallen snow, and unbridged lakes and rivers freeze into winter roads. April and May can be wet and slushy, making transport difficult: the river ice is too thin for vehicles but too thick for boats.

May and June are peak danger periods for encephalitis-carrying ticks, though June and July are worse for biting insects; by August the air has cleared of mosquitoes. In early October the temperature is still quite mild and the deciduous vegetation takes on a glorious russet palette (particularly in the east); this beautiful season comes a month earlier in the mountains of Altay (for more information see the Climate section in the Facts about Siberia & the Russian Far East chapter).

Some rural accommodation is unheated and therefore only open in summer. Ski resorts get particularly busy at new year and in March; the resorts can offer considerable out-of-season rates from April to May before prices rise again in summer (though a few close altogether).

Maps

Maps exclusively covering Siberia are hard to find, so aim to pick up a good one of Russia as a whole (see Maps in the European Russia Facts for the Visitor chapter for more details).

Siberian bookshops often sell maps of neighbouring cities or regions so if you see a map or plan of a place you may be going to, pick it up because it's possible you won't find it when you get there.

What to Bring

Unless embarking on extreme wilderness trips, refer to the equivalent section in the European Russia Facts for the Visitor chapter to find out what to bring.

CONSULATES
Irkutsk

Mongolia (☎ 3952-342 145, fax 342 143, e irconsul@angara.ru) ul Lapina 11. Open 9.30am to noon and 2.30pm to 5pm Monday,

Customs Warning

Recently we have received a steady stream of stories from travellers who, upon leaving Russia, experienced the confiscation of their dollars and other foreign currencies by customs officers. Problems can arise if you don't have a currency declaration form, or if you have a form that hasn't been officially stamped; such confiscations have become a virtual business for many inspectors, with the most typical reports coming from the Trans-Siberian route to Mongolia. Arriving in the night without a stamped declaration leaves you with a stark choice: you can lose all your foreign currency, or you can get off the train (thereby forfeiting onward tickets) and change your money into roubles. If you choose the latter the roubles can apparently be exported without the original declaration form, but by the time the exchange is made, you'll have missed your train and will need new tickets (which will be hard to rebook). In addition, you'll be lumbered with a poor exchange rate and annoying bundles of roubles that need to be changed back upon arrival in Ulaan Baatar. Just to add to the fun, you'll be stuck in dismal Naushki, the border town, where there's no hotel. In one of the worst incidents in recent times, some 70 people were herded off a train at Naushki and locked in a room for much of the night.

Our advice is to make sure on entering Russia that you receive a customs form – fill it out and insist it gets stamped. Don't leave the airport customs area, or your train at a border crossing, unless the form has been stamped front and back (they'll put hand-drawn rings around the sum of money you declare, too). Keep this document safely (and a photocopy as backup) and present it when you leave Russia, along with a new customs declaration showing that you are taking out less money than you brought in. Should you have *more* than when you arrived, spend the excess before getting near the border.

Tuesday, Thursday and Friday. A two-week tourist visa, processed in a week, costs US$25; pay US$50 and it gets done in two days. Visas for longer stays require invitation letters.

Ulan Ude

Mongolia (ul Profsoyuznaya off ul Lenina). Open Monday, Wednesday and Friday. Apply for visas from 10am to 1pm; collect them from 3pm to 5pm. A one-month tourist visa (valid for three months) costs US$25 if you wait a week and US$50 for same-day service.

Kyzyl

Mongolia (☎ 3942-210 445) ul Internatsionalnaya 9. Open 10am to noon and 2pm to 4.30pm Monday to Thursday, 10am to 1pm Friday. For two-day processing a single-entry, 20-day visa costs US$25; a double-entry, one-month version is US$50; and a transit visa US$15. Prices are doubled for same-day service.

Khabarovsk

China (☎ 4212-34 75 50, fax 32 83 90) Lenin Stadium 1. Visa applications accepted 10.30am to 1pm Monday, Wednesday and Friday. For processing in a week, pay R900 for a single-entry visa; one-day is R1800.

Japan (☎ 4212-32 69 07, fax 32 72 12, **e** consul@ japan.khv.ru) ul Pushkina 38A

Vladivostok

South Korea (☎ 4232-22 77 29, fax 22 73 18) Aleutskaya ul 45A

Japan (☎ 4232-26 74 81, fax 26 75 41) Verkhne-portovaya ul 46
USA (☎ 30 00 70, fax 26 02 48) Pushkinskaya ul 32

MONEY

Most cities in the region have at least a couple of banks with ATMs that will accept credit and debit cards, including Visa, MasterCard, Maestro, Electron and others. While Alfa and OBK banks seem to be the most consistent, it's wise to keep a fairly sizable stash of cash in case the ATMs aren't available, or won't work, or will only dispense R1500 at a time (resulting in significant bank charges).

US dollars are still the way to go. Euros are sometimes accepted in big cities, but the exchange rates are not so good; other currencies are virtually unchangeable. Bank tellers can be finicky about what banknotes they will accept: if a bill is defaced in any way (written on, torn, dirty, badly worn) it will be handed straight back. Carrying around wads of cash isn't the security problem you might imagine. Divide your money into three or four stashes hidden out of view about your person, and take solace in the fact that nowadays there are a lot of Russians with plenty more money on them than you.

You might see signs saying that travellers cheques are accepted (American Express and, to a lesser extent, Thomas Cook), but any attempt to use them will probably result in a Chaplinesque scene starring you pointing desperately at the sign and the stone-faced teller shaking her head 'no'. The most likely bank to cash them is Sberbank, with branches in all the major cities.

Costs

As a general rule of thumb, mid-sized towns are cheaper than remote villages or big cities. Novosibirsk and Yekaterinburg are noticeably poorer value than other Siberian cities, except for northern oil-boom towns like Salekhard and Khanty Mansysk. In the Russian Far East and very remote far north outposts, prices rise considerably due to additional transportation costs.

You should be able to find accommodation for under R100 a night in small towns and villages, while in the main towns and cities the average price of a room will be R300 to R600. For the top hotels anything from US$50 to US$200 a night is common.

Dining out is also variable. In Tuva it's hard to find any restaurant with full meals over R20 (that's cheaper than self catering), and in most towns a basic *stolovaya* (canteen) can fill you up for under R40. In big cities, meals in classier restaurants range from R120 to R200 (much more in Novosibirsk, Khabarovsk and Vladivostok). Beer drinkers can save a fortune by sticking to local draught ales (R10 to R25 per half-litre in most cafés, R50 in a snazzy bar), rather than the imported beers (R70 to R160) found in top restaurants and expat bars.

If you use the *platskartny* ('hard' class, or 3rd class) carriages of overnight trains you will reduce your hotel bills. It can be no great challenge to live on US$20 per day – if you don't spend too long in big cities. However, if you stick to the main towns, eat Western-style meals in upmarket cafés and travel on *kupeynyy* (2nd class) trains, US$40 per day is a more realistic minimum.

DIGITAL RESOURCES

The following sites will be useful when planning your trip. (For more information see also the listings in the equivalent section of the European Russia Facts for the Visitor chapter.)

General

W **www.russianfareast.com** Predominantly concerned with business travellers and investment, but it provides a number of useful links for tourists.

W **www.mnh.si.edu/arctic/features/croads** Offers a virtual tour of the Washington-based National Museum of Natural History's *Crossroads of Continents* exhibit – a look at Siberian and Alaskan peoples.

W **www.traveleastrussia.com** This Seattle-based adventure-tour site has plenty of useful Russian Far East information.

Trans-Siberian

W **www.transsib.ru/Eng** Far and away the best Trans-Siberian site, regularly updated with tons of useful information and a huge photo library (there's a German-language version at W www.trans-sib.de).

W **www.washingtonpost.com/wp-srv/world/sib eriadiary** *Washington Post* journalist Robert G Kaiser and photographer Lucian Perkins crossed Siberia in August 2001, filing these fascinating stories along the way.

W **http://kbzd.irk.ru** A photographic essay of the Circum-Baikal railway.

W **www.whereishayden.org** Postings from a Kiwi's 2001 global tour, including thoughtful, fun accounts of Siberia from Vladivostok westwards along the BAM.

W **www.F8com/fp/Russia** Although it's from 1995, this high-quality Trans-Siberian photojournalism is still good background reading.

BOOKS

See the European Russia Facts for the Visitor chapter for general reading.

Guidebooks

Apart from the Lonely Planet publications listed in the European Russia Facts for the Visitor chapter, other useful guidebooks include *Trekking in Russia & Central Asia*, by Frith Maier, detailing many interesting Siberian hikes, including the Circum-Baikal railroad, the Altay and Sayan Mountains. For in-depth details on the BAM route as well as Magadan and Yakutsk, see Trailblazer's *Siberian BAM Guide*, by Athol Yates & Nicholas Zvegintzov.

Travel

The Trans-Siberian railway has been a rich source of inspiration for many writers. Eric Newby's classic *The Big Red Train Ride* is a frequently hilarious account of hopping on and off the *Rossiya* between Moscow and

SIBERIA & THE RUSSIAN FAR EAST

Nakhodka; it's outdated but still provides plenty of colour and detail.

For a more current read, there's Colin Thubron's *In Siberia*, a fascinating, literate (but often sombre) account of the author's journey from the Urals to Magadan on the Sea of Okhotsk, with detours to Tuva, Yakutsk, and the Entsy village of Potalovo and Pokrovskoe (where he meets 'Rasputin').

Paul Theroux, another great travel writer, includes a caustic account of a late-1970s Trans-Siberian journey in *The Great Rail Bazaar*. His mood is little better 10 years later, when he boards the Trans-Mongolian as the prelude to an exhaustive rail exploration of China, recounted in *Riding the Iron Rooster*.

Hopelessly in love with the Trans-Siberian is Lesley Blanch, whose *Journey into the Mind's Eye* is a ripe, semi-autobiographical account of her romantic addiction to Russia.

Paddy Linehan's *Trans-Siberia – Inside the Grey Area*, although not especially polished, gives a fair idea of the sort of experiences you're likely to encounter on a typical Siberian trip.

During the late 1980s, Brad Newsham was 'toting a bale of misery' around Japan and China and, via the Trans-Mongolian, to Moscow; he describes his woes, and little else, in *All the Right Places*. At around the same time, Mary Morris, also labouring under a cloud of self-created gloom, was following a similar self-absorbed route, related in *Wall to Wall: From Beijing to Berlin*.

A good antidote to modern-day whingeing is Peter Fleming's *One's Company*, originally published in 1933, in which a tumble down an embankment on board the Trans-Siberian is described with admirable sang-froid. Going even further back, *Recollections of Tartar Steppes and Their Inhabitants*, by Lucy Atkinson, recounts this British woman's travels through Siberia and Central Asia in the 1860s.

During the summer of 1991, German journalist Frederick Kempe followed the Tom River north from Novokuznetsk to the Ob and on to the Arctic Sea, a journey recalled in *Siberian Odyssey: A Voyage into the Russian Soul*. Italian journo Tiziano Terzani's *Goodnight Mr Lenin* captures the death of communism and Terzani's efforts to return to Moscow from the Far East during that tumultuous time.

The best book about cycling across Siberia is *Between the Hammer and the Sickle* by Simon Vickers, although it's out of print. *Around the Sacred Sea* is an interesting and nicely illustrated account of an epic horseback ride around Lake Baikal.

Tuva or Bust!, by Ralph Leighton, is not so much a travelogue as a 'pre-travelogue'. It describes Leighton and Nobel physics laureate Richard Feynman's growing obsession with Tuva, which began with a geography game at dinner in 1977 and developed through subsequent years as the pair tried to unravel Soviet bureaucracy in order to visit the region. Although Leighton doesn't actually get to Tuva until the book's epilogue, you still learn a lot about the place; Feynman died in 1988, just before the final go-ahead for their trip was received.

General

Benson Bobrick's *East of the Sun* is an excellent, very readable history of the conquest and settlement of Siberia and the Russian Far East, good on gory details.

A more academic treatment is given in *The Russian Far East: A History*, by John J Stephan. *A History of the Peoples of Siberia*, by James Forsyth, covers the same ground but from the perspective of the indigenous tribes; it's rather heavy going. Those with a more casual interest might prefer Fred Mayer's *The Forgotten Peoples of Siberia*, a beautiful photographic essay on the living conditions of the reindeer-herding Koryaks, the walrus-hunting Chukchi and others.

Anna Reid's *The Shaman's Coat* is another historical account of the indigenous peoples of the region.

To the Great Ocean, by Harmon Tupper, is *the* book to read on the history of the Trans-Siberian Railway; it's out of print, but may be available in libraries.

The animal and plant life of Siberia and the eastern regions comes under scrutiny in *The Realms of the Russian Bear*, by John Sparks, and *The Nature of Russia*, by John Massey Stewart, both written with the novice naturalist in mind, both lavishly illustrated, and both out of print (again, these should be available in libraries).

Also heavy on photographs is *Baikal, Sacred Sea of Siberia*, a pictorial tribute to the great lake with a text by travel writer and novelist Peter Matthiessen.

MEDIA

For a general overview of the Russian media, see the European Russia Facts for the Visitor chapter.

Every major town and city throughout Siberia and the Russian Far East has its own newspaper and periodicals, and each region and territory has its own TV channel, usually a mix of local news, imported soaps and badly dubbed movies.

The *Vladivostok News* (**W** http://vn.vlad news.ru) is an online newspaper, updated weekly. The *Krasnoyarsk Times* is an English-language paper available free from top hotels and restaurants in Krasnoyarsk. The *Sakhalin Times* is also free and is available at main expat haunts in Yuzhno-Sakhalinsk. Otherwise, don't expect to find any English-language papers or magazines on sale.

PHOTOGRAPHY & VIDEO

See the European Russia Facts for the Visitor chapter for general comments.

Taking photographs in Siberia presents problems in deep winter: at extremely low temperatures, camera batteries won't function, film becomes very brittle, and if cameras are exposed to cold and humidity for too long, they acquire a frosty coating which can later work its way inside and cause havoc within the camera body.

In most towns print films can be purchased and processed in about an hour, though quality varies. Widespread computer clubs have CD burners, making it easy to transfer digital photos. However, APS film is virtually unobtainable, and in all Siberia we only found slide film at Skaska in Irkutsk (200ASA Kodak Ektachrome, R220 for 36 exposures).

TIME

The regions of Siberia and the Russian Far East are spread across eight time zones, strangely disorienting if you're travelling steadily across them.

When it's noon in Moscow, it's...

2pm in Tyumen & Tobolsk
3pm in Omsk, Novosibirsk, Tomsk & Altay
4pm in Novokuznetsk, Abakan, Krasnoyarsk & Tuva
5pm in Bratsk, Irkutsk & Ulan Ude
6pm in Chita, Blagoveshchensk & Yakutsk
7pm in Khabarovsk, Vladivostok & Sakhalin
8pm in Magadan
9pm in Kamchatka

Long-distance train timetables, most train station clocks and some air timetables are on Moscow time.

HEALTH

'Ticks? No problem!' my hiking guide told me. But when we rendezvoused in Severobaikalsk, he looked prepared for Chernobyl, wearing – despite the heat – head-to-toe protection and a Kamarnik face-cover hat. He was horrified to see me arrive without gloves: was I suicidal? He had also *assumed* that everyone was inoculated against encephalitis. Despite donning the claustrophobic protection, I found three ticks on me which I fortunately flicked off before getting bitten. Other travellers were less fortunate, attacked while strolling around Baikal and near Novosibirsk's Akademgorodok. So don't be fooled: if locals say ticks are no problem, they're speaking in a *relative* sense.

Mark Elliott

From May to July, tick-borne encephalitis is a risk anywhere in rural Russia, while Japanese encephalitis (caused by mosquito bites) is a danger from May to September in the rural areas bordering Mongolia, China and North Korea. The risk involved in catching encephalitis should not be taken lightly: read under 'Ticks' in the health section of the European Russia Facts for the Visitor chapter. If visiting rural areas you should consider the immunisation available for both types of encephalitis.

DANGERS & ANNOYANCES

Specific natural hazards include bears and volatile volcanoes if trekking in Kamchatka, and tick-borne encephalitis in virtually all rural areas (but particularly in Ussuriland). Siberia and the Russian Far East are pretty safe as far as human dangers are concerned, with the possible exception being Irkutsk, a popular stopover for Trans-Mongolian and Trans-Manchurian passengers. We've had reports of bag theft (especially around the Irkutsk train station) and the occasional mugging, so take care, especially at night.

PUBLIC HOLIDAYS & SPECIAL EVENTS

See the European Russia Facts for the Visitor chapter for general Russian holidays and events.

February-March

Tibetan Buddhist New Year (Tsagaalgan) A moveable feast lasting 16 days, Tsagaalgan celebrates the lunar new year and hence advances by about 10 days annually. It's mainly celebrated at family level in Buryatia and Tuva, where it's known as Shagaa.

June

Tun-Payram Khakass (opening-of-summer-pastures festival) With traditional food, costumes and sports, this festival is celebrated in Askiz, usually on the first or second Sunday of the month, and then in villages.

July

Maitreya Buddha Festival Held at Ivolginsk *datsan* (monastery) near Ulan Ude.

Buryatia Folk Festival Celebrated at the hippodrome near the ethnographic museum in Ulan Ude.

Ysyakh Yakut (opening-of-pastures festival) Here you can eat traditional food amid local costumes and sports.

August

Naadym Tuvan A summer festival with *khuresh* (Tuvan wrestling), long-distance horse racing and throat-singing.

December–January

Russian Winter Festival Features tourist-oriented *troyka* (horse-drawn sleigh) rides and folklore performances at Irkutsk.

ACTIVITIES

The Siberia and Russian Far East region is little more than a wilderness upon which humanity has scarcely made a scratch – as such, it's ideal adventure-holiday terrain. Mountaineering, rafting, fishing and so on have always been popular with Russians, and many small towns have well-established outdoor clubs.

But one vital thing to be aware of is that you can't just turn up and expect to participate straight away – instead, make initial contact with the specialist agencies listed under the respective Activities sections. Even if you arrive at the clubs armed with addresses and phone numbers, it can take two or three days to make contact with anyone (and then maybe an extra couple of days for them to figure out exactly what it is you want of them). So give people as much advance warning as possible; even if you can't hammer out all the details, give them an idea of your interests. Above all, be flexible and patient, and don't expect things to always go smoothly.

Trekking

The best trekking is found where the dense taiga is broken by mountains, rivers and other physical features. Kamchatka, with its awesome volcanic landscapes, and the very beautiful Altay Mountains are great places to explore; hikes around Lake Baikal (some of which are only accessible by boat) are also rewarding. Many towns along the BAM line make good bases for heading out into the wilds; the western part of the line passes through quite mountainous terrain, complete with high-altitude lakes and hot springs, and abandoned Gulag camps hidden in high canyons.

Mountain Climbing

Possibilities for climbing exist in the Altay Mountains (south of Biysk on the Kazakhstan and Mongolian borders), the spectacular Ergaki Mountains (south of Abakan), the Sayan Mountains (on the Mongolian border), in the Baikalsky range (on Lake Baikal's western shore) and among the volcanoes of the Kamchatka Peninsula. Frith Maier's book *Trekking in Russia & Central Asia* has information on worthwhile climbs and their levels of difficulty.

Rafting & Canoeing

With over 53,000 Siberian rivers, there's plenty of potential for waterborne adventuring. Rafting trips can be arranged with agencies in Vladivostok, Komsomolsk-on-Amur and Kamchatka, and short-distance rafting in the Altay region is possible on a 'turn up' basis. For the most spectacular (and dangerous) stretches, you'll need plenty of planning; professional rafting specialists based in Omsk and Barnaul can help.

Skiing

The Siberian winter is such that high mountains are unnecessary for skiing: near any town there'll be a hill or even a steep river bank with a basic tow-lift for skiers, enabling you to easily nip home afterwards and largely negating the need for *lizhny baza* (ski resorts). However, a few good resorts do exist, including those at Sayanogorsk, Solnechny Springs near Severobaikalsk, and the Gorny Vozdukh (Mountain Air) tourist centre outside Yuzhno-Sakhalinsk; all have modern equipment for rent. Cross-country skiing is also popular.

Fishing

The region is an angler's paradise: rivers are swollen with grayling and various species of salmon, and gigantic 20kg to 30kg *taimen* swim in Tuva's isolated Todzha district. Kamchatka is a particular draw, with steelhead fishing in the peninsula reckoned to be the best in the world; check out **w** www.wild salmoncenter.org for details. Be prepared: organised fishing trips in Siberia and the Russian Far East can be heart-stoppingly expensive. While it's possible to go it alone and just head off with rod and tackle, most regions have severe restrictions on fishing so you'd be wise to at least check these out before departure.

ACCOMMODATION

Although you'll find a few overpriced, dilapidated hotels, on the whole the accommodation situation is improving and is now pretty much on a par with European Russia. In the Far East cities of Khabarovsk and Vladivostok – already visited by large numbers of Japanese and Koreans – there are many good, upmarket hotels with first-class amenities (in one case, thermostatically controlled, heated toilet seats) and correspondingly high prices.

If you're looking for something cheaper, head for the smaller towns or consider a homestay; many of the travel agencies in the region can arrange these. Inexplicably, twin rooms are occasionally cheaper than singles, and in small towns it's often possible to pay half again when only one person is staying (though you may end up sharing with a stranger). See the Accommodation section in the European Russia Facts for the Visitor chapter for further possibilities and agency recommendations.

FOOD

It's a great myth that there is no good food in Siberia. In fact, increased prosperity has brought with it better dining options, particularly in the big cities. In Novosibirsk, Krasnoyarsk, Irkutsk, Khabarovsk and Vladivostok, for example, you can now dine very well indeed on a previously unimaginable range of cuisines. Local Russian delicacies and recipes are well represented and, if you're tired of them, there'll always be a Chinese or perhaps Mongolian or Caucasian-style restaurant to fall back on. Of course, sushi, the trans-Russian craze, is popular (but pricey).

The best cafés rarely make much attempt to advertise their presence, with many hidden in hard-to-find entrances at the back of apartment blocks. Others are in cellar rooms beneath street level, their small signs often making them initially indistinguishable from similarly positioned disreputable brawl bars. Upmarket restaurants are often far from the centre in hard-to-find suburban back streets.

In smaller towns the choice will be far narrower, perhaps limited to standard Russian meals such as *pelmeni* and *kotlet*; in villages there may be no hot food available at all (though there's almost always do-it-yourself pot noodles available from kiosk shops). The choice is particularly abysmal in Tuva (beyond Kyzyl); locals often take their own food when visiting the provinces!

Local dishes that always pop up are *myaso po Sibirski*, Siberian-style beef topped with cheese, and *vyrezka po tayozhnomu* (taiga tender loin), cubed steak cooked with herbs. The Siberian staple is *pelmeni*: small, boiled doughy packets stuffed with meat and usually served heaped on a plate with sour cream or butter, or in a stock soup. *Manti* is the steamed, palm-sized version (two or three make a good, greasy meal), known as *pozy buuzy* in Buryatia and *pyan-se* (a peppery version) in the Russian Far East. Bite carefully, blow to cool and suck out the liquid, otherwise you may soak your shirt in hot lamb juice, as poor, embarrassed Mikhail Gorbachev did when visiting Ulan Ude!

Fish is plentiful, especially in late summer and autumn when *losos* (salmon) and *osyotr* (sturgeon) are far more likely to grace the table than meat. Around Baikal, these fish are supplemented by *omul* (a cousin of salmon and trout), endemic to the lake and considered a great delicacy. Russians serve it smoked, broiled or salted on a slice of bread as an appetiser, in the same manner as that most ubiquitous of Siberian appetisers, *ikra* (caviar); you'll most often see the red (salmon) caviar, saltier and much cheaper than the black sort.

A moderate warning: several travellers have become extremely ill on fish (Russians tend to overcook it, but don't always store it properly).

Seafood replaces freshwater fish in the Pacific coast region, especially around Vladivostok. Standard items on the menu include *kalmary*, *kraby* and *grebeshki* (scallops).

On the whole, relatively few Siberians eat out because of lack of money and the fact that restaurant meals seldom match those dished up at home, which are prepared using fresh ingredients from the dacha, forest or river. If you are lucky enough to be invited back to a Siberian family household to eat, chances are it will be one of the best meals of your trip.

Homes, roadside vendors and the well-stocked markets are your best bet for tasting the great range of wild mushrooms, *paporotnik* (fern tips), *shishki* (cedar nuts) and various soft fruits (red currants, raspberries) laboriously gathered by locals from the forest. The fruits in turn are made into jams which you can add to tea; native Tuvans often drink tea weak and milky, while Altay tea has butter and *talkan* (a sort of ground muesli) added to taste. The Bashkirs, the Kazakhs of southernmost Altay and the Sakhans of the Sakha Republic drink *koumys*, rapidly perishable fermented mare's milk.

Getting There & Away

Many visitors come to Siberia on the Trans-Siberian Railway, but the region can also be accessed via a wide range of air connections and several overland routes from China, Kazakhstan and Mongolia. In fact, two extra crossing points along the Mongolian border are slated to open within a couple of years, ensuring that Siberia's beautiful Tuva and Altay republics will no longer be 'dead-end' destinations.

AIR
European Russia
All major cities and large towns in the region have an airport with direct Moscow flights (often one or more per day), generally 30% cheaper for advance bookings or evening departures. Beware: most such flights use either Domodedovo or Vnukovo airports in Moscow; if you're connecting to Moscow's Sheremetevo-2 International Airport, allow a few hours to cross town.

Many cities also have weekly flights to St Petersburg, weekend summer flights to Sochi, and other connections to Caucasus, Volga and Ural airports.

Costs The following are economy one-way fares (return fares are usually double):

from	to	cost (R)	duration (hrs)
Moscow	Novosibirsk	3300	4
Moscow	Petropavlovsk-Kamchatsky	9300	9
Moscow	Khabarovsk	8300	8½
Moscow	Vladivostok	9300	9
St Petersburg	Novosibirsk	4500	4
St Petersburg	Krasnoyarsk	4500	4¾
St Petersburg	Irkutsk	5000	7½
St Petersburg	Petropavlovsk-Kamachatsky	9350	13½

Europe
Lufthansa (W www.lufthansa.ru) flies from Frankfurt to Perm, Kazan, Samara and Yekaterinburg; from any of these, it's a shorter land journey into Siberia than from Moscow.

Krasair (W www.krasair.ru), out of Krasnoyarsk, and **Siberia Airlines** (W www.s7.ru), out of Novosibirsk (via Omsk or Barnaul), offer direct services to Hanover and Frankfurt,

with one-way/return prices averaging US$410/460. To get to Germany as cheaply as possible, consider flying to Kaliningrad (US$220 from Krasnoyarsk) and taking a bus across Poland. For Ukraine, a direct Novosibirsk–Kiev flight costs US$151, and there are summer flights from Novosibirsk to Larnaka (Cyprus), Barcelona (Catalonia), and Burgas/Varna (Bulgarian Black Sea coast).

Turkey, the Caucasus & the Middle East
Summer charter flights to Turkey, especially Antalya, are offered from several major airports, but rarely show up on timetables. Weekly flights to Baku, Azerbaijan, operate from Tyumen (US$175), Krasnoyarsk (US$205) and Novosibirsk (US$180); the latter also has twice-weekly flights to Yerevan, Armenia (US$220), as well as weekly services to Tel Aviv, Israel (US$425).

The USA
Anchorage-based **Magadan Airlines** (☎ 907-248 2994, fax 248 2893) flies weekly from Anchorage to Magadan (one way US$685 plus 5% VAT, cheapest return US$902 plus 5% VAT), via Petropavlovsk-Kamchatsky (US$1300, 4 hours). These flights are often subject to long delays.

Note that Russia is on the other side of the International Date Line from the USA: when it's noon Tuesday in Kamchatka, it's 3pm Monday in Alaska (making a 21-hour difference).

Asia

Seoul in South Korea is one of the best international travel hubs for Siberia and the Russian Far East, with weekly flights to Khabarovsk (US$440) and at least twice-weekly services to Novosibirsk (US$299), Vladivostok (US$252 to US$286) and Yuzhno-Sakhalinsk (US$403). There are also flights connecting Pusan to/from Vladivostok and Yuzhno-Sakhalinsk.

For Japan, Vladivostok Air flies three times a week from Vladivostok to Niigata (US$263), Osaka (US$399) and Toyama (US$330). From Yuzhno-Sakhalinsk there are twice-weekly connections to Hakodate and weekly flights to Sapporo (both US$370). From Khabarovsk there are weekly flights to Niigata (US$224) and from July to September, a service to Aomori (US$224).

China connections include Irkutsk to Beijing (US$180 to US$470) and Shenyang (from US$152); Khabarovsk to Harbin (US$157) and Guangzhou (US$257); Novosibirsk to Beijing (US$256) and Ürümqi (US$113); and Vladivostok to Harbin (US$90).

Mongolia and Central Asia

Mongolia's capital, Ulaan Baatar, is poorly served with just two flights a week to/from Irkutsk (US$170). However, there are dozens of connections to Central Asia: from Novosibirsk you can reach Almaty (US$160) and Öskemen/Ust Kamenogorsk (US$74) in Kazakhstan; Andizhan (US$125) and Tashkent (US$135) in Uzbekistan; Dushanbe (US$145) and Khujand/Khodzhent (US$140) in Tajikistan; and Bishkek (US$170) in Kyrgyzstan. Tyumen, Omsk and Krasnoyarsk have a slightly smaller range of similar destinations.

LAND
Train

Of course, the way to travel by train is on the Trans-Siberian Railway from Moscow, or Japan (via ship or plane to Vladivostok), or along the Trans-Mongolian branch line to/from Beijing (see the boxed text 'Trans-Siberian Railway' in the Getting Around Siberia chapter for more details).

There are also direct trains into Siberia from St Petersburg; from Kharkiv in Ukraine to Vladivostok, every two days; and in summer from Crimea, the Caucasus and the Russian Black Sea coast, going at least as far east as Irkutsk.

Although the main line from Moscow to Central Asia avoids Siberia (instead travelling via Samara on the Volga), several other lines head into Kazakhstan. Destinations from Novosibirsk or Novokuznetsk (via Barnaul on the Turkestan–Siberia, or 'Turk–Sib', route) include Almaty, Qaraghandy/Karaganda and Leninogorsk (Kazakhstan).

If you don't happen to have a Kazakh visa (and a double-entry Russian visa) be warned: east–west trains on the Omsk–Chelyabinsk route travel through Petropavl/Petropavlovsk in Kazakhstan, including the weekly service Novosibirsk–Berlin Lichtenburg No 070/059.

See the Russian Far East chapter (specifically the Getting There & Away sections for Vladivostok and Khabarovsk) for options on travelling overland to China.

SEA

To reach Japan, there are ferries from Vladivostok to Fushiki (on Japan's main island of Honshu), and from Korsakov (on Sakhalin) to Wakkanai (on Hokkaido). For full details, see the Vladivostok and Yuzhno-Sakhalinsk Getting There & Away sections in the Russian Far East chapter.

TRAVEL AGENCIES & ORGANISED TOURS

It is reasonably easy to travel independently if you stick to the main Trans-Siberian routes. Nonetheless, you may be very grateful for the assistance of an agent for booking tickets, finding alternative accommodation options, and providing personalised guided visits of the region – especially if you don't speak Russian. You will find at least one agency listed for several of the major cities in this section of the guide; contact them well in advance as most are relatively small and overstretched.

In the wilderness areas, even determinedly independent travellers might consider at least some elements of a tour – trekking trails exist, but the great distances can be disorientating. You might walk for days without meeting another soul, so a knowledgeable guide is better than Hansel-and-Gretel-style breadcrumbs for finding your way out of a taiga forest!

Most of the agencies we recommend will prepare tailor-made itineraries for individuals or relatively small groups. Although Siberian and Far East 'tours' are not necessarily upmarket, you may be glad to pay that bit extra to have permits pre-arranged, jeeps or pack horses prepared to get you up unmarked muddy trails, and food waiting for you at isolated camps where supplies are otherwise unavailable. If a day rate of US$60 per person sounds steep for camping, bear in mind it often includes transport, cooks, guides, and considerable back-up staff.

Curiously, the best agencies are not always located in the areas they serve: for example, one of the recommended outfits for extreme mountaineering, trekking and expedition rafting in the Altay and Sayan mountains is **K2 Adventures** (w http://extreme.k2.omsknet.ru), ironically based in pan-flat Omsk. For the Altay, **Sibalp** (e sibalp@online.nsk.su) in Novosibirsk is obliging, English-proficient and very experienced, while **Sputnik-Altai** (w http://arw.dcn-asu.ru/~sputnik) in Barnaul is very well connected.

LenAlpTurs (w www.russia-climbing.com) in St Petersburg is a great choice for the Belukha area. For Tuva and Khakassia, compare local agencies with cosmopolitan **Paradise Travel** (w www.siberiaparadise.com) in Krasnoyarsk and imaginative **Abakan Tours** (e parkotel@khakasnet.ru) in Abakan. Nizhny Novgorod–based **Team Gorky** (w www.teamgorky.ru) runs trips to the Altay, as does **Wild Russia** (w www.wildrussia.spb.ru) in St Petersburg, which also has a Kamchatka tour.

If you speak Russian or are learning the language, it's a great cultural experience to simply go into a regional travel agency and join a local group heading for a wilderness region. This can be especially good value when visiting Altay from Barnaul or Novosibirsk: it's quite possible to get by on around US$100 a week, including full board, visits, treks and transport; standards, however, can be very ropey, itineraries inflexible and last-minute availability unpredictable. Bring your vodka glass.

While a few of the agencies listed here can arrange Trans-Siberian packages, for more options check out the listings in the European Russia Getting There & Away chapter.

Overseas Agencies

The USA The following may be useful:

Far East Development (☎ 206-282 0824, fax 281 4417, w www.traveleastrussia.com) 2001 Western Ave #300, Seattle WA 98121. Eco-adventure tour company specialising in Far East Russia.

Ouzel Expeditions (☎ 907-783 2216, w www.ouzel.com) PO Box 935, Girdwood, Alaska 99587. Specialises in Kamchatka fishing trips.

Society Expeditions (☎ 800-548 8669, w www.societyexpeditions.com) 2001 Western Ave #300, Seattle, WA 98121. Can arrange cruises of the northern Pacific rim, including Kamchatka, the Kuril Islands and Sakhalin.

Zegrahm Expeditions (☎ 800-628 8747, w www.zeco.com) 1414 Dexter Ave N #327, Seattle, WA 98109. Offers a 17-day cruise from Sapporo, Japan, to Kamchatka, including a stop on the Kuril Islands.

Japan A couple of Tokyo agents specialise in Trans-Siberian tours and can also arrange ferry tickets to Vladivostok:

Euras Tours (☎ 03-5296 5783, fax 5296 5759, w www.motcis.com) 2F Kandatsukasa-cho Bldg, 2-2-12 Kandatsukasa-cho, Chiyoda-ku, Tokyo 101 0048).

MO Tourist CIS Russian Centre (☎ 03-5296 5783, fax 5296 5759, w www.motcis.com) 2F Kandatsukasa-cho Bldg, 2-2-12 Kandatsukasa-cho, Chiyoda-ku, Tokyo 101 0048.

China To purchase train tickets from Beijing to Russia, contact the following:

Beijing Tourism Group (BTG, ☎ 8610-6515 8562, fax 6515 8603) Beijing Tourist Building, 28 Jianguomen Wai Dajie, Beijing. Formerly known as the China International Travel Service (CITS).

Monkey Business (☎ 8610-6591 6519, fax 6356 6517, w www.monkeyshrine.com) 12 Dong Da Qiao Xie, Beijing. Offers tours on the Trans-Manchurian and Trans-Mongolian railways, with stops in Ulaan Baatar, Irkutsk and/or Yekaterinburg. Some have complained of inflated prices, but it remains a popular option.

Moonsky Star Ltd (☎ 852-2723 1376, fax 2723 6653) Chung King Mansion, E-4-6, Nathan Road 36-44, Kowloon, Hong Kong. Monkey Business's Hong Kong partner caters to clients wishing to start their journey in that city.

Getting Around

Getting around in Siberia and the Russian Far East isn't so much travel as a series of expeditions. In fact, foreign visitors to the region have traditionally regarded getting around – in the form of a trip on the Trans-Siberian Railway – as constituting the whole experience. Spare a thought for those poor unfortunates who had to do it on the hoof before the first railway tracks were laid. For them the journey from A, somewhere west of the Ural Mountains, to B, somewhere in Siberia, could easily consume a year or more of their footsore lives. The distances involved are vast. From Yekaterinburg at the western limits of Siberia to Vladivostok on the Pacific coast is about the same distance as from Berlin to New York, while even a relatively short overland hop, such as the one from Irkutsk to its near neighbour Khabarovsk, is still roughly equivalent to the distance from London to Cairo. And you were wondering about taking a bus?

Information in this chapter is largely specific to Siberia and the Russian Far East. For more general information on travel in Russia, see the European Russia Getting Around chapter.

AIR

Because of the vast distances involved and the limited extent of the road and rail network, flying is sometimes the only practical way of getting around. Aircraft take on the role of buses, especially on short-haul flights. Passengers frequently have to carry their own baggage aboard and dump it at the rear before scrumming for seats.

Almost every small town has an airport but don't expect much; most of these places have fewer facilities than the average bus shelter. If nothing else, it will at least have flights to the nearest big town or city, and from there you'll be able to make nationwide connections. Recent years have seen the emergence of small, regional airlines, but most use old Aeroflot machines with a fresh coat of paint (see the boxed text 'Airline Safety in Russia' in the European Russia Getting Around chapter).

It is no problem buying a ticket these days with *avia kassa* (ticket offices) all over most large towns and cities. While it's possible to book major flights (eg, Moscow to Petropavlovsk-Kamchatsky on Aeroflot) with overseas agencies, reservations for shorter flights on one of the smaller regional airlines will be problematic, if not impossible. For such cases it's best to go through a Russian-based agency. Reservations cost nothing so it's worth making them for whatever dates you might think possible.

Tickets for internal flights can be booked online through ⓦ www.biletplus.ru, but as they are not electronic tickets you'll need to have them delivered to a Russian address or visit the company's office in Novosibirsk (its location has changed three times in as many years and it plans to do so again, so check carefully!).

For sample fares see the Getting There & Away sections in the following Siberia and Russian Far East chapters.

TRAIN

The railway is the main artery of life in Siberia and the Russian Far East, sustaining and nurturing the towns and cities along its length. For the traveller, this makes the railway the ideal mode of transport because it connects almost every place of any significance. (Towns that were once wealthy and important shrivelled and all but died after the railway bypassed them.)

The same types of train run in Siberia and the Far East as in European Russia – see the European Russia Getting Around chapter. All mainline intercity services run on Moscow time, with only local *elektrichka* (suburban trains) generally listed in local time. For help in cracking the timetable code, see the boxed text 'Reading A Train Timetable' in the European Russia Getting Around chapter.

One important thing to bear in mind is that during the peak summer travel period (from the end of June to the end of August) securing a berth at a few days' notice from one major Siberian town to another (say from Novosibirsk to Irkutsk, or Irkutsk to Vladivostok) can be tricky. This is when lots of Russians are on the move for their summer holidays, so, if you have a rough idea of your itinerary it's sound advice to use a local travel agency in order to book tickets in advance.

Costs

Fares vary from train to train, and there have been regular price hikes. The fares given here are for high-season 2nd-class/*kupe* tickets (one way), current at the time of writing.

from	to	cost (R)	duration (hrs)
Irkutsk	Ulan Ude	341	8
Irkutsk	Khabarovsk	1766	60
Khabarovsk	Komsomolsk	476	8
Khabarovsk	Vladivostok	751	13
Khabarovsk	Novosibirsk	2506	96
Moscow	Irkutsk	3286–3720	88
Moscow	Khabarovsk	3120–4630	144
Moscow	Vladivostok	2850–4665	157

BUS

Long-distance buses complement rather than compete with the rail network. They generally serve areas with no railway (notably Altay and Tuva) or routes on which trains are slow, infrequent or overloaded (eg, Novokuznetsk to Biysk and Khabarovsk to Birobidzhan). Buses generally charge a (sometimes hefty) fee for larger bags.

Minibuses (known as *marshrutki*, Russian for fixed-route) are quicker than the rusty old buses and rarely cost much more. Within cities they're everywhere, and in certain towns they're prepared to stop between bus stops, which can save quite a walk. Where roads are good and villages frequent, shared taxis can be twice as fast as buses, and well worth the double fare.

CAR & MOTORCYCLE

There is nothing remotely approaching a continuous Trans-Siberian highway, but a few intrepid souls have been known to rise to the challenge of driving, even cycling, across the country. Most famously, *Corriere della Sera* journalist Luigi Barzini documented the road trip he made from Beijing to Paris in 1907 led by Prince Scipione Borghese. The journey took them two months during which time they frequently resorted to driving along the railway rather than the mud tracks that constituted Siberian roads.

Today, the main road, such as it can be called, still peters out in the swamps 400km east of Chita and doesn't re-emerge as a drivable road roughly until Skovorodino, some 700km to the east. Even the most dedicated transcontinental expedition drivers generally put their 4WDs onto trains for this section (see **w** www.markandmichelle.com /transsib.htm to see what this involves!). In winter and with extreme perseverance, you might just make it from Bratsk across to Magadan in around three months. The website **w** www.4x44u.com/pub/k2/am4x44u/events /adventure/teuindex.htm tells the tale of how it was done in 1995–96 but things are even harder nowadays since it's now illegal for foreigners to use GPS equipment in Russia.

Bearing in mind the numbing monotony of the landscape, the frequently dire quality of the roads, lack of adequate signposting, keen-eyed highway police on the lookout for a bribe, and the difficulty of obtaining petrol, not to mention spare parts, there are few advantages for a motorist in Siberia. Besides, the majority of settlements cling tenaciously to the lifeline of the railway and there are few off-the-beaten-track places that can easily be reached by road.

This said, not every Siberian road is appalling. The glorious Altay Mountains, Khakassia and parts of the Russian Far East around Khabarovsk and Vladivostok have basic skeletons of reasonable asphalt. As buses are rare, to make the most of the views and tempting side trips, it's worth chartering a private vehicle (with driver). This can be surprisingly good value, especially in Altay where private drivers charge R3 per kilometre for a Lada Zhiguli. This price assumes you arrange things yourself (eg, by asking around in the village shop). Professional taxi drivers want more and you'll pay up to R8 per kilometre if you make arrangements through an agency. In Tuva you can expect to pay R170 to R200 per hour (plus negotiated waiting time) for an indestructible UAZ 4WD minivan – necessary for some of the rougher rural routes.

Note that you'll always have to pay return mileage if renting 'one way', and that many local drivers want to get home the same night, even if that's at 3am.

BOAT

Siberia and the Russian Far East were first opened up by boat, but with such a short navigation season (mid-June to September), long-distance river transport is now limited

[Continued on page 500]

The Trans-Siberian Railway

Extending 9289km from Moscow to Vladivostok on the Pacific coast, the Trans-Siberian Railway and connecting routes comprise one of the most famous, romantic and potentially enjoyable of the world's great train journeys. Rolling out of Europe and into Asia, through eight time zones and over vast swathes of taiga, steppe and desert, the Trans-Siberian – the world's longest single-service railway – makes all other train rides seem like once around the block with Thomas the Tank Engine.

Don't look for the Trans-Siberian Railway on a timetable, though. The term is used generically for three main lines and the numerous trains that run on them. The trains most people use are the daily *Rossiya* No 1/2 service linking Moscow and Vladivostok (or the better *Baikal* No 9/10 service from Moscow to Irkutsk for part of the way); the weekly No 3/4 Trans-Mongolian service via Ulaan Baatar to Beijing; and the weekly No 19/20 Trans-Manchurian service also from Moscow to Beijing but via Harbin in China.

For the first four days' travel out of Moscow's Yaroslavl station, the Trans-Siberian, Trans-Manchurian and Trans-Mongolian routes all follow the same line, passing through Nizhny Novgorod on the way to Yekaterinburg in the Ural Mountains and then into Siberia. Many travellers choose to break their journey at Irkutsk to visit Lake Baikal (we recommend you do) but, otherwise, the three main services continue on round the southern tip of the lake to Ulan Ude. From here Trans-Siberian trains continue to Vladivostok, while the Trans-Mongolian ones head south for the Mongolian border, Ulaan Baatar and Beijing. The Trans-Manchurian service continues past Ulan Ude, then turns southeast for Zabaikalsk on the Chinese border.

History

Beginnings Prior to the Trans-Siberian Railway, crossing Siberia was a torturously slow and uncomfortable business. In fact, it was quicker to travel from St Petersburg to Vladivostok by crossing the Atlantic, North America and the Pacific, than by going overland.

In the 19th century, as the region's population grew, and both Japan and China began coveting Russia's Far Eastern territories, the Russian Empire realised it needed better communication links with its extremities. Ideas for a railway across Siberia were floated, but it wasn't until 1886 that Tsar Alexander III finally authorised the building of a 7500km line from Chelyabinsk (then Russia's eastern railhead) to Vladivostok, to run along the route of the old Siberian post road. In May 1891, Tsarevich Nicholas, visiting Vladivostok, emptied a wheelbarrow of dirt, so signifying that work on the new railway had begun.

Construction A route was cut across the steppe and through the taiga with hand tools. The labour force was made up of exiles and convicts (offered reduced sentences as an incentive), soldiers and imported, paid Chinese labourers. Due to the terrain, climate, floods and landslides, disease, war and bandit attacks, not to mention shoddy materials and bad planning, the railway took 26 years to build. But it remains the most brilliant engineering feat of its time.

The railway was divided into six sections, with construction taking place simultaneously along the route. The Ussuri line (Vladivostok to Khabarovsk) was built between 1891 and 1897, followed by the western Siberian line (Chelyabinsk to Novosibirsk), built between 1892 and 1896, and the mid-Siberian line (Novosibirsk via Irkutsk to Port Baikal), built between 1893 and 1898. Within seven years, the Trans-Siberian Railway stretched 5200km from Moscow to the western shore of Lake Baikal.

Baikal was initially crossed by two icebreakers built at Newcastle-upon-Tyne in England and sent in pieces to be assembled in Irkutsk. The huge, four-funnelled *Baikal* was the larger of the two, and her decks were laid with three lines of track that could accommodate an entire express train and its load. The smaller ship, the *Angara*, was used for passengers.

By 1904, it was finally possible to take a train all the way from St Petersburg to Vladivostok, via the East China line across Manchuria. However, propelled by fears that they might lose control of Manchuria to the Japanese, the Russians embarked upon the alternative Amur line, from Sretensk

The Trans-Siberian Railway

to Khabarovsk. Finished in 1916, with the bridge over the Amur River at Khabarovsk, it was the final link in the world's longest railway.

Early Services Following Russia's orgy of self-publicity at the Paris Universal Exposition of 1900, the earliest Trans-Siberian travellers were lured on to the rails even before the line was fully completed. To attract overseas clientele, the *State Express* (as it was then known) was presented at the exposition as a palace on wheels with sleeping carriages, a gymnasium car, a restaurant car with a large tiled bathroom, reading lounge and piano, and even a fully functioning church car crowned with a belfry – in a mock-up landscape of stuffed seals, papier-mache icebergs and mannequins of native hunters. The same year saw the publication of the official *Guide to the Great Siberian Railway*.

The primary reason for the construction of the railway had been to further the economic and social development of Siberia, and the bulk of passengers were emigrants escaping overpopulation in European Russia. Their travelling conditions were a far cry from the sumptuousness on offer to the international set – 'stables on wheels' was one eyewitness description. But a few weeks of hardship on the rails was far preferable to crossing Siberia on foot, and in 1908 alone 750,000 peasants rode east.

Post-Revolution Civil war interrupted the development of the railway. When the Reds finally prevailed, upgrading the Trans-Siberian Railway was a major priority in their plans for economic rebirth by linking the iron-ore reserves of the Ural region with the Kuznetsk coalfields and the great industrial plants being developed throughout western Siberia.

In the 1920s, the railway was extended southwest from Novosibirsk to Almaty in Kazakhstan (the present-day Turkestan–Siberian Railway, known as the Turk–Sib). In 1940, a branch line was built between Ulan Ude and Naushki, on the border with Mongolia. By 1949 it had connected with Ulaan Baatar, the Mongolian capital. The line from Ulaan Baatar to Beijing was begun four years later and completed by 1956.

Although work on the alternative Trans-Siberian Railway, the Baikal Amur Mainline (BAM), began in the 1930s, this 'Hero Project of the Century' wasn't officially opened until 1991 – for details see the boxed text 'The Hero Project of the Century' in the Siberia chapter.

Despite the ascendancy of the aeroplane and the demise of the Soviet system, the importance of the Trans-Siberian Railway has not diminished; it's the glue that holds Russia together. Rail is still the only viable option for heavy freight, a fact underlined by tentative plans made for a Trans-Korean line raising the possibility of travelling all the way by train from Seoul to the far west of Europe.

Booking Tickets

There's no such thing as a stopover ticket. If you are travelling from Moscow to Beijing, and plan on spending a night or two in Irkutsk and Ulaan Baatar, you'll need three separate tickets: Moscow–Irkutsk, Irkutsk–Ulaan Baatar and Ulaan Baatar–Beijing. The tickets will all be for a specific berth on a specific train on a specified day.

Tickets can be booked a month in advance and you'd be wise to do this over the busy summer months when securing berths at short notice on certain trains can be difficult. Many travel agencies will be able to make advance bookings, but for anyone with flexible travel plans, independent rail travel within Russia is easy enough, and tickets for the Moscow–Vladivostok route in particular are rarely hard to get.

On the other hand, tickets to China are rarely easy to get in Ulaan Baatar without the help of a local tourist agency or government official. On the Trans-Manchurian route, Shanhaiguan and Tianjin are worth a couple of days' stopover, and getting off at either of these cities shouldn't be a problem as they are both relatively close to Beijing and connected by frequent daily services.

For full details of travelling on the Trans-Siberian routes, read Lonely Planet's *Trans-Siberian Railway* guide book. For general information on buying tickets and travelling on trains in Russia see the Getting Around chapters of both the European Russia and the Siberia and Russian Far East chapters of this book.

[Continued from page 497]

to the rivers Ob/Irtysh (Omsk-Tara-Tobolsk-Salekhard), Yenisey (Krasnoyarsk-Igarka-Dudinka) and Lena (Ust Kut-Lensk-Yakutsk). You can also make one-day hops by hydrofoil along several sections of these rivers, along the Amur River (Khabarovsk-Komsomolsk-Nikolaevsk) and across Lake Baikal (Irkutsk-Severobaikalsk-Nizhneangarsk). Other Baikal services are limited to short hops around Irkutsk/Listvyanka unless you charter a boat (around US$100 per day) in either Irkutsk or Listvyanka.

Ferries from Vanino cross the Tatar Strait to Sakhalin, but it can be murder trying to buy a ticket in the summer months; although sailings are supposed to be daily, in reality there is no set schedule. There are also irregular sailings from Korsakov, on Sakhalin,

across to Yuzhno-Kurilsk in the Kuril Island chain.

Out of Vladivostok there is a range of ferries to nearby islands and beach resorts farther south along the coast. For the truly adventurous, with a month or so to spare, it's possible to hitch a lift on one of the supply ships that sail out of Nakhodka and Vladivostok up to the Arctic Circle towns of Anadyr and Providenia.

Beware that boat schedules can change radically from year to year (especially on Lake Baikal) and are only published infuriatingly near to the first sailing of each season. When buying tickets for a hydrofoil *(raketa* or *voskhod)* try to avoid *ryad* (rows) 1–3 as spray will obscure your view and although enclosed, you'll often get wet. For more detailed information, see the respective regional sections in the Siberia and Russian Far East chapters.

Siberia Сибирь

From the Ural Mountains to the great Lena River, Siberia is huge, but much more manageable than one might imagine. Taken as a series of overnight train hops, the continent slips painlessly by while tempting mountain-bound side trips offer cultural as well as scenic interest. Food is improving, prices are dropping and in summer you'll need a swimsuit not a fur coat.

Tyumen & Omsk Regions
Тюмень и Омская Области

Though few travellers seem to bother stopping there, the cities of Tyumen and Omsk are both pleasant, cosmopolitan places, Tara and Pokrovskoe are intriguing, and Tobolsk is one of Siberia's most appealing historic towns.

TYUMEN
ТЮМЕНЬ
☎ 3452 • pop 507,000 • Moscow time plus 2 hours

Founded in 1586, Tyumen was the first Russian fort in Siberia but is now the booming capital of an oil rich *oblast* (region) stretching all the way to the Arctic Circle. The city has a youthful bustle and businesslike drive, with new constructions and traffic jams, yet it maintains a pleasant, liveable feel, created by tree-lined streets, stylish watering holes and picturesque old buildings.

Orientation & Information

The train station is 1.5km south of ulitsa Respubliki, the main street that runs across town from the Trinity Monastery in the northwest to well beyond the bus station in the southeast.

There are dozens of exchange bureaus and ATMs in the city centre, including those at Hotel Vostok and Quality Hotel. The **post office** (*ul Respubliki 56*) is on the corner of Tsentralnaya ploshchad. The **telephone office** (*ul Respubliki 51; open 24hr*) has an Internet salon, charging R24 per hour; queue at

Highlights

- Gaze at Lake Baikal from lovely Listvyanka or meditational Olkhon Island
- Admire the 'wooden lace' architecture of old Tomsk
- Meet shamans and *khöömei* throat-singers in the Tuva Republic
- Stroll around the kremlin and splendidly decrepit old town of Tobolsk
- Drink *koumys* in a Kazakh herder's yurt near Kosh-Agach
- Hike, raft or ride a horse to reach one of Altay's mountain lakes

Tyumen p503
Omsk p508 Tomsk p514 Severobaikalsk p568
Novosibirsk p511 Krasnoyarsk p546
Barnaul p520
Baikal p556 Abakan p532 Irkutsk p558
Kyzyl p539 Ulan Ude p572
Altay Republic p517
Khakassia Republic & Tuva Republic p531

★★★★★★★★★★★★★★★★★★★★★★

window 1. Alternatively, the Internet café **Profi/Web Khauz** (*ul Respubliki 61; open 11am-8pm daily*), up two flights of dark, graffitied stairs and along a balcony, has an hourly rate of R20.

City maps with bus routes are sold at **Novkina Bookshop** (*ul Respubliki 155; open 10am-7pm Mon-Fri, 10am-5pm Sat*). The specialist map kiosk **Melodika** (*open 8.30am-5.30pm Mon-Fri*), hidden away in the northbound bus shelter outside the blue-glass tower at 147 ulitsa Respubliki, has an unparalleled selection of hard-to-find city maps for most places in Siberia and the Urals.

SIBERIA

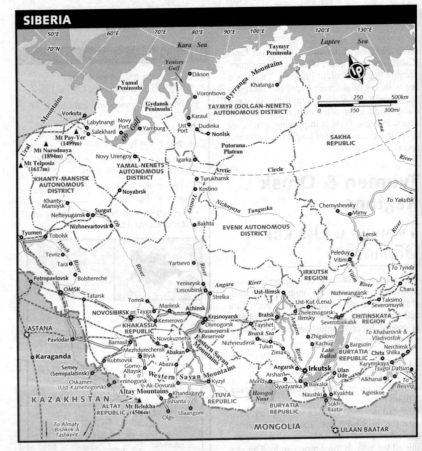

SIBERIA

Things to See

Tyumen's charm lies in random exploration of the old streets on the northern stretches of ulitsas Lenin and Respubliki, especially on cross streets such as ulitsas Turgenyeva and Semakova. Though interspersed with brand-new structures, there are plenty of atmospheric, carved wooden homes and 19th century stucco-fronted mansions. Several old buildings contain humdrum museums, including **Marsharov Mansion Museum** (*ul Lenina 24*), **House Museum of 19th & 20th-Century History** (*Istoriya Adnovo Dma; ul Respubliki 18*) and the **Town Hall Museum** (*ul Respubliki 2*), all charging R15 admission.

On ulitsa Respubliki's northern side is the baroque, multidomed **Znamensky Cathedral** (*ul Semakova 13*), built in 1786. A short walk

to the northeastern end of ulitsa Semakova is rewarded with a good sunset view down the river towards the walled, kremlin-esque **Trinity Monastery** (*Cvyato Troitskiy; ul Kommunisticheskaya 10*), partly reconstructed and containing a striking black-domed cathedral. Take bus No 14 or 30 from ulitsa Respubliki to Krestovozdvizhenskaya Church, then walk five minutes along the promenade (ulitsa Respubliki's extension).

In the city centre, the **Fine Arts Museum** (*Izobrazitelnykh Iskusstv muzey; ☎ 46 91 15; ul Ordzhonikidze 47; admission R15; open 10am-6pm Tues-Sun, last entry 5pm*) has an impressive and eclectic collection, ranging from ornate window frames saved from the city's old wooden houses to tiny, intricately carved bone figures.

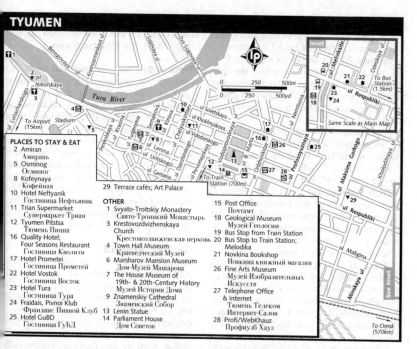

TYUMEN

PLACES TO STAY & EAT
2 Amiran
Амирань
5 Osminog
Осминог
8 Kofeynaya
Кофейная
10 Hotel Neftyanik
Гостиница Нефтяник
11 Trian Supermarket
Супермаркет Триан
12 Tyumen Pitstsa
Тюмень Пицца
16 Quality Hotel;
Four Seasons Restaurant
Гостиница Кволити
17 Hotel Prometei
Гостиница Прометей
22 Hotel Vostok
Гостиница Восток
23 Hotel Tura
Гостиница Тура
24 Fraidais, Pivnoi Klub
Фрайдайс Пивной Клуб
25 Hotel GuBD
Гостиница ГуБД

29 Terrace cafés; Art Palace

OTHER
1 Svyato-Troitskiy Monastery
Свято-Троицкий Монастырь
3 Krestovozdvizhenskaya
Church
Крестовоздвиженская церковь
4 Town Hall Museum
Краеведческий Музей
6 Marsharov Mansion Museum
Дом-Музей Машарова
7 The House Museum of
19th- & 20th-Century History
Музей Истории Дома
9 Znamenskiy Cathedral
Знаменский Собор
13 Lenin Statue
14 Parliament House
Дом Советов

15 Post Office
Почтамт
18 Geological Museum
Музей Геологии
19 Bus Stop from Train Station
20 Bus Stop to Train Station;
Melodika
21 Novkina Bookshop
Новкина книжный магазин
26 Fine Arts Museum
Музей Изобразительных
Искусств
27 Telephone Office
& Internet
Тюмень Телеком
Интернет-Салон
28 Profi/WebKhauz
Профиуэб Хауз

Near Hotel Vostok is a large **Geological Museum** (*Muzey Geologii; Nefti i Gaza, ul Respubliki 142*), immediately south of which is a unique modern war memorial in the shape of a gigantic metal candle.

Places to Stay

At the train station (upstairs, accessed from outside) are very basic **resting rooms** (*komnaty otdykha; dorm beds/singles R83/193*), with shared seatless toilets.

Hotel GuBD (*☎ 24 74 34; ul Sovetskaya 124; dorm beds/singles from R120/140*) is a much better and more central cheapie option. Basic rooms share squat toilets and a shower room – single women may find the military clientele off-putting bath-mates! However, the more expensive rooms (beds R250 to R350) have fancy sofas and private if temperamental cranky showers.

Hotel Neftyanik (*☎ 46 01 45; ul Cheluskintsev 12; singles R400-550, twins R700-900*) is an ugly concrete slab, but has by far the best position of the city's hotels for visiting the old town. The pricier rooms are nicely renovated and offer the best value in town.

Hotel Prometei (*☎/fax 25 14 23; ul Sovetskaya 61; singles R565-815, twins R920*) has a mixed bag of rooms which are OK but less appealing than cheaper equivalents at Hotel Neftyanik.

Hotel Vostok (*☎/fax 22 61 24; ul Respubliki 159; rooms from R598*), in a lively area out of the city centre, has repainted but tired Soviet-era rooms, with TV and fridge and an evens chance of hot water. The room rates include a meatball breakfast.

Hotel Tura (*☎/fax 22 99 69; ul Melnikaite 103A; singles/twins R735/1260*) is a small, well-managed hotel, with rooms that are OK once you get over the swirly carpets. Rates include breakfast.

Quality Hotel (*Kvoliti Otel Tyumen; ☎ 49 40 40, fax 49 40 50; e quality@sbtx.tmn.ru; ul Ordzhonikidze 46; singles/doubles R2520/2940*) is a typical international hotel, complete with muzak and pinging elevators. Its restaurant and patisserie-café are surprisingly good value. Room rates include breakfast.

Places to Eat & Drink

Amiran (*off ploshchad Nikolskaya; shashlyk per stick R50; open 4pm-11pm summer*) is on

SIBERIA

an unsophisticated terrace high above the River Tura, near the Trinity Monastery, and has generous barbecued lamb brochettes.

Tyumen Pitstsa (*ul Lenina 61; bliny from R7, pizza slices R15.60*), opposite the City Park, looks pretty ragged but is the cheapest of several pizza-and-bliny places with generous pizza slices that are unexpectedly good when fresh.

Four Seasons (☎ 49 40 53; *ul Orzhonokidze 46; most mains R170-460*), in the Quality Hotel, is formal but not forbidding with prices that are relatively affordable unless you plump for foie gras (R504) and lobster (R1575).

Trian Supermarket (*ul Bolodarskogo 23; open 24hrs*), around the corner from Hotel Neftyanik, sells hot, spit-roast chicken. Hotel Prometei also has a good **supermarket**, with by-the-scoop salads, cheap draft beer and tables at which to enjoy them.

Beside Hotel Tura is the fast-food joint **Fraidais** ('Fridays'; *ul Melnikaitye 103; pizza slices R14; open 10am-11pm*) and the stylish bierkeller **Pivnoi Klub** (*ul Melnikaitye 103; meals R65-140, beers from R40; open 10am-11pm daily*), where you should try the Thai fish cakes (R70).

Kofeynaya (☎ 46 60 83; *ul Semakova 19; espresso R35; open 8am-11pm daily*) offers the serenade of a real espresso machine while you drink a latte or macchiato, luxuriate over an ice-cream sundae and read the local papers.

During the summer months, popular **terrace cafés** appear outside the **Art Palace** (*cnr uls Respubliki & Gorkogo*), a cinema-concert complex nearing completion at the time of writing.

Osminog (☎ 45 12 47; *ul Lenina 4; cover charge R50-70; bistro open 11am-6pm, disco 11pm-6am*) is the city's trendiest disco and has an attached daytime bistro serving reasonable food.

Getting There & Away

Air There are several travel agencies that sell air tickets, including **Tyumenaviatrans** (☎/fax 25 05 32; *ul Pervomayskaya 58A; open 8am-8pm daily*), opposite the train station, with English-speaking flight-booking staff; one at Hotel Vostok (see Places to Stay); and **Agentstvo Vozdyshnkh Soobshchenii** (*ul Republika 156*), from where minibus No 35 leaves for the airport every 15 minutes. Domestic flight destinations include Moscow (from R3024, twice daily) and Salekhard (R3748, daily). International services fly to Baku (US$175) and Tashkent (US$125); both flights depart on Wednesday only.

Train & Bus From the **train station** (*ul Pervomayskaya*), there are regular rail services to all Trans-Siberian Railway destinations, including Moscow (35 hours), Yekaterinburg (4½ hours), Omsk (R385, 12 hours; departs 8.47pm) and Novosibirsk.

The **bus station** (*ul Permyakova*) is a short walk north of the big overpass where ulitsa Permyakova crosses ulitsa Respubliki. Buses for Tobolsk (R189, three hours, eight daily) go via Pokrovskoe (R61, 1¾ hours), for which you could also take Yarkovo-bound services (four daily). At least seven buses per day go to Yalutorovsk (R57, 1½ hours).

Getting Around

The most useful buses run along ulitsa Respubliki, although southbound through the old town's one-way system they use ul Lenina for one stretch. Most useful of these are Nos 30 and 14, both starting beyond the Krastovozdvizhenskaya Church (for Trinity Monastery), and No 25 starting from the train station. All three pass the Hotel Vostok, only finally turning off ulitsa Respubliki at the big ulitsa Permyakovo overpass, where they turn south. For the bus station get off before this at the Dom Kultury Stroitel bus stop or you'll be carried far out of your way.

At the time of writing, many city roads are being upgraded causing considerable diversions and delays so leave plenty of time.

TOBOLSK
ТОБОЛЬСК
☎ 34511 • pop 98,000 • Moscow time plus 2 hours

With its handsome kremlin, wooden houses and photogenic, crumbling churches, Tobolsk is the most memorable old city in Siberia.

An early visitor to the city was Yermak Timofeevich, whose band of Cossack mercenaries sacked the nearby Tatar stronghold of Sibir in 1582 and built Tobolsk's original fort five years later. Although the locals were Muslim Tatars, Tobolsk became the seat of Siberia's first bishopric in 1620, set up to stamp out incest, wife-renting and spouse-stealing by sexually frustrated Cossacks.

Due to its strategic location at the confluence of the Irtysh and Tobol Rivers, Tobolsk became the region's politico-military hub and from 1708 to 1839 the governors of Siberia resided here. Its strategic importance started to wane in the 1760s, when it was bypassed by the new Great Siberian Trakt (or Post Road), but it remained a significant centre of learning and culture right up to the early 20th century. This was reinforced by the arrival of educated Decembrists in the 1830s. Other guests included Fyodor Dostoevsky (en route to exile in Omsk) and deposed Tsar Nicholas II and his family, who spent several doomed months here in 1917.

Tatars still form 30% of the city's population, many living in the quaint if mosquito-blighted old town, with its 19th-century mosque. A handy Tatar greeting is *istimissis* (hello); thank you is *rakhmat*.

Orientation & Information

The heart of Tobolsk is its splendid kremlin set on a steep rise above the photogenic old town, which extends southwards across the boggy Irtysh valley. North of the kremlin ulitsa Oktjabrskaya and ulitsa Semena Remezova/Komsomolsky prospekt lead into a contrastingly ugly sprawl of Soviet-era concrete, which has its drab centre 3km from the kremlin around the Hotel Slavyanskaya, a block to the west of which is the bus station. The train station is some 10km further north.

You can change cash at the reception of the Hotel Slavyanskaya and at **Gazprombank** (*ul Oktjabriskaya*), beside Hotel Sibir. Just north of the big traffic circle on Komosomolsky prospekt are the post office and **Internet Club** (*open 8am-10pm daily*), next door, which charges R25 per hour.

Slavyanskaya Tourist Agency (☎ 9 91 14, fax 5 58 76; e sputnik@tob.ru; 2nd floor, Hotel Slavyanskaya), accessed through the hotel's casino, can arrange English-language city tours.

Kremlin

Within the tower-studded 18th-century walls of the kremlin (*grounds open 8am-8pm*) are the disused **Gostiny Dvor** (Trading Arcades), the blue-domed **St Sofia Cathedral** (1686) and the **Pokrovsky Cathedral** (1740s). Also inside the grounds is the **bell tower** built for the Uglich bell, which announced the murder of Ivan the Great's son Dmitry (1591) and signalled the start of a failed revolt against Tsar Boris Godunov. In a mad fury Godunov

ordered the bell publicly flogged, de-tongued and banished to Tobolsk for treacherous tolling. Behind a row of 11 cannons the elegant Arkhereisky mansion now houses the intriguing **Museum of the Spiritual Cultures of Western Siberia** (*admission R18; open 10am-5pm Tues-Sun*), with interesting nooks, viewpoints and style mood-swings between exhibition rooms.

Outside the Kremlin

At the time of writing, the small **Fine Art Museum** (*1887; ul Oktjabrskaja*), across from Hotel Sibir, was under renovation. Next door, through two unmarked doors, is **Minsalim Folk Trade** (☎ 6 26 50; ul Oktjabrskaja 2), an art-and-craft shop behind which the delightful Minsalim Timergazeev, a spiritual Tatar eccentric, carves miniature bone models using Heath Robinson–esque elastic-band technology.

Old Town

Wooden stairs lead down from the kremlin's southern gate to the dilapidated old town, full of picturesque ruined churches and angled wooden homes sinking into the soggy marshland.

Ulitsas Lenina, Mira and Kirova (once a wooden carriageway to the then huge river station) converge at a small square. Here you'll spot the little 1918 **Victory Chapel**, and the grand **Mendeleev Mansion** (*ul Mira 10*). Also on this square is a less-eye-catching old house (now an office building of Tobolsk Rayon), which was the exile-home of the last tsar before his fateful journey to execution in Yekaterinburg. Upstairs, one room has been restored to its original appearance as the **Kabinet-Myzey Imperatora Nikolaya II** (☎ 6 37 13; cnr uls Kirova & Mira; admission R15, with guide R110).

Two blocks to the east of the square, behind swirling wrought-iron gates, lies the attractive **Mikhail Arkhangel Church** (*ul Lenina 24*), with a colourfully restored interior. Tatianna Larina, in Pushkin's epic *Eugene Onegin*, is said to have been modelled on Natalia Fonvezena, wife of an exiled Decembrist, who prayed here when not cultivating pineapples in her hothouse.

The nearby **Tsentr Sibirsko-Tatarskoi Kultur** (☎ 6 27 13; ul Yershova 30) is a Tatar cultural centre, with occasional exhibitions and musical shows plus a dull museum upstairs.

SIBERIA

Two blocks south, beyond the red-brick mosque (☎ 6 27 48; ul Pushkina 27) weave through the muddy lanes of attractive Tatar cottages to reach the splendid baroque shell of the **Krestovazdvizhinskaya Church**.

Places to Stay & Eat

The train station has **resting rooms** (komnaty otdykha; dorm beds/twins R78/205), with showers for R12.50 extra.

Hotel Sibir (☎ 6 23 90; ul Oktyabriskaya 1; singles/twins R270/520, lyux suites R800), perfectly situated a stone's throw from the kremlin, has standard rooms with toilet and chintzy suites with modern shower, historical photos on the wall and a hint of a canopy over the queen bed. It sells map-brochures and has a good-value restaurant, but the staff are fussy in checking your original visa registration. Room rates include breakfast.

Hotel Slavyanskaya (☎/fax 9 91 01; Mikrorayon 9, cnr uls Komsomolskaya & Mendeleev; singles R660-950, doubles R1210-1470) is a comfortable Western-standard hotel-restaurant-casino complex offering unexpected value for money. Room rates include breakfast, and there's a swimming pool in the basement. The cheaper rooms are those above the noisy nightclub.

Akcharlak (☎ 5 16 83; 4th M/R Bldg 9, back entrance; mains R20-90) is a restaurant serving Tatar/Central Asian cuisine. Book ahead to reserve the 'divan' room, with its decorative water pipe and cushions on the floor, or to order a traditional plate of kanina (boiled horse).

Getting There & Away

There are convenient overnight trains to/from Yekaterinburg (No 241 or 242, R420 kupe, 12 hours) and Omsk (No 273, R494 kupe, 12 hours), and several daily trains northbound to Surgut and Nizhnevartovsk. For Tyumen, buses (R189, five hours, eight daily) are cheaper and more frequent than trains, plus you can stop off at Pokrovskoe (3¼ hours) en route; the last Tobolsk–Tyumen bus leaves at 6pm. Eight buses per day to various destinations pass Abalak.

Every eight days from June to September the **river station** (☎ 9 66 17) operates ferries down the Irtysh and Tobol Rivers to Salekhard (R1264 berth, four to five days). Tickets are in short supply from Salekhard (southbound) in June and from Tobolsk

(northbound) in August and September, but trips are also possible in a series of hydrofoil day-hops: Tobolsk–Khanty–Mansiysk (R706, twice per week), then to Beryezovo (R545, daily), then to Salekhard (R480, four weekly), from where you could travel by bus to Vorkuta and then by train to cities in European Russia. Southbound ferries from Salekhard continue past Tobolsk to Omsk via Tara, or there are hydrofoils on alternate days from Tobolsk to Tevriz and Tevriz to Omsk via Tara.

Getting Around

Bus No 4 goes to/from the train station through the new town to the kremlin. Bus Nos 1 and 10 travel past the kremlin and loop around the old town, passing near the river station; bus No 3 passes the mosque instead.

AROUND TOBOLSK
Abalak
Абалак

For 25km from Tobolsk, a quiet road skirts the border of the ancient Tatar kingdom of Isker to the region's holiest **monastery** at Abalak. It was built on the site of a miraculous materialising icon, which was last spotted in Australia, long after the Soviets had turned the church into a tractor barn. Today, the monastery is working again, with a copy of the icon over the door. If you walk the 249 steps down the opposite riverbank, you can see charming views over the bend in the Irtysh River. Buses from Tobolsk to Yuzhno Begishebskie, Baigara and Zagbazdina stop at the Abalaka bus stop after 40 minutes. It's an obvious 1.5km walk to the monastery.

Pokrovskoe
Покровское

The home village of Rasputin (see the boxed text 'The Priest of Sex' in the St Petersburg chapter) is basically two long streets. From the bus stop on the main Tobolsk–Tyumen road, walk 10 minutes southeast down ulitsa Severnaya, then right along ulitsa Sovetskaya, the cottage-lined historic post road. Rasputin's family home formerly stood at No 78 but has been replaced by another house. The museum opposite at No 79 is rarely open, but if you call at the ramshackle cottage at No 102 and can raise him from his hangover (as Colin Thubron did in In Siberia), you'll soon be sipping vodka breakfast with Rasputin himself;

well, a dead-ringer anyway. Viktor Prolubshikov has the lank long hair, peasant smock and hypnotic, piercing eyes of his claimed forebear. For a bottle of booze he'll happily pose for photos and regale you (in slurred Russian) with half-believable yarns. Just be ready to dive in case he tries to snog you!

There are frequent buses to/from Tyumen (R61, 1¾ hours) and Tobolsk (R118, 3½ hours, eight per day).

OMSK
ОМСК

☎ 3812 • pop 1.3 million • Moscow time plus 3 hours

Omsk, 568km east of Tyumen, grew rapidly from a 1716 Cossack outpost, replacing Tobolsk as the seat of Siberia's governor general by 1824. Until overrun by the Red Army in 1919, it was the civil war seat of Admiral Kolchak's anti-Bolshevik government, and has long been a dumping ground for exiles, including Dostoevsky, who nearly died from a flogging while jailed here from 1849 to 1853.

Although it is ringed by heavily industrial suburbs, the compact central area is dotted with parks, little museums and a surprising collection of quirky public sculptures along the unusually charming main street – ulitsa Lenina, of course. You can see all the city's sights in a day and then get on with enjoying some of Siberia's most appealing, decently priced dining.

Orientation & Information

The Irtysh River divides the city. On the western bank are the airport and the bus station. The historic centre, 4km north of the train station, is on the eastern bank at the confluence of the Irtysh with the much smaller Om River. The Om is crossed by ulitsa Lenina and by parallel prospekt Marksa and ulitsa Gagarina on the city's two bridges, Yubileyny most and Komsomolskiy most.

The main **post office** (ul Gertsena 1) is north of the city centre. A good Internet café is **Perekryostok** (cnr uls Lenina & Maslennikova; open 24hrs), with an hourly rate of R40. For excellent city maps, head to the bookstall at the station (upstairs).

K2 Adventures (☎/fax 3812-69 30 75; w http://extreme.k2.omsknet.ru/eng/; office 5, ul Neftezavodskaya 14) is hard to beat for rafting trips and mountaineering on the toughest rivers and peaks of Siberia and Central Asia. Its staff are very experienced and have a network of partner-guides across the region, notably in Altay and the Sayan Mountains. As the office itself is quite difficult to find, it's best to call and get the English-speaking staff to come and find you.

Things to See

On the otherwise drab, concrete western bank of the Irtysh River is a giant war-memorial figure and, just before the bus station, the dramatic new **Khristo-Rozhdestbenskiy Cathedral**, crowned with multiple gilded domes. Just north of the Yubileyny Bridge is the cute, painstakingly rebuilt little 1908 **Serafimo-Alexievskaya Chapel** which looks like it fell off a kremlin.

The architectural fun of upper ulitsa Lenina (little changed since 1905) continues past the ornate Drama Theatre to ploshchad Dzerzhinskogo.

Housed in the former imperial governor's mansion, the **History Museum** (Omskiy Gosudarstvenny Istoriko-Kraevadcheskiy muzey; ☎ 31 47 47; ul Lenina 23A; admission R10; open 10am-7pm Tues-Sun) has good ethnographic sections on Kazak, Tatar and Russian peasant life, plus an art gallery.

Beside the old town **duma** on ploshchad Lenina is the **Liberov Centre** (☎ 30 16 45; ul Dymskaya 3; admission R6; open 10am-5pm Tues-Sun), with a piano room/gallery and a dozen works by renowned artist Alexey Liberov.

West of the Yubileyny Bridge walk through the park and along the promenade, then take the first path to the right after a small derelict factory to reach the **Literature Museum** (☎ 24 29 65; ul Dostoevskogo 1; admission R20; open 10am-6pm Tues-Sun). Its limited attractions include interesting old city photos and some Dostoevsky doodles from the time the writer spent here. A block west beside a cannon-guarded Yukos townhouse is the **Military Museum** (ul Taube 7; admission R10; open 10am-5pm Tues-Sun), with a garden full of bristling artillery.

The city has several fine churches, including **St Nicholas Cathedral** (Svyato-Nikolsky Sobor; ul Truda 31), plus a rare Old Believers' **House Chapel** (ul Shchetinkina 10; services 3pm Sat & 7.30am Sun) in a 90-year-old turquoise wooden house tucked behind Omsk bank in a patchy area of old buildings east below ulitsa Gagarina.

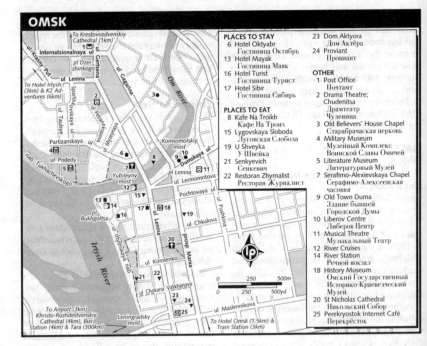

OMSK

PLACES TO STAY
6 Hotel Oktyabr
Гостиница Октябрь
13 Hotel Mayak
Гостиница Маяк
16 Hotel Turist
Гостиница Турист
17 Hotel Sibir
Гостиница Сибирь

PLACES TO EAT
8 Kafe Na Troikh
Кафе На Троих
15 Lygovskaya Sloboda
Луговская Слобода
19 U Shveyka
У Швейка
21 Senkyevich
Сенкевич
22 Restoran Zhyrnalist
Ресторан Журналист

23 Dom Aktyora
Дом Актёра
24 Proviant
Провиант

OTHER
1 Post Office
Почтамт
2 Drama Theatre;
Chudenitsa
Драмтеатр
Чуденица
3 Old Believers' House Chapel
Старабрачаская перковь
4 Military Museum
Музейный Комплекс
Воинской Славы Омичей
5 Literature Museum
Литературный Музей
7 Serafimo-Alexievskaya Chapel
Серафимо-Алексеевская
часовня
9 Old Town Duma
Здание бывшей
Городской Думы
10 Liberov Centre
Либеров Центр
11 Musical Theatre
Музыкальный Театр
12 River Cruises
14 River Station
Речной вокзал
18 History Museum
Омский Государственный
Историко-Краеведческий
Музей
20 St Nicholas Cathedral
Никольский Собор
25 Perekryostok Internet Café
Перекрёсток

Places to Stay

As usual the cheapest beds are the train station's **resting rooms** (*komnaty otdykha; dorm beds from R85*).

Hotel Sibir (☎ 31 25 71; *ul Lenina 22; singles/twins from R300/600*) has a great central position, but it's tatty and you may need a torch to find your room. Enter the hotel from its side entrance.

Hotel Omsk (☎ 31 07 21, fax 31 52 22; *ul Irtyshskaya Naberezhnaya 30; singles R350-550, twins R600-800*), about 1.5km south of the city centre towards the train station, is a big, bright place with river views.

Hotel Irtysh (☎ 23 27 02; **e** *sin@omsk net.ru; ul Krasny Put 155; singles R550-700, twins R680-800*) is similar to Hotel Omsk but farther from the city. The rates for its unfashionably renovated rooms include breakfast.

Hotel Mayak (☎ 31 54 31; *ul Lermontova 2; singles R390-980, twins R500-1180*), within the rounded end of the Art Deco river station, is the best value in town. All of its rooms are small but come with private bathroom, and the more expensive rooms are built to Western standards. Some of the hotel's friendly staff speak English.

Hotel Turist (☎/fax 31 64 14; *ul Broz Tito 2; singles R635-880, twins R895-1145*), also near the river station, is in an impersonal grey tower block with fine views but slightly less appealing rooms than Hotel Mayak.

If it's completely renovated as planned, the top choice may become the central 1905 **Hotel Oktyabr** (☎ 24 28 67; *ul Parizansk 2*).

Places to Eat

If you want a quick croissant and coffee, good bakery-cafés include **Lygovskaya Sloboda** (*ul Lenina 20*) and **Proviant** (*ul Marksa 10*); both are open 10am to 10pm daily.

U Shveyka (☎ 31 36 46; *ul Marksa 5; lunch special R120; open noon-3am daily*) is all beams and grandfather clocks. Actually, it's much nicer than you'd guess from the ugly exterior of the building it shares with a pizzeria and roast chicken joint (which has live music from 9pm to midnight Wednesday to Sunday).

Kafe Na Troikh (*mains R50-130; open 24hrs*), beside Yubileyny Bridge, has the decor of a neo-50s diner, complete with tongue-in-cheek communist memorabilia. It's marred by karaoke after 6pm.

SIBERIA

Chudenitsa (☎ 23 49 79; ul Nekrasova 8; kharcho R30, mains R60-100; open 24hrs), beside the Drama Theatre in a place marked simply 'Kafe', offers genuine Georgian cuisine.

Restoran Zhyrnalist (☎ 31 47 79; ul Lenina 34; meals R70-140; open noon-1am daily) is very atmospheric, with a pianist tinkling in the candle light, gramophones on the ceiling, and menus and wine lists presented as ye olde 'newspapers' (fun if awkward to decipher). Its fine Russian cuisine makes it worth the effort.

Senkyevich (☎ 51 09 81; ul Sezdovskaya 1; open noon-midnight) overlooks the river-beach in a super-stylish contemporary glass-and-steel building. It contains a café, sushi bar (R60 per nigiri), laid-back grill-bar and an airy French restaurant complete with a Parisian musical trio.

Dom Aktyora (☎ 31 32 54; ul Lenina 45; mains R85-140; open noon-midnight daily) has mood lighting, jazz and dozens of signed photos of the local stars who you might see eating there. It serves Russian dishes, pizza and beer.

Getting There & Away

Omsk's **airport** (ul 12 Dekabrya) is on the western bank of the Irtysh River. Useful flight destinations include Moscow (R3900 to R4500, several daily), St Petersburg (R3300, daily) and Irkutsk (R3100, three times weekly). Weekend-only flights to Frankfurt start at US$320 (one way). Air tickets can be purchased at one of the numerous ticket agencies at the river station.

From Omsk's train station there are handy overnight trains to Novosibirsk (No 88, R526, 9½ hours), Tyumen (No 273, R385, 11½ hours) and Yekaterinburg (No 25/55, R553, 12 hours); the Tyumen-bound train continues east to Tobolsk (R494 kupe, 12 hours). Buy tickets at the train station or at the handy, usually queue-free rail-ticket booth at the river station.

The bus station, about 3km west of the city centre, has buses to Tara (R127, six to eight hours, eight daily).

From the **river station** (information ☎ 39 81 25; tickets sold 7am-1pm, 2pm-7pm upstairs), ferries cruise up the Irtysh River to Tobolsk (two days), with departures every eight days. Hydrofoils to Tevriz via Tara (R120.40) leave every second day. Pleasure river-cruises (R40) use a separate jetty/ticket booth near the Yubileyny Bridge.

Getting Around

Trolleybus No 4 runs from the train station along prospekt Marksa to ploshchad Lenina. It then crosses the Om, passes the post office and continues up Krasny Put to Hotel Irtysh. Trolleybus No 7 links the train and bus stations.

TARA
TAPA
☎ 38171 • pop 26,000

Founded in 1594 as a defensive outpost for Tobolsk, the town of Tara recovered from a devastating 1669 fire to become a major trade centre. It was later eclipsed by Omsk, 300km to its south, becoming a dozy provincial backwater and a place of exile for several Decembrists. Soviet planners ringed an obligatory Lenin statue with a few small concrete eyesores on ploshchad Marksa and destroyed five of the city's six great 18th- and 19th-century churches. However, a gentle charm remains, making Tara the best stopoff if you take the river route between Omsk and Tobolsk.

Within a block of ploshchad Marksa, at the end of ulitsa Sovetskaya, you'll find the **Spaskaya Church** (1761; cnr uls Spaskaya & Kuybesheva), a small **museum** (pl Marksa; admission R3; open 9am-3pm Sun-Fri), **Hotel Irtysh** (pl Marksa; beds R50-214) and a short section of reconstructed ostrog (timber fortress) **wall**. Starting a block northeast of the square (down a short, steep bank beside a silver-toadstool-shaped memorial) is the most attractive area of wooden cottages with its little **mosque**. This 'lower town' straggles 3km along the wide river valley to the river station where ferries and the Omsk-Tevriz hydrofoils dock.

To walk to ploshchad Marksa from the hidden bus station, turn left down ulitsa Izbisheva. After two blocks cross ulitsa Lenin – which is the main road from Omsk – beside the little market and then continue three blocks farther, turning left when you spot the ostrog. Buses to Omsk (R127, six hours) leave five times during the daytime plus overnighters.

Around Tara

The town of **Bolshereche** (102km from Tara), famed for its little zoo, boasts a trio of small, carved wooden trader's houses (one with preserved interior), near the post office on ulitsa Sovetskaya. **Hotel Rus** (☎ 9 18 51; ul 50i let VLKSM 7; beds R70-130) is opposite the market. The Omsk–Tara buses stop in the town.

SIBERIA

Novosibirsk & Tomsk Regions

Новосибирская и Томская области

Novosibirsk, 530km east of Omsk and Siberia's biggest city, is a useful transport hub with plenty of cosmopolitan bars and eateries, but it's relatively expensive and of negligible architectural interest. If you're looking to break a long Siberian journey, Tomsk is a much more pleasant choice.

NOVOSIBIRSK
НОВОСИбИРСК

☎ 3832 • pop 1.45 million • Moscow time plus 3 hours

Founded in 1893, Novosibirsk wouldn't exist if not for the Trans-Siberian Railway. Until 1925 it was known as Novonikolaevsk, after the last tsar. Suffering badly during the civil war (1918–21) and its immediate aftermath, when some 60,000 citizens died of typhus, Novosibirsk quickly recovered. Its phenomenal growth into Siberia's biggest metropolis began in the 1920s when it was purpose-built as an industrial and transport centre, between the coalfields to the east and the mineral deposits of the Ural Mountains to the west.

In the 1930s the building of the Turkestan–Siberian (Turk–Sib) Railway south from Novosibirsk to Almaty in Kazakhstan made the city a crucial transport link between Russia and Central Asia. In 1958 Novosibirsk was chosen as the location for an experimental city of scientists, Akademgorodok (see the Around Novosibirsk section later).

Orientation & Information

Despite its daunting scale, the 'capital of Siberia' has a manageably simple centre focused on ploshchad Lenina. The city's main axis, Krasny prospekt runs through this square linking most major points of interest.

You can change money in the lobbies of Hotel Sibir and Hotel Novosibirsk. The main **post office** (ul Lenina 5; open 8am-7pm Mon-Fri, 8am-6pm Sat-Sun) is attached to the **telephone office** (ul Sovetskaya 33; open 9am-9pm daily), which offers long-distance telephone calls, and Internet access for R26 per hour. There's also a handy **Internet Klub**

(ul Trudovaya 1; open 24hr), with an hourly rate of US$1, hidden beneath an apartment block near ploshchad Lenina: start walking towards the station then chicane through the first alley to the right and just believe!

The **PVU** (old OVIR visa office; ☎ 29 04 85; ul Oktyabrskaya 78; open 3pm-5pm Mon & 10am-noon Thur only) is behind the large Globus Theatre.

Dom Knigi Bookshop (Krasny pr 51; open 10am-8pm daily) sells a good range of maps.

Sibalp (☎ 46 31 91, fax 54 13 74; e sibalp@ online.nsk.su; office 515, pr Karla Marksa 2) is a helpful travel service offering homestays, city tours and Altay escapades. Its English-speaking staff will meet clients at their hotel.

The service bureau **Intourist** (☎ 23 02 03), in the lobby of Hotel Sibir (see Places to Stay), arranges tours, and can book train and air tickets.

Things to See & Do

Behind statues of Lenin and his traffic-directing supporters stands Novosibirsk's huge silver-domed **Opera & Ballet Theatre** (☎ 18 07 59; pl Lenina). It has a grand interior and performances here (October to June only) are one of the city's highlights.

In an elegant mansion across ploshchad Lenina is the well-presented **Local Studies Museum** (Kraevedchesky muzey; ☎ 18 17 73; Krasny pr 23; admission R12; open 10am-5.30pm Tues-Sun), with Altay shaman coats, cutaway pioneer houses and some splendid religious artefacts.

The **Art Gallery** (Kartinnaya galereya; ☎ 22 20 42; Krasny pr 5; admission R30; open 10am-6pm Tues-Fri, 11am-6pm Sat-Sun) includes Braque-esque works by Nikolai Gritsyuk and numerous distinctive semi-impressionist mountainscapes by celebrated Russian painter Nikolay Rerikh.

The pretty little **Chapel of St Nicholas** (Chasovnya Svyatitelya Nikolaya; pr Krasny) was said during tsarist time to mark the geographical centre of Russia. Built in 1915 to celebrate (two years late!) 300 years of the Romanov dynasty, but demolished in the 1930s, it was rebuilt in 1993 for Novosibirsk's centenary.

The 1898 brick, Byzantine-style **Alexander Nevsky Cathedral** (Alexandr Nevskogo sobor; Krasny pr 1A) has gilded domes and colourful new murals, and was rededicated in 2002. Other notable churches include the

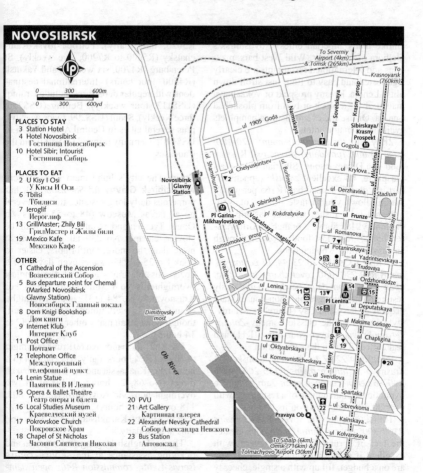

NOVOSIBIRSK

PLACES TO STAY
3 Station Hotel
4 Hotel Novosibirsk
   Гостиница Новосибирск
10 Hotel Sibir; Intourist
   Гостиница Сибирь

PLACES TO EAT
2 U Kisy I Osi
   У Кисы И Оси
6 Tbilisi
   Тбилиси
7 Ieroglif
   Иероглиф
13 GrillMaster; Zhily Bili
   ГрилМастер и Жилы били
19 Mexico Kafe
   Мексико Кафе

OTHER
1 Cathedral of the Ascension
   Вознесенский Собор
5 Bus departure point for Chemal
   (Marked Novosibirsk
   Glavny Station)
   Новосибирск Главный вокзал
8 Dom Knigi Bookshop
   Дом книги
9 Internet Klub
   Интернет Клуб
11 Post Office
   Почтамт
12 Telephone Office
   Междугородный
   телефонный пункт
14 Lenin Statue
   Памятник В И Ленину
15 Opera & Ballet Theatre
   Театр оперы и балета
16 Local Studies Museum
   Краеведческий музей
17 Pokrovskoe Church
   Покровское Храм
18 Chapel of St Nicholas
   Часовня Святителя Николая
20 PVU
21 Art Gallery
   Картинная галерея
22 Alexander Nevsky Cathedral
   Собор Александра Невского
23 Bus Station
   Автовокзал

photogenic 1914 blue-and-gold-domed **Cathedral of the Ascension** (*Voznesensky sobor; ul Sovetskaya 91*) and **Pokrovskoe Church** (*ul Oktyabrskaya 9*) in an old wooden house, with an attached icon-maker's workshop.

Places to Stay
Homestays (*R450-600*) are available through travel agency Sibalp (see earlier) and, more haphazardly, with women who loiter outside the train station after 9pm with 'Kvartira' (Apartment) signs around their necks.

Novosibirsk hotels are very poor value by Siberian standards and most (including the Ob, Tsentralnaya, Oktyabrskaya and the nicely renovated Vostok) will only accept foreigners when booked through a travel agency. This leaves only three walk-in options.

The cheapest (though almost always full) is the **station hotel** (*☎ 29 23 76; 2nd floor, Novosibirsk Glavny train station; twins/triples R300/350, lyux rooms R1500*).

Hotel Novosibirsk (*☎ 20 11 20, fax 21 65 17; Vokzalnaya magistral 1; singles/twins from R835/1471*), opposite the Novosibirsk Glavny train station, is a typical Soviet-era 23-storey tower. The most basic rooms share a toilet and washbasin between pairs of rooms. Room rates include breakfast.

Hotel Sibir (*☎ 23 02 03, fax 23 87 66; e centre@gk-sibir.sibnet.ru; ul Lenina 21; singles/doubles US$44/73*) has pleasantly renovated ensuite rooms (including breakfast) and, given the alternatives, is a reasonable option. Better still get a night train to somewhere else.

SIBERIA

Places to Eat

Unlike many Siberian cities, Novosibirsk's plethora of Irish pubs, Wild West bars, pizzerias and international restaurants are clearly signposted and easy to find: just stroll down ulitsa Lenina, Krasny prospekt or Vokzalnaya magistral for a block or two from ploshchad Lenina. Or use the events/listings pamphlets available at major hotels.

Zhily Bili *(ul Lenina 1; mains R70-180; open 11am-11pm daily)* serves real Russian food in a Disney-esque 'Siberian village' atmosphere. Its excellent *zakuski* (appetisers) cart is a glorified salad bar (R165 per plate), which allows you to taste dozens of well-prepared local dishes without dashing to a dictionary! It's above a branch of **GrillMaster** *(burgers R23)* fast-food, accessed through an easy-to-miss wooden door.

U Kisy I Osi *(☎ 20 23 44; ul Lenina 86; mains R90-230, R30 cover charge from 8pm; open 10am-11pm daily)* occupies a gloriously restored high-ceilinged old shop-house. Mannequins of Kisy and Osy (Laurel-and-Hardy-style heroes of the classic comedy *Zolotoy Telyonok*) watch over your bliny (R11) and real coffee (R30) in the café section.

Ieroglif *(☎ 22 57 12; cnr ul Potaninskaya & Krasny pr; Chinese mains R135-200, sushi R40-85 per piece; open noon-2am daily)* is a hypnotic Oriental temple of a restaurant, with over 20 different brews on its 'tea list'.

Tbilisi *(basement, ul Sovetskaya 63; mains R160-300; open 11am-11pm daily)* creates the feel of a rural Caucasian tavern, with excellent if pricey Georgian cuisine. If you are on a budget, fill up with a single, cheesey *khajapuri* (flaky pastry cheese turnover; R80).

Mexico Kafe *(☎ 10 34 20; Oktyabrskaya magistral 49; mains from R160; open noon-1am daily)* serves you tacos, burritos and the whole enchilada as you sip margaritas (R190) in an El Paso basement. From Wednesday to Saturday nights you'll be serenaded by live Hispanic music.

Getting There & Away

Air Novosibirsk has two airports. Two weekly flights (Monday and Wednesday) to Kyzyl (R2850) depart from the central Severny airport. However, most airlines use Tolmachyovo airport, 30km west of the centre off the Omsk road. Flights include another Kyzyl service (R2200) on Saturday, Magadan

(R6600, three weekly), Moscow (R3300 to R5025, three daily), Petropavlovsk-Kamchatsky (R5600 to R7200, five weekly), St Petersburg (R4700, six weekly) and Yakutsk (R4500, four hours). International destinations with regular departures include Ürümqi (US$112, four weekly), Beijing (US$256, three weekly), Seoul (US$299, twice weekly), plus several cities in Central Asia (US$75 to US$170), Germany (around US$400) and the Caucasus.

Train The city's huge main train station, **Novosibirsk Glavny** *(ul Shamshurina)*, has numerous daily long-distance trains. Several go as far as Moscow (48 to 55 hours via Omsk, Tyumen and Yekaterinburg), with the slower, cheaper No 239 taking one night more the more comfortable, easier to book No 25 (R2370 *kupe*, even days). Of a dozen possible trains to Omsk the handiest overnighter is No 87 (nine hours, daily). For Krasnoyarsk, No 84 (13¾ hours overnight, even days) is well timed and rarely full, though slower than many other options (12 to 14 hours).

For Altay the handy No 601 runs overnight to Biysk (10¾ hours, daily) via Barnaul (5½ hours). For Khakassia and Tuva go to Abakan direct (No 68, 23 hours, daily) or in two overnight hops via Novokuznetsk (No 605, 118 or 032, 9½ hours). The Turk–Sib Railway to Almaty, Kazakhstan (32 to 37 hours) runs at least daily.

There's English-language information and ticketing assistance at the **service centre** *(servis tsentr; commission R40; open 8am-7.30pm daily)*, inside the NG train station, and at Intourist in Hotel Sibir.

Bus Useful buses from the **bus station** *(Krasny pr 4)* serve Barnaul (R125, five to six hours, 20 daily) and Tomsk (R147, 5½ hours, eight daily). For about double the price, taking a shared taxi will get you to these towns much faster. A direct bus to Gorno-Altaysk (Altay Republic) leaves daily at 10.30am.

The well-organised, linguistically Russian-only **travel agency** *(ul Frunze 5)*, on the top floor, runs a twice weekly overnight bus to Turbaza Katun (on the Chemal road in the Altay Republic). However, since foreigners need to register in Gorno-Altaysk before exploring the region, this is only really useful for the return leg of the trip.

Getting Around

The metro's north–south line runs beneath Krasny prospekt and across the river to ploshchad Karla Marksa. A three-stop line intersects at Sibirskaya/Krasny prospekt and serves ploshchad Garina-Mikhaylovskogo, near Novosibirsk Glavny train station. Buses/minibuses are generally handier than the metro for getting around the city centre.

From the train station, take trolleybus No 2 to Severny airport, minibus No 122 to Tolmachyova airport, bus No 11 for the bus station via ploshchad Lenina and minibus No 1015 to central Akademgorodok.

AROUND NOVOSIBIRSK

Akademgorodok

Академгородок

Most big Siberian cities have an Akademgorodok, an originally elite Soviet academic township of research institutes, where scientists attracted by special perks could work in peaceful surroundings. Novosibirsk has Siberia's biggest, nestled in taiga forest almost 30km from the city centre, close to the beaches of the 'Ob Sea' (Obskoe More), the 200km-long reservoir behind a nearby dam on the Ob River.

The main point of interest is the **open-air museum** (admission by invitation only), 4km along the Akedemgorodok–Klyuchi road. It contains ancient kameny baba, a brilliant Yakutian wooden church and a partly restored ostrog (military stockade) fortress. Sadly, like all the museums of Akademgorodok, access is officially by invitation only, though you can glimpse most of the points of interest by looking through the high gates. Several guided tours inexplicably elect to take tourists instead to the **Mineralogy Museum** (Musey Mineralagii; ☎ 33 28 37; ul Koptyuga; guided visit R100; open by arrangement), which, apart from the hilariously self-parodying guides, offers nothing you won't see in cheaper, easier to visit equivalents in Tyumen, Krasnoyarsk or Ulan Ude.

Beside the main Novosibirsk–Akademgorodok road, some 2km north of the latter, is a **Railway Museum** (admission free; open 11am-5pm Sat-Thur). Here, there are colourfully painted locomotives and carriages of assorted ages parked in sidings beside Seyatel, an elektrichka station. You can look at, but no longer climb aboard, the trains – too many drunk visitors were apparently dumping 'souvenirs' in the toilets!

TOMSK
ТОМСК

☎ 3822 • pop 473,000 • Moscow time plus 3 hours

Founded in 1604 and gearing up for big 400th anniversary celebrations, Tomsk, 267km northeast of Novosibirsk, is a delightful city combining endless examples of fine wooden mansions, some grand century-old commercial buildings and a dynamic, modern outlook. Tomsk's relatively intact architecture was in part preserved by a ghastly commercial miscalculation. The city fathers refused to have the Trans-Siberian Railway pass through, fearing noise, dirt and disruption. Instead they found economic isolation, and the once important trading centre dwindled. However, it was revived as a university city in the late 19th century and now has half a dozen major academic establishments – hence the youthful, intellectual atmosphere during term time (September to June).

Orientation & Information

The bus station and Tomsk 1 (main) train station sit together about 2.5km southeast of the centre. The main axis is prospekt Lenina, where you'll find many banks with ATMs and the **post office** (pr Lenina 95). The fairly hip Internet café **M@KDEL** (ul Yakovleva 2; open 24hrs) has Internet access for R20 per hour. To get there, take bus No 11 from the train station or bus No 8 from pr Lenina. You're very near when you see a brick water tower.

Accurate bus maps are sold at the news kiosk in the bus station. Excellent city maps are available from Hotel Sputnik's reception desk and at **Dom Knigi Bookshop** (pr Komsomolsky 49; open 10am-7pm Mon-Fri, 11am-6pm Sat-Sun).

Graft Tur (☎ 52 63 99, fax 52 82 59; ul Gagarina 35; e tour@graft.ru; open 10am-7pm Mon-Fri, 11am-5pm Sat), not far from Hotel Sibir, is a helpful tour agency, with English-speaking staff. **Tomskturist** (☎ 52 81 79; pr Lenina 59; e tatjana@tomskturist.ru; open 9am-7pm Mon-Fri, 11am-4pm Sat), in a lovely wooden house opposite the university, can arrange individual walking tours of the city, with English-, French- and German-speaking guides (R1000 per guide for four hours).

Things to See

Tomsk's greatest attraction is its 'wooden lace' architecture – the carved windows and

SIBERIA

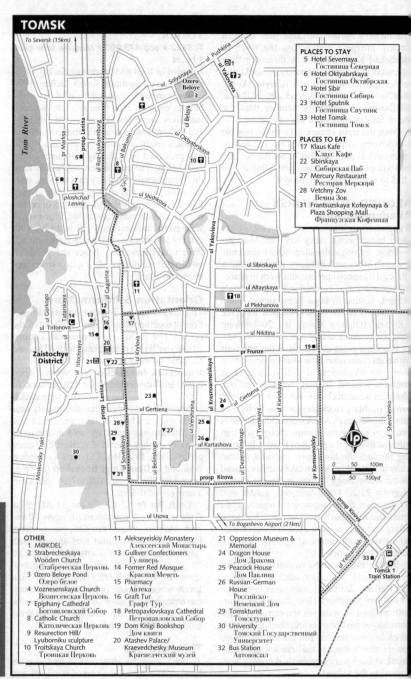

TOMSK

To Seversk (15km)

Tom River

ul Pushkina

ul Solyanaya

ul Yakovleva

Ozero
Beloye

ul Belaya

pr Marksa

prosp Lenina

ul Roz-Lyuksemburg

ul Bakunin

ul Oktyabrskaya

ploshchad
Lenina

ul Shishkova

ul Yakovleva

ul Sibirskaya

ul Altayskaya

ul Plekhanova

ul Gorkogo

Tatarskaya

ul Gagarina

ul Krylova

ul Nikitina

pr Frunze

ul Trifonova

ul Istochnaya

Zaistochye
District

prosp Lenina

ul Krasnoarmeiskaya

ul Vershinina

ul Gertsena

ul Gertsena

ul Kievskaya

ul Dezerzhinskogo

ul Tverskaya

ul Shevchenko

Moskovsky Trakt

ul Sovetskaya

ul Belinskogo

ul Kartashova

prosp Kirova

prosp Komsomolsky

pr Kirova

0   50   100m
0   50   100yd

ul Usova

To Bogashevo Airport (21km)

ul Yelizarovkh

Tomsk 1
Train Station

PLACES TO STAY

5 Hotel Severnaya
   Гостиница Северная
6 Hotel Oktyabrskaya
   Гостиница Октябрская
12 Hotel Sibir
   Гостиница Сибирь
23 Hotel Sputnik
   Гостиница Спутник
33 Hotel Tomsk
   Гостиница Томск

PLACES TO EAT

17 Klaus Kafe
   Клаус Кафе
22 Sibirskaya
   Сибирская Паб
27 Mercury Restaurant
   Ресторан Меркюри
28 Vetchny Zov
   Вечны Зов
31 Frantsuzskaya Kofeynaya &
   Plaza Shopping Mall
   Французская Кофейная

OTHER

1 M@KDEL
2 Strabrecheskaya
   Wooden Church
   Стабречевская Церковь
3 Ozero Beloye Pond
   Озеро белое
4 Voznesenskaya Church
   Вознесенская Церковь
7 Epiphany Cathedral
   Богоявленский Собор
8 Catholic Church
   Католическая Церковь
9 Resurection Hill/
   Lyuborniku sculpture
10 Troitskaya Church
   Троицкая Церковь
11 Alekseyeiskiy Monastery
   Алексеевский Монастырь
13 Gulliver Confectionery
   Гуливерь
14 Former Red Mosque
   Красная Мечеть
15 Pharmacy
   Аптека
16 Graft Tur
   Графт Тур
18 Petropavlovskaya Cathedral
   Петропавловский Собор
19 Dom Knigi Bookshop
   Дом книги
20 Atashev Palace/
   Kraevedchesky Museum
   Краеведческий музей
21 Oppression Museum &
   Memorial
24 Dragon House
   Дом Дракона
25 Peacock House
   Дом Павлина
26 Russian-German
   House
   Российско-
   Немецкий Дом
29 Tomskturist
   Томсктурист
30 University
   Томский Государственный
   Университет
32 Bus Station
   Автовокзал

racery on myriad old log-and-timber houses. Traditionally, these were left unpainted to show off the double coloured patterns created by using different woods. There's a notable concentration in the Zaistochye 'Tatar' district around the sad shell of a brick **red mosque** *(1904; ul Tatarskaya 4)*, which was sacrilegiously used as a vodka factory in the Soviet era. Access is via steps beside the lovely old house at prospekt Lenina 56, passing **Gulliver Confectioners** *(ul Trifonova 24)*, whose speciality is chocolate-covered dried pears at R29 per packet.

Grander, more showy wooden mansions stand along ulitsa Krasnoarmeiskaya, including the spired, bright turquoise **Russian-German House** *(1906; ul Krasnoarmeiskaya 71)*, the **Dragon House** *(ul Krasnoarmeiskaya 68)* and the fan-gabled **Peacock House** *(ul Krasnoarmeiskaya 67A)*.

Resurrection Hill is the bare site of the city's original fortress, which dates to 1604. From the hilltop viewpoint you can supposedly spot seven churches and cathedrals, but you may have to search the skyline a bit! There are plans to build a history museum on the site, but for now there's a fun sculpture, called **Lyuborniku**, of a panicked lover escaping through a window in his underwear.

For more atmosphere, take cobbled ulitsa Bakunin (named for a 19th-century anarchist) from the viewpoint past the renovated Catholic Church and walk up the street between wooden homes to the Gothic **Voznesenskaya Church**, with five gold-tipped black spires. The park, about 100m beyond, is home to the **Ozero Beloye pond**, and is popular for its beer-terraces and has horse-cart or sleigh rides according to the season.

Tomsk has plenty more to explore, and many more fine churches, including the 1911 **Petropavlovskaya Cathedral** *(ul Altayskaya 47)*, whose icon of St Nicholas works miracles for a donation. The grand 1784 **Epiphany Cathedral** *(pl Lenina)* and cute, wooden **Starorecheskaya Church** *(ul Yakovleva)* have both been recently renovated.

Prospekt Lenina South of ploshchad Lenina, prospekt Lenina sweeps through the appealing commercial district, most attractive between ulitsa Nakhanovicha and the the main university's leafy grounds. The grand 1842 ochre-and-white **Atashev Palace** *(pr Lenina 75)* was built for a gold miner, converted to a

church (hence the incongruous steeple tower) and now houses the **Kraevedchesky Museum** *(admission R15-30 per exhibition; 11am-6pm Tues-Sun)*, with limited displays.

The haunted brick building (built in 1898) opposite was closed as a church school following the murder of a pupil, becoming a prison for the NKVD (later the KGB). Descend into the building's eerie dungeon, now an **Oppression Museum** *(☎ 51 29 35; pr Lenina 44, rear entrance; open 10am-6pm Mon-Wed & Fri-Sat)*. Nearby, lighten the mood by peeping into the 1908 **pharmacy** *(aptek; pr Lenina 54; open 8am-8pm daily)*, which has an original, well-preserved Art Nouveau interior.

Places to Stay

Hotel Severnaya *(☎ 22 23 24; pr Lenina 86; dorm beds from R125, singles/doubles from R300/440)*, although unappealingly run-down, is often full.

Hotel Sibir *(☎/fax 22 64 52; pr Lenina 91; standard singles/doubles from R302/528)* is small, reasonably cosy and has a central if noisy position. Most *lyux* (luxury) rooms aren't worth the extra roubles, but beautifully rebuilt rooms at Nos 302, 402 and 409 are uniquely good value for R750. A good gift shop in the lobby sells birch-bark crafts and bargain *matryoshka* dolls.

Hotel Tomsk *(☎ 52 41 15; pr Kirova 65; singles/twins R500/600)* has comfortable rooms with hot shower, and a handy position opposite the bus and train stations. Staff will stamp visa registrations. Although it's a little inconvenient for the city centre, there are dozens of eating options and a nightclub within a stone's throw.

Hotel Oktyabrskaya *(☎ 51 21 51; ul Karla Marksa 12; singles from R600)* overlooks the river, near ploshchad Lenina. Its smart if unrenovated rooms are all en suite. There are virtually no doubles or twins.

Hotel Sputnik *(☎ 52 66 60; ul Belinskogo 15; singles/doubles R800/1120)* also has cheaper rooms without bathrooms.

Places to Eat

There are almost a dozen fast-food 'bistros' dotted about town, and more choices on and around prospekt Lenina than you can eat through in a week.

Klaus Kafe *(ul Plekhanova 11; meals R30-80; open 11am-midnight daily)* is a cutesy, kitsch little place specialising in fruity sundaes, and serving casked wine at R40 per glass.

Vetchny Zov *(☎ 23 41 67; ul Sovetskaya 47; bliny R17-160, mains R80-150; open 24hrs)* does great traditional Russian food and imaginative new variants. Its English-language menu includes elk cutlets, bear with foxberries and Casanova salad!

Mercury Restaurant *(☎ 52 73 93; ul Belinskogo 38; mains R70-200; open 6pm-midnight Mon-Sat & lunches winter only)* is a new, up-market place, but not as pricey as the dramatic nouveau-baronial interior would suggest.

Frantsuzskaya Kofeynaya *(pr Lenina 63; open 10am-2am daily)* is a decent coffeehouse on the bottom level of the Plaza shopping mall.

Sibirskaya *(☎ 53 00 47; ul Novosobornaya 2; mains R100-200, Guinness R140 per pint; open noon-3am daily)* is Tomsk's British pub, with international food, a menu in English and a family of welcoming photo-icons (Princess Di, Prince Charles, a red London bus). Weekend live music ranges from jazz-blues to heavy rock.

Getting There & Away
From Tomsk's **Bogashevo Airport** (22km southeast) there are two flights per day to Moscow (from R3100).

The No 037 train going to Moscow (Kazan Station/Kazansky vokzal) arrives in Omsk at 4.20am (R850, odd days). An overnight Krasnoyarsk-bound *platskartny*-only carriage (R225, 13 hours, odd days) is also attached to Novokuznetsk-bound train No 609. On even days there are direct trains to Abakan (24 hours) via Achinsk, and Barnaul (No 647, 15 hours).

For Novosibirsk, buses (R147, 5½ hours, eight daily) are more frequent and convenient than the poorly timed overnight trains; shared taxis (R300, 3½ hours) are faster than both. There are direct daily buses to Biysk (R350, 13 hours) departing at 8am; Barnaul (R200, nine to 10 hours), departing at 11.45am and 8.10pm; and Yarskoe (seven daily) via the village of Kolorovo (30 minutes), where there's an attractive old riverside church.

Getting Around
The very infrequent bus No 119 runs between ploshchad Lenina and the airport. From the train station, bus No 7 cuts along prospekt

Frunze, goes up prospekt Lenina, then east again on ulitsa Pushkina. Bus No 11 shows you the wooden houses along ulitsa Krasnoarmeiskaya, bus No 29 does the same for ulitsa Tatarskaya, while bus No 4 goes west from the train station and then runs north the length of prospekt Lenina. Bus No 40 goes to Seversk (or Tomsk 7), the secret nuclear city whose main monument is reportedly a Geiger counter. Don't imagine you can actually visit

Altay Republic & Altay Territory
Республика Алтай и Алтайский Край

Inhabited sparsely since Stone Age times 'Altay' straddles corners of Kazakhstan, Mongolia and China as well as southern Siberia. Within the Russian Federation it's divided administratively between the almost flat Altay Territory and the mountainous Altay Republic. The landscapes vary from steppe to taiga to glaciers to semidesert, with over 7000 lakes, many wild rivers and beautiful waterfalls. The jagged, permanently snowcapped southern mountains culminate in Siberia's highest peak, Mt Belukha (4506m), and since 1998 have been included on the Unesco list of natural World Heritage sites. The 19th-century Russian mystical artist Nikolay Rerikh painted the region obsessively and considered it one of the world's charmed places. His view is echoed by Russian New Age groups who call it *shambala* or *belovodie*, a source of great spiritual energy.

Of the Altay Republic's population of 200,000, the partly Christianised ethnic Altay people represent only about 30%, although they form majorities in certain villages such as Ulagan and Balyktuyul. In the Altay language, hello is *yakhshler*, thank you (very much) is *(dyan) biyan/biyan bolzyn* and beautiful is *charash*. Most Altay people are now village dwellers, but many homes still incorporate a traditional *ail* as an outhouse, extra room or summer kitchen. Altay tea is served milky: add *talkan*, a bran-rich flour, and it turns into a sort of porridge.

About 5% of Altay's population are Muslim ethnic Kazakhs. While they're keen on *koumys* (fermented mares milk) they don'

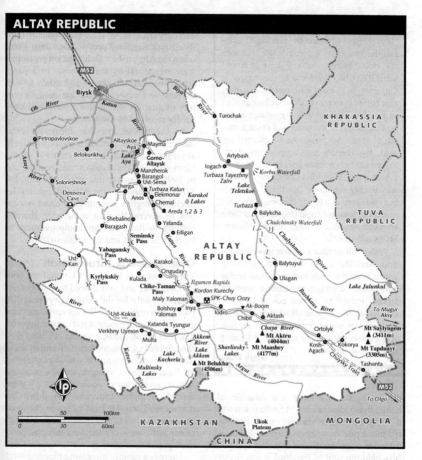

ALTAY REPUBLIC

generally drink vodka, making Kazakh settlements less hazardous at night than Altay ones! Some nomadic Kazakh herders still live in traditional felt yurts, notably south of Kosh-Agach. In the Kazakh language, hello is *salamat sizbe*, thank you is *rakhmat* and a handy term for yak meat is *sarlyk*.

The mainstays of Altay's rural economy are sheep, goats, cattle, yak, horses and Maral deer – bred for their aphrodisiac antlers. Altay is locally famous for honey (notably from Ust-Koksa), for Syrmak carpets and for herbal balms made from *zolotoy koren (Rhodiola rosea)*. The region's new boom is tourism.

History

Palaeolithic (Stone Age) finds at the Denisova and Ust-Kan caves and at Ulalinskaya Stoy-anka (an archaeological site near Gorno-Altaysk) show proto-human habitation of the region for 300,000 to one million years! Altay is dotted with *kurgans* (burial mounds) in which grave artefacts have been wonderfully preserved by rain or melting snow which seeped in, then froze, encasing them in ice for centuries. Such finds point to at least three separate Scytho-Siberian cultures existing in the 6th to 2nd centuries BC: Pazyryk (whose classic *kurgan* are 5km from Balyktuyul), Tuetka (on the Chuysky Trakt) and Ukok (high in the mountains near the Chinese border). A celebrated tattooed Ukok mummy is due to be returned to Gorno-Altaysk from St Petersburg in 2004.

There are many more *kurgan* from the later Turkic period (after the 6th century AD).

SIBERIA

Rural Rides

'Taxis?! Here? At five in the evening?!' To locals the idea seemed preposterous. But with rain clouds blotting out any sense of mountainscape, I had no desire to stay longer in Onguday. So I picked the nicest looking *magazin* (shop) in town, strode in looking as alien as possible, beamed a few greetings in the best Russian I could muster and made a couple of token purchases. As I explained my plan, the friendly blue-aproned assistants looked aghast – nobody goes to Aktash in the evening! It's 160km! But I persisted. I knew it was terribly expensive (for them, anyway), but I was prepared to pay the necessary 1000 roubles as long as I could stop here and there en route. Any ideas? '1000 roubles? Hmmm. That's different.'

Within half an hour a car was revving at the door and the driver appeared graciously sober. Even the burly-looking fellow beside him looked much less threatening when he smiled. Indeed he turned out to be none other than the amiable director of the local museum. He would come along for the ride and explain some Altay history – if I didn't mind. Wow, bingo!

Mark Elliot

★★★★★★★★★★★★★★★★★★★

Archaeologists find these less valuable, although those like the ones at Shiba (6km west of Tuetka) are more visually impressive (but still just a pile of stones!). Originally carved in human form holding a cup that symbolically held the soul of the dead, a few mysterious *kameny baba* (standing stone idols), most accessibly near the Chuysky Trakt, have avoided being carted off to museums. There are also many groups of petroglyphs (rock drawings) of debatable origin, but these fascinating albeit faint scratches are easy to miss even when you're staring right at them!

From 1635 the Altay nation was under the rule of the Dzhungarians (Oyrats) from western Mongolia. Meanwhile, advancing Russia protected its new border with fortresses such as those at Biysk and Kuznetsk, behind which the Demidov clan expanded its metallurgical empire. In these new Russian lands (known as the Altay Territory) they opened copper mines and smelters at Kolyvan in 1725 and Ust-Barnaulskaya (now Barnaul) in 1730–44. These became so profitable that in

1747 the tsars nationalised the whole Altay Territory (ie, grabbed it for the Romanov family). Biysk remained prey to raids until 1756, when the Altay tribe's Dzhungarian protectors were wiped out by the Chinese. In a panic Altay switched allegiance and asked to join the Russian Empire, a move that caused a century of quarrels with China which were only finally resolved in 1864.

In the Soviet era that formerly semi-independent state remained administratively separate from the Altay Territory as the Gorno-Altayskaya Autonomous region, and in 1991 it became a full republic within the Russian Federation (the Altay Republic). Its liberal tax regime has attracted paper relocation of several Russian companies, thereby helping to fund the rapid improvement in tourism facilities and road infrastructure.

Orientation & Information

The old areas of Biysk and Barnaul are both worth a look, and you'll need to visit Gorno-Altaysk if only for the compulsory Altay Republic visa registration. But the real attractions are the lakes and mountains. For relaxing with a beer at sunset the best choice is Lake Teletskoe, touted as a 'second Baikal' and in some ways more picturesque. If you want glimpses of local culture, rugged valleys, varying scenery and plenty of ancient stones it's quite feasible to potter independently down the memorable Chuysky Trakt by bus or chartered Lada (see the boxed text 'Rural Rides'). To get closer to the snow-crested mountaintops, however, you'll have to hike.

There is a rapidly increasing range of rural accommodation, but don't get over excited: beyond a few top places in Chemal, Artybash and Aya village, showers and sit-down toilets remain virtually unimagined luxuries.

Maps Decent 1:500,000 maps of the Altay Republic are sold in Biysk. More detailed 1:200,000 (1cm:2km) maps of parts of the Altay are sold at Dom Knigi Bookshop in Novosibirsk (see that section), but ask for them specifically as they're not on show. The Vysotnik Turbaza in Tyungur sells a 1:100,000 topographic hiking map of the Belukha area.

Hiking & Horse Riding

Popular hiking destinations include the numerous groups of small mountain lakes (such as Multinsky, Shavlinsky, Karakol and Akkem), beautifully framing views of higher peaks. Beware that compared to Nepal or New Zealand, hiking in Altay can be a pretty strenuous and largely self-sufficient experience. Even on popular trails there are usually no villages or teahouses en route and although there are some wilderness huts and *zimniks* (winter refuge huts), you'll generally need to be fully equipped with tent, sleeping bag and all provisions. However, several agencies (notably Sibalp in Novosibirsk, Sputnik-Altay in Barnaul and **Lenalpturs** (☎ 812-279 0716, fax 279 0651; **e** *info@ russia-climbing.com*) in St Petersburg/Tyungur) can arrange everything for you, including base camps with cooks waiting, and save you time by jolting you through the duller forested foothills by jeep, 4WD or even by raft. It's best to make arrangements well in advance.

Tyungur, the tiny but tourist-focussed hiking centre for the Mt Belukha area, is one place where you have a decent chance of finding guides, renting tents and equipment and organising a trip without much preparation. As an alternative to hiking, a do-it-yourself horse trip will cost a typical R300 per horse per day, but factor in extra horses for your guides and baggage, plus an extra payment for their return if you're planning on only walking 'one way'.

Note that some local guides seem to see hiking as a masochistic A-to-B slog rather than a pleasure, and their calculation of journey times may be based on a gruellingly arduous pace. Be prepared to take longer. Especially in the peak July/early August period cloud can suddenly hide the views and rain can wash away the trails, possibly adding days to your trek. Leave plenty of time and don't hike without a guide unless you're very experienced.

Rafting

Altay offers all grades of white-water rafting. A two-hour fun-splash (R150 per person) down the Katun River from Manzherok is easy to arrange one day in advance at Turbaza Katun and at several places around Aya Bridge (see the Along the Katun River to Chemal section). Rafting from Tyungur to Lake Akkem is easy to arrange, too, but going beyond to Inya or rafting the Ilgumen rapids both take several days and require experience (grades 4 to 5), support and good equipment.

Rafting the fiendishly difficult Chulyshman River is a full-blown expedition; talk to staff at K2 Adventures in Omsk or Altour in Barnaul (see those sections for details).

BARNAUL
БАРНАУЛ
☎ 3852 • pop 575,000 • Moscow time plus 3 hours

Almost since its foundation in 1730 (as Ust-Barnaulskaya) Barnaul has been a prosperous industrial city. It has great cafés, good museums, a fair sprinkling of historic buildings and, though far from the mountains, hosts the nearest major airport to the Altay Republic.

Orientation & Information

Prospekt Lenina runs 8km northwest from the river station through ploshchads Sovetov and Oktyabrya. It's paralleled by Sotsialisticheskiy prospekt and Krasnoarmeyskiy prospekt, which almost converge at ploshchad Pobedy, behind whose large war memorial are both the bus and train stations.

The **post office** (*pr Lenina 54; open 8am-7pm daily*), at ploshchad Sovetov, has an Internet room around the back. Web access is also available at **Amitel** (*pr Lenina 53*) and **Nikolsky** (*ul Chkalova 57A; open 21hrs 10am-7am daily*), beside Hotel Rus, which charges R26 per hour.

Maps of bus and tram routes (R15) are sold at the train station, but are cheaper at **Penaty Bookshop** (*pr Lenina 85*), which stocks good city and regional maps, Altay atlases and picture books. **Ekstrim** (*Komsomolskiy pr 75; open 9am-7pm daily*) sells good climbing, fishing, camping and mountain-bike gear.

Sputnik-Altay (☎ 36 77 50, fax 36 72 75; **w** *http://arw.dcn-asu.ru/~sputnik; 2nd floor, Sotsialisticheskiy pr 87; open 9am-1pm & 2pm-6pm Mon-Fri*) is a highly professional, well-connected specialist travel agency for the Altay. It can book accommodation, slot you into good-value Altay tours or arrange tailor-made excursions. Marina speaks good English.

The white-water-rafting specialist **Altour** (☎ 23 16 98, fax 23 03 69; **w** *www.rafting .barnaul.ru/english; apartment 138, ul Chkalova 89*) has its office hidden in an unlikely concrete apartment block.

Things to See

It's pleasant to stroll the varied, tree-shaded southern end of prospekt Lenina. Climb the

SIBERIA

BARNAUL

PLACES TO STAY & EAT	OTHER

PLACES TO STAY & EAT

9 Hotel Barnaul
   Гостиница Барнаул
10 U Matryony
   У Матрёны
11 Hotel Kolos
   Гостиница Колос
14 Hotel Tsentralnaya
   Гостиница
   Центральная
17 Granmulino
19 Hotel Rus; Nikolskiy
   Гостиница Рус
   Никольский
21 Rok'n'Roll
   Рок и Рол
23 Hotel Altay
   Гостиница Алтай
25 Imperator (Ruski Chai)
   Император

OTHER

1 Art Gallery
2 Art Gallery
3 Art Gallery
4 Art Gallery
5 Aerokassa
   Центральное Агенство
   воздушных
6 Penaty Bookshop
   Пенаты
7 Bus Station
   Автовокзал
8 War Memorial
   Памятник Войны
12 Ekstrim
   Экстрим
13 Main Post Office
   Почтамт
15 Amitel
   Клуб
16 Sputnik-Altay
   Спутник-Алтай
18 Nikolskiy Church
   Никольский Храм
20 Altour
   Алтур
22 Lenin the Toreador
   Памятник Ленину
24 Pokrovskoe Cathedral
   Покровское Собор
26 Obelisk
   Площадь Демидов
27 Kraevedchesky Museum
   Краеведческий музей
28 Philharmonia
   Филармония
29 Altay Art & Literature Museum
   Музей Истории Литературы
   Искусства и Культуры Алтая
30 River Station
   Речной вокзал
31 BARNAUL Sign
   барнаул

SIBERIA

hill of a former celebrity-graveyard (end of Sotsialisticheskiy prospekt) for great river views over the gigantic Hollywood-sized БАРНАУЛ **(Barnaul) sign**. Heading north along prospekt Lenina, you'll pass an amusing cloak-throwing **statue** of Lenin as a *toreador* (bullfighter), lurking in the trees, and the brick **Nikolskii Church** *(1904; pr Lenina)*, which has recently been re-spired. Further on, around ploshchad Oktyabrya, are several **art galleries** *(pr Lenina 84, 105 & 111)*, but the best collection is at No 88.

Classical ploshchad Demidov around an 1825 **obelisk** (still bullet pocked from a 1918 skirmish) was once exaggeratedly dubbed a 'slice of St Petersburg'. Now the slice is itself sliced in half by the tram tracks of Krasnoarmeiskiy prospekt, but, at the time of writing, the **almshouses** on its eastern flank were undergoing painstaking renovations. A construction boom is nibbling away the last pockets of attractive wooden architecture, but some examples remain, including on ulitsa Nikitina (either side of Krasnoarmeiskaya prospekt). The bulbous-domed, brick **Pokrovskoe Cathedral** *(ul Nikitina 135-7)* is the most appealing of the city's many churches and has a fine, gilded interior.

Fronted by artillery-pieces opposite the sadly dilapidated Philharmonia, the **Kraevedchesky Museum** *(ul Polzunova; open 10am-4pm Wed-Sun)*, between Krasnoarmeyskaya prospekt and prospekt Lenina, is Siberia's oldest museum. To its east is the impressive **Altay Art & Literature Museum** *(ul Tolstogo 2; admission R20; open 10am-6pm daily)*, occupying a restored, furnished 1850s mansion.

Places to Stay & Eat

The train station has decent **resting rooms** *(komnaty otdykha; beds in doubles/quads per 12 hrs R157/136, 24hrs R283.50/236.25)*, with clean, shared hot showers.

Hotel Altay *(☎ 23 92 47; pr Lenina 24; singles/twins R200/300, suites R1000)*, near the Lenin statue, has a slightly musty early-Stalinist grandeur. Basic rooms have phone and fridge but shared bathrooms. Its suites have private showers with water heaters.

Hotel Tsentralnaya *(☎ 36 84 39; pr Lenina 57; singles without bathroom R190, singles/twins R320/460, suites up to R2100)*, on ploshchad Sovetov, is a decently renovated Soviet-era tower.

Overpriced in comparison are the unappealing **Hotel Barnaul** *(☎ 62 62 22; pl Pobedy 3; singles/twins R450/500)*, and the marginally better **Hotel Kolos** *(☎ 22 86 05; ul Molodozhnaya 25; singles/twins R292/376)*, with very cramped rooms. Both are near the train station.

Hotel Rus *(☎ 35 43 82; 2nd floor, ul Chkalova 57A; singles/twins/triples R352/300/378)* is a small, new hotel, which has rooms with private bathroom. It's central and great value but often full. It's easy to miss – enter by a small door beside the Traktir Nikolskiy restaurant and Internet café, then go upstairs.

There are dozens of appealing eateries with several summer terraces along prospekt Lenina. Elsewhere, **Imperator** *(aka Ruski Chai; Krasnoarmeiskiy pr 131; open 2pm-2am daily)* occupies a magnificent old wooden-lace building.

Rok'n'Roll *(ul Anatoliya 68; meals R40-80; open 9am-11pm daily)*, visible from Hotel Altay, is Barnaul's hip answer to the Hard Rock Café, with menu items named using Beatles lyrics.

U Matryony *(☎ 62 46 07; Krasnoarmeiskiy pr 131; mains 25-105; open 10am-11pm daily)* has a pseudo-cottage interior and serves great bliny (R7 to R40).

Granmulino *(☎ 36 36 00; ul Peschanaya 83; breakfast from R50; open 24hrs)*, a stylishly modern café, is *the* place for real espresso (R25) and tiramisu (R70).

Getting There & Away

The site of reported UFO landings in January 2001, Barnaul's airport is in the city's northwestern suburbs. There are flights to Moscow (R3200 to R4930, daily), Krasnoyarsk (R2450, three weekly), Vladivostok (from R5500, weekly) via Irkutsk, and Kyzyl (R2800) at 4am. Air tickets from both Barnaul and Novosibirsk's Tolmachyovo airport (much wider choice) can be purchased from the main **Aerokassa** *(☎ 36 81 81; ul Sovetskaya 4; open 8am-7pm daily)*. Bus no 112 to the airport leaves outside and the Aerokassa can organise R300 per passenger car transfers direct to Tolmachyovo.

Trains leave daily to Moscow (Kazan Station/Kazansky vokzal, 60 hours), Krasnoyarsk (23 hours) and Almaty in Kazakhstan (32 hours), on even days for Tomsk and Novokuznetsk, and on Friday and Sunday only for Bishkek in Kyrgyzstan.

SIBERIA

Buses are more convenient for Biysk (R95, 3½ hours, one to two per hour) and Novosibirsk (R125, five to six hours, 20 daily), while for twice the price, shared taxis take half the time. There are also direct buses to Gorno-Altaysk (R152, 6 hours, five daily), Belokurikha (R153, 5½ hours, six daily) and Chemal (R204, seven hours, daily).

From the river station at the southern end of prospekt Lenina, river boats serve only local destinations, such as Bobrovka (R25, two hours, three per day Monday to Friday, seven per day Saturday and Sunday), Rassakazikha (R30, 2½ hours, one per day Monday to Friday, three Saturday and Sunday) and Kokuiskoe (R35, three hours, weekends according to demand).

Getting Around

From the *rechnoy vokzal* (river station) the infrequent bus No 144 serves the airport; the frequent buses Nos 1 and 10 go straight up prospekt Lenina; and handy bus No 43 swings past ploshchad Demidov, turns north up Krasnoarmeiskaya prospekt, then passes ploshchad Pobedy for the stations before rejoining prospekt Lenina at ploshchad Oktyabrya.

BIYSK
БИЙСК
☎ 3854 • pop 236,000 • Moscow time plus 3 hours

Biysk, 160km southeast of Barnaul, is the nearest railhead to the Altay Mountains and, like Barnaul, is a place you may need to change transportation on the way to/from the mountains.

In 1709, 70 Russian soldiers with five cannons built a fort at the junction of the Biya and Katun Rivers. This didn't impress the Dzhungarian Mongols, who sent 3000 men to burn it down. Biysk was re-established 20km to the east in 1718, and after the peace of 1756, was rapidly developed as a prosperous trade entrepot protected by a big, Vauban-style star-shaped fortress.

Today, the small but impressive old town at the eastern end of ulitsa Tolstogo is hidden behind a vast, unprepossessing curtain of Soviet-era concrete. Nonetheless, if you have an hour or two between transport connections hop on an eastbound bus No 23 or 35 to see the grand 1916 **theatre** (*ul Sovetskaya 25*), the five-domed **Uspenskaya Church** (*ul Sovetskaya 13*) and the excellent **museum**

(*ul Lenina 134; open 10am-4.30pm Tues-Sat*), housed in a great 1912 Art Nouveau merchant's house with original fittings.

Sberbank (*ul Lenina 244; open 9am-1pm & 2pm-7pm Mon-Sat*) changes money. **Dom Knigi Bookshop** (*ul Lenina 246; open 10am-6.30pm Mon-Sat*) sells maps and Altay photobooks, including Viktor Sadchikov's bilingual *Biysk*. The helpful **travel agency** (☎ 22 75 84; e *zlatogor@mail.ru*), attached to Hotel Tsentralnaya, has at least one English speaker, sells air tickets and can advise you on accommodation options and tours in the Altay Republic.

Hotel Tsentralnaya (☎ 22 83 07; *basic singles/twins R220/360, R350/500*) has a selection of decent rooms with private bathroom and cheaper unrenovated ones. It's three stops east of the two stations by tram No 1 or 3.

Hotel Khimnik (aka *Polieks*; ☎ 23 64 40; *pl 9i Yanvara 3; doubles/twins from R300/400, lyux rooms R450-600*) has good-value *lyux* rooms but is inconveniently far from the old town. To get there, catch a westbound bus No 23.

The Hotel Tsentralnaya has a good supermarket in the basement and is surrounded by summer cafés. Diagonally across the road, **Kalinka** (*Krasnoarmeiskaya ul 81*) shop has a stylish but good value restaurant and a currency exchange booth.

The bus and train stations face each other across a large square at the north end of ulitsa Mitrofanova, 2km east of the Hotel Tsentralnaya, 4km from the historic centre. There is a useful overnight train to Novosibirsk (11 hours). Buses leave frequently to Gorno-Altaysk (2½ hours, last at 8pm), Barnaul (R95, 3½ hours, last at 7.30pm) and Belokurikha (R56, two hours, last at 6.40pm), though shared taxis are much faster. Handy if slow daily buses to Novokuznetsk (R148, six to seven hours, four each morning) are the best option for connecting to the overnight train to Abakan. The 3.10pm daily bus to Turochak (six hours) offers the first leg of an alternative route to Artybash on Lake Teletskoe, but you'll be stuck in Turochak for one night en route.

BELOKURIKHA
БЕЛОКУРИХА
☎ 38577 • pop 18,000 • Moscow time plus 3 hours

Ski resort in winter, health spa in summer, a reputation for illicit sexual encounters and an almost 100% occupancy rate in the 5000-plus expensive hotel/sanatorium rooms – with such an image one expects Belokurikha to be more interesting than the drab straggle of concrete blocks that is the reality. The forested valley and streamside footpaths at the western end of ulitsa Myasnikova/ Slavskogo are pleasant enough. It may be worth a day trip from Biysk, 75km to the north, to see locals at play among street artists, candy floss and stuffed bears on wheels.

GORNO-ALTAYSK & MAYMA
ГОРНО-АЛТАЙСК И МАЙМА
☎ 38541 • pop 48,000

The capital of the Altay Republic mars a once attractive narrow valley with its uninspired Soviet-era concrete edifices. Straggling 7km to Mayma (an officially separate appendage on the M52), the main street is prospekt Kommunistecheskiy, paralleled for 2km in the city centre by ulitsa Churos Gurkina. The bus station is between the two, 1500m west of the main square (officially ulitsa Palkina) with its Lenin statue and the miserable Hotel Gorny Altay.

Before heading elsewhere in the Altay Republic you should register your visa and list your planned destinations at the office of **MVD** (☎ 6 20 12; pr Kommunistecheskiy 95; open 8am-1pm & 2pm-5pm Mon-Fri). Enter through the door marked 'Автоколонна 1931', climb to the top floor, and it's the first door on the left. No English is spoken but the staff are helpful, and the procedure should take only 15 minutes. From the bus station, it's four stops on any west-bound bus; hop off at the Zhil Masif bus stop.

Sberbank (ul Churos Gurkina 13; open 9am-4pm daily) changes dollars, euros and Kazakhstan tenge, and has a 24-hour ATM. Near the bus station is a **post office** (pr Kommunistecheskiy 61; open 9am-6pm Mon-Fri), with two Internet-linked computers charging R42 per hour.

The star attraction of the interesting **Regional Museum** (Kraevedchesky muzey; ☎ 2 78 75; ul Churos Gurkina 46; admission R15; open 10am-4.30pm Wed-Sun) is a reconstructed 2000-year-old Pazyryk grave pit. In the top-floor art gallery, view some fine Rerikh canvasses and discover that Churos Gurkin was no talentless artist.

Places to Stay & Eat
Turbaza Stanitsya Yunkh Turistov (☎ 2 61 81; ul Zarechnaya 1; dorm beds R40) is cheap,

peacefully situated and a good option – if you're happy to use the river as a bath. There is a shared kitchen for use by guests. To get there from behind the bus station, follow the tiny lane between the Dom Obuvi shop and ulitsa Choros Gurkina 77 to the river, take the narrow riverside path five minutes to the right, cross the rickety footbridge and then double back through a row of garages to the end of the track.

Hotel Gorno Altaiavtodor (☎ 6 22 56; 4th floor, pr Kommunistecheskiy 182; beds R180) is a clean, new place with good, hot shared showers. It's above government offices opposite Kunbadysh Market, one bus stop west of the MVD visa office. Ring the entry-phone buzzer at the rear door and say 'Gastinitsa' (which means 'hotel').

Hotel Gorny Altay (☎ 9 50 86; ul Palkina 5; dorm beds/singles/twins R119/320/333) is a rotting establishment and should only be a last resort. It's a 20-minute walk up prospekt Kommunistecheskiy from the bus station, on the main square facing a park; Lenin points to its door.

In Mayma, there's a comfortable two-room **hotel** (gastinitsa; ☎ 2 28 86; behind ul Lenina 5; singles/twins R300/460), across from the market, with shared hot showers and sit-down toilets. It's above a hidden half-brick building through black metal gates.

Ul Sur (lower level, ul Choros Gurkina 50; meals R20; open noon-10pm daily) serves some Altay traditional foods, such as kochu (bland mutton and barley stew), washed down with strident, part-fermented chegen (sour milk; R5 per glass).

Kafe Natalya (☎ 2 43 93; ul Churos Gurkina 30; meals R30-60, cover charge R20 from 7.30pm; open 10am-11pm daily), a cosy, brasserie-style eatery, is Gorno-Altaysk's nicest. Delicious point-and-pick dishes include Ossetian chicken with garlic paporotnik (Siberian fern shoots).

Kafe Pristen (☎ 2 28 75; ul Lenina 62; mains R25-75, cover charge R30 from 9pm; open 11am-3am daily) is in Mayma, 2km south of the market. It serves a good, cheesey Myaso po Sibirski (beef topped with cheese) at heavy wooden bench tables overlooked by hunting trophies.

Getting There & Away
There is no railway, but a useful booth within the bus station allows you to pre-book train

trips, including the popular overnight Biysk–Novosibirsk service. Buses serve most main Altay villages at least daily (including Aktash at 7.10am and 10.40am, Ust-Koksa at 7.20am, Onguday at 3.30pm and Ust-Kan at 1.05pm), with additional shared taxis/ minibuses leaving for most destinations before 7am. Buses to Barnaul (R152, six hours, five daily) and Biysk (2½ hours, nine daily) take twice as long as shared taxis, but cost half the price. Chartering your own taxi is generally much cheaper from the Mayma market (eg, R60 to Lake Aya versus R200 from Gorno-Altaysk!). For helicopter rentals call **Narz-Altay-Avia** (☎ *38844-2 21 73*).

Getting Around

From the bus station any eastbound city bus will pass the Hotel Gorny Altay, while any westbound bus will pass the MVD office and Hotel Gorno Altaiavtodor. The frequent bus No 101 (R8) terminates at Mayma market, where buses 102 and 117 (also R8) turn south and continue via the Kafe Pristen.

LAKE TELETSKOE & ARTYBASH
ОЗЕРО ТЕЛЕЦКОЕ И АРТЫБАШ
☎ 38843 ● pop 4500

Deep, delightful Lake Teletskoe is Altay's serene answer to Lake Baikal, a great place to simply relax and breath. Ridge after forested ridge unfolds as you scuttle along on one of the myriad little pleasure boats that buzz out of Artybash village, the lake's sleepy but surprisingly artistic tourist hub. Horse rental is easy to arrange and scuba rental is possible at Pensionate Edem. If you don't want to charter your own boat you can take the tourist ferry to the 12m **Korbu Waterfall** from the *turbaza* jetty (R180, four hours return), with departures at 10am and 3pm daily, weather permitting.

Reaching the phenomenal 160m **Chulchinsky Waterfall**, well beyond the lake's southern end, is a much greater boat-and-trek adventure. Death-defying rafting down the Chulyshman River to this point requires a helicopter drop-off, bags of experience and some very professional backup as this is one of the world's great white-water challenges.

Places to Stay & Eat

The villages of Artybash and Iogach face each other across a bridge that marks the lake's westernmost extent.

In Iogach, the fifth house down ulitsa Naberezhnaya from the bridge, is **Hotel Tay-ozhnaya** (☎ *2 74 45; beds R150-250*), where some attractive new rooms have lake views and all share a bearable outside toilet. Pay R100 extra to use the sauna/bathhouse.

However, most accommodation is on the Artybash side. In the main village many cottages rent good-value, lakeside rooms: look for signs marked 'Слаю Дом' and 'Сдаётся Дом' (house for rent), notably along ulitsa Teletskaya, eg, at Nos 30, 32, 59, 95, 101 and 103. All charge around R150 per person, though especially at weekends many want a minimum group of three to six people.

Stary Zamok (☎ *2 64 60; doubles R1000-1200*), farther down ulitsa Teletskaya in a kitschy little 'castle', is the village's best-value upmarket accommodation. The pricier rooms have private bathroom with hot shower, and shared terrace, sitting and dining room. Three meals per day cost an extra R450.

A 10-minute walk beyond just where Artybash officially ends, huts start to multiply. **Pensionat Edem** (☎ *2 64 34; doubles/twins R1000/1400*) is popular, but is set back from the lake without views. Rates include half-board.

Turbaza Zolotoe Ozera (☎ *2 64 40; beds R120-250 June & Sept, R170-300 July & Aug*), about 3km east of the bridge, is big, institutional and not very appealing, but it has hundreds of rooms, is handy for the main jetty and has a reasonable **restaurant** (*mains R43-72; open noon-2am daily*), which serves lake fish.

Beyond Turbaza Zolotoe Ozera, a wide grassy camping area gets very noisy on weekends. There are more huts here, including the cheap if cheerless **Gorizont** (*dorm beds from R95, quads from R400*). A 10-minute walk from here you'll find more peaceful places such as **Blinovy** (☎ *2 64 75; doubles R500*), offering shared huts with washbasin, toilet and nonlockable doors.

There are two *turbaza* farther down the lake, only accessible by boat, though these are easily chartered from Artybash or Iogach.

Getting There & Away

The direct bus from Gorno-Altaysk (R86, 2½ hours), departing at 1.10pm, arrives in Artybash around the same time as the 11am service, which makes a long detour to Turochak. Buses and faster shared taxis returning to Gorno-Altaysk have all left Artybash by 8am, though hitching is possible. From the southern end of the lake, reached by chartered boat from Artybash (or by semi-regular mini-ferry some Thursdays), it's a hitch by truck or 4WD, or a five-day hike to Balyktuyul, north of Aktash on the Chuysky Trakt. Or you could hike to Edigan, south of Chemal, as described in Lonely Planet's *Trekking in Russia & Central Asia*.

ALONG THE KATUN RIVER TO CHEMAL

Riverside camping grounds, *turbaza* and hotels are mushrooming along the Katun River between Gorno-Altaysk and Chemal. Although scenery is much less spectacular than that of the southern Chusky Trakt, this touristy area is pleasant enough for a night's journey break with lots of accommodation that is comfy by Siberian standards. Despite pretty, rocky river banks, **Aya** is rather overdeveloped and its popular but pitiful little lake is not worth the diversion. Nonetheless, Aya Most (the village's access bridge) along with the institutional **Turbaza Katun** are the easiest places to sign up for a quick dose of **white-water rafting** (R150 per person for two hours, R430 for seven hours) without much pre-arrangement. **Manzherok** is surrounded by pine woods and there's an easy short hike to a small, swimmable lake via Ozernoe (2km southeast). At the roadside some 9km south of Manzherok village, **Arzhaan Suu** is a gushing cold-water spring at the roadside, shrouded in souvenir sellers during summer. At **Barangol**, the riverside café of **Tsarskaya Okhota** is appealing if often crowded and from here you could cross the long suspension bridge and hike 3km to a waterfall. At **Ust-Sema**, the Chuysky Trakt (see later in this section) diverges from the Katun River. Dominated by cliffs, attractive **Anos** village remains unspoilt, thanks to its position across the Katun from the Chemal road. Easiest access is via a pedestrian-only suspension bridge. Nearby **Elekmonar** is the starting point for multiday hikes or horse rides to the attractive **Karakol Lakes** amid picturesque bald mountaintops.

Chemal is a fairly cute if oversized village with a couple of 'museum yurts', a sweet little church and the picturesque wooden chapel of the **Ioanno Bogoslavski convent** (*admission by donation; open 7am-10am & 4pm-6.30pm daily*). Rebuilt in 2000–01 to the original 1849 design, the chapel is reached by a dizzying suspension footbridge across the swirling waters of a small river canyon.

Places to Stay

The greatest concentration of accommodation is around Aya Bridge, a curious narrow toll-bridge, across which it's a 3km detour to Aya village, where many cottage owners rent **private rooms**.

The tiny, laughably dull Lake Aya has a musty, package-tour-style **hotel** (*rooms from R1050*), each of its rooms with private bathrooms.

Every kilometre or two south of Aya Bridge you'll find more resorts, including the comfortable **Avrora** (☎ 38844-2 43 88; km 461; doubles from R1400) and the associated no-frills **Turbaza Bars** (km 465; hut twins R200) in an attractive river bend.

About 800m beyond a riverside bust of Siberian engineer Vyacheslav Shushkov, **Turkomplex Manzherok** (☎ 38844-2 43 99; km 469; hut beds from R125, doubles from R500) sits behind a mock-Cossack stockade in a pine grove by the Katun. Its good-value doubles have private shower and toilet.

In Barangol, **Tsarskaya Okhota** (☎ 38844-2 64 10; e ram@alt.ru; basic hut beds from R485, double cottages with private bathroom R2990) has an eye-catching, castle-style entrance but the accommodation is steeply overpriced and inadequately maintained.

The only accommodation in Anos is the Sibalp-run **guesthouse** (☎ 3832-46 31 91; e sibalp@online.nsk.su; beds R170), which is a real bargain. It's mostly reserved for groups, so bookings are essential.

Many homes in Elekmonar and especially Chemal rent private rooms (from R150 per person). The travel agency **Sibir-Altay travel agency** (☎ 03832 18 44 85; ul Frunze 5, Novosibirsk) has a catalogue featuring two dozen such cottages which can be booked outright. Or for similar cottages surf to the Russian-only site w www.zel-dom.narod.ru. Chemal also has several more luxurious hotels. At the northern edge of the village near the river is the good-value **Hotel Chemal** (☎ 38841-2 23 45; ul Naberezhnaya 9; beds from R200 with shared hot shower, lyux doubles with private bathroom R1800).

There are three more hotels in a wooded valley 6km south of Chemal and all are, helpfully, named Areda. The first you'll come to

SIBERIA

is the family-run **Areda 3** (☎ *38841-2 21 22; twins/doubles R2000/2500)*, with splendid suites, huge beds, modern bathrooms and nice river views, plus a stylishly cosy bar. Beyond, the slightly older **Areda 2**, with less appealing double rooms and apartments, **Areda 1** (☎ *38 841-2 21 32;* e *kokstravel@alt.ru; doubles from R1600)* is professionally run but larger and more impersonal than Areda 3.

If you have no accommodation booked the best way to find somewhere that has space yet suits your taste and budget is to charter a taxi/ private car at Mayma market and check out the myriad, ever-multiplying options for yourself.

With stops, reckon on R60 to R100 to the Lake Aya area, R250 as far as Ust-Sema, and R400 to Chemal. You'll pay much more from Gorno-Altaysk.

Getting There & Away

A private bus from Novosibirsk direct to Tur-baza Katun (R490/600 one-way/return), 7km north of Anos, departs at 11.30pm Thursday and Saturday, returning at 11am Friday and Sunday. Tickets are sold at **Sibir Altay** *(office 515, 5th floor, ul Frunze 5; open 10am-6pm Mon-Fri, 11am-3pm Sat)*, and the buses leave from outside the agency.

There are also buses to Chemal from Bar-naul (R204, seven hours) at 7.40am daily, Biysk (4½ hours) at 10.30am and 3.20pm daily and Gorno-Altaysk (two hours) at 1.35pm and 6.40pm daily. For Mayma and the northern section of the route as far as Ust-Sema you can also use any of the Chuysky Trakt buses (see that section, later)

CHUYSKY TRAKT
ЧУЙСКИЙ ТРАКТ

South of Ust-Sema, the dramatic and now well-paved Chuysky Trakt (M52) is a scenic kaleidoscope of passes, canyons and mountain vistas leading eventually to peak-rimmed steppeland dotted with Kazakh yurts. Plans are mooted to open the Mongolian frontier beyond Tashanta in 2004, but for now only local citizens can cross here.

The large village of **Onguday** (literally '10 gods' for the 10 surrounding peaks) is a possible base for visiting the *kurgans* at Karakol, Tuetka and Shiba. To Onguday's northwest, a dead end side road to **Kulada village** passes through **Bichiktu-Boom** (with some traditional tepee-shaped Altay *ails*) and an attractive valley which offers hiking and

free-camping possibilities. **Kulada** itself is built around a rocky knob and is a holy place in Burkhanism, a curious Altay religion founded in 1904 by shepherd Chet Chelpan, fusing Orthodox Christianity, Buddhism and folk traditions. Banned by the communists in 1933, the religion is now almost extinct. Southeast of Onguday the Chuysky Trakt crosses the beautiful, serpentine **Chike-Taman Pass**, descends close to the Ilgumen rapids and passes through **Maly Yaloman**, whose microclimate allows local villagers to grow cherries, apples and naughty weeds. Around **Bolshoi Yaloman**, 12km up a rough side track, are said to be several *kameny baba*. A faceless but much more accessible trio stand right beside the Trakt just beyond the southern end of **Inya** village.

Ringed by a low wall beside the slip road for the SPK-Chuy Oozy restaurant (see later in this section) at km 714 is a very accessible group of petroglyphs, though you'll have to look very carefully to pick out the lightly scored little antelope figures. There's another group at Kalbak Tash crag, a five-minute walk north of km 721. The road then wiggles scenically through the Chuya Canyon either side of **Aktash** (km 790). This nondescript little garrison town makes a possible base for an excursion via the disreputable town of **Ulagan** (Ust-Ulagan), through a lovely high valley to **Balyktuyul**. Here you'll find a wooden Altay church and, 5km beyond near the jeep track to Balykcha, the excavation sites of classic Pazyrik *kurgan*.

The Northern Chuysky Range south of Ak-tash offers several opportunities for treks and challenging mountaineering on peaks topped by Mt Aktru (4044m) and Mt Maashey (4177m), views of which are framed idyllically across the Shavlinsky Lakes.

The Chuysky Trakt's best views are between Aktash and Kosh-Agach. Wide distant panoramas of perennially snow-topped peaks across valleys known as the Kurayskaya and Chuyskaya Steppe (km 821 to km 840 and km 870 onwards) are interspersed by more great canyons and a chocolate pudding of a mountain at km 856. There's little to see in **Kosh-Agach** except perhaps its tiny wooden **Xazret Osman Mosque** *(ul Sovetskaya 62B)*. However, yurts picturesquely dot the steppeland beyond, which rises towards the dramatic twin peaks of Mt Saylyugem (3411m) and Mt Tapduayr (3305m).

When you are registering your visa in Gorno-Altaysk check whether any proposed destinations beyond Kosh-Agach still fall into a 'border-zone' for which permits are required.

Places to Stay & Eat

In accommodation beyond Chemal the only stars are the ones you'll see on the way to the toilet. Minimalist hotels in Onguday, Kosh-Agach and beside the Trakt 3km north of Aktash give change from R100.

Kordon Kurkechy (*tent site R35, hut twins R120*) is in a fabulous position perched above Ilgumen Rapids at the confluence of the Ilgumen and Katun Rivers (800m off the road at km 680). The place is popular, impossible to book and several kilometres from the nearest village, so it's wise to have a tent as backup in case all the huts are full. Note that food is not available. There's a *kameny baba*, a 3km walk from here.

Most of the villages have a couple of grocery shops, and there are basic daytime *stolovaya* (cafeterias) in Aktash and Onguday and a couple of tatty bars in Kosh-Agach. The best hopes of a hot meal are the roadside truck stops **Ak Boom** (*km742; spicy laghman R16*) or **SPK-Chuy Oozy** (☎ *38545-2 54 31; km714; standard Russian meals R15-25*). The latter has a beautifully furnished *ail* for traditional banquets, but it's only open by advance arrangement.

Getting There & Around

There are daily buses from Gorno-Altaysk to Onguday at 3.30pm, and Aktash (R200) at 7.10am and 10.40am. On alternate days the 7.10am bus continues to either Ulagan or Kosh-Agach. Only Kosh-Agach has professional taxis, but for R1000 you can probably find someone sober enough to drive you between Onguday and Aktash (see the boxed text 'Rural Rides' earlier in this chapter).

From Aktash, for R600 return with photo stops, reliable ethnic Kazakh driver **Tole Jabataev** (☎ *2 34 45; ul Kraynyaya 10*) can take you to sample fresh *koumys* with yurt-dwelling nomad-herders beyond Kosh-Agach. He speaks no English, but for R100 extra you can stay at his home, taste his *talkan* and pluck his *topsuur*.

TOWARDS TYUNGUR

Tiny Tyungur sits in an appealing valley and, although it lacks viewpoints itself, is the nor-

Don't Drink with Strangers

As with Tuvans, alcohol has a disastrous effect on Altay people, whose gentle smiles can turn to unpredictable violence within a bottle. In Ulagan my companion, being from Aktash (over 30km away!) and thus himself a 'foreigner', was very reluctant to ask directions. 'They might be drunk,' he hissed with a throat-slitting gesticulation! I laughed. But he wasn't joking. Arriving in Balyktuyul he took the extraordinary precaution of going to the village office to find a sober local to escort us to visit the church. The fellow who came along appeared to find the request quite normal. I started to get paranoid but then we chanced upon a ludicrously optimistic lone hitchhiker from Belarus. He loved the place, hitched everywhere and later made it all the way to Balykcha – astounding, as there's barely even a jeep track. He was very positive. 'The place is quite safe if you're careful.' 'So no trouble with drunks?' 'Oh, that's different,' he counselled excitedly. 'Don't drink with Altay people. Last night my friend got drunk and needed more vodka money. I wanted to sleep. I said, 'Go to bed.' But his rapidly drawn gun said, VODKA NOW!'

Mark Elliott

★★★★★★★★★★★★★★★★★★

mal staging point for treks and climbs towards Mt Belukha (4506m), Siberia's highest peak.

The access road to Tyungur branches off the northern Chuysky Trakt at Cherga and crosses a delightfully isolated, mostly forested area via Baragash. After the high grasslands of **Ust-Kan**, there's a brief glimpse of the distant white-tops from the Kyrlykskiy Pass as the road descends into the Koksa Valley. Though less dramatic than the Chuysk Trakt, the landscape is attractive, with bucolic meadows framed by hills and bluffs. The valley meets the Katun River at **Ust-Koksa**, where the daily bus from Gorno-Altaysk terminates in a small square. Walk one block north and two blocks east to find the delightful wooden **Pokrovskoe Church** (*ul Nagornaya 31*). From the village it's a R400 taxi ride to Tyungur, with brief mountain views glimpsed from Katanda.

Across the Katun River beyond Multa, the Multinsky Lakes offer yet more great hikes.

SIBERIA

Another village in the area is **Verkhny Uymon**, where you can visit the Museum of Old Belief (Muzey Staroobryadchetva) and the rather disappointing Nikolay Rerikh House-Museum (there's a better selection of his work in Gorno-Altaysk's Regional Museum).

Places to Stay & Eat

Ust-Kan has a **hotel** *(beds R80)* at its bus station, and there's a small hut-camp 4km east of town near an archaeological cave site.

In Ust-Koksa, the grocery shop **Lada** *(ul Sovetskaya 71; beds R150)*, with multi-coloured roof, has decent rooms upstairs, let down by a meet-the-neighbours shared squat toilet. Often full of kids, **Talan Turbaza** *(☎ 38848-2 28 44; ul Argunskogo; beds R150-200)* is a 10-minute walk from the square: cross the Koksa River by a suspension footbridge, turn right, walk five minutes along the river bank, then take the first main track on your left. The most comfortable accommodation in Ust-Koksa is an unmarked three-room **guesthouse** *(ul Sovetskaya 58; beds R181)* with kitchen and real bathroom, but to get the key you must visit the **Komkhoz office** *(☎ 38848-2 23 93; ul Nagornaya 23)* during work hours.

In Tyungur, cross the suspension bridge from the village. Keep left to reach the simple but very well organised **Turbaza Vysotnik** *(☎ 38848-2 20 24; beds in fixed tent R30, beds in hut R80)*. Sheets or sleeping bags cost R20 extra. It has a helpful English-speaking manager and a good café, which is the nearest you'll find to an international traveller hangout in Altay. Even if the place is full, staff will rent you a tent to sleep in. Still, it's worth booking huts, guides and tours in advance through the St Petersburg travel agency **LenalpTours** *(☎ 812-279 0716; fax 279 0651; e info@russia -climbing.com)*. Almost anything you'll need for mountaineering or treks into the wilderness is available for rent here, and they even sell a passable topographical map of the area.

A five-minute walk to the right of the Tyungur bridge is the more comfortable but less traveller orientated **Turbaza Uch Sumer** *(Kucherla/Tyungur; ☎ 38848-2 94 24, fax 2 28 72; basic twin huts R200, beds in ail-style minihotel with indoor toilet R400)*. The owners offer many tour options, and also have **cabins** *(twins R800)*, with outside toilet, at Lake Kucherla and elsewhere in the mountains.

Getting There & Away

Ust-Koksa's airport may be renovated by the time you read this. At the time of writing, flights were planned from Novosibirsk, along with helicopter trips to Mt Belukha and back (US$1400 for up to 20 people).

Buses run from Gorno-Altaysk to Ust-Kan (5½ hours), departing at 1.05pm, returning at 8am, and to Ust-Koksa (8½ hours), departing at 7.20am, returning at 7.45am. Shared taxis in the early morning are much faster, but after 8am you're likely to be stuck in Ust-Koksa until the following day.

No buses serve Tyungur but from Usk-Koksa (64km, partly paved), a taxi costs only R400. If you have a big group, you may persuade the Gorno-Altaysk to Ust-Koksa bus to keep going for about R700! Taxis plying the Ust-Koksa–Verkhny Uymon route charge R400 return with waiting time; buses only run twice a week. The Turbaza Vysotnik in Tyungur can generally arrange transfers to Biysk for R3000 per car, or R500 per person for groups in a minibus.

HIKING FROM TYUNGUR
Preparation

Decent tents, climbing equipment and even sleeping bags can be rented from the Vysotnik Turbaza in Tyungur. You can also arrange guides and horses here, buy a local map and have some chance of meeting other travellers to form a trekking group (it would be unwise to hike alone). It's worth emailing ahead with your requests, and to inquire about guides – if you speak some Russian ask about joining an existing Russian group (much cheaper at around US$20 per person per day). If hiking independently, buy food supplies in Ust-Koksa or earlier, as Tyungur has minimal supplies.

Routes

Only experienced groups of hikers should attempt these un-signed trails without a guide. Renting pack horses will make the treks more pleasant and horsemen often double as guides (though none speak any English). The popular five- to 12-day Akkem-Kucherla loop starts across the 1513m Kuzuyak Pass or by rafting 20km down the Katun River to the mouth of the Akkem River (you'll see some *kameny baba* en route). To get to the lovely Lake Akkem you can either trudge up the rather dull, forested river valley (two days) or take a four- to five-day high loop to the east, with many good mountain views en route. At **Lake Akkem** there is a hydrometeorological station, some ugly metal-drum-style lodges and an area suitable for camping some 20 minutes' walk along the lake. There's also a rescue post, whose staff can arrange helicopter evacuation (at a huge price – reckon on US$5000 minimum).

Stupendous panoramas of Mt Belukha are the reward for crossing the boulder-strewn Kara-Tyurek Pass (3060m), which loops from Lake Akkem to **Lake Kucherla**; it takes one day if you don't get lost, and is tricky for horses. Several other hikes are worthwhile from this more peaceful lake, before returning down the Kucherla River valley to Tyungur (two days).

From the confluence of the Akkem and Katun Rivers it's also possible to hike along the Katun River to Inya (three days) on the Chuysky Trakt. If you want to see Mt Belukha in a (long) day's hike from Tyungur, walk east along the Katun's northern bank and climb steeply up to Mt Bayda. Before setting off on any of these adventures, be aware that you're heading for real wilderness. Discuss your plans carefully with staff at one of the *turbaza* in Tyungur, or join one of the many organised groups by booking well ahead with one of the trekking companies listed in the introduction to the Altay section earlier.

Climbing Belukha

Ascents of Belukha (grade 3A-5A) are only for experienced mountaineers but don't require special permits. A two-week package (US$365) available from Vysotnik Turbaza includes guides, food and acclimatisation climbs for individuals or small groups. Add US$70 for transfers from Barnaul. Specialist mountaineering groups such as K2 Adventures in Omsk have successfully guided mountaineers up the toughest 'Bottle' ascent.

NOVOKUZNETSK
НОВОКУЗНЕЦК

☎ 3843 • pop 560,000 • Moscow time plus 4 hours

Although administratively in Kemerovo region (note the time change), Novokuznetsk is a key transit point between Altay and Khakassia (for Tuva). Founded on the right bank of the Tom River in 1617, the frequently enlarged Kuznetsk fortress became one of the most important guardians of imperial Rus-

sia's southeastern frontier. Renamed Stalinsk until 1961, the city's left bank developed from 1932 as a gigantic steel town (now the city centre). Today, despite some areas of ultramodern construction, Novokuznetsk retains its pompous early-Stalinist boulevards fanning out to towering smokestacks.

Things to See

Prospekt Metallurgov is a good example of Novokuznetsk's memorable 'Brave New 1930s' feel. The **Regional Museum** (*Kraevedcheskiy musey; pr Metallurgov 35; admission R10; open 10am-6pm Tues-Sat*), on this main prospekt, is an easy stroll due north from the cohabiting bus and train stations.

To visit the remnants of old Kuznetsk, take minibus No 5 from the stations past the excellent **art museum** (five stops), the old wooden-spired Biznes Tsentr (eight stops) and across the river to Sovetskiy ploshchad. Opposite this unremarkable square is the beautiful white, turquoise and gold **cathedral** (*1792; Preobrazhenskoi sobor; open 8am-2pm & 4pm-7pm daily*). Follow the road that leads steeply up and around beside the cathedral (a 10- to 15-minute walk) to reach the copper-domed Barnaul gate of the **fortress** (*ul Geologicheskaya; admission R6, plus camera R10; open 10am-5pm daily*). Its painstakingly restored stone ramparts are impressively massive and topped with cannons but represent only 20% of its former (1810) extent. There's an excellent little gift shop upstairs within the gate and an exhibition in the renovated barrack house.

Return to Sovetskiy ploshchad and walk five minutes south down ulitsa Dostoevskogo, which, after crossing beneath the rail bridge, becomes an attractive area of wooden homes set in riverside gardens. Here you'll find the quaint, artistically presented **Dostoevsky Museum** (*ul Dostoevskogo 40; admission R10; open 9am-5pm Mon-Fri, 10am-3pm Sat*), the log cabin where the writer stayed for three weeks in 1856–57. To enter, ask for the key from the house at ulitsa Dostoevskogo 29.

Places to Stay & Eat

Hotel Metallurg (☎ 6 46 18; pr Metallurgov 19; dorm beds from R100, twins without bathroom from R300, rooms with bathroom R500-1200) is centrally located beside the main post office.

SIBERIA

Hotel Novokuznetsk (☎ 46 51 55; ul Kirova 53; twins from R605, suites up to R2116) is a somewhat smarter alternative to the Metallurg. It's on a large traffic circle, 1.5km up prospekt Bardina from the stations; catch minibus No 5.

There are many cheap cafés near the stations, but for a little more style try Oregon (behind ul Kirov 75).

Getting There & Around
There's a nightly train to Abakan (No 696, R266, 11 hours). Slow, bumpy but very useful buses run to Biysk (R140.50, six to seven hours, four daily), two continuing to Belokurikha.

To get around the city, there's the frequent minibus No 5.

Khakassia Republic & Southern Krasnoyarsk Territory
Хакасия и Южный Красноярский Край

The Ireland-sized Khakassia Republic rises from lake-dotted taiga through a vast agricultural plain to richly forested mountains on the Tuvan border. Geographically it is inextricably linked with Southern Krasnoyarsk Territory. For both areas, transport connections focus on Abakan.

Like culturally similar Altay and Tuva, Khakassia is one of the cradles of Siberian civilisation. Kameny baba and thousands of kurgans pock the landscape, many over 3000 years old, though the most visually impressive date from the Turkic period (6th to 12th centuries). The Khyagas (Yenisey Kyrgyz) Empire, from which the name Khakassia is derived, ruled much of Central Asia and central Siberia from around AD 840 until its golden age ended abruptly with the arrival of Jenghis Khan and company.

Most Khyagas later migrated to what is now Kyrgyzstan. Those who remained were picked on by neighbours until, in 1701, they asked to join the Russian Empire. Compared to neighbouring Tuva, Russian colonisation in relatively fertile Khakassia was comprehensive. Outnumbered eight-to-one, the shamanist-Khakass people have been largely Christianised and integrated into Russian society, although the area around Askiz remains something of a Khakass cultural stronghold.

ABAKAN
АБАКАН
☎ 39022 • pop 163,000 • Moscow time plus 4 hours

Khakassia's capital is a pleasant, leafy but terminally dull 20th-century transport hub. It started life as a Russian fort in 1707, but until the 1930s remained insignificant compared to suave neighbouring Minusinsk, which was the region's centre of European civilisation.

Ulitsa Shchetinkina, the main north–south axis, has its southern end at ulitsa Pushkina. The bus station is about 800m east of ulitsa Shchetinkina along ulitsa Pushkina, while the train station is 400m to the west.

Money can be changed at **OBK Bank** (open 9am-7pm Mon-Fri, 9am-6pm Sat), where there's an ATM, too.

The **main post office** (ul Shchetinkina 20) is opposite Pervomayskaya ploshchad. The modern **Elektrorosvyazrkh Telephone Office** (ul Sovetskaya 45) has an air-conditioned **Internet** salon (open 8am-11pm), with an hourly rate of R38.

The **PVU** (old OVIR visa office; ☎ 6 36 54; ul Sovetskaya 35; open 9am-noon Mon & Fri, 2pm-5pm Wed) is entered around the back of the building through a metal gate. It's upstairs through the second door on the left.

Outside the **Univermag department store** (ul Pushkina) you can often find an itinerant stall selling good city maps.

Abakan Tours (☎ 6 60 33, fax 6 74 42; e parkotel@khakasnet.ru, attention: Sergei Metchtanov; open 9am-noon & 1pm-5pm Mon-Fri), at Hotel Park-Otel, is one of the most flexible, imaginative and helpful English-speaking travel agencies in Siberia. Sergei speaks good English and can arrange competitive personalised excursions throughout Khakassia and Tuva, including Salbyk (US$25 to R30 per car with guide) and the Shushenskoe-Sayanogorsk loop (US$45).

Things to See & Do
A superb forest of ancient totem stones welcomes you to the otherwise disappointing **Khakassia Museum** (☎ 6 78 74; ul Pushkina

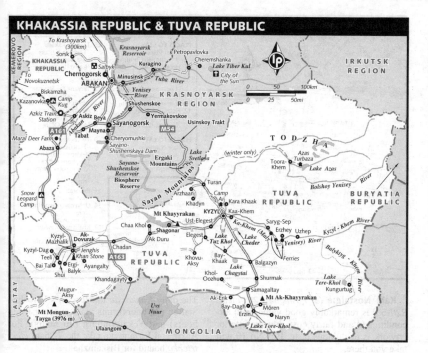

KHAKASSIA REPUBLIC & TUVA REPUBLIC

86; open 10am-6pm Tues-Sun). For better exhibits visit the Martyanov Museum in Minusinsk (see that section later).

Up unappealing prospekt Druzhby Narodov (bus No 15) an impressive new **cathedral** was under construction at the time of writing. However, if you speak decent Russian and fancy a more traditional spiritual fix, shaman **Tatyana Kobezhikova** (☎ 5 85 00; apartment 13, ul Shchetinkina 30) offers consultations in her modest home. She can also take you on various shamanic excursions, best organised through her colleagues at **The Russia Experience** (W www.trans-siberian.co.uk), who will arrange translators and boats/ rafts to get you to the more isolated riverside holy spots.

The city's **zoo** (ul Pushkina; admission R25; open 9am-4pm daily summer, 10am-4pm winter) is 3km west of the centre where ulitsa Pushkina turns north and joins ulitsa Sovetskaya.

Places to Stay

Hotel Abakan (☎ 6 30 26; pr Lenina 59; singles with shared bathroom R98, singles/ twins with private bathroom R279/520), behind a misleadingly grand facade, has simple but perfectly acceptable rooms. The cheap singles share new, clean communal showers.

Hotel Khakassia (☎ 6 37 02; pr Lenina 88; singles R240-336, twins R528-744), opposite the post office, has en suite rooms similar to those of the Hotel Abakan with no-frills Soviet-era facilities.

Hotel Druzhba (☎ 5 02 44; pr Druzhba Narodov 2; beds from R220, twins R980) is a last resort, with no hot water. The friendly staff were embarrassed to show the rooms.

Hotel Park-Otel (☎ 6 74 42, fax 6 37 60; e abtour@khakasnet.ru; ul Pushkina 54A; suites R600-900) is delightful, with just six plush, slightly ageing suites, all with marble bathtub. It's behind the 'Kristal' shop.

Hotel Sibir (☎ 6 77 11; pr Druzhba Narodov 9; rooms R200-1400), well maintained, has mostly upper-end suites. Access is via a path through a play area in the courtyard of the complex at ulitsa Druzhba Narodov 7.

Places to Eat

The **central market** is on ulitsa Shevchenko across from the bus station, with many cheap **cafés** nearby, and more on ulitsa Pushkina close to the train station.

SIBERIA

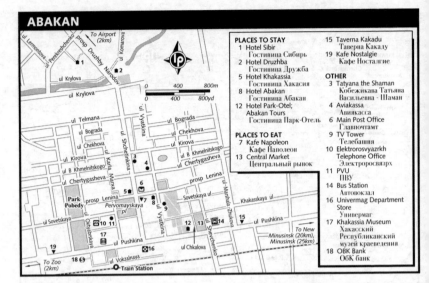

ABAKAN

PLACES TO STAY
1 Hotel Sibir
   Гостиница Сибирь
2 Hotel Druzhba
   Гостиница Дружба
5 Hotel Khakassia
   Гостиница Хакасия
8 Hotel Abakan
   Гостиница Абакан
12 Hotel Park-Otel;
   Abakan Tours
   Гостиница Парк-Отель

PLACES TO EAT
7 Kafe Napoleon
   Кафе Наполеон
13 Central Market
   Центральный рынок

15 Taverna Kakadu
   Таверна Какаду
19 Kafe Nostalgie
   Кафе Ностальгие

OTHER
3 Tatyana the Shaman
   Кобежикава Татьяна
   Васильевна - Шаман
4 Aviakassa
   Авиакасса
6 Main Post Office
   Главпочтамт
9 TV Tower
   Телебашня
10 Elektorosvyazrkh
   Telephone Office
   Электросвязрх
11 PVU
   ПВУ
14 Bus Station
   Автовокзал
16 Univermag Department
   Store
   Универмаг
17 Khakassia Museum
   Хакасский
   Республиканский
   музей краеведения
18 OBK Bank
   ОБК банк

Kafe Nostalgie *(ul Pushkina 126; meals R20-50)* is remarkably good value, well air-conditioned and fairly cosy, but the interior artwork is of dubious taste. Bus No 10 will take you there.

Taverna Kakadu *(☎ 5 03 36; ul Pushkina 36A; cover charge R20 after 8pm; open 11am-4pm & 5pm-2am daily)* has a pirate-themed interior and good Russian food, but can get overheated in summer. To get here, catch bus No 12.

Kafe Napoleon *(☎ 5 49 81; ul Shchetinkina 18; mains R80-130, cover charge R50 evening)* is the city centre's best restaurant, decorated with guns, swords and a startled turkey. Some of the attentive staff speak English.

Getting There & Away

Air Abakan's airport is about 2km northwest of the city centre. You can buy tickets from **Aviakassa** *(ul Chertygasheva 104; open 8am-1pm & 2pm-6pm daily)*. There are flights to Kyzyl (R2100) on Wednesday, Krasnoyarsk (R2400, five weekly), Novosibirsk (R3250) on Wednesday, Moscow (R5300, three weekly) and Vladivostok (R6100) on Wednesday and Saturday.

Train There are overnight connections to Novokuznetsk (No 696, R296, 11 hours), Krasnoyarsk (No 24, R578, 10½ hours) and Taishet (connecting to the BAM, 18½ hours).

The daily *Khakassia* to Moscow's Yaroslavl Station (75 hours) runs via Novosibirsk (24 hours) and Yekaterinburg (46 hours). For Askiz and Kazanovka take the 7.25am *elektrichka* bound for Biskamzha.

Bus From the **bus station** *(ul Shevchenko)* there are services to Krasnoyarsk (R215, nine to 10 hours, three to five daily) via Divnogorsk, and to Kuragino (R56, 2½ hours) at 1.40pm, 3.20pm and 5.30pm daily, Shushenskoe (R50, 1¾ hours, eight daily), Sayanogorsk (R61.50, 2¼ hours, nine daily) and Abaza via Askiz (R90, three hours, nine daily). Very frequent minibuses run to new Minusinsk (R10, 25 minutes), but for old Minusinsk you're better off taking big bus No 120 (R8, 40 minutes), which has departures three times per hour until 6.30pm, and then hourly until 9.30pm.

Road transport for Tuva leaves from outside the train station, with recommended early morning shared taxis to Kyzyl and Ak-Dovurak (R400 to R500 per seat, five to six hours) and snail-paced buses only to Kyzyl (R220, nine to 11 hours) departing at 8.30am, noon and 7pm daily – book ahead from a **booth** *(open 6.30am-noon & 2pm-7pm daily)* inside the station.

Getting Around

Bus No 15 runs from the airport and then down prospekt Druzhba Narodov and ulitsa

Shchetinkina, then east along ulitsa Pushkina, terminating a block northeast of the bus station. Bus Nos 10 and 21 run from the zoo all along ulitsa Pushkina then loop around to the post office. Frequent bus No 11 also follows Pushkina then ulitsa Shchetinkina, passing the Hotel Sibir, then turning right on ulitsa Perekreshchenko just before reaching the new cathedral.

AROUND ABAKAN
Minusinsk
Минусинск
☎ 39132 • pop 75,000

Old Minusinsk, 25km east of Abakan, has an attractive if compact 18th- to 19th-century core, across the protoka Minusinskaya waterway from a domineering concrete new town.

Just after the bridge, jump off bus No 120 or 10 at the pastel yellow **Spaskaya Church** (1803; ul Komsomolskaya 10), which is on the corner of a square. A block northwest is the award-winning **Drama Theatre** (1882; cnr ul Podinskaya). East of the church, diagonally across the square, is the excellent **Martyanov Museum** (☎ 2 00 54; ul Lenina 60; admission R25, 1½hr guided tour R100; open 10am-6pm Wed-Sun). Here, in among the splendid archaeological, cultural and regional exhibits, you will come across the original mineralogical displays of 19th-century pharmacist-founder Martyanov, and the preserved little library where Lenin used to study when exiled in Shushenskoe. The gift shop sells town maps.

Walk a block along ulitsa Lenina, then two blocks to the northeast up ulitsa Kravchenko to ulitsa Oktyabrskaya. This is the north corner of the overgrown ploshchad Lenina, and it's where several crumbling buildings have maudlin echoes of former grandeur. Continue along ulitsa Oktyabrskaya to sniff out several Lenin-related, attractively preserved buildings and the atmospheric **Stary Gorod** restaurant.

Hotel Amyl (☎ 2 01 06; ul Lenina 74; beds from R180, singles/twins R350/500) is half a block southeast of the Martyanov Museum. It has an historic if tatty facade, rooms with private bathroom and plans for much needed renovations.

City bus No 10 runs between the new town and the inconvenient **bus station** (ul Krasnykh Partizan) via ulitsa Gogolya and the old town centre.

Salbyk
Салбык

Of all Khakassia's standing stones, the most impressive group is the Stonehenge-sized remnant of Salbyk 'royal' kurgan, excavated in 1956, which is 5.6km (of unsurfaced road) south of the km 38 post on the Chernogorsk–Sorsk road. About 2km before Salbyk you'll see the large, grassy dome of the unexcavated 'Princess' kurgan, which it once resembled. A taxi from Abakan costs at least R450 return. Bring buckets of mosquito repellent.

Vissarion Villages

Vissarion (the 'teacher') and his apostles live atop a mountain at the the religion's nascent Jerusalem, 'City of the Sun/Abode of Dawn', (see the boxed text 'The Messiah of Siberia' in the Facts about Siberia & Russian Far East chapter). Access is from the pleasant market town of **Kuragino**, but after Cheremshanka (about 100km east) it's part cart track (weekly jeep each Sunday for the faithful), part trek (three to four hours). Somewhat more accessible, **Petropavlovka** village has a particularly attractive wooden Vissarion church and believers are usually happy to welcome and accommodate you, feed you great vegetarian food and discuss plenty of interesting philosophy. Plan ahead by contacting the **Info Tsentr** (☎ 39136-2 35 94; ⓦ www.vissarion.ru; open 8.30am-noon & 1pm-7pm daily) in Kuragino: ask a taxi for Motorskoe Obshchizitye (R15).

Kuragino has the basic **Hotel Tuba** (ul Partizanskaya 108, cnr ul Traktovaya; beds in triples/doubles R86/127, beds in rooms with attached toilet R150) near the river, a block from the bus station. Buses run to Abakan via Minusinsk (R50, two hours, three daily) but all leave in the morning. The bone-shattering bus to Cheremshanka via Petropavlovka (2½ hours) departs at 4pm daily and returns at 6am the next day. A taxi costs R500 if you can find one.

Shushenskoe
Шушенское
☎ 39139 • pop 20,000

As every good Soviet knows, Shushenskoe (**Shu**-shen-ska-ya) played host to Lenin for three (relatively comfortable) years of exile. But fewer know that the young atheist's 1898 wedding was held in the local church, much

SIBERIA

to his later embarrassment. For Lenin's 1970 birth centennial much of the village centre was reconstructed to look as it had in 1870, and the commercial area of town was moved a respectful distance to ulitsa Polukoltsevaya.

The reconstructed centre isn't as busy as it once was, but it retains its **Lenin Memorial Museum** (ul Novaya 1; admission R60 plus R30 per camera; open 9am-5pm daily), now as an open-air ethnographic museum comprising several streets of well-kept 'old' Siberian houses. Many of these houses are convincingly furnished, costumed craftsmen sit around carving spoons and the gift shop sells maps and some tempting Lenin-abilia.

Shushenskoe is the headquarters of the **Sayano-Shushenskiy Biosphere Reserve** (☎ 3 23 00; e sayan@public.krasnet.ru; ul Zapovednaya 7) – listed by Unesco – with an office and small museum at the eastern end of ulitsa Pionirskaya (see also the Sayanogorsk section later), the southeasterly continuation of ulitsa Polukoltsevaya from the bus station.

Turbaza Iskra (☎ 3 21 51; dorm beds R110), across the river by a footbridge behind the Lenin Memorial Museum, offers simple accommodation in old huts.

Hotel Turist (☎ 3 28 41; ul Pushkina 1; singles/doubles with toilet R247/340 with shower & toilet R370/440) fails to hide the worn, mustiness of its Soviet era rooms with carelessly placed Laura Ashley–esqe wallpaper. It's across the road from the post office, a 10-minute walk from both the Lenin Memorial Museum (southwest via ulitsa Pushkina) and the bus station (southeast along ulitsa Polukoltsevaya).

Medved (☎ 3 12 61; ul Pervomayskaya 50; meals R17-45, beers from R20; open 11.30am-2.30pm & 9pm-5am daily) is an atmospheric café, 100m from the bus station.

Buses serve Abakan (R50, 1¾ hours, eight daily), Sayanogorsk (two hours, two daily), Krasnoyarsk (10½ hours) at 8am (irregular), and Kyzyl (R200, seven to nine hours) at 10am, for which you should book ahead.

Sayanogorsk & Around
Саяногорск
☎ 39042 • pop 57,000

Central Sayanogorsk is an ugly huddle of concrete towers, but the forested mountains and valleys behind are well worth exploring.

SAF Agency (☎ 7 38 11, fax 2 66 42; e gladski@khakasnet.ru), behind Hotel Merid-

ian, can fix rural accommodation and tours of the marble factory; none of its staff speak English. SAF can also whisk you up to **Gladenkaya Ski Resort** (Russian only w www .gladenkaya.khakassia.ru; huts R235-1400 per person; open Nov-Apr only), which has well-equipped hut accommodation with bio-toilets. You can hire Western-brand ski equipment, and, at the time of writing, new runs were under construction.

South of Sayanogorsk, a steep, forest-clad valley is mirrored photogenically when viewed from the low dam just beyond Mayna (catch bus No 2 from Sayanogorsk). An attractive new church sponsored by a local wrestling champion adds to the scene. Down a side road, 3km west of the low dam, lies Zharki Sanatorium (see Places to Stay & Eat) and some quiet alpine valleys beyond, with nice hiking opportunities.

The main road south dead-ends after Cheryomushki at the very impressive Sayano-Shushenskaya Dam, Russia's biggest, and the world's fourth in terms of energy production. Book ahead with SAF if you want to tour the turbine rooms; bring a passport photocopy.

The enormous reservoir that the dam created stretches all the way to the Tuva Republic. It's surrounded by largely untouched wilderness, now constituting the Sayano-Shushenskiy Biosphere Reserve. Sightings of its estimated 20 to 25 snow leopards are exceedingly rare, but guided visitors are 'virtually assured' to spot ibex year-round according to the reserve's headquarters in Shushenskoe, which can arrange trips, permits, translators etc for around US$100 per person per day. Abakan Tours in Abakan (see that section earlier) can also help you make arrangements and has even organised three-day boat rides right down the lake to Shagonar in Tuva: start planning weeks or months ahead.

Places to Stay & Eat The Hotel Meridian (☎ 2 27 66; ul Sovetskiy 30; apartments singles/doubles R350/700), with its splendid apartments (including breakfast), is superb value and reason enough to stay in Sayanogorsk. Its excellent **restaurant** (mains R40-70) serves imaginative meals. Access is around the back of the hotel, past a cloak-room, upstairs and across a meeting room!

Zharki Sanatorium (☎ 4 23 78; beds R250, lyux singles/doubles R700/1500) has a range of mud baths, paraffin treatments and hydro/

gas massage machines, which look like they belong in a 1970s James Bond movie. Its *lyux* rooms have been rebuilt to Western standards.

At the time of writing, a plush new **hotel** was under construction at Babik (not Bablik, which means 'womaniser'!), 4km west of Sayanogorsk. Already operational are a few six-bed motel-style **rooms** (R600); book through SAF agency (see earlier). Babik is beside a peaceful stream, and would make a nice base for gentle hikes.

Getting There & Around Sayanogorsk's bus station is 1km west of the Hotel Meridien (a R10 taxi trip), with services to Shushen-skoe (two hours) at 10.10am and 5.30pm daily, Abakan (R61.50, 2¼ hours, nine daily), and Krasnoyarsk (R255, 10½ hours, twice daily). There's also a bus to Askiz (R52, 2½ hours) which returns at 10.30am on a lovely route through some archetypal Russian villages and following a foothill ridge with wide views over the plains below.

Taxis from Sayanogorsk charge R200 return to the high Sayano-Shushenskaya Dam. You could use city bus No 2 (R4, 30 minutes, every 40 minutes) from ulitsa Sovetskiy as far as 'Tsentralny' in Cheryomushki. Transfer to the free GES tram (10 minutes, hourly on the half-hour), or hitch the last 4km.

SOUTHWEST KHAKASSIA

Askiz (Аскиз; ☎ 39045, pop 24,000) is the most Khakass town of Khakassia, though it's really only interesting during the Pasture-Opening Festival (Tun Payran). This special event features wrestling, horse-racing, archery and much merriment but its dates (usually in June) are infamously changeable.

About 30km west of Askiz is the very quaint Khakass village of **Kazanovka**. Near the village, in a lovely rural setting, close to a series of sacred bluffs, is the excellent **Camp Kug** (e luna@paradise-travel.ru; full board per person US$25). This is a great place to relax or break a journey and, occasionally, to see Khakass cultural performances (given when there's a tour group). The camp has comfortable *ail*-yurts with washbasins and chemical toilets plus shared hot showers. If you book ahead through Sayan Ring Travel in Krasnoyarsk (see that section) the fee includes a guided walk through some of the shamanic spots nearby. When there are no guests, the camp is virtually deserted, so

should you be passing by without a reserva-tion first call on **Viktoria Kulimeyevna** (☎ 9 45 31) in Kazanovka village. It may be possi-ble to get the 'bed only' last-minute rate of R300 per person. To get to the camp, cross the river at the far western end of Kazanovka, turn right immediately (a sign says 'Музей') and follow the bumpy track for 4km, bearing right at the only fork in the track. It's alterna-tively possible to walk directly to Camp Kug in an hour from Kazanovka's isolated little train station (over 3km east of Kazanovka it-self), but you'll probably need a guide, espe-cially to find the bridge across the river.

Between Askiz and the town of Abaza, there are hundreds of ancient **standing stones**, notably at km 109/307, where re-markable concentrations stand right by the roadside. The **Maral Deer Farm** (admission R35) at km 163/253 is at its most interesting in May/June when you can watch the cutting of the animals' antlers (if you're not squea-mish). In summer all the deer are away on distant slopes, though the corral and antler-drying barn are still worth a visit.

Further south is **Abaza**, which has the passable **Hotel Kedr** (☎ 2 98 70; ul Parkovaya 2A; singles/twins R353/411); all rooms have shared toilet.

Abaza's forward-thinking adventure tourist outfit **Rodnik** (☎ 2 32 81; w http://come.to/rodnik; ul Filatova 8-1) runs the excellent, ecofriendly **Snow Leopard Camp** (Turbaza Snezhny Bars; US$35 per day), a two-hour drive south of here. It's set in thick, tick-free woodland 1.6km west of the mountainous Abaza–Ak Dovurak road (km 296/120). The daily rate includes full board, *banya* and an English-speaking guide. Organised hikes and horse treks can take you to associated hunting lodges and tent camps (R350 per night) dotted around high lakes in the cedar forests above. From Abaza the only sensible way to get to Snow Leopard Camp is by taxi or on one of Rodik's transfer minibuses (patient single trav-ellers may be able to join a Rodik staff car more cheaply). Getting to km296/120 from Ak Dovurak is feasible by Abakan-bound share taxi (R400 as you'll pay the Abaza fare), but heading the other way is virtually impossible without backtracking to Abaza.

USINSKOY TRAKT

First built in 1910, the Usinskoy Trakt (be-tween Minusinsk and Kyzyl in Tuva) skirts cute little fruit-growing villages, then winds dramatically across the Sayan Mountains for brilliant, if somewhat distant, views of the crazy, rough-cut Ergaki Mountains (km 598 to km 601 and km 611 to km 614). Former hero of Chechnya/Krasnoyarsk, governor Alexander Lebed, died near here in 2002 when his helicopter snagged power lines and crashed. A big cross strewn with flowers marks the spot. Many locals stop here to pay their respects, and it is a relatively easy point from which to hitch should you hop off the bus. There are fabulous views from the ridge, 1.5km up the steep track towards the radar station above. Squint and you may see why the profile of one of the mountains is known as the 'sleeping princess'. At km 609, 4km after Lake Oyskoe, a small track to the right leads 2.5km to the ultrabasic **Alenya Rechka Campsite** (book through Shushenskoe), which rents saddled horses at R50 per hour.

The classic view of the Ergaki Mountains is from **Lake Svetlaya**, a popular three- to four-hour walk off the Trakt. Start at km 622/445, where there's a little guarded parking corral and a guide who is sometimes available to show you the way to (R350). At the time of writing a couple of huts were under construction, but it's wise to bring a tent and all food supplies.

Buses (R220, nine to 11 hours, three daily) and shared taxis (R400 to R500, five to six hours) travel along the Trakt from Abakan's train station to Kyzyl.

Tuva Тува

Tuva (spelt Тыва in Tuvan) has forests, mountains, lakes and vast undulating waves of beautiful, barely populated steppe. It is culturally and scenically similar to neighbouring Mongolia. Somewhat surprisingly, Tuva has developed a global cult following. Philatelists fall for the curiously shaped 1930s Tannu Tuva postage stamps. For world music aficionados it's in fact the unbelievable self-harmonising of Tuvan throat singers. For millions of armchair travellers it's Ralph Leighton's book *Tuva or Bust!*, which tells the story of how irrepressible, curious Nobel Prize–winning physicist Richard Feynman spends years following a quirky, never-to-be-achieved obsession of reaching Soviet-era Kyzyl. Now that visitors are finally allowed in, Leighton's organisation **Friends of Tuva** (W www.fotuva.org) keeps up the inspirational work with an unsurpassed collection of Tuvan resources and links on its website.

About two-thirds of the republic's 310,000 population are ethnic Tuvan: Buddhist-shamanist by religion, Mongolian by cultural heritage, and Turkic by language. In Tuvan *ekii* is 'hello,' *eki* is 'good' and *...ghaide?* is a handy way to ask someone directions. Hopefully they'll answer by pointing! Tuvan Cyrillic has a range of exotic extra vowels and place names can have different Russian and Tuvan variants.

At the time of writing, Tuva's borders with Mongolia were closed to foreigners. However things are in flux; a Mongolian consulate has opened recently in Kyzyl and, by the time you read this, the frontier at Khandagayty (for Ulaangom near Lake Uvs Nuur) may be open. The Erzin border crossing will almost certainly stay closed.

History

First inhabited at least 40,000 years ago, Tuva was controlled from the 6th century by a succession of Turkic empires. In the 1750s it became an outpost of China, against whose rule the much-celebrated Aldan Maadyr (60 Martyrs) rebelled in 1885. Tibetan Buddhism took root during the 19th century, coexisting with older shamanist nature-based beliefs; by the late 1920s one man in 15 in Tuva was a lama.

With the Chinese distracted by a revolution in 1911, Russia stirred up a separatist movement and took Tuva 'under protection' in 1914. The effects of Russia's October Revolution weren't felt much in Tuva until 1921, when the region was briefly a last bolt-hole of the retreating white Russians. But they were swiftly ejected into Mongolia by 'Red Partisans', to whom you'll see monuments in Kyzyl and Bay Dagh. Tuva's prize was renewed if nominal independence as the Tuvan Agrarian Republic (TAR), better known as Tannu-Tuva. However, to Communist Russia's chagrin, Prime Minister Donduk's government dared to declare Buddhism the state religion and favoured reunification with Mongolia. Russia's riposte was to install a dependable Communist, Solchak Toka, and, later, to force Tuvans to write their language in the fundamentally inappropriate Cyrillic

Tuvan Culture

Colourful *khuresh* is a form of wrestling similar to Japanese sumo but without the ring, the formality or the huge bellies. Multiple heats run simultaneously, each judged by a pair of referees, flamboyantly dressed in national costume. They'll occasionally slap the posteriors of fighters who seem not to be making sufficient effort. Tuvans also love Mongolian-style long-distance horse races but are most widely famed for their *khöömei* throat-singers. *Khöömei* is both a general term and the name of a specific style in which low and whistling tones, all from a single throat, somehow harmonise with one another. The troll-like *kargyraa* style sounds like singing through a prolonged burp. *Sygyt* is reminiscent of a wine glass being rung by a wet finger: quaintly odd if you hear a recording but truly astonishing when you hear it coming out of a human mouth. Accompanying instruments often include a jew's-harp, a bowed two-stringed *igil* or a three-stringed *doshpular* (Tuvan banjo).

It's increasingly easy to get CDs of Tuvan music in the West. Kaigal-ool and his group Huun Huur Tu (literally, 'Sun Propeller'), along with the inventive Alash, are perhaps the most interesting performers. Better known Kongar-ol Ondar has collaborated with Frank Zappa and worked on the soundtrack for the Oscar-nominated film *Genghis Blues*. You can even listen to *khöömei* online at W www.fotuva.org/soundsheet/index.html.

Despite this, many visitors manage to visit Tuva without hearing a note. If someone asked you if you could sing, you'd probably modestly decline. Given a few beers or a football crowd, however, the reality may be different. In Tuva, it's similar with *khöömei*. If you ask directly, you're unlikely to find anyone who claims they can do it. But one evening over a couple of beers, I pulled out my harmonica and played a couple of amateurish blues riffs. My Tuvan friend lamented, 'the only instrument I have is my throat'. With that he let rip with a blast of spine-tingling *sygyt*. At last – some live *khöömei*!

Mark Elliot

★★★

alphabet, creating a cultural divide with Mongolia. Having 'voluntarily' helped Russia in WWII, Tuva's 'reward' was incorporation into the USSR. Russian immigration increased, Buddhism and shamanism were repressed and the seminomadic Tuvans were collectivised; many Tuvans slaughtered their animals in preference to handing them over.

Today, some people have reverted to traditional pastoralism but, unlike in neighbouring Mongolia, yurt camps are often hidden away in the remoter valleys, largely because gangs of ruthless rustlers have scared herders off the most accessible grasslands. Buddhist-shamanist beliefs survived the oppressions rather better. Even avowed atheists still revere local *arzhaan* sacred springs, offer food to fire spirits and tie prayer ribbons to cairns and holy trees using the colours of the national flag: blue for sky, yellow for Buddhism and white for purity and happiness.

Festivals

Vastly less touristy than the Mongolian equivalent, **Naadym**, held on a weekend around 14 August, is Tuva's most dramatic festival. It's your best chance to hear *khöömei* concerts (for more details on *khöömei*, see the boxed text 'Tuvan Culture' above), to drink the local firewater, *araka*, at the horse races and to see if Mongush Ayas wins the *khuresh* (traditional wrestling) as usual. Similar elements accompany the **International Khöömei Symposium** (held roughly every three years) and the brilliant but as yet one-off **Dembildey festival**. More significant for locals is **Shagaa**, Buddhist New Year (January or February), with ceremonial purification ceremonies, gift giving and temple rituals.

Dangers & Annoyances

Meeting locals is the key to experiencing Tuva but be aware that many friendly Tuvans react to alcohol by becoming disproportionately aggressive. A proliferation of knives and weapons among Tuvans doesn't help. Chadan in Western Tuva is particularly notorious and even in tiny, apparently peaceful villages, steer well clear of drunks, travel with trusted, sober Tuvans and avoid drinking vodka with local 'friends'. While researching this chapter, this author witnessed a bar brawl, was ambushed (and rescued!) twice and suffered an attempted strangling. Next day the perpetrators were friendly again and remembered nothing! Be streetwise and consider going to bed early!

SIBERIA

Food

Almost every rural household keeps a vat of *khoitpak* (fermenting sour milk), which tastes like ginger beer with a sediment of finely chopped brie. Any *khoitpak* that is not drunk is distilled into alcoholic *araka*. As in Altay, roast *dalgan* (a cereal, the same as the bran-rich flour *talkan*) can be added to your salted milky tea, or eaten with *oreme* (sour cream). Tuvans are said to have learnt from Jenghis Khan a special way to kill their sheep without wasting any of the animal's blood. Collected with miscellaneous offal in a handy intestine, this blood gives the local delicacy, *han* sausage. You may be less than disappointed to find that restaurants rarely if ever serve it. Not that there are any restaurants anyway! Beyond Kyzyl, truck stops, *pelmeni* steamers and the temperamental village *stolovaya* are your best hope for a hot meal unless you're staying with families. Kyzyl residents take their own supplies when travelling to the provinces.

KYZYL
КЫЗЫЛ
☎ 39422 • pop 95,000 • Moscow time plus 4 hours

Tuva's capital may claim grandly to be the 'centre of Asia', but architecturally it's a disappointingly unexotic grid of typical Soviet-era concrete. Fortunately the central area's streets are pleasantly tree lined. There are quietly picturesque views across the rivers from the Centre of Asia monument and more peacefully from the Park Kultury-i-Odykha. Look across from the latter to a tiny temple that sits alone on the empty north-bank steppe, backed by a horizon crowded with arid, low mountains.

The town was founded in 1914 as Belotsarsk (White Tsarville). Whether to be pedantic or humorously ironic, the Soviet regime changed the name to Kyzyl, a Tuvan word which simply means 'red'.

The most memorable attractions in Kyzyl are ephemeral – meeting shamans, hearing throat-singing or catching a wrestling competition.

Orientation & Information

Made to look slightly oriental with well-chosen wooden flourishes, a distinctive white concrete theatre sits in a sizable square marking the city centre where the main streets ulitsas Kochetova and Chuldum cross.

Your hotel should register your visa for you. If they're reluctant to do this, visit **PVU** (*former OVIR; ul Kochetova 31; open 2pm-6pm Mon-Wed*), above Sberbank; registration is sometimes checked elsewhere in Tuva.

Rana at the **Tourist Department** (☎ *3 51 09; fax 1 17 67;* e *mineconom@tuva.ru; ul Chuldum 18, Government House, room 207*) is extremely obliging, speaks excellent English and does her best to provide introductions, sort out transport difficulties and offer what information is available. To reach her office, show your passport at the security check and keep saying 'Turism'. Departmental emails are laboriously printed out from a central computer and can get lost in transit. Mark the subject line 'Attention Tourist Department'.

Hidden off the central square in an unmarked courtyard, **OBK Bank** (*ul Shchetinkina-Kravchenko 37a; open 9am-6pm Mon-Fri, 10am-2pm Sat*) has a useful ATM and changes dollars. Cashing travellers cheques can take a day or two.

Facing the theatre is the main **post office**, which has a single Internet-connected computer and attached **telephone office**. There's another Internet computer in the **Biznis Tsentr** (*open 9am-noon & 1pm-6pm Mon-Fri*) of Hotel Odugen (see Places to Stay later). **Aldynai** (☎ *5 30 05;* e *aldynai@tuva.ru*) is a friendly English teacher who doubles as translator in the summer (and has just written an English-Tuvan phrasebook).

Tsentr Asii (☎/*fax 3 23 26;* e *asiatur@ tuva.ru*) is a helpful, experienced travel agency based in Hotel Odugen, which can arrange air tickets, vehicle charters and trips to Turbaza Erzhey. It also sells good postcards and a few CDs of throat-singing.

Alash Travel (☎ *3 48 26;* w *www.tuva.ru /alash/; ul Kochetova 62/2*) has been recommended by readers and offers some pretty adventurous rafting trips in places such as Todzha.

Generally reliable **Abakan Tours** (see the earlier Abakan section) claim that they can better prices offered by local companies for transport and some individual tours within Tuva. It can't harm to compare!

Bookshop **Deloyve Melochi** (*ul Krasnoarmeyskaya 100; open 9am-6pm Mon-Fri, 10am-3pm Sat*), in the basement, occasionally stocks decent republic and city maps (R40). The entrance to the bookshop is off to

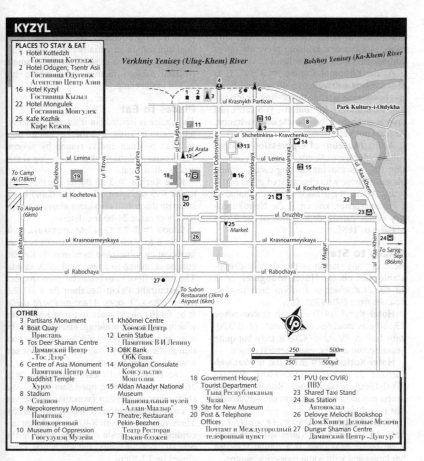

KYZYL

PLACES TO STAY & EAT
1 Hotel Kottedzh
  Гостиница Коттэдж
2 Hotel Odugen; Tsentr Asii
  Гостиница Одугенж
  Агентство Центр Азии
16 Hotel Kyzyl
  Гостиница Кызыл
22 Hotel Mongulek
  Гостиница Монгулек
25 Kafe Kezhik
  Кафе Кежик

Verkhniy Yenisey (Ulug-Khem) River

Bolshoy Yenisey (Ka-Khem) River

Park Kultury-i-Otdykha

To Camp
Ai (18km)

To Airport
(6km)

To Subon
Restaurant (3km) &
Airport (6km)

To Saryg-
Sep
(86km)

Market

0   250   500m
0   250   500yd

OTHER
3 Partisans Monument
  Памятник
4 Boat Quay
  Пристань
5 Tos Deer Shaman Centre
  Даманский Центр
  „Тос Дээр"
6 Centre of Asia Monument
  Памятник Центр Азии
7 Buddhist Temple
  Хурээ
8 Stadium
  Стадион
9 Nepokorennyy Monument
  Памятник
  Непокоренный
10 Museum of Oppression
  Гёогузунэн Музейи

11 Khöömei Centre
   Хоомэй Центр
12 Lenin Statue
   Памятник В И Ленину
13 OBK Bank
   ОбК банк
14 Mongolian Consulate
   Консульство
   Монголии
15 Aldan Maadyr National
   Museum
   Национальный музей
   „Алдан-Маадыр"
17 Theatre; Restaurant
   Pekin-Beezhen
   Театр Ресторан
   Пэкин-бээжен

18 Government House;
   Tourist Department
   Тыва Республиканьн
   Чазаа
19 Site for New Museum
20 Post & Telephone
   Offices
   Почтамт и Междугородный
   телефонный пункт

21 PVU (ex OVIR)
   ПВУ
23 Shared Taxi Stand
24 Bus Station
   Автовокзал
26 Delovye Melochi Bookshop
   Дом Книги Деловые Мелочи
27 Dungur Shaman Centre
   Даманский Центр „Дунгур"

the side; take the third door on the right. For US$8 plus postage these can also be purchased through US-based **Tuva Trader** (W www.scs-intl.com/trader/)

Things to See & Do

If you map a map, cut out Asia and balance the continent on a pin, the pinprick will be Kyzyl. Well, only if you've used the utterly obscure Gall's stereographic projection. However, that doesn't stop the town perpetuating the 'Centre of Asia' idea first posited by a mysterious 19th-century English eccentric and still marked with a concrete globe-and-obelisk **monument** on the river bank, at the end of ulitsa Komsomolskaya.

A few paces west along the promenade are the eye-catching totem poles and reception

yurt of the **Tos Deer Shaman Centre** (☎ 3 20 23; ul Krasnykh Partizan 18a). It's highly photogenic but the shamans are very touchy about you taking snaps. Some evenings, if someone has stumped up the cash, there are sunset ceremonies here. Medico-spiritual consultations for highly arbitrary fees are available by day and Natasha, one of the young trainee shamans, speaks decent English. However, some locals claim that powers are greater at the much less atmospheric **Dungur Shaman Centre** (☎ 3 19 09; ul Rabochaya 245).

The interesting **Aldan Maadyr National Museum** (☎ 3 00 96; ul Lenina 7; admission $2; open 11am-5pm Tues-Sun) has many fine 6th- to 12th-century stone figures, photos from the independence era, a furnished yurt,

SIBERIA

exhibitions of local stone carvers and so much more in storage that it will eventually move to a big new building presently under construction on ulitsa Kochetova.

At the **Khöömei Centre** (☎ 3 34 24; ul Shchetinkina-i-Kravchenko 46, ground floor) it is possible to arrange throat-singing lessons but, frustratingly for tourists, you can't just drop in and hear a five-minute demonstration. At least not yet.

A tiny **Museum of Oppression** (Gööguzuneng Muzeyi; ul Komsomolskaya 5; admission R8) has moving, if dog-eared, copied photos of those who disappeared in the Stalin years. Across the grass the tall new statue of a Tuvan warrior, known as the **Nepokorennyy** (Undefeated), depicts one of the Aldan Maadyr of 1885.

Places to Stay

Near the bus station is the slightly disreputable, but cheap, **Hotel Mongulek** (☎ 3 12 53; ul Kochetova 1; dorm beds/singles/doubles from R70/120/200).

Hotel Kyzyl (ul Tuvinskikh Dobrovoltsev 13; singles/doubles with toilet R170/320, with bath & TV R290/420) is tatty but quite bearable and a safer, more central option.

Hotel Kottedzh (☎ 3 05 03; ul Krasnykh Partizan 38; singles R350-1300, doubles R700-1800) is fairly cosy. Rooms all have toilets and most have a decent shower. Breakfast is included.

Hotel Odugen (☎ 3 25 18; ul Krasnykh Partizan 36; singles R270, suites with bathroom R700-1400), next door, is a similar standard but larger and with some river-view rooms.

Camp Ai (beds US$20, with meals US$25), 18km north of town, is much the nicest place to stay. Relatively luxurious felt yurts are set in an attractive riverside location, and there are petroglyphs nearby to discover. Yurts have private washbasins and chemical toilets and there are shared hot showers and a café (open to camp guests only). Book ahead through **Sayan Ring Travel** (☎ 3912-65 26 50, fax 65 26 49; w www.siberiaparadise .com; ul Lenina 24) in Krasnoyarsk or call **Artur** (☎ 3 89 00), the local manager, based in Kyzyl. Shaman shows and throat-singing demonstrations are arranged when Sayan Ring tour groups are staying. A taxi from Kyzyl should cost R100 to R120 but you may need to give the driver directions. To get to the camp, cross the Yenisey bridge 2km west

of the centre; 1.6km after the river turn right (signed to Kara-Khaak), continue for 13km, then turn left on an initially paved road. This becomes a track as it skirts around a small, isolated asphalt factory from where it's 2.2km to the camp.

Places to Eat

The choice is limited but it's better than anywhere else in Tuva. The **market** has a range of fresh produce and is ringed by several cheap cafés and shashlyk grills serving skewered, grilled meat.

Kafe Kezhik (☎ 3 29 04; ul Druzhby 151; mains R35-60; open 10am-3am daily) has a smartish disco-ball restaurant above a significantly cheaper 24-hour cafeteria.

Subon (☎ 5 12 12; ul Moskovskaya 100; bus No 6 to Yuzhny; mains R30-60) is in an unappealing suburb and its nominally Korean cuisine is limited to a few good spicy salads. The dance-floor brawls can be even spicier.

Restaurant Pekin-Beezhen (☎ 1 03 22; mains R90-120; open 11am-midnight daily) is by far the nicest place to eat in Kyzyl. It's within the theatre building: enter through the oriental portal on ulitsa Kochetova. One portion of their punchy 'sour and keen' (hot and sour) soup is enough for three.

The Hotel Kyzyl's **café-restaurant** (☎ 3 16 59; mains R20-55R; open 8am-1am) has a short menu of Russian favourites and serves a curious cinnamon 'cappuccino' (R15). There may be a R5 to R40 cover charge according to live music offerings. Despite the official opening hours, the kitchen is often closed by 10.30pm.

Getting There & Away

The airport is 7km southwest of the centre by bus No 1A. Though frequently cancelled or rescheduled, there are supposedly flights to Krasnoyarsk (R2440, four per week) and Novosibirsk (R2850, three to four per week), and weekly flights to Irkutsk (R3300), Barnaul (R2800), Abakan (R2100) and Moscow (R5850). Helicopters serve Todzha (R2100).

For Abakan, shared taxis (R400 to R500 per seat, 5½ hours) are well worth the difference over the grindingly slow, overbooked buses (R220, nine to 11 hours, three per day), if only to see the fabulous views of the Ergaki Mountains en route. Cars congregate behind Hotel Mongulek and departures are most frequent before 8am and around 1pm.

From the bus station, there are services to Saryg-Sep (R46, two hours, two per day), Erzin (R96, 6½ hours, once daily), Khandagayty (seven hours, three to seven per week), Chaa-Khol (4½ hours, three per week), Ak-Dovurak (R100, seven hours, two or three per day, with one continuing to Teeli) and Turan (R16, 2½ hours, once daily continuing to either Arzhaan or Khadyn). Shared taxis are inevitably faster, with at least a few cars daily to Shagonar, Chadan and Ak-Dovurak.

Agencies want around R200/hour to rent a six- to eight-seater UAZ (Wazik) all-terrain van, useful for the rough roads of the southeast. Lada Zhigoulis are cheaper per kilometre and do fine on the paved main road to the west. **Voyazh Taxi** (☎ 1 11 15) charges R350 to Tuz Khol plus R50 per hour waiting time. Note that renting vehicles outside Kyzyl can be difficult and sometimes ends up more expensive than paying the extra mileage.

Book ahead for the summer hydrofoil, which shoots the Yenisey rapids up to Toora-Khem in Todzha (R564, 10 hours upstream, seven hours back) on alternate days. Take your passport to the **ticket office** (end ul Tuvinskikh Dobrovoltsev; open 2pm-4.30pm as well as some mornings) beside the quay and try to get window seats No 19, 25 or 31.

Getting Around
For the airport, take bus No 1 or 1A from ulitsa Kochetova. Within the centre all bus routes head along ulitsa Kochetova (bus stop Pochta for the theatre). Routes 1, 2 and 10 pass the bus station.

AROUND KYZYL
Five minutes' drive south of Kyzyl a giant statue of a herder on the hill to the left surveys the city. Prayer rags photogenically deck the small freshwater spring beyond, the closest such *arzhaan* to the capital. To get a taste for the steppe, relatively easy excursions include to the salt lakes **Cheder** or **Tuz Khol**. The latter is crowded with comically mud-blackened health-vacationers and so salty that you float Dead Sea–style! It's 20km off the main road down sandy, unsurfaced access tracks. There is no public transport here, but charter and company buses do make the trip.

On the Usinskiy Trakt, 74km north of Kyzyl, **Turan** is an attractive village of old wooden homes, one of which contains a cute little **museum** (ul Druzhby 44). A daily bus

heads to Turan from Kyzyl (2½ hours), and continues to either Arzhaan or Khadyn. The big-sky, straight road from Turan to Arzhaan and Khadyn passes through Tuva's 7th-century-BC **Valley of the Kings**, though the four pancake-shaped burial mounds are mere lumps in the grassland. Archaeologists believe that a chief and his mistress were buried near the centre of each mound. Their servants were buried around them, and the horses were buried around the servants. A model in Kyzyl's Aldan Maadyr National Museum shows the layout.

SOUTHEASTERN TUVA
ЮЖНО ЗАПАДНАЯ ТУВА
Along the Ka-Khem (Maly Yenisey) River
Southeast of Kyzyl, steppe gives way to agricultural greenery around low-rise **Saryg-Sep**, on the Ka-Khem River. It has a basic, friendly **hotel** (per Bukhtueva 18; dorm beds R53). This is as far as you can go by public bus (R46 from Kyzyl bus station, two hours). Upstream of Saryg-Sep are some charmingly situated, but surreally isolated, riverside accommodation options reached via a mud road on which 10km/h is optimistic after rain. A nice option is three-hut **Turbaza Vasilyevka** (☎ 39432-2 22 53; twins including use of the banya R150) in a peaceful flower-filled meadow at Bilbey. This is 33km from Saryg-Sep (22km beyond asphalt's end), on the south bank of the Ka-Khem where the track crosses the river using a small rope-ferry (R50 per jeep, only one at a time!). Some 12km beyond Bilbey along the southern-bank track a second ferry (R50 per car) crosses back to the attractively situated Old Believers' village of **Erzhey**. Backtrack 2km along the north bank (quicker to walk than drive) to the find the attractive **Turbaza Erzhey** (full board $30), which can be booked via the Tsentr Asii agency in Kyzyl (see Orientation & Information under Kyzyl earlier in this chapter). Although it's possible to reach Saryg-Sep by bus, the rest of this route is only reliably accessible by rented four-wheel-drive vehicle. It is generally cheaper and easier to arrange rentals in Kyzyl than in Saryg-Sep. Hitchhiking back to Saryg-Sep from Erzhey is very slow but feasible if you're prepared to pay what can be outrageous fees – we were asked R800 per person! The easiest option is to book a package with Tesntr Asii.

There are more *turbaza* and isolated hunting lodges sprinkled through the region, but access east of Erzhey is by boat only. The Ka-Khem is formed by the confluence of the Balyktyg-Khem and Kyzyl-Khem Rivers. The Kyzyl-Khem River is considered ideal for rafting, if you can afford the helicopter drop-in. The even more dangerous grade 5 rapids on the Balyktyg-Khem isolate **Kungurtug**, which is connected to Kyzyl only by unreliably scheduled helicopter (R3000, four times per week). Relatively nearby is Lake Tere-Khol, in which is an island covered by the mysterious ruins of an 8th-century Uyghur fortress-palace. So far only locals and archaeologists have seen it.

From Kyzyl to Erzin

The paved M54 offers a wonderfully varied scenic feast with archetypal Central Asian grassland, then parkland-style rolling woodlands after **Balgazyn** thickening to pine forest beyond the two tiny cafés at **Shurmak**. Between two low passes (a few kilometres west of Shurmak) marked with shamanic cairns and prayer-rag ticker tape is a picturesque meadow with occasional herders' yurts. The landscape gets starkly drier descending past **Samagaltay** and **Bay Dagh**, a former camel-breeding centre where memorials commemorate the last scuffles of the civil war in 1921. Between km 1023 and km 1024, radar posts look down on the junction of a smooth, scenic but unpaved road to **Mören**, 18km away. The village has no hotel but yurt-dwelling cattle herders in the glorious, hard-to-reach valleys beyond can accommodate a handful of visitors. The experience is unforgettable but as yet needs careful planning via the headmaster of Mören school or the Tourist Department in Kyzyl. These grassy valleys are backed by sharply rugged peaks, including **Ak-Khayyrakan**, 10km from Mören on steep, unpaved tracks. Its spiritual energy is focused on a much revered spring, the start of whose seasonal flow is aided each summer by multiple shamanic ceremonies. You can camp nearby.

The asphalt main road ends at **Erzin**, which has a clean, basic, mural-brightened **hotel** *(ul Komsomolkaya 31; dorm beds/twins R50/ 120)* near the bus stand. Up the street at No 22 is a photogenic competitor for the world's smallest Buddhist temple competition.

A network of sandy tracks continue 20km south past Dali-esque rocky outcrops to Lake Tore Khol (not to be confused with the lake of the same name near Kungurtug), a popular local picnic spot. Although at the edge of the desert zone, herded horses trotting through the shallows gives the area a slight feel of the Camargue. Across the water is Mongolia. There's no border crossing for foreigners.

TODZHA (TODZHU)
ТОДЖА (ТОДЖУ)

'If you haven't seen Todzhu you haven't seen Tuva' sighs a popular local saying. Most Tuvans haven't. Mainly lake-dappled forest, this roadless northeastern lobe of the republic has a distinctly different culture traditionally based on reindeer herding. Above unnavigable rapids, salmon-like *taimen* grow to 15kg (even 30kg by some reports) safe from any fisherman unable to fork out US$8500 for helicopter rental.

Without time and extensive planning casual visitors are limited to the area around Toora-Khem village, where you must register immediately with the police upon arrival. The village has a basic hotel and is accessible by scheduled helicopter from Kyzyl (R2100) or up the beautiful Bolshoy Yenisey (Biy-Khem) River by somewhat claustrophobic hydrofoil.

Some 40 minutes' drive down a tough jeep track from Toora-Khem, the main attraction is serene, forest-edged Lake Azas famed for its water lilies. Beautifully positioned at the lakeside is the basic, astonishingly isolated **Azas Turbaza** *(beds R30; meals R30; open mid-June–mid-Sept)*. Well before leaving Kyzyl ask the tourist office to warn the manager of your arrival date so that he buys food in preparation and is ready to pick you up from the boat dock (transfer about R30 per person).

At Azas you can row on the lake, walk to Green Lake (Noghaan Khol) and imagine that the bears in the woods are only aural mirages.

WESTERN TUVA
ЗАПАДНАЯ ТУВА

Western Tuva is considered wild and lawless, and even other Tuvans are nervous to travel without a local companion. It is nonetheless a splendid and (compared with Mongolia) accessible area of roller-coaster grassland scenery. Visible for 25km, **Mt Khayyrakan** is a spiky ridge blessed by the Dalai Lama in 1992, memorialised at km 107 opposite the On Kum roadside *stolovaya* (eat while you can!). **Shagonar** (Shagon Arigh in Tuvan), 111km west of Kyzyl, was an attractive old town of neat wooden homes until was drowned by the southernmost nose of the Sayano-Shushenskoe reservoir in the 1980s. The 'new' Shagonar is a hopelessly depressing grid of concrete towers, though there is a little museum in one of the few Siberian-style cottages. The **hotel** *(☎ 39436-2 24 33; ul Sayano-Shushinskaya 3, Apt 56; singles/ twins with indoor toilet R168/274)* is surprisingly acceptable if you dare to climb the horror-film stairwell to get there (you have to go to Flat 57 to request the key when the hotel door is locked). There are a few shared taxis daily between Shagonar and Kyzyl.

Chaa Khol, 74km from Shagonar, is nicer but while the three-room **hotel** *(ul Lenina 37; beds R70)* has the luxury of a shared cold bath, the toilet-hole is outside. There are three buses a week between Chaa Kol and Kyzyl. Around 15km north of here (possible by car), carved into a rocky lakeside headland, is a heavily defaced old Buddha. The circling raptors, wide silent landscapes and the precarious scramble to find it are the real attraction. When the Sayano-Shushenskoe reservoir is full, the waters may drown the Buddha's niche altogether.

Chadan (Chadaana)
Чадан
☎ 39434 • pop 8700

Full of wooden cottages, Chadan was formerly Tuva's spiritual centre but today is nicknamed the 'Chicago of Tuva' and its population has a reputation for weapon-wielding. Restoration has haltingly started on the chunky ruins of the once great **Ustuu Khuree** temple, hidden in serene woodland 6km down tracks from the Bazhin-Alaak turning at the eastern edge of Chadan. There's an appealing little **museum** *(admission R5; ul Lenina 33; open 9am-4pm Mon-Fri)* and an annual July music festival (featuring everything from *khöömei* to hard rock). You can stay at the **aalchylar bazhyngy** *(guesthouse; ul Pobedy 1; beds/ twins R46/102)*, which has an outside toilet-hole. Make sure you are very careful on the streets at night.

There are a few shared taxis daily between Kyzyl and Chadan. Five kilometres west of Chadan a road branches south to **Khandagayty**, where the Mongolian border may soon open. A glorious but atrociously difficult track from here skirts the frontier west to **Mugur-Aksy** and high, bald, glacier-topped Mt Mongun-Tayga (3976m). Bring food, a reliable guide, ample extra fuel and spare parts, especially if you plan a truck or jeep convoy across the mountains from Mugur-Aksy to Kosh Agach in Altay (impossible after rain).

Ak-Dovurak
Ак-Довурак
☎ 39441 • pop 13,300

Tuva's unlovable second city, Ak-Dovurak, is dominated by the world's largest open-pit asbestos mine. The main sight is the **Jenghis Khan Stone**, a well-preserved moustachioed stone idol *(kameny baba in Russian or kizhigozher in Tuvan)*. It stands in a field 400m to the right of the Ayangalty road, 8km from Kyzyl-Mazhalik and 500m beyond the turning to Bizhiktig Haya. Taxis ask R200 return from Ak-Dovurak. In Ak-Dovurak, accommodation is available at the **Hotel MPP ZhKKh** *(☎ 12 55; ul Tsentralnaya 6; twins with bathroom R200)*, which has real toilets. It's upstairs in the rear of the building show giant Soviet-era mural faces the east side of a bright new café, **Mirazh** *(ul Tsentralnaya 2; meals R10-20; open 9am-5pm & 6pm-11pm daily)*.

Shared taxis leave around 6am or 7am to Abakan train station (R500 per seat, six hours) using the 95% asphalt yet very infrequently travelled A161 via Abaza. The route is extremely beautiful as far as the Khakassian border on the dramatic Sayanskiy pass (2206m), which is topped by fields of alpine flowers and affords a fine panorama. Further north the thick forest makes the scenery more monotonous. Northbound you could hop off at Snow Leopard Camp (for more details, see the Southwest Khakassia section earlier in this chapter). However, southbound transport from there is limited to hitchhiking.

From Kyzyl, there are two or three buses a day to Ak-Dovurak (R100), one of which continues to Teeli. There are also a few shared taxis a day between Kyzyl and Ak-Dovurak. Heading towards Teeli, there are two buses a day.

City buses link the centre of town via the bus station (1.5km) to marginally nicer **Kyzyl Mazhalik** across the Shui River.

Teeli & Kyzyl-Dag
Тээли и Кызыл-Даг
Teeli ☎ 39442
Low-rise Teeli is a scenic 38km west of Ak-Dovurak. There are no sights per se, and as anywhere in Western Tuva there is something of a wild west edge to life here. Nonetheless, it's the most attractive village in the region to have any public accommodation. Teeli's **Chonar Dash Hotel** (*ul Lenina 25; beds R46-71*), with outside long-drop, is one long block from the bus station.

From Teeli or Ak-Dovurak the most popular excursion is to Kyzyl-Dag, which has a small oriental-roofed Buddhist temple and is famous for carvings in agalmatolite (self-hardening soapstone). Craftsman **Sergei Kochaa** (*ul Kamnerezov 9*) also processes sheepskins, makes saddles and claims to be the only surviving maker of traditional smoked-leather *körgerzhik* (kidney-shaped drinking vessels), displayed in many museums), though his prices for samples and practical demonstrations can be arbitrarily excessive. Some 7km away is the spiritually powerful **Aghylygh-Shat** mystical burial site, but approaching without the necessary shamanic ceremonies can get you cursed or worse.

One bus daily runs between Kyzyl and Teeli (R116, eight hours) via Ak-Dovurak. In addition here are twice-daily Ak-Dovurak–Teeli buses (R20, 50 minutes) which, according to the day, continue to Bai Tal, Shui or Kyzyl-Dag (Wednesday and Sunday) making day trips possible.

Krasnoyarsk Territory
Красноярский край

Vast, mineral-rich Krasnoyarsk Territory stretches from the borders of Tuva right up to the Arctic islands of Severnaya Zemlya. At its centre, the territory's capital, Krasnoyarsk, sits astride the mighty Yenisey River and is the major regional transport hub. Southern Krasnoyarsk Territory, however, is easier to visit from Abakan in the Khakassia Republic

and is covered separately in the Khakassia Republic & Southern Krasnoyarsk Territory section earlier in this chapter.

KRASNOYARSK
КРАСНОЯРСК
☎ 3912 • pop 871,000 • Moscow time plus 4 hours
A forested backdrop of jagged foothills and contours all its own give Krasnoyarsk, 760km east of Novosibirsk, a much more appealing setting than typical big, flat Siberian cities. Architecture isn't a particular strength but amid the predominantly unaesthetic concrete of the post-WWII industrialisation, you'll still find some outstandingly well-embellished timber mansions. Pleasant river trips and the nearby Stolby Nature Reserve as well as the region's best concert halls, theatres and museums make Krasnoyarsk a most agreeable place to break a trans-Siberian journey.

Orientation & Information
The Yenisey River splits the city in two. The city centre is on the north bank, while the zoo, funicular and access to Stolby Nature Reserve are west of the city, along the south bank.

A variety of city maps are sold at the river station or more cheaply at bookshops such as **Russkoe Slovo** (*ul Lenina 28; open 10am-2pm & 3pm-7pm Mon-Fri, 10am-3pm Sat*), which also stocks a 1:200,000 regional map.

The website **w** http://tlcom.krs.ru is a useful introduction to the city. **OBK Bank** (*pr Mira 7A; open 9am-7pm Mon-Fri, 9am-6pm Sat*) gives good rates for US$ cash and changes travellers cheques. There's an ATM here and in Hotel Krasnoyarsk.

Ulitsa Lenina has some fine wooden mansions (such as Nos 88 and 67) but the **post office** (*ul Lenina 49*) isn't one of them. The **long-distance telephone office** (*pr Mira 102*) is round the corner from **KrasAir** (*open 8.30am-7.30pm daily*), the main air ticket office. For Internet access, try **Port** (*☎ 27 72 18; ul Surikova 2; open 24hr*), which has its entrance on ulitsa Dubrovinskogo.

SIAT (*ul Vzlyotnaya 9; bus No 50; open 8am-8pm Mon-Fri, 8am-1pm & 2pm-6pm Sat & Sun*) sells Sibaviatrans tickets to/from Igarka, Turukhansk and Khatanga.

Sayan Ring Travel (*☎ 65 26 50, fax 65 26 49; w www.gotosiberia.ru; ul Lenina 24*) is a friendly travel agency with a couple of staff who speak English. They specialise in relatively luxurious tours of Khakassia and Tuva, where they run a pair of yurt-hotels, but these can be booked independently when not full with tour groups.

Travel Academy (☎ 27 74 40, fax 27 62 52; e geomuseum@krsk.ru; pr Mira 37) runs specialised geological tours. The office is upstairs in the fine, cavernous but generally appointment-only Geological Museum.

Dyula Tur (☎ 59 14 00; e litamail@mail.ru) has branches in Hotel Krasnoyarsk and the river station. It can book flights and organises an annual trip to the North Pole in March or April.

Museums

A wonderfully incongruous 1912 Egyptian temple–style building with glorious Art Nouveau interiors houses one of Siberia's top museums. This completely renovated **Regional Museum** (Kraevedchesky muzey; ☎ 27 69 70; ul Dubrovinskogo 84; admission R20; open 11am-7pm Tues-Sun) walks you through various historical room interiors arranged around a Cossack explorer's s' the fine ethnographic section .. which compares the historical fi of shamans from various tribal g appealing gift shop sells old coins and medals.

The **Surikov Museum-Estate** (Muzey-usadba V I Surikova; ☎ 23 15 07; ul Lenina 98; admission R20; open 10am-6pm Tues-Sat) preserves the house, sheds and vegetable patch of 19th-century painter Vasily Surikov (1848–1916). The heavy-gated garden forms a refreshing oasis of rural Siberia right in the city centre. More of Surikov's work is on show at the cute **Surikov Art Museum** (ul Parizhskoy Kommuny 20; open 11am-6pm Tues-Sun).

The **Geological Museum** (Muzey Geologii Tsentralnoy Sibiri; ☎ 27 62 62; pr Mira 37; admission R70; open Mon-Fri by appointment) is one of the best of its kind but if you want to visit (like President Putin in 2002) you have to call ahead and arrange a guided tour (in Russian only).

The **Literature Museum** (Literaturnyy Muzey; ☎ 27 62 01; ul Lenina 66; admission R7; open 10am-5pm Tues-Sun) is within a glorious 1911 wooden mansion opposite an antique fire-station. Beers cost R20 in the attached bar.

Churches

The **Catholic Chapel** (Rimsko-Katolicheskiy Kostyol; ul Dekabristov 2) is twin spired if not inspired – a 1911 church whose European neo-Gothic style is unusual for Siberia. More attractive churches include the fancy **Pokrovsky Cathedral**, the tall, elegant **Blagoveshchensky Church** and the **Troitskaya Church** across the Kacha Stream. Clearly visible on the crest of a hill to the north is the pointy little **Chasoviya Chapel** that features on the Russian 10-rouble note. Several new churches and a big mosque are under construction.

Lenin Memorabilia

In April 1897, the goateed wonder stayed in Krasnoyarsk at ulitsa Markovskogo 27. A pensive statue beside the house is now almost lost in weeds and building works. A big, much prouder, Lenin stands opposite the popular city park. Permanently docked below an ugly concrete exhibition centre is the boat **SV Nikolay** (admission R12; open 10am-6pm Tues-Sun), which transported our Vlad to Shushenskoe. Aboard, Lenin is now merely a forgotten mannequin in steerage class, while the better berths display a witty collection of musical boxes and 20th-century household objects.

Stolby Nature Reserve & Roev Ruchey Zoo

Strange volcanic rock pillars, called stolby, litter the woods in the 17,000-hectare Stolby Nature Reserve (Zapovednik Stolby). The standard way to get there is to walk for 7km down a track that starts opposite Kafe Turist, 200m east of Turbaza Yenisey. (Beware of ticks between May and July.) Alternatively, an easier way to get a panoramic view of the reserve is by taking the **chair lift** (R40 one way), which operates year-round on request, from Kafe Bobrovyylog, at the end of ulitsa Sibirskaya. To get there, take bus No 50 to the Bazaikha Stream (ie, ulitsa Sverdlovskaya 173), then walk about 15 minutes south, following occasional signs. From the top of the chair lift, it's a two-minute stroll to a great viewpoint, from where trails lead steeply down into the reserve.

About 0.5km west of Turbaza Yenisey, Siberian species rare and not so rare, along with happily humping camels, inhabit the new, relatively humane **Roev Ruchey Zoo** (bus No 72 or 50; admission R20; open 10am-6.30pm daily).

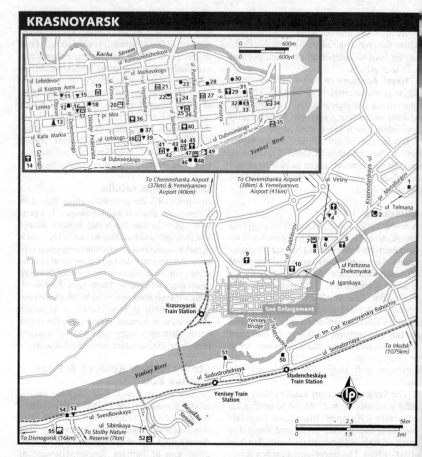

KRASNOYARSK

Places to Stay

Several of the cheapies, including **Hotel Seber** (☎ 22 41 14; ul Lenina 21) and **Hotel Ogin Yeniseyya** (☎ 27 52 62; ul Dubrovinskogo 80; singles R11/hour), generally don't take foreigners. One that usually will is the decent-value if unpronounceable **Krasnoyarskstroy-strategiya** (☎ 27 66 12; pr Mira 12; dorm beds/singles/twins R177/282/380); the entrance is on ulitsa Karatanova.

Hotel-ship Mayak (☎ 29 04 81; ul Dubrovinskogo; single/twin berths R220/320, luxe berths R450) is behind the river station. Although the place is well positioned and atmospheric, it's noisy and not very secure: the windows of several cabin rooms don't lock effectively and each faces a semi-public walkway.

Hotel Polyot (☎/fax 27 34 74; ul Aero-vokzalnaya 16; singles/twins from R400/580) close to the bus station has some nicely renovated rooms but each is different and the prices don't always reflect the variation in standards. The R550 singles are generally better than R780 versions. Rates include breakfast.

Turbaza Yenisey (☎ 69 81 10; bus No 50; doubles from R300, suites R1500) is actually a hotel. Handy for the zoo and Stolby reserve, it has a nice river view from its minuscule terrace and the doubles have clean, shared toilets.

Hotel Krasnoyarsk (☎ 27 37 54, fax 27 02 36; e hotelkrs@ktk.ru; ul Uritskogo 94; singles/doubles from R630/870) is big and well kept, handily central and has English-

KRASNOYARSK

PLACES TO STAY		42	Kofeinya
1	Hotel Yakhont		Кофеиня
	Гостиница Яхонт	53	Kafe Turist
8	Hotel Polyot		Кафе Турист
	Гостиница Полёт		
12	Hotel Seber	**OTHER**	
	Гостиница Себер	2	Mosque
31	Hotel Krasnoyarsk-		Мечеть
	stroystrategiya	3	New Georgian Church
	Гостиница Красноярскт-		Гружинский Церковь
	ройстратегия	5	New Baptist Church
32	Hotel Oktyabrskaya		Храм-Дом Молитвы
	Гостиница Октябрьская	6	SIAT
37	Hotel Krasnoyarsk		Сибавиатранс
	Гостиница Красноярск	7	Bus Station
43	Hotel Ogin Yeniseyya		Автовокзал
	Гостиница Огин Енисейя	9	Chasoviya Chapel
48	Hotel-ship Mayak		Часовия
	Гостиница Маяк	10	Troitskaya Church
50	Hotel Turist		Троицкая Церковь
	Гостиница Турист	13	Lenin Statue
51	Siberian Safari Club		Памятник Ленину
	Сибирский Сафари	14	Catholic Chapel
	Клуб	17	Telephone Office
54	Turbaza Yenisey		Междугородный
	Турбаза Енисей		телефонный пункт
		18	KrasAir
PLACES TO EAT			КрасЗр
4	He Goryuy	19	Surikov Museum-Estate
	Не Горюй		Музей-усадьба В. И.
11	Bar Chemodan		Сурикова
	бар Чемодан	20	Kinopark Pikra
15	Ritaz		Кинопарк Пикра
	Ритаз	21	Literature Museum
16	Kantri; Severyanka		Литературный Музей
	Кантри	22	Post Office
25	Kafe Razole; Pikra 16		Почтамт
	Кафе Разоле;	23	Lenin House
	Пикра 16		Дом Ленина
39	Shashlyk Grills & Beer Bars	24	Pokrovsky Cathedral
	(Summer Only)		Покровский Собор

26	Geological Museum; Travel Academy
	Музей Геологиу
	Центральной Сибири
27	Surikov Art Museum
	Художественный музей
	имени В. И. Сурикова
28	Russkoe Slobo Bookshop
	Русское Слово
29	Blagoveshchensky Church
	благовещенский
	Церковь
30	Paradise Travel
	Парадайз
33	OBK Bank
	ОбК банк
34	Philharmonia
	Филармония
35	S V Nikolay
	СВ Николай
36	Karambol
	Ночной клуб Карамболь
38	Opera-Ballet Theatre
	Театр оперы и балета
40	Zolotaya Podkova
	Ночной клуб Золотая
	Подкова
41	Regional Museum
	Краеведческий музей
44	Port (Internet Café)
	Интернет Кафе Порт
45	Church under Construction
46	Hydrofoils to Divnogorsk
47	Buses to Divnogorsk
49	River Station; Dyula Tur
	Речной вокзал; Дюла Тур
52	Chair Lift; Kafe Bobrovyylog
	Фуникюларь; Кафе
	бобровыйлог
55	Roev Ruchey Zoo
	Зоопарк Роев Ручей

speaking receptionists. Rates include a buffet breakfast.

Hotel Turist (☎ 36 14 70, fax 36 61 23; w http://tlcom.krs.ru/tourist/index.html; ul Matrasova 2; singles/doubles from US$20/ 40) is directly across the long Yenisey Bridge from the city centre. Rooms, with toilet and shower, are reasonable enough but at night the dubious disco sets the whole Soviet-era tower vibrating.

Siberian Safari Club (☎ 61 33 35/58, fax 61 27 66; w http://tlcom.krs.ru/safari/index htm; ul Sudostroitelnaya 117A; bus No 36; singles US$25-35, doubles US$70) is an intimate, 17-room Western-standard hotel with English-speaking staff and a classy terrace restaurant. Booking is advisable (R183 to R573 fee) but the cheapest single rooms are

superb value. It's a 10-minute walk from the nearest bus stop.

Hotel Oktyabrskaya (☎ 27 19 16, 27 05 81; w www.tlcom.krs.ru/october; pr Mira 15; doubles from R1500) is professionally run with mostly Western-style renovated rooms. Rates include breakfast.

Hotel Yakhont (☎ 24 44 53; ul Telmana 44A; trolleybus No 7; rooms US$80) is pricey and inconveniently suburban but the rooms are impressively modern and there's endless juvenile amusement in mispronouncing the name.

Places to Eat & Drink
There are plenty of eateries along prospekt Mira, and many summer cafés on the promenade near the river station. On summer

SIBERIA

evenings, lively shashlyk grills and beer bars give the concrete, fountain-filled square outside Hotel Krasnoyarsk a piazza feel. The grocery store **Ritaz** (*ul Lenina 112; open 9am-8pm*) has a cheap café and bakery.

Kafe Razole (*pr Mira 37; meals R25-60, beers R12-65; open 10am-4pm & 5pm-11pm daily*) is a pleasant basement where you pay under R15 for a packet cappuccino and a chocolate éclair. In the same block **Pikra 16** (☎ 65 25 60; mains R70-140; open noon-midnight daily) has wooden pew-seats under its classy old brick arches.

He Goryuy (☎ 58 70 76; cnr uls 78 Dobrovolocheskoy Brigady & Vesny; bus No 50 or 97; mains R40-60; open noon-3am daily) is worth the trek to the unlikely Novaya Zlemka suburb for pillow-sized *khajapuri*s (R50) in a cheap but atmospheric stone-walled pub-café.

Kantri (*Country; pr Mira 102A; lunches R120, small beers from R34*) is a Wild West saloon pub beneath the much cheaper café **Severyanka** (*open 24hr*).

Kofeinya (☎ 23 26 96; ul Dubrovinskogo 82; mains R120-190; open 8am-midnight daily) is pricey but has menus in English, real coffee and an interesting range of traditional dishes, including soup-in-a-roll.

Bar Chemodan (☎ 23 02 59; ul Oboron 2B; mains R140-400, Guinness per pint R165; open noon-midnight daily) is the most stylish pub-restaurant in town, with over a hundred whiskies and a Siberian-retro mock-historical ambience.

Entertainment

Krasnoyarsk is a great place for opera or ballet, with up to five shows per week at the large **Opera-Ballet Theatre** (☎ 27 86 97; ul Perensona 2; tickets from R60) during October to June. The **Philharmonia** (☎ 27 49 30; pl Mira 2B) has three concert halls showcasing folk, pop and classical music.

Popular city-centre nightclubs include **Karambol** (*ul Perensona 20; open 10pm-6am*), **Zolotaya Podkova** and the **Kinopark Pikra** (☎ 27 75 31; ul Perensona 29A), a cinema-bar-club complex that's easy to spot thanks to a plane that crashes through its front wall!

Getting There & Away

Air Apart from the weekly Khatanga (R6700 via Norilsk) service from Cheremshanka airport, 43km northwest of the city, on Wednes-

day, almost all flights use Yemelyanovo airport, 3km beyond Cheremshanka. From Yemelyanovo, there are services to a vast network of domestic destinations, including Moscow (R4500 to R6000, three per day), St Petersburg (R5000 to R5280, four per week), Norilsk (twice daily), Khabarovsk (R3960 to R4200, three per week), Irkutsk (R2650, five per week), Yekaterinburg (R3730 to R4150, two to six per week) and Kyzyl (R2440, four per week). KrasAir has weekly flights to Tashkent (US$150), Hanover (US$400 one way, US$445 to US$550 return) and Frankfurt (from around US$475) via Barnaul. A cheaper way to get to Germany would be to fly Kaliningrad (R6690, three per week) then to take a bus across Poland.

Train Overnight hops include Abakan (No 24, *kupe* R578, 10½ hours), Tomsk (No 107, odd days in summer), Lesosibirsk (No 667, *platskart* R193, 11½ hours) and Novosibirsk (No 055, 12½ hours, even days). No 055 is the best choice for Yekaterinburg (33 hours) and Moscow (60 hours). Train No 092 takes 30 hours to Severobaikalsk. Six or more trains daily take around 18 to 19 hours to Irkutsk.

To save a trip to the train station, buy tickets at the handy **booking office** (open 8am-1pm & 2pm-7pm Mon-Fri, 9am-1pm & 2pm-5pm Sat, 9am-1pm & 2pm-3pm Sun) in the river station.

Bus From the main **bus station** (☎ 23 05 12; ul Aerovokzalnaya 22; trolleybus No 2 or bus No 50) there are services to Yeniseysk (R188, 7½ hours, four daily), Abakan (nine hours, two daily), Shushenskoe (10½ hours, once daily) and Sayanogorsk (R255, 10½ hours, once daily).

Regular No 106 buses to Divnogorsk (R21, one hour, two per hour until 8pm) use a small stand at the western side of the river station. Descend the steps halfway for the ticket window, all the way for buses.

Boat From Krasnoyarsk's spired **river station** (☎ 27 44 46; open 8am-7pm daily), passenger boats ply the Yenisey to Dudinka via Yeniseysk (17 hours), Turukhansk (38 to 40 hours) and Igarka (R1234 to R2974, 74 to 79 hours). There are three to four boats per week, departing at 7am, from the end of May to early October. The *Bliznyak* continues to Ust Port (R1369 to R3309, 92 hours) and

Karaul (R1445 to R3495, 99 hours). Return (upstream) journeys take 50% longer. Last-minute tickets are usually available. For Yeniseysk, the hydrofoil (R389, alternate days between June and mid-August) arrives at a less antisocial time.

Hydrofoils to Divnogorsk use quay No 2 or 4 near Hotel-ship Mayak and depart at 10am, noon, 2pm, 4pm and 6pm daily in summer, returning an hour later. Buy tickets (R38) on board.

Getting Around
Bus No 135 (R26, three to four hours, 20 per day) from the bus station serves Yemelyanovo airport, passing right beside the smaller Cheremshanka airport 3km before arrival.

Within the centre, almost all public transport runs eastbound along ulitsa Karla Marksa and returns westbound on ulitsa Lenina. Any eastbound bus marked 'Matrasovo' will veer south, stopping at both ends of the long Yenisey Bridge, which is handy for Hotel Krasnoyarsk and Hotel Turist.

Frequent, if slow, trolleybus No 7 trundles from the train station via ulitsa Karla Marksa, up ulitsa Surikova and on eventually (after half an hour) past the mosque to Hotel Yakhont. The remarkably useful bus No 50 starts beyond the zoo, passes the Turbaza Yenisey and comes through the centre of town, winding on to the bus station, SIAT and a loop beyond. Bus No 50A repeats the first half of the route then turns left along ulitsa Lenina to the train station.

AROUND KRASNOYARSK
Divnogorsk
Дивногорск
☎ 39144 • pop 29,000 • Moscow time plus 4 hours
Even if you don't like dams, Divnogorsk, 16km southwest of Krasnoyarsk along the Yenisey, makes a scenic river-boat excursion from Krasnoyarsk and offers a cheaper accommodation alternative to that city, especially if you're heading to Abakan.

From Divnogorsk's little jetty, it's 5km to the foot of the impressive 90m-high dam. The powerhouse museum has closed, but the 4m-tall red-faced Lenin portrait remains photogenic. Taxis meet boats on arrival and want R100 for a return trip to the dam, or R200 to continue to the top. This lets you look down

into the reservoir and allows you to see the inclined plane on which moving basins transport ships across the dam.

Hotel Biryuza (☎ 2 37 61; 2nd floor, ul Lenina 55; singles R150-200, twins R180-250), by the riverside, is five minutes' walk from the jetty. It offers nice views and a rudimentary shower in the better rooms.

From Krasnoyarsk, both buses and high-speed river boats give attractive and rather different views of the tree-lined Yenisey gorge. Divnogorsk's bus station is a steep walk from the jetty, high above the river in the market area. Buses to Abakan leave at 1pm and 9.45pm, with a third at 11.05am continuing to Shushenskoe.

NORTH ALONG THE YENISEY
Every couple of days in summer, elegant passenger ships with wood panelling and shiny brass fittings depart Krasnoyarsk for a 2000km Yenisey River odyssey. The trip is meditational more than scenic, with days merging as the sun barely manages to bob below the Arctic horizon. Most routes terminate at Dudinka (from R1420, 4½ days north, six days back). However, Dudinka and nearby Norilsk were 'closed' to foreigners by decree in October 2001. The farthest you can go without a permit now is Igarka (R1234 to R2974, four days; arrives 3am), but that's still above the Arctic Circle.

It may be possible to get Dudinka permits as part of a 10-day 'luxury tourist cruise' on the good ship Anton Chekhov, which costs US$950 to US$1150 per person in a double cabin with shower and toilet. However, its management is in flux: inquire at Dyula Tur or Sayan Ring Travel in Krasnoyarsk for the latest details.

Yeniseysk
Енисейск
☎ 39115 • pop 16,000 • Moscow time plus 4 hours
For a shorter jaunt from Krasnoyarsk, head for historic Yeniseysk, 340km northwest along the river. Founded in 1619, this was once Russia's great fur-trading capital, with world-famous 18th-century August fairs and 10 grand churches gracing its skyline. Eclipsed by Krasnoyarsk, despite a burst of gold-rush prosperity in the 1860s, the town is now a delightfully peaceful backwater with a good **Regional Museum** (ul Lenina 106; admission

SIBERIA

R8; open 9am-5pm Mon-Sat), many old wooden houses, the faded commercial grandeur of ulitsa Lenina, and four remaining religious edifices. Most appealing are the walled **Spaso-Pereobrazhensky Monastery** (ul Raboche-Krestyanskaya 105, enter through the green gate), built in 1731 but now a shell, and the nearby **Uspensky Church** (ul Raboche-Krestyanskaya 116; donation required) with an unusual metal floor and splendid antique icons.

Hotel Yenisey (☎ 2 31 49; ul Khuzinskogo 2; dorm beds R105, singles R195-480), near the quay, has burping old toilets and washbasins in the best rooms.

To get to Yeniseysk, you can either take one of the passenger ships heading north from Krasnoyarsk or use hydrofoils (R389, 10 hours, alternate days). There are also four buses per day to/from Krasnoyarsk (7½ hours) and hourly buses to Lesosibirsk.

Lesosibirsk
Лесосибирск
☎ 39145 • pop 77,000 • Moscow time plus 4 hours

For most travellers, Lesosibirsk is simply the railhead for Yeniseysk, 36km farther north. It's basically an uninteresting timber mill but it does have the breathtaking new **Kresto-vozdvizhenskiy Church** (south of ul Gorkogo 81), with gleaming clusters of golden domes. Take bus No 2 or 8 to its southern terminus and you'll be in front of **Hotel Kedr** (☎ 39145-2 28 52; ul 60 Let VLKSM 7; singles/twins R300/500), which offers bearable rooms with hot water.

To Yeniseysk there are hourly buses (R25, 45 minutes) from the bus station plus one direct from the train station departing 15 minutes after the arrival of the nightly train from Krasnoyarsk. Bus No 13 links the bus and train stations but very infrequently.

Igarka
Игарка
☎ 39112 • pop 9000 • Moscow time plus 4 hours

Sulking dejectedly at the mouth of the frigid Protoka River, the ragged timber port of Igarka, 1405km north of Yeniseysk, was developed as Gulag 503. Up to 35,000 exiles laboured on a nonsensical, never-to-be-completed train line that Stalin had carelessly doodled across a map to Salekhard.

Today the town is dying, with its dismal climate and hopeless employment prospects. The melt-thaw moods of the permafrost on which the town is built relentlessly undermine the foundations of those buildings that have survived being burnt down by alcoholics (many of whom have fallen catastrophically unconscious, cigarette in hand). Yet hidden incredibly in the ruins from permafrost and economic collapse is a museum that beat London's National Portrait Gallery for commendation as European Museum of the Year in 2002. This **Permafrost Museum** (Vechnoy Merzloty muzey; ☎ 2 41 10; w www.museum.ru/M1405; ul Bolshoy Teatr 15A; admission R127; open 9am-12.45pm & 2pm-5pm Sun-Fri) is small but unforgettable, allowing you to descend 10m through the frozen mud and ice strata into a fairy-tale world of crystalline condensed breath. It has associated sub-museums (separate admission charges) and a Gulag memorial.

Hotel Morskoe Port (LPK) (☎ 2 43 12; ul Chkalova 3; dorm beds from R150), near the museum, is cosy. **Hotel Zapolyare** (☎ 2 16 11; 1st Microrayon 7A; singles/twins from R288/432), 4km away amid crumbling concrete apartment blocks and handier for the main shop, has a bar/restaurant and showers. Bus No 1 (via the art gallery) and No 2 link the museum and both hotels.

Tickets for Sibaviatrans (SIAT) flights to Krasnoyarsk (R2310, 3½ hours, three to seven per week) are sold at the bank beside Hotel Zapolyare, but it's wise to book ahead from Krasnoyarsk. The airport is on an island linked to town by boat, bus or helicopter (R100/person), according to the state of the ice. For details on passenger ships from Krasnoyarsk, see the start of the North along the Yenisey section earlier.

Dudinka & Norilsk
Дудинка и Норильск
☎ 39112 • pop 33,000 (Dudinka), 290,000 (Norilsk) • Moscow time plus 4 hours

Both Dudinka and Norilsk have been closed to foreigners since October 2001, and you will need a permit to visit either place, which is virtually impossible to get without local contacts.

Dudinka is an unattractive port town of dilapidated pastel-coloured apartment blocks and cranes, sporting a brace of war memorials. The best hotel is **Severnoe Siyatsie** (☎ 5 60 79; ul Matrasova 14; singles R300).

Norilsk, 80km east of Dudinka, is an improbably large nickel-processing city, which is responsible for acid rain over a wide area of Siberian tundra. The city has a distinctive green mosque (1997) and a museum with exhibits about the city's construction and gulag horrors. The good-value **Hotel Norilsk** (☎ 4 99 30; ul Talnakhskaya 39A; singles R280), off ulitsa Sovetskaya, examines permits and visas in minute detail.

Norilsk has twice-daily air connections with Krasnoyarsk, as well as services to Moscow and several Urals cities, and a weekly hop to the tiny Taymyr outpost of Khatanga.

Beyond Norilsk

The gigantic Taymyr (Dolgan-Nenets) Autonomous District stretches to mainland Russia's most northerly point. The whole region is extremely sparsely populated, with sad, decaying settlements scattered along the ever-widening yawn of the Yenisey Gulf. Ethnic Russians overwhelmingly outnumber the minuscule population of indigenous Dolgan and Nenets peoples.

Inland, magnificent waterfalls and canyons lead up to the flat, barren and frigidly windswept Putorana Plateau. However, you'll need time, money and plenty of mosquito repellent to explore, hunt or fish here. Agencies offering tours include K2 in Omsk and Dyula Tur in Krasnoyarsk; tours generally avoid Norilsk by flying via the tsarist exile village of Turukhansk and continuing by fearsomely expensive rented helicopter.

To the North Pole

Khatanga acts as a launching point for annual excursions in March or April to the top of the world. A fly-in, fly-out trip booked through Dyula Tur in Krasnoyarsk (see under Orientation & Information in Krasnoyarsk earlier for contact details) costs around US$3000 if there's sufficient demand. For an organised expedition, the German **DAV Summit Club** (☎ 089-642 400, fax 642 401 in Germany; W www.dav-summit-club.de) offers 18-day 'Exnor' adventures for around US$8000 departing from Germany or Austria.

If just getting to the Pole isn't enough, experienced drysuit divers can plunge beneath it with UK-based **Divercity Ltd** (☎ 01908 647300 in the UK; W www.divercityscuba .com), whose annual two-week expeditions cost around US$8500.

The Western BAM
Западный БАМ

The Baikal-Amur Mainline (BAM), starting at Tayshet 417km east of Krasnoyarsk and ending at Sovetskaya Gavan on the Pacific coast some 3100km later, is an astonishing victory of belief over adversity. Much of this 'other' trans-Siberian line was cut through virgin taiga and pesky mountain ranges in the 1970s and '80s by volunteer labourers (see the boxed text 'The Hero Project of the Century'). Expecting a bright new future, many stayed on to populate the towns that grew sparsely along the lonely line, but most of these have proved economic disappointments. Most thriving is Severobaikalsk (see Lake Baikal later in this chapter), a hub for North Baikal, which is the BAM's biggest draw for travellers.

The main attraction of the BAM is that it crosses virtually virgin territory: you're travelling across parts of Siberia and the Far East that few other foreigners have ever seen. While not particularly absorbing in themselves, the towns along the line can serve as bases for exploration of the surrounding wilderness, and there are good opportunities for adventure tourism. For details on Eastern BAM towns Tynda, Komsomolskna-Amur, Vanino and Sovetskaya Gavan, see the Russian Far East chapter later in this book.

Although there are through trains to Tynda from Moscow and Krasnoyarsk, the official start of the BAM is **Tayshet**, where there are station resting rooms should you have a long time to wait between trains. Between **Bratsk** and **Ust-Kut** (from which there are irregular boat services along the Lena River to Yakutsk) is the claustrophobic 1960s iron-ore processing town of **Zheleznogorsk-Ilimsky** (train station Korshunikha Angarskaya), whose sole, modest attraction is the **Yangel Museum** (admission R5; open 9am-4pm Mon-Fri) celebrating a local astroscientist friend of Yuri Gagarin.

There are fine mountain views between **Kunerma** and **Goudzhekit**. The latter is a delightfully tiny spa between bald, high peaks that stay snow dusted until early June. To find the small **hotel** (beds in heated huts R100-440) walk to the right out of the station then turn left after five minutes to the end of the track. Book via tour agency Khozyain in

The Hero Project of the Century

In the 1930s, work was begun on a second trans-Siberian line, the Baikal-Amur Mainline (Baikalo-Amurskaya Magistral, or BAM). This line was to extend from Tayshet on the existing Trans-Siberian Railway, around the northern tip of Lake Baikal, and on to the previously inaccessible, timber-rich Lena Basin and its coal, iron-ore and gold mines. Abandoned in WWII and stripped so its tracks could be used to lay a relief line to the besieged city of Stalingrad (now Volgograd), it was essentially started all over again in 1974. In the meantime, the line had gained in strategic importance as an alternative to the existing Trans-Siberian Railway, which was felt to be too vulnerable to attack by a potentially hostile China.

The BAM was called the 'Hero Project of the Century', and the youth of the Soviet Union was called to rally to the challenge. Their response is evident in the names of some of the towns along the line (such as Estbam, Latbam and Litbam, named for the workers from the Baltic states who built them) and in the striking absence of elderly people in these communities today. The BAM towns grew with the new railway, which was forced through virgin wilderness. Overcoming Siberia's swamps and mountains, its seemingly infinite number of rivers and, in particular, its vast swathe of permafrost pushed the cost of the project to a staggering US$25 billion (by comparison, the Trans-Siberian Railway is estimated to have cost the equivalent of US$500 million).

Officially opened in 1991, the line still isn't finished – the incomplete Severomuysk tunnel is currently bypassed by a temporary line that is extremely susceptible to landslides. There is little traffic on the line and many of its settlements have become ghost towns.

Severobaikalsk (see that section for contact details for Khozyain).

The line between **Severobaikalsk** and **Nizhneangarsk** offers many flashes of dazzling Lake Baikal views. It continues to **Dzelinda**, another spa, though less attractively situated and tougher to access than Goudzhekit. Accommodation in huts is available here from R350 (book through Khozyain). Trains on to Tynda will continue to switchback up and over the **Severomuysk Pass** until the 15km-long tunnel is finally opened (possibly in 2003 or 2004). This is the most spectacular section of the Western BAM.

BRATSK
БРАТСК
☎ 3953 • pop 281,000 • Moscow time plus 5 hours

Historical Bratsk started as a 17th-century fortress but, along with 40 other villages, it is now at the bottom of the Bratsk Sea. This artificial lake was created in 1955 by a gigantic dam and hydroelectric station, Bratskaya Gidro Elektro Stantsiya, whose vast energy capacity industrial Bratsk was built to harness. The city rose out of virgin taiga through the labour of patriotic volunteer workers who initially lived under canvas, enduring winter temperatures as low as -58°C and swarms of summer midges that nearly blotted out the sun. Or so the legend goes.

Orientation & Information
Bratsk is a confusing necklace of disconnected 'subcities' around the west and north shores of the Bratsk Sea. Factories and smelters ring the polluted southern centre of Bratsk Tsentralny, a place you'll love if you're looking for that perfect photo of crushingly depressing Soviet-era town planning. Here miserably monotonous nine-storey apartment blocks painted in sludgy grey-turquoise mass around a lifeless square and dejected Lenin statue. Some 30km to the north, the quiet, low-rise Padun area is a different world, with neat wooden houses and a quaint church nestling by the lake. Padun merges into the more bustling Energetik area at the western end of the dam. Gidrostroitel is another predominantly industrial district, 4km east of the dam. The best available city maps are printed in the telephone directory.

In Tsentralny you can change money at the Hotel Taiga. There are **post** and **telephone offices** *(ul Lenin)* opposite the theatre, and a great cybercafé *(open 10am-7pm)*, within the Luiza nightclub at the rear of the Bratsk Hotel, charging R25 per for Internet access.

In Energetik the Internet club **Strelka** *(20R/hr; open 24hr)* is through an unmarked door at the rear of the Santa Barbara kiosk-shop, almost opposite the market: walk one block from the Hotel Turist to the end of ulitsa Kholodnova and it's on your left (ring the buzzer).

Two delightful travel agencies in Tsentralny have English- and German-speaking staff and can arrange a variety of city or adventure excursions. **Taiga Tours** (☎ 41 39 51, fax 41 65 22; [e] taiga-tours@bratsk.net.ru) is upstairs in the Hotel Taiga. **Lovely Tour** (Lavli Tur; ☎ 44 32 90; [e] lovely@bratsk.net.ru; ul Sovetskaya 3) is close to the Lenin statue.

Things to See
The huge Bratsk Dam is over 1km long, with the BAM running across the top. From the terminus of bus No 8 (called GES) it's an obvious 10-minute downhill walk to a decent viewing area. To get inside the powerhouse, however, you'll need an official guide, arranged in advance through Lovely Tour (from US$20 plus transport) or Taiga Tours. Bring a photocopy of your passport.

Bratsk's other attraction is the open-air **Angara Village** (admission R12; open 10am-5pm Tues-Sun, longer hours in summer), a beautifully situated lakeside ethnographic museum featuring a rare wooden watchtower and many other buildings rescued from drowning in the Bratsk and Ust-Ilimsk Dam projects. In the woods behind is a particularly well presented series of Tungus/Evenki chum (tepee-shaped conical dwelling) and shaman sites. Angara Village is about 3km off the main road, roughly halfway between Padun and Tsentralny. There are direct buses on school holidays. Otherwise get off minibus No 118 or 107 at the lonely Sibirsky Traktyr roadside restaurant and walk east along a narrow, asphalted taiga lane for around 25 minutes.

Places to Stay & Eat
Hotel Lyuks (☎ 36 31 46; ul Nabesrezhnaya 62, Padun; singles/doubles R300/600) is a bargain, though slightly tattier than in its heyday when it was an exclusive Communist Party retreat: Khrushchev, Brezhnev, Yeltsin and even Jacques Chirac have stayed here. It has a superb lakeside position and a flower garden with swooping swallows and swifts. Most rooms are suites with views, big double beds, massive bathrooms and separate dining areas.

Hotel Bratskgesstroy (☎ 36 43 91; ul Gidrostroiteley 89A, cnr ul Pursey, Padun;

beds from R230), one block north, is a slightly less exciting alternative. Standard rooms share bathrooms between pairs of rooms, but for R300 per person you get a large suite.

Energetik is less attractive than Padun but handier for restaurants, Internet cafés and transport connections. **Hotel Turist** (ul Naymushina 24, Energetik; singles/twins R473/734) is a typical concrete tower just two bus stops from the dam. Take bus No 8 from the Padunskie Porogie train station.

Should you need to stay in Tsentralny, the **Hotel Taiga** (☎ 41 40 00; ul Mira 35, Tsentralny; doubles/twins US$64/90) seems overpriced for its rebuilt but unstylish rooms.

The **Bratsk** (☎ 43 84 36; ul Deputatskaya 32, Tsentralny; singles/twins R604/827) has mostly rooms with bathroom, although there are also a few waterless twins at R264 per bed.

Right beside Hotel Turist is the food shop **Sibirsky Gastronom** (ul Naymushina 24, Energetik; open 9am-2pm & 3pm-9pm) and mood-lit **Kafe Pitstsa** (open 9am-8pm & 9pm-2am) attached. **Kalipso** (☎ 37 67 81; ul Naymushina 54, Energetik; bus stop GES; mains R40-85; open noon-3am) is the nicest café in Energetik, with a nautical interior and a terrace that almost overlooks the lake.

Getting There & Away
There are five flights per week to Irkutsk, four to Moscow and weekly services to Yekaterinburg, Omsk, Khabarovsk and St Petersburg.

There are three main train stations. Padunskie Porogie is closest to Energetik and Padun. For Tsentralny, get off at Anzyobi station and transfer by bus or elektrichka. If you simply ask for 'Bratsk' you might be sold a ticket to Gidrostroitel, which is a few kilometres east of the dam, but easily connected to Energetik and Padun by bus No 4.

Eastbound there are daily trains to Severobaikalsk (R480 kupe, 18 hours) and Tynda/Neryungri, where you'll have to change for Komsomols-na-Amure. A daily train loops round via Tayshet to Irkutsk (R620 kupe) and at least one daily service goes all the way to Moscow (R2330 kupe, R1350 platskart).

Faster than the train to Irkutsk are morning and night buses from Tsentralny (R325, 12 hours) and summer hydrofoils (R580, 13 hours, three per week) down the Angara. Hydrofoils leave from the rechnoy vokzal (river station, several kilometres southeast of Tsentralny by infrequent city bus (six per day).

SIBERIA

Getting Around

Minibus No 118 (R15) shuttles regularly between Hotel Turist in Energetik and Tsentralny bus station (45 minutes), via Padun bus station. Bus No 1 runs between Energetik and Padun, looping past Hotel Bratskgesstroy westbound only. Bus No 8 starts beside the Kalipso café and wiggles around Energetik's Mikro-Rayon 7 estate to a no-man's-land bus stop near Padunskie Porogi train station. From the stop, walk across the major road towards the big chimney then down some steps to find the initially invisible station.

UST-KUT & LENA
УСТЬ-КУТ И ЛЕНА
☎ 39565 • pop 70,000 • Moscow time plus 5 hours

Almost from the time it was founded in 1631, Ust-Kut has been the launching point for journeys along the great Lena River, notably to Yakutsk almost 2000km downstream (see the Russian Far East chapter later). Today the town is a 15km-long ribbon hugging the Lena's north bank, with a compact high-rise centre at Lena/Osetrovo, where the main train and river ports face each other across an overgrown square. Attractive old Ust-Kut, 8km to the west, was founded in 1631 at the junction with the Kuta River. It was formed by pioneer explorer Yerofey Khabarov, who developed one of Siberia's fabled, but in fact rare, salt mines. This operated commercially from 1639 to 1650 but was reactivated as a prison camp from the 1860s until WWI. Old Ust-Kut was also the temporary expeditionary base for Vitus Bering (of Bering Strait fame).

Things to See & Do

The area around ulitsa Sovetskaya in old Ust-Kut is interesting to wander through (take westbound bus No 1 from Lena train station), as is the walk to the sanatorium (bus No 2 to the end, then across the suspension footbridge; the last service back is at 8pm). At sunset even a riverside stroll behind Lena's high-rises can be very pleasant. The little **museum** (top floor, ul Rebrova-Denisova 9; admission R8; open 10am-5pm Tues-Sat), 200m east of the river station, has local artworks, historical artefacts, a hemp-weaving loom and some entrancingly enthusiastic staff members. Alternatively, it would be an interesting adventure to take one of the daily Lena river hydrofoils to a random village –

stop early enough and you can get back the same day.

Places to Stay & Eat

Upstairs at the river port building are basic **resting rooms** (beds R80-130). Across from Lena train station is the **Lena Hotel** (☎ 5 15 07; ul Kirova 88; singles/doubles with toilet & shower R550/650). The **sanatorium** (☎ 2 32 92; bus No 2 then walk; singles/twins R472.50/598) fills up with noisy kids but its setting is pleasant and peaceful if not entirely pristine, close to the site of the former saltmine ponds. Except for a dingy restaurant (with music blaring) attached to the Lena Hotel, and a small **café** at the station, dining is limited to a couple of summer beer and shashlyk tents along the riverbank near the Osetrovo river terminal.

Getting There & Away

Ust-Kut's small airfield (infrequent bus No 101 from Lena station) has flights to Irkutsk (six per week) and weekly flights to Mirny via Lensk. Tickets are sold in the Lena Hotel.

Old Ust-Kut is a tiny halt on the BAM. It's much easier to use central Lena station. Useful overnight trains to Severobaikalsk (7½ hours) via Goudzhekit (seven hours) leave nightly around midnight. At least two westbound trains a day stop here, including one which goes all the way to Moscow.

From late May to September, ferries cruise all the way to Yakutsk (R3818, 4½ days, twice a month) – check departure details carefully as some use the Vostochny port, a long way east of the main Osetrovo river terminal. Bus No 1 passes Osetrovo and continues to Vostochny. Regular hydrofoils from Osetrovo (☎ 2 63 94) run to Peleduy (R1168, 14 hours, once daily), from where you can continue (daily except Sunday) to Lensk. However, Lensk–Yakutsk hydrofoils were suspended at the time of writing.

Lake Baikal
Озеро Байкал

Lake Baikal, known as the 'Pearl of Siberia', is a crystal clear body of the bluest water, ringed with mountains and surrounded on most sides by rocky, tree-covered cliffs. Considered the 'kitchen' of Siberian weather, its

Baikal's Environmental Profile

Most of Lake Baikal remains pristine, as untouched and beautiful as it was before human beings came to settle its shores. In the middle and northern reaches of the lake the water is so clean that you can easily see fish some 30m to 40m below the surface. There are also freshwater Nerpa seals, bears, sable and other mammals that can be seen along the shore.

In a few areas, however, the lake has suffered from industrial pollution. In the very southern tip, at Baikalsk, a pulp and paper plant has been dumping its effluent into the lake for nearly four decades. Although production there is sagging, and the plant will probably close down soon if investors are not found to keep it running, there is still a plume of pollution that will take years to clean up. In addition, the Selenga River, which empties out a watershed the size of France into Baikal, brings unwanted organic and inorganic wastes from mines, overgrazed pastureland and deforested steppe upriver in Mongolia and Buryatia. Nevertheless, Baikal is a large lake, and these contaminated areas remain more or less isolated.

Several parks and national nature reserves protect some two-thirds of Baikal's shoreline, including the Tunka National Park, one of Russia's newest, just southwest of the lake. There are a couple of long-term threats to Baikal's health, though. Uranium at the Khiagda deposit site in Buryatia may well be developed in the next year or so, unless local people and environmental groups are able to stop this mine from being built. If the mine does open, then Baikal's claim as one of the few areas in Russia that does not suffer from any problems of radioactivity may change.

In addition, oil was recently discovered west of Baikal. There are plans to build a 2000-mile pipeline to China across southern Baikal's shores. Once again, a number of local residents and environmental groups are worried that this pipeline could cause major damage. The region is seismically very active, and there are worries that a pipeline could easily spill vast amounts of oil into the Baikal ecosystem. Also, there are plans to close the Tunka National Park, so as to allow the construction of this pipeline through the heart of the park. For the environmentalists of the region, there will be no shortage of work in the near or even distant future.

Gary Cook, Earth Island Projects

★★★

meteorological mood swings are transfixing spectacles as whole weather systems dance for your delectation.

Shaped like a banana, Baikal is 636km from north to south, 60km wide and 1637m deep near the western edge. That makes it the world's deepest lake, though 25 million years ago it was three times deeper. Incredibly, it contains nearly one-fifth of all the world's fresh water, more than North America's five Great Lakes combined.

Most tourism is based in the southwest, notably in attractive Listvyanka village, and the south coast is dramatically visible from the Trans-Siberian trains. Around the Selenga Delta are several forgotten, historical villages. Beyond magical Olkon Island on the west coast and the dramatic Barguzin Valley on the east, all roads fizzle out in the forested mountain wilderness. The attractive far north region around Severobaikalsk is only accessible by air, boat, a very long loop on the BAM or, in midwinter, by driving up the ice!

IRKUTSK
ИРКУТСК
☎ 3952 • pop 591,000 • Moscow time plus 5 hours

Cosmopolitan Irkutsk, 1090km southeast of Krasnoyarsk, is the nearest big city to glorious Lake Baikal. With beautiful churches, grand 19th-century architecture and some good examples of wooden houses, it's well worth a stop. Be aware, however, that accommodation facilities can be stretched in summer, when it's probably worth booking ahead.

Irkutsk was founded in 1651 as a Cossack garrison to establish authority over the indigenous Buryats. In the 1700s Irkutsk was the springboard for expeditions to the far north and east as far as Alaska, which was referred to at the time as the 'American district of Irkutsk'.

Irkutsk became eastern Siberia's trading and administrative centre. From here, Siberian furs and ivory were sent to Mongolia, Tibet and China in exchange for silk and tea. Its most illustrious 19th-century residents

SIBERIA

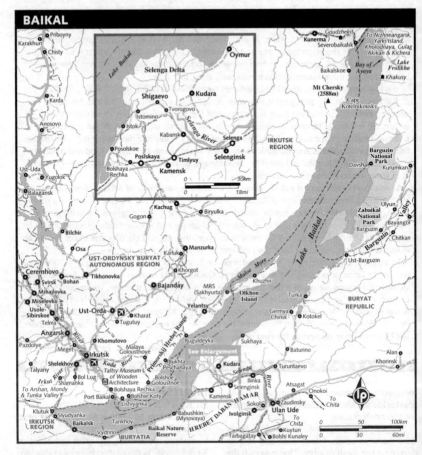

were Decembrists and Polish rebels who formed a rough-hewn aristocracy who valued education, the arts and political awareness.

Three-quarters of the city burnt down in the disastrous fire of 1879 but the Lena Basin gold rush of the 1880s quickly restored its fortunes. The newly rich built brick mansions and grand public buildings, many of which still stand today. Irkutsk became known as the 'Paris of Siberia' and its well-to-do merchants did not welcome news of the October Revolution. The city became a centre of resistance to Bolshevism and only succumbed to the Red tide in 1920, with the capture and execution of Admiral Kolchak, head of the White army. Soviet-era planning saw Irkutsk develop as a sprawling industrial and scientific centre, which it remains today.

Orientation

The city's commercial centre is grand ulitsa Karla Marksa. Paralleling the Angara River, the main axis is ulitsa Lenina, which runs from the administrative centre of ploshchad Kirova to the Krestovozdvizhenskaya Church, where it becomes ulitsa Sedova. Nearly 6km south of the church the continuation of this road reaches the Angara dam near the Sib-Expo area and hydrofoil station.

The attractive, bustling train station is across the Angara River from the city centre. The centre is bypassed by ulitsa Lermontova, being the main west-bank axis, which leads down towards Yubileyny and the west end of the dam (9km). In this unexotic area you will find many of the cheaper homestays.

Good city maps, including a compact tourist map (R25) and a more comprehensive map with bus routes (R39) are sold at Hotel Angara. Kiosks at the airport sell highly detailed *atlas goroda* (street atlases) for around R120.

Information

There's an ATM at Hotel Angara on ulitsa Sukh-Batora. The 24-hour exchange bureau at Hotel Intourist changes US dollars and gives cash advances on all major credit cards. **Alfa-Bank** *(bulvar Gagarina 38; open 8.30am- 7.30pm Mon-Fri, 9am-6pm Sat)* cashes travellers cheques and has an ATM with 24-hour access.

The tin-pot 'main' **post office** *(ul Stepana Razina 23; open 8am-8pm Mon-Fri, 9am-8pm Sat & Sun)* is smaller than the branch at ulitsa Karla Marksa 28. The main **telephone office** *(ul Proletarskaya 12)* is opposite the circus, and a good **Internet Klub** *(ul Sverdlova 37)* around the corner stays open all night if there's enough business; access is R15. Other Internet cafés include the graffiti-trendy **38 Net** *(ul Marata 38)*, which charges R36 per hour from 10am to midnight, and R25 per hour from midnight to 9am, and several branches of **Web-Ugol** *(open 10am to 10pm daily)* including ulitsa Lenina 13, ulitsa Lermontova 104 and ulitsa Chekhova 19 (limited opening). Web-Ugol charges R30 per hour.

A superb website with history, maps, tourist information and more is W www.icc .ru. The website W kbzd.irk.ru/Eng/shedule .htm has a very useful, regularly updated schedule for the boats, buses and Circumbaikal trains out of Irkutsk.

One of the very few places in Siberia to stock slide film is **Skazka** *(ul Litvina 2; open 9am-8pm Mon-Sat)*, which charges R220 for 36-exposure Kodak Ektachrome 200 ASA film. Entry is via an un-numbered building opposite ulitsa Karl Marksa 23.

Local tour operators are useful not only for organising excursions (of which there are many), but also for booking hotels and train tickets. Note that most have only one or two overstretched English speakers, so you may need some patience.

BaikalComplex (☎ 38 92 05, W www.baikal complex.irk.ru) Youry Nemirovsky is helpful and well organised, offering homestays and trips tailored for Western travellers. Call Youry to arrange a meeting.

Green Express (☎ 56 49 64, e info@green express.ru) ul Baikalskaya 291, 7th floor. This professional outfit has its own charming hotel in Listvyanka, yurts on Olkhon Island and many mountain-bike, horse-riding and other tour options. It's open from 9am to 6pm Monday to Friday. The address is somewhat misleading: follow the directions on the map.

Maria (☎ 34 14 92, fax 25 80 10, W www.baikal -maria.irk.ru) Kievskaya ul 2, office 211, upstairs to right from a door on ul Karla Marksa. Named for the Virgin Mary, this friendly but rather disorganised bunch can show you dozens of photos of interesting places to visit and may even remember where some of them are!

Baikaler (☎ 51 19 79, W www.baikaler.com). If you can track him down, Jack Sheremetoff speaks good English and can arrange trips and nice if outlying homestays (US$10 B&B or US$15 full board). Call him to arrange a meeting.

Museums

Irkutsk's pleasant if fairly standard **Regional Museum** *(Kraevedchesky muzey;* ☎ 33 34 49; *ul Karla Marksa 2; foreigner admission R60; open 10am-6pm Tues-Sun)* is within a fancy 1870s brick building that formerly housed the Siberian Geographical Society, a club of Victorian gentlemen-explorers. Equivalent museums in Chita and Krasnoyarsk are more impressive but don't miss the amazing 1884 Aleut fish-skin coat. The gift shop is good for birch-bark boxes and jewellery made from Siberian minerals like purple chaorite. Across the road, an **obelisk** commemorates the 10th anniversary of the arrival of the famous Trans-Siberian Railway. Among the portraits it sports is that of Count Muravyov-Amursky. To historians he's the China-bashing governor general who retook the Amur. To alcoholics he's the face of wicked Gubernskoe beer.

Beyond the Pilgrim's Theatre, through big heavy gates, is the **Volkonsky House Museum** *(*☎ *27 75 32; per Volkonskogo 10; admission R50; open 10am-6pm Tues-Sun)*. This is the preserved house of Decembrist Count Sergey Volkonsky, whose wife Maria Volkonskaya was the subject of Christine Sutherland's book *The Princess of Siberia*. The grey mansion is set in a courtyard with renovated stables, barn and servant quarters (beware of the dog). Downstairs is an (over-) renovated piano room; upstairs is a photo exhibition including portraits of the 1820s women who romantically followed their husbands into exile. In a smaller Decembrist

SIBERIA

IRKUTSK

To Khuzhir (Olkhon Island (293km)

To Kazinsky Church (700m)

U'shakovka River

To Znamenskaya Monastery (1.5km)

400m
400yd
200
200

To Oktyabrskoy Revolyutsii

ul Timiryazeva

ul Dzerzhinskogo

ul Baikalskaya

To Airport (2km)

ul Babushkina

ul Dekabrskikh Sobytiy

ul Kalia Libenkhta

ul Karla Marksa

ul Chekhova

ul Uritskogo

ul Litvinova

ul Bogdana Khmelnitskogo

Kievskaya ul

ul Sverdlova

ul Gorkogo

ul Sukhe-Batora

pl Kirova

ul Lenina

ul Marata

ul Stepana Razina

ul Chkalova

ul Surikova

Angara River

ul Pyatoy Armii

ul Sverdlova

ul Gorkogo

ul Gorkaya

ul Lapina

ul Lenina

ul Karla Marksa

bul Gagarina

ul 3 July

ul Sedova

ul Dzerzhinskogo

Stadium

Youth Island

Angara River

To Ulan Ude (456km)

To Irkutsk Dam

Train Station

ul Vokzalnaya

To Lermontova

To Web Ogol (3km); Hotel Selena (3.5km); Hotel Akademicheskaya (5km); Hotel Ikar (7km); & Angara Dam (10km)

To City History Museum (1.8km) & American House (2.5km)

Circus

To City Centre (6km, see main map)

Baikalsky Trakt

pr Marshala Zhukova (651m)

To Listvyanka (651m)

Angara Dam

Tsentralny Park Kultury i Otdykha

ul Baikalskaya

ul Sovetskaya

ul Sovetskaya

ul-Baikalskaya

To Hotel Retro 2 (1.7km) & Airport (4km)

To Hydrofoil Station & SibExpo Area (5km, see inset); Listvyanka (66km)

To Hydrofoil Station (see inset)

1km
0.5mi
0

SIBERIA

IRKUTSK

PLACES TO STAY
6 Hotel Uzory
   Гостиница Узоры
12 Hotel Arena
   Гостиница Арена
15 Hotel Angara
   Гостиница Ангара
18 Hotel Agat
   Гостиница Агат
19 Hotel Intourist
   Гостиница Интурист
22 Hotel Rus
   Гостиница Рус
42 Hotel Gornyak
   Гостиница Горьняк
44 Hotel Retro 1
   Гостиница Ретро 1

PLACES TO EAT
11 U Shveyka
   У Швейка
28 Kafe Na Dnye
   Кафе На Дне
31 Laguna
   Лагуна
32 Vernisazh
   Вернисаж
33 Snezhinka
   Снежинка
38 Kyoto
   Кйото
41 Club 1952 Restaurant
   Клуб 1952
51 Figaro Pizza
   Фигаро Пицца

OTHER
1 Bogoyavlensky Cathedral
   Богоявленский Собор

2 Spasskaya Church
   Спасская церковь
3 Regional Administrative
   Игилдвитп
   Дворец пионеров
4 Polish Chapel
   Полская Костёль
5 Bus Station
   Автовокзал
7 Volkonsky House
   Museum
   Дом Волконского
8 Titanik Night Club
   Ночной клуб Титаник
9 Trubetskoy House
   Museum
   Дом Трубецкого
10 Jewish Cultural Centre
   Хэсэр Ха-яд
13 Telephone & Telegraph
   Office
   Телефон и Телеграф
14 Internet Klub
   Интернет Клуб
16 Hydrofoil to Bratsk
17 Troitskaya Church
   Троицкая церковь
20 Alfa Bank
   Алфа-банк
21 Main Post Office
   Почтамт
23 38 Net
   38 Нэт
24 Art Gallery
   Художественный
   музей
25 Central Air Agency
   Центральное Агенство
   воздушный сообщений

26 Web Ugol Web
   Угол
27 Old Pharmacy
   Аптек
29 Central Market
   Центральный рынок
30 Department Store
   Универмаг
34 Skaska Photo-shop
   Сказка
35 Post Office
   Почта
36 Maria Tour Agency
   Агенство Мария
37 Stratosphera Night Club
   Ночной клуб
   Стратосфера
39 Mongolian Consulate
   Консульство Монголии
40 Web Ugol Web
   Угол
43 Okhlopkov Drama
   Theatre
   Драматический театр
   имени Охлопкова
45 bulvar Gagarina Landing;
   Pleasure Cruises
46 Obelisk
47 Kraevedchesky Museum
   Краеведческий
   музей
48 Sh17 Bar
   O17
49 Philharmonic Hall
   Филармония
50 Krestovozdvizhenskaya
   Church
   Крестовоздвиженская
   церковь

house nearby is the similar **Trubetskoy House Museum** (☎ 27 57 73; ul Dzerzhinskogo 64; admission R40; open 10am-6pm Thur-Mon).

The grand old **Art Gallery** (cnr uls Lenina & Sverdlova; foreigner admission R50; open 10am-6pm Wed-Mon) has a valuable if poorly lit collection ranging from Mongolian thanka to pseudo-Impressionist canvasses. Balding babushka attendants urge you to lift burlap veils to peep at the 19th-century watercolours, but more artistically appealing are the bold works by the local artist Yevtey Simonov.

Small but well presented, the **City History Museum** (ul Tchaikovskogo 5; bus No 11; admission R30; open 10am-6pm Thur-Tues) shows various eras through shop-window-style displays.

Churches
Ploshchad Kirova was once dominated by the magnificent Annunciation Cathedral. Where it stood is now a hulking concrete **regional administrative building** (the ex-Communist Party headquarters) but there's a trio of churches just to the east. The 1881 Catholic **Polish Chapel** (Polskaya Kostyol) is stylistically identical to the Catholic Chapel in Krasnoyarsk, but that doesn't stop tour guides insisting that it's 'Siberia's only Gothic church'. Much more attractive is the fairytale ensemble of the **Bogoyavlensky Cathedral** on the riverbank nearby and the more modest **Spasskaya Church** in between.

Set in a leafy garden behind a noisy traffic circle, the **Znamenskaya Monastery** is 1.5km up the mostly unappealing riverbank (trolleybus No 3). Built in 1762, it was restored

SIBERIA

by exiled nuns and reopened after WWII. In the gold sarcophagus, the treasured relics of Siberian missionary St Innokent are a supposed source of miracles for believers. Graves outside include that of Russia-Alaska merchant-explorer Grigory Shelekhov.

The gilded interior of the baroque **Krestovozdvizhenskaya Church** (*ul Sedova 1*), dating from 1758, is worth a look. Walk around the exterior to see examples of the unusual intricate brickwork, a rare rounded style which you can see here and at Posolskoe across Lake Baikal but almost nowhere else.

Two stops northeast from the bus station by tram No 4, the gigantic, unfinished **Kazansky Church** is a feast of Day-Glo blue domes. If it weren't for its odd position between a market and a tumble-down factory, this would be one of the city's major landmarks.

Other Attractions

Don't miss strolling along ulitsa Karla Marksa and soaking up some of the 19th-century charm of its architecture.

Near the market on ulitsa Chekhova, peep inside the lovely old **pharmacist's shop** (*Apteka; cnr uls Chekhova & Dzerzhinskogo*), which still has an early-20th-century cash register.

While this is not Tomsk, there are several areas of older wooden houses, notably on ulitsa Babushkina and ulitsa Karla Libernikha between uls Karla Marksa and Timiryazeva.

Moored near the dam is the **Angara steamship**, an ice-breaker ferry brought in kit form from England. It once carried Trans-Siberian Railway passengers across Lake Baikal (the trains went on her bigger sistership, which sank years ago). Officially closed to visitors, Angara is currently used as a drinks store for a nearby summer café, but the impressive engines still work as you'll see should the café owner decide to befriend you.

Places to Stay

Tourist agencies such as BaikalComplex and Baikaler (see under Information earlier for contact details) arrange **homestays** in Irkutsk and villages around Lake Baikal. Prices start at US$10 for a bed, though US$20 to US$25 for full board is more common; the cheaper places can be 10km or more from the city centre. Without the help of a tourist agency, finding hotel accommodation in summer can be tricky and time consuming. Cheaper hotels rarely take phone reservations and, despite the vast choice, summer occupancy rates are very high.

Budget Most of the rock-bottom dosshouses around the bus station refuse foreigners, though the rather better, new traders' guesthouse **Uzory** (*☎ 27 92 39; cnr uls Oktyabrskoy Revolyutsii & Engelsa; singles/twins with clean shared toilet R300/500*) is an exception.

Arena (*☎ 34 46 42; ul Zhelyabova 8A; singles/twins R750/1100*), flanking the circus, has tattier basic rooms from R220/430 in a separately managed *obshchitye* section (*☎ 33 46 63*) entered from ulitsa Sverdlova 39 through a warren of brown metal doors.

Hotel Agat (*☎ 29 73 25; ul Piyatoy Armii 12, entrance No 2; bed in twins R500*) would seem hopelessly overpriced anywhere else in east Siberia, despite the clean shared toilet and shower. But the quiet central position next to the Troitskaya Church may merit the expense.

Hotel Profsoyuz Profsoyuznaya (*Profsoyuznaya; ☎ 35 79 63; ul Baikalskaya 263; bed in twins R189*), in the distant SibExpo area, is cheaper, bigger and very acceptable, if somewhat institutional. It has hot showers.

On the west bank, the crumbling, wedge-shaped **Selena** (*☎ 39 78 59; ul Igoshima 1; beds/singles/doubles R230/450/580*) overlooks the river, five minutes' walk west of the Geological Institute and Web Ugol Internet café at ulitsa Lermontova 104.

Farther south in Akademgorodok, **Hotel Akademicheskaya** (*☎ 46 34 72; ul Lermontova 271A; bus No 3, bus stop Gosuniversitet; singles/twins with shower R650/800*) is set back across a grassy area from ulitsa Lermontova 265 (check the map on **w** www .irkutsk.org/fed/pic/akad.jpg). It also has simpler R410 doubles and an unfortunately named Internet café called Virus.

American House (*☎ 43 26 89; e slida@ irk.ru; ul Ostrovskogo 19; beds US$15, with breakfast US$20*) is an English-speaking homestay-guesthouse in a low-rise muddy street, a R50 taxi ride west of the train station. From the city centre take bus No 11, which crosses the river, climbs a hill, then turns left onto ulitsa Tchaikovskogo, passing the City History Museum. Get off one stop further south, walk a block east (steeply down ulitsa Kayskaya), then north on ulitsa Ostrovskogo.

Hotel Gornyak (*☎ 24 37 54; ul Lenina 24, enter from ul Dzerzhinskogo; singles/twins*

R600/1100) is a bargain-value small hotel with newly renovated rooms with bathroom.

Mid-Range Upstairs within an eye hospital, 30 minutes' bus ride down the Angara's west bank, **Hotel Ikar** *(☎ 56 41 44, fax 42 20 35; Tsentr Mikrokhirugiy Glaza, ul Lermontova 337; trolleybus No 1 or minivan No 3; rooms US$25-40)* seems the oddest choice. Nonetheless rooms are brand new, clinically clean and worth the foreigner price; they're a giveaway if you get the R200 per person local price.

Comfortable and great value, **Hotel Rus** *(☎ 24 27 15, fax 24 07 33; w http://rus .baikal.ru; ul Sverdlova 19; singles/doubles with breakfast R922/1117)* is usually booked solid.

Hotel Angara *(☎ 25 51 05, fax 25 51 03; w www.angarahotel.ru; ul Sukh-Batora 7; singles/doubles with breakfast from R990/ 1430)* is very central and has some good renovated suites for US$100 and upwards. But don't be fooled by the fancy foyer or by the Internet pictures, which show only the best upgraded accommodation. The cheapest 3rd-floor rooms are disgracefully shabby. Many higher standard rooms are passable by old Soviet-era standards but are very overpriced by today's standards.

Hotel Intourist *(☎ 25 01 67, fax 25 03 14; bulvar Gagarina 44; singles/twins with breakfast R2000/2200)* has river views and nice new beds but older-style showers. Single-occupancy twins for R1140 might be available if you ask nicely.

Top End The following three hotels are all on ulitsa Baikalskaya, in the SibExpo trade-fair area, which is near the airport and hydrofoil station, some 6km from the centre.

The white and blue-glass **Baikal Business Centre** *(☎ 25 91 08, fax 35 83 83; w www .bbc.ru; singles/twins US$100/150)* is almost international standard, though the private bathrooms have showers but no bathtubs.

Rooms are better at the nearby **Sun Hotel** *(☎ 25 59 12/10; w www.xemi.com/sunhotel; tram No 5; singles/doubles/twins US$95/ 125/140)*, where rates include a buffet breakfast.

Next door, **Hotel Solnyshonok** *(singles/ doubles US$45/ 60)* is slightly simpler and excellent value. The Sun Hotel handles bookings and also provides complimentary breakfasts for Solnyshonok guests.

Irkutsk's most exclusive options are the restored historic house-hotels **Retro 1** *(☎ 33 32 51; ul Karla Marksa 1)* and **Retro 2** *(☎ 27 15 34; ul Yardintsyeva 1, off ul Sovetskaya)*. Prices range from R850 to R3720, with Internet reservation available via the Hotel Rus website.

Places to Eat

Across from the modern, lively central market is the good-value **Kafe Na Dnye** *(ul Chekhova 21; meals R35-50, Pilsner Urquel per pint R27; open 11am-11pm)* with billiards, camouflage netting and a taste for Fat Boy Slim. Try the *riba-pa-Irkutskaya* (R46), a Baikal version of fish and chips.

Laguna *(☎ 27 59 75; ul Litinova 20; mains R40-75; open noon-midnight Mon-Sat)* is good value, disco-free and sometimes presents free garlic-and-cheese bread appetisers while you wait.

Vernisazh *(ul Uritskogo; open 10am-late daily)* has a grocery shop with salad bar and cheap snacks, a stylish but surprisingly reasonable café and a grand banqueting restaurant upstairs. All three are within a fine, restored mansion on Irkutsk's pedestrianised street.

Figaro Pizza *(☎ 27 06 07; ul Sovetskaya 58; pizzas R100-270, beers from R50; open 10am-midnight daily)* is the most authentic pizzeria in town, three blocks southwest of the market.

U Shveyka *(☎ 24 26 87; ul Karla Marksa 34; snacks R40-70, mains R50-150; music cover charge R30 after 8pm; open noon-midnight daily)* is an air-con cavern with elk-head old-world atmosphere and a good summer terrace.

Snezhinka *(☎ 34 48 62; opposite ul Karla Marksa 25; mains R100-230, espresso R55; open 11am-11pm daily)* is stylishly upmarket with bilingual menus, lunch specials and a real Italian coffee machine.

Club 1952 *(☎ 33 62 82; ul Lenina 15; mains R90-200; open noon-3am Wed-Sat, noon-midnight Sun)* is suave yet cosy, with a menu in English.

Kyoto *(Kioto; ☎ 55 05 05; sushi set R280; open 10am-2am daily)* has the Japanese ambience just right, but the rice all wrong.

Entertainment

On summer evenings there's a *passagiata* of local strollers on the grassy area behind the fine **Okhlopkov Drama Theatre**. Tucked into the side of the nearby stadium, bar **Sh17** (*beers from R40; open 6pm-1am daily*) has an extraordinary submarine interior.

The **Circus** (☎ 33 61 39; *ul Zhelyabova; seats R80, R100 & R200; open Sat & Sun Oct-June*) has eye-boggling Cirque du Soleil–style performances, but avoid the cheapest seats, where you'll get poor views and a regular splashing.

The **Philharmonic Hall** (☎ 24 50 76; *ul Dzerzhinskogo 2*) stages regular classical musical shows.

Stratosphera Night Club (ⓦ *www.strata-club.ru; ul Karla Marksa 15; cover R100; open 6pm-6am Fri-Sun*) is the weekend hotspot, with bowling alley, two-storey disco and three-storey drinks prices.

Titanik Night Club (*ul Oktyabrskoy-Revolyutsii 20B; open 9pm-6am Tues, Wed, Fri-Sun*) near the bus station, also hosts occasional Salsa/Merengue evenings of the **La Palma** (☎ 46 44 08; ⓦ *www.la-palma.narod.ru/*) dance club.

Getting There & Away

Air For air tickets, foreigners are expected to use the helpful **Central Air Agency** (☎ 20 15 17; *ul Gorkogo 29; open 8am-7pm daily*). International flights serve Mongolia and China; destinations include Ulaan Baatar (US$170, Wednesday and Saturday), Beijing (R12,100, two per week) and Shenyang (R5140, Tuesday and Saturday). There's a plethora of domestic destinations, including Moscow (R3700 to R4800, daily), St Petersburg (R5000, three per week), Novosibirsk (R3300, daily), Bratsk (R1370, five per week), Khabarovsk (R3300, six per week) and Krasnoyarsk (R2650, five per week) and Kyzyl (R3300, Saturday).

Train The best, if most expensive, train for Moscow is the No 9/10 *Baikal* (R3700 *kupe*, 77 hours) while *platskart* berths on slower trains such as No 240/250 (87 hours) cost R1530 via Tayshet (12 hours) and Krasnoyarsk (19 hours).

There are several alternate-day trains for Vladivostok (including No 002, R3300 *kupe*, 72 hours; No 230, R2100 *kupe*, 75 hours) via Khabarovsk (58 to 60 hours). Trains for Beijing (R3050 to R3400) pass through Irkutsk on Wednesday (direct) and Saturday (via Mongolia). Fast train No 006 to Ulaan Baatar leaves Friday and Saturday mornings and is a full 10 hours quicker than the daily No 264

(R1760; 35 hours). In any case, heading east consider stopping in Ulan Ude, eight hours by handy overnighters but well worth travelling by day to enjoy the views of Lake Baikal: take train No 012 (7.15am even days) or No 78E (R330 *kupe*, 8.40am odd days).

Buy tickets at the **international ticket window** (*mezhdunarodnaya kassa;* ☎ 28 28 20), even if you are buying a domestic ticket. Or pay an agency (see under Information earlier).

Bus Useful destinations include Listvyanka (R70, 1¾ hours, four per day), Bratsk (R325, 12 hours, 7.30am and 7.30pm), Arshan (R177, 8am and 11am), Mondy (three per week) and Khuzhir on Olkhon Island (R257.50, eight hours, 8.10am daily in summer). The bus station **ticket office** (*open 6am-7pm daily*) is quietest after 6.30pm, and it's well worth buying tickets a day or more ahead.

Hydrofoil From the hydrofoil station there are Raketa hydrofoil services across Lake Baikal to Severobaikalsk and Nizhneangarsk (R990, 12 hours, one or two per week from mid-June to September), Listvyanka, Bolshie Koty and other lakeside villages on an ever-changing summer-only schedule. In summer, there are three hydrofoils a week to Bratsk (R580, 13 hours) from a jetty near the Angara bridge in the city centre.

Getting Around

Trolleybus No 4 (R5) from ulitsa Lenina passes Figaro Pizza and Hotel Retro 2 and terminates at the airport. Rare trolleybus No 6 (to the dam) or taxis are the only way to go directly from the airport to the SibExpo area and hydrofoil station without having to go first into the city centre.

Within the central area, walking is often the best idea as one-way loops make the bus routes confusingly convoluted. From the train station, bus No 7 crosses the Angara to ploshchad Kirova, then loops round the centre and out past the Znamenskaya Monastery. Bus No 16 continues down ulitsa Lenina, past the Krestovozdvizhenskaya Church and (eventually) the dam, passing within 500m of the SibExpo hotels before looping back past the hydrofoil station to the Angara steamship. If you've got all day, tram No 5 from the Sun Hotel trundles to the Central Market, whence tram No 4 goes past the bus station to the Kazansky Church.

On the west bank both minibus No 12 from the train station (rare) and bus/minibus No 3 from the Central Market (frequent, to Yubilieyny) cover the whole length of ulitsa Lermontova.

AROUND IRKUTSK
Taltsy Museum of Wooden Architecture
Талцы Музей Деревянного Зодчество

About 47km southeast of Irkutsk, 23km before Listvyanka, Taltsy *(foreigner admission R80 plus camera fees, locals R20; open 10am-6pm daily summer, 10am-4pm winter)* is an impressive collection of old Siberian buildings set in a delightful riverside forest. Amid the renovated farmsteads are two chapels, a church, a watermill, some Tungusi graves and the eye-catching 17th-century Iliminsk Ostrog watchtower. Four daily Listvyanka–Irkutsk buses stop on request at the apparently deserted entrance access road, from where it's only a minute's walk to the ticket booth. Hitching to Taltsy from Listvyanka is easy.

LISTVYANKA
ЛИСТВЯНКА
☎ 3952 • pop 2500 • Moscow time plus 5 hours

These days little Listvyanka is listed in virtually every Trans-Siberian brochure. You might expect it to be overwhelmed with visitors, but for now it remains quainter than one dares to expect.

Hugging the Baikal banks, ulitsa Gorkogo is the main road from Irkutsk but it's quiet enough to double as a strolling promenade. It links Listvyanka's picturesque concentrations of old wooden cottages that tumble down three separate valleys: ulitsa Gudina and ulitsa Chapaeva (either side of the ferry landing and bus terminus) and the wider Krestovka Valley (ulitsa Ostrovskoe/Gornaya), 15 minutes' walk farther south. See ⓦ www .irkutsk.org/fed/maps/listmap.jpg for a basic map.

Things to See & Do
Boat rides, cute cottages and gentle strolls are the village's strong points, with accessible viewpoints around and above Hotel Baikal. At the top of ulitsa Chapaeva, inspiring local artist Vladimir Plamenevsky has a splendid little **gallery** *(☎ 11 25 52; ul Chapaeva 76;* *admission R10; open on request)*. Fishing boats are easy to rent from the port just west of the ferry terminal for R800 per hour. Krestovka has pretty **Svyato-Nikolskaya Church** and a nearby **song theatre** *(performances 9pm Sat & Sun)*.

If you're with a tour, you may be herded into the **Baikal Limnological Institute** *(ul Akademicheskaya 1; admission US$3; open 10am-5pm daily)* south of Krestovka at km 4, whose two pitiful rooms of marine exhibits are an outrageous case of tourist fleecing. Vast improvements are supposedly planned. Ten minutes' walk towards Irkutsk, where the road curves west, is a tiny **aquarium** *(admission R30; open 11am-6pm daily)* containing two cramped but smiley freshwater Nerpa seals.

Places to Stay
Listvyanka has dozens of private guesthouses and homestays, most without signs. Even in summer it's generally quite possible to find a cheap room without reservation, but if you want luxury (ie, a sit-down toilet) it really pays to reserve, which is most easily done through an Irkutsk tourist agency (see Information in that section earlier).

Room rentals for R150 to R500 can be found at many houses on attractive ulitsa Chapaeva, including Nos 6, 7, 24, 65 and notably 76, where there are huts attached to the art gallery, including one with an attached hot shower and toilet for R450. Ulitsa Gudina has more options, including **Briz** *(☎ 25 04 68; ul Gudina 71; rooms R300-450)* with shared chemical toilet. Showers cost R50 extra. The **unmarked house** at ulitsa Gudina 75 is a step up, with showers, toilet and terrace in the best US$40 upstairs rooms. English is spoken and breakfast is included; book via BaikalComplex in Irkutsk.

National Park Hostel *(☎ 11 25 20, ul Gorkogo 39; beds R240)* has three shared triple rooms and a kitchen above the Pribaikalsky National Park information centre.

Priboy *(aka Baikal-Listvyanka; ☎ 11 23 93; ul Gorkogo 101; dorm beds R150, twins R600-800)* is a small concrete 'hotel' near the ferry terminal with lake views, shared toilet and no showers.

Baikalskie Terema *(☎ 11 25 99; ⓔ info@ greenexpress.ru; ul Gornaya 16; singles/ doubles including breakfast R2500/2700)* is much the snazziest option for Western comforts. Pine-furnished, it sits attractively on a hill above Krestovka. You pay only half price if you plan to stay less than 12 hours, which works well if you arrive on the last bus from Irkutsk and continue next day by boat to Bolshie Koty. The terrace restaurant has a good, imaginative menu.

The Intourist **Hotel Baikal** (☎ 25 03 91; fax 25 01 55; ul Akademicheskaya 13; singles/doubles $120/128), five minutes' walk above the Limnological Institute, is inconvenient for the ferries and has ludicrously overpriced walk-in rates. It is used mainly by package tours. From the terrace in front, views are free and nicer than from most of the hotel's tree-shaded rooms. It's about a 40-minute walk from the ferry terminal; there is no public transport, although hitching is possible.

Places to Eat

Near the port are a couple of **cheap eateries**, the odd shashlyk barbecue and numerous vendors pedalling delicious smoked omul fish. Apart from those at the hotels, the most atmospheric restaurant is **Proshlii Vek** (☎ 11 25 54; ul Lazlo 1; mains R70-100; open noon-midnight daily). It's 2km south of the ferry terminal on the main lakeside road, and has a thoroughly tempting English menu.

Getting There & Away

Five daily buses run from Listvyanka ferry terminal to Irkutsk (R70, 1¾ hours), one continuing to Angarsk. All pass the Limonological Institute and Taltsy museum. Hitchhiking is quite easy towards Irkutsk.

Between mid-May and late September, hydrofoils run several times per week to Irkutsk (around R80) and Bolshie Koty (R30), with more frequent services at weekends. The schedule changes every summer but is usually posted on W http://kbzd.irk.ru/Eng/shedule.htm.

A battered old ferry lumbers across to Port Baikal six times a day, with the last return at 8pm.

AROUND LISTVYANKA
КРУГОБАЙКАЛЬСКАЯ
ЖЕЛЕЗНАЯ ДОРОГА

From 1900 to 1904 the Trans-Siberian Railway tracks from Irkutsk stopped at Port Baikal, across the mouth of the Angara from Listvyanka. From here ice-breaking steamships carried passengers and trains across the lake to Mysovaya (Babushkin), where the rails continued. Extending the track south around the lake (the Circum-Baikal line) required a tunnel or bridge almost every kilometre, a job done so impressively it earned the nickname the 'Tsar's Jewelled Buckle'.

With the damming of the Angara River in the 1950s, the original Irkutsk to Port Baikal section was submerged and replaced with an Irkutsk–Kultuk shortcut, leaving Port Baikal to wither at the dead end of a rarely used branch line. Today trains run between Port Baikal and Slyudyanka (just beyond Kultuk) only four times a week, and do so westbound at night. The eastbound journey is becoming popular with tourists as in summer it travels during the day, allowing spectacular views between the mind-boggling succession of tunnels. Schedules change regularly but if, as is usually the case, the train arrives in Port Baikal after the last (8pm) ferry to Listvyanka (the nearest town) you'll need to camp, seek out a local homestay or charter a fishing boat across. Alternatively join BaikalComplex's organised 'Circumbaikal Experience' from Irkutsk.

It's also possible to walk sections of the train line. The whole route would take four to six days but although there are many areas for camping at either end, these thin considerably in between. Several remote villages along the line have well-equipped lakeside resorts, but these need to be reserved in advance through Irkutsk agencies.

A ferry heads across to Listvyanka six times a day.

Bolshie Koty
Большие Коты

Founded by 19th-century gold miners, and named 'Bolshie Koty' for their 'Big Boots', this picturesque fishing village makes an easy day trip by boat from Irkutsk or Listvyanka. The little **museum** opposite the jetty will let you peruse its pickled crustaceans and stuffed rodents for R20. Otherwise, the village is a great place to stroll, snooze and watch fish dry.

Several homestay options are available, all of which are basic. Sweet, bearded babushka Anna Zuyeva's **furnished potting-shed** (ul Baikalskaya 55; beds R50) is unbeatable for price or position, with a window looking straight out across Lake Baikal. **Alex and Nina Kazlov** (☎ 3952-45 76 50; ul Zarechnaya 11b; beds R75) can take over a dozen people.

Other homestays are a similar standard but much more expensive. Great fresh-smoked *omul* are sold at the port when boats arrive, and there are a couple of basic food shops.

Hydrofoils originating in Irkutsk depart Listvyanka (R30, 25 minutes) around seven times per week, with most services at weekends. Each waits nearly two hours before returning, which is enough for many people. There's no road, but hiking trails follow the lake shore, making a spectacular, if sometimes hair-raising, coastal hike back to Listvyanka (beware of ticks in May and June).

Bukhta Peschanaya
Бухта Песчаная

The name means 'Sandy Bay' and the place is as far as you can go on a waterborne day trip from Irkutsk (3½ hours, three weekly). Popular with Russians for its sandy beaches and dramatic capes, it has a holiday-camp atmosphere. Given plenty of advance warning, Irkutsk travel agencies can book accommodation in twin huts with shared facilities from R458 per person full board.

OLKHON ISLAND
ОСТРОВ ОЛЬХОН

pop 1200

If you put spiritual calm over physical comfort, Olkhon is likely to inspire you. The long, undulating island is subtly beautiful and considered to be one of five global poles of shamanic energy. The oft-photographed **Shaman Rocks** are on a little curl of turquoise beach behind **Khuzhir**, the island's main village. While neither huge nor spectacular, they make a perfect meditational focus for the ever-changing cloudscapes across the picturesque Maloe More (Little Sea). The island's dry southern end is rolling grassland – great for off-road mountain biking. This transforms near Khuzhir into thick woodland and at the northern tip there's a fair chance of spotting freshwater Nerpa seals.

On the mainland, while waiting at MRS (aka Sakhyurta) for the ferry, scramble up a little harbourside knoll for cliff-top lake views.

Places to Stay & Eat

Bike rental, organised excursions and helpful advice are available from **Nikita's Guest House** (*ul Kirpichnaya 6, Khuzhir; full board per person US$15*), which is very near the Shaman Rocks and rates as Siberia's only real

travellers hangout. Rooms are attractive if basic, there's a *banya* (bathhouse), and delicious garlic-supercharged meals are served at a convivial communal dining area. Get off the bus on ulitsa Baikalskaya just before the *gastronom* (grocery shop), turn left onto ulitsa Pushkina, walk for five minutes and the second left is ulitsa Kirpichnaya. Nikita's is about 150m down the street, on the right behind the little tourist information booth that he's creating. The tiny **village hotel** (*ul Lesnaya; beds R70*) is a block behind the war memorial, though finding someone with the key is a great palaver. A dismal **turbaza** (*full board R450*) at the north edge of Khuzhir is a last resort.

Green Express (see under Information in Irkutsk earlier in this chapter) has two yurt-style camps designed for their tours, but available to independent travellers – if you can find them. The camps are tucked into roadless coves several kilometres north of Khuzhir towards the tiny hamlet of Kharansti. **Fun Camp** (*beds per person with breakfast R321*) is more isolated and less charming than **Harmony Camp** (*beds R600, with meals R1410, banya R300*).

There's a summer *turbaza* at MRS should you miss the last ferry to Olkhon, and Yelantsy has a small hotel and two cafés.

Getting There & Away

From mid-June to August there's a daily Irkutsk–Khuzhir bus (R257.50, eight hours including the ferry). The route is 75% paved and is scenically unexciting until around Yelantsy. Bus frequency drops to twice a week in September. In winter buses run only as far as Yelantsy (daily) or MRS (occasionally), whence you have to hitch or take a taxi across the ice. When the ice is partly formed or partly melted, the island is completely cut off for a few weeks at a time. With a little warning Nikita can usually find you a ride in a private car to Irkutsk (R600 per seat, R2000 for the whole car, 5½ hours).

SOUTH BAIKAL

Even if you don't stop, it's worth travelling the scenic south coast by day to watch the lake glide by the train window. The biggest town, **Slyudyanka**, while unexciting, is a starting point for the Circum-Baikal Railway (see The Circum-Baikal Railway earlier in this chapter). It's also the best place to switch from train to minibus if you want to head west for

Arshan (120km), a resort town backed by attractive mountains. The same road leads to the spectacular Tunka Valley beyond Mondy, where the Mongolian border is firmly shut.

Back on the coast, **Baikalsk** is the site of the controversial Baikal-polluting pulp mill (see the boxed text 'Baikal's Environmental Profile' earlier), but it's better known to locals as the region's best ski base. On winter weekends ski-lift prices double and accommodation needs to be booked well ahead.

The most historic villages of South Baikal are close to the Selenga Delta, and have largely been forgotten since the delta was bypassed by the Trans-Siberian Railway. Most notable is **Posolskoe**, site of Imperial Russia's first trans-Baikal diplomatic mission to the Mongolian khan in 1651. By the 1680s its monastery was spearheading the evangelism of Buryatia. Closed in the 1920s, the sad hulk of the monastery's once-great Spaso-Preobrazhensky Church still dominates what is now a quiet little wooden-cottage fishing village. It stands on a slight rise overlooking a long, pebbly Baikal beach and wide shallows that attract wading birds. Since 2000 the monastery has once again been active and the monks seem happy to show visitors up the rickety bell tower for even better lake views (donation requested).

Reaching Posolskoe is easiest by twice-daily minibus from Ulan Ude (R70, 3½ hours, last return at 6pm). The bus loops via the interesting old towns of **Kabansk**, which has a museum and a big Soviet 'flame' monument, and **Tvorogovo**. The latter has an impressive old ruined church at the roadside, though it lacks Posolkoe's great lakeside setting. A Posolskoe–Kabansk bus leaves at 3pm. From Kabansk, shared taxis (R6) run frequently to Timlyuy station on the Trans-Siberian Railway.

EASTERN BAIKAL

North of the Selenga Delta the main population centres of East Baikal are dotted along the rough road via Turka to the beautiful, wide Barguzin Valley, from where Jenghis Khan's family is said to have originated. This route passes **Baturino** with its lonely old Sretenskaya church. It also provides access to a few lakeside *turbaza*, but although for much of its length it follows the boat, views are rare and not always worth the discomfort. The largest settlement, the timber town **Ust-Barguzin**, is a concrete disappointment and all the less appealing now that the weekly Irkutsk hydrofoil service has been suspended (though it may be reinstated eventually).

In contrast, the big inland valley beyond Barguzin is very picturesque, with standing stones and wide panoramas of distant peaks towering above the endless meanders of the Barguzin River. Farther north all roads stop. The virtually impenetrable **Barguzin National Reserve** (Barguzinsky zapovednik) is Russia's oldest reserve, with over 263,000 hectares of protected flora and fauna. There's a lonely scientific hamlet at **Davsha**, which can only be reached by boat (no regular public service) from Ust-Barguzin, where you'd need to arrange permits to enter the reserve. Only on ice roads in winter, or by chartering a boat, can you continue to Khakusy or the BAM towns of North Baikal.

Buses from Ulan Ude run daily to Barguzin (R170, 11 hours, departs at 8.35am) and Ust-Barguzin (R143, 7½ hours, departs 8am).

SEVEROBAIKALSK
СЕВЕРОБАЙКАЛЬСК

☎ 30139 • pop 35,000 • Moscow time plus 5 hours

Severobaikalsk rose out of virgin taiga almost overnight with the arrival of the BAM in the early 1970s. Although the centre is a depressingly typical regiment of prefabricated apartment blocks, it's just a short walk across the train tracks to peace, quiet and some memorable Baikal viewpoints. With English-speaking help at hand, the town makes a convenient base from which to explore the beautiful yet little-visited North Baikal area.

Information

Set behind the Torgovy Tsentr shopping centre on Tsentralny ploshchad is **Sberbank** *(open 8.30am-5.30pm Mon-Thur, 8:30am-1pm Fri)*, where you can change money, and the **telephone office** *(per Proletarskiy; open 24hr)*. Around the corner from the **post office** *(Leningradsky pr 6)*, Internet access is available in a local **youth club** entered from the back of Leningradsky prospekt 6A.

Tour agency **Baikal Service** *(☎/fax 2 39 12; e baikals@burnet.ru)* is a professional outfit with its own boat, hotel, permit arrangements and tour programme, but they don't speak English. **Khozyain** *(☎/fax 2 45 12; e hozjain@*

mail.ru; Leningradsky pr 5, Apt 43) coordinates accommodation at the hot springs of Dzelinda, Goudzhekit and Khakusy.

Rashit Yakhin/BAM Tour (☎/fax 2 15 60; w www.gobaikal.com, ul Oktyabrya 16/2) is an experienced full-time travel-fixer, former guide and ex-BAM worker. An immobilising stroke in the mid-1990s has rendered his decent spoken English a little hard to follow, but he is quick to reply to emails and is always keen to please. He also has a brilliant apartment to rent for US$10 a night.

More informal assistance is offered by witty, widely travelled **Petr Ishkin** (☎ 2 42 05; e petr_great@hotmail.com; pr 60 let SSSR 16, Apt 136) and proverb-spouting John Cleese lookalike **Vladimir Yatskovich** (☎ 2 01 11; e Y_V_N@hotmail.com; ul Polygrafistov 5, Apt 112). Both are local school teachers with great English and time on their hands in summer. Vladimir offers a family homestay for US$10 to US$12, including meals.

All of the agencies and individuals mentioned here, except Khozyain, can help you arrange boat trips, but check very carefully what is and is not included in any deal you arrange.

Things to See & Do

There are lovely lake views from a small summer shashlyk stand at the eastern end of town (minibus No 3 passes nearby, or walk 10 to 15 minutes from the station). A steep path leads down from there onto a scenic, surprisingly deserted, pebble beach.

If you're interested in the history of the BAM, you may enjoy the friendly little **BAM Museum** (☎ 2 76 44; ul Mira 2; minibus No 3; admission R20; open 10am-12.30pm & 1.30pm-5pm Tues-Sun), 1.5km east of the central square. It also has a few Buryat artefacts, an associated art gallery and at least one staff member who speaks basic English.

It's pleasant to take a boat ride out onto the lake. Arrange trips with any of the guide or tour agents listed under Information earlier. If you dare brave the chilly waters, the yacht club **Belyi Parus** (☎ 33467; e nordsail@mail.ru; Severobaikalsk port) rents windsurfers (ails parusniye), waterskis (vodnye Lyzhi) and wet suits.

Places to Stay

The cheapest deal, apart from the station resting rooms, is the friendly, clean but basic **Hotel Cherenbas** (☎ 2 36 54; ul Mira 44; dorm beds R150-200), which has a kitchen for self-catering. Despite the address, it is not accessed (or visible) from ulitsa Mira; instead, follow the directions on the map.

Hotel Podlemore (☎ 2 31 79; pr 60 let SSSR 26A; rooms from R330) is a brand-new, if jerry-built, red-and-yellow tower beside the train station. Rooms are very good value with hot water in the attached showers and great 7th-floor views of Baikal, but light sleepers may be disturbed by the rail yard noise.

Santa Barbara (ul Neptuna 5; ☎ 3 35 00; double suites R1170) is discreetly unmarked in a silver-turreted brick house behind daunting gates. The two plush suites are great value if you want pampering. It's across the tracks from Hotel Podlemore.

A cheaper business house-hotel is almost complete at ulitsa Neptuna 3: contact **Alex Rudkovskiy** (e ru_alex@hotmail.com) for details.

The **BAM Cottages** (ul Sibirskaya 14; rooms per person US$19), along the ridge from the Santa Barbara, are overpriced. Their best feature are peeps of view down across the dacha-lined waterfront.

Hidden in a pine grove at the otherwise unpromising northeast end of town, Baikal Service (see under Information earlier) has some surprisingly peaceful Hansel and Gretel–style **cottages** (minibus No 1; rooms per person US$25) plus better value US$12 beds in the 'student' house with shared fridge and good hot shower. The cottage rates include breakfast.

Places to Eat

The no-frills **Zakusochnaya** (Leningradsky pr 5; open 8.30am-7.30pm; borshch R12) within the video shop often looks closed but actually offers a handwritten menu and the cheapest draught beer in town. It's beside the handy **Olimp 2 food store** (open 9am-1pm & 2pm-midnight daily).

Across the road is **Kafe Ayana** (☎ 2 12 24; pr Leningradsky 6; pozi per plate R30, cover R30 at weekends; open 9am-6pm & 7pm-1am daily), serving the steamed dumpling-sized balls of soft pasta-like dough filled with minced lamb and onion known as pozi. Around the corner of the same building is the nicer, generally quieter **Kafe Tyya** (mains R30-45, draught local ale per ½ litre R18).

Smart, but prone to DJ attack, is **Kafe Nostalgie** (ul Proletarski 7, 2nd floor; mains

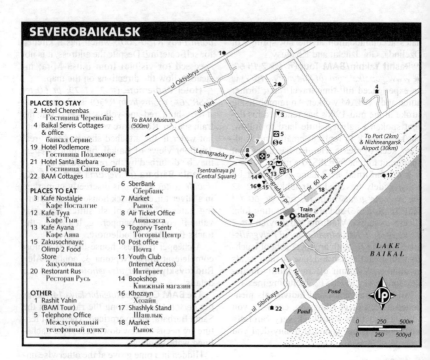

SEVEROBAIKALSK

PLACES TO STAY
2 Hotel Cherenbas
    Гостиница Череньбас
4 Baikal Servis Cottages
    & office
    байкал Сервис
19 Hotel Podlemore
    Гостиница Подлеморе
21 Hotel Santa Barbara
    Гостиница Санта барбара
22 BAM Cottages

PLACES TO EAT
3 Kafe Nostalgie
    Кафе Ностальгие
12 Kafe Tyya
    Кафе Тыя
13 Kafe Ayana
    Кафе Аяна
15 Zakusochnaya;
    Olimp 2 Food
    Store
    Закусочная
20 Restorant Rus
    Ресторан Русь

OTHER
1 Rashit Yahin
    (BAM Tour)
5 Telephone Office
    Междугородный
    телефонный пункт
6 SberBank
    Сбербанк
7 Market
    Рынок
8 Air Ticket Office
    Авиакасса
9 Togorvy Tsentr
    Тогоргы Центр
10 Post office
    Почта
11 Youth Club
    (Internet Access)
    Интернет
14 Bookshop
    Книжный магазин
16 Khozain
    Хозяин
17 Shashlyk Stand
    Шашлык
18 Market
    Рынок

To BAM Museum
(500m)

Leningradsky pr

Tsentralnaya pl
(Central Square)

To Port (2km)
& Nizhneangarsk
Airport (30km)

Train
Station

*LAKE
BAIKAL*

Pond

Pond

ul Oktyabrya

ul Mira

pr 60 let SSSR

ul Neptuna

ul Sibirskaya

0   250   500m
0   250   500yd

R40-75; open 10am-4pm & 7pm-1am daily)
serving dishes such as *omul* with mushrooms
(R70).

Rus (☎ 2 39 14; w *www.sbaikal.pp.ru/mpz
.htm; pr 60 let SSSR 28; open noon-2am
Wed-Sun)* is the other upmarket restaurant
option.

Getting There & Away
From Nizhneangarsk airport (30km northeast
of Severobaikalsk) scenic low-altitude flights
cross Lake Baikal to Ulan Ude (R965, six per
week) and Irkutsk (R1335, two per week). Be
aware that flights are prone to long delays
and cancellations because of turbulent
weather over the lake. The **air ticket office**
(☎ 2 27 46; *Tsentralny pl; open 9am-noon &
1pm-4pm Wed-Fri & Sun-Mon)* is within the
Dom Kultury Zhelezne Dorognikov.

Train No 75 heads for Moscow on odd-
numbered days. Overnight trains for Lena and
Bratsk continue either to Krasnoyarsk (even-
numbered days) or loop round to Irkutsk (odd
days). These are nonstop to Goudzhekit
(R94.10, 35 minutes), though *elektrichka*
(R11, one hour, three per day) would be vastly
cheaper. Eastbound No 76 (odd-numbered

days) and No 98 (Wednesday and Sunday in
summer) go all the way to Tynda, No 956
runs to Novaya Chara (15½ hours, daily) and
there are morning *elektrichka* to Uoyan and
Kichera.

From mid-June to the end of August a hydrofoil service runs the length of Lake Baikal
between Nizhneangarsk, Severobaikalsk and
Irkutsk (R990, 12 hours, one or two per
week). Unfortunately, the precise timetable is
only announced days before the service begins, making advance planning difficult. The
boat calls at the port beside the yacht club,
2km northeast of the town centre.

A minibus to Baikalskoe leaves some
mornings at 7am.

Getting Around
Hourly on the hour a minibus (R20) shuttles
from Severobaikalsk's Tsentralnaya ploshchad, past Severobaikalsk port (2km) to
Nizhneangarsk (passing its port, the town and
the airport). At weekends these don't always
show up. Minibus No 3 connects the new,
low-rise Zarechnie suburb via the museum, then continues to
the station, loops right around to the far side

Cruise Control?

Pashka, the jovial captain, was already roaring drunk when I got aboard his trawler. But it seemed a bargain.

'Really? You'll take me to see the petroglyphs for R150?'

'*Davai*, no problem, problem *nyet*' he slurred slapping my back heavily with a friendly (albeit tar-blackened) palm. The boat lurched out to sea, round a cape, into a lovely little bay.

He grunted something unintelligible.

'There,' translated the first mate who was slightly more sober.

It was a small cave, but how to reach it? Before I could ask, the boat picked up speed and Pashka slammed the sizable craft onto the shingle beach with a sickening metallic screech.

I had to jump down some three metres from the prow to explore. The cove was lovely, and the soot-blackened cave had plenty of smashed vodka bottles. But no sign of anything more ancient.

Anyway, I was more concerned how to re-board the boat. '*Nyet* problem.' The crew lowered a noose. This was a makeshift foothold and somehow they winched me aboard as the engines strained frantically to pull the boat free.

With clouds of black smoke and the motors wheezing they managed it. Before long I'd been promoted to pilot, steering a course to enjoy the sunset while funnels of vodka were administered. By the time we spluttered back into port I'd had much more fun than seeing a few scratched rocks. Pashka was happy too. With the R150. And especially with the tip – one dollar. He'd never seen a greenback before!

Mark Elliot

of the tracks, passing (eventually) almost beside the Santa Barbara hotel. Minibus No 1 passes near Baikal Service, the train station and then makes a big loop from Tsentralnaya ploshchad.

AROUND SEVEROBAIKALSK
North of Severobaikalsk

Though much smaller than Severobaikalsk, **Nizhneangarsk**, 30km northeast around the lake, is the original administrative centre of northern Baikal, with a small **museum** in the high school, which traces the history of the settlement back to the 17th century. The town itself is fairly attractive; it's effectively two long parallel streets of mainly wooden buildings stretching 4km from the port to the airport. Towards the northern end an appealing new wooden **hotel** (☎ 63 28; ul Rabochaya 10) was nearing completion when we visited. An hourly minibus runs between Severobaikalsk's Tsentralnaya ploshchad to Nizhneangarsk.

North of Nizhneangarsk, beyond the barrier strip of Yarki island, Lake Baikal opens up again with a new, shallower, marshy persona. This is most photogenically viewed from tiny **Dushkachan** hamlet. Some 12km beyond, and 500m off the road through trees away from the lake, **Kholodnaya** is an attractively mountain-backed but economically unravelling village of Evenki people.

A track starting 3km north of the Kholodnaya turn-off is the start of a forest hike to remnants of the small mica-mining **Akokan Gulag** (1931–33). After an hour you reach the 'officers' huts'; above is the main camp with a collapsed watchtower and a kitchen area whose three *Marie Celeste* cauldrons await use. About 15 minutes' climb beyond, a little mini-railway has tiny bucket wagons and a magical pile of mica remnants. It leads up to the collapsed mine entrance.

A few minibuses each week serve Kholodnaya, and both hamlets have rail halts where *elektrichka* stop briefly. However, realistically the only practical way to visit is to charter a taxi.

Nikolai Sorokin, a taxi driver at Severobaikalsk train station, speaks no English but manages to guide foreigners to the site, show them animal tracks and point out gulag secrets all for R500 to R700, including transport and anti-tick hat.

Baikalskoe
Байкальское

The gorgeous little fishing village of Baikalskoe, some 60km south of Severobaikalsk, has a timeless quality, an old bridge and an absurdly picturesque lakeside location. From the fishing port, past the cute wooden church, walk 20 minutes up the cliff-side path towards

SIBERIA

the radio mast for particularly superb views. Continue to the bay beyond for possible camping opportunities. Among the rocks below are supposedly some shamanic petroglyphs (pictured in the Severobaikalsk museum), though you'll need a decent guide to spot them (see the boxed text 'Cruise Control?' earlier).

Baikalskoe has no hotel, and only one minibus plies the dead-end road from Severobaikalsk (departing most days at 7am, returning around 3pm). A taxi for the one-hour drive costs from R500 according to waiting time, with a stop at the viewpoint halfway. For around US$150 return, Baikalskoe fishermen may be persuaded to take you 65km south down the lake to effectively uninhabited Cape Kotelnikovsky. It is said to be distantly backed by some of the most spectacular mountains in Siberia. However, at the time of writing the remote little hot spring and *turbaza* there had closed down.

East Across Lake Baikal

Baikal's mountain backdrop looks most spectacular from about 3km offshore and boat trips are highly recommended. Going all the way across doesn't add a lot scenically but you could visit shaman-haunted, fjord-like **Ayaya Bay**, where reindeer have been reintroduced, and perhaps take a mud-soaked 7km hike up to biologically unique Lake Frolikha. Clean up afterwards at the idyllically isolated hot-spring *turbaza* of **Khakusy** *(beds R100)*, where accommodation is in wood-fire-heated huts.

You need a permit to visit (these areas are a restricted reserve) but prebooked tours generally include this and if you come for the day, the requirement might be overlooked. Check well in advance as permits can take several days to organise.

It's possible to negotiate cheap charters with fishermen at Severobaikalsk, Nizhneangarsk or Baikalskoe, but think carefully before taking a boat that's small or seems unreliable, as storms can come from nowhere and getting help in the middle of icy-cold Baikal is virtually impossible. For a reliable charter, contact the charming **Viktor Kuznetsov** *(☎ 5 10 05, fax 5 10 30; e frolicha@ mail.ru)*. Based in Nizhneangarsk, his boat *Jeanne* (R4500 per day, R450 per hour) has basic berths for five people, offering shelter from unpredictable weather and a decent turn of speed. It's possible to visit Ayaya and Khakusy on a long day trip. Note that in May

to early June, when the ice is half melted, these places are totally cut off. Once the ice thickens you can drive across.

Southern Buryatia
Южная бурятия

The Buryatia Republic crouches on the Mongolian border like a cartographic crab squeezing Lake Baikal with its right pincer. The indigenous Buryats are a Mongol people, and now represent only around 25% of the region's population. Jenghis Khan's mother is said to have hailed from the Barguzin Valley (see under Lake Baikal earlier). While forest-dwelling Western Buryats retained their shamanic animist beliefs, Eastern Buryats from the southern steppe-lands mostly converted to Tibetan-style Buddhism during the 19th century. These areas remained a bastion for the religion throughout the Soviet era, although every Buryat *datsan* (temple) was systematically wrecked by the Communists' anti-religious mania of the 1930s. Recently many have been rebuilt, and Ivolginsk is now the centre of Buddhism in Russia.

Beyond their republic, Buryats also live in Mongolia and northern China and represent some 65% of the Aginskiy Autonomous District southeast of Chita, which is another bastion of Siberian Buddhism. Ust-Ordinskiy is another Buryat district, albeit more heavily Russianised. Rumblings in March 2002 about incorporating it into the Irkutsk Region rang alarm bells. Precious metals have been discovered in the region and some sniff a ploy to prize the land out of Buryat control in time for a possible gold rush.

Buryat is a Turkic language, though very different from Tuvan and Altay. Dialects vary considerably between regions but almost everyone speaks decent Russian. Hello is *sainbena/sambaina*, thank you is *bai yer la*.

ULAN UDE
УЛАН УДЕ
☎ 3012 • pop 380,000 • Moscow time plus 5 hours
Although Ulan means 'Red,' Ulan Ude, 456km by train east of Irkutsk, is pleasantly green and sits in an attractive cradle of rolling hills at the junction of the Selenga and Uda Rivers. Founded as Verkhne Udinsk in 1775,

it prospered as a major stop on the tea-caravan route between Troitskosavsk (now Kyakhta) and Irkutsk.

Because of sensitive border installations and a secretive aircraft factory (with a private airport that still doesn't appear on maps), the city and region was closed to tourists until 1987. This may explain why so few foreigners visit what is one of the most charming towns in eastern Siberia.

Orientation & Information

Most traffic bypasses the city centre, using busy ulitsa Baorsoeva and ulitsa Baltakhinova, which leaves tree-lined ulitsa Lenina surprisingly calm for a main commercial thoroughfare. Good city maps are hard to find, but your best bet is the **bookshop** (*ul Lenina 30; open 10am-6pm daily*).

There are **exchange bureaus** in the Geser and Buryatia hotels; the Buryatia also has an ATM.

Until the main **post office** (*ul Lenina 61; open 8am-7pm Mon-Fri, 9am-6pm Sat & Sun*) has rebuilt its Internet room, web access is easiest at the busy **telephone office** (*ul Borsoeva; open 8am-10pm; Internet access R30/hr*).

Friendly English-speaking tour agencies include **Buryat-Intour** (upstairs in Hotel Baikal) and **Naran Tur** (in Hotel Buryatia). They can arrange trips to *datsan*, Old Believers' villages and a host of other destinations.

Things to See

Much 19th-century opulence is still visible in the attractive commercial buildings on and around ulitsa Lenina, notably the renovated 1838 **trading arcades** now filled with boutiques, and enclosing the central department store. Many styles of wooden houses are to be found in the old town area south of ulitsa Kirova. Balanced by a grand opera house, even the Stalinist central square, ploshchad Sovetov, is manageably proportioned and, decapitated in its midst, the world's largest **Lenin head** is less domineering than comically cross-eyed.

Ulitsa Lenina ends at the attractive white-washed **Odigitria Cathedral**, built between 1741 and 1785 and rescued from near collapse in the late 1990s. In somewhat better condition is the **Troitskaya Church**, hidden away off ulitsa Dimitrova and backed by a park with a Ferris wheel and Gaudi-esque fountain.

Given the pricing structure of the **Historical Museum** (*ul Profsoyuznaya 29; admission per floor R70; open 10am-5.30pm Tues-Sun*) you might consider seeing only its top storey, which has a dazzling collection of *thanka*, Buddhas and icons salvaged from Buryatia's monasteries and temples on the eve of their destruction. Other floors have more standard collections of historical photos, maps and artefacts.

The **Ethnographic Museum** (*Etnografichesky muzey; bus No 8; admission R45; open 10am-5pm daily June-Aug*) is 6km from the centre but well worth the trip. It lacks the pretty lakeside setting of equivalents in Bratsk and Irkutsk but has an extensive and informative outdoor collection of local architecture plus some reconstructed burial mounds, the odd stone totem and plenty of old wooden houses, and features occasional craft demonstrations. The centrepiece is a splendid wooden church and a whole strip of Old Believers' homesteads. From the Muzey bus stop, walk west for a kilometre along an asphalt lane through the woods. The museum gates and ticket booth are obvious (to the right) as you pass.

The **Buryatia Literary Museum** (*Literaturnyy Muzey; ul Sovetskaya 27; admission R12; open 10am-6pm Tues-Sat*) is in an attractive 1847 wooden house containing photos, books and a small but rare collection of ancient Buddhist manuscripts. Its 108-volume Atsagat Ganzhur (Chant Book) is inscribed in multicoloured Tibetan script on a special black lacquer made, so it is claimed, from blood, pounded sheep's vertebrae and sugar.

The **Fine Arts Museum** (*Khudozhestbennyy Muzey; ul Kuybysheva 29; admission R10-15 per exhibition; open 10am-5pm Tues-Sun*) has small, regularly changing exhibitions from its extensive permanent collection and might display anything from Buryat Buddhist art to Russian portraiture and photos of the moon. Look for the powerful work of AV Kazansky.

The **Nature Museum** (*Muzey Pripody Buryatii; ul Lenina 46; admission R10; open 10am-6pm Wed-Sun*) has more and bigger stuffed animals than ever. A scale model of Baikal gives a great sense of just how deep the lake is.

The new **Geological Museum** (*Geologcheskiy Muzey; ul Lenina 59; admission R5*) is modest but well presented and knocks spots

ULAN UDE

To Airport (7km),
Ivolginsk Datsan (7km),
Ivolginsk (39km) &
Kyakhta (240km)

Footbridge

Train Station

Market

To Ethnographic Museum,
Turbaza Salyut (8.5km),
Baatarai Urgoo Restaurant (9.5km),
& Atsagat Datsun (54.5km)

Pl Sovetov

ul Gagarina

ul Revolyutsii 1950

ul Borsoeva

ul Smolina

ul Lesnaya

ul Sukhe-Batora

ul Ranzhurova

ul Kommunisticheskaya

ul Profsoyuznaya

ul Sovetskaya

ul Lenina

ul Smolina

ul Kalandarishvili

ul Kirova

ul Shmidta

ul Svobody

ul Kuybysheva

ul Sverdlova

ul Banzarova

ul Linkhavoyna

ul Naberezhnaya

pr Pobedy

ul Balashinova

ul Kommunisticheskaya

ul Kalinina

ul Dimitrova

ul Kuybysheva

Market

Selenga River

Uda River

To Bolshoy Kunaley
& Kuytun (70km)

PLACES TO STAY
1 Hotel Odon;
   Restoran Odon
   Гостиница Одон
4 Hotel Geser
   Гостиница Гэсэр
9 Hotel Baikal
   Гостиница байкал
13 Hotel Buryatia;
   Aerokassa Booth
   Гостиница бурятия
17 Hotel Barguzin
   Гостиница баргузин
26 Hotel Zolotoy Kolos
   Гостиница Золотой
   Колос

PLACES TO EAT
2 Samovar
   Самовар
10 Buterbrodnaya Baikal
   Бутербродная байкал
11 U Druzhei
   У Дружеи
15 Drakon
   Дракон
18 Ulger
   Ульгэр
22 Zolotoy Drakon
   Золотой Дракон

OTHER
3 Telephone & Internet Office
   Телефон Интернет
5 Main Post Office
   почтамт
6 Lenin Head
   Голова Ленина
7 Geological Museum
   Музей Геллогии
   Бурятии
8 Opera House
   Театр оперы и балета
   Бурятии
12 Historical Museum
   Исторический музей
14 Mongolian Consulate
   Консульство Монголии
16 Main Bus Station
   Центральный автовокзал
19 Nature Museum
   Музей природы
20 Buryatia Literary Museum
   Литературный Музей
   Бурятии
21 Bookshop
   Книжный магазин
23 Trading Arcades;
   Торговые ряды
   Central Department Store
   ЦУМ
24 Fine Arts Museum
   Художественный музей
25 Troitskaya Church
   Троицкая Церковь
27 Banzarova Bus Station
   Местный автовокзал
28 Odigitria Cathedral
   Одигитриевский собор

0   125   250m
0   125   250yd

off the Minerology Museum in Akademgorodok near Novosibirsk.

Places to Stay

The **Hotel Zolotoy Kolos** (ul Sverdlova 43; singles/twins R105/180), a vaguely disreputable traders hostel, has only its price to recommend it.

Even cheaper, pleasantly rural but inconveniently far from the centre is a trio of *turbaza* close to the turning for the Ethnographic Museum. Best of these is children's camp **Salyut** (☎ 44 78 80; bus No 8; dorm beds R100) at km 9 (look for the big red-and-yellow sign), which has a few rooms with attached toilet and washbasin in the green-and-white hut at the back.

Hotel Odon (☎ 34 29 83; ul Gagarina 43; singles R163-269, twins R305-485) is uninspiring but only five minutes' walk from the train station.

Hotel Barguzin (☎ 21 57 46; ul Sovetskaya 28; singles/twins with shower R275/430, doubles R630), well-positioned for the old town, has faded corridors and a bear guarding the foyer. The doubles have their own water heaters.

Hotel Buryatia (☎ 21 18 35, fax 21 17 60; e hotel@burnet.ru; ul Kommunisticheskaya 47A; singles/twins from US$12/18) is a big, Soviet tower with decent rooms, but no hot water in summer. When we stayed, we found that the room cleaners had a tendency to put items into the back corners of wardrobes and drawers, perhaps hoping that we would leave them behind.

Hotel Baikal (☎ 21 37 18; ul Erbinova 12; singles/twins/luxe R320/480/670) is surprisingly good value and right on ploshchad Sovetov.

Hotel Geser (☎/fax 21 61 51; e hotel_geser@mail.ru; ul Ranzhurova 11; singles/doubles with breakfast R930/1240) is a former Party hangout and the most comfortable place in town, with water heaters in each room. The restaurant is very reasonably priced.

Places to Eat

There are many summer cafés near the river, around the opera house and beside the trading arcades. To fill up for a pittance, join the beer-breakfast locals at **Buterbrodnaya Baikal** (ul Kommunisticheskaya 45; snacks R3-12; open 8am-3pm & 4pm-9pm daily).

U Druzhei (ul Kommunisticheskaya 44; mains R30-80, kebabs R45; open 11am-11.30pm daily), across the street from Buterbrodnaya, is refreshingly air-conditioned and looks much more attractive at night, when it has a cosy, candlelight atmosphere.

Samovar (☎ 26 41 88; ul Gagarina 41; mains R60-120; open 11am-11pm daily) has flavours of old Russia, costumed friendly staff and graciously quiet music. Simple but tasty grilled aubergine slices form the one vegetarian choice. Portions are small.

Drakon (☎ 21 52 83; ul Smolina 38; mains R25-50; open 11am-11pm daily) has a curious jousting-cavern interior.

Zolotoy Drakon (☎ 21 21 09; ul Kirova 8; mains R30-75, Xo-Go fondue R100-200; open 11am-4pm & 5pm-11pm daily), not to be confused with Drakon, serves nominally Chinese cuisine at very good prices.

Restoran Odon (☎ 44 29 89; mains R130-240; open 10am-1am daily), in Hotel Odon, is more authentically Chinese but there's a noisy disco later in the evening.

Ulger (☎ 21 80 66; ul Lenina 46; mains R60-100; open 11am-4pm & 5pm-11pm daily) is in the rear of the Natural History Museum. It has a shady terrace, and wishfully named menu items like Texan chilli, French chicken and Pork Exotica.

At **Baatarai Urgoo** (Yurta; ☎ 44 74 92; Barguzin road; bus No 8; pozi for 4 R59.30; open noon-11pm daily) Jenghis Khan would have felt right at home sitting upon the raised throne watching a two-metre dragon curl down the central chimney flue. This unique spaceship-shaped palace-yurt is out of town but only 10 minutes' walk beyond the turning for the Ethnographic Museum. It's not to be missed, though a snack or a beer may suffice – the Buryat food is not memorable.

Getting There & Away

There are useful (and very scenic) flights to Nizhneangarsk (for Severobaikalsk and North Baikal; R965, six per week) but for most other destinations you'll save money by flying from Irkutsk. You can buy tickets departing from any airport in Siberia from the **Aerokassa booth** in Hotel Buryatia.

Beijing-bound trains pass through Ulan Ude on Wednesday (via Chita) and Saturday (via Mongolia). Fast trains to Ulaan Baatar pass through on Friday and Saturday at 2.15am and waste vastly less time at the

SIBERIA

border than the daily *Angara*, which takes 24 hours and costs R1220 *kupe*. It departs at 6am from Ulan Ude and returns at 7pm from Ulaan Baatar (US$20). Irkutsk and Chita are both easy overnight hops. Buy your tickets at the **mezhdunarodnaya kassa** *(international ticket window; open 9am-noon & 1pm-7pm)* even if you are buying a domestic ticket.

From the **main bus station** on ulitsa Sovetskaya, services run to Kyakhta (R126, five hours, three per day) via Novoselenginsk and daily to Ust-Barguzin and Barguzin. For Posolskoe, take a minibus from ulitsa Sovetskaya outside the bus station. For Ivolginsk and the *datsan* (marked 'Kalenova') use the **Banzarova bus station** *(cnr uls Banzarova & Lenina)*. Minibuses to Irkutsk and Arshan leave when full from the courtyard at the train station, usually around 7pm or 9pm.

Getting Around

From ploshchad Sovetov take minibus No 55 (R5, 20 minutes, three to four per hour) for the airport or bus No 10 for the train station. From the market, bus No 56 and tram No 7 go up ulitsa Baltakhinova and ulitsa Kommunisticheskaya and past Hotel Odon. Bus No 8 drives by the city park, the big train-carriage works, the hippodrome, a large new *datsan*, and eventually passes within a kilometre of the Ethnographic Museum, continuing past Turbaza Salyut to terminate just beyond the Baatarai Urgoo restaurant (last bus back to town is at 8.20pm).

AROUND ULAN UDE

The hilly steppe around Ulan Ude is pimpled with forgotten **Hun castles** so ancient that they are effectively invisible in the flower-filled grass. Naran Tur (see Orientation & Information under Ulan Ude earlier) can show you one such area but butterflies, flowers and the guide's enthusiasm are the biggest attractions of the trip. There are relatively accessible **Old Believers' villages** at Saratovka (35km), Kuytun (70km) and Bolshoi Kunaley (70km), with costumed shows put on for tour groups. The cheapest tours cost around US$35: book through either of the agencies listed under Orientation & Information earlier.

The most popular attractions are the *datsan*, which give a good introduction to the local form of Buddhism despite being somewhat 'tinny' and far less visually impressive than the Tibetan-style equivalents in the Chita region.

First founded in 1741, **Tamchinski Datsan** was Buryatia's first Buddhist monastery, but the main temple has only partially been rebuilt since it was destroyed in the 1930s, and is now surrounded by the disappointing small town of Gusinoe Ozero (not Gusinoozersk) on the Naushki–Ulan Ude rail train line. **Atsagat Datsan** was once the centre of Buryat Buddhist scholarship with an important scriptorium. Fine examples of Atsagat manuscripts are displayed in Ulan Ude's Literary Museum. Like Tamchinski, it was completely destroyed in the 1930s, but is now crawling back to life and has a tiny **Ayvan Darzhiev museum** *(hut 4; admission R5; open sporadically)* commemorating the Atsagat monk who became a key counsellor to the 13th Dalai Lama. The photogenically gaudy little monastery sits on a lonely grassy knoll set back from km 54 of the old Chita road, which runs on the northern bank of the Uda. The only bus from Ulan Ude to pass Atsagat is the Romanovka-bound service at 8.20am, which leaves from the main bus station. It returns about 1pm from Atsagat, but check with the driver before you get off the bus.

Ivolginsk Datsan
Иволгинский Дацан

This centre of Siberian Buddhism *(Ivolga Datsan in Buryat; admission free, camera fee R25 in grounds, R50 per photo inside temple)* was founded in 1946. The complex includes a glassed-in Bodhi Tree and is pleasantly set in a wide green valley edged by the Khamar-Daban Mountains. Remember to walk and spin the prayer wheels in a clockwise direction, keeping your right side respectfully towards the temple.

There are direct buses from Ulan Ude's Banzarova bus station (No 104, R35, one hour, departing 6.50am, noon, 4.20pm and 7pm). Returning it's easier to take a shared taxi (R8 per seat) to uninteresting Ivolginsk (Ivolga) town, whence very frequent minibuses shuttle to Ulan Ude (No 130, R30, three to four per hour). To visit the *datsan* library with its rare silk-wrapped Tibetan and Mongolian texts, you may need to join a tour (US$15 per person through Buryat Intour in Ulan Ude).

TOWARDS MONGOLIA

Until recently the only option for travellers heading to Mongolia was the train. Although

Visiting Ivolginsk Datsan

The Ulan Ude bus arrived well before the 9am start of ceremonies, tempting me to stroll beyond the monks' outhouses where the bushes flap with endless prayer flags. This proved unwise. Legions of resident mosquitoes here have grown fearless, accustomed to sipping their monk-blood cocktails swat-free. Loudspeakers played a hypnotic tape-loop of *Om Mani Padme Om*, which after half an hour started sounding like *Oh money, money Oh!* This was a suspicion apparently confirmed by the donation boxes tucked under every prayer wheel and by the discordant chunter of cash registers interrupting the babble of hell-for-leather chants in the main temple. Butter candles cost R5, wishes cost R10; just write down your desire, get a receipt and post the slip of paper in the box marked 'Yuroo'.

Mark Elliot

there are faster weekend expresses, the daily Ulaan Baator–bound train from Irkutsk is excruciatingly slow, spending a mind-numbing 11 hours to clear the borders. It's a single carriage appended to train No 264; a through ticket costs R1220. It would cost barely half that if you bought a ticket for three separate sections of the journey (via Naushki and Sükh Baatar), though *from* Mongolia there's no such saving.

From 2002, a more interesting option has opened up. The land border has finally opened in the once opulent old tea-route city of Kyakhta. This is accessible by bus from Ulan Ude via the intriguing Decembrist town of Novoselenginsk, but once at the border you'll need your wits about you as it's a smuggler's free-for-all.

For now this is the only 'new' Mongolian crossing. But farther west, the routes from Tuva (at Kandagayty) and Altay (at Tashanta) are expected to open within a couple of years. Keep asking!

Novoselenginsk
Новоселенгинск
Moscow time plus 5 hours

Stockades and little wooden houses on ludicrously overwide dust-blown roads give this 19th-century town a memorable Wild West feel. The 200-year-old colonnaded house beside the Bestuzhev bust is the **Decembrist Museum** (*muzey Dekabristov; ☎ 9 67 16; ul Lenina 51; admission R10; open 9am-5pm Wed-Sun*). Lower floors retain 19th-century furnishings, while upstairs are maps and photos relating to the Decembrist exiles who added a layer of culture to remote outposts like these after their failed 1825 uprising. The star exhibit is a long-armed naive-style crucifixion scene rescued from the town's ravaged but now partly restored church.

Novoselenginsk moved across the Selenga River to its present position around 1800. All that remains of original Staroselenginsk, abandoned due to frequent floods, is the Staroselenginsk-Spasky Church (1789) sitting totally isolated on the picturesque grassy far bank. There are very photogenic views from low cliffs, 20 minutes' walk east along ulitsa Kyubysheva from the *pozi* 'saloon' cum bus station. The 6m-tall whitewashed obelisk nearby commemorates the last foreign tourists who visited: Glaswegian missionaries Robert Yuille and Martha Cowie back in 1829. There's no hotel in Novoselenginsk, but no need to linger either when you can easily connect with Kyakhta and Ulan Ude by bus (three times daily in either direction).

Kyakhta
Кяхта
☎ 30142 • pop 18,300 • Moscow time plus 5 hours

Kyakhta lacks the cinemascope landscapes of Novoselenginsk but retains three once-grand churches, a great museum and a surprisingly good hotel. Formerly called Troitskosavsk, Kyakhta was a town of tea-trade millionaires whose grandiose cathedral was reputed to have had solid silver doors embedded with diamonds. By the mid-19th century, as many as 5000 cases of tea a day were arriving via Mongolia on a stream of horse or camel caravans, which returned loaded with exported furs. This glorious state of affairs was brought to an abrupt end with the completion of the Trans-Siberian Railway. Almost overnight, all trade was redirected via Vladivostok and Kyakhta withered into a remote border garrison town, bristling with weapons instead of gilded spires.

Modern Kyakhta is effectively two towns. The main centre is around the impressive

SIBERIA

shell of the **Troitskiy Cathedral** (1817), hidden in the overgrown central park. **Ryady Gostinye**, trading arches that date from 1853, flank the nearby main square beside which is the bus terminus. Leading northeast, ulitsa Lenina is lined with many early-20th-century buildings, including the delightfully eccentric **Museum** *(ul Lenina 49; admission R40; open 10am-6pm Tues-Sat)* with its original 1922 hardwood exhibition cases full of pickled foetuses and pinned butterflies and imaginative displays of treasures salvaged from Soviet-plundered churches and *datsan*.

Kyakhta's alternative centre, the smaller Sloboda district, is 4km south (R30 by taxi from the main centre). Here a dwarfish Lenin glares condescendingly at the extraordinarily grand but sadly ruined **Voskresenskaya Church** (1838) with its splendid Italianate cupola. Behind Lenin is the big but rather mutilated **Zdanie Gostinogo Dvora** (Historic Customs Warehouse, dating from 1842) with appended Communist-era spire. The brand-new frontier station for crossing into Mongolia is set back from here.

Places to Stay Beside the active Uspensky Church, **Hotel Druzhba** *(☎ 9 13 21; ul Krupskaya 8; dorm beds from R150, suites R300)*, 10 minutes' walk south of Kyakhta's main centre, has superb-value suites with hot water, sitting room and king-size bed.

Hotel Turist *(ul Lenina 21 cnr ul Sovetskaya; beds R135)*, with shared cold showers, is more basic. It's in a chocolate-box wooden house near the market.

Eating options are very limited but include **Buryatskaya Kukhnya** *(ul Menina; pozi 9R each)*, a small, very basic yet disco-balled room tucked behind the trading arches. **Kafe Viola** *(upstairs at ul Lenina 40; meals from R25)*, near the market and beside the taxi stand, is the nearest the town has to a restaurant.

Getting There & Away Ulan Ude–Kyakhta buses (R126, five hours) depart 9am, 11am and 3pm daily in either direction and take a scenic route. Buses stop for a 20-minute meal break in Novoselenginsk; if you want to have a brief look at this town, the two hours between morning buses is long enough.

The Kyakhta road border is open between 9am and noon and 2pm and 6pm. There's an official R11 paperwork fee and some staff

speak English or French. Since you can't cross the border on foot, you need to negotiate passage with private drivers. Start as close as possible to the front of the queue as only a handful of vehicles get through each hour. The going rate is R100 per passenger across no-man's land, but it's well worth negotiating a ride all the way to Sükh Baatar train station (around R30 extra) rather than becoming prey to rip-off taxi drivers in Altan Bulag, the uninteresting Mongolian border village. Nightly trains from Sükh Baatar to Ulaan Baatar (US$7 *kupe*, paid in Tugrik; departs 9.05pm) are rarely full.

Naushki
Наушки

Minibuses shuttle the 35km between Naushki and Kyakhta to connect with trains. Outside the station is a small park and two kiosks to the right: that's about it. If you arrive in Naushki en route for Mongolia and suddenly realise that your original currency declaration registration form wasn't stamped on entry to Russia, or you don't have a form at all, you face a tough choice: have customs confiscate all your dollars, or get off here and try to change it all into roubles. Rates will be bad but at least you should be allowed to take roubles out of Russia, which you can change back again to dollars in Ulaan Baatar. Of course it's better to notice this ahead of time and dump the dollars in Ulan Ude! For more information, see the boxed text 'Customs Warning' in the Siberia & the Russian Far East Facts for the Visitor chapter, earlier in this book. Naushki has no hotels – the nearest are in Kyakhta.

The fare from Naushki to Sükh Baatar is R230 *kupe* in what is often a one-carriage train. If it is officially 'full', a suitably tipped *provodnik* (carriage attendant) may still be able to get you aboard for the one-hour hop across no-man's land.

CHITA
ЧИТА
☎ 3022 • pop 370,000

Founded in 1653 as a Cossack stockade, Chita, 560km east of Ulan Ude and the capital of Chitinskaya Region, developed into a rough-and-tumble silver-mining centre. After 1827, however, it was force-fed a dose of urban culture by the arrival of more than 80 exiled Decembrist gentlemen-rebels. At the end of the civil war in 1920, Chita became the capital of the short-lived Far Eastern Republic, whose parliament building is now garishly over-renovated at ulitsa Amurskya 61. Light engineering grew to form the backbone of the regional economy, but these days the wealth you see is as likely to come from border trade and shady deals. As the gateway to the East Chinese Railway (opened in 1901), the city is now flooded with Chinese traders, and has a very large military presence. Closed to foreign visitors until the late 1980s, non-Chinese tourists remain rare.

Orientation & Information

Three blocks north of the main Chita 2 train station, uls Butina and Leningradskaya form the sides of the wide pedestrianised expanse of ploshchad Lenina, where a pink-granite Vladimir Ilych looks decidedly constipated. Perpendicular, the attractively tree-lined ulitsa Lenina parallels the train tracks from either side of the square. Ulitsa Babushkina parallels both, four blocks further north, and is the best bet for searching out restaurants and museums. Several hotels are located off ulitsa Profsoyuznaya, a block southeast of ulitsa Leningradskaya.

You can change US dollars, euros and Chinese yuan at **Promstroibank** (ul Petrovskaya 41), a block southeast of the train station. There's an ATM in Hotel Zabaikale.

Hidden by trees, the main **post office** (west cnr pl Lenina; open 8am-7pm Mon-Fri, 8am-6pm Sat & Sun) is in a quaintly spired wooden building. The **telephone office** and Internet café **Magellan** (ul Chaikovskogo 24; open 9am-8pm Mon-Fri, 9am-5pm Sat), which charges R50 per hour for Internet access, are half a block from the north corner of the square. Cheaper if slightly less reliable Internet access is available at **Klub Internet** (ul 9 Yanvarya 34; open 10am-2pm & 3pm-7pm Mon-Sat), inside the Ekran shopping centre, which charges R30 per hour plus R4 per MB.

The **bookshop** (Dom Knigi shopping centre, ul Amurskaya 58) sells out-of-date city maps for R7, excellent regional maps (R46) and hiking route-plans.

For English language help, it pays dividends to visit the university's **foreign languages faculty** (ul Butina 65, cnr ul Babushkina) and befriend students who want to practise their English.

Flamingo (☎ 23 55 59; Lenina 120) is a travel agency with English-speaking staff but

Panama City Tur (☎ 32 80 99; e panamatour@land.ru; Chaikovskogo 24; open 9am-1pm & 2pm-6pm Mon-Fri, 10am-2pm Sat) is better organised. Panama City runs weekly tours to Alkhanai (see Around Chita later in this chapter) and it owns good-quality hotels in Chita and Aginskoe which you can reserve by email.

Things to See

If all Chita's architectural gems were less widely dispersed the city might be considered one of Siberia's more appealing. However, each attractive area is too diffuse to give a great impact overall. Even the lovely **Archangel Michael** log church (1771) is hemmed in by apartment blocks. It houses a small but interesting **Decembrist's Museum** (Muzey Dekabristov; ☎ 3 48 03; ul Dekabristov 3B; admission R30; open 10am-6pm Tues-Sun). Still, there are many delightful old **wooden houses**, including ulitsa Lenina 104, ulitsa Babushkina 80 and ulitsa Chkalova 125 and 83, and much early-20th-century architecture, lending a grand air to sections of ulitsas Lenina, Amurskaya and Akhokhina.

Reopened after 12 years' restoration, the excellent **Regional Museum** (Kraevedchesky muzey; ☎ 3 35 30; ul Babushkina 113; admission R25; open 10am-6pm Tues-Sun) is in an early-20th-century mansion. Beyond the gratuitous stuffed elk, you'll find some pretty interesting local exhibits, including a very thorough examination of the heritage and architectural renaissance of the city and region.

Walk three sides of a block, then go upstairs through a furniture store (honestly!) to get to the **Art Museum** (Oblastnoy khudozhectvennyy muzey; ☎ 3 85 36; ul Chkalova 118; admission R10; open 10am-6pm Tues-Sun), which shows frequently rotated exhibitions by local artists, both talented and abysmal.

The **Military Museum** (Muzey istorii voysk ZaBVO; ☎ 2 41 32; ul Lenina 86; admission R5; usually open 10am-4.30pm Wed-Sun) has an exhibit about the recent exhumation of a nearby mass grave, which contained local victims of Stalin's purges. You can see the big guns for free by walking up the passage between the museum and the impressive **Officers' Club** building next door. Lenin medals sold from the museum gift-stand make great souvenirs.

SIBERIA

Places to Stay

Despite the plentiful options, hotels fill up fast so call ahead or get a room as soon as you can.

Hotel Metelitsa (*dorm beds R100, singles/twins R437/468*) is accessed through some gates at the western side of Chita 2 (main) train station. Showers cost R30 extra.

Hotel Taiga (☎ *26 23 32; 4th floor, ul Lenina 75; dorm beds R150*) has the next cheapest beds. Sheets are clean and guests are usually segregated by gender, but there's no shower and by 11.30pm the front door may be locked.

Hotel AChO (☎ *26 23 97; ul Profsoyuznaya 19; twins/triples R300/360, deluxe rooms R1032-1720*), short for Administratsii Chitinskoi Oblastu, is vastly better than the Metelitsa and Taiga. The deluxe rooms have been rebuilt to Western standards.

Best of several essentially similar, typical Soviet-era choices is **Hotel Chitaavtotrans** (☎ *23 50 11; ul Kostyushko-Grigovicha 7; singles/twins with shower R280/400*), a block north of ploshchad Lenina via ulitsa Butina. Others include **Hotel Zabaikale** (☎ *26 45 20; ul Leningradskaya 36 on pl Lenina; singles/doubles without bath R266/331, with bath R451/640*), the smarter **Hotel Ingoda** (☎ *23 32 22; ul Profsoyuznaya 23; singles/twins R420/820*) and the disappointing **Hotel Dauria** (☎ *90 12 20; ul Amurskaya 80/Profsoyuznaya 12; singles/twins R510/719*) above the pricey Kharbin Chinese Restaurant.

Turist (☎ *23 17 18; ul Babushkina 42A; singles/doubles R350/600*), a cockroach-plagued place, is a last resort. Take trolleybus No 1 or 5 from the train station.

Panama City Motel (☎ *44 31 31, fax 44 43 93;* e *panamatour@land.ru; cnr uls Krasnoe Zvedy & ul Shilova; doubles R1150-1650*), in its own class, has Western standards and two good restaurants; booking are essential. It's 5km north of the centre; to get there, take bus No 2 or 3 from ulitsa Amurskaya, halfway between the train station and ploshchad Lenina.

Places to Eat

Even by secretive Siberian standards, Chita is adept at keeping its better dining options hidden in unexpected corners. Good cheap *pozi* are available at **Priyatel Poznaya** (*ul Zhuraleva 40; open 9am-6pm Mon-Fri*), which lurks within the office of the Chita customs department!

The cheap, central *stolovaya* **Bistro Annushka** (*ul Lenina 108; open 10am-10pm daily*) is entered by the more easterly of the building's two unmarked orange doors.

Chita's fast-food joint **Gril Master** (*ul Chekhov 5; cheeseburgers from R40; open 11am-11pm daily*) is up the 'closed' lane beside the Military Museum.

The city's best little coffee bar is incongruously plonked within the **Expostroi Hardware Store** (*ul Chkalovo 144; espresso R15, open 10am-7pm Mon-Sat*).

Pivnoi Tayum (☎ *26 34 65; ul Babushkina 127; mains R40-90; open noon-midnight daily*) is a nautically themed pub-restaurant. It is entered downstairs from ulitsa Zuraleva.

Kafe Kollazh (☎ *97 81 38; ul Babushkina 90; mains R45-80; open 11.30am-11pm daily*) has a terrace and a cosy interior with birch-bark art and soft French music. Its *gorbusha appetitnaya* (R56) is a deliciously flavoured salmon steak topped with crispy cheese crust, lemon and herbs. At lunch time, meals are discounted by 15%.

Kafe Minimo (☎ *323 338; ul Babushkina 62; mains R50-100; open noon-midnight daily*) is worth a try for genuine if somewhat underspiced Georgian food. Access is through the eagle arch behind the 24-hour Vecherniy grocery store.

Mey Vey (*ul Babushkina 173; mains R120-180; open 11am-midnight daily*) is not beautiful but has the most consistently recommended food of the six central Chinese restaurants. Enter from the rear of what appears (from ulitsa Babushkina) to be an unmarked office building set back behind some trees.

Getting There & Away

The *Vostok* train (No 020) to Beijing (R2900 *kupe*) leaves from Chita very early Wednesday morning; there's also a nightly service to the border town of Zabaikalsk (R330 *kupe*, 14 hours) via Olovyannaya for Tsugol Datsan (arrives 3am!). Other useful destinations include Ulan Ude (R410, 9½ hours overnight), Blagoveshchensk (No 250, R930, 34½ hours, odd days) and Tynda (No 078, R790, 27 hours). A helpful Service Centre in the station can help obtain tickets for a R36.65 commission.

There's no real **bus station**, just a trio of ticket kiosks facing the train station. Confusingly, each sells tickets for different departures so check all three. For Alkhanai take buses bound for Aksha (at 8am and noon) and get off at Duldurga (extra direct bus at 5pm). To Aginskoe there's an 8am bus Tuesday to Sunday (from the far left kiosk) and a 2pm bus Monday to Friday (right kiosk).

AROUND CHITA

Ropey public transport and former secrecy has kept foreign tourists to an absolute minimum in Chita region, but there's plenty to see. **Alkhanai**, three hours south of Chita, is reckoned by local Buddhists to be the religion's fifth most important holy mountain, albeit not especially high. A devotional six- to seven-hour return trek takes pilgrims to a small stupa and a window rock that is considered the Gate of Shambala, the spiritual paradise. Panama City Tur (see Orientation & Information under Chita earlier) organises tours departing 2pm each Friday (R400 for transport plus R300 to R1000 per night for accommodation in yurts or huts) but things are much more peaceful midweek. Take a bus from Chita to nearby Duldurga (three buses per day), where there are three hotels, then take a taxi or walk.

More interesting is the *datsan* (dating from 1816), centrepiece of the Institute of Buddhism at **Aginskoe**, capital of the Aginskiy Buryat Autonomous District. Aginskoe is 90km northeast of Durdurga but the road is so rough, it's best to return to Chita first. Just 4km from the temple is the excellent **Hotel Sapsam** (☎ 30289-3 45 90; e *panamatour@land.ru; doubles R930-1200*). It has a yurt-style Mongolian café and the Chernaya Zhemchuzhina restaurant, rated, incredibly, among Russia's 100 best!

If you liked Aginskoe, you'll love **Tsugol Datsan**, an essentially similar Tibetan-style edifice (dating from 1801) but in a smaller village backed by rolling grassland. However, it's 20km from the nearest station at Olovyannaya, where the daily trains roll in at 3am. Taxis from Aginskoe want around R800 return with a brief wait, or go first to Magoitoi by shared taxi.

Easier to reach is the crumbling old cathedral in **Kalinino** village, 15km from the old Decembrist city of Nerchinsk, and not far from Nerchinsk station on the Trans-Siberian Railway.

Russian Far East
Дальний Восток

The Russian Far East is the geographical term for the territories along the Pacific seaboard, including Khabarovsky Territory; Amur Region; Sakha Republic; Primorsky Territory; Magadan Region; Kamchatka; and the Kuril Islands, which arc down to Japan, enclosing the Sea of Okhotsk and the large, claw-shaped island of Sakhalin.

The region has long attracted Russian explorers and those seeking their fortune. Recently, foreign business has also flooded in, although it's little visited by regular travellers. Still, the Far East has much to offer, including the chance to find out about the many native peoples and to indulge in thrilling adventures: reindeer sledging across the frozen Sakha Republic; summitting live volcanoes on Kamchatka; or scuba-diving off Sakhalin.

Khabarovsky Territory
Хабаровский Край

Khabarovsk, the Russian Far East's largest and most vibrant city, is the capital of Khabarovsky Territory, which covers 788,600 sq km from the Chinese border along the Amur River to the frozen northern reaches on the Sea of Okhotsk.

KHABAROVSK
ХАБАРОВСК
☎ 4212 • pop 617,800 • Moscow time plus seven hours

The first major city you come to after the monotonous taiga and isolated settlements of eastern Siberia is Khabarovsk. What a relief it is. Lying at the broad confluence of the Amur River and its tributary, the Ussuri, the city almost has the air of a coastal resort. With the region's major airport, it is also the hub that you will most likely pass through while travelling around the Russian Far East.

The main street in Khabarovsk is ulitsa Muravyova-Amurskogo, a lively, tree-lined boulevard with attractive 19th-century brick

Highlights

- Discover the many native cultures of the Sakha Republic in the capital Yakutsk
- Shield your ears as the noon-day gun is fired at Vladivostok's restored city fortress
- Scrub off the grime from your long journey along the BAM railway at Tynda's public *banya*
- Stroll along ulitsa Muravyova-Amurskogo in Khabarovsk, enjoying the old-world architecture
- Climb a live volcano, cruise beautiful Avacha Bay, and track down Even reindeer-herders in Kamchatka

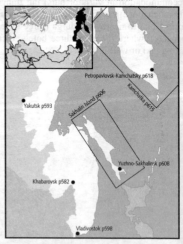

Petropavlovsk-Kamchatsky p618
Kamchatka p615
Yakutsk p593
Sakhalin Island p606
Yuzhno-Sakhalinsk p608
Khabarovsk p582
Vladivostok p598

★★★★★★★★★★★★★★★★★★★★

architecture. Among the crowds are Asian faces, unsurprising considering the city is 25km from China. But Khabarovsk is distinctly European in atmosphere; the closest examples of Asian culture are at the city's admirable Regional History Museum and in the Japanese, Korean and Chinese restaurants.

History

Khabarovsk was founded in 1858 as a military post by eastern Siberia's governor general,

RUSSIAN FAR EAST

140°E   160°E   80°N   CHUKCHI   SEA   Chukotka   USA 60°N
Peninsula   St Lawrence
Wrangel   Providenia   Island
Island   Bering
Strait

EAST
SIBERIAN   Chukotka
SEA   Autonomous   Anadyr   BERING

ARCTIC   OCEAN   Okrug   SEA

Novosibirskie
Islands
LAPTEV   Commander
SEA   Koryak   Islands
Avtonomnaya
Magadan   Okrug
Oblast   Kamchatskaya
Shelekhov   Oblast
Tiksi   Gulf   Ust-Kamchatsk
Sakha   Republic   ▲ Klyuchevskaya
(4750m)
Oimyakon   Esso   Milkovo

ARCTIC CIRCLE   Magadan   Kamchatka   Petropavlovsk-
Peninsula   Kamchatsky
Olenek   Lena   Yakutsk   Okhotsk

Mirny   Lensk   Aldan   SEA   Paramushir
OF   Island
OKHOTSK

Khabarovsky
Kray   Okha

STANOVOY MOUNTAINS   Nikolaevsk-   Nogliki   Simushir
na-Amur   Island
Neryungri   Zeisk   Sakhalinskaya
Reservoir   Oblast   Urup
UDOKAN   Tynda   Komsomolsk-   Sakhalin   Island
MTNS   Amurskaya   na-Amur   Island   Iturup
Oblast   Baikal-Amur   Vanino   Yuzhno-   (Etorofu)
Skovorodino   Mainline   Troitskoe   Sovietskaya   Sakhalinsk   Island
Severobaikalsk   Gavan   Kholmsk   Korsakov   Shikotan
Belogorsk   Moneron   Kunashir   Island
YABLONOVY MOUNTAINS   Island   Wakkanai   Island
Lake   Blagoveshchensk   Birobidzhan   Khabarovsk   Rebun Is   Habomai
Baikal   Rishiri   Islands
Irkutsk   Chita   Yevreyskaya   Island   Hokkaido
Ulan Ude   Avtonomnaya   Lake   Ternei   Sapporo
Oblast   Khanka   Primorsky
Gaivaron   Kray
Harbin   Spassk-Dalny   SEA
Vladivostok   OF
Ussuriysk   JAPAN
Slavyanka   Nakhodka   40°N

Ulaan Baatar   Tokyo
NORTH
MONGOLIA   KOREA   JAPAN
CHINA
Pyongyang

Seoul
Beijing   SOUTH
KOREA

0   500   1000km
0   300   600mi

KHABAROVSK

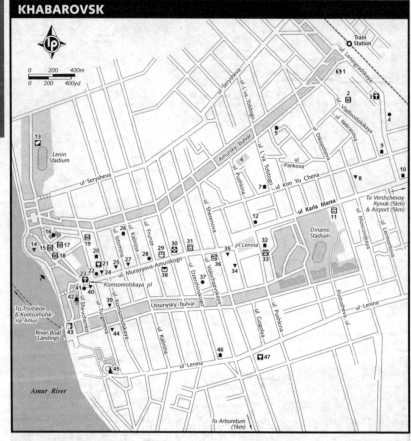

Count Nikolay Muravyov (later Muravyov-Amursky), during his campaign to take the Amur back from the Manchus. It was named after the man who got the Russians into trouble with the Manchus in the first place, 17th-century Russian explorer Yerofey Khabarov.

Khabarovsk remained a garrison, a fur-trading post and an Amur River landing until the Trans-Siberian Railway arrived from Vladivostok in 1897. During the civil war, it was occupied by Japanese troops for most of 1920. The final Bolshevik victory in the Far East was at Volochaevka, 45km to the west.

In 1969 Soviet and Chinese soldiers fought a bloody hand-to-hand battle over Damansky Island in the Ussuri River. The fighting stopped just short of all-out war but it set in motion a huge military build-up. Since 1984,

tensions have eased, and there's now substantial cross-border trade. Damansky and several other islands were handed back to the Chinese in 1991.

The Japanese are also back – this time for business and pleasure. They make up four-fifths of all foreign visitors here and their presence in town is demonstrated by the Japanese-style hotels and the restaurants that specialise in Japanese food. South Koreans are also arriving in large numbers, opening many businesses.

Khabarovskians are 80% native Russian-speakers, including small communities from Korea and the Caucasus. The only indigenous people here in any numbers are the Nanai, whose capital is Troitskoe, three hours down the Amur.

KHARBAROVSK

PLACES TO STAY
5   Hotel Versal
    Гостиница Версаль
7   Hotel Amethyst
    Гостиница Аметист
9   Hotel Zarya
    Гостиница Заря
10 Hotel Turist
    Гостиница Турист
16 Hotel Intourist; Unikhab; Korea
    House; Intour-Khabarovsk
    Гостиница Интурист
20 Hotel Sapporo
    Гостиница Саппоро
26 Maly Hotel
    Гостиница Малая
32 Hotel Tsentralnaya; B52
    Гостиница Центральная
42 Parus; Business Centre
    Парус; Бизнес-Центр
46 Hotel Amur
    Гостиница Амур

PLACES TO EAT
8   Green Plaza
    Зелёная Плаза
14 Kafe Utyos; Count Nikolay
    Muravyov-Amursky Monu-
    ment
    Кафе Утёс; Памятник
    Графу Николаю Муравёву-
    Амурскому
24 Restoran Sapporo
    Ресторан Саппоро
25 Tsentralnaya Gastronom
    Центральный
    Гастроном
27 Bistro Erofey
    Бистро Ерофей

34 Kafe Sion
    Кафе Сион
35 Kasam
    Касам
39 Russky Restaurant
    Русский Ресторан
40 Syangan
    Сянган
44 Stary Khabarovsk
    Старый Хабаровск

MUSEUMS
2   Museum of History of the Far
    Eastern Railway
    Музей Истории Дальневост-
    очной Железной Дороги
15 Regional Museum
    Краеведческий Музей
17 Military Museum
    Военный Музей
18 Far Eastern Art Museum
    Художественный Музей
19 Archeology Museum
    Археологический Музей

OTHER
1   Sberbank
    Сбербанк
3   Church of Christ's Birth
    Христорождественская
    Церковь
4   Train Ticket Office
    Железнодорожные кассы
6   Market
    Рынок
11 Theatre of Musical Comedy
    Театр Музыкальной Комедии
12 Knizhny Mir Bookshop
    Книжный Мир

13 Chinese Consulate
    Китайское Консульство
21 Traktyr
    Трактир
22 Far Eastern State Research
    Library
    Библиотека Дальнего-
    Восточного Исследовательск-
    ого Института
23 Khram Uspennya Bozhiei
    Materi
    Храм Успения Божей Матери
28 House of Pioneers; Souvenir
    Shop
    Дом Пионеров
29 Kino Gigant
    Кино Гигант
30 Department Store
    Универмаг
31 Drama Theatre
    Драматический театр
33 Main Telephone Office
    Центральный Переговорный
    Пункт
36 Internet Tsentr
    Интернет Центр
37 Dalgeo Tours
    Далгео Тур
38 Main Post Office
    Главпочтамт
41 Amur Steamship Company
    Параходная Компания
    Амур
43 River Boat Ticket Office
    Касса Речного Вокзала
45 WWII Memorial
    Памятник Второй
    Мировой Войне
47 Rio

Orientation

The train station is 3.5km northeast of the
Amur waterfront at the head of broad
Amursky bulvar; the airport is 5km northeast
of the centre. Running more or less parallel
down to the river is the busiest street, ulitsa
Muravyova-Amurskogo, which becomes ulitsa
Karla Marxa east of ploshchad Lenina, the
central square.

There are numerous maps of Khabarovsk
available – try the bookshop **Knizhny Mir** (ul
Pushkina 56; open 9am-8pm daily), which
also stocks a good range of maps for the entire Russian Far East.

Information

Currency exchange offices can be found
across the city. The **exchange bureau** at Hotel
Intourist (Amursky bulvar 2; open 9.30am-

10pm daily) changes travellers cheques. **Sberbank** (Amursky bulvar; open 9.30am-7pm
Mon-Fri, 10am-5pm Sat, 10am-2pm Sun),
across from the train station, has good rates.

The **main post office** (ul Muravyova-
Amurskogo 28) is open from 8am to 8pm
weekdays, and from 9am to 6pm on weekends. The **main telephone office** (ul Pushkina 52) is open from 8.30am to 10pm daily.
Internet Tsentr (☎ 32 23 14; ul Muravyova-
Amurskogo 44; open 8am-10.30pm daily)
charges R42 an hour.

For details of the Chinese consulate, see
the Siberia & the Russian Far East Facts for
the Visitor chapter.

Travel Agencies The friendly **Intour-
Khabarovsk** (☎ 31 23 17, fax 32 76 34;
w www.intour.khv.ru; Hotel Intourist, Amursky

bulvar 2) has plenty of experience in dealing with foreigners – usually large groups with planned itineraries. It offers an impressive range of day trips in the area, as well as longer trans-Siberian packages. Staff can book individual rail and plane tickets for a commission of US$4. The 2½-hour city tour with a guide and car is US$30.

Another very helpful agency offering a similar range of tours is **Dalgeo Tours** (☎ 74 77 84, fax 32 67 02; e dalgeo@dgt.khv.ru; 34A ul Dzerzhinskogo). They can arrange homestays for US$35 per person, including breakfast.

Ulitsa Muravyova-Amurskogo

A stroll along ulitsa Muravyova-Amurskogo is recommended, to admire the graceful **architecture** that survived the civil war. Start at ploshchad Lenina, where the pretty fountains are a magnet for locals relaxing in the evening, and where Lenin still looks down from the front of a handsome 1903 red-brick building.

The striking old **duma**, or local parliament building (ul Muravyova-Amurskogo 17), became the House of Pioneers (Dom Pionerov) in Soviet times. Today it houses one of the city's best souvenir shops and has a gallery for local artists downstairs.

A statue of Mercury tops **Tsentralnaya Gastronom** (ul Muravyova-Amurskogo 9), a glamorous 1895 mint-green Style Moderne building with a food store and decent café – see Places to Eat later. The **Far Eastern State Research Library** (ul Muravyova-Amurskogo 1), with its intricate red-brick facade, was built in 1900 to 1902.

The centrepiece of Komsomolskaya ploshchad is the monument to the Bolshevik heroes of the civil war, while to one side is the newly reconstructed Orthodox church **Khram Uspennya Bozhiei Materi**, a replica of one destroyed during communist times. On the corner of ulitsa Shevchenko on the south side of the square is the headquarters of the **Amur Steamship Company**, with its round, church-like tower.

The Waterfront & River Trips

Steps from Komsomolskaya ploshchad lead to the waterfront and a strip of beach that's very popular with sunbathers on hot days. South, there's a string of summertime food stalls and the landing stages for the suburban river boats. Farther on, as you climb the steps back up to ulitsa Lenina, you'll encounter Khabarovsk's bombastic **WWII memorial**.

A pleasant **city park** stretches 1.5km downriver (northwards). On the promontory is a cliff-top **tower** in which a troupe of WWI Austro-Hungarian POW musicians was shot dead for refusing to play the Russian Imperial anthem. It now contains a café – see Places to Eat later.

Opposite the tower is a statue of **Count Nikolay Muravyov-Amursky**. Muravyov's remains actually lie in Montparnasse cemetery in Paris, the city in which he died in 1881. The **monument** at the foot of the cliff below the tower marks the spot where the city's founders first stepped ashore.

For a short local ferry trip along the Amur, check out the schedules at one of the prichal (landings) by the beach. Some good choices might be the trip downstream to Green Island (Ostrov Zelyony) from landing No 5, upstream to Vladimirovka or around the back channels to Priamurskaya, both from landing No 3. Boats run from May to October.

Museums

The excellent **Regional History Museum** (Kraevedchesky muzey; ☎ 38 93 54; ul Shevchenko 11; admission R84; open 10am-6pm Tues-Sun) was founded in 1894. It includes displays on the natural history of the Far East (with the obligatory stuffed Amur tiger), fascinating artefacts and costumes of the indigenous peoples, an archaeology section and a recent history section with a striking 360-degree panorama depicting the 1922 civil war battle at Volochaevka.

The **Far Eastern Art Museum** (Dalnevostochny Khudozhestvenny muzey; ☎ 32 83 38; ul Shevchenko 7; admission R95; open 10am-5pm Tues-Sun) next door has a patchy assortment of religious icons, Japanese porcelain and 19th-century Russian paintings on the upper floor. The lower floors are given over to displays of ethnic handicrafts, a contemporary gallery and a good **souvenir shop** (open 10am-5pm daily).

Across the road, the highlight of the **Military Museum** (Voenny muzey; ☎ 32 63 50; ul Shevchenko 20; admission R60; open 10am-5pm Tues-Sun) is the luxury officers-only rail carriage dating from 1926. It's located in the courtyard at the back, along with the tanks and rockets. Ask nicely, and the guards may let you peek inside.

Another must for train buffs is the small but interesting **Museum of History of the Far Eastern Railway** (☎ 38 95 13; ul Vladivostokskaya 40; admission free; open 8.30am-5.30pm Mon-Fri). Call ahead and the helpful curator will give you a guided tour of the displays, which include some evocative photographs, maps and models. The museum is about five minutes' walk south of the station.

The small **Archaeology Museum** (Muzey Arkheologii; ☎ 32 41 77; ul Turgeneva 86; admission R84; open 10am-6pm Tues-Sun) is housed in a turn-of-the-20th-century brick mansion and contains clear reproductions and diagrams of the petroglyphs at Sikachi-Alyan (see Around Khabarovsk later in this chapter).

Other Attractions

Among the few churches that survived the Soviet years is the **Church of Christ's Birth** (Khristorozhdestvenskaya tserkov; ☎ 38 06 71; ul Leningradskaya 65). Its simple wooden construction hides a kaleidoscopic interior of coloured glass and glitzy icons. Services are held from 7am to 9am and 5pm to 7pm daily, though this schedule tends to change on church holidays.

The **Arboretum** (Dendrary; ul Volochaevskaya; open 9am-6pm daily) is a 12-hectare botanical garden with samples of all the trees and shrubs of the Russian Far East. Tram Nos 1, 2 and 6 run down here from the station.

Places to Stay – Budget

The cheapest rooms at the **Hotel Zarya** (☎ 32 70 75, fax 31 01 03; ul Kim Yu Chena 81/16; singles/doubles R195/500, with bathroom R280/700) have shared bathrooms, but they're often full. The staff are friendly and there's a café and sauna on the premises.

Hotel Turist (☎ 31 03 27, fax 78 36 40; ul Karla Marxa 67; singles/doubles US$18/24) is a typical 1970s Soviet hotel, but its boxy rooms are well maintained and have decent facilities, and it's reasonably close to the train station.

More moderately upgraded Soviet-era bastions are **Hotel Tsentralnaya** (☎ 32 47 59, fax 32 41 88; ul Pushkina 52; singles/doubles R850/900), which always seems to be full when we show up, and **Hotel Amur** (☎ 21 71 41, fax 22 12 23; ul Lenina 29; singles/doubles from R630/640), which have acceptable old-fashioned rooms with TV and fridge.

Places to Stay – Mid-Range & Top End

A once-budget place upgraded almost beyond recognition is **Hotel Versal** (☎ 30 55 50, fax 65 92 90; Amursky bulvar 46a; singles/doubles with breakfast US$40/60). The regular rooms are small, but comfortable. There's a travel agency in the hotel that might be able to help with local tours.

Hotel Amethyst (☎ 32 54 81, fax 32 46 99; e amethyst@hotel.kht.ru; ul L'va Tolstogo 5a; singles/doubles from US$60/100) is a boutique-style hotel with just 16 spacious, nicely decorated rooms. The staff are great and there's a pleasant café and sauna.

The **Hotel Intourist** (☎ 31 23 13, fax 32 65 07; w www.intour.khv.ru; Amursky bulvar 2; singles/doubles from US$70/78) might be huge, but its service and rooms are good, and most of the package tourists who stay here seem to like it. Many rooms have great views of the Amur and rates are slightly cheaper in winter.

At the **Hotel Sapporo** (☎ 30 67 45, fax 30 60 75; e sapporo@gin.ru; ul Komsomolskaya 79; singles/doubles US$95/105), the rooms are straight out of a Japanese business hotel, to suit the requirements of visitors from across the Sea of Japan – thus standards are high and you'll need to book well in advance. Its sauna (R400 for two hours) is recommended.

Maly Hotel (☎ 30 58 02, fax 30 59 39; ul Kalinina 83a; singles/doubles US$110/180) is another small and pristine place (just 10 rooms) done out to Japanese specifications. It's set in a quiet compound off the main street and has a very good Japanese restaurant attached.

Parus (☎ 32 72 70, fax 32 57 07; e guest@parus.vic.ru; ul Shevchenko 5; singles/doubles US$100/130) is connected to a business centre and is about as luxurious as you're going to get. There's a nicely decorated and equally pricey bar and restaurant, too.

Places to Eat

Restaurants The cosy and slightly kitsch **Russky Restaurant** (☎ 30 65 87; Ussuriisky bulvar 9; mains around R200; open noon-midnight daily) has great food and good live traditional music. While here, try the speciality: sturgeon sizzling on a hot stone plate. Everyone gets a complimentary shot of vodka, too.

Stary Khabarovsk (*Ussuriysky bulvar 6; mains R150-250; open noon-2am daily*), in the pink and mint-green building across the road from Russky Restaurant, trades on nostalgia for tsarist times. The food's OK and the light-pop live music is not too hard on the ears.

If you're hanging out for something spicy, head for **Green Plaza** (☎ 30 19 28; *ul Moskovskaya 6; mains around R200; open noon-2am daily*). It does traditional Korean food very well, such as *bibimba* with all the trimmings.

Syangan (☎ 31 13 28; *ul Muravyova-Amurskogo 2; mains around R200; open noon-midnight daily*) is a glitzy Chinese restaurant, the kind of place where the big round tables, if not hosting tour groups, are occupied by giggling office girls or gangsters in the midst of a deal.

Kafe Utyos (*ul Shevchenko 15; mains R100-200; open noon-midnight daily*), in the tower in the park overlooking the river, is one of the nicest places for a drink or meal; it serves Russian and Japanese food.

Kafe Sion (☎ 74 77 95; *ul Gogolya 21; mains R150-200; open noon-midnight daily*) is a small basement place serving nicely prepared and presented Russian dishes; it also has live music after 9pm.

The 3rd-floor Japanese restaurant is the main draw at **Restoran Sapporo** (☎ 32 82 40; *ul Muravyova-Amurskogo 3; mains R300-500*). Its sushi and other Japanese specialities aren't bad, with the lunch-time set menu from R250 being the best value.

The Hotel Intourist has **Unikhab** (☎ 31 23 15; *Amursky bulvar 2*), a swish Japanese restaurant on the 11th floor, with a reasonably priced menu of standards such as sushi and tempura, and **Korea House** (☎ 31 22 34), serving Korean cuisine; traditional rice dishes start at R150.

Cafés & Self-Catering With practically all you could want in sumptuous surroundings, **Tsentralnaya Gastronom** (*ul Muravyova-Amurskogo 9; open 8am-10pm daily*) is the place for trans-Siberian supplies; upstairs is a cute self-service café where lunch shouldn't cost more than R60.

For fresh produce, try the **market** (*8am-7pm daily*) on Amursky bulvar between ul L'va Tolstogo and ul Pushkina.

There are lots of cheap places for snacks on ulitsa Muravyova-Amurskogo, including

outdoor kiosks serving shashlyk and pastries. Try **Bistro Erofey** (*ul Muravyova-Amurskogo 11*) or **Kasam** (*ul Muravyova-Amurskogo 50*), which has a menu with photos and does very nice bliny.

Entertainment

The bar/restaurant/casino **B52** (☎ 32 47 59; *ul Pushkina 52*) at Hotel Tsentralnaya is indeed central, but better is **Rio** (☎ 23 84 20; *ul Lenina 49; cover charge R200*), the city's largest club on two levels.

Traktyr (*ul Komsomolskaya 19*) is a popular bar serving the local brew, Amur Pivo.

For more highbrow entertainment you will need to brush up on your Russian to appreciate the dramatic offerings at the **Drama Theatre** (*Teatr Dramy; ☎ 23 55 33; ul Dzerzhinskogo 44*) and the **Theatre of Musical Comedy** (*Teatr Muzkomedii; ☎ 21 14 09; ul Karla Marxa 64*). Alternatively, you can wrestle with dubbed dialogue at the movies at **Kino Gigant** (☎ 32 58 28; *ul Muravyova-Amurskogo 19*).

Shopping

For a good range of souvenirs, try the shop and gallery at ulitsa Muravyova-Amurskogo 17, or the shop on the ground floor of the Far Eastern Art Museum, which has a collectors' area including rare stamps.

The **Veshchevoy Rynok** (Oriental Bazaar) is one of the biggest traders' markets in the Far East. From about 10am to early afternoon, hordes of Chinese and Russian traders fill this vacant lot with stall after stall of cheap merchandise. Take trolley No 1 to the ulitsa Vyborgskaya stop, where cabs are usually waiting to take you the next 3km to the market for R50.

Getting There & Away

Air Domestic flights include Moscow (R8280, 8½ hours, three daily), Yuzhno-Sakhalinsk (R3100, 1½ hours, two daily), Irkutsk (R3320, three hours, four weekly), Yakutsk (R4650, three hours, four weekly), Vladivostok (R2080, 1¾ hours, three weekly), Magadan (R4430, 2½ hours, weekly) and Nikolaevsk-na-Amur (R2635, 1½ hours, daily).

There are international flights to Harbin (US$157) and Guau (US$257) in China, Seoul (US$350-440) in Korea, and Niigata (US$215) and (July to September) Aomori (US$224) in Japan.

The foreign airlines all have offices on the upper floor of the airport's international terminal. **Intour-Khabarovsk** (☎ *31 21 54, fax 32 76 34)* at Hotel Intourist can also book seats and issue tickets.

All international flights are subject to a US$25 departure tax, is to be paid in roubles at the terminal's information desk prior to checking in. Foreigners making domestic flights should check in at the old international terminal, which is the classical-looking building with the portico, to the left of the new one.

Train Heading west, apart from the No 1 *Rossiya*, which departs for Moscow (R4630, 130 hours) and Irkutsk (R1766, 60 hours) on even-numbered dates, there's also the daily No 43 service to Moscow (R3120) and the No 7 to Novosibirsk (R2506). Heading east, Vladivostok is best reached on the daily No 6 Okean service (R751, 13 hours), which has a good restaurant car.

Other daily services include the No 226 to Tynda and Neryungri (R790, 29 hours) and the No 67 to Komsomolsk-na-Amur (R476, eight hours), both on the BAM (Baikal-Amur Mainline), the latter with connections to Sovetskaya Gavan and Port Vanino for the ferry across to Sakhalin.

Tickets can easily be purchased at the station, or the quieter **ticket office** *(ul Leningradskaya 56B; open 8am-8pm daily)*, where you'll pay a R30 booking fee.

Boat From Khabarovsk's river station boats sail down the Amur to Fuyuan in northern China (see the Around Khabarovsk section later). Between May and October, hydrofoils run north on the Amur between Khabarovsk and Komsomolsk (R290, six hours) and Nikolaevsk (R1458, 16½ hours). There's also a combined bus/hydrofoil service to Nikolaevsk; the bus (R200) leaves daily at 11pm from the river station, arriving at Komsomolsk's river station in time to catch the daily 7.30am boat (R1121) from there to Nikolaevsk. The **ticket office** *(open 8am-12.30pm & 1.30pm-4pm daily)* is across from the green river boat station.

Getting Around

Trolley bus No 1 (R5) runs regularly from the airport to ulitsa Muravyova-Amurskogo, taking around 30 minutes to cover the 5km to the city centre; minivans also do the journey. A taxi to/from the Hotel Intourist should cost no more than R200.

The easiest way to get into the city centre from the train station at the eastern end of Amursky bulvar is by way of tram No 1, 2, 4 or 6 (R5), which cross ulitsa Muravyova-Amurskogo along ulitsa Sheronova.

AROUND KHABAROVSK
Fuyuan (China)
Фуюань
From mid-May to mid-October, every other day at around 8am, a hydrofoil departs from the river station at Khabarovsk for Fuyuan (R870, 1½ hours), a small town on the Chinese bank of the Amur River. To do this trip you'll need a Chinese visa and a double/multiple entry Russian visa. There is a Chinese consulate in Khabarovsk (see the Siberia & the Russian Far East Facts for the Visitor chapter for details), but you'd be wise to prearrange your visa to be safe. From Fuyuan you can take a bus to Jiamusi and then on to Harbin. Intour-Khabarovsk (see Travel Agencies in the Khabarovsk section) can arrange day trips for US$190 and sort out the visa paperwork for you if you give them notice.

Troitskoe & Sikachi-Alyan
Троицкое и Сикачи-Алян
Troitskoe, 130km northeast of Khabarovsk on the Amur River, is home to about 22,000 indigenous Nanai. The hydrofoil to Komsomolsk stops at Troitskoe (R128, three hours) on the way, but without a guide you would be hard-pressed to get the most out of your visit; a day trip here including a visit to the local museum, lunch and a folk music concert is around US$100 for a minimum of three people.

The main attraction at Sikachi-Alyan, 40km downriver of Khabarovsk, is the petroglyphs. These enigmatic stone carvings, dating from the 11th century BC, can be found on the basalt boulders at the water's edge. From June through to October, the river is infested with swarms of mosquitoes that can easily bite through cotton.

In the village you'll also find the recently opened **Ecological Tourist Complex**. Here, there are small displays about Nanai culture and occasional music performances by locals. Half-day trips are around US$70, again for a minimum of three people.

KOMSOMOLSK-NA-AMUR
КОМСОМОЛЬСК-НА-АМУРЕ
☎ 42172 • pop 305,000 • Moscow time
plus 7 hours

In the middle of a great swamp 290km north
of Khabarovsk, Komsomolsk-na-Amur (or
Komsomolsk – 'City of Youth') is the largest
city on the Baikal-Amur Mainline (BAM).
Established in 1932 to strengthen the Soviet's
Far Eastern defences, this once-closed city
became the site for steelworks, an aircraft
factory and huge shipbuilding yards, turning
out icebreakers and submarines. These industries continue, albeit at a much reduced
rate from the glory days of the Soviet Union.

If you're travelling the BAM, Komsomolsk
is a good place to stop, likewise if you're
heading north along the Amur to Nikolaevsk.
It's also a base for gentle rafting expeditions
through the nearby **Komsomolsky Nature
Reserve**, a 64,400-hectare area around the
Gorin River that is rich in bird life. **Nata Tour**
(☎/fax 3 03 32; e natatour@kmscom.ru), run
by helpful people and found on the ground
floor of the Hotel Voskhod (see Places to Stay
& Eat later), offers such trips (from US$45 a
day) as well as other tours in the area.

For a city so young and isolated, Komsomolsk is a striking place with parade-wide
boulevards, some once-grand architecture and
fading monuments to Soviet glory. Among the
most impressive are the **war memorial** and
the **First Builders memorial**, both close by the
river station. Also, both the **Regional Museum** (☎ 4 22 60; pr Mira 8; admission R25;
open 10am-1pm & 2pm-6pm Mon-Fri, 11am-
6pm Sat & Sun) and the **Fine Art Museum**
(☎ 4 22 60; pr Mira 16; admission R30; open
10am-5.45pm Tues-Fri, 11am-5.45pm Sat &
Sun) show how proud the locals are of their
newly born city. Nata Tour can help arrange
visits to the museum at the **Yuri Gagarin Aircraft Factory** (☎ 6 85 54; open by appointment), outside the centre of town.

Places to Stay & Eat
Hotel Voskhod (☎ 3 03 36; pr Pervostroiteley 31; singles/doubles R458/646) is pricey
considering it has boxy, old-fashioned rooms.
At least it has hot water in summer, which is
more than can be said for the basic **Hotel
Amur** (☎ 9 09 84; pr Mira 15; singles/doubles
without bathrooms R210/270).

There's a **market** at ploshchad Metallurgov and a **bistro** (ul Lenina 18) in the 24-hour

food store nearby. Other cheap meals can be
had at the **Pelmennaya** (ul Lenina 21; open
11am-8pm Mon-Fri, 11am-6pm Sat). The
fanciest place in town is the flash **Rodnik**
(☎ 3 33 96; pr Pervostroiteley 15; meals
around R200; open noon-3am daily), around
500m south of Hotel Voskhod, which serves
its own tasty beer, Flora (R60 per litre).

Getting There & Away
Train Nos 67/68 run daily overnight from/to
Khabarovsk (R476, 9½ hours). Heading east,
there are services to Port Vanino and Sovetskaya Gavan (R410, 15 hours), while to the
west a daily train heads to Tynda along the
BAM (R845, 37 hours).

Between early June and the end of August
it's possible to travel to/from Khabarovsk
(R290, six hours) and Nikolaevsk-na-Amur
(R900, 13 hours) by way of the Amur River,
using the daily hydrofoil service.

Within the city, tram No 2 runs from outside the Hotel Voskhod to the river station.

VANINO & SOVETSKAYA GAVAN
ВАНИНО И СОВЕТСКАЯ ГАВАНЬ
The main reason for heading some 500km
east of Komsomolsk is if you plan to take the
daily ferry from Vanino to Kholmsk, on
Sakhalin (around R780, 16 hours). Unfortunately, the weather can play havoc with the
sailing schedule; your best bet is to pitch
up at the train station where boat tickets are
sold (and where there can be nightmarishly
long queues during the summer season).
Once you are on the ferry it's not too bad, and
there is a bufet if you've not got your own
provisions.

Should you require a bed for the night in
Vanino, there's **Hotel Vanino** (☎ 42176-5 12
28; ul Chekova 1; rooms US$40), conve-
niently placed above the station.

The stop after Vanino is Sovetskaya Gavan,
usually shortened to Sovgavan. Russia's third-
largest naval base on the Pacific was founded
in 1853 and originally named Imperatorskaya
Gavan (Emperor's Harbour), changing to
'Harbour of the Soviets' in 1926. Aside from
a complex of concrete bunkers and gun emplacements constructed prior to WWII in an-
ticipation of war with the Japanese, there's
very little to see here.

Train Nos 251/252 connect Vanino and
Sovgavan with Vladivostok (R864, 24 hours)
via Khabarovsk and Komsomolsk.

NIKOLAEVSK-NA-AMUR
НИКОЛАЕВСК-НА-АМУРЕ
☎ 42135 • pop 40,000

Named after the tsar, Nikolaevsk was founded in 1850 as a fortress at the mouth of the river during Nikolay Muravyov's push down the Amur into Manchu territory. When Sakhalin, just 20km across the Tatar Strait, was transformed into a penal colony in 1875, Nikolaevsk became a staging post for the shiploads of convicts being sailed there. Following the trail of the prisoners, Anton Chekhov spent a night in Nikolaevsk in 1890, recording in his journal that he couldn't find a bed for the night.

Despite its remote location, by 1910 the town had become quite cosmopolitan, boasting Chinese, Japanese and British consulates, an American club set up by Californian and Bostonian traders, and a brothel staffed by French women. All of this was turned upside down when the Bolsheviks rode into town in 1920 and, as their first action, massacred every Japanese person they could find.

Although not particularly worth going out of your way for, a quaint air hangs over Nikolaevsk today, with its tree-lined streets squeezing between many wooden houses. There's a small **Regional Museum** (☎ 2 32 47; ul Gorkogo; admission R62; open 10am-1pm & 2pm-6pm Wed-Fri, 10am-5pm Sat & Sun) and a **cultural centre** (☎ 2 36 59; ul Sovetskaya 69) for the local indigenous people, where song-and-dance performances are occasionally held; there's a small exhibition hall here also.

At the municipally run **Hotel Servis** (☎ 2 21 79; ul Sibirskaya 117; singles/doubles from R340/616) they're likely to stick you in their most expensive room (with its useless big fridge and TV, for which you'll be charged extra) unless you're firm. The hotel is around a 20-minute walk west of the harbour, along Nikolaevsk's main road, ulitsa Sovetskaya, then two blocks north down ulitsa Volodarskogo to ploshchad Lenina.

The **restaurant** at Hotel Servis isn't too bad. The only other place of note to eat is the simple café **Maestro** (ul Kantera 2), which becomes a karaoke bar at night.

Getting There & Away
From June to October, hydrofoils connect Nikolaevsk with Komsomolsk (R900, 13 hours) and Khabarovsk (R1458, 16½ hours). During February and March the ice on the river is usually – though not always – thick

enough for it to serve as a temporary road. Year-round there are daily flights to Khabarovsk (R2635, 1½ hours).

BIROBIDZHAN
БИРОБИДЖАН
☎ 42162 • pop 90,000 • Moscow time plus 7 hours

The pleasantly leafy city of Birobidzhan, 180km west of Khabarovsk, is not an essential stop, but has an interesting history. The big Hebrew letters spelling out the station's name are one of the scarce present-day indications of Birobidzhan's status as capital of the Jewish Autonomous Region (Yevreyskaya Avtonomnaya Region).

This 36,000-sq-km swampy, mosquito-infested territory on the Bira and Bidzhan Rivers (tributaries of the Amur), was opened to settlement in 1927, when the Soviet authorities conceived the idea of a homeland for Jews in the sensitive border region of the Far East. Some 43,000 Jews, mainly from Belarus and Ukraine but also from the US, Argentina and even Palestine, made the trek. The harshness of the land and climate (temperatures can drop as low as -40°C here) meant only a third stayed.

Despite being proclaimed the Jewish Autonomous Region in 1934, the anti-Semitism and persecutions of later Soviet years killed off the project. All Jewish institutions in the region, including the schools and synagogue, were shut down and the use of Hebrew was banned. Since 1991, and the establishment of diplomatic ties between Russia and Israel, there has been a further outpouring of Jews.

Today, although probably less than 10,000 Jews account for only 7% of the region's population, there's a tiny but noticeable revival of Jewish culture in the town. Apart from the synagogue, there's a cultural centre, a newspaper in Yiddish (the polyglot language of Eastern European Jews), and Hebrew and Yiddish are taught in schools.

Orientation & Information
The city's main streets run east–west, parallel to and squeezed between the railway line and the River Bira to the south. From the train station, the streets are ulitsa Kalinina, ulitsa Lenina, ulitsa Sholom-Aleykhema (the main axis), ulitsa Pionerskaya and prospekt 60 let SSSR with its twin squares, ploshchad Lenina and ploshchad Sovietov.

At the **main post and telephone office** (pr 60 let SSSR 14) you can access the Internet.

Things to See & Do

The **Regional Museum** (Kraevedchesky muzey; ☎ 6 83 21; ul Lenina 25; admission US$2; open 9am-1pm & 2pm-6pm Tues-Fri) has a room devoted to the Jewish history of the region, as well as the obligatory menagerie of stuffed animals, including an Amur tiger.

A better place to go if you want to find out about the town's Jews is **Freid** (☎ 4 15 31; ul Sholom-Aleykhema 14A), a Jewish community centre with its main entrance at ul Lenina 19, easily spotted because of the giant menorah outside. Freid means 'happiness' in Yiddish. A new synagogue is being built next to here, but for the time being there's the tiny pale-blue painted **prayer hall** at ulitsa Mayakovskogo 11 – follow ulitsa Sholom-Aleykhema east into ulitsa Komsomolskaya, then into ulitsa Sovietskaya, and Mayakovskogo is left at the end.

Places to Stay & Eat

The **komnaty otdykha** (singles without bathrooms R150, four-bed dorms R80) is on the top floor of the station.

Hotel Vostok (☎ 6 53 30; ul Sholom-Aleykhema 1; singles/doubles US$16/32), Birobidzhan's only hotel, offers acceptable accommodation. Its restaurant sometimes serves Jewish-style cuisine for visiting tour groups.

Next to the hotel is the town's lively market, where you'll find plenty of food for a picnic. Otherwise, try **Restaurant Birobidzhan** (☎ 6 84 19; ul Golkogo 10), on the corner of ulitsa Lenina. Reasonable Russian dishes cost around R70.

Getting There & Away

You might find it difficult getting a ticket on the Rossiya or any of the other long-distance trains that pause in Birobidzhan – the easier option is to take the twice-daily elektrichka (suburban train) service to/from Khabarovsk (R50, three hours).

Buses from the bus station next to Birobidzhan's train station and Khabarovsk station are more frequent, but slightly more expensive (R75). You can also take a tour to Birobidzhan from Khabarovsk with either Dalgeo Tours or Intour-Khabarovsk. See Information in the Khabarovsk section earlier for details.

Amurskaya Region
Амурская Област

There are two main reasons for visiting the Amurskaya Region, which stretches from the Stanovoy mountain range bordering the Sakha Republic in the north to the Amur River separating Russia from China in the south. One reason is to cross into China from the region's capital, Blagoveshchensk. The other is to travel the BAM and visit Tynda, a major junction on the alternative trans-Siberian route.

BLAGOVESHCHENSK
БЛАГОВЕШЧЕНСК

☎ 4162 • pop 210,000 • Moscow time plus 6 hours

Blagoveshchensk is less than half a kilometre across the Amur River from the Chinese town of Heihe. Blagoveshchensk has a stormy history, beginning in 1644 as a military outpost under the name Ust-Zaysk. It was seized by the Manchurians 45 years later, while the Russians, under the command of Nikolay Muravyov, took it back in 1856 and gave it its present name: Blagoveshchensk means 'Good News'.

By the end of the century, Blagoveshchensk was thriving on Sino-Russian commerce, larger and of greater importance than either Vladivostok or Khabarovsk. But in 1900, as a means to avenge European deaths in the Chinese Boxer Rebellion, Cossacks slaughtered the thousands of Chinese people in the city. During the years of the Cultural Revolution, the Chinese subjected Blagoveshchensk to 24-hour propaganda blasted from loudspeakers across the river.

Nowadays, there is once again a lively cross-border trade, encouraged by the free-trade zone that was declared between the Chinese and Russian cities in early 1994. There's an exchange of people also, with plenty of visiting Chinese tourists and the shortage of labour in the Russian Amur region being remedied by importing Chinese workers. For most Western visitors the town will be of principal interest as a possible gateway into China.

Blagoveshchensk retains faint traces of tsarist elegance, particularly around ploshchad Pobedy, on the Amur waterfront, around 4km south of the train station. A bust of

Chekhov on the wall of the ornate red and white building on the south side of the square records that the writer passed through here in June 1890, on his way to Sakhalin. Nearby is the large and well laid-out **Regional Museum** (*Amursky Oblastnoi Kraevedchesky muzey*; ☎ 42 24 14; *ul Lenina 165*; *admission R40*; *open 10am-6pm Tues-Sun*) in another smartly kept building dating from the turn of the 20th century The northern reaches of ulitsa 50 let Oktyabrya, the town's central artery heading from the train station to ploshchad Lenina on the river, are lined with dilapidated wooden houses. Closer to the river are shopping malls packed with Chinese-made goods. You will find Internet access at **Amur Net** (*ul Amurskaya 205*; *open 8am-8.30pm Mon-Fri, 10am-7.30pm Sat*), one block west of ulitsa 50 let Oktyabrya.

Places to Stay & Eat

Among the town's several hotels, the **Druzhba** (☎ 49 99 40, fax 49 98 77; **W** *www.hotel druzhba.ru*; *ul Kuznechnaya 1*; *singles/doubles R650/1000*) is the best, with good service and rooms. Here you will also find a reasonable Chinese restaurant and the Amur Tourist tour agency, which may be able to help you with any travel plans you have in the region. Note that the Druzhba's website is in Russian only.

The **Zeya** (☎ 42 49 06, fax 44 68 00; *ul Kalinina 8*; *singles/doubles R660/1020*), on the west side of ploshchad Pobedy, is also a friendly place with well-kept rooms.

A good place to eat traditional Russian dishes is **Russkaya Izba** (☎ 44 66 61; *ul Lenina 48*; *meals around R200*; *open 11am-11pm daily*). It's a small place and is cutely done up with wooden fixtures and polished samovars.

Getting There & Away

Blagoveshchensk is 110km off the Trans-Siberian, on a branch line from Belogorsk. Train Nos 185/ 186 run between Vladivostok and Blagoveshchensk, passing through Khabarovsk (R477, 18 hours). There are also direct trains to Moscow (Nos 249/250), with the No 81/82 trains to/from Tynda (R823, 16 hours) running every other day.

Boats for China (R340) leave at regular intervals during the day from the customs point, located 500m east of the Druzhba hotel along the waterfront.

TYNDA
ТЫНДА
☎ 41656 • pop 70,000 • Moscow time plus 6 hours

At the junction of the BAM lines heading north, south, east and west, Tynda is *the* BAM town and a place you'll likely be spending some time in while travelling along Siberia's alternative rail route. The BAM construction company's headquarters are here, and it's from Tynda that the as-yet-unfinished AYaM (Amuro-Yakutskaya Magistral) railway will extend towards Yakutsk. For now, and the foreseeable future, passenger trains only go 200km farther north to Neryungri in the Sakha Republic (see later).

Tynda's most striking landmark is its train station, a gleaming modernist affair. The local **museum** (☎ 2 16 90; *ul Sportivnaya 22*) was under reconstruction in a new location when we visited; it will contain eight rooms with displays not only on the railway, but also the native Evenki people, around 200 families of which live in the nearby village of **Zarya**. You'll find the museum in the old school, 200m west of the giant Ferris wheel, across the pedestrian bridge linking the station with the town centre, on the hill to the north. You won't fail to notice the golden domes of the new Orthodox cathedral, **Svetoi Troitsi Sabor**, on Tynda's main thoroughfare, ulitsa Krasnaya Presnaya.

It's well worth timing your visit to take advantage of Tynda's public **banya** (*bathhouse*; ☎ 7 44 98; *ul Amurskaya*; *admission R60*; *open 2pm-8.30pm Thur & 10am-8.30pm Sat for women, 2pm-8.30pm Fri & 10am-8.30pm Sun for men*). This clean and well-patronised place is the real McCoy, with a hellishly hot steam room and a pool for a bracing swim; a bunch of freshly cut birch branches costs R15. (See the boxed text 'Steaming: The Joys of the Banya' in the European Russia Facts for the Visitor chapter for more on *banya* etiquette.) The *banya* is located just beyond the great sledgehammer-wielding statue at the eastern end of ulitsa Krasnaya Presnaya, 50m south of the telephone office where you'll find **Internet access** (*ul Krasnaya Presnaya 53*; *10am-1pm & 2pm-6pm Mon-Fri*).

For help with organising tours in the area, including visits to the reindeer-herding camps of the Evenki, contact **Nadezhda Nizova** (☎ 2 96 55, fax 2 13 58; **e** *td_nadejda@amur.ru*; *ul Festivalnaya 1*). She only speaks Russian.

Places to Stay & Eat

On the station platform is the **Vagon Gostinitsa** *(24hrs R130, 12hrs R80)*, basically a parked *kupe* (compartment) carriage. It's clean enough and will do for a short stay, as will the rather more comfortable **komnaty otdykha** *(☎ 7 32 97; beds in 2-bed/4-bed rooms R176/164, lyux rooms R280)* inside the station building.

The clean and simple **Hotel Nadezhda** *(☎ 2 70 21; 4th floor, ul Festivalnaya 1; singles/doubles with shared bathroom R220/ 440)* is a good deal if you want to be in the centre of town. If it's full, you can fall back on the nearby **Hotel Yunost** *(☎ 2 31 60; ul Krasnaya Presnaya 9; singles/doubles from R259/518)*, which has a range of acceptable, unspectacular rooms, the more expensive with attached bathrooms.

If you want to stay where VIPs bed down when they're in Tynda, take a taxi (it's far too complicated to find on foot) to the **Hotel Orbita** *(☎ 33 64; singles/doubles R450/900)*, in a villa hidden in the woods at the western end of town. They don't take kindly to surprise visits, so book ahead.

Eating options are less abundant. The Yunost restaurant was closed for reconstruction when we visited. The self-service **kafe** in the station *(8am-7pm daily)* does OK, cheap canteen food. For a bit more class, try **Teremok** *(☎ 2 01 91; ul Krasnaya Presnaya 59a; meals around R90; open noon-3pm & 6pm-2am daily)*, a café/bar complex at the eastern end of the main street. The lively daily **market** behind Hotel Nadezhda is a good place to replenish food supplies for your train travels.

Getting There & Away

Train Nos 75/76 link Tynda with Moscow and Nos 77/78 on odd-numbered dates with Novosibirsk via the western BAM. There's also a twice-weekly service southwest, to the Caucasus town of Kislovodsk (Nos 97/98). Heading east, there's the daily Tynda-Komsomolsk service on train Nos 963/964 (R845, 37 hours) along the BAM, and services to Khabarovsk on the Nos 225/226 (R789, 30 hours). Going south, services run from/to Blagoveshchensk on the Nos 81/82 (R823, 16 hours). All these trains have through-carriages going north to Neryungri.

Buses run from in front of the train station south to the town of Bolshoy Never on the Trans-Siberian Railway.

Sakha Republic
Саха Республика

Covering over 3.1 million sq km of some of the most inhospitable, yet mineral-rich terrain in the whole Russian Federation is the Sakha Republic, formerly known as Yakutia. Almost half of it is within the Arctic Circle and almost all within the permafrost zone. Only one million people (of whom 30% are Yakuts) live in this vast area, most in settlements along the 4400km-long Lena River and its tributaries.

There are amazing contrasts. Small communities of Evenki and Chukchi still hunt for a living on the Arctic coast, while in the regional capital Yakutsk, modern buildings rise out of the permafrost, symbols of the republic's vast wealth (99% of Russia's diamonds are mined here). January temperatures can plummet to below -50°C, while June and July are stifling hot, the taiga and tundra infested with mosquitoes. August is perhaps the best month to visit, but you may have to contend with smog from rampaging forest fires.

Yakutsk is fascinating, but the far north people and landscapes are the reason to visit the area. You need to spend money and time on excursions, principally along the Lena River, originating in the mountains to the west of Lake Baikal and flowing to the Arctic. It's navigable for five months of the year, but during the other months, it's frozen to a depth of 5m, serving as an icy route for conventional wheeled traffic.

Sakha has its own visa regulations; you'll need listed on your Russian visa all the towns you wish to visit, and if you're planning on a stay of over 13 days, you'll also need an AIDS and hepatitis certificate. If you don't have the correct papers, you might have a problem checking into some hotels. However, we found there were no visa checks on flying into Yakutsk. Your safest course would be to make suitable arrangements with a local travel agent – if only for accommodation on your first night.

YAKUTSK
ЯКУТСК
☎ 41122 • pop 198,000 • Moscow time plus 6 hours
For somewhere that's over 1000km from anywhere much, Yakutsk comes as a pleasant,

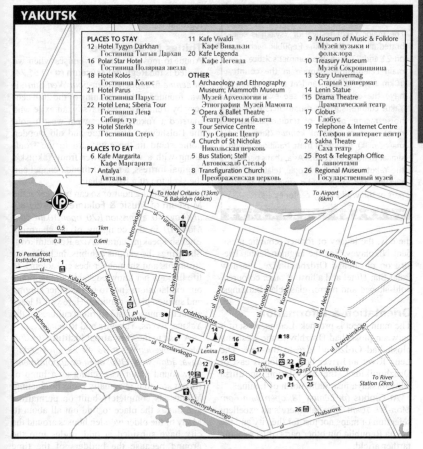

YAKUTSK

PLACES TO STAY
12 Hotel Tygyn Darkhan
   Гостиница Тыгын Дархан
16 Polar Star Hotel
   Гостиница Полярная звезда
18 Hotel Kolos
   Гостиница Колос
21 Hotel Parus
   Гостиница Парус
22 Hotel Lena; Siberia Tour
   Гостиница Лена;
   Сибирь тур
23 Hotel Sterkh
   Гостиница Стерх

PLACES TO EAT
6 Kafe Margarita
   Кафе Маргарита
7 Antalya
   Анталья

11 Kafe Vivaldi
   Кафе Вивальди
20 Kafe Legenda
   Кафе Легенда

OTHER
1 Archaeology and Ethnography
   Museum; Mammoth Museum
   Музей Археологии и
   Этнографии Музей Мамонта
2 Opera & Ballet Theatre
   Театр Оперы и балета
3 Tour Service Centre
   Тур Сервис Центр
4 Church of St Nicholas
   Никольская церковь
5 Bus Station; Stelf
   Автовокзал5 Стельф
8 Transfiguration Church
   Преображенская церковь

9 Museum of Music & Folklore
   Музей музыки и
   фольклора
10 Treasury Museum
   Музей Сокровищница
13 Stary Univermag
   Старый универмаг
14 Lenin Statue
15 Drama Theatre
   Драматический театр
17 Globus
   Глобус
19 Telephone & Internet Centre
   Телефон и интернет центр
24 Sakha Theatre
   Саха театр
25 Post & Telegraph Office
   Главпочтамп
26 Regional Museum
   Государственный музей

To Hotel Ontario (13km)
& Bakaldyn (46km)

To Airport
(6km)

ul Turgeneva

ul Petrovskogo

0   0.5   1km
0   0.3   0.6mi

To Permafrost
Institute (2km)

ul Kulakovskogo

ul Dezhneva

ul Oktyabrskaya

ul Lermontova

ul Kirova

ul Kotolenko

ul Kurashova

ul Kalandarishvili

pl
Druzhby

ul Ordzhonikidze

ul Petra Alekseeva

ul Yaroslavskogo

pl
Lenina

ul Dzerzhinskogo

ul Dzerzhinskogo

pr
Lenina

pl Ordzhonikidze

ul Chernyshevskogo

To River
Station (2km)

ul Khabarova

---

and sometimes surreal, surprise. As the base for trips to the rest of the republic, it's a place you're going to have to spend some time in. The city built on stilts above the permafrost also has a fair number of interesting museums, not to mention good hotels and restaurants.

One of the oldest cities in the Far East, Yakutsk was founded in 1632 as a Cossack fort, and later served as a base for expeditions to the Pacific coast. The most unrepentant dissidents (including Decembrists and Bolsheviks) were exiled here. It was a 'jail without doors'. There was no need for bars or locks: isolated amid millions of square kilometres of bug-infested, swampy forest that became one great deep-freeze for eight months of the year, no-one was going anywhere. Some tried, but

their bodies usually turned up in spring, uncovered by the melting snow. Hence the runaways became known as 'snowdrops'.

When it became apparent in the late 19th century that the Yakutian earth had more to give up than just corpses, the fortunes of the town underwent a dramatic change. Prospectors, adventurers and mining companies needed a base from which to exploit the newly discovered mineral wealth of the Lena River basin, and Yakutsk became a kind of 'Wild East' version of Dodge City. Supplied by Lena shipping, the town was a boozy, bawdy rest-and-recreation centre for the region's gold-miners, who rolled in to blow their wages on drink and women.

Today, money is more noticeably being spent on striking modern architecture around

Ysyakh

The major Yakut festival of Ysyakh is celebrated all over the Sakha Republic each year on 21 and 22 June, the summer solstice. The main celebrations happen in the country 10km from Yakutsk, and at them you will have the opportunity to see examples of Yakut culture, such as round-circle dancing, horse racing, playing of traditional instruments and drinking of *koumis* (fermented mares' milk). If some of these traditions sound similar to those of Central Asia, that's because the Yakuts are a Turkic people, related to the Kazakhs and Kyrgyz, who emigrated to this part of the world many centuries ago.

★★★★★★★★★★★★★★★★★★★★★★

the city, the legacy of former republic president Nikolayev. See the angular Sakha Theatre on ploshchad Ordzhonikidze, the new Polar Star Hotel and a host of other coloured, bold-shaped and mirror-glass-clad buildings.

Orientation & Information

The main street is prospekt Lenina, most of it between ploshchad Druzhby to the west and ploshchad Ordzhonikidze to the east. The Lena River and river boat station is east of Ordzhonikidze, the bus station on ulitsa Oktyabrskaya just 500m north of Lenina.

At **Globus** (*pr Lenina 18; open 9am-6pm Mon-Fri, 10am-3pm Sat*) there's an excellent selection of maps not just for the city and the Sakha Republic but other parts of Russia and farther afield.

There are many places to change money along prospekt Lenina, all giving decent rates. The **main post and telegraph office** (*pl Ordzhonikidze*) has a couple of Internet terminals. More can be found at the **Telephone & Internet Centre** (*pr Lenina 10; open 11am-2pm & 3pm-9.30pm daily*).

Tour Service Centre (☎ 25 11 44, fax 25 08 97; ⓦ www.yakutiatravel.com; ul Oktyabrskaya 5) is run by experienced, helpful Vyacheslav Ipatiev. The English-speaking staff can arrange all kinds of tours of Yakutsk and Sakha, and their website is a mine of helpful information. They've also established a network of homestays throughout the republic that could make for a fascinating trip.

Siberia Tour (☎ 42 26 52; ⓔ siberia_tour@mail.ru; office 216, Hotel Lena, pr Lenina 8)

is another reputable agency offering city and regional tours.

Things to See & Do

About to move into new premises when we visited is the **Regional Museum** (☎ 42 51 74; pr Lenina 5/2; open 10am-5pm Wed-Sun). It was founded at the beginning of the 20th century by Yemelyan Yaroslavsky, an exile who married a Yakut and later went west to join the Bolsheviks. His statue and old wooden home stand in the courtyard in the front, along with a wooden tower from Yakutsk's original fortress, a new Orthodox chapel and the skeleton of a baby whale.

A fascinating hour or so can be spent at the **Museum of Music & Folklore** (☎ 44 51 80; ul Kirova 10; admission R70; open 10am-5pm Mon-Fri) in the company of its charming English-speaking curator Aiza Reshetnikova. She brings the various exhibits, including instruments and shamans' robes and totems, to life through her knowledgeable and humourous explanations (not to mention her singing and spirited piano playing). Here you'll learn about the musical and spiritual cultures of the Yakuts, Evens, Yukagirs and Russians.

A visit to the **Permafrost Institute** (Institut Merzlotovedeniya; ☎ 33 44 23; ul Merzlotnaya; admission R300; open by appointment) may sound about as exciting as a lump of frozen soil, but is actually quite fascinating. Yakutsk is completely built on permafrost and this is the place to find out all about it. Many of the older wooden houses around the city have subsided at odd angles into the ground because the builders of the time didn't know how to stop the ground thawing from the weight and heat of the building above. Here, and at the associated institute in Igarka (see the Siberia chapter), researchers discovered that the only way to keep a building steady and upright was to sit it on stilts bored 10m into the ground; look carefully around Yakutsk and you'll see that all modern buildings have an insulating gap between their ground floor and the earth.

The highlight of the institute (for which you'll need to wrap up warmly) is descending into the underground laboratory, 12m deep in the frozen earth, where the temperature stays constant at around -5°C and you can see 10,000-year-old deposits of vegetation. The baby mammoth 'Dima', discovered in 1977 on the Kolyma River (and now at St Petersburg's Museum of Zoology) was stored here for a while; a model of it is in the cavern. There's also a chance to view an English video about the work of the institute.

The **Archaeology and Ethnography Museum** and **Mammoth Museum** (ul Kulakovskogo 48; admission R100; open 10am- 1pm & 2pm-5pm Mon-Fri, 11am-1pm & 2pm-4pm Sat) are in the same building. Both have fresh new displays; at the Mammoth Museum there's a 4m-high full mammoth skeleton.

Usually reserved only for visiting VIPs, the **Treasury Museum** hidden away in the building behind the Hotel Tygyn Darkhan, is a repository of some of Sakha's amazing riches, including whopping diamonds, gold ingots and many beautiful pieces of jewellery. There are plans to open it up to the public, but in the meantime the Tour Service Centre (see Orientation & Information earlier) can arrange for you to get in.

Places to Stay
Homestays for US$12 a night, including breakfast, can be arranged through the Tour Service Centre – see Orientation & Information.

Hotel Kolos (☎/fax 24 18 05; ul Kurashova 28/1; singles/doubles R500/690) is a basic budget hotel where the staff are friendly and you can stay for 12 hours for half-price, if you wish.

Several hotels are grouped together close to ploshchad Ordzhonikidze. Best value is the **Hotel Lena** (☎ 42 48 92, fax 42 42 14; pr Lenina 8; singles/doubles with breakfast from R340/680), which has reasonably comfortable rooms. Next door, **Hotel Sterkh** (☎ 24 27 01, fax 24 28 05; pr Lenina 8; singles/doubles with breakfast R735/1100) is more plush, with suite-like rooms done out in rather shiny fabrics.

Hotel Parus (☎ 42 37 27, fax 42 53 09; pr Lenina 7; singles & doubles R1500) is a bit more elegant. The bathrooms are spacious, with surprisingly good tiling, and there's a bar and sauna.

It can get noisy with traffic along Lenina, so if you're wanting something quieter, consider the **Hotel Ontario** (☎ 26 50 58; Sergelyakhskoe shosse; singles/doubles with breakfast US$16/22), about a 20-minute drive from the city centre. It may look like a traditional Yakut log building, but inside it's all modern Western conveniences, with a good restaurant.

Top of the range is the sleek, comfy **Hotel Tygyn Darkhan** (☎ 43 51 09, fax 43 53 54; e darkhan2001@mail.ru; ul Ammosova 9; singles/doubles from US$60/90). At the time of research, the **Polar Star Hotel** (pr Lenina), slated to be Yakutsk's finest, was under construction.

Places to Eat
Hotel Tygyn Darkhan's reasonably priced restaurant is the place to sample local dishes such as fillet of horse meat, smoked fish and koumis.

Excellent pizza – R25 by the slice, R70 to R120 for a whole one – can be had at the stylish **Kafe Vivaldi** (ul Ammosova 9; open 10am-10pm daily), inside the building next to Hotel Tygyn Darkhan. It sometimes has live jazz music in the evenings.

Antalya (☎ 43 55 28; pr Lenina 23; meals R200; open noon-3pm & 6pm-1am daily) is a classy place serving good Russian cuisine. Next door is the popular **Kafe Margarita** (☎ 43 55 14; pr Lenina 23; meals R150; noon-5pm & 6pm-midnight daily), with cosy wooden booths and a smaller menu.

For a cheap meal, try **Kafe Legenda** (pr Lenina 11; open 10am-midnight daily); it serves tasty Central Asian food such as shashlyk and the rice dish plov.

Entertainment
Yakutsk's main nightclub is **Stelf** (ul Oktyabrskaya; admission R50), above the bus station. Of the several theatres, the most accessible programs are at the grand **Opera & Ballet Theatre** (pr Lenina 46). The strikingly modern **Sakha Theatre** (pl Ordzhonikidze) has performances in Yakutian; for Russian drama, try the **Drama Theatre** (pr Lenina 21), which has the obligatory statue of Pushkin outside.

Getting There & Away
There are daily Moscow flights (R7000 to R9000, six hours) and four-weekly connections to Khabarovsk (R4700, four hours) and Irkutsk (R3100). There are less frequent flights to Vladivostok (R4700), Blagoveshchensk (R5400), Krasnoyarsk (R4520) and Novosibirsk (R4500).

During summer there are twice-monthly sailings by ship between Yakutsk and Ust-Kut, nearly 2000km upriver. See the Ust-Kut section in the Siberia chapter for further details. Note that, while it takes only 4½ days to sail to Yakutsk, the journey in the opposite direction, which is against the current, takes a whole week.

The other option, for the devotee of off-the-beaten-track travelling, is to take the bus. There's a very rough 1200km highway between Yakutsk and Bolshoy Never on the Trans-Siberian line, passing through Neryungri and the BAM town of Tynda. Buses to Neryungri (R1500, 24 hours) run on an irregular schedule – check at the bus station.

AROUND YAKUTSK
Bakaldyn
Бакалдын

In the taiga, 46km northwest of Yakutsk, is Bakaldyn, a family-run Evenki ethnographical complex and base for reindeer-pulled sledge rides. Day trips here are around US$50, and seven-day sledge tours in winter can be arranged too. See Orientation & Information in the Yakutsk section for tour agency details.

Even without the snow it's still a great place to learn more about the Evenki culture and shamanism in an appropriate setting. You can trek through the forest to find grazing reindeer, learn how to lasso one, and try on the amazingly lightweight but warm reindeer coats and hats – the height of Yakut winter fashion!

Sottintsy
Соттинцы

At this village on the Lena River, some 60km north of Yakutsk, is the **Druzhba Historical Park** with a collection of original wooden buildings, both Yakutian and Russian. There are hydrofoils that will take you part of the way here, but they don't run to a regular schedule any more and the park itself, a state-run enterprise, also has erratic opening times. If you want to visit here, it's best to make arrangements through one of the Yakutsk tour agencies (see the Yakutsk Orientation and Information section).

LENA PILLARS
ЛЕНСКИЕ СТОЛБЫ

The main scenic reason for visiting Sakha is to sail to the Lena Pillars (Lenskie Stolby), huge, tower-like sandstone formations that line the river for an 18km stretch, about 140km south of Yakutsk. Two-night/three-day excursions by boat usually leave Yakutsk on Friday night and cost around R4500, not in-

cluding food. You'll have around five hours of free time at the Pillars, in which you can climb them for a sweeping view of the river. Bookings for the boat are best arranged through one of the Yakutsk tour agencies (see earlier).

OIMYAKON
ОЙМЯКОН

Known locally as the 'pole of cold', the reason for visiting this remote village, a breeding station for reindeer, horses and silver foxes 650km north of Yakutsk, is that it holds the record as the coldest inhabited spot on earth. Temperatures have been recorded as low as -71°C (in the nearby valleys they go down to -82°C). At such times, according to Yakut lore, if you shout to a friend and they can't hear you, it's because all the words have frozen in the air. But when spring comes, all the words thaw and if you go back at the right time you can hear everything that was said months ago. The best time to visit is in March, when the temperatures are a relatively balmy -25°C. Again, the Yakutsk tour agencies can help you get here.

NERYUNGRI
НЕРЮНГРИ

Just over 30 years old, Neryungri is Sakha's second-largest town (population 70,000) and notable as the home of one of the world's largest open-cut coal mines – apparently more interesting than it sounds. It's also about as far as you can currently travel on the AYaM railway that heads north out of Tynda (see the Tynda section earlier in this chapter) and which will, eventually, connect with Yakutsk. For transport details, see the Tynda section – many trains heading there have carriages that continue to Neryungri.

Primorsky Territory
Приморский Край

Primorsky Territory, bounded by the Ussuri and Bikin Rivers and shielded from the sea by the Sikhote-Alin Mountains, is also known as Ussuriland. The southern forests are the world's most northerly monsoon forests and home to black and brown bears, Siberian boar, the rare Siberian tiger and the virtually extinct Amur leopard, plus hundreds of species of local migratory birds.

VLADIVOSTOK
ВЛАДИВОСТОК

☎ 4232 • pop 900,000 • Moscow time plus 7 hours

Sprinkled across a series of peaks, peninsulas and islands, Vladivostok is one of the most attractively located cities in all of Russia. Its Golden Horn Bay (bukhta Zolotoy Rog), named after Istanbul's similar-looking natural harbour, is home to the Russian Pacific Fleet, which put Vladivostok firmly off limits to all foreigners (and most Russians) during Soviet times.

Once again open to everyone, the eastern terminus of the Trans-Siberian is a bustling commercial city of seedy charm, where you're as likely to rub shoulders with burly 'business men' in sushi bars as with off-duty sailors or battalions of Chinese, Japanese and Korean tourists. It's now possible to explore the early-20th-century fortifications that made this such a crucial garrison at the Far Eastern end of the Russian Empire, clamber through a Soviet submarine or lounge on island beaches that were once the sole preserve of the navy.

Tour agencies offer an impressive range of outdoor adventures, but with the city suffering torrential rainstorms each summer and power cuts in the depths of winter, you don't always need to head to the countryside to experience the rough life in Vladivostok. Steadily, though, the old cosmopolitan flair is returning, as witnessed in the city's most fashionable cafés.

History

Founded in 1860, Vladivostok (meaning 'Lord of the East') became a naval base in 1872, when the residence of the governor general of Primorsky Region moved here from Nikolaevsk-na-Amur to the north.

Tsarevitch Nicholas II turned up in 1891 to inaugurate the new Trans-Siberian rail line. By the early 20th century, Vladivostok teemed with merchants, speculators and sailors of every nation in a manner more akin to Shanghai or Hong Kong than to Moscow. Korean and Chinese, many of whom had built the city, accounted for four out of every five of its citizens.

After Port Arthur fell in the Russo-Japanese War of 1904–05, Vladivostok took on an even more crucial strategic role, and when the Bolsheviks seized power in European Russia in 1917, Japanese, Americans, French and English poured ashore here to support the tsarist counterattack. Vladivostok held out until 25 October 1922, when Soviet forces finally marched in and took control.

Stalin deported or shot most of the foreign population of the city, and further developed it as a port and shipbuilding centre. The northern suburb of Vtoraya Rechka became a transit centre for hundreds of thousands of prisoners waiting to be shipped up to labour, and most likely perish, in the gold fields of Kolyma.

From 1958 to 1992 the city was closed – during this period, foreign trans-Siberian travellers began or ended their journey in Nakhodka, 220km northeast of Vladivostok. The US consulate was one of the first to re-open in 1992 – 50 years after it had been forced to shut – signifying the continued strategic and trade importance of the city. Japanese and Korean cars are now vigorously traded (and driven!) here, along with all manner of other goods.

Orientation

The heart of central Vladivostok is where ulitsa Aleutskaya intersects with ulitsa Svetlanskaya, the city's main waterfront axis. The majority of hotels are west of ulitsa Aleutskaya, all within 10 minutes' walk of the train station. Running north, ulitsa Aleutskaya feeds into other major roads to become the main highway out of the city.

City maps are available in GUM department store and several bookshops along ulitsa Svetlanskaya. The best bookshop for English titles (there are only a few classic novels though) is **Dom Knigi** *(ul Aleutskaya 19)*.

Information

There are currency exchange desks all over town; **Sberbank** *(ul Aleutskaya 12; open 9am-7pm Mon-Sat, 10am-5pm Sun)* has good rates and accepts travellers cheques and credit cards.

The **main post office** is on ulitsa Aleutskaya, opposite the train station. Envelopes, stamps, post boxes etc are on the 1st level (the stairs are on the left, immediately as you enter the building), while on the ground level is the international **telephone, fax and telegraph office**, open 24 hours. There's an Internet service here, too. Also for Internet access, try **Glyubina** *(☎ 22 57 81; ul Sukhanova 101/3A; open 24hrs)*, or the post office at ulitsa Svetlanskaya 41.

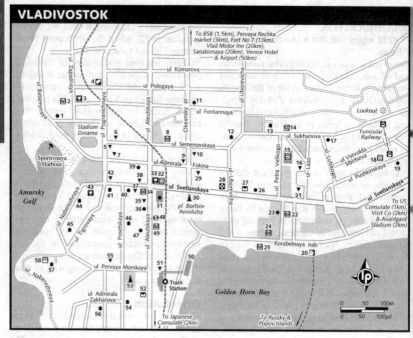

VLADIVOSTOK

The *Vladivostok News* (**w** vn.vladnews.ru) is an online newspaper in English. *Pyutevoditel Vladivostok* (Guide to Vladivostok) is a small advertising-based guide with some information in English; you'll find it at kiosks around town, but it's mainly for students of bad English spelling and grammar.

To extend your visa at **PVU** (*ul Fontannaya 49*) costs around US$70. For details of consulates, see that section of the Siberia & the Russian Far East Facts for the Visitor chapter.

Travel Agencies The following agencies can arrange visas, train tickets, homestays and tours.

Dalintourist (☎ 22 29 49, fax 22 80 55; **w** www.dalintourist.ru; ul Admirala Fokina 8) specialises in trips to the Sikhote-Alin Nature Reserve and to see the tiger family at Gaivoron.

Vizit Co (☎/fax 26 91 72; **w** www.tour-vizit.vladivostok.ru; ul Svetlanskaya 147) is a great all-round agency specialising in trans-Siberian train trips as well as the full range of local tours.

Lucky Tour (☎ 22 33 33, fax 26 78 00; **w** www.luckytour.com; ul Sukhanova 20) also has lots of trans-Siberian trip experience,

as well as organising tours to Kamchatka (including heliskiing) and white-water rafting on rivers near Vladivostok.

City Centre & Waterfront

Vladivostok Station, originally built in 1912 and smartly renovated since, is an exotic architectural concoction; the ceiling in the main hall is decorated with some bold murals. Across the road stands an unusually animated **Lenin** who, curiously, as if he'd known all along how things were going to turn out, points towards Japan, whose business Vladivostok now so assiduously courts. Pop into the nearby **post office** and go upstairs to see some impressive Soviet-era mosaic murals on the walls.

Ulitsa Aleutskaya is lined with once-grand buildings. The house at No 15 (the yellow building next door to the offices of the Far Eastern Shipping Company) was the home of actor Yul Brynner.

Ploshchad Bortsov Revolutsy has the impressive **Monument to the Fighters for Soviet Power in the Far East** as its centrepiece. The square, a focal point for performers and protesters of all kinds, and Alexander

VLADIVOSTOK

PLACES TO STAY
12 Hotel Hyundai; Tsarsky;
    Sky Bar
    Гостиница Хундай
13 Hotel Renessans
    Гостиница Ренессанс
41 Hotel Versailles; Versal
    Гостиница Версаль
44 Hotel Ekvator
    Гостиница Экватор
45 Hotel Vladivostok; Hotel Visit
    Гостиница Владивосток;
    Гостиница Визит
46 Hotel Moryak
    Гостиница Моряк
54 Hotel Primorye; Pizza M
    Гостиница Приморье и
    Пицца М
56 Hotel Chayka
    Гостиница Чайка
57 Hotel Amursky Zaliv
    Гостиница Амурский
    Залив

PLACES TO EAT
5   Ali Baba Fast Food
    Али-Баба
6   Stary Gorod
    Старый Гоголь
7   Paparatstsi
    Папараци
9   Mauro Gianvanni
    Мауро Джанванни
10 Kafe Krishna; Kafe Ekspress
    Кафе Кришна; Кафе
    Экспресс
16 Pitstsabar Zhemchuzhina
    Пиццабар Жемчужина
21 Pizza M
    Пицца М
29 Edem
    Эдем
35 Kafe Ldinka
    Кафе Льдинка
37 Studio Coffee
    Студио Кофе
38 Cafe Montmartre
    Кафе Монмартр

42 Prestizh
    Престиж
51 Gudok
    Гудок
55 Nostalgia
    Ностальгия

MUSEUMS
2   Vladivostok Fortress
    Museum
8   Border Guards'
    Museum
    Музей Боевой Славы
    Погранвойск
22 Annex of Arsenev Regional
    Museum
    Музей им В К Арсеньева
    филиал
24 Submarine Museum
    Подводная Лодка-Музей
25 Krasny Vympel
    Корабль-Музей
    Красный Вымпел
34 Arsenev Regional
    Museum
    Объединённый Крае
    ведческий Музей Им
    Арсеньева
49 Primorsky Art Gallery
    Приморская Картинная
    Галерея

OTHER
1   Aquarium
    Аквариум
3   Bezdonnaya Bochka
    Бездонная Бочка
4   Korean Consulate
11 OVIR
14 Glyubina
    Глубина
15 Gorky Theatre
    Театр Имени М
    Горького
18 Pushkinsky Theatre
    Пушкинский
    Театр

19 Far Eastern State Technical
    University (DVGTU)
20 Coastal Ferries Station
    Вокзал Прибрежных
    Морских Сообщений
23 Triumphal Arch
    Триумфальная Арка
26 Bookshops
    Книги
27 Post Office; Internet
    Access
    Почтамт
28 GUM
    ГУМ
30 Monument to the Fighters
    for Soviet Power in the Far
    East
    Памятник Борцам за
    Власть Советов на
    Дальнем Востоке
31 White House
    Белый Дом
32 Philharmonic Hall
    Филармония
33 Blue Star
    Синяя Звезда
36 Dom Knigi
    Дом Книги
39 Dalintourist
40 Flotsky Univermag
    Флотский
    Чивермаг
43 Kino Okean
    Кино Океан
47 The Brynner House
    (No 15)
    Дом Бриннера
48 Sberbank
    Сбербанк
50 Marine Terminal; Crazy;
    Biznes Intur Servis
    Морской Вокзал
52 Post, Telephone and
    Internet Office
    Главный Почтамт
53 Lenin Statue
58 Zabriskie Point
    Забриски Поинт

Solzhenitsyn's first stop-off point on his internationally heralded return to Russia in 1994, hosts a market every Friday. The monolithic slab at the square's western end is the **White House** (Bely dom), home to the regional administration.

Heading east from the square, you'll soon pitch up at the S-56 submarine. Having sunk 10 enemy ships during WWII, it now serves as a **museum** (*Memornalnaya Podvodnaya Lodka S-56;* ☎ *21 67 57; Korabelnaya nab;*

adults/children R50/25; open 10am-1pm & 2pm-8pm daily), and while the mainly photographic collection isn't too enthralling, clambering around inside is fun. Opposite floats the *Krasny Vympel*, the Soviet Pacific Fleet's first ship launched in 1923, now also a missable **museum**.

Arsenev Regional Museum

The eclectic Arsenev Regional Museum (*Kraevedchesky muzey Arseneva;* ☎ *41 11 73;*

ul Svetlanskaya 20; adults/children R70/35; open 9.30am-6pm Tues-Sun), named after a late-19th-century ethnographer, is worth a browse. The ground floor has the customary array of stuffed wildlife, including a rare Amur leopard as well as two Siberian tigers – one in a deadly scrap with a bear. The 2nd floor has ethnographic and historical displays, including a small section on the Brynner family, while on the top floor there's more on the city's recent history and temporary art exhibitions.

There's also a missable section of the museum across town *(Vistavka; ul Petra Velikogo 6; admission R70)*. Inside the same building is a great little shop stocking model cars and planes, and outside is a new reconstruction of a **triumphal arch** built originally for Tsar Nicholas II in 1902.

Vladivostok Fortress Museum & Other Forts

Every day at noon, a giant gun is fired at the Vladivostok Fortress Museum *(Myzey Vladivostokskaya Krepost; ☎ 25 88 96; ul Batereynaya 4A; admission R70; open 10am-6pm daily)*, one of only three places in Russia where this happens (the others are St Petersburg and Kaliningrad). Huge crowds of Asian tourists gather for this big bang; if you want to explore the renovated fort and its interesting museum in peace, it's recommended you turn up at a quieter time. You'll find the museum just up the hill from the aquarium.

The museum has models of the other forts around the city and across the nearby islands, most now in ruins but still impressive in their technical construction and locations.

Turtsentr Briz *(☎ 22 19 92, fax 22 84 43; e breze@mail.ru)* runs tours to **Fort No 7**, 14km north of the centre. The tour has an English-speaking guide and includes an exploration of the fort's underground tunnels. To visit on your own, take a bus along prospekt Stoletiya Vladivostok to the Zariya stop and then follow what looks like a dirt road uphill to the right. For information on the forts, check **w** www.dvgu.ru/rus/region/culture/fort.

Other Attractions

The best view of Golden Horn Bay is from the lookout at the top of ulitsa Sukhanova, beside the buildings of the DVGTU (Far Eastern State Technical University). If you don't feel like climbing the hill (about 20 minutes from the waterfront), a **funicular railway** *(funikulyor; R5; open 7am-8pm daily)* runs from beside the elegantly restored **Pushkinsky Theatre** on ulitsa Pushkinskaya. Opposite here is the handsome main building of DVGTU.

The **Primorsky Art Gallery** *(Primorskaya kartinnaya galereya; ☎ 41 11 95; ul Aleutskaya 12; admission R100; open 10am-1pm & 2pm-6.30pm Tues-Sat, 11am-5pm Sun)* is something of a surprise, with a large number of 17th-century Dutch paintings and some excellent works by Russian artists, including Repin and Vereshchagin.

The **Border Guards' Museum** *(Muzey boevoy slavy pogran-voysk; ☎ 21 20 74; ul Semenovskaya 17–19; admission R20; open 9am-1pm & 2pm-5pm Tues-Sat, closed last Fri of month)*, spread over three floors, is marginally interesting; the best part is using the high-definition binoculars on the top floor to spy on what's happening at the waterfront.

At the western end of ulitsa Svetlanskaya is a small **park** leading to a narrow strip of sandy beach before the chilly waters of the Amursky Gulf (Amursky zaliv). A few hundred metres north of the beach, past the sports stadium, is a medium-sized **Aquarium** *(Okeanarium; ul Batareynaya W4; admission R70; open 10am-8pm Tues-Sun)* with some interesting local species, shells, turtles and stuffed birds.

Harbour & Island Boat Tours

To catch ferries to the nearby Russky and Popov Islands, part of the archipelago that stretches southwards from Vladivostok towards North Korea, go to the **coastal ferries station**, 100m east along ulitsa Korabelnaya Naberezhnaya from the submarine museum. Many locals have dachas (summer houses) on these islands and there are secluded beaches where you can camp.

There are several daily services to Russky (R40 return, 30 minutes), but only one to Popov (R65 return, 1½ hours). Russky Island, once sole property of the Pacific Fleet, was said to have been stocked with sufficient firepower to blast Vladivostok to kingdom come. There are still parts that are off-limits, and if you want to explore safely it's best to arrange a trip here with one of the travel agencies mentioned earlier. They all run trips around the harbour – a great way to view the Russian Pacific Fleet, the container vessels and giant icebreakers up close.

Alternatively, try the fishing boats beside the **Marine Terminal**; if the skippers aren't busy they may be willing to take you for a harbour tour for around US$20 an hour.

Places to Stay

Vladivostok is poorly served by budget accommodation; if funds are tight it's best to arrange a homestay for around US$25, including breakfast, with one of the travel agencies listed earlier. Also note that the cheaper hotels get very busy during the summer months with package-tour groups from China and Korea – if you want a bed at this time, it's wise to book well ahead.

Another word of caution about the budget to medium-priced hotels: in recent winters, Vladivostok has experienced a severe energy shortage, which has meant that hot water is a rarity, and even cold water disappears on occasion. If you're visiting during this time, check what the situation is, keep your bathtub full and ask the receptionist about saunas around town.

City Centre It may look pretty seedy, but the rooms at the **Hotel Ekvator** (☎ 41 20 60; ul Naberezhnaya 20; singles/doubles R980/ 1800), with the typical Russian-style comforts of giant TVs and fridges, aren't too bad. You might also want to try the better-looking **Hotel Chayka** (☎ 41 43 87, fax 41 38 50; ul Bestyuzheva 29; singles/doubles R750/ 1000), which was predictably full when we showed up.

A good deal is **Hotel Primorye** (☎ 41 14 22, fax 41 34 05; e admin@hbotel.prim orye.ru; ul Posetskaya 20; singles/doubles from R1000/1200), which is handy for the train station. Its newly renovated rooms are quite comfortable and the staff friendly.

Hotel Vladivostok (☎ 41 28 08, fax 41 20 21; w www.vladhotel.vl.ru; ul Naberezhnaya 10; economy twins/standard doubles R1500/ 1800), the former flagship of the Soviet era, has reasonable enough rooms, half with great views over the Amursky Gulf.

A couple of floors of Hotel Vladivostok are leased-out to other operating companies, including the 4th floor, where you'll find **Hotel Visit** (☎ 41 34 53, fax 41 06 13; w www.vizit.vl.ru; singles/twins/doubles with breakfast R1900/2200/2400). Here, the refurbished rooms come with a few more comforts than in the main hotel (such as

minibars and complimentary toiletries), but are otherwise pretty much the same.

Hotel Moryak (☎/fax 49 94 99; ul Poset-skaya 38) was under renovation when we last visited and is sure to move from its budget position to more of a mid-range level.

Hotel Amursky Zaliv (☎ 22 55 20, fax 22 14 30; ul Naberezhnaya 9; singles/doubles from US$32/64), a rambling place dug into the cliff side (the top floor is at street level), is packed with noisy Chinese tour groups from May to September. The cheaper rooms are overpriced, but the renovated ones with balconies overlooking the bay are not too bad.

Hotel Renessans (☎ 40 68 66, fax 40 68 70; ul Sukhanova 3; singles/doubles US$50/ 60) is a new boutique-style hotel with just 12 comfortable rooms. The furnishings tend towards nouveau-Russian garishness, but otherwise it's a quiet, well-located place.

A couple of kilometres down the peninsula from the city centre is the presentable **Hotel Gavan** (☎ 49 53 63, fax 49 53 64; w www .gavan.ru; ul Krygina 3; economy singles/ doubles US$60/70, standard singles/doubles with breakfast and use of pool US$95/105). If you're going to stay all the way out here, it's worth spending a bit more on the standard rooms so that you can freely use the 25m pool; also ask for a room overlooking the harbour. To get here, take bus No 60, 61, 62 or 69 from the city centre.

Rooms at the **Hotel Versailles** (☎ 26 42 01, fax 26 51 24; e versal@mail.primorye.ru; ul Svetlanskaya 10; singles/doubles R3600/ 4500) are sumptuous, but frequently booked out with upmarket tour groups.

The city's top choice is the **Hotel Hyundai** (☎ 40 72 05, fax 40 70 08; e marketing .vbc@gin.ru; w www.hotelhyundai.ru; ul Se-menovskaya 29; double or twin rooms with breakfast US$200), offering plush accommodation and services to full international four-star specifications.

Sanatornaya & the Airport For a respite from Russia, may we suggest the **Vlad Motor Inn** (☎ 33 13 51, fax 33 07 17; w www .vlad-inn.ru; ul Vosmaya 11, Sanatornaya; singles & doubles US$157.50). This Canadian/ Russian joint venture, 20km north of the centre in the leafy coastal suburb of Sanatornaya, is comfortable, quiet and very Western. The rates include free airport transfers, and the hotel has an excellent restaurant which is almost worth a trip out here on its own. Sanatornaya is six stops from the city on the local train or a 30-minute bus ride.

A stone's throw from the airport is the **Venice Hotel** (☎ 30 76 00, fax 30 76 02; ul Portovaya 39; singles/twins/doubles R1980/2520/2880), a new place certainly worth considering if you have an early flight or arrive too late to get into the city. The rooms are not too big, but spotless and with modern furnishings. It also has a good restaurant – a better place to hang out for your flight than the airport.

Places to Eat

Restaurants The long-established **Nostalgia** (☎ 41 05 13; ul Pervaya Morskaya 6/25; meals R350; open 8am-11pm daily) restaurant and café serves fine, good-value traditional Russian cuisine. The small dining room recreates tsarist elegance, with its crimson upholstery and gilt-framed pictures, while the café is more relaxed.

Gudok (☎ 41 29 98; ul Aleutskaya 2A; mains around US$10; open noon-1am daily) is a grandly decorated dining room at the northern end of Vladivostok Station. It offers a wide range of dishes, including Russian favourites. The atmosphere is enhanced (or marred, depending on your tastes) by the cabaret-style live music.

Pitstsabar Zhemchuzhina (☎ 26 53 97) and **Pizza M** (☎ 26 50 96), both at ulitsa Svetlanskaya 51A, are two modern pizzerias around the corner from each other near the Gorky Theatre. Locals say that the pizzas at Zhemchuzhina (meaning Pearl) taste better; they're certainly a little pricier, with small ones starting at R200 as opposed to R120 at Pizza M, which offers its pizzas in thick- or thin-crust versions. There's another branch of **Pizza M** (☎ 41 34 30; ul Posetskaya 20) attached to Hotel Primorye.

Stary Gorod (☎ 20 52 94; ul Semenovskaya 1/10; meals around R350) is tucked away in a tumbledown part of town. It's a newly opened place with some fake village-style decor (including a waterfall and a room covered with fish tanks). The Russian cuisine is quite acceptable and the live music is not too intrusive.

Mauro Gianvanni (☎ 20 57 62; Okeansky pr 9) is a modern Italian café that has a short menu of pasta dishes (which come in small portions) and a much longer list of cocktails.

Edem (☎ 26 19 90; ul Admirala Fokina 22; mains from US$7; open 11am-midnight Sun-Thur, 11am-3am Fri & Sat) has pricey, fresh sushi and sashimi. The atmosphere in the cellar-like space can be weird, especially if there are gangsters taking long lunch breaks, but in the evenings it's a lively place.

For top-quality meals (R300 to over R700 for main courses), try the elegant **Versal** (☎ 26 93 92) at the Hotel Versailles, **Tsarsky** (☎ 40 73 24) at the Hotel Hyundai, or the restaurant at the Vlad Motor Inn out at Sanatornaya, which does some mean American-style sandwiches and killer steaks. (See Places to Stay earlier for location details.)

Cafés About as trendy as it gets for Vlad is the relaxed, modern **Studio Coffee** (☎ 41 28 82; ul Svetlanskaya 18; open 24hrs). It does a good range of drinks (including alcohol), cakes and snack-type meals such as spaghetti with meatballs and excellent hamburgers (R95) and salads (R35).

Cafe Montmartre (☎ 41 27 89; ul Svetlanskaya 9/6; open 9am-4am daily), opposite and tucked away in a courtyard, is an equally stylish and popular place, but the service can be slow. It has a good range of breakfast deals.

The media-theme at **Paparatstsi** (☎ 22 86 67; ul Admirala Fokina 5; mains US$3; open 9am-2am daily) translates into pleasing contemporary decor and there are local glossy mags to flick through as you savour your cappuccino.

Around the corner is **Ali Baba Fast Food** (☎ 26 48 87; ul Pogranichnaya 6/3; open 9am-11pm daily), a dusky pink-painted place serving good, cheap Middle Eastern–style pitta-bread sandwiches (the French fries were a bit limp though).

Kafe Ldinka (ul Aleutskaya 21; mains US$1.50; open 10am-10pm daily), a throwback to Soviet times in terms of decor, is still a good café to linger over drinks, ice cream or a bowl of pelmeni (Russian-style ravioli dumplings).

Kafe Krishna (Okeansky pr 10/12; mains US$1.50; open 11am-7pm daily) offers cheap vegetarian food of the lentil variety. Next door, but at the same address, is the modern Russian **Kafe Ekspress** (☎ 22 55 77), where the service is indeed zippy.

Self-Catering Open 24 hours is **Prestizh** (ul Svetlanskaya 1), a Western-style supermarket with a good bakery. For fresh fruit and vegetables, there are daily stalls along ulitsa Posetskaya, behind the post office. There's also a lively waterfront market every Friday at ploshchad Bortsov Revolutsy.

Entertainment

Gorky Theatre (*Teatr Gorkogo;* ☎ 26 48 91; *ul Svetlanskaya 49*) is the city's main venue for drama. For classical music, try the **Philharmonic Hall** (*Filarmoniya;* ☎ 26 08 21; *ul Svetlanskaya 15*).

The modern multiplex cinema **Kino Okean** (☎ 41 42 92; *ul Naberezhnaya 3*) shows dubbed recent US releases. Tickets range from R30 to R80 depending on the time of day and seat. It has a spacious bar upstairs.

The popular local football team, Luch, play at **Stadium Dinamo** (*ul Pogranichnaya*) on Wednesday at around 5.30pm, from September to May. Tickets are R60 and, if the match leaves you less than thrilled, the view from the stands across the Amursky Gulf provides fine compensation. There are also **speedway** races at Avantgard stadium (ulitsa Svetlanskaya) on Monday and Friday evenings.

Bars & Clubs For most clubs there is a cover charge between R100 and R300.

BSB (☎ 30 08 00; *Kransogo Znameni pr 67*) is the city's best club, playing a good mix of contemporary music, and on some Saturdays there are live rock bands. The crowd here is studenty and relaxed.

The cavern-like **Bottomless Barrel** (*Bezdonnaya Bochka;* ☎ 22 13 83; *ul Fontannaya 2; open noon-4am daily*) boasts Vlad's best choice of beer and is a pretty popular place, particularly on weekends, when you should book a table if you don't want to be left standing at the bar.

Zabriskie Point (☎ 21 85 72; *ul Naberezhnaya 9; cover charge R300; open 8pm-4am daily*) is a dark and weirdly decorated rock and jazz club down at sea level on the corner of the Hotel Amursky Zaliv. It shows movies and rock videos on its cinema-style screen, and if there's a live act on, it's perhaps worth paying the steep cover charge and drink prices; otherwise give it a miss.

Other options (but be prepared for a concentrated assault of Russian high-energy disco) include the cosy and louche **Blue Star** (*Sinyaya zvezda; ul Svetlanskaya 13*); and

Crazy (*4th floor, Morskoi Vokzal*), where the only crazy things are the price of drinks and the quality of dancing.

For a quiet drink, try either **Studio Coffee** or **Paparatstsi** (see Places to Eat earlier), or the **Sky Bar** on the 12th floor of the Hotel Hyundai.

Shopping

Nostalgia (*ul Pervaya Morskaya 6/25*) has the best range of traditional handicrafts, but it's pricey. There's no shortage of other places hawking the usual range of lacquered boxes, matryoshka dolls, painted trays and jewellery. For something a bit quirkier, try the **antique shop** (*ul Svetlanskaya 20; open 8.30am-6pm daily*) next to the Arsenev Regional Museum.

A wander around **GUM** (*ul Svetlanskaya 35*) is recommended more for the Art Deco elegance of the building than the quality of its stock.

Flotsky Univermag (*ul Svetlanskaya 11*) is an army and navy supplies store, selling buttons, badges and other small bits of military insignia.

Getting There & Away

Air There are direct flights that go to Moscow (R9300, nine hours, twice daily), Khabarovsk (R2480, 1¼ hours, five weekly), Irkutsk (R3565, four hours, six weekly), Yuzhno-Sakhalinsk (R3410, 1¾ hours, daily), Magadan (R5735, three hours, weekly), Yakutsk (R3940, twice weekly) and Petropavlovsk-Kamchatsky (R4340, four hours, five weekly).

Vladivostok Air flies three times a week to Niigata (US$270), and less regularly to Osaka (US$380) and Toyama (US$300) in Japan, Seoul (US$220) and Pusan (US$220) in South Korea, and Harbin (US$90) in China. Korean Air has two flights a week to/from Seoul (US$280). China Airlines also flies twice a week to Shanghai.

Train At the time of writing, the No 1 service, the *Rossiya*, leaves for Moscow (R4665, 6½ days) on even-numbered days, passing through Irkutsk (R3230), but be sure to check, as this may change. A cheaper service is the No 317, which has *kupe* tickets to Moscow (R2850.30) and Irkutsk (R1978.60).

Other trains west include the daily No 5 *Okean* overnight to Khabarovsk (R740), the

No 7 *Sibir* to Novosibirsk (R2650), and the No 53, which departs on even-numbered days to Kharkiv (Kharkov), in Ukraine, and which has *platskart* (3rd-class, dorm carriages) should you wish to save money. The daily No 251 to Sovgavan (R864) is the service you'll need to catch if you're heading north to Vanino for the ferry to Sakhalin or to Komsomolsk and west along the BAM.

On Monday and Thursday the No 185 also connects Vladivostok with Harbin (R1100) in the Heilongjiang province of northern China, from where there are daily connections to Beijing. The train crosses the border at the Chinese town of Suifenhe and also stops at Mudanjiang.

Tickets for long-distance trains are sold in the office beside the main platform. Go downstairs from the main entrance, turn left and go back into the building. If there are long queues here you can also buy tickets at the **Service Centre** (☎ 21 04 04; open 8am-noon & 1pm-5.30pm Mon-Fri), at the southern end of the building, for a commission of R50, plus R30 if you need information on the trains first. The major travel agents (see Travel Agencies earlier) will also happily buy tickets for you for similar fees.

Boat The **Biznes Intur Servis** (☎ 49 73 91, fax 41 18 29; e bis@ints.vtc.ru; w www.bis intour.com; 3rd floor, Morskoi Vokzal, 1 Okeansky pr) handles bookings for the fairly regular ferries (it claims to offer them every Monday and Saturday, but check first) between Vladivostok and the Japanese port of Fushiki from late February to early January. Once or twice a year there are also sailings to Pusan in South Korea.

The voyage to Fushiki takes 42 hours, with the cheapest berth being in an outside cabin on the third deck (US$190) and rising to US$740 for a two-room luxury cabin with TV and fridge. All meals are included in the price. The ship is rarely full, so chances are you'll have a cabin to yourself. The food's not bad, but the crossing can be rough, so be prepared to eat little and suffer seasickness.

Getting Around

To/From the Airport For the cheapest (but least direct and longest) connection between the airport and the city centre, take a local train from the central station three stops to Vtoraya Rechka. There's a bus station 150m

east of the railway along the main street, ulitsa Russkaya. From there, take the infrequent bus No 101, the express airport service (R22, 45 minutes). Count on about two hours for the whole journey. Coming from the airport it's the reverse procedure; or you may find a minivan taxi that will be going to the city centre.

Car transfers arranged through a travel agency will cost around US$25, while the airport taxi gang will attempt to charge you double.

Public Transport Trolleybuses and trams cost R5 a ride; pay either the conductor or the driver when you get off. From in front of the train station, tram Nos 4 and 5 run north then swing east onto ulitsa Svetlanskaya, to the head of the bay; tram No 7 stays on ulitsa Aleutskaya, running north past the market.

For local ferry information, see Harbour & Island Boat Tours earlier.

AROUND VLADIVOSTOK
Slavyanka
Славянка

A popular day trip for locals is to take the ferry from the terminal on ulitsa Korabelnaya Naberezhnaya across the Amursky Gulf to the port of Slavyanka, 50km south towards the North Korean border. The small town is quite attractive, but nothing to go out of your way for – it's its surrounding beaches that are the real draw, and on hot summer days they're packed. However, if you go far enough south it is possible to find seclusion.

Lake Khanka & Gaivoron
Озера Ханка и Гаиворон

Around 235km north of Vladivostok is the 4000-sq-metre Lake Khanka, home to around 350 different species of birds every summer. Its shallow waters – only around 4m in the deepest parts – famously bloom with giant lotus flowers.

A few kilometres from the eastern shore of the lake is Gaivoron, the location of a Russian Academy of Sciences biological research reserve, home to a family of rare Amur tigers. Dr Victor Yudin (☎ 42352-7 42 49) will happily show you his four tigers, the original two – Kuchir and Nurka – given to him as orphaned cubs in 1991. This is the only guaranteed chance you'll have of seeing these magnificent beasts up close. They're kept safely behind an electrified high-wire fence in a two-hectare compound, beside which Yudin has several caged bears and other orphaned animals passed on to him by locals.

Gaivoron is 15km north of Spassk, a run-down town on the main train line between Khabarovsk and Vladivostok. A round-trip drive from Vladivostok takes at least eight hours; travel agencies can arrange this for around US$200 a car.

Partizanskaya River
Партизанская Река

Vladivostok tour agencies also offer day rafting trips to the Partizanskaya River, a couple of hours' drive north of the city. This is a generally gentle run; more experienced rafters should look into the longer trips along the Kema River farther north, with class 3 and occasional class 4 rapids.

SIKHOTE-ALIN NATURE RESERVE
СИХОТЕ-АЛИНСКИЙ ЗАПОВЕДНИК

The main draw of this 344,000-hectare forested reserve, headquartered in the coastal town of Ternei (a 10-hour ride northeast of Vladivostok), is the chance to find out about the Russian-American Siberian Tiger project. Chances of spotting tigers in this wilderness are very slim, but there are plenty of birds around Blagodtnoye Lake, and seals on the coast.

Besides tigers, the reserve, which stretches along the Pacific coast and back into the Sikhote-Alin Mountains, has crystal-clear salmon streams, a Savannah-like oasis and dramatic beaches of large, round stones that whistle as the aloe-green waves pour over them.

Permission to visit the reserve has to be obtained from the reserve director – this is best arranged through one of the Vladivostok tour agencies listed earlier; they'll also sort out transport and accommodation for you.

NAKHODKA
НАХОДКА

Nakhodka, which means 'discovery', was little more than a landing until after WWII (and was, in its infancy, called Amerikanka). Now it's a major fishing port, spread around a sheltered bay stumbled upon by a storm-tossed Russian ship in the 1850s (hence the present name).

The town prospered as a result of being the only Soviet-era Pacific port open to foreign ships. It was also the eastern terminus of the Trans-Siberian Railway, though few foreigners ever saw more than just the road from the train station to the quay as they were quickly ushered on board the ferry for Japan.

The main reason for heading out this way is to inspect the dramatic coastal rock formations near the city; to do this, arrange a car and guide with one of the Vladivostok tour agencies.

Sakhalinskaya Region
Сахалинская Область

The main island of the Sakhalinskaya Region (Sakhalin Region), which also includes Moneron Island and the disputed Kuril chain, is Sakhalin. Geographically, the 948km-long island is an offshore extension of the Sikhote-Alin Mountains in the southeast corner of Russia, though it looks just as much a northern extension of Japan. In fact, Russia and Japan have been wrangling over the territory for more than a century.

The first Japanese settlers came across from Hokkaido in the early 1800s, attracted by seas that were so full of fish, whales and seals that, in the words of an early explorer, 'the water looked as though it was boiling'. The island already had occupants in the form of the Nivkhi, Oroki and Ainu peoples but, just as this didn't give pause to the Japanese, the Russians were equally heedless when they claimed Sakhalin in 1853, as part of their campaign to secure the Amur region. Japan agreed to recognise Russian sovereignty in exchange for the rights to the Kuril Islands (incidentally, also inhabited by Nivkhi, Oroki and Ainu).

Inspired by its extreme remoteness from European Russia, in 1882 the tsar made the island into one huge penal colony. Anton Chekhov visited in 1890 and wrote up his observations in A Journey to Sakhalin. They can be summarised in one extract: 'I have seen Ceylon which is paradise and Sakhalin which is hell.'

Japan restaked its claim to hell, seizing the island during the Russo-Japanese War and getting to keep the southern half, which they

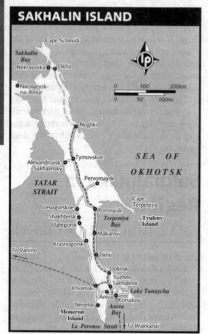

SAKHALIN ISLAND

Cape Schmidt

Sakhalin Bay

Nekrasovka ● ○ Okha

● Nikolaevsk-na-Amur

0   100   200km
0   50   100mi

● Nogliki

SEA OF OKHOTSK

● Tymovskoe

Alexandrovsk- ○
Sakhalinsky

● Pervomaysk

TATAR STRAIT

Lesogorskoe ●
Shakhtersk ●
Uglegorsk ●

Poronaisk ●

Terpeniya Bay

Cape Terpeniya

Tyuleny Island

● Makarov

Krasnogorsk ●

To Vanino →

● Tikhii

Dolinsk ●
Yuzhno-Sakhalinsk ●

Kholmsk ●   Lake Tunaycha

Aniva ● × Korsakov

Nevelsk ●   *Aniva Bay*

Moneron Island

Le Perouse Strait | To Wakkanai

called Karafuto, under the terms of the peace settlement (the Treaty of Portsmouth, 1905). In the final days of WWII, though, the Soviet Union staged a successful invasion of the island. Sakhalin became a highly militarised eastern outpost of the Soviet empire, loaded with aircraft, missiles and guns. Just how sensitive Sakhalin had become was illustrated in 1983, when the off-course Korean Airlines flight 007 was shot down by the Russians. All 267 on board were killed instantly. The Americans charged the Russians with the deliberate mass murder of innocents, while the Russians accused the USA of callously putting those lives at risk by sending flight 007 on a spying mission over the island.

Nowadays, Russia, the USA and Japan work shoulder to shoulder extracting oil while investors from around the Pacific rim eye Sakhalin's other natural riches – gas, coal, uranium and silver, as well as timber, furs and a fine fishery.

Almost three-quarters of Sakhalin is wild, mountain terrain, covered with pine forests and strands of bamboo. The majority of the island's 630,000 people live in the capital, Yuzhno-Sakhalinsk, and the two southern

ports, Kholmsk and Korsakov. While Sakhalin has a rugged beauty, it's also very difficult to explore because of the lack of a decent transport system and roads. You'll need time, money and a disregard for comfort to see the best that Sakhalin has to offer.

YUZHNO-SAKHALINSK
ЮЖНО-САЖАЛИНСК
☎ 4242, 42422 for five-digit numbers • pop 179,000 • Moscow time plus 7 hours

The capital of Sakhalin, Yuzhno-Sakhalinsk is a compact, not unattractive city nestled at the foothills of the Susunai mountains. There isn't much to do here, but its tour companies, decent (but expensive) hotels and restaurants make it the obvious starting point for further exploration of the island.

Yuzhno-Sakhalinsk was founded in 1881 as Vladimirovka, named after a major who directed the island's compulsory labour. At that time it was little more than a hamlet, composed of a few farmsteads worked by convicts. The main Russian settlements were farther north, on the coast of the Tatar Strait – places that were more accessible from the mainland. It was the Japanese who developed Vladimirovka, renaming it Toiohara and, during their 40 years of occupation, building it into a thriving township and centre of regional administration.

After the Japanese were booted out in 1945, the USSR tried to whip up enthusiasm on the mainland and get people to migrate to southern Sakhalin, with the intention that the island should be decisively and irreversibly Russified; Toiohara became Yuzhno-Sakhalinsk (literally 'Southern Sakhalin').

For 45 years the town developed unexceptionally as a centre for light industry and food processing (specifically fish) before attracting widespread international recognition in 1990 as the site of the 'Sakhalin experiment'.

A newly appointed governor from Moscow, Valentin Fyodorov, a former economics professor, vowed to create capitalism on the island. He privatised retail trade, distributed land and turned Yuzhno-Sakhalinsk's Communist Party headquarters into a business centre. The experiment was not an unqualified success, with the majority of people claiming to have been left poorer by the free-market reforms. Fyodorov called it a day and hightailed it back to Moscow in 1993.

The demise of the Soviet Union and the influx of thousands of expat oil-industry people and their entourages have achieved what Fyodorov couldn't. New businesses are opening up all the time and there are several shiny new joint-venture buildings in the town.

Orientation

The town's main axis, running roughly north–south, is ulitsa Lenina with ploshchad Lenina and the train station at its midpoint. Kommunistichesky prospekt runs east from the square, with the island's main administrative buildings strung along it.

Information

The central **post office** *(open 8am-7.30pm Mon-Fri, 9am-4pm Sat & Sun)* is in the northeast corner of ploshchad Lenina. The **telephone office** *(ul Lenina 220; open 8am-9pm daily)* is next door.

Currency can be exchanged at several banks around town, as well as in the basement of the **Sakhalin Centre** *(Kommunistichesky pr 32; open 10am-4pm Mon-Fri)*, where you'll also find a cash machine dispensing both dollars and roubles.

Lunny Svet *(☎ 72 63 92; ul Lenina 182A; open 9am-10pm daily)* offers Internet access (one hour minimum for R40) on the ground floor.

The best map of the city is the *Yuzhno-Sakhalinsk Map of City* published by Eikon Co; ask one of the tour agencies if they have it. Also useful are the fortnightly English-language newspaper the *Sakhalin Times* (distributed at the major hotels and joint-venture companies around town), and the monthly Russian-language *Bybor Dosuga*, a pocket-size guide to what's on in the city.

None of the city's bookshops have much in the way of English-language books, but you could try **Evrika** *(ul Sakhalinskaya 8; open 10am-7pm daily)*, which stocks coffee-table type volumes on the island.

Tour Agencies The **Sakhalin-Kurils Tour & Tourist Information Agency** *(☎/fax 72 81 91; W www.geocities.com/iatur; ul Dzerzhinskogo 23)* specialises in eco-tours and adventure tours all over the region, including caving and rafting on Sakhalin, diving around Moneron Island and trips to the Kuril Islands. It can also arrange homestays in Yuzhno-Sakhalinsk for US$30 per night, with breakfast.

Intourist Sakhalin *(☎ 42 13 53, fax 72 73 43; W www.intourist-sakhalin.ru; ul Dzerzhinskogo 36, office 112)* is another long-running agency offering group and individual tours around the island.

Sakhalin Travel Group *(☎ 72 72 88; W http ://stg.sakhalin.su; 31 Kommunistichesky pr)* has experience at getting oil people to remote sites and should be able to assist with transport and English-speaking guides.

All of these agencies are quite pricey; but the people on Sakhalin are very friendly and, if you offer to foot the bill for petrol, a local may offer to show you around.

Things to See & Do

The pagoda-like roofs of the **Regional Museum** *(☎ 72 75 56; Kommunistichesky pr 29; admission R15; open 11am-5pm Tues, 11am-6pm Wed-Sun)* are a strong visual reminder of Sakhalin's Japanese heritage – the building was home to the Karafuto administration before the Soviet Union took over the whole island in 1945.

On the ground level are displays about the island's natural and climatic features, its prehistory and some fascinating ethnography, including fish-skin robes and seal-hide tunics worn by the Ainu. The Siberian and Far Eastern penchant for taxidermy is also well in evidence, with the larger part of a whole colony of seals stuffed and on display. Upstairs you can learn about Sakhalin's history, and there are temporary art and photography exhibitions.

In the gardens in front of the museum stand three squat pieces of ancient artillery; for those with an interest in things that go bang, the **Officers' Club** *(Dom Ofitserov)*, one block east, has a yard full of armoured vehicles and tanks. Other remnants of Soviet days along Kommunistichesky prospekt include colourful wall murals either side of the **Chekhov Theatre** and the cinema **Oktyabr Kino**.

The regional **Art Museum** *(☎ 72 29 25; ul Lenina 137; admission R20; open 11am-6pm Tues-Sun)* is in another building dating from the Japanese era. Its permanent collection was under wraps when we visited, but the small temporary exhibition was not too bad.

Anton Chekhov's trip to Sakhalin is celebrated at the **AP Chekhov Book Museum** *(☎ 42 33 49; ul Kurilskaya 42; admission R10; open 11am-6pm Tues-Sat)*. This small museum has copies of the writer's books and letters, evocative photographs from the period

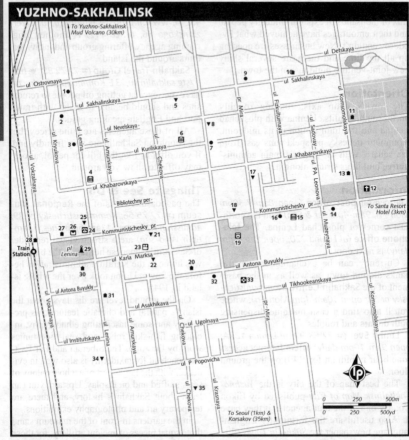

YUZHNO-SAKHALINSK

and some modern paintings and drawings summing up the plight of the prisoners of the Sakhalin penal colony.

Places to Stay – Budget & Mid-Range

The city has a shortage of hotels (blame it all on those oil projects) so advance booking, for which there is generally a fee of between 10% and 20% of the room cost, is essential, particularly in the summer.

Moneron (☎ 72 34 53, fax 72 34 54; Kommunistichesky pr 86; singles/doubles R302/578), a big Wedgwood-blue building on ploshchad Lenina's northern side, has small, clean rooms with lingering smells and shared bathrooms. Bathrooms are also shared at the **Rybak** (☎ 72 37 68, fax 72 27 12; ul Karla

Marksa 51; singles/doubles US$40/76), across the square, making it too expensive for what's on offer. At neither are you guaranteed hot water in the summer months.

The colourful **Oriental** (☎ 72 19 72, fax 46 30 54; e orientalsakhalin@mail.ru; ul Sakhalinskaya 2A; singles/doubles with breakfast US$50/75) has been renovated in a cosy way and has a café and billiard table in the lobby. You'll also find city maps and postcards on sale here.

Lada (☎/fax 42 38 37; ul Komsomolskaya 154; singles/doubles from R1530/2050) is acceptable for an old-style hotel, and will do if nothing else is available.

Eurasia (☎ 72 35 60, fax 72 32 32; e eurtur@sakhmail.sakhalin.ru; ul Vokzalnaya 54; singles/doubles R1700/2100), next door to

YUZHNO-SAKHALINSK

PLACES TO STAY
10 Oriental
   Ориенталь
11 Gagarin
   Гагарин
13 Lada
   Лада
20 Natalya
   Наталя
27 Moneron
   Монерон
28 Eurasia
   Евразия
30 Rybak
   Рыбак
31 Hotel Sakhalin-Sapporo
   Гостиница Сахалин -
   Сапоро

PLACES TO EAT
5 Slavyanka
   Славянка
8 Holiday Palace; Vecher;
   Aska
   Холидей Палас, Вечер,
   Аска
17 Kafe Vechernee
   Кафе Вечернее

18 Sakhalin Centre; Pacific Cafe;
   Kona Bar
   Сахалин центр
21 Blini Stand
22 Saigon
   Сайгон
25 Kafe Kolobok
   Кафе Колобок
34 Okhotskoe More
   Охотское море
35 777

OTHER
1 Sakhalin Fantastic
2 Bowling Centre
   Боулинг центр
3 Lunny Svet
   Лунный свет
4 Art Museum
   Художественный
   музей
6 Chekov Book
   Museum
   Книги А П Чехова -
   музей
7 Sakhalin-Kurils Tour & Tourist
   Information Agency
   Сахалин - Курилы тур

9 Evrika
   Эврика
10 St Innokenty
   Church
   Св Иннокентия
   церковь
14 Officers' Club
   Дом Офицеров
15 Regional Museum
   Краеведческий
   музей
16 Sakhalin Travel
   Group
19 Chekhov Theatre
   Драматический театр
   им Чехова
23 Oktyabr Kino
   Кино Октябрь
24 Telephone Office
26 Post Office
   Почтамп
29 Lenin Statue
   Статуя Ленина
32 Intourist Sakhalin
   Интурист Сахалин
33 TSUM Department
   Store & Market
   ЦУМ

the train station, is a friendly, clean and modern place.

Places to Stay – Top End
The new, popular **Gagarin** (☎ 46 30 64, fax 46 30 61; e gagarin@karafuto.ru; ul Komsomolskaya 133; singles/doubles US$80/100) has large, comfortable rooms, a sauna and pleasant bar.

Natalya (☎ 3 66 83, fax 46 27 01; ul Antona Buyukly 38; singles/doubles with breakfast R2350/3900) offers what are essentially mini-apartments, nicely fitted out with a large bedroom and bathroom, TV and VCR, and a kitchen – great if you're here for a long stay.

Hotel Sakhalin-Sapporo (☎ 72 15 60, fax 72 38 89; ul Lenina 181; singles/doubles with breakfast US$126/148) looks much better inside than out, with the rooms all upgraded to Japanese tourist standards.

Santa Resort Hotel (☎ 46 28 24, fax 50985-6 55 55; e santa@sakhalin.ru; ul Venskaya 3; singles/doubles with breakfast US$165/200), in a peaceful and green spot a few kilometres east of the centre, has the most facilities, including a spa, tennis court and two restaurants. The rooms are huge and all

have balconies. In winter it's a good ski base, with a downhill slope and chairlifts nearby.

Places to Eat
In the Sakhalin Centre, **Pacific Cafe** (Kommunistichesky pr 32; meals around R250), run by the French-US remote-operations services group Universal Sodhexo, is your all-Western standard self-serve café, offering decent sandwiches, burgers and hot meals. It's supposed to be open 8am to midnight daily, but the best choice of food is available at lunch time during the week, when you'll also find a pastry counter and real coffee on sale in the lobby.

Kafe Kolobok (ul Lenina 218; meals R80; open 8am-7pm daily) is the modern Russian version of a stolovaya (cafeteria). You can get a good selection of traditional dishes here, from borsht to bliny – it's all cheap and hearty. Another inexpensive place for a snack is the **bliny stand** in front of the Oktyabr cinema, which has an amazing range of fillings for these Russian pancakes.

The self-consciously Russian **Slavyanka** (☎ 42 96 67; ul Sakhalinskaya 45; meals around R300; open noon-4pm & 5pm-10pm daily) is decorated with painted wooden spoons, matryoshka dolls and the like. A balalaika trio plays some nights from 9pm. The Russian cuisine is great, although the portions can be a bit small.

The bright, relaxed **Okhotskoe More** (☎ 72 54 79; ul Lenina 248; meals R300; open noon-1am daily) specialises in fish dishes and has an English menu.

Kafe Vechernee (☎ 3 64 36; pr Mira 112; meals R300; open 11am-1am daily) is a good, reasonably priced café with excellent soups and some Korean dishes.

The standard Russian food on offer at **Saigon** (☎ 72 40 23; ul Karla Marksa 2; meals R200; open noon-midnight Mon & Wed-Fri, noon-5pm Tues, 6pm-midnight Sat & Sun) has little to do with Vietnam, although the decor makes a stab at evoking the Far East, with liberal use of bamboo. It offers a business lunch (R100) and at night the synth-pop trio has the locals grooving.

Fine Korean food can be found at **Seoul** (☎ 55 13 42; pr Mira 245; meals R1000; open noon-3pm Mon-Fri & 7pm-1am Tues-Sun), which also has an attached nightclub if you feel like dancing off the *kimchee* afterwards.

Of the hotel restaurants, the one at Hotel Sakhalin-Sapporo is good but pricey (US$56 for steak!); you can get a real cappuccino at the adjoining café/bar. At the Santa Resort Hotel, the **Ruby** restaurant has European cuisine, while the **Zhemchyzhina** (Pearl) offers Japanese food made by a Japanese chef – at both, mains will cost R400 to R500.

Entertainment

The main expat hang-out is the convivial **Kona Bar** (Sakhalin Centre, Kommunist-ichesky pr 32; open 11am-11pm daily), done out in Hawaiian style. Come here if you don't mind oil talk and paying over the odds for a beer (R76).

A popular late-night spot is the **Holiday Palace** (☎ 72 86 22; ul Dzerzhinskogo 21). The large disco (minimum cover R100) attracts a young crowd. There's also a casino, sauna, the snazzy Russian restaurant **Vecher** (☎ 42 05 39), with a decent lunch-time buffet for R170, and the Japanese/Korean restaurant **Aska** (☎ 3 76 36). A smaller restaurant/disco complex is **777** (☎ 42 94 62; ul Chekova 71), but it's much more expensive to get in (R350 for men, R250 for women).

Upstairs at **Lunny Svet** (ul Lenina 182; admission R70) is the place to go for a boogie, striptease and a decent meal. Or if you prefer your entertainment more wholesome, try the **Bowling Centre** (☎ 77 23 12; ul Sakhalin-skaya 157; open noon-3pm daily).

Getting There & Away

Air There are daily flights to/from Khabarovsk (R2850, 1¼ hours), Moscow (R6000 to R8000, nine hours) and Vladivostok (R3000, two hours), as well as less-regular flights to Blagoveshchensk, Yekaterinburg, Irkutsk, Krasnoyarsk, Novosibirsk, Omsk and St Petersburg.

Sakhalin Air flies twice a week to/from Hakodate (US$365) and weekly to Sapporo (US$365), both on the Japanese island of Hokkaido, twice weekly to Seoul (US$385) and weekly to Pusan (US$385), both Korea. The foreigners' departure hall is through a small door 15m to the left of the main entrance. There's an international departure tax of around R500, payable on checking in.

Train The farthest point north on the island reached by the railway is Nogliki – see that section later in this chapter.

Boat Daily ferries head to Vanino on the mainland from Kholmsk (see the earlier section on Vanino for further details). Kholmsk is connected to Yuzhno-Sakhalinsk by numerous buses (R70, 1½ hours).

From Korsakov, 35km south of Yuzhno, regular ferries run to Wakkanai on Hokkaido between May and October. The cheapest one-way ticket is US$150; bookings can be made through **Sakhalin Fantastic** (☎/fax 42 09 17; e sfl@sakhalin.ru; ul Lenina 154). There are also regular buses from Yuzhno to Korsakov, but they terminate a fair way from the port – you'll have to catch another bus to it.

Getting Around

Although Yuzhno is compact enough to walk around, *mikriki* (minivan buses) run regular routes about the city, many departing from in front of the train station on ploshchad Lenina. Bus Nos 63 and 68 run to the airport (R7, 25 minutes). A taxi from the train station to the airport will cost around R200.

SOUTHERN SAKHALIN
Lake Tunaycha
Озеро Тунайча

One of the nicest places to go to from Yuzhno-Sakhalinsk is the Lake Tunaycha region in the extreme southeast, where there's an archipelago of lakes, some only separated from the sea by narrow causeways a few metres wide. Many birds come here during the migrating seasons and the coastline is favoured by seals. Amber gets washed up on the beaches, and it's a favourite place for locals to go crab-hunting and camping.

To get to Tunaycha, drive southwards out of Yuzhno-Sakhalinsk, past the right-hand turn for the airport, and at the next crossroads turn left towards Okhotskoe. It's about 45km.

Yuzhno-Sakhalinsk Mud Volcano
Южно-Сажалинский Грязевой Вулкан
Sakhalin doesn't actually have any volcanoes, but this six-hectare field of volcanic mud appeared in the midst of the forest, some 30km north of Yuzhno-Sakhalinsk near the village of Klyuchi, in 1959. Another big eruption of mud occurred in 2002, following an earthquake in the region, and the ground here still bubbles with small fumaroles. It's a striking spot and, although you can drive up here along a hill track, it would also make for a good hike for a couple of hours, as long as you had a guide.

Korsakov
Корсаков
Thirty-five kilometres due south of Yuzhno-Sakhalinsk is the grimy port of Korsakov, centre of the island's hugely profitable fishing industry, and the place to come for the ferry to Wakkanai on Hokkaido (see Getting There & Away under Yuzhno-Sakhalinsk earlier). There's no other reason to come here, but if you have to stay, **Hotel Alfa** (*☎/fax 42435-4 10 10; ul Krasnoflotskaya 31; singles/doubles with breakfast US$75/110*) is a modern place, with a cosy bar, that's comfortable enough.

Kholmsk & Nevelsk
Холмск и Невелск
Southern Sakhalin's other major port, Kholmsk, is 40km due west of the capital. The only reason to come here is if you're taking a ferry to or from Vanino on the mainland. **Hotel Kholmsk** (*☎ 42433-5 28 54, fax 5 18 24; ul Sovietskaya 60; singles/doubles from R300/400*) is a decent place to stay in case of delays or schedule changes to the ferry. Kholmsk's bus station is in front of the passenger shipping terminal.

From Kholmsk, you can take a bus to other fishing towns along the south coast, including Nevelsk, from where charter boats sail to Moneron Island (see later). **Hotel Nevelskaya** (*☎ 42436-6 23 36; ul Lenina 2A; singles & doubles R350*), across from the bus station, is comfortable and clean if you're inclined to spend the night.

NORTHERN SAKHALIN
Despite the oil and gas wealth that lies offshore, the north of Sakhalin is littered with the decaying remnants of communist times; it's a place best visited by those with a taste for destruction.

Although there are around three flights a week to Okha (R4000, 1½ hours), the main route north is by train, running up the spine of the island past rusting factories, ghost towns and long stretches of desolate taiga, parts of which are dead following forest fires.

Tikhii
Тихиш
Driving north two hours from Yuzhno-Sakhalinsk brings you to Tikhii, where the Zhdanko Mountains drop into the ocean in volcanic-rock formations and hardened lava flows. Among the most dramatic of Sakhalin coastlines, the area can be explored on day hiking tours (around US$150 with food and guides) or longer camping trips; contact **Sakhalin-Kurils Tour & Tourist Information Agency** (*☎/fax 72 81 91; ᴡ www.geocities.com/iatur; ul Dzerzhinskogo 23*).

Aleksandrovsk-Sakhalinsky
Александровск-Сахалинск
About two-thirds of up the island, the train stops at Tymovsk (the station for the town of Tymovskoe). Here, a bus usually waits before departing for Aleksandrovsk-Sakhalinsky on the west coast (R52, two hours). This small town, one of the first Russian settlements on Sakhalin, was where Chekhov spent most of his time during his visit in 1890; the house in which he stayed is now a museum, but you will see little more there than at the Chekhov Museum in Yuzhno-Sakhalinsk. The rugged coastline here is also an attraction.

Nogliki
Ногликш
The train terminates at this drab town, which hardly seems to have benefited from the billions of dollars being sunk just offshore, in the form of giant oil-drilling platforms anchored

into the shelf to keep them from being tossed around in the icy, fast-moving waters.

Only if you miss the bus north, or if you're connected with the oil industry, might you want to stay here. The cheap option is **Hotel Severyanka** (☎ 42444-2 28; doubles R367.50), in the grey, wooden building 100m directly ahead from the train station, past the **bufet**, which is as good a place to hang out and get some food as anywhere else in town.

The centre of Nogliki is about 5km from the station (minivans and shared taxis for R7 run there regularly). **Hotel Nogliki** (☎ 42444-9 68 05, fax 9 68 65; ul Sovetskaya 6; singles/ doubles US$82/97) is comfortable; the inflated prices are because of its oil-industry guests. The café here suffices and has an English menu.

From Yuzhno-Sakhalinsk, the best train to catch is the daily No 1 leaving at 9.05pm (R650, 14½ hours); the No 2 returns to Yuzhno at 4.40pm.

Okha & Nekrasovka
Оха и Некрасовка
On Monday, Tuesday and Thursday a 6WD Kamaz bus usually (but not always) waits for the train to arrive in Nogliki before taking off along the dirt road 250km north (R250, five to seven hours) to Okha. The northernmost town on the island, and another base for the oil industry, it's possibly the ugliest town in Russia; the giant apple and geometrical stencils on the prefab buildings don't help.

One possible reason for heading this way is to visit the village of Nekrasovka, 28km west of Okha. Home to around 1200 Nivkhi, of whom there are said to be less than 2000 left on the whole island, Nekrasovka was created in the 1970s as a state fish farm – the Nivkhi are traditionally fisherfolk. There's a small museum here and it may also be worth visiting during the traditional holiday festivals in early January and mid-to-late June. But at any other time it's depressing.

If you are planning to head up this way, it's best to arrange a tour with one of the Yuzhno-Sakhalinsk agencies listed in that section earlier, who should be able to help you make the most of the trip.

MONERON ISLAND
Остров Монерон
In the Tatar Strait, 50km southwest of Sakhalin, is the largely uninhabited Moneron

Island. Around the 30-sq-km island is a marine park, where the subtropical waters are a boon to divers and snorkellers. Many species of birds flock here too, including the long billed guillemot and black-tailed gulls.

The island, reached by charter boats from Nevelsk (see Southern Sakhalin earlier), is best visited on a group tour; inquire at the Yuzhno-Sakhalinsk tour agencies about diving tours here.

KURIL ISLANDS
КУРИЛСКИЕ ОСТРОВА
Discovered and first charted in 1739 as part of Russia's Great Northern Expedition, the Kurils are a chain of 56 islands, arced like stepping stones between the southern tip of Kamchatka and the northern Japanese island of Hokkaido. Geographically, the islands seem to form a link between Russia and Japan, but politically they are more of a wedge, driving the two powers apart.

A treaty of 1855 divided possession of the chain between Russia and Japan; the latter received the islands of Habomai, Shikotan, Kunashir and Etorofu. A second treaty, in 1875, gave Tokyo sovereignty over the whole lot in exchange for recognising the Russians' right to Sakhalin. But then, in the last days of WWII, the Soviets reneged on the deal and invaded the Kurils. For three years the new Russian settlers and the existing Japanese residents lived side by side, but in 1948 Stalin ordered all the Japanese to leave. The Kurils have been a diplomatic minefield between the two nations ever since and, technically, Japan and Russia have never concluded a peace treaty after WWII because of them.

The islands, which form part of the Pacific 'Ring of Fire', are actually the tips of a volcanic mountain range. Among the peaks protruding from the sea are around 40 active volcanoes, many of which erupt frequently and violently. Of these, Mt Tyatya is considered the most picturesque. The islands are stunningly beautiful, with circular azure-blue lagoons, steaming rivers and hot springs, and some spectacular cliff formations, notably the Stolbchaty Cape.

The main centres of habitation are Severo-Kurilsk on Paramushir Island, Kurilsk on Iturup Island and Yuzhno-Kurilsk on Kunashir, the southernmost and most accessible of the island chain. Here you'll find the **Energiya Hotel**, where most tour groups will be put up.

Getting There & Away

This can be tricky. First you need separate permission to visit the islands; any of the Yuzhno-Sakhalinsk tour agencies should be able to arrange this for you (it takes about a week) and organise a guided tour.

There are flights around four times a week from Yuzhno-Sakhalinsk to Yuzhno-Kurilsk on Kunashir (R4000, one hour 40 minutes). However the islands are often wreathed in a thick fog, making airborne approaches impossible, so you have to be prepared to hang around for days waiting for the weather to improve.

The alternative is to sail on one of the irregular boats that depart from Korsakov, Sakhalin's southern port, taking a day to reach Yuzhno-Kurilsk. It's not a ferry service but fare-paying passengers are taken – for enquiries, contact the **sea terminal information desk** *(☎ 42435-2 23 52; per Reydovy 2)* in Korsakov.

Magadan

Магадан

☎ 41322 • pop 152,000 • Moscow time plus 8 hours

Once known as the 'gateway to hell', Magadan's awful origins spring from the great terrors of the Stalin era. In 1932 gold was discovered in the Kolyma region. A new administration, Dalstroy, was brought into being, under the auspices of the NKVD, to excavate the gold and other precious metals. The same year, the first prisoner-laden ships arrived at a bare, swampy site on Nagaeva Bay, on the inhospitable northern shore of the Sea of Okhotsk. The prisoners built docks and piers for the following ships, administrative blocks for their overseers and barracks for their guards. Eventually – though not before winter had come and thousands had died from working knee-deep in deathly cold waters and mud – they built their own flimsy accommodation.

Completed, the newly named town of Magadan served as a marshalling point for the human cargo destined for the hinterland gold fields of Kolyma. For more information, see the boxed text 'Russia's Auschwitz'.

The town's trade in human lives began to end in the 1950s, with the death of Stalin. The watchtowers and high, barbed-wire-topped fences came down, and the headquarters of Dalstroy were destroyed, as were the wooden barracks. All were replaced with civic brick buildings – ugly but innocuous. Today Magadan remains bleak, but no more so than most other northern Siberian settlements. Gold is still mined here, as are silver, tin and coal.

If your interest is not in contemporary Russian history, the main reason to come here is to take advantage of the fishing and ecotour possibilities opening up in the area. For more information on these, contact **DVS-Tour** *(☎ 2 32 96, fax 2 11 95; W www.dvs-tour.ru; pr Lenina 3)*. Staff here can also show you round what is left from the Dalstroy era.

On the approach into town from the airport, 60km northeast, you'll pass the striking **Mask of Sorrow** monument, built in memory of those who perished in Magadan's camps. In the town itself, conventional sights include a **Regional Museum** *(pr Karla Marksa 55)* with exhibits portraying life in the camps as well as the usual range of stuffed animals, and a **Geological & Mineralogical Museum** *(ul Portovaya 16)*.

Places to Stay & Eat

The gloomy **Hotel Magadan** *(☎ 9 95 57, fax 9 93 20; ul Proletarskaya 8; singles/doubles from R300/500)*, conveniently located across from the bus station, is reasonably cheap and has a bar.

For more comfort, try **Hotel Business Center** *(☎ 5 89 44, fax 5 82 23; ul Proletarskaya 84V; singles/doubles R450/700)*, 2km south of the bus station, which has clean, well-furnished rooms; or the more modern **Hotel VM-Tsentralnaya** *(☎ 4 13 22, fax 9 76 43; ul Lenina 13; singles/doubles with breakfast US$24/31)*. Both of these hotels have restaurants.

Getting There & Away

The main way in and out of Magadan is by air. There are weekly connections to Moscow, Khabarovsk (R5070, 2½ hours, twice weekly) and Vladivostok (three hours, weekly). There's also a weekly flight to Anchorage, Alaska, which goes via Petropavlovsk-Kamchatsky; for details, see Getting There & Away in the Petropavlovsk-Kamchatsky section later in this chapter.

Those interested in more extreme travel might want to contemplate a road trip to

Russia's Auschwitz

If Kolyma isn't a name as chillingly recognisable as Auschwitz, Belsen or Dachau, it is not because the horrors there were any less awful, but because they were perpetrated by a secretive government on its own citizens and because they took place in an isolated, ice-locked region, 9000km from Moscow.

At any one moment, the camps in Kolyma held about half a million occupants. Kolyma consumed prisoners – those who survived the journey there. Prisoners were shipped up, thousands at a time, from Vladivostok, where they'd been waiting in transit camps after crossing Russia crammed into cattle cars so tightly that some died of suffocation. The sea passage took a further eight or 10 days and was, if anything, an even more deadly journey. One ship left Vladivostok too late in the year and became stuck fast in the ice, finally reaching the Kolyma coast nine months later. Not one of its thousands of prisoners survived. Those aboard another prison ship revolted and the guards held them back with hoses, filling the hold with water. It was 40°C below zero. The 3000 prisoners were delivered to Magadan entombed in ice.

From Magadan's harbour the already wasted prisoners, little more than living skeletons, were marched along the infamous 'road of bones' to one of the region's 100 or more camps. Many of these were simply named by their distance from the start of the march: the 23km camp, the 72km camp, the 220km camp.

Once in the camps, most of the prisoners dug for gold 14 hours a day, barely sustained by a daily diet of 700g of bread and an evening bowl of cabbage soup. High daily quotas were set for the amount of gold they had to recover; in the attempt to meet them, prisoners often died of exhaustion. It's estimated that for every kilogram of gold mined, one man died.

★★★

Magadan along the Kolyma Highway from Yakutsk, more than 1500km to the east. Known as the 'road of bones' (for the prisoners who died building it), the highway really only appears as a through road in winter. It's a very rough journey and most travellers follow the route by hitching rides with truck drivers. Check out the website **w** www .turtleexpedition.com for notes on a road journey made from Magadan to Yakutsk.

Kamchatskaya Region
Камчатская Областъ

An adventure traveller's dream, the 1000km-long Kamchatka Peninsula is one of Russia's most scenically spectacular regions, a place to climb up or heliski down active volcanoes, fish for wild salmon, or trek into the wilderness in search of bears or reindeer herds. Dubbed the 'land of fire and ice', Kamchatka, separated from the mainland by the Sea of Okhotsk, is hyperactively volcanic, with terrain that bubbles, spurts and spews in a manner that suggests that here, Creation hasn't quite finished yet.

The region has 200-plus volcanoes in varying stages of activity, some long extinct and grassed over with aquamarine crater lakes, others among the world's most volatile (see the boxed text 'Kamchatka's Volcanoes' later). The volcanoes are often surrounded by lava fields, and these lunar-like, pocked cinder landscapes served as the testing grounds for Russia's moon-walking vehicles. The thermal activity deep below the Earth's surface also produces numerous hot springs and geysers, with the most spectacular examples found in the Valley of the Geysers in the Kronotsky National Park.

Away from the volcanoes, Kamchatka is covered by mixed forests and plains of giant grasses, home to a vast array of wildlife, including between 10,000 and 20,000 brown bears and herds of reindeer, as well as pristine rivers that are the spawning grounds for many types of salmon.

Don't skimp on time or expense in visiting Kamchatka, as the best scenic attractions are well away from Petropavlovsk-Kamchatsky, the regional capital. To get to most places, a helicopter flight will be necessary or some serious hiking has to be embarked upon, requiring nights of wilderness camping. Even at the height of summer the weather can be fickle and travel plans can change from day to day. The help of a local tour agency or guide is crucial.

As a legacy of the Soviet era, when it was very much off limits, foreign visitors are still supposed to have an invitation specifically for Kamchatka. In practice you're unlikely to run into problems, especially if you're on a tour where all the paperwork is being taken care of. To avoid possible problems, include Petropavlovsk-Kamchatsky as one of your proposed destinations when applying for your visa and hope it makes it onto the issued document.

History

The man credited with the discovery of Kamchatka, in 1696, was the half-Cossack, half-Yakut Vladimir Atlasov who, like most explorers of the time, was out to find new lands to plunder. He established two forts on the Kamchatka River that became bases for the Russian traders who followed, looking to exact tithes of furs from the locals.

The native Koryaki, Chukchi and Itelmeni warred with their new self-appointed overlords, but fared badly and their numbers were greatly diminished. Today, the remnants of the Chukchi nation inhabit the isolated northeast of Kamchatka, while the Koryaki live on the west coast of the peninsula with their territorial capital at Palana. There's also a community of Even, related to the Evenki of the Sakha Republic (see earlier in this chapter), based around Esso, the central Kamchatka village they migrated to 150 years ago. Some of these peoples still maintain a traditional existence as reindeer-herders and sea hunters, the animals being a source of food and raw materials for clothing. While much of their culture and language have been lost, the tradition of storytelling through mime, dance and song has survived; see the boxed text 'The Dancers of Esso' later in the chapter.

Kamchatka was long regarded as the least hospitable place in the Russian Empire – a land of primeval wilderness inhabited by a few primitives, half a year's journey away and with nothing to offer beyond a dwindling supply of furs. When Alaska was sold off in 1867, Kamchatka might also have been up for grabs if the Americans had shown enough interest. Some 53 years later there was a taker – an American named Washington Baker Vanderlip. He was offered a 60-year conces-

sion by Lenin but the two couldn't come to terms and the deal never went through.

During the Cold War, Kamchatka took on new strategic importance and foreign interest was definitely no longer welcome. It became a base for military airfields and early-warning radar systems, while the coastline sheltered parts of the Soviet Pacific Fleet. Isolated regions of Kamchatka also served as target areas for missile testings. No foreigners, nor even nonresident Russians, were allowed anywhere near the peninsula.

Today the peninsula is open to all, but, with the Soviet-era subsidies long gone, more people are leaving than arriving. The most recent figures show that 380,200 people live in Kamchatka – less than one per square kilometre. Petropavlovsk-Kamchatsky is the second-most expensive place in the Russian Federation (after even more remote Anadyr on the Arctic Chukotka Peninsula) for the average basket of food.

Getting Around

Locals say that on Kamchatka there are no roads, only directions. This isn't strictly true (there are two daily buses from Petropavlovsk

Kamchatka's Volcanoes

The Kamchatka Peninsula is the northern link in the 2000km Kuril–Kamchatka island arc. This region contains 68 active volcanoes, over 10% of the total found on land anywhere on Earth. This arc is part of the 'Ring of Fire', a string of volcanoes that encircles the Pacific Ocean.

The native peoples of Kamchatka are intimately familiar with the peninsula's history of continuous, violent rebirth. They have always feared the volcanoes, whose peaks they believed to be inhabited by mountain spirits known as gomuls. By night, the gomuls took to the sky and hunted whales, returning home with leviathans impaled on each finger. They would then roast the whales. This is why the volcanoes lit up at night.

Until the late Pliocene (approximately 2.5 million years ago), what is now Kamchatka was little more than a pool of magma waiting beneath the floor of the Pacific Ocean. When this magma finally erupted, it formed submarine mountain ranges. These eventually reached the ocean surface, where they formed an island chain much like the Aleutian Islands of today. Eventually this volcanic activity slowed, and as the Pleistocene epoch dawned, the balance of power was put back in the hands of the Pacific. Waves washed over Kamchatka, levelling its relief.

New basaltic flood eruptions eventually brought Kamchatka back above the sea, forming vast volcanic plateaus that connected the islands into a single landmass linked to Asia. A period of relative peace followed. A visitor to Kamchatka at the time would have found a steaming, hilly landscape resembling present-day Iceland.

This calm was only temporary. Kamchatka's plateaus swelled with the pressure of gas-saturated magma, struggling to break loose. When water reached the magma through giant fissures in the earth, a new round of eruptions released vast floods of lava and ash, levelling the mountainous landscape and turning Kamchatka into a dull grey flatland.

As the huge magma reservoirs emptied, the Earth's surface began to sink, forming giant depressions. This gave birth to the peninsula's present landscape, where deep rift valleys cut between mountain ridges and plateaus.

Today's volcanism is a repeat, on a smaller scale, of these earlier events. Modern volcanoes are located atop the rifts that fed early volcanic belts, but cover smaller areas and are more moderate in their eruptive powers. Nevertheless, the volcanic power of Kamchatka's 29 active volcanoes is still spectacular. Mt Klyuchevskaya is the highest active volcano in Eurasia (at 4750m) and one of the largest in the world. On average it erupts 60 million tonnes of basalt a year, or 2.5% of the material ejected by all 850 active land volcanoes. When it erupted in October 1994 it sent so much ash into the air that international flights from North America to Southeast Asia were disrupted. The peninsula's most reliable volcano is Karymsky, which has been erupting continuously since 1996.

The animals of Kamchatka have turned the harsh volcanic environment to their advantage. Brown bears are often seen bathing in the peninsula's sulphurous hot springs (sometimes competing with humans for the privilege). Like humans, bears cherish the hot springs' curative properties – the sulphurous water drives off fleas, ticks and other infestations. Bears also appear to be genuinely fearless of volcanoes. During the eruption of Mt Karymsky in 1997, a volcanologist who ventured to the summit during a quiet period reported seeing fresh bear tracks near the edge of the crater; what a bear was doing at the summit of a volcano during an eruption is anyone's guess.

For more information, visit **W** www.KamchatkaPeninsula.com.

Andrew Logan

to Esso, which, depending on the condition of the road, take eight to 12 hours to get there), but it's a fact that if you use road transport you won't get very far.

Small planes fly from Petropavlovsk-Kamchatsky go to some of the larger settlements, such as to Ust-Kamchatsk, a small fishing town at the mouth of the Kamchatka River, but generally it's helicopters you'll be flying in around here. These operate like minibuses, ferrying mainly tourists, scientists, volcanologists and hunters between remote settlements, isolated cabins and scenic wonders.

For a one-hour ride in the smallest Mi-2 helicopter (which takes a maximum of six people) you're looking at US$400. To use one of the 20-seater Mi-8 choppers would set you back a minimum of US$3000 for three hours. Even areas that are close enough not to necessitate helicopter transfers often, because of the lack of paved roads, require some kind of tracked all-terrain vehicle, or at least a 4WD – and these don't come cheaply either. The tour agencies listed under Organised Tours can help arrange both helicopters and suitable road transport.

Organised Tours While independent travel on Kamchatka isn't impossible, taking a tour so you can split the transportation costs, or hiring a guide makes sense. It's also the safest option; many locals have died exploring Kamchatka, whether overcome by sulphurous fumes on the volcanoes, crashing through thin crusts into boiling pits below, or being mauled by a bear. This is not a place to explore on your own.

Some advance preparation is necessary – you can't just turn up and be assured of finding a place on a tour. Even when you've arrived, conditions are constantly changing. The volcano you were planning to climb may be erupting, and bad weather can cancel a helicopter flight or a boat trip at any moment. You'll need to be flexible.

Based in Petropavlovsk-Kamchatsky, the following agencies are usually the same ones the foreign agencies contract, so going to them directly is almost always cheaper. Also see the Siberia & the Russian Far East Getting There & Away chapter for overseas agents that cover Kamchatka.

The Lost World (*☎/fax 4152-19 83 28; w www.travelkamchatka.com; 4/1-4 Frolova ul)* is a highly professional operation with lots of experience. It specialises in smaller group tours and offers many different itineraries, including experiences such as winter dog-sledge tours out of Esso to meet the reindeer-herders, and major treks through central and southern Kamchatka.

Kamchatintour (*☎ 41522-7 10 34, 7 37 76, fax 4152-11 80 07; e inform@kamchatintour.ru; ul Leningradskaya 124b)* is another long-running, reliable agency. It offers many shorter tours and can put together individual itineraries.

Lena & Friends (*☎ 4152-11 22 38, fax 11 21 98; w www.lenaandfriends.com; ul Sovetskaya 18)* also runs the full range of activity-based (skiing, rafting) and cultural tours on the peninsula. Its 14-day tour is US$1000.

Alpindustriya-Kamchatka (*☎ 41522-3 02 46, fax 7 24 89; e malkov@mail.iks.ru; pr 50 let Oktyabrya 22; open 11am-7pm Mon-Fri, 11am-4pm Sat)* is mainly a camping equipment store where you can rent gear, a real plus if you don't want to be lugging this stuff with you across Russia. It can also arrange various excursions, including horse-riding trips in the hot springs area of Paratunka for R150 per hour.

The Wild Salmon Centre (*☎ 4152-11 63 26, fax 41531-6 97 14; e wsc.mail.iks.ru; office 319, ul Naberezhnaya 30)* can arrange fishing tours and sort out the necessary permits.

Also, based in St Petersburg, **Wild Russia** (*☎/fax 812-25 93 30; w www.wildrussia.spb.ru; Nevsky pr 22/24)* offers 11-day tours to Kamchatka, starting at US$1180.

PETROPAVLOVSK-KAMCHATSKY
ПЕТРОПАВЛОВСК-КАМЧАТСКИЙ
☎ 41522, 4152 for six-digit numbers • pop 205,500 • Moscow time plus 9 hours
Strung out for 25km around Avacha Bay, Petropavlovsk-Kamchatsky is Kamchatka's administrative centre. As beautiful as Avacha Bay is, it's the two volcanoes, Mt Avachinskaya and Mt Koryakskaya, looming over the city that will first grab your attention. Avachinskaya last erupted in 1991, but the town's residents, living in jerry-built Soviet structures, fear earthquakes far more than they fear the smoky mountains.

One of the oldest Far East cities, Petropavlovsk was founded in 1741 by Vitus Bering, the Danish-born Russian captain who discovered the straits that bear his name. The town was named for Bering's two ships, the *Svyatoy Pyotr* (St Peter) and *Svyatoy Pavel* (St Paul); 'Kamchatsky' was added to distinguish it from all the other Petropavlovsks. It became the tsars' major Pacific sea port and was used as the base for explorations that turned up the Aleutian Islands and Alaska. A slow developer, in 1866 the settlement still consisted of little more than a cluster of log cabins and a small, green-domed church.

There were unlikely visitors in 1779, when Captain Clerke sailing under the British flag entered Petropavlovsk harbour in command of the *Discovery* and the *Resolution*. These

RUSSIAN FAR EAST

PETROPAVLOVSK-KAMCHATSKY

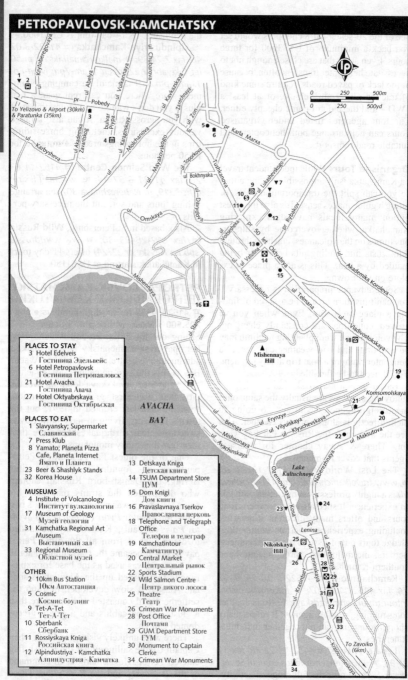

To Yelizovo & Airport (30km) & Paratunka (35km)

0   250   500m
0   250   500yd

AVACHA BAY

Mishennaya Hill

Lake Kultuchnoye

Komsomolskaya pl

pl Lenina

Nikolskaya Hill

To Zavoiko (6km)

PLACES TO STAY
3 Hotel Edelveis
  Гостиница Эдельвейс
6 Hotel Petropavlovsk
  Гостиница Петропавловск
21 Hotel Avacha
  Гостиница Авача
27 Hotel Oktyabrskaya
  Гостиница Октябрьская

PLACES TO EAT
1 Slavyansky; Supermarket
  Славянский
7 Press Klub
9 Yamato; Planeta Pizza
  Cafe, Planeta Internet
  Ямато и Планета
23 Beer & Shashlyk Stands
32 Korea House

MUSEUMS
4 Institute of Volcanology
  Институт вулканологии
17 Museum of Geology
  Музей геологии
31 Kamchatka Regional Art
  Museum
  Выставочный зал
33 Regional Museum
  Областной музей

OTHER
2 10km Bus Station
  10км Автостанция
5 Cosmic
  Космис боулинг
9 Tet-A-Tet
  Тет-А-Тет
10 Sberbank
  Сбербанк
11 Rossiyskaya Kniga
  Российская книга
12 Alpindustriya - Kamchatka
  Алпиндустрия - Камчатка

13 Detskaya Kniga
  Детская книга
14 TSUM Department Store
  ЦУМ
15 Dom Knigi
  Дом книги
16 Pravaslavnaya Tserkov
  Православная церковь
18 Telephone and Telegraph
  Office
  Телефон и телеграф
19 Kamchatintour
  Камчатинтур
20 Central Market
  Центральный рынок
22 Sports Stadium
24 Wild Salmon Centre
  Центр дикого лосося
25 Theatre
  Театр
26 Crimean War Monuments
28 Post Office
  Почтамп
29 GUM Department Store
  ГУМ
30 Monument to Captain
  Clerke
34 Crimean War Monuments

were formerly the ships of Captain James Cook, the famed explorer who had met his death in Hawaii two years earlier. Clerke was continuing Cook's work, with an intended expedition to the Arctic, but shortly after setting out from Petropavlovsk he was stricken with consumption and returned there to die that same year. Some 75 years later, in August 1854, more British sailed into Avacha Bay, this time accompanied by the French and intent on conquest of a less benign nature. This seaborne Crimean War invasion was successfully and unexpectedly repulsed by the small Petropavlovsk garrison.

During the Soviet era the town retained its military role and became a sizable Pacific Fleet submarine base, however its present prosperity is owed completely to the fishing industry. Rusting Petropavlovsk trawlers bring in a million tonnes of fish a year, of which nearly half is sold to Japan for hard currency.

Orientation

Petropavlovsk is strung along one main axis, the road that runs in from the airport 30km east. It enters the city limits as prospekt Pobedy and changes its name no less than 11 times as it snakes around the rippling contours of the bayside hills before finishing up at a small fishing harbour, Rakovaya (Seashell) Bay, on the southern edge of the town. Although nominally ploshchad Lenina is the centre of town, there is no one focal point, but instead a succession of little knots strung along the main artery.

Information

There is a **main post office** (ul Leninskaya 56) and a **main telephone and telegraph office** (ul Vladivostokskaya 5).

You can change money at **Sberbank** (ul Lukashevskogo 2; open 9am-9pm Mon-Fri, 9am-5pm Sat & Sun). Hotel Petropavlovsk has a cash machine in its lobby which accepts overseas cards.

The Internet can be accessed round the clock at the **Planeta** (Planeta shopping centre, ul Lukashevskogo 5) and across the road at **Tet-A-Tet** (ul Lukashevskogo 4); both charge R60 per hour.

The best bookshops, with maps and postcards, are **Dom Knigi** (pr 50 let Oktyabrya 7), **Rossiyskaya Kniga** (pr 50 let Oktyabrya) and **Detskaya Kniga** (pr 50 let Oktyabrya 17).

Things to See & Do

A **boat tour** of Avacha Bay is a must – it's the best way to view one of the most beautiful natural harbours in the world and the fascinating rock formations around it. The agencies listed earlier can all organise such tours, usually held on large boats that can make it out into the sometimes-rough waters of the Pacific and to the tiny island of Starichkoe, a haven for bird life.

Pop into the **Regional Museum** (☎ 12 54 11; ul Leninskaya 20; admission R100; open 10am-5pm Wed-Sun), housed in an attractive half-timbered building overlooking the bay, to view a well-presented history of Kamchatka. There are good examples of native clothing and implements, and an excellent exhibition of wood-block prints depicting local customs, legends and landscapes.

If you don't speak Russian, a visit to the **Institute of Volcanology** (☎ 5 95 46; bulvar Piypa 9; open 10am-6pm Mon-Fri), which has a one-room exhibition on Kamchatka's volcanoes, is best arranged with an interpreter so you can understand the detailed lecture that comes with the tour.

Somewhat more accessible to non-Russian speakers is the **Museum of Geology** (☎ 3 98 67; ul Beringa 117; admission free; open 9am-4pm Mon-Fri), which has several rooms packed with cabinets bearing many examples of Kamchatka's minerals and ores.

Overlooking Avacha Bay is the onion-domed Orthodox church **Pravaslavnaya Tserkov** (ul Staritsna). It is a newly constructed building and quite attractive both inside and outside.

It's pleasant to stroll around the original heart of the city from ploshchad Lenina (sometimes called ploshchad Teatralnaya) up Nikolskaya Hill, where there's a small chapel and several **monuments** to those who fell in the failed Crimean War invasion in 1854. Descending from the hill to ulitsa Leninskaya, there's a small obelisk, a **monument to Captain Clerke**, erected by a British delegation in 1913, in front of the classically styled regional administration building (ul Leninskaya 14).

Places to Stay & Eat

None of the hotels in Petropavlovsk are particularly flash, but all include breakfast in their rates. The tour agencies mentioned earlier should be able to arrange homestays and flat rentals from around US$15 per night.

Hotel Edelveis (☎ 5 33 24, fax 5 74 19; e idelves@mail.iks.ru; pr Pobedy 27; singles & doubles from US$27) has small, but quite acceptable, renovated rooms and a café.

Hotel Avacha (☎/fax 11 08 08; w www .iks.ru/~avacha; ul Leningradskaya 61; singles/ doubles US$38/60) has a reasonably central location and is often used by tour agencies.

Hotel Oktyabrskaya (☎ 11 26 84, fax 11 26 80; e hoteloct@svyaz.kamchatka.su; ul Sovetskaya 51; singles/doubles US$48/54), in the prettiest part of town, has clean rooms and polite staff.

Just about the best choice (and certainly the most expensive) is Hotel Petropavlovsk (☎ 5 03 74, fax 11 03 14; e adm@olghot. kamchatka.su; pr Karla Marxa 31; singles/ doubles US$78/84), a squat concrete block facing the volcanoes. The rooms are reasonably pleasant. Its cheerful café-bar serves decent, well-priced food from an English-language menu, but service can be slow.

Slavyansky (☎ 11 05 16; pr Pobedy 22; open noon-5pm & 6.30pm-2am daily) is a smart restaurant with an extensive menu including many seafood dishes. In the evening there's often live music. Next door is a supermarket (open 9am-9pm daily), where you can pick up most self-catering supplies.

Korea House (☎ 12 11 93; ul Leninskaya 26) does decent Korean food, while Yamato (☎ 16 77 00; Planeta shopping centre, ul Lukashevskogo 5) is not too bad at rustling up Japanese dishes; it also has good-value set lunches for under R150.

In the same complex as Yamato is Planeta (☎ 3 36 53; open 10am-11pm daily), serving tasty pizzas, while next door Press Klub (☎ 6 09 38; ul Lukashevskogo 5), in the Argumenty i Fakty newspaper building, has good food, atmosphere and cocktails.

In summer, beer and shashlyk stands set up along the small beach beside ploshchad Lenina.

Entertainment

Cosmic (☎ 9 49 90), a bowling and disco complex next to the Hotel Petropavlovsk, is the liveliest place in town. Entry to the disco ranges from R50 to R150 depending on the night, while a bowling lane for the hour starts at R600.

Shopping

For local crafts and souvenirs, try GUM (ul Leninskaya 54; open 9am-7pm Mon-Fri,

10am-4pm Sat) or the Kamchatka Regional Art Museum (☎ 12 37 07; ul Leninskaya 36; admission R60; open 10am-6pm daily), which is more of an art gallery and art-supply shop. The central market at Komsomolskaya ploshchad, opposite the Hotel Avacha, is also good for a browse.

Getting There & Away

There are flights to/from Moscow (R9300, nine hours, daily), Khabarovsk (from R3700 to R4100, three hours, daily), Vladivostok (R3700, three hours, four weekly) and St Petersburg (R9340, 10 hours, weekly). Also, a weekly flight from Anchorage, Alaska (US$1300, four hours) stops en route to Magadan (R5100, one hour 20 minutes).

Getting Around

Buses (R5) run from the avtostantsiya desyaty kilometr ('10km station'), on prospekt Pobedy at the northern end of town, to the Regional Museum. Mikriki provide most of the rest of the town's transportation.

All buses and mikriki for the airport (R10, 45 minutes) depart from the 10km station; take anything marked 'Aeroport' or 'Yelizovo', which is the name of the settlement close by the airport. To get into town from the airport, catch any bus at the stop just across the parking lot from the main entrance. A taxi will cost around R300.

AROUND PETROPAVLOVSK-KAMCHATSKY
Paratunka
Паратунка

At Paratunka, west of Avacha Bay and 25km south of Yelizovo, the airport town, is a scattering of sanatoria and small resorts all trumpeting the curative effects of the local hot springs. Tour companies often build a stay here into their programs and, if you're looking for somewhere quiet and leafy as a base, then it's worth inquiring about the options. One place you may end up at is the Army Sanatorium (☎/fax 4152-11 16 95) – not nearly as dreadful as it sounds, sporting comfortably renovated rooms (but rather bland canteen meals).

Also based out in Paratunka is musician/ farmer Sasha Yasterebov, an eccentric, talented fellow whom it's possible to visit for a tour of his modest mosquito-infested homestead where he gathers the local plants to make tasty repasts. An evening meal here in a tepee will end up with a rousing sing-song and piano recital from Sasha and his son – all huge fun. To visit, make arrangements with one of the tour agencies listed earlier under Organised Tours.

Mikriki (R15 to R20) leave regularly from both Petropavlovsk and Yelizovo for the public hot springs in Paratunka – giant outdoor concrete pools which are not particularly attractive. With private transport and a local guide it's better to head for a set of natural springs some 15km farther south, on the slopes of **Goryachaya**.

Mt Avachinskaya & Mt Koryakskaya

Торы Авачинская и Коряская

It's possible to ascend the slopes of Mt Avachinskaya (2741m) and Mt Koryakskaya (3456m), the two volcanoes that loom over Petropavlovsk. The foot of both slopes begins about 30km from the town, but there's no public transportation there, so you need to enlist the help of a local agency. The 2km ascent of Avachinskaya takes from six to eight hours depending on your hiking experience; go with a guide because of fissures in the glaciers, high winds and thick fog that often covers the steep upper slopes of the mountain in the late afternoon. Koryakskaya is more difficult and should not be attempted by climbers who are inexperienced.

Activities

If you charter a car south of central Petropavlovsk along the bay to Zavoiko, you will eventually hit a **black-sand beach**, one of the area's nicest, and a good spot from which to spot puffins and other sea birds in the bay. At the northern end of Avacha Bay, Mokhovaya is a village where you may be able to witness **sea lions** – they gather around the local fish factory looking for a free lunch from the waste the factory dumps back in the bay.

For rafting, the **Bystraya River** is the easiest to get to; the most-travelled section is the 120km southwest-flowing stretch between the village of Malki, 80km west of Yelizovo, and the Ust-Bolsheretsk bridge just before the Bystraya empties into the Sea of Okhotsk. The name means 'fast', but there are only a few rapids, and the journey takes a leisurely two days.

NORTHERN KAMCHATKA

Valley of the Geysers & Uzon Caldera

Долина Гейзеров

About 150km north of Petropavlovsk and most commonly accessed by helicopter is the spectacular Valley of the Geysers (Dolina Geyzerov). Discovered in 1941 by geologist Tatyana Ustinova and her local guide Anisifor Krypemin, the 6km-long valley cut through by the Geysernaya River is part of the protected Kronotsky State Biospheric Reserve. Here, around 200 geothermal pressure valves sporadically blast steam, mud and water heavenwards. The setting is exquisite and walking tours along duckboards take you past some of the more colourful and active geysers. The valley is closed for a 40-day period between May and June because of migrating birds.

Krechet (☎ 6 43 47, fax 11 16 33; Ⓦ www .krechet.com) has the concession to fly helicopters into the valley, and other agencies use their services as part of their tours. To make a day trip of not less than six hours, including flights over several volcanoes, a guided tour of the geysers and a hearty lunch at a log cabin in the valley, costs US$200. It's possible to stay overnight in the valley *(full board US$96)*, which will enable you to trek to one of the reserves' waterfalls.

For an extra US$50 per person, Krechet can tack on the Uzon Caldera to the Valley of the Geysers flight. The caldera is the remains of an ancient volcano, now a 10km crater with steamy lakes, enormous mushrooms and prolific berry bushes (thus well attended by the local bears).

Milkovo

Милково

Some 300km north of Petropavlovsk, close to the Kamchatka River, is the down-at-heel fishing and agricultural town of Milkovo, where you'll find a surprisingly interesting **museum** *(admission R100; open 11am-1pm & 2pm-6pm Wed-Sun)*. Sitting across from a small pond, this Siberian-style wooden building in the shape of a cross was constructed by local artist Mikhail Ugrin and decorated with the help of his wife. Inside you'll find a fascinating collection of native artefacts, such as shamans' hats and clothes, and pictures depicting the traditional lives of the area's Itelmen people.

If Ugrin (☎ 41533-2 18 80) isn't around, his daughter Olssa (☎ 41533-2 26 48) may be able to show you around the museum and village. Other things to see include a replica of a Cossack *ostrog* (fort), also built by Ugrin and partly burnt down several years ago; some totem poles carved by Ugrin representing local legends; and the art gallery containing pictures from across Russia as well as plans of the burnt fort.

The **Hotel Dolina** (☎ 41533-2 28 92), on the main square, is nothing to write home about, but clean enough once you get over the lack of toilet seats and flimsy bedding. On the opposite side of the square from the hotel, a striking wall painting is another example of Ugrin's community art. There's a **café** beside the bus stop; there are at least two buses daily from Petropavlovsk (R300, four hours).

Esso
3ссо

A farther 240km from Milkovo, the village of Esso (population 3000) is as pretty a place as you could wish to find at the end of the road – which it is. Known as the Switzerland of Kamchatka, the villagers – who live in wooden cottages, many painted pale blue and surrounded by flourishing vegetable and flower gardens – use the very un-Swiss method of thermal heating their greenhouses from the local hot springs to grow tomatoes year-round.

Evenki people migrated here 150 years ago from what is now the Sakha Republic, becoming the distinct Even people in the process. Here they met the local Itelmen and Korayak people and Russians. Although Esso remains a mixed community, the nearby village of Anavgay is 100% Even. You can find out much about the history of the area's peoples in the local **museum** (☎ 41542-2 13 19; admission without/with guide R50/80; open 10am-6pm daily), a small but nicely designed wooden building set beside the burbling river that flows through Esso. Here also is a picturesque wooden bridge and a souvenir shop (admission R5) selling local handicrafts.

Other than checking out the outdoor **hot springs pool** and maybe seeing the dance group Nulgur (see the boxed text 'The Dancers of Esso' later), the main reason for coming here is to fly in a helicopter and track down one of the three Even-managed **reindeer herds**. A flight into a nomadic camp, where you should be able to watch the Even round up, catch and slaughter at least one of their 1500-strong herd of reindeer, is an unforgettable experience. The high alpine scenery, carpeted with wild flowers (and alive with mosquitoes) in summer is worth the flight alone. Such trips must be arranged through an agency, as should flights out to **Kozyrevsk**, the base camp from which to launch an ascent of the region's giant volcano **Klyuchevskaya** (4688m).

Popular with Kamchatka residents as a holiday base, Esso has several small, simple hotels, but chances are that you'll end up at the **Turistichesky Priyut** (☎ 41542-2 17 30; ul Zelyonaya 10; US$25 per person without meals), a cosy *pension*-style place with tiptop fixtures and fittings, and good food.

The Dancers of Esso

One of the best reasons for making the long road trip to Esso is the chance to see a performance by the folk dance group Nulgur. Made up of 20 members, including Evens, Itelmens and Korayaks, the group has been together since the mid-1990s and performs the traditional dances and songs of the native people of Kamchatka.

Although they are sometimes on tour (and have attended events in Germany and New York in the past), Nulgur perform and practise regularly at Esso's cultural building, the ugly Le Corbussier–style concrete block up on the hill. This is no tourist-trap show, but an enthusiastic performance of surprisingly sensual, evocative dances. Some of the Even dances mimic the movements of the reindeer that are central to their culture. The Korayak's seagull dance incorporates the bird's call into the music. You'll hear throat singing and see spirited bounding to the beat of reindeer-skinned hand drums.

A highlight of the show is the appearance of Mikhail, who joined the group in 1999 when he was just three-and-a-half years old. Since then, this tiny but skilled dancer has swiped up a gold medal at an international competition in Novosibirsk.

A two-daily bus runs here from the 10km station in Petropavlovsk (R300), taking eight to 12 hours depending on the condition of the largely unsealed road.

SOUTHERN KAMCHATKA
Mt Mutnovskaya
Тора Мутновская

One of the most active of Kamchatka's southern group of volcanoes is Mt Mutnovskaya (2322m), which is also one of the easiest to summit. Depending on where you start from, the hike to the top can take between two and four hours. Don't, however, underestimate how gruelling a hike this can be if the weather is against you. The effort is worth it; Mutnovskaya's bubbling, steaming caldera feels like another planet, and for the really fearless it's possible to go to the very crumbly edge of the beast. No wonder engineers are working on tapping the volcano's thermal power to generate electricity for Kamchatka.

Don't be surprised to see snow up here at the height of summer. In fact, it's possible to go snowboarding from June to August in **Rodnikovoe**, about 15km north of Mt Mutnovskaya in the Vilyucha River valley.

LAKE KURILSKOE
ОЗЕРО КУРИЛСКОЕ

Farther south, towards the tip of the peninsula, you'll find Lake Kurilskoe (in the Yuzhno-Kamchatsky State Reserve), the spawning ground for over a million salmon each year and, consequently, home to Steller's sea eagle, a bird with a wingspan of around 2.5m. You will be able to see brown bears here, but an experienced guide is indispensable; in 2000 a lone Japanese photographer was eaten by a bear here.

Belarus

Facts about Belarus

Belarus can never lay claim to being a press darling. If anyone in the West has heard of Belarus at all, what they've heard has been negative: the last dictatorship in Europe! A Soviet Union time capsule! Radiation and political oppression! Rusty tractors and tacky 1970s fashion!

The only time a positive spotlight shone on the country was following its upset victory over the Swedes in the 2002 Winter Olympic hockey tournament. For many television viewers around the world, that game was their first introduction to a country shrouded in mystery and hearsay.

True, the current government of Belarus is backward and repressive in almost all ways, yet tourists will be undisturbed by its wicked machinations. While Belarus' reputation as a living museum of the USSR is much exaggerated (capitalism and a love for modern comforts have taken root too deeply for that), visitors can indeed get a better taste of what life resembled in the 'good old days' than in today's Russia. The rule of law is more strongly felt here, and the clean city streets are lined with more Soviet iconography and statues than you can shake a sickle at. The capital, Minsk, is a shining testament to neoclassical Stalinist architecture but straining to become cosmopolitan and Westernised – it's communism with a cappuccino.

Other parts of Belarus may even prove more interesting to visitors than its capital, Minsk. Brest is a lively border town with a pleasant, timeless charm; Hrodna boasts a rich Catholic influence; Vitsebsk has some lovely old sections and carries on the traditions of its favourite son, Marc Chagall. The countryside – where you can see some of the planet's last remaining collective farms in full (in)action! – is bereft of tourists, and historic towns such as Njasvizh and the reconstructed village at Dudutki make a relaxing day's excursion from the capital.

Stretches of nature are never far away. National parks protect Europe's oldest untouched forests and the continent's largest marshland. While the land is unspectacularly flat, some parts of the country retain a haunting beauty, especially when fields of birch groves are interspersed with wooden villages that seem frozen in 19th-century isolation.

Many of the foreigners who have ventured here so far (descendants of former Jewish residents, Slavophiles, human rights investigators, humanitarian aid workers) have done so for a specific purpose, but there is room for the casual tourist interested in exploring a (slowly) developing Eastern European country. Visa and border regulations are relatively simple (less stringently enforced than Russia's), and the legendary Belarusian hospitality makes up for any minor irritants you might encounter.

HISTORY
Arrival of the Slavs
Evidence of human occupation in Belarus goes back to the early Stone Age. Eastern Slavs from the Krivichi, Dregovichi and Radimichi tribes were here in the 6th to 8th centuries AD during the Slavic expansion, and those who settled on the territory of modern Belarus formed a number of principalities, including Polatsk (first mentioned in 862), Turov (980), Pinsk and Minsk. With Prince Vladimir's annexation of Polatsk, the principalities fell under the general control of Kyivan Rus. The economy was based on slash-and-burn agriculture and river trade, particularly on the Dnjapro (Dnepr in Russian).

Lithuanian & Polish Control
When Kyivan Rus was smashed by the Mongol Tatars in 1240, many Belarusian towns became Tatar vassals. In the 14th century, Belarus was gradually taken over by Lithuania. It was to be 400 years before Belarus came under Russian control, a period in which Belarusians became linguistically and culturally differentiated from the

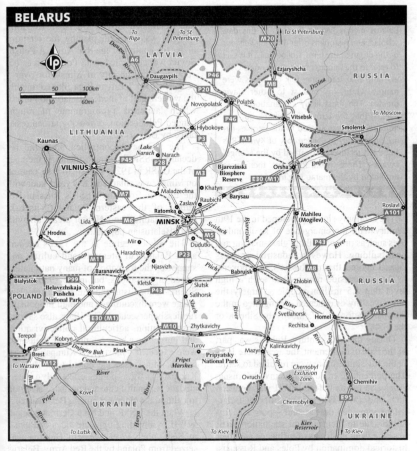

Russians to their east and the Ukrainians to their south.

Lithuania permitted its subject peoples a fair degree of autonomy, even using Belarusian as its own state language during the early years. Even after Lithuania became Roman Catholic following the uniting of its crown with Poland's in 1386, the Belarusian peasantry remained Orthodox. However, they were effectively reduced to serf status by agricultural reforms that took place in the 16th century.

In 1596, the Polish authorities arranged the Union of Brest, which set up the Uniate Church (also known as Ukrainian Catholic or Greek Catholic), bringing much of the Orthodox Church in Belarus under the authority of the Vatican. The Uniate Church insisted on the pope's supremacy and Catholic doctrine, but permitted Orthodox forms of ritual.

For the next two centuries of Polish rule, Belarus largely stagnated. Poles and Jews controlled trade was and most Belarusians remained peasants. After the three Partitions of Poland (1772, 1793 and 1795–96), Belarus was absorbed into Russia.

Tsarist Rule

Under Russian rule a policy of Russification was pursued, and in 1839 the Uniate Church was abolished, with most Belarusians turning to Orthodoxy. The Russian rulers and the Orthodox Church regarded Belarus as 'western Russia' and tried to obliterate any sense of a separate Belarusian nationality. Publishing in the Belarusian language was banned.

Why White?

Belarus means 'White Russia'. To this day, scholars and historians offer differing versions of the origin of the term. Colloquially, it is said to refer to the people's fair complexions. Others note that traditional folk costumes were mainly white, in contrast to other Slavic dresses. The most likely explanation, however, is that the term *bely* ('white', but also 'pure, clean') was applied to the peoples living on the only major territory of Kyivan Rus to be left relatively unscathed by the Mongol ravages. These 'white Russians', then, were untainted by the marauding invaders.

★★★★★★★★★★★★★★★★★★★★★

The economy slowly developed in the 19th century with the emergence of small industries such as timber-milling, glass-making and boat-building. However, industrial progress lagged behind that of Russia's, and poverty in the countryside remained at such a high level that 1.5 million people – largely the more wealthy or educated – emigrated in the 50 years before 1917, mostly to Siberia or the USA.

During the 19th century, Belarus was part of the Pale of Settlement, the area where Jews in the Russian Empire were required to settle. The percentage of Jews in many Belarusian cities and towns before WWII was between 35% and 75%. The vast majority of Belarusians remained on the land – poor and illiterate. Due to their cultural stagnation, their absence from positions of influence and their historical domination by Poles and Russians, any sense among Belarusian speakers that they were a distinct nationality was very slow to emerge.

Nonetheless, Belarusian intellectuals were part of a wave of nationalism in the area that begat a flourishing of cultural awareness in Russia's Baltic territories, and it was in the 19th century that the concept of Belarusians as a distinct people first emerged. The early years of the 20th century saw the first newspapers published in Belarusian.

World Wars & Soviet Rule

During WWI there was considerable fighting between Russia and Germany on Belarusian soil, and consequently much destruction. In March 1918, under German occupation, an independent Belarusian Democratic Republic was declared, but already by January 1919 the Belarusian Soviet Socialist Republic (BSSR) was formed, placing the territory under the control of the Red Army. A Polish-Soviet war continued, with Polish forces occupying even the city of Minsk for over a year. The 1921 Treaty of Riga allotted roughly the western half of modern Belarus to Poland, which launched a programme of rough-handed Polonisation, provoking armed resistance by Belarusians.

The Bolshevik-controlled area, the redeclared BSSR, became a founding member of the USSR in 1922. This small area, centred on Minsk, was enlarged a few years later with the transfer from the USSR's Russian Republic of the eastern Polatsk, Vitsebsk, Orsha, Mahileu and Homel areas, all with large Belarusian populations.

The Soviet regime in the 1920s encouraged Belarusian literature and culture and supported the formation of many nationalist-tinged organisations, but in the 1930s under Stalin, nationalism and the Belarusian language were discouraged and their proponents ruthlessly persecuted. The 1930s also saw industrialisation, agricultural collectivisation, and purges in which hundreds of thousands were executed – most in the Kurapaty Forest, outside Minsk (see the boxed text 'Burying Kurapaty'). These purges effectively obliterated the nationalist elite and put a decisive stop to cultural development among Belarusians.

When the USSR and Nazi Germany began WWII by invading opposite sides of Poland in September 1939, western Belarus was seized from Poland by the Red Army. Belarus again found itself on the front line when the Nazis turned around and invaded the USSR in 1941. The resulting occupation was savage and partisan resistance widespread until the Red Army drove the Germans out, with massive destruction on both sides, in 1944. There were big battles around Vitsebsk, Barysau and Minsk, where barely a stone was left standing. At least 25% of Belarus' population (more than two million people) died between 1939 and 1945. Many of them, Jews and others, died in 200-plus concentration camps; the third-largest Nazi concentration camp was set up at Maly Trostenets, where over 200,000 Jews and others were executed.

Western Belarus remained in Soviet hands at the end of the war. The first postwar Five-Year Plan succeeded in repairing most of the

Burying Kurapaty

In 1988, excavations led by Zjanon Paznjak (leader of the Belarusian Popular Front) near the district of Kurapaty on the outskirts of Minsk revealed more than 500 mass graves containing the remains of up to 250,000 bodies of men and women executed by the NKVD (the KGB's precursors) during Stalin's terror purges between 1937 and 1941. At the time of their discovery, these revelations became a central focus of the re-emerging nationalist movement, emphasising as it did Belarusian suffering at the hands of the Soviet regime.

While government commissions were set up to investigate these crimes, and while numerous vigils, demonstrations and ceremonies have been held at the site since its discovery, the government under Alexander Lukashenka has undertaken a thorough cover-up of the excavation's findings. One commission laid the blame on Nazi murderers, not the NKVD, and called into question the number of bodies in the area – one estimate is as low as 7000.

Lukashenka himself has never visited the site, a 20-minute drive from his residence, while Bill Clinton in 1994 unveiled there a small memorial, destroyed by vandals in 2001. Open debate on the subject is not tolerated. Instead, Lukashenka authorised massive reconstruction of the Minsk ringroad, which would run through Kurapaty and preclude the erecting of any further memorials. At the time of writing, construction was underway and the area was off-limits for civilians. Belarusian museums and official history books are bereft of information about the NKVD atrocities.

Local residents prefer not to discuss the touchy and unresolved issue of Kurapaty, and many are afraid to visit and be seen by police. Still, in January 2002, a small group laid a granite bench there, replacing the vandalised 1994 memorial. This humble step was the act of volunteers and is seen as a hopefully temporary substitute for a large-scale memorial that has been talked about since the late 1980s.

★★

war damage, and industrialisation began again, with Minsk developing into the industrial hub of the western USSR and Belarus becoming one of the Soviet Union's most prosperous republics.

Protest & Independence

The 1986 Chernobyl disaster in Ukraine hit Belarus even worse than Ukraine itself, with around one quarter of the country seriously contaminated. This was one of the few issues that crystallised political opposition among a traditionally placid population in an area considered to be among the most rigidly communist of the Soviet republics.

In 1988 the Belarusian Popular Front was formed to address the issues raised by the Chernobyl disaster, the discoveries at Kurapaty and the declining use of the Belarusian language. The leader of the Popular Front since its inception has been archaeologist Zjanon Paznjak, now residing in the USA after seeking political asylum.

In response to the growth of nationalist feeling, on 27 July 1990 the republic issued a declaration of sovereignty within the USSR. That same year, Belarusian was declared the republic's official language (though the Rus-

sian language rejoined it in 1995). The leadership instituted its own financial system and state currency.

After the failed anti-Gorbachev coup in August 1991, the Supreme Soviet (parliament) issued a declaration of full national independence on 25 August. The country's name was changed to the Republic of Belarus. With no history whatsoever as a politically or economically independent entity, Belarus was one of the oddest products of the disintegration of the USSR.

Post-Independence Politics

Stanislau Shushkevich, a physicist supported by the Popular Front who had campaigned to expose official negligence over Chernobyl, was chosen head of the Supreme Soviet (effectively, head of state) which nonetheless remained dominated by the communist old guard. In December 1991 Belarus became a founding member of the Commonwealth of Independent States (CIS), with Minsk its headquarters.

With the Communists advocating closer ties with Russia and regaining popularity during economically difficult times, Shushkevich came into increasing conflict with them.

Finally, he was dismissed in January 1994 over trumped-up corruption charges.

In July 1994, in Belarus' first direct presidential election, Alexander Lukashenka, a non-Party former collective-farm director (a common derogatory nickname for him is *kolkhoznik*, from *kolkhoz*: collective farm) won with a majority. Lukashenka, who had supported the 1991 anti-Gorbachev coup in Moscow and led the anticorruption investigation that unseated Shushkevich, had campaigned on promises to reverse inflation, raise wages, stop privatisation and corruption, break the Mafia and move closer to Russia.

Lukashenka's style of presidency has been autocratic and authoritarian and he clashed frequently with parliament. Finally, in a bid to increase his powers, in 1996 he held what the West still regards as an illegitimate referendum. This referendum – with the dubious support of the populace – effectively stripped the authority of the parliament, now to be appointed by Lukashenka, and made the entire government subservient to the president (see Government & Politics later in this chapter).

From the beginning of his first term, Lukashenka proved antagonistic, even combative, in his attitude towards the West. In September 1995, an air balloon manned by two Americans taking part in an international race accidentally drifted into Belarusian airspace and was shot down by a military helicopter. Both pilots were killed, and it took three weeks before Lukashenka issued an official apology. In the interim, he took time to praise his country's efficient air force.

In 1997, Lukashenka ordered the Soros Foundation – a nonprofit organisation created by billionaire George Soros to encourage a free society – to pay US$3 million in supposed taxes despite the fact that it had donated US$13 million to schools and hospitals; instead of paying, the foundation closed and left the country. In August that same year Lukashenka had a Russian TV journalist arrested for purportedly entering the country illegally, holding him in prison without trial for two months. He aimed higher in June 1998, when ambassadors from a number of European Union (EU) nations and the USA were ignominiously locked out of their residence complex at Drozby, a suburb of Minsk (Lukashenka said the building was in need of repairs).

Official elections were held in November 2001, despite international criticism and opposition calls of their illegality. Lukashenka again won a majority and is now scheduled to stay in power until (at least) 2006.

The country has become, politically, an isolated island in the centre of Europe. After Monaco's and Yugoslavia's accession to the Council of Europe, Belarus will be the only European country without membership of this organisation which monitors democracy and human rights. It is considered too far outside European democratic norms for inclusion. Lukashenka's isolationist policies have shown little regard for what the 'outside world' thinks, save for Russia, with whom the president has been trying with varying degrees of success to forge closer ties (see under Government & Politics).

However, Lukashenka was incensed when, in autumn 2002, he was denied a visa to attend the NATO summit meeting in Prague and later denied an entry visa to both the EU and the USA – all in protest of his country's poor human rights record.

GEOGRAPHY

Belarus has an area of 207,600 sq km, slightly smaller than the UK. It borders Russia in the north and east, Latvia and Lithuania in the northwest, Poland in the west and Ukraine in the south.

It's a low-lying country, with the highest hill, Dzerzhinskaja in the central west, reaching only 345m. The terrain consists of low ridges dividing broad, often marshy lowlands with many small lakes. The largest lake (79.6 sq km) is the Narach, north of Minsk. In the south are the Pripet Marshes, Europe's largest marsh area, though they have largely been drained for agriculture.

The country's major river is the Dnjapro, which traverses through 700km of Belarus. The north of Belarus is drained by the Dzvina River which flows from Russia to Latvia (where it's known as the Daugava), while the Nioman flows north through Hrodna into Lithuania.

CLIMATE

Belarus has a continental climate, which becomes marginally less temperate as you move from southwest to northeast. Average January temperatures are between -4° and -8°C, with frosts experienced for five to six months of

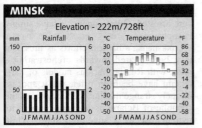

MINSK

Elevation - 222m/728ft

the year. The warmest month is July, when temperatures can reach up to 30°C, but the average temperature is 18°C. Rainfall is moderate at an average 670mm a year, with June to August the wettest months. There's snow cover continuously from December/January to March/April.

ECOLOGY & ENVIRONMENT

The 1986 disaster at Chernobyl has been the defining event for the Belarusian environment, if not for the republic as a whole. Some 70% of Chernobyl's released radioisotopes fell on Belarus (primarily in the Homel and Mahileu districts in the south and east, but caesium-137 fallout was registered in many other regions of the country), contaminating about a quarter of its territory where some 2.2 million people lived. Some 1.8 million still live in these areas; many are unwilling or unable to relocate elsewhere, primarily as government aid has been grossly insufficient.

The after-effects of Chernobyl once took 20% of the annual state budget, but under Lukashenka, this percentage has steadily declined (at the time of writing it was about 8%). Financial benefits to people living in contaminated areas have been gradually cut, and the government is now actively downplaying the dangers inherent in living in these areas, instead actually encouraging resettlement. In fact, scientists and officials who dare speak out about the continuing dangers and consequences of the accident have been intimidated and jailed on trumped-up charges. The best-known case is that of Yuri Bandazhevsky, the former dean of a Homel medical institute, who linked the accident with continued health defects – some fatal – in children. After several years of being hounded by secret police and removed from his post, in 2001 he was jailed on bribery charges and sentenced to eight years in a labour camp. His case has attracted international attention.

The dangers of exposure to radiation for the casual tourist are negligible, however, even for those who briefly visit areas that experienced some fallout (these regions are not covered in this book).

The decades of Soviet rule were not much better for the nation as a whole, with environmentally unfriendly factories spewing pollution in the rush to industrialise. Since the USSR's break-up and the resultant closing of many factories, pollution levels have dropped steadily throughout the 1990s, though air in the larger cities, especially in the eastern sectors of the republic (for instance, around Polotsk) is polluted by emissions from aging factories and outdated cars. The flipside is that most of the countryside is unspoiled, and old farmsteads have slowly been reclaimed by new forests. The marshland area known as Polesye, in the south of the country, is dubbed locally as the 'lungs of Europe' as air currents passing over it are re-oxygenated and purified by the marshes and swamps.

FLORA & FAUNA

The forests are a mixture of coniferous and deciduous trees, with conifers such as pine and spruce dominating in the north, and deciduous trees such as oak and beech in the south. Silver birch is common everywhere, growing in dense groves.

The Belavezhskaja Pushcha National Park, on the western border with Poland, is Europe's largest piece of surviving primeval mixed forest. Once used as private hunting grounds for Polish and Russian royalty, the forest has always been renowned for its European bison, Europe's largest mammal (see also Brest in the Elsewhere in Belarus chapter).

Other animals found throughout wooded areas include elk, deer, boars, lynx, wolves, foxes, squirrels, martens and hares. Beavers, otters, minks and badgers can be found in and around Belarus's 20,000 streams and 10,000 small lakes, the largest populations in isolated southern swamp regions and along the Dzvina River's northern marshes, near Polatsk.

The Pripet River is Europe's largest migratory circuit of waterfowl; some 250 bird species live, nest or pass through the region. White (and more rarely black) storks are visible in the villages in southern Belarus, and other commonly spotted birds include owls, hawks, grouse, woodcocks, cuckoos and partridges.

BELARUS

BELARUS

GOVERNMENT & POLITICS

In theory, Belarus is a democracy with an executive president, chosen in direct popular elections. The president chooses a prime minister, who is responsible for many of the day-to-day affairs of government. The country's parliament is the National Assembly, consisting of two chambers. In practice, however, the country is run by the sitting president, Alexander Lukashenka.

On 24 November 1996, 70% of Belarus gave Lukashenka the power he had always wanted. In a nationwide referendum, which has never been officially recognised by the West, Belarusians said yes to a new constitution, effectively extending Lukashenka's term from five to seven years. The new rules allowed Lukashenka to dissolve parliament and fill it with nodding donkeys. (The referendum also voted down measures that would set up a free market system, and gave approval to switching the national Independence Day from 27 July – when the first constitution was passed in 1991 – to 3 July, the day of Soviet liberation of Minsk at the end of WWII.) Opposition parliamentarians, who were already being booted from their rostrums the following day, called the vote a farce.

Since then, the opposition has been reduced to a few – often bickering – groups, which hold rallies in the capital but have been unable to galvanise popular support. The general public views these groups as unruly and is wary of their seemingly anti-Russian stance. Moreover, participation in a banned rally can lead to imprisonment or a heavy fine. Currently, there is no properly organised opposition offering a workable alternative to Lukashenka's government, and the climate of political oppression does not favour its creation.

Lukashenka subsequently cracked down on media, halted or reversed economic reforms, stifled political opposition and played chicken with the West – harshly condemning it while at the same time making moderate reforms to attract the funding he needed to keep the country running. He also pays pensions and military salaries on time and subsidises farmers, ensuring the support of those who form the backbone of his electorate. He has effectively eliminated any real opposition and most voices of dissent. The list of firings, arrests and imprisonments imposed on those who cross him is long; even in early 2002, 14 journalists protesting the closing of yet another independent newspaper in Hrodna were arrested. Other opponents have simply disappeared.

Lukashenka's biggest efforts as president have been geared towards orchestrating a union with Russia. Various models of partnership have been on offer, yet it appears uniquely strange that the political goal of the Republic of Belarus is to work towards its own demise as a sovereign state. While Lukashenka and Boris Yeltsin signed some non-binding pacts of cooperation, Vladimir Putin has been lukewarm to the idea of union. Putin publicly humiliated Lukashenka after a summit meeting in 2002 by calling attention to Belarus' ostentatious, sometimes contradictory demands on Russia. Putin offered full annexation, but Lukashenka balked at Belarus becoming a mere Russian province. Lukashenka was shown to want his bliny and to eat it too – that is, a closer and economically beneficial union with Russia, while maintaining power over his little dominion.

Despite these setbacks, the Belarus press brims with optimistic reports of an eventual union with what many regard as the motherland. The country is divided into six administrative regions centred on the cities of Minsk, Brest, Hrodna, Vitsebsk, Homel and Mahileu.

ECONOMY

Belarus, despite attempts at reform in the early 1990s, has devolved continually under Lukashenka's spectacularly unsuccessful attempts at 'market socialism'. On paper, positive growth is shown (the economy grew by 4.1% in 2001, and industrial output was up by 5.4%) but this is largely due to the government pumping money into key industries.

On paper, some 42% of all businesses are private, yet included in this figure are hundreds of enterprises owned by directors of state-run big businesses or organisations. In practice, it is a major feat for anyone to open a small business in Belarus – either they are forced to pay thousands of dollars in bribes in order to get the required permits, or are refused an operating license outright. In 1994, there were over 3200 small private businesses operating in the Pervamaiski district of central Minsk alone; in 2002, that figure was just over 200. A law in April 2002 outlawed the existence of all non state-run sidewalk beer stands. Along Minsk's main drags, outdoor beer terraces disappeared overnight, leaving only a few government-run, more expensive options. Incredibly, half of all Belarusian enterprises operate in the red.

Agriculture accounts for about 20% of the country's Gross Domestic Product (GDP) and occupies more than half the land, with livestock (chiefly cattle and pigs) responsible for 60% of agricultural produce; potatoes, grain, sugar beet and flax are the main crops.

Industry contributes over 40% of the GDP. More important are the mineral and chemical processing industries such as the fertiliser plants at Salihorsk and Hrodna and the oil refineries at Novopolatsk and Mazyr. Some of Belarus' major export items include potassium fertilizers, chemicals, wood fibreboards, refrigerators, tractors and trucks. Some US$600 million worth of finished products sit in storage houses as factories produce much more than they can distribute and sell; many industries remain in operation only through government support and to keep labourers employed.

The country is almost totally dependent on Russia for oil and gas supplies, and in part on Lithuania for electricity. It is, however, rich in peat, which is used as fuel for power stations and in the manufacture of chemicals. It also has substantial deposits of potassium salts, used in fertiliser.

Belarus' economic policies have turned Western lending agencies, such as the IMF and the World Bank, against the country, leaving it even more heavily dependent on Russia. Foreign investment was a meagre US$16 million in the first quarter of 2002 (the government's aim was to attract US$400 million in 2002). Inflation for food items at the close of 2001 was just under 50%; for nonfood products it was just under 30%.

As a legacy of the Soviet era, unemployment in the country is very low: in 2001, 2.3% were officially unemployed. However, complicated methods of registration and lack of proper benefits more than likely put people off from going through the procedure. While the average monthly wage in early 2002 was US$95, a substantial proportion of the populace earns much less than that.

POPULATION & PEOPLE

The population of Belarus is 9.95 million people, with 81.2% Belarusian, 11.4% Russian, 4% Polish and 2.4% Ukrainian. This results in a rather homogenous population, with many sharing physical attributes such as fair hair and piercing blue eyes. The only sizeable, non-Slavic minority in the country is Roma (formerly referred to as gypsies; no figures available), who live primarily in some towns and cities in the south and southeast. Their presence is not well tolerated and there is virtually no mixing between the groups.

There was once a huge Polish and Jewish population as well as a substantial German minority – all of whom were either killed or fled during WWII, or were sent off to Siberia in its aftermath. Prior to WWII, 10% of the national population was Jewish and in cities such as Minsk, Hrodna, Brest and Vitsebsk, and towns such as Mir, Jews made up between one-third and three-quarters of the population. They now account for less than 1% of the population.

The overall population density of the country is low (an average of less than 50 persons per square kilometre). As with other countries in the region, the death rate far exceeds the birth rate: in Belarus it is over 50% higher.

EDUCATION

Most high schools and universities now teach exclusively in Russian, though there are still many Belarusian elementary schools. In Russian-language schools, Belarusian is taught much less frequently than Russian in Belarusian-language schools. In Minsk, the number of Belarusian-language schools shrank from 220 in 1994 to 11 in 2002. At the time of writing, there were 22 Jewish Sunday schools in operation.

ARTS

Few cultural artefacts survive from the early Slavic settlements of the 6th to 8th centuries, which were followed by long periods of foreign rule, first by Lithuania and later by the Polish and Russian empires. Without control of its own destiny, Belarusian cultural identity was, outside the rural framework, subdued and often suppressed, with only brief periods of revival in the 16th, 19th and 20th centuries.

Literature & Drama

The hero of early Belarusian literary achievement was Francyska Skaryny (after whom many main streets in Belarus are named). Born in Polatsk but educated in Poland and

Italy, the scientist, doctor, writer and humanist became the first person to translate the Bible into the Belarusian language. This, as well as other editions by Skaryny between 1517 and 1525, was one of the first books to be printed in all of Eastern Europe. In the late 16th century, the philosopher and humanist Simon Budny printed a number of works in Belarusian, including controversial editions such as *Justification of a Sinner Before God*. The 17th-century Belarusian poet Symeon of Polatsk was the first writer to introduce the baroque style of literature to Russia.

The 19th century saw the beginning of modern Belarusian literature, with works by writers and poets such as Maxim Haradsky, Maxim Bohdanovish, Janka Kupala and, most notably, Jakub Kolas. Many of these writers were active in the influential nationalist newspaper *Nasha Niva* (Our Cornfield), which had to be published in Lithuania from 1906 to 1916, as nationalist literature in Belarus was banned by the tsar at the time. Haradsky's novel *Two Souls* (1919) and Kupala's play *The Locals* (1922) are poignant expressions of the repressed state of Belarus after WWI and during the revolution. Kolas is considered to be the pioneer of classical Belarusian literature, and both he and Kupala are revered for having promoted the literary and poetic use of Belarusian.

A period of cultural revival in the 1920s saw the rise of many talented poets and writers, including Jazep Pushcha and satirist playwright Kandrat Krapiva. Another mini revival occurred in the 1960s, with works by V Karatkevich and Vasyl Bykov, who wrote several books depicting Belarus in wartime and the efforts of partisans.

Music

Belarusian folk music is well known and visitors to the country shouldn't miss a performance. Modern folk music originated from ritualistic ceremonies – either based on peasant seasonal feasts or, more commonly, on the traditions of church music (hymns and psalms), which became highly developed in Belarus from the 16th century. The band Pesnyary have since the 1960s been extremely popular for having put a modern twist on traditional Belarusian folk music. Other modern bands that utilise folk songs as a base include Troitsa and Stary Olsa; both sing in Belarusian.

Classical music in the modern sense only developed in Belarus within the last 100 years, with composers such as Kulikovich Shchehlov and Yevheny Hlebov, the latter composing the operas *Your Spring* (1963) and *Alpine Ballad* (1967).

Popular modern groups from Belarus include the hard rock NRM; the equally hard but more melodic Palats; Krama, who sing in both Russian and Belarusian; and the well-known Lyapis Trubetskoi, whose catchy light rock-pop has found many fans.

SOCIETY & CONDUCT

Though a majority of Belarusian city dwellers deride President Lukashenka and his oppressive policies, you might sense that the Belarusian people nonetheless like a firm leader, and this is not far from the mark. Throughout history the Belarusian people have been the underclass in their own country, with little distinct culture or history of their own. As such, Belarusians are quiet and somewhat reserved. Less demonstrative and approachable than Russians, they are just as friendly and generous, if not more so, once introductions are made.

One of the first things foreigners notice in Belarus, especially those familiar with Russia, is the cleanliness of the cities and towns. Even in Soviet times, Belarusians had the reputation of being exceptionally neat and tidy. Central streets are kept immaculate – by the swarms of overnight street sweepers but also by citizens. Even tipsy teens assiduously use rubbish bins for their beer bottles. People are also loath to walk on park grass or cross streets where they're supposed to use an underpass. This undercurrent of respect (ie, fear) of the law is felt in many aspects of society, and this sometimes bleeds into a reluctance to do anything deemed out of the ordinary or not by the book. It has also fostered a slight wariness of strangers, which may likely dissipate after a few beers.

In further comparison to their Russian cousins, Belarusians tend to be harder workers, more aspiring in their personal goals, more polite and less likely to swear. However, in the service industries, you are likely to encounter blunt, even rude service.

RELIGION

Belarus, like Ukraine, has always been a crossing point between Latin and Eastern Orthodox Christianity, Polish Catholics to the west and Orthodox Russians to the east. Some 80% of the populace is Eastern Orthodox. In 1990 the Belarusian Orthodox Church was officially established.

As a legacy of centuries of Polish rule, 20% of the population (about two million people) is Roman Catholic, of whom 15% are ethnic Poles. Their presence can be especially felt in Hrodna, where they hold services in Polish.

In the early 1990s the Uniate Church – an Orthodox sect that looks to Rome, not Moscow – was re-established and now has a following of over 100,000, many of them Ukrainians living in Belarus. There's also a small Protestant minority, the remnant of a once large German population. The number of Baptist churches has grown to over 200 and there are small pockets of Tatars, who practise Islam, as well as scattered urban Jewish communities, although most of the latter have emigrated. At the beginning of the 20th century, there were 704 synagogues in Belarus – by 1995, there were but 15.

LANGUAGE

The centralised Soviet system subjected Belarus to a process of Russification, with the result that well over 80% of Belarusian school pupils were taught exclusively in Russian. In 1984, Belarusians ranked last of all Soviet republics in terms of their citizens' ability to speak the national language.

Today, Russian predominates in nearly all aspects of social life. Even those whose mother tongue is Belarusian tend to communicate to each other in Russian, or in a mix of both languages. In cities, speaking Belarusian publicly is sometimes seen as a bold declaration of nationalism and can cause heads to turn.

Though some teenagers can be seen making an effort to utilise their nation's language as often as possible, and while local dialects are frequently heard in villages and small towns, one senses an implicit pressure to stick to Russian. Lukashenka himself has an infamously poor command of Belarusian and makes nearly all his public speeches in Russian only. There is little state support for keeping the language alive and flourishing, and many citizens are apathetic, if slightly embarrassed about the subject.

Though there are several Belarusian newspapers, most are peppered with Russian-language articles. While much signage is in Belarusian (see later), usage often appears indiscriminate: a Belarusian-language billboard can include a few Russian words; in the Minsk metro, some signs are in Russian, others in Belarusian. Even on Belarusian-language national TV, broadcasters have been known to sprinkle their sentences with Russian words and make grammatical errors in Belarusian.

In 1990, shortly before independence, Belarusian was announced as the country's only official language. Just as a resurgence of the national tongue seemed ready to blossom, Lukashenka decreed in 1995 that Russian was also to be the official language, and most ordinary citizens heaved a sigh of relief and reverted to Russian. Today, only about 11% of school children are instructed in Belarusian.

Belarusian belongs to the Eastern Slavonic branch of Indo-European languages. It is closely related to both Russian and Ukrainian, though its written form shares with Ukrainian only its ancestor in the now extinct language called Ruthenian. It began to differ from Old Russian (also called Church Slavonic) in the Middle Ages. It's normally written with the Cyrillic alphabet, but there does exist a written form using accented Latin characters. This latter is dubbed Lacinka, and it is different than transliterated Belarusian. While Russian and present-day Belarusian are very close, there are significant pronunciation and spelling differences, and some case endings and many words are completely different; a Russian-speaker would at best understand 60% of spoken Belarusian heard for the first time.

Another complicating factor in the preservation of a unified version of Belarusian is that the language spoken today is actually a modernised version following reforms undertaken during the Soviet period in the early 1930s, when the language was brought closer to Russian.

Belarusian, like Ukrainian but not Russian, has the letter i, pronounced *ee* (this replaces the Russian и). It also has the unique letter ў, pronounced like 'w' in the word 'west'. Transliteration is also different, with й transcribed as *j*, ю as *ju*, я as *ja* and ё as *io*. Г is pronounced and transcribed *h*, as in Ukrainian. The Russian letter o often becomes a in Belarusian – making, for example, Komsomolskaya into Kamsamolskaja, which looks closer to its pronunciation in any case. The

Russian Gogolya becomes Hoholja in Belarusian. You'll see an apostrophe used in written Belarusian to separate a consonant from the syllable that follows it.

To honour the local language we use the form of transliteration described above, as confusing as it may seem. It may be noble to try a little Belarusian, but you're likely to be greeted with consternation and confusion.

At the time of writing, although Russian is by far more often spoken in all walks of life, a significant amount of signage – at bus/train stations, metro stops, streets, museums etc – remains in Belarusian.

Belarus	Беларусь
beh-lah-ROOS	
Hello.	Добры джень.
DOB-ree DZHEN	
Goodbye.	Да пабачэньня.
DA pah-bah-CHEN-nyah	
yes	так
tahk	
no	не
nye	
Please.	Калі ласка.
kah-LEE LAHS-kah	
Thank you.	Дзякуй.
DZYAH-koo-ee	
good	добры
DOHB-ree	
bad	дрэнны
DREHN-nee	

entrance	уваход
uva-KHOD	
exit	выхад
VY-khad	
left-luggage	камера
room	захоўвання
KA-mera za-KHAU-	багажа
vannya ba-GA-zha	
on even days	па цотных
pa TSOT-nykh	
on odd days	па няцотных
pa nya-TSOT-nykh	
daily	штодзюнна
shtod-ZYO-nna	
departure	адпраўленне
ad-prau-LEN-nje	
arrival	прыбыще
pry-BY-tssje	
information	даведка
da-VED-ka	
Monday	панядзелак
pan-ya-DZEL-ak	
Tuesday	аўторак
AUT-orak	
Wednesday	серада
se-ra-DA	
Thursday	чацвер
CHATS-ver	
Friday	пятніца
PYAT-nitsa	
Saturday	субота
su-BO-ta	
Sunday	нядзеля
NYAD-ze-lya	

Facts for the Visitor

HIGHLIGHTS

Belarus is a country with few traditional attractions on offer to tourists. The best way to enjoy Belarus is to sample city life but spend as much time as possible in the countryside or in small towns, getting to know the locals. Urbanisation is a relatively new phenomenon for the country and the heart of the nation still resides in the least populous areas. Minsk itself, aside from its miniscule rebuilt old town, has an impressive grandeur to it, but is ultimately an uninviting city with few sites of great interest to visitors.

Outside Minsk, Vitsebsk offers a more relaxed alternative to city life and boasts a great art museum. Hrodna has a truly stunning Polish Catholic cathedral. No visitor should pass up the opportunity to see Brest's amazing fortress-cum-war memorial. The reconstructed village of Dudutki, where you can experience 19th-century Belarus for a few hours, is another must. A visit to the Belavezhskaja Pushcha National Park or any other of Belarus' national parks is also highly recommended – there's nothing like wild nature to serve as an antidote to the sometimes oppressive air in the country's larger cities.

SUGGESTED ITINERARIES

Two Days
This will afford enough time to see only Minsk, and a brief side-trip to Dudutki.

One Week
Visit Minsk, Dudutki, Njasvizh as well as Brest and the Belavezhskaja Pushcha National Park.

One Month
In addition to the above, visit other centres such as Vitsebsk, Polatsk and Hrodna, and an extended stay in one of the country's national parks is recommended.

PLANNING
When to Go

It's always low season in Belarus, which means never having to worry about crowds. There are, however, tour groups that book up summer excursions in the country's national parks months in advance. With summer being the warmest but wettest season and with winter a grey freeze, the best time to visit is typically from May to June or from August to September.

Maps

Good maps are widely available in Minsk and sparingly in the other cities. Small, user-friendly maps of Minsk, Hrodna, Brest and Vitsebsk are published by Interpresservis and cost about BR1800 each. They double as handy bus, trolleybus and metro maps as well, and are easy to find in bookshops and kiosks in those cities. Trivium publishes an excellent 1:750,000 scale map of Belarus and a very detailed 1:20,000 scale Minsk map (with a 1:10,000 city centre map). These cost about BR2500 each.

RESPONSIBLE TOURISM

Everyone comments on the cleanliness of the streets of Belarus' cities and towns – keep up the tradition by disposing of your rubbish in appropriate places only. If you insist on talking politics, avoid brash statements that may seem obviously true to you, such as 'I can't believe that people here actually support that petty dictator of yours!' Many people realise the conditions in which they live and may make criticisms of their own, but are nonetheless touchy when the same critiques are delivered by outsiders.

TOURIST OFFICES

There are no tourist information offices in the formal sense in Belarus, but there are some hotel service bureaux and excursion offices that may be helpful. Otherwise, travel agencies are your best bet – see Travel Agencies in the Minsk chapter for more details. Outside Belarus, information on the country is rare; however, there is a good deal of information available on the Internet. (See Digital Resources later in this chapter.)

VISAS & DOCUMENTS

Belarusian visa regulations change frequently, so check the Belarusian US embassy website at **w** www.belarusembassy.org for more information.

All foreigners visiting Belarus need a visa, and arranging one before you arrive is essential. Visas are not issued at border points except at the Minsk-2 international airport – however, you will still need to show hotel reservations or your personal or business invitation.

BELARUS

To get a visa, you will need a photograph, an invitation from a private person or a business, or a confirmation of reservation from a hotel, and your passport. There are three types of visas: tourist, issued if you have a tourist voucher or hotel reservation; visitor, if your invitation comes from an individual; and business, if your invitation is from a business. Tourist and visitor visas are issued for 30 days, while business visas are valid for 90 days and can be for multientry.

Belarus now requires foreigners to possess medical insurance from a pre-approved company covering their entire length of stay in the country. This is over and above any other pre-existing insurance the traveller might have. Your local Belarusian embassy will tell you which local insurance companies are acceptable. Costs are reasonable (US$15 for a 60-day stay). Insurance is also sold at border-entry points, and is not required for holders of transit visas. Though proof of insurance is rarely asked for at border points, it's best to have it to avoid potential complications.

Once you enter the country you must be officially registered. Hotels do this automatically for a small fee. They'll give you small pieces of papers with stamps on them, which you keep to show to customs agents upon departure. In theory, you'll be fined if you don't provide proof of registration; in practice, this is rarely asked for. If you've received a personal invitation, you'll need to seek out the nearest *passportno-vizovoye upravleniye*, or passport and visa department (PVU). The **PVU main office** (☎ 017-231 91 74; *vul Francyska Skaryny 8*) is in Minsk.

Transit Visas

All persons passing through Belarusian territory are required to possess a transit visa, which can be obtained at any Belarusian consulate upon presentation of travel tickets clearly showing the final destination as being outside of Belarus. The possession of a valid Russian visa is no longer enough to serve as a transit visa. Be sure to check your train or bus routing, as you could be removed and not allowed to travel onwards. Transit visas are not available at the border.

Applying for a Visa

By far the simplest – although the most expensive – way to get a visa is to apply through a travel agency. Alternately, you can take a faxed confirmation from your hotel to the nearest Belarusian embassy and apply for one yourself.

Tallinn, Riga and Vilnius have numerous travel agencies specialising in Belarusian visas. In Vilnius, the most convenient point to jump off, try **Viliota** (☎ 370 2-65 22 38, fax 65 22 36; *Russian only* **W** www.viliota.lt; *Basanaviciaus gatve 15*), where you can get a visa hassle-free with a photo of yourself and US$70 to US$100.

Many Belarusian travel agencies (see Travel Agencies in the Minsk chapter) can send you an invitation. The Host Families Association (HOFA) (see under Homestays in this chapter for details) can do the same.

Getting an invitation from an individual can be a long, complex process. Your friend in Belarus needs a *zapreshenne* (official invitation) form from their local PVU office and should then send it to you. With this, you apply at the nearest Belarusian embassy.

Visa costs vary from embassy to embassy. Typically, single-entry visas cost about US$50 for five working-days service and US$90 for next-day service; double-entry visas usually cost double that. Transit visas typically cost from US$20 to US$35.

Visa Extensions

Nontransit visas cannot be extended beyond the 30-day limit for tourists, or the 90-day limit for holders of business visas; you will need to apply for a new visa. Try at the **Belintourist office** (☎ 017-226 98 85; *pr Masherava 19A*) or the **Ministry of Foreign Affairs** (☎ 017-222 26 74; *vul Lenina 19*), both in Minsk.

EMBASSIES & CONSULATES
Belarusian Embassies & Consulates

Belarus' diplomatic representation abroad includes the following:

Canada
  Embassy: (☎ 613-233 9994) Suite 600, 130 Albert St, Ottawa, Ontario K1P 5G4
France
  Embassy: (☎ 01 44 14 69 79, fax 01 44 14 69 70) 38 Blvd Suchet, 75016 Paris
Germany
  Embassy: (☎ 030-5 36 35 929, fax 5 36 35 923; consular department ☎ 030-5 36 35 934, fax 5 36 35 924) Am Treptower Park 32, 12435 Berlin

Embassy representative: (☎ 0228-201 13 10, fax 201 13 19; consular department ☎ 0228-201 13 30, fax 201 13 39) Fritz-Schäffer-Strasse 20, 53113 Bonn

Latvia
Embassy: (☎ 732 34 11, fax 732 28 91) Jezus baznicas iela 12, Riga 1050
Consulate: (☎ 54-37 573, fax 52 945) 18-Noyabrya 44, Daugavpils

Lithuania
Embassy: (☎ 2-25 16 66, fax 25 16 62) Mimdaugo gatve 13, Vilnius
Consulate: (☎ 2-23 22 55, fax 23 33 22) Muitines gatve 41, Vilnius

Poland
Embassy: (☎ 022-617 23 91, fax 617 84 41) ulica Atenska 67, 03-978 Warsaw
Consulates: (☎ 0583-41 00 26, fax 41 40 26) ulica Yackova Dolina 50, 80-251 Gdansk; (☎ 085-44 55 01, fax 44 66 61) ulica Warshiskeho 4, 15-461 Bialystok

Russia
Embassy: (☎ 095-924 70 31, fax 928 66 33) Maroseyka ulitsa 17/6, 101000 Moscow
Consulates: (☎ 095-928 78 13, fax 928 64 03) Armyansky pereulok 6, 101000 Moscow; (☎ 812-273 00 78) ulitsa Robespierra 8/46-66 St Petersburg

UK
Embassy: (☎ 020-7937 3288, fax 7361 0005) 6 Kensington Court, London W8 5DL

Ukraine
Embassy: (☎ 044-290 02 01, fax 290 34 13) vulitsya Sichnevogo povstannya 6, 252010 Kiev

USA
Embassy: (☎ 202-986 1604, fax 986 1805) 1619 New Hampshire Ave NW, Washington, DC 20009
Consulate: (☎ 212-682 5392, fax 682 5491) 708 Third Ave, New York, NY 10017

Embassies & Consulates in Belarus

The following addresses are all in Minsk, telephone area code ☎ 017.

France (☎ 210 28 68, fax 210 25 48) ploshcha Svabody 11
Germany (☎ 284 87 14, fax 284 85 52) vulitsa Zakharava 26
Latvia (☎/fax 284 74 75) vulitsa Darashevicha 6
Lithuania (☎ 234 77 84, fax 234 72 00) vulitsa Varvasheni 17
Poland (☎ 213 41 14, fax 236 49 92) vulitsa Rumjantsava 6
Russia (☎ 250 36 66, fax 250 36 64) vulitsa Staravilenskaja 48
UK (☎ 210 59 20, fax 229 23 06) vulitsa Karla Marxa 37

Ukraine (☎/fax 222 38 04) vulitsa Kirava 17
USA (☎ 210 12 83, fax 234 78 53) vulitsa Staravilenskaja 46

CUSTOMS

Upon arrival, you may be given a *deklaratsia* (customs declaration form) to fill out. You are allowed to bring in and out of the country currency up to US$1500 without filling in a form. You are allowed to carry one video camera per person. If you are given a form to fill out, keep it until your departure as you may be asked to show it.

For more detailed information, see the Belarusian US embassy website at **w** www.belarusembassy.org, or contact the **State Customs Office** (☎ 017-234 43 55; *vul Khoruzhoy 29, Minsk*), or the **local customs office** (☎ 017-220 38 22; *vul Ostrovskoho 2A, Minsk*).

MONEY

All prices are listed in Belarusian roubles (abbreviated to BR) in this book.

Currency

The official currency is the Belarusian rouble, which replaced the Soviet rouble in May 1992. It was intended to be a transitional monetary unit, to be used only until the economy stabilised and the Belarusian *taler* could be issued.

Belarusian roubles are better known as *zaichiki* or 'rabbits', named after the one rouble note issued in 1992 that featured a leaping rabbit. The extinct rabbits have since been replaced and devalued many times, and the currency has been the subject of many jokes. In 2001 researchers found it was actually cheaper to use 1 rouble notes than purchase toilet paper.

There is no coinage in Belarus, but notes range from 1 to 20,000 roubles. This means you'll always be left with a fistful of bills after every purchase. It may be difficult to get change with a 10,000 or the rarely seen 20,000 notes.

Exchanging Money

Minsk has a plethora of ATMs (along all major streets, inside metro stations, night clubs etc), which accept all major credit cards and dispense roubles. Many banks and *obmin valjuty* (exchange kiosks) also give cash advances on credit cards. In smaller cities, exchange kiosks are not difficult to find. Most hotels have around-the-clock exchange services.

Exchange Rates

The following exchange rates were correct at the time of research.

country	unit		Belarusian rouble (BR)
Eurozone	€1	=	BR2072
Latvia	lat1	=	BR3355
Lithuania	lita1	=	BR600
Poland	1 zl	=	BR501
Russia	RR1	=	BR62
UK	UK£1	=	BR3087
Ukraine	10 hv	=	BR3638
USA	US$1	=	BR1941

Costs

For travellers to Belarus, the major cost will be accommodation. For foreigners, there is now very little choice available, as hotel prices more than doubled in early 2002. It is very hard to find budget accommodation, with singles running at a minimum of US$25 to US$50; for what you get, prices are unrealistically inflated.

In Minsk, dining in all but the cheapest cafés will also cost you more than you'd think – about BR17,000 for an average-sized meal. Almost everything else is inexpensive, however. You can travel to most corners of the country from Minsk for under BR15,000. Local buses cost BR120. Museums in Minsk charge foreigners up to 35 times more than locals (BR5000), but in other cities admission costs around BR160. A night at the opera will cost only a few dollars, and hanging out drinking beer is very cheap by Western standards.

POST & COMMUNICATIONS
Post

The word for post office is *pashtamt*. Addresses are written as in Russia, basically in the opposite direction to the West, with the country first and the name last.

Posting a 20g letter within Belarus costs BR62 and to any other country BR466. The best way to mail important, time-sensitive items is with Express Mail Service (EMS), offered at most main post offices, or better (but more expensive) one of the multinational services such as UPS, DHL or TNT in Minsk (see that chapter for details).

Telephone

Local Calls There are two kinds of pay phones in Belarus – the old-style, grey boxes, which have been refitted to accept phonecards instead of kopecks, and the newer, blue pay phones that accept another type of phonecard. Local calls can be made from both, but intercity and international calls, or local mobile numbers that require the ☎ 8 prefix can only be made from the blue phones, which are few and far between. Both types of phonecard can be purchased from post offices and some newspaper kiosks, and range in price from about BR3000 to BR10,000.

Useful numbers include:

AT&T Direct ☎ 8 800 101
City Code information ☎ 053
Directory information ☎ 09
Minsk Infoline ☎ 085; English-language
  operators ☎ 221 84 48 – 9am to 5pm daily
Police ☎ 02

Intercity & International Calls Intercity and international phone calls can be made in one of three ways: from a private phone; from *perehovorny punkt* (long-distance telephone offices), often found near or in main post and telegraph offices; or through the new, bluecard phones, found in most hotels, all post offices and on some street corners along praspekt Francyska Skaryny in Minsk.

To dial within Belarus, dial ☎ 8, wait for the new tone, then dial the city code and the number. To dial abroad, dial ☎ 8, wait for the new tone, then dial ☎ 10, country code, city code and the number. If you can't get through, try placing your call with an **international operator** *(Minsk ☎ 017-233 29 71)*.

To phone Belarus from abroad, dial ☎ 375 followed by the city code and home number.

Email & Internet Access In Minsk, accessing the Internet is easy – there are several clubs and cafés for that purpose, and some post and telephone offices boast terminals.

All other urban centres also have Internet access points, though some might require advance booking to use a computer. Smaller towns and villages will likely be bereft of public computers, however.

DIGITAL RESOURCES

Belarus is very well represented on the Web – it's possible to spend hours reading up on

View across to Mt Cheget on the way up to Mt Elbrus

Locomotive, Krasnoyarsk

Tundra ice, northeastern Siberia

Koryaksky Volcano, Kamchatka

Beluga whale *(Delphinapterus leucas)*

Freezing winter weather in the village of Listvyanka, Lake Baikal

more than you'd have thought possible on the country.

w www.inyourpocket.com While the print version of its Minsk guide has not been published for several years, information is occasionally added to its website. Even if its information isn't the most up-to-date, its irreverent comments are spot-on.

w www.ac.by/country This site regroups over 3000 sites in various languages related to every last detail of Belarusian society, history, sports, business, clubs...

w www.belarus-misc.org An excellent site written by patriotic expats, this has all the dirt you need about the country's hedgy politics and abuses of human rights as well as about Lukashenka's bad grammar!

w www.belarustoday.info What used to be the country's only English newspaper is no longer being printed, but is now a great site featuring up-to-date news from Belarus, including the kind of stuff you're not likely to read in the local, state-sponsored press!

BOOKS
Some of the books mentioned in the European Russia Facts for the Visitor chapter deal with the whole former USSR and include portions relating to Belarus.

Guidebooks
Minsk – A Historical Guide (1994), by Guy Picarda, has detailed historical information and plenty of travel information on Minsk, including walking tours of the city and motoring tours of the surrounding region.

There are several Russian-language softcover guidebooks, published annually, on sale in bookshops. The English-language *Minsk What & Where*, a free annual magazine available at travel agencies, contains helpful general information on the city's museums and places to eat.

History & Politics
What few books there are solely about Belarusian history are difficult to find (though Amazon.com always has a few in stock), and are simply nonexistent inside Belarus.

Canadian history professor David Marples has written two excellent books that assess the enduring consequences of the Soviet regime, the Chernobyl disaster and Lukashenka's regime, taking into account Belarus' unique sociopolitical context: *Belarus: From Soviet Rule to Nuclear Catastrophe* (1996),

and *Belarus: A Denationalized Nation* (1999).

Belarus: At a Crossroads in History, by Jan Zaprudnik, although published in 1993, is one of the best reads on the conditions affecting the newly independent nation. *Belorussia: the Making of a Nation*, by Nicholas Vakar, covers history up to the 1950s, including the origins of folk traditions. *Belarus at the Crossroads* (1999), edited by Sherman W Garnett and Robert Legvold, is an excellent collection of essays examining the country's current political position as seen from American, Russian and Lithuanian perspectives.

Out of Fire, edited by Ales Adamovich, Janka Bryl & Vladimir Kolesnik, is a shocking collection of first-hand stories of the brutal atrocities committed during WWII, although told with a decidedly Soviet slant. *Defiance: The Bielski Partisans*, by Nechama Tec, tells the story of Jewish WWII partisans in the forests of western Belarus.

Kurapaty: Articles, Comments and Photographs, by opposition leader Zjanon Paznjak, is a controversial 1994 exposé of the Soviet slaughter of Belarusians at Kurapaty, just outside of Minsk. For the flipside of WWII atrocities, read Martin Dean's 1999 *Collaboration in the Holocaust: Crimes of the Local Police in Belorussia and Ukraine, 1941–44*.

NEWSPAPERS & MAGAZINES
President Lukashenka's administration has been battling the free press for years, forcing many independent papers out of business by refusing to grant operating licenses, imposing exorbitant fines for supposed violations, and driving them out of their operating premises; however, there still exist several independent papers. They regularly publish scathing critiques of the president, and articles are sometimes so venomous that many moderate readers find them off-putting.

State-run newspapers such as *Sovetskaya Belorussia* dominate the market, usually featuring at least once a week a photo of Lukashenka on the cover striking a commanding pose, framed by headlines bellowing about how the country is in good hands and following the right path. Popular among the independent press is *Belorusskaya Gazeta*, which features many articles about the sorry political path the country is actually on, and *Vecherny Minsk* (Evening Minsk), an apolitical paper with listings of cultural events.

BELARUS

Newspaper kiosk vendors will inform you which papers are *gosudarstveniy* (government) or *nyezavisimiy* (independent). There are no English-language newspapers.

RADIO & TV

State-owned Radio Minsk, heavy on classical concerts, can usually be picked up anywhere along the dial on the plastic radio hanging on your hotel room wall. The most popular station is FM 104.6, Radio BA, the first private radio station in the country. FM 108 is Belarus State Radio.

Most TV channels are from Russia. There is a national Belarusian TV channel, where you can see exciting reports on Lukashenka's every move, and there are a few local stations across the country as well, with a mix of Belarusian and Russian-language programming.

PHOTOGRAPHY & VIDEO

Film (predominantly only colour print) can be widely purchased in Minsk and at photo-developing shops in most large department stores.

TIME

Belarus is one hour behind Moscow time, ie, GMT/UMC plus two hours. At midnight on the last Sunday in March the country shifts to 'summer time', setting clocks ahead one hour, and on the last Sunday in September sets them back again.

ELECTRICITY

Belarus' electrical system is the same as Russia's: standard voltage is 220V, 50Hz AC. Sockets require a continental or European plug with two round pins.

HEALTH

Most of the information given in the Health section of the European Russia Facts for the Visitor chapter also applies to Belarus, including the incidence of tick encephalitis and Lyme disease in rural areas in summer. Certain immunisations, such as tetanus, typhoid and diphtheria, should be current. Unboiled tap water is not recommended to drink, although for showering and brushing teeth it should pose no problems. Village well water, especially in the south of the country, is also not recommended to drink. Bottled mineral water is easily found across the country.

Chernobyl

Belarus suffered most from the 1986 Chernobyl disaster, with 70% of the fallout landing on its territory. Some 20% of the country's forests and well over 250,000 hectares of agricultural land remain contaminated. The plight of residents in the worst-hit southeastern areas only gradually became clear with increasing reports of cancer and related diseases, birth anomalies and so on. Scientists say that because thyroid cancer and other disorders take time to develop, the full extent of the health effects from the disaster won't be known until at least 2006 – and until the government allows a free flow of information about the topic.

The risk to short-term visitors from the aftermath of the Chernobyl nuclear disaster is considered insignificant. The areas in Belarus to stay away from, at least for long-term exposure, are the southeastern regions. Some experts say that being in the most exposed areas for one week is the equivalent of getting one chest X-ray. The city of Homel and south of Mahileu were heavily exposed.

Some regional museums display maps that show the levels and areas of contamination in the country, but these can at best be used as guidelines. It's widely believed that in drawing up such maps, the government purposely did not classify certain towns and cities as contaminated, even when neighbouring villages (in some cases 1km or 2km away) were considered tainted, in order to avoid having to compensate areas with large populations.

WOMEN TRAVELLERS

Women travelling on their own is a rare sight in these parts, and would be looked upon as an oddity ('Oh, those foreigners!'), but those wishing to do so should encounter no particular problems or harassment. The restaurants listed in this book would all serve as appropriate hang-outs for single women, but in bars and pubs, women alone may be mistaken for prostitutes and may be approached as such. On the streets, you need not dress conservatively, however; young women here often express their femininity through fashion styles that would be considered provocative or sexy in the West. As this is the norm, they are not pestered in public places for it. Travellers should be aware that traditional sex roles are quite firmly in place here, with both sexes straining to act in ways seen to be in accordance with their genders.

The **Discussion Women's Club** (☎ 017-263 77 36; e beluwi@minsk.soram.com), in Minsk, is a nongovernmental organisation (NGO) that regularly hosts forums and meetings about women's issues in Belarus.

GAY & LESBIAN TRAVELLERS

Homosexuality is less tolerated in Belarus than in Russia. Although sex between consenting women is legal in Belarus from the age of 14 and between consenting men from 18, the state is not supportive of gay initiatives and organisations, and prevented the Gay Pride parade from occurring in September 2000. However, there is a lively and popular gay bar in Minsk, Babylon (see Entertainment in the Minsk chapter), and the **Belarus Lambda League** (Minsk; ☎ 017-221 92 05; e uwb@user.unibel.by), can also provide assistance and advice.

DISABLED TRAVELLERS

Wheelchair-bound travellers will find that many locations in Minsk are accessible: metro entrances and underground walkways, hotels and some museums. Still, Belarusian society is not used to serving disabled tourists and is much less equipped than in the West. Hotel, restaurant and museum staff will usually be happy – if caught unawares – to help.

An organisation called **MOOIZ** (☎ 017-223 14 73; Amuratorskaja vul 4, Minsk) has developed special programs for the blind and sight-impaired. Call for further information.

SENIOR TRAVELLERS

Belarus offers no particular impediments for senior travellers, nor does it offer much that's specifically geared to them. A general respect for the elderly that exists in Belarusian society will see that seniors in need of temporary assistance will usually be offered it by passersby. Discounts are often available to seniors on public transport and in some museums and concert halls.

USEFUL ORGANISATIONS

The dynamic independent youth organisation called **Next Stop – New Life** (☎ 017-221 27 22, fax 221 81 79; w nextstop.org.by; Fizkulturnaja vul 26A, Minsk) organises festivals and youth exchanges, outreach programs, cultural events and ecological summer camps.

The **Children of Chornobyl Fund** (☎ 017-234 21 53; e childr@user.unibel.by; Star-Avilenskaja vul 14, Minsk) organises help groups for children and adults directly affected by Chernobyl. By way of donations it distributes medicines, sets up camps and workshops, and provides help for elderly persons who have been displaced as a result of the disaster.

DANGERS & ANNOYANCES

The level of crime in Belarus, partially thanks to the omnipresence of police on city centre streets, is relatively low, far below those of Western countries. As a foreigner you have a slightly higher chance of being targeted – don't flash your money around or put yourself in a vulnerable situation. For further information and general advice, see Dangers & Annoyances in the European Russia Facts for the Visitor chapter.

BUSINESS HOURS

Most shops inconveniently close for lunch for an hour in the afternoon, anytime between noon and 4pm. Most shops are open every day, with slightly shorter hours on weekends.

PUBLIC HOLIDAYS & SPECIAL EVENTS

The night of 6–7 July is a celebration with pagan roots called *Kupalye*. Similar to St John's Day, celebrated in the Baltic States and Scandinavia on 24 June, young girls gather flowers and throw them into a river as a method of fortune-telling, and everyone else sits by lakeside or riverside fires, drinking beer.

In mid-July in Vitsebsk is the Slavyansky Bazar, a major musical event that gathers Slavic singers and performers from many countries (see Vitsebsk in the Elsewhere in Belarus chapter). The Belarusian Musical Autumn is an international folk dance and folk and classical-music festival, which takes place in different Minsk locales during the last ten days of November.

The main public holidays, which may or may not be recognised due to presidential whims, are:

New Year's Day	1 January
Orthodox Christmas Day	7 January
International Women's Day	8 March
Catholic Easter	March/April
Orthodox Easter	March/April

Radunitsa	Ninth day after Orthodox Easter
International Labour Day	1 May
Victory Day (1945)	9 May
Day of the Coat of Arms & the State Flag of the Republic of Belarus	Second Sunday in May
Independence Day	3 July
Dzyady (Memory Day)	2 November
Anniversary of the October Revolution	7 November
Catholic Christmas Day	25 December

ACTIVITIES

Because most of Belarus is flat as a board, hiking isn't exactly a major pastime. National parks boast some pretty walking trails, however, and the region around Lake Narach (see later) makes for some particularly scenic forest walks.

The flatness of Belarus does make it a good, easy option for long-range **cycling** expeditions, though. Cycling from Minsk to Njasvizh would take you through some small villages and picturesque countryside, and the region around Lake Narach is worth exploring on two wheels.

Minsk's favourite **swimming** and tanning area is Minskae Mora (Minsk Sea), a small lake 17km north of the capital. This little getaway place has a free public beach, and offers pedal-boat and catamaran rental. Over a dozen buses make the 45-minute trip daily from Minsk's central bus station; by car, head north along the P28 and watch for the signs after the village of Ratomka.

Some 160km north of Minsk, along the P28, is the town of Narach, which sits on the banks of the country's largest lake, Lake Narach (79 sq km). It's a popular outdoor recreational area, with a large **tourist complex** (☎ 297-4 74 43; *vul Turistkaja*), where boat rentals and many summer-oriented activities can be organised.

With over 10,000 small lakes and streams totalling more than 90,000km in length, **fishing** is obviously a national pastime.

For more activities, see Spectator Sports in the Minsk chapter.

COURSES

The linguistic faculty of the **Belarusian State University** (*Filahahichny fakultet BDU*; ☎ 017-222 31 42; e sb@phyl.bsu.unibel.by; *vul Francyska Skaryny 4*) organises seminars on Belarusian linguistic issues. It also func-

tions as a good source of information on where to take courses in Belarusian and Russian in Belarus.

WORK

Most foreigners working in Belarus are affiliated with either an embassy, a joint business venture or a university such as the **Institute of Foreign Languages** (*vul Zakharava 21, 220662 Minsk*). Transient seasonal work for foreigners doesn't exist in Belarus.

ACCOMMODATION
Camping

Farmers and villagers are generally generous about allowing campers to pitch a tent on their lot for an evening, although they may be astounded to see non-natives so far out in the countryside. Outside national parks you may camp in forests and the like, provided you don't make too much of a ruckus. Camping within cities is forbidden and there are no Western-style camping grounds.

Hotels

While accommodation standards in Belarus tend to be lower than those in the West, they are generally decent. Unless stated otherwise, prices include rooms with a private bathroom (toilet and shower). Cheaper hotels usually have rooms with three beds, without bathroom facilities, that cost about half as much as single rooms per person.

When checking in, you'll need to surrender your passport, generally for under an hour, while the staff registers you. Usually, you are expected to leave your key at the front desk or with the *dezhurna* (floor lady), who'll keep it in supposed safety while you're out gallivanting.

Homestays

Opting for homestays is catching on, and more travel agencies are organising them. Usually, the host family also acts as your personal guide and a source of information. Agencies dealing with homestays in the Minsk area include:

Gateway Travel (☎ 02-9745 3333, fax 9745 3237) 48 The Boulevarde, Strathfield, NSW 2135, Australia
Host Families Association (HOFA; ☎/fax 812-275 1992, e alexei@hofak.hop.stu.neva.ru, w webcenter.ru/~hofa) 5-25 Tavricheskaya ulitsa, St Petersburg, Russia

Apartments

In Minsk, it's possible to rent centrally located, spacious and clean apartments for a lot less than any hotel charges – usually US$15 to US$25 per day for a spacious one-room apartment. The only downside is not receiving official registration, which is automatically organised at hotels. You can either take a chance that border guards will not check for this upon your departure (they rarely do, but you'd be liable for a fine if caught), or register yourself at the PVU.

The friendly and efficient **Harmony Agency** (☎ 29-282 60 08, 017-283 10 78; W *www.russianlady.net/apartment1*), which conveniently doubles as a reliable dating and matchmaking service, has several excellent options in the centre of Minsk.

FOOD & DRINK

The Belarusians love their mushrooms, and mushroom-gathering is a traditional expedition in Belarus. It's hard to avoid the fungus, as they pop up in one way or another everywhere. *Hribnoy sup* is a mushroom and barley soup, and *kotleta pokrestyansky* is a pork cutlet smothered with a mushroom sauce.

Draniki are potato pancakes – a very traditional Belarusian dish. *Kolduni* are delicious, thick potato dumplings stuffed with meat, while *kletsky* are dumplings stuffed with either mushrooms, cheese or potatoes.

Try Belarusian *kvas*, a popular elixir made of malt, flour, sugar, mint and fruit. *Belovezhskaja* is a bitter herbal alcoholic drink. Most popular among alcoholic beverages are, of course, vodka and beer.

ENTERTAINMENT

As the nation's capital, Minsk is also the country's entertainment centre, with all kinds of concerts, plays and performances staged most days. However, other major urban centres, such as Vitebsk and Brest, have their fair share of entertainment options too. The Belarusian Ballet is one of the best in Eastern Europe and shouldn't be missed. Belarusian folk choirs are popular, with a long tradition of performing. Nightlife is always a popular option, particularly in Minsk where most of the dance clubs and many bars stay open to the wee hours to appease the endless joie de vivre coursing through the veins of Belarusian clubbers. For listings of cultural events and activities, see Entertainment in the Minsk chapter.

SPECTATOR SPORTS

Dinamo Minsk is Belarus' top soccer club and plays frequently in its home stadium in central Minsk, but there's no denying that ice hockey is the number one spectator sport in the country, especially since Lukashenka has gone all-out to help popularise it. After Belarus was placed fourth in the ice hockey tournament at the 2002 Winter Olympics, the sport was given an extra boost. Cross-country skiing is another popular winter sport.

In Olympic events, Belarus has, in the past, been a major power in the biathlon, gymnastics, shooting and rowing. Vitaly Shcherbo, considered one of the world's finest gymnasts, is a six-time Olympic gold medallist and has won 14 world championship medals. The two reputedly strongest men in the world, Alexander Kurlovich and Leonid Taranenko, are also Belarusian.

For a comprehensive list of websites related to sporting associations and opportunities in Belarus, check W www.ac.by /country/sports.

SHOPPING

Folk art is the main source of souvenirs, which include carved wooden trinkets, ceramics and woven textiles. Unique to Belarus are wooden boxes intricately ornamented with geometric patterns composed of multi-coloured pieces of straw. These are easily found in city department stores and in some museum gift shops.

Getting There & Away

Travel into Belarus is unrestricted at all main border points, provided you have a valid visa. Land travel in either direction is possible between Belarus and Russia to the east, Lithuania and Latvia to the north, Poland to the west and Ukraine to the south. All international flights arrive and depart from Minsk (see the Air section later).

AIR

International flights entering and departing Belarus do so at the **Minsk-2 airport** (☎ 279 10 32), about 40km east of Minsk. Some domestic flights as well as flights to Kiev, Kaliningrad and Moscow depart from the smaller **Minsk-1 airport** (☎ 222 54 18), only about 3km from the city centre.

Belavia (☎ 017-210 41 00; w http://belavia .hypermart.net; vul Njamiha 14, Minsk), Belarus' national airline, has direct connections to a number of destinations, including London (US$390 return), Berlin, Frankfurt, Prague, Rome, St Petersburg, Stockholm, Tel Aviv, Vienna and Warsaw (all once to three times a week). It also flies several times a week to Boston, Chicago and New York (all via Shannon, Ireland), and Beijing, Delhi and Tokyo (all via Moscow). Belavia also offers daily flights to Kiev and Moscow (both US$165 return), and weekly flights to a number of other cities in Russia. Belavia has offices in Berlin (☎ 30-2023 20 25), London (☎ 020-7393 1202) and Moscow (☎ 095-923 10 84).

A number of other airlines service Minsk. Airline offices in the capital include:

Austrian Airlines (☎ 017-289 19 70) praspekt Masherava 19
El Al Israeli Airlines (☎ 017-211 26 06) Kamsamolskaja vulitsa 8-18
LOT Polish Airlines (☎ 017-226 66 28) praspekt Masherava 7
Lufthansa Airlines (☎ 017-284 71 29) praspekt Francyska Skaryny 56

LAND
Border Crossings

Long queues at border crossings are not uncommon. The most frequently used bus crossings are those on the quick four-hour trip between Vilnius (Lithuania) and Minsk, and the seven-hour trip between Minsk and

Warning

The information in this chapter is particularly vulnerable to change: prices for international travel are volatile, routes are introduced and cancelled, schedules change, special deals come and go, and rules and visa requirements are amended. You should check directly with the airline or a travel agency to make sure you understand how a fare (and the ticket you may buy) works and be aware of the security requirements for international travel.

The upshot of this is that you should get opinions, quotes and advice from as many airlines and travel agencies as possible before you part with your hard-earned cash. The details given in this chapter should be regarded as pointers and are not a substitute for your own careful, up-to-date research.

Bialystok (Poland). Buses stop at the border for customs and passport controls.

If you're driving your own vehicle, there are about 10 main road routes into Belarus through border stations. To avoid possible complications, drivers should enter by one of these official routes. International driving permits are recognised in Belarus. Roads in Belarus are predictably bad, but main highways are decent. Fuel is available on the outskirts of most major cities, but may be difficult to find elsewhere.

International trains cross into/out of Belarus at more than 10 crossing points and from five different countries.

To/From Estonia

There is a weekly Eurolines bus from Tallinn to Minsk, passing through Pskov in Russia and Vitsebsk, as well as a twice weekly train via Riga and Vilnius.

To/From Latvia

The main road and rail crossing lies between Polatsk and Daugavpils (four to five hours) along the Dzvina River valley.

To/From Lithuania

There are two train lines converging on Vilnius from Belarus. The busiest is the Minsk–Vilnius line (four to five hours, several trains daily), which passes through Maladzechna. The Warsaw–Vilnius direct line passes through Hrodna. There are many daily buses between Vilnius and Minsk, between Vilnius and Lida and between Kaunas and Hrodna.

To/From Poland

The main train route into Belarus from Poland is the Brest crossing; the Polish border station is the town of Terespol. Dozens of trains pull through each day, including the frequently used Warsaw–Minsk–Moscow route.

The other rail and road crossing is between Hrodna and Bialystok, the same crossing used by some of the St Petersburg–Vilnius–Warsaw trains. Two buses a day run between Minsk and Bialystok (seven hours).

To/From Russia

The main northern rail and road crossing from Minsk to St Petersburg (via Vitsebsk) is the Belarusian border town of Ezjaryshcha and the Russian town of Lobok. Both the train and main road (M1) between Minsk and

Moscow cross the border between Orsha (Belarus) and Smolensk (Russia), near the Russian town of Krasnoe.

To/From Ukraine

There are only three main entry points to Ukraine from Belarus, the busiest being the train and road link between Homel and Chernihov (Ukraine); the nightly Minsk–Kiev train uses this route. South of Mazyr (Belarus) is a road link to the town of Ovruch, and from Brest, the M12 leads to Kovel.

ORGANISED TOURS

Very few travel agencies abroad specialise in trips to Belarus. See the European Russia Getting There and Away chapter for agencies specialising in Russian travel, but which may include Belarus in their itineraries. There are a number of agencies inside Belarus, such as Belintourist and Sakub, which would be more than happy to organise personalised individual or group tours, starting from your country of origin. (See Travel Agencies in the Minsk chapter.)

Getting Around

Travel within Belarus, although not always easy, is completely unrestricted. The country is linked by a system of train lines, bus routes and roads, and the cities themselves are navigable by trolleybus, tram, city bus and, in Minsk, a metro. Local transport can often be crowded, grungy and slow.

AIR

There are several regional airports in Belarus, but at the time of writing the only domestic flight left operating regularly in the country was the Minsk–Gomel route, run by **Gomel Avia** (☎ 017-222 54 18). Contact the office of the Belarus national airline, **Belavia** (☎ 017-229 28 38; vul Njamiha 14, Minsk), for the current status of domestic flights in Belarus.

BUS

Buses are often the better option to trains for travellers on most routes, due to more convenient departure times, faster journey times and frequencies. It's possible to get to most destinations inside Belarus for just a few dollars. A five-hour trip from Minsk to Polatsk costs just BR8000; both the seven-hour trip from Minsk to Turov and the (approximately) 6½-hour trip between Hrodna and Brest will set you back BR10,000.

TRAIN

Trains between major cities are reasonably frequent and cheap. A typical train ticket between Minsk and Polatsk (6¼ to eight hours) or Minsk and Brest (five to six hours) on a *kupe* (2nd-class sleeper) costs under BR14,000. Local electric trains are even cheaper, but much slower. Train stations are called *zhelznadarazhniy* or *vokzal* (station).

Sometimes getting information about how to get from one city to another can be overwhelming – not only will schedules be written in Belarusian, the information on them may contradict what you're told at the information counter. You should also be sure to note the duration of your chosen train, as there might be several types of trains making the same journey, each with a different duration.

CAR & MOTORCYCLE

With spare parts rare, road conditions rugged and getting lost inevitable, driving or riding in Belarus is undeniably problematic. However, it is always an adventure and the best way to really see the country. Make sure you know a bit about general mechanics before setting off, and don't take a shiny, new car and expect it to stay that way; it may also tempt car thieves. Also be aware that truck drivers sometimes drive at night without headlights.

The E30 (M1) highway dissects Belarus and is the major route between Warsaw and Moscow; it's in relatively good shape. For more information on road conditions, rules and regulations, fuel, repairs and motorbikes, see the Getting Around European Russia chapter. Road police are not very forgiving (though they can usually be made so with the offer of a few dollars), so be sure to obey all legal limits and make sure you have have all the necessary documents handy.

Road Rules

You will be instructed by signs to slow down when approaching GAI (road police) stations; not doing will get you a substantial fine. GAI signs may be in Russian (UFQ) or Belarusian (LFQ).

Rental

Cars can be rented in Belarus with or without a driver, but it may be cheaper to bargain with a taxi driver if you just want to go to one way and back for a day trip. The going rate for a city taxi is BR450 per kilometre, and drivers will be happy to take you outside the city for a reasonable price. Rates for car rental average at around US$15 per hour or US$50 to US$200 per day depending on the type of car and whether or not you have a driver.

For details of some car-rental agencies, see the Getting There & Away section in the Minsk chapter.

HITCHING

Hitching is never entirely safe in any country in the world, and Lonely Planet does not recommend it. Nevertheless, in Belarus it is a very common method to get around the country, especially for students. Avoid hitching at night or alone. Women should exercise caution.

LOCAL TRANSPORT

Local transport in Minsk is reasonably efficient; in Brest average; and in other cities infrequent. In any event it will be quite crowded.

Bus and trolleybus tickets *(kvitok* or *bilet)* cost BR120. You can buy them at most kiosks around bus stops. Single-trip plastic metro *zhetony* (tokens) are sold in Minsk's metro stations for BR150. Monthly passes for all modes of transport are also available and

there are ticket inspectors on all but the metro. The fine for fare evasion is very small.

An A sign indicates a bus stop, T indicates a tram stop, Tp a trolleybus stop, and M a metro station.

ORGANISED TOURS

Once you're in the country and you wish to have a tour or excursion arranged, contact Belintourist or the other travel agencies listed in the Minsk chapter.

Minsk Мінск

☎ 017 • pop 1.71 million

There's a palpable pride about Minsk, the pride of a survivor. It has come back from the dead several times in its almost millennium of existence (the city's official birthday is 3 March 1067). It was frequently destroyed by fire throughout the centuries, sacked by Crimean Tatars in 1505, trampled to ruin by the French in 1812, and damaged by the Germans in 1918 and the Poles in 1919–20. Its greatest suffering came in WWII, when half the city's people died, including almost the entire population of 50,000 Jews. Virtually every building here has been erected since 1944, when Minsk's recapture by the Soviet army left barely a stone standing.

Moscow architects were given a blank slate after the war and they decided to make out of Minsk's ruins a model Soviet city. The excess of monumental classicism was supposed to give the impression of worker utopia. The wide boulevards, expansive squares and the grandiose proportions of the buildings in the city centre do initially impress, but after a while these same elements take on an oppressive weightiness. Aside from a minuscule reconstructed Old Town and an equally tiny unreconstructed old section, the city has no cosy corners or alleyways as antidotes to the concrete grandeur. However, there are several pleasant parks as well as a lovely promenade along the Svislach River, which courses through the city and acts as the city's main strolling grounds and jogging path. Evenings, when buildings are beautifully illuminated, offer a softer view of the city.

Over the past 50 years Minsk has watched its population triple with the pouring in of industry. Before independence, it was the industrial powerhouse of the western USSR. Although Minsk is the nominal capital of the Commonwealth of Independent States (CIS), a decision made in the hope of turning the city into a 'Brussels of the East', it is little more than a figurehead. It has developed something of a bustling, metropolitan atmosphere, but the dearth of tourists and peoples of visible minorities give it a disconnected, insular feel. Minsk is, however, a safe city, thanks partially to the fact that there are more police here per capita than in any other European city). It's also ultra-clean and best enjoyed as most youths do – hanging out in the parks, and kicking back with a few beers.

Highlights

- Walk along some of the ex–Soviet Union's cleanest, grandest, most Soviet-looking streets
- Down a Belarusian pint in the shadow of the KGB building
- Buy your very own poster of Lukashenka in the shops, or just hang out in the city's parks
- Sample homemade *samagon* (moonshine) in the recreated 19th-century village of Dudutki
- Wander leisurely through the lush, sprawling palace fortress grounds at Njasvizh

✪ Minsk p652

ORIENTATION

The city of Minsk stretches about 15km from north to south and east to west, the Brest–Moscow highway crossing it from southwest to northeast. The highway is called praspekt Francyska Skaryny in the centre.

Vulitsa Lenina is one of the main streets intersecting praspekt Francyska Skaryny. North of vulitsa Njamiha, Lenina becomes

MINSK

praspekt Masherava. Both the main train and bus stations are two blocks southeast of ploshcha Nezalezhnastsi.

Maps

Interpresservis publishes a colourful Minsk map (BR1800), with a handy public transport scheme on one side. Trivium publishes a very detailed 1:20,000 scale Minsk map (with a 1:10,000 centre map), listing every city street and costing about BR2500. These are easily found in kiosks and bookshops.

INFORMATION
Tourist Offices

There are no Western-styled tourist information offices anywhere in Belarus, so travel agencies are your best source of information (see later in this section for details).

Money

There are money-exchange bureaus in every hotel, in most big shops, lining major streets and around the bus and train stations. Many are able to offer cash advances on major credit cards. The most popular foreign currencies are US dollars and the euro. Typically, exchange bureaus in main hotels offer the most varied services, including cashing travellers cheques. The one in the lobby of Hotel Jubileynaja (see Places to Stay) is open 24 hours.

Along praspekt Francyska Skaryny you'll find a bevy of hard-currency exchange kiosks. ATMs are now omnipresent but do not dispense US dollars. There is an **exchange kiosk** (vul Njamiha 8; open 9.30am-9.30pm Mon-Sat, 9.30am-7pm Sun) inside the Na Nemige shopping centre.

Post, Telephone & Fax

Minsk's **central post office** (pashtamt; pr Francyska Skaryny 10; open 8am-8pm Mon-Sat, 10am-5pm Sun) is at the eastern end of ploshcha Nezalezhnastsi. It is worth visiting if only for the impressive neobaroque, domed interior. For express delivery, use the state-run **Express Mail Service** (EMS; ☎ 227 85 12) on the post office's 2nd floor, or the Western couriers **DHL** (☎ 228 11 08), **TNT** (☎ 236 80 00) or **UPS** (☎ 227 22 33), all of which have offices in major hotels, including the Hotel Jubileynaja and the Hotel Complex Oktjabrsky. From the post office, you can also send faxes (BR500 per page to Europe, BR1500 to North America). You can receive faxes at

☎ 375-17-226 05 30, upon presentation of your passport. They'll cost you just BR100 per page, and staff will hold them for one month.

Also at the central post office is one of the numerous **telegraph offices** (tsentralny telegraf; open 7am-11pm daily), where you can make national and international calls. Another convenient telegraph office is **Beltelekom** (☎ 236 71 24; vul Enhelsa 14; open 24 hrs).

Email & Internet Access

Options for accessing the Internet increase all the time. There is round-the-clock Internet access at **Beltelekom** (☎ 219-06 79; vul Enhelsa 14), although you must call to reserve a terminal as they are usually prebooked, especially between 10am and 11pm. You have a better chance of getting online at **HP Invent** (☎ 226 42 43; vul Njamiha 8; open 9am-11pm daily), an Internet salon in the Na Nemige shopping centre. Both places charge about BR1800 per hour and have printing facilities.

Travel Agencies

Belintourist (☎ 226 98 85, fax 226 94 21; w www.belarustourist.minsk.by; pr Masherava 19A; open 8am-8pm daily) has can-do staff who are able to arrange a variety of city and national tours. The agency mainly deals with groups, but individuals can be accommodated. A city tour runs at around US$45 per group; trips to Khatyn cost around US$65. Its staff can also get about US$10 knocked off the price of a room at the next-door Hotel Jubileynaja if they book it.

U Zheni (☎ 211 26 05; w www.uzheni .com; vul Kamsamolskaja 8/18) deals mainly with Jewish tourists who come to explore their family's roots. It offers at least 10 Jewish-themed tours (plus others) of the country, ranging from a few hours to several days. Its staff are extremely resourceful and helpful, and can also get discounts at some Minsk hotels.

Sakub (☎ 202 10 20; w www.sakub.com; vul Surganova 64) is another completely flexible and very inventive company, which is happy to take individual and group requests, and can arrange all kinds of transport quickly and offer visa support.

Bookshops

The two main bookshops are **Tsentralnaja Kniharnya Mahazin** (☎ 227 49 18; pr Francyska Skaryny 19; open 10am-8pm Mon-Fri,

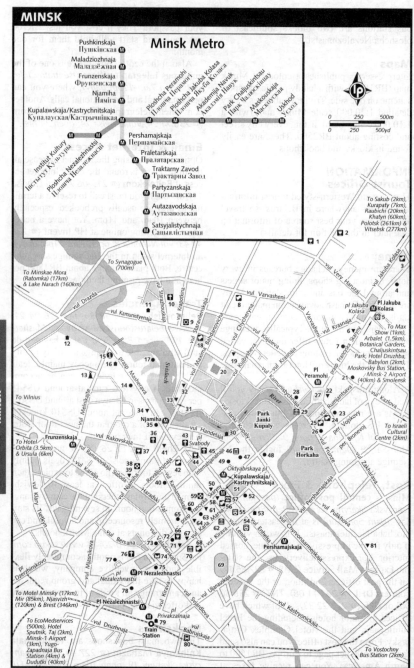

MINSK

Minsk Metro

Pushkinskaja
Пушкінская Ⓜ

Maladziozhnaja
Маладзёжная Ⓜ

Frunzenskaja
Фрунзенская Ⓜ

Njamiha
Няміга Ⓜ

Kupalawskaja/Kastrychnitskaja
Купалаўская/Кастрычніцкая Ⓜ

Ploshcha Peramohi
Плошча Перамогі Ⓜ

Ploshcha Jakuba Kolasa
Плошча Якуба Коласа Ⓜ

Akademija Navuk
Акадэмія Навук Ⓜ

Park Chaljuskintsau
Парк Чалюскінцаў Ⓜ

Maskouskaja
Маскоўская Ⓜ

Uskhod
Усход Ⓜ

Institut Kultury
Інстытут Культуры Ⓜ

Ploshcha Nezalezhnastsi
Плошча Незалежнасці Ⓜ

Pershamajskaja
Першамайская Ⓜ

Praletarskaja
Пралетарская Ⓜ

Traktarny Zavod
Трактарны Завод Ⓜ

Partyzanskaja
Партызанская Ⓜ

Autazavodskaja
Аўтазаводская Ⓜ

Satsyjalistychnaja
Сацыялістычная Ⓜ

MINSK

PLACES TO STAY
11 Hotel Belarus; Avis
 Гасцініца беларус
12 Hotel Planeta; Attant-m
 Гасцініца Планета
16 Hotel Jubileynaja; Intercars
 Гасцініца Юбілейная
30 Zhuravinka
 Журавінка
53 Hotel Complex Oktjabrsky
 Гостиничный комплекс
 Октябрский
79 Hotel Ekspress
 Гасцініца Экспресс

PLACES TO EAT
6 Café Gourmand
 Кафе Гурман
19 Café Gourmand
 Кафе Гурман
22 Stary Mlyn
 Стары Млын
32 Kitaiskoye Zhemchug
 Китайское Жемчуг
33 Karchma Stavravilenskaja;
 Children of Chornobyl Fund
 Карчма Ставравіленская
 фонд Дети Чёрнобыла
34 Tractkir Na Parkavoi
 Трактір на паркавой
41 Air Grip
50 McDonald's; Tsentrainy
 Universam
58 Pechki Lavochki; Patio Pizza;
 El Rincon Espanol
 Патио Пицца Печки-
 Лавочки Испанскій
 Куток
61 Beze
64 Express Kiritsa
 Экспресс КЗрЗца
67 Café Traktir Na Marxa
 Трактир На Маркса
71 Grunwald
 Грунвалд
81 Astra
 Астара

EMBASSIES
3 Latvian Embassy
8 Lithuanian Embassy
18 US & Russian Embassies
24 German Embassy
25 Polish Embassy
42 French Embassy
56 UK Embassy
68 Ukraine Embassy

OTHER
1 Reactor
 Реактор
2 Aquarium
 Акварыум

4 Lufthansa
 Луфтганса
5 Belarusian State Philharmonia
 Беларуская Дзяржаўная
 філармонія
7 Podzemka
 Падземка
9 Synagogue
 Сінагога
10 St Mary Magdeline Church
 Царква св. Мары
 Магдалены
13 Jewish Ghetto Monument
14 Svetoch
 Светоч
15 Belintourist Office
 Белінтурыст
17 Sports Palace
 Палац Спорта
20 National Academic Opera &
 Ballet Theatre
 Дзяржаўны акадэмічны
 вялікі тэатр оперы і
 балета
21 Palats Mastatsva
 Палац мастацтва
23 Institute of Foreign Languages
 Інстытут замежных моў
26 Goethe Institute
27 Ploshcha Peramohi & Victory
 Obelisk
 Плошча Перамогі
28 Former Apartment Building of
 Lee Harvey Oswald
29 Museum of the First Congress
 of the Russian Social
 Democratic Worker's Party
 Дом Музей 1 з езда
 Расійскай сацыял-
 демакратычнай партыі
31 Old Town (Traetskae
 Prodmestse)
 Траецкае прадмесце
35 LOT Airlines
 Авиалнии Дел
36 SS Peter & Paul Church
 Петрапаўлаўская царква
37 Rakovsky Brovar
 Ракоўскій я
38 Na Nemige; HP Invent
 На Німге
39 Belavia
40 U Zheni & El Al Airlines
 Авиалнии У жени и Зл Ал
43 Holy Spirit Cathedral
 Свято Духов савор
44 Vinarnya U Admirala
 Винария у адмирала
45 Bernardine Church
 бернад бернааійнская царква
46 Museum of the Great Patriotic
 War
 Музей гісторы Вялікай
 Айчыннай вайны

47 Trade Unions' Culture Palace;
 Zio Pepe
 Палац культуры
 прафсаюзаўж Зио Пэпэ
48 Circus
49 Palats Respubliki
 Палац Рэспублікі
51 Tsentralny Skver
 Центральны Сквер
52 Presidential Administrative
 Building
54 State Puppet Theatre
55 Janka Kupala Belarusian
 National Theatre; Ministry of
 Foreign Affairs
57 Beltelekom
59 GUM Department
 Store
 Дзяржаўны універсальны
 магазін
60 Tsentralnaja Kniharnya
 Mahazin
 Централное Кнігаря
 Магазин
62 Belarusian State Art
 Museum
 Дзяржаўны мастацкі
 музей беларусі
63 Train Ticket Office
 Чыгуначныя білетныя
 касы
65 KGB Building
 КДб
66 Stary Mensk
 Стары Менск
69 Dinamo Stadium
 Стадыён Дынама
70 Belarus National Museum of
 History & Culture
 беларускі Дзяржаўны
 краязнаўчы музей
72 Mastatsky Salon
 Мастацкі Салон
73 Theatre Ticket Office
 Тэатральная каса
74 Central Post & Telegraph
 Office
 Глаўпаштампт
75 PVU (Main Office)
 ОВПС
76 Church of St Simon & Elena
 Касцёл Сымона і Елены
77 Belarusian Government
 Building
 Дом ураду беларусі
78 Belarusian State University;
 Next Stop - New Life
 беларускі дзяржаўны
 універсітэт; Следующая
 остановка - Новая Жизнь
80 Central Bus Station
 Аўтобусны вакзал
 Подземка

10am-6pm Sat), which has a good selection of dictionaries, postcards, souvenirs, English-language coffee-table books and posters of Lukashenka; and **Svetoch** *(☎ 223 15 03; pr Masherava 11; open 10am-7pm Mon-Sat)*, which has all of the above, plus a larger map selection.

Cultural Centres

The following are good places to catch up on current events, swap stories with expats or just get your hands on a good book, newspaper or magazine.

Goethe Institute (☎ 236 34 33) vul Frunze 5. Open 9am to 6pm Monday to Thursday and 8am to 4.30pm Friday.

Scientific Methodics Centre (☎ 236 79 53) Institute of Foreign Languages, vul Zakharava 21. In place of the defunct British Council, this reading room includes foreign-language books and journals. Call for opening hours.

Laundry

As in Russia, there are no launderettes. Hotels usually provide a laundry service, or you can make a deal with the cleaning ladies.

Toilets

Public toilets – when you can find them – are better left unfound, unless you're partial to those gaping holes in the ground. Your best bets are at large hotels, restaurants and McDonald's. Always keep some spare tissues with you as toilet paper can be a rare sight.

Left Luggage

There are lockers at the bus station and downstairs at the train station.

Medical Services

Medical service is, predictably, well behind Western Europe and in some cases behind other parts of the Commonwealth of Independent States (CIS). No reliable, Western-run clinics operate, but **EcoMedservices** *(☎ 220 45 81; vul Tolstoho 4; open 24 hrs)* comes the closest. Drop-ins are possible, but you'll need to reserve a time with a doctor. Consultations cost between BR9000 and BR21,000. Also contact your embassy to see who they recommend.

Emergency

Emergency contact numbers are: fire ☎ 01, police ☎ 02, ambulance ☎ 03 and gas ☎ 04.

Dangers & Annoyances

Any run-in with the authorities can result in much unpleasantness for tourists. Thus, do not photograph the Presidential Administrative Building (people have had their film ripped out of their cameras for doing so), and avoid participating in opposition rallies and protests, unless you're willing to chance being arrested or questioned.

Minsk has relatively little street crime, unless you count jaywalking, for which the police will quite eagerly fine you!

PRASPEKT FRANCYSKA SKARYNY

Minsk's main street was named after the 16th-century national hero who was the first printer to utilise the printing press in the Old Slavonic and Belarusian languages. Today, the thoroughfare is hectic and huge: it tripled in width when it was rebuilt after WWII and extends over 11km from the train station to the outer city limits. The busiest section – and where the best architectural examples of Soviet monumentalism can be seen – is sandwiched between ploshcha Nezalezhnastsi and ploshcha Peramohi, with the block between vulitsa Lenina and vulitsa Enhelsa doubling as a popular evening youth hangout.

The stubbornly austere, expansive **ploshcha Nezalezhnastsi** (Independence Square; ploshchad Nezavisimosti in Russian) is dominated by the Belarusian Government Building (behind the Lenin statue) on its northern side, and the equally proletarian Belarusian State University on its southern side. At the time of writing, a massive reconstruction project was underway, and once completed, promises to make the square look more inviting.

Breaking the theme of Soviet classicism that dominates the square is the red-brick Catholic **Church of St Simon & Elena** (1910), next to the Belarusian Government Building. Its tall, gabled bell tower and attractive detailing are reminiscent of many brick churches in the former Teutonic north of Poland. It's named after the two children of the Polish nobles who had it built. It was used as a cinema studio in the Soviet era, and it became a key opposition meeting place in the last years of the USSR.

Northwest of the square, along praspekt Francyska Skaryny, are many of Minsk's main shops and cafés. An entire block on this street is occupied by a yellow neoclassical building with an ominous, temple-like Corinthian portal – the **KGB building** *(pr Francyska Skaryny 17)*. On the opposite side of the street is a long, narrow park with a bust of Felix Dzerzhynsky, the founder of the KGB's predecessor, the Cheka, a native of Belarus.

Between vulitsa Enhelsa and vulitsa Janki Kupaly is the city's most impressive square, still referred to by its Russian name **Oktyabrskaya Ploshchad**. Here you'll find the impressively severe **Palats Respubliki** (Palace of the Republic), opened in 2001 after some 15 years in construction. The city's premier concert hall, it resembles a massive mausoleum on the outside, and is decorated in 1960s-style gaudy splendour inside.

Also on this square is the classical-style, multicolumned **Trade Unions' Culture Palace**, which houses exhibition spaces as well as a nightclub and two eateries. Next to this is the highly recommended **Museum of the Great Patriotic War** *(☎ 277 56 11; pr Francyska Skaryny 25A; admission BR5000; open 10am-5pm Tues-Sun)*. The 28 well-designed rooms display the horrors of WWII and go a long way towards explaining Belarus' apparent obsession with WWII, which transformed the land and people of the country. Particularly harrowing are the photos of partisans being executed in recognisable central Minsk locations. The museum also graphically depicts the Nazi atrocities against Jews during the war, giving special attention to the Maly Trostenets concentration camp where over 200,000 Jews from Minsk and surrounding cities were murdered.

Across the street is **Tsentralny Skver** (Central Square), a small park on the site of a 19th-century marketplace. People gather around the small statue of a boy and a swan, play guitar and drink beer until the last metro. Behind this, well-lit and peering through the trees is the **Presidential Administrative Building**, where Lukashenka makes most of his wise decisions. It's also his residence and as such is well guarded. It's best seen from afar.

As praspekt Francyska Skaryny crosses the Svislach River, it passes two of the city's main parks, **Park Janki Kupaly** on the southwestern bank opposite the **circus**, and the larger **Park Horkaha**, where there's a children's section with rides, attractions and fast-food kiosks. Just across the bridge, in a green wooden house by the banks of the river is the **Museum of the First Congress of the Russian Social Democratic Workers' Party** *(☎ 236 68 47; pr Francyska Skaryny 31; admission free; open 10am-6pm Thur-Tues)*, where the Russian Social Democratic Workers' Party – Russia's original Marxist party – held its illegal founding congress in 1898. Today, you can wander around the small museum inside, just as Fidel Castro did in 1972.

Diagonally opposite is the **apartment building** *(Kamunistychnaja vul 4)* where Lee Harvey Oswald – the future alleged assassin of US President John F Kennedy – lived (and was spied on by the KGB) for a few years in his early 20s. This is one of the city's prettiest streets, good for riverside strolling.

Just 100m north of here, **Ploshcha Peramohi** (Victory Square; ploshchad Pobedy in Russian) is hard to miss. A giant victory obelisk rises up from the centre of the busy intersection, the eternal flame at its feet. Parades on 9 May (Victory Day) and 7 November (Anniversary of the October Revolution) often end up here. The eternal flame is accessible from the underground passageway.

Farther north is **Ploshcha Jakuba Kolasa**, another expansive square, this one softened by pleasant parkland and a sitting area near the oversized monument to the Belarusian writer after which it's named.

Praspekt Francyska Skaryny continues northeastward, becoming a bit of a student ghetto around metro Akademija Navuk; various faculties of the State University are located nearby, as well as the impressive, multicolumned **National Scientific Academy** *(pr Francyska Skaryny 66)*. Beyond the hohum **Botanical Gardens** *(pl Kalinina; admission BR500; open 10am-6pm daily early May–late Oct)* and the adjacent, sprawling, forest-like **Chaljuskintsau Park**, the praspekt's shops, cafés and commercial buildings get replaced by residential ones.

OLD TOWN (TRAETSKAE PRODMESTSE)

The congested overpass that now carries vulitsa Lenina over vulitsa Njamiha near the Njamiha metro station was the site of Minsk's main marketplace in the 12th century. In May 1999 the metro entrance was the site of a brutal stampede in which 53 people died. The tragedy occurred when hundreds of young people ran into the pedestrian tunnel to

Jewish Belarus

Around the corner from Hotel Jubileynaja in Minsk, on the corner of vulitsas Zaslavskaja and Melnikajte is the haunting **Jewish Ghetto Memorial**, which marks the site of a pit where on 2 March 1942 – in one day – 5000 Jews were shot and buried. It depicts bronze figures, people of all ages, descending a staircase to face certain death. Sadly, this is a fitting reminder of the fate of the vast majority of the over one million Jews living in what is now Belarus at the start of WWII. Though they made up more than half the population of Minsk, Hrodna, Brest, Vitsebsk and many other towns at the turn of the 20th century, the number of Jews in Belarus today is 26,600 (estimated by the Hebrew University in Jerusalem in 2000).

Belarus' Jewish community dates from the 14th century, when Brest and Hrodna grew as cultural centres, and when Jews were encouraged to settle in these areas by the liberal Lithuanian rulers. After control switched to Russia in the late 18th century, Belarus was part of the Pale of Settlement where Jews were forced to live; however, a series of brutal pogroms in 1881 and uncontained anti-Semitism and cultural persecution thereafter caused many to flee west. Most of those who remained were massacred in and around the 164 ghettos formed by the Nazis in every corner of the country.

Today, the community is tiny and continues to shrink. There are two **synagogues** (vul Krapotkina 22 & vul Daumana 13B), some of the few active ones left in the country. For more information, contact the **Israeli Cultural Centre** (☎ 230 18 74; Uralskaja vul 3; open 9am-5pm Sun-Fri), which has a small library of history books, old maps and documents, mostly in Russian.

escape a sudden thunderstorm at a beer festival. There is now an official memorial at the site, as well as dozens of touching personal memorials pasted by loved ones onto the wall of the metro entrance.

Ploshcha Svabody to the southeast became the new city centre in the 16th century. The baroque, twin-towered Orthodox **Holy Spirit Cathedral**, off the northern end of the small square, stands defiantly on a small hill overlooking its rather bleak surroundings. It was once part of a Polish Bernardine convent (founded in 1628) along with the former **Bernardine Church** next door, which now houses city archives. The former monastery buildings farther to the right (east) have been restored and now house a music academy affiliated with the classical-looking conservatory building at the far southwestern end of ploshcha Svabody.

There are several side streets in the triangle formed by vulitsas Lenina, Handelaja and Internatsjanalnaja, on which some houses remain from the pre-WWII period. They are mainly in poor condition, but their small-scale charm offers a welcome respite in a city whose past is little felt.

Across the vulitsa Lenina overpass sits the attractively restored 17th-century **SS Peter & Paul Church** (vul Njamiha), the city's oldest church (built in 1613, restored in 1871), awkwardly dwarfed by the morose concrete structures surrounding it. It's worth dropping in to see the unusual icons.

A minuscule area on the eastern bank of the Svislach River, bordered by vulitsa Maxima Bahdanovicha, has been rebuilt in 17th- and 18th-century style to recreate the look and feel of what much of Minsk once looked like. This Old Town is known as Traetskae Prodmestse (Trinity Suburb). It is the city's most photographed area, and there are a few cafés, bars, restaurants and craft/gift shops to tempt you for a lazy hour. Two blocks northeast is the ominous-looking **National Academic Opera & Ballet Theatre**, set in a leafy park.

The nicest small church in the city is about 500m north of here near Hotel Belarus. The attractive little **St Mary Magdeline Church** (Tsrakva Svyati Mary Magdaleny; vul Kisjaleva 42) was built in 1847 in the ancient Orthodox style, with a pointed octagonal bell tower over the entrance and a single sweeping dome over the cruciform plan.

MUSEUMS & ART GALLERIES

There is so much history and culture at the **Belarus National Museum of History & Culture** (vul Karla Marxa 12; admission BR5000; open 11am-7pm Thur-Tues), most visitors leave with their heads spinning (the mostly Belarusian-only explanation panels don't ease the confusion much). It takes you on a journey into the turbulent history of the nation, beginning with a replica of the printing press used by national hero Francyska Skaryny and ending on the top floor, usually reserved for ethnographic displays or period installations.

More interesting is the **Belarusian State Art Museum** (☎ 227 71 63; vul Lenina 20; admission BR5000; open 11am-7pm Wed-Mon). Here you'll find the country's largest collection of Belarusian art, in two rooms devoted to works depicting depopulated agrarian bliss from the 1920s and 1930s. There are also some minor European paintings and ceramics. Among the museum's most impressive works are the unusual *Birch Grove* by Arkhip Kuindji; the beautiful *Achilles Mourning the Body of Patrocles* by Nikolai Ge; and two sculptures by Mykhail Klodt, models for the Anichkov Bridge statues in St Petersburg. In addition, there are some works by Ilya Repin, Isaak Levitan, Mikhail Vrubel and Konstantin Makovsky.

A block north of ploshcha Peramohi is the **Palats Mastatsva** (Art Palace; ☎ 213 35 49; vul Kazlova 3; admission free; open 10am-7pm Tues-Sun), an art gallery with interesting temporary exhibitions of modern art. The **Mastatsky Salon** (Art Gallery; ☎ 227 83 63; pr Francyska Skaryny 12; open 10am-8pm Mon-Sat) also features rotating exhibits of local artist.

PLACES TO STAY

With few exceptions, hotels in Minsk follow a predictable mould – unremarkable and overpriced. Budget travellers face a thin choice, as many hotels in the city centre charge at least US$55/70 per night for a single/double room.

Camping & Motels

There are no longer any official camping grounds near Minsk, though the authorities are not tough on those who wish to pitch their tent unobtrusively in outlying wooded areas.

Motel Minsky (☎ 506 51 40; rooms BR15,000 per person) is 17km southwest of the city centre on the Brest highway (Brestskoe shosse; E30/M1) at the 727km marker, shortly beyond the Ptich Reservoir (Vodokhranilishche Ptich). It's a favourite recreation spot as the area around the reservoir is restful and pretty (if you disregard the highway, that is). The tatty motel, a popular truck stop, has small rooms, a restaurant and no visible pluses.

To get here, take one of six daily buses (BR2500, 30 minutes) departing from the Yugo-Zapadnaja bus station to the town of Dzerzhinsk, stopping outside the motel on the way. A taxi to/from the city should cost about BR10,000.

Hotels – Budget

Hotel Ekspress (☎ 225 64 63; pl Privakzalnaja 4; bed in 4-person dorm BR20,000, shared doubles BR26,000 per person, luxury doubles BR118,000), attached to the eastern end of the train station, is a no-frills affair, save for a few 'luxury' rooms (which would not be considered so luxurious in more upscale hotels!). It may be your best bet, especially if you're in a group of three or four and don't mind the absence of showers. All rooms have toilets.

Hotel Sputnik (☎ 229 36 19; vul Brilevskaja 2; singles/doubles from BR40,000/57,000) has some of the city's least expensive rooms – if you can navigate yourself through the brazenly impolite service at the front desk and actually get information about availability. There are many kinds of rooms to choose from, but none are memorable. At least you can commiserate at the friendly, adjacent Indian restaurant, Taj.

Hotel Druzhba (☎ 266 24 81; vul Tolbukhina 3; singles/doubles BR55,000/81,000, triples with shared toilets BR60,000), near the Chaljuskintsau Park metro station, has spartan rooms and a slightly seedy atmosphere, but its triple rooms are one of the best deals in the city (despite the toilet being located in the corridor).

Hotels – Mid-Range

Hotel Orbita (☎ 252 32 08, fax 257 14 20; pr Pushkina 39; singles/doubles from US$35/50), rising above a concrete suburb near Pushkinskaja metro station, boasts friendly, attentive service (something you'll end up appreciating) and dull but decent rooms.

Ursula (☎ 255 13 94; vul Petra Hlebki 11; singles/doubles US$47/70), a cosy, 21-room hotel, is the closest you'll get to a Western-style B&B. Rooms are clean and pleasant. Only the location, about 6km from the centre, might prove inconvenient to some: from Metro Pushkinskaja, it's at least a 10-minute ride (north) on bus No 28, 46 or 49.

Hotel Jubileynaja (☎ 226 90 24, fax 226 91 71; pr Masherava 19; singles/doubles

US$47/58, renovated singles/doubles from US$62/75), with its snazzy, full-service lobby, may come as a welcome contrast to its dull, grey exterior but is sadly no indication of the rooms therein. The renovated rooms have merely been given an extra coat of paint and a few 'Euro-standard' fixings; all rooms in the hotel except the luxury suites are the same brand of mediocre.

Hotel Planeta (☎ 226 78 55, fax 226 77 80; pr Masherava 31; singles/doubles from US$70/ 80), about 200m away from the Jubileynaja, has an equally pretty, marbled lobby but more comfortable and modern rooms. Each room has slightly different furniture and bed sizes – ask to see a few before you choose. It prides itself on its business facilities.

Hotels – Top End

IBB Hotel (☎ 270 39 94, fax 270 39 95; pr Gazety Pravda 11; singles/doubles US$67/ 104) is a business-level, Western-standard oasis in the southwestern corner of the city, although its location (just off the praspekt Dzerzhinskovo highway to Brest) might be a drawback.

Hotel Belarus (☎ 209 76 93, fax 239 12 33; e belarus@hotel.minsk.by; Starazhouskaja vul 15; singles US$55-80, doubles US$80-100, suites from US$160) has several renovated floors, but aside from having the best city views of any Minsk hotel (ask for a room facing the centre), there is nothing noteworthy about this otherwise stodgy 23-storey giant.

Hotel Complex Oktjabrsky (☎ 222 32 89, fax 227 33 14; vul Enhelsa 13; singles/ doubles from US$80/95, suites from US$135- 190), for years until now considered the tops in central Minsk, has a rather humorous formality to it, perhaps due to its location right behind the Presidential Administrative Building. Rooms are starchily tasteful and comfortable.

Zhuravinka (☎ 206 69 00, fax 227 55 42; vul Janki Kupaly 25; singles/doubles US$112/ 167), currently the city's top lodgings, is a sparkling new complex sporting a bowling alley, pool, fitness centre and restaurant where you can hobnob with the Belarus elite (or with those who fancy themselves as such).

PLACES TO EAT

Pleasant dining in the capital remains a challenge, but at least you'll have an interesting time trying to find your favourite spot; each eatery tends to be an experience unto itself. There's lots of good food in the city, but usually it'll end up costing more than you'd expected once you add the garnish (an extra charge, normally) and beverages. Your best bets are the places in this section listed under Belarusian Cuisine.

Restaurants

Belarusian Cuisine The city's best restaurant, hands-down, is **Stary Mlyn** (☎ 284 44 40; pr Francyska Skaryny 40; mains BR5000- 8000; open noon-midnight daily). Boasting four rarities in Minsk restaurants – cosy atmosphere, creative and mouthwatering food, friendly service and reasonable prices – this place offers an array of delicious meat and fish dishes, and dozens of salads. It's almost impossible to go wrong here.

'Peasant food' has become quite a back-to-roots fad in Belarus's big cities. A good bet for this traditional cuisine is **Traktir Na Parkavoi** (☎ 223 69 91; pr Masherava 11; mains BR6000-15,000; open noon-midnight daily), a pleasant early-20th-century country kitchen tucked behind a row of cement blocks. The popular **Rakovsky Brovar** (see Entertainment later in this chapter) serves similar though less tasty fare in an equally rustic but more touristy setting.

Café Traktir Na Marxa (☎ 226 03 61; vul Karla Marxa 21; mains BR3000-7000) is another excellent choice, which serves decent Belarusian food such as draniki. The relaxed atmosphere in this cellar café-cum-bar is better than the food. And it's a good place to hang out and have a few beers.

Pechki Lavochki (☎ 227 78 79; pr Francyska Skaryny 22; mains from BR6000; open 8am-midnight daily) has a large selection of traditional grub, some of it grilled over coal. It also serves breakfast, a relative rarity in the city.

Mediterranean Cuisine Nearly an entire block is taken up by three adjacent restaurants, all of them under the same ownership. Sandwiching Pechki Lavochki (see earlier) are **Patio Pizza** (☎ 227 17 91; pr Francyska Skaryny 22; pizzas BR5000-13,000, salad bar BR12,000, mains BR10,000-22,000; open noon-midnight daily), with good pizzas, a salad bar and a good choice of Italian dishes, and **El Rincon Español** (☎ 227 23 31; pr Francyska Skaryny 22; mains from BR11,000;

open noon-2am daily), which serves fine if pricey Spanish cuisine such as paella. The latter also features occasional live music.

Zio Pepe *(☎ 227 02 95; pr Francyska Skaryny 25; pizzas from BR3500-5500; open noon-4am daily)*, in the Trade Unions' Culture Palace, serves OK thin-crusted pizzas and other Italian fare in an always-crowded, smoky basement. It also does home deliveries.

Ethnic Cuisine The leader in this category is **Taj** *(☎ 229 35 92; vul Brilevskaja 2; mains BR6000-13,000; open noon-midnight daily)*, serving up delicious North Indian food in a subdued atmosphere – subdued, that is, until the belly dancer appears. There's a good selection of vegetarian dishes (all around BR6000), and the menu has English explanations and photos.

Astara *(☎ 289 97 61; vul Pulikhava 37; mains BR5000-11,000; open 10am-11pm daily)* does spicy Azerbaijani kebabs and salads that are worth the cab ride out here. The tacky atmosphere may be even more memorable – an outlandish floor show is assured on weekends, and if the crowd likes it too much, goons doubling as security guards are on hand to assure that no-one has too good a time (exclamations of joy are big no-nos).

Kitaiskoye Zhemchug *(☎ 234 94 41; vul Staravilenskaja 10; mains from BR12,000; open noon-11pm daily)*, one of the few Chinese eateries that have sprouted recently, is seriously overplush, but serves authentic dishes.

Top End There are several ostentatious restaurants in Minsk where you can drop cash alongside rich, shady characters, but the best place for a splurge is **Grunwald** *(☎ 210 42 55; vul Karla Marxa 19; starters BR5000-12,000, mains BR13,000-26,000; open 10am-11.30pm daily)*. The decor is slightly medieval and the atmosphere relaxed, and the superb food is a mix of European and Belarusian (delicious soups and *draniki*, filling enough for a meal). Its menu is a dazzling array of inventive fish and meat dishes.

Cafés

There are a number of good places to hang out, sip espresso and watch life go by. In the Old Town, try **Karchma Stavravilenskaja** *(☎ 289 37 54; vul Staravilenskaja 2; open 11am-midnight daily)*, along the riverfront,

which has a breezy summer terrace and a low-key interior. Its food is good, if overpriced, but it's the beer and coffee that most head here for.

Air Grip *(☎ 226 90 98; vul Njamiha 3; open 10am-11pm daily)* is set up on one of the city's busiest streets, but the terrace is ultra-popular with poseurs and Italian tourists, who appreciate the excellent espresso and gelato.

Beze *(☎ 206 59 06; pr Francyska Skaryny 18; 10am-1am daily)* is an upscale place decked out like a Viennese café and specialises in coffees, ice-cream cocktails and plastic-flavoured pastries.

Café Gourmand has two locations. One is a sweet, brightly decorated little café *(☎ 284 70 78; pr Francyska Skaryny 47)*, whose speciality is delicious *pelmeni* (stuffed ravioli) of all colours and stripes; the other, larger location *(☎ 236 67 74; vul Chycheryna 6)* is more of a restaurant but is a favourite expat haunt. Both are open from 8am to 11pm daily and have a small breakfast menu.

Fast Food

For those desperate moments, there are six **McDonald's** and **McDrive's** (the drive-through version) in Minsk, the main one *(☎ 217 65 28; pr Francyska Skaryny 23)* doubling as one of the city's main youth hangouts. Yes, all their toilets are decent.

Express Kiritsa *(☎ 226 17 08; pr Francyska Skaryny 18; meals under BR8000; open 11am-11pm daily)*, a more interesting alternative to McDonald's, is a cafeteria where all the food, happily swimming in grease, is visible (a pointer's delight).

Self-Catering

Kamarowski Rynok *(vul Very Haruzaj 6; open daily 8am-4pm)*, northwest of the Ploshcha Jakuba Kolasa metro station, is an immense minicity of market mayhem. Inside you'll find nuts, spices, breads, dried fish, meat carcasses – the lot.

There are dozens of grocery shops throughout the city; the best stocked is **Tsentralny Universam** *(☎ 227 88 76; pr Francyska Skaryny 23; open 9am-11pm daily)*.

ENTERTAINMENT
Bars

Rakovsky Brovar *(☎ 206 64 04; Vitsebskaja vul 10; open noon-midnight daily)* is the best place for a Belarusian pint. Because of its four brewed-on-site beers, both light and dark, this is the city's most popular place for suds-lovers. Its food is largely unsurprising, however.

Stary Mensk (☎ 289 14 00; pr Francyska Skaryny 14; open 8.30am-11.30pm daily) is a tiny watering hole (in-the-wall!), but has two things going for it – from its terrace, you can get sauced while trying to focus on the KGB building on the opposite side of the street, and inside there are more photos of pre-WWII Minsk than you'll find at any museum.

Vinarnya U Admirala (☎ 206 53 32; pl Svabody 10A; open 24 hrs), a pleasantly cave-like wine cellar, is another good, though pricier option for tippling.

Clubs

Discos are widespread, but as prices are prohibitive for ordinary Belarusians, you're likely to encounter a predictable crowd – leather jackets, short skirts, wads of cash. You're almost guaranteed an 'erotic show' around midnight, too, and many hotel clubs are filled with sex workers. Most clubs have a cover charge of between BR3000 and BR10,000.

Reactor (☎ 288 61 60; vul Very Haruzaj 29; open 10pm-5am Tues-Sun), which often has live music, is very well regarded and attracts a young crowd.

Aquarium (☎ 231 20 53; vul Kulman 14; open 10pm-5am daily), one block north of Reactor, maintains a reputation for having the best live shows in the city and a fairly relaxed environment.

Max Show (☎ 232 00 38; pr Francyska Skaryny 73; open 9pm-6am daily), northeast of the city centre, is another popular option, with the occasional outlandish male and female strip shows.

Babylon (☎ 8-029 677 04 45; vul Tolbu-khina 4; open 10pm-6am Tues-Sun) is the city's premier gay club, and probably the least pretentious and most fun-spirited club in town. Here people of all persuasions gather just to have a down-to-earth good time. It's on the 3rd floor of a commercial building.

Classical Music, Opera & Ballet

Minsk has quite a lively cultural life and its Belarusian Ballet is one of the best companies in Eastern Europe, second only to Moscow's Bolshoi Ballet during the Soviet years. Ballets and operas are regularly performed at the bulky **National Academic Opera & Ballet Theatre** (☎ 234 06 52; pl Parizhskoy Kamuni 1), whose main season runs from September to April.

The **Belarusian State Philharmonia** (☎ 284 44 27; pr Francyska Skaryny 50) also has an excellent reputation – it features folk ensembles as well as a symphony orchestra, and performs everything from classical to jazz.

To buy advance tickets or to find out what's playing in Minsk, head to the **theatre ticket office** (teatralnaja kasa; pr Francyska Skaryny 13); tickets for pretty much every performance in all theatres, with some exceptions, can be bought here. Same-day tickets are usually available only from the theatres.

Belarusian folk song and dance shows are staged periodically and are well known for their rich traditions – check the listings at the theatre ticket office, or ask at the Belintourist office. The Belarusian Musical Autumn in the last 10 days of November is a festival of folk and classical music and dance.

Other popular theatres include the **Janka Kupala National Academic Theatre** (☎ 227 17 17; vul Enhelsa 7), and the **State Puppet Theatre** (☎ 227 05 32; vul Enhelsa 20), one of the few places you can head to with the kids.

SPECTATOR SPORTS

Dinamo Minsk, Belarus' top soccer club (often appearing in European competitions), has the 55,000-capacity **Dinamo Stadium** (☎ 227 26 11; vul Kirava 8). The **Ice Sports Palace** (☎ 252 50 22; vul Prititskoho 27) and sometimes the **Sports Palace** (☎ 223 44 83; pr Masherava 4) host stellar ice-hockey matches.

About 20km northeast of Minsk is the large **Raubichi Sports Complex** (☎ 507 44 11; Raubichi village; open year-round). It's at its busiest during winter, with cross-country skiing and ski trampolines; local and world championships are held here, too. During summer, there's swimming, tennis courts and small-boat rentals.

SHOPPING

Souvenirs are often sold in hotel lobbies, or you can find a decent selection at the city's main department store **GUM** (☎ 226 10 48; pr Francyska Skaryny 21).

Mastatsky Salon (☎ 227 83 63; pr Francyska Skaryny 12) has a good selection of porcelain and wooden souvenirs.

Most days, a small outdoor **tourist market** operates in the small space between the Trade Unions' Culture Palace and the Museum of the Great Patriotic War.

There's a small **antique kiosk** (☎ 213 31 27; vul Kazlova 3), inside the Palats Mastatsva, but an even more interesting one at **Arbalet** (☎ 269 16 32; pr Francyska Skaryny 83A), where the colourful owner is almost as interesting as his odd collection of objects.

There are many places to get cheap, pirated CDs, including the **Na Nemige shopping centre** (☎ 220 97 47; vul Njamiha 8), but the best-stocked store is **Podzemka** (☎ 288 20 36; pr Francyska Skaryny 43).

GETTING THERE & AWAY
Air
Most international flights use **Minsk-2 airport** (☎ 279 10 32), built in 1989, which is about 40km east of the city off the Moscow highway. A few shorter flights to neighbouring countries use **Minsk-1 airport** (☎ 222 54 18), at the end of vulitsa Chkalava, about 3km south of ploshcha Nezalezhnastsi. Flights to Moscow and St Petersburg use both airports. For more information on international flights to/from Minsk and the contact details of airlines serving the country, see the Belarus Getting There & Away chapter.

Belarus's national airline, **Belavia** (☎ 210 41 00; w http://belavia.hypermart.net; vul Njamiha 14), has an office near Na Nemige shopping centre. For international flight information call ☎ 225 02 31.

Bus
Minsk has several bus stations. Most buses for international destinations leave from the **central bus station** (tsentralny avtovokzal; ☎ 004 or ☎ 227 37 25; Babrujskaja vul 12), about 200m east of the train station. No matter what station you leave from, you can buy all advance tickets at this location. Call to find out what station your bus leaves from, as destinations are shared among different stations. Other stations are in awkward, outlying areas, so it's best to take a taxi to reach them.

From the central bus station there are two buses a day to both Bialystok (BR16,000, seven hours) and Kaunas (BR14000, 5½ hours), one a day to Klaipeda (BR21,600,

eight hours) and five daily to Vilnius (BR8000, four hours). One bus a day runs to Riga (BR19,000, 10½ hours), and a once weekly bus goes to Tallinn (BR39,000, 18 hours).

Domestic trips include about four daily to Narach (BR6500, four hours), and around 13 daily to Minskae Mora (BR2500, 45 minutes).

The **Vostochny bus station** (☎ 248 58 21) is about 3km southeast of the centre; bus No 8 and trolleybus No 13 travel between the central station and Vostochny. Daily buses leaving Vostochny bus station include those to Homel (BR9000, seven hours), Pinsk (BR9000, seven hours) and Warsaw (BR36000, 11 hours). There are also eight buses daily to Mahileu/Mogilev (BR6400, four hours).

From the **Moskovsky bus station** (☎ 264 93 13), about 1km northeast of Chaljuskintsau Park, buses and minibuses each leave at least once daily to Polatsk (BR8000, five hours) and Vitsebsk (BR10,500, five hours to 6½ hours).

Intercars (☎ 226 90 22; Russian only w www.intercars.ru), inside Hotel Jubileynaja, sells tickets for long-distance buses to Amsterdam (US$105), Paris (US$140), Rome (US$200) and other European destinations. It offers a 10% student discount.

Train
Minsk is on the main Moscow–Warsaw–Berlin line, and there are at least 15 trains daily to Moscow (BR33,700, 12 hours), two to Warsaw (BR45,000, nine to 12 hours), and one daily to Berlin (BR105,000, 18 hours). Most Moscow trains stop at Smolensk (BR15,000, usually four hours).

Daily, at least two trains go to St Petersburg (BR58,000, 16 hours) via Vitsebsk, two to Vilnius (BR10,000, four hours), three to Kaliningrad (BR51,000, 15 hours) and one to both Kiev (BR25,000, 12 hours) and Prague (BR115,000, 25 hours). There are twice weekly trains to Tallinn (BR67,000), passing through Riga and Vilnius; another train goes to Riga on odd-numbered dates (BR29,000, 13½ hours). Every other day (dropping to twice weekly in winter) there are trains to Odessa (BR87,000, 27 hours) and Simferopol (BR87,000, 22 hours), passing through Kiev.

Domestic trains include about eight daily to Brest (BR14,000 to BR17,000, 4½ to 10 hours), some of which continue on to Warsaw.

Each day, three trains go to Hrodna (BR11,000, five to eight hours), two to Polatsk (BR6600 to BR10,800, 6¼ to eight hours), three to Homel (BR12,000, 4½ hours), and about three to Vitsebsk (BR9000, 4½ to six hours), including those trains that continue on to St Petersburg.

For some help in reading train station timetables, see the Language section in the Facts about Belarus chapter. The times in red are for weekends and holidays only; those in black are for every day.

Buying Tickets Ticket counters are on either side of the main entrance hall of Minsk's **train station** (*pl Privakzalnaja*; ☎ 005, 596 54 10). However, for non-CIS international destinations such as Prague and Warsaw, counter No 13 sells tickets only on the day of departure (open only from 8pm to 8am daily). Ask at counters No 14 and 15 for train information. Tickets for the slow electric trains to suburban destinations are sold in the smaller building just west of (to the right if facing) the train station.

To save a trip to the station, and to book international tickets in advance, book through any of the city's travel agencies (see earlier in this chapter), or at the **international ticket office** (☎ 225 30 67; *vul Voronyanskoho 6*). To purchase tickets for domestic and CIS destinations, you can also use the **ticket office** (☎ 225 61 24; *pr Francyska Skaryny 18; open 9am-8pm Mon-Fri, 9am-7pm Sat-Sun*), which is usually quieter than the train station.

Car & Motorcycle
The Brestskoe shosse, the road from Minsk to Brest (E30/M1), is one of the best in the country – an excellent two-laner all the way. Minsk to Smolensk has a few narrow, slow stretches, though patches of forest alleviate its tedium.

Car-rental agencies in Minsk include **Avis** (☎ 234 79 90, fax 239 16 13), upstairs at Hotel Belarus, and **Atlant-M** (☎/fax 226 73 83), inside Hotel Planeta. Rates start at around US$55 per day.

GETTING AROUND
To/From the Airport
The taxi drivers who lurk around Minsk-2 airport are vultures who all want about US$40 for the 40-minute ride into the city (it should cost about US$15 to US$20). You can

try to bargain them down, or else wait for one of the hourly buses that cost BR2000 (90 minutes) and take you to the central bus station. There are also regular minibuses that make the trip in under an hour and cost only BR3500.

Metro
Minsk has two metro lines, intersecting at the Kupalawskaja/Kastrychnitskaja station. Ploshcha Nezalezhnastsi metro station has one entrance at the train station, with that metro line following praspekt Francyska Skaryny across the city.

Note that some metro stations still have their old or Russian names up on signs – namely Ploshcha Nezalezhnastsi, which is in places still marked as Ploshchad Lenina; Ploshcha Peramohi, which is alternatively marked as Ploshchad Pobedy; and Kastrychnitskaja, which is almost always still referred to as Oktyabrskaya.

For BR150, *zhetony* (plastic metro tokens) can be bought at all station entrances. The metro operates from 6am to 12.30am daily.

Bus & Trolleybus
Extremely crowded buses and trolleybuses, operating from 5.30am to 1am daily, serve all parts of the city. You will find trolleybus Nos 1, 2 and 18 plying praspekt Francyska Skaryny between ploshcha Nezalezhnastsi and ploshcha Peramohi.

Around Minsk

DUDUTKI
ДУДУТКІ
Near the sleepy, dusty village of Dudutki, 40km south of Minsk (15km east after a cutoff from the P23 highway), is an open-air **museum** (☎ 213-7 25 25, 017-269 09 60; unguided admission BR9000; open 10am-8pm Tues-Sun May-Oct), where 19th-century Belarusian country life is recreated. Guided tours are offered for BR33,000 per person; an English-speaking guide costs US$25 per group. If you only make one day trip from Minsk let this be the one.

Traditional crafts, such as carpentry, pottery, handicraft-making and bakery, are on display in old-style wood-and-hay houses. You can wander around the grounds, taking in the fresh air, spying on a working farm as it was a century ago. Nearby is a working windmill which you can climb. You can also go horse riding or just rest on bales of hay. Best of all, though, is the meal you can order – tastier and less expensive than anywhere in Minsk, as it's prepared on the premises using traditional recipes and techniques. Homemade cheeses, bread, *draniki*, *kolduni*, and pork sausages all go down so well, especially with a shot of local *samagon* (moonshine) – make sure you're not the one driving home! A scrumptious, full-course meal will cost only about BR10,000.

Getting There & Away

Public transport to Dudutki by public transport is iffy. About three daily buses go to Ptich from Minsk's Yugo-Zapadnaja bus station, letting you off at the village of Dudutki, a 2km walk to the museum complex. Travel agencies will be happy to organise excursions for you, but you'd do just as well without a guide on the premises, to wander around unhurriedly. Hailing a cab from central Minsk and convincing the driver to wait for you for a few hours there will cost about BR60,000.

KHATYN
ХАТЫНЬ

The hamlet of Khatyn, 60km north of Minsk, was burned to the ground with all its inhabitants in a 1943 Nazi reprisal. The site is now a sobering memorial centred around a sculpture modelled on the only survivor, Yuzif Kaminsky. Also here are the **Graveyard of Villages**, commemorating 185 other Belarusian villages annihilated by the Germans; the **Trees of Life** (actually concrete posts) commemorating a further 433 villages that were destroyed but rebuilt; and a **Memory Wall** listing the Nazi concentration camps in Belarus and some of their victims.

Khatyn is about 5km east of the Minsk–Vitsebsk road (M3). The turn-off is about 15km north of Lohoysk, opposite the village of Kazyry. There's no reliable public transport out there, but a taxi will cost around BR60,000 for the return journey from Minsk. Trips organised through Minsk's Belintourist run during the summer and cost about US$65 for up to three people.

Don't confuse Khatyn with the Katyn Forest near Smolensk, where the NKVD (the predecessor of the KGB) murdered thousands of 'enemies of the people' and Polish officers in the 1930s and 1940s.

MIR
МІР
☎ 01770

About 85km southwest of Minsk and 8km north off the Minsk–Brest road is the small town of Mir where, overlooking a pond, sits the 16th-century Mir Castle, once owned by the powerful Radzivills princes. Since 1994, it has been under Unesco protection. Built predominantly of stone and red brick, it's a walled complex with five towers surrounding a courtyard. The exterior detailing was intended to be aesthetic as well as defensive. At the time of writing, the castle was under restoration, but one tower is already open as an **archaeological museum** *(admission BR250; open 10am-5pm Wed-Sun)*.

Due to its Unesco recognition, Lukashenka signed a decree in 2002 to turn Mir into one of Belarus' prettiest villages, and consequently much reconstruction is underway. Most tourists, however, will find the area, including the castle, decidedly ho-hum, especially compared to Njasvizh.

Getting There & Away

From the central bus station in Minsk there are about 10 buses a day heading to the town of Navahrudak (Novogrudok in Russian), stopping in Mir (BR6000, two to 2½ hours) shortly after they turn off the main highway. For an alternative way of getting to Mir, see Getting There & Away in the Njasvizh section, following.

NJASVIZH
НЯСВІЖ
☎ 01770

Njasvizh, 120km southwest of Minsk, is one of the oldest sites in the country, dating from the 13th century. It reached its zenith in the mid-16th century while owned by the mighty Radziwill magnates, who had the town re-designed and rebuilt with the most advanced system of fortification known at the time. Over the centuries, war, fire and neglect diminished the town's status and today it's a random mix of painted wooden cottages and bland housing, but with enough fine pieces of 16th-century architecture and a great park to happily occupy you for a few hours.

There's a small but interesting **Local History Museum** *(☎ 5 58 74; Leninskaja vul 96; admission BR250; open 8am-5pm daily)*, a healthy 2km walk from the bus station, with everything from farm tools to maps and photos depicting life over the centuries in Njasvizh.

From the bus station, walk southeast (to your right) down Savetskaja vulitsa for six blocks to the 16th-century **town hall**, one of the oldest of its kind in the country.

Facing away from the town hall, cross vulitsa Savetskaja one block to Leninskaja vulitsa and the impressive **Farny Polish Roman Catholic Church**. Large and sombre, it was built between 1584 and 1593 in early baroque style and features a splendidly proportioned facade. The building facing it is a former **printing house** where, in the late 16th century, the philosopher Simon Budny printed some controversial works in the Belarusian language. Budny's statue stands out front.

Just beyond the Farny Church is the redbrick arcaded **Castle Gate Tower**. Built in the 16th century, it was part of a wall and gateway controlling the passage between the palace fortress and the town. There's an **excursion bureau** (☎ 2 13 67; unguided admission to fortress BR450; open 8am-5pm daily) in the gate tower, where you pay to enter the palace fortress grounds. Guided tours are available.

Farther on is a causeway leading to the **Radziwill Palace Fortress** (1583), designed by the Italian architect Bernardoni, who was also responsible for the Farny Church. The Bolshevik army looted the palace in November 1917. In Soviet times it was turned into a sanatorium, but is now undergoing painfully slow restoration to turn it into a full-fledged museum. Only a few halls have been preserved.

Unesco protection and money would best go to this fine architectural ensemble than Mir; the splendid, lush parkland and nearby lake make for fitting surroundings. Across another causeway, you can reach a nice picnic area by the banks of Lake Dzinkava, where there is also pedal and rowboat rental.

Places to Stay & Eat

Hotel Njasvizh (☎ 5 53 67; Belaruskaja vul 9; singles/doubles BR40,000/66,000), behind the town hall, is a friendly place with a shabby baroque quality and a sleepy restaurant. Rooms here are clean and adequate.

You can probably find something decent to eat at **Kafe Njasvizh** (Savetskaja vul 15; open 11am-7pm Tues-Sun).

Getting There & Away

From Minsk's central bus station, one or two buses bound for Kletsk daily stop at Njasvizh (BR6700, 2½ to three hours) along the way. Alternatively, take one of the six daily electric trains to Baranavichy and get off at the Haradzeja stop, about two hours (12 stops) from Minsk. This station is between Mir, 15km to the north, and Njasvizh, 15km to the south. At least 15 buses a day make the 30-minute trip from Haradzeja to Njasvizh. There are also two buses daily running between Njasvizh and Mir, stopping in Haradzeja en route.

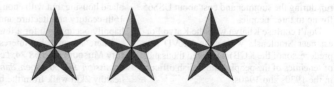

Elsewhere in Belarus
Па Беларусі

Outside Minsk, Brest and Hrodna, Belarus sees relatively few tourists. Yet there is still much to entice the traveller off the beaten path. In cities such as Hrodna and Polatsk many historic vestiges remain, and many small villages are still lost somewhere in the 19th century. The countryside is serene with swathes of forest, clusters of lakes and tangles of streams, drawing many campers and hikers from the cities.

BREST
ВРЭСТ
☎ 0162 • pop 350,000
Brest, snug up on the border with Poland, has always had a more cosmopolitan and Western feel than anywhere else in the country, Minsk included. Locals boast that within Belarus, Brest is a world apart.

Brest is on one of the busiest road and rail border points in Eastern Europe, less than 200km from Warsaw and 346km from Minsk. Some sections have the bustle associated with a border town, but mostly the pace is laid-back and comfortable. This, along with the friendliness of the locals, some great places to eat and some lovely, tree-lined streets of wooden houses, gives the city a true charm, unique in Belarus. As a bonus, here is one of the wonders of the Soviet era – Brest Fortress, a larger-than-life war memorial. Those with extra time should not miss the Belavezhskaja Pushcha National Park, 60km to the north.

First mentioned in 1019 and originally known as Bereste, Brest was sacked by the Tatars in 1241 and tossed between Slavic, Lithuanian and Polish control for several decades until it finally settled under the control of the Grand Duchy of Lithuania. The Uniate Church was set up here in 1596 at the Union of Brest, forming a branch of Orthodox Christians who were faithful to Rome as a way of bridging the largely Slavic populace and their Polish rulers. The peace was short-lived, as Russians invaded in 1654, supported by the Slavic peasants and farmers, and a series of wars featuring a Swedish invasion levelled Brest.

The Treaty of Brest-Litovsk (as the city was named until WWI) was negotiated here in March 1918, buying time for the new Soviet government in Russia by surrendering Poland, the Baltic territories and most of Ukraine and Belarus to German control. As a result, Brest was well inside Poland from 1919 to 1939, and became the front line when Germany attacked the USSR on 22 June 1941. The two hugely outnumbered regiments in

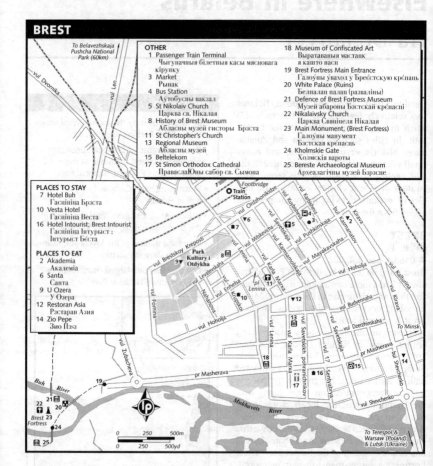

BREST

OTHER
1 Passenger Train Terminal
Чыгуначныя білетныя касы мясновага кірунку
3 Market
Рынак
4 Bus Station
Аўтобусны вакзал
5 St Nikolaiv Church
Царква св. Нікалая
8 History of Brest Museum
Абласны музей гісторы Брэста
11 St Christopher's Church
13 Regional Museum
Абласны музей
15 Beltelekom
17 St Simon Orthodox Cathedral
ПраваслаЮны сабор св. Сымона

18 Museum of Confiscated Art
Вырататаныя мастацк я кашто насп
19 Brest Fortress Main Entrance
Галоўны ўваход у Брэёстскую крэпань
20 White Palace (Ruins)
Белпалан палан (развалíны)
21 Defence of Brest Fortress Museum
Музей абароны Бэстскай крэпасці
22 Nikalaivsky Church
Царква Свянцеля Нікалая
23 Main Monument, (Brest Fortress)
Галоўны манумент
Бэстская крэпасць
24 Kholmskie Gate
Холмскія вароты
25 Bereste Archaeological Museum
Археалагічны музей Бэрэсце

PLACES TO STAY
7 Hotel Buh
Гасцініца Брэста
10 Vesta Hotel
Гасцініца Веста
16 Hotel Intourist; Brest Intourist
Гасцініца Інтурыст ;
Інтурыст Бéста

PLACES TO EAT
2 Akademia
Акадэмія
6 Santa
Санта
9 U Ozera
У Озера
12 Restoran Asia
Рэстаран Азія
14 Zio Pepe
Зио Пэзэ

Brest's fortress held out for almost a month – a heroic defence for which Brest was named one of the former Soviet Union's 11 'Hero Cities' of WWII.

Orientation & Information

Central Brest, about 2 sq km, fans out southeast from the main train station to the Mukhavets River. Vulitsa Savetskaja is the main drag and has several pedestrian sections with some ho-hum cafés and bars (for better eating options see Places to Eat later). Brest Fortress lies at the confluence of the Buh and Mukhavets Rivers, about 2km southwest of the centre down praspekt Masherava.

Brest Intourist (☎ 20 05 10; pr Masherava 15; open 9am-6pm Mon-Fri) inside Hotel Intourist is superfriendly and can make organ-

ising tours much easier. Nearby, **Beltelekom** (☎ 22 13 15; pr Masherava 21) offers Internet access for BR1800 an hour; long-distance calls can be made from here as well.

To get you excited about your visit, see w www.brestonline.com, a great English-language site with lots of useful information and lovely photos.

Museums

The Regional Museum has several branches throughout the city. Its **History of Brest Museum** (☎ 23 17 65; vul Levatevskaha 3; admission BR160; open 10am-5pm Wed-Sun) has a small exhibit on the city in its different guises throughout history. Check the painting of Brest-Litovsk in medieval times to see what a vibrant European city it was during that period. Another branch, also called the **Regional Museum** (☎ 23 91 16; vul Karla Marxa 60; admission BR160; open 10am-5pm Tues-Sat), has an odd exhibit on the history of science, and a small display on Chernobyl.

The most interesting branch is the **Museum of Confiscated Art** (☎ 20 41 95; vul Lenina 39; admission BR160; open 10am-5pm Tues-Sun), a display of valuable international art pieces (paintings, sculptures, ceramics) seized by Brest border guards as they were being smuggled out of the country. It is no doubt the most eclectic art collection in Belarus, and is well worth a visit. It often has interesting temporary exhibits.

Churches

Brest boasts many lovely churches. On the main street you'll find the breathtakingly detailed 200-year-old **St Nikolaiv Church** (cnr vuls Savetskaja & Mitskevicha), with traditional Orthodox aesthetics. On ploshcha Lenina, a **statue** of Lenin faces east towards Moscow, but it appears to be pointing accusatorily across the street to sthe Catholic **St Christopher's Church** (1856). Next to Hotel Intourist is the gold-and-white 17th-century **St Simon Orthodox Cathedral** (pr Masherava), with a richly gilded interior.

Brest Fortress

If you are going to see only one Soviet WWII memorial in your life, make it Brest Fortress (Brestskaja krepost; ☎ 20 41 09; pr Masherava; admission free; open 9.30am-6pm Tues-Sun). The scale of the fortress itself is so massive and the heroism of its defenders so vast, even the Soviet additions of a giant stone face and glistening obelisk are dwarfed in comparison.

It's at the western end of praspekt Masherava, about a 30-minute walk from the centre; the hourly bus No 17 travels between here and Hotel Intourist.

Between 1838 and 1842 the entire town of Brest was moved east to make way for this massive fort built at the confluence of the Buh and Mukhavets Rivers. During the interwar period it was used mainly for housing soldiers and had lost most of its military importance. Nevertheless, two regiments bunking here at the time of the sudden German invasion in 1941 defended the aged fort for an astounding month. The whole structure withstood incredible attacks, including at least 500 cannon fires and 600 bombs. What is left of the fortress is too overwhelming to be poignant, but too emotional to be gauche.

At the main entrance, a looped recording of soldier songs, gunfire and a radio broadcast informing of the German attack echo from a large, star-shaped opening in a huge concrete mass on top of the old brick outer wall. Inside, the enormous central monument comes into view – a stone soldier's head projecting from a massive rock, entitled 'Valour'.

As you step into the centre, to your right are the brick ruins of the **White Palace**, where the 1918 Treaty of Brest-Litovsk was signed. Farther to the right is the **Defence of Brest Fortress Museum** (☎ 20 03 65; admission BR200; open 9.30am-6pm Tues-Sun). Its extensive and dramatic exhibits demonstrate aptly the plight of the defenders.

Behind the Valour rock is the attractive, damaged shell of the Byzantine **Nikalaivsky Church**, the oldest in the city, which dates from when the town centre occupied the fortress site. Once part of a large monastery before being turned into a soldier's garrison club, it was gutted during the 1941 siege but is undergoing restoration and holds regular services.

To the south is the **Kholmskie Gate**; its bricks are decorated with crenulated turrets and its outer face is riddled with hundreds of bullet and shrapnel holes. Beyond the gate is the small **Bereste Architectural Museum** (☎ 20 55 54; admission BR160; open 9.30am-6pm Tues-Sun).

Places to Stay

Komnata Otdykha (Rest Room; ☎ 27 39 67; beds in 8-person dorm BR3500), for true and proud penny-pinchers, is a sort-of hostel on the 2nd floor of the train station's main building. It is – without doubt – the cheapest accommodation in Belarus. Toilets are shared, there are bathrooms but no showers, and you can be assured of colourful characters as roommates. It's not recommended for lone female travellers.

Hotel Buh (☎ 23 64 17; vul Lenina 2; singles/doubles from BR35,000/58,000) is set in a stately building with neoclassical entryway and pagan-themed murals. The staff will try to get you to choose one of the hotel's renovated rooms (20% more expensive), but the prerenovated ones have more charm. If your room faces the street, it'll be noisy.

Hotel Vesta (☎ *23 71 69, fax 23 78 39; vul Krupskoi 16; singles/doubles BR49,000/63,000*), probably the most pleasant hotel in Belarus, is the best choice in town. Rooms are as quaint and comfortable as your granny's home (and all have TV and fridge), and the surrounding streets are peaceful and green.

Hotel Intourist (☎ *25 20 82/3; vul Masherava 15; singles/doubles BR48,000/83,000*) is a typical Soviet product of the 1970s – dark and dreary. Although some staff can be rude, rooms are decent. The statues of prancing children near the car park at least provide a dash of joy to the surroundings.

Places to Eat

Restoran Asia (☎ *26 63 25; vul Hoholja 29; mains around BR7000; open noon-11pm Tues-Sun*) is a good bet, with a wide selection of spicy Korean and Chinese dishes.

Zio Pepe (☎ *20 50 53; bul Shevchenko 4; mains BR3000-6000; open noon-6am daily*), one of the country's many all-purpose restaurants, is a nightclub (after 9pm), bowling alley, bar, casino and eatery all rolled into one. If the chrome-and-black lights don't give you indigestion, the thin-crust pizzas are very good, as are its other Italian dishes.

Akademia (☎ *23 69 21; vul Kasmanatov 42A; mains around BR4500; open noon-6am daily*) is similar to Zio Pepe, but with more of a lounge feel for all the cool types who come here. Meals are standard but tasty. Half of the space is a pool hall (BR6000 per hour), the city's nicest.

U Ozera (☎ *23 57 63; Park Kultury i Otdykha; starters BR3000-7500; mains BR7000-17,000; open 11am-1am daily*) wins hands-down in terms of location, perched as it is by a pond in the city's prettiest park. The terrace sits under willow trees. You can get simple, cheap shashlyks as well as very tasty, more elaborate fish and meat meals.

Santa (☎ *26 36 05; vul Ordzhonikidze 7; mains BR14,000-35,000; open 11am-11pm daily*) is the place to go if you have a taste for kangaroo, ostrich, shark, tiger shrimp, Canadian lobster or other exotic (if not mildly illegal!) dishes. Its excellent food almost makes the Clint Eastwood–style service bearable. Almost.

Getting There & Away

Bus The bus station (☎ *004 or 23 81 42; vul Mitskevicha*) is in the centre of town, next to the city's main market. There are at least two daily buses or minibuses to Hrodna (BR10,500, four to 6½ hours). There are also about five buses daily to Warsaw (BR12,000, five hours) and at least one per day to Lviv (BR11,500, nine hours). There is a service once a week to Prague (BR100,000, 15 hours).

Train Brest's impressive, classical **train station** (☎ *005*) is a busy place, as Brest is an important border crossing on the Warsaw–Minsk–Moscow line. There are at least five trains a day to Warsaw (BR15,000 four to five hours). Five daily trains head to Moscow (BR45,000, 12 to 15 hours), all stopping at Minsk (BR45,000, five to six hours) and Smolensk. There are also much slower electric trains to Minsk three or four times a day (BR14,000, around 10½ hours), as well as one daily express train called *Bereste* (BR17,000, 4½ hours).

At least three daily trains go to Prague (BR100,000, 17 hours), one daily to Vienna (BR100,000, 18 hours), Berlin (BR90,000, 15 hours) and St Petersburg (BR47,000, 22 hours) and trains on odd-numbered dates to Kiev (BR26,000, 15 hours) and Kaliningrad (BR48,000, 19 hours).

Other domestic trains include a daily train to Hrodna (BR9200, 8½ hours), two a day to Vitsebsk (BR17,000, 10 to 20 hours), at least two a day to Homel (BR13,500, 12 hours), and at least one daily to Brest (BR12,000 to BR17,000, 13 to 20 hours).

For all trains leaving Brest for Poland, you have to go through customs at the station, so get there early. Tickets for trips outside Belarus are purchased from the *mezhdunarodnie kassi* (international ticket windows) in the main hall of the ticketing building.

Tickets for domestic electric trains (to Minsk, Hrodna, Homel or Vitsebsk) are sold in the *passazhirsky pavilon* (passenger train terminal) behind the train station, away from the city.

AROUND BREST
Belavezhskaja Pushcha National Park

Some 1300 sq km of primeval forest survive in the Belavezhskaja Pushcha National Park (*information* ☎ *1631-56 370, 56 396*), which stretches north from the town of Kamjanjuky, about 60km north of Brest. Another section of the forest – which is all that remains of a canopy that eight centuries ago covered northern Europe – is in Poland, which administers the national park jointly with Belarus. Some oak trees here are over 600 years old, some pines at least 300 years old.

Some 55 mammal species, including deer, lynx, boars, wild horses, wolves, elks, ermines, badgers, martens, otters, mink and beavers live here, but it is most celebrated for its 300 or so European bison, the continent's largest land mammal. These free-range *zoobr* – slightly smaller than their American cousins – were driven to near extinction (the last one living in the wild was shot by a hunter in 1919) and then bred back from 52 animals that had survived in zoos. Now a total of about 2000 exist, most of them in and around western Belarus, Lithuania, Poland and Ukraine.

There's a nature museum and *volerei* (enclosures), where you can view bison, deer, boars and other animals (including the rare hybrid Tarpan horse, a crossbreed of a species that was also shot into near extinction). The national park went from obscurity to the front page in late 1991, as the presidents of Belarus, Russia and Ukraine officially signed the death certificate of the USSR with a document creating the Commonwealth of Independent States (CIS) at the Viskuli dacha here. This country estate remains the occasional residence of Lukashenka.

The national park never sees individual tourists, partially as the area is a border zone and visitors not in a prearranged group need special permission to be there; the park staff wouldn't know what to do with them. You can organise excursions around the park with the park headquarters itself, but these are best booked through Brest Intourist (see Orientation & Information under Brest earlier in this chapter). It's about US$60 for a small group. There are two small hotels on-site (doubles BR38,000).

HRODNA
ГРОДНА

☎ 0152 • pop 310,000

Hrodna (Grodno in Russian), 282km west of Minsk, survived the war better than anywhere else in Belarus and has more intact historic buildings to prove it. As such, there are some picturesque corners. Hrodna has a substantial Polish Catholic population, and its presence gives it a welcome whiff of multiculturalism.

Still, the city has a gritty, somewhat menacing feel, and its service industry is below that of other major Belarusian cities.

Settled since ancient times and first mentioned in 1128, it was an important town under the Princedom of Polatsk and became a crucial outpost on the fringes of Kyivan Rus. Absorbed by Lithuania in the late 14th century, Hrodna fast became a major defensive fort and trading centre. Control quickly shifted to the Polish crown.

After Poland was carved up in the 1770s, the city went to Russia before being taken by Napoleon on his march to Moscow in 1812. After being overrun in WWI, the city found itself back under Polish control until 1939. It was one of the first cities to be besieged by the invading Germans in 1941. It fell easily, suffering far less damage than it did when the Soviet forces came back through at the end of WWII. In the interim, the once multiethnic population of Hrodna, including a large Jewish contingency, was wiped out.

Today, it's an industrial and cultural centre and, with its proximity to both Lithuania (42km away) and Poland (24km), has a few more private enterprises (based on trade) than in the rest of the country.

Orientation & Information

The city centre is about 2km southwest of the train station and occupies an elevated portion of land overlooking a shallow bend in the Nioman River to the south. The bus station is 1km south of the train station, and 1km east of the centre, down vulitsa Karla Marxa.

The **main post office** (☎ 72 00 60; vul Karla Marxa 29) also harbours a currency exchange booth and the tiny and crowded **Internet Club** (☎ 72 01 79; open 8am-8pm Mon-Fri, 10am-4pm Sat-Sun), with an hourly rate of BR3200. City maps can be bought at **Ranitsa Book Store** (☎ 72 17 05; vul Mastovaja 33).

Vulitsa Savetskaja

The mostly pedestrianised vulitsa Savetskaja is a favourite strolling venue – a pleasing cobblestoned strip of curious shops and cafés behind faded pastel facades. At the northern end is the city's main department store, and the southern end spills into the wide, hectic **ploshcha Savetskaja**, which in turn extends southwards into a long tree-lined 'park' running down the middle of the street.

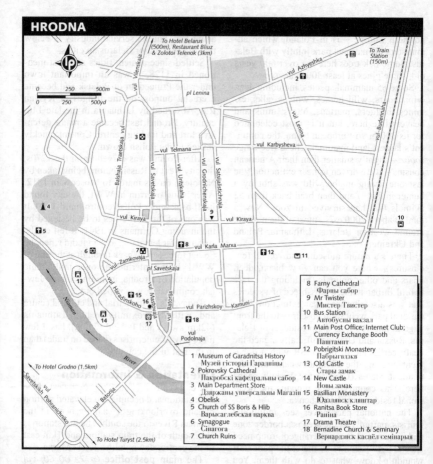

HRODNA

To Hotel Belarus (500m), Restaurant Bliuz & Zolotoi Telenok (3km)

To Train Station (150m)

vul Azhyeshka

vul Vilenskaja

pl Lenina

vul Lenina

vul Budemaha

vul Telmana

vul Karbysheva

Balshaja Traetskaja vul

vul Saveckaja

vul Uritskaha

vul Grodnicherskaja

vul Satyalsichnaja

vul Kiraya

vul Kiraya

vul Karla Marxa

vul Zamkovaja

pl Savetskaja

Nioman

vul Haradinskoho

vul Mastovaja

vul Batoria

vul Parizhskoy Kamuni

vul Podolnaja

To Hotel Grodno (1.5km)

River

To Hotel Turyst (2.5km)

vul Batoria

Savetskikh Pohranichnikov

To Hotel Grodno (1.5km)

1	Museum of Garadnitsa History
	Музей гісторыы Гарадніпы
2	Pokrovsky Cathedral
	Пакробскі кафедральны сабор
3	Main Department Store
	Дзяржаны універсальны Магазін
4	Obelisk
5	Church of SS Boris & Hlib
	Варысаглебская парква
6	Synagogue
	Сінагога
7	Church Ruins
8	Farny Cathedral
	Фарны сабор
9	Mr Twister
	Мистер Твистер
10	Bus Station
	Аўтобусны вакзал
11	Main Post Office; Internet Club; Currency Exchange Booth
	Паштампт
12	Pobrigitski Monastery
	Пабрыгдлкв
13	Old Castle
	Стары замак
14	New Castle
	Новы замак
15	Basillian Monastery
	Юаалінск кляштар
16	Ranitsa Book Store
	Раніпа
17	Drama Theatre
18	Bernadine Church & Seminary
	Вернадзінск каспёл семінарыя

Churches & Museums

Near the train station is the attractive 1904–05 **Pokrovsky Cathedral** (vul Azhyeshka 23), a candy-striped house with blue-and-gold domes. Nearby is the **Museum of Garadnitsa History** (☎ 72 16 69; vul Azhyeshka 37; admission BR160; open 10am-6pm Tues-Sat). This tiny city history museum has almost nothing in it, but it's nice to walk around the 18th-century wooden home it's housed in, and it's the best place in town to pick up handcrafted items and souvenirs.

At the northeastern corner of ploshcha Savetskaja proudly stands what is likely the most impressive church in Belarus, the Catholic **Farny Cathedral** (☎ 44 26 77; pl Savetskaja 4). Started in the late 17th century, it was continually built up during the 18th century, as foreign masters (especially Kristof Peykher from Königsberg) designed altars and drew frescoes. Inside is a row of splendidly ornate altars leading to a huge main altarpiece constructed of multiple columns interspersed with sculpted saints. Another church once stood on the opposite side of the square. It was damaged in WWII and later razed by the Soviet regime; fragmented foundation **ruins** now mark the spot.

The 16th-century Catholic **Bernadine Church and Seminary** (Parizhskoy Kamuni 1) is also worth visiting. The church was built predominantly in the Renaissance style in the 16th century, and the bell tower was redone with a defiant baroque flair 250 years later, and again after damage in WWII. It stands atop a hill opposite the bizarre, spiderlike

ELSEWHERE IN BELARUS

Drama Theatre *(vul Mastovaja 35)*, looking much like a spacecraft about to lift off.

About 500m west of the bus station is the **Pobrigitski Monastery** *(vul Karla Marxa 27)*, built in 1651, which has some lovely ornaments on its facade, as well as some 18th-century wooden buildings inside the complex.

Along vulitsa Balshaja Traetskaja is a dilapidated and abandoned 19th-century synagogue, the largest still standing in Belarus. Just beyond the synagogue, take a left turn down a shaded lane and across a wooden bridge through the park, which will take you to an obelisk marking the 850th anniversary of the city's first mention in chronicles (1128). From there head south (left) and you'll find on a hillside by the riverbank the very attractive **Church of SS Boris and Hlib** *(☎ 72 31 45)*, a small, unassuming wood-and-stone church. The stone sections date from the 12th century, making it the second-oldest surviving structure in the country after St Sophia Cathedral in Polatsk. There are weekend services.

Castles

There are two castles facing each other: the Novi Zamak (New Castle) to the southeast and the Stari Zamak (Old Castle) to the northwest. Each houses a branch of the Historical and Architectural Museum. Between the castles is a wooden carving of Vytautas the Great, the Lithuanian leader responsible for the **Stari Zamak** *(☎ 72 18 51; admission BR570; open 10am-6pm Tues-Sun)*, which was built in the 14th century on the same site as the Kyivan Rus settlers had established a few centuries earlier. The only original remains are the sections of wall to the left as you enter, from which there are nice views across the river. The main building which houses the museum dates from 1678; the extensive exhibits in the museum focus on the wars that ravaged Hrodna.

On the opposite side of the bluff overlooking the river is the **Novi Zamak** *(Governor's Palace; ☎ 44 72 69; admission BR160; open 10am-6pm Tues-Sun)*, built in 1737 as the royal palace for the Polish King August III. Originally built in opulent rococo, it was gutted by fire when the Soviets retook Hrodna from the Germans in 1944 and rebuilt in a subdued classical style. In the early 20th century, it was converted to a hospital and taken over by the Communists as their headquarters.

Places to Stay

Hotel Belarus *(☎ 44 16 74, fax 44 41 45; vul Kalinovskoho 1; singles/doubles BR40,500/62,500)* is probably the hotel to choose out of the city's limited hotel options. The staff are friendly and the rooms decent. It also offers several luxury rooms for double the standard-room price. Single males can expect regular late-night calls from sex workers offering their company. Bus No 15 from the train station goes to the hotel.

Hotel Turyst *(☎ 26 99 48, fax 26 98 73; pr Janki Kupaly 63; singles/doubles from BR40,000/55,000)* is a more modern option to Hotel Belarus, but it's in a dull, grey-concrete suburban area 4km southeast of the city centre. To get there, take bus No 1 from the bus station or No 26 from ploshcha Savetskaja.

Hotel Grodno *(☎ 22 42 33, fax 44 17 53; vul Popovicha 5; singles/doubles BR45,000/60,000)* is in a typical 1970s high-rise; rooms are clean and functional, if a bit austere. From ploshcha Savetskaja, take trolleybus No 1 or bus No 3, the latter originating from the train station.

Places to Eat

Mr Twister *(☎ 47 09 89; vul Karla Marxa 10; mains BR3000-7000; open 11am-midnight daily)*, a tacky bar-café, is virtually your only choice in the city centre. It serves passable fare while a soothing mix of techno and heavy metal blares from the speakers.

About 4km northwest of the centre, beyond Hotel Belarus, are Hrodna's two top eateries. **Restaurant Bliuz** *(☎ 33 29 74; vul Vrublevskoho 1A; mains BR3500-9000; open noon-2am daily)*, with a slightly jazzy atmosphere, serves the city's best dishes and most inventive recipes. Across the street is the ultra-formal **Zolotoi Telenok** *(☎ 33 36 10; vul Leninskoho Kamsamola 29A; mains BR6000-10,000; open noon-midnight daily)*, with good, standard cuisine, fake lace curtains and live music. It's a favourite of the over-40 crowd who love to boogie down under the big mirror ball each Saturday night. Trolleybus No 9 runs from the centre, north along vulitsa Kalinovskoho.

Getting There & Away

Bus From the **main bus station** *(☎ 72 37 24)*, there are about 14 daily buses to Minsk (BR10,300, five to six hours) and at least two buses or minibuses per day to Brest (BR10,500, four to 6½ hours). To Lithuania,

Hrodna's Favourite Daughter

A petite young athlete from Hrodna caught the world's attention at the age of 16 when she performed moves never seen before at the gymnastics competition of the 1972 Munich Olympics. Olga Korbut won an amazing three gold medals that year. At the 1976 Montreal Olympics, she scored another gold and sealed her reputation as one of the century's most spectacular gymnasts.

Lithe and poetic on the balance beam, a powerhouse on the parallel bars, and often sporting a coy, albeit self-confident smile, Korbut seemingly effortlessly performed aerial somersaults and backflips, some of which had never been done before. Certain moves are still named after her, such as the Korbut Flip. She was given the USSR's top honours in sport, named Athlete of the Year by many organisations around the world, and honoured as Woman of the Year by the United Nations in 1975.

From 1977, she turned her attention to coaching. In 1991, she emigrated to the USA, and today lives in Atlanta, Georgia. In 2002, Korbut got some bad press when she was arrested on shoplifting charges and investigated after counterfeit money was discovered in her former home. Korbut denied having stuffed the US$19 of merchandise in her purse and charges were eventually dropped. So, too, was the counterfeiting investigation.

While Hrodna gave Korbut a hero's welcome when she returned from her Olympic victories, there has yet to be a street named after her, or a monument placed in her honour. You'd think that the town council could spare one of the streets named after obscure and forgotten Communist Party officials for its most famous 20th-century resident. But in these parts, people who emigrate are still not looked upon favourably.

there are two daily buses to Kaunas (BR8200, four hours) and three weekly buses to Vilnius (BR7000, five hours). Express buses run by **Intaks** (☎ 72 02 30) go daily to Warsaw (BR16,000, six hours) and four times a week to St Petersburg (BR40,000, 20 hours). The Intaks ticket counter is outside the main building, facing the platforms; it also sells tickets for express minibuses to Brest.

Train From Hrodna's **train station** (☎ 44 85 56) there are at least three trains a day to Minsk (BR11,000, five to eight hours), one daily to Brest (BR9200, 8½ hours) and one on odd-numbered days of the month to Vitsebsk (BR13,000, 12 hours).

Hrodna lies on the main St Petersburg–Warsaw line. About two trains a day cross the border to Warsaw (BR19,000, seven hours), stopping in Bialystok along the way. Three trains a week go to St Petersburg (BR47,000, 21 hours) via Minsk and Vitsebsk. One train a day runs to Moscow (BR42,500, 17 hours) and one a day to Berlin (BR96,000, 17 hours), from Vilnius.

POLATSK
ПОЛАЦК
☎ 02144 • pop 87,000
Polatsk, 261km north of Minsk, is a sleepy riverfront town with a rich history. It was the

birthplace of the Belarus nation as well as that of the country's national hero, Francyska Skaryny, who published the first Bible in a Slavonic language in 1517–19. Today, however, its lovely monastery and a cathedral are the only things of interest to tourists.

The Princedom of Polatsk, first mentioned in 862, was one of the earliest Slavic settlements. It was absorbed by the Kingdom of Lithuania in 1307 and later by Poland, which introduced Catholicism. Polatsk prospered as a river port, but was continually flung back and forth between the feuding Muscovy tsars and the Polish crown, being reduced to rubble more than once. Ivan the Terrible had his day here in 1563 when he had the entire city council drowned or impaled for daring to show too much independence. A spark of nationalist fervour that arose out of Polatsk in the late 19th century ended with WWI and was sealed with the Soviet takeover. The new city of Novopolatsk, a grey concrete industrial centre, has grown up right next to Polatsk, making the immediate surroundings rather unattractive.

Orientation
The centre lies 1km south of the train and bus stations (along vulitsa Hoholja). The main axis is the east–west vulitsa Karla Marxa, which has ploshcha Francyska Skaryny at its

Towering Lena Pillars, sandstone formations near Yakutsk

Vladivostok Central Station, eastern terminus for the Trans-Siberian Railway

Reconstructed 10th- and 13th-century Russian Orthodox churches near the Dzvina River

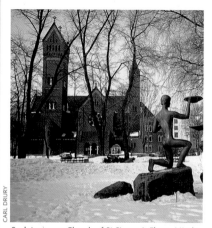

Sculpture near Church of St Simon & Elena, Minsk

McDonald's sign on Stalinist architecture, Minsk

Couple enjoying the winter sun, Minsk

JONATHAN SMITH

CARL DRURY

JONATHAN SMITH

CARL DRURY

astern end and ploshcha Lenina at its west-
rn end. The oldest and most interesting area
s along vulitsa Lenina, parallel to and one
treet south of vulitsa Karla Marxa. The train
and bus stations are 1km north of the city
centre.

For general information about Polatsk, it's
best to inquire at travel agencies in Minsk.

St Sophia Cathedral

At the western end of vulitsa Lenina, on top
of a small hill, is the finely moulded facade
of the St Sophia Cathedral, its twin baroque
bell towers rising high over the Dzvina River.
It's the oldest surviving monument of architecture in Belarus and one of two original
11th-century Kyivan Rus cathedrals (the
other is in Novgorod) modelled and named
after the St Sophia Cathedral in Kiev. Its orig-
nal appearance, however, has long gone.
Damaged by fire in the 15th century, it was
turned into an armoury, which was subsequently destroyed by retreating Russians in
1710. About 40 years later the Poles reconstructed it – inside and out – as a baroque
Catholic cathedral.

The interior is a **museum** *(admission
BR260; open 10am-5pm Tues-Sun)*, with a
model inside showing the cathedral's original
Byzantine appearance. Parts of the 11th-
century foundations can be seen in the
vaulted basement. Out front is a large stone
on which a cross was carved in the 12th century by Prince Boris, who etched Christian
symbols on every formerly pagan rock or
stone he could find.

St Efrasinnia Monastery

This monastery *(☎ 4 56 79; vul Efrosini Polot-
skoi 59; admission free; open noon to 4pm
daily)* was founded in 1125 by St Efrasinnia
(1110–73), Belarus' first saint and the first
woman to be canonised by the Orthodox
Church. She was the founder of the city's
first library and had a strong independent
streak, shunning numerous offers of marriage
to establish her own convent here and to commission the **Holy Saviour Church**. Still
standing, it's one of the finest examples of
early 12th-century religious architecture in
Belarus, and the small, dark interior is mes-
merisingly beautiful. At the time of writing,
the fine frescoes, also dating from the 12th
century, were being restored. The saint's
embalmed remains are in a glass-covered

coffin inside. Her remains were returned to
the monastery in the early 1990s from Kiev,
where they had been buried in the Monastery
of the Caves in 1187.

The small **Church of the Transfiguration**
(Spaso-Preobrazhenski Sabor), on the right
as you enter the grounds, was originally built
in the 17th century, although the current facade dates from 1833. It also houses a small
gift shop.

In the centre of the ensemble stands the
large **Kresto-Vozdvizhenskom Cathedral**
(1897). The impressive interiors, where most
services are held, contain, in finely gilded
cases, the sanctified remains of 239 saints,
as well as miracle-performing icons. The
monastery restarted religious services in
1990 and today, there are 90 female monks
living here.

To get to the monastery, you can either
walk due north from ploshcha Lenina on
vulitsa Frunza for a brisk half-hour, watching
for the complex on your right, or take the infrequent buses No 4 or 17 three stops from
the northern end of ploshcha Lenina. The
monastery is used to accepting visitors onto
its grounds outside official opening hours,
but not all of its buildings may be open.

Places to Stay & Eat

If you're really stuck for cash, there's a converted **train wagon** *(☎ 4 62 37; BR3000)* at
the train station, with no showers. They may
eventually open a hostel of sorts in the beige-
pink building next to the main building; call
for details.

Hotel Dzvina *(☎ 4 22 35; vul Karla Marxa
13; singles/doubles BR48,000/BR60,000)* is
the only hotel in town, with average but adequate rooms. Its **restaurant** serves a mediocre
meal, which will do nicely in a pinch.

Frantsisk *(☎ 4 64 83; vul Karla Marxa
17/6; mains BR3000-5000; open 11am-5am
daily)*, the best restaurant in town, is a dingy,
cavernous place attached to a casino. It boasts
unusually stern service, but has a good selection of salads and mainly meat dishes. The
most intriguing item on the menu is the last
one – condoms. This may say more than you
wish to know about the place.

Getting There & Away

The modern-looking building next to (east
of) the older train station sells long-distance
train tickets, while tickets for the five daily

electric trains connecting Polatsk and Vitsebsk (BR4700, two hours) are sold inside the train station itself. Most long-distance routes are served by through-trains.

Two trains a day run to Minsk (BR6600 to BR10,800, 6¼ to eight hours), and one train daily goes to Moscow (BR29,000, 13 hours) via Smolensk (BR17,100, five hours). Trains to Riga run on even-numbered days of the month (BR50,300, eight hours) via Daugavpils.

The bus station is 100m east of the train station, with about four daily buses to both Minsk (BR8000, five hours) and Vitsebsk (BR3500, two hours), one daily to Homel (BR15,600, 12 hours). Left-luggage lockers are available.

Getting Around

Getting around this town is an easy stroll, even with a moderate backpack; the half-hour walk out to the monastery will be as far as you'll need to go.

VITSEBSK
ВІЦЕБСК

☎ 0212 • pop 350,000

Vitsebsk (Vitebsk in Russian), 277km north of the capital, is in some ways the most interesting Belarusian city outside Minsk, mainly due to its grand artistic heritage. Marc Chagall was born here, studying under an unheralded master, Yudel Pyen, who opened the country's first art school here in 1897; the artists Vasili Kandinsky and Kasimir Malevich also spent some time in what was then a dynamic city. Ilya Repin, one of Russia's best-loved painters, also lived in the region – he bought the Zdravnevo estate on the outskirts of the city and lived there from 1892 to 1896.

Today, this artistic heritage is kept alive by the wonderful Art Museum, the original art school, and by a group of artists called Kvadrat who continue the avant-garde spirit with their abstract (and often humorous) carvings and paintings. Furthermore, the hugely popular Slavyansky Bazar (Slavic Bazaar) is held here in mid-July, bringing together dozens of singers and performers from various Slavic countries for a weeklong series of concerts. The annual event attracts thousands of visitors, creating a huge city-wide party.

Aside from this, the city boasts what even Minsk cannot – a sense of the past. Several small areas of pre-WWII houses lend a delicate elegance to the relatively hilly city sitting at the confluence of three rivers, the dramatic Dzvina, and the smaller Vitba and Luchesa.

Its past, however, is as painful as that of other Belarusian cities. Its history goes back to the 6th-century Varangian explorers from Scandinavia who began to settle at strategic river junctions on their migration south. Part of the Princedom of Polatsk, Vitsebsk was also pulled into the sphere of Kyivan Rus, then fell under the Lithuanian and Polish umbrella before being finally pinched by Moscow.

It was burned to ashes by Ivan the Terrible in the mid-16th century, and was savagely razed in WWII, when only 118 people out of a prewar population of 170,000 survived. Each year, on 26 June, the city celebrates the day in 1944, when the Red Army liberated it from the Nazis. Though less developed than Minsk, Vitsebsk has a down-to-earth quality that visitors will appreciate.

Orientation & Information

The remnants of the old town lie along a picturesque, steep ridge about 2km northeast of the train station and across the Dzvina River. Heading due east from the station is the main thoroughfare, vulitsa Kirava, which becomes vulitsa Zamkovaja after it crosses the river, and vulitsa Frunze after it crosses vulitsa Lenina, the main north–south thoroughfare.

There is a handy **Internet Club** (☎ 37 29 66; open 24hrs) on the 2nd floor of the train station; the hourly rate is BR1600.

Museums

There's an intriguing mix of old and new in the **Art Museum** (☎ 36 22 31; vul Lenina 32; admission BR1000; open 11am-6pm Wed-Sun), with temporary exhibitions of mainly local artists, as well as 18th- to 20th-century European works, including those by Repin and Vladimir Egorovic Makovsky. A highlight is the collection of very moving realist scenes of early 20th-century Vitsebsk street life by Yudel Pyen. Of the 793 paintings he donated to the city before he died, only 200 have survived, most of them held here.

A few houses away, past the **town hall** distinguished by its clock tower, is the **Regional Museum** (☎ 36 47 12; vul Lenina 36; admission BR160; open 11am-6pm Wed-Sun), with up to five rotating exhibitions plus a

Marc Chagall

Surrealist painter and visionary Marc Chagall (1887–1985) took his first views of the world when he was born in Vitsebsk on 7 July 1887. He spent from 1897 to 1910 in a small **wooden house** (☎ 36 34 68; vul Pokrovskaja 11; admission BR160; open 11am-7pm Tues-Sun), now kitted out with early-20th-century Jewish knick-knacks and photos. To get there, turn left when exiting the bus or train station, walk one block, then turn right onto vulitsa 1-ja Krasina. After a block you'll see a fanciful **monument** to the artist; turn left here onto vulitsa Pokrovskaja.

Chagall left Vitsebsk to go on to greater fame in St Petersburg and Moscow, finally settling in Paris from 1923, where he lived until his death, churning out fantastically poetic and often humorous murals and artwork. Many of his pieces reflect the Jewish country life of his childhood, largely influenced by his upbringing in Vitsebsk.

Nestled in a pretty park, the **Chagall Museum** (☎ 36 03 87; vul Punta 2; admission BR500; open 11am-7pm Tues-Sun) has two floors filled with 300 original, colourful lithographs (all donations), as well as reproductions of some of his famous paintings, including the infamous murals he did for the Moscow Jewish Theatre, considered so mesmerising that they were banned from the stage for distracting the audience.

There would be more originals at the museum had Soviet authorities accepted Chagall's offer to donate some to the city of his birth; they didn't think much of his art and declined. To get to the museum from Vitsebsk's Regional Museum, head north along vulitsa Lenina or the nicer vulitsa Suvorava to vulitsa Uritsoho, make a left and walk to the end; the museum will be on your right.

★★★

permanent one full of 11th- to 14th-century artefacts from the city.

The **Museum of the Belarusian Army** (☎ 22 39 72; vul Voinov Internatsionalistov 20; admission BR500; open by appointment), set up by veterans of the Afghan War, has some touching exhibits on the history of war on Belarusian soil from the 6th century, as well as of Belarusians participating in foreign wars. The museum is difficult to find on your own; take a BR4000 taxi from the centre.

For information on other city museums, see the boxed text 'Marc Chagall'.

Churches

While Vitsebsk does not have many churches of note, there is a pair of very different Russian Orthodox churches on the eastern bank of the Dzvina, near the main bridge on vulitsa Zamkovaja. These are reconstructions built in 1998 of 10th- (wooden) and 13th-century (white stone) styles. Both hold regular services; the atmospheric wooden church is especially worth visiting.

Places to Stay

Hotel Dvina (☎ 37 71 73; vul Ilinskoho 2; singles/doubles BR9500/19,000), a student residence on the western banks of the Dzvina, on the northern side of the main bridge, may be the last great deal for foreigners left in Belarus. All of the bare rooms have toilet and showers.

Vetrazh (☎ 21 72 04; pr Cherniahovsky 29/1; singles/doubles BR51,000/65,000), with 300 beds, is a standard service hotel just south of the city centre (tram No 4 from the bus and train stations goes there). Staff seem to find cheaper rooms if you're persistent.

Hotel Oridan (☎/fax 36 24 56; vul Savetskaja 21/17; singles/doubles BR120,000/224,000), in the quiet old town, is much more intimate and upscale than Vetrazh. Extremely comfortable and modern, the hotel also boasts an excellent (and expensive) restaurant.

Places to Eat

Gulliver (☎ 23 50 37; vul Pushkinskaja 2; mains BR2500-6000; open noon-midnight daily) boasts a pleasant terrace doubling as an informal bar, and cheap fill-up meals.

Traktir Vitebsky (☎ 37 01 07; vul Suvorava 2; mains BR5000-7500; open noon-midnight daily) is the best place to eat in town, with its charming, cavelike rooms, and a great menu, chock-full of inventive, tasty dishes. It does a mean gazpacho for BR2500.

Kafe Teatralnaja (☎ 36 99 66; vul Zamkovaja 2; mains BR5000-10,000; open noon-6am daily), near Gulliver, is a slightly artsy place. It attracts a varied crowd to its dark, underground sprawl, which blossoms into a

ELSEWHERE IN BELARUS

...y disco after 11pm. Its menu is also large and sprawling, comprising Belarusian and European dishes; it even has a decent vegetarian menu.

Getting There & Away

Vitsebsk is on one of the major railway lines heading south from St Petersburg into Ukraine. There are about three trains a day to Minsk (BR9000, 4½ to six hours) and St Petersburg (BR20,000, 10 to 13 hours). On even-numbered days of the month trains run to Kiev (BR24,000, 16 hours).

Two trains daily cross the border into Russia stopping at Smolensk (BR10,000, three to four hours), with one continuing to Moscow (BR18,000, 11 hours).

Domestic trains, other than those to Minsk, include at least one daily to Brest (BR12,000 to BR17,000, 13 to 20 hours) and every odd-numbered day of the month to Hrodna (BR13,000, 12 hours). Domestic electric trains connect Polatsk and Vitsebsk (two hours, BR4700) about four or five times daily, but most southbound or westbound trains stop at Polatsk.

There's at least one daily bus and one mini-bus to Minsk (BR10,500, five to 6½ hours). Buses head once or twice daily to Polatsk (BR3500, two hours), and three times a week to Tallinn (BR38,000, 13½ hours).

Getting Around

While Vitsebsk is larger than most other regional centres, and while the main sites are several kilometres from each other, the city is still quite possible to explore on foot. The older parts of Vitsebsk especially make for some of the most pleasant urban strolls in Belarus. Buses ply the 1.5km main drag from the bus and train stations into town; get off just after crossing the Dzvina and you'll be just 500m from the Art Museum.

PRIPYATSKY NATIONAL PARK
ПРИПЯТСКИЙ НАЦИОНАЛЬНЫЙ ПАРК

Covering 750 sq km of land in the so-called lowlands, 250km south of Minsk, is this national park (☎ 02353-75 644, 75 173; Leninskaya ul 127, Turov village) comprised mainly marshes, swampland and floodplains. As unattractive as 'swamp' might sound, the landscape here is quite striking and provides a contrast to the endless stretches of flat, dry fields that cover most of Belarus.

A unique ecosystem has developed here wherein air currents passing over wetlands comprised of marshes, swamps and bogs are re-oxygenated; locals dub it the 'lungs of Europe'. Flora and fauna particular to wetlands are found here, including over 800 plant species (38 rare or threatened), some 45 mammal species and over 140 species of birds.

The **park headquarters and museum** (☎ 02353-75 644; Leninskaja vul 127) are located in the village of Turov. Staff can arrange a variety of activities in the park with advance notice, from guided day tours (BR114,000 for up to 10 people) to extended fishing, hunting and boating expeditions deep in the marshlands. Cruises on the Pripet River are also available, costing from BR27,000 per person. Staff can also organise custom-made tours depending on your budget, but make sure you get guarantees of the services you require beforehand. There are several guesthouses to choose from, ranging from BR18,000 to BR120,000 per room; ask at the park headquarters for accommodation details.

Day tours of the national park usually include a trip around Turov, too. Founded in the 10th century, the village is a dusty dot on the map, with a rich history as one of the main principalities in Kyivan Rus. Many supernatural legends are associated with the town.

Getting There & Away

Transport is tricky. Two daily buses make the gruellingly long trip to Turov from Minsk's Vostochny bus station (BR10,000, seven hours). By car, take the P23 south from Minsk until the M10 for 26km, drive east on the M10 for 26km, south on the P88 for 25km, then head west for 6km to Turov. Staff at the park headquarters can also arrange private transport to or from anywhere in Belarus; it might cost up to US$100 for a one-way ride from Minsk to Turov for up to three people.

Language

Who Speaks What?

Just about everyone in Russia speaks Russian, although there are dozens of other languages spoken by ethnic minorities. Russian and most of the other languages are written in variants of the Cyrillic alphabet. It's easy to find English-speakers in the big cities, but not so easy in small towns (sometimes not even in tourist hotels). Russian grammar may be daunting, but your travels will be far more interesting if you at least take the time to learn the Cyrillic alphabet, so that you can read maps and street signs.

Before you head off, get a copy of Lonely Planet's detailed and useful *Russian phrasebook* and a small dictionary such as the *Pocket Oxford Russian Dictionary*.

RUSSIAN
Cyrillic Alphabet

The Cyrillic alphabet resembles Greek with a few additional characters. Every language that uses Cyrillic has its own slightly different variant. The alphabet table on the following page shows the letters of the Russian alphabet and the Roman-letter equivalents used to transliterate them in this language guide.

Pronunciation

The sounds of a, o, e and я are 'weaker' when the stress in the word does not fall on them – eg, in вода (*voda*, water), the stress falls on the second syllable, so it's pronounced *vada*, with the 'a' representing both the unstressed pronunciation for o and the stressed pronunciation for a. The vowel й only follows other vowels in so-called diphthongs, eg, ой *oy*, ей *ey*. Note that Russians usually print ё without the dots, a source of confusion in pronunciation.

The 'voiced' consonants б, в, г, д, ж and з are not voiced at the end of words, eg, хлеб (bread) is pronounced *khlyep* (not *khlyeb*), or before voiceless consonants. The г in the common adjective endings -его and -ого is pronounced 'v'.

Soft & Hard Sign

Two letters have no sound but function by modifying other sounds. A consonant followed by the 'soft sign' ь is spoken with the tongue flat against the palate, as if followed by the faint beginnings of a 'y' – it's represented in this section by an apostrophe. The rare 'hard sign' ъ after a consonant inserts a slight pause before the next vowel.

Transliteration

There's no ideal system for rendering Cyrillic in the Roman alphabet; the more faithfully a system indicates pronunciation, the more complicated it is. The transliteration system used in this language guide differs from that used in the rest of the book (which follows the US Lib-rary of Congress System I – good for deciphering printed words and rendering proper names); it's intended to assist you in pronouncing Russian letters and sounds, with an emphasis on practicality. Most letters are transliterated in accordance with the pronunciation guide in the Cyrillic alphabet table on the following page. A few exceptions are listed below:

е	written as **e** (except at the beginning of words, when it's written as **ye**)
ай	written as **ay**
ей	written as **ey**
ий	written as **iy**
ой	written as **oy** (when stressed), as **ay** (when unstressed)
ый	written as **y**
ж	written as **zh**
х	written as **kh**

Useful Words & Phrases

Two words you're sure to use are Здравствуйте (*zdrastvuyte*), the universal 'hello' (but if you say it a second time in one day to the same person, they'll think you forgot you already saw them!), and Пожалуйста (*pazhalsta*), the multipurpose word for 'please' (commonly included in all polite requests), 'you're welcome', 'pardon me', 'after you' and more.

Good morning.
    *dobraye **utra***   Доброе утро.
Good afternoon.
    dobry den'   Добрый день.
Good evening.
    dobry vecher   Добрый вечер.

The Russian Cyrillic Alphabet

Cyrillic	Roman	Pronunciation
А, а	a	as the 'a' in 'path' (in stressed syllables) as the 'a' in 'about' (in unstressed syllables)
Б, б	b	as the 'b' in 'but'
В, в	v	as the 'v' in 'van'
Г, г	g	as the 'g' in 'god'
Д, д	d	as the 'd' in 'dog'
Е, е *	e	as the 'ye' in 'yet' (in stressed syllables) as the 'yi' in 'yin' (in unstressed syllables)
Ё, ё **	yo	as the 'yo' in 'yonder'
Ж, ж	zh	as the 's' in 'measure'
З, з	z	as the 'z' in 'zoo'
И, и	i	as the 'i' in 'litre'
Й, й	y	as the 'y' in 'boy'
К, к	k	as the 'k' in 'kind'
Л, л	l	as the 'l' in 'lamp'
М, м	m	as the 'm' in 'mad'
Н, н	n	as the 'n' in 'not'
О, о	o	as the 'o' in 'more' (in stressed syllables) as the 'a' in 'path' (in unstressed syllables)
П, п	p	as the 'p' in 'pig'
Р, р	r	as the 'r' in 'rub' (rolled)
С, с	s	as the 's' in 'sing'
Т, т	t	as the 't' in 'ten'
У, у	u	as the 'u' in 'put'
Ф, ф	f	as the 'f' in 'fan'
Х, х	kh	as the 'ch' in 'Bach'
Ц, ц	ts	as the 'ts' in 'bits'
Ч, ч	ch	as the 'ch' in 'chin'
Ш, ш	sh	as the 'sh' in 'shop'
Щ, щ	shch	as 'sh-ch' in 'fresh chips'
ъ	(no symbol)	'hard sign' (see p.677)
Ы, ы	y	as the 'y' in 'busy'
ь	'	'soft sign'; (see p.677)
Э, э	e	as the 'e' in 'ten'
Ю, ю	yu	as the 'yu' in 'yule'
Я, я	ya	as the 'ya' in 'yard' (in stressed syllables) as the 'yi' in 'yin' (in unstressed syllables)

* Е, е is transliterated Ye, ye when at the beginning of a word

** Ё, ё is often printed without dots

Goodbye.
da svidaniya   До свидания.
Goodbye (informal).
paka   Пока.
How are you?
kak dela?   Как дела?
Yes.
da   Да.
No.
net   Нет.

Thank you (very much).
(bal'shoye) spasiba
(Большое) спасибо.
Pardon me.
prastite/pazhalsta
Простите/Пожалуйста.
No problem/Never mind.
nichevo (literally 'nothing')
Ничего.
I like (it).
mne nravitsya
Мне нравится.
Can you help me?
pamagite pazhalsta
Помогите, пожалуйста.
May I take a photo?
mozhna fatagrafiravat'?
Можно фотографировать?

Pronouns

Normally, the polite form вы (*vy*, 'you' plural) is used in conversation. The informal ты (*ty*, 'you' singular) is for talking to children, relatives and close friends.

I
ya   я
you (singular informal)
ty   ты
he, she, it
on, ana, ano   он, она, оно
we
my   мы
you (polite plural or singular)
vy   вы
they
ani   они

Names & Introductions

In introducing yourself you can use your first name, or first and last. Russians often address each other by first name plus patronymic (a middle name based on their father's first name) – eg, Natalya Borisovna

(Natalya, daughter of Boris), Pavel Niko-laevich (Pavel, son of Nikolay). This requires careful attention when someone is being introduced to you!

What's your name?
kak vas zavut? Как вас зовут?
My name is ...
menya zavut ... Меня зовут ...
Pleased to meet you.
ochen' priyatna Очень приятно.
my husband
moy muzh мой муж
my wife
maya zhina моя жена
my boyfriend
moy paren' мой парень
my girlfriend
maya devushka моя девушка

Language Difficulties

I don't speak Russian.
ya ni gavaryu pa ruski
Я не говорю по-русски.
I don't understand.
ya ni panimayu
Я не понимаю.
Do you speak English?
vy gavarite pa angliyski?
Вы говорите по-английски?
Can you write it down, please?
zapishite pazhalsta
Запишите, пожалуйста
translator
perevotchik
переводчик

Countries

Where are you from?
atkuda vy? Откуда вы?
Australia
afstraliya Австралия
Canada
kanada Канада
France
frantsiya Франция
Germany
germaniya Германия
Great Britain
velikabritaniya Великобритания
Ireland
irlandiya Ирландия
New Zealand
novaya zelandiya Новая Зеландия
USA, America
se she a/amerika США/Америка

Getting Around

How do we get to ...?
kak dabrat'sa k ...?
Как добраться к ...?
When does it leave?
kagda atpravlyaetsya?
Когда отправляется?

The usual way to get to the exit in a crowded bus is to say to anyone in the way, Вы выходите? *(vy vykhoditi?)*, 'Are you getting off?'.

bus
aftobus автобус
taxi
taksi такси
train
poyezt поезд
tram
tramvay трамвай
trolleybus
traleybus троллейбус
fixed-route minibus
marshrutnaye маршрутное
taksi такси

railway station
zhileznadarozhny vagzal
железнодорожный (ж. д.) вокзал
stop (bus, tram etc)
astanofka
остановка
ticket, tickets
bilet/bilety
билет/билеты
ticket/tickets (city bus, trolleybus/tram)
talon/talony
талон/талоны
metro token, tokens
zheton/zhetony
жетон/жетоны
map
karta
карта
transport map
skhema transparta
схема транспорта

Accommodation

A *lyux* (as in 'deluxe') is a suite with a sitting room in addition to the bedroom and bathroom. A *polu-lyux* ('half deluxe') is less spacious.

How much is a room?
skol'ka stoit nomer?
Сколько стоит номер?
Do you have a cheaper room?
u vas est' dishevle nomer?
У вас дешевле номер?

hotel
gastinitsa   гостиница
room
nomer   номер
key
klyuch   ключ
boiling water
kipyatok   кипяток
toilet paper
tualetnaya   туалетная бумага
bumaga
towel
palatentse   полотенце
blanket
adeyala   одеяло
too hot/stuffy
zharka/dushna   жарко/душно

The ... isn't working.
... ne rabotaet   ... не работает.
toilet
tualet   туалет
tap/faucet
kran   кран
heating
atapleniye   отопление
light
svet   свет
electricity
electrichestva   электричество

Around Town

House numbers are not always in step on opposite sides of the street. Russian addresses are written back to front (country first, then postal code, city or town, street address, and name at the bottom).

Where is ...?
gde ...?   Где ...?
I'm lost.
ya zabludilsya/   Я заблудился/
zabludilas' (m/f) заблудилась.

to (on) the left
naleva   налево
to (on) the right
naprava   направо

Signs	
Вход	**Entrance**
Выход	**Exit**
Мест Нет	**No Vacancy**
Справки	**Information**
Открыт	**Open**
Закрыт	**Closed**
Касса	**Cashier/Ticket Office**
Больница	**Hospital**
Милиция	**Police**
Туалет	**Toilet**
Мужской (М)	**Men**
Женский (Ж)	**Women**

straight ahead
pryama   прямо
near
daleko   далеко
far
bliska   близко
north
sever   север
south
yuk   юг
east
vastok   восток
west
zapad   запад
(go) back
nazat   назад
here, there
tut, tam   тут, там

avenue
praspekt   проспект (просп.)
church
tserkof'   церковь
circus
tsirk   цирк
lane
pereulak   переулок (пер.)
museum
muzey   музей
square/plaza
ploshchat'   площадь (пл.)
street
ulitsa   улица (ул.)
theatre
teatr   театр
toilet
tualet   туалет

Belarusian

Russian is by far the most dominant language in Belarus. No matter how noble it may be of you to try a little Belarusian, be aware you're more likely than not to be greeted with consternation and confusion – it's far less problematic to use Russian.

Belarusian belongs to the Eastern Slavonic branch of Indo-European, closely related to both Russian and Ukrainian, though its written form shares with Ukrainian only its ancestor in the now extinct language called Ruthenian. It began to differ from Old Russian (also called Church Slavonic) in the Middle Ages. It's normally written with the Cyrillic alphabet, but there does exist a written form using accented Latin characters. This latter is dubbed Lacinka, and it is different than transliterated Belarusian. While Russian and present-day Belarusian are very close, there are significant differences in pronunciation and spelling, and some case endings and many words are completely different; a Russian-speaker would at best understand 60% of spoken Belarusian heard for the first time.

Belarusian, like Ukrainian (but not Russian), has the letter i, pronounced ee (this replaces the Russian и). It also has the unique letter ў, pronounced like 'w' in the word 'west'. Transliteration is also different, with й transcribed as j, ю as ju, я as ja and ё as io. Г is pronounced and transcribed h, as in Ukrainian. The Russian letter o often becomes a in Belarusian – making, for example, Komsomolskaya into Kamsamolskaja, which looks closer to its pronunciation in any case. The Russian Gogolya becomes Hoholja in Belarusian.

You'll see an apostrophe used in written Belarusian to separate a consonant from the syllable that follows it.

Belarus	beh-lah-**roos**	Беларусь
Hello.	**dob**-ree **dzhen**	Добры джень.
Goodbye.	da pah-bah-**chen**-nyah	Да пабачэньня.
Yes.	tahk	Так.
No.	nye	Не.
Please.	kah-**lee lahs**-kah	Калі ласка.
Thank you.	**dzyah**-koo-ee	Дзякуй.
good	**dohb**-ree	добры
bad	**drehn**-nee	дрэнны

Belarusian on Signs

Entrance	uva-**khod**	Уваход
Exit	**vy**-khad	Выхад
Information	da-**ved**-ka	Даведка
left luggage room	ka-mera za-**khau**-vannya ba-**ga**-zha	камера захоі вання
on even days	pa **tsot**-nykh	па потных
on odd days	pa nya-**tsot**-nykh	па няцотных
daily	shtod-**zyo**-nna	штодзюнна
departure	ad-prau-**len**-nje	адпраіленне
arrival	pry-**by**-tssje	прыбышце
Monday	pan-ya-**dzel**-ak	панядзелак
Tuesday	**aut**-orak	аіторак
Wednesday	se-ra-**da**	серада
Thursday	**chats**-ver	чацвер
Friday	**pyat**-nitsa	пятн ца
Saturday	su-**bo**-ta	субота
Sunday	**nyad**-ze-lya	нядзеля

bank			travellers cheques	
bank	банк		*darozhnye cheki*	дорожные чеки
currency exchange			small change	
abmen valyuty	обмен валюты		*razmen*	размен
money			post office	
den'gi	деньги		*pochta*	почтамт

stamp
   marka   марка
postcard
   atkrytka   открытка
telephone
   telefon   телефон
fax
   faks   факс/телефакс
... telephone office
   ... *telefonyy punkt* ... телефонный пункт
intercity
   mezhdugorodny   междугородный
international
   mezhdunarodny   международный

Shopping

I need ...
   mne nuzhna ...   Мне нужно ...
Do you have ...?
   u vas est'...?   У вас есть ...?
Please show me.
   pakazhiti   Покажите,
   pazhalste   пожалуйста.
How much is it?
   skol'ka stoit?   Сколько стоит?

bookshop
   knizhny   книжный магазин
   magazin
department store
   univirsal'ny   универсальный
   magazin   магазин
market
   rynak   рынок
newsstand
   gazetny kiosk   газетный киоск
pharmacy
   apteka   аптека
shop
   magazin   магазин
good/OK
   kharasho   хорошо
bad
   plokha   плохо
open/closed
   otkryta/zakryta   открыто/закрыто

Time, Days & Date

What time is it?
   katory chas?   Который час?
At what time?
   f katoram chasu? В котором часу?
hour
   chas   час
minute
   minuta   минута

am/in the morning
   utra   утра
pm/in the afternoon
   dnya   дня
in the evening
   vechera   вечера
local time
   mesnaye vremya местное время
Moscow time
   maskovskaye   московское время
   vremya
When?
   kagda?   Когда?
today
   sevodnya   сегодня
tomorrow
   zaftra   завтра
yesterday
   vchera   вчера
day after tomorrow
   poslezaftra   послезавтра

Monday
   panedel'nik   понедельник
Tuesday
   ftornik   вторник
Wednesday
   sreda   среда
Thursday
   chetverk   четверг
Friday
   pyatnitsa   пятница
Saturday
   subota   суббота
Sunday
   vaskrisen'e   воскресенье

(Centuries are written in Roman numerals.)

century, centuries
   в., вв. *(v, vv)*
year, years
   г., гг. *(g, gg)*
beginning/middle/end
   начало/середина/конец
   (nachala/seredina/kanets)
AD (literally 'our era')
   н.э. *(n.e – nasha era)*
BC (literally 'before our era')
   до н.э. *(do n.e – da nashey ery)*
10th century AD
   X в. н.э. *(disyaty vek nashey ery)*
7th century BC
   VII в. до н.э. *(syed'moy vek da*
   nashey ery)

Emergencies

I'm sick.
  ya bolen (m)   Я болен.
  ya bal'na (f)   Я больна.
I need a doctor.
  mne nuzhen vrach   Мне нужен врач.
Help!
  na pomashch!/   На помощь!/
  pamagite!   Помогите!
Thief!
  vor!   Вор!
Fire!
  pazhar!   Пожар!
hospital
  bal'nitsa   больница
police
  militsiya   милиция

Numbers

How many?
  skol'ka?   Сколько?

0	*nol'*	
1	*adin*	
2	*dva*	
3	*tri*	
4	*chetyri*	
5	*pyat'*	
6	*shest'*	
7	*sem'*	
8	*vosem'*	
9	*devyat'*	
10	*desyat'*	
11	*adinatsat'*	
12	*dvenatsat'*	
13	*trinatsat'*	
20	*dvatsat'*	
21	*dvatsat' adin*	
30	*tritsat'*	
40	*sorak*	
50	*pyat'desyat*	
60	*shest'desyat*	
70	*sem'desyat*	
80	*vosimdesyat*	
90	*devyanosta*	
100	*sto*	
200	*dvesti*	
300	*trista*	
400	*chetyrista*	
500	*pyat'sot*	
1000	*tysyacha*	
10,000	*desyat' tysyach*	

one million
  (adin) milion   (один) миллион

FOOD

restaurant
  restaran   ресторан
café
  kafe   кафе
canteen
  stalovaya   столовая
snack bar
  bufet   буфет
buffet/smorgasbord/Swedish Table
  shvetskiy stol   шведский стол
take away
  s saboy   с собой

Types of snack shop include:

блинная *(blinaya)* serves *bliny* (pancakes
with savoury or sweet fillings)
бутербродная *(buterbrodnaya)* serves small
open sandwiches
закусочная *(zakusachnaya)* serves miscellaneous snacks
пельменная *(pil'mennaya)* serves *pelmeni*
(meat ravioli)
пирожковая *(pirashkovaya)* serves
pirozhki (deep-fried meat or vegetable
turnovers)
чебуречная *(chiburechnaya)* serves Armenian or Georgian *chebureki* (spicy,
deep-fried mutton pies)
шашлычная *(shashlychnaya)* serves *shashlyk* (charcoal-grilled meat kebab)

At the Restaurant
Ordering

Except at the fanciest restaurants (or foreign
restaurants) waiters will probably not speak
English.

waiter
  afitsiant   официант
waitress
  afitsiantka   официантка
menu
  minyu   меню
hot
  garyachiy   горячий
cold
  khalodnyy   холодный
more
  yishchyo   ещё

What's this?
shto eta?
Что это?

I'd like ...
ya by khatel/khatela ... (m/f)
Я бы хотел/хотела ...

May we order?
mozhna zakazat?
Можно заказать?

Please bring ...
prinisiti, pazhalsta ...
Принесите пожалуйста ...

That's all.
vsyo
Всё.

Bon appetit!
priyatnava apitita!
Приятного аппетита!

The bill/check, please.
schyot, pazhalsta
Счёт, пожалуйста.

Menu Decoder
Breakfast

If you are staying in a hotel, breakfast (завтрак, *zaftrak*) can range from a large help-yourself buffet spread to bread, butter, jam, tea and a boiled egg or nothing at all. Items you might find include:

блины *(bliny)* or блинчики *(blinchiki)* – thin pancackes, usually filled with jam, cheese or meat

каша *(kasha)* – Russian-style buckwheat porridge

сырники *(syrniki)* – fritters of cottage cheese, flour and egg

творог *(tvarog/tvorag)* – cottage cheese

кефир *(kifir)* – yogurt-like sour milk, served as a drink

яйцо *(yaytso)* – egg

всмятку *(fsmyatku)* – soft-boiled

крутое *(krutoye)* – hard-boiled

омлет *(amlet)* – omelette

яичница *(yaishnitsa)* – fried

сметана *(smitana)* – sour cream

Lunch & Dinner

обед *(ahbet)* – early-afternoon meal, usually substantial

ужин, *(uzhyn)* – evening meal, lighter than *ahbet*.

Meals (and menus) are divided into courses:

закуски *(zakuski)* – appetisers, often grouped into cold *zakuski* (холодные закуски) and hot *zakuski* (горячие закуски)

первые блюда *(pervyya bluda)* – first courses, usually soups

вторые блюда *(vtariya bluda)* – second courses or 'main' dishes

горячие блюда *(garyachiya bluda)* – hot courses (same as second courses)

сладкие блюда *(sladkiya bluda)* – sweet courses or desserts

Main dishes may be further divided into:

фирменные *(firmeniye)* – house specials

национальные *(natsianalniye)* – national or ethnic dishes

порционные *(portsioniye)* – special orders

мясные *(myasniye)* – meat

рыбные *(rybniye)* – fish

птица *(ptitsa)* – poultry

овощные *(ovashniye)* – vegetable

Cooking Styles

Words you might spot on the menu are:

варёный *(varyonyy)* – boiled

жареный *(zharinyy)* – roasted or fried

отварной *(atvarnoy)* – poached or boiled

печёный *(pichyonyy)* – baked

фри *(fri)* – fried

Appetisers

The fancier appetisers (*zakuski*, закуски), rival main courses for price. A few *zakuski* worth trying are:

икра *(ikra)* – caviar

блины со сметаной *(bliny sa smitanay)* – pancakes with sour cream

грибы в сметане *(griby fsmitani)* – mushrooms baked in sour cream

рыба солёная *(ryba salyonaya)* – salted fish

семга копчёная *(syimga kapchyonaya)* – smoked salmon

салат из помидоров *(salat iz pamidorof)* – tomato salad

салат из огурцов *(salat iz agurtsof)* – cucumber salad

салат столичный *(salat stalichnyy)* – salad comprised of vegetable and beef bits, potato and egg in sour cream and mayonnaise

Soup

Rich soups may be the pinnacle of Slavic cooking. There are dozens of varieties, often served with a dollop of sour cream. Most are made from meat stock. The Russian word for soup sounds the same, суп. Among the most common soups are:

борщ *(borshch)* – beetroot with vegetables and meat

лапша *(lapsha)* – chicken noodle

окрошка *(akroshka)* – cold or hot soup made from cucumbers, sour cream, potatoes, egg, meat and *kvas* (a beer-like drink)

рассольник *(rasol'nik)* – pickled cucumber and kidney

солянка *(salyanka)* – thick meat or fish soup with salted cucumbers and other vegetables

уха *(ukha)* – fish soup with potatoes and vegetables

харчо *(kharcho)* – Caucasian-style garlicky mutton

щи *(shchi)* – cabbage or sauerkraut (many varieties)

Poultry & Meat

птица, *ptitsa)* – poultry

курица *(kuritsa)* – chicken (the meat)

цыплёнок *(tsyplyonok)* – a pullet

мясо *(myasa)* – meat

баранина *(baranina)* – mutton

говядина *(gavyadina)* – beef

свинина *(svinina)* – pork

The list of possible dishes (and possible names) is huge, but following are some common meat and poultry dishes:

антрекот *(antrikot)* – entrecote, boned sirloin steak

бифстроганов *(bifstroganaf)* – beef stroganoff, beef slices in a rich sauce

бифштекс *(bifshteks)* – 'steak', usually a glorified hamburger filling

голубцы *(galuptsy)* – cabbage rolls stuffed with meat

жаркое *(zharkoye)* – meat or poultry stewed in a clay pot, usually with mushrooms, potatoes and vegetables

котлета *(katleta)* – croquette of ground meat

котлета по-жарская *(katleta pa-zharskaya)* – croquette with minced chicken

котлета по-киевски *(katleta pa-kiefski)* – chicken Kiev, fried boneless chicken breast stuffed with butter (watch out, it squirts!)

пельмени *(pil'meni)* – pelmeni, Siberian-style meat dumplings

плов *(plov)* – pilaf, rice with mutton bits, from Central Asia

сосиска *(sosiska)* – sausage

цыплёнок табака *(tsyplyonak tabaka)* – chicken Tabaka, Caucasian-style grilled chicken

шашлык *(shashlyk)* – skewered and grilled mutton or other meat, adapted from Central Asia and Transcaucasia

Fish

Fish is рыба *(ryba)*.

омуль *(omul')* – omul, like salmon, from Lake Baikal

сёмга *(syomga)* – salmon

судак *(sudak)* – pike perch

форель *(farel')* – trout

осётр *(asyotr)*, осетрина *(asitrina)* or севрюга *(sivryuga)* – sturgeon

осетрина отварная *(asitrina atvarnaya)* – poached sturgeon

осетрина с грибами *(asitrina zgribami)* – sturgeon with mushrooms

Vegetables

Vegetables are овощи *(ovashchi)*; greens are зелень *(zelin')*. A garnish is гарниры *(garniry)*.

горох *(garokh)* – peas

грибы *(griby)* – mushrooms

капуста *(kapusta)* – cabbage

картошка *(kartoshka)* or картофель *(kartofil')* – potato

морковь *(markof')* – carrots

огурец *(agurets)* – cucumber

помидор *(pamidor)* – tomato

Fruit

Fruit is фрукты *(frukty)*.

абрикос *(abrikos)* – apricot

арбуз *(arbus)* – watermelon

виноград *(vinagrad)* – grapes

груша *(grusha)* – pear

дыня *(dynya)* – melon

яблоко *(yablaka)* – apple

Other Foods & Snacks

On every table are stacks of bread (хлеб, *khlep*). The best is Russian 'black' bread, a vitamin-rich sour rye. Russians are mad about wild mushrooms (грибы, *griby*); in late summer and early autumn they troop into the woods with their buckets. Other items are:

бутерброд *(buterbrod)* – small open sandwiches

варенье *(varyenya)* – jam

масло *(masla)* – butter

перец *(pyerits)* – pepper

рис *(ris)* – rice

сахар *(sakhar)* – sugar

сметана *(smetana)* – sour cream

соль *(sol')* – salt

сыр *(syr)* – cheese

хачапури *(khachapury)* – rich, cheesy bread, usually served hot

яйцо *(yaytso)* – egg

Desserts

Perhaps most Russians are exhausted or drunk by dessert time, since this is the least imaginative course.

блинчики *(blinchiki)* – pancakes with jam or other sweet filling

кисель *(kisel')* – fruit jelly (Jell-o in American jargon)

компот *(kampot)* – fruit in syrup (probably from a tin)

оладьи *(alad'l)* – fritters topped with syrup or sour cream

пирожное *(pirozhnaye)* – pastries

мороженое *(morozhenoe, marozhinaye)* – ice-cream

Vegetarian Food

Menus often have a category like vegetable (овощные), milk (молочные), egg (яичные) and flour (мучные) dishes, but don't get your hopes up.

I'm a vegetarian.

| Я вегетарианка. | *ya vigitarianka* (f) |
| Я вегетарианец. | *ya vigitarianits* (m) |

I can't eat meat.

| Я не ем мясного. | *ya ni em myasnova* |

without meat

| без мяса | *bez myasa* |

only vegetables

| только овощи | *tol'ka ovashchi* |

DRINKS
Nonalcoholic

water	
вода	*vada*
boiled water	
кипяток	*kipyatok*
mineral water	
минеральная вода	*mineralnaya vada*
soda water	
газированная вода	*gazirovanaya vada*
coffee	
кофе	*kofe*
tea	
чай	*chai*
with sugar	
с сахаром	*s sakharam*
with jam	
с вареньем	*s faren'im*
milk	
молоко	*malako*
juice	
сок	*sok*
lemonade	
лимонад	*limanad*
soft drink	
безалкогольный напиток	
bezalkagol'nyy napituk	

Alcoholic

alcohol	
алкоголь	*alkagol'*
vodka	
водка	*votka*
sparkling wine (Champagne-style)	
советское	*savyetskaya*
шампанское	*shampanskaya*
red/white wine	
красное/белое	*krasnaya/belaya*
вино	*vino*
brandy	
коньяк	*kan'ak*
beer	
пиво	*piva*
kvas (beer-like drink)	
квас	*kvas*
medavuka (mead)	
медовуха	*medavukha*

To your health!

За ваше здоровье!

za vashe zdarov'e!

Glossary

You may encounter some of the following terms and abbreviations during your travels in Russia and Belarus. See also the Language chapter.

aeroport – airport
aerovokzal – airline terminal
ail – hexagonal or tepee-shaped yurt
apteka – pharmacy
ataman – Cossack leader
avtobus – bus
avtomat – automatic ticket machine
avtostantsiya – bus stop
avtovokzal – bus terminal

babushka – literally grandmother, but used generally in Russian society for all old women
balalaika – traditional Russian musical instrument, usually with a triangular body and three strings
BAM (Baikalo-Amurskaya Magistral) – Baikal-Amur Mainline, a trans-Siberian rail route
bankomat – automated teller machine (ATM)
banya – bathhouse
bashnya – tower
baza otdykha – literally, 'relaxation base'; often used to describe lodges and sanatoriums
benzin – petrol
biblioteka – library
bilet – ticket
biznesmen, biznesmenka – literally, 'businessman', 'businesswoman'; often used to mean a small-time operator on the fringe of the law
bolnitsa – hospital
boyar – high-ranking noble
bufet – snack bar selling cheap cold meats, boiled eggs, salads, bread, pastries etc
bulochnaya – bakery
bulvar – boulevard
buterbrod – open sandwich
byliny – epic songs

CIS – Commonwealth of Independent States; an alliance (proclaimed in 1991) of independent states comprising the former USSR (less the three Baltic States)

dacha – country cottage, summer house
datsan – Buddhist monastery
deklaratsia – customs declaration

detsky – child's, children's
Detsky Mir – Children's World, name for many toy shops
devushki – young women
dezhurnaya – woman looking after a particular floor of a hotel
dolina – valley
dom – house
dorogoy – expensive
duma – parliament
dvorets – palace
dvorets kultury – literally, 'culture palace'; a meeting, social, entertainment, education centre, usually for a group like railway workers, children etc

elektrichka – suburban train
etazh – floor (storey)

GAI (Gosudarstvennaya Avtomobilnaya Inspektsia) – State Automobile Inspectorate (traffic police)
gallereya – gallery
gastronom – speciality food shop
gavan – harbour
gazeta – newspaper
glasnost – literally, 'openness'; the free-expression aspect of the Gorbachev reforms
glavpochtamt – main post office
gora – mountain
gorod – city, town
gostinitsa – hotel (R)
gostiny dvor – trading arcade
granitsa – border
gril-bar – grill bar, often limited to roast chicken
Gulag (Glavnoe Upravlenie Lagerey) – Main Administration for Camps; the Soviet network of concentration camps
GUM (Gosudarstvenny Univermag) – State Department Store

i – and
ikra – caviar
imeni – 'named after' (often used in names of theatres and libraries, eg, Moscow's Konsertny zal imeni Chaykovskogo is the Tchaikovsky Concert Hall)
inostranets – foreigner
Intourist – old Soviet State Committee for Tourism, now privatised, split up and in competition with hundreds of other travel agencies

istochnik – mineral spring
izba – traditional, single-storey wooden cottage
izveshchenie – notice of permission (for visas)

kafe – café
kameny baba – standing stone idol
kamera khranenia – left-luggage office
kanal – canal
karta – map
kassa – ticket office, cashier's desk
kater – small ferry
Kazak – Cossack
kemping – camp site; often has small cabins as well as tent sites
KGB (Komitet Gosydarstvennoy Bezopasnosti) – Committee of State Security
khleb – bread
kholm – hill
khram – church
kino – cinema
kipyatok – boiled water
kladbishche – cemetery
klyuch – key
kniga – book (plural *knigi*)
kokoshniki – colourful tiles and brick patterns
kolkhoz – collective farm
kolonna – column, pillar
koltsevaya doroga – ring road
kombinat – complex of factories
Komnaty otdykha – resting rooms found at all major train stations and several smaller ones
Komsomol – Communist Youth League
kopek – kopeck; the smallest, worthless unit of Russian currency
korpus – building (ie, one of several in a complex)
kray – territory
krazha – theft
kreml – kremlin, a town's fortified stronghold
kruglosutochno – around the clock
krugovoy – round trip
kulak – Stalinist name for a wealthier peasant
kupe – compartment (on a train)
kurgan – burial mound
kvartira – flat, apartment
kvitantsia – receipt

lavra – senior monastery
lednik – glacier
les – forest

lyux – a kind of hotel suite, with a sitting room in addition to bedroom and bathroom; a *polu-lyux* suite is the less spacious version

Mafia – anyone who has anything to do with crime, from genuine gangsters to victims of their protection rackets
magazin – shop
manezh – riding school
marka – postage stamp or brand, trademark
marshrut – route
marshrutki, marshrutnoe taxi – minibus that runs along a fixed route
mashina – car
matryoshka – set of painted wooden dolls within dolls
mavzoley – mausoleum
mestnoe vremya – local time
mesto – place, seat
mezhdugorodnyy – intercity
mezhdunarodnyy – international
mikriki – minivan
militsia – police
mineralnaya voda – mineral water
monastyr – monastery
more – sea
morskoy vokzal – sea terminal
Moskovskoe vremya – Moscow time
most – bridge
muzey – museum; also some palaces, art galleries and nonworking churches
muzhskoy – men's (toilet)

naberezhnaya – embankment
nomenklatura – literally, 'list of nominees'; the old government and Communist Party elite
novy – new

obed – lunch
oblast – region
obmen valyuty – currency exchange
obmenny punkt – exchange point (bureau, counter)
obyavlenie – handwritten bulletin
okrug – district
ostanovka – bus stop
ostrov – island
OVIR (Otdel Viz I Registratsii) – Department of Visas and Registration; now known under the acronym PVU, although outside Moscow OVIR is still likely to be in use
ozero – lake

pamyatnik – monument, statue
Paskha – Easter

passazhirskiy poezd – intercity stopping train

pereryv – break (when shops, ticket offices, restaurants etc close for an hour or two during the day; this always happens just as you arrive)

perestroika – literally, 'restructuring'; Mikhail Gorbachev's efforts to revive the Soviet economy

pereulok – lane

peshchera – cave

pivo – beer

plan goroda – city map

plyazh – beach

ploshchad (Russian), ploshcha (Belarusian) – square

pochta, pochtamt – post office

poezd – train

poliklinika – medical centre

polu-lyux – less spacious version of a *lyux*, a kind of hotel suite with a sitting room in addition to the bedroom and bathroom

poluostrov – peninsula

polyana – glade, clearing

posilka – parcel

posolstvo – embassy

praspekt (Belarusian), prospekt (Russian) – avenue

prichal – landing, pier

priglashenie – invitation

prigorodnyy poezd – suburban train

prodazha – sale

produkty – food store

proezd – passage

prokat – rental

propusk – permit, pass

prospekt (Russian), praspekt (Belarusian) – avenue

provodnik (m), provodnitsa (f) – carriage attendant on a train

PVU (*passportno-vizovoye upravleniye*) – passport and visa department, formerly OVIR (an acronym which is still likely to be in use outside Moscow)

rabochy den – working day (Monday to Friday)

rayon – district

rechnoy vokzal – river station

reka – river

remont, na remont – closed for repairs (a sign you see all too often)

restoran – restaurant

Rozhdestvo – Christmas

rubl – rouble

ruchnoy – handmade

rynky – food markets

rynok – market

sad – garden

samolyot – aeroplane

sanitarny den – literally, 'sanitary day'; the monthly day when shops, museums, restaurant, hotel dining rooms etc are shut down for cleaning

schyot – bill

schyotchik – taxi meter

selo – village

sever – north

shlagbaum – checkpoint, barrier

shosse – highway

shtuka – piece (many produce items are sold by the piece)

skhema transporta – transport map

skoryy poezd – literally, fast train; a long-distance train

sneg – snow

sobor – cathedral

Sodruzhestvo Nezavisimykh Gosudarstv (SNG) – Commonwealth of Independent States (CIS)

soviet – council

spravka – certificate

spusk – descent, slope

Sputnik – former youth-travel arm of Komsomol; now just one of the bigger tourism agencies

stanitsa – Cossack village

stary – old

stolovaya – canteen, cafeteria

sutok – period of 24 hours

suvenir – souvenir

taiga – northern pine, fir, spruce and larch forest

taksofon – pay telephone

talon – bus ticket, coupon

tapochki – slippers

teatr – theatre

teatralnaya kassa – theatre ticket office

telegramma – telegram

traktir – tavern

tramvay – tram

troyka – vehicle drawn by three horses

tserkov – church

tsirk – circus

TsUM (Tsentralny Univermag) – name of department store

tualet – toilet

tuda i obratno – 'there and back', return ticket
turbaza – tourist camp

ulitsa (Russian), vulitsa (Belarusian) – street
univermag, universalnyy magazin – department store
ushchelie – gorge, canyon
uzhin – supper

valyuta – foreign currency
vanna – bath
vareniki – dumplings with a variety of possible fillings
velosiped – bicycle
venik – birch branch
vezdekhod – all-terrain vehicle
vkhod – way in, entrance
voda – water
vodapad – waterfall
vodny vokzal – ferry terminal
vokzal – station
vorovstvo – theft
vostok – east
vrach – doctor

vulitsa (Belarusian), ulitsa (Russian) – street
vykhod – way out, exit
vykhodnoy den – day off (Saturday, Sunday and holidays)

yantar – amber
yezhednevno – every day
yug – south
yurt – nomad's portable, round tent-house made of felt or skins stretched over a collapsible frame of wood slats

zakaz – reservation
zakaznoe – registration (of mail)
zakuski – appetisers
zal – hall, room
zaliv – gulf, bay
zamok – castle, fortress
zapad – west
zapovednik – (nature) reserve
zavtrak – breakfast
zheleznodorozhnyy vokzal – train station
zhenskiy – women's (toilet)
zheton – token (for metro etc)

Thanks

Many thanks to the following travellers who wrote to us with helpful hints, useful advice and interesting anecdotes:

Nick Adlam, Eric Adler, Alexandre Akopian, Bas Aldewereld, Henryk Alff, Lukas F Allemann, Kevin Allen, Mark Allen, Mike Allen, Andre & Jane Ancomas, Ifigeneia Andredaki, Rachel Angus, Jonathan Arkins, Hilmir Ásgeirsson, Glenn Ashenden, Kris Ayre, Alex Baechle, J Bailey, Johannes Banzhof, Marcel Bartels, Olga Bekhtereva, Bev & Chris Bennett, Sturla Berg-Olsen, Hans H Bergschmidt, John Bisges, Dan Bode, Thomas Boren, Anna Borjeson, Peter Borowski, Antoine Boulart, L Bowers, Alan Bowtell, Jean-Claude Branch, Mark Brandt, Peter Brechbuehler, Aaron Brodsky, Bev Broger, Adam Brooke, Rita Brookhouse, Doug Brooks, Edmund Brown, Kevin Brown, Marl Allen Brown, Karin Bruce, Noel Burke, James Bush, Merial Buxton, Harry Cadle, Steven Caron, Alister Carroll, S M Chan, John Chang, Rebekka Chaplin, Samuel Charache, Fiona Charlesson, Farid Chetouani, Pravit Chintawongvanich, Magnus Christiansson, Elspeth Christie, Jenni Clark, Fiona Clarkson, Joe N Clavan, Julian Clee, Jan Adriaan Coebergh, Cheryl Collins, Terry Collins, Rachel Colpus, Mrs Cook, Ron Cook, Phil Coote, Matthew Cordery, Carl Court, Bob Cromwell, Daniel Darby, Tyler Dash, Michiel de Graaff, Jens Jakob de Hansen, Rob de Raaij, Tom De Vecchi, Marcel de Vroed, Jozien de Wit, Terry Deague, Jean-Patrick Debbeche, Matthew DeCoursey, Hafan Deg, Nicolas Delerue, Leroy Demery Jnr, Johan Denis, Katherine Desormeau, Sherry & Mike DiBari, Mark Dirksen, Ponor Doline, Lloyd Donaldson, Ian Douglas, V Downes, Mark Dudman, Ivonne Duiser, Debbie Edwards, Garth Eichel, Pierre Elias, Mary Ellis, Hugh Elsol, Andrey V Emeliyanov, Emma Emily, Chris Enting, Peter Epanchin, Yury Epstein, Erling N Eriksen, Dr Christina Evaghoras, Brett Factor, Paul Farrell, Eli Feiman, Andreas Fertin, Dietmar Fischer, Mark Fisher, Catherine Fixe, Wendy Fletcher, Mark Forrest, Minna Fossi, Jill Fournier, Simon Francis, Adam Franz, Guido Freitag, Ricardo A Fridman, Mischa Gabowitsch, Giles Galahad, Jane Galvin, Felicity Gatchell, Didier Gayraud, Simon & Georgie, Howard Gethin, Dave Gibbs, Serge Gielkens, Marta & Philip Giesbertz, Monique Gijsbrechts, Brad Gledhill, Eric Glerum, Kate Glover, Tavis Gorman, Jack Graham, Mark Grant, Melissa Graves, Ed Graystone, Micael Gustavsson, Lars Gyllenhaal, Brian Aslak Gylte, Tim Hall, Roy F Halvorsen, Dave Hamlin, Ben Hampson, Jenny Mai Handford, Paul Hannon, Lau & Ludmila Hansen, Soren Vestergaard Hansen, Anna Harmala, Terry Hart, Phil Hayward, Claire Heald, Marc Heerbrant, Ron Helfrich, Peter J Henderson, Jim Hendrickson, Jane Hepburn, Tony Hermans, Kaj Heydorn, Alistair Hind, Charles Hirsch, Erwin Hirt, John Hogan, Vance Holliday, Paul Hubers, Alina Hughes, Laura Hughes, Stephen Humphrey, Julia Humphreys, Katrin Ilg, Lindsay Image, Mr Inva, Stephen Ireland, Belle Jackson, Graham Jackson, Jessica Jacobson, Rafik Jallad, Linda & Clive Jameson, Rok Jarc, Marie Javins, John Jay, Emil Jelstrup, Christian Jongeneel, Kevin Jordan, Anne Juhl, Kerry Just, Roman Kaczaj, Paul Kail, Max Kamenetsky, Stefan Kamola, Jennifer Kavanagh, Randy Kempa, Stephen Kenmar, Toby Kenyon, Dave Kiely, Alexander Kierdorf, Heather Kimmel, Brian King, Teja Klobucar, Brent Knazan, Karen Koblitz, Marnix Koets, Ruth & David Koffman, Ctibor Kostal, Jay Krajic, Corine Kruijsen, Andrey Kurbatsky, Joanna Kurosz, Roger Landau, Joann Landingham, Lee Leatham, John A Lee, Alexandre Leigh, Steffen Lempp, Phil Lewis, Scott Lewis, Henry Lipiec, Breukink Lisette, Ian Lockett, Sabine Loebbe, David Love, Peter Lowthian, Francesco Lulli, Darren Lydom, P A MaCaitlem, Tim Macmillan, Lachlan MacQuarrie, Iwona Madura, Attila Mag, J Mak, Constantine Mandylas, Joel H Marks, Federico Marquart, Cathy & Kevin Marston, Bill Martin, Fabrice Mathieu, Vanda Mathis, Anu Mathur, Brent Maupin, Phil Mayor, Kirsty McCluskey, Damian McCormack, Edmund McCosh, Eric McEachen, Robert McIlveen, John McIntyre, Marty McLennan, Chajim Meinhold, Pietro Meroni, Franz H Messerli, Kathy Meyer, Stephen Miles, Nicolas Minec, Hamed Ministar, Tobias Moerschen, Thomas Molnard, John Monfries, Shane Monks, N Moore, Chris Mourney, Terry Nakazono, Bob Nansen, John Neil, Stuart Nicholson, Bernhard Niebaum, Madelen Nilsson, Lore Nizet, Jacques Noel, Bruce Nolin, Eric Norton, Markus Nuremberg, Erin K O'Brien, Mary Beth O'Donovan, Momo Ohta, Lars Olberg, Zuzana Olzova, Ingrid M Opdahl, Aino Oura, Paul Ozorak, Sandra Pagano, Elizabeth Pahl, Chris Palmer, Lars Pardo, Julia Parfitt, Tanya Partem, Irina Pavlova, Rachel & Mike Peake, Val Pearson,

Michael Pedersen, Maarten Peeters, Piritta Pelkonen, Cristian Pérez de Laborda, Piergiorgio Pescali, Sven Peters, Alex Phillips, Michael Pike, Anna Judith Piller, Alex Podres, Jacques Poitras, Aase Popper, Chris Porritt, Katarina Potznerova, Colleen Poulter, James Pritchard, Paul Prowting, Paolo Puccetti, Sophia Pugsley, Jemma Pullen, Mark Quandt, Philippe Quix, Wasyl Radelicki, Kristine Ramming, Jean-Renaud Ratti, Thadeusz Rawa, Christopher Reeves, Dietrich Rehnert, David Reid, Peter Relyveld, Susan Renkert, Reuben Rich, Anton Rijsdijk, Marion Rimmer, Wayne Rimmer, Daniele Rinaldi, Nils Rinaldi, David Robinson, Lorraine Robinson, D A Roseman, Jeff Rosenberg, Jaroslaw Rudnik, Patti Ryan, Barry Sachais, David Salas, Richard Salveter, Stefan Samuelsson, Andrea Sansoni, Fred Sargent, Suzanne Sataline, Nathon Sato, Rachel Savidge, Samit Sawhny, Dietmar Schaeper, Peter Schaer, Joe Schill, Tim Schmith, Matthias Schmoll, Christiana Schmullius, Pascal Schoenmaekers, Brian Schroeter, Robert Schwandt, Jack Schwartz, Runes Schwartz, Patrick Sclater, Alice Scott, Allan Sealy, Adam Sebire, Tim Shabarekh, Joshua Sharkey, Jack Sheremetoff, Michael Sherman, Nicholas Sherman, Karl Sigiscar, Frank Sitchler, Andrew Smith, Barney Smith, Jonathon Smith, Lisa Smith, Vic Sofras, Gerard Souness, Nicola & Steve Spencer, Walter Spoerle, John Staveley, Timo Stewart, George Strain, Wendy Stronge, Birgit Suhr, Holger Supper, M Szwedziuk, Steve Talley, Steve Talley, Terence Tam, Ivan Tassev, Neil Taylor, Rob Taylor, Anja Thijssen, Erik S Thomson, Fred Thornett, Anders Thorsell, Emma Tidy, David Towers, Dan Tully, Julle Tuuliainen, Esther van Bloemen, Carlijn van Dehn, Anthony van der Craats, Paul van Gelder, Dick van Mersbergen, Jany Venditto, Soren Vestergaard, Clem Vetters, Ferdinand Vieider, Max von Hahn, Stijn Vossen, Malcolm Wake, Helen Walker, Sophie Walker, Naomi Wall, Jonathan Wallace, Mike Wallace, Anne Warburton, Jane Ward, D G Waring, Colin Watkins, Chris Webb, James Webb, Lindsay Webb, Mandy Webster, Renee Webster, Wayne Welborn, Liz & Todd Werner, Diana Wernicke, Thomas Whitcroft, Anna White, Einar Wilhelmsen, Dominic Williams, Peter J Wilsmhurst, David & Jocelyn Wilson, Tracy Wilson, Chris Winchester, Matt Woodhouse, Whui Mei Yeo, Elie Younes, Andrew Young, Steve Yover, Alexander Zhuravlev

LONELY PLANET

You already know that Lonely Planet produces more than this one guidebook, but you might not be aware of the other products we have on this region. Here is a selection of titles that you may want to check out as well:

St Petersburg Map
ISBN 1 86450 179 0
US$5.99 • UK£3.99

St Petersburg
ISBN 1 86450 325 4
US$15.99 • UK£9.99

Russian Phrasebook
ISBN 1 86450 106 5
US$7.95 • UK£4.50

Eastern Europe
ISBN 1 74059 289 1
US$27.99 • UK£15.99

Estonia Latvia & Lithuania
ISBN 1 74059 132 1
US$24.99 • UK£14.99

Moscow
ISBN 1 86450 359 9
US$18.99 • UK£10.99

Poland
ISBN 1 74059 082 1
US$19.99 • UK£12.99

Romania & Moldova
ISBN 1 86450 058 1
US$16.99 • UK£10.99

Georgia, Armenia & Azerbaijan
ISBN 0 86442 680 1
US$19.99 • UK£12.99

Trans-Siberian Railway
ISBN 1 86450 335 1
US$15.99 • UK£12.99

Finland
ISBN 1 74059 076 7
US$21.99 • UK£13.99

China
ISBN 1 74059 117 8
US$29.99 • UK£17.99

Available wherever books are sold

You already know that Lonely Planet produces more than this one guidebook but you might not be aware of the other products we have on this region. Here is a selection of titles that you may want to check out as well:

St Petersburg Map
ISBN 1 86450 178 2
US$5.99 UK£3.99

St Petersburg
ISBN 1 74059 339 1
US$... UK£...

Russian Phrasebook
ISBN 1 86450 243 6
US$... UK£...

Eastern Europe
ISBN ...
US$... UK£...

Estonia, Latvia & Lithuania
ISBN ...
US$... UK£...

Moscow
ISBN ...
US$... UK£...

Poland
ISBN ...
US$... UK£...

Romania & Moldova
ISBN ...
US$... UK£...

Georgia, Armenia & Azerbaijan
ISBN ...
US$... UK£...

Trans-Siberian Railway
ISBN ...
US$... UK£...

Finland
ISBN ...
US$... UK£...

China
ISBN ...
US$... UK£...

Available wherever books are sold

Index

Abbreviations

Belarus – B   Russia – R

Text

Boxed Text

MAP LEGEND

CITY ROUTES

Freeway	Freeway		Unsealed Road
Highway	Primary Road		One Way Street
Road	Secondary Road		Pedestrian Street
Street	Street		Stepped Street
Lane	Lane		Tunnel
	On/Off Ramp		Footbridge

REGIONAL ROUTES

	Tollway, Freeway
	Primary Road
	Secondary Road
	Minor Road

BOUNDARIES

	International
	State
	Disputed
	Fortified Wall

HYDROGRAPHY

	River, Creek		Dry Lake, Salt Lake
	Canal		Spring, Rapids
	Lake		Waterfalls

TRANSPORT ROUTES & STATIONS

	Train		Ferry
	Underground Train		Walking Trail
	Metro		Walking Tour
	Tramway		Path
	Funicular Railway		Pier or Jetty

AREA FEATURES

	Building		Market		Beach		Forest
	Park, Gardens		Sports Ground		Cemetery		Plaza

POPULATION SYMBOLS

◎ CAPITAL	National Capital	● CITY	City	● Village	Village
◉ CAPITAL	State Capital	● Town	Town		Urban Area

MAP SYMBOLS

■	Place to Stay	▼	Place to Eat	●	Point of Interest

Airport	Embassy, Consulate	Palace, Stately Home	Synagogue
Bank	Fountain	Police Station	Taxi
Buddhist Temple	Hospital	Post Office	Telephone
Bus Station	Internet Cafe	Pub or Bar	Theatre
Cable Car, Funicular	Monument	Ruins	Tomb
Cathedral, Church	Mosque	Shopping Centre	Tourist Information
Cinema	Museum	Swimming Pool	Trolleybus

Note: not all symbols displayed above appear in this book

LONELY PLANET OFFICES

Australia
Locked Bag 1, Footscray, Victoria 3011
☎ 03 8379 8000 fax 03 8379 8111
email: talk2us@lonelyplanet.com.au

USA
150 Linden St, Oakland, CA 94607
☎ 510 893 8555 TOLL FREE: 800 275 8555
fax 510 893 8572
email: info@lonelyplanet.com

UK
72 – 82 Rosebery Ave, London EC1R 4RW
☎ 020 7841 9000 fax 020 7841 9001
email: go@lonelyplanet.co.uk

France
1 rue du Dahomey, 75011 Paris
☎ 01 55 25 33 00 fax 01 55 25 33 01
email: bip@lonelyplanet.fr
www.lonelyplanet.fr

World Wide Web: www.lonelyplanet.com *or* AOL keyword: lp
Lonely Planet Images: www.lonelyplanetimages.com